The Greenwood Encyclopedia of
American Poets and Poetry

Advisory Board

The Greenwood Encyclopedia of

AMERICAN POETS AND POETRY

Volume 1

A – C

Jeffrey Gray, Editor
James McCorkle and Mary McAleer Balkun,
Associate Editors

GREENWOOD PRESS
WESTPORT, CONNECTICUT • LONDON

Library of Congress Cataloging-in-Publication Data

The Greenwood encyclopedia of American poets and poetry / Jeffrey Gray, editor ; James McCorkle and Mary McAleer Balkun, associate editors.
　　p. cm.
　Includes bibliographical references and index.
　ISBN 0–313–32381–X (set : alk. paper) — ISBN 0–313–33009–3 (v. 1 : alk. paper) —
ISBN 0–313–33010–7 (v. 2 : alk. paper) — ISBN 0–313–33011–5 (v. 3 : alk. paper) —
ISBN 0–313–33012–3 (v. 4 : alk. paper) — ISBN 0–313–33013–1 (v. 5 : alk. paper)
1. American poetry—Encyclopedias. 2. Poets, American—Biography—Encyclopedias.
I. Gray, Jeffrey, 1944– II. McCorkle, James. III. Balkun, Mary McAleer.
PS303.G74　2006
811.00903–dc22　　　2005025445

British Library Cataloguing in Publication Data is available.

Library of Congress Catalog Card Number: 2005025445
ISBN: 0–313–32381–X (set)
　　　0–313–33009–3 (vol. 1)
　　　0–313–33010–7 (vol. 2)
　　　0–313–33011–5 (vol. 3)
　　　0–313–33012–3 (vol. 4)
　　　0–313–33013–1 (vol. 5)

First published in 2006

Greenwood Press, 88 Post Road West, Westport, CT 06881
An imprint of Greenwood Publishing Group, Inc.
www.greenwood.com

Printed in the United States of America

∞

The paper used in this book complies with the
Permanent Paper Standard issued by the National
Information Standards Organization (Z39.48–1984).

10　9　8　7　6　5　4　3　2　1

Copyright Acknowledgments

Contents

List of Entries

List of Poets

Pre–Twentieth-Century Poets

Abbey, Henry
Adams, Henry Brooks
Adams, John
Adams, John Quincy
Albee, John
Alcott, Amos Bronson
Alcott, Louisa May
Aldrich, Anne Reeve
Aldrich, Thomas Bailey
Allen, Elizabeth Akers
Allston, Washington
Alsop, George
Austin, Mary
Balbuena, Bernardo de
Bangs, John Kendrick
Barlow, Joel
Bates, Charlotte Fiske
Bates, Katharine Lee
Beers, Henry Augustin
Belknap, Jeremy
Bell, Robert Mowry
Bierce, Ambrose
Bleecker, Ann Eliza
Bloede, Gertrude
Blood, Benjamin
Bodman, Manoah
Boucher, Jonathan
Brackenridge, Hugh Henry
Bradford, William
Bradley, Mary Emily Neeley

Bradstreet, Anne Dudley
Braithwaite, William Stanley
Brooks, Charles Timothy
Brooks, Maria Gowen
Bryant, William Cullen
Byles, Mather
Byrd, William, II
Carleton, Will
Cary, Alice
Cary, Phoebe
Cawein, Madison
Chandler, Elizabeth Margaret
Channing, William Ellery
Channing, (William) Ellery
Child, Lydia Maria
Church, Benjamin
Cleghorn, Sarah Norcliffe
Colman, Benjamin
Cooke, Ebenezer
Cooke, Rose Terry
Coolbrith, Ina
Cotton, John
Cradock, Thomas
Cranch, Christopher Pearse
Crane, Stephen
Dana, Richard Henry
Dandridge, Danske
Danforth, Samuel
Davies, Samuel
De Vere, Mary Ainge

Deland, Margaret
Dickinson, Emily
Doane, George Washington
Dodge, Mary Mapes
Drake, Joseph Rodman
Dreiser, Theodore
Duché, Jacob
Dudley, Thomas
Dunbar, Paul Laurence
Dwight, Timothy
Eastman, Elaine Goodale
Emerson, Ralph Waldo
English, Thomas Dunn
Equiano, Olaudah
Evans, Nathaniel
Faugeres, Margaretta Bleecker
Fenollosa, Ernest
Fenollosa, Mary McNeil
Fergusson, Elizabeth Graeme
Field, Eugene
Fields, Annie
Fields, James Thomas
Fiske, John
Fordham, Mary Weston
Forten, Sarah Louisa
Freneau, Philip
French, Mary
Fuller, Margaret
Garland, Hamilin
Garrison, William Lloyd

Williams, Roger
Willis, Nathaniel Parker
Wilson, John
Wolcott, Roger

Wood, William
Woodworth, Samuel
Woolsey, Sarah Chauncey (also Chauncy)

Woolson, Constance Fenimore
Work, Henry Clay
Wright, Susanna

Twentieth- and Twenty-first–Century Poets

Ackerman, Diane
Adair, Virginia Hamilton
Adams, Léonie
Addonizio, Kim
Ai
Aiken, Conrad Potter
Alexander, Elizabeth
Alexander, Meena
Alexander, Will
Alexie, Sherman
Algarín, Miguel
Ali, Agha Shahid
Alvarez, Julia
Ammons, A.R.
Anania, Michael
Andrews, Bruce (Errol)
Angelou, Maya
Antin, David
Arensberg, Walter Conrad
Armantrout, Rae
Ash, John
Ashbery, John
Atwood, Margaret (Eleanor)
Auden, W.H.
Baca, Jimmy Santiago
Baker, David
Bang, Mary Jo
Baraka, Amiri
Barnes, Djuna
Becker, Robin
Bell, Marvin
Benedikt, Michael
Benét, Stephen Vincent
Bennett-Coverly, Louise
Berg, Stephen
Bernard, April
Bernstein, Charles
Berrigan, Ted
Berry, Wendell
Berryman, John
Berssenbrugge, Mei-mei
Bidart, Frank

Bierds, Linda
Birney, Earle
Bishop, Elizabeth
Bishop, John Peale
Blackburn, Paul
Blackmur, R.P.
Blaser, Robin
Bly, Robert
Bogan, Louise
Bök, Christian
Boland, Eavan
Bontemps, Arna
Booth, Philip
Boyle, Kay
Brainard, Joe
Brathwaite, Edward Kamau
Brautigan, Richard
Brock-Broido Lucie
Brodsky, Joseph
Bromige, David
Bronk, William
Brooks, Gwendolyn
Brossard, Nicole
Broumas, Olga
Brown, Sterling A.
Bruchac, Joseph
Buckley, Christopher
Bukowski, Charles
Burkard, Michael
Byer, Kathryn Stripling
Bynner, Witter
Cage, John
Campo, Raphel
Carroll, Jim
Carroll, Paul
Carruth, Hayden
Carson, Anne
Carver, Raymond
Cassity, Turner
Castillo, Ana
Cather, Willa
Ceravolo, Joseph

Cervantes, Lorna Dee
Cha, Theresa Hak Kyung
Chandra, G.S. Sharat
Chappell, Fred
Chin, Marilyn
Chrystos
Ciardi, John
Clampitt, Amy
Clifton, Lucille
Codrescu, Andrei
Cofer, Judith Ortiz
Cole, Henri
Coleman, Wanda
Collier, Michael
Collins, Billy
Coolidge, Clark
Cooper, Jane
Corman, Cid
Corn, Alfred
Corso, Gregory
Cortez, Jayne
Coulette, Henri
Cowdery, Mae Virginia
Crane, Harold Hart
Crapsey, Adelaide
Crase, Douglas
Creeley, Robert
Crews, Judson
Cruz, Victor Hernández
Cullen, Countee
cummings, e.e.
Cunningham, J.V.
Dahlen, Beverly
Davidson, Michael
Davison, Peter
Delgado, Juan
Dennis, Carl
Dent, Tory
Derricotte, Toi
Deutsch, Babette
De Vries, Peter
Dewdney, Christopher

Di Prima, Diane
Dickey, James
Digges, Deborah
DiPalma, Ray
Disch, Tom
Dobyns, Stephen
Donaghy, Michael
Dorn, Edward
Doty, Mark
Dove, Rita
Dragonette, Ree
Drucker, Johanna
Dubie, Norman
DuBois, W.E.B.
Dugan, Alan
Duhamel, Denise
Dumas, Henry Lee
Dunbar-Nelson, Alice
Duncan, Robert
Dunn, Stephen
DuPlessis, Rachel Blau
Dylan, Bob
Eady, Cornelius
Eberhart, Richard
Economou, George
Edson, Russell
Eigner, Larry
Eliot, T.S.
Elmslie, Kenward
Emanuel, Lynn
Enslin, Theodore
Equi, Elaine
Erdrich, Louise
Eshleman, Clayton
Espada, Martín
Evans, Abbie Huston
Evans, Donald
Everson, William (Brother
    Antonious)
Everwine, Peter
Fairchild, B.H.
Fearing, Kenneth
Feldman, Irving
Ferlinghetti, Lawrence
Field, Edward
Finch, Annie
Finkel, Donald
Finkelstein, Norman
Fitzgerald, Robert
Forché, Carolyn

Foster, Edward Halsey
Francis, Robert
Fraser, Kathleen
Friebert, Stuart
Friend, Robert
Frost, Carol
Frost, Robert
Fulton, Alice
Galassi, Jonathon
Gallagher, Tess
Galvin, James
Gander, Forrest
Gardner, Isabella
Garrigue, Jean
Geisel, Theodore (Dr. Seuss)
Gerstler, Amy
Gibran, Kahlil
Gidlow, Elsa
Gilbert, Jack
Gilbert, Sandra
Ginsberg, Allen
Ginsberg, Louis
Gioia, Dana
Giovanni, Nikki
Giovannitti, Arturo
Gizzi, Michael
Gizzi, Peter
Glatt, Lisa
Glück, Louise
Goldbarth, Albert
Goldsmith, Kenneth
Gonzalez, Ray
Goodison, Lorna
Graham, Jorie
Grahn, Judy
Greger, Debora
Gregg, Linda
Gregor, Arthur
Grenier, Robert
Grimké, Angelina Weld
Grossman, Allen
Guest, Barbara
Guest, Edgar A.
Gunn, Thom
Gwynn, R.S.
H.D. (Hilda Doolittle)
Hacker, Marilyn
Hadas, Rachel
Hagedorn, Jessica
Hahn, Kimiko

Haines, John
Hall, Donald
Hamby, Barbara
Harjo, Joy
Harper, Michael S.
Harrison, Jim
Harryman, Carla
Hartman, Charles
Hass, Robert
Hayden, Robert
Heaney, Seamus
Hecht, Anthony
Hejinian, Lynn
Heller, Michael
Herrera, Juan Felipe
Heyen, William
Higgins, Dick
Hilbert, Donna
Hillman, Brenda
Hirsch, Edward
Hirschman, Jack
Hirshfield, Jane
Hoagland, Tony
Hogan, Linda
Hollander, John
Hollo, Anselm
Holman, Bob
Hongo, Garrett
Honig, Edwin
Howard, Richard
Howe, Fanny
Howe, Susan
Hudgins, Andrew
Hughes, Langston
Hugo, Richard
Ignatow, David
Inada, Lawson Fusao
Jackson, Richard
Jacobsen, Josephine
Jarrell, Randall
Jeffers, Robinson
Johnson, Fenton
Johnson, Georgia Douglas
Johnson, Helene
Johnson, James Weldon
Johnson, Ronald
Jones, Rodney
Jordan, June
Joris, Pierre
Joseph, Allison

Joseph, Lawrence
Justice, Donald
Kaufman, Bob
Kees, Weldon
Kelly, Robert
Kennedy, X.J.
Kenyon, Jane
Kerouac, Jack
Kilmer, Alfred Joyce
Kim, Myung Mi
Kinnell, Galway
Kinzie, Mary
Kirby, David
Kiyooka, Roy (Kenzie)
Kizer, Carolyn
Klein-Healy, Eloise
Kleinzahler, August
Klepfisz, Irena
Kloefkorn, William
Knight, Etheridge
Knott, Bill
Koch, Kenneth
Koertge, Ron
Komunyakaa, Yusef
Kooser, Ted
Kostelanetz, Richard
Kowit, Steve
Kramer, Aaron
Kroetsch, Robert
Kumin, Maxine
Kunitz, Stanley
Kyger, Joanne
Lansing, Gerrit
Laughlin, James
Lauterbach, Ann
Laux, Dorianne
Lax, Robert
Lea, Sydney
Lee, Li-Young
Lehman, David
Leib (Brahinsky), Mani
Leithauser, Brad
Levertov, Denise
Levin, Phillis
Levine, Philip
Levis, Larry
Lewis, Janet
Lieberman, Laurence
Lifshin, Lyn
Lindsay, Vachel

Locklin, Gerald
Loden, Rachel
Logan, John
Logan, William
Lorde, Audre
Louis, Adrian C.
Lowell, Amy
Lowell, Robert
Loy, Mina
Lummis, Suzanne
Lux, Thomas
Mac Cormack, Karen
Mac Low, Jackson
Mackey, Nathaniel
MacLeish, Archibald
Major, Clarence
Mariani, Paul
Martin, Charles
Masters, Edgar Lee
Mathews, Harry
Matthews, William
Matthias, John
Maxwell, Glyn
Mayer, Bernadette
McCaffery, Steve
McClatchy, J.D.
McClure, Michael
McGrath, Campbell
McGrath, Thomas
McHugh, Heather
McKay, Claude
McPherson, Sandra
Menashe, Samuel
Meredith, William
Merrill, James
Merton, Thomas
Merwin, W.S.
Messerli, Douglas
Mezey, Robert
Miles, Josephine
Millay, Edna St. Vincent
Miller, Vassar
Mills, Ralph J., Jr.
Miłosz, Czesław
Momaday, N. Scott
Montague, John
Moore, Marianne
Mora, Pat
Morgan, Robert
Morley, Hilda

Moss, Howard
Moss, Stanley
Moss, Thylias
Muldoon, Paul
Mullen, Harryette
Mura, David
Muske-Dukes, Carol
Myles, Eileen
Nash, Ogden
Nelson (Waniek), Marilyn
Nemerov, Howard
Nichol, b(arrie)p(hilip)
Niedecker, Lorine
Nims, John Frederick
Noguchi, Yone
Norse, Harold
North, Charles
Notley, Alice
Nye, Naomi Shihab
Oates, Joyce Carol
O'Hara, Frank
Olds, Sharon
Oliver, Mary
Olson, Charles
Oppen, George
Oppenheimer, Joel
Ortiz, Simon J.
Ostriker, Alicia
Padgett, Ron
Paley, Grace
Palmer, Michael
Pankey, Eric
Parini, Jay
Parker, Dorothy
Pastan, Linda
Patchen, Kenneth
Peacock, Molly
Perelman, Bob
Perillo, Lucia
Phillips, Carl
Phillips, Dennis
Piercy, Marge
Piñero, Miguel
Pinkerton, Helen
Pinsky, Robert
Plath, Sylvia
Plumly, Stanley
Ponsot, Marie
Pound, Ezra Loomis
Pratt, Minnie Bruce

List of Topics

Topical Entries Grouped by Subtopics

American Poetics
Closure
Deep Image
Intentional Fallacy
Line
Linear Fallacy
Objective Correlative
Open Form
Poetic Forms
Prosody and Versification
Sentimentality
Sublime
Symbolism
Variable Foot

Ethnic, Cultural, and Political Influences
African American Poetry
African American Poetry Collectives
African American Slave Songs
Angel Island Poetry
Asian American Poetry
Black Arts Movement
British Poetry
Canadian Poetry
Caribbean Poetry
Chicano Poetry

Chinese Poetry
Corridos
East European Poetry
Feminist Poetics
French Poetry
Gay and Lesbian Poetry
Harlem Renaissance
Hawai'ian Internment Camp Poetry of Japanese American Internees
Irish Poetry
Japanese Poetry
Latin American Poetry
Latino Poetry
Minstrelsy
Modernismo
Native American Poetry
Negritude
Poetry and Politics, including War and Anti-War Poetry
Puerto Rican Poetry
Yiddish Poetry

Genres, Movements, and Schools
Agrarian School (the Agrarians)
Almanac Poetry (Seventeenth-Century)
Beat Poetry
Black Arts Movement

Black Mountain School
Children's Poetry
Concrete Poetry
Confessional Poetry
Corridos
Dada
Devotional Poetry
Digital Poetry
Ecopoetics
Ekphrastic Poetry
Elegy
Epic
Ethnopoetics
Expatriates
Experimental Poetry and the Avant-Garde
Feminist Poetics
Fireside Poets
Fluxus
Free Verse
Fugitives
Genteel Versifiers
Graveyard Poetry
Ideogram
Imagism
Language Poetry
Light Verse
Literary Independence Poem

Preface

Content and Structure

The Greenwood Encyclopedia of American Poets and Poetry is the largest reference work on American poetry ever assembled. Its span extends from the earliest appearance of poetry in what was to become the United States (and to some extent the Americas at large) to poetry at the beginning of the twenty-first century. Within this compass we include more than nine hundred essays, not only on the most recognized names but also on hundreds of others: early poets whose work was significant but little-known at the time, and later poets who, in a world of poetry now unrecognizably expanded, are emerging into prominence, either regionally or nationally.

The reader will also find topical entries on key schools, movements, poetic theories, practices, and terms. Since the *Encyclopedia* is not a dictionary of general literary terms, literary terms are included only if they were coined in the New World, or if they apply to American poetic practice. Thus, the entry on **sublime** will address the American sublime rather than the general concept. Similarly, the reader may assume that an entry on **ekphrastic poetry** or the **long poem**, for example, will principally concern instances and practitioners of these genres or approaches within American poetry. This is also true of entries such as **British poetry**, **Irish poetry**, and the like, which do not address all poetry from Ireland but rather Irish poetry's influence on and relation to American poetry and poetics.

Access

Entries are presented alphabetically regardless of period or type. While this is the simplest and perhaps most convenient arrangement, we also offer a total of five lists of entries that give readers other ways to get their bearings within this large encyclopedia:

1. An alphabetical list of all entries
2. A list of pre–twentieth-century poets
3. A list of twentieth-century poets
4. A list of topics
5. A list of the topics grouped under sub-headings

In this way, readers who may be interested, for example, only in those poets writing before the twentieth century may scan the list of names featured. For readers interested in certain American poetry subjects, the topics list prevents those entries from escaping notice among the hundreds of poet entries, and the reader can thus easily locate information on **Native American poetry**, **negritude**, **New Criticism**, **New Formalism**, the **New York School**, and many more subjects.

Following the A–Z entries in the volumes is a comprehensive bibliography of general sources on American poetry. Each entry in the A–Z section also includes further reading resources.

As further navigational aids, words or names in **boldface** indicate cross-references to guide the reader to related entries, and an index provides extensive access to the encyclopedia's contents.

Scope

A canon becomes a canon by leaving something out. Although copiously inclusive (if not canon-averse), *The Greenwood Encyclopedia of American Poets and Poetry* is nevertheless not "complete." If our inclusions are greater than any reference work on the subject thus far, our exclusions are equally, and inevitably, legion.

The problem is not so much the past, which, precisely because it recedes, appears mappable, but the present, which is vast, vibrant, and uncontainable, perhaps particularly so in America where few constraints remain to limit voices that demand hearing. Even if the editors attempted to represent all of the several thousand living, English-writing poets listed in the current *Directory of American Poets*, the *Encyclopedia* would still not be complete, since many more thousands of poets—hardly mute or inglorious—are writing in little magazines and on the Internet, some of whom will eventually assume prominent places in the landscape of poetry.

As examples of this uncontainability, consider the two categories in our title—"American" and "poetry"—and their tempting but slippery slopes. First, we live in the "Americas," and while even the Anglophone world increasingly understands "America" to mean what José Martí called "Nuestra America"—that is, an entity much larger than the United States—our purpose has been to represent predominantly Anglophone poetry, poetry of the Northern Hemisphere and parts of the Caribbean. While we have also attempted to account for important inter- and intra-American influences in all directions, the *Encyclopedia* is designed for English-speaking readers, who would not expect to find full treatments of Brazilian and Peruvian poets, for example, in an encyclopedia of American poetry.

Constructions of the Americas aren't the only geographical/cultural problem. Most Americans are by definition immigrants, and to understand their writing is to examine their histories and ethnicities. Thus, we have included entries that attempt to account for influences from abroad—for example, **Irish poetry**, **French poetry**, **Chinese poetry**, **Japanese poetry**, and so forth. This too is a nearly limitless slope; our choice was to do some of it as well as we could and leave much undone, or not to do it at all. We chose the former path.

The second category of the title—poetry—is not geographical but literary and generic. What constitutes "poetry"? For an encyclopedia that, initially at least, will appear in print, we should begin by acknowledging a bias toward that medium. The problem is, again, not the past but the present: poets now emerging who present their work principally on sound recordings or who are principally performers, and whose audiences know their work largely through performance, are underrepresented here. Song and performance are not neglected, however, in such entries as **performance poetry**, **jazz**, **minstrelsy**, **slam poetry**, **sound poetry**, **African American slave songs**, and so on. While we may not agree with Whitman that "the singers do not beget, only the Poet begets," with some musical exceptions, our leaning has been toward the enormous tradition of *printed* poetry from America's beginnings to the present time.

The other area that a print bias may only obliquely acknowledge is not sonic but visual: the Internet. If there are tens of thousands writing poetry in print, there may be several times that number writing online. Among poets with a very large Internet presence, one would have to list, among many others, Richard Denner, Luis Garcia, John Oliver Simon, Belle Randall, Paul Hunter, Charles Potts, John Bennett, Mark Halperin, and Joe Powell. These poets, while not represented here, may be Googled readily. (And we do include an entry on **Digital Poetry**.)

A last comment is necessary on the most interesting problem of all: the synchronic leaning of the twenty-first–century world. Our sympathies as writers and editors may tend toward the diachronic, but the culture at large and literature studies in particular, as college class enrollments reveal, show a much greater interest in the present than in the past. The *Encyclopedia*'s imbalance in the number of twentieth-century and contemporary poets represented here vis-à-vis those of earlier periods reflects this interest–existing as much among established scholars as among students—along with several other factors:

The enormous growth in both population and in print technology and distribution over the past century

The pronounced flourishing of poetry following the upheavals of literary modernism early in the twentieth century, and the successive waves of poetry since then, particularly from the 1960s, often extending but sometimes challenging the precepts and practices of modernism

The burgeoning of poetic practice in the United States over the past forty years as a result of poetry workshops at universities across the nation, a situation earlier poets, for good or ill, could not avail themselves of

Because of this "excess" (as William Carlos Williams called poetry), our criteria for inclusion of twentieth-century poets have had to be different from those of earlier periods. Where now tens of thousands of writers publish books, formerly only a handful did. Some of our entries are on early poets who published only a few poems and never a book, a circumstance that seems quaint from today's perspective, suggesting either humility, a different set of priorities, or simply a level of economic and technological constraint difficult to comprehend in our own time.

Acknowledgments

In compiling the *Greenwood Encyclopedia of American Poets and Poetry*, we have often received counsel—from our advisory board but also from many colleagues and contributors, who offered suggestions about inclusions, exclusions, and lengths of entries. While we have not been able to accommodate all such suggestions, many suggested entries *have* been included to the greater benefit of the work as a whole.

Among our contributors are the most distinguished scholars, critics, and poets of the field. We owe thanks to our advisory board, some of whom are also contributors, for their many suggestions and helpful leads over the past couple of years, often connecting the right entry to the right writer. At Greenwood, we are much indebted to George Butler, who got the project off the ground, and to Mariah Gumpert and Anne Thompson for keeping this vast mission on track. For support from Seton Hall University's English Department, we thank former chair Martha Carpentier and secretary Rebecca Warren. We are particularly grateful for the work of our assistants from that department: Jocelyn Dumaresq, Sherry Chung, Peter Donahue, and Caitlin Womersley. We are indebted to our editorial staff, including colleagues such as Jeanne McNett, John Wargacki, and Robert Squillace, who helped in reading and editing entries; and Melissa Fabros, who was indispensable in creating and maintaining the EOAP website. We also wish to thank John A. Balkun, Lei Jun, and Cynthia Williams. There are far too many contributors to thank in this small space but among those who wrote a great many entries, helped critique entries, or matched writers with entries, we must mention Steven Gould Axelrod, Charles Bernstein, Burt Kimmelman, Don Marshall, Marjorie Perloff, Tad Richards, Linda Russo, and John Shields.

Introduction

I dwell in possibility—
A fairer house than prose—

Emily Dickinson

From Beginnings to the Nineteenth Century

Poetry in the New World began centuries before Spanish explorers and English settlers crossed the Atlantic. It began in many indigenous languages and it served variously religious, ceremonial, curative, magical, and commemorative purposes. Many poems that have survived, through oral tradition and later through transcription, are difficult to date, having been composed long before European settlement. Moreover, there is a question whether Western ideas of poetry are applicable to early Amerindian forms, which differed greatly in their performance, their contexts, and their concept of authorship. Perhaps the earliest native poem to appear in English was a Cherokee "war song," coerced into neoclassical style and meters by a Virginian named Henry Timberlake—a poem that, in turn, the English poet Robert Southey borrowed for his epic *Madoc*. Most of the Europeans and their descendants who wrote poetry in the Americas did not investigate these indigenous sources, the famous exception being Longfellow's "The Song of Hiawatha," which was based on legends of the Objibwa and other tribes. European settlers and travelers, even—or particularly—those who took an interest in conserving native cultures, were more interested in narrative. By the eighteenth century numerous Native Americans began to publish in English, but the first Native American to publish a book of poetry in English was the Cherokee John Rollin Ridge (Yellow Bird), whose poems were published posthumously in 1868.

For printed texts in Spanish, poetry began with the publication of Gaspar Pérez de Villagra's *Historia de la Nueva México* in 1610, an epic poem about the violent subjugation of Native Americans, particularly the destruction of the Acoma pueblo of New Mexico. For English texts, poetry in America would seem to begin with Anne Bradstreet's *The Tenth Muse Lately Sprung Up in America* in 1650. However, since Bradstreet's book was printed in London, and Bradstreet herself was, like Edward Taylor, an expatriate, some scholars give the honor of primacy to Philip Pain's *Daily Meditations*, published in Massachusetts in 1666. But little is known of Pain beyond the fact that he was drowned in a shipwreck. Since he too may have been born in England, the title of first *native-born* poet in English then passes to Sarah Whipple Goodhue, whose *The Copy of a Valedictory* (1681), a book of spiritual guidance written for her family, contains only a few verses.

As these uncertainties illustrate, a search for the foundations of American poetry in English—with which the bulk of the present work is concerned—leads to a series of displacements. As the defining condition for most inhabitants of the New World, displacement may also be an apt condition for a poetry that has by turns sought, flouted, and labored to invent tradition. It is a condition that may account—though nothing can fully account—for the strange vicissitudes poetry has passed through in the centuries since these beginnings.

There were no professional poets in colonial times. What poets there were saw themselves as instruments of a muse or of God's will. None devoted the majority of his or her time to authorship. (Michael Wigglesworth and Edward Taylor, as prominent examples, were both

Puritan ministers.) Poets often published anonymously, or they circulated their work in manuscript.

This conception of the role of the poet would change greatly. By the eighteenth century, while religious topics remained popular, the spiritual anxieties of the early colonials were eclipsed by more worldly concerns. The passage of the Stamp Act in 1765, for example, provoked a boom of anti-British ballads. The same period produced America's first published black poet, Jupiter Hammond, whose broadside "Evening Thought" was printed in 1760, and, more famously, Phillis Wheatley, the first African American to publish a *book* of poems. Although Wheatley died young, her work became widely known, particularly in the 1830s when it was reprinted and circulated by abolitionists. The Revolutionary era is more noted for its tracts and nation-building essays than for its poetry, but in addition to Wheatley it produced a number of important poets, including Philip Freneau, "the poet of the revolution" and precursor to the American Romantics.

By the early nineteenth century, in part owing to the states' newly won independence, poets began to see themselves as original voices espousing original views. This generation—of William Cullen Bryant, John Greenleaf Whittier, Oliver Wendell Holmes, Henry Wadsworth Longfellow, and James Russell Lowell—constituted the first coherent U.S. answer to the recurrent (and still familiar) charge that the new nation had no culture. While the neoclassicism of some of these poets continued into the mid-century, the concern for man in nature gained steady ascendancy, particularly in the prodigy William Cullen Bryant, who at age seventeen published his most celebrated poem, "Thanatopsis."

The mid-nineteenth century witnessed what we now know as the "American Renaissance," although the term, supplied by F.O. Mathiessen, is a misnomer since the flowering to which it refers was not a *re*-birth but a birth, one to which earlier literature now seems precursory. The flowering had its most tangible beginnings in Emerson's repudiation of the past in his 1836 essay "Nature" and in his declaration of literary independence in "The American Scholar" the following year. It reached its zenith in the 1850s with the publication of some of the most important books in all American literature—by Melville, Hawthorne, Emerson, Thoreau, Stowe, Whitman, and Douglass. Although the revolution was mostly in prose, many feel that it is only from this period that one can speak of a distinctively American poetry, largely because of the example of Whitman.

Emerson was the philosophical giant of the period, combining the influences of the German idealist philosophers, the Bhagavad-Gita, and the Unitarian belief in the innate goodness of man. He argued for submission to "universal being" and effacement of the personal ego

("I become a transparent eyeball; I am nothing; I see all"). Earlier peoples, he thought, saw "God and Nature face to face." Why shouldn't we? Moreover, given the infinite untapped power within, why shouldn't we shape our own destinies? These were not the sentiments of a Bradstreet or a Wigglesworth.

The runaway industrialization that followed the triumph of the North in the Civil War might seem to have stifled the Emersonian urge to seek one's soul in the pine woods. From a congeries of farms and villages before the war, the United States became, after the war, a nation in which most of the population lived in cities. However, just as in England industrialization incited more than it dampened the turn toward nature, so it did, at least for poets, in the United States. Besides, Emerson had already predicted a poetry that would take up the subject of the nation's growth and expansion—a poetry that dealt not only with Nature but with the vigor and vulgarity of the growing nation: "I ask not for the great, the remote, the romantic," he insisted; "I embrace the common, I explore and sit at the feet of the familiar, the low."

In similar terms, Alexis de Tocqueville foresaw a vigorous American literature, predicting that it would be "fantastic, incorrect, overburdened, and loose, almost always vehement and bold." The object of American authors would be "to stir the passions more than to charm the taste." Most important, and whether he meant it as praise or blame, de Toqueville predicted that the subject of American poetry would not be history—America had none, after all—or even nature, but the *self*.

From their very different perspectives, these two observers, uncannily, predicted the arrival of Walt Whitman. (That Whitman may have *deliberately* set out to fulfill Emerson's prophecy makes the "prediction" less uncanny.) Emerson had written "All objects fall into the subject"; Whitman was the first American poet to develop this claim for a subjectivity that contains the object world. The gesture of "Song of Myself" (the final 1881 title of a variously titled sequence) is an embrace of no less than *everything*. For Whitman, there is nothing outside of the self. (And in another sense, nothing *inside*, since the self is dispersed throughout Nature: "I effuse my flesh in eddies, I drift it in lacy jags.") Whitman assimilates the world; he breathes it, it becomes him, and he breathes it out again. In spite of his reference to the interchangeable atoms of bodies in the first lines of the "Song," the self is not atomic in Whitman; it is a rhythmic process, as are the poems also, "vaguely wafted in the night air, uncaught, unwritten."

The poetics of process that Whitman introduced has remained integral to American poetry. Even the modernists who spurned or ignored Whitman—as many of Whitman's own contemporaries did also—discovered the poem as process and, in Ezra Pound's case, came to terms with Whitman in verse, conceding that "it was [he] that broke the new wood."

Emily Dickinson's language experiments—also deeply influential on later poetry—began around the same time, though, for the most part, her poems did not see the light of day until after her death. Formally, even more than thematically, they took a very different direction than Whitman's. Dickinson's extreme concision and quirky use of traditional forms contrast with Whitman's expansiveness and prolixity. Dickinson's aberrations from form, however, including her odd and slant rhymes, which although puzzling to her few contemporary readers, who thought she was merely making "mistakes," found a receptive public after her death—both immediately after and particularly sixty years after, when her complete poems were finally published in their original versions and when readers who had lived through the modernist era found her elliptical style and paradoxical content much to their liking.

Twentieth-Century Views

The first anthology of American poetry did not appear until 1793, nearly two centuries after English began to be spoken in the New World, with Elihu Smith's *American Poems.* Smith included fifteen poets, of whom only two are read today: Joel Barlow and Philip Freneau. The second anthology of American poetry appeared half a century later, in 1840, and was titled *Gems of American Poetry.* Of the many poets included, only one is known today and not very well known at that: Clement Moore.

The twentieth- and twenty-first century views of the nineteenth century are only slightly less problematic. I have emphasized the importance of Whitman and Dickinson, but for readers in the first half of the twentieth century Longfellow, Whittier, and Poe were the poets to read. Longfellow's poems were particularly loved, as they embodied the Romantic beliefs of the time, particularly the belief—consistent with that of Emerson and Whitman—in the innate nobility of nature and its human and animal denizens. Although few read "The Song of Hiawatha" today, the poem evokes (while it sentimentalizes) Native American landscapes and reveals the tragic price of "taming" the wilderness. Longfellow's metrical ability—more than these sentiments—made him the life-long ideal of Robert Frost. Notwithstanding either of these features, however, the popularity of Longfellow's work dwindled. After World War II, American readers found Whitman and Dickinson more to their taste. It is perhaps not a coincidence that Dickinson's complete poems were not published in their entirety until 1955, and that in 1955 a new edition of *Leaves of Grass* was published, the same year as Randall Jarrell's re-appraisal of Whitman in *Poetry and the Age* and Allen Ginsberg's hallucinatory Whitmanic poem "Howl."

As the somewhat top-heavy contents of this encyclopedia demonstrate, the twentieth century was the American century for poetry. Most obviously, poetic modernism—which, considered as a period of innovation, stretches from 1900 to 1930, but which, as a set of attributes and poetic approaches, extends at least up to World War II, if not to the present—was largely the product of American writers living in the United States and Europe. Modernist practice included an avoidance of abstraction, an abandonment of Victorian conventions of form and sentiment, and a drive to forge a language commensurate to the ruptures that the twentieth-century world was experiencing, particularly during and after World War I. Some modernist techniques—Imagism, logical and rhetorical ellipsis, collage, and intertextual allusion—trained a generation of readers and have, in some measure, characterized U.S. poetry ever since.

Modernism, however—whether that of Ezra Pound and T.S. Eliot, or of Wallace Stevens, Marianne Moore, Gertrude Stein, H.D., and William Carlos Williams—has also been held accountable for the situation of poetry today, which is at once effervescent with its workshops and festivals, websites and slams, and, at the same time, alienated from readers in a way unimaginable a century ago, when ordinary literate people read Kipling, Houseman, and Browning for pleasure, not to mention Keats, Shelley, and Byron. It is sometimes said that the modernists—or the "mad lads," as the English poet Philip Larkin called them—forced, by dint of their difficulty, a split between poetry and public, as Charlie Parker did in jazz or Picasso in painting.

It is true that many readers who were moved by a Masefield or a Houseman poem found little comfort in Stein or Eliot. Yet poetry's ambition to push beyond popular modes was not merely "modern." Emerson's essay "The Poet" suggests the ambition to find a new poetic language, as do Whitman's prefaces to *Leaves of Grass,* Poe's essays on poetics, and Dickinson's letters. In both the nineteenth and the twentieth centuries, under the pressure, which Whitman described, of creating a poetry adequate to a new land and new, proliferating constructions of the self and the world, poetry has been serious and demanding. Melville, Whitman, Dickinson, and Longfellow in the nineteenth century were as conscious as Pound, Moore, Stevens, and Williams in the twentieth that representation, like consciousness, is complex, and that the world is mediated through memory and sensibility as well as through language. Moreover, in both the nineteenth and early twentieth centuries, more than today, American poetry had a large audience that aspired to be "elite," an audience that would willingly sustain the effort required by texts laden with learned allusion and unfamiliar frames of reference. In 1922, after all, *The Waste Land* was a best-seller. Few understood it, but many, if not most, sensed its importance.

Poetry, Process, and the Mid-Century

By the time of the generation that followed the modernists, the poetry of process introduced by Whitman had become the ethos of the time—not only in the Black Mountain poets or the Beat Generation or those poets influenced by ethnopoetics, but also in "mainstream" poetry such as that written by Robert Lowell, Elizabeth Bishop, or Randall Jarrell. Even Robert Frost, whose career extended—as did Eliot's, Pound's, and Williams's—well into that next generation, differs from the Georgian poets with whom he was early associated because of his emphasis on process, notably in the conversational digressions that run through many of his poems.

Matters become cloudy, however, from the 1950s onward and are likely to remain so. Marjorie Perloff has noted that forty years after high modernism it was clear who was important and who not, whereas forty years (at this writing, more than fifty) after the mid-century, no such clarity has emerged. Wildly different views circulate on the question of whose work will prove enduring. And even this criterion, once thought indispensable, is no longer seen as a key question. It is nevertheless possible to make an observation. From the mid- to late 1950s, books such as Robert Lowell's *Life Studies,* the last installment of William Carlos Williams's *Paterson,* Allen Ginsberg's *Howl,* and John Ashbery's *Some Trees* (though the latter was not seen as important until some time later) were suggesting the direction of the ensuing decades. The move would be in two directions, usually but not necessarily complementary. The first, following William Carlos Williams, was a movement toward an open form—an open "field," as Charles Olson called it in 1950; a prizing of spontaneity; the embrace of plain speech; and an urge to tap the unconscious. And the second was an effort to turn Eliot's impersonalism upside down, to explore the personal (again), but to take it further, to write—in the case of the confessional poets—poetry about matters that had never been treated in poetry before: mental instability, institutionalization, marital trauma, surgeries, and suicide, and about private *spaces* that poetry had not previously inhabited, such as kitchens, bedrooms, automobiles (in one famous instance the prowling car of a voyeur, in another that of a pediatrician).

The "tranquilized fifties," as Lowell called them in a poem, were hardly tranquil (though Americans themselves may often have been, as Lowell's word also suggests, sedated). The bloody wars for independence in Algeria, Congo, and Cyprus, and the continued unrest in newly independent Pakistan and India and in newly communist China; the Cuban revolution; the birth of Israel and independent Ireland; CIA interventions in Guatemala and Iran; the boom following World War II and the cultural and economic displacement of the British Empire by the United States; the Korean War; the Cold War and its global repercussions in Southeast Asia and Latin America; the McCarthy hearings in the United States, and the 1954 legislation outlawing school segregation, foreshadowing civil rights struggles of the next decade and more—all of these undermine the image, familiar from the sitcoms of the era, of the pacified suburbs, crew-cut conformists, and the U.S. government's policy of "containment."

By the 1960s and 1970s, cultural and intellectual life in the United States began to change profoundly—not only in the ways visible in newscasts of civil rights marches, the Berkeley protests, Kent State, or Woodstock, but, importantly for literature, with the advent of a perception that had not much occupied the modernists: the idea that it mattered who is writing and who is reading, that there is not a "neutral" writer and reader, that reality is not "out there," and that indeed the poet's (and reader's) history, gender, or race might influence or even determine how a text is read. In other words, the critique of objectivity, which had begun in the sciences early in the century and that had been inherent in the literature, began to filter through to the culture at large.

American Poetry in the World

As viewed from abroad, U.S. poetry had a reputation throughout the twentieth century as somewhat academic, elite, and not politically or socially engaged. This impression was due in large part to the influence of modernism. The United States was, many international readers thought, the land of the novel—of Melville, Faulkner, and Hemingway—not the poem. Given the strong conservative political stances of the key modernist poets, or the progressive politics of many poets of the 1930s and 1950s, this depoliticized view may seem hard to credit. One can nevertheless see how a reader of Pablo Neruda or Ernesto Cardenal or Nazim Hikmet–a reader accustomed to poems that actually address the government, that criticize policies, that speak out for political victims—might have found Eliot's Prufrock or Pound's Mauberly not merely effete (as of course Eliot and Pound intended them to be; these were satires, after all) but beside the point. For Latin America, whose poets remained enamored of Whitman and José Martí, much of modernist poetry fell into the category of what Neruda (thinking of Mallarmé) called the poetry of "closed rooms." The New World was, after all, still open, with rivers and mountains and species still unnamed, and thus not only the impetus of French and Spanish surrealism, but also the Adamic view of the poet as an originary voice infused with a naming power exerted a more profound influence on these poets than did the collage and allusion of Williams or Eliot or the innovative typography of e.e. cummings.

This situation accounts for an interesting reversal in poetry after 1950 in North America, when poets began to turn away from English or even French sources to locate models in Spain and South America; Poland, Italy, Germany, and Russia; and China and Japan. Bly's journal *The Fifties* (later *The Sixties*) introduced Machado, Neruda, Vallejo, and Aleixandre to many who had not read these poets. Cid Corman's journal *Origin* presented Chinese and Japanese texts, ancient and modern. Lowell's *Imitations* published Montale, Ungaretti, and Rilke. Other journals—too numerous to mention—brought Trakl, Golub, Miosz, Herbert, and others.

What many U.S. poets—among them W.S. Merwin, James Wright, Robert Bly, and Galway Kinnell—found in these non-anglophone poets was Whitman coming back toward them, now speaking Spanish, Polish, and Russian. Particularly Spanish: Lorca, Neruda, and Vallejo all wrote odes to Whitman and saw in Whitman's wide vision, catalogues, and cosmic effusion of self a poetics applicable to Third World concerns. The U.S. poets found in the poetry from abroad a freedom of association and a fresh logic of image that seemed to have moved on from its origins in 1930s French surrealism. From García Lorca onward, the poetry began to sprout new dimensions and purposes. It was not random or merely dream-like; it had political and cultural force and could even be mobilized to revolutionary ends (as it was in Vallejo's "Spain, Take This Cup from Me," or Aimé Césaire's *Notebook of a Return to My Native Land.*)

Are North American poets today more politically engaged? Dissent was often palpable in Lowell, Jeffers, Williams, Pound, and has been in many poets since, of very different stamps–Oppen, Reznikoff, Rukeyser, Ginsberg, Sexton, and, of the living (at this writing) Bly, Baraka, Berry, Koumounyakaa, Forché, and many more. Certain anthologies—Carolyn Forché's *Against Forgetting: Twentieth-Century Poetry of Witness* comes to mind first—suggest poetry's return to commitment and to engagement with material struggles in the world, an engagement that many readers had found wanting in earlier U.S. poetry. After all, in spite of all the names mentioned, the poem of private experience, confessional or not, and whether a cause for celebration or regret, has been the dominant genre from the New Critical age to the present.

Poetry and Continuity

The landscape of American poetry is now almost unfathomably varied, and choices such as engagement vs. withdrawal, populist vs. patrician—rhetorical oppositions to begin with—seem of little help. Is there a "continuity of American poetry" as Roy Harvey Pearce thought there was in a book of that title in the 1960s? If there is, it may be different than the one Pearce imagined. Richard Ellman, in his preface to the 1976 *Oxford Book of American Verse*, thought the labels that then-recent poets had adopted—Black Mountain, Projectivist, New York School, Beat—were not likely to survive, but those terms are now common currency. In fact, it is arguable that those groups had in common a Whitmanic mission: to make poetry more *immediate*, fresh, and—for some of them—pre- or supra-rational. They struggled for a poetry that defamiliarizes through discovery, not only in content and form but, as Charles Olson suggested, in the poet's stance toward reality.

Of other groups that have emerged since those that Ellman mentions, one should note the Language-based poets, among whom there is a similar drive to bypass the usual mental channels of composition and to inhibit the accustomed response of writer and reader, not by deranging the senses or even by subjective exploration but more often by anti-subjective, programmatic means—by constraints put upon the writing process. Still, the impulse is recognizable: not to "write what you know," as the writing seminars teach, but to delve into what you do not know, indeed to avoid the known—a "tranquilized" terrain established by repetition if not by coercion.

But to mention Language poets is to mention their purported mirror opposites, the New Formalists, and indeed a plethora of groups and individuals whose poetics may be "subjective" or non- "formal" or non-. Today, in America and in the Americas, whatever the mode, medium, or the topic, someone, somewhere, is writing it. And there is a journal, or more likely several, in which to publish it. This condition of repletion (or, for some, glut) may not augur well for continuity, much less for clarity. But if one inquires after the large Whitmanic ethos—the ethos that values not explaining the world but absorbing and inhabiting it, not resisting contradiction but containing it, not to translate but to be untranslatable—it is more palpable than ever, though we often scarcely recognize it, under our boot soles.

The Greenwood Encyclopedia of
American Poets and Poetry

A

ABBEY, HENRY (1842–1911)

The poetry of Henry Abbey is not well known today. But in an 1898 review of his book *The Poems of Henry Abbey* (1886), a reviewer at the *New York Times* mentions that, as the book was then in its third edition, the poems must be appealing to someone. Perhaps the reason for Abbey's appeal had to do, as the writer suggests, with the comfortable and familiar tone of his poems, and with a broad sympathy expressed in plain speech that "common" men and women could relate to.

Born in Rondout, New York, on July 11, 1842, Henry Abbey went to school at Kingston Academy and the Hudson River Institute. Around 1862 he started work as the assistant editor of the *Rondout Courier*, and he published his first book of poems, *May Dreams*, in the same year. Later Abbey moved to New Jersey, where he was the assistant editor at the *Orange Spectator*. In 1869 he published another collection, *Stories in Verse*, following this book with *Ballads of Good Deeds* in 1872. In 1879 Abbey compiled his first edition of *The Poems of Henry Abbey*, selecting poems from his previous volumes, and in 1884 he published another original collection, *The City of Success and Other Poems*. Abbey died in 1911.

Abbey self-published his compilation *Poems*, a fact that his *New York Times* reviewer notes not with derision but with respect, postulating that any author who could avoid the complicated workings of the publishing indus-try and still enjoy popular success deserves praise. His poems received acclaim from other publications as well, such as the *Boston Courier* and the *New York Herald*. A common feature of the poems is an amiable warmth, a quality one might use to describe a steadfast if unremarkable friend: Even as many reviewers concede that Abbey was no great artistic master, and though his scope and depth are limited, the reviewers largely agree that his level of feeling is great and describe the poems with words such as "simple," "sweet," "earnest," "moralistic," and even "wholesome."

Abbey's forms vary, but he returns to the same themes: moral decisions and the heroes who make good ones, suffering and the insights it can deliver, and the power of good to sway evil minds. "The Drawbridge-Keeper," included in *Ballads of Good Deeds* and published also in *Harper's Weekly*, achieves its moral purpose through a dramatic vignette in six-line rhymed stanzas. Opening the bridge to let a ship through, the drawbridge-keeper Drecker suddenly hears a train coming, and begins to close it again. Then Drecker's little boy, who has been standing beside him, falls into the water. Drecker must decide if he should keep working to close the bridge or jump into the river to aid his "darling boy." Abbey's speaker interrupts the narrative to address the reader: "Which should he do? Were you as he was tried, / Would not your love outweigh all beside?" Abbey's speaker goes on to say that Drecker, "being of great soul and true," continues to do his duty to save the train, while his beloved son drowns. The climax of the action is followed by a two-stanza comment on the nature of nobility, which may be found in the lowliest in society as often as in the highest.

"The Drawbridge-Keeper" reads like a fable in its final moral and its scant detail, but Abbey explores similar issues of morals and egalitarianism in a more complex and rich way in his long narrative poem "Karagwe, an African" (*Stories in Verse*). Divided into two main parts, which are further segmented into numbered sections of variously lined blank-verse stanzas, Abbey deals here with the ravages of slavery on the souls and lives of African Americans. The noble slave Karagwe tries to protect his beloved Ruth from a white neighbor; saves his master's daughter's life; and helps his master, Dalton Earl, regain the land he is cheated out of, even when Earl betrays him. Karagwe's goodness is undisputed, and his floggings are clearly marked as unjust and unproductive—unlike some of the suffering in Abbey's other poems, such as "Ballad of Consolation" (*The City of Success*), in which a woman whose three babies die is shown in a dream that the deaths were meant to spare her the greater suffering of watching the boys grow up to be hanged as criminals. But other characters in "Karagwe," such as Ruth, are given more complexity, as she, perhaps the most exploited and helpless figure in the poem, strikes unforgivingly and stealthily back. The poem ends with a statement similar to that in "The Drawbridge-Keeper," in which the speaker proclaims that he looks not to figures of noble blood for models of moral behavior, but to whoever "rounds a prudent life with noble deeds."

In his lifetime, Abbey's poetry was sometimes labeled "cheerful" for its examples of the triumph of good, as for instance in "Nathan and Mithridanes" (*Ballads of Good Deeds*), which recounts a story from Boccaccio's *Decameron*. Nathan, who has accumulated wealth, decides to give it to the poor. Noting the respect Nathan receives for his deed, Mithridanes decides to do the same but, perceiving that Nathan is still more respected, resolves to kill his rival. On his way to do so, Mithridanes meets up with Nathan, who claims to be his own servant and offers to lead Mithridanes to his victim. Mithridanes confides in Nathan his plan for murder; when they arrive, Nathan reveals himself, and Mithridanes, full of regret, begs for Nathan's forgiveness, which is easily given; "Thus malice passed / And peace had triumphed with open arms."

Abbey's poems, with their simplified situations and often predictable rhymes, nonetheless reveal a great capacity for hope and joy. One of Abbey's somber moments, though, comes in the poem "Faciebat," in which the speaker could be Abbey himself, looking critically at the thinness of his own poems: "For, looking down the ladders of our deeds, / The rounds seem slender." We cannot help, Abbey says, but compare our own best efforts to our grand ideals, "the excellence we would attain."

Further Reading. *Selected Primary Sources:* Abbey, Henry, *Ballads of Good Deeds, and Other Verses* (New York: D. Appleton & Co., 1872); ———, *The City of Success and Other Poems* (New York: D. Appleton & Co., 1884); ———, *The Poems of Henry Abbey* (Kingston, NY: Henry Abbey, 1886); ———, *Stories in Verse* (New York: A.D.F. Randolf & Co., 1869). ***Selected Secondary Sources:*** "Extracts from Some Newspaper Notices," *The City of Success and Other Poems* (New York: D. Appleton & Co., 1884); "New Publications: Two Books of Verse, Father Tabb's and Henry Abbey's" (*New York Times* [4 February 1895]: 3).

Cheri Johnson

ACKERMAN, DIANE (1948–)

Diane Ackerman, perhaps better known now for her creative nonfiction, is an accomplished lyric poet, having won several poetry awards, including the Lavan Poetry Prize in 1985. In 1994 the New York Public Library honored her as a "Literary Lion." Often considered a practitioner of **ecopoetics**, Ackerman also uses conventions of **confessional poetry**, grounded by intense sensory detail and natural metaphors. Her poetry has expanded the boundaries of poetic material in the United States by adding scientific description to nature observation and social commentary. In her prose study *A Natural History of the Senses*, Ackerman maintains that "much of our experience in twentieth-century America is an effort to get away from . . . textures, to fade into a stark, simple, solemn, puritanical, all-business routine that doesn't have anything so unseemly as sensuous zest" (xviii). Her poetry can be conceived as an antidote to American sensory deprivation.

Ackerman was born in 1948 in Waukegan, Illinois, to a family that owned a franchise restaurant. After graduating from local schools, she attended Boston University and received a BA from Pennsylvania State University in 1970. At Cornell University she earned an MFA in 1973 and a Ph.D. in 1979. She taught at the University of Pittsburgh and Washington University before taking a position at the *New Yorker*. In addition to her poetry, Ackerman has published several popular nonfiction books on the natural world, psychology, and human evolution.

Ackerman's early poetry carries two distinguishing traits: an omnivorous intellectual interest and a gift for detailed description. In "Quixote," from *Wife of Light* (1978), the poet boasts, "They spend their lives like dull brass coins, / while I crack open a world or two." The poems address topics ranging from an appreciation of a stallion's prowess to speculation about St. Augustine's response to the theory of relativity. A central theme in this volume is the experience of being a woman, providing meditations on fertility and menstruation, portrayals of sexual pleasure and jealousy, and thoughts about the mental world of George Sand. Her next volume, *Lady Faustus* (1983), solidified her place alongside **Mary Oliver**, **Gary Snyder**, and **James Wright** as a nature poet. The first three sections of the book treat three elements: water, air, and earth, which the poet experiences in scuba diving, piloting an airplane, and working in her garden. These sections move from the wild ocean, through the mediation of mechanical flight, to the controlled environment of the garden, tracing a course from the natural to the constructed environment. The last four sections of the volume continue this progression, moving from scientific experiments and natural history exhibits to the social realm of spectator athletics in poems such as "Patrick Ewing Takes a Foul Shot" and "Soccer at the Meadowlands." Yet the fact of nature never leaves the made environment, and the final poem, addressed to soccer star Franz Beckenbaur, advises us to "scrape culture off being's hot milk" in order to "know a deeper dream."

The title poem of *Lady Faustus* indicates another theme in Ackerman's poetry: the social constraints on women's intellect, as evidenced by the double allusion to Marlowe's *Dr. Faustus* and **Sylvia Plath**'s "Lady Lazarus." The poet is driven by curiosity, "burning with a lidless flame." The speaker longs to travel, study nature, and learn "the fate of us all." Such an intellect in a woman has often been seen as a social threat. Ackerman's dramatic poem *Reverse Thunder* (1988) addresses the intellectual oppression of women through the fictionalized biography of **Sor Juana Inés de la Cruz**, "an extraordinary woman who had the bad fortune to live during an era which demanded that its women be ordinary." Juana Inés de la Cruz lived in Mexico during the second half of the seventeenth century and built an intellectual community in her convent, studying the new science, learning languages, and engaging in theology, until Church pressure put an end to her scholarship. In the play, Juana also has a lover, Giorgio. When she is told that he has died at sea, and when the archbishop imprisons her to purify her of her intellect, Juana wastes away. The dual tragedy that kills Juana displays the connection between the control of women's bodies and the oppression of their minds.

Ackerman's next collections, *Jaguar of Sweet Laughter* (1991) and *I Praise My Destroyer* (1998), continue to explore her principal themes. The earlier volume includes extended observations of Antarctica and the Amazon basin along with a short cycle of love poems, "Tales from a Sonnetarium." Throughout, Ackerman's innovative descriptive metaphor follows **William Carlos Williams**'s guideline "no ideas but in things." A penguin's cry "sounds like an harmonica or an oncoming train"; the call of an Amazonian bird is "part throb, / part Moog synthesizer." *I Praise My Destroyer* picks up the theme of death and the poet's relation to it. The title poem asks, "How can it all end?" The answer, "We Die," determines the book's central philosophical problem.

Origami Bridges (2002), Ackerman's most recent poetic collection, could be considered an episodic **long poem**, in the tradition of **H.D.** or **Ezra Pound**. It follows the poet through a course of psychotherapy, from her early engagement with the therapist's published papers to a poem of farewell, in which she explains she will miss the therapist "because caring and missing / is the way of our kind." The analysand progresses from being afraid to engage "A Tournament of Fears" to being able to list the particular tragedies, large and small, that contribute to her emotional crises. In addition to overcoming fear, the poet integrates aspects of her personality and memories, her "Secret Society of Selves." Variously named "the girls," "the bitches," and "the angels," these personae are united, but the poet cannot say how. For his part, the therapist plays the "you" to whom most of the poems are addressed. However, his persona is sometimes a mask for others, such as the poet's father, his "mind blanked / by death's long train whistle." Ackerman's poems thus detail the various roles both participants in therapy must play. Furthermore, the sequence becomes a *Bildungsgedicht*, a work about the poet's literary development. Lyrics in such poems as "How the Poet Got Her Stripes" tell how a young girl first learns to love writing. The sequence also describes creative self-doubt and the fickle poetic muse, who seems to abandon the poet but "reappears / drunk and demands to be fed." A final unifying device, the cycle of seasons described throughout the work, along with continued vivid, natural imagery, remind the reader that Diane Ackerman, even in philosophy, remains grounded in the sensuous earth.

Further Reading. ***Selected Primary Sources:*** Ackerman, Diane, *I Praise My Destroyer* (New York: Random House, 1998); ———, *Jaguar of Sweet Laughter* (New York: Random House, 1991); ———, *Lady Faustus* (New York: William Morrow, 1983); ———, *Origami Bridges: Poems of Psychoanalysis and Fire* (New York: HarperCollins, 2002); ———, *Reverse Thunder* (New York: Lumen Books, 1988); ———, *Wife of Light* (New York: William Morrow, 1978). ***Selected Secondary Source:*** Ackerman, Diane, *A Natural History of the Senses* (New York: Random House, 1990).

Benjamin Harder

ADAIR, VIRGINIA HAMILTON (1913–2002)

Virginia Hamilton Adair published her first poetry collection, *Ants on the Melon*, in 1996 at age eighty-three.

Beliefs and Blasphemies appeared in 1998 and *Living on Fire* in 2000. Although this may seem a late start, the fact is that throughout the 1930s and 1940s, Adair published in the *Atlantic Monthly*, the *New Republic*, and the *Saturday Review of Literature*; and although she then stopped publishing, she continued to write poetry. Consequently, her three collections reveal a lifetime of poetic creation. **Robert Mezey** writes in the Afterword to *Ants* that Adair believed "that poetry was an intimate and essential part of life and had nothing to do with ambition or celebrity" (152). Adair's significance within an American poetic tradition lies in the intimacy and the dailiness that her poems convey as well as in her use of the personal to capture the awesome.

Adair, born Virginia Hamilton in New York City, grew up in New Jersey. As a student at Mount Holyoke, she competed in the prestigious Katherine Irene Glascock Intercollegiate Poetry Contest, winning twice and placing second once. She graduated from Mount Holyoke in 1933, received an honorary doctoral degree in 1999, and attended Radcliffe for her MA. While at Radcliffe, Adair met and, in 1937, married Douglass Adair, then a Harvard law student and later a noted professor and historian at William and Mary College, where he also served as editor of the *William and Mary Quarterly*. The Adairs spent a decade in Williamsburg, where she raised their three children and occasionally taught literature courses at William and Mary. In 1955 the family moved to Claremont, California, where Adair lived until her death in 2002. She taught for twenty-two years at California Polytechnical University in Pomona. During this time two events occurred that directly relate to Adair's poetry: In 1968 in an upstairs bedroom, her husband shot himself while Virginia cooked in the kitchen, and toward the end of her life, the poet went blind as a result of glaucoma.

However, *Ants*, like *Fire*, extends beyond Adair's personal joys and tragedies as she investigates the processes of loving, experiencing, aging, and dying. For Adair the occasion of the personal initiates a move toward philosophical inquiry into the nature of being and meaning, both of which entail interacting with and understanding the world we inhabit. For instance, "The Dark Hole" opens with three-year-old Douglass III digging on the beach and asking innocent questions about the war (in this case World War II): "'Who won?' / 'We did,' his mother tells him. 'We have the bomb'" (*Fire*, 21). By the end of the poem the speaker laments the inadequacy of language to represent "the confusion of jubilation and horror" that marked Hiroshima and Nagasaki (21). "The Survivors," dated 1945, presents the shattering of belief and certainty in the aftermath of war; and chaos, destruction, and death underpin "Ants on the Melon." In *Beliefs and Blasphemies* Adair develops one theme, religion, through poems that move from childish belief and

certainty to adult questioning. Adair questions, parodies, and challenges Christian myths, and in several poems she presents a Zen-like deism. The poems manifest a range of voices: "Sermon on the Sermon," "Seven Deadly Sins," "Judas," and "Pro Snake" exhibit playfulness and humor; "Communion," "His Mother," and "Veronica" sound blatantly feminist; and "If and What," "Yeshua," "For Yeshua," and "Making Truth" emerge as revisionist, as does "The Genesis Strain" from *Ants*.

Many of the best poems in *Ants on the Melon* and *Living on Fire* address Adair's husband's death and, in the poems of Part IV of *Living*, titled "Mindsight," her blindness. In her profile of Adair for the *New Yorker*, Alice Quinn writes, "Some of her most harrowing poems are love poems written just after the suicide of her husband" (173). The images are indeed harrowing—"a shattered tower," an image "forever across the bed," "eyes turned to glass," "zeros of absence" ("The Ruin," "Exit Amor," "The Year After" from *Ants*; and "The Passage" from *Fire*). These poems contain bewilderment and passion, according to Quinn, and each strives to answer the question "Why?" The question, however, can resonate only in "the unanswering sky" as unrelenting grief strains against the terseness of these love poems.

Through the language of poetry Adair orders her thoughts, confronts her emotions, and makes sense of her world: "I never know what I think until I read it in one of [her] poems" (Quinn, 135). Adair's poems affirm the importance of poetry in the daily life we all lead.

Further Reading. ***Selected Primary Sources:*** Adair, Virginia Hamilton, *Ants on the Melon* (New York: Random House, 1996); ———, *Beliefs and Blasphemies* (New York: Random House, 1998); ———, *Living on Fire* (New York: Random House, 2000). ***Selected Secondary Source:*** Quinn, Alice, "Dancing in the Dark" (*New Yorker* [25 December 1995, 1 January 1996]: 132–138).

Catherine Cucinella

ADAMS, HENRY BROOKS (1838–1918)

Professor, historian, and descendent of presidents, Henry Adams is usually recognized for any of these things before he is remarked upon for his poetry. But Adams published two notable poems—"Buddha and Brahma" and "Prayer to the Virgin of Chartres"—in addition to his prose works, including his autobiography, *The Education of Henry Adams* (1907), *History of the United States of America During the Administrations of Jefferson and Madison* (1889–1891), and others.

After graduating from Harvard in 1858, Adams traveled in Europe. In 1870 he joined the faculty at Harvard, teaching medieval history. He had a happy marriage with Marian Hooper until Marian's father died in 1885; months later, a depressed Marian committed suicide. Adams traveled the world to assuage his grief, and on these travels he found inspiration for his poems. At his various homes in the United States, he surrounded himself with nieces and friends' children. In 1904 Adams published *Mont-Saint-Michel and Chartres*, a presentation of church architecture in the eleventh through thirteenth centuries, and a discussion of the cult of the Virgin. One of his "nieces-in-wish," a young singer named Aileen Tone, took care of him in his last years. He died on March 27, 1918.

Both of his notable poems Adams sent to friends, claiming he had written them only because he was bored. In 1895 he sent John Hay the philosophical "Buddha and Brahma," written while Adams was in Japan. In blank verse, with few rhythmical variations, the poem nonetheless poses challenging ideas. A young Buddhist asks his teacher Siddartha if the world is eternal. Siddartha simply contemplates the flower in his hand. Unsatisfied, the young man seeks out his father, a Brahman. When asked the same question, the older man responds with a twofold answer—"Think not! Strike!"—a response qualified by the acknowledgment that the truest reality lies in thought.

Adams sent Elizabeth Cameron, a married friend, a copy of his other poem, "Prayer to the Virgin of Chartres," published in 1920 by one of his young friends, Mabel La Farge. The poem, Adams says, will not interest Cameron at all, and she should throw it in the fire. But the "Prayer" is often considered to have more artistic merit than "Buddha and Brahma"; its meter is also iambic pentameter, but with more variation, including skillful use of the enjambed line and the caesura. The poem is written in rhymed quatrains and shares subject matter with *Mont-Saint-Michel*. Throughout his life, Adams respected women's qualities over men's. In his "Prayer," Adams extols the loving virtues of the female divine figure over the indifference of a male god. In the interjected stanzas that make up "Prayer to the Dynamo," the poem's speaker "worships" the male divinity in brutal clipped language: "Seize, then, the Atom! rack his joints!" The speaker regrets the time spent with this god, and marks his return to the Virgin with pleas to help him live a better life: "Help me to see!"

Further Reading. *Selected Primary Sources:* Adams, Henry, "Buddha and Brahma" (*Yale Review* V [November 1915]: 82–89); ———, *Henry Adams and His Friends, a Collection of His Unpublished Letters*, ed. Harold Dean Carter (Boston: Houghton Mifflin Co., 1947); ———, *Letters to a Niece and Prayer to the Virgin of Chartres*, with "A Niece's Memories," by Mabel La Farge (Boston: Houghton Mifflin Co., 1920). ***Selected Secondary Sources:*** Byrnes, Joseph F., *The Virgin of Chartres, An Intellectual and Psychological History of The Work of Henry Adams* (East Brunswick, NJ: Associated University Presses, Ltd.,

1981); Hume, Robert A., *Runaway Star: An Appreciation of Henry Adams* (Ithaca, NY: Cornell University Press, 1951); Levenson, J.C., *The Mind and Art of Henry Adams* (Cambridge, MA: Riverside Press, 1957).

Cheri Johnson

ADAMS, JOHN (1704/5–1740)

One of the first American poets to exhibit the influence of the British neoclassicists (Richard Blackmore, John Dryden, Alexander Pope), John Adams was also an essayist and minister. In addition to having a hand in the reconfiguration of the Puritan Congregational Church, Adams was the first American translator to publish a Bible verse in an American periodical. He knew several languages, and much of his published work consists of translations. His other works include a metrical version of the Book of Revelation.

Sources disagree on the exact date and place of Adams's birth, but he was baptized on March 26 in Boston and was most likely born there, although he probably spent much of his childhood in Nova Scotia. In 1717 Adams returned to the United States to attend Harvard, and in 1726 he published for the first time a translation of a Horatian ode in the *New England Courant*. In the following two years he joined **Mather Byles**, as well as his uncle, Matthew Adams, in writing essays and poems for a series called "Proteus Echo" in Samuel Kneeland's *New England Weekly Journal*. The series was disbanded, at least partly so that Byles and Adams could continue their work in the ministry, and in 1727 Adams moved to Rhode Island to assist the minister at a troubled Congregational Church congregation. There he was ordained in 1728. He stayed until 1730, when he was dismissed for reasons that are not entirely clear. It is known that in the rift that took place in the Puritan church at this point in American history, Adams called for new, more liberal ideas, particularly concerning who would be allowed to take Holy Communion. After leaving Rhode Island, Adams spent four years at Harvard, probably pursuing his master's degree or tutoring. On January 23, 1740, after suffering a period of delirium, Adams died in Boston at the age of 34.

Adams published many poems in periodicals during his lifetime, and after his death most of these were collected into *Poems on Several Occasions* (1745), a volume for which his uncle Matthew wrote an effusive introduction. Little critical study has been applied to the analysis of Adams's works, and the appraisals of his artistry and talent that do exist are often lukewarm. However, Adams is a notable figure in that his work marks a break from the models of early American poetry such as that of **Anne Bradstreet**, who was influenced primarily by religious poets. Although religion is often Adams's subject, his mining of forms and sounds found in satirical writers such as Pope opened up new directions for American poetry. *Poems on Several Occasions* is arranged in five sections and includes Adams's Revelation translation and other biblical translations, six translations of Horatian odes, and more secular poems concerning sadness, joy, and comments on society. Many of the poems differ from the versions originally published in newspapers, which has led to speculation on the nature and extent of their editorship; but Adams's authorship of the poems is not widely questioned. Adams shares with his contemporary **Cotton Mather** the idea that a poet's ultimate inspiration is God, and he addresses the respective values of poetry and religion in poems such as "An Address to The Supreme Being, For His Assistance in My Poetical Compositions." In rhymed couplets of iambic pentameter, almost certainly a nod to Pope, Adams makes it quite clear that while he wholeheartedly believes poetry is important, that importance lies mostly in its ability to praise or clarify religion: "Thro' all my Works, let Order clearly shine."

Adams also addressed secular subjects, as in his *Proteus Echo* contributions. "Proteus Echo" was the persona of an educated and well-traveled old bachelor, settling down into his retirement and remarking on his thoughts and surroundings. In the first essays of the series, Mather Byles, in the voice of this persona, introduces the other members of the old man's "club" in a manner found in other contemporary periodicals of the time, such as the *Tatler.* Signing only with cryptic initials, Adams pens essays and exuberant verse in the guise of old Proteus. In his poems written upon the deaths of friends and their loved ones, Adams expresses his most genuine emotion, as in "A Consolatory Letter to a Near Relative on the Death of His Consort, July 2, 1973," probably written for his uncle Matthew upon the death of his wife, and in a poem for his father, in which Adams regrets the older man's blindness but envisions his sightedness in heaven.

Further Reading. *Selected Primary Sources:* Adams, John, *Poems on Several Occasions, Original and Translated* (Boston: [by Rogers and Fowle] for D. Gookin, 1745); Adams, John, Matthew Adams, and Mather Byles, *Proteus Echo*, 1927–1928, ed. Bruce Granger (Delmar, NY: Scholars' Facsimiles & Reprints, 1986). ***Selected Secondary Source:*** Franklin, Benjamin V., *The Other John Adams, 1705–1740* (Cranbury, NJ: Associated University Presses, 2003).

Cheri Johnson

ADAMS, JOHN QUINCY (1767–1848)

At the age of fifty-three, the man who would become the sixth president of the United States wrote with regret in his diary that he had made a living by practicing law, and pursued public office because he felt it was his duty to do so, but that if he could have, he would have devoted his life to literature. This diary, which he began at the age of eighteen and continued steadily throughout his life, attests to Adams's dedication to the written word, as does a volume of poems, *Poems of Religion and Society* (1850); a 7,300-line translation of Christopher Wieland's *Oberon, a Poetical Romance* (1940), a historical epic in verse; and Adams's nickname, "Old Man Eloquent."

Adams was born on July 11, 1767, in Braintree, Massachusetts (now called Quincy). His father, John Adams, was to become the second president of the United States in 1796. At the age of eleven, the young Adams accompanied his father to France, where he studied the language. He became secretary to the Minister of Russia at the age of fourteen. In 1787 he graduated from Harvard, and his graduation address was printed in *Columbia Magazine.* He began to practice law in 1790, and four years later he was nominated by George Washington, impressed with the published articles of Adams, as Minister to the Dutch Republic. In 1797 Adams married Louisa Catherine Johnson and traveled with her to Prussia to serve as Minister Plenipotentiary; it was during his stay here that Adams learned German and then completed his massive translation of Wieland's *Oberon.* In 1802 Adams became a Massachusetts state senator, and in 1816 he was sworn in as James Madison's secretary of state. In 1825 Adams became president, serving one term. He was involved in such issues as treaties with the Creek Indians of Georgia and the Panama Congress. In 1831 Adams was elected to the House of Representatives, where he served for the rest of his life. In the same year Adams wrote his epic *Dermot MacMorrogh or The Conquest of Ireland.* On February 21, 1848, at the age of 81, Adams collapsed in his House seat and died two days later, survived by his wife and one of his three sons.

Adams published many articles on politics and history, but he considered *Dermot MacMorrogh* his greatest literary achievement. Two thousand lines long and written in two months, the work met with a difficult reception, due at least partially to Adams's politics. His unwavering stance on the right to free speech and his opposition to the "Gag Rule," a policy designed to squelch the anti-slavery movement, earned him bitter opponents.

Adams spent two years translating and revising *Oberon,* which consists of twelve sections or "books." It is written, like the original version, in octaves, but Adams imposed a stricter rhyme scheme than Wieland's. Adams did not publish his translation, however; as he was finishing it, he discovered that an Englishman, William Sotheby, had already published one, and Adams admired Sotheby's version enough to file his own away. Adams's *Oberon,* which begins with a religious pilgrimage, also includes elements of violence, love, and magic, and often takes on a dramatic, excitable tone, particularly in its impassioned addresses: "Save, save them, O thou faithful squire!—in vain— / Their madness hears not e'en the thunder roll!"

Adams's shorter poems are often passionate as well, but they reveal a spirit of quiet contemplation that must have pervaded Adams's busy public life. In one of his best-known poems, the apostrophic sonnet "To the Sun-Dial, Under the Window of the Hall of the House of Representatives of the United States," Adams speaks of the dial's "warning voice." The dial, Adams says, reminds him and others to live each moment as well as possible, even as that moment passes away.

Written in the alternating rhyme style of his version of *Oberon*, another of Adams's better-known poems, "The Wants of Man," begins with a quote from a song: "Man wants but little here below, / Nor wants that little long." Adams's speaker politely disagrees, then commences with a sweetly tongue-in-cheek and exhaustive list of his desires, rolling out each item with rich detail and in a pleasant singsong style, like the wish list of an eager, eloquent child. Adams uses comfortable rhythms and rhymes, in addition to alliteration, and moves from listing material pleasures like "Black sable furs, for winter's frost" to such gifts as an affectionate wife and singing daughters, to a sharp eye and praise from the world, ending with the desire not to forget God amidst all of it.

Further Reading. *Selected Primary Sources:* Adams, John Quincy, *Oberon, A Poetical Romance in Twelve Books, Translated From the German of Christopher Wieland (1799–1801)* (New York: F.S. Crofts & Co., 1940); ———, *Poems of Religion and Society* (New York: Auburn, Derby and Miller, 1850). ***Selected Secondary Sources:*** Clark, Bennett Champ, *John Quincy Adams, "Old Man Eloquent"* (Boston: Little, Brown, and Co., 1932); Jones, Kenneth, *John Quincy Adams: 1767–1858* (New York: Oceana Publications, Inc., 1970).

Cheri Johnson

ADAMS, LÉONIE (1899–1988)

Léonie Adams was a unique American synthesizer of the Metaphysical, Elizabethan, and French symbolist poetic traditions. Adams, like **John Crowe Ransom**, favored Metaphysical poets such as John Donne and George Herbert and embraced the virtues of irony and complexity. Faithful to traditional prosodic techniques of meter, stanza, and rhyme, she dwelt on the classic poetic themes of love, mortality, and beauty. Her tense, meditative nature lyrics brought her the attention of **Allen Tate** and **Louis Untermeyer**, who became committed advocates of her work. By mid-century, she was considered one of America's great lyric poets, along with **Edna St. Vincent Millay**, **Elinor Wylie**, and close friend **Louise Bogan**. Adams achieved her greatest fame early in her career, publishing work sparingly after 1933, but her compact oeuvre offers readers a dreamlike elegance bolstered by meticulous craft.

Born in Brooklyn, New York, on December 9, 1899, Léonie Fuller Adams was the fifth of Charles Frederic and Henrietta Rozier Adams's six children. The well-established Adams family provided their daughter with a comfortable, if sheltered and restricted, upbringing. She was forbidden to ride the New York subways until her matriculation at Barnard College necessitated the commute, and still her lawyer-father usually escorted the eighteen-year-old Adams to her classes. While at Barnard, Adams began exercising her poetic aspirations in secret, and she made her debut appearance in the *New Republic* with "April Mortality" in 1921. The following year she graduated with an AB and magna cum laude honors. After graduation, Adams held editorial positions at Wilson Publishing Company and the Metropolitan Museum of Art. Adams continued to write, publishing *Those Not Elect* in 1926.

In this first collection, Adams deploys a learned wit and deft irony alongside solemn drama in the subjective dialogue "Death and the Lady." The poem, recalling Mary Elizabeth Coleridge's poem of the same name, features a lady who, after spurning Death to savor her youth and "lively breath," is now at her own twilight petitioning Death's favor. Death, himself fickle, retorts, "Beauties I claim at morning-prime / . . . the lackluster in good time." Allen Tate's review in the *Nation* aptly outlines Adams's muses: "Her sensibility, metaphysical in Johnson's sense, has isolated a world somewhere between eighteenth-century decoration and the fresh intensity of a lyric by Thomas Heywood or Greene. . . . There are perhaps five poems in this book of almost ultimate perfection" ("Distinguished Minor Poetry" [3 March 1926]: 237–238). The strength of *Those Not Elect* propelled Adams to become one of the first poets to receive the Guggenheim Award in 1928, which allowed her to craft the pieces for her next volume, *High Falcon & Other Poems* (1929), in Paris. *High Falcon* sees some of Adams's most consistent successes and reveals her affinity with the later Yeats. Here Adams further tunes her lyrical prowess while mining her favorite grounds, human evanescence and the rural autumn landscape, in sonnets such as "Twilight of the Wood."

In 1933 Adams married critic and essayist William E. Troy and produced *This Measure* (1933) as a single-poem chapbook illustrated by George Plank. She would not publish another major collection for almost twenty years, as she struggled to find the new direction that she felt poetry had to take. Endorsed by a loyal coterie of poets, Adams remained highly esteemed despite her lengthy silence, and she became an established presence in American poetry anthologies as one of the finest twentieth-century American women poets. Adams succeeded Robert Lowell in the position of U.S. Poet Laureate in 1948, when the appointment was titled "Consultant in Poetry to the Library of Congress." During her tenure, Adams composed her final volume, *Poems: A Selection* (1954).

Appearing nineteen years after *This Measure*, *Poems: A Selection* won Yale University's Bollingen Prize in poetry along with Louise Bogan's *Collected Poems, 1923–1953* (1954). Poems such as "Goodbye Those Children" demonstrate Adams's finely honed acuity and sensitivity as she memorializes a child's starfish memento, "Singular, crusted with itself, as when / Its thorns curled shrinking from the wondering touch." The volume resonates with such moments of poignant quietude, and Kenneth Rexroth considered the collection "something like some early Pre-Raphaelite verse, but it is most, in my opinion, like Muslim poetry" (quoted in Bower, 25).

Adams retreated from the poetry scene but remained active as a university English teacher and lecturer, serving at Columbia University for nearly twenty years until 1968. For her last publishing venture, Adams compiled her late husband's essays for editor Stanley Edgar Hyman's *William Troy: Selected Essays*, which received the 1968 National Book Award in Arts and Letters. Contemporary readers may find her poems difficult and her highly stylized diction emotionally distant. Nevertheless, Bruce Bawer touts Adams's catholicity: "The remarkable thing, in any event, is not that Adams learned from so many teachers, but that she was able to borrow in a highly specific way from each of them, and to create thereby a kind of verse that was very much her own" (25). Though her work is well remembered, if largely unread, the refined discipline and sensitive craft of Adams's lyrics make them a rich and uncharted mine.

Further Reading. *Selected Primary Sources:* Adams, Léonie, *High Falcon & Other Poems* (New York: John Day, 1929); ———, *The Measure* (New York: Knopf, 1933); ———, *Poems: A Selection* (New York: Funk & Wagnalls, 1954); ———, *Those Not Elect* (New York: McBride, 1925). ***Selected Secondary Sources:*** Bawer, Bruce, "Léonie Adams, Poet" (*New Criterion* 7.2 [October 1988]: 21–26); Bonacci, Bette Bradford, "Image and Idea in the Poetry of Léonie Adams," Ph.D. diss., University of Michigan, Ann Arbor; abstract in *Dissertation Abstracts International* 38 [1978]: 4813A–4814A; Fowlie, Wallace, "Remembering Léonie Adams" (*New Criterion* 7.2 [October 1988]: 16–20); Redd, Tony, "Léonie Adams," in *Dictionary of Literary Biography: American Poets, 1880–1945* (Detroit: Gale Research Co., 1986)

Melissa Gabot Fabros

ADDONIZIO, KIM (1954–)

Though Kim Addonizio is often categorized as a **confessional poet**, her work, even when it draws on her individual experiences, transcends the personal to look, often longingly, at the broader reaches of human existence. Known for her charged performances of her own work, Addonizio's poetry is both accessible and direct and recalls the oral tradition of storytelling. Her poetry betrays her obsessions with writing about love, suffering, and death, and her poems recall **Sharon Olds** in their particularizing of these obsessions in terms of gender.

Born in 1954 in Washington, D.C., Kim Addonizio was raised in Bethesda, Maryland, and was educated at San Francisco State University, where she received both her BA and MA. A second-generation Italian American who describes herself as an "ex-Catholic," Addonizio has been married and divorced twice, and has one daughter, Aya. She currently lives in Oakland, California, where she teaches writing in private lessons and maintains an online journal focused primarily on her writing process.

Addonizio's first full-length collection of poetry, *The Philosopher's Club* (1994), is an early example of the themes to which she repeatedly returns in her later works. In quiet reflections on mortality and love, such as "The Last Poem about the Dead" and "What the Dead Fear," Addonizio continues the elegies and eroticism displayed in the fifteen poems included in her section of *Three West Coast Women* (1987), which also contains work by Laurie Duesing and **Dorianne Laux**. Although containing many **free-verse** poems, *The Philosopher's Club* shows experimentation with **poetic forms**, particularly the sonnet, a practice that all but disappears in her later collections, only to reappear in her most recent work.

Addonizio describes her second collection, *Jimmy & Rita* (1997), as a verse novel. It tells the story of the doomed relationship between the title characters as they deal with alcohol and heroin abuse and attempt to support themselves through prostitution, theft, and drug dealing. More so than in her previous collections, the poems here demonstrate an oral dimension, as the narrative is revealed through a series of dramatic monologues in the voices of the main characters, interspersed with poems spoken by an omniscient narrator.

Tell Me (2000), a finalist for the National Book Award, continues the concerns of Addonizio's earlier collections, focusing primarily on relationships, love, and intimacy. As in her other books, she draws on personal experience to find some common human ground in poems such as "Generations," about her search for her heritage, in which she reaches beyond her individual search to a more universal hunger to know one's roots. Addonizio's fine sense of metaphor is on display in many of these poems, particularly "The Body in Extremis," in which the body of a dying loved one is rendered first as a factory and then as a vase of flowers, with the final admission that metaphor itself is too flimsy to bear the weight of that particular grief. Addonizio's long-lined pieces, bordering on **prose poems**, often quietly build to a crescendo as she writes candidly of the conflicted pleasure and loneliness of bars and one-night stands.

In her most recent collection, *What Is This Thing Called Love* (2004), while Addonizio remains enamored with love itself, she is also pragmatic about its transience; in her poems, love is "a side trip. / It wasn't love for eternity, or any such crap." Like **Anne Sexton**'s *Love Poems*, Addonizio's most recent collection employs eroticism and an accessible voice to turn an unflinching eye on the disappointments of love, the pleasures of sex, and the pain of mourning. Although she returns to forms previously employed in *The Philosopher's Club*, such as the sonnet and the pantoum, *What Is This Thing Called Love* adds still others, including the sonnenizio, **Billy Collins**'s paradelle, and the **blues**.

In addition to her poetry, Addonizio is well known for her writing *about* poetry. *The Poet's Companion: A Guide to the Pleasures of Writing Poetry* (1997), which Addonizio co-authored with Dorianne Laux, focuses on the craft and process of writing poetry and includes thematically arranged writing exercises and examples from numerous contemporary poets. Cast in a conversational tone, the handbook includes pragmatic information about how to send poetry to **literary magazines** and how to cope with rejection, as well as lessons on "Meter, Rhyme, and Form" and "Voice and Style."

Although Addonizio began writing as a poet and remains primarily committed to poetry, she has also written fiction intermittently for nearly as long and has published one collection of stories, *In the Box Called Pleasure* (1999), and a novel, *Dirty Beautiful* (2005), about two California women and the child one of them is about to have. Like her early short fiction in *Crimes of Passion* (1984), Addonizio's recent fiction is driven more by voice than by plot. Like *Jimmy & Rita*, *In the Box Called Pleasure* explores characters on the edge of losing all they have, and like much of her poetry, her stories investigate sex, although their approach is more clinical than erotic.

Addonizio is at work on another collection of stories.

Further Reading. *Selected Primary Sources:* Addonizio, Kim, *Crimes of Passion* (Berkeley, CA: exempli gratia, 1984); *Dirty Beautiful* (New York: Simon & Schuster, 2005); ———, *In the Box Called Pleasure* (Normal, IL: FC2, 1999); ———, *Jimmy & Rita* (Rochester, NY: BOA Editions, 1997); ———, *The Philosopher's Club* (Rochester, NY: BOA Editions, 1994); ———, *Tell Me* (Rochester, NY: BOA Editions, 2000); ———, *What Is This Thing Called Love* (New York: W.W. Norton & Co., 2004); Addonizio, Kim, and Dorianne Laux, *The Poet's Companion: A Guide to the Pleasures of Writing Poetry* (New York: W.W. Norton & Co., 1997); Addonizio, Kim, Laurie Duesing, and Dorianne Laux, *Three West Coast Women* (San Francisco: Five Fingers Poetry, 1987). *Selected Secondary Sources:* Shoaf, Diann Blakely,

Review of *Jimmy & Rita* (*Ploughshares* 23.1 [Spring 1997]: 212–214); Ullman, Leslie, Review of *Tell Me* (*Poetry* 179.4 [January 2002]: 234–238); Van Cleave, Ryan G., "Kim Addonizio: A Poet with Duende" (*Iowa Review* 32.3 [Winter 2002–2003]: 122–128).

Jennifer Perrine

AFRICAN AMERICAN POETRY

African American poetry has a long history. **Phillis Wheatley**, an African-born household slave in Boston, was only the second woman of any race from the original thirteen colonies to publish a volume of verse when her first book appeared in 1774. She famously took on the Enlightenment notion that Africans were the polar opposite of moral beings. One of the chief points that such late Enlightenment figures as Hegel, Hume, and Jefferson made to support this claim is that Africans did not produce "high" art. In much the same way that African American slavery negatively defined freedom for white Europeans and North Americans, a supposed black cultural illiteracy delineated a white transnational literacy. Simply by writing skillful poems inflected by Milton and British neoclassicism, Wheatley caused an uproar that is hard to imagine now.

Wheatley's combination of neoclassicism, Protestantism, and proto-republican rhetoric gave her writing an American cast quite unlike the poetry of her literary models. While what is now her best-known work, "On Being Brought from Africa to America," represents her kidnapping as a "mercy" (before going on to make a plea for the recognition of "Negro" humanity), "To the Right Honourable W I L L I A M, Earl of DARTMOUTH" invokes the metaphors of tyranny and slavery favored by Jefferson and other North American partisans in a far different manner. Wheatley asserts that she understands the issues at stake in the struggle between the crown and colonists not in spite of her status as black female slave born in Africa, but because of that status. She also makes the logical but still radical claim that as someone kidnapped and sold into bondage far from home and family, she profoundly understands unreasonable tyranny and unjust slavery. Her poem suggests that the enslaved Africans and their descendants are the most American of Americans. At the same time, this radical democratic claim rests on a notion that African Americans have a distinct history and a psychology stemming from that history. Her poetry, with its formal and thematic engagement with race, universalism, and nation, set an agenda with which those who followed would grapple.

In the nineteenth century the increasing number and circulation of such abolitionist publications as the *Liberator* and the *North Star* and the emergence of a sympathetic popular press in the Northeast offered platforms for occasional verse by African American poets. These poems were generally polemical or topical, written in hymn meter and ballad- or hymn-like quatrains or stanzas of iambic couplets, engaging secular and sacred song, and street rhyme. They dealt with such topics as slavery, the Fugitive Slave Act, and the heroism and sacrifice of the black Civil War soldiers. At the same time, like those of Wheatley, they mixed a grassroots American rhetoric, an African American consciousness, and an attempted high literary syntactical tour de force. The slave poet of North Carolina **George Moses Horton**, for example, combined popular metrical forms and rhyme patterns, particularly those of the hymn and ballad; quatrains of rhyming couplets; and a studiously literary diction. Horton wrote powerful antislavery pieces, with the poet himself cast as a Romantic hero straining Prometheus-like against authority. However, his struggles are not against the gods or human limitations in general but against the slave system.

At the same time that such lyrics appeared in the press, an African American tradition of the **epic** developed in response to the "mainstream" notion that the production of the epic was a fundamental test of the spirit of a people. One can see George Vashon's 1854 epic of the Haitian Revolution, "Vincent Ogé," and, later, Albery Whitman's 1884 book-length *The Rape of Florida* as at least implicitly nationalist, promoting a sense of black nationhood as well as establishing African Americans as moral beings deserving of citizenship. Such poems established the epic as an important form in African American literature, anticipating later long poems and poetic sequences that attempted to sound a distinct African American voice.

Such a sounding was complicated by the nineteenth-century saturation of American popular culture with problematic versions of African American's folkore. The blackface **minstrel** show, born in New York City during the early part of the nineteenth century and featuring stock characters and stock routines, became a national phenomenon, inflecting even the most sympathetic literary re-creations of African Americans and their culture. It was soon joined by a form of popular literature that has sometimes been called plantation literature, arising largely as a response to *Uncle Tom's Cabin*. This literature typically featured contented slaves fanatically devoted to "Marse" and "Mistress" on plantations portrayed as a romantic feudal alternative to the harshness and dislocations of modern urban life. Versions of plantation fiction remained popular after the Civil War and, indeed, gained a new popularity in the Reconstruction and post-Reconstruction eras. The problem, then, was not that African Americans were marginal to high and popular culture in the United States but that, by the late nineteenth century, stylized versions of their bodies, voices, speech, music, dance, stories, and fashion were everywhere. African American artists and intellectuals generally found these stylizations to be degrading, endlessly recycling images of African Americans as, by turn, stupid, docile, servile, brutish, outlandishly pretentious, cowardly, thieving, and lazy.

At the same time, this era saw the birth of the **blues**, ragtime, and **jazz**, forms that would enter American popular music over the next couple of decades. These genres of music, and their consumption by non–African American audiences, had an uneasy relationship with earlier forms of minstrelsy. Nonetheless, part of the myth of much jazz and blues performance was a notion of black secular authenticity, of seeing beneath or taking off the mask.

In other words, the position of African Americans relative to the body politic of the United States was as intimate strangers and that of African American expressive culture relative to "mainstream culture" was as intimate strangeness, a strangeness of masking and unmasking that paradoxically was at the root of popular culture. These paradoxical positions intensified after the end of the Civil War with the rise and fall of Reconstruction, when both black and white Americans perceived that a great challenge facing the postbellum United States was how the South and the great mass of freedmen and freedwomen would be integrated into the nation. The discussion of this challenge turned on the familiar question of the capacity of African Americans for true citizenship. Socially engaged black writers confronted the difficult contradiction of helping to move the former slaves toward political, economic, and cultural participation while promoting the group solidarity that the defense of full black citizenship entailed.

Frances Ellen Watkins Harper was among the most important of these writers. Much of her early abolitionist poetry drew on the rhetoric and tropes of sentimental literature and millenarian Protestantism, mixing jeremiad with True Womanhood. She sold tens of thousands of volumes of her poetry, largely on intersecting abolitionist, temperance, feminist, and civil rights lecture circuits. She was also among the first black poets to consider how one might draw directly on the resources of African American vernacular speech and culture in work aimed significantly, if not primarily, at a black audience without seeming to collaborate with minstrel or plantation stereotypes. During Reconstruction, Harper wrote a series of poems intended for use in black literacy classes. The idea was to provide poems that when read aloud sounded more like the speech of the students, providing them with what might be thought of as halfway texts, more familiar and less daunting than so-called standard literature. Harper did not literally try to re-create folk speech on the page. She also avoided most of the emerging conventions of "dialect literature." Instead, Harper employed a "standard" orthography, drawing occasionally on the rhythms, syntax, and diction of black vernacular speech to create a distinctly African American poetry rooted in the culture of the black folk and aimed at a black audience while avoiding identification with minstrelsy and plantation literature.

The ascent of the poet **Paul Laurence Dunbar** into literary prominence as the first truly professional black poet came as the remnants of the hopes and promises of Reconstruction were wiped out in the 1890s, despite the fact that the Thirteenth, Fourteenth, and Fifteenth Amendments remained part of the Constitution. The infamous 1896 *Plessy v. Ferguson* and 1898 *Williams v. Mississippi* Supreme Court decisions legitimated a legal, political, and cultural dualism in which African Americans were Americans and not Americans, citizens and not citizens, humans and yet not full humans. Dunbar's influence remained strong well into the twentieth century not merely because of his professional success, but because of the representation of this dualism in his poetry. Dunbar's version of dualism is expressed as a split between surface and core, between the grinning face and the concealed heart, most famously in "We Wear the Mask" (*The Collected Poetry of Paul Laurence Dunbar*, 1993):

We wear the mask that grins and lies,
It hides our cheeks and shades our eyes,—

This poem offers a strategy for dealing with problems of expressing an African American subjectivity in a time when distorted and demeaning versions of the black subject were everywhere present in American high and popular cultures. The proposal of a split between mask and authentic self allowed Dunbar to depict the moment of Jim Crow, both registering a protest and providing a defense against the contamination of minstrelsy in his vernacular work. In this scheme, the high poems and dialect poems existed in symbiotic relationship. In such poems as "We Wear the Mask" and "Sympathy" (with its famous line "I know why the caged bird sings"), Dunbar assumed a neo-Romantic stance, staking a claim to true literacy and true artistry while figuring the aesthetic, political, and existential limits of the Jim Crow era for African Americans by suggesting that these poems are his "real" work that nobody is willing to see. The dialect poems serve as an exhibit of the defensive masking and restrictions forced on the poet by Jim Crow—restrictions that are enforced as much by friendly but patronizing critics and the reading public as by laws and vigilante violence.

At the same time, what the high poetry reveals about the self behind the mask or the apparently happy bird within the cage suggests that another interpretation of the dialect poems is possible. In some of these poems, such as "An Ante-Bellum Sermon" or "When Dey 'Listed Colored Soldiers," one does not have to dig very deep to find a message of black pride and resistance.

However, even poems that seem to fall more squarely in the sentimental and humorous dialect traditions can be reread differently, such as "When Malindy Sings," which can be seen as arguing for the superiority of the African American musical tradition over the European "classical" art music tradition. Thus, the high poetry suggests a possible interpretive strategy that reclaims the dialect poetry while foregrounding an awareness of the dangers and costs of writing such dialect poetry in the face of the versions of the African American body, voice, and expressive culture that permeated high and popular culture in the United States. The dialect poetry in turn provides concrete examples of what the mask or the cage look and sound like, giving an increased urgency and force to the high poems.

This synergistic opposition of "high" and "low" remained a potent paradigm for the New Negro era of the early twentieth century, with its concern for representing "authentically" the racial self without being imprisoned by racist expectations, especially as the plantation/minstrel types migrated into the new media of film and radio. In many respects, the **Harlem Renaissance** took Dunbar's symbiotic dualist split between high and low as a way of figuring multiple subjectivities within the context of the continuation and even intensification of Jim Crow (and the saturation of high and popular culture in the United States with minstrel/plantation-derived images) and inflected it with the various movements (modernism, feminism, socialism, black nationalism, etc.) that transformed the political and cultural landscape of the United States following World War I. One trend within Harlem Renaissance poetry is a continuation of the radical democratic impulse that can be traced back to Wheatley. As **Countee Cullen** pointed out when questioned about his use of Greek myth, Keats wrote of Endymion even though he was far removed from the ancient Greeks. So why should it be strange if Cullen did likewise? In short, he claimed full cultural citizenship, rejecting pseudo-biological racist notions of artistic propriety and property. In his poetry Cullen assumed the split between high and low proposed by Dunbar and then rose above it by eliminating the low.

Another powerful strain in the Harlem Renaissance was an engagement with feminism. There was long a tendency to paint such black women poets as **Georgia Douglas Johnson**, Gwendolyn Bennett, and even Anne Spencer as prim and proper Victorians, aesthetically, morally, and politically. However, these women splintered the dualism of Dunbar into at least a triple consciousness, with the black woman seen as both inside and outside the fields of the feminist movement and the black political and cultural upsurge. This multiple subjectivity can be seen in both the earnest iambic couplets of Johnson's "Heart of a Woman," revising the cage of Dunbar's "Sympathy" to figure the sexual, intellectual, and economic gender oppression without forgetting the original racial context of Dunbar's poem, and the bitter parodic pastiche of Spencer's "At the Carnival," in which the speaker wishes for the death of a young girl at the moment of a glorious physical and emotional triumph that emerges from a haze of cynical irony before the girl, a high diver at the carnival, can be drawn into the everyday world of the speaker.

Another complex of related tendencies might be thought of as nationalist. Two key theorists, editors, and promoters of the idea of a "New Negro Renaissance," Alain Locke and **James Weldon Johnson**, promoted a culturalism much influenced by the Irish literary renaissance. In this model black artists would transmute the raw material of the folk culture into a distinctive African American high culture. Such art would cement the status of African Americans as a people, giving them the cultural and political capital necessary to force their way into citizenship. It was this model that informed Johnson's series of poems based on the folk sermon and eventually collected in *God's Trombones* (1927). Like Frances Harper in the 1870s, Johnson did not try to literally re-create vernacular speech on the page, an effort that he felt would be immediately converted to the familiar register of minstrel/plantation slapstick humor and pathos. Instead, he attempted to give the "flavor" of vernacular diction, syntax, rhythms, humor, and imagery to verse that for the most part followed "standard" literary language, syntax, and metrics.

The most famous literary representation of the New Negro was Jamaican-born **Claude McKay**'s 1919 sonnet "If We Must Die" (*Complete Poems*, 2003), which ends with the couplet

Like men we'll face the murderous, cowardly pack,
Pressed to the wall, dying, but fighting back.

Appearing in the context of a wave of racist violence in 1919, McKay's call for armed self-defense sounded an arresting New Negro self-assertion. Closely associated with the Communist Party of the United States of America (CPUSA), the Comintern, and the leftist nationalist African Blood Brotherhood, McKay anticipated the later movement of black literature in the 1930s, merging a radical internationalism with a diasporic nationalism in which the black exile in the colonial metropolis imagines a return to a black home. Interestingly, McKay, who began his career writing in a Jamaican vernacular, employed "standard," even slightly archaic European poetic diction and modes—again merging a vision of a "high" universalist art with a black identity.

The final strain of Harlem Renaissance poetry predicated on the notion of African Americans as a people or nation is associated most prominently with **Langston Hughes**, Waring Cuney, and **Sterling A. Brown**. These poets wrote verse in a variety of modes. However, they are most famous for their use of vernacular black diction and forms adapted from folk and popular culture, especially the blues. Hughes pioneered this approach in such poems as "The Weary Blues" and "Bound N'oth Blues." In "The Weary Blues" an alienated black speaker observes a blues pianist-singer in a Harlem dive and through the speaker's interaction with the music becomes one with the singer by the end of the poem. Something of the same process takes place in Brown's "Ma Rainey." There the black artist takes the experiences and culture of the people and creates a work of art that allows the people to see itself and make intellectual and emotional sense of its collective experience. The audience then validates the artist—and so the cycle continues. Although Hughes and Brown differed about the nature of folk culture and popular culture, both offered a vision of the black artist and African American art in which the artist is more like a medium through which the people speak than an alchemist who stands above the folk.

These stances associated with Brown and Hughes took on an even higher profile in the 1930s and 1940s, when an enormous proportion of African American poets moved within the orbit of the communist Left because of the impact of the economic crisis and the ideological and practical commitment of the CPUSA and its cultural apparatus to "Negro Liberation" and the promotion of African American artists. Like earlier black writers, Hughes, Brown, and Cuney—joined by Richard Wright, Frank Marshall Davis, **Robert Hayden**, **Melvin Tolson**, **Margaret Walker**, and **Gwendolyn Brooks**—negotiated the difficult problem of the relationship between high literary culture and popular culture and the question of how one might talk by, for, and of the people rather than simply writing about them. The poetry of this Left milieu can be divided roughly into two related periods that each featured an interest in the connections between history, documentary, folklore, race, nation, citizenship, and culture. The first half of the decade saw the promotion of a counterculture rooted in folk and proletarian culture that was imagined to be outside bourgeois high culture and mass culture. Brown's and Cuney's vernacular poems, drawing on the folk blues, work songs, badman songs and stories, and so on, and extolling some version of the folk artist, exemplify this countercultural spirit.

The Popular Front era during the second half of the decade arose in response to the international threat of fascism. It saw popular culture as an arena in which "the People" and progressive artists could battle against reaction. The Popular Front poet par excellence was Langston Hughes in such works as his revolutionary "poetry-play" *Don't You Want to Be Free* and the poems "Broadcast on Ethiopia" and "Air Raid over Harlem," which drew on newsreels, newspaper articles, radio broadcasts, folk and urban blues, vaudeville, and other media, as well as various strains of "high" literature. Similarly, Frank Marshall Davis in "Portrait of the Cotton South" weaves together the colloquial hard-boiled diction of pulp literature and gangster movies, popular journalism, Whitmanic catalogues, and the mock epic, suggesting that the challenge of the contemporary painter was to achieve the immediacy and impact of the tabloid photographer.

This use of the themes, forms, and voices of popular and folk culture remained as the United States moved from the Depression through World War II into the high Cold War. At the same time, such black writers as Hayden, Brooks, Tolson, and Margaret Danner engaged the "high" modernism of the early twentieth century in an increasingly open way. It is true that in many respects, the black neo-modernists practiced a Popular Front neo-modernism. One finds in the work of Brooks, Hayden, Tolson, and Danner a fascination with history, community, and popular culture and an ambiguous, if not adversarial, relationship to the often racist and anti-Semitic white high modernists. Much like Wheatley, Brooks, in her poem "Kitchenette Building" from the 1944 *A Street in Bronzeville*, argues that the experience of African Americans gives them a particular insight into the condition of modernity in the twentieth century. While Brooks echoes **T.S. Eliot**'s "Gerontion," she renders the ghetto housing of Chicago's South Side, the kitchenette apartment, as an icon of the all-too-real city.

In this period Hughes, too, promoted a black modernism, but of a different sort. He endorsed bebop as a model of a black avant-garde rooted in popular black culture and experience, claiming in a prefatory note that his 1951 *Montage of a Dream Deferred* was organized formally with the "conflicting changes, sudden nuances, sharp and impudent interjections, broken rhythms" of bebop in mind. Hughes's notion of a black avant-garde in dialogue with black popular culture and black experience exerted enormous influence on black experimental writing in the 1950s and 1960s, and the growth of the **Black Arts Movement**.

To a considerable extent the Black Arts Movement emerged out of these circles of black avant-gardists associated with what came to be known as the New American Poetry in the 1950s and early 1960s. Some black avant-gardists, especially **Bob Kaufman** in San Francisco and Ted Joans and **Amiri Baraka** (then LeRoi Jones) in New York, had been central figures in the literary countercultures of what became known as the "New American Poetry." Baraka in particular was not only a leading poet but also a tireless editor and cultural organizer who mediated between the various countercultural groups, doing much to make the idea of a "New American Poetry" possible. Others, such as

the participants in the Umbra Poets Workshop in New York, including Tom Dent, Calvin Hernton, David Henderson, **Ishmael Reed**, **Lorenzo Thomas**, and Askia Touré, were perhaps less prominent as individuals, but as a group were a crucial part of the new artistic bohemia. The existence of the Umbra Poets Workshop and On Guard, a radical political action organization of African American artists and intellectuals, serves as a reminder that even at the height of their participation in the general artistic counterculture, black artists met and attempted to work out the nature of black art and aesthetics, and the role of the African American artist in the time of decolonization, the Nonaligned Movement, the Cuban Revolution, the Civil Rights Movement, and Malcolm X.

The Black Arts Movement of the 1960s and 1970s was a network of nationalist African American artists and intellectuals. As in the linked Black Power Movement, its participants held a variety of political and aesthetic positions. Despite this range of beliefs, there was a generally held concept that African Americans were a nation with the right to determine their own destiny. Black Arts activists also shared a belief in a need for the development or recovery of an authentic national black culture. There was enough common ground to produce national conferences, journals, organizations, and widely read anthologies. Virtually every sizable African American community, and many college campuses, saw the rise of new black theaters and performance spaces and organizations of nationalist-minded visual artists, writers, dancers, and musicians.

Poetry was a dominant Black Arts genre, rivaled only by drama and music. Poetry was easily performed at street rallies, demonstrations, political meetings, and other communal events. Poetry also lent itself to the multimedia productions, combining spoken, visual, and musical elements, which characterized the movement. As in the 1930s, one can generally distinguish between poetry promoting a model of African American culture that was simultaneously popular and avant-garde, encompassing, say, James Brown and John Coltrane, and more alternative models that posited a neo-African counterculture that largely rejected even African American popular culture (including the blues) as part of an ideological accommodationism that needed to be transcended. The first position is seen most clearly, at least initially, in the work of Baraka and other poets associated with the Northeast, including Neal, Touré, and **Sonia Sanchez**. The second position was most powerfully advanced by such midwestern poets as Haki Madhubuti (Don L. Lee) and **Nikki Giovanni**.

Black Arts splintered in the mid-1970s as Marxists, cultural nationalists, and liberals battled over the direction of the movement. What survived of it increasingly became just another tendency among several sometimes overlapping strains of African American literature and art—though one might argue that the memory of the time when Black Arts was central lingered.

One current might be thought of as a new textualism in which poems exist more powerfully on the page than in performance. One might further divide this group into a more formally conservative strain, which would include much of the work of **Michael S. Harper**, **Rita Dove**, Anthony Walton, and Sherley Ann Williams, and a more self-consciously avant-garde line, which would include poetry from **Clarence Major**, **Harryette Mullen**, and Kevin Young. Interestingly, both the more conservative strain and the more avant-garde drew a great deal on the idea of the blues and jazz as a black classical tradition, though in many respects as a textual tradition rather than as a guide to performance after the manner of many Black Arts activists. However, generally the avant-gardists, especially the younger poets, distinguished themselves from the more conservative textualists in their relative ease with a wide range of popular culture forms and genres, from cartoons to hip-hop, in this respect having more in common with Baraka than with Michael Harper.

Unquestionably, the most influential response to the Black Arts era was the rise of woman-centered literature that emerged from and critiqued Black Arts/Black Power and second-wave feminism. Typically, even the poetry most straightforwardly feminist and critical of Black Arts visions of gender, such as Sherley Ann Williams's *The Peacock Poems*, generally retained a Black Arts concern with community and a distinct tradition of African American expressive culture, though distinguishing between the interests of men and women within that community. The work of **Audre Lorde**, whose early literary career was nurtured by the Black Arts Movement, is often in this register, as seen in the love poem "Letter for Jan" (*The Black Unicorn*, 1978). Here it is "being a woman full of loving" for another woman that has impregnated the speaker with the "black song" that wishes for utterance.

One line of poetry issuing directly from the Black Arts Movement came from Black Arts veterans such as Baraka, Sanchez, **Jayne Cortez**, and Touré, whose work critiqued certain aspects of the movement (sometimes, as in Baraka's case, from a Marxist perspective) while honoring the basic Black Arts impulse and maintaining much of the same performative multigeneric style as their earlier work. For example, in Sanchez's prose poem "Just Don't Never Give Up on Love" (*Homegirls and Handgrenades*, 1984), a youngish black woman who is a parent, poet, intellectual, writer of book reviews, tired, harried, and perhaps troubled in love, encounters an elderly black woman, Mrs. Rosalie Johnson. As in the work of Williams, there is a bonding of black women across generations, a sharing of African American

women's experience and culture, and a reinvigoration of a troubled and dissatisfied female subject. Yet in the final analysis one finds the restatement of a certain Black Arts vision in which the fallen or degraded black man is set against the vision of a "good" man. The speaker is reinvigorated by Mrs. Johnson's story of the redemptive powers of a good black man. One can see this poem as a reconstruction of the idea of community within the Black Arts boundaries, combined with a positive engagement with feminism.

Yet another sort of woman-centered stance can be found in the early work of Ntozake Shange, a stance that engages Black Arts in a spirit of critical support, seeing sexism as a weakness in the movement but not fundamental to it. For example, in her 1977 "taking a solo/a poetic possibility/a poetic imperative," Shange makes a plea for formal and thematic diversity and individual subjectivity within black poetry while retaining a Black Arts sense of community, tradition, and movement. As a crucial part of this plea, she expresses the need for self-representation of black women's subjectivities. In the poem Shange not only favorably quotes or mentions prominent male Black Arts poets, but also emphatically includes the work of black women. She also expands the notion of the black literary tradition to include some Latina/o and Asian American writers, drawing an analogy to jazz's ability to incorporate elements that are not "black," as the term is understood in the United States, and still remain a black art form.

This expansion at least indirectly touches on a demographic shift in the African American community that has had an enormous impact on notions of black art and identity. Changes in immigration laws in 1965 made emigration from Africa, Asia, the Caribbean, and Latin America to the United States far easier. At roughly the same time, there were parallel migrations from Africa and its diaspora to urban areas in Europe and North America outside of the United States. Many black communities in the United States became deeply multiethnic and multilingual, with close personal ties to African and diasporic populations across the globe.

One result of this demographic and cultural movement is that the already pronounced interest of African American poets in the connections between Africa and its diaspora took on a new urgency. Amiri Baraka, in post–Black Arts poetry that criticized certain aspects of the earlier movement from a Marxist perspective, nonetheless wrote frequently about the organic connections between Africa and the diaspora in poems like *Wise, Why's, Y's* (1995), an epic meditation on African American history that can seen as part of the line reaching back to early black epic.

At the same time, this migration has led to a renewed conversation about the question, how might one characterize the bedrock of black culture in the face of these changes? One response is that the older notions of African Americans as a nation or people are severely inadequate. The poetry of **Jay Wright** has increasingly created or drawn on existing hybrids of Native American Indian, African, African American, Caribbean, Mexican, and European spiritual and cultural practices, suggesting that such practices have long been inextricably linked. Wright does not deny the impact and heritage of Africa; in fact, he places the influence of Africa at the center of so-called New World identities. Similarly, Willie Perdomo interrogates the connection between his identity as a Puerto Rican in New York and as an African American. He takes up the obsessive U.S. question of "what are you?" in his collection *Where a Nickel Costs a Dime*. Perdomo, whose work is heavily marked by hip-hop and the rap-influenced performance poetry scene, finds his identity as an artist in the present as much as in the past, in the common urban culture of hip-hop and racial and national oppression as much as in traditional Puerto Rican or African American culture as they have often been conceived.

Undoubtedly, among the most important products of this movement of people and culture is the development of rap and hip-hop. Although the precise dating of the birth of rap is difficult, it seems clear that it arose first among young African Americans (many of them immigrants or the children of immigrants from the Caribbean) and Puerto Ricans in the Bronx during the 1970s, drawing on, among other things, soul, R&B, disco, Jamaican dub and toasting, and Black Arts merging of spoken word and music. This new form became popular to an extent only dreamed of by previous spoken word artists in the United States and has in many respects defined the field in which all poets in the United States have written over the last thirty years. Some black poets have become even more rigorously textual in an effort to write against rap; some have associated themselves with the rhythms, tropes, and sensibilities of hip-hop; and some have taken a middle course. None have been able to ignore it. The hugely popular genre of **performance poetry** and the related phenomenon of **slam poetry** derive directly from hip-hop in many respects, with some artists, such as Mos' Def, crossing back and forth between performance poetry and hip-hop.

Of course, the age of rap has occasioned new versions of the old debates about literacy, culture, and citizenship, about how the African American community and the African American subject, the black voice and the black body are (and should be) represented in popular culture. Hip-hop has both renewed arguments over the relation of popular culture to high culture, of art to audience, and recontextualized them for the age of cultural globalization in which older notions of race, culture, and nation persist, recalling, perhaps, an earlier moment of global upheaval and exchange when a young Phillis Wheatley was transported from Africa to New England either through mercy or tyranny.

Further Reading.   *Selected Secondary Sources:* Hutchinson, George, *The Harlem Renaissance in Black and White* (Cambridge, MA: Harvard University Press, 1995); Nielsen, Aldon, *Black Chant: Languages of African-American Postmodernism* (New York: Cambridge University Press, 1997); Redmond, Eugene, *Drumvoices: The Mission of Afro-American Poetry: A Critical History* (Garden City, NY: Anchor, 1976); Sherman, Joan, *Invisible Poets: Afro-Americans of the Nineteenth Century* (Urbana: University of Illinois Press, 1988); Smethurst, James, *The New Red Negro: The Literary Left and African-American Poetry, 1930–1946* (New York: Oxford University Press, 1999); Thomas, Lorenzo, *Extraordinary Measures: Afrocentric Modernism and Twentieth-Century American Poetry* (Tuscaloosa: University of Alabama Press, 2000).

James Smethurst

AFRICAN AMERICAN POETRY COLLECTIVES

Black artists in America have always felt a need to connect with the community while simultaneously perfecting their craft. Writers as far apart in their missions as Alain Locke and Richard Wright have recognized the need to speak from and to the black community in order to make their writing valid. African Americans have also always known the importance of being a part of a community of artists, while also understanding the artists' need to distance themselves from the demands of the present in their writing and their ideas.

In the 1960s Larry Neal, **Amiri Baraka**, Askia Toure, Tom Dent, Calvin Hernton, and others set forth the goal of establishing a poetry that would speak to and about black people and would set forth the criteria of the new poetry of the **Black Arts Movement**. In 1962 Tom Dent with Calvin Hernton and David Henderson started the Umbra workshop in New York's Lower East Side, out of which emerged poets such as Joe Johnson, Ray Patterson, Steve Cannon, **Ishmael Reed**, **Lorenzo Thomas**, and others. The Umbra workshop encouraged poetry as performance as well as writing, and set an example for the type of cultural nationalist organization/ poetry collective that would foster much of the black poetry written in the later twentieth century. Through literary and dramatic workshops, such as the Black Arts Repertory Theatre School of Amiri Baraka in Harlem, the Free Southern Theatre, BLKARTSOUTH, and the Congo Square Writers Union in Mississippi and New Orleans, Tom Dent, John O'Neal, Kalamu ya Salaam, Nayo Barbara Watkins, Quo Vadis Gex, Raymond Breaux, and many other young writers executed new forms of cultural nationalism. Black theaters and poetry grew to form working ties with the communities that were their source. The meaning of community theater and poetry evolved.

The poets of the post–Black Aesthetic Movement shifted toward an interest in the religion, folklore, and languages of theAfrican diaspora and opened up the world of African American writers to new presses. These writers included South African poet Keorapetse Kgositsile, who joined the Uptown Writers Movement, which grew out of the Umbra Workshop. They also included many women poets who came out of the black art and womanist movements of the 1970s, such as **Sonia Sanchez**, **Nikki Giovanni**, **Jayne Cortez**, Mari Evans, **Lucille Clifton**, and **June Jordan**, whose voices continue to demand an ear for the density of music, language, and vision, as influenced by black women in American and diasporic societies in the second half of the twentieth century.

A number of significant presses and journals dedicated to the publishing of African American writers began with the Civil Rights Movement of the 1960s, 1970s, and 1980s. Some of these offered prizes and a few developed collectives. Haki Madhubuti, along with Johari Amini (Jewel C. Lattimore) and Carolyn Rodgers, started Third World Press in 1967 in Chicago, which published the works of **Gwendolyn Brooks**, **Dudley Felker Randall**, Amiri Baraka, Sonia Sanchez, Mari Evans, **Margaret Walker**, and many others. In 1965 Randall, with the cooperation of younger poet Melba Boyd Davis, founded the Broadside Press in Detroit, promoting the works of black writers and the Civil Rights Movement. In the 1970s Naomi Long Madgett took over Lotus Press, Inc., also in Detroit, which soon became a leading publisher of black poetry. In 1993 Madgett started the Poetry Series of Michigan State University and introduced the Naomi Long Madgett Prize for Excellence in a manuscript by an African American poet. In 1975 Alvin Aubert, Professor Emeritus at Wayne State University, founded and edited the journal *Obsidian*, now *Obsidian II*, aimed at publishing works in English by and about writers of African descent worldwide. The Detroit Writers Guild was founded by Peggy Moore in 1983 and grew to include more than 600 members in its heyday.

Southern University in Baton Rouge became a leader in African American literature with the founding of its landmark journal *Callaloo*, edited by Charles H. Rowell, in 1976. *Callaloo* is a literary-critical journal covering African American, African, and African diasporic arts. Published by The Johns Hopkins University Press, the journal has sponsored a Poetry Series since 1983 and has published such poets as Brenda Marie Osbey, **Yusef Komunyakaa**, **Elizabeth Alexander**, Natasha Trethewey, and Kevin Young.

Lorenzo Thomas, in his book *Extraordinary Measures: Afrocentric Modernism and Twentieth-Century American Poetry*, points out the many strong communities of poets that have appeared across the country since the 1980s and 1990s, including the Carolina African-American Writers' Collective in Durham, North Carolina, the Cave Canem Collective in Pittsburgh, the Dark Room Collective in Boston, and the Eugene B. Redmond Writers Club in East St. Louis.

As Lenard D. Moore writes in "The Art of Black Writers Collectives," "Black writers have always known the importance of community, even though many write in isolation. For some, though, writers' collectives provide a way to connect with their community while offering an important link to fellow authors." Moore founded the Carolina African-American Writers' Collective in 1995, which provided a sense of social and aesthetic solidarity for writers such as Janice W. Hodges and Beverly Fields Burnette, who did not feel welcomed into most poetry collectives in the region and found little support in most historically black colleges and universities (HBCUs). Later members included Christian A. Campbell, L. Teresa Church, Candice M. Jenkins, Mendi Lewis Obadike, and Evie Shockley, among others. The group's interaction led to more experimentation in the poets' writing and to the expression of a wider range of experience.

Other examples of collectives include the Eugene B. Redmond Writers Club, founded by Eugene B. Redmond in East St. Louis in 1988, whose founding members included Sherman Fowler, Michael Roy, and Michael Fontaine; and the Dark Room Collective, which began as a reading series just after the death of James Baldwin in 1987, as poets in Cambridge and New York City met to honor the older writer's life. The reading series featured the work of such poets as the 1992 Nobel laureate **Derek Walcott** and brought together poets from the community. Founded by Sharan Strange and Thomas Sayers Ellis, the Dark Room Collective also included Vera Beatty, Major Jackson, Natasha Trethewey, and Kevin Young. This collective continued to meet from 1988 to 1998, affording these and other members an opportunity to travel, to read their work together, and to share their experiences as growing writers.

An important collective whose work continues at present is Cave Canem, which began as a weeklong summer workshop/retreat for African American poets under the leadership of **Toi Derricotte** and **Cornelius Eady**. The idea was to offer a safe haven for young poets. The summer workshops continue to meet, with lessons, critiques, and readings for fellows, faculty, and guest poets. Cave Canem also offers regional workshops, an annual book prize for a previously unpublished African American poet, public readings, and the publication of an annual anthology of poems by participating fellows and faculty. Faculty of the workshops have included Elizabeth Alexander, Cyrus Cassells, Cheryl Clarke, Lucille Clifton, Toi Derricotte, Cornelius

Eady, Nikky Finney, **Michael S. Harper**, Yusef Komu-nyakaa, **Harryette Mullen**, **Marilyn Nelson**, Sonia Sanchez, Tim Siebles, Patricia Smith, Afaa Michael Weaver, Al Young, and Kevin Young. Winners of the Cave Canem Book Prize have included Natasha Tre-thewey (1999), Major Jackson (2000), Lyrae Van Clief (2001), Tracey K. Smith (2002), Kyle Dargan (2003), and Amber Flora Thomas (2004).

Kalamu ya Salaam, co-founder of the 1970s BLKARTSOUTH in New Orleans, continues encourag-ing young poets to write, critique, perform, and conduct community instructional workshops in his organization the Nommo Literary Society, which was founded in Sep-tember 1995. Kalamu and the Nommo poets work across the state and nation, using text, light, and sound to teach and perform. Poetry collectives continue to pro-mote the work of African American writers, to critique their work by fellow writers and audiences, to create publishing opportunities, and to increase the level of connection between community and writers across the country.

Further Reading. *Selected Secondary Sources:* Bryan, Violet Harrington, *The Myth of New Orleans in Literature: Dialogues of Race and Gender* (Knoxville: University of Tennessee Press, 1993); Hood, Susan, "The Genesis of a Poet: An Interview with Sharan Strange '81" (*Radcliffe Quarterly* [Spring 1999]); Moore, Lenard D., "The Art of Black Writers Collectives" (*Black Issues Book Review* [July–August 2002]); Thomas, Lorenzo, *Extraordinary Measures: Afrocentric Modernism and Twentieth-Century American Poetry* (Tuscaloosa: University of Alabama Press, 2000).

Violet Harrington Bryan

AFRICAN AMERICAN SLAVE SONGS

Often regarded as the most important body of sacred songs created in America, African American slave songs as they have been passed down are likely to have had their roots in the mid- to late eighteenth century. It is certain that they predate the period when they were first formally transcribed, in the 1840s, but their precise time of origin, specific sources, and processes of composition remain mysterious and have been subjects of debate since these songs were first captured by figures such as Fredricka Bremer, Lucy McKim, and **Thomas Went-worth Higginson**.

Described by early observers as wild, uncanny, other-worldly, barbaric, rhythmic, and dissonant, the slave songs also were criticized for being directly related in imagery, diction, and structure to white Protestant hymns. These similarities were used by musicologists such as George Pullen Jackson, Richard Wallascheck, Newman White, and Edmund S. Lorenz to demonstrate the fundamental lack of "originality" in the slave songs

and thus to diminish their importance. White hymns of the day undoubtedly influenced the slaves, who would have encountered them while being evangelized into Christianity, but it was evident to other early recorders such as William Francis Allen that this material had become something unmistakably different through the slaves poets' imaginative transformations. Numerous observers noted their distinctiveness from the language and performance of white church music in the use of such features as rhythmic arm movements, coordinated foot shuffling, shouts of loud abandon, ecstatic displays of jubilation, uncanny imagery, and vernacular diction.

The poetic qualities of the slave songs were noted by observers such as Allen, Ware, and Garrison, who com-mented that the slave songs "will dash heroically through a trochaic tune at the head of a column of iambs with wonderful skill" (iv) and expressed surprise that no systematic effort had been made to preserve them. Hig-ginson described the slave songs as being fundamentally poetic. Just a few years later, the songs reached the level of wider public attention that Allen and Higginson had hoped for through the intervention of key figures at some of the newly founded historically black colleges and universities (HBCUs). Richard P. Fenner, a music professor at what was then the Hampton Institute, issued a collection of what he referred to as *Cabin and Planta-tion Songs*. Under the direction of George Leonard White, the Jubilee Singers of Fisk University were formed. In national and international tours between 1871 and 1878, they performed the slave songs to rapt audiences, including a recital for Queen Victoria.

The slave songs are sometimes divided into the cate-gories of "spirituals" and "seculars"; however, such divi-sions are of limited value since the songs often depict a highly permeable boundary between the sacred and the earthly. The actual themes of the songs provide insight into how the slaves understood the nature of their own existence. The songs refer, for example, to the slaves' particular types of physical labor, such as shucking corn; to the Old Testament, with particular focus on the Exo-dus narrative, and to figures such as Daniel, Jacob, Noah, Joshua, and Moses as the primary means of inter-preting the New Testament, in a reversal of the Chris-tianity typical of the slaveholders; and to the sufferings of Mary and the crucified Jesus in the New Testament. The songs often represent biblical figures as being in direct contact with the slaves, who had the ability to carry on an active dialogue with them. They reveal the belief in God's ability to intervene and free the slaves, as He had delivered Daniel and the Hebrew slaves, whose situation the African American slaves compared to their own. The songs frequently suspend the laws of physics, so that the poetic personae move freely in time and space. They depict "home" as heaven, or as a metaphor for the state of future freedom to be achieved, either in the United States or upon a return to Africa. The songs slyly parody slaveholding culture in coded language and vernacular that were not meant to be understood by the overseers. Particularly, they depict the religious hypocrisy of the slaveholding culture by the selective interpretation of key aspects of scripture. The imagery of crossing water, flying through the air, traveling on the railroad, or going over the River Jordan is used to covertly spread information on ways to escape detection when attending the forbidden slave meetings, sometimes known as "shouts," or fleeing to freedom across the Ohio River.

The slave songs generally have been appreciated and studied for their musical significance, influence, and beauty, especially insofar as they served as the foundation of gospel, **jazz**, and the **blues**. They sometimes are discussed for their role in the formation and expression of African American Christianity; they offer keys to the ways in which the slaves became Christianized and demonstrate how the adoption of Western religious beliefs aided in their survival and sustenance. The songs also are discussed as a record of coded communication among the slaves in their efforts to elude detection by slaveholders when arranging shouts, meetings, escape routes, and plans; giving warnings of "pattyrollers"; or offering one another the support and encouragement to carry on. Frederick Douglass credited the spiritual "Run to Jesus, Shun the Danger" as the inspiration that made him decide to escape slavery. Nat Turner often is credited as having been the author of one of the most famous spirituals, "Steal Away," which may have been used as the rallying cry for the secret meetings that led to the 1831 slave insurrection that he led. Harriet Tubman, another major figure in African American history, used spirituals such as "Go Down Moses" and "Swing Low, Sweet Chariot" as effective means of communication in operating the underground railroad, and is reputed to herself have been the creator of some of the slave songs.

The roots of the African American slave songs partially lie in African customs, community, and oral communication, but the songs also reflect the immediate circumstances of slavery and plantation life in the United States. What F. Abiola Irele terms the African Imagination provided common ground and enabled the black and unknown bards, as they were called by **James Weldon Johnson**, to blend vestiges of their ancestral homelands with American influences to produce something unique. Although they came from widely diverse geographical and linguistic backgrounds in Africa, the slaves would have shared music and dance as key elements in marking significant events and in establishing individual and community identity. Other characteristic elements of the spirituals that are African survivals include the direct address of ancestors and spirit guides (extended in the context of western Christianization to include biblical figures); inherently significant repetition that often took the form of triads; the antiphonal structure known as call-and-response, where a leader led a call followed by the echoing chorus of the group; the absence of Western dualism; the depiction of Satan as a trickster figure; a concept of time in which the future is viewed as a direct and immediate extension of the present, with past and present as dominant modes of consciousness; the description of human relationships and connections as being maintained even in absence and after death; and an emphasis on the importance of community for every individual.

While the issue of Africanisms has been a source of critical debate since the slave songs were first preserved and written about, there is clear evidence that the slave songs are a hybrid of African references, customs, and ontology grafted on direct and immediate experiences of American slave culture. These influences include the adoption of Christianity, which is seen in the slave songs to have been melded to African customs and suited to the slaves' psychological and emotional needs and worldview; commentary on the daily routines and rhythms of particular kinds of enforced labor; reflections on current political events that traveled by word of mouth via the slave songs; the development of fluency in English; and the construction of a community across barriers of language and culture with other slaves who might share no common links beyond their African roots, the experience of being snatched away from home, a shared location, and their present status in life. Logic as well as concrete evidence shows that when transplanted unwillingly to their new surroundings, the slaves carried with them elements of their cultures of origin by which to retain a sense of personhood and forge a new sense of community after the loss of all past connections.

The slave songs rarely are considered **lyric poetry**, and typically do not appear in the major anthologies of either African American or American literature, except in special categories such as "vernacular poetry," "African American folk songs," "oral verse," "plantation songs," or simply "spirituals." However, the absence of the slave songs from discussions of American lyric poetry is a serious oversight that is a reflection more of the formation and exclusions of the American poetry canon than of the inherent features and literary value of the slave songs themselves. Their importance to the **African American poetry** tradition can be traced through their direct and indirect influence on countless African American poets, including James Weldon Johnson, **Paul Laurence Dunbar**, **Melvin Tolson**, Calvin C. Hernton, **Margaret Walker**, Waring Cuney, **Sterling A. Brown**, **Robert Hayden**, **Sonia Sanchez**, and **Amiri Baraka**. Brown attributed a significant measure of their importance to the fact that they were self-defining, rather than an external description of the African American experience. Alain Locke considered them not only to be a racial product but to possess universal meaning for all of American culture.

The lyrics of the slave songs have a compelling power, sophistication, and complexity that are consistent with traditional expectations for poetry. "Nobody Knows the Trouble I've Seen," "Oh Mary, Don't You Weep," "My Lord What a Mornin'," "Go, Tell It on the Mountain," "Roll, Jordan, Roll," "Were You There When They Crucified My Lord," "Lay This Body Down," "Wade in the Water," and "Many Thousand Go," among numerous other examples of classic slave songs, are an integral part of America's literary treasures. As early and later commentators have argued, the humble and anonymous nature of their authors should not prevent a full appreciation of the songs' exquisite imagery and emotional pathos. Considered as lyric poetry, they are a record of the slave poets' ability to overcome adversity; they illuminate the strength of slave society in achieving unprecedented cultural production under circumstances of dire repression. Viewing the slave songs primarily as music or historical footnotes is a misprision of their significance as living cultural artifacts, contemporaneous records of the daily experiences of individuals and their society, a major body of poetry born of long suffering, and timeless expressions of the human refusal to be destroyed by inhumanity. The finest examples stand up to anything produced in the American poetry tradition. Referred to by **W.E.B. DuBois** as the sorrow songs, they were, he justly claimed, "the most beautiful expression of human experience born this side of the seas" (186). *See also* **Bible and American Poetry**.

Further Readings. *Selected Primary Sources:* Allen, William Francis, Charles Pickard Ware, and Lucy McKim Garrison, comps., *Slave Songs of the United States* (1867; reprint Bedford, MA: Applewood Books, n.d.); Armstrong, Mrs. M.F., and Helen Ludlow, eds., *Hampton and Its Students. With Fifty Cabin and Plantation Songs Arranged by Thomas P. Fenner* (New York: G.P. Putnam's Sons, 1874); Dett, R. Nathaniel, ed. *Religious Folk-Songs of the Negro as Sung at Hampton Institute* (Hampton, VA: Hampton Institute, 1927); Hogan, Moses, ed., *The Oxford Book of Spirituals* (New York: Oxford University Press, 2002); Johnson, James Weldon, and J. Rosamond Johnson, eds., *American Negro Spirituals* (New York: Viking Press, 1925, 1926; reprint Cambridge, MA: Da Capo Press, 1973); Work, John, ed., *American Negro Songs* (New York: Crown Publishers, 1940; reprint New York: Dover Publications, 1998). *Selected Secondary Sources:* Cone, James H., *The Spirituals and the Blues* (New York: Seabury Press, 1972); DuBois, W.E.B., "The Sorrow Songs," in *The Souls of Black Folk* (1903; reprint Boston: Bedford Books, 1997); Epstein, Dena J., *Sinful Tunes and Spirituals* (Urbana: University of Illinois Press, 1977); Fisher, Miles Mark, *Negro Slave Songs in the United States* (New York: American Historical Association, 1953, 1981; reprint New York: Carol Publishing Group, 1990); Higginson, Thomas Wentworth, "Negro Spirituals," in *Army Life in a Black Regiment and Other Writings* (Fields, Osgood & Co., 1870; reprint New York: Penguin Books, 1997); Levine, Lawrence W., *Black Culture and Black Consciousness* (New York: Oxford University Press, 1977); Lovell, John, Jr., *Black Song: The Forge and the Flame* (New York: Macmillan, 1972).

Lauri Ramey

AGRARIAN SCHOOL (THE AGRARIANS)

Although the group known as the Agrarians (also known as the Nashville Agrarians, the Vanderbilt Agrarians, and the Southern Agrarians) was in part an offshoot of the **Fugitives**, most members of the group were not poets, and the group's collective output was published as a volume of essays, *I'll Take My Stand: The South and the Agrarian Tradition* (1930). A sequel volume with a different lineup of essayists, *Who Owns America? A New Declaration of Independence*, appeared in 1936. The contributors to *I'll Take My Stand*, identified first as "Twelve Southerners" on the book's title page and cover, were intellectuals whose professional areas of expertise included psychology, history, political science, economics, theater, poetry, and critical theory. Each contributor's individual essay presents a different perspective on what the group considered a major problem: the increasing industrialization of the South. In short, *I'll Take My Stand* argues that industrial life is harmful to individuals and society, whereas agrarian life is beneficial to both on a number of levels. The collection's individual essays emphasize different aspects of Southern life circa 1930 (including art, religion, family farming versus wage work, subsistence farming versus cash crop farming, and race relations) to produce a multifaceted series of arguments in favor of traditional farming-centered lifestyles as opposed to absorption into a system of modern industrial wage labor.

The best-known figures in the group, **John Crowe Ransom**, **Allen Tate**, Donald Davidson, and **Robert Penn Warren**, forged impressive literary careers as poets and critics, and their individual successes no doubt contributed to the long-standing tendency to associate the Agrarians with poetry despite the group's focus on prose. This association has often led to the facile assumption that the group's ideas were intended to be merely theoretical, or that the economic and sociological commentary of a group of poets is automatically impractical. In fact, several of the Agrarians hoped that their essays would contribute to a bloodless Agrarian revolution that would transform American politics and culture, and two of the nonpoet Agrarians were well qualified to offer such commentary: Henry Blue Kline worked as an industrial economist, and Herman Clarence Nixon's academic specialty was the intersection of economics, political science, and sociology.

Although the interests and opinions of the contributors diverged widely in the decades following the publication of *I'll Take My Stand*, at the time the collection was published they shared a set of concerns and principles that opposed the prevailing models of political and economic thought. All of the contributors thought of Southern traditions as fundamentally more humane than modern industrial alternatives, and all of them were reacting against a national tendency to think of the South as a morally, intellectually, and culturally inferior region. When the prominent essayist and critic H.L. Mencken (whose 1917 anti-South essay "The Sahara of the Bozart" portrays the South as a cultural desert) and numerous other public figures heaped derision on the region in the wake of the 1925 Scopes "Monkey" trial in Dayton, Tennessee, Ransom and other Southern intellectuals took umbrage.

Not only were all twelve original Agrarians Southerners, most of them had some connection to Vanderbilt University in Nashville, Tennessee, and hence noticed the fallout of the events in Dayton even more than they might have otherwise. As Thomas Daniel Young explains in *Waking Their Neighbors Up: The Nashville Agrarians Rediscovered*, although *I'll Take My Stand* is primarily concerned with the relative values of two very different economic systems, the book was conceived as a response to the widespread ridicule of the South that resulted from the media circus surrounding the Scopes trial. Ransom, Tate, and Davidson, along with fellow Vanderbilt professors John Donald Wade, Frank Lawrence Owsley, and Lyle Lanier, met frequently to discuss the possibility of a concerted response, a rebuttal of the prevailing idea of Southern inferiority.

When *I'll Take My Stand* appeared in 1930, reviews were generally not enthusiastic. In the interim between the book's conception and its publication, the economic climate of the nation had taken a sharp turn for the worse. The Great Depression was hardly a fortuitous time to propose turning away from industrialism and the other aspects of capitalism that were widely perceived as positive qualities of modernization. Thus, the unfavorable critical responses were no surprise. What is somewhat surprising is that many critics apparently misunderstood the collection and condemned it as impractical, improvident, or inimical to progress, and thus *morally* backward. Appeals to progress that assumed industrial expansion was inherently linked to improved quality of life missed the major point of the collection, namely that those two things do not necessarily go hand in hand. The heated negative treatment of the book's central arguments was not entirely a bad thing, however,

in that it drew attention to the Agrarians' ideas about economic and social alternatives to the mainstream of American socioeconomic values. Andrew Nelson Lytle expresses the difference succinctly in his essay by declaring, "A farm is not a place to grow rich; it is a place to grow corn" (*I'll Take My Stand*, 205). Once *I'll Take My Stand* had generated critical controversy, several of the Agrarians went beyond this essay-based opposition and extended their arguments through a well-attended series of debates between individual Agrarians and opponents throughout the South.

Lytle's essay invites a discussion of the great problem of *I'll Take My Stand*: its embrace (not merely a reluctant acceptance) of racial segregation. Two paragraphs after making his pithy comment about the nonmonetary priorities of farming life, Lytle uses a startling metaphor to describe the hidden threat or surprise inherent in industrialism: "That is the nigger in the wood-pile" (205). To twenty-first–century readers, such a figure of speech comes as a jolt and detracts from the main line of the Agrarian argument by reminding us that the original Agrarians (all of whom were white males) were generally not interested in bettering the lot of African Americans, and for the most part their humanistic concerns did not extend beyond their own race or their own gender. Robert Penn Warren's "The Briar Patch" is the essay that deals most extensively with segregation, and its treatment of race relations has been controversial in two major ways: Although the essay generally defends the segregated Southern status quo, some contributors (especially Davidson) thought that it was too progressive, too liberal, and therefore at odds with the values of the rest of the collection. It is worth noting that although Warren's essay does discuss improving conditions for black workers, it does so primarily by emphasizing how such changes would directly benefit whites.

The second controversy regarding the essay was less intense and longer lasting: Though Warren increasingly distanced himself from "The Briar Patch," which he wrote when he was a graduate student at the beginning of a literary career that would last until his death in 1989, the essay's place in *I'll Take My Stand* ensured that it would be read by generations of critics even though Warren would rather have had it be forgotten. In the decades after 1930, Warren and Davidson occupied the most extreme positions of any Agrarians with regard to race relations: In 1956 Warren published *Segregation: The Inner Conflict in the South* (a sort of travelogue presenting Warren's examination of segregation in the Deep South), and in 1965 he published *Who Speaks for the Negro?*, a collection of interviews with African Americans, including prominent figures such as Martin Luther King, Malcolm X, and Stokely Carmichael. By then Warren had recanted his earlier segregationist views and he spoke of his nonfiction writings on race relations as the most important work he had ever done. Davidson, on the other hand, remained a lifelong segregationist. Davidson's somewhat-infamous poem "Sequel of Appomattox" stands as a convenient reminder of his unapologetic segregationist and Confederate sympathies. In it, ghostly Confederate cavalrymen call out, "Remember, I was your master; / Remember, you were my slave."

The legacy of the Confederacy haunts *I'll Take My Stand*, both in some essays' metaphorical use of Confederate rhetoric in arguments against the economic, social, and personal encroachments of Northern industrialism and in the collection's title itself. The second part of the title (*The South and the Agrarian Tradition*) is inoffensive, but the phrase "I'll Take My Stand" is a quotation from the Confederate marching song and anthem, "Dixie." Although the rhetoric of Confederate resistance shows up in several of the collection's essays, the title created some discord among contributors right from the beginning. Tate included a footnote expressing his disagreement with the book's title in his essay "Remarks on the Southern Religion," and in later years several of the contributors came to dislike the title, in part because they felt that it detracted from the essays' serious arguments, most of which had little to do with the Confederacy. Although some essays do refer directly to the Civil War and frame the rising tide of industrialism as a Yankee assault on Southern values, for the most part the title's "Dixie" reference functions as a sort of shorthand for a philosophical willingness to resist industrialization.

Nine of the twelve contributors to *I'll Take My Stand* also wrote essays for *Who Owns America?*; however, there were also a dozen new contributors, including one woman (Mary Shattuck Fisher, who contributed an essay called "The Emancipated Woman"). Many critics acknowledge the second collection as a sequel but continue to refer to the Twelve Southerners of the first collection as the Agrarians. The new contributors' relationship to the original group was and is somewhat difficult to define, in part because the original Agrarians existed as a group primarily between the covers of *I'll Take My Stand*. Depending on one's perspective, referring to the contributors of *Who Owns America?* as Agrarians is either a valid way of expanding the definition of the term (thereby including a wider range of essayists and ideas beyond those of the original twelve contributors) or the equivalent of a music group that continues touring for decades under the same name even though many or most of the original members have been replaced by new ones.

In recent decades, critics, scholars, and creative writers have increasingly come to regard *I'll Take My Stand* as a book that was ahead of its time. Paul V. Murphy has argued that the Agrarians' ideas influenced many aspects of the social and political conservative movements of recent decades, and several critics have compared *I'll Take My Stand* to **Henry David Thoreau**'s *Walden*. Both books urge readers to think deeply about the personal and economic costs of going along with the mass of men in pursuit of conventional economic success, both books were underappreciated in their own time, and both books now appear increasingly prescient and relevant to later generations of readers. In the years after *I'll Take My Stand*, the individual contributors went their separate intellectual ways. Ransom, one of the prime movers, turned his back on Agrarian ideas and eventually publicly disowned *I'll Take My Stand*. Tate, who had expressed the strongest reservations about the title, never abandoned his belief in Agrarian ideas; like a number of the other contributors, he viewed the increasingly mixed effects of industrialization on the South as proof that the Agrarians had been right.

In part because of the accelerating pace of the growth and industrialization of the South, the Agrarians' ideas strike some contemporary thinkers as being more relevant now than ever. **Wendell Berry**, whose poetry, novels, and essays have earned him considerable renown, is the most notable champion of Agrarian ideals today. Berry's writings often build on Agrarian themes and sometimes directly explain the significance and practicality of the ideas the Agrarians advocated, as in his 1999 essay "Still Standing," which argues that despite the racism inherent in *I'll Take My Stand*, its major elements are sound and in fact prefigure the activities of numerous present-day community-based agriculture groups. (Berry also practices what he preaches: He lives on a Kentucky farm and uses horses rather than tractors to work the land.) Many critics regard Berry as a contemporary Agrarian, a writer who remains committed to the Twelve Southerners' belief that rural life and a close connection to the environment offer significant dividends that American society tends to overlook.

Further Reading. ***Selected Primary Sources:*** Agar, Herbert, and Allen Tate, eds., *Who Owns America? A New Declaration of Independence* (Wilmington, DE: Intercollegiate Studies Institute, 1999); Twelve Southerners, *I'll Take My Stand: The South and the Agrarian Tradition* (Baton Rouge: Louisiana State University Press, 1977). ***Selected Secondary Sources:*** Berry, Wendell, "Still Standing" (*Oxford American* [January/February 1999]); Conkin, Paul K., *The Southern Agrarians* (Nashville, TN: Vanderbilt University Press, 2001); Duncan, Christopher M., *Fugitive Theory: Political Theory, the Southern Agrarians, and America* (New York: Lexington Books, 2000); Malvasi, Mark G., *The Unregenerate South: The Agrarian Thought of John Crowe Ransom, Allen Tate, and Donald Davidson* (Baton Rouge: Louisiana State University Press, 1997); Murphy, Paul V., *The Rebuke of History: The Southern Agrarians and American Conservative Thought* (Chapel Hill: University of North Carolina Press, 2001); Young, Thomas Daniel, *Waking*

Their Neighbors Up: The Nashville Agrarians Rediscovered (Athens: University of Georgia Press, 1982).

Sean Heuston

AI (1947–)

Ai has stood at the forefront of the activist poetry scene since the appearance of her first book, *Cruelty*, which caused a critical uproar when it appeared in 1973. Her poetry exposes exploitation and injustice as it probes the underside of life. The titles of her collections make clear her subject area. After *Cruelty*, her books include *Killing Floor* (1979), *Sin* (1986), *Fate* (1991), *Greed* (1993), and *Vice* (1999). She has also written a novel and articles. Ai's work is a part of the contemporary realist strain that has its roots in the work of the confessional poets of the 1950s, but that became less personal and more socially involved in the 1980s and 1990s. Her poetry is direct, to the point of sometimes seeming to assault the reader; her characters are vastly different from one another, sharing only, for the most part, a world of pain and deprivation. Some accept the limits unfairly imposed on them, while others fight those limits and occasionally overcome them. Ai's work brings to an audience of poetry readers some of the excitements of fiction; her narratives provide characterization, political analysis, and even suspense.

Ai was born Florence Anthony in Texas on October 21, 1947; her nom de plume is a Japanese word meaning "love." Of mixed African American, Native American, Irish, and Japanese ancestry, Ai has explored in her poems the multiple strands of her racial heritage. She received an MFA. from the University of California at Irvine in 1971. Her awards and honors include a Guggenheim fellowship (1975), two National Endowment for the Arts fellowships (1978, 1985), a Lamont poetry selection, and an American Book Award. She has taught creative writing at Wayne State University, George Mason University, Oklahoma State University, and the University of Colorado at Boulder, among other institutions.

Ai is best known for her dramatic monologues, which give voice to poverty-stricken and abused individuals who are motivated by the desire to live and experience. The speakers she chooses or invents are often powerless against violence from within and without. They struggle against poverty, bad luck, and the system that degrades and denies them. Most of them are women, and most of them are living (or dying) on the margins. The poems make the reader aware of social inequities in an immediate, shocking way, and the specific characters cannot be brushed aside lightly. One remembers "The Cockfighter's Daughter," for instance, long after finishing this story of violence and survival, and sees the speaker driving away with the fighting cock, the symbol of her own strong spirit.

Ai's first book, *Cruelty* (1973), establishes her subject matter, women and violence, and a central theme—the violence inherent in intimate relationships. The women of *Cruelty* are both victims and perpetrators; for example, the woman describes her desire in "Twenty-Year Marriage": "I'll pull, you push, we'll tear each other in half." Although Ai creates women who can dish it out as well as take it, she also has many protagonists who are overcome or annihilated as a result of their confrontations.

Killing Floor (1979) was a Lamont poetry selection and is very different in style from *Cruelty*; its poems are longer and more unified, and the voices of the speakers are more blunt and explicit. Some are historical figures, such as Marilyn Monroe and Leon Trotsky, who speaks on three different occasions in the title poem while his assassination date approaches.

Sin (1986), *Fate* (1991), and *Greed* (1993) continue to engage shockingly real individuals who are either popular or notorious icons or unknown ravaged psyches. *Sin*, which won the American Book Award, provides fully developed dramatic monologues that give new life to the form. Ai's portraits have some of the same effects as Diane Arbus's photographs: Everyone becomes a freak, and the reader will be wary of mirrors. In *Fate*, James Dean and Mary Jo Kopechne share space with the Cockfighter's Daughter and other marginalized figures of rural and urban life. In *Greed*, J. Edgar Hoover and Jack Ruby appear, and in "Finished" an abused wife shoots her husband and uncompromisingly sums up her own situation: "I shot him, I say, he beat me."

Vice: New and Selected Poems (1999) picks up some of the most powerful poems from the earlier collections and adds seventeen new works. This book received the National Book Award for Poetry for 1999. The poems from previous collections have been carefully culled, and the new poems round out the collection with monologues of local and foreign terrors. An especially hardhitting dramatic monologue, "Rwanda," tells the story of a girl whose terrorist neighbor kills the family and rapes her; the violation results in a child whom the speaker does not kill because her mother's bones tell her killing is wrong. The poem ends with the speaker in despair, because—unlike some of Ai's other traumatized women—she can do nothing to avenge herself.

Ai has been called "the foremost poet of urban terror," but in fact the terror knows no bounds: Rural and urban, foreign and domestic—all the characters are subject to the same drives and constraints. The poems provide the pleasure and suspense of narrative as the reader follows these tortured stories to their sometimes explosive conclusions. The guns, knives, and blood that so frequently appear in her work remind readers that civilization is not even skin deep.

Further Reading. *Selected Primary Sources:* Ai, *Cruelty* (Boston: Houghton Mifflin, 1973); ———, *Fate* (Boston: Houghton Mifflin, 1991); ———, *Greed* (New York:

Norton, 1993); ———, *Killing Floor* (Boston: Houghton Mifflin, 1979); ———, *Sin* (Boston: Houghton Mifflin, 1986); ———, *Vice: New and Selected Poems* (New York: Norton, 1999). **Selected Secondary Source:** Harrison, Pat, "The Many Voices of the Poet Ai" (*Radcliffe Quarterly* [Spring 2000]).

Janet McCann

AIKEN, CONRAD POTTER (1889–1973)

Perhaps no word is more often applied to the poetry of Conrad Aiken than "neglected." He is one of the most prolific of modern American poets, having published over forty books in his lifetime, most of which are poetry, but including also novels, short stories, drama, criticism, and an autobiography. He received many honors, including a Guggenheim, a National Book Award, and a Pulitzer, and he was one of the first modern American poets to receive a full-length study, Houston Peterson's *The Melody of Chaos* (1931). Contemporaries such as **R.P. Blackmur**, **Hayden Carruth**, Malcom Cowley, James Joyce, **T.S. Eliot**, and **Marianne Moore** have recognized Aiken's value as a poet in his own time, but it is a widespread theme, and point of regret, in much of the existing critical attention to Aiken, that he has, by reviewers and critics, largely been ignored, underestimated, or, at best, misunderstood.

Born in Savannah, Georgia, to socialite parents, Aiken faced the horror, at age eleven, of finding both of his parents dead in their home. Aiken's father had shot his wife in a rage, then killed himself. Aiken would later write in his autobiographical essay *Ushant* (1952) that, "finding them dead, [he] found himself possessed of them forever" (302). The oldest of four children, Aiken himself went to the police station to report the incident. He was then separated from his younger brothers and sister, who were adopted by a wealthy man. Conrad, after being shuffled between relatives, was finally settled in New England, where in 1903 he published a magazine with other boys at the Peabody Grammar School in Cambridge, and at Middlesex School in Concord became the editor of its literary magazine *Anvil*. In 1907 Aiken went to Harvard, and in 1911 he was named Class Poet. At Harvard Aiken joined a group—the classes of 1910–1915—of some of the most influential writers and intellectuals of the twentieth century: T.S. Eliot, John Reed, Walter Lippman, **e.e. cummings**, and Robert Benchley. Aiken befriended Eliot and studied with **George Santayana**.

Conrad Aiken's association with this group may offer a partial explanation for his relative obscurity in comparison with heralded figureheads of poetic movements such as Eliot and cummings. Although it was Aiken who introduced typescripts of Eliot's "The Love Song of J. Alfred Prufrock" to an enthusiastic **Ezra Pound**, Aiken's conservative language and prosody did not mesh with popular modes of writing in the 1920s, which valued stylistic experimentation and oddities and the reflection of the flux of modern life. In his criticism, Aiken even attacked **Imagism** and realism. Aiken's early poetry in particular, usually written in blank verse and including traditional rhymes and rhythms, often pegs him as an heir to the Romantics, as does his interest in creating an imaginative order as a solace to replace the moral emptiness of modern life.

Aiken published his first volume of poetry, *Earth Triumphant and Other Tales in Verse*, in 1914, when he was twenty-five. Aiken would include none of these poems in either his *Selected Poems* (1929) or *The Collected Poems* (1953, 1970), considering none of them salvageable. The poems are widely considered even by Aiken's admirers to be amateurish and overly mannered. The book appeared after his marriage to his first wife, Jesse McDonald, with whom he had three children. He would marry twice more, to Clarissa Lorenz, who saved him from a suicide attempt in 1932 and later wrote a book about their marriage, *Lorelei Two: My Life With Conrad Aiken* (1983); and, in 1937, to the artist Mary Hoover. By 1929 Aiken had published several volumes of poetry, enough to compile *Selected Poems*, for which he won the 1930 Pulitzer Prize. In the same year, he became a mentor to the young aspiring novelist Malcolm Lowry, with whom Aiken was to establish a lifelong, if tumultuous, connection, marred at times by Lowry's jealousy of Aiken and their influence on each other as drinkers and carousers.

Throughout his life, Aiken made his living primarily by writing. In 1934, the same year he won a Guggenheim, he began writing a series of essays for the *New Yorker* on world issues, called the "London Letters," under the pen name of Samuel Jeake, Jr. In 1950 Aiken served as the Chair of Poetry for the Library of Congress. In 1952, the same year *Ushant* was published, the *Wake* dedicated an issue to a discussion of Aiken's work, including a list by Malcom Lowry postulating reasons why Aiken had suffered critical neglect, the common theme among them being that his work was never amenable to the current idea of what poetry ought to do and be. This aspect of Aiken's work, Lowry and others thought, had often led critics to give it only casual critical attention, or to simply repeat what previous critics had said. Nonetheless, Aiken's *Collected Poems* earned him a National Book Award in 1954, and in 1958 he was awarded the Gold Medal for Poetry from the National Institute of Arts and Letters. Aiken lived in a variety of places, owning houses in England, Cape Cod, and, in his last twelve years, Savannah, next door to the house in which he had discovered his dead parents. He continued to write and publish poetry throughout his life. Suffering from a skin disease and a heart condition, Aiken died at the age of eighty-four.

Although often known more for his fiction than for his poetry—including stories such as "Silent Snow, Secret Snow" in his collection *Among the Lost People* (1934) and his psychoanalytic stream-of-consciousness novel, *Blue Voyage*, most likely influenced by James Joyce's *Ulysses*—Aiken considered himself, as he says in *Ushant*, primarily devoted to poetry. Aiken worked seriously and held himself to a high standard; he often revised poems that had already been published in volumes, before including them in later editions. His early poems, particularly those written before the 1930s, his major period, are included in such volumes as *Turns and Movies and Other Tales in Verse* (1916), *Jig of Forslin: A Symphony* (1916), *Nocturne of Remembered Spring* (1917), *Punch: The Immortal Liar* (1921), and others. Aiken's use of the language of story and music in his titles is reflected clearly in the poems themselves. Often the books are composed of long poems broken up into untitled, numbered sections, like chapters, in the case of the narrative portrait in *Punch*, or like musical movements, as in *House of Dust: A Symphony* (1920). The stories Aiken tells in verse are often concerned with the seemingly countless ways human beings can see and interpret the world. In *Punch* Aiken gives this common theme in his work an extended and dramatic structure, as various voices inspect the same "facts" about the title character from their individual perceptions, each in an attempt to decide for him- or herself—or for his or her listeners—what Punch is: fool or hero or devil.

In *John Deth: A Metaphysical Legend and Other Poems* (1930) Aiken further explores the possibilities of human consciousness, creating mythical figures to represent concepts from Sigmund Freud's *Beyond the Pleasure Principle* (1920). Aiken, who was greatly influenced by Freud, saw, in the concepts and terms of psychoanalysis, metaphors that could reveal insights into how human beings live their lives. At Harvard Aiken had joined its magazine the *Advocate*, for which he wrote poems whose themes of consciousness—such as "Le Penseur" (1910), in which a statue acquires life, then complains of being alone—would show up in more sophisticated ways in later poems, such as in his well-known "Telelestai" in *Priapus and the Pool and Other Poems* (1925).

Connected to Aiken's drive to explore a multiplicity of perceptions of the world is his use of musical forms and ideas. Between the years of 1914 and 1921, when he was in his late twenties, Aiken wrote his "symphonies," which make up *The Divine Pilgrim*. The poems are indebted for their style and vocabulary to, among others, Algernon Swinburne, Robert Browning, **Edgar Allan Poe**, and Oscar Wilde; but Aiken employed a new form, the symphonic, in which poetry's capacity for musical resonance is exploited. In addition to explicitly stated ideas and meanings, tone and sound are used to add layers of depth to a reader's understanding. Musical tones and rhythms are so evident in the poems as to require a complete exegesis to take them into account. Meaning lies not in a particular word, phrase, or line, but in the order of things and in the cumulative effect of sensory overtones of the language. Aiken's method is sometimes also called impressionistic. In *Senlin* (1918) the title "character" regards his reflection in the world around him (Is he the single ant, or the desert? Does his childhood lie in that small white hearse?) in order to answer the question of who he is and where he comes from. His scattered impressions form a sort of musical chorus, a multiplicity of voices in one, speaking from various parts of his psyche.

Aiken's style in the "symphonies" is often described as sweet and mellifluous, and he is sometimes compared to composers, notably Chopin and Debussy. Aiken may have been influenced by Walter Pater, who in 1877 included the phrase, in his "The School of Giorgione," that "all art constantly aspires toward the condition of music" (140). Aiken's poems have been criticized for lacking an intellectual firmness, but in his own criticism, Aiken often decried aesthetics of poetry that did not find musicality necessary or even valuable. His poems abound in colors and elements of nature that are somehow simultaneously rich and unspecific, leaving a shimmering effect, even ethereal or elusive. But in *Preludes for Memnon* (1931) and *Landscape West of Eden* (1934), Aiken turned toward a more analytic and ruminative style in which to continue his contemplation of the nature of consciousness. *Preludes for Memnon* is often seen as the core of Aiken's work, and the volume that establishes him as a major poet. As in *Senlin*, the speaker sees himself and his experience reflected in the world around him, in one case, in the wintry landscape: "The mind too has its snows, its slippery paths."

In both *Preludes for Memnon* and in *Time in the Rock, Preludes to Definition* (1936), Aiken also deals with the inadequacies of religion for developing the self and describing reality, and calls for a replacement of the religious search for faith with the kind of intense and self-reflective inspection of the world that his speakers so often practice.

After the publication of *Preludes to Definition*, Aiken felt, as many of his contemporaries and critics did, that the book was the crowning achievement of his career. He felt somewhat lost about what he should do next. Living at the time in England, and feeling threatened by the advent of World War II, Aiken returned with his new wife Mary in 1939 to the United States and experienced a revival of interest in the spirit and history of his home country. Exploring the themes of ancestors, roots, and uprootedness, Aiken wrote poems such as "Mayflower," "The Kid," and "Hallowe'en," which deal with American issues and their connections to Europe, as well as his still-prevalent themes of perception and consciousness. Aiken continued to mine American legends, folk tales, and scenes for the rest of his life's work, later adding to these the theme of "home." At an earlier point in his life, Aiken believed that feeling too "at home" might induce complacency and stifle interest in learning new things. However, in later poems—"A Letter from Li Po" (*A Letter from Li Po and Other Poems*, 1955) and "The Crystal" (*Sheepfold Hill*, 1958)—while often speaking with the voice of an exile, Aiken postulated that an "at home" feeling could exist simultaneously with a probing mind and spirit. Aiken continued to write poems, including three books of poetry for children, until his death in 1973.

Further Reading. *Selected Primary Sources:* Aiken, Conrad Potter, *Collected Poems*, 2nd ed. (New York: Oxford University Press, 1970); ———, *Earth Triumphant and Other Tales in Verse* (New York: St. Martin's Press, 1975); ———, *Ushant: An Essay* (New York: Little, Brown and Co., 1952). *Selected Secondary Sources:* Denney, Reuel, *Conrad Aiken* (Minneapolis: University of Minnesota Press, 1964); Harris, Catherine Kirk, *Conrad Aiken: Critical Recognition, 1914–1981: A Bibliographic Guide* (New York: Garland Publishing, 1983); Hoffman, Frederick J., *Conrad Aiken* (New York: Twayne Publishers, 1962); Marten, Henry, *The Art of Knowing: The Poetry and Prose of Conrad Aiken* (Columbia: University of Missouri Press, 1988); Martin, Jay, *Conrad Aiken: A Life of His Art* (Princeton, NJ: Princeton University Press, 1962).

Cheri Johnson

ALBEE, JOHN (1833–1915)

John Albee wrote poetry and essays in the vein of the Transcendentalists, the nineteenth-century writers and philosophers who adhered to an idealistic system of thought that posited a belief in the essential unity of all creation, the innate goodness of humanity, and the superiority of insight over logic and experience in pursuit of the deepest truths. As a student at the orthodox seminary of Andover, he had been stirred to unrest like so many young men of the time by **Ralph Waldo Emerson**'s radical idealism. A member of the Boston intelligentsia, Albee espoused the wonders of nature in his work, particularly the glory of his beloved coastal region of New Hampshire.

Albee was born in Bellingham, Massachusetts, on April 3, 1833, the son of John and Esther Thayer Albee. In May 1852 Albee called upon Ralph Waldo Emerson to inquire as to how one might receive the best kind of education. Upon arrival, he met **Henry David Thoreau** and was able to observe the dynamic of the two writers' relationship. Albee recorded his observations in his *Remembrances of Emerson* (1901), noting that Thoreau "was much at home with Emerson: and he remained through the afternoon and evening;

and I left him still at the fire side, he appeared to me to belong in some way to the household" (18–19). Regarding Albee's inquiry, Emerson recommended a college education; Thoreau angrily objected, criticizing both education and educational institutions. Albee concluded that Emerson deliberatey chastised Thoreau to amuse himself, laughing heartily when his casual remark that most branches of learning were taught at Cambridge was answered with Thoreau's caustic "Yes indeed, all of the branches and none of the roots" (*Remembrances*, 22). Taking Emerson's advice, Albee attended Harvard University as a student of Divinity but devoted his time to studying philosophy, nature, and literary and linguistic research. While pursuing these, he divided his life between traveling abroad and working his farms, one by the ocean in New Castle, New Hampshire, and the other in the New Hampshire mountains near Chocorua. He married Harriet Ryan, founder of the Channing Street Home for Sick and Destitute Women, who died in 1873 from consumption. Albee served as lecturer at the Concord School of Philosophy and elsewhere. His output in poetry and prose includes *Literary Art*, 1881; *Poems*, 1883; *New Castle, Historic and Picturesque*, 1884; and *Prose Idyls*, 1892. He died in New England on March 24, 1915.

Albee's writings center primarily on nature, particularly the wildlife and lore of the New England seacoast around New Hampshire. Having farmed the terrain there, he felt a part of the rocky soil and salty brine. This intimacy with the rhythmic cycle of the earth and water allowed him to write about the minutest aspects of life, from the murmur of the tide to the buds of the earth. His poem "Dandelions" bears this out as he follows the life span of the foliage from "Some morn it opes a little golden sun" until "it findeth wings and lightly flies, / A Spirit form, till on the sight it dies." This cyclical pulse is captured in Albee's poems about human mortality as well. From the "sweet repose" found in "A Soldier's Grave" to the portentous call of death from "Bos'n Hill," the poet conveys the notion of death as an undisturbed slumber that is to be not feared but anticipated.

Albee's interest in his adopted New Castle likely led him to invest in an area hostelry that he named the Wentworth Hotel (now Wentworth by the Sea). To aid visitors in exploring the region, he wrote the only history of New Castle, published in 1884 as *New Castle, Historic and Picturesque*. His delving into local myths and legends inspired him that same year to write "Saint Aspenquid," a poem that appeared in a collection of New England folk stories by Samuel Adams Drake. The poem opens with the elderly seventeenth-century Native American chief Passaconaway bidding farewell to his people gathered on Agamenticus, the highest point in the seacoast region. Although the poem is based loosely on the historic Penacook leader who refused to go to war with the first New England settlers, his Jesuit alter ego is a literary fabrication. Albee's poem turns on the imagined notion that the supernatural "saint" advised his followers to cooperate with the European traders despite his vision that the situation would prove hopeless for his race no matter what their actions. The poem's closing lines, "But mind the counsel many years have taught, / The last I give: remember it and live" strike a noble, uplifting chord, although the historic tribe would be devastated by disease, leaving at the end of the century only a few hundred survivors to face exile in Canada.

Though Albee's works are largely out of print and difficult to find, the impetus of his oeuvre, the peaks and waves along the mighty New England shores, stands as testament to his idyllic vision.

Further Reading. *Selected Primary Sources:* Albee, John, *Literary Art* (1881); ———, *New Castle, Historic and Picturesque* (1884); ———, *Poems* (1883); ———, *Prose Idyls* (Boston: Houghton Mifflin, 1892); ———, *Remembrances of Emerson* (New York: R.G. Cooke, 1901). *Selected Secondary Source:* Cooke, George Willis, *The Poets of Transcendentalism: An Anthology* (Hartford, CT: Transcendental Books, 1971).

Roxanne Y. Schwab

ALCOTT, AMOS BRONSON (1799–1888)

Amos Bronson Alcott was a Transcendentalist philosopher, educator, and writer. He once observed in his own journal that he had "written too little verse to claim the poet's inspiration" (Shepard, 501), and thus his most enduring contributions to American poetry came through his influence on others. In his friendships with **Ralph Waldo Emerson** and the other Transcendentalists, he helped articulate the American Romantic impulse that inspired **Jones Very**, **James Russell Lowell**, **Walt Whitman**, and others. Emerson credited Alcott with enormous influence on his own thinking, for they shared a commitment to intuitive inspiration and a dissatisfaction with social convention.

Alcott was born on November 29, 1799, at Spindle Hill, his family's home in Wolcott, Connecticut. As a young man he traveled through the South as a peddler, then returned to New England to pursue the vocation to which he would dedicate much of his life: teaching. Alcott identified the traditional methods of recitation and rote memorization as insufficient; he believed education should prepare the soul of the child to aspire. He gained varied experience through teaching at several schools in Connecticut and Boston, as well as briefly in Pennsylvania (he had also taught for a few months while traveling through Virginia). In 1834 he opened the Temple School in Boston. During this phase of great activity in teaching, Alcott published two essays on education: *Observations on the Principles and Methods of Infant Instruc-*

tion (1830) and *On the Doctrine and Discipline of Human Culture* (1836). In these essays he insisted that adults must tailor their pedagogy to the special needs of the child's mind and conscience.

Alcott became notorious for his own pedagogy when he published *Conversations with Children on the Gospels* (1836–1837). The book described Socratic exchanges at the Temple School in which Alcott had encouraged his students to explore such unorthodox topics as the physiology of birth and the circumcision of Christ. The outcry over this book, along with Alcott's admission of an African American child, resulted in dwindling enrollments, and he was forced to close the school in 1838. Five years later he helped to found Fruitlands, a small commune at which he experimented with agriculture and education, but the effort foundered after only a few months. He was appointed Concord superintendent of schools in 1859 and served until 1865, returning to assist on a voluntary basis in 1875–1876. In 1879 he established the Concord School of Philosophy with William Torrey Harris, Frank Sanborn, and others, and remained active in it until his death in 1888.

Alcott's most widely known writings were his "Orphic Sayings," two series of prose poems that appeared in the Transcendentalists' journal the *Dial* in July 1840 and January 1841. These brief paragraphs expressed Alcott's philosophy on such topics as "Bread": "Wouldst enter into life? Beg bread then. In the kingdom of God are love and bread consociated, but in the realm of mammon, bread sojourns with lies, and truth is a starvling." Alcott's often abstruse remarks were greeted with much derision by critics of Transcendentalism, who cited his abstract impenetrability as typical of the movement's impracticality. Washington Irving's *Knickerbocker* published cruel parodies of the sayings, congratulated the *Dial*'s editors when none of Alcott's work appeared in the magazine's second issue, mocked his writing in the third issue, and proposed publicly that he adopt (as a more suitable "organ" for his thoughts) a hand organ to play in the streets while begging. This reception did not prevent Alcott from contributing further to the *Dial* or from writing poetry, but he crafted no more "Orphic Sayings" for the magazine.

Alcott occasionally published his verse in local papers such as the Boston *Commonwealth*. His early poems evinced a longing for wisdom and virtue, as in "The Return," where he ennobled the thinker's struggle to overcome despair. Nearer the end of his life, he immortalized his friends and family in *Sonnets and Canzonets* (1882), a collection of portraits in which he celebrated the lives of such figures as Waldo and Lidian Emerson, **Margaret Fuller**, Elizabeth Peabody, **Ellery Channing**, and his own third daughter (whose death had also been dramatized in *Little Women*, the autobiographical novel authored by his second daughter, Louisa May). At Emerson's funeral a few months after the collection appeared, Alcott read "Ion: A Monody," another sonnet that voiced an aching solitude and mourned the loss of the many friends whom he had survived.

Alcott's writings, however, provide only a partial record of his significance to Transcendentalism. Many Transcendentalists referred to the incomparable experience of attending one of Alcott's "Conversations," a discussion series on topics in philosophy, literature, or history. In his own journal, Emerson lamented that Alcott's conversation, formal and informal, could not be captured on the page. Alcott and other acquaintances believed that the last chapter of Emerson's *Nature* (1836), with its remarks to a poet, were written with Alcott in mind, and Alcott's friend and biographer F.B. Sanborn has observed that Alcott may have inspired several of the descriptions of the true intellectual in James Russell Lowell's poems.

Further Reading. *Selected Primary Sources:* Alcott, Amos Bronson, *Conversations with Children on the Gospels* (1836; reprint New York: Arno Press, 1972); ———, *Essays on Education* (Gainesville, FL: Scholars' Facsimiles & Reprints, 1960); ———, *The Journals of Bronson Alcott*, ed. Odell Shepard (Boston: Little, Brown and Co., 1938); ———, *The Letters of A. Bronson Alcott*, ed. Richard L. Herrnstadt (Ames: Iowa State University Press, 1969); ———, "Orphic Sayings" (*Dial* 1.1 [1840]: 85-98); ———, "Orphic Sayings" (*Dial* 1.3 [1841]). *Selected Secondary Sources:* Bedell, Madelon, *The Alcotts: Biography of a Family* (New York: Clarkson N. Potter, 1980); Dahlstrand, Frederick C., *Amos Bronson Alcott: An Intellectual Biography* (Rutherford, NJ: Fairleigh Dickinson UP, 1982); Sanborn, F. B., and William T. Harris, *A. Bronson Alcott: His Life and Philosophy* (2 vols, Boston: Roberts Brothers, 1893); Shepard, Odell, *Pedlar's Progress: The Life of Bronson Alcott* (Boston: Little, Brown and Company, 1937).

Tara L. Robbins

ALCOTT, LOUISA MAY (1832–1888)

Although poetry is not the genre for which Louisa May Alcott is best known, it is the genre in which she first published at the age of eighteen, when her poem "Sunset" appeared in *Peterson's Magazine* (Vol. XX, No. 3, 1851) under the pseudonym Flora Fairfield. Throughout her lifetime, Alcott wrote poetry but published relatively little, especially after the publication of her most famous novel, *Little Women*, in 1868. Her poetry provides insights into the time in which she lived and the family and friends who were important to her. No collection of Alcott's poetry was published during her lifetime, but many of her poems were published posthumously in Ednah Cheney's *Louisa May Alcott: Her Life, Letters and Journals* (1889).

Louisa May Alcott was born in 1832 in Germantown, Pennsylvania, to Bronson and Abigail "Abba" Alcott. The Alcott family moved several times, but they lived primarily in Concord or Boston. **Amos Bronson Alcott**'s career as a Transcendentalist philosopher and educator kept the family poor, but Abba provided for the family by working in a variety of jobs outside the home while her husband traveled and lectured. Louisa's unconventional education included attending her father's schools and learning from the Alcott's friends and neighbors, including **Henry David Thoreau**, the abolitionist Frank Sanborn, the preacher Theodore Parker, and **Ralph Waldo Emerson**, whom she idolized. To help support her family, Louisa began working as a teenager by teaching Emerson's children, taking in sewing, and once working as "companion," which she later recounted in "How I Went Out to Service." After her first book, *Flower Fables*, was published (1855), Alcott continued to publish poetry and juvenile stories along with her "blood and thunder" stories, which were published anonymously or under the pseudonym A.M. Barnard. These gothic thrillers and lurid romances earned Alcott money that helped pay her family's bills, and Alcott determined to continue to earn money so that her family would not live in poverty. Her first real literary success came with the publication of *Hospital Sketches* (1863), based on her experiences working as a nurse in a Georgetown Civil War hospital at the age of 30. In 1867 Alcott became the editor of a children's magazine, *Merry's Museum*, but it was the publication of *Little Women* that allowed Alcott to pay all of her family's debts and to experience some peace and independence, though she never did break her close ties to her family. After *Little Women*, her continued success as a writer of short stories and novels for children provided her financial security and enabled her to take care of her parents and other family members as well. For the most part, Alcott stopped publishing her "lurid novels" and her poetry after the success of *Little Women*, although she published an adult novel, *Work*, in 1873 and *A Modern Mephistopheles* in 1877, which was published anonymously. Louisa May Alcott was a social reformer who supported abolition, temperance, and women's suffrage. She never married, but she did raise Lulu, the daughter of May, Louisa's youngest sister, who died in 1879 just seven weeks after giving birth. Along with raising Lulu, Alcott's final years were devoted to caring for her father, who had a stroke in 1882. Alcott died March 6, 1888, two days after her father's death.

Alcott's poetry reveals information about the important events and people of her lifetime, including her family and such notables as Thoreau and **Nathaniel Hawthorne**. Her poetry includes a range of topics and tones, beginning with nature in "To the First Robin," the first poem she wrote, at the age of eight, to the poems in which she wrote about the loss of people she loved, to her satirical poetry after the publication of *Little Women*. As an example of her satire, "The Lay of the Golden Goose" concerns a little goose whose father was "A mild Socratic bird," a goose who was laughed at by the owls, "Hooting above the rest, / No useful egg was ever hatched / From transcendental nest." The goose who went through many years of struggle before being suddenly lauded is, of course, Louisa herself, who became disconcerted by the constant demand of the periodical editors after the publication of *Little Women*. In "A Wail Uttered in the Woman's Club," which refers to the Concord Women's Club, Alcott asks the women of the club to "Forget awhile your Woman's Rights, / And pity author's wrongs," and takes aim at both the male philosophers of Concord and at the literary tourists who constantly "Embalm the chickweed from their yards, / And photograph their cats."

While her brilliant wit comes through in poems satirizing society, Alcott's sorrow and warmth is found in the many poems she wrote about people she cared for. "Thoreau's Flute," for example, is a beautiful poem written about Henry David Thoreau, a neighbor of the Alcotts in Concord. The poem came to her one night when she was caring for a wounded soldier at the Union City Hotel Hospital in Georgetown. Sophia Hawthorne brought the poem to the attention of the *Atlantic Monthly*, where it was published anonymously in 1863. In the poem Alcott writes that although "The Genius of the wood is lost" he "still will be / A potent presence, though unseen." Thoreau had been a strong presence in her young life, teaching her botany on long walks in the woods. Her poem "Transfiguration," a tribute to her mother after she died in November 1877, was first published anonymously in *A Masque of Poets* (1878), a "noname series" by Roberts Brothers. In the poem Alcott refers to her mother's faith, hope, patience, and loyalty, and to her "great, deep heart that was a home for all." Another example of a poem about the loss of a loved one appears in *Little Women*, attributed to the character of Jo, who is writing about her sister Beth, who is ill. The poem, "My Beth," was actually written by Alcott as she watched her sister Lizzie die in 1858.

"My Beth," along with the other poems in *Little Women*, may be Alcott's best-known pieces, yet they are but a small sample of the many poems she wrote during her lifetime, which included poetry for children, poetry for family and friends to commemorate birthdays and memorials, poems to satirize society, and poems to honor people she admired, such as "With a Rose That Bloomed on the Day of John Brown's Martyrdom," a poem honoring the abolitionist John Brown after his execution at Harper's Ferry. Although Jo, in *Little Women*, claims her poetry is "bad poetry," and Alcott claimed to know little about poetry, she wrote many poems that illustrate her humor, her talent, and her perspective on the world in which she lived.

Further Reading. *Selected Primary Sources:* Alcott, Lousia May, *Little Women*, With an Introduction by Ann Douglas (New York: Signet Classic, 1983); Cheney, Ednah, *Louisa May Alcott: Her Life, Letters and Journals* (Boston: Roberts Brothers, 1889); Gray, Janet, ed., *She Wields a Pen* (Iowa City: University of Iowa Press, 1997); *L. M. Alcott: An Intimate Anthology*, New York Public Library's Collector's Edition (New York: Doubleday, 1997); ***Selected Secondary Sources:*** Boyd, Anne E., *Writing for Immortality* (Baltimore: Johns Hopkins University Press, 2004); Stern, Madeleine B., ed., *Critical Essays on Louisa May Alcott* (Boston: G.K. Hall & Co., 1984); ———, *Louisa May Alcott: A Biography* (New York: Random House, 1996).

Deborah Brown

ALDRICH, ANNE REEVE (1866–1892)

Like her contemporary **Emily Dickinson**, Anne Reeve Aldrich wrote lyric poetry centered on the themes of love, death, nature, and God. Her eloquent, concise, and deceptively simple verses reveal a touching voice on the verge of artistic maturity.

Aldrich, a relation of poet James Aldrich, was born in New York, New York, on April 25, 1866. She realized her interest in writing in her early childhood, creating stories and verses when she was not romping outdoors. Upon her father's death, when she was eight years old, Aldrich was taken to the country by her mother, who assumed responsibility for her education before assigning the task to a series of tutors. The young pupil excelled at language skills, translating French and Latin authors for amusement, but struggled over elementary arithmetic equations that could leave her in tears. Following a note of encouragement coupled with her first poetry rejection from Scribner's, the fifteen-year-old continued reading everything from early English poems and plays to medieval literature and wrote voraciously, destroying her work from month to month. By age seventeen she had contributed pieces to *Lippincott's*, *Century*, *Scribner's*, and other literary periodicals. Fonder of the social whirl of the city than of bucolic solitude, Aldrich returned to New York a few years later. Her first book, *The Rose of Flame*, was published in 1889 but was criticized for its immature, unbridled emotionalism. Her next book, a novel titled *The Feet of Love*, came out in 1890. Aldrich died in New York City on June 28, 1892, before her last lyrical volume, *Songs about Love, Life and Death* could be released. Its posthumous publication demonstrated that amid the words of suffering, the poet conveyed a moving maturity.

In Dickinsonian fashion, Aldrich looks to the world around her for symbols to express her deepest longings. Her poem "A Song about Singing" speaks not just for the tuneful bird but for the voluble artist as well, who sees the nightingale as a kindred spirit "[w]ho never sings so well as when / The rose thorns bruise his heart."

Despite her passion for metropolitan society, Aldrich conveys a kinship with the natural world. Her identification with the suffering nightingale communicates her realization that those upon whom special gifts are bestowed must use them for the good of humankind, with little thought for personal consolation. She recognizes that all blessings are bestowed by God, yet the deity of Aldrich's verses seeks not human perfection but the desire to increase one's spirituality, as demonstrated in her poem "The Eternal Justice." While some view Judgment Day as threatening, she is grateful to be judged by "He who knows the whole." Aldrich attests that the heavenly Father is "wholly just" and that those who believe in him will "live untouched by fear." She is certain that the Almighty, having marked all souls with original sin, seeks only that his people work toward salvation. To this end, the purpose of earthly life is to achieve salvation through the comfort that we can provide to others in pain, no matter what the cause. This notion of ministering to the needs of fellow beings is fully expressed in Aldrich's lyric "Fraternity," in which, "in our anguish-darkened land," we must draw close to each other in commiseration, whispering the password, "Yeah, I understand!"

Many of Aldrich's verses center on suffering through loss of hope, love, or life. In the world of agony she depicts, however, there is always the promise of aid and solace to be found in the warmth of the light. The poet's words convey that beacon, reminding the listener that distress is but a temporary affliction.

Further Reading. *Selected Primary Sources:* Aldrich, Anne Reeve, *The Feet of Love* (New York: Scribner's, 1890); ———, *The Rose of Flame* (New York: Scribner's, 1889); ———, *Songs about Love, Life, and Death* (New York: Scribner's, 1892). *Selected Secondary Source:* Willard, Frances Elizabeth, *American Women* (Detroit: Gale, 1973).

Roxanne Y. Schwab

ALDRICH, THOMAS BAILEY (1836–1907)

Thomas Bailey Aldrich is remembered more as a less-than-famous American man of letters than as a beloved bad boy from Portsmouth who made good. Aldrich's legendary rapier-like wit is evident in his caustic comment about Horace Scudder, his successor at the *Atlantic Monthly*, who, Aldrich contended, was greater than the biblical Moses because "while Moses dried up the Red Sea once, Scudder dried up the *Atlantic* monthly." His wit is also notable in a remark about his descendants (both the Bailey and Aldrich families), who could trace their roots to colonial America. He quipped, "I could boast of a long line of ancestors, but won't. They are of no possible benefit to me, save it is pleasant to think that none of them were hanged for criminals or shot for traitors."

Aldrich was born in 1836 in Portsmouth, New Hampshire. Although he spent some time in New Orleans, he returned to Portsmouth between 1849 and 1852, where his most popular story, "The Story of a Bad Boy," takes place. At age sixteen, Aldrich, after his father's death, took off to New York to work at his uncle's bank. There, at nineteen, he launched his career as a poet and critic and as editor of such magazines as *Home Journal*, *Illustrated News*, and *Saturday Press*. After a hitch as a correspondent in the Civil War, Aldrich returned to the "bohemian" New York literary scene.

Aldrich's first success came at age nineteen with the sentimental poem "The Ballad of Babie Bell" in 1855. This poem was a part of his first volume of verse, *The Bells: A Collection of Chimes*. His success propelled him into the midst of New York City's literati, among whom he was noted principally for his wit. In the same year, Aldrich became a junior literary critic of the magazine *Evening Mirror* and then sub-editor of *Home Journal*. Married to Lilian Woodman in 1865 as a resident of Boston, he became friends with such luminaries as **William Dean Howells**, Mark Twain, **James Thomas Fields**, **Henry Wadsworth Longfellow**, and **James Russell Lowell**. His reputation as a wit and writer of note and accomplishment made him a good choice to succeed Howells as the editor of the *Atlantic Monthly*, the most important literary magazine of its time.

Aldrich's most important work, *The Story of a Bad Boy*, is an autobiographical recount of his own childhood spent at his grandfather's "Nutter House" on Court Street in Portsmouth. The house is now the Thomas Bailey Aldrich Memorial. Mark Twain was in attendance at the memorial ceremony at Portsmouth Music Hall in 1908. The story itself is about the life of "Tom Bailey," who was no "faultless young gentleman," but rather a "real human boy such as you may meet anywhere." The comparison of Tom to Twain's "Tom Sawyer" is clear, as is Aldrich's purpose for his novel: to entertain rather than to instruct. For this shift in the author's intent alone Aldrich merits a closer examination, as the story renders the first realistic portrayal of a boy in American literature. In the story, Tom and his friends set off some old cannons on the wharf at midnight, rousing the entire town; steal an old mail coach and push it into the Fourth of July bonfire; and spend a night "shipwrecked" on a river island, which sounds suspiciously close to an incident in *The Adventures of Huckleberry Finn*. Aldrich also penned *An Old Town by the Sea*, an 1883 evocative literary picture of this New England region at the end of the nineteenth century. Aldrich died at the age of seventy in 1907.

Further Reading. *Selected Primary Sources:* Aldrich, Thomas Bailey, *Marjorie Daw and Other People* (Boston: Houghton Mifflin, 1901); ———, *The Poems of Thomas Bailey Aldrich* (Boston: Houghton Mifflin, 1885); ———, *A Sea Turn and Other Matters* (Boston: Houghton Mifflin, 1902); ———, *The Story of a Bad Boy* (Boston: Houghton Mifflin, 1927); ———, *The Writings of Thomas Bailey Aldrich* (Cambridge, MA: Printed at the Riverside Press, 1897–1907). *Selected Secondary Sources:* Bellman, Samuel I., "Riding on Wishes: Ritual Make-Believe Patterns in Three 19th-Century American Authors: Aldrich, Hale, Bunner," in *Ritual in the United States: Acts and Representations*, ed. Don Harkness (Tampa, FL: American Studies Press, 1985); Gribben, Alan, "'I Did Wish Tom Sawyer Was There': Boy-Book Elements in *Tom Sawyer* and *Huckleberry Finn*," in *One Hundred Years of Huckleberry Finn: The Boy, His Book, and American Culture*, ed. Robert Sattelmeyer et al. (Columbia: University of Missouri Press, 1985); Samuels, Charles E., *Thomas Bailey Aldrich* (New York: Twayne Publishers, 1965); West, Mark I., "Rediscovering Thomas Bailey Aldrich's *The Story of a Bad Boy*" (*Teaching and Learning Literature* 7.5 [May–June 1998]: 39–44).

David Fritz

ALEXANDER, ELIZABETH (1962–)

Born in 1962 in Harlem, New York, Elizabeth Alexander received a BA from Yale University, a MA from Boston University, and a Ph. D. from the University of Pennsylvania. Her first book of poems, *The Venus Hottentot* (1990), announced the emergence of a potentially major new talent on the American literary landscape. Alexander's subsequent publications, *Body of Life* (1996) and *Antebellum Dream Book* (2001), have demonstrated a steadiness of focus and consistency of tone that, depending on the reader, may seem reassuringly familiar or monotonously obsessive. In either case, what appears indisputable is that Alexander's work, above all else, pays homage to the female body of color inscribed within American and European cultural history. It is her singular and most compelling theme.

As a woman of mixed blood from a prominent Harlem family, Alexander often links the question of women of color and their bodies to intraracial and interracial issues. Issues of class and caste, however, are apparently taken for granted—another way of saying that Alexander's work, like that of **Rita Dove** or Alice Walker (but unlike that of **Lucille Clifton** or **Gwendolyn Brooks**, for example), is mainstream in some of its methods and concerns. To this extent her work is in a tradition that includes not only Dove and Walker but also a **Harlem Renaissance** poet such as Anna Julia Cooper or, in the nineteenth century, **Frances Ellen Watkins Harper**. These poets all privilege the lives of women of color as their themes and, formally, they all depend on narrative and lyrical methodologies. For Alexander in particular, issues of skin color and gender drive her paeans to women like Josephine Baker, the Venus Hottentot, and Frieda Kahlo. These three women—an African, an African American, and a Mexican—function for Alexander as exemplars of those who could not escape their historical epoch, which linked, in different ways, their status as "artists" to their bodies.

In many respects, this legacy—the body bound to the woman artist—is one that Alexander struggles with throughout all three collections of poems. One could argue, for example, that Alexander's multiple variations on the "body" merely reinforce the objectification of the female body. In her 2001 collection of poetry, *Antebellum Dream Book*, Alexander links the experience of the body within the body—pregnancy—with her own mixed-race body, the white body inside the black body ("Clean" and "After the Gig: Mick Jagger") and the black body inside the white body ("Race"). In the first two poems, the body belongs to the narrator, however subject to external forces. To reject or excise any part of it would be to undermine her identity. Thus, in the poem "Clean," the narrator dreams of excreting a bar "of Lever Brothers soap, / a huge white lovely cake," but doing so causes her stomach to shrink until it is empty. In "Race" the black body inside the white body is both literal—a black man married to a white woman—and figurative: the man "passes" as white. Thus pregnancy, a central theme in *Antebellum Dream Book*, is another manifestation of the body-in-body theme—as sexual and racial politics—that dominates the first two books, *The Venus Hottentot* and *Body of Life*. Collectively, the Escher-like blending of bodies in all three books suggests that the question of racial identity is not something to turn away from, especially for one who is racially "mixed." On the contrary, Alexander's own body becomes emblematic of American culture in general. She not only sings America, she *is* America. Yet it would be a mistake to suggest that Alexander's poetic output represents a reification of that cliché of multiculturalism, the "melting pot." On the contrary, Alexander is careful to delineate the differences—indeed, the conflicts—both without and within the mixed-race bodies that constitute Americans and Americana.

The tension between the actual people who populate the United States and a culture that, too often, whitewashes the ethnic and racial differences of the populace is the theme in Alexander's first two books. Whereas *The Venus Hottentot* concerns itself with the cultural and political representations of the body, especially the black female body, *Body of Life* develops the confessional mode already implicit in the first book. Thus "Stravinsky in L.A.," from *Body of Life*, turns on the conundrum of celebration and appropriation, with the speaker hoping to one day understand "these people, rhythms, jazz, Simon Rodia, / Watts, Los Angeles, aspiration." By juxtaposing this meditation on the problem of representing the "other" with the problem of self-representation ("The Josephine Baker Museum"), Alexander stakes out the divide between American realities and American representations of those realities via the immigrant and the expatriate. The ambivalence of their experiences vis-à-vis their "host" countries (e.g., Stravinsky in America, Baker in France) represents for Alexander the ambivalence of being "black."

What it means to be a woman appears, in Alexander's poetry, to be less contested. In the private sphere, Alexander has no problem refusing idealized "models" of what American women "should" look like. In a poem like "Butter," she celebrates the sheer pleasure of eating. This exuberance has been won, Alexander implies, by women who sacrificed their bodies for men and a culture founded on spectacle and objectification. Thus, in "Painting," from *The Venus Hottentot*, the famed artist Frieda Kahlo confesses that she has "cropped the black hair Diego loves." The poem follows the logic of this editing of the body to its cruel conclusion: self-immolation. "Painting" encapsulates the role women of color once played, and often still play, under patriarchy: that which must be cropped, shaped, molded. Alexander's response to the winnowed, whittled-down woman is to drive in the opposite direction: a celebration of all the body's appetites.

Further Reading. ***Selected Primary Sources:*** Alexander, Elizabeth, *Antebellum Dream Book* (St. Paul, MN: Graywolf, 2001); ———, *Body of Life* (Chicago: Tia Chucha, 1996); ———, *The Venus Hottentot* (Charlottesville: University Press of Virginia, 1990). ***Selected Secondary Sources:*** Phillip, Christine, "An Interview with Elizabeth Alexander" (*Callaloo* 19.2 [1996]: 493–507); Rose, Tricia, "Call and Response" (*Village Voice Literary Supplement* 109 [October 1992]: 11–12); Trethewey, Natasha, "The Far, Deep Things of Dreamland: An Interview with Elizabeth Alexander" (*Poets & Writers* 29 [November/December 2001]: 28–33).

Tyrone Williams

ALEXANDER, MEENA (1951–)

Meena Alexander is a much-acclaimed writer in the late twentieth- and early twenty-first–century wave of South Asian American Literature. Variously noted as a poet, novelist, memoirist, and literary critic, Alexander considers poetry the genre closest to her heart. She writes poetry with a critical self-awareness of language and an emphatic precision of image. Having lived in India, Sudan, England, and the United States, Alexander is acutely conscious of the roles that place, memory, and language play in identity formation. Her writing, drawing on experiences among diverse ethnic and religious communities on four continents, maps a geographical and psychological landscape of postcolonial diaspora. In particular, her work offers a perceptive examination of the construction of gender within the postcolonial condition.

Alexander was born into a socially prominent Syrian Christian family in Allahabad, India, on February 17, 1951. The family relocated in Khartoum, Sudan, in 1956 when Alexander's father took up a job with the Sudanese government. From age five to eighteen, Alexander lived with her parents in Khartoum, traveling between Sudan and India. In 1969 she graduated from Khartoum University with a Bachelor of Arts degree. Then she left her Sudanese home and pursued graduate studies at the University of Nottingham in England. After earning her Ph.D. in 1973 from Nottingham, she returned to India and worked first at Delhi University and later at universities in Hyderabad. During her return to India, Alexander published her first collections of poetry: *The Bird's Bright Ring* (1976), *I Root My Name* (1977), and *Without Place* (1978). Alexander's early poetry favors Indian themes and imagery, often depicting the sociopolitical effects of British rule in India with sharp and concrete images of native flora, fauna, and cultural emblems.

Late in 1979, after several months as a visiting fellow at the Sorbonne in Paris, Alexander immigrated to the United States and settled in Manhattan. By the late 1980s she had not only contributed numerous scholarly articles to literary journals and feminist anthologies, but also published the poetry collections *House of a Thousand Doors* (1988), *The Storm* (1989), and *Night-Scene, the Garden* (1989) as well as the critical study *Women in Romanticism* (1989). In this period, her poetry becomes more fervently feminist. Her first book published in the United States, *House of a Thousand Doors*, based on the memories of her grandmother, introduces the story of postcolonial migrant women that constitutes most of her later work. The enigmatic grandmother image, through *The Storm* and *Night Scene, the Garden*, is developed as a bridge between differences in race, age, and sex. Also ubiquitous is the voice of the lyric female "I," as when she addresses the women of Delhi, saying, "You do not see how centuries of dream are flowing from your land / And so I sing knowing poetry to be like bread."

In the 1990s Alexander turned out more books in prose than in poetry, writing two novels, *Nampally Road* (1991) and *Manhattan Music* (1997); a memoir, *Fault Lines* (1993); a book of prose and poetry, *The Shock of Arrival: Reflections on Postcolonial Experience* (1996); and a book of poetry, *River and Bridge* (1996). Her first novel, *Nampally Road*, was a 1991 *Village Voice Literary Supplement* Editor's Choice. It in many ways anticipates *Manhattan Music*, which also delineates the struggle of a displaced diasporic Indian woman to redefine herself and the world around her. Alexander's memoir

Fault Lines drew critical acclaim and was chosen as one of *Publishers Weekly*'s Best Books of 1993 (its revised version was published in 2003, with a chapter titled "Lyric in a Time of Violence" in response to 9/11). The book is a collage of memories, with remote and disparate events seemingly cut and pasted together, a procedure whereby Alexander represents "a woman cracked by multiple migrations." A few years later, she created the persona of a "no-nation woman" in *The Shock of Arrival*, asking the poignant and yet perhaps intentionally platitudinous questions "Where am I?" "Who am I?" and, hardest of all, "When am I?" Focusing on the endemic confusion accompanying the Americanization of the "no-nation woman," Alexander not only highlights the themes that occur in her earlier work but, as Lavina Dhingra Shankar puts it, "yoke(s) together complex imbrications of postcolonial identities with American ethnicities" (291).

Alexander's latest volumes of poetry are *Illiterate Heart*, which won a 2002 PEN Open Book Award, and *Raw Silk* (2004). *Illiterate Heart* is the more theoretical of the two books, many of the poems illustrating how gender is shaped by language under colonial and patriarchal pedagogy. The title poem, about learning English as a child, exposes the inscription of the twofold tyranny on the female body, describing the disintegration of the body: "O the body in parts, / bruised buttress of heaven." In *Raw Silk* Alexander continues to write about identity, language, and the dislocation of immigrants, particularly as regards the Indian diaspora in the United States and the problem of "home" and "abroad" in the aftermath of September 11. *See also* **Feminist Poetics**.

Further Reading. *Selected Primary Sources:* Alexander, Meena, *Fault Lines* (New York: Feminist Press, 1992); ———, *House of a Thousand Doors* (Washington, DC: Three Continents, 1989); ———, *Illiterate Heart* (Evanston, IL: Triquarterly, 2002); ———, *Manhattan Music: A Novel* (San Francisco: Mercury House, 1997); ———, *Nampally Road* (San Francisco: Mercury House, 1991); ———, *Night-Scene, The Garden* (New York: Red Dust, 1992); *Raw Silk* (Evanston, IL: Triquarterly, 2004); ———, *The Shock of Arrival: Reflections on Postcolonial Experience* (Boston: South End Press, 1996); ———, *The Storm: A Poem in Five Parts* (New York: Red Dust, 1989). *Selected Secondary Sources:* Cheung, King-Kok, ed., *Words Matter: Conversations with Asian American Writers* (Honolulu: University of Hawaii Press, 2000); Fadem, Maureen E. Ruprecht, "The Movement Toward Self Definition" (*Jouvert* 7.2 [2003], http://social.chass.ncsu.edu/jouvert/v7i2); Shankar, Lavina Dhingra, "Postcolonial Diaporics 'Writing in Search of a Homeland': Meena Alexander's *Manhattan Music, Fault Lines*, and *The Shock of Arrival*" (*LIT* 12.3 [2001]: 285–312).

Jun Lei

ALEXANDER, WILL (1948–)

Will Alexander is a poet, novelist, essayist, and playwright whose works, influenced by surrealism, use a startling and visionary vocabulary in order to reveal communication as a cosmological and alchemical activity. As he writes in "Towards the Endless Vertex Summit" (1994), he wishes words to be "magnetized / by anti-delusional boron & flailing x-ray procedure" (43). Alexander's subject matter is often rooted in obscure topics or philosophies, used as literal topics as well as fertile ground for metaphor. Alexander's works involve history, science, mathematics, philosophy, social identity, geography, spirituality, architecture, and a gamut of creative forms, often assembled in both his verse and prose as clauses within clauses within clauses. This compositional approach has the effect of removing the author's own presence from the work while also bewildering readers unwilling to make a sustained effort to read the poems. However, what is often perceived as nonsense or lack of specificity, is never thorough and can usually be read—albeit with some exertion—as a statement responding to the predicament of oppressed people and cultures, as in the exquisite volume *Asia & Haiti* (1995) and other works. In this latter regard, Alexander's work suggests elements of **negritude**, a concern with cross-fertilization of influence, and a language configured through hybrid literary forms. His poems constitute a call for reconsideration of ornate speech and radical verbal aesthetics, in response to the leveling forces of popular media. His verbal pyrotechnics do not, however, negate his culturally engrained meanings. To aid readers, he often includes extensive glossaries in his books.

Alexander's writings first appeared in little magazines in the mid-1980s. By the 1990s he had become known to wider audiences through the publication of his books and the inclusion of his work in several anthologies. His paintings have been included in numerous exhibitions and have appeared both within and on the covers of several of his collections. Nevertheless, he has remained obscure—if not hermetic. A freelance educator who has held professorial residencies at several universities, Alexander has lived his entire life in Los Angeles, where he presently holds the title of "Lead Artist" and "Artist-in-Residence" at Theatre of Hearts/Youth First, an organization that provides multidisciplinary arts workshops for at-risk children and teenagers. Alexander's proximity to the hub of the entertainment industry and to suburban California culture, combined with his own upbringing in one of the least privileged areas of the city (South Central) and his awareness of revolutionary struggles throughout history, provide an unstated but powerful impetus for Alexander's incendiary writing.

While all of his works reveal his pluralistically informed perspective, several essays make clear his position in relation to literary praxis and the larger cultural landscape. In "Alchemy as Poetic Kindling" (1993) Alexander praises the "alchemical poet," who, "by magically ingesting demons, is able to enunciate prophetic enigmas, is able to take as riddle a fount, which pours forth tenacious wanderings from an essentially rebellious interior" (195). Alexander explicitly refers to a number of poets in this category, including Hölderlin, Shelley, and Artaud. Like these and certain negritude poets (notably, Aimé Césaire), Alexander rejects the rational in favor of liberated forms that allow expansive deliberation. "From each quotidian annihilation," Alexander writes, "comes a fruit of a higher and greater energy, of a fire of fertile and surreptitious turquoise" (195). In "On Anti-Biography," Alexander describes himself as "a martyr of drills, of spates of specific lingual flooding, casting at times, a mist or mirage, like a caravan of yaks, transporting tungsten and water" who is "guarded by ferns, legs plowing land, the face and the mind guided by stars" (1). Terrestrial concerns are elevated to the realm of the fantastic, adding new dimensions to a bedouin mythos that has previously been explored in **African American poetry** by writers such as **Bob Kaufman**, **Nathaniel Mackey**, and Sun Ra. In a brief autobiographical sketch, *My Interior Vita*, which appeared as part of a 1999 issue of the journal *Callaloo* focusing on his work, Alexander explains that the planet for him is Africa—which he reads through the anti-assimilationist lenses of Diop, Jackson, Van Sertima, and Damas. Also in this essay, he relates his belief that knowledge and language are alchemical procedures. His work is intended to reveal "an inward light whose source is simultaneous with the riveting connection between flashes of lightning" (371), in which language is a "supraphysical" tool that has the potential to conquer "the mortality of the temporal" (372).

Alexander's unusual poetics was established in his earliest publications. His first collection published by a major press was *Asia & Haiti*, a book divided into two sections for the two geographical regions of the title. The book explores the tyranny faced by people in both regions, to which a pair of poems spoken by voices of the dead respond. In "Asia" the collective voice of monks slaughtered near Lhasa do not condemn Mao's bloody intervention in Tibet but rather show the eternal power of the monks' spirits in words, the tone of which is contemplative, explanatory, and inquisitive. In "Haiti" the voices of anonymous victims of the Duvalier regimes are more volatile, rising to cast a Voudoun spell for the purpose of reclaiming their humanity. Alexander details an act of judgment and retaliation, a crime and a curse. The spiritual framework reflected in both sections is a means by which to incite transformation in the reader.

Once asked how his vocabulary had become so expansive, Alexander replied that when he was young,

he obtained the biggest dictionary he could find and read it from cover to cover, pausing to write down the most interesting words and meanings in a notebook. This anecdote suggests Alexander's keen respect for language and words as power at a young age. His studious approach to expression is complemented by his copious readings of philosophical and mystical texts. Alexander is interested in embracing and revealing the relationships between personal psychological landscapes and the universe at large, by means of a keen vision, a deeply informed imagination, and an outrageous prosody.

Further Reading. ***Selected Primary Sources:*** Alexander, Will, *Above the Human Nerve Domain* (Columbus, OH: Pavement Saw, 1999); ———, "Alchemy as Poetic Kindling" (*Talisman* 11 [1993]); ———, *Asia & Haiti* (Los Angeles: Sun & Moon, 1995); ———, *The Stratospheric Canticles* (Berkeley, CA: Pantograph, 1995); ———, "Toward the Endless Vertext Summit" (*Juxta* 1 [1994]); ———, *Toward the Primeval Lightning Field* (Oakland, CA: O Books, 1998); ———, *Vertical Rainbow Climber* (Aptos, CA: Jazz Press, 1987). ***Selected Secondary Sources:*** Eshelman, Clayton, "A Note on Will Alexander" (*American Poet* [Winter 2000–2001]: 15); Mullen, Harriet, "Hauling up Gold from the Abyss: An Interview with Will Alexander" (*Callaloo* 22.2 [Spring 1999]: 391–408).

Christopher Funkhouser

ALEXIE, SHERMAN (1966–)

Since the beginning of his publishing career in 1992, Sherman Alexie has produced books of poetry and short fiction, novels, screenplays, and soundtrack materials for films. His depictions of his personal life and of his Native American heritage and culture, of contemporary Indian life both on and off the reservation, have made him a leading voice in contemporary American literature.

Born October 7, 1966, to Sherman Joseph Alexie, a member of the Coeur d'Alene tribe, and Lillian Agnes Cox Alexie, a Spokane, Sherman Joseph Alexie, Jr., grew up a registered member of his mother's tribe on the Spokane reservation in Wellpinit, Washington. His early education was at the reservation school, but he transferred to nearby Reardan, Washington, to attend high school and increase his chances of a college career. In 1985 Alexie was awarded a scholarship to Gonzaga University in Spokane, where he quickly grew uneasy with the social structure of the student body and began to drink. He left Gonzaga after two years, relocated in Seattle, and eventually enrolled in classes at Washington State University in Pullman. One of these was a poetry class led by Alex Kuo, who inspired Alexie's first writings and then encouraged him to become an author. Within two years after Alexie left Washington State, his talent and energy, coupled with Kuo's inspiration and encouragement, led to an explosion of creativity that resulted in the publication of four books of poetry in quick succession: *I Would Steal Horses* (1992), *The Business of Fancydancing: Stories and Poems* (1992), *Old Shirts & New Skins* (1993), and *First Indian on the Moon* (1993). Since then Alexie has authored both chapbooks and full-length collections of poetry, books of short stories, novels, and screenplays, and he has been the recipient of many awards, including a poetry fellowship from the National Endowment for the Arts.

The Business of Fancydancing, like many of Alexie's poetic works, is a mixture of prose and verse forms. The starkness of life on the reservation—the effects of racism and alcoholism, the omnipresence of commodity food and HUD housing, the escapes of powwow and basketball—serves as the book's central focus. The poem "13/16" probes, among other things, the construction of identity, how the mathematics of blood leads to the individual's identification and tribal enrollment number. Little by little, all seems to become lost through compromises that are often too minute to see or too mundane to recognize. This process of loss is further explored in the poem "Evolution," in which Buffalo Bill sets up a pawn shop on the edge of the reservation and accepts all that the Indians have to offer, from their belongings to their bodies. When all is pawned, Buffalo Bill changes his shop to a museum and charges the Indians admission to see what they once owned. Alexie portrays the irony inherent in the actions not only of Buffalo Bill but also of the Indians. The poems in *The Business of Fancydancing* offer little hope of improvement in either Indian lives or Indian-U.S. relations.

First Indian on the Moon continues Alexie's manipulation of form by including traditional-looking verse, prose poems that are more nearly stories than poems, and pieces that blend verse and prose. "Scalp Dance by Spokane Indians," a **prose poem**, in part relates the story of Paul Kane's painting by the same title. The speaker, the woman who posed for the central figure in the painting, claims that the painting is a lie. Kane has portrayed her as the distraught widow of a man killed by the Blackfoot when she had, in fact, never been married. Furthermore, Kane refused to allow his subjects to smile although laughter and humor, the speaker argues, create more accurate portraits of the Native American subject. In this piece, Alexie, like many of his fellow Native American authors, participates in the act of revising imperialist discourse. Nevertheless, *First Indian on the Moon* displays a degree of both restraint and optimism not apparent in *The Business of Fancydancing*. Alexie is kinder to the white woman on the train in "On the Amtrak from Boston to New York City," written largely in quatrains, than he is to either whites or Indians in poems such as "Evolution." Although the woman's sense of history seems to reach back only to Walden Pond and two-hundred-year-old houses that dot the passing landscape, Alexie's speaker, riding with her on the train, does not counter, as he might have, with a Native American history that includes not only a greater span of time but also a litany of the wrongs perpetrated against tribal peoples by Euro-American culture.

After forays into short fiction—for example, *The Lone Ranger and Tonto Fistfight in Heaven* (1993)—and two novels, *Reservation Blues* (1995) and *Indian Killer* (1996), *The Summer of Black Widows* (1996) continues Alexie's development in verse and prose poetry toward an edgy and often uneasy optimism. The tension one senses in the collection is generated by a desire to hope and a frank realization of all that has been lost to such hope in the past. "The Exaggeration of Despair" contains a catalogue of desperate situations in which Native Americans find themselves, lost characters born out of these situations, and evils perpetrated on Native Americans by whites and even by their own kin; Alexie's speaker flies in the face of all these harsh realities of past and present and opens the door to possibilities in the wind.

Despite branching out into various roles in the world of film (screenwriter, producer, director), Alexie continues to work as a poet. He published *One Stick Song* in 2000 and reigned as World Heavyweight Poetry Champion from 1998 to 2001, a title determined by the results of live bouts held annually as part of the Taos Poetry Circus in New Mexico. Alexie's beginnings as a writer were in the form of poetry. Although certain narrative elements help him to construct the poetry, he has said, his focus has always been on the images—often the clash of images—seen through his life experiences and the troubled relationship between the tribal and nontribal in American history, society, and culture.

Further Reading. ***Selected Primary Sources:*** Alexie, Sherman, *The Business of Fancydancing* (Brooklyn, NY: Hanging Loose, 1992); ———, *First Indian on the Moon* (Brooklyn, NY: Hanging Loose, 1993); ———, *I Would Steal Horses* (Niagara Falls, NY: Slipstream, 1992); ———, *One Stick Song* (Brooklyn, NY: Hanging Loose, 2000); ———, *The Summer of Black Widows* (Brooklyn, NY: Hanging Loose, 1996). ***Selected Secondary Sources:*** Gillan, Jennifer, "Reservation Home Movies: Sherman Alexie's Poetry" (*American Literature* 68.1 [March 1996]: 92–110); McFarland, Ron, "'Another Kind of Violence': Sherman Alexie's Poems" (*American Indian Quarterly* 21.2 [Spring 1997]: 251–265).

Michael Cody

ALGARÍN, MIGUEL (1941–)

Miguel Algarín began publishing his poetry in the 1970s and has continued to write into the twenty-first century. Early in his career he became one of the prominent members of a Nuyorican community of poets that included Sandra María Esteves, Lucky Cienfuegos, and Pedro Pietri. As a Nuyorican (a Puerto Rican in and of New York City), Algarín translates the grit and beauty of New York City's urban elements into rhythmic poetic forms. To be Nuyorican, Algarín often observes, is to negotiate a hybrid identity, as many do who migrate to the United States. His poetry creates a discourse of survival and healing from the disruptive forces of American culture. Influenced by the Beat Generation poets, Algarín's poetry is concerned with social issues that plague not only Nuyoricans but also other groups underrepresented nationally and internationally. Algarín's work is often written to be performed, for he sees spoken poetry as a method of social action. For example, it is not uncommon for Algarín to read his poetry to musical accompaniment or to share the stage with local performance artists. The language of his poetry switches deftly between English and Spanish, sometimes resulting in lines that are in Spanglish. The hybridity of language, he finds, is reflective of the ways in which Nuyoricans have blended their Puerto Rican roots with American cultures and practices, and it serves to remind his audience that his poetry is of the people and for the people.

Miguel Algarín is a poet, editor, translator, theater producer, and community leader. He has also been a professor of English for over 30 years and has translated the poetry of Pablo Neruda from Spanish into English. Algarín has published five volumes of poetry and has edited three anthologies of poetry and plays. In the 1960s and 1970s he collaborated with key poets and playwrights from both the **Black Arts Movement** and the Nuyorican community such as **Amiri Baraka** and **Miguel Piñero**. In 1973 Algarín founded the Nuyorican Poets' Café in New York City—a multicultural venue for traditionally underrepresented artists, playwrights, poets, and musicians. As a community performance space, the Café provides a location and an opportunity for words to jump from the page to the stage. In recent years the Nuyorican Poets' Café has been influential in cultivating the genres of Spoken Word and **Slam Poetry**.

Algarín considers the Nuyorican Poets' Café to be one of his greatest achievements. Oral transimission of poetry gives the poet an immediate rather than a delayed and distant response from his audience. Moreover, it allows members of the community who are illiterate to experience poetry firsthand. Algarín's first volume of poetry, *Mongo Affair* (1978), frequently elucidates the mission of poetic performance. In "Happy New Year, January 1, 1976," Algarín considers alternative systems of making meaning. Like the Café's mission, Algarín's poetry is an act of translation and transmission.

The orality of Algarín's work is indebted to both previous and current traditions of poetry, visual art, and music. For example, it is not uncommon for Algarín to praise Van Gogh's art or Richard Wagner's music in his poems while borrowing their artistic practices. Like **Walt Whitman**, Algarín often meditates on visions of the self in relation to the universe. He translates Whitman's Transcendentalist sensibilities to his observations on urban communities and social action. Frequently, African American and Latin jazz music or traditional Puerto Rican music are celebrated, elegized, or emulated in the poetry. Through Algarín's incorporation of Western and non-Western music and poetic traditions, the meter of his poetry is dynamically hybrid, rhythmic, and melodic.

Algarín's themes are frequently those of displacement and the voiceless members of society. The title poem of Algarín's first volume, "Mongo Affair," offers this warning to Puerto Ricans who emigrate to New York City to seek a better life for themselves and their families: "don't believe the deadly game / of northern cities paved with gold and plenty." His second volume of poetry, *On Call* (1980), broaches the subject of violence against women, human brutality, and denial of the American Dream to emigrants and American citizens alike.

While often political, Algarín's poetry also celebrates hope. His third volume, *Body Bee Calling from the 21st Century* (1985), portrays visions from and for the future. Mixing Transcendentalist and Buddhist philosophy with science, the content of *Body Bee* explores the intersections of science and poetry for future generations. Algarín's vision of the twenty-first century is a world where humanity exists within a paradoxical matrix of technology and human emotion. What lies in the space between machine and human for Algarín is love, and it is love that bridges and heals the gap between people of different nations and beliefs.

Generally, Algarín's work seeks to explore and cross cultural divides. Algarín acts as his own translator in his bilingual third volume *Time's Now/Ya es Tiempo* (1985), which presents Spanish and English versions of the poetry side by side. His fourth volume, *Love Is Hard Work* (1997), continues to weave together concerns of the Nuyorican community with oral poetic forms. A section of this volume, "Nuyorican Kaddish," is reminiscent of the poetry of **Alan Ginsberg**, who befriended Algarín and attended shows at the Nuyorican Poets' Café. Algarín borrows Ginsberg's "Kaddish" form to mourn, binlingually, the death of Nuyoricans in his community. Overall, Algarín's work has been and continues to be a blend of musical, poetic, and oral traditions. Political poet, performance artist, and community leader, Miguel Algarín wields his words and his pen to the hybrid, urban beats of Nuyorican aesthetics. *See also* **Beat Poetry**.

Further Reading. *Selected Primary Sources:* Algarín, Miguel, *Action: The Nuyorican Poets Café Theater Festival*, ed.

Miguel Algarín and Lois Griffith (New York: Simon & Schuster, 1997); *Aloud: Voices from the Nuyorican Poets Café*, ed. Miguel Algarín and Bob Holman (New York: Henry Holt and Co., 1994); ———, *Body Bee Calling from the 21st Century* (Houston: Arte Publico Press, 1982); ———, *Love Is Hard Work: Memorias de Loisaida* (New York: Scribner Poetry, 1997); *Mongo Affair* (New York: Nuyorican Press, 1978); ———, *Time's Now/Ya es Tiempo* (Houston: Arte Publico Press, 1985); ———, "Nuyorican Literature" (MELUS 8 [Summer 1981]: 89–92); *Nuyorican Poetry: An Anthology of Puerto Rican Words and Feelings*, ed. Miguel Algarín and Miguel Piñero (New York: Morrow, 1975); ———, *On Call* (Houston: Arte Publico Press, 1980). **Selected Secondary Sources:** Flores, Juan, *From Bomba to Hip-Hop: Puerto Rican Culture and Latino Identity* (New York: Columbia University Press, 2000); Hernández, Carmen Dolores, *Puerto Rican Voices in English: Interviews with Writers* (Westport, CT: Praeger, 1997); Sanchez-Gonzalez, Lisa, *Boricua Literature: A Literary History of the Puerto Rican Diaspora* (New York: New York University Press, 2001).

Zina Rodríguez

ALI, AGHA SHAHID (1949–2001)

One of the foremost Anglo-Indian poets of his generation, Agha Shahid Ali introduced the *ghazal*, a classical Urdu poetic form, to a wide audience in English through his own groundbreaking poems and through his editing of *Ravishing DisUnities: Real Ghazals in English* (2000), an intercultural collection of *ghazals* by 105 poets. His introduction includes a *ghazal* primer in which he discusses the strictures of the form. Louis Werner notes that Ali intended to bring the *ghazal* to the same level of popularity as the haiku, another poetic form that crossed from East to West. Ali himself jumped that divide by becoming a master of formal Western prosody, especially canzone, syllabics, Sapphics, and villanelle. His postcolonial intermingling of Eastern and Western languages and culture, both vernacular and traditional, and his astute political conscience infused a **New Formalist** aesthetic with a geopolitical awareness rooted in the tragic history of his homeland and in his exile from its language and landscape. His relocation to the United States and the acclaim given his work by such poets as **James Merrill** and **John Ashbery** identify Ali as an American poet. His poetry is characterized by contrapuntal rhetoric, musicality, and brilliant imagery.

Born in New Delhi on February 4, 1949, two years after the partitioning of India and Pakistan, Ali grew up Muslim in Kashmir, fluent in three languages: Urdu, Kashmiri, and English. In the 1960s he lived in Muncie, Indiana, while his parents were doctoral students at Ball State University. There he wrote his first poems in English. After returning to Delhi, he became friends with the *ghazal* singer Begum Akhtar. Through her singing he experienced the power of the lyrics of the Urdu poet Faiz Ahmed Faiz, whose work he translated twenty years later. Ali was educated at the University of Kashmir, Srinagar, and the University of Delhi; he then completed a Ph. D. in English at Pennsylvania State University (1984) and an MFA in creative writing at the University of Arizona (1985). In addition to writing and editing, he held faculty positions at colleges and universities in India and the United States, including SUNY–Binghamton, Princeton University, Hamilton College, Baruch College, the University of Utah, and Warren Wilson College, and directed the MFA program in creative writing at the University of Massachusetts–Amherst. He received fellowships from the Pennsylvania Council on the Arts, the Bread Loaf Writers' Conference, the Ingram-Merrill Foundation, the New York Foundation for the Arts, and the Guggenheim Foundation and was awarded a Pushcart Prize. His penultimate collection, *Rooms Are Never Finished* (2001), was nominated for a National Book Award. He died from brain cancer in Amherst, Massachusetts, on December 8, 2001.

Ali's first two collections, *Bone Sculpture* (1972) and *In Memory of Begum Akhtar and Other Poems* (1979), were published in Calcutta, as was *The Beloved Witness: Selected Poems* (1992); six other collections were published in the United States, including a chapbook, *A Walk Through the Yellow Pages* (1987). In addition, he authored *T. S. Eliot as Editor* (1986) and translated from Urdu the poems of Faiz Ahmed Faiz in *The Rebel's Silhouette* (rev. ed. 1995).

In his introduction to *The Rebel's Silhouette*, Ali draws an essential distinction between his mother tongue (Urdu) and his first language (English), thus claiming both the language and canon of colonial heritage. Because his embrace of English includes American vernacular and popular culture, his aesthetic develops from the interpenetration of three sources. This aesthetic of hybridity is apparent in his use of translation to transpose thematic, formal, and mytho-cultural elements of Urdu and Persian literature in his poetry written in English. In his first major U.S. collection, *The Half-Inch Himalayas* (1987), themes of exile and memory predominate in interwoven images of New Delhi, Philadelphia, Houston, and the poet's dreams of his homeland, both miniaturized and enlarged by distance. "Postcard from Kashmir" opens, "Kashmir shrinks into my mailbox / my home a neat four by six inches," yet this country that comes to him in miniature becomes an expansive subject of his poetry. *A Nostalgist's Map of America* (1991) continues the themes of memory, loss, and longing. "In Search of Evanescence" is a disjunctive narrative of a road trip from Pennsylvania to Arizona; however, its terrain is more mythic than historical or geographical. Density is created through a contrapuntal rhetoric in which several motifs of death occur simultaneously: the death of a friend, of tribes, of American and Kashmiri landscapes, and of a language. There is a hybrid juxtaposition of allusions to historical, political, and cultural losses. For example, "Eurydice" relocates the tragic Greek figure to the Nazi death camp of Belsen, "Beyond the Ash Rains" merges landscapes of ancient Iraq/Mesopotamia with those of America, and "I See Chile in My Rearview Mirror" refigures the political and environmental brutalization of the Americas as rearview images overlaid on a cross-country journey. Amitav Ghosh observes that in *The Country Without a Post Office* (1997) and *Rooms Are Never Finished*, Ali's vision of Kashmir enlarges to become identified with the idea of death. In the former volume his personal experience with strife in Kashmir brings him into communion with the displaced and oppressed throughout the ages. The ache of loss is manifest in the pile of undelivered letters in the title poem: "that archive for letters with doomed / addresses, each house buried or empty." Ali invokes two of his literary guides in this volume: **Emily Dickinson**, whose fabled and distant "Cashmere" contrasts with the contemporary political reality of his Kashmir; and James Merrill, who influenced Ali's exploration of Western forms. Christopher Merrill notes that by linking the fate of his native land to his mother's death in *Rooms Are Never Finished*, Ali complicates his engagement with Urdu and English literary traditions, religion, and politics. Notable for its variety of forms, including the difficult canzone, "Lenox Hill," this volume moves from engaged witness and meditation toward prayer. A posthumous collection, *Call Me Ishmael Tonight* (2003), is a tour de force of the classical *ghazal* form that he pioneered in *Ravishing DisUnities*. Merrill speculates that with the *ghazal*, Ali may play a part in reshaping American poetry. At the least, his poems are standard-bearers for the form.

Further Reading. ***Selected Primary Sources:*** Ali, Agha Shahid, *Call Me Ishmael Tonight: A Book of Ghazals* (New York: W.W. Norton & Co., 2003); ———, *The Country Without a Post Office* (New York: W.W. Norton & Co., 1997);———, *The Half-Inch Himalayas* (Hanover, NH: Wesleyan University Press, 1987); ———, *A Nostalgist's Map of America* (New York: W.W. Norton & Co., 1991); ———, ed., *Ravishing DisUnities: Real Ghazals in English* (Hanover, NJ: Wesleyan University Press, 2000); ———, *Rooms Are Never Finished* (New York: W.W. Norton & Co., 2001). ***Selected Secondary Sources:*** Ghosh, Amitav, "'The Ghat of the Only World': Agha Shahid Ali in Brooklyn" (*Annual of Urdu Studies* 17.1 [2002]: 1–19); Merrill, Christopher, "After You" (*Tin House* 3.3 [Spring 2002]: 17–21); Werner, Louis, "A Gift of Ghazals" (*Saudi Aramco World* 52.4 [July–August 2001]: 38–45).

J.C. Todd

ALLEN, ELIZABETH AKERS (1832–1911)

Elizabeth Akers Allen, aka Florence Percy, was considered a minor Victorian poet even by her contemporaries. Allen published what was then commonly termed "household poetry," embodying **sentimental** and traditional values, expressed competently, but with no attempt at innovation in style or content. Her typical verse consisted of rhyming heroic couplets or regular rhyming quatrains, and she seldom deviated from these basic forms. Her poems appeared regularly in popular periodicals such as the *Atlantic Monthly*. Nine collected volumes of her poetry were published in her lifetime.

Allen was born Elizabeth Chase on October 9, 1832, in Strong, Maine. Her own accounts of her childhood describe an unhappy life of relative privation. Her father was domineering and frequently absent; her mother was left to care for the family in spite of her failing health. After her mother's death, Elizabeth lived unhappily for a time with relatives, and then with her father and stepmother. Neither situation provided her with the independence and comfort that she desired. At fourteen, she accepted work in the offices of the Portland (Maine) *Transcript*, and she eventually rose to the position of assistant editor, a job she held intermittently from 1855 to 1865. During this period, she supported herself in part by writing prose for several newspapers, and in 1856 she published her first volume of poetry, *Forest Buds from the Woods of Maine*. In 1874 she became the literary editor of the *Portland Daily Advertiser*. Throughout her life she remained quite prolific and commercially successful in her writing, though her unpublished 1904 memoir, *History of One Woman's Financial Experiences*, indicates that she never found the personal satisfaction in marriage or family life that she sought. She died in Tuckahoe, New York, on August 9, 1911.

Reviews of Allen's work that appeared in the *Nation* in 1866 and 1886 were generally complimentary. The 1866 review of *Poems* suggests that while not unpleasing in the context of her work, Allen's melancholic tone was relatively uninteresting in comparison with that of Tennyson. The reviewer also compares Allen's "The Mountains" unfavorably with poems by Longfellow. Nevertheless, the larger message of the review is that her continued popularity with her readers was assured, and the fiduciary concentration of Allen's memoir indicates that any review that promoted sales was likely to have pleased her.

At this point in Allen's career, a dispute developed over the authorship of what is still her best-known poem, "Rock Me to Sleep," which she wrote in Rome in 1859 and first published anonymously in the Philadelphia *Saturday Evening Post* in 1860. After its publication, several prominent New York–area men published a pamphlet claiming that one of them, the Hon. Alexander M.W. Ball of the New Jersey legislature, was the poem's author; another of them testified to having heard

Ball read the poem as his own in 1856. Ball's version contained the six stanzas originally published, plus nine more that did not appear but which he claimed were part of the original. A lengthy letter to the editors of the *New York Times*, published on May 27, 1867, and signed only "W," disputes Ball's claims on the grounds of the dissimilarity of style and form between the published and unpublished stanzas, and of the inconsistency in quality between Allen's extant body of work and Ball's. The author also offered comparative evidence that Ball had plagiarized the work of another poet, Sarah Helen Whitman, in his attempt to establish that he regularly wrote poetry of a quality comparable with Allen's. Though no further reports exist of a formal settlement of the argument, "Rock Me to Sleep" appeared in *Poems*, Allen's 1866 collection, and since that time has been attributed to her. Though not considered by reviewers to be Allen's best work, it was certainly her most popular and was eventually set to music. Evidence of the work's enduring appeal exists in Laura Ingalls Wilder's recollection of a local woman's 1882 performance of the musical version, in her novel *Little Town on the Prairie* (1941).

In 1886, upon the release of *The Silver Bridge and Other Poems*, Allen's work was again reviewed in the *Nation*. Her reputation remained consistent as an important minor poet of the day, and the reviewer praises her style as having "ripened" since the popularity of "Rock Me to Sleep," which he characterizes as "too easy sing-song." But this mention is considerably briefer than the 1866 review, and Allen is only one of several poets discussed in the column. Though brief, this notice depicts Allen as part of a vibrant culture of poetry, particularly for women poets. She continued to publish individual pieces and compilation volumes for the rest of her life. More than 300 of her poems appeared in the *Atlantic Monthly* alone. Today her work is seldom anthologized, and the collections have fallen out of print, but individual poems still appear on popular lists of romantic poetry, poetry about children, and sentimental poetry.

Further Reading. *Selected Primary Sources:* Percy, Florence [Elizabeth Akers Allen], *Forest Buds from the Woods of Maine* (Boston, 1856); ———, *Poems* (Boston, 1866); ———, *The Silver Bridge and Other Poems* (Boston, 1886). *Selected Secondary Sources:* Cary, Richard, "The Misted Prism: Paul Akers and Elizabeth Akers Allen" (*Colby Library Quarterly* 7 [1966]: 193–227); "Mrs. Akers—Miss Cary" (*Nation* 2 [18 Oct. 1866]: 306–307); "Who Wrote 'Rock Me to Sleep'?" (*New York Times* [27 May 1867]).

Nicole Roussos

ALLSTON, WASHINGTON (1779–1843)

Known primarily for his paintings, which earned him the moniker of the "American Titian," Washington Allston also produced poetry, including many sonnets, that often takes art as its subject. His literary circle included Washington Irving and Samuel Taylor Coleridge, whose portrait by Allston hangs in the National Gallery.

Washington Allston was born on a plantation in Waccamaw, South Carolina. The son of a Revolutionary War captain who died in 1781, he was schooled in Charleston and left for New England to finish his education in 1787. In Newport, Rhode Island, he befriended William Ellery Channing, uncle of the poet of the same name, and Edmund Dana, brother of the poet and editor **Richard Henry Dana** (who in turn was father of the novelist of the same name, famous for *Two Years Before the Mast*). After four years at Harvard University, he returned to Charleston and studied painting with Edward Greene Malbone and Charles Fraser. He was at the time engaged to Channing's sister, Ann.

In 1800 he sailed with Malbone to study at the Royal Academy in London. There he sat under Benjamin West and Henry Fuseli from 1801 to 1803. For the next five years Allston traveled throughout Europe, befriending many European artists and writers. In 1808 he returned to the United States and married Ann. The couple settled in Boston, where he completed his first collection, *Sylphs of the Season*, in 1813, garnering great acclaim from Coleridge. Soon thereafter he returned to England, bringing Ann and his then student Samuel F.B. Morse along. There he fell ill, which resulted in debilitation for his remaining years. After he received treatment in Bristol, where he had a very successful show of his paintings, Ann died in 1815. Allston then became a devoted Anglican, an influence that would pervade his work.

Before his return to the United States in 1818, he was unanimously elected to the Royal Academy. In Boston he opened a studio. He published a few essays in Dana's journal, the *Idle Man*, and in 1827 had shows at the Boston Athenaeum. He began work on "Belshazzar's Feast," which was never finished despite his dedicating the next thirty-five years to it. He married Ruth Dana, cousin to Ann and sister to Richard Henry and Edmund Dana. The couple settled in Cambridgeport, Massachusetts. Nearly ten years later, in 1839, he showed forty-five paintings in Boston to enormous acclaim. **Margaret Fuller** lauded Allston's work in an essay that appeared in the *Dial* that same year. His brother-in-law, Richard Henry Dana, would publish posthumously Allston's *Lectures on Art, and Poems* in 1850.

Coleridge is quoted as saying that Allston was surpassed by no man of his age in artistic and poetic genius. Among American painters, that may not be in dispute. Allston's poetry, however, perhaps because of his ties to the Old World, echoes much of the verse of the English Romantics, with the difference that, for him, a meditation on a work of art is more likely to inspire awe than any mountain. That sense of smallness in the universe ("a speck in space" in his "A Word: Man") that is prevalent in Romantic poetry, one's being humbled before beauty, appears in much of Allston's work.

Whatever questions of national identity Allston may have grappled with, his poetry is firmly tied to England—"thou noble land, / Our Fathers' native soil!"—and the Western tradition. In the same poem from which this apostrophe comes, "America to Great Britain," Allston stakes a claim to "the blood of England in our veins!" and ends the lyric with a voiced declaration from the blood, "We are One."

Indeed, his approach, from addressing the Sistine Chapel to eulogizing his ally Coleridge, forgoes any claim to school or fashion. In his meditation on art ("high gift of Heaven!") Allston explains that, for him, art is "life to life responding," and as such was obligated to maintain that wide scope. This sensibility occasions some lapses into the archaic, including "thy" and "thee" and the contractions "'twas," "e'en," and "o'er." But in pursuit of a line that participates in the greater tradition, Allston, for all his pretenses, never loses sight of his final goal, praising, as he does from the beginning in *The Sylphs of the Seasons*, "The soul's creative might."

Further Reading.   *Selected Primary Sources:* Allston, Washington, *Lectures on Art, and Poems* (New York: Baker & Scribner, 1850); ———, *Sibylline Leaves* (London: Rest Fenner, 1817); ———, *Sylphs of the Seasons* (London: W. Pope, 1813). ***Selected Secondary Sources:*** Flagg, J.B., *Life and Letters of Washington Allston* (New York, 1892); Fuller, Margaret, *Literature and Art* (New York: Fowles and Wells, 1852); Peabody, Elizabeth Palmer, *Last Evening with Allston, and Other Papers* (Boston: D. Lothrop and Co., 1886).

Anthony Lacavaro

ALMANAC POETRY (SEVENTEENTH-CENTURY)

The term "almanac," originating in medieval times, referred to a table showing calculations for the movement of heavenly bodies, which was considered important knowledge for agriculture. Later, almanacs for shorter spans were produced, eventually for single years—calendars, in other words. Eventually other agricultural information was added, such as weather lore. The form gave rise to some poetically important works. In England Edmund Spenser's series of eclogues *Shepheardes Calendar* (1579) took its title from a similar French work, and consists of twelve poems with seasonal variations. Most true almanacs were utilitarian, however; by the end of the seventeenth century, they included humor, usually coarse, and occasional satire. Later, maxims set in verse appeared in most American almanacs, including Benjamin Franklin's *Poor Richard's Alma-*

nac (1732–1758), inspired by England's *Poor Robin*. German almanacs of the eighteenth and nineteenth centuries contained works by the best German poets. The American almanac, however, remained chiefly a storehouse of general information. The Davy Crockett almanacs, issued in 1835 and 1856, included "tall tales," helping to preserve a significant aspect of oral culture.

The information encoded within almanacs, like the underpinnings of poetry itself, came long before the written word. Verse and the calendrical lore of the sky and the weather have many interconnections; poetry has appeared in printed almanacs since the technology of printing made their wide distribution possible beginning in the sixteenth century. The earliest United States almanac on record was published in Philadelphia in 1687. Benjamin Franklin published *Poor Richard's Almanac* for twenty-five years, beginning in 1732, under the pseudonym "Richard Saunders." Poetry in American almanacs never reached the level attained in French and German almanacs of the eighteenth and nineteenth centuries, in which the most celebrated Continental poets were published. *The American Almanac and Repository of Useful Knowledge* was published in 1828–1861 in Boston. *The Old Farmer's Almanac*, founded by Robert B. Thomas, has been published in the United States since 1793 and has always included brief weather-related verse in its calendar pages.

Besides Franklin, notable colonial producers of almanacs were the Leeds family; Isaiah Thomas, father and son; William, Cornelia, and Andrew Bradford; Samuel Danforth; and Nathanael Low. All incorporated verse into their almanacs. Though American almanacs, as literature, were generally pale imitations of their English and Continental counterparts, they had their strengths. The verse they featured ranged from religious admonition to satire on politics or human foibles, occasionally taking the form of parodies of the material of the almanac itself, such as supposed astrological correspondences. "Almost from its beginning in 1639," Marion Barber Stowell writes, "the colonial almanac bears the unmistakably original stamp of, first, its Harvard College compilers and, before long, its eccentric and humorous Yankee author-printers" (vii). Samuel Eliot Morison called the *Cambridge Almanac* "the annual poetry magazine of Harvard College" (quoted in Stowell, vii). offering as it did the opportunity for young college men to test their mettle with classically inspired verse about weather, seasons, astronomy, and agriculture. Other than these educated pastorals, humor, often satiric, is the most common style of almanac verse.

Samuel Danforth's 1647 almanac included verse with seasonal prognostications:

August: Many this month I doe fore-see
Together by the eares will bee:

Indian and English in the field
To one another will not yield.

The New England Almanac for 1686 includes Danforth's "Ad Librum," a poem about Copernican science. Stowell writes, "[Danforth's] stanzas typify a quality of much early American verse: a deliberate striving after ancient Greek and Roman virtues, clothed in appropriately Anglo-Saxon, rustic dress" (237).

Benjamin Franklin borrowed freely from popular poets, without payment or attribution. Franklin's work is well known for reworking and paraphrasing much-loved English poets, including Shakespeare, Dryden, and Pope. As Poor Richard, he writes in 1748, "Why . . . should I give my Readers bad lines of my own, when good ones of other people's are so plenty?" and in 1733, "Jove, Juno leaves, and loves to take his range; / From whom man learns to love, and loves to change."

Benjamin Banneker, the black polymath, produced almanacs for various publishers between 1792 and 1797, and these often included verse and excerpts from the famous works of the day, along with Banneker's astronomical calculations. A poem in the 1795 editions, signed only "G.H." and possibly by Gerard Hopkins, a minister of the Society of Friends, compares Banneker to Isaac Newton in heroic couplets:

What tho' thy skin be of the blackest hue,
Such as the sable sons of Afric' shew . . .
Talent thou hast superior to most,
No matter what complexions they boast

Most American almanac poetry has been pedestrian, imitative, admonitory, or crudely satiric. Titan Leeds included this moral epigram in his 1728 almanac: "Good friendly drinking I account not evil, / But much carousing makes a man a devil."

In a pleasing image, Dr. Nathaniel Ames II (his father and son also contributed to almanacs) wrote in 1748,

Consuming Winter's gone, the Earth hath lost
Her snow-white robes, and now no more the frost
Candies the grass

Further Reading. ***Selected Primary Sources:*** Franklin, Benjamin, *Poor Richard's Almanac* (many eds.); Meine, Franklin J., ed., *The Crockett Almanacks: Nashville Series 1835–1838* (Chicago: Caxton Club, 1955). ***Selected Secondary Sources:*** Sagendorph, Robb, *America and Her Almanacs: Wit, Wisdom & Weather 1639–1970* (Boston: Little, Brown and Co., 1970); Stowell, Marion Barber, *Early American Almanacs: The Colonial Weekday Bible* (New York: Burt Franklin & Co., 1977).

Gail Shivel

ALSOP, GEORGE (1636–?)

George Alsop wrote some of wittiest poetry produced by seventeenth-century colonial British American writers. Alsop's poems cover a range of topics. They explore the anxieties of life in the colonies for English men and women living in an environment quite different from England's, they extol the virtues of England's colonial ventures at a time when such ventures were the source of great controversy, they help bring to life England's identity as nation whose trade extends around the globe, and they provide a window into the way monarchy served as a crucial foundation for English social hierarchies. All of this Alsop accomplished in an inventive style that combined ribald language with innovative imagery, a style that bordered on bad taste and often crossed that border with impunity.

Little is known of Alsop's life. Scholars believe he was born in 1636 to Peter and Rose Alsop of London. His promotional tract on Maryland, *A Character of the Province of Mary-Land*, where his only extant poetry appears, indicates he knew Latin and French. For reasons that are not entirely clear, Alsop indentured himself in 1658 to four years of service as a bondservant in Maryland. The Royalist sentiments expressed in his book suggest that he did this to flee persecution while Cromwell was in power. He remained in Maryland two years after his service was to have ended, perhaps because of illness. His occupation during his indentureship and immediately afterward remains a mystery. He returned to Restoration England in 1663 or 1664 and, once settled, became an Anglican minister. *A Character* indicates that he had a reputation for writing poetry even before he went to the colonies, but we have nothing to confirm this other than Alsop's own words. And no writing by Alsop after *A Character* has been found. Indeed, other than scattered references to Alsop in letters and in his father's will, and an account of his being attacked by Quakers, we know nothing of Alsop's later life, not even when he died.

A Character of the Province of Mary-land was first published in London in 1666 Alsop divides *A Character* into four chapters, the first describing the geography and environment of Maryland, the second offering a glimpse of the colony's government and people, the third explaining the value of the indentured servant for both the servant and the colony, and the fourth detailing the various Maryland products that could be used in England or sold on the international market. In addition to these chapters, *A Character* includes introductory materials addressed, respectively, to the proprietors, investors, and readers, as well as an appendix on the Native Americans in Maryland and letters that Alsop sent home from the colonies. The poems are, for the most part, untitled and appear at the ends of the chapters, as was customary for poetry in promotional tracts of the time. The status of these poems as simply part of the tract, rather than as separate expressions published elsewhere or even segregated from the prose within the work itself, show how colonial writers often saw—and used—verse, not as distinct from prose but as equally if not better able to convey the complexities of the New World. For Alsop, at least, poetry served as a natural vehicle to promote the English empire.

"Traffique is Earth's great Atlas" is perhaps the best-known poem. A ten-line poem of rhymed couplets, it expresses the view in clear, evocative language that commerce is the lifeblood of nations and individual workers while it encourages Maryland to join the circuit of exchange in goods. Although "Heaven's bright Lamp, shine forth some of thy Light" remains less known to readers of colonial British American scholars, this poem, included in a letter to his friend "Mr. T.B.," provides a fascinating representation of the conceptual turmoil brought about by the English Civil War. In bold and forceful language, the poem casts England as a modern-day Sodom, where commoners have replaced true nobility in places of distinction. The poem's royal sympathies make this an especially interesting poem since so few poems—or prose, for that matter—supporting the Royalist position came out of colonial British America. Alsop's most provocative and challenging poem is the first to appear in the volume. "The Author to His Book" twists a series of standard figures of speech to fit the colonial situation and, in the process, helps the typical English reader of the period to re-imagine his or her identity. The poem begins with the standard trope of the author as mother to the book, but in this case the black print of the book casts doubts on the purity of the author's—and the book's—national identity. The book's black print combined with its production outside England leads English critics to worry that it might threaten the nation's health with its foreign wit, so the innocent book is executed by its critics. In telling such a story, Alsop mocks those who would challenge the Englishness of those who have spent time outside England. While there is no direct mention of Alsop's poetry or any part of *A Character* by early modern British or British American writers, some of the incidents and even the language of **Ebenezer Cooke**'s *The Sot-weed Factor* (1708) echoes those in Alsop's work.

Further Reading. ***Selected Primary Sources:*** Alsop, George, *A Character of the Province of Mary-land* (London: 1666). ***Selected Secondary Sources:*** Egan, Jim, "'To Bring Mary-land into England': English Identities in Colonial American Writing," in *Finding Colonial America: Essays Honoring J.A. Leo Lemay*, ed. Carla Mulford and David S. Shields (Newark: University of Delaware Press, 2001, 125–136); Lemay, J.A. Leo, *Men of Letters in Colonial Maryland* (Knoxville: University of Tennessee Press, 1972); Pebworth, Ted-Larry, "The 'Character' of George Alsop's Mary-land" (*Seventeenth-Century News* 34 [Summer–Fall 1976]: 64–66).

James Egan

ALVAREZ, JULIA (1950–)

Julia Alvarez occupies a prominent place among Latina writers, a group that has emerged into prominence in late twentieth- and early twenty-first–century American literature. Her poetry finds much of its power in its intensely personal nature and its recognition of timeless forms of experience. Alvarez's poetry was recognized in 1995 by the *American Poetry Review* when she received its Jessica Nobel-Maxwell Poetry Prize. However, Alvarez is perhaps best known as a novelist, especially for her first novel, *How the García Girls Lost Their Accents* (1991), which in 1999 was chosen by New York librarians as one of the "21 Classics for the 21st Century." Her more recent novels have included historical subjects, as in *In the Time of the Butterflies* (chosen as a 1994 Notable Book by the American Library Association), a fictional treatment of the martyrdom of four sisters in the struggle against Dominican dictator Rafael Trujillo.

Alvarez refers to herself ironically as "a Vermont writer from the Dominican Republic." In fact, she was born in New York City to Dominican parents, who soon after her birth returned to the Dominican Republic, where the family remained until she was ten years old. In 1960 the family was forced to return to the United States because her father, a physician, was in danger of being arrested for his involvement in a plot to overthrow Trujillo. When Trujillo was overthrown only a year later, the Alvarez family remained in the United States but were able to reestablish their connections with relatives and friends in the Dominican Republic, where Julia and her sisters visited often. She attended public school in Queens, New York, where she found adjustment to the new culture difficult. She was sent to boarding school at age thirteen; she then attended Connecticut College and Middlebury College, where she received a BA in English in 1971. While still an undergraduate, she began writing and publishing poetry and succeeded in winning poetry prizes at both colleges. She also published translations from the Spanish of poems by Pablo Neruda. After Alvarez earned an MA in Creative Writing at Syracuse University in 1975, she began more than a decade of temporary academic jobs before joining the faculty of Middlebury College in 1988.

Alvarez's first book of poetry was *Homecoming*, published in 1984; it was reissued with additions in 1996 as *Homecoming: New and Collected Poems*. Many of the poems are about childhood experiences, including a group called "Housekeeping" with such titles as "Dusting," "Hairwashing," and "How I Learned to Sweep." The poems are nostalgic for childhood's innocence, yet they sketch that innocence through an adult's eyes. They suggest that a rejection of childhood's dependence and naiveté is necessary to find one's own adult voice and to explore life's complex possibilities. Especially poignant are the unspoken confrontations between mother and daughter: filial love counterpointed by a struggle for separate identity and escape from parental expectations. A second group of poems in the volume is a sonnet sequence titled "33," written during Alvarez's thirty-third year. This sequence traces the emotional landscape of a woman who feels the despair of past love, experiences the loneliness of love's absence, and wonders if love can ever compensate for past disappointments. The poems are notable for their forceful honesty and self-deprecating humor. Alvarez describes their form as "free verse sonnet" structure, fourteen lines of iambic pentameter with frequent enjambment, pervasive use of slant rhyme, and no fixed rhyme scheme. She indicates that she was drawn to the sonnet tradition because it is "one in which women were caged in golden cages of beloved." But the form can be subverted: "The cage can turn into a house if you housekeep it in the right way."

In her second collection of poems, *The Other Side / El Otro Lado*, published in 1995, Alvarez explores questions of gender difference, cultural disparity, and the profound influence of language. The implications of the bilingual title are taken up by the opening poem, "Bilingual Sestina," which meditates on the poet's sensuous experience of her native Spanish, the way in which her adopted English seems at times not to offer a real equivalence, and in either language, "how frail a word / is when faced with the thing it names." The title poem, whose twenty-one cantos of varying lengths and verse forms range among the narrative, the dramatic, and the meditative, tells of a visit by the poet, now a Dominican Vermonter, to the Dominican Republic. There she explores her childhood associations in contrast to the life she has created in the United States.

As Alvarez's poetry explores the terrain of the mother-daughter relationship, the delicate but sometimes unsatisfying encounters of lovers, and the broader communal experience that she finds among sisters, aunts, and others, experience takes on a mythical dimension. Even in the poems' evocation of frustration and despair, there remains the half-humorous perspective of the adult looking upon herself as the naive child. *See also* **Latin American Poetry; Latino Poetry.**

Further Reading. *Selected Primary Sources:* Alvarez, Julia, *Homecoming: New and Collected Poems* (New York: Plume, 1996); ———, *How the García Girls Lost Their Accents* (Chapel Hill, NC: Algonquin, 1991); ———, *In the Time of the Butterflies* (Chapel Hill, NC: Algonquin, 1994); ———, *The Other Side / El Otro Lado* (New York: E.P. Dutton, 1995); ———, *Something to Declare* (Chapel Hill, NC: Algonquin, 1998). ***Selected Secondary Sources:*** Ghosh, Bishnupriya, and Brinda Bose, eds., *Interventions: Feminist Dialogues on Third World Women's Literature and Film* (New York: Garland, 1997); Rosario-Sievert, Heather, "Conversation with Julia Alvarez" (*Review: Latin American Literature and Arts* 54 [Spring 1997]: 31–37); Sirias, Silvio, *Julia Alvarez: A Critical Companion* (Westport, CT: Greenwood, 2001).

James S. Leonard

AMERICAN SUBLIME. *SEE* SUBLIME

AMMONS, A.R. (1926–2001)

With nineteen books of poetry spanning the entire latter half of the twentieth century, A.R. Ammons was one of the most prolific and distinctive American poets of his time, creating an oeuvre as diverse as it is broad, ranging from the epigrammatic collection *The Really Short Poems of A.R. Ammons* to the 200-page *Tape of the Turn of the Year*. As a master of the long poem, he is often described as a principal heir of the tradition of **Walt Whitman**. While, like Whitman, Ammons holds a place in the American poetic canon as a nature poet—for meditations on the relation of self and the natural world such as his famous "Corsons Inlet"—he is also credited with integrating into American poetry the discourse of the sciences. Critic (and close friend of Ammons) Harold Bloom declared, in a book-jacket blurb for Ammons's 1972 *Collected Poems*, "No contemporary poet, in America, is likelier to become a classic than A.R. Ammons."

The third child of Lucy Dell McKee Ammons and W.M. Ammons, Archibald Randolph Ammons was born in rural Whiteville, North Carolina, on February 19, 1926. Raised with two sisters, Ammons remained the family's only son after the death of his two infant brothers. Growing up during the Great Depression, Ammons's early childhood on his family's tobacco farm was difficult and impoverished and yet pastoral. The hardship and the infant deaths are featured in his most poignant elegies, "Nelly Myers" and "Easter Morning." After graduating from high school in Whiteville, Ammons worked in a North Carolina shipyard before enlisting in the Navy in 1944. Stationed on the U.S.S. *Gunason* in the South Pacific, Ammons began writing poetry, his first efforts being comic pieces about his fellow shipmates. Ammons served as a "ping jockey," taking sonar readings for a destroyer escort until his discharge in 1946, when the G.I. bill allowed him to be the first in his family to attend college. He enrolled at Wake Forest University with the intention of becoming a doctor, but pursuing further medical training proved prohibitively expensive, and Ammons graduated with a BS in general science.

While in college, Ammons met Phyllis Plumbo, his college Spanish instructor, and they later married in 1949. The couple lived in Cape Hatteras, North

Carolina, where Ammons took a position as an elementary school principal just before enrolling in the master's program in English at the University of California–Berkeley. Although Ammons's interest in poetry went as far back as the teenage verse written while he was in the Navy, it was at Berkeley that Ammons found his mentor in poet-scholar **Josephine Miles**. As much a neighbor as a teacher, Miles advised Ammons on publishing and encouraged his efforts, from his earliest work until her own death in 1983. Only four units shy of his degree, Ammons left the Berkeley program in 1952 to take an office position at his father-in-law's scientific glass manufacturing factory while continuing, with Miles's support, his pursuit of poetry. Like **Wallace Stevens** and **William Carlos Williams** before him, Ammons at first earned his living outside the literary world, typing poems on the backs of carbon-copy memoranda. Isolated, in southern New Jersey, from any literary community, Ammons published his first book, *Ommateum; with Doxology* (1955), through a vanity press in 1955.

The publication of *Ommateum* was scarcely noticed; most of the volumes were sent as gifts to friends and business associates. Titled after the scientific name for the compound eye of an insect, the volume is quite unlike Ammons's later poetry. Charged with highly symbolic language and set in an abstract wasteland, the poems of *Ommateum* were thought strange by their few readers and critics. However, the volume establishes trends that are refined in later works, particularly that bridging of the rhetoric of poetry and science for which Ammons would become known.

Writing in anonymity for the rest of the 1950s, Ammons started to make a name for himself in literary circles in the early 1960s. Resigning from the glass factory in 1962, Ammons devoted himself full-time to his literary pursuits. He befriended William Carlos Williams and began publishing regularly in journals such as the *Hudson Review.* Championed by that journal's editor, Frederick Morgan, he eventually won a scholarship to the Breadloaf writers' conference in Vermont, where he met **Robert Frost** and **Howard Nemerov**. Guided by Nemerov and **Denise Levertov**, Ammons started aggressively to pursue a career in poetry, beginning with a position as rotating poetry editor at the *Nation.*

Ammons was to wait nine years before the publication of his next book, *Expressions of Sea Level* (1964), by Ohio State University Press. Titled after an experience in the Navy, this volume helped to establish Ammons's reputation as a noteworthy new poet. That same year Ammons accepted a temporary instructor position at Cornell University in Ithaca, New York, which was to become the lifetime home of Ammons and his wife and son. His one-year contract at Cornell evolved into a nearly thirty-year tenure. Though originally a South-erner, Ammons's vision of nature is very often of the same northeastern terrain shared by Emerson, Dickinson, and Frost.

The appearance of *Expressions of Sea Level* followed by the twin publication of *Corsons Inlet* (1965) and the book-length poem *Tape for the Turn of the Year* (1965) placed Ammons and his poetic vision firmly into the American literary scene. *Expressions at Sea Level* introduced the poet's fascination with drift and motion as a poetic conceit. What becomes his characteristic use of the colon is fully realized in this collection, deployed in nearly every poem. These early poems intimate the full range of Ammons's palette, from the elegiac remembrance of "Nelly Myers" to the study of spider webs in "Identity." The poems also introduce the public to Ammons's life-long interest in the mutual engagement of systems and the individual.

Corsons Inlet solidified Ammons's reputation as America's premier nature poet. Its title poem, which became his best-known and most anthologized poem, is inspired by Ammons's long residence in southern New Jersey. "Corsons Inlet" offers a serene introspection into the drift and dissolution of self and nature during a walk along the dunes of the Jersey shore. Originally titled "A Nature Walk," the poem recalls Robert Frost's own solitary "walking" poems and is the one most often used to classify Ammons as an American post-Romantic poet. Charles Altieri places Ammons alongside **Robert Bly** and **Gary Snyder** as a contemporary Coleridgian, one for whom "concrete universals" demand that the poet "synthesize his particulars into a single organic emotional whole" (*Enlarging the Temple: New Directions in American Poetry during the 1960's*, 16). However, Ammons's vision never arrives at a transcendental apogee; "The overall is beyond me," the poem's narrator insists. What Ammons unfolds during the walk along Corsons Inlet is a congregation of particularities. Grace arrives with "no finality of vision," as the narrator yields to an existence among the pulsing networks of transactions and exchanges of living and dying, shore and sand.

Published at the same time as *Corson's Inlet, Tape of the Turn of the Year* is Ammons's first book-length poem. In the form of diary entries typed on a roll of adding-machine tape between December 6, 1963, and January 10, 1964, the poem chronicles the changing of the year in a singular convergence of Whitman's expansive impulse and Dickinson's contracted brevity. *Tape* also signals a shift in American poetry toward postmodernism *avant la lettre*. Ammons's playful and discursive intertwining of the minutiae of suburban life with the mythic conceit of Homer's *Odyssey* makes the piece one of the first major post–World War II poetic productions to blur the line between high art and the commonplace. Along with *Corsons Inlet, Tape for the Turn of the Year* helped to establish Ammons as a serious innovator of postwar American poetry. The experiment of writing on adding-machine tape recalls **Jack Kerouac**'s *On the Road*, written on twenty rolls of teletype paper pieced together. Although Ammons has often been fixed in the Emersonian-Whitmanian poetic tradition, early work such as *Tape for the Turn of the Year* also reveals a love of experimentation that anticipates postmodern poetic innovations. The poet **John Ashbery** says of Ammons's poetry, "Much has been written about the relation of the so-called 'New York School' of poets to the painting of Jackson Pollock, but in a curious way Ammons's poetry seems a much closer and more successful approximation of 'Action Painting' or art as process" (Bloom, 59).

A fascination with expression as action rather than statement characterizes much of Ammons's work. *Collected Poems 1951–1971* (1972) spans twenty years, representing a capstone to only part of a career, as Ammons continued to publish new books for more than twenty-five years after its publication. This collection most clearly captures Ammons's espousal of poetry as action, as is aptly demonstrated in poems such as "Four Motions for the Pea Vines" (1965), in which "expansion and / contraction: the unfolding, / furling" describe the action of the poem as much as anything external to it.

In fact, there are no fewer than five poems in *Collected Poems* that use "motion" in the title. Even Ammons's penchant for the colon suggests this embrace of incomplete but forward momentum over the period's resting "still point." Flowing, rising, falling, spiraling are only a few of the modes of motion that Ammons traces. He explains his modus operandi in the essay "Surfaces": "The bringing of all the forces into momentary symmetry of actions allows one to participate in an apparently easy, effortless harmony of things" (*Set in Motion*, 21)

Collected Poems also indicates a shift away from the nature poetry for which Ammons had become recognized. While never breaking away from his engagement with nature, Ammons's poetry of the late 1960s to early 1970s reveals him as a poet of ideas and abstraction, in the tradition of Wallace Stevens, rather than one of images and sentiment. Although Ammons claims no predecessor, Stevens's influence cannot be ignored. Ammons's short monologue "King of Ice"(1970), which announces "I will never believe in ice" seems at once to refer to Stevens's "The Emperor of Ice-cream" and to be in direct dialogue with Stevens's assertion that "One must have a mind of winter" from his "The Snowman." However, Ammons most often plays out his philosophical meditations in what he called "talkathons," such as "One::Many," and later in longer works such as "Essay on Poetics," "Extremes and Moderation," and "Hibernaculum." Fashioned after Alexander Pope's poetic treatise, Ammons's "Essay on Poetics," built from prose couplets, at once elaborates and demonstrates his poetic principles, going as far as crafting another poem within

"Essay on Poetics" to explicate. In addition, *Collected Poems* presages the rise of French semiotics and deconstruction. In 1962 he notes in "Motion" that "The word is / not the thing: / is a construction of, / a tag for, the thing."

Many critics see *Collected Poems* as the dividing line of Ammons's career. After the publication of *Collected Poems*, Ammons expanded on his "talkathons,"repeatedly embracing the format of the book-length poem over the next quarter century. His next book of this type, *Sphere: the form of a motion* (1974), Ammons dubbed "my long deconstructive poem." The grandest of the "Harold Bloom poems," *Sphere* debuted in sections in the high-theory journal *Diacritics*. Ammons and Bloom shared a great friendship while at similar points in their careers, and Bloom's high regard for Ammons's work brought the poet national attention. Ammons dedicated "The Arc Inside Out" to Bloom and wrote a poem, "For Harold Bloom," as preface to *Sphere*. Made up of 155 sections of four free-verse tercets each, *Sphere* is more rigorously formal than the drifting lines characteristic of *Expressions of Sea Level* and "Corson's Inlet." Inspired by the first images of earth from outer space (such as "The Blue Marble" [1972] photograph taken by the Apollo 17 mission), *Sphere* seeks out the full boundary of Whitman's vistas "to found / a federation of loveship." Ammons's interest seemed to shift in *Sphere* from seeking possibility to unifying diversity. *Sphere* clearly demonstrates its debt to Whitman, though couched in Ammons humor, when he puns, "I am not a whit manic / to roam the globe."

After the critical acclaim of *Collected Poems* and *Sphere*, Ammons's next book was uncharacteristically poorly received. *Snow Poems* was critically snubbed and remains one of Ammons's most underappreciated works. Dedicated "for my country," *The Snow Poems* (1977) recalls its predecessor *Tape for the Turn of the Year* in marking the days of Ithaca's long winters, from the first flakes of November to the last sleet of May. Made up of unnumbered and untitled poems, the work was written around 1976, the bicentennial of the United States; Ammons had envisioned writing a poem for every state in the union. Such a project might account for the wide variety of poem types in the collection, running the course from the lewd to the sublime. Although not well regarded when first published, *Snow Poems* seems to mark a frontier of and perhaps a limit to Ammons's aggressive poetic experimentation.

After *The Snow Poems*, Ammons returned to his lyrics and elegies, establishing his position as Emerson's heir; postmodern elements are underplayed in the later works. The most famous and traditional of these later lyrics would be "Easter Morning," found in *A Coast of Trees* (1981), which finds Ammons going "back to my home country in these fresh far-away days." In the poem Ammons tenderly recalls the death of his infant brother and his rural beginnings in North Carolina. He mourns the "life that did not become, / that turned aside and stopped." Eventually, the poet finds his way toward consolation, articulated in plain but resonant elegance.

In 1991 Ammons collected a book of terse, ironic verses called *The Really Short Poems of A.R. Ammons.* Lucid and humorous, *The Really Short Poems* marks a strong contrast to Ammons's proclivity for extended and contemplative studies of the flow of form and being. Culled from forty years of publishing, Ammons's short poems are shockingly minimal, never longer than a page and most less than twelve lines long. Ammons manages to encapsulate the vagaries of human frailty and absurdity with quick-witted pun and precision, as in the single-line poem "Coward" (1991): "Bravery runs in my family." In addition, he remains as attuned to nature's ironies and paradoxes as ever. Haiku-like pieces such as "Small Song" (1991) deliver wisdom with a delicate and light hand. Indeed, Ammons's observations of nature's ephemera betray the eastern sensibility he found in poets such as Lao Tse, whose writing resonated with Ammons from his earliest days as a poet.

Ammons returns to nature in his next book, but the nature of *Garbage* (1993) is far from the *ikebana*-style nature of *The Really Short Poems of A.R. Ammons.* Inspired by a giant smoldering trash heap seen from Highway I-95 in Florida, *Garbage* earned a second National Book Award for Ammons. He began *Garbage* in the 1980s, but health problems delayed its completion. Dedicating the book "to the bacteria, tumblebugs, scavengers, wordsmiths—the transfigururers, restorers," Ammons fulfills a promise made in his early poem "Still," where he declares that he will find what is lowly "and put the roots of my identity / down there." Ammons sees garbage as "the poem of our time because / garbage is spiritual." In *Garbage,* he embraces heaps of refuse as the building blocks of the universe. Ammons's monologue ranges through eighteen sections of meditative **free verse** couplets, contemplating mortality, nature, and humanity's place in a cosmology where waste—organic or spiritual—is never trash. His faith in the conservation of matter recoups the straggly, unsightly ends of life—age, decay, disappointment, worldly antipathy—and knits them into a text that points toward comfort and connection, circumventing the alienation usually associated with a wasteland.

Glare (1997) is the last book published in Ammons's lifetime and his last great long poem, ensuring Ammons's reputation as a master of that genre. Projecting a novelistic ambition, Ammons returns to the experimental impetus that *Tape for the Turn of the Year* announced. *Glare* consists of two sections, "Strip" and "Scat Scan." The sections of "Strip" are typed chronologically but were reordered for publication; the first section is followed by the last, the second section is fol-

lowed by the penultimate one, and so on until the middle sections meet. At 70, Ammons looks back at his life with breezy freshness and sympathetic humor. Though crotchety at the outset about the cramped space of his "tape" and the state of his health, the poet of *Glare* breaches the "crises of fear," and his expression of hope enacts its own fulfillment.

Widely considered one of the last great American poets of the twentieth century, Ammons swept nearly all the major poetry prizes: the Bollingen, Bobbit, the National Book Award twice (for *Collected Poems* and *Garbage*), the Frost Medal, and the National Book Critics Circle Award, though the Pulitzer unaccountably eluded him. He was also the first American poet to receive a MacArthur fellowship. After retiring from Cornell University in 2000, Ammons passed away in the spring of 2001; he remains among the most cherished poets of the American canon.

Further Reading. ***Selected Primary Sources:*** Ammons, A.R., *A Coast of Trees* (New York: W.W. Norton and Co., 1981); ———, *Collected Poems* (New York: W.W. Norton and Co., 1972); ———, *Garbage* (New York: W.W. Norton and Co., 1993); ———, *Glare* (New York: W.W. Norton and Co., 1997); ———, *The Really Short Poems of A.R Ammons* (New York: W.W. Norton and Co., 1991); ———, *Set in Motion: Essays, Interviews, & Dialogues,* ed. Sofia Burr (Ann Arbor: University of Michigan Press, 1996); *The Snow Poems* (New York: W.W. Norton and Co., 1977); ———, *Sphere: A Form of Motion* (New York: W.W. Norton and Co., 1974); ———, *Tape for the Turn of the Year* (New York: W.W. Norton and Co., 1965). ***Selected Secondary Sources:*** Bloom, Harold, ed., *Modern Critical Views: A.R. Ammons* (New York: Chelsea House, 1986); Gilbert, Roger, "A.R. Ammons," in *Dictionary of Literary Biography, Vol. 165: American Poets Since World War II,* 4th ser., ed. Joseph Conte (New York: Bruccoli Clark Layman,1996, 3–24); Kirschten, Robert, ed. *Critical Essays on A.R. Ammons* (New York: G.K. Hall, 1997); Vendler, Helen, "The Titles: A.R. Ammons, 1926–2001" (*Poetry* 179.1 [October 2001]: 31–44).

Melissa Gabot Fabros

ANANIA, MICHAEL (1939–)

Michael Anania's first significant publications came out of his involvement with a remarkable gathering of writers at SUNY–Buffalo in the 1960s. Like the work of his teacher **Charles Olson**, Anania's most accomplished volumes, including *The Color of Dust* (1970), *Riversongs* (1978), and *The Sky at Ashland* (1986), take the human experience of space as a principal subject matter. In his earliest works, historical narratives of the American West provide a context for this interest; later works explore how the spaces, events, and rituals of urban Chicago communicate the city's history. He complements his attention to history and setting with a lyricism that reviewers often recognize as inspired by another **Black Mountain School** poet, **Robert Creeley**. If Anania's work is an elaboration of the "**projective verse**" poetics outlined by Olson, he makes that approach his own by engaging with his particular surroundings, and by means of a linguistic playfulness that can be attributed to his reading of the philosopher Ludwig Wittgenstein.

Born in Omaha, Nebraska, Michael Anania was raised by his mother, Dora, after his father, Angelo, died when Anania was only nine years old. In his novel *The Red Menace* (1975), he documents the experience of living as a boy in an Omaha housing project during the early years of the Cold War. He studied at the University of Nebraska at Lincoln and at the Municipal University of Omaha (now the University of Nebraska at Omaha), where he received a BA in 1961. A graduate student at SUNY–Buffalo from 1961 to 1964, he later taught at SUNY–Fredonia and Northwestern University. Now an Emeritus Professor of English at the University of Illinois at Chicago, where he began teaching in 1968, Anania is an influential force in the city's literary community. In addition to directing the Ph.D. program in creative writing at UIC for many years, he has worked as an editor for the Swallow Press and *TriQuarterly*, and helped to found or direct several local and state initiatives in the arts, including the Poetry Center of Chicago, the Read Illinois Program, the Illinois Center for the Book, the Illinois Arts Council, the Illinois Cultural Resources Coordinating Council, and the Arts Club of Chicago.

His best-known poem remains "The Riversongs of Arion, I–X," the opening sequence of *Riversongs*. "Arion" refers to the hero of a Greek myth, who escapes the capture of pirates with a song so powerful it summons a dolphin to save him. Anania's Arion is a modern-day explorer who becomes stranded on the banks of the Missouri River just south of Omaha, and just opposite from what he imagines was the campsite of Lewis and Clark in 1804. In his notes to the poem, Anania acknowledges the influence of American studies scholar Henry Nash Smith, whose *Virgin Land* (1950) was for years the definitive text on the literature of the American West. But Anania does not romanticize the westward movement of European Americans, nor does he indulge in nostalgia for an uncultivated expanse of land that stretched mythically from the frontier to the Pacific. Instead, he mediates between the present and the past in order to correct the historical record. He exposes as racist caricatures the popular depictions in films and novels of Sacajewea as the "Indian maid" of Lewis and Clark, and he acknowledges the destruction of the Native American societies through Arion's recognition that the surviving members of the "Oto, Ponca, and Pawnee" tribes have little choice but to work as migrant laborers who "move west each morning in open trucks / to get a year's beet sugar in."

Anania's wit is most evident in his collection of essays, *In Plain Sight: Obsessions, Morals, and Domestic Laughter* (1991), which reflects on literary precursors, contemporary poets, and, above all, Chicago. The opening sentence of "Excesses and Boondoggles" explains an attitude about history that runs through all of his writings about urban space: "To live in a city . . . is to live with a city's past, not as an idea or an academic exercise but as a day-to-day fact of life, something you can brush elbows with or lean up against waiting for a bus" (27). Embodied in our experience of space, the history of a place often remains hidden in plain sight.

Like his essays, Anania's most recent volume of poetry, *In Natural Light* (1999), brings into relief events, things, and ideas that have faded from view as a result of their familiarity. He achieves this recovery in spare lyrics that reveal the narrative dimension of any experience, and from there show how events exceed the "ideas" or "academic exercises" used to frame them. In a single sentence over seven short lines, "Eclogue" inverts the sequence of **Ezra Pound**'s Imagist classic "In a Station of the Metro." Anania begins with the "sudden" quality of "the gradual lives of flowers," and then compares them to faces seen in the light of a "B" train stop, "taking, as you always / do, the 'A' train." Casting this poem in second person, and positioning "you" on the train moving through the station, Anania reverses the direction of Pound's original metaphor. Here, the juxtaposition does not fix the appearance of faces in the image of petals on a bough; instead, the routine of taking the "A" train is identified as the event that makes possible the instant in which the faces are revealed to resemble flowers. Anania's title is an especially deft touch. In a poem that conveys a sense of the duration apparent in flowers or faces in a train station, he counters the urban inflection of Pound's title with "Eclogue," the name for a form of pastoral poetry.

The volume's final sequence, "Fifty-two Definite Articles," makes explicit Anania's enthusiasm for Wittgenstein. The grammatical play of the title prepares the reader for a catalogue of items introduced with "the," which range in content from "*the swan*" to "*the aging proponent*" to "*the description of rivers*." Presented as italicized headings, these "articles" precede aphoristic stanzas that recall the procedure of Wittgenstein's *Philosophical Investigations*. Under the double heading of "*the advent observer*" and "*the lurking suspicion*," the philosopher himself appears, under a desk, with twentieth-century thought "wadded like gum / above his head." With this image, Anania puns implausibly; ideas appear to be over the head of Wittgenstein. In a cramped space far removed from the western expanses of his *Riversongs*, Anania fashions an irreverent simile for twentieth-century thought, investing it with resilience, good humor, and a sense of its lively history.

Further Reading. *Selected Primary Sources:* Anania, Michael, *The Color of Dust* (Chicago: Swallow Press, 1970); ———, *In Natural Light* (Wakefield, RI: Moyer Bell, 1999); ———, *In Plain Sight* (Wakefield, RI: Moyer Bell, 1991); *Riversongs* (Urbana: University of Illinois Press, 1978); ———, *Selected Poems* (Wakefield, RI: Moyer Bell, 1994); ———, *The Sky at Ashland* (Wakefield, RI: Moyer Bell, 1986).

Jim Zeigler

ANDREWS, BRUCE (ERROL) (1948–)

Bruce Andrews has published more than forty books of poetry and criticism, numerous articles, and a monograph in the social and political sciences. He is probably best known for his continued involvement with **Language poetry** as a poet and a critic, and for starting, along with **Charles Bernstein**, the seminal **small press** Xerox magazine *L=A=N=G=U=A=G=E* in 1978. This publication, together with West Coast magazines such as **Robert Grenier** and **Barrett Watten**'s *This*, formed the core of early Language poetry and helped to shape the movement's investigation of the materiality of language over the three years of its run. Andrews's own poetry and poetics have continued to explore the materiality of language and genre through performance, sound, shape, collaboration with a wide range of practitioners, and alternative approaches to both prose (see Alan Golding's "Bruce Andrews' Poetics and the Limits of Genre" [1999]) and poetry.

Andrews was born in Chicago in 1948 but grew up around Washington, D.C. He was educated in political science at Johns Hopkins, where he received bachelor's and master's degrees, and was granted a Ph.D. from Harvard in 1975 for his dissertation on American public policy and the Vietnam War. He is currently a professor of political science at Fordham University in New York City, where he has lived since 1975.

Andrews started actively writing poetry in the late 1960s and early 1970s while still in graduate school in Baltimore. This early work was inflected by his growing discomfort with the use and abuse of language by the dominant American culture and by what he terms, in an interview with Kevin Davies and Jeff Derksen, "the abuse of public authority, the abuse of the public sphere" (6) that was occurring over the course of the Vietnam War and, in particular, during the Nixon years in the White House. For Andrews the use to which language was being put in order to prop up a flawed and disturbed public policy, while he was actively engaged in a critical study of that very same public policy, was too much to endure. As a consequence, he began to explore what might happen when language was pushed to the point of failing, so that the kinds of abuse being carried out with language by the structures of public authority might be made visible.

During the Nixon administration, what was left unsaid was at least as important as what was said, and poems like "Bananas are an example" (1972) (entire text of the poem) seek to point this out. The poem gives us a concrete image, but no context for that image. We are left with the unanswerable question, "Of what are they an example?" This phrasal level of interruption of the syllogistic movement of language is just what **Ron Silliman** refers to in his work on **Gertrude Stein** as the building blocks of the new sentence and permeates much of Andrews's poetic work from the 1970s to the present. For Andrews, the disruption of syllogistic movement and the retarding of the accrual of meaning to the phrasal and subphrasal levels is essentially a political act, one that exposes the abuses that the forces of public authority perpetrate on individuals and seek to obfuscate through the furthering of the myth of the transparency of language.

By the time Andrews had moved to New York he had already published five small books of poetry: *Edge* (1973), *Corona* (1973), *a capella* (1973), *Appalachia* (1974), and *Melancholy* (1975); much of these texts has been reprinted in his *Executive Summary* (1991). These works were characterized by short lines, almost **Imagist** in nature, sometimes at the level of the phrase and other times at the level of single words such as "warblings / betwixt" from "Appalachia" (*Executive Summary*, 32). This investigation of the materiality of language through small, incomplete phrasal units continued through the late 1970s, culminating in the large sequence of performance scores and songs *Love Songs* (1982), which collects pieces from his collaborations with dancer and choreographer Sally Silvers, with whom he has continued to work to the present day. These performance scores and plans are often visual in nature, reflecting performers' movement through the space of performance with the movement of the words on the page, which radically depart from a left-justified textuality. In some cases this departure from normative textual presentation dispenses with the poetic line altogether, as in "NO 73," with italicized capital letters (*A, E, I, L, T, F,* and *G*) distributed askew down the page in a roughly two-inch-wide centered column. The letters suggest words, but never quite coalesce into full semantic units.

With the publication of *I Don't Have Any Paper So Shut Up (or, Social Romanticism)* (1992) Andrews's poetic praxis began exploring a different way to foreground the mechanisms of language and thereby allow for a reading practice to make visible the inherent politics of transparent communication. The book is a series of one hundred pieces, each six hundred words long, written during the mid-1980s. Gone are the solitary words dispersed over the face of the page. The language here is dense, and prose-like, built from fragmentary phrases of dynamic, phonically and politically charged language. Moments like "USA = immaculate / conception air assault sticks in million dollar baby's mouth" (63) or "Spoken / like true clothes-hamper twins inform the womb: reindeer / are druggies" (74) read like collaged tabloid headlines or political sloganeering transformed into a spin doctor's nightmare. The text is intentionally difficult both in its fragmentary nature and in its offensive phrasing. Nevertheless, the humor emerges. There is something both disturbing and hilarious about the juxtapositions—reindeer junkies and Arthur Rankin and Jules Bass's Animagic (puppet-mation) Rudolph Christmas specials.

Furthering this more dense linguistic assault is *Lip Service* (2001). The complicated procedures that Andrews put his language through in this reworking of Dante's *Paradiso*, detailed in his essay "Paradise and Method" (1996), involved sorting and re-sorting a large volume of language collected on cards in the late 1980s. Using methodology from his essay "Tips for Totalizers" (1996), the sorted language was then worked into a structure that mimicked Dante's stanzas and cantos. The one hundred sections of the book correspond directly to the thematic and formal structure of Dante's work using a fragmentary technique similar to that of *Shut Up* with the addition of poetic lineation based mostly on the phrase.

The companion piece to *Lip Service*, *The Millennium Project* (2001), although less visible in terms of its critical response, is arguably more important in terms of its radical formal experimentation with textual units, furthering Andrews's early investigations into the visual space of the page. It is an 11 by 5 electronic matrix of poetry with each intersection or node containing between 12 and 14 electronic pages of poetry, for a total of 666. These pages are arranged chronologically along the longer axis and thematically/formally along the shorter. The pieces themselves are all right-justified—a format that eliminates much of the visual play on the page of many previously published sections. The work allows navigation through the matrix following both axes, giving the reader a very different kind of textual experience from that of navigating through a standard codex. The work no longer has a strictly linear progression from one page/text to another. Rather, *The Millennium Project* problematizes our normative relationship with a multipage text with the insertion of choice into the mix. What Andrews has done is to produce a large text that is organized three-dimensionally with a high degree of freedom with respect to the ways in which the text *allows* us to read. This, coupled with his phrasal level of linguistic disruption and pointedly humorous neologisms, makes *The Millennium Project* his most concerted attack on linguistic and textual hegemony to date.

It is important to note that in addition to his collaborations with Sally Silvers, Andrews has made a long-term practice of collaborating with various other practitioners in both performance and text. The textual end of this practice can be broken down into two distinct forms: verbo-visual collaborations, often with text by Andrews and visual material supplied by a collaborator, and collaborative textual projects. Of the first form, works like *eXcla* (1993) with Maggie O'Sullivan, *Tizzy Boost* (1993) with **Kenneth Goldsmith**, and *BothBoth* (1987) with Bob Cobbing are indicative of a certain kind of **visual poetry** conversation. Still more interesting are his strictly textual collaborations like the seminal Language poetry collaboration *Legend* (1980) with Charles Bernstein, **Steve McCaffery**, **Ray DiPalma**, and Ron Silliman, or the card-based piece *Joint Words* (1979) with John M. Bennett. The latter, although smaller than Robert Grenier's *Sentences* (1978), is an equally important exploration of poetic alternatives to the codex form.

For Andrews all of this practice is in an attempt to reach a kind of paradise wherein language is not, and cannot be, used as a tool of oppression or a means through which an empowered system sustains itself beyond its usefulness, a paradise that in his "Paradise and Method" is "Strangeness estranging us from the familiarity of already pregiven union" (236). His defamiliarized language is always poised to coalesce into comprehensibility, but resists the clarity required of a tool for power structures. As Andrews puts it, again in "Paradise and Method," his work is "[a] disturbing of the peace as a basis for peace" (237). The consistent and almost brutal fragmentation of language does more than just halt the syllogistic movement, as Silliman would have it; rather , as Jerome Sala says, "What was fragmentary becomes monolithic" (28). At a certain point, language becomes an undifferentiable mass, becomes the masses.

Further Reading. *Selected Primary Sources:* Andrews, Bruce, "Appalachia," in *Executive Summary* (Elmwood, CT: Potes & Poets, 1991); ———, "Bananas are an example" (*Paris Review* 53 [1972]: 162), ———, *Ex Why Zee: Performance Texts, Collaborations with Sally Silvers, Word Maps, Bricolage & Improvisation* (New York: Roof Books, 1995), ———, *Factura* (Madison, WI: Xexoxial, 1987); ———, *Give Em Enough Rope* (Los Angeles: Sun & Moon Press, 1987); ———, *I Don't Have Any Paper So Shut Up (or, Social Romanticism)* (Los Angeles: Sun & Moon Press, 1992), ———, *Lip Service* (Toronto: Coach House Books, 2001); ———, *Love Songs* (Baltimore, MD: Pod Books, 1982); ———, *The Millennium Project* (Princeton, NJ: Eclipse, 2001, http://www.princeton.edu/eclipse/projects/Millennium/title.html); ———, "Paradise and Method," in *Paradise and Method: Poetics and Praxis* (Evanston, IL: Northwestern University Press, 1996; reprint *Aerial* 9 [1999]: 221–240]); ———, *Paradise and Method: Poetics and Praxis* (Evanston, IL: Northwestern University Press, 1996; ———, *Wobbling* (New York: Roof, 1981); Andrews, Bruce, and John M. Bennett, *Joint Words* (Columbus, OH: Luna Bisonte Prods., 1979); Andrews,

Bruce, and Charles Bernstein, eds., *The L=A=N=G=U=A=G=E Book* (Carbondale: Southern Illinois University Press, 1984); Andrews, Bruce, Charles Bernstein, Ray DiPalma, Steve McCaffery, and Ron Silliman, *Legend* (New York: L=A=N=G=U=A=G=E/ Segue, 1980); Andrews, Bruce, and Bob Cobbing, *BothBoth* (London: Writers Forum, 1987); Andrews, Bruce, Kevin Davies, and Jeff Derksen, "Bruce Andrews Interview: May 1990, Vancouver" (*Aerial* 9 [1999]: 5–17); Andrews, Bruce, and Kenneth Goldsmith, *Tizzy Boost* (Great Barrington, MA: The Figures, 1993); Andrews, Bruce, and Maggie O'Sullivan, *eXcla* (London: Writers Forum, 1993). **Selected Secondary Sources:** Cabri, Louis, "Louis Cabri on the Bruce Andrews/Rod Smith PhillyTalks December 1998 at the Kelly Writers House" (http://www.writing.upenn.edu/~afilreis/88/phillytalks-andrews-smith.html); Golding, Alan, "Bruce Andrews' Poetics and the Limits of Genre" (*Aerial* 9 [1999]: 196–207); Lawrence, Nick, ed., *Jacket* 22 (special section on Bruce Andrews) (http://jacketmagazine.com/22/index.html); Sala, Jerome, "Talking about *Shut Up*" (*Aerial* 9 [1999]: 28–31); Smith, Rod, ed., *Aerial* 9 (special issue on Bruce Andrews) (Washington, DC: Aerial/Edge, 1999).

William R. Howe

ANGEL ISLAND POETRY

In the first half of the twentieth century, Chinese immigrants detained in the West Coast immigration station of Angel Island expressed the fear, uncertainty, and injustice of their situation through poems, which they carved or wrote on the barrack walls in which they were held. These poets, the majority of whom did not sign names to the 135 discovered poems, have become collectively known as the Anonymous Angel Island Poets. Their writing is a unique vehicle not only to understanding the condition of Chinese immigrants seeking new lives in the United States, but also to tracking the themes of alienation, labor, and race that are an inextricable part of American literature and history.

The authors of the Angel Island poetry arrived in the San Francisco Bay at the height of tensions between the Chinese and white populations. For decades, the Chinese had been instrumental in building the new Western frontier, most famously the railroads. The Chinese were also a critical part of the labor force in mining, agriculture, and fishing. In fact, as of 1852 one-quarter of California's entire workforce were Chinese.

When the transcontinental railroad was completed in 1869, many Chinese (and others) were put out of work, creating competition for jobs. A recession after the Civil War made economic conditions even more severe. Poverty and unemployment grew, and some white groups singled out Chinese immigrants as targets for their frustrations. Employers kept workers racially divided by keeping separate, lower pay scales for their Asian labor-

ers and ensuring that workers did not form unions. The city of San Francisco passed several racist laws, including the Sidewalk Ordinance, which prohibited Chinese from carrying their laundry on poles; and the Queue Ordinance, which forced Chinese prisoners to chop their hair short, a humiliating punishment.

The harshest of these racist laws was the Chinese Exclusion Act, passed by Congress in 1882. The Chinese Exclusion Act marked the first time that a specific ethnic group was prohibited from immigration.

Chinese laborers attempting entry into the United States via Angel Island, "the Ellis Island of the West," were often detained for weeks or months, and in some cases up to two years. Upon arrival at Angel Island, would-be immigrants were forced to pass a series of difficult physical and interrogative tests. Many were quarantined or sent back to China for ailments that were treatable and that affected almost exclusively the Chinese, adding yet another barrier to Chinese immigration. All potential immigrants had to pass an oral examination that included detailed questions about their home towns or villages and family history, questions that most individuals would not have been able to answer without studying "coaching papers" en route to the United States and destroying these as their boat entered the bay.

For those would-be immigrants whose cases were pending, or who awaited detention, the first encounter with the United States was one of great uncertainty and disappointment. The detainees had hoped for better lives in the United States than could be offered by their home country. For Chinese, as for many Americans, the West represented opportunity and upward mobility. But the poems of Angel Island demonstrate that these detainees learned about injustice toward immigrants very quickly. Many exhibit the stirrings of a Chinese American sensibility, an awareness of their rights as immigrants and the sting of the violation of those rights. "America has power, but not justice," one poem complains; "in prison, we were victimized as if we were guilty."

Men and women were housed separately while in detention, meaning that some husbands and wives did not see or communicate with each other for months. The majority of Chinese immigrants to the United States at this time were men; the relatively fewer women immigrants, because of socioeconomic factors and the lack of a formal education, apparently did not write poems; the writing was found only in the men's barracks. One man, pining for his wife and son, writes, "When the moonlight shines on me alone, the nights seem even longer."

Most of the immigrants were Cantonese, and the majority of the poems can be traced to the Pearl River Delta region in Guangdong Province, southern China. The poems were written in pencil or ink, and then carved into the wall. Some were written with a brush and later carved.

The poems are written in the classical Cantonese style, structured in four lines with five or seven characters per line. This style, perfected during the T'ang dynasty, was well known to most Chinese, even those with a limited education (as was the case for many of the Angel Island detainees). Its structure—with introduction, development, and conclusion, each in a line or pair of lines—could in a small space frame the detainees' situations. One poem, describing "the low building with three beams [which] merely shelters the body," longs for the day when the writer will be successful: "I will not speak of love when I level the immigrant station!" Revenge fantasies such as this may have helped detainees feel that they had some agency in a humiliating and confining situation. For the same reason, as well as out of adherence to classical Cantonese tradition, many of the poems refer to legendary figures from Chinese literature and history, most commonly the great King Wen. The poets compare their trials to those endured by mythical heroes. One detainee asks, "When Ziqing was in distant lands, who pitied and inquired after him?"—an allusion to the famous figure also known as Su Wu, who had been held prisoner by a nomadic people for nearly twenty years but never renounced his loyalty to the Han emperor. Another writes, "Even though Su Wu was detained among the barbarians, he would one day return home."

These allusions to legendary figures are a way of framing the larger spiritual significance of the poets' imprisonment. In a rare, signed "Poem by One Named Xu, From Xiangshan, Consoling Himself," the poet asks, "Rich or poor, who is to say it is not the will of heaven? / . . . From ancient times, heroes were often the first ones to face adversity."

Many of the poems display a sorrowful awareness of the natural world outside, which continues its usual cycles while the poet remains imprisoned. Male prisoners, unlike the women and children, were not permitted to leave the barracks to walk the grounds in groups, so their poetry refers only to what could be seen from the window—moon and fog and clouds—and to sounds that penetrated the barrack walls. "Yu from Taishan" writes, in "Random Thoughts Deep at Night," of the "forms and shadows," "the whistling of wind," and the grief and bitterness that spur him to compose a poem of these materials. The fog of San Francisco Bay, particularly, is a recurring image, seemingly a correlative for the poets' inward state. Another poet writes, "My grief, like dense clouds, cannot be dispersed."

These poems also illuminate the "double consciousness" commonly felt by immigrants: a sense of being held between two worlds, in a sort of purgatory. The poets have left behind their families and often their previous occupations ("leaving behind my writing brush and removing my sword," writes one scholar, "I came to America"), and in many poems there is the sense that, trapped on Angel Island, these men hardly recognize themselves. The changes they have experienced are as baffling and vast as the ocean over which they have traveled. "I have infinite feelings that the ocean has changed into a mulberry grove," writes another poet. "My body is detained in this building," and he sees no recourse but to throw away his writing-brush in despair.

The Angel Island poems were noticed and documented by two former detainees: "Smiley Jann," detained in 1931, who copied ninety-two poems in a manuscript called "Collection of Autumn Grass: Volume Collecting Voices from the Hearts of the Weak"; and Tet Yee, detained a year later, who copied ninety-six poems, seventy-eight of which are also in Jann's book. However, the Angel Island poems were nearly lost in the 1970s when the barracks were slated to be razed. Intervention came in the form of Angel Island park ranger Alexander Weiss, who in 1970 noticed the Chinese writing carved into the barrack walls. Thinking that they might have been carved by immigrants, he contacted Dr. George Araki, a professor at San Francisco State University. Araki, along with photographer Mak Takahashi, visited the site and took pictures of the carved characters. In 1976 Barrack 37 was designated as a historical site.

Collectively, the Angel Island poems confer an understanding of these detainees as men of worth in the face of a nation that has ridiculed and ostracized them. Beyond this, the anonymous poets of Angel Island hold an important cultural and literary legacy for Chinese American writers who have followed. The narrator in Maxine Hong Kingston's novel *China Men* (1980) fantasizes that her father has inscribed an anonymous poem into the barrack wall at Angel Island. Other novelists, such as Shawn Wong in *Homebase* (1979) and Fae Myenne Ng in *Bone* (1993), feature protagonists who have passed through the island.

The displaced, grieving, and hopeful poets of Angel Island left a literary and cultural legacy that has—like the immigrants themselves, and their descendants—endured against difficult odds.

Further Readings. ***Selected Primary Sources:*** Hom, Marlon K., *Songs of Gold Mountain: Cantonese Rhymes from San Francisco Chinatown* (Berkeley: University of California Press, 1987); Lai, Him Mark, Genny Lim, and Judy Young, *Island: Poetry and History of Chinese Immigrants on Angel Island 1910–1940* (Seattle: University of Washington Press, 1980). ***Selected Secondary Sources:*** Lee, Robert G., *Orientals: Asian Americans in Popular Culture* (Philadelphia: Temple University Press, 1999); Polster, Karen, "Opportunity in the Borderlands: Labor and the American Dream in Chinese American Literature," in *Imagined Communities: Nationalism and Ethnicity in Twentieth-Century American Immigration Literature* (Ph.D. diss., University of California–Riverside, 2000).

Andria Williams

ANGELOU, MAYA (1928–)

Poet and social activist Maya Angelou's contribution to contemporary American poetry stems from her commitment to using literature to advocate for social justice and civil rights. In their emphasis on oral storytelling, **jazz**, **blues**, and the black vernacular as a mode of expression, Angelou's poems bridge the gap extending from the Black Aesthetics or **Black Arts Movement** of the 1960s and the neorealism movement of the 1970s to the present. Angelou's poetry, notable for its accessibility, uses clear, direct language to explore racial, class, and gender oppression. As Lyman B. Hagen states in *Heart of a Woman, Mind of a Writer, and Soul of a Poet: A Critical Analysis of the Writings of Maya Angelou*, "Angelou's poems are a continuum of mood and emotion" (118).

Born Marguerite Johnson in St. Louis, Missouri, Maya Angelou grew up in St. Louis; Stamps, Arkansas; and San Francisco, California. Her brother called her "Maya" when she was a child, and the name Angelou stems from Enistasious Angelous, an ex-husband (Pettis, 11). As northern coordinator for the Southern Christian Leadership Conference in the late 1950s and early 1960s, Angelou advocated for civil rights for African Americans. From the 1970s to the present, she has published eleven books of poetry. She is presently the Reynolds Professor of American Studies at Wake Forest University in Winston-Salem, North Carolina.

Just Give Me a Cool Drink of Water 'Fore I Diiie: The Poetry of Maya Angelou (1971), nominated for the Pulitzer Prize, focuses on topics such as love, addiction, and community. In "They Went Home" the speaker is a woman who loves married men; she feels a sense of loss due to the temporal and fleeting nature of her relationships. "Letter to an Aspiring Junkie" features a gritty realism in which Angelou addresses the issue of drug abuse in urban American communities. Similarly, *Oh Pray My Wings Are Gonna Fit Me Well* (1975) contains poems with personae revealing their interior emotional lives. For example, the speaker in "Pickin Em Up and Layin Em Down" boasts about short-lived romantic relationships with women in San Francisco, Birmingham, and Detroit. Angelou uses a blues format in this poem to reflect the perspective of the poem's speaker and to connect with the African American oral tradition.

The poems of *And Still I Rise* (1978) chiefly concern survival against adversity and the search for selfhood. The title poem, "Still I Rise," is the most famous of this collection, taking up the issues of self-definition and resistance to oppression from an African American perspective: "Bringing the gifts that my ancestors gave, / I am the dream and the hope of the slave." The connection between the self and society frames Angelou's *Shaker, Why Don't You Sing?* (1983), in which "A Good Woman Feeling Bad" appropriates the blues as a means of recounting a history of pain, sadness, and loss. In another poem, "Caged Bird," the speaker explores the tension between freedom and captivity. The phrase "caged bird" alludes to the African American **Paul Laurence Dunbar**'s poem "Sympathy." Dunbar's poem also inspired the title of Angelou's autobiography, *I Know Why the Caged Bird Sings* (1970). Other poems comment on socioeconomic issues, such as "Contemporary Announcement," which documents poverty and unemployment. The speaker laments, "I lost my job two weeks ago / and rent day's here again." "Weekend Glory" features a working-class black speaker critiquing the materialism of the upper classes. The speaker, rejoicing in being employed, having friends, and enjoying life, notes, "My life ain't heaven / but it sure ain't hell." The poem represents working-class self-definition, assertiveness, and identity. Angelou explores the importance of sexuality in "Shaker, Why Don't You Sing," using singing as a metaphor for unity.

Angelou has sometimes collaborated with visual artists, as in the volume *Now Sheba Sings the Song* (1987), which emphasizes the significance of black women's song, spirit, and history, illustrated by Tom Feelings. Angelou's collection *I Shall Not Be Moved* (1990) continues in the vein of poetry about the self and its relation to society. Her poem "Human Family" celebrates differences and similarities among individuals of varying racial and ethnic backgrounds: "We are more alike, my friends, / than we are unalike." "Seven Women's Blessed Assurance" is a poem with multiple speakers; seven female speakers of diverse ages and physical appearances celebrate their identities and their relationships with men. The title poem of *On the Pulse of the Morning* (1993) is an exploration of the importance of unity, peace, justice, and diversity. Written for a particular event, William Jefferson Clinton's 1993 presidential inauguration (Pettis, 11), the poem received national and international recognition.

Several of Angelou's poems also appeared in the 1993 film *Poetic Justice*, directed by John Singleton. "A Conceit" and "Alone" (from *Oh Pray My Wings Are Gonna Fit Me Well*), "A Kind of Love, Some Say" and "Phenomenal Woman" (from *And Still I Rise*), and "In a Time" (from *Just Give Me a Cool Drink of Water 'Fore I Diiie*) are featured in this film about a young African American woman's quest for selfhood in South Central Los Angeles. Angelou also appeared in the film as the character Aunt June.

The recent republishing and repackaging of Angelou's work stems from the popularity of her poetry with the general public. Angelou's *Phenomenal Woman: Four Poems Celebrating Women* (1994) contains previously published poetry, including "Phenomenal Woman" and "Still I Rise" from *And Still I Rise*, "Our Grandmothers" from *I Shall Not Be Moved*, and "Weekend Glory" from *Shaker, Why Don't You Sing?* Angelou read the title poem of *A Brave and Startling Truth* (1995), a plea for peace, justice, equality, and unity, at an anniversary celebration for the United Nations in honor of the international organization's fiftieth anniversary.

Due to her prolific output and high-profile appearances in film and television, Angelou remains an important force in contemporary American poetry. Her influence also extends to drama and prose. Like other contemporary African American women writers such as **Nikki Giovanni** and **Sonia Sanchez**, Angelou has helped to redefine contemporary American poetry through her emphasis on race, class, and gender diversity.

Further Reading.   ***Selected Primary Sources:*** Angelou, Maya, *And Still I Rise* (New York: Random House, 1978); ———, *A Brave and Startling Truth* (New York: Random House, 1995); ———, *The Complete Collected Poems of Maya Angelou* (New York: Random House, 1994); ———, *I Shall Not Be Moved* (New York: Random House, 1990); ———, *Just Give Me a Cool Drink of Water 'Fore I Diiie: The Poetry of Maya Angelou* (New York: Random House, 1971); ———, *Now Sheba Sings the Song* (New York: Penguin, 1994); ———, *Oh Pray My Wings Are Gonna Fit Me Well* (New York: Random House, 1975); ———, *On the Pulse of the Morning* (New York: Random House, 1993); ———, *Phenomenal Woman: Four Poems Celebrating Women* (New York: Random House, 1994); ———, *Poems: Maya Angelou* (New York: Bantam, 1986); ———, *Shaker, Why Don't You Sing?* (New York: Random House, 1983); Singleton, John, and Veronica Chambers, *Poetic Justice: Film Making South Central Style* (featuring Maya Angelou poetry) (New York: Dell, 1993). ***Selected Secondary Sources:*** Hagen, Lyman B., *Heart of a Woman, Mind of a Writer, and Soul of a Poet: A Critical Analysis of the Writings of Maya Angelou* (Lanham, MD: University Press of America, 1997); Pettis, Joyce, *African American Poets: Lives, Works, and Sources* (Westport, CT: Greenwood Press, 2002).

Sharon L. Jones

ANTHOLOGIES, TWENTIETH-CENTURY

As the traditional book form for collecting verse, the anthology has exerted enormous influence in literary history. This influence broadened further with the modern popularization of anthologies for the teaching of literature at all levels, from elementary schools to universities. Currently, "anthologies" embrace not only collections of poetry (the original sense of the word), but "selections" from nearly any genre. It must be noted from the outset that "anthology" became an umbrella term for all kinds of textual collections only in the twentieth century. Before this period, a published gathering of verse could have a multitude of designations: *miscellany* (early English collections), *pageant, galaxy, beauties, paradise, cabinet, gathering, collection, book, gallery, treasury, gems, specimens, encyclopedia, omnibus, school, sampler, digest, reader*, and so on. Likewise, anthologists often played with the botanical etymology of *anthology* (Greek, "gathering of flowers," i.e., "bouquet"): *florilegium* (a medieval Latin calque), *garland, blossoms, leaves, garden, nosegay*, and *posy* (with a pun on "poesy"). Considering the thousands of collections these diverse titles represent, the role of anthologies in poetic **canon formation** is crucial, though sometimes unacknowledged. Since it has now become a dead metaphor, the term "anthologies" will conveniently stand here for all kinds of poetic collections, however titled.

Because anthologies can be overwhelmingly popular books, their role as literary documents has sometimes been brought into question. For instance, in their still useful *A Pamphlet Against Anthologies* (1928), Laura Riding and Robert Graves contend that there is a long-standing "confusion between true anthologies, that confine themselves to literary rescue-work or have some excuse as works of criticism, or as private albums, and are not numerous, and the all too numerous trade-anthologies that turn poetry into an industrial packet-commodity" (17–18). But there is also a middle ground, where anthologies can be both serious as well as widely disseminated—contemporary college literature anthologies being one obvious example. Similarly, in surveying the history of American poetry anthologies, Alan Golding finds a need for synthesis between two mutually opposed perspectives on these canons of poetry, namely "the view that writers make canons (the aesthetic model) and the view that critics, teachers, and the academy do so (the institutional model)" (xv). Clearly, the "true anthology" of Riding and Graves adheres to Golding's aesthetic model, which has now been largely displaced in literary studies by the institutional model, as in the influential work of John Guillory.

Nevertheless, as Golding has suggested regarding American poetry, the history of anthologies shows that both the aesthetic and institutional viewpoints have been at work (if not at odds) since written poetic collections first appeared in the earliest literatures around the globe, in Egypt, China, India, Arabia, and Japan. Sometimes the collections gathered by the poets themselves have held sway; at other times the most influential anthologists have been institutional figures. In the West, the tradition of gathering poems into an aesthetically motivated collection was first formalized by a Greek poet, Meleagar, who around 100 B.C. brought the "flowers" of his own and his friends' poetry together in his *Garland* (*Stephanos*, "floral crown"). A reconstruction suggests that this lost collection was divided into several thematic sections, each with concentrically arranged rings of short poems. Later authors and editors adapted and imitated the *Garland* until its great institutionalization around 900 A.D., when the Byzantine Christian educator Constantine Cephalus gathered the poems of Meleagar and many others into an encyclopedic compendium that eventually became known as the *Greek Anthology*, the inspiration for all later collections of that name.

Often the choices anthologists must make are difficult to attribute to either aesthetic or institutional motivations. For purely material reasons of space, even the largest poetic collections such as the *Greek Anthology* have historically preferred the shorter poem, though the lyric is far from being an aesthetically or institutionally prestigious genre in the West. The inclusion of long selections of prose in today's anthologies, which can encompass thousands of pages in a single volume, is an unusual development made physically possible by technological improvements in papermaking and printing. As Riding and Graves point out, another modern anachronism is that anthologies are automatically intended for a wide audience. For instance, it is not clear whether Meleagar ever intended his *Garland* to circulate beyond his immediate group of poet-friends. But when it did, others like Constantine Cephalus saw the institutional potential for the form. Poets also saw the aesthetic possibilities. In 39 B.C., Virgil completed his *Eclogues*, an artfully varied and intricately structured set of ten bucolic poems that announced the "humble beginnings" of his career as a poet. Although the title *Eclogues* (which may not be Virgil's) became closely associated with the pastoral poetry there exemplified, it shares the root word of "anthology" and originally meant "selections."

The dominant poetic form of the *Greek Anthology* is the pithy epigram, which suggests why poems from the *Anthology* were widely employed to teach classical Greek. Although it was immediately popular when it was rediscovered and printed in the Renaissance, the *Greek Anthology* reached its broadest audience in English between 1849 and World War I, when there appeared dozens of critical editions, popular translations, and often-reprinted selections for students. From this era, W.R. Paton's five-volume edition for the Loeb Classical Library (1916–1918) remains the most complete English translation of the over 4,000 epigrams of the *Greek Anthology*. Such sprawling size, not to mention the large number of frankly erotic poems, naturally led to the re-selection of the *Greek Anthology* by many hands. One of these modern selections was given to **Edgar Lee Masters** and inspired his *Spoon River Anthology* (1915), whose title must thus be understood not in today's sense of mere "collection," but as an allusion to a classic aesthetic setting intended to dignify an otherwise slight poetic genre (in Masters's case, the sardonic epitaph).

The tip toward the contemporary sense of "anthology" as a basic-category "collection" was already well under way by the turn of the twentieth century, however. Before this time, the term "anthology" still echoed its English classical forebear, and was thus applied in English titles primarily to translations of poetry from other languages. Around the year 1900 (and encouraged by the centennial), there were a number of ambitious collections that attempted to anthologize the *native* language, including the thirty-three–volume *The Universal Anthology*, published simultaneously in England and the United States (ed. Richard Garnett et al., 1899), part of the then-pioneering "great books" movement, marked by such other series as *The World's Great Books* (1899–1901) and *The Harvard Classics* (1909). However, these collections were devoted more to prose than poetry. A more poetic anthology series also published in both Britain and America around this time was *The British Anthologies* (ed. Edward Arber, 1899–1901). This ten-volume set organized British literature into ten successive periods (from 1401 to 1800), but each volume was also given the name of a major author from that era (*The Shakespeare Anthology*, *The Milton Anthology*, etc.). Here the categories of literary period and major author were added to the more traditional anthology concept bequeathed by the *Greek Anthology* of "poetry of a given language." As poetic collections titled "anthologies" proliferated in the twentieth century, still more categories were added: collections of a given genre (besides the epigram), themes and topics other than love and death (such as places), selections of purely contemporary verse (e.g., annuals and gatherings from periodicals), and seasonal anthologies (giftbooks and holiday-themed gatherings). Gradually, "anthologies" extended to all kinds of prose as well.

Since the most collectible prose pieces often have an epigrammatic if not poetic quality, anthologies, if considered as personal collections (what Riding and Graves call "private albums"), must also include the traditional "commonplace book." Dating from the sixteenth century in Europe, these individual compilations of memorable quotations and other passages copied in the course of one's reading formed a journal of intellectual or spiritual development, and could be interspersed with one's own reflections, imitations, or original compositions. Commonplace books by figures such as Robert Burns and Thomas Jefferson have been published posthumously, as have those by modern poets such as **W.H. Auden** and **Wallace Stevens**. But because most commonplace books were not kept by well-known authors and remain unpublished, it is difficult to categorize these personal anthologies as either "aesthetic" or "institutional." The commonplace book was one of several types of anthologies imported by early American writers, such as Martha Moore, who kept a commonplace book (only recently published) during the Revolutionary period. Earlier, **Anne Dudley Bradstreet**'s *The Tenth Muse Lately Sprung Up in America* (1650) also exhibits the "occasional" feel of the commonplace book.

The foremost of anthologies imported to America, however, was certainly the collection of sacred texts known as the Bible. Indeed, one of the central Reformation debates that led many settlers to the American colonies concerned which individual works were worthy of inclusion in "the canon of scripture," with some Protestants (at considerable risk) refusing to bind the Catholic Church's "apocryphal" books into their copies of the Bible. Thus the preferred scripture brought to America by the Puritans, the Geneva Bible (1560), was very much understood as a deliberate collection of texts. Printed in Roman type and the first English Bible to have numbered verses, the Geneva Bible fit easily in the hand and was thus intended for household use. This popular version of the Bible also illustrates another Reformation underpinning: the vernacular translation of the scriptures, in a calculated break with the Latin Vulgate, which was declared the only canonical version by the Council of Trent (1646). In America, the first book both written and printed in English was an anthology of biblical translations by prominent Puritans: **The Bay Psalm Book** of 1640, a metrical version of the book of Psalms.

A third kind of imported anthology in early America was the immensely popular collection of devotional poetry intended for musical performance. While "anthology" has traditionally referred to both collected texts and gatherings of musical pieces, in this case the words were often published without musical arrangements. This encouraged the masters of many secular "singing schools" (a popular weekly pastime of later eighteenth-century America) to compose their own original music. But the words for many songs still came from England. One of the most popular of these devotional anthologies, the *Hymns and Spiritual Songs* of Isaac Watts, went through at least thirty-seven editions before 1775, many published in America. *Divine Songs*, a shorter collection by Watts intended for children (and also without music), likewise went through many editions by 1780. Also popular was Watts's earlier *Horae Lyricae* (1706), a thematically arranged collection of edifying secular verse.

During the colonial era, there was no desire to duplicate influential secular English anthologies such as Richard Tottel's *Miscellany* (1559) or *England's Helicon* (1602). These, of course, were closely associated with the English Cavalier poetry rather than the Metaphysical verse that provided a model for Puritan poets like **Edward Taylor**. Taylor's *Preparatory Meditations* (begun in 1682 and continued throughout his long life, though rediscovered only in the 1930s) was an entirely personal collection of scripturally based poems in which Taylor vividly grappled with spiritual mysteries such as the Incarnation and the Lord's Supper. Although Taylor wrote for decades in the frontier town of Westfield, Massachusetts, on the Connecticut River, a highway for native groups, there is scarcely any mention of them in his large corpus. Among English, Dutch, and French settlements alike, there was no perceived need, in line with recuperative collections like Thomas Percy's *Reliques of Ancient English Poetry* (1765), to gather the continent's indigenous verse. After all, a New Canaan implied that the natives were debased Philistines to be displaced if not utterly exterminated. A very different attitude was found in the earlier Spanish colonies of Central and South America, where Spanish missionaries actively recruited informants to gather local texts into such collections as the Florentine Codex (1547–1579) and the *Cantares Mexicanos* (1550–1581), an anthology of Aztec (Nahuatl) poems. It can be assumed, however, that the Western model of the anthology may have significantly influenced the construction of these collections. In oral literatures, whether in America or elsewhere, the container is the memory, not the book, and the focus is on actively performing and passing down rather than collecting and preserving in static form.

With the Treaty of Paris in 1783 came the first drive to define a truly American literature, and the first anthologies titled "American" began to appear. (For a bibliography of early American anthologies, see Pattee.) In a brief but comprehensive account of American poetry anthologies, Alan Golding divides this history into four successive phases (3–28): the phase of simple preservation (the late eighteenth century), the phase of "historicizing and moralizing" (through the mid-nineteenth century), the phase of "universal excellence" (following the Civil War), and the phase of revisionism (beginning around the turn of the twentieth century and continuing to the present). As Golding finds, there is significant overlap between the phases, and each represents an impulse that can be found in many of today's anthologies.

With much of the printing capacity of the new nation devoted to serial publication, the bulk of American poetry was being published in subscribed periodicals, which were highly ephemeral. In what Riding and Graves would praise as "literary rescue-work" of such "fugitive" pieces, Elihu Hubbard Smith gathered his *American Poems, Selected and Original* (1793). But the "American" of this collection was relative to Smith's own political and geographical biases; his collection, much like Meleager's two millennia earlier, featured primarily his friends, in this case the Connecticut Wits. Readers used another practical way to preserve the poetry published in such periodicals as the *American Museum*, edited by Matthew Carey (1787–1792): The separate issues were often collected and custom-bound into volumes that were thus virtual anthologies. Carey also issued a selection of his own assembled from the *American Museum*: *Beauties of English Poetry British and American* (1791).

Golding's second phase, anthologies that historicize and moralize, continued the conservative trend of the earliest "rescue-work" anthologies. The immensely popular anthologies of this phase include Samuel Kettel's *Specimens of American Poetry* (1829) and the anthologies edited by Rufus Griswold, such as *The Poets and Poetry of America* (1842). The motivation of these anthologists, which carried over into such collections as Henry T. Coates's *Fireside Encyclopedia of Poetry* (1878), was to provide a sense of the historical sweep of United States poetry and to edify the reader, whatever the quality of individual poets or poems. Even in these first mass-market anthologies, the educative influence of the personal commonplace book was still being felt: One editor, George B. Cheever, invoked the form directly in his *The American Common-Place Book of Poetry* (1831).

A more aesthetic sensibility began to mark the anthologies of Golding's third phase, pioneered by Charles A. Dana's *Household Book of Poetry* (1858). Now notable American poets began to issue anthologies: **William Cullen Bryant**, *A Library of Poetry and Song* (1870); **Ralph Waldo Emerson**, *Parnassus* (1874); and **John Greenleaf Whittier**, *Songs of Three Centuries* (1875). The watchword for these collections was the oft-cited criterion of "poetic merit," which now overlaid (or justified) the blander historicizing and moralizing of the previous generation. Bryant's enormously popular anthology, for instance, was organized in topical sections, with "Poems of Childhood and Youth" first, and "Humorous Poems," though hardly containing objectionable selections, held until the end. "Poetic merit" was also often equivalent in these collections to the traditional verse epitomized by the **Fireside Poets** themselves (Bryant, Whittier, **Henry Wadsworth Longfellow**, **James Russell Lowell**, and **Oliver Wendell Holmes**), who were taken to be the first American equals of British versifiers.

It was still some time before a more ambitious sense of a "progress of poetry" culminating in the present-day United States would start to animate the modern anthologist. One turning point was **Edmund Clarence Stedman**, whose *An American Anthology, 1787–1900* (1900) was one of the first to include a more modern appreciation of (and many more selections from) such figures as **Edgar Allan Poe**, **Herman Melville**, and **Walt Whitman**. Coupled with the first stirrings of the "great books" movement noted earlier, Stedman's status as a critic seems to have suggested the possibilities of the "critical" anthology to various literary scholars at American universities, such as Thomas R. Lounsbury, who edited the *Yale Book of American Verse* (1912). Lounsbury and other critics easily recognized that Stedman's simple chronological arrangement, as opposed to Bryant's thematic sections, could powerfully illustrate literary history, the critical paradigm then in the ascendant.

Golding points to Stedman's sweeping *American Anthology* as the first in a long wave of such revisionism, which eventually would take two very different forms: on the one hand, a carefully perfected, "difficult" and studied poetry, and on the other, the poetry of unmodified experience that embodied a more radical break with the past—the "cooked" versus the "raw," according to **Robert Lowell**'s notorious distinction. These two contradictory forms of modernism clashed in the so-called anthology wars of the 1950s and 1960s, when the "cooked" was championed by *New Poets of England and America* (edited by **Donald Hall**, Robert Pack, and **Louis Simpson**, 1957) and the "raw" by Donald M. Allen's *The New American Poetry* (1960). In his introduction to *New Poets of England and America*, **Robert Frost** enunciates the "cooked" aesthetic with statements like "school and poetry come so near being one thing" and "the reader is more on trial here than [the poets] are" (10–11). In the introduction to his "raw" anthology, by contrast, Allen calls his selected poets "our avant-garde . . . closely allied to modern jazz and abstract expressionist painting" (xi), and groups them into now-familiar categories such as the **Black Mountain School**, the **San Francisco Renaissance**, the Beats (*see* **Beat Poetry**), and the **New York School**. Like the Cold War that inspired the name, the anthology wars had no winners, and a deep revisionist divide still exists between proponents such as Helen Vendler of a contemporary lyric voice well-schooled in the literary tradition, and the more "raw" and radically innovative **Language poetry**.

Whatever their school, proponents of any kind of poetry in the contemporary era may create an anthology dedicated to it. Perhaps the largest division among anthologies today, then, is not among proliferating specialized collections, but between these and the encyclopedic collections that try to encompass them—the ever-more-comprehensive classroom anthologies from Norton and many other textbook publishers. The history of the latter kind of anthologies, and their impact on the canonization of given poets and poems, has been the subject of increasing attention (see Golding; Rasula; Csicsila), but much remains to be discovered.

On the other hand, Anne Ferry has found that early anthologies encouraged poets to conceive of selecting and collecting their own works. This suggests that future investigations of the anthology must also take into account this kind of autocollection as well, especially since classroom anthologies by their nature obscure the aesthetic patterns that poets may incorporate into their collected works. Most readers of anthologies, and perhaps many anthologists, have remained only dimly aware that gathering, selecting, and arranging poems into a coherent, not to say beautiful, collection can be a literary art unto itself.

Further Reading. *Selected Primary Sources:* Allen, Donald M., ed., *The New American Poetry* (New York: Grove [London: Evergreen], 1960); Blecki, Catherine La Courreye, and Karin A. Wulf, eds., *Milcah Martha Moore's Book: A Commonplace Book from Revolutionary America* (University Park: Pennsylvania State University Press, 1997); Hall, Donald, Robert Pack, and Louis Simpson, eds., *New Poets of England and America* (New York: Meridian, 1957); Masters, Edgar Lee, *The Spoon River Anthology: An Annotated Edition*, ed. John E. Hallwas (Urbana: University of Illinois Press, 1992); Paton, W.R., trans., *The Greek Anthology* (5 vols., Loeb Classical Library) (Cambridge, MA: Harvard University Press [London: Heinemann], 1916–1918; reprint 1960); Pattee, Fred Lewis, "American Poetry Anthologies before 1861" (*Colophon* 16 [1934]: n.p.). *Selected Secondary Sources:* Csicsila, Joseph, *Canons by Consensus: Critical Trends and American Literature Anthologies* (Tuscaloosa: University of Alabama Press, 2004); Ferry, Ann, *Tradition and the Individual Poem: A Study of Anthologies* (Stanford, CA: Stanford University Press, 2001); Golding, Alan, *From Outlaw to Classic: Canons in American Poetry* (Madison: University of Wisconsin Press, 1995); Rasula, Jed, *The American Poetry Wax Museum: Reality Effects, 1940–1990* (Urbana, IL: NCTE, 1996); Riding, Laura, and Robert Graves, *A Pamphlet Against Anthologies* (1928; reprint New York: AMS Press, 1970).

Christopher M. Kuipers

ANTIN, DAVID (1932–)

David Antin has had one of the most varied artistic careers in twentieth-century American culture. Yet for all his contributions to the fields of contemporary art, science, and mathematics, Antin is best known for his "talk poems," which he began composing in front of audiences and then publishing in 1972. As an undergraduate and graduate student he worked in the physical sciences and mathematics as well as linguistics. Indeed, Antin translated and edited several books on the sciences and mathematics early in his career.

Born in New York City on February 1, 1932, Antin began seriously writing and publishing his poetry in 1955 and, with his increasing interest in contemporary art, became an art critic in 1964. Antin's interest in art led to a position as educational curator at the Institute of Contemporary Art in Boston. In 1968 Antin became a faculty member in the Visual Arts Department at the University of California–San Diego. For four years Antin was director of the UCSD Mandeville Art Gallery before beginning a career as a full-time teacher in 1972, focusing on postmodernism in art and literature.

Antin's first four books of poetry, *Definitions* (1967), *Autobiography* (1967), *Codes of Flag Behavior* (1968), and *Meditations* (1971), display Antin's interest in surrealist, nonlinear strategies of writing. These books are also much more political in content than the talk poems that would follow, though it has been argued that the talk poems, like **Language poetry** and its assault on narrative and subject-position norms, reinvent the sphere of the political, making these works more politically engaged than xplicitly political poems. In short, these poems are evidence of Antin's early interests in the relationship between the political and social spheres and the cultural sphere—especially linguistics and art. These interests coincide with those that would later be taken up by the language writers in the early 1970s. But while these writers' explorations led in the general direction of linguistics and writing—with the important exception of some of the Canadian writers like **Steve McCaffery** and the mythopoetics of **Jerome Rothenberg**—Antin would wind up pursuing experimental oral poetry. One can see in these early books signs of the direction Antin would pursue in the early 1970s.

In overtly political poems such as "the marchers," "poem found in the street," "oswald, ruby and mrs. johnson," all from *Codes of Flag Behavior*, or the long surrealist poems that comprise much of *Definitions* (e.g., "trip through a landscape"), Antin, like most of the **Beat poets** (**Allen Ginsberg**, **Jack Kerouac**, etc.) and most members of the **Black Mountain School** (with the notable exception of **Robert Creeley**), is writing against what he considers the eviscerated **Deep Image** poetics of such poets as **James Wright** as well as the lyrical self-regard of a **Robert Lowell**. There are few discrete poems in these early books, suggesting that from the very beginning Antin thought more like a New Novelist than a traditional poet.

Given his early association with Rothenberg, who was interested in the serial and communal values of indigenous American tales, songs, and poems, it is not surprising that Antin's poetry of the 1960s and 1970s displays an interest in related poetic values and strategies. Indeed, the poems in all these early books, including the nonlinear prose of *Autobiography*, suggest that Antin was more interested in collage effects and experimental narrative possibilities than in the evocation of emotion associated with the traditional lyric. These aesthetic interests may be related to Antin's background in mathematics and the physical sciences and his career as an art critic and curator, insofar as these fields tend to value method and procedure over conclusions and products.

In 1972 Antin's various experiments with form and narrative coalesced in the proto–talk poem book *Meditations*. It is here that we see Antin groping toward a conception of the page analogous to the function of the canvas in Abstract Expressionism. Abstract Expressionists like Jackson Pollock conceived of the so-called all-over technique as one that facilitated the erasure of painterly perspective and liminality. This procedure accepted the flat plane of the canvas as an irreducible "given." In certain poems in *Meditations*, particularly "the first hundred" and "the second hundred," Antin blends technical/technological explanation with prose lyricism, meshing traditional narrative with paratactic procedures in order to reduce expectations about what one "sees" on the page and, more important, how one proceeds "across" the page. Note, for example, this section from "the first hundred":

> never see again all right i could try again question at
> an acute angle try to follow all gestures to their antece-

The stop-and-starts (evident at the end of the quotation), the lack of punctuation to indicate pauses and hesitations, the decapitalization of the narrator ("I") to a letter unprivileged within the narrative, all point to the techniques developed more fully and satisfactorily in Antin's "talk poems." As the title of the book suggests, these proto–talk pieces remain largely the ruminations of a brilliant, eccentric intellect. Their oral possibilities remain latent, as yet unarticulated.

In that same year, 1972, Antin would, however, publish his first collection where the talk poem format is fully developed across the entire page (the margins serving as the "frame" of the "canvas"). *Talking*, a collection of three talk poems, nevertheless contains a "found" poem; "November Exercises," which opens the collection, provides a transition from the traditional lyric or dramatic expressionist poem that defined one facet of postmodern poetry. The found poem, a work that is by definition anti–self-expressionist, subverts the ego of the narrator and frustrates normative reading habits that tend to conflate author and persona. Yet Antin's talk poems are extremely personal, even autobiographical, even as they subvert the conventions of "talking," the "personal," and narrative strategies. However, to the extent that the talk poems are almost all monologues—with important exceptions like "November Exercises"—it becomes clear that Antin's work is avant-garde to the extent it straddles the line between proto-**modernism** and **postmodernism**. That is, to the extent Antin's concerns revolve around the medium in which he works—language—he may be considered a modernist poet. However, to the extent Antin invokes a form of communication that simultaneously honors and undercuts William Wordsworth's famous dictum that a poet is simply a man speaking to other men, Antin is a postmodernist. This border zone that Antin occupies, situated between the spheres of life carved out by modernity, has, historically, been occupied by avant-gardes. Is David Antin an exemplary member of the **avant-garde** in contemporary poetry, or is he an old-fashioned storyteller in the guise of an aesthetic innovator?

It depends, of course, on how one understands the meaning of the term "avant-garde." Indeed, conflicts over exactly how to interpret "avant-garde" belong as much to its history as the movements themselves. Yet, arguably, one common thread running through the history of avant-garde art is that all avant-gardes attempt to overcome the various aesthetic, social, economic, and political effects of modernity. Because one of the effects of modernity is the separation of art and life—which functions as an analogue to the separation of church and state—avant-gardes attempt to violently reintegrate art with life. From this perspective, then, the avant-garde is inconceivable before modernity—hence the contradictions and paradoxes that have marked the histories of both modernity and avant-garde practice. In terms of the specific issue of "talk" and writing, one can trace the drive toward "reintegration" of art and life back to Dante's deployment of the vernacular in his epic poems. In terms of modernism, that aesthetic movement of the late nineteenth and early twentieth centuries, **Gertrude Stein** is an important predecessor of David Antin. In Stein we have a writer concerned first and foremost with the materials with which she works, a writer who attempts to reintegrate "talk" and "writing" via black dialect into her work. Yet, like even the most radical of the modernist writers, Stein still conceives of the "work" as primarily a "book" of writing. Orality still serves texuality.

In his talk poems, Antin adopts the avant-garde tenet that life and art must be integrated in order to produce a body of work that, certainly when performed, appears "just like" ordinary talk. However, the monologue is itself a theatrical genre, and so it alone would resist the total conflation of the talk poems with ordinary talk. But another factor that compounds the problem of Antin's avant-garde strategy is what occurs when he transcribes and prints the talk poems. A representative examination of work from *Talking* (1972), *Talking at the Boundaries* (1975), *Tuning* (1984), and *What It Means to Be Avant-Garde* (1993) provide examples of the merits and flaws of Antin's project in relation to its avowed avant-gardism.

In separate interviews with Barry Alpert (1975) and **Charles Bernstein** (2002), Antin indicated that the talk poems, for all their flirtation with cerebral concerns, have an ethical, democratic charge that he does not find in most contemporary poetry. For Antin, "life" is taken as the parameter for what "art" should aspire to, and in this regard Antin's concerns are in line with those of the historical avant-gardes. Given the privileged place assigned to "life," Antin's talk poems should, ideally, reproduce the general messiness, incoherency, and interruptedness that constitute the context and form of most talk. In the context of Antin's project, this would mean, at minimum, spontaneous, unscripted audience participation, not only "after" Antin is finished "talking" but also "during" his talk poems. For rare is the conversation that a listener does not, or is not tempted to, interrupt or accentuate (e.g., "I see," "You're right," "uh huh"). In his interview with Antin, Alpert broached precisely the question of audience participation, though he only wondered if the question-and-answer session after one of Antin's talks could not constitute a poem itself. Antin replied that inasmuch as he still conceived of his talks as poems, and inasmuch as his conception of poetry demanded "the freedom to move out into invention and discovery," he was uncomfortable with this form of audience participation. Antin expressed concern that "the claims of the people you're addressing . . . may begin to exert too much of a pull" on the artist. This conception of his role as a poet has a direct bearing not only on how and where Antin performs his poems, but also on the forms in which he transcribes them. Antin's refusal to capitalize and punctuate is both an avant-garde gesture aimed at bringing art (in this case, the transcribed poem) as close to life (ordinary talk) as possible and a modernist move to keep art and life separate. For despite his use of erratic spacing (meant to mimic pauses), reading the poem (and reading is no more or less a part of life than talking) is difficult—like "good" modernist art—due precisely to the absence of capitalization and punctuation. Perhaps recognizing the paradox of his entire enterprise, Antin's struggles with the question of interruption are thematized in some of his talk poems.

Toward the end of the first talk poem in *Talking at the Boundaries*, "what am I doing here," Antin, who throughout the piece has been attempting to argue that "all talking is poetry and that not all poetry is talking," by which he means there can also be a "poetry of the cry," says that poetry is "uninterruptable discourse." Since "not all poetry is talking," Antin appears to imply that talking is interruptable, with the lone exception of talking that is poetry. At the beginning of this poem Antin says that poetry is art added to talking. Thus the art that is added to talking appears to facilitate, if not justify, its uninterruptability. The anxiety underlying Antin's attempts to wed talking to poetry but not the reverse is itself a symptom of a basic possibility haunting the talk poem performance. Is there any reason Antin's audience members could not, in theory, do what he does? One would think that the talk poem would need to be open to interruption in order to fulfill its democratic, to say nothing of its avant-garde, aspirations. Otherwise it might, as monologue, acquire the monolithic status traditionally ascribed to modernist autonomous art. Perhaps this is why Antin, in the title poem of *What It Means to Be Avant-Garde*, concedes that he may be a "poor avant-gardist." He is, he says, concerned with the "present," not the past or the future, which defines the avant-garde.

In his 2002 published interview with Bernstein, Antin notes that while he continues to "do" his talk poems, he has been composing what he calls "Micro-Films." These cinematic products consist of a series of words and images that function as short films in popular genres (sci-fi, film noir, etc.). These "marginal," parodic, artistic practices suggest that Antin remains a paradigmatic postmodern, if not avant-garde, artist.

Further Reading. ***Selected Primary Sources:*** Antin, David, *Autobiography* (New York: Something Else Press, 1967); ———, *Code of Flag Behavior* (Los Angeles: Black Sparrow, 1968); ———, *Definitions* (New York: Caterpillar Press, 1967); ———, *Meditations* (Los Angeles: Sun and Moon Press, 1971); ———, *Selected Poems: 1963–1973* (Los Angeles: Sun and Moon Press, 1991); ———, *Talking* (New York: Kulchur Foundation, 1972); ———, *Talking at the Boundaries* (New York: New Directions, 1976); ———, *Tuning* (New York: New Directions, 1984); ———, *What It Means to Be Avant-Garde* (New York: New Directions, 1993). ***Selected Secondary Sources:*** Aji, Helene, "David Antin: The Hermeneutics of Performance" (*Review of Contemporary Fiction* 21:1 [Spring 2001]: 95–105); Alpert, Barry, "David Antin: An Interview Conducted by Barry Alpert" (*Vort* 7.4 [1975]: 29–30); Altieri, Charles, "The Postmodernism of David Antin's *Tuning*" (College English 48 [1986]: 9–26); Bernstein, Charles, and David Antin, *A Conversation with David Antin* (New York: Granary Books, 2002); Garber, Frederick, "The Talk-Poems of David Antin" (*North Dakota Quarterly* 55.4 [Fall 1987]: 217–238); Sayre, Henry, "David Antin and the Oral Poetic Movement" (*Contemporary Literature* 23 [1982]: 428–450).

Tyrone Williams

ANXIETY OF INFLUENCE

The critic Harold Bloom in *The Anxiety of Influence* contends that great or "strong" poetry necessarily results from the poet's struggle against an influential precursor—a father-figure of sorts. Bloom's theory, which attempts to unify the complex intertextual relationships that run through the continuum of Western poetry, has generated deep critical controversy. The heart of the argument, first published in 1973, is succinctly summarized by Bloom in the first chapter of the text:

Poetic influence—when it involves two strong, authentic poets—always proceeds by a *misreading* of the prior poet, an act of *correction* that is actually and necessarily a *misinterpretation*. The history of fruitful poetic influence, which is to say the main tradition of Western poetry since the Renaissance, is a history of anxiety and self-serving caricature, of distortion, of perverse, willful revisionism without which modern poetry as such could not exist. (30) [italics Bloom's]

Hence, in Bloomian terms, misreading is an integral part of the creative process in which an aspiring poet must struggle against his or her precursor's genius to achieve originality. For Bloom, this does not involve a conscientious method by which strong poets may develop; rather, it is the only way great poetry is made. By extension, all literary texts must therefore be strong misreadings of previous works, while critical assessment of any poem invariably begins and ends by viewing it in terms of its precursors. Bloom's entry on **Wallace Stevens** in his book *Genius* serves as a representative example of his approach in that he centers his critical analysis on Stevens's relationship to **Walt Whitman**, whom Bloom has often deemed to be the "center of the American canon":

> I am not suggesting that the Good Gray Poet of Brooklyn, Manhattan, and Camden, New Jersey, was the Pennsylvanian aesthete's real Me, but rather that what was strongest in Stevens's poetry found the genius of the shore in the bard of Night, Death, Mother, and the Sea, the fourfold unison that peals forth in Stevens as urgently and frequently as it does in Whitman and Hart Crane. (365–366)

In his preface to the second edition of *The Anxiety of Influence* (1997), Bloom disputes the notion that his revolutionary theory of poetics derives from Freudian roots.

> I never meant by "the anxiety of influence" a Freudian Oedipal rivalry, despite a rhetorical flourish or two in this book. A Shakespearean reading of Freud, which I favor over a Freudian reading of Shakespeare or anyone else, reveals that Freud suffered from a Hamlet complex (the true name of the Oedipal Complex) or an anxiety of influence in regard to Shakespeare. (xxii)

Although some literary theorists dispute or even dismiss the approach outright, Harold Bloom's theory of anxiety of influence remains relevant for intertextual critics, standing among a handful of theories that helped shape the conversation about literature—specifically poetry—from the last quarter of the twentieth century to the present.

Further Reading. *Selected Primary Sources:* Bloom, Harold, *The Anxiety of Influence*, 2nd ed. (New York: Oxford University Press, 1997); ———, *Genius* (New York: Warner Books, 2002); ———, *A Map of Misreading* (New York: Oxford University Press, 1975); ———, *The Western Canon* (New York: Riverhead Books, 1994).

John P. Wargacki

ARENSBERG, WALTER CONRAD (1878–1954)

Although best known as a pioneering collector of modern art, Walter Conrad Arensberg was also a poet who progressed rapidly from conventional verse to Dada during the 1910s. Independently wealthy, he used his fortune to promote modernism in both art and literature. He was the chief patron of Marcel Duchamp and the eponymous center of the "Arensberg Circle" in New York, which brought together the **avant-garde** artists and writers now loosely categorized as the New York **Dada** movement, including the poets **William Carlos Williams**, **Mina Loy**, and **Wallace Stevens**. He funded and helped to launch a number of little magazines, including the important *Others*. He published two books of poems, *Poems* (1914) and *Idols* (1916), and contributed increasingly experimental poems to various little magazines throughout the 1910s. Although his poetic efforts ceased when he and his wife Louise moved to California in 1922, the couple continued to build their famous art collection, which is now housed at the Philadelphia Museum of Art.

Arensberg was born the son of a wealthy industrialist in Pittsburgh in 1878. At Harvard he majored in English, edited the *Harvard Monthly*, and was chosen Class Poet at graduation in 1900. He took several classes with Wallace Stevens, and the two became close friends. After graduating, he traveled in Europe, did a year of graduate work in English, and tried his hand at journalism before deciding to devote himself to writing poetry. His first book, *Poems* (1914), shows him to be an accomplished craftsman of conventional rhyme and meter.

Arensberg's life and poetry were changed by the Armory Show of 1913. Held at the 69th Regiment Armory in New York at Lexington Avenue and 25th Street, the Armory Show was a huge exhibition of American and European art that introduced the American public to Postimpressionism and Cubism. It is generally credited with inspiring the modernist revolution in American art and literature. Arensberg, at least, was utterly transformed by the exhibition. He purchased the first works of modern art in his famous art collection directly from the Armory Show, and he and his wife immediately moved to New York from Boston to be at the center of avant-garde activity. As their collection grew, they started opening their apartment to visitors interested in modernism. The "Arensberg salon" became a gathering place throughout the 1910s for writers and artists, including Duchamp, Francis Picabia, Albert Gleizes, Charles Demuth, Man Ray, Joseph Stella, Marsden Hartley, and **Djuna Barnes**, along with Loy, Williams, and Stevens.

Arensberg's second collection, *Idols*, appeared in 1916. He never published another book of poems, but over the next few years he published increasingly experimental Dada pieces in little magazines, a number of which he financed and helped edit: *Others*,

Rogue, The Blind Man, Rongwrong, TNT, 391. Then, in an equally abrupt shift, he and his wife moved to California in 1922, disbanding their "salon" and devoting their quiet new life to art collecting. Arensberg ceased writing poetry, devoting his literary energies instead to cryptographic readings designed to prove that Francis Bacon had written Shakespeare's plays.

The poems of Arensberg's first book, *Poems,* are redolent of the nineteenth century, with Keatsian diction, traditional forms, and titles that sound like souvenirs of the Grand Tour: "The Pieta of Michel Angelo," "For a Picture by Leonardo da Vinci," "Venus of Melos." A section of translations points to his interest in French **symbolism**, with examples of Mallarme, Laforgue, and Verlaine. Hints of his more iconoclastic, independent turn of mind can be found in the quatrain "The Masterpiece," which praises "the supreme poet who imagined God." That line combines philosophical interest and nose-thumbing wit in a way that anticipates Dada and underscores his closeness to Stevens, whose central poetic quest was for a "supreme fiction" that would replace the idea of God.

Arensberg's second (and last) book of poems, *Idols,* announces his commitment to modernism in the title of its first poem, "For Forms That Are Free." The book begins with a strong group of poems in **free verse**, many of which first appeared in *Others.* The best of these is "Voyage à L'Infini," a meditation on appearance and reality that begins by suggesting that the swan "[i]s like a song with an accompaniment / Imaginary." The poem bears comparison with Stevens's "Sunday Morning," not only in its theme (the interplay of imagination and reality) but also in its last lines: "At night / The lake is a wide silence, / Without imagination," echoing the "wide water, without sound" of Stevens's poem.

Arensberg's Dada writings during the rest of the 1910s have been collected by **Jerome Rothenberg** in *The Revolution of the Word.* Although Arensberg's alignment with Dada was publicized in a prose piece called "Dada Is American," published under his name in *Littérature* in 1920, Francis Naumann has shown that Arensberg probably did not write this piece. "Vacuum Tires: A Formula for the Digestion of Figments" (1919) is a prose poem that shows the influence of **Gertrude Stein**, as in this excerpt: "Notwithstanding the thermometer into which the conductor spits, the telephone meets in extremes. A window will change the subject for standing room only." Similarly, "Ing" (1916), a witty exercise in the relations between sound and meaning, shows a kind of dream logic in passages such as "Soporific / has accordingly a value for soap," and Steinian punning in phrases such as "sew pieces / And *p* says: Peace is." Arensberg's delight in puzzles and in puzzle solving suggests the quality of mind that drew him to cryptography, chess (another

obsession), and the cerebral art of Marcel Duchamp. He has a place in the history of American poetry for his roles as "poet, patron, and participant" (Naumann) in the New York avant-garde of the 1910s.

Further Reading. *Selected Primary Sources:* Arensberg, Walter Conrad, *Idols* (Boston: Houghton Mifflin, 1916); ———, *Poems* (Boston: Houghton Mifflin, 1014); Rothenberg, Jerome, ed., *The Revolution of the Word* (with collected Dada writings by Arensberg) (New York: Seabury, 1974, 3–8). *Selected Secondary Sources:* Naumann, Francis M., "Cryptography and the Arensberg Circle" (*Arts Magazine* 51 [May 1977]: 127–133); ———, *Making Mischief: Dada Invades New York* (New York: Whitney Museum, 1996); ———, "Walter Conrad Arensberg: Poet, Patron, and Participant in the New York Avant-Garde 1915–1920" (*Philadelphia Museum of Art Bulletin* 76 [Spring 1980]: 1–32).

Glen MacLeod

ARMANTROUT, RAE (1947–)

Beneath Rae Armantrout's bemused and microscopic gaze, the metaphors we live and die by are made to seem suddenly tangible and, by the same stroke, absurdly contingent. She is a satirist of **Dickinsonian** scale, alert to the contradictions in the stories we tell ourselves as individuals and as a society. Her poems do not sneer at or condescend to the persons who populate them, nor do they presume to counsel the reader as to the right conduct of his or her life. Rather, they offer witty and incisive testimony—often in a fragmentary form that solicits and repays active interpretation on the part of the reader—about the nature and texture of contemporary existence, especially as lived in a Southern California landscape dominated by military bases, shopping malls, churches, and freeways.

Mary Rae Armantrout was born in Vallejo, California, on April 13, 1947. Her father made his career in the Navy for most of his life, and her mother managed candy stores, turning to Pentecostalism after her husband's death in the early 1980s. Armantrout's formative years were spent in San Diego, and she attended San Diego State University for two years before completing her degree in English at the University of California at Berkeley in 1970, where she studied with **Denise Levertov** and came to be acquainted with Donald Allen's *New American Poetry* anthology as well as with many of the poets—**Ron Silliman** perhaps most important among them—with whom she'd be identified throughout her career, including the major West Coast figures of language-centered writing (**Robert Grenier, Bob Perelman, Lyn Hejinian**, David Melnick, and others). Armatrout's first magazine publication was in **Clayton Eshleman**'s *Caterpillar*; "from then on," she recalls in her short memoir *True* (1998), "I would, with some trepidation, call myself a writer." In 1975 Armantrout completed an MA in Creative Writing from San Francisco State University. In 1971 she and Charles Korkegian married and in 1979, shortly after their return to San Diego, their son Aaron was born. Armantrout taught for a while at California State University before taking up first an adjunct position (in 1981) and later an associate professorship (2003) at the University of California at San Diego, where she presently directs the New Writing Series.

The six-part poem "Tone," from Armantrout's debut volume, *Extremities* (1978), is a good example of the poet's abiding practice—which is evident still in the title poem of *The Pretext* (2001) as in many of the poems from *Up to Speed* (2004)—of building up a poem through the juxtaposition of short sections, varied in perspective, mode of address, and content, through which a common thread—often signaled by the repetition of a keyword—is discovered by the poet (and, through her, the reader) to run. In this case, the keyword is also the poem's title, "Tone." An opening section, formatted as prose (as will be the third and sixth sections), narrates a scene of self-staging ("I'm smiling languidly. Acting.") for a lover's behalf. Later, in section 3, the speaker questions the string of associations that link a concern for small details to class and gender: "Is it bourgeois to dwell on nuance? Or effeminate?" The answer supplied takes the form of a question: "Or should we attend to it the way a careful animal sniffs the wind." The next section cites, without providing an overt reference to, a line from Denise Levertov's poem "The Ache of Marriage": "the ark of the ache of it." In the fifth section the subject is not a lover but a maternal figure: "But Mama's saying she's alright / 'as far as breathing and all that.'" That maternal tone—bespeaking a form of suffering that a worried interpreter, such as a dutiful daughter, might hear as including all but the most rudimentary of acts ("breathing and all that")—hangs in the air as the sixth section, just two sentences long, brings the poem to a provisional conclusion: "When you're late I turn slavish, listen hard for your footstep. Sound that represents the end of lack." Common to these six glimpses—exactly scaled and held just long enough for us to begin to surmise the situations they describe—is a concern for small differences, for matters of tone as much as of overt content, and for the delicate inflections of which our core relationships—erotic, filial—are comprised.

"Anti-Short Story," also from *Extremities*, is typical of Armantrout's poetry in that it expresses a persistent restlessness with and skepticism about narrative conventions. The poem is only three lines long (such brevity would lead early interpreters of Armantrout to liken her frequently to **Objectivist** poet **Lorine Niedecker**) and consists of three statements, beginning with "A girl is running." This statement is quickly interrupted, perhaps by a new speaker: "*Don't* tell me / She's running for her bus." A blank line separates this from the poem's last enigmatic exclamation: "All that aside!" A narration has begun, a conclusion has been leapt to, and the exchange has then been canceled out as irrelevant to a story perhaps still to come.

Acute observation of social relationships and exacting depiction of the natural and manmade backdrops against which those relationships unfold or unravel are hallmarks of Armantrout's work from the sparse early first books to the ampler books from *Necromance* (1991) through *Up to Speed* (2004). Her lyric compression, subtle handling of rhythmical variations, and unerring ear for "found" and overheard language from ordinary life link Armantrout to the tradition of **William Carlos Williams** as extended by **Robert Creeley** and Denise Levertov. Her name has often been linked with language-centered writing (or **Language poetry**) of the 1970s and 1980s, and it is true that her work took root and achieved its first distinction within that artistic and social milieu. But she is perhaps best situated among the extraordinary cohort of women writers—Lyn Hejinian, **Fanny Howe**, **Rachel Blau DuPlessis**, Laura Moriarty, **Alice Notley**, **Rosmarie Waldrop**, and many others—who rose to prominence in the last fifteen years of the twentieth century and brought about the most radical expansion of possibilities for female authorship and authority since the generation of **Mina Loy**, **Gertrude Stein**, and **H.D.** in the first wave of modernism.

Further Reading. ***Selected Primary Sources:*** Armantrout, Rae, *True* (Berkeley, CA: Atelos, 1998); *Veil: New and Selected Poems* (Middletown, CT: Wesleyan University Press, 2001). ***Selected Secondary Sources:*** Beckett, Tom, ed., *A Wild Salience: The Writing of Rae Armantrout* (Cleveland: Burning Press, 1999); Burt, Stephen, "'Where Every Eye's a Guard': Rae Armantrout's Poetry of Suspicion" (*Boston Review* 27.2 [April/May 2002]).

Steve Evans

ASH, JOHN (1948–)

John Ash, in the course of his career, has moved in exile from a moribund British empire, to the heart of the great American metropolis, and then to the ruins of no less than Byzantium. Unique for his expertise in ancient urban cultures and his simultaneous involvement in Manhattan art, music, and literary circles, he has created a poetry of classical learning with an avant-garde flare, enthralled by abandoned histories yet on the postmodern edge. His impassioned vision of what was lost in Anatolia gives his fascination with American pop artifacts a dark edge of instant nostalgia, a sense of what we, also, stand to lose or leave behind. An arbiter of taste and a tireless host, he is missed now by the **New York School**, with whom, from Istanbul, he stays in touch.

Born in 1948 in Manchester, England, Ash early appreciated Byzantium not as decadent but as "an unparalleled fusion of spiritual refinement and overwhelming material splendor . . . great and mysterious, something also neglected and slandered, something that seemed to demand my sympathy and understanding" (*A Byzantine Journey*, 4) Graduating from the University of Birmingham, he taught writing in Manchester grade schools and, for one year, in Cyprus. His early **British poetry** collections include *The Casino* (1978), *The Bed* (1981), *The Goodbyes* (1982), and *The Branching Stairs* (1984). In 1984, when Manhattan—a New Byzantium—called, his vibrant personality and literary talent helped him navigate New York City's established, ambitious, gossipy social and artistic circles. Tall, slender, and bespectacled, a dark forelock falling over his expansive brow, the elegant young poet charmed the party-going literati of New York. In the mid-1980s, a younger generation of New York School poets centered around **John Ashbery**, **Kenneth Koch**, and **James Schuyler**. Ash's work attracted their attention, and his presence helped catalyze many emerging writers. He won honors including a Guggenheim fellowship, an Ingram Merrill grant, and a Whiting Foundation Writers Award; found work assisting Kenneth Koch with manuscripts; taught at Iowa and Berkeley; and wrote reviews for *Art Forum* and *Art in America*. In his first New York collection, *Disbelief* (1987), "The Sky My Husband" celebrates romantic skyscapes and landscapes: "The sky my arches and my aqueducts in ruins / The sky my waning moon my child." The poem was set to music by Aaron Jay Kernis. Poems in *The Burnt Pages* (1991) reminded Ashbery of Sir Thomas Browne's musing on ruins that suddenly become our own cities; "Twentieth Century" apostrophizes, "you are leaving us / with resurrections of dead gods who remain dead."

For roughly a decade, like **W.H. Auden** in Greenwich Village, Ash influenced many poets and writers, especially those who attended a salon-workshop in his Fifteenth Street walk-up; the weekly meeting was quickly christened "Ash Wednesday." Among those sharing work-in-progress were the late Gerrit Henry, Jaime Manrique, Maggie Paley, Marc Cohen, Susan Baran, Ted Castle, Jane DeLynn, Roberta Allen, Eugene Richie, and Rosanne Wasserman; **Harry Mathews** visited with drafts of his novel *Cigarettes.* After publishing *A Byzantine Journey* (1995), a travelogue searching Anatolia for remains of empire, Ash relocated to Istanbul. *Selected Poems* in 1996 showcased his first five books. His latest collection is *Two Books: The Anatolikon / To the City* (2002); in the latter's title poem, Ash envisions an eternal version of Auden's "City without Walls": "It is the City, the only City. / Though it has many names, there is no need to name it."

Although his international sensibility annoys some British critics, who complain that he ignores contemporary British problems, others hold Ash dear both for his early allegiance to New York School styles and his later, Turkish departures from them. For their part, New Yorkers responded to his postmodern, elegaic, eclectic poems—at once witty, surreal, and nostalgic—evoking Cavafy, George Trakl, St. John Perse, and Ronald Firbank, and composers David del Tredici and Robin Holloway. Ash covers the range of New York School interests—music, art, cinema, architecture—adding his unique taste for things Byzantine. John Gery finds that his work reflects the merry, rambling, urban-*flaneur* style familiar in Ashbery, though with terser, more biting satire (137). But Ash's Americanization most clearly appears in a Whitmanesque embrace of democratic masses, human or inanimate: As Ash predicts in "Advanced Choreography for Beginners" (*The Branching Stairs*), the future lies in establishing "a new lyricism in which all these things will find their place / equally like buildings on the loop of a promenade." Ash says, "Americans in general are much more open than the English. English politeness can be unbearable. In New York you can say exactly what you feel and people won't think you're weird. They're all doing it too" ("The Writer's Almanac," June 28–July 4, 1999, http://writers almanac.publicradio.org/docs/99_06_28.htm). Michael Schmidt's *Lives of the Poets* praises Ash's humor and reluctance to moralize. Ash celebrates the past with the same delight and disbelief with which he views New York: In Byzantium, he writes, fans of rival chariot teams wore their hair long "'in the Hunnish fashion' / and wore the colours of their teams" ("Language Poem: 2000 BC–2000 AD," *The Anatolikon*). Robert Kelly praises Ash's ability to restore entire histories through imagery. "The Anatolikon" begins with Ash being asked why he wants to go to such a place. He replies that he likes its name: "It means 'opium' and 'fortress.'" The poem ends with images of "distances and ghosts! Lakes that vanish, and smiling mouths of strangers!" and an argument for travel: "*The road is lovely as if there were no death.*"

Today, writing poems and travel articles, teaching, and exploring unstudied Anatolian locales, Ash continues to inhabit the remains of that empire. Prophetically positioned at an epicenter of our twenty-first–century geological, political, and religious disturbances, he may be showing us, in the ruins of Byzantium, the fate of the American empire as well.

Further Reading. ***Selected Primary Sources:*** Ash, John, *A Byzantine Journey* (New York: Random House, 1995); ———, *Selected Poems* (Manchester: Carcanet, 1996); ———, *Two Books: The Anatolikon / To the City* (Manchester: Carcanet, 2002). ***Selected Secondary Sources:*** Gery, John, "Ashbery's Menagerie and the Anxiety of Influence," in

The Tribe of John: Ashbery and Contemporary Poetry, ed. Susan M. Schultz (Tuscaloosa, University of Alabama Press, 1995, 126–145); Kelly, Robert, "Review of *The Anatolikon* by John Ash" (*Rain Taxi Review of Books Online Edition* [Winter 2000/2001], http://www.raintaxi.com/online/2000winter/ash .shtml); Messo, George, "Extract from *Being Here—John Ash in Conversation with George Messo*" (NER 1.1–2: 121–131, http://www.bilkent.edu.tr/~leech/nerjournal/johnash.htm).

Rosanne Wasserman

ASHBERY, JOHN (1927–)

John Ashbery is one of the leading postwar poets writing in English and the most famous member of the **New York School** of poets (which includes **Frank O'Hara**, **Kenneth Koch**, **Harry Mathews**, James Schuyler, and **Barbara Guest**). By general critical consensus, he is the most important of all postmodern poets. His influence on American, British, Irish, and indeed world poetry is hard to overestimate. Aside from his central importance in the fields of postmodernism, contemporary writing, and poetics, he is also, quite simply, a popular poet read by many for the pleasure of his beautiful, funny, and mysterious verse.

Born in Rochester, New York, in 1927, Ashbery studied at Harvard, where he met fellow poet and friend Frank O'Hara. Subsequently he studied at Columbia and then at New York University. He worked as a copywriter for Oxford University Press and McGraw-Hill until 1955, when a Fulbright scholarship enabled him to study in France. He left for Paris with the intention of writing a doctoral thesis on the work of experimental French writer Raymond Roussel. Roussel's formulaic mode of composition, combining a surrealist automatism with a more structural understanding of language as a mechanism, has proven to be a strong influence on Ashbery's own unusual compositional techniques. However, the work on Roussel was never completed. Perhaps strangely for a poet so closely associated both with the New York arts scene and American sensibilities in general, Ashbery chose to remain in Paris for the next ten years. During this time he wrote art criticism for the European edition of the *New York Herald Tribune* and for *Art International.*

Ashbery has published over twenty volumes of verse, but his career began slowly. He jokingly notes that his first proper collection, *Some Trees* (1956), which won the Yale Series of Younger Poets prize, awarded half-heartedly by Auden, took ten years to sell out of its first print run of one thousand copies. His next collection, *The Tennis Court Oath* (1962), written while he was in Paris, seems almost to have been published against Ashbery's better judgment. He has since called it an unfinished series of notes rather than a properly conceived collection, and admitted he thought about giving up poetry entirely dur-

ing this period. Pieces from the collection, however, had been distributed among the avant-garde of New York, with the long poem "Europe" in particular having a massive impact. Thus it was as a hero of the avant-garde that Ashbery returned to New York, the city he has chosen, on the whole, to call home ever since.

His next three collections, *Rivers and Mountains* (1966), *The Double Dream of Spring* (1970), and *Three Poems* (1972), began to establish first a national and then an international reputation for Ashbery, culminating in his *annus mirabilis* of 1975, when he was awarded all three major American prizes—the Pulitzer Prize, the National Book Critics Circle Award, and the National Book Award—for *Self-Portrait in a Convex Mirror*. That Ashbery could publish a collection to such acclaim and, in the same year, publish the almost totally ignored *The Vermont Notebook*, a collaboration with the artist Joe Brainard, is perhaps typical of his ability to be simultaneously popular and experimental.

Since the successes of the mid-1970s Ashbery has continued this peculiar double career path. He is the recipient of numerous awards and prestigious posts. The collection *A Wave* (1984) won the Lenore Marshall Poetry Prize and the Bollingen Prize. Ashbery was the first English-language poet to win the Grand Prix de Biennales Internationales de Poésie (Brussels), and he has also won the English Speaking Union Prize, the Feltrinelli Prize, the Ruth Lilly Poetry Prize, two Ingram Merrill Foundation grants, the MLA Common Wealth Award in Literature, the Harriet Monroe Memorial Prize, the Frank O'Hara Prize, the Shelley Memorial Award, and fellowships from the Academy of American Poets, the Fulbright Foundation, the Guggenheim Foundation, and the MacArthur Foundation. He is a former chancellor of the Academy of American Poets and is currently the Charles P. Stevenson, Jr., Professor of Languages and Literature at Bard College.

Despite these many accolades, Ashbery remains something of an outsider, still able to produce challenging works such as *Flow Chart* (1991) that form a central dialogue with the rich contemporary culture of experimental poetry and poetics in the United States but that also seem to alienate as many readers as they impress. Since the publication of this epic work, Ashbery has published a collection almost every two years: *Hotel Lautréamont* (1992), *And the Stars Were Shining* (1994), *Can You Hear, Bird* (1995), *Wakefulness* (1998), *Girls on the Run* (1999), *Your Name Here* (2000), *Chinese Whispers* (2002), and most recently *Where Shall I Wander* (2005). However, some critics feel that his last important collection of lyrical pieces is *April Galleons* (1987).

Ashbery can be said to have had many careers in addition to his "double dream" of poetry. He has had an illustrious career in arts journalism and until 1972 was editor of *Art News*. He is art critic for *Newsweek* and frequent contributor to the *New Yorker*. Selections of his art criticism have been published in *Reported Sightings: Art Chronicles, 1957–1987* (1989). Ashbery has also made a major contribution to academia. He has taught at Brooklyn College, CUNY, Harvard, and Bard College and has produced a significant body of criticism and translations from the French. His Harvard lectures are collected in *Other Traditions: The Charles Eliot Norton Lectures* (2000), and his literary criticism and other essays are gathered in *Selected Prose* (2004). Other significant projects include interventions on the experimental drama scene centered around the St. Marks Poetry Project in New York in the 1950s, published as *Three Plays* (1982), a novel, *A Nest of Ninnies* (1969), with James Schuyler, and his editing of *The Best American Poetry* (1988).

For a writer of such importance and influence there is surprisingly little major critical work devoted to Ashbery's poetry. His work is famously difficult, and most of the critical commentary on his work has focused on the source and significance of this difficulty; however, his career is, in fact, coherent and easily summarized. In his poetry, he has systematically recorded the process of his consciousness, his self-conscious reflections on this process, and the interactions of this process with various discourses, events, people, places, arts, languages, and things.

Ashbery once observed that he thought of himself as basically an empirical poet, a true assertion if we define empiricism as knowledge through observation. However, the knowledge garnered from Ashbery's observations remains flawed and often obscure, while the act of observing itself regularly upends the certainties of knowing and can even change the object one is observing, particularly if that object is oneself. This is complicated by postmodern self-referentiality, the fact that the poet's day-to-day life, recorded through its effects on his recording consciousness, consists primarily of that act of recording, and by a radical understanding of language not as a mode of communication but as a thing unto itself that often fails at communication. One begins to see that the origin of Ashbery's difficulty is the origin of the difficulties of contemporary life itself. Ashbery's poetry seems to say that to exist is complex, to talk about it necessary and difficult, and that, in talking about life, life itself is modified in significant ways.

His major theme, repeated and extended in multifarious and sometimes tedious forms, is that we live in a world without reliable belief systems but we are still dominated personally and culturally by a desire to believe. In "Down by the Station Early in the Morning," from the *A Wave* (1981), the poet writes, "It all wears out. I keep telling myself this, but / I can never believe me, though others do. Even things do" (14). Here the *it*, a classically obscure deictic pointer to no one thing in par-

ticular, comes to refer to the ability of the artist to transform his personal experience into aesthetically significant and accurate recollections. The poet cannot redeem the past by preserving fragments of it, but only wear it out by going over it again and again. Paradoxically, because belief in the poet as seer has also worn out, the poet cannot believe his own bad news. Other people, however, still seem capable of belief and trust, enough to take seriously the poet's message. That this message is basically that they should not take the poet seriously is one of Ashbery's many conundrums.

"Down by the Station" then goes on to reconstruct significant episodes from thepoet's past, including the station of the poem's title, before focusing, bathetically, on a particular type of shoe leather "that no longer exists. / And nothing does, until you name it, remembering." Even in such a case, he argues, it may only have existed because of "the perceptual dysfunction you've been carrying around for years" (14).

In contrast to the conundrum that began the poem, we have here a radical skepticism combined with an understanding of language's slippages, lies, and deferrals, which is classically postmodern. Do words name things that already exist, or do things only exist through the unreliable mediation of language? Like so many postmodern writers Ashbery seems to favor the latter position. However, he goes one step further in suggesting that existence is something beyond language, so that giving something a name is not enough to guarantee it presence.

The publication in 1975 of both the much-acclaimed *Self-Portrait in a Convex Mirror* and *The Vermont Notebook* offers two extremes of Ashbery's art. On the one hand we have the oblique but profound reflections on the art of self-making to be found in the long title poem "Self-Portrait in a Convex Mirror," where the painter Parmigianino, whose self-portrait the poem considers, stands in for the poet himself. In this poem the mannerist distortions of the self's image of itself when seen in the convex mirror represent the act of self-regard typical of Ashbery's work, in which the mirror reflects only what the artist wishes: "Which was enough for his purpose: his image / Glazed, embalmed, projected at a 180-degree angle" (68).

If the exhilarating but confrontational experiments of *The Tennis Court Oath* gave too little to the reader, the almost direct statements of poetic intent to be found in the poems of *Self-Portrait* seemed, to Ashbery himself, to give almost too much. These poems have an intellectual lucidity markedly different from the ludic work of most, if not all, of Ashbery's twenty-odd collections. A number of poems deal directly with his anxiety over his "job" as a poet. In "As One Put Drunk into a Packet Boat" (the original title of the collection), Ashbery writes with a paradoxical clarity of the dangers posed to his subjectivity *by* clarity. Stopped by "a look of glass," he walks on, disturbed: "was I the perceived? / Did they notice me, this time, as I am . . . ?" (1). In the title poem, his commentary on Parmigianino seems to reflect criticism of his own poetry as all surface effect, as he observes how Parmigianino's work has "begun to grow stale as no answer / Or answers were forthcoming" (76).

In contrast to *Self-Portrait*, we have the work of *The Vermont Notebook*, made up of lists and obscure games with words that shy away from semantic profundity in favor of linguistic innovation. Although the poems of *Self-Portrait* vouchsafed Ashbery's public importance and garnered him the most prizes, it is the work of *Notebook*, *The Tennis Court Oath*, *Three Poems*, and *Flow Chart* that had the most impact on the contemporary avant-garde.

If Ashbery's poetry is divisible into two complementary but quite different strands, the criticism has also fallen along these two lines. There are those like Harold Bloom and Helen Vendler who see Ashbery as the latest in a long line of Romantic soul makers, using the process of poetic artifice to forge an inner life then projected out to the world at large. Indeed, it is useful to think of Ashbery as a modern-day combination of Keatsian beauty and Wordsworthian self-analysis, although Bloom's description of Ashbery as "an antithetical transcendentalist, bearer of an influx of the Newness that he cannot know himself" (*John Ashbery*, 17) is perhaps closer to the mark. For all the influences of the European avant-garde writers such as Roussel, Lautréamont, Breton, and Apollinaire, Ashbery is a quintessentially American poet. If Ashbery's close friend and fellow poet Frank O'Hara could be seen as the inheritor of the tradition of poetry of the everyday handed down by **William Carlos Williams**, Ashbery is generally seen as a follower of **Wallace Stevens**'s more skeptical, transcendental approach. The Transcendentalist adage "know thyself" so central to the American experience is certainly important for Ashbery's work, although not, perhaps, for the reasons Bloom gives. The poem "Wet Casements" from *Houseboat Days* (1977) begins with a statement of Romantic solipsism, as the poet speaks of seeing, as though through rain-streaked windows, "the look of others through / Their own eyes" and of "Their self-analytical attitudes overlaid by your / Ghostly transparent face." The poet is trying to establish criteria for self-analysis, not of the soul so much as one's appearance to others, perhaps a postmodern surface-oriented version of the soul. The ghostly face operates as a typically Romantic meta-commentator, placed on top of the blurred, rainy self-reflection. The special role of the poet comes to the fore in the second stanza, where the poet's anger at losing the name of a nameless, symbolic "you" creates a work of art, specifically a bridge resembling the one "of Avignon." The poet's quest to know himself,

especially to know himself as a poet, is fulfilled through a literal act of bridge building. In reaching out to the people with an emotion-based art form, he will come to know himself in full, and he shall at last see his face reflected "not in the water but in the worn stone of my bridge" (28). The notion of finding one's soul and of projecting oneself in art, however tongue-in-cheek, locates Ashbery within the Romantic tradition.

This late-Romantic view, however, ignores what many consider most important in Ashbery: his experimental approach to language, particularly hackneyed language, whether Romantic or not, as in the above example of sampling the most cliché French song ("Sur le Pont d'Avignon"). In other words, if in the Romantic tradition of soul making the signifier *soul* is emphasized, in Ashbery's work it is the *making* that is all important, and that construction occurs through the material of language.

Susan Schultz has pointed out, in her essay "Returning to Bloom: John Ashbery's Critique of Harold Bloom," that a shift away from the Bloomian view of Ashbery as a late-Romantic, so-called Orphic poet began with the work of S.P. Mohanty and Jonathan Monroe in the late 1980s, with their stress on the democratic and discursive nature of Ashbery's poetry. Rather than see his work as a private and solipsistic quest for personal meaning, they looked to the language Ashbery was using and its political and subjective implications. Ashbery the poet was a social construct, which he then set out in works like *Three Poems* and *Self-Portrait* to deconstruct through the use of richly varied and complexly patterned discursive modes and speech acts. In other words, the persona of the Romantic poet was a poetic grand narrative forcing Ashbery into certain patterns of experience and expression he might wish to rebel against, and in this situation he was no different from any subject living in the modern world of consumerism and sign systems.

Another poem from *Houseboat Days*, "Daffy Duck in Hollywood," illustrates this predicament with an exhilarating mixture of speech patterns. The poem begins lyrically enough, "Something strange is creeping across me," before descending into a multiplicity of registers, including that of a famous self-referential Warner Brothers cartoon in which Daffy finds himself trapped in the frame by the cartoonist. Completely incongruous with the register we might associate with Daffy Duck is the description of the "lineaments" of Daffy's face in "yon hubcap" as "*déconfit*." We may still detect here the artist's self-reflection and self-analysis, but Ashbery has Daffy Duck speaking archaic English and French, and referring to "*Amadigi de Gaula*" and "Rumford's Baking Powder." The poet is not soul making here but using the self as a vehicle for critical interventions on the multiple discourses that combine to form even a cartoon self.

This second view, of Ashbery's persona as a sophisticated tool in a radical reappraisal of subjectivity, its expression and control, is taken even further by the work of Charles Altieri and his application of the Wittgensteinian aspectual self to Ashbery's ongoing process of the depiction of a consciousness in the midst of depicting a consciousness (826–827). Wittgenstein explains that an aspectual self is the self as "as," combining a real utterance with a self-consciousness built on the fact that one could have said otherwise. This "virtual subjectivity" is not the traditional figure of the Romantic, questing poet looking for his or her true self, but rather a radically "daffy" postmodern subject of uncertainty, caught in the process of creating and recreating its own self through the various material means made available to it. This is the essence of postmodern ontology, and Ashbery has been the most successful writer of the age in expressing this state in literary form.

It would be wrong to consider Ashbery's work as a whole without making mention of his many poetic innovations. While Ashbery does not seem, on the surface, as innovative as some contemporary American poets, he has always been a self-conscious experimenter with poetic form. As Ashbery has himself pointed out in *Three Poems*, the early part of his career resembled a kind of laboratory for poetry. He says in the long **prose poem** "The New Spirit," "I thought that if I could put it all down, that would be one way. And next the thought came to me that to leave all out would be another, and truer, way." If *The Tennis Court Oath* is an example of leaving it all out, then *Three Poems* and *Flow Chart* are, in their length and use of prose or extended hypertactic lines, majestic examples of putting it all down.

While it may be said of Ashbery that, at times, it is hard to distinguish one poem from another and to differentiate the significant from the insignificant, it is hard to mistake Ashbery's work for anyone else's, whether in style, tone, or overall methodology. Consider, for example, the opening lines of "Late Echo" from *As We Know* (1979), where Ashbery writes, "Alone with our madness and favourite flower / We see that there really is nothing left to write about." The poem illustrates a series of Ashberyian techniques that feature in most, if not all, of his major works. Title abuse is typical of Ashbery, with titles often added later or at random. What in fact is a "late echo," if it exists at all? Whatever it is, the title and the poem that follows indicate the temporal zone of belatedness, which is where most of Ashbery's poems take place. Not only is the poem an echo of mimetic art, late for its appointment with meaning, but we feel as if we had arrived late into a rather bizarre conversation. What Marjorie Perloff has called pronominal shifters in *Frank O'Hara: A Poet Among Painters* also feature frequently in Ashbery's work. In this instance we wonder immediately who the "we" is—is it Ashbery and his friends, or

are we included? Is it humanity? The concomitant question then follows, who is Ashbery to speak for others, anyway? In fact, Ashbery as a "real" human being rarely, if ever, speaks in his work; instead, all pronominal indicators—he, she, I, we—are linguistic devices to mount different aspects of self within different language games. In other words, "our" favorite flower has little to do with John Ashbery's.

Geoff Ward has noted that Ashbery is a poet who renounces the image in favor of syntax, and his favorite syntactic device is the argument. His poems rely on a narratology of logical sequences, which, however, once they have hold of you, either tail off, suggest links that make no sense, or transport you from one set of ideas to another in the twinkle of a conjunction. "Late Echo" appears to be lucid, but of course, in between its logical, syntactic signposts, Ashbery is intent on distracting us from the pursuit of the argument.

All of this leads us to the alternative logic of Ashbery's work. Many have incorrectly suggested that his work is surreal, while others have come closer to the truth by suggesting that his work has a dream logic. In fact, Ashbery's poems pursue a cognitive process of associative thinking that we all indulge in every day, awake or asleep. Ashbery puts together the associative way the mind works, with its reliance on the conventions of linguistic and aesthetic communication, and uses one to undermine the other, although there is no hierarchical order. Sometimes language and grammar win, sometimes consciousness and association.

Given these considerations, it is not as easy as it is with other poets to identify the themes of Ashbery's work. In the first instance the form/theme dichotomy is regularly deconstructed by the poet so that the decision, say, to write two 10-line stanzas a day to produce "Fragment" comes to form part of the poem's ruminations on rooms, spaces, and death. In addition, Ashbery's poems make massive leaps over short periods of time, decentering the poem and making it impossible to summarize a single meaning. The leaps are further problematized by his random selection of titles and his processual aesthetic, which records ideas as they pass through the mind and language rather than as they appear at the end of a period of rumination. What can be said of his work, however, is that it is the most sustained body of postmodern poetry that exists. This, along with his commitment to experimentation, makes Ashbery one of *the* central writers of our age.

Further Reading. *Selected Primary Sources:* Ashbery, John, *As We Know* (New York: Penguin, 1979); ———, *Flow Chart* (Manchester: Carcanet, 1991); ———, *The Mooring of Starting Out: The First Five Books of Poetry* (New York: Ecco Press, 1997); ———, *Self-Portrait in a Convex Mirror* (Manchester: Carcanet, 1977); ———, *Three Books*

(New York: Penguin, 1993); ———, *Three Poems* (New York: Ecco Press, 1989); ———, *A Wave* (Manchester: Carcanet, 1984). **Selected Secondary Sources:** Altieri, Charles, "John Ashbery and the Challenge of Postmodernism in the Visual Arts" (*Critical Inquiry* 14 [Summer 1988]: 805–830); Bloom, Harold, ed., *John Ashbery: Modern Critical Views* (New York: Chelsea House, 1985); Herd, David, *John Ashbery and American Poetry* (Basingstoke: Palgrave Macmillan, 2001); Lehman, David, *Beyond Amazement: New Essays on John Ashbery* (New York: Cornell University Press, 1993); Shoptaw, John, *On the Outside Looking Out: John Ashbery's Poetry* (Cambridge, MA: Harvard University Press, 1994); Schultz, Susan, ed., *The Tribe of John* (Tuscaloosa: University of Alabama Press, 1995); Ward, Geoff, *Statutes of Liberty: The New York School Poets* (Basingstoke: Macmillan, 1993; rev. ed. 2000); Watkin, William, *In the Process of Poetry: The New York School and the Avant-Garde* (Lewisburg, PA: Bucknell University Press, 2001).

William Watkin

ASIAN AMERICAN POETRY

Asian American poetry is a body of writing comprising and organizing literary expressions of North Americans of Asian ancestry. As such, it constitutes a vital part of American literature as a fluid, multicultural, and multiracial field. Composed of writings appearing in English and produced by persons wholly or partially of Asian—especially Asian Pacific or South Asian—ancestry who have inhabited the United States or Canada and who have designated their literary output as poetry, Asian American poetry can be seen as both a *conception* with a fairly precise period of origin and a *tradition* with complex and in some cases still undiscovered roots.

As a component of Asian American literature, Asian American poetry traces its conception to the late 1960s and early 1970s when, in the footsteps of the Civil Rights Movement and in the spirit of racial and ethnic power struggles, women's liberation, community activism, and emerging demands for the recognition of ethnic studies, Americans of Asian ancestry sought to unite peoples of common racial characteristics, Pacific Rim geographies, and similar histories or experiences of discrimination and prejudice in the United States (and later in Canada) under the inclusive, coalitional label *Asian American.* Implicit in the new designation was a rejection of the term "Oriental," a label encumbered with exoticism and a lengthy history of racial and gender stereotypes. Specifically, in the late 1960s and early 1970s, social activists and restive artists on both coasts of the United States envisioned an Asian American literature that lay outside of and frequently in opposition to the dominant literary traditions promulgated through the publishing industry and sustained by academic institutions.

For some, Asian American poetry was to be dedicated to pursuing the nexus between art and social change. This was to be a poetry of the people, or at least of recognizable communities, to be pursued in the spirit of empowerment and social justice, cultural and historical survival, emerging self-definitions, and, when necessary, militant struggle. Frequently, it was linked to oral traditions and marked by a subject matter relating to issues of oppression and liberation and by a style that conveyed energy and spontaneity. While to greater or lesser degrees it could draw upon traditional ideas of craft, it rejected the association of poetry with artistic difficulty, privilege, and a narrow reading elite. Poetry was to be a vehicle of change rather than a library artifact whose primary purpose was to be admired and studied. On both the East and West coasts, scores of Asian American writers, many of them young and most of them relatively unheralded, engaged in producing this poetry.

For others, Asian American writings were to be distinguished primarily by particularities of language, intonation, idiom, and voice—aspects of identities forged within an inhospitable social environment. Thus, if the writings, including poetry, did not always serve as direct stimuli for social change or embrace liberationist politics, they were nevertheless infused with historical memory and situated outside the mainstream of American literary tradition. Over time, Asian American literary output gained visibility through newspapers, magazines, journals, and literary anthologies. On the East Coast, for example, the anthology *Yellow Pearl*, a product of New York City's Basement Workshop, a community of artists, writers, musicians, urban planners, and activists, was published in 1972. Despite humble beginnings, the Basement Workshop ran a successful creative arts program, established the Asian American Resource Center, conducted numerous community improvement and self-help activities, and published *Bridge*, a path-setting literary magazine.

On the West Coast, literary activity flourished widely, often in campus and community magazines and newspapers. In San Francisco the first Asian American literary magazine, *Aion*, appeared, and the writers associated with the Kearny Street Workshop, as well as students engaged in the Third World Strike at San Francisco State University, helped set a socially engaged, activist tone. In subsequent years, all along the West Coast students and community activists helped promote Asian American literary activity by holding writing conferences and staging poetry readings. The interdisciplinary anthologies *Roots: An Asian American Reader* (1971) and *Counterpoint: Perspectives on Asian America* (1976) included literature sections that situated Asian American poetry within the framework of Third World struggle. Poet and editor Janice Mirikitani helped place Asian American poetry within the context of liberationist struggles through her editorial work on *Time to Greez! Incantations from the Third World* (1975) and through the publication of *Awake in the River* (1978), her first volume of poetry. As early as 1973, writer and performance artist **Jessica Hagedorn** was one of four featured poets in *Four Young Women*, a collection edited by **Kenneth Rexroth**, which was soon followed by her own collection of prose fiction and poetry, *Dangerous Music* (1975). During this period Hagedorn's fellow Filipino/a American poets, including Al Robles, Luis Syquia, Sam Tagatac, Jeff Tagami, Virginia Cerenio, and Jaime Jacinto, contributed to a growing body of literature, most of it highly democratized and geared toward the cultural politics of the working class. Other literary anthologies of the era dedicated to the marriage of writing and political progressivism included Volume 3 of *Yardbird Reader* (1974) and the anthology *Third World Women* (1972).

The ferment of literary activity sustained in substantial part by the era's radical politics helped to consolidate the conception of an Asian America. However, in terms of inaugurating a recognized literary tradition, the period's seminal event was the publication of *Aiiieeeee! An Anthology of Asian-American Writers* (1974), edited by Frank Chin, Jeffery Paul Chan, **Lawson Fusao Inada**, and Shawn Hsu Wong. Although it limited itself to prose fiction and drama, and although it published only writings of Chinese Americans, Japanese Americans, and Filipino/a Americans, the anthology purported to offer "fifty years of our whole voice," a declaration less significant for its accuracy than for its recognition of a literary production that was decades old yet still unrecognized in literary circles. Since Asians inhabited the North American continent before the establishment of the United States, and since substantial numbers of them had lived and worked in America during the nineteenth and early twentieth centuries, the claiming of a literary tradition resonated with other efforts to declare both presence and history. Equally important, while North American Asians themselves had historically relied on categories of identity based on nation of origin, thereby implicitly acknowledging the histories of conflict and the varieties of linguistic and cultural differences that served to separate them, the editors of *Aiiieeeee!* asserted the existence of a coalitional literary tradition able to mediate ethnic and cultural differences by grounding itself in and against a common history of oppression in North America. Other literary anthologies of the time seeking to represent earlier literary output and contributing to this coalitional literary tradition included *Asian-American Authors* (1972), edited by Kai-yu Hsu and Helen Palubinskas, and *Asian-American Heritage: An Anthology of Poetry and Prose* (1974), edited by David Hsin-Fu Wand.

During these formative years, literary criticism was understandably sparse. The 1971 appearance of *Amerasia Journal*, initially published by students at Yale University and thereafter securing a permanent home with UCLA's Asian American Studies Program, was a vital first step in defining an entire disciplinary field and thereby providing a foundation from which critical studies of literature eventually might emerge. But in the meantime, the anthologies and the sporadic initial efforts to construct a critical discourse on Asian American literature helped fashion an environment that could embrace single-authored volumes of poetry under the rubric Asian America rather than, as previously had been the habit, as achievements of individual authors contained wholly under existing national identities. Such a critical environment was vital, since not only did individual-author books appear with greater frequency during the 1970s, but even earlier published volumes now found themselves connected to the corpus of Asian American poetry. Galvanizing the development of this tradition was the 1971 publication of Lawson Fusao Inada's first book, *Before the War: Poems as They Happened*. Although Inada's collection of understated, jazz-like, seemingly impromptu verse was not the first single-author volume of poetry to be published in the United States by an American of Asian ancestry, his was the first to be recognized amid the growing discussions of Asian American literature. His identifications with jazz and with the racial minorities residing in and around West Fresno, California, made Inada a new, distinguishable voice in Asian American poetry. His subsequent poetry collections, including *Legends from Camp* (1992) and *Drawing the Line* (1997), have continued to highlight his importance to the field.

Although Inada quickly became an icon of Asian American poetry, numerous other writers also contributed to the growth of a recognized literary tradition. Poets such as the aforementioned Janice Mirikitani and Al Robles, along with activist writers like Nellie Wong, were overt in their efforts at politicizing poetry. Some, like Lonny Kaneko, Diana Chang, James Masao Mitsui, Fay Chiang, and Wing Tek Lum, used poetry as a vehicle for lyrical explorations of culture, history, and identity. Others, such as Jessica Hagedorn, **Mei-Mei Berssenbrugge**, **Arthur Sze**, and later **Theresa Hak Kyung Cha** and **Kimiko Hahn**, were keenly interested in experimenting with and exploring poetry from a variety of performative, linguistic, and intellectual perspectives. Some of the writings proved daunting to the general reader accustomed to linear narratives and transparent lyrics, but all of them helped expand the range and meaning of Asian American poetry.

As various writers and writings helped to consolidate a sense of tradition, efforts to recuperate a poetic legacy grew as well. The early anthologies recognized that a portion of this poetic legacy resided in the later nineteenth and earlier twentieth centuries. The Japanese German writer **Sadakichi Hartmann**, who became a naturalized American citizen in 1894, published six collections of poetry in English in a wide-ranging literary career. Long before multiculturalism became a media byword, Hartmann produced poetry resonating variously with **Walt Whitman**'s poetics of democracy, French symbolism, and Japanese haiku (also called hokku or haikai), tanka, and dodoitsu. Hartmann's contemporary, **Yone Noguchi**, sojourned in the United States from 1893 to 1904 and again from 1919 to 1920, acquiring fluency in English and eventually gaining acclaim for seven collections of poetry. Like Hartmann's, Noguchi's early poetry was influenced by Western models, his first volume, *Seen and Unseen* (1897), a clear effort to produce lush, fin de siècle verse. But Noguchi also sought to explore aesthetic relationships between East and West, and he soon transformed his poetry with shorter lines, an emphasis on nature, and the use of Japanese words and memories. His experiments with Japanese hokku would call increased attention to linguistic precision and the power of the image, concerns that readily converged with the Imagism of Ezra Pound and with the advent of modernism.

The early Asian American literary anthologies also recognized the brilliant and idiosyncratic poet **Jose Garcia Villa** from the Philippines, who wrote poems suffused with both mysticism and sensuality, gaining initial acclaim for his book *Have Come, Am Here* (1942). Subsequent volumes included *Appassionata: Poems in Praise of Love* (1942); the experimental *Volume Two* (1949), wherein the poems' tonal values were regulated by a landslide of commas; and *Poems Fifty-Five: The Best Poems of Jose Garcia Villa* (1962). Villa's poetry would stand in stark contrast to that of his countryman, Carlos Bulosan, later to be celebrated for his Depression-era memoir of migrant Filipino workers, *America Is in the Heart* (1946). Bulosan dedicated substantial portions of his romantic, sometimes sentimental, but also soaringly lyrical poetry to descrying the grueling life of the immigrant subaltern from the Philippines; the social, economic, political, and legal forces that circumscribed that existence; and the unmet yearnings for both material and emotional nourishment that such meager conditions produced.

From the start, attempts at recovering poetic legacies have recognized that Asian American poetry is not limited to works produced by professional writers who gained recognition, however marginal, from literary authorities. Indeed, writers who were acknowledged by the literary academy constitute only a fragment of its beginnings. Asian American community members and scholars alike appreciated the value of the poems carved on the walls of the immigration station at **Angel Island** in San Francisco Bay by early Chinese immigrants who endured protracted periods of detainment, as their papers ostensibly were being processed. Often expressing their loneliness, pain, homesickness, and sense of betrayal, the poets instinctively understood the connection between art and politics. An invaluable bilingual anthology of poems and narratives entitled *Island: Poetry and History of Chinese Immigrants on Angel Island, 1910 to 1940*, edited and translated by Him Mark Lai, Genny Lim, and Judy Yung, was published in 1980. Altogether the editors translated 135 poems, of which 69 were chosen for publication, many of them taken from the walls of the decaying barracks of the immigration station. *Island* remains important not only as a legacy of history but as a record of an aesthetic sensibility in the process of being shaped, for these poems were the issue of nonprofessional writers emerging from a tradition of Chinese literacy but prepared to use poetry as a natural medium of expression for Asians in America forced to endure hardship and discrimination. A body of Cantonese verse originating in San Francisco exists as well, thanks to the recovery efforts of Marlon Hom, whose *Songs of Gold Mountain: Cantonese Rhymes from San Francisco Chinatown* was published in 1987.

Similarly, early Japanese American literary production was not limited to Hartmann or Noguchi. Prior to World War II, both issei (first-generation Japanese immigrants to America) and nisei (second-generation Japanese Americans) found publishing outlets for their poetic efforts in a variety of community newspapers, including San Francisco's *Nichibei Times*, New York's *Nichibei*, and Los Angeles' *Rafu Shimpo*, as well as in nisei literary magazines such as *Reimei* and *Leaves*. Poetry societies existed in a variety of communities. During the internment camp period, literary publications such as *Topaz Trek* and *Poston Chronicle* helped sustain literary efforts. Toyo Suyemoto and Iwao Kawakami, along with Hisaye Yamamoto, who would become best known for her fiction, were just a few of the Japanese American poets writing and publishing during the 1940s. Mitsuye Yamada wrote ironic, understated poems about the internment experience that would be published decades later in her first volume of poetry, *Camp Notes and Other Poems* (1976). Poems written by issei and nisei were gathered together in another landmark publication, the bilingual *Ayumi: A Japanese American Anthology* (1980), edited by Mirikitani. *Poets Behind Barbed Wire* (1983), edited and translated by Jiro Nakano and Kay Nakano, featured tanka poems written by four Hawai'i issei sent to mainland internment camps. *May Sky: There Is Always Tomorrow: An Anthology of Japanese American Concentration Camp Kaiko Haiku* (1997), edited by Violet Kazue de Cristoforo, helped connect the poetry produced in the internment camps with the prewar poetry societies in California's vast Central Valley. In 1996 Juliana Chang edited *Quiet Fire: A Historical Anthology of Asian American Poetry, 1892–1970*. Featuring selected poems from twenty-nine writers, the majority of whom were writing before the close of World War II, the anthology suggests the range and diversity of the Asian American poetic heritage and argues the need for further research.

As the poetic output and tradition developed along these multiple lines on the mainland United States, Asian American literature in Hawai'i operated on a different register. Because Hawai'i was multiracial, multiethnic, and multicultural in ways that the mainland could scarcely know, and because other Americans tended to view it as a vacation destination rather than a complex of interacting communities, the more salient traditional distinction was between those who were "local" and those who were not. The locals understood Hawai'i as a separate place and a separate sensibility, not merely as a resort and an escape. Hawai'i for the locals also was steeped in history; it was more than the beautiful surface of a tourist brochure. Moreover, the categories of national origin and ethnicity often proved unreliable among a large, mixed-race population.

Writings by and critical studies of what mainlanders would call ethnic or minority writers of Hawai'i had been conducted in advance of those on the mainland. At the same time, however, Hawai'ian educational institutions, buttressed by social and political policy, historically had remained unreceptive to notions of a specifically ethnic literary perspective. Such institutions were far more comfortable with approved or standard linguistic expressions and with reigning ideas of literary authority and canon—but often to the detriment of genuinely local experiences and indigenous expressions. Not surprisingly, the conceptual importance of Asian American literature gained ground as modern theories of postcolonialism emerged. Today, the Hawai'ian sovereignty movement, which has called for a recognition of the legacies of Western imperialism and a restoration of rights and lands to indigenous Hawai'ians, not only serves as a vital reminder of the material stakes of postcolonial struggle but as a reminder of the successive non-indigenous settler regimes that have constructed cultural hegemonies within Asian American literature itself.

For a number of Island writers, the 1978 Talk Story Conference, the first of a number of similar meetings to be held in this and subsequent years, constituted an important step in the process of literary reconceptualization. The conference led to the publication of *Talk Story: An Anthology of Hawai'i's Local Writers*. In the same year, Darrell Lum and Eric Chock inaugurated *Bamboo Ridge, The Hawai'i Writers' Quarterly*, which subsequently became an important channel for showcasing the talents of local writers and expanding the field of Asian American literature. From such beginnings, local writers began to challenge the mainland and Caucasian-dominated literary establishment, which included the University of Hawai'i, the Hawai'i Literary Arts Council, and the State Foundation of Culture and the Arts. Among the promi-

nent Asian American poets identified with Hawai'i are Wing Tek Lum, Albert Saijo, Eric Chock, **Cathy Song**, Juliet Kono, Carolyn Lau (Carolyn Lei-Lanilau) and the native **Garrett Hongo**. Lois-Ann Yamanaka gained attention through her use of pidgin and her acerbic character portraits in *Saturday Night at the Pahala Theater* (1993), and Richard Hamasaki through his multigeneric *From the Spider Bone Diaries: Poems and Songs* (2002).

As in Hawai'i, the conceptual development of Asian American literature in Canada proceeded along a separate course. Indeed, only gradually did it become clear that Asian American literature actually might encompass all English-language North American literature. When, in the 1960s and 1970s, a number of Canadian writers, including **Roy Kiyooka**, **Fred Wah**, Joy Kogawa, and Gerry Shikatani, published volumes of poetry, they were encouraged to identify themselves simply as Canadian rather than as Asian Canadian or Asian North American poets. Perhaps because the numbers of minorities in Canada did not rival those in the United States, the frictions of race did not develop in precisely the same way—even though Japanese Canadians, like Japanese in the United States, were forced to endure a brutal relocation during World War II. While Asian American poetry on the United States mainland arises conceptually from a faith in literature as an instrument of social change whose allegiances are to community, race, and to some extent class, Asian North American poetry in Canada arises from, then sets out to reshape, an existing canon of linguistically conventionalized Canadian literature. In 1981 Shikatani and co-editor David Aylward produced *Paper Doors: An Anthology of Japanese Canadian Poetry*, a title suggesting the incipient effort to define poetry outside the customary parameters of Canadian literature. The charge was taken up further by Cyril Dabydeen, who edited *Another Way to Dance: Asian-Canadian Poetry* (1990), and Diane McGifford and Judith Kearns, who edited *Shakti's Words: An Anthology of South Asian Canadian Women's Poetry* (1990).

Two of the most celebrated Asian Canadian poets, Kiyooka and Wah, have gravitated toward language experiments and away from ethnographic narratives. This has been their way of simultaneously declaring their connection to nation and their minority position as citizens and writers. Poet and editor Roy Miki remains prominent among those who have championed such language experimentation. In other respects, Asian Canadian poetry has spread in a variety of directions. Evelyn Lau's poetry, including *You Are Not Who You Claim* (1990), *Oedipal Dreams* (1992), and *In the House of Slaves* (1994), has explored the darker regions of sexuality, drugs, violence, and prostitution. South Asian Canadian poetry is an expansive category, which naturally includes writers encompassing wide geographical and cultural boundaries. Bangladesh-born Himani Bannerji, Guyana-born Cyril Dabydeen, India-born Uma Parameswaran, and Sri Lankans Rienzi Crusz and Michael Ondaatje are among the notables.

By the late 1970s and especially the mid-1980s, Asian American poetry not only extended beyond the geographical borders of the mainland United States but also began to coalesce in the collective mind of the academy as a recognizable and formidable body of work, even as its purposes and methods became increasingly diverse. An important anthology devoted exclusively to poetry was *Breaking Silence: An Anthology of Contemporary Asian American Poets* (1983), edited by **Joseph Bruchac**. While the title seemed to ignore the plethora of poetry that had preceded this volume, in actuality it was a testimony to the self-defining presence of Asian American poetry, a body of work, the title suggested, that now was actively engaged in resisting the silencing that had greeted its previous efforts. The range and diversity of the poetry of its fifty contributors suggested, however, that the silence was to be broken in different ways.

As the 1980s advanced, individual Asian American poets were embraced through various forms of institutional recognition, often garnering major awards. Starting with the appearance of Garrett Hongo's *Yellow Light* (1982), a series of poetry volumes appearing in rapid succession shed national light on producers of Asian American poetry. The Discovery/*The Nation* Award having previously been won by Hongo, **Richard Hugo** named Cathy Song winner of the Yale Series of Younger Poets Prize for her first volume, *Picture Bride* (1983), and **John Ashbery** selected **John Yau**'s avant-garde *Corpse and Mirror* (1983) as winner of the National Poetry Series. Even though Yau, an art critic, had begun publishing poetry in the mid-1970s, and fellow poet **Ai** had published her first two volumes of poetry by the turn of the decade, including the Lamont Award–winning *Killing Floor* (1978), the concentration of awards in the 1980s meant a situational shift for Asian American poetry. Whereas it had once seemed assuredly marginalized, one segment of it, at least, now found itself embraced by the literary establishment.

As canon revision gained momentum and multiculturalism became a catchphrase in education, the process continued. **David Mura** won the National Poetry Series for his book *After We Lost Our Way* (1989), and Hongo's *The River of Heaven* (1988) and **Li-Young Lee**'s *The City in Which I Love You* (1990) (following the intense literary excitement generated by his first volume, *Rose*, in 1986) were each named winner of the Lamont Award. For the poetry cognoscenti, **Marilyn Chin**, author of *Dwarf Bamboo* (1987), *The Phoenix Gone, the Terrace Empty* (1994), and *Rhapsody in Plain Yellow* (2003), and **Kimiko Hahn**, author of *Air Pocket* (1989), *Earshot* (1992), *The Unbearable Heart* (1995), and other volumes, were notably exciting

writers. Chin has been acclaimed for the richness of her allusions and for a satiric voice that transforms conventional narratives of acculturation and exile, and Hahn for her emotional depth and intellectual acuity, as she probes issues of women's subjectivity in dialogue with feminist and Marxist discourses while borrowing freely from Asian literary genres. Chitra Banerjee Divakaruni published a series of novels and short story and poetry collections, as did **G.S. Sharat Chandra** and the versatile and prolific **Meena Alexander**.

Not lost on these writers, most of whom were old enough to have had direct experience with or memory of the activism that had heralded the conceptual beginnings of Asian American literature, was the danger of co-optation. Many of the award-winning poets maintained commitments to principles of social justice and change, but it was clear that the recognition they received for their work was for their formal achievements—in a word, their works' artistry—and that this recognition entailed a diminished faith among the public at large in poetry as an instrument of social change. Many of these writers understood quite well that the recognition they gained placed them in a liminal space vis-à-vis the historical principles of ethnic studies.

Since the late 1980s, along with the numerous individually authored books of poetry, Asian American poetry (or combined poetry and prose) anthologies have proliferated. This fact testifies to the poetry's enhanced status in the literary marketplace and to its multiple constituencies, as demonstrated, for example, in such titles as *The Forbidden Stitch: An Asian American Women's Anthology* (1989), *Chinese American Poetry: An Anthology* (1989), *Living in America: Poetry and Fiction by South Asian American Writers* (1995), *Returning a Borrowed Tongue: Poems by Filipino and Filipino American Writers* (1996), *Watermark: Vietnamese American Poetry & Prose* (1998), and *Echoes Upon Echoes: New Korean American Writings* (2003). The return to writing marked by nation of origin does not constitute a rupture within the concept of Asian American poetry. Rather, it is a continuing recognition that within that broad framework, poetic production can acknowledge both similarities of experience and the diversities that enlarge cultural understandings, while precluding facile generalizations and stereotypes.

Nonetheless, two of the most influential anthologies have been multinational, coalitional ones. *The Open Boat: Poems from Asian America* (1993), edited by Hongo, and *Premonitions: The Kaya Anthology of New Asian North American Poetry* (1995), edited by Walter K. Lew, reveal differing conceptions of Asian American poetry. Hongo's anthology uses the open boat as a metaphor for poets writing in English whose ancestry lies in a wide range of cultural, geographical, and national Asian identities, whose political alignments are various, and whose sensitivity to language is paramount. Lew, in contrast, constructs an anthology filled with experimental writings and cross-disciplinary forms whose editorial purpose is to redefine Asian American poetry as a field of fluid, interpenetrating discourses, as opposed to a body of work marked primarily by ethnographic subject matter or conventional ideas of literary craft. Both editors situate their contributors within the framework of Asian American poetry and both remain hospitable to the poetic tradition of political resistance, but both also show their interest in acknowledging the variety of impulses the current poetry reflects.

In the early twenty-first century, the Asian American poetry scene has proliferated to the point that generalizations frequently unravel under careful scrutiny. Nevertheless, race, ethnicity, national origin, class, sexuality, and gender continue to be self-consciously inscribed in the writings, and to varying degrees poets remain aware of the cultural and political ideologies that preceded them. Timothy Liu continues his intense explorations of sexuality begun in the early 1990s, and anthologies such as *On a Bed of Rice: An Asian American Erotic Feast* (1995), *The Very Inside: An Anthology of Writings by Asian & Pacific Islander Lesbians & Bisexual Women* (1994), and *Take Out: Queer Writing from Asian America* (2001) have helped construct new literary paradigms for Asian America. Poets such as Kyoko Mori, Adrienne Su, Rick Noguchi, Tran Thi Nha, Vince Gotera, Alan Chong Lau, Barbara Tran, Dwight Okita, Hilary Pham, Stephen Shu Ning Liu, Russell Leong, Amy Uyematsu, Eugene Gloria, Leah Ann Roripaugh, Shirley Geok-lin Lim, and Maxine Hong Kingston explore issues of identity, conflict, history, race, class, and gender in a variety of engaging ways. So did the Kashmir poet **Agha Shahid Ali**, whose posthumous *Call Me Ishmael Tonight* (2003) brought to a close a luminous career. Walter K. Lew and **Myung Mi Kim**, following in the path of Theresa Hak Kyung Cha, grapple with issues of language and epistemology. The author of several volumes of poetry, including *Under Flag* (1991), *Dura* (1998), and *Commons* (2002), Kim rearranges language in startling patterns that call attention to the ideologies at work in conventional language practices and foreground the possibility of reconceptualizing the world, with its legacies of oppression and imperialism, through language. Koon Woon, in *The Truth in Rented Rooms* (1998), confronts the perils of living life in brutal urban centers, amidst drugs and prostitution, despair and mental derangement. Ha Jin, like a growing number of transnational poets, sets his poems either here or abroad. And as never before, there are multitudes of engaging newer works, including Eric Gamalinda's *Zero Gravity Poems* (1999), Rick Barot's *The Darker Fall* (2001), Oliver de la Paz's *Names Above Houses* (2001), Mong-Lan's *Song of the Cicadas* (2001), Wei Shao's *Pulling a Dragon's Teeth* (2003), Aimee Nezhukumatathil's *Miracle Fruit* (2003), and Wang Ping's *The Magic Whip* (2003).

Connectors to the literary tradition of the past thirty years are evident in journals and literary reviews, such as New York's *Asian Pacific American Journal* and the Colorado-based, multicultural *Many Mountains Moving*. They are evident as well through the academic periodicals *Amerasia Journal, Journal of Asian American Studies,* and *MELUS*, the first two of which remain devoted to the larger field of Asian American studies and the third to the study of the multiethnic literatures of the United States. Now out of publication, journals such as *Asian America: Journal of Culture and the Arts, Journal of Ethnic Studies,* and *Critical Mass* contributed variously to the literary and critical discourses constituting Asian America. New York's Asian American Writers' Workshop and Hawai'i's Bamboo Press continue to promote and publish the poetry of new and established writers. Popular on college campuses and in community gatherings, Spoken Word, also known as **performance poetry**, evokes memories of the oral/aural traditions of the 1960s and 1970s, often with the same blend of radical politics and affiliations with identifiable minority communities. While strongly influenced by rap, many Spoken Word artists are creatively aligned with writers like Jessica Hagedorn, who thirty years ago intuited the vital links among poetry, politics, and performance. Asian American poetry undoubtedly will continue to pursue a variety of directions in years to come. On the whole, however, its practitioners are unlikely to lose sight of the forces that first named, defined, and substantiated it— and in so doing secured its place within the political and cultural life of the continent.

Further Reading. ***Selected Secondary Sources:*** Bruchac, Joseph, ed., *Breaking Silence: An Anthology of Contemporary Asian American Poets* (Greenfield Center, NY: Greenfield Review Press, 1983); Chang, Juliana, ed., *Quiet Fire: A Historical Anthology of Asian American Poetry, 1892–1970* (New York: Asian American Writers' Workshop, 1996); ———, "Reading Asian American Poetry" (*MELUS* 21.1 [1996]: 113–132); Chin, Frank, et al., eds., *Aiiieeeee! An Anthology of Asian-American Writers* (Washington, DC: Howard University Press, 1974); Davis, Rocio G., and Sami Ludwig, eds., *Asian American Literature in the International Context: Readings on Fiction, Poetry, and Performance* (Munster: Lit, 2002); Hongo, Garrett, ed., *The Open Boat: Poems from Asian America* (New York: Anchor, 1993); Huang, Guiyou, ed., *Asian American Poets: A Bio-Bibliographical Critical Sourcebook* (Westport, CT: Greenwood Press, 2002); Lai, Him Mark, et al., eds., *Island: Poetry and History of Chinese Immigrants on Angel Island, 1910 to 1940* (San Francisco: San Francisco Study Center, 1980); Lew, Walter K., ed., *Premonitions: The Kaya Anthology of New Asian North American Poetry* (New York: Kaya, 1995); Tabios, Eileen, ed., *Black Lightning: Poetry-in-Progress* (New York: Asian American

Writers Workshop, 1998); Trudeau, Lawrence J., ed., *Asian American Literature: Reviews and Criticism of Works by American Writers of Asian Descent* (Detroit: Gale Research, 1999); Zhou, Xiaojing, "Rearticulating 'Otherness': Strategies of Cultural and Linguistic Differences in Asian American Women's Poetry," in *Asian American Studies: Identity, Images, Issues Past and Present*, ed. Esther Mikyung Ghymn (New York: Peter Lang, 2000, 151–177); ———, "Asian American Poetry: Diaspora and National Identity" (*Revista Canaria de Estudios Ingleses* 43 [2001]: 59–81).

George Uba

ATWOOD, MARGARET (ELEANOR) (1939–)

Best known for her novels, Margaret Atwood is one of Canada's most prominent and prolific contemporary writers. Atwood's fame, however, also rests on her voluminous contributions to the genres of poetry, the short story, and the essay. In the latter connection, her writings have appeared in a range of scholarly material, from college and university textbooks to important literary journals and anthologies. Publishing in several genres and in many venues, Atwood has become the most productive writer of her time in Canada. Her fiction has been widely translated, adding to her international renown.

Atwood was born to Carl and Margaret Killam Atwood in 1939 in Ottawa. The position of her father as a prominent entomological researcher had a profound effect on the eventual career of his daughter. Margaret Atwood discovered her interest in nature and natural phenomena at a very early age due to the site of her father's research, which was often the woods of Ontario and Quebec, where the family mostly spent their summers. One of the other major influences on Atwood's literary career was the work of the Romantic poet William Blake, whom she took an interest in through her teacher, the renowned critic and literary scholar Northrop Frye, while she was an undergraduate at University of Toronto.

The influence of Blake marks Atwood's first collection of verse, *Double Persephone* (1961), which in turn sets the tone and theme for the rest of her poetry. Not as conspicuous in their treatment of environmental and sociocultural issues as most of her later poetry, the poems in this collection almost unanimously highlight the perpetual contrast and inherent conflict between nature and the ways adopted by human beings to dominate it. *The Circle Game* (1966), for which Atwood received the prestigious Governor General Award in 1967, and which brought the poet to the attention of the literary world, developed the theme of contrast between humans and nature to the fullest. Conflict, in general, constitutes the backbone of most of Atwood's poetry, and in *The Circle Game* it extends to the strife that exists between genders, between art and nature, and between Canadians as a distinct nation and non-Canadians,

among other oppositions. The highly metaphoric use of language in most of the poems in this collection, most notably in poems like "Playing Cards" and "An Attempted Solution for Chess Problems," highlights the limitations men and women set for themselves in their interactions with the world, in the same way laws and regulations governing children's games are restricted to the games and not applicable to the world outside. By juxtaposing the artificiality of language and the constructive quality of art in general, on the one hand, with nature, on the other, Atwood reveals the arbitrariness of the rules that govern people's lives.

Atwood's next collection of poems, *The Animals in That Country* (1968), carries on the theme of conflict between humans and nature with a particular emphasis on environmental issues. The title poem in this collection contrasts nature and history with the way humankind has recognized them, addressing the distinct positions animals hold in different cultures; hence, the killing of the fox in England, with the huntsmen "around him, fixed / in their tapestry of manners," and, in Spain, the "elegant death" of the bull, "his name / stamped in him, heraldic brand" are contrasted with Canadian treatment of animals: In Canada, the animals are simply animals, and "Their deaths are not elegant."

Although most of the poems in *The Animals in That Country* address the more general issues of environment and the discrepancies between human beings and nature, some of the poems deal with more specific subjects, such as the alienation of people in a technological environment; in "What happened," for example, wires, no matter how sensitive, are unable to "transmit the impact of / our seasons, our catastrophes," while we inhabit them. Humans are far from each other, the poems suggest, but also far from their true nature.

A related subject occupies *The Journals of Susanna Moodie* (1970), which recounts the struggles of a pioneer woman in Canada. The conflict within the persona between her attachment to city life and the actual hardship of living on the prairies is the dominant theme, portrayed in poems such as "The Two Fires," in which, the speaker says, the fires have "left charred marks / now around which / I try to grow." This collection, unlike most of Atwood's books, is illustrated, so that the poetic imagery of natural phenomena such as fire and water, or man-made phenomena such as architecture and art, is heightened by the accompanying drawings.

In a general sense, all of Atwood's poems deal with a search for identity in deeper pre- or trans-human sources. In *Procedures for Underground* (1970) the power of the unconscious to shape the persona is taken to an unprecedented level; the artist becomes a shamanistic figure in touch with natural forces, advising that from the trees and rocks one can gain "wisdom and great power, / if you can descend and return safely."

As its title suggests, in her next collection of verse, *Power Politics* (1971), Atwood commits herself primarily to the elucidation of the relationship between the sexes and the definitions of gender roles in both personal and public spheres. Her caustic tone is prevalent throughout this collection of verse. Addressing the male partner, the speaker comments that "[l]ike eggs and snails [he has] a shell" to suggest his inaccessibility, adding that, like an invasive weed, he is "bad for the garden, / hard to eradicate."

The poems in *You Are Happy* (1974) continue the thread of feminist concerns, with only the concluding poems of the collection reflecting the optimism of the title. Thus in "Late August" the moment of joy is invited to linger, as "The air is still / warm, flesh moves over flesh."

The poems in her next collection, *Two-Headed Poems* (1978), capture the idea of two-sidedness as an inherent duality existing in all of us, personally and collectively. The title of the collection, however, refers more specifically to the dual, irreconcilable state of being a woman and a writer at the same time. This duality is best represented in the title piece, in which the narrator's two heads speak sometimes individually, sometimes together, and, "[l]ike all Siamese twins, they dream of separation." These poems also deal with the victimization of women in a patriarchal society, juxtaposing, as does Atwood's famous novel *The Handmaid's Tale* (1986), the constraints of women with the relative freedom of men.

True Stories (1981) suggests the trajectory of Atwood's work, beginning from this volume to expand from feminist concerns to still broader political issues, such as Amnesty International, and the injustice and abuse to which human beings in general are subjected. *True Stories* often becomes a sort of poetry of witness, recounting atrocities, mass burials, a self-mutilating woman, a suicidal friend. As observed by Linda Wagner-Martin, in these later poems Atwood has actively become a spokesperson for human rights (72). By contrast, *Murder in the Dark: Short Fictions and Prose Poems* (1983), which is either her tenth book of poetry or her seventh novel, depending on how the reader places the genre, is wittier, lighter, more postmodern, and offers shorter takes on a variety of topics, including male cooking and the art of writing.

Morning in the Burned House (1995), Atwood's twelfth book of poetry, is divided into five parts, with each part dealing specifically with one aspect of the narrator's life. The poems deal with both the past and the future, as metaphorically indicated by the two parts of the title "the Burned House" and "Morning." The poems range from the elegiac to the satirical and include a mystical meditation called "In the Secular Night," in which the speaker wanders through her house in search of God, reflecting that, several hundred years ago, her state of mind would have been seen "as mysticism / or heresy. It isn't now."

Further Reading.   *Selected Primary Sources:* Atwood, Margaret, *The Animals in That Country* (Toronto: Oxford University Press, 1968); ———, *The Circle Game* (Toronto: Anansi, 1998); ———, *Double Persephone* (Toronto: Hawkshead Press, 1961); ———, *The Journals of Susanna Moodie* (Toronto: Macfarlane Walter & Ross, 1970);); ———, *Morning in the Burned House* (Toronto: McClelland & Stewart, 1995); ———, *Murder in the Dark* (Toronto: Coach House Press, 1983); ———, *Power Politics* (Toronto: Anansi, 1971); ———, *Procedures for Underground* (Toronto: Oxford University Press, 1970); ———, *True Stories* (Toronto: Oxford University Press, 1981); ———, *Two-Headed Poems* (Toronto: Oxford University Press, 1978); ———, *You Are Happy* (Toronto: Oxford University Press, 1974). ***Selected Secondary Sources:*** Davey, Frank, *Margaret Atwood: A Feminist Poetics* (Vancouver: Talonbooks, 1984); Hollis, Hilda, "Between the Scylla of Essentialism and the Charybdis of Deconstruction: Margaret Atwood's *True Stories*," in *Various Atwoods: Essays on the Later Poems, Short Fiction, and Novels*, ed. Lorraine M. York (Toronto: Anansi, 1995); Hönninghausen, Lothar, "Margaret Atwood's Poetry 1966–1995," in *Margaret Atwood: Works & Impact*, ed. Reingard M. Nischik (Toronto: Anansi, 2000, 97–119); Sullivan, Rosemary, *The Red Shoes: Margaret Atwood Starting Out* (Toronto: Harper Flamingo, 1998); Wagner-Martin, Linda, "'Giving Way to Bedrock': Atwood's Later Poems," in *Various Atwoods: Essays on the Later Poems, Short Fiction, and Novels*, ed. Lorraine M. York (Toronto: Anansi, 1995).

Manijeh Mannani

AUDEN, W.H. (1907–1973)

Wystan Hugh Auden, a defining poet of the twentieth century, embodied many of the contradictions of his times and embraced those contradictions in his art, suggesting that it was only through a clear-eyed grappling with the competing obligations of individual love, civic responsibility, and ultimately, religious faith that art could contribute to a just society. The complex arc of his career, which he began as a British leftist avant-garde experimentalist and concluded as a United States citizen and Christian traditionalist, encompassed numerous other artistic identities, including celebrated public intellectual, literary critic, teacher, opera librettist, and unrivaled master of poetic form. Though widely admired throughout his career, he frequently challenged his audience's expectations for his work, and his commitment to matching the power of rhetoric to honest moral purpose provoked substantial controversy when he deemed some of his earlier work, including a number of his best-loved poems ("Petition," "Spain," and "September 1,

1939"), intellectually dishonest and excised them from his oeuvre, refusing to allow them to be reprinted. Influenced in his own early poetry by ancient Icelandic sagas, Hardy, **Dickinson**, Hopkins, **Frost**, and **Eliot**, and adopting countless other modes and styles over a career in which, he was proud to claim, he'd composed work in every existing poetic form, Auden would in turn play a crucial role in the evolution of twentieth-century poetry, influencing both his peers and several generations of younger poets who are still assimilating his legacy.

Auden was born in 1907 in York, a city in the north of England whose Viking heritage always pleased him, since he believed his own ancestry to be Scandinavian, and his enthusiasm as a boy for Norse sagas and mythology would prove to be one of the strongest and earliest literary influences on his own poetry. His father was a prominent physician in Birmingham, the gritty industrial capital of the British Midlands, to which Auden's family moved while he was a child, and in which he and his two older brothers would be raised in an upper-middle-class household defined by the extensive scientific and classical library of his father, and the piano on which his devout mother would play Anglican hymns. As described by Christopher Isherwood, Auden's oldest friend and closest literary collaborator, these two influences—his father's mode of scientific inquiry and his mother's tuneful religiosity—would serve as the twin pillars of Auden's mature art. "Auden is essentially a scientist," wrote Isherwood in 1937, as well as "a musician and ritualist" (Spender, 74). From his father, Auden "acquired the scientific outlook and technique of approach," and from his mother he learned "to be preoccupied with ritual in all its forms"(Spender, 74). Recalling their work together on the experimental verse dramas *The Dog Beneath the Skin* (1935) and *The Ascent of F6* (1936), Isherwood noted that Auden's childhood "high Anglicanism" had evaporated in the adult, atheist poet, "leaving only the height," and jocularly observed, "When we collaborate, I have to keep a sharp eye on him—or down flop the characters on their knees. . . . If Auden had his way, he would turn every play into a cross between grand opera and high mass" (Spender, 74).

This blend of the analytical and the reverential found its early idealized object in the geology and landscape of the Pennines and North Yorkshire moors, which the young Auden would visit on family excursions and holidays. What attracted the nascent poet was less the wind-swept natural beauty of the region than the lonely detritus of earlier doomed efforts at human habitation and mastery of the land, especially the crumbling ruins of ancient Roman walls, and the abandoned and rusting machinery and water-filled tunnels of a once-thriving mining industry that was already moribund by the time of Auden's childhood. "Tramlines and slagheaps, pieces of machinery, / That was, and still is, my ideal scenery," Auden would reflect in 1937's "Letter to Lord Byron," and "Allendale," a poem he wrote in 1924 at the age of seventeen, sounds a representative note of the young poet's sensibilities, combining his dual enthusiasms for archaic, saga-inspired diction and a similarly antiquated industrial landscape.

The early imaginative world of hushed and sepulchral industrial outbuildings, rail lines snaking through stony valleys, and unfathomable tunnels disappearing beneath ominous fells would set the defining tone for much of Auden's early work, in which this atmospheric but inscrutable landscape is matched by an equally intense rhetorical obscurity. In much of the poetry Auden wrote in the late 1920s and early 1930s, a strong sense of communicative urgency, often in the face of some unspecified but omnipresent danger, is countered by a powerful syntactic difficulty and evasiveness, giving early poems like "The Letter" (1927) a paradoxically insistent reticence, pointing toward its urgent concerns but, in the words of the poem, "always afraid to say more than it meant." In a poem like "The Secret Agent" (1928), this landscape of enigmatic foreboding gets mapped onto another of Auden's favorite early tropes, that of the poet as spy, reporting vital information from behind enemy lines but doomed to remain unheard or misunderstood by his readers.

Auden's image of the poet as hero-spy, engaged in a hazardous but crucial mission of detection and warning for an oblivious public, provides one of the governing motifs for his lengthy and difficult experimental work, *The Orators*, published in 1932, which mixes poetic and prose genres as it grafts that cloak-and-dagger ambience onto the decidedly more prosaic—though, in Auden's account, just as ominous—environment of the British public school. Building on Auden's own unhappy childhood experiences as a boarder at Gresham's School in Norfolk, the world of *The Orators* swings dizzyingly back and forth between the repressive and hierarchical milieu of the boarding school and that of a dashing and strong-willed airman who, from his privileged but dangerous vantage point in the skies, is able to survey and diagnose the ills of the world below. *The Orators* operates on at least three levels of discourse. First, it serves as a kind of solipsistic dialogue with the poet himself, full of private jokes and obscure allusions to intimate moments in Auden's own life that even his closest friends couldn't have been expected to understand. Second, it functions as a coterie document, speaking in a kind of privileged and difficult code to a select band of the like-minded. This reflects Auden's role at the time as the center of a group of young writers, artists, and friends that included Isherwood, Stephen Spender, Louis MacNiece, Cecil Day-Lewis, and Edward Upward, all of whom shared a certain post-Eliotic aesthetic sensibility alongside their progressive leftist politics. It also reflects Auden's attempt to write from a position of honesty about his homosexuality to those who would understand the poem's private, fraught symbolism, but not in a way that would risk exposure and attract the attention of the uninitiated, the unsympathetic, or the police. Third, *The Orators* also inaugurates Auden's ambition, which would gather force through the 1930s, to use his poetry to comment on issues of public and political concern; the school/battlefield serves as a clear figuration for an unhealthy body politic, and the entire multilayered text stands in answer to the question posed at its beginning by the headmaster to his students: "What do you think about England, this country of ours where nobody is well?"

While the figure of the heroic but dispassionate airman/artist in *The Orators* suggests that the twenty-four-year-old Auden was attracted by the idea of what he called "the truly strong man" as an answer to the enervation of his cultural moment, as the decade advanced, Auden's political thinking developed beyond this simplifying idealization and his poetry reflected this new complexity. He spent a year living in Berlin following his graduation from Oxford in 1928 and, joined there by Isherwood (who would famously memorialize those waning days of Weimar decadence in his *Berlin Stories*), he had seen the early ugly stirrings of Nazism firsthand. As the political face of Europe darkened, Auden's poems reflected both anxiety and an urge to respond productively to the threat gathering in Germany, Italy, and Spain. Throughout the 1930s Auden's poetry would oscillate between the dueling demands of private desire and his sense of broader political obligation to a world sliding toward catastrophe. In poems like "Lullaby" (1937) and "As I Walked Out One Evening" (1937), he explores the province of individual, ephemeral, erotic love, while in poems like "O What Is That Sound" (1932) and, most famously, "Spain" (1937), he addresses the looming specter of European Fascism. In poems such as "A Bride in the 30s" (1934) he suggests an inescapable link between the two.

As his poetry, along with the plays he was writing with Isherwood, became increasingly and more explicitly political, Auden rose to prominence not only as heir to T.S. Eliot as the most notable poetic voice of his generation, but as a standard-bearer for the British literary Left. Yet even as his work, like that of many of his artistic generation, reflected a serious engagement with Marxist ideals, and even as he traveled to Spain in 1936 to volunteer as an ambulance driver on the side of the anti-Fascists, Auden was never the ideologue that many of his fellow young artists were. Even "Spain," which speaks in stirring cadences of the necessity of "the struggle" against Franco, takes a characteristically complex, intellectual view of the conflict, suggesting its ancient roots in the evolution of European culture, and framing the Spanish Civil War as a grand dialectic of abstractions.

While Auden never wavered in his conviction that the evil of Fascism demanded resistance, as the 1930s came to an end and the unchecked advances of Franco, Mussolini, and Hitler made world war seem inevitable, he grew increasingly uncomfortable both with his public role as celebrity propagandist and with the idea that art itself had any role to play in a world in which, it seemed, no words he could write would stop the war from coming.

This growing ambivalence about poetry's place in the political world is expressed in one of his most famous poems, "Musee des Beaux Arts" (1938), which uses a reading of Brueghel's painting "The Fall of Icarus" to present the reader with the same dilemma the poet himself was facing: What is art's response, and responsibility, to human suffering? Does art merely witness, and record, the inevitability of suffering for posterity, such that it can be reflected upon in somber tranquility, like a painting in a museum? Or should it—*can* it—compel its audience to take action to remedy, or prevent, that suffering? The poem doesn't provide an easy answer to this question, and it was in the shadow of both this personal artistic crisis and the wider global crisis that Auden made the most dramatic and consequential decision of his career: He would leave England and emigrate to the United States.

Auden had always been a traveler, having made extensive, inquisitive trips not only across Western Europe but also to more far-flung locales like Iceland and China, which produced, respectively, the travelogues *Letters from Iceland* (1937) and *Journey to a War* (1939). And even while living in England he had rarely stayed in one place for very long. But his move to the United States was more than the latest example of the personal restlessness that had kept him on the move for much of his life. It was, in Auden's eyes, a firm break not only with the country of his birth, which had come to seem to him claustrophobic and parochial, but with the poetic identity that had made him famous. It would be a clean, blank page on which he could grapple with the problem of poetry's relation to the wider world and forge a new poetics in response to the melancholy truth asserted in the very first poem he would write upon his arrival in New York in January 1939, "In Memory of W.B. Yeats," which famously claims "[P]oetry makes nothing happen." Auden's departure, along with Isherwood, who had come to similar conclusions and accompanied him to New York (he would eventually settle in Los Angeles as a novelist, screenwriter, and prominent advocate of Vedantism), caused considerable consternation and anger back in Britain, where it was seen by many as a betrayal, at the nation's darkest hour, of the political ideals Auden had spent much of the 1930s seeming to represent. But if his apparent abandonment of his home provoked a bitterness that would color his British reputation for decades afterward, it also marked the beginning of a new, specifically American identity and career for Auden.

In New York, where he would live until the year before he died in 1973, Auden set about figuring out the kind of poetry the new realities of his changed life and a war-haunted world demanded, and he looked to his new home for guidance and inspiration. He saw in the polyglot bustle of the metropolis, and in the open expansiveness of the country he soon began to explore as he embarked on a series of short-term teaching jobs at high schools and colleges from Massachusetts to Pennsylvania to Michigan, a constructive model for this new poetry. For Auden, the United States offered a useful emblem, and a conducive working environment, for his developing notion that art's true function was not to compel people into specific political action, but to get them to engage with moral and intellectual complexity such that they would be led to act more justly in the world outside the poem. If poetry "makes nothing happen," it could still be "a way of happening," as he puts it in the Yeats elegy, not by telling its readers what to think, but by teaching them *how* to think, and forcing them to grapple with the problem of moral, intellectual, and existential choice. Articulating these ideas in lyric parables like "Atlantis" (1941) and in the long philosophical poem "New Year Letter" (1941), Auden frames America in specifically poetic terms, as a site of unresolved dialectic in which the traveler/reader/citizen must learn "the ways / To doubt that you may believe" and where he or she gains "the gift of double-focus"— the capacity to see the world from more than a single ideological perspective.

The years following his move to the United States were especially productive for Auden, as he wrote prolifically and gradually ensconced himself at the center of the American literary establishment. Through the 1940s he published a series of very long, cerebral poems on public, literary, and, increasingly, spiritual themes, including *For the Time Being* (1942), *The Sea and the Mirror* (1944), and *The Age of Anxiety* (1946), along with influential lyrics like "The Unknown Citizen," "Refugee Blues," and "September 1, 1939" (all 1939), "The Fall of Rome" (1947), "A Walk after Dark" (1948), and "The Shield of Achilles" (1952), that cemented his American and international reputation as a preeminent public intellectual, giving voice to the anxious moral climate of a world traumatized by global disaster. In one of his best-known poems of this period, "In Praise of Limestone" (1948), Auden makes an imaginative return to the sacred landscape of his youth, finding in the bleak, forlorn countryside of childhood memory an idealized figure for the

hope and forgiveness that had eluded him, and his generation, in the long dark years since he'd left that scenery behind: "[W]hen I try to imagine a faultless love / Or the life to come, what I hear is the murmur / Of underground streams, what I see is a limestone landscape." He was also an energetic and influential critic, editing numerous collections of other writers' work and publishing countless essays and book reviews in the major literary journals and newspapers, as well as teaching and lecturing extensively across the country, thereby helping to institutionalize the late-century phenomena of the academic creative writing program and the celebrity poetry reading. Under the influence of his partner, Chester Kallman, whom he'd met during his first year in New York, he also exercised a new enthusiasm for opera, which produced, among other notable libretti, a major contribution to the modern operatic repertoire, Stravinsky's *The Rake's Progress* (1951).

During this time, Auden also became an American citizen, and he took a civilian commission in the U.S. Army to visit Germany at the end of the war to survey the damage wrought by the Allied bombing on the cities he'd once happily visited, and reveled in, as a young man. This experience, and the devastation he witnessed, troubled him so deeply that he refused to speak of it upon his return to New York, and accelerated his doubts about the power of art to forestall, or withstand, human misery. Another important, and related, development in Auden's American life and work was his reconversion to the Christianity of his childhood. In poems written soon after his arrival in America, such as "In Memory of Sigmund Freud" (1939), "At the Grave of Henry James" (1941), and the elegy for Yeats, the latent spiritual sensibility Isherwood had diagnosed in his friend asserted itself in the poems' treatment of their subjects as something akin to intellectual saints, to whom the poet looks for guidance and worldly intercession. But increasingly, under the influence of a Kierkegaardian notion of the necessity of faith as a grounding for moral choice, Auden's poems moved toward an open embrace of Christianity as a source of meaning and order in a tragic and irrational world. Auden's turn toward religion, while still displaying the same restless questioning and intellectual rigor that characterized all his work, didn't please some of his readers, who preferred the mix of irony and idealism in his early poems to the mix of faith and philosophy in the later work. This newfound spirituality, coupled with a perceived retreat toward what the critic **Randall Jarrell**, a disappointed former champion of Auden's work, derisively and influentially termed a "comfy" domesticity—typified in his 1966 volume *About the House*, containing a meditative sequence of poems on each room in his little summer home in Kirchstetten, Austria—contributed to a critical conception of Auden's final decades as being somewhat diminished in comparison to the brashness and formal innovation of his earlier career. This consensus has been undergoing a challenge in recent years, as critics have pointed to substantial thematic, formal, and moral continuities between the early and later phases of Auden's career, and have suggested that the same rigorous commitment to truthfulness that governed his early, reticent poetry, "always afraid to say more than it meant," gives his later work, which insisted on confronting the evolution of his own perspective and ideas, a similar quality of brave and bracing honesty.

Whatever the vicissitudes of critical opinion, it is difficult to overstate the significance of Auden's arrival in the United States to the course of American poetry. His American contemporary **Richard Eberhart** noted at the time, "Auden's coming to America may prove as significant as Eliot's leaving it," and his judgment proved prophetic. From his public role as critic, reviewer, and arbiter of important literary awards like the Yale Younger Poets Prize, to the private encouragement he offered the many young writers he welcomed into his shabby Greenwich Village apartment, Auden exercised an immense influence over the development of postwar poetry in the United States. As a voice on a page, a teacher, and, in many cases, an individual mentor who helped foster their beginning careers, Auden played a crucial role in the work and lives of an entire generation of younger American poets who came to artistic maturity in the years following his arrival in New York, including poets as diverse and numerous as **Ginsberg**, **Plath**, **Wilbur**, **Schuyler**, **Merwin**, **Hollander**, **Rich**, **Merrill**, **O'Hara**, and **Ashbery**. In remaking himself into an "American" poet, he helped the poets who followed him discover what American poetry in the late twentieth century, and beyond, could be.

Further Reading. *Selected Primary Sources:* Auden, W.H., *Collected Poems* (New York: Random House, 1991); ——, *The Dyer's Hand* (New York: Random House, 1990); ——, *The English Auden* (London: Faber & Faber, 1988; ——, *Juvenilia: Poems 1922–1928* (Princeton, NJ: Princeton University Press, 2003); ——, *Selected Poems* (New York: Random House, 1979). *Selected Secondary Sources:* Boly, John, *Reading Auden: The Returns of Caliban* (Ithaca, NY: Cornell University Press, 1991); Carpenter, Humphrey, *W.H. Auden: A Biography* (Boston: Houghton Mifflin, 1981); Fuller, John, *W.H. Auden: A Commentary* (Princeton, NJ: Princeton University Press, 1998); Hecht, Anthony, *The Hidden Law: The Poetry of W.H. Auden* (Cambridge, MA: Harvard University Press, 1993); Hynes, Samuel, *The Auden Generation* (Princeton, NJ: Princeton University Press, 1982); Mendelson, Edward, *Early Auden* (New York: Farrar, Straus and Giroux, 2000); ——, *Later Auden* (New York: Farrar, Straus and Giroux, 1999); Spender, Stephen, ed., *W.H. Auden: A Tribute* (New York: Macmillan, 1975).

Aidan Wasley

AUSTIN, MARY (1868–1934)

Seen as a regional writer of the Southwest, Mary Austin always addressed the human connection to nature in her essays, novels, short stories, dramas, and poems. Nature is so influential that, for Austin, the connection to the environment is reflected in each of a person's social actions. Austin's poetry also draws upon her extensive knowledge of Native American expressions, or what she called in her poetry a "re-expression" of cultures governed by natural cycles.

Born on September 9, 1868, in Carlinville, Illinois, Mary Hunter was a creative and rambunctious child of a Civil War veteran, George Hunter, and Susan Savilla Graham, whose ancestors were the town founders. As a small child, Mary was captivated by the large walnut tree at her home. She would later claim in her autobiography, *Earth Horizon*, that under this tree she first found spirituality. Indeed, she would spend the rest of her life in a spiritual quest through the natural environment. When she was age ten, Mary's father and sister both died. At sixteen, Austin attended Blackburn College, where she spent two years taking mostly science courses. She loved writing but felt that she could teach the craft to herself. When she graduated at eighteen, she followed her brother, James, reluctantly, to Southern California, abandoning her home and the rest of her family. Her sense of powerlessness at this point in her life would result in the feminist themes of her writing. She married Stafford Wallace Austin on May 19, 1891, and the couple moved to the southern side of Owens Valley, California. Mary Austin stayed in Owens Valley for fourteen years, and it is there that she learned about Native Americans, in particular the Paiutes and Shoshones, cultural influences that are featured extensively in her writing. The next year, Austin published her story, "The Mother of Felipe" in the *Overland Monthly*, and she gave birth to her daughter, Ruth. Despite many serious setbacks—a developmentally disabled daughter, an estranged relationship with her husband, and a hopeless relationship with her mother—Austin was publishing poems, sketches, and short stories by the turn of the century. These publications brought her into literary circles and also gave her the opportunity to build a house in the California coastal town of Carmel in 1906. Austin would go on to publish several more works, including *The American Rhythm*.

In *The American Rhythm*, a study of Amerindian poetry, Austin notes how the rhythm of life for Native Americans is tied to nature. They believe that their songs, dances, and prayers can affect the course of nature. If all people were more in touch with their environment, Austin suggests, they would recognize their own role in nature's creative force, and everyday life could be turned into art. Austin believed this transformation would happen, and that it would take place first in the American Southwest, where the very land, the mountains, and the rivers were inspiring. In the presence of these features all people would come to see their spiritual connection to nature. Many of her poems, including her earliest, reflect this belief.

Austin's only published poetry collection appeared in 1928 and was titled *The Children Sing in the Far West.* Some of these poems were written many years earlier, when the young Austin was teaching school,and she would often have her class read them. The poems are simple and can be memorized and recited easily. "The Sandhill Crane," for example, playfully describes how the "minnows scuttle away in fear, / When the sandhill crane goes walking." Though many of the animals are frightened by the stalking crane, its actions are part of nature and the cycle of life. In another poem, "Whisper of the Wind," the poet struggles to find a word to describe the wind; once she thinks she has it, it skips away from her again. The poem suggests at once the ephemerality of language and the inexpressibility of nature.

Though Austin published over thirty novels in addition to other essays and sketches, the poet and critic Mark Van Doren thought that she should abandon other forms of writing and focus on poetry. The originality of Austin's poems can be felt in "Western Magic," in which she creates an unforgiving picture of the rugged desert terrain, and notes that it is unsuited for the "fairy-folk" of European folklore, who would perish from thirst and whose wings would get torn on the cacti. Instead of fair-

ies, the desert is inhabited by entities from Native American lore, such as Spider Woman, who mends the sky, Johano-ai, Pelado Peak, and the Rainbow Boy. And even older than the mythic figures, Austin thought, are the real insects and animals that live in the desert of the Southwest: the black beetle, prairie dog, snake, and tecolote (owl).

Perhaps her most vivid example of the theme of one's mystic connection to nature is her poem "When I Am Dead." Here the speaker explains that, once dead, she will no longer be worn down by physical experience but will be free to consort with the birds and the flowers and with others who have perished. Austin was truly interested in the betterment of society, but she believed that this betterment could be achieved only by discovering what T.M. Pearce calls "the fundamental patterns in human relationships" (123), which are the patterns of life and death and the earth's seasons. Every pattern has its own rhythm, and, for Austin, a rebirth can occur only if one becomes conscious of the rhythms of nature.

Further Reading. ***Selected Primary Sources:*** Austin, Mary, *The American Rhythm* (New York: Harcourt Brace, 1923); ———, *Children Sing in the Far West* (Boston: Houghton Mifflin, 1932); ———, *Earth Horizon: An Autobiography* (Boston: Houghton Mifflin, 1932). ***Selected Secondary Sources:*** Brooks, Paul, *Speaking for Nature* (New York: Houghton Mifflin, 1980); Pearce, T.M., *Mary Hunter Austin* (New York: Twayne, 1965).

Earl Yarington

AVANT-GARDE. *SEE* EXPERIMENTAL POETRY AND THE AVANT-GARDE

B

BACA, JIMMY SANTIAGO (1952–)

Jimmy Santiago Baca's remarkable life fuels his imagination, and knowing about it is essential for understanding his poetry. His childhood was filled with chaos and sorrow: He was abandoned by his parents, briefly raised by his elderly grandparents, and then sent with his brother to live at an orphanage, until he ran away at the age of thirteen. The barely literate Baca then survived as a street fighter and drug dealer. At twenty-one he was convicted on felony drug charges and sent to Florence State Prison in Arizona. During his six years of incarceration, a wheelchair-bound World War II veteran who corresponded with Baca as part of a church program turned his life around. Unable to read the only letter he had ever been sent, Baca eventually determined it was from this veteran, a man named Harry, and was inspired to teach himself to write. Harry gave Baca a dictionary, and they continued to correspond. Learning to read, write, and engage with poetry became Baca's way of coping with prison life. Baca saturated himself with the poetry and images of William Wordsworth and **Emily Dickinson** to protect himself from the savage, violent images that surrounded him in prison, and to attain a measure of peace, redemption, and self-identity.

Immigrants in Our Own Land, Baca's first collection of poems, was published initially in 1973 and reissued in 1991. These are Baca's prison poems of isolation and sal-vation. They also concern his childhood and abandonment, particularly the poem "Ancestor," in which he still speaks of his father with admiration and wonder, since "to meet him, you must be in the right place, / even his sons and daughter, we wondered," but also with sadness, for "they were hands that had not fixed our crumbling home, / hands that had not taken us into them."

The poetry in Baca's next collection, *Martin and Meditations on the South Valley* (1987), focuses on identity. Here Baca looks to his subconscious to recall aspects of the Chicano, Indian, and Mestizo cultures within his poetry. In *Martin* Baca offers a different view of the Chicano experience than the usual rural description. His own experience had been that of a slick city kid, like millions of others who live without any literary models to reflect their experiences. Baca wrote *Martin* to give them dignity. In "V" the speaker says, "[N]othing to do, no where to go, / comb my hair in the blue tinted office windows," and "entangled in the rusty barbwire of a society I do not understand, / Mejicano blood in me spattering like runoff water." Baca clearly expresses the isolation of city-dwelling Chicanos.

November 1989 brought Baca the Wallace Stevens Award for his *Black Mesa Poems*. This collection moves Baca in a more positive direction as he continues to exalt his heritage in "Greene Chile," remembering a visit to his grandmother: "bandanna round her forehead, /

mysterious passion on her face," and the possibilities for the future in "A Daily Joy to Be Alive," when he reminds himself that "I do not live to retrieve / or multiply what my father lost" and ends with the inspired "I can see treetops!" *Healing Earthquakes* (2001) was a departure for Baca from his usual poetry. Baca uses his powerful **lyrical** style to describe an intense journey through the human soul to create a romance that is explored through a series of poems in book form. Baca introduces a man and woman before they meet, and the reader then follows the couple's extensive range of emotions from beginning love to devastating breakup. In this series of poems, Baca manages to create characters with whom the like-minded reader is able to identify. Baca's latest collection of poems, published in 2004, focuses on a deeply spiritual part of himself, using the Rio Grande as his metaphorical midwife to define and reinterpret his life in *Winter Poems Along the Rio Grande*. Living in isolation by the Rio Grande and using it as inspiration enables Baca to feel close to nature and its regenerative powers.

The remarkable story of Baca's life and his ability to rise above seemingly insurmountable odds is the kind of story that can and has inspired others. However, that is not why Baca decided to write his autobiographical novel, *A Place to Stand* (2001). He wrote the book because he wanted his sons to know the full story of his personal transformation and not to be confused by rumors and gossip. Baca could never get information about his father's or grandmother's history from them, but he wanted his sons to have the knowledge of his history so they could gain both courage and honor in order to live better lives. Baca's story continues to encourage and inspire young writers. Baca's latest book is a collection of short stories, *The Importance of a Piece of Paper* (2004), that focuses on disenfranchised characters struggling for a place in the world, a topic never far from Baca's poetry. Many of these stories revolve around the conflict between old world traditions and new world realities.

After emerging from prison, Baca went on to receive a BA in English from the University of New Mexico in 1984 and then a Ph.D. in literature in 2003. Since receiving his first award in 1986, the National Endowment for the Arts Literary Fellowship, Baca went on to receive the Vogelstein Foundation Award in 1987; the Pushcart Prize in 1988; the American Book Award for Poetry and the Wallace Stevens Endowed Chair at Yale University in 1989; the International Hispanic Heritage Award and the Berkeley Regents Chair at the University of California–Berkeley in 1990; the Southwest Book Award in 1993; the Endowed Hulbert Chair at Colorado College in 1995; the Humanitarian Award in Albuquerque in 1997; and the Barnes and Noble Discover Author as well as the International Prize for *A Place to Stand* in 2001. The

professional accolades that Baca has received for his work certainly validate the power of his poetic voice, but this recognition is secondary to his desire to share his experiences with others so that they, too, can achieve their dreams.

Further Reading. *Selected Primary Sources:* Baca, Jimmy Santiago, *Healing Earthquakes* (New York: Grove Press, 2001); ———, *Immigrants in Our Own Land* (New York: New Directions, 1991); ———, *The Importance of a Piece of Paper* (New York: Grove Press, 2004); ———, *Martin and Meditations on the South Valley* (New York: New Directions, 1989); ———, *A Place to Stand* (New York: Grove Press, 2001). ***Selected Secondary Sources:*** Crawford, John, and Annie O. Esturoy, "Jimmy Santiago Baca," in *This Is About Vision: Interviews with Southwestern Writers*, ed. William Balassi, John Fr. Crawford, and Annie O. Eysturoy (Albuquerque: University of New Mexico Press, 1990, 181–193); Haba, James, ed., *The Language of Life: A Festival of Poets* (New York: Doubleday, 1995).

Alisa M. Smith-Riel

BAKER, DAVID (1954–)

One of the ablest poets of an able generation that includes **Carolyn Forché**, **David St. John**, and **Elizabeth Spires**, David Baker is best described as a poet who defies categorization. Defined to some extent by his native midwestern locale, he is not bound by it; his preoccupation with the landscape of personal memory is balanced by an ongoing engagement with American literary history. Indeed, American Romantic writers rank as his most notable influences and subjects. Although his poetry tends toward formalism, he is hardly an adherent of the **New Formalism**. Clearly influenced by the **New Criticism**'s conception of the "well-made poem," he nevertheless continues to test the versatility of the **lyric** form.

Baker was born December 27, 1954, in Bangor, Maine, and grew up in Missouri. Son of a surveyor and mapmaker, he earned his baccalaureate and master's degrees from Central Missouri State University and completed his doctoral studies at the University of Utah in 1983. Baker's works include six volumes of poetry and two book-length critical studies entitled *Meter in English* (1996) and *Heresy and the Ideal* (2000). He currently teaches at Denison University in Ohio.

Deftly assimilating influences as diverse as **Walt Whitman** and **W.S. Merwin**, Baker is primarily a poet of lyric epiphanies, one who skillfully exploits the tension between syllabic regularity and rhythmic flexibility in each line. In his first collection, *Laws of the Land* (1983), he displays a gift for select imagery and vibrant metaphor. For example, in "Antonyms: Morning and Afternoon Near the Osage River," Baker scans the landscape with an eye for detail, sorting out "scores of arrowheads, from thumbnail-size bird points / to spearheads long as boots." Describing with lapidary elegance artifacts sifted from the mineral earth, the poet resurrects the culture of an indigenous people long vanished. *Haunts* (1985) consolidates and expands the artistic gains of Baker's previous volume, revisiting his abiding themes of life, death, time, and mutability. In "The Catfish," the young speaker's father slits the white-bellied bottom-feeder into the spring: "Out slide all the black and bloody entrails." As the dark viscera uncoil, the boy notices "a green sack," eggs suspended like pulsing nebulae in a primal ooze. Through a commingling of Eros and Thanatos, Baker's protagonist experiences his first intimations of the eternal paradox.

The lengthy title poem of Baker's third volume, *Sweet Home, Saturday Night* (1991), ostensibly pays homage to Lynrd Skynrd's "Sweet Home, Alabama," and draws on his own skill and experience as an accomplished country rock and **jazz** guitarist. The setting is a roadhouse on Route 63 in Missouri, dubbed the "Com-On-Inn." Here Baker often resorts to the spoken vernacular, as his playing drives a beer-soaked, jeans-and-satin crowd to an orgiastic frenzy, a veritable saturnalia that gives way to Dantesque phantasmagoria: "I vamp down to G, plucking and teasing / a note so loud it will ignite." The poet lends Orphic utterance to the still, sad music of humanity, his Gretsch fretting plaintively as he works the ache of those strings into callused fingers. In a polyphonic interlude, he remembers his grandmother's life of toil at a J.C. Penney fabric counter and hearkens once more to her sturdy admonition, "*Sore hands make a strong heart,* and shows me again her pin- / swollen fingers and her calluses gray as nickels." Baker's nine-part, multi-layered poem becomes a vast paean, a trope for all laboring class people who crave a weekend's escape from the daily grind.

Although cunningly wrought and replete with felicity of phrasing, *After the Reunion* (1994) proves a transitional volume that rehearses themes more fully realized in *The Truth about Small Towns* (1998). In the latter book, Baker explores the transient landscape of middle America, observing in the title poem, "the remnant industry of a dying town's itself." "Dust to Dust" is a series of five lyric vignettes describing a stretch of brick road laid by men of the Works Progress Administration during the Depression. No three-ton tandem roller embedded into sand the kiln-fired clay surface that the speaker strolls upon decades later; instead, men went down on their knees and hand-tamped the bricks: "They tapped in bricks from the limekiln one season. / They turned each one one-quarter twist the next." The poet remembers his own father returning from the road crew each evening "burned and hurt" and notes how his own life is still attuned to each tremor of passing traffic: "Four blocks down the road gives way to asphalt blacktop. / But here the block stamp MACON BRICK hasn't rubbed off." Within the indelible phrase "MACON BRICK" lies a rubric for the fusion of clay and spirit, the durable masonry that "wrecked the knees" of many fathers, yet offered the speaker both a way out of poverty and a pattern for "one thing made so well."

Baker's sixth volume of poetry, *Changeable Thunder* (2001), extends his obsession with the twenty-first century's slow but inexorable encroachments on the landscape and townships of the American Midwest. However, his vision expands to include seminal figures from the nation's shaping past, encompassing such theological, philosophical, and aesthetic forebears as **Edward Taylor**, **Samuel Sewall**, **Cotton Mather**, **Ralph Waldo Emerson**, and **Walt Whitman**. "Romanticism" pursues the evolution of American literary history by exploring an extraordinary notation found in the journals of Emerson: "I visited / Ellen's tomb & opened the coffin." Ellen Tucker, Emerson's bride of less than eighteen months, succumbed to tuberculosis at the age of twenty; she had been dead scarcely a year when he walked from Boston to the family vault in Roxbury and broached the locked casket with a brass key. What he saw is not recorded, but Baker participates in his fellow poet's terrible confrontation, devising an elliptical lyric structure that manipulates a continuous parallel between Emerson's loss and his own brush with mortality. Recovering from a fever, he notices how an almost other-worldly evanescence still clings to the Ohio landscape barbed with hoarfrost and bramble. Baker envisions the Concord sage pacing off his own aesthetic and philosophical tract of ground, printing the rimed and oozing sod with a deft, sure-footed measure. However, Baker is chagrined when his young daughter happens abruptly on the dessicated, "slug-riddled" carcass of a deer, an event resulting in her loss of innocence. Baker's ability to embody more than one vessel of consciousness, his gift for striking imagery, and his knowledge of the myriad phonetic connotations inherent in poetic diction suffuse "Romanticism" with an aura of immediate experience. **Marilyn Hacker** has called David Baker "the most expansive and moving poet to come out of the American Midwest since **James Wright**." The comparison does honor to both poets when Baker is at the top of his form.

Further Reading. *Selected Primary Sources:* Baker, David, *After the Reunion* (Fayetteville: University of Arkansas Press, 1994); ———, *Changeable Thunder* (Fayetteville: University of Arkansas Press, 2001); ———, *Haunts* (Cleveland: Cleveland State University Poetry Center, 1985); ———, *Heresy and the Ideal: On Contemporary Poetry* (Fayetteville: University of Arkansas Press, 2000); ———, *Laws of the Land* (Boise, ID:

Ahsahta Press, 1981); ———, ed., *Meter in English: A Critical Engagement* (Fayetteville: University of Arkansas Press, 1996); ———, *Midwest Eclogue* (New York: W.W. Norton, 2005); ———, *The Truth about Small Towns* (Fayetteville: University of Arkansas Press, 1998). **Selected Secondary Sources:** Byrne, Edward, "To Remember and to Articulate the Past: David Baker's *Changeable Thunder* and *Heresy and the Ideal: On Contemporary Poetry*" (*Valparaiso Poetry Review* 3.2 [Spring/ Summer 2002], http://www.valpo.edu/English/vpr/ byrnereviewbaker.html).

Floyd Collins

BALBUENA, BERNARDO DE (1562?–1627)

Bernardo de Balbuena stands out in Hispanic letters for having written all his works while away from Spain, in the recently discovered continent of America. Like the Chroniclers of Indies, Balbuena used his pen to glorify his country while describing and praising the New World. Therefore, the dilemma surrounding Balbuena is whether he was a Spanish or an American poet. Indeed, the latter predominates, as the epithets given to him can attest: the "First American Poet" and "Patriarch of American Poetics." Angel Rama called Balbuena the "Founder of Poetic Mannerism," and others classified him as "Pioneer of the American Baroque." For Octavio Paz, Balbuena was responsible for the birth of American nature and wildlife poetry, and Anita Arroyo argues that he conquered the natural habitat of America both physically and spiritually through his poetic strength. Balbuena is an example of assimilation to the adoptive land (Luis Adolfo Domínguez), the first "human transplant" from the Old to the New World that became his homeland until his death. However, as stated in his poetry and in letters written to the various kings of Spain during his lifetime, he wanted to go back to his motherland and be buried there.

Balbuena was born in Valdepeñas, a small town in the province of Ciudad Real in the region of La Mancha, Spain, between 1562 and 1563. While the exact date of his birth is still problematic, that of his death is not: Balbuena died on October 11, 1627, in Puerto Rico and was buried in the Chapel of Saint Bernardo in the Cathedral of San Juan. He embarked for the New World in 1584 and settled in San Pedro Lagunillas in the New Galicia, where his father was already living. Balbuena was not taken to Mexico when he was a two-year-old toddler, contrary to conventional understanding; he was raised by his mother, Francisca Sánchez de Velasco, in Valdepeñas. José Rojas Garcidueñas established the fact in his second edition of Balbuena's biography.

In the early seventeenth century Balbuena became the first transatlantic literary figure to publish his works in both Madrid and Mexico. Indeed, Balbuena traveled various times between the two cities while in the process of publishing his **pastoral** novel, *Siglo de oro en las selvas de Erífile* (*Golden Age in the Woods of Erífile*, 1608). He went often to Mexico City to participate in poetry contests that he usually won. In 1606, upon finishing a law degree at the University of Mexico, Balbuena sailed back to Spain to earn a doctorate in theology from the University of Sigüenza. Balbuena, poised for high ecclesiastical position in the New Spain or in Peru, sought favors from the crown and the church. However, his desires were not fully granted, and he had to accept more humble appointments in Santo Domingo, and as abbot of Jamaica and bishop of Puerto Rico.

Bernardo de Balbuena is primarily known for his *Grandeza mexicana* (*Mexican Grandeur*), published in Mexico in 1604. This **long poem** includes an introductory royal octave, the verses of which serve as titles for the eight chapters that comprise the work. Each chapter is written in triplet stanzas ending with a quartet. The poem is a descriptive letter for a Spanish lady, Isabel Tobar y Guzmán, who had requested his opinion about the city where she was planning to live. At the same time that Balbuena admires Mexico City, he glorifies Spain for conceiving it as the crown jewel of the Hapsburg Empire overseas. Balbuena's depictions of Mexico and the New World are Eurocentric insofar as any allusions to native, indigenous, or *criollo* realities are either masked by European airs or are absent. In fact, the only mention of a Native American appears at the end of the poem referring to "the ugly Indian," whose newly appointed purpose in life was to collect and load the gold onto caravels sailing back to Spain. Balbuena exalts the city planning, the fine architectural design, the elegance of the people, the pomp and circumstance of daily life, and every other realm of human endeavor, just as Hernán Cortés had done decades earlier in his long and eloquent letters to Charles V (Charles I of Spain). Whereas the conquistador marveled at the solid construction of Aztec dwellings, temples, and towers that were destroyed, Balbuena praises their reconstruction. He memorializes the transformation of Tenochtitlan, the Aztec capital built in the middle of a lake on a high plateau, into a European metropolis, or a New Arcadia. The addendum to *Grandeza mexicana* comprises Balbuena's *Compendio apologético en alabanza de la poesía* (*Apologetic Compendium in Praise of Poesy*), a comprehensive theoretical treatise on the aesthetic foundations of poetry.

His second work, *Siglo de oro . . .* , in the classic form and content of Sannazaro and written in a genre that had lost its momentum, presents the fantastic underground, dreamlike passage of the protagonist from the shadows of Old Europe onto the brightness of a new territory: Mexico City. Consisting of twelve eclogues, the sixth one marks the transition and symbolic birth of a new race with its roots still deeply set in the ways of the Counter-Reformation.

Finally, his 1624 poem, *El Bernardo o Victoria de Roncesvalles* (*Bernardo or the Victory at Roncesvalles*), is a monumental **epic** in the tradition of Vergil, Ovid, Ariosto, and Boyard. With forty thousand stanzas composed in royal octaves, *El Bernardo* is dedicated to the eighth-century Spanish legendary hero Bernardo del Carpio, who is thought to have defeated Roland and the Twelve Peers of France in the famous Battle of Roncesvalles. Here, the poet creates a metaphor after his own name, Bernardo: the soldier who conquered with the power of the sword and the writer who, eight hundred years later and in recently discovered lands, was conquering readers with the power of the written word.

Siglo de oro. . . and *El Bernardo* were published in Madrid alongside works of Balbuena's contemporary writers who never crossed the ocean. Among others, Miguel de Cervantes in his *Viaje del Parnaso* (*Voyage to Parnassus*, 1614) and Lope de Vega in his *Laurel de Apolo* (*Apollo's Laurel*, 1630) praised Balbuena for his erudite renditions. He, who witnessed the reign of the Habsburg kings Phillip II, Phillip III, and Charles II, became the first author to reconcile Spain's old glories and its imperial ventures over the vanquished Meso-American civilization. Bernardo de Balbuena is recognized among other Spanish Golden Age writers for making accessible to the people of Spain an idealized geography along with the saga that unfolded on the other side of the Atlantic.

Further Reading. ***Selected Primary Sources:*** Balbuena, Bernardo de, *El Bernardo. Poema heroico* (Madrid: Gaspar y Roig, 1852; facsimile Guadalajara, Jalisco: UNED, 1989); ———, *La Grandeza mexicana y Compendio apologético en alabanza de la poesía*, ed. Luis Adolfo Domínguez (México: Porrúa, 1997); ———, *Siglo de Oro en las selvas de Erífile*, ed. José Carlos González Boixo (Xalapa: University of Veracruzana, 1989). ***Selected Secondary Sources:*** Hintze de Molinari, Gloria, "Intertextualidad manierista en la *Grandeza mexicana* de Bernardo de Balbuena" (*Revista de Literaturas Modernas* 24 [1991]: 197–210); Madrigal, Luis Iñigo, "*Grandeza mexicana* de Bernardo de Balbuena o El interés, señor de las naciones" (*Revue Suisse des Litteratures Romanes* 22 [1992]: 23–38); Perelmuter, Rosa, "¿Merece la pena leer *El Bernardo*? Lectura y lectores del poema épico de Bernardo de Balbuena" (*Revista Iberoamericana* 61.172–173 [1995]: 461–466); Sabat-Rivers, Georgina, "Las obras menores de Bernardo de Balbuena" (*Revista de Crítica Literaria Latinoamericana* 22.43–44 [1996]: 89–101).

Asima FX Saad Maura

BANG, MARY JO (1946–)

Always wry, and never linear, Mary Jo Bang's poems leap from image to image, from idea to idea, like watergliders on quickly moving streams. Because of the speed and quirky disjointedness of her poems, Bang, who is the author of four collections of poetry, has become known as a member of the elliptical school, the poetic movement that emerged in the last decade of the twentieth century. Although her poems are highly stylized, they are not empty of meaning; Bang's work probes deeply into the **postmodern** experience and has grown increasingly theoretical and inquisitive over the course of her career. Intense areas of interest include romantic love, the construction of female subjectivity, and pictorial art. Arch, whimsical, enigmatic and dreamlike, Bang's poems are as much about voice as they are about content; one of her most significant contributions is the invention of a voice that is deeply representative of its cultural and historical era. Bang is a popular and well-recognized poet, whose work is emblematic of the postmodern **lyric** consciousness.

Bang was born on October 22, 1946, in Waynesville, Missouri, where she was raised by her mother and stepfather. Bang's beginnings were humble; neither of her parents had completed high school. She overcame family resistance to pursue a college degree at Northwestern University, where she majored in sociology, graduating summa cum laude in 1971. She completed a master's at Northwestern in 1975. Bang received certification as a physician's assistant from St. Louis University and later pursued a career as a professional photographer in Chicago, having received a second BA in 1989 in photography from Westminster University in London. A relative latecomer to the professional life of poetry, she received her MFA in poetry at Columbia in 1998. Bang has taught at the University of Montana; she is currently associate professor at Washington University in St. Louis. She has served as poetry co-editor of *Boston Review* since 1995. Her poems have appeared in innumerable journals, including *American Letters & Commentary*, *Denver Quarterly*, the *Nation*, the *New Republic*, the *New Yorker*, *Paris Review*, *Ploughshares*, and *Yale Review*. Her honors and awards include the "Discovery"/*Nation* award, the Katherine Bakeless Nason Prize for Poetry, the Great Lakes College Association New Writers Award, a Hodder Fellowship at Princeton, and an Alice Fay di Castagnola Award, Poetry Society of America.

Bang's first book, *Apology for Want*, appeared in 1997, the recipient of the Bakeless first book award. More accessible than her later work, some of the poems in her debut collection could be described as personal or autobiographical. By the same token, they do adumbrate the more experimental future of her work: The poems skip rapidly from one idea to another. The first poem in the collection, "Waking in Antibes," moves from trilobites to Ganesha to the Virgin Mary to graffiti. While the early work demonstrates some of the shape-shifting quality that is so characteristic of Bang, many of the poems are more tightly controlled, depicting personal incidents or anecdotes through lyric. Physical infirmities or disasters recur here as subjects; Bang describes a child with Down syndrome, a drug addict with an abscessed arm, a house fire, and a heart operation. Bang examines the role of the poet in relation to these subjects: Is the poet a witness or a voyeur?

Bang's fanciful second book, *Louise in Love* (2001), tells the story of the fictional title character. More rhythmic than her first collection, and considerably less realistic, the poems construct a universe for Louise that is familiar but slightly off: "The girl in the icy-blue coat gave them her eyes / only to take them right back." It's a realm of beautiful objects illuminated by desire, inspired by the silent film star Louise Brooks. In this non-narrative narrative, which seems influenced by **John Berryman**'s *Dream Songs*, Louise vacillates in her desire for her lover, the pithy Ham: "Facts, said Ham, too often confide an edifice / with no hint of what hides behind." What happens is less important than how it is told: "They moved blindly backwards / and away from the text that failed to find their eyes."

The Downstream Extremity of the Isle of Swans (2001), Bang's third collection, draws its title from Samuel Beckett's *Ohio Impromptu*. As Bang's work has progressed, it has grown more difficult to gain entrance to; her third collection demonstrates a poetic practice in which the sound and texture of the word is valued more than the meaning. "Comfort is brazen. / Caution a train" (6). **John Ashbery** is clearly an influence, as is **Gertrude Stein**. Her fourth volume, *The Eye Like a Strange Balloon* (2004), finds its focus in **ekphrasis**; each of the poems in the collection is about a different work of art. The artworks she describes are as various as Willem de Kooning, Cindy Sherman, Picasso, and David Lynch, but the description is characteristically off-kilter and absurd. She deploys the artworks principally as a means to examine subjectivity and to address the unanswerable question of how mortality affects us: for her, art "is the depth of whatever has deepened / an abbreviate existence" (2). Bang's work can clearly be connected to a field of poets influenced by the experiments of the **New York School**; however, her quirky tyle and idiosyncratic diction are a creation entirely her own.

Further Reading. *Selected Primary Sources:* Bang, Mary Jo, *Apology for Want* (Hanover, NH: Middlebury College Press, 1997);———, *The Downstream Extremity of the Isle of Swans* (Athens: University of Georgia Press, 2001); ———, *The Eye Like a Strange Balloon* (New York: Grove Press, 2004); ———, *Louise in Love* (New York: Grove Press, 2001). ***Selected Secondary Sources:*** Bendall, Molly. "Review of *Louise in Love*" (*Prairie Schooner* 77.3 [Fall 2003]: 185); Burt, Stephen, "Happy as Two Blue-Plate Specials" (*New York Times* [21 November 2004]: 26); Conley, Susan,

"Review of *Apology for Want*" (*Ploughshares* 23.4 [Winter 1997]: 214); Kaufman, E.M., "Review of The Eye Like a Strange Balloon" (*Library Journal* [15 January 2005]: 116); Zaleski, Jeff, "*Louise in Love*" (*Publisher's Weekly* 247.45 [6 November 2000]: 84).

Amy Newlove Schroeder

BANGS, JOHN KENDRICK (1862–1922)

John Kendrick Bangs made a name for himself writing comic, often savage, spoof fantasy. This specialty led to the coining of the term "Bangsian Fantasy," or a fantasy set in the afterlife. Philip Jose Farmer's *Riverworld* series draws its inspiration from this genre.

Bangs was born in Yonkers, New York, in May 1862. His father, Francis N. Bangs, was a prominent New York attorney. His grandfather, the Reverend Nathan Bangs, DD, served as America's first historian of the Methodist Church and the first editor of a Methodist paper. Additionally, the elder Bangs served as president of Wesleyan University in Middletown, Connecticut. Following an education comparable to that of other wealthy northeastern sons, Bangs graduated from Columbia University with a degree in philosophy. He studied law in his father's office for a year and a half, but his true interest in literature found him writing humorous sketches. These served as an entrée to *Life* magazine, where he was named editor. Shortly after his marriage, Bangs traveled abroad in 1887, published his first book, *Roger Camorden, a Strange Story*, and, with classmate Frank Dempster Sherman, produced a volume of humorous and satirical pieces entitled *New Waggings of Old Tales*.

Returning to America, he retired from *Life* to devote himself to larger projects, including travesties on *The Taming of the Shrew* and *Mephistopheles*, that brought him greater popularity. Turning to children's literature, the father of three boys published *Tiddledywink Tales* in 1891, the first in a series of four books that launched him as a contributor of juvenilia to numerous literary syndicates. His first widely successful work, *Coffee and Repartee*, premiered in 1893, followed by books at regular intervals, including the first in *The Idiot* series, that were a liberal reader's delight. Turning his unsuccessful 1894 run for mayor of Yonkers into the entertaining *Ten Weeks in Politics*, Bangs attributed his defeat to his refusal to transform his house into a beer garden for some local German serenaders. He graciously accepted a position on the board of education, wryly observing that "politics and humor do not mix, unless you happen to be a cartoonist." Combining his keenly accurate wit with a charismatic presence, Bangs also lectured on the topic of humor, most notably delivering an address on "The Evolution of the Humorist from Adam to Bill Nye." The turn of the century found him working as editor of *Harper's Weekly* while continuing prolifically to churn out novels, collections, nonfiction offerings, and additions to his *Idiot* series, including *The Idiot at Home* (1902), *The Inventions of the Idiot* (1904), *The Genial Idiot* (1908), and *Half-Hours with the Idiot* (1917). Bangs died in New York in 1922.

Though Bangs was known primarily for his humorous spoofs, he also penned verses, primarily found in his volume *Cobwebs from a Library Corner* (1899). Even as he addresses seemingly solemn topics, there is usually a biting edge in the lyrics' tone and phrasing. For instance, in his poem "To a Withered Rose," Bangs cannot help but counter the anticipated gravity of the fading bloom with a sharp reflection, "was it not thy happy lot / To live and die a rose?" As in most Bangsian humor, the piercing observation urges the listener to ponder the truth of the wry words.

His focus on the afterlife, the great unknown, allows him to undertake ruminations on the world's complexities with the simplicity of understatement. Like his contemporary Mark Twain, his wit is revealed as he reflects on past experiences with the knowledge gained through those events. His ability to perceive what many overlook is particularly evident in his verse titled "May 30, 1893." In this poem a group of children come to play on a former battlefield, not knowing it was where "once the cannon's breath / Laid many a hero cold and stark in death." By chance the children leave a wreath of wildflowers over the unmarked, forgotten site of a fallen soldier.

Bangs takes up the writer's task—to see that which is unseen. As in most intelligent humor, there is also the touch of sorrow underscoring the humanity and, thus, increasing the listener's ability to identify with the subject and the speaker.

This proverbial nature is most clearly expressed in Bangs's poem "The Little Elf." When the poem's narrator mets an elf and inquires why he is so small, the elf with evident glee replies, "I am quite as big for me." Bangs believed that "humor is as necessary to the home as is the cooking stove. I mean good, healthy humor. It eases the mind and it becomes an educator; it fills and makes pleasant many a long night; it gives encouragement to the wanderer; it relieves the tired mother of the burden of her cares; it encourages men and women to look on the bright side of life, and the bright side is the only side which should be exposed to view." Hence, his verses unveil an aspect of life and its complexities too often missed.

Further Reading. ***Selected Primary Sources:*** Bangs, John Kendrick, *The Bicyclers, and Three Other Farces* (New York: Harper, 1902); ———, *Coffee and Repartee* (New York: 1893); ———, *A House-Boat on the Styx* (New York: Harper, 1902); ———, *Mr. Bonaparte of Corsica* (New York: Harper, 1895); ———, *The Pursuit of the House-Boat. Being Some Further Account of the Divers Doings of the Associated Shades,*

under the Leadership of Sherlock Holmes (New York: Harper, 1897).

Roxanne Y. Schwab

BARAKA, AMIRI (1934–)

For more than four decades Amiri Baraka (known as LeRoi Jones until 1968) has used his ability and inclinations as a writer to fight the injustices of racism, capitalism, imperialism, and Western hegemony. Few North American poets of the past century have achieved Baraka's level of public recognition or have incited the controversy he has. His pronouncements customarily explore the most pressing political issues of the day, incorporating critical analysis, independent thinking, and personal introspection. Baraka's maverick insights and political orientation, in conjunction with a willingness to speak the unspeakable with force and acuity, are the basis of all of his work.

From the beginning of his career Baraka has worked in multiple written forms, including drama and prose; complemented performances of his work with musical accompaniment; and produced and exhibited paintings and drawings that often include text. At times Baraka has been a proponent of violence; early on some of his utterances were self-admittedly anti-Semitic, a viewpoint he says he has neither condoned nor written from since the 1970s, though the matter arose powerfully in recent years as a result of his 2001 poem "Who Blew Up America?" Because of these inflammatory issues, the discussion surrounding Baraka's work is ofen highly charged. Yet Baraka's versatility and influence as an artist are virtually unmatched, even if they are often overlooked in favor of his divisive points of view.

The overt ideological and societal concerns presented by Baraka puts him in a small literary cadre that includes **Beat** generation author **Allen Ginsberg**. From the beginning of his literary career in New York City during the late 1950s, Baraka held great appreciation for, and intellectually identified with, Ginsberg. Both authors had been born in Newark, New Jersey, where Baraka was raised and has lived most of his life. After attending Newark public schools, then Rutgers and Howard Universities, Baraka enlisted in the Air Force in 1954, without having received a college degree. His service career was educational, though not as a result of his military training. "But in every way, like it or not, pleasant or not," Baraka writes in *The Autobiography of LeRoi Jones/Amiri Baraka*, "the service was my graduate school or maybe it was undergraduate school" (114). As a result of his position as a part-time librarian at a base in Puerto Rico, he had access to classical books and music, which he voraciously consumed before his discharge as "undesirable" in 1957. At this juncture, he settled in Greenwich Village, where he lived and produced several important works until 1965.

Though Baraka mainly worked apart from Ginsberg, and often held differing perspectives on contemporary social issues, there was an intrinsic connection between the two men. This connection is illuminated by Baraka in his 1997 testimony to Ginsberg, "Blues for Allen," which identifies their shared objective as "that fundamental struggle for an American poetry. For our speech and consciousness as part of the energy and power of the United front against the dead and their ghosts" (5).

Among his other early guides Baraka acknowledges— as did Ginsberg—the projectivist poets and another New Jerseyan, **William Carlos Williams**, whose emphasis on attention to the local and writing in one's own "speech" reverberates throughout Baraka's poems. Numerous other creative, thoughtful, and culturally historic figures have also inspired his efforts. Baraka's deep understanding of writers such as **W.E.B. DuBois**, Paul Robeson, and Mao Tse Tung, and musical artists such as Miles Davis, Albert Ayler, and Sarah Vaughan is projected in his own expressions and has influenced his methods and purpose. In terms of his poetry, Baraka is also clearly indebted to the multifaceted agenda and inclinations toward resistance promoted by the authors associated with **negritude**, who had been influenced in part by the **Harlem Renaissance**. The type of deep, acerbic affirmations depicted in works such as Aimé Césaire's *Notebook of a Return to the Native Land* reverberate in Baraka's writing. The constantly evolving inscription of personal soul searching, discovery, and defiance of oppression that characterizes negritude are prominent in his work. Such expression for Baraka takes shape, as it has historically, in the re-invention of contemporary speech, the invocation of African art, and the oral transmission of language as its fundamental axis.

This trans-African effect and sensitivity, with its emphasis on black art, minimal in his first two volumes, gained force when Baraka's poetic and cultural disposition shifted drastically in the mid-1960s. After the assassination of Malcolm X, Baraka left behind the family he had started with his first wife, Hettie Jones, with whom he had two children, as well as his predominantly white and Eurocentric artistic milieu, in favor of cultivating African-American communities and afrocentric arts. He founded the **Black Arts Movement** and the Black Arts Repertory Theater in Harlem (1965) before permanently returning to Newark the next year and establishing Spirit House, a black cultural center at which theatrical works and artistic publications were produced until 1974. At this time he rejected black nationalism for its narrowness in scope; his ideological horizons became reformed in order to address the broader evils of the capitalist system. Essentially, Baraka began to view the oppressive circumstances faced by people everywhere as a matter of class instead of race.

Baraka has since raised five children with his wife Amina, continues to edit and produce numerous volumes of writing, organize events, and involve himself with socially oriented initiatives. Because of his predisposition toward **small press** and self-publishing, it is difficult to determine with precision the number of books of poetry Baraka has produced, but in all he has authored more than forty known titles as essayist, poet, dramatist, historian, and critic. Beyond his prodigious output as a writer, Baraka also has edited several influential poetry anthologies, including *Black Fire: An Anthology of Afro-American Writing* (with Larry Neal, 1968) and *The Moderns: An Anthology of New Writing in America* (1963). He has always promoted poetic arts by establishing independent publishing groups and magazines throughout his career. He was publisher of Totem Press and *Yugen* magazine in the 1950s, and then *Floating Bear* and *The Cricket* in the 1960s. At present, his efforts as an editor involve the production of the political arts newspaper *Unity and Struggle*, as well as his own small press imprint, RAZOR.

Baraka was employed as a professor in the Africana Studies Department at SUNY–Stony Brook from 1979 to 1999 and has also taught at Yale, Columbia, Rutgers, and other universities. During his career he has been the recipient of numerous awards, including fellowships from the Guggenheim Foundation (1965), the Rockefeller Foundation, and the National Endowment for the Arts (1981), and the American Book Awards' Lifetime Achievement Award (1989). In 2002 he was inducted into the American Academy of Arts and Letters.

Music has always been the primary source of inspiration for Baraka. From his earliest works onward—including his influential prose studies on the form, *Blues People* (1963) and *Black Music* (1968)—he has shown profound reverence for, and identification with, **jazz** and **blues** musicians, who are collectively referred to as "the priests of pure wisdom, in essence a voice of the people" in an editorial that appeared in the first edition of a short-lived magazine co-edited by Baraka and Larry Neal, titled *The Cricket* (1968). "Music is my life," writes Baraka in his autobiography. "It opens me into the deeper sensitivity of the world, what it is really about, past our worlds" (314). This relationship with, and appreciation for, sound—its power and politic—provides Baraka with, as **Nathaniel Mackey** observes, a "dual role of impulse (life-style or ethos as well as technique)" (24). Baraka's understanding of music has always added a beneficial component to his writing and has permitted the verbal structures and improvisations found in his work. For example, each segment of the 1995 collection *Wise, Why's, Y's*, a long poem about African American history written in the style of the African griot, is tuned to a specific piece of music identified at its outset. These poems, as usual, call for awareness and movement against systemic colonialism and racism with typical urgency of voice. The motivations of the poem include establishing the lineage of African American artists with whom he shares affinities, including **Langston Hughes**, Zora Neale Hurston, and Duke Ellington.

Beginning in the 1960s, Bakara began to perform his works with musical accompaniment. He has collaborated and produced recordings with the leading artists of his time, including the New York Art Quartet, Sun Ra Arkestra, Max Roach, and David Murray. Since the 1990s he has performed and toured widely with a group of local musicians, Blue Ark. Since the 1990s Baraka has developed an extensive sequence of deliberately short poems, given the designation "Low Coups" and posited as "the African American version of the haiku," which are sung and presented in a musical setting during performances. These works are direct, aphoristic, sometimes crude or irrational, and, as usual, sociopolitically charged. Several works written in this style were used as captions in Baraka's 2003 collaboration with the visual artist Theodore A. Harris, examples of which appeared in the journal *Callaloo*.

The greatest uproar surrounding Baraka's work involved the poem "Somebody Blew Up America," written a month after the September 11, 2001, terrorist attacks in New York and Washington. The poem, which begins with the assertion that all reasonable people reject both domestic and international terrorism, but that "one should not/be used/to cover the other," raises questions about who may be defined as a terrorist and who is responsible for the traumas and atrocities of the past few hundred years ("who got fat from plantations / who genocided Indians"). The most inflammatory passage was that in which Baraka suggested that the Jews knew the attack on the trade towers was coming, since, as Baraka suggests, they stayed at home on September 11. "Somebody Blew Up America" also implicates the KKK, high financiers, politicians, government agencies, the mass media, and others guilty, in Baraka's view, of crimes against humanity, including those who persecuted Jews ("who put the Jews in ovens / and who helped them do it"). The poem itself, while perhaps not the literary achievement of Ginsberg's "Howl," became, at least briefly, a text of comparable notoriety. The chief rhetorical device of the poem is the catalogue of questions rather than of direct charges. Baraka has effectively used this interrogative approach—said by Mackey to suggest an "uncertainty principle" (44)—since his very first collection, *Preface to a Twenty Volume Suicide Note*, in which questions like "Where are the beasts?" and "Are you singing?" punctuate the poem "The Clearing." Indeed, compared with aggressive lines found in early works, such as in his second volume, *The Dead Lecturer*'s "Black Dada Nihilismus" (e.g., "Rape the white girls. Rape / their fathers. Cut the mothers' throats"), the poet's inquiries in "Somebody Blew Up America," are

probing and speculative rather than blunt. Nevertheless, some of these questions—including who "told 4000 Israeli workers at the Twin Towers / to stay home that day," or who warned off Ariel Sharon from visiting—drawing upon rumors circulating throughout the New York metropolitan area and on the Internet, and widely embraced in the Arab world, are certainly troubling.

Nearly a year later, after reading the poem at the Geraldine R. Dodge Poetry Festival in September 2003, Baraka, who had been appointed poet laureate of New Jersey two months earlier, became a subject of scrutiny and attack on a level unmatched by any of his—or anyone else's—previous poetic exploits. The judgment that Baraka was again making pronouncements critical of Jews was spread widely; the controversy was reported in newspapers and on television across the continent. Baraka's defense was that his indictment was directed at all forms of oppression, exploitation, and injustice, including the actions and policies of Israel and the United States' own political strategies and allegiances. Ultimately, the governor of New Jersey asked Baraka to apologize and resign as poet laureate. When Baraka refused to do so, the state legislature drafted a bill allowing them to terminate the existence of his position. He nonetheless honored his initial agreement with the state, to promote poetry in schools and in the public sphere, without receiving the compensation stipulated in his contract.

Since the publication of *The Dead Lecturer*, Baraka's poems have always meant to agitate, probe, and disturb; cultivating these strategies to invoke such effects has been among his primary intentions as a writer. He is unafraid to use outrageous or irrational means to convey a point he wishes to make, re-think, or repudiate. Whether or not a reader construes Baraka's views to be accurate or inaccurate, it is clear that he has taken on the poet's duty to investigate, to question with sense and impulse, the world in which he lives. At his own expense, he draws attention to what he sees as his work's most charged elements. Each of his many initiatives exists to promote, project, and otherwise support revolutionary art.

Further Reading. *Selected Primary Sources:* Baraka, Amiri, *The Autobiography of LeRoi Jones/Amiri Baraka* (Chicago: Lawrence Hill, 1997); ———, "Blues for Allen" (*Blacklisted Journalist* [July 1998], http://www.blackmagic.com/pages/ blackj/column35.html); ———, *The Dead Lecturer* (New York: Grove Press, 1964); ———, *The LeRoi Jones/Amiri Baraka Reader* (New York: Thunder's Mouth Press, 1991); ———, *Preface to a Twenty Volume Suicide Note* (New York: Totem/Corinth, 1961); ———, *Somebody Blew Up America & Other Poems* (Philipsburg, St. Martin: House of Nehesi, 2003); ———, *Transbluesency: The Selected Poems of Amiri Baraka/LeRoi Jones (1961–1995)* (New York: Marsilio,

1995); ———, *Un Poco Low Coup* (Newark, NJ: Razor Editions, 2003); ———, *Wise, Why's, Y's* (Chicago: Third World Press, 1995); Baraka, Amiri, with Theodore A. Harris, "Our Flesh of Flames" (*Callaloo* 26.1 [2003]). **Selected Secondary Sources:** Harris, William J., *The Poetry and Poetics of Amiri Baraka: The Jazz Aesthetic* (Columbia: University of Missouri Press, 1985); Harris, William J., and Aldon Lynn Neilsen, "Somebody Blew Off Baraka," (*African American Review* 37.2–3 [Summer/Fall 2003], Amiri Baraka issue); Mackey, Nathaniel, "The Changing Same: Black Music in the Poetry of Amiri Baraka," in *Discrepant Engagement: Dissonance, Cross-Culturality, and Experimental Writing* (New York: Cambridge University Press, 1994).

Christopher Funkhouser

BARLOW, JOEL (1754–1812)

Joel Barlow celebrated America as a model of progress in commemorative, philosophical, and epic poems. A key figure in American politics noted for his varied and entrepreneurial talents, Barlow was a poet, army chaplain, lawyer, journalist, real estate agent, merchant, and diplomat. Barlow is now perhaps best known for his nostalgic poem of childhood *The Hasty-Pudding* (1796) and his depiction of the horrors of war in *Advice to a Raven in Russia*, written in 1812 but not published until 1938.

Joel Barlow was born on March 24, 1754, in Redding, Connecticut. In 1772 Barlow attended Moor's Indian School, founded by Eleazar Wheelock, who described Barlow as a "middling scholar" possessed of "sober, regular, and good Behavior." In August 1774 Barlow enrolled at Dartmouth College but later transferred to Yale College. The Revolutionary War interrupted Barlow's college years, and in 1776 he fought in the Battle of Long Island. After graduating from Yale in 1778, Barlow served as chaplain for the Third Massachusetts Brigade. In January 1781 Barlow secretly married Ruth Baldwin despite her father's objections to Barlow's limited prospects.

In 1787 Barlow's *The Vision of Columbus* was published and successfully received. With newfound celebrity, he became an agent for the Scioto Land Company and set sail for Paris in 1788, with Ruth joining him in 1790. Though the company proved fraudulent, Barlow was not legally embroiled. Strained finances, however, caused him to extend his stay. During his next seventeen years abroad, Barlow became a persuasive pamphleteer and successful merchant who associated with key reformists including Thomas Paine, Mary Wollstonecraft, Joseph Priestly, Thomas Jefferson, William Godwin, and General Lafayette. As consul to Algiers, 1795–1797, Barlow negotiated the release of over 100 American seamen held hostage and enslaved for ten years by maritime highjackers. In 1804 the Barlows returned to America and settled in a mansion, Kalorama ("beautiful view"), which became a gathering place for Washington's inner circle. In 1811 President James Madison sent Barlow to France as minister plenipotentiary to negotiate a treaty with Napoleon. Barlow was summoned to the Russian front, a 1,400-mile, three-week journey. The meeting was jettisoned as Napoleon's campaign collapsed, and in the attempt to outrun the fleeing troops, Barlow's envoy traveled for ten days in sub-zero temperatures. Barlow died of pneumonia in Zarnowiec, near Cracow, Poland, on December 26, 1812.

Barlow belonged briefly to a group known as the "Connecticut Wits," who collaborated on satirical, polemical verse; the group's members included Yale graduates **Timothy Dwight**, **John Trumbull**, **David Humphreys**, Noah Webster, and **Lemuel Hopkins**. Their best-known poem is a mock-heroic **epic**, *The Anarchiad: A Poem on the Restoration of Chaos and Substantial Night* (1786–1787), directed against Daniel Shays and the general political unrest following the Revolution.

In Barlow's own work, he continued to address political themes and moral issues. *The Vision of Columbus* (1787), a philosophical poem in nine books with over 5,000 lines of heroic couplets, opens with Columbus in prison at the end of his life and relays his vision for a New World, with lessons on geography and history. J.A. Leo Lemay notes that this work "marks the first important use of American Indian mythology in poetry" (10). It boasted a subscription list of 769 prominent names, including King Louis XVI of France, the Marquis de Lafayette, Benjamin Franklin, George Washington, and approximately 200 members of the Revolutionary Army. Living abroad and witnessing the French Revolution had radically changed the views of the once conservative Yale student. *The Columbiad* (1807), published twenty years after *The Vision*, is more consonant with Barlow's deistic beliefs and Jeffersonian republicanism. Dedicated to his good friend Robert Fulton, who assisted with the engravings, the elaborate volume cost $10,000 to publish and sold for $20 a copy. Based on *The Vision*, *The Columbiad* was not, however, deemed successful because of its strained poetics and uneven control. Barlow did make several interesting changes, though, such as replacing the angel who guides Columbus with the mythological figure of Hesper, the genius of the Western world. Cecelia Tichi points outs that "the Christian trinity is replaced by a 'holy triad' of 'EQUALITY, FREE ELECTION, and FEDERAL BAND'" (28). In each version, Milton's *Paradise Lost* and Virgil's *Aeneid* were important influences. Other sources include William Robertson's *History of America* (1777) and Garcilaso de la Vega's *The Royal Commentaries of Peru* (1688). Barlow proved more successful in "The Hasty Pudding" (1793), a mock-heroic, mock-**pastoral** work divided into three cantos that trace the growing, preparation, and eating of this native New England dish: "First in your bowl the milk abundant take, / Then drop with care along the silver lake / Your flakes of pudding; here at first will hide / Their little bulk beneath the swelling tide" (III, 332–335). From such light-hearted lines, "Hasty Pudding" has often been characterized as a nostalgic, witty poem, occasioned by Barlow's visit to Savoy, where he was offered a bowl of cornmeal mush. Lemay finds the poem far more substantive, as it "reflects late eighteenth-century **avant-garde**, radical thought" and addresses "politics, language, religion, and myth," while considering the "nature of men and the bases for culture" (3).

Barlow wrote his final poem, *Advice to a Raven in Russia* (1812), after witnessing the horrors of Napoleon's ill-fated Russian campaign. It begins with the speaker questioning the raven: "Black fool, why winter here? These frozen skies, / Worn by your wings and deafened by your cries, / Should warn you hence, where milder suns invite" (1–3). When the carnage increases, Napoleon's legacy is made clear: "War after war his hungry soul requires, / State after state shall sink beneath his fires" (73–74). As these lines and the surrounding circumstances attest, Joel Barlow was an impassioned, ambitious figure who risked personal safety and family happiness to promote America as an ideal through poetry and prose and in his political and diplomatic endeavors.

Further Reading. *Selected Primary Sources:* Barlow, Joel, *Advice to the Privileged Orders in the Several States of Europe, Resulting from the Necessity and Propriety of a General Revolution in the Principle of Government. Part 1* (New York: Childs & Swaine, 1792) and *Part 2* (New York: Childs & Fellows, 1794); ———, *The Columbiad: A Poem* (Philadelphia and Baltimore: Conrad, Lucas and Co., 1807); ———, *The Conspiracy of Kings; A Poem: Addressed to the Inhabitants of Europe, from Another Quarter of the World* (London: J. Johnson, 1792); ———, *The Hasty-Pudding: A Poem, in Three Cantos* (New Haven, CT: 1796); ———, *A Poem: Spoken at the Public Commencement at Yale College, in New Haven; September 12, 1781* (Hartford, CT: Hudson & Goodwin, 1781); ———, *The Prospect of Peace. A Poetical Composition, Delivered in Yale-College* (New Haven, CT: Thomas & Green, 1778); ———, *The Vision of Columbus; A Poem in Nine Books* (Hartford, CT: Hudson & Goodwin, 1887); Barlow, Joel, with David Humphries, John Trumbull, and Lemuel Hopkins, *The Anarchiad: A New England Poem* (New Haven, CT: Pease, 1861). *Selected Secondary Sources:* Lemay, J.A. Leo, "The Contexts and Themes of 'The Hasty-Pudding'" (*Early American Literature* 17 [1982]: 3–23); Tichi, Cecelia, "Joel Barlow" (*Dictionary of Literary Biography: American Writers of the Early Republic* 37 [1985]: 18–31); Woodress, James Leslie, *A Yankee's Odyssey: The Life of Joel Barlow* (New York: J.B. Lippincott, 1958).

Susan Clair Imbarrato

BARNES, DJUNA (1892–1982)

An eclectic and experimental writer, Djuna Barnes figures prominently in twentieth-century **avant-garde** and **modernist** literature. Best known as a novelist, Barnes was also a prolific and imaginative journalist, illustrator, playwright, and poet. Her fictional and visual work bears witness to her interest in folklore, medieval and Renaissance literature, music and art history, as well as her concern for questions of gender identity and sexuality. Barnes's extraordinary taste for wordplay and for experimentation with language, genre, and subject matter have won her the admiration of some of the most important writers and intellectuals of her age, but have also led to a mis-recognition of her work among the reading public and literary critics, who have considered it obscure and often obscene.

Djuna Barnes was born in 1892 in Cornwall-on-Hudson, New York. She did not receive any formal schooling until she moved to New York City in 1912. There she attended the Pratt Institute and the Art Students League and started working as a journalist and illustrator for various newspapers and magazines. She often illustrated her feature articles, which are characterized by an understanding and empathy for her subjects, as well as an ironical tone and insightful comments.

Living in Greenwich Village, Barnes came into contact with the most important figures of the resident bohemian and intellectual circles, including Carl van Vechten, Edmund Wilson, Eugene O'Neill and **Edna St. Vincent Millay**. In 1915 Barnes published her first volume, *The Book of Repulsive Women*, a collection of eight "rhythms" and five drawings in Beardsleyan style, as part of the series *Bruno's Chap Books*. Moreover, Barnes's collaboration with the Provincetown Players, of which Eugene O'Neill and Edna St. Vincent Millay were also members, led to the production between 1916 and 1923 of some of her numerous short plays, written for magazines and journals under the pseudonym of Lydia Steptoe. During these years Barnes also published some stories in Margaret Anderson and Jean Heap's *The Little Review*.

After a brief marriage Barnes moved to Paris in 1920 to work as a correspondent for *McCalls Magazine*, where she remained until the beginning of World War II. During those years she traveled across Europe and to Africa before briefly returning to New York. While in Paris she also wrote for the *New Yorker*, *Vanity Fair*, and the *New York Tribune*. She also met many literary expatriates, including James Joyce, **T.S. Eliot**, **Ezra Pound**, **Gertrude Stein**, Samuel Beckett, Man Ray, **Mina Loy**, Sylvia Beach—the first publisher of Joyce's *Ulysses*—Janet Flanner, silverpoint artist Thelma Wood—who became her lover—as well as Natalie Barney and Peggy Guggenheim, who became her patrons for many years to come.

The 1920s were an extremely productive decade for Barnes. In 1923 she published *A Book*, a collection of **lyrical** poems, short stories, drawings, and one-act plays, which was revised and reprinted in 1929 as *A Night among the Horses*. The year 1926 saw the publication of her most famous work, *Nightwood*, an extremely complex novel that rejects traditional narrative forms and challenges sex and gender norms. In 1928 *Ryder* and *Ladies Almanack* came out. The former is a bawdy parody of the genres of the *Bildungsroman* and the picaresque novel, interspersed with references to American and European folklore and music, written in mock Elizabethan English and illustrated with Barnes's own drawings, stylistically reminiscent of the illustrations in medieval books of hours. *Ladies Almanack*, published anonymously, shares some of the formal characteristics of *Ryder*, including the drawings, but focuses on a group of female characters gathered around the figure of "Dame Musset," the lesbian heroine of the book.

For a long time Barnes's poems were neglected by critics and the literary world because of the inaccessibility and rarity of the printed copies available, but also because of prejudices toward Barnes as an eccentric and obscure figure—prejudices that were easily projected onto her writing. The exception was *Nightwood*, which T.S. Eliot introduced into the modernist canon. *Nightwood*'s prose, as Eliot recognized, owes much to Barnes's poetic talent, and indeed she wrote poems all her life, even though very few of them have been published. Much as it is difficult to find common traits, her poems are characterized by the juxtaposition of traditional meter and rhythm with jarring images, a satire of middle-class conventions, and an interest in mechanisms of the construction of identity through the body. Her writing is emblematic, focusing on specific objects and visual images, which become tools to explore the potentialities and ambiguities of language.

In *The Book of Repulsive Women*, the five drawings that were placed at the back of the original edition accompany five of the eight poems in the current edition. In line with the style of the drawings, which recalls the work of Aubrey Beardsley, the texts in this volume refer back to the tradition of European **symbolism**. The female bodies portrayed in the book are decaying, grotesque, and excessive, defying normative "femininity." The bodily fluids and sounds, the inability of these bodies to keep within boundaries, are vital and productive but also expose the aberration inherent in the cultural representation of the female body and identity. Thus, in "Seen from the 'L,'" the body of the central figure is represented as blooming, fleshy, and vital, but this also constitutes a "repulsive truth." The reiteration of images and sounds, the juxtaposition of musical rhythms and visual patterns which would traditionally not fit the subject matter are also part of a strategy of repetition by which

gender categories and imagery are subverted and acquire new meaning.

Between 1911 and 1923 Barnes wrote approximately thirty poems, only a few of which were collected in *A Book*. These poems, lyrical and austere in tone, speak of memory, loss, and love. The attention to minor natural events and to small objects and animals endows some of the poems with an idyllic atmosphere. However, reassuring genres and tropes are constantly subverted through the juxtaposition of threatening images and the exploitation of the potential ambiguities of language: In "Pastoral," grapes bleed and ferns hide hissing adders; in "Lullaby," both the title of the poem and its rhythm, recalling nursery rhymes, are distorted by the final lines in each stanza, which undermine the meaning of the preceding lines. A few of the poems have been interpreted as the account of an initially happy love story, passing through moments of pain, and ending with the death of the loved one, who will metaphorically transform itself through poetry, and survive in the memory of the lover.

After returning to New York immediately before World War II, Barnes lived a secluded life in relative poverty, refusing any contact with the press and the literary world, often positively hindering the publication of her works. However, she continued writing poetry, most of which remains unpublished. In 1958 she published *The Antiphon*, a **verse drama** on the topic of family incest, first staged in Stockholm in 1962. Djuna Barnes died in her Greenwich Village apartment in 1982. *Creatures in an Alphabet* (1982), a modern "bestiary" in rhyme with Barnes's own drawings, and *Smoke, and Other Early Stories* (1982) were published posthumously.

Further Reading. *Selected Primary Sources:* Barnes, Djuna, *A Book* (New York: Boni & Liveright, 1923); ———, *The Book of Repulsive Women* (New York: Bruno's Chapbooks, 1915; reprint Los Angeles: Sun & Moon Press, 1994); ———, *The Book of Repulsive Women and Other Poems* (Manchester: Carcanet Press, 2003); ———, *Creatures in an Alphabet* (New York: Dial Press, 1982); ———, *Ladies Almanack* (Dijon, France [privately printed]: 1928; reprint Lisle, IL: Dalkey Archive Press, 1992); ———, *Nightwood* (London: Faber & Faber, 1936; reprint London: Faber & Faber, 1995); ———, *Ryder* (New York, Boni & Liveright, 1928; reprint Lisle, IL: Dalkey Archive Press, 1990); ———, *Selected Works of Djuna Barnes* (London: Faber & Faber, 1962); ———, *Smoke and Other Early Stories* (London: Virago, 1985). ***Selected Secondary Sources:*** Broe, Mary Lynn, ed., *Silence and Power: A Reevaluation of Djuna Barnes* (Carbondale: Southern Illinois University Press, 1991); Caselli, Daniela, "'Elementary, my dear Djuna': Unreadable Simplicity in Djuna Barnes's *Creatures in an Alphabet*" (*Critical Survey* 13.3

[2001]: 89–112); Herring, Phillip, *Djuna: The Life and Work of Djuna Barnes* (London: Viking, 1995); Kime Scott, Bonnie, "Barnes Being 'Beast familiar': Representations on the Margins of Modernism" (*Review of Contemporary Fiction* 13.3 [1993]: 41–52); Plumb, Cheryl, *Fancy's Craft: Art and Identity in the Early Works of Djuna Barnes* (Selinsgrove, PA: Susquehanna University Press, 1986).

Laura Scuriatti

BATES, CHARLOTTE FISKE (1838–1916)

Charlotte Fiske Bates began writing poetry early in her life and by the last quarter of the nineteenth century had established herself as a prominent figure in the New England literary scene. Like other women writers of her day, Bates began her career as a contributor to children's magazines before breaking into more prestigious literary journals. Her publishing activity in the *Atlantic Monthly*, *Century*, *Harper's*, and *Scribner's Monthly* spanned thirty years, from 1869 to 1899. Her first and only collection of poetry was *Risk, and Other Poems* (1879), although she edited *The Cambridge Book of Poetry and Song* (1882) and assisted **Henry Wadsworth Longfellow** in the compilation of two minor collections. Several of her poems were published in Edmund Clarence Stedman's *An American Anthology* (1900), the most popular and comprehensive literary anthology of the time. Unlike her contemporary **Emily Dickinson**, Bates's popularity would flourish during her lifetime and fade into obscurity with the turn of the century.

Bates was born in New York City on November 30, 1838, to Harvey and Eliza Bates. Her father died shortly after her birth, and in 1847 she and her mother moved to Cambridge, Massachusetts, where Bates was educated in the public schools. She showed an early and immediate interest in poetry and published her first poem at the age of twenty in *Our Young Folks*, a juvenile magazine. She taught privately for twenty-five years, also giving public lectures and readings of her poems. In 1891 Bates married Adolphe Rogé, a playwright from New York City, from whom she took the penname Madame Rogé. Their marriage was brief, as he died five years later, and Bates readjusted to single life until her death in 1916. Bates greatly admired Henry Wadsworth Longfellow and worked as his assistant, translating ten poems from the French for "Poems of Places" and assisting in the compilation of *The Seven Voices of Sympathy* (1881). According to Edmund Clarence Stedman, Bates pioneered the popularity of "birthday books" in the 1880s and 1890s with her inventive compilation of *The Longfellow Birthday Book* (1881), a volume interspersed with Longfellow's verse. Used to record the names, births, and deaths in one's family, birthday books are now highly valued among genealogists.

Like most of her contemporaries, Bates produced **genteel** lyrics influenced by the strict conventions of Victorian verse and the themes of eighteenth-century **sentimentality** and Romanticism. Her work is dominated by themes of romantic love, death, fame, moral and religious piety, and nature. The title poem from *Risk, and Other Poems* reflects a recurring pattern in her lyrics, in which the speaker presents a conflict and nature offers reconciliation. In "Risk," the tensions of anger and jealousy that divide two young lovers turn to forgiveness when they encounter a majestic oak tree. In her poems extolling nature, the season of autumn prevails, and Bates offers remarkably vivid portrayals of leaves, vines, and flowers. One of her most popular poems was "Woodbines in October" (1877), published in *Scribner's*, in which the speaker makes a striking observation while admiring the blood-red vines: "The Heart of Autumn must have broken here / And poured its treasure out upon the leaves." Similarly, the poem "Presage" (1880), which appeared in the *Atlantic Monthly*, compares the hint of autumnal color in a spring leaf to the facial features of children, who "wear the strange presage of their latest year." Later in her life, especially after the death of her husband, Bates turned to themes of religious piety and moral duty in poems like "Solace" (1894), "On and Off" (1898), and "Supreme Moments" (1899). One of the last poems she published, "At Fourscore" (1899), expresses a relentless zest for life even as she faces death.

Bates began publishing at the height of women's literary emergence in America, and reviews of her work indicate that she was well liked by critics and readers. This was in part a result of her adherence to accepted "feminine" sensibilities in her poetry. Because women writers were contradictorily celebrated and denounced, their poems accepted for publication inevitably reflect conventions deemed appropriate by male editors. But Bates exercised creativity within these narrow confines, and occasionally, there is evidence of feminist subversion in her work.

Significantly, the poems Bates wrote in the 1880s and 1890s reflect a preoccupation with both fame and voice, or lack thereof. In *Century*, Bates contributed three poems that deal variously with these themes; "The Quatrain" and "The Couplet" both question the possibility of fame in the vast "abyss" of world and time, while "A Dumb Beauty" (1884) compares a beautiful woman, lacking a voice, to a rose. Similarly, in "Genius Within Hearing of Death" (1892), published in *Century*, Bates personifies Genius as Motherhood, whose "unborn" creations "long for birth" as Death approaches. The poem articulates a sense of urgency and regret as Genius passes into Heaven leaving "no voice behind." In "The Perils of a Poet" (1886), published in *Century*, Bates portrays a twenty-year-old female poet named Lorinda who has many suitors until her poems are published, when she laments, "That verse which has attracted fame has been repelling lovers!" By the end of the poem, Lorinda has completely changed her voice, abandoning "the edicts of her youth" and turning to themes "of battles, heroes, minsters." Not only do her lovers return, but critics say her poetry is "much *stronger.*" Despite their appearance as light humor pieces, these poems poignantly articulate the "anxiety of authorship" (Gilbert and Gubar) female poets endured, often writing to please their audience rather than to define, or redefine, the sphere of their artistry.

Recognition of female poetic achievement was a primary concern for Bates. In her preface to *The Cambridge Book of Poetry and Song* (1882), she states her aim as "first, to represent the genius of woman as fairly as that of man." Her impulse to anthologize women's voices was perhaps premonitory; Bates was a poet of significant achievement who has become forgotten as **modernist** themes have taken precedence over nineteenth-century sensibilities in the study of American poetry.

Further Reading. *Selected Primary Sources:* Bates, Charlotte Fiske, *The Longfellow Birthday Book* (Boston: Houghton Mifflin, 1881); ———, ed., *The Cambridge Book of Poetry and Song: Selected from English and American Authors* (New York: Thomas Y. Crowell, 1882); ———, *Risk, and Other Poems* (Boston: A. Williams & Co., 1879); Longfellow, Henry Wadsworth, *The Seven Voices of Sympathy*, ed. Charlotte Fiske Bates (Boston: Houghton Mifflin, 1882). ***Selected Secondary Sources:*** Gilbert, Sandra, and Susan Gubar, *The Madwoman in the Attic: The Woman Writer and the Nineteenth-Century Literary Imagination* (New Haven, CT: Yale University Press, 1979); Stedman, Edmund Clarence, ed., *An American Anthology, 1787–1900* (Boston: Houghton Mifflin, 1900); Walker, Cheryl, *American Women Poets of the Nineteenth Century: An Anthology* (New Brunswick, NJ: Rutgers University Press, 1992).·

M. Beth Keefauver

BATES, KATHARINE LEE (1859–1929)

Katharine Lee Bates, poet and educator, produced more than a dozen books of poetry and prose and published widely in literary magazines for more than four decades. Writing at the height of **modernism**, Bates eschewed the **Imagism** of **Ezra Pound** in favor of the increasingly unfashionable **sentimentality** of the **Fireside Poets**. As a result of its antiquated style, the majority of her poetry has received very little attention. Today, she is remembered almost exclusively for her classic poem "America the Beautiful," which, set to the tune of the hymn "Materna," has become one of the nation's most beloved patriotic songs.

Bates was born in Falmouth, Massachusetts, in 1859. Despite struggling with poverty, her family valued education, and, in 1876 her brother paid for her to attend the newly opened women's college at Wellesley. As a sophomore Bates published a poem in the *Atlantic Monthly*, which later received the compliments of **Henry Wadsworth Longfellow**. Five years after she graduated, in 1885, Wellesley invited her to return as a faculty member in English. For nearly forty years, Bates contributed substantially to the higher education of women and the intellectual life of Wellesley College. Her historical study, *American Literature* (1897), reveals the breadth of her knowledge of American literary history and is noteworthy for the balanced and sympathetic attention it gives to women writers. At Wellesley, Bates surrounded herself with a circle of independent, free-thinking women, such as her colleague, Vida Scudder, and her lover and companion, Katharine Coman. While never an ardent activist herself, in 1890 Bates helped Scudder and Coman found the College Settlement Association, which later grew into Denison House in Boston, a community center dedicated to social welfare in immigrant neighborhoods.

In 1893, while traveling to Colorado to give a guest lecture, Bates witnessed the dramatic scenery that would inspire her poem "America the Beautiful." First published as "America" in the *Congregationalist* on July 4, 1895, the poem drew an immediate and overwhelming public reaction. Audiences were so enthusiastic about the poem's vision of brotherhood that the subsequent song was almost adopted as the national anthem. Themes of patriotism and national heritage occupy a substantial portion of Bates's writing. In her collection *America the Beautiful and Other Poems* (1911), she continually celebrates America's independent spirit, embodied in its first settlers, and hails the country's singular natural beauty.

However, on the whole, Bates's poetry evokes a more complex form of nationalism. Even in "America the Beautiful" she prays, "God mend thine every flaw." Bates elaborates these social "flaws" throughout the remainder of the collection. "The Slave's Escape" highlights the hypocrisy of American colonials who forcefully transported African slaves across the Atlantic. As the patriots fought to transform America into a model of freedom, the slaves could only hope to escape to a better place. Thus, Bates's nationalism imagines America as "The Land of Hope," a country filled with the possibility of change and marked by a desire for continuous improvement. Her ethos strongly resembles the doctrines of Progressive Era social reformers like Jane Addams and was probably reinforced by Coman's and Scudder's ongoing activist work.

With its sentimental style and didactic tone, Bates's poetry often resembles nineteenth-century abolitionist verse. In *The Retinue and Other Poems* (1918) she uses this outdated form to confront the distinctly modern problem of World War I. "How long shall bomb and bullet think for / human brains?" she asks in the poem "How Long?" Bates mourns the human carnage of war and imagines founding a nation in love rather than pain: "To build the state on thee, / And shape the deed of nations by thy yet / untested law!" The poems participate in a long tradition of anti-war poetry and offer an intricate emotional account of the domestic costs of a foreign war. Yet, ultimately, the collection expands beyond America's national borders. Poems like "Russia," "To Italy," and "Jerusalem" reveal enormous sympathy for the plight of citizens in Europe and the Middle East. While her poems retain a backward rhetorical style, her sentiments of international cooperation are perfectly attuned to the cosmopolitanism of her age.

In fact, travel poems account for a substantial portion of Bates's corpus. Like her contemporary **Sara Teasdale**, Bates traveled extensively and produced many "postcard" poems to document her experiences. Her prose work *Spanish Highways and Biways* (1900), originally written for the *New York Times*, offers a romanticized portrait of the Spanish people and customs that poignantly captures Bates's abiding love for travel and learning. The poem "Vacation" from *Fairy Gold: Poems* (1916) playfully expresses this zeal: "My school is out for a summer of rest, / And now for the schoolroom I love the best!"

Bates's companion in many of her travels was her lover, Katharine Coman, with whom she lived and worked for twenty-five years. In 1915 Coman died from a long and painful struggle with cancer. When Bates retired from Wellesley in 1920, she dedicated herself to writing poetry full-time. Out of her grief and longing for Coman, Bates produced *Yellow Clover: A Book of Remembrance*, which Judith Schwarz calls "one of the most anguished memorials to the love and comradeship between two women that has ever existed" (59). The flower, yellow clover, long represented an intimate tie between the two women, as Bates describes in the title poem: "This vagabond, unvalued yellow clover, / To be our tenderest language." Unrequited passion and mourning dominate the emotionally charged collection. "My sorrow asks no healing," Bates concludes in "Yellow Clover," "it is love." At Wellesley, the Clover Club, an organization of lesbian faculty and staff, was later formed in honor of Bates's work.

Throughout the 1990s, numerous hagiographic portraits of Bates and her famous poem appeared, mainly marketed to primary and secondary school students. Among these works, *America the Beautiful: The Stirring True Story Behind Our Nation's Favorite Song* (2001) stands out as the most balanced and historically accurate account.

Further Reading. *Selected Primary Sources:* Bates, Katharine Lee, *America the Beautiful and Other Poems*

(New York: Thomas Y. Crowell, 1911); ———, *American Literature* (New York: Macmillan, 1897); ———, *The Retinue and Other Poems* (New York: E.P. Dutton, 1918); ———, *Spanish Highways and Biways* (New York: Macmillan, 1900);———, *Yellow Clover: A Book of Remembrance* (New York: E.P. Dutton, 1922). ***Selected Secondary Sources:*** Robinson, Lillian S., "Katharine Lee Bates," in *American National Biography*, Vol. 2 (New York: Oxford University Press, 1999); Schwartz, Judith, "*Yellow Clover*: Katherine Lee Bates and Katharine Coman" (*Frontiers* 4.1 [1979]: 59–67); Sherr, Lynn, *America the Beautiful: The Stirring True Story Behind Our Nation's Favorite Song* (New York: Public Affairs, 2001).

Melissa Girard

BAY PSALM BOOK (1640)

The Whole Booke of Psalmes Faithfully Translated into English Metre, commonly known as the *Bay Psalm Book* (first printing 1640), was the first book printed in the British American colonies, at the printing press established in Cambridge, Massachusetts, by Stephen Daye. The collaborative effort of several New England divines, it became the standard worship songbook for generations of New England Congregationist churchgoers until well into the eighteenth century; as such, it may be considered one of the most influential and widespread of colonial American poetry publications. It was reprinted over fifty times, including in England. Indeed, its fame was lasting enough that James Fenimore Cooper could base the character of psalm singer David Gamut in *The Last of the Mohicans* (1826) on the *Bay Psalm Book*.

The roots of metrical psalmody extend deep into the Reformation, as worship services were affected by vernacular translations of the Bible as well as by the rise of congregational singing. Early influences include Lutheran hymnody of the 1520s and especially the later Calvinist insistence on close adherence to scripture, in effect "versifying" the text. The major leap forward in English psalmody came with Thomas Sternhold's first metrical version of selected psalms in 1549, which was soon extended by John Hopkins and others to include the entire book of Psalms. The first complete version appeared in 1562 and was reprinted over two hundred times. However, dissatisfied with the looseness of the translation, Henry Ainsworth produced a closer, literal rendering, which appeared in 1612 with accompanying tunes drawn from English, Dutch, and French psalters.

Perhaps because of Ainsworth's Separatist associations, the founders of Massachusetts Bay determined to create their own metrical psalm book. It seems clear that Thomas Weld, John Eliot, Richard Mather, **John Cotton**, **John Wilson**, **Nathaniel Ward**, Peter Bulkeley, and Thomas Shepard were principally involved, but there may have been up to thirty different translators on the project. In addition to the psalms themselves, this first edition is especially memorable for its anonymously authored preface (traditionally attributed to Richard Mather, but Zoltán Haraszti argues for John Cotton). Whatever its limitations, the preface may be considered the earliest attempt at articulating aesthetic principles in the British American colonies. In it, the author carefully lays out the justification for and principles behind the translation. Employing scripture citation and typological rationale, the author addresses three problems: whether psalms or hymns are permissible (the conclusion is for psalms only); whether English meter is permissible (yes); and whether psalms are to be sung solo or congregationally (the latter). These answers do not, however, preclude individuals from composing and performing hymns for private devotion. With little leeway, the translators shunned paraphrase and aimed at close adherence to the Hebrew text. The author concludes with the defense that if "the verses are not always so smooth and elegant as some may desire or expect; let them consider that Gods Altar needs not our polishings: Ex. 20. for wee have respected rather a plaine translation, then to smooth our verses with the sweetnes of any paraphrase, and soe have attended Conscience rather than elegance, fidelity rather than poetry." Cotton's *Singing of Psalmes a Gospel-Ordinance* (1647), published in conjunction with the second printing, repeats and elaborates on these and other arguments.

In 1651, for the third printing, the book underwent major revision by Harvard president Henry Dunster and Richard Lyon with the new title of *The Psalms Hymns and Spiritual Songs of the Old and New Testament, faithfully translated into English metre.* While Dunster and Lyon hewed to the same basic aesthetic principles, they also undertook translations of all the various songs scattered throughout the Bible. This version came to be known as the *New England Psalm Book* and was the text for remaining printings for the next century. After that, its influence began to decline, as evidenced by the emergence of the practice of "lining out" as congregations began to lose command of the various tunes, and then by the "Regular Singing" controversy. In the early eighteenth century, the psalm book experienced stiff competition as congregations elected to turn to a new English version by Nahum Tate and Nicholas Brady and then to the popular hymns of Isaac Watts. Thomas Prince's "revised and improved" edition of the *Bay Psalm Book* in 1758 may be considered the last.

Until the 1690s, the *Bay Psalm Book* did not include musical notation for the tunes, but the "[a]n admonition to the reader" at the conclusion of the first edition indicates that "[t]he verses of these psalms may be reduced to six kindes" with various tunes supplied from Thomas Ravenscroft's settings assembled for the Sternhold-Hopkins psalter. The vast majority are in common measure (8/6/8/6), with several in both long (8/8/8/8) and short meters (6/6/8/6), some in "hallelujah" meter, and one in a unique form. Some sense of the work may be gleaned from the rendering of the opening lines of the Twenty-third Psalm: "The Lord to mee a shepheard is, / want therefore shall not I, / Hee in the folds of tender-grasse, / doth cause mee downe to lie."

When considered as poetry, the *Bay Psalm Book* has met with considerable critical disdain and castigation. Moses Coit Tyler complained of "[s]entences wrenched about end for end, clauses heaved up and abandoned in chaos, words disemboweled or split up quite in two in the middle and dissonant combinations of sound that are the despair of such poor vocal organs as are granted to human beings"; Harold S. Jantz caustically derided one psalm as "utter rhythmic and syntactic wreckage," although he admitted that occasionally the translators managed to produced "fairly reputable verse." In fairness, however, it should be noted that these psalms were intended chiefly to be sung; still, no one has bothered to champion the verse except on grounds of historical significance.

Further Reading. *Selected Primary Sources:* *The Bay Psalm Book: A Facsimile Reprint of the First Edition of 1640,* ed. Zoltán Haraszti (Chicago: University of Chicago Press, 1956). ***Selected Secondary Sources:*** Haraszti, Zoltán, *The Enigma of the Bay Psalm Book* (Chicago: University of Chicago Press, 1956); Stallings, Louise Russell, *The Unpolished Altar: The Place of the Bay Psalm Book in American Culture* (Ph.D. diss., Texas A&M University, 1977).

Michael G. Ditmore

BEAT POETRY

The term "Beat" entered the American literary lexicon in the late 1940s, when Herbert Huncke, New York hustler and writer, used the word to describe the defeated condition of street-savvy, world-weary people. **Jack Kerouac** embraced the idea of Beat immediately as being the perfect definition of an emerging sensibility in America during and following World War II. Later, the definition of Beat grew to include the pseudo-religious notion of "beatific." Although critical observers derisively imposed the title "Beatnik" on them, Beat writers themselves never cultivated the bearded and bereted caricature created to accompany that name. Disenchanted with prevailing ideals of all kinds—social, political, and literary—and not knowing they were a "movement," mid- and postwar writers engaged in a vigorous rejection of norms and embarked on multi-focal journeys of discovery. In the case of the Beats, like-minded people opened themselves to experiences of all kinds: sexual, pharmaceutical, spiritual. These experiences subsequently were articulated in a new and spontaneous poetry, marked not only by its scandalous subject matter but also by its slang and coarse diction, its **jazz** rhythm, its neo-Romanticism, and its experiments with form. While other poetic movements emerged at the same time and for the same reasons, these collective experiments, goals, and methods are most particularly associated with the so-called Beat generation. However, the poets of the **San Francisco Renaissance**, with whom the Beats had significant interaction in spite of the transcontinental separation, were closely related. Other poets whose work is closely connected to some aspects of Beat writing (but less so to each other) are those more accurately identified with the **New York School**, the **Black Mountain School**, and **confessional poetry**.

Beat writing developed in New York City in the cultural mix and tolerance of Greenwich Village. The core Beat writers are the poets **Allen Ginsberg**, Jack Kerouac, and **Gregory Corso**, and the prose writer William S. Burroughs. Ginsberg and Kerouac met through Burroughs and Lucien Carr in 1944, when Ginsberg was still a student at Columbia University and Kerouac already had dropped out. Six years later, Ginsberg and Corso met in a Greenwich Village bar soon after Corso's release from prison. Ginsberg, Kerouac, Burroughs, and Corso, along with the many others who are collected under the Beat umbrella—such as LeRoi Jones (**Amiri Baraka**), who became the organizing force behind the **Black Arts Movement**, and **Diane di Prima**, who established various publishing and performance venues for poets to disseminate their work—came from widely disparate economic and ethnic backgrounds but were drawn together not only by regional proximity and a desire to write, but also by an iconoclastic impulse. This impulse was all-encompassing, and though generalized and vague at first, it became more clearly defined as the Beats lived, traveled, worked, and corresponded with each other. Jones and di Prima co-founded *The Floating Bear*, a free mimeographed literary periodical in which many notable poets were first published. In its thirty-eight issues, new work by **Edward Dorn**, **Charles Olson**, **Robert Creeley**, **Frank O'Hara**, **John Ashbery**, and **Joel Oppenheimer**, along with Ginsberg, di Prima, and many others, appeared for the first time. Their lives became a literary petri dish, and they embraced **William Carlos Williams**'s philosophy that there is no subject unsuitable for poetry.

They reached back to the British Romantics, especially William Blake and Percy Shelley, and to **Walt Whitman** for the inspiration and permission to seek and to articulate experience. Further, they saw **Hart Crane** as their more immediate literary ancestor. Whitman and Crane both advocated the use of common speech rather than an elevated vocabulary in poetry, and as an extension of that, they believed that an American rhythm was essential to American poetry. Crane isolated jazz as that rhythm, and the Beats encoded jazz as a tenet of their

work. Kerouac expressed the desire to be known as a jazz poet and employed improvisation in his jazz and **blues** poetry. The constant movement of the journey, the Beat relocations and road trips, is an extension of the poetry's integral rhythm. Another vitally important contribution these British and American forefathers made to the Beat equation was a life of liberated sexual activity. Even more significant is both Whitman's and Crane's queer life. Crossing boundaries such as monogamy and heterosexuality, in the name of freedom, experience, and preference, became a norm itself. The difference was that, although Whitman and Crane veiled their sexual orientation or activity because of the times in which they lived, the Beats wrote explicitly and graphically, naming and describing body parts and acts, and initiating the development of queer activism. Ginsberg declares at the end of "America," "I'm putting my queer shoulder to the wheel." Making this kind of brazen revelation, along with others about communism and anarchism, in 1950s America was a courageous thing to do: Homosexuality was illegal, and political witch hunts were attempting to strangulate dissent. To stress that point, Corso wrote of "earth's grumpy empires" in the mushroom cloud–shaped "Bomb" (1960).

Ginsberg's *Howl and Other Poems* (1956) and Kerouac's *Mexico City Blues* (1959) were written in 1955; Corso's *Gasoline* appeared in 1958. These three books are the seminal works of Beat poetry. The first line of "Howl" is the most immediately recognized line from the period: "I saw the best minds of my generation destroyed by madness, starving hysterical naked." Evident here is the extended line, which harkens back to Whitman and is echoed in Olson's theory of **projective verse**, freed from the constraints of traditional metrics at the same time that it speaks with unabashed directness of indiscreet subjects such as madness and nudity. The performance of this poetry requires the participation of the body as much as the inflection of the voice because the reader has to measure the breath so carefully. Thus the body becomes subject and vehicle, is both form and content, in much Beat poetry. The Beats recognized that everything is experienced through the body, that it is the only way to take in information about the world. Elise Cowen wrote of a "whole city of body." They expanded the Romantic focus on feeling to include physical responses and contracted the leisure of recall so that the poem was generated in the urgency of experience. Beat poetry is nothing if not subjective. Kerouac was committed to what Ginsberg called a spontaneous bop prosody, requiring that poetry be composed in immediacy rather than tranquility. He also argued against subsequent revision, convinced that what came first was best.

As important as the body's rhythms, functions, and responses are to Beat poetry, the Beats also saw a clear relationship between drugs and the creative process.

They fearlessly and energetically consumed anything chemical for the revelations drugs could induce and for the new experiences to record, which predictably resulted in many substance abuse problems. If there was something to ingest, smoke, or inject, they tried it—generally more than once—and often wrote feverishly while under the influence. Kerouac's *Mexico City Blues* was written in three weeks, Ginsberg's "Kaddish" in forty hours, both of them fueled by drugs. The Beats were experience junkies as much as they were attached to their drugs of choice, and they used drugs pragmatically, at times simply because it was an efficient means of generating the energy they needed to do the things they wanted or felt compelled to do. They were not people who lolled about in a drug-induced haze. The Beats had an astonishing momentum and churned out an enormous body of work. They were, as Burroughs said of Kerouac, writers—that is, they wrote.

The final factor in the creation of Beat poetry is religion, most specifically Buddhism, although the Beat icon of the angel is to be found everywhere. They were spiritual seekers, having cast off the dominant religious practices of their nation along with its other dominant ideologies and prescribed attitudes about everything else. The exploration of Eastern religion was earnest, not faddish, as writers on both coasts sought other ways of being and perceiving. Ginsberg described them as "angelheaded hipsters burning for the ancient heavenly connection to the starry dynamo in the machinery of night" ("Howl"). While Kerouac struggled to accommodate Roman Catholicism and Buddhism, Ginsberg and di Prima, and **Gary Snyder**, **Philip Whalen**, and **Michael McClure** in San Francisco, are among those whose commitment to Eastern thought has been lifelong. The language and concepts of Buddhism are apparent in their poems, chanting a "mantra of American language" in Ginsberg's "Wichita Vortex Sutra" (1973), longing to get off "that slaving meat wheel" in Kerouac's "211th Chorus" of *Mexico City Blues*, and thinking to "step off the roof light as air" into "Blue Nirvana" in di Prima's *The New Handbook of Heaven* (1963).

The public emergence of what had been percolating for a decade took place in October 1955 at San Francisco's Six Gallery. That night, six unknown poets shared the stage: Philip Lamantia, Michael McClure, Gary Snyder, Philip Whalen, and Allen Ginsberg read; **Kenneth Rexroth** acted as emcee; and Jack Kerouac (who declined the invitation to read) went out for wine to serve the audience. **Lawrence Ferlinghetti** was in the crowd, and when he recovered from Ginsberg's stunning performance of the unfinished "Howl," he sent a note asking to publish the manuscript at City Lights Books. The book was published the following year and almost immediately precipitated an obscenity trial. The poem itself had fixed Ginsberg's reputation among

receptive poets, but the trial raised the poem's profile to an extent otherwise impossible. Ferlinghetti successfully defended against the charge, the poem was found to have the redeeming social value necessary for it not to be judged obscene, and Ginsberg became a star. Word was out, and writers all over the country heard it and were galvanized by it.

"Howl" is almost unarguably the most influential American poem written to date. But Ginsberg himself pointed to Kerouac as the most influential poet because of his impact on both Ginsberg and **Bob Dylan**, and therefore by extension his global effect. Fifty years after the Six Gallery reading, critics are taking the Beats far more seriously than they did half a century ago. Their lives and their work were dismissed, vilified, and ridiculed in the early years. The only attention came in the form of reviews, and academic critics were generally vehemently negative. A collection or two of essays was all the scholarship that could be generated for two decades; however, the poets published themselves and each other, establishing **small presses** if they had to while advocates established imprints and journals to serve as venues for innovative work. Criticism lagged behind popularity because the closed culture of the academy was diametrically opposed to Beat culture, regardless of its resonance among the masses. The poets kept writing, biographies began to appear, and gradually—as more attuned critics and scholars came to the fore—the work became more respected. Where once a negative review would have been the limit of critical notice, now there are whole books devoted to an analysis of the work of individual writers.

The greater number of women entering academic life has resulted in the retrieval and reexamination of women's writing. In the case of the Beats, the prevailing anti-feminist attitude of the 1940s and 1950s was a major factor in the general neglect, but it was compounded by the fact that many women writing at the time were also intimately involved with male writers. These women frequently found their goals subsumed by their men's. Being both writer and nurturer made things difficult but not impossible, and they were women bent on making their own art. These women had to negotiate opposing sets of rules, rejecting prevailing social constraints for women but also entering into a Beat agreement to be cool with everything. Coolness presented a problem when their male companions made those same assumptions about a woman's place. Not only did the Beat men consider the women's writing as secondary to their own but they also expected somebody to tend the home while they were busy being geniuses. Somehow, the women had to find a precarious balance between practicing the code of cool and resisting the re-imposition of male dominance at the same time they determined to write their own work. Female Beat writers can be identified as an important stage in the progress of feminism. In recent years, **Joanne Kyger** (who was married to Gary Snyder), Joyce Johnson (who was involved with Jack Kerouac), Elise Cowen (involved for a time with Ginsberg), Janine Pommy Vega (married to the painter Fernando Vega), and Hettie Jones (married to Baraka), while never completely unknown, are emerging from the shadows of their partners into the popular imagination and the critical consciousness.

Further Reading. Campbell, James, *This is the Beat Generation: New York—San Francisco—Paris* (London: Secker & Warburg, 1999); Johnson, Ronna C., and Nancy M. Grace, eds. *Girls Who Wore Black: Women Writing the Beat Generation* (New Brunswick, NJ: Rutgers University Press, 2002); Knight, Brenda, *Women of the Beat Generation: The Writers, Artists and Muses at the Heart of a Revolution* (Berkeley: Conari Press, 1996); Myrsiades, Kostas, ed., *The Beat Generation: Critical Essays* (New York: Pater Lang, 2002); Parkinson, Thomas, ed., *A Casebook on the Beat* (New York: Crowell, 1961); Peabody, Richard, *A Different Beat: Early Work by Women of the Beat Generation* (London: Serpent's Tail, 1997); Stephenson, Gregory, *The Daybreak Boys: Essays on the Literature of the Beat Generation* (Carbondale: Southern Illinois University Press, 1990).

A. Mary Murphy

BECKER, ROBIN (1951–)

Robin Becker is heir to the poetic tradition of **Adrienne Rich**, **Audre Lorde**, and **Judy Grahn**. Like **Muriel Rukeyser**, Becker writes as an involved outsider. While she is a **feminist poet**, Becker's most radical feminist poems do not evoke a world where women must exist in opposition to men. Like that of Grahn, Becker's voice is imbued with irony, clarity, and intelligence. Much of her poetry is a **lyric** evocation of family and of the pains and tragedies that accompany family entanglements. In this regard, some of her work could be considered **confessional**, yet Becker is both more intimate than **Sylvia Plath** and less explicit than **Anne Sexton**. While writing of the deaths of loved ones, no trace of self-indulgence affects the voice of the poet, which is curious and alert, reminiscent of **Elizabeth Bishop** or **Marianne Moore**.

Born in Philadelphia, Pennsylvania, Becker received a BA and an MA from Boston University. She taught seventeen years at Massachusetts Institute of Technology and is now an Associate Professor of English and Women's Studies at Pennsylvania State University. Her books include *Horse Fair* (2000); *All American Girl* (1996), winner of the Lambda Literary Award in Lesbian Poetry; *Giacometti's Dog* (1990); *Backtalk* (1982); and *Personal Effects* (1977). Her book reviews and poetry have appeared widely; she was awarded the Virginia Faulkner Prize for Excellence in Writing and has won an NEA fellowship.

Although some critics found *All-American Girl* to be a collection of devastating poems contending with loss and survival, the sly, ironic voice of Becker rarely subsides to despair. It combines the careful writing of the modernists with the story-telling quality of Rita Dove. Although Becker focuses on the chaos that accompanies life in *All-American Girl*, the voice of the poetry is detached. As families dissolve, and the loose fragments of childhood rush down the drain, Becker tells stories as tiny and brilliant as moons seen through a telescope. There is no savior, but there is a contemplative space from which the writer can observe the brittle shards of life dissolving. Tragedy, for Becker, does not so much randomly disrupt a life as contain it, creating the fabric of the day to day. *All-American Girl* is an ironic title implying that a girl might create identity out of vast, incongruent forces. The speaker's voice evokes both the frontier myth of living on the edge, where creation of identity is possible, and the colonial idea that we carry identity from one country to the next.

Becker writes hauntingly of being an outsider and a survivor. Her readers move into a wintry landscape where family members commit suicide, relationships are upended, women fall in and out of love, yet our narrator survives and thrives. We are taken to Boston, to the Southwest, to Jerusalem. Everywhere we take ourselves, we are smitten, undone, yet life itself is redemption.

As Jew and lesbian, Becker writes of the "outsider-ness" experienced by these personae. *Horse Fair* features a long poem in the voice of Charlotte Salomon, an artist who did not survive the concentration camps. Against that monumental event in history, ordinary crumbling relationships seem inconsequential. Instead of reaching for the obtuse, the academic, Becker calls on Hebrew myths to enrich the work. Yiddish stories and Jewish history contextualize her poetry.

In his praise for *The Horse Fair*, the poet **Mark Doty** states, "What I love in Robin Becker's poems is how much the world is with her; characters, histories, animals, places and things crowd onto these pages, inscribing them with the cries of the living. Becker is against the silence." An example of this crowded energy, in which characters, histories, and animals are equally urgent, is the poem "Meeting the Gaze of the Great Horned Owl," from *The Horse Fair*, in which Becker writes, "I moved my arms—slowly—in an awkward imitation /of flight." Where another poet might have focused on the owl as a representation of the natural world, Becker allows herself to become the owl, which in turn reminds her of death, and specifically of her sister's suicide. She wants her sister back, she writes, so that she might show her "how one small percussive surprise in the trees can turn you / from one self to another, this one with wings." The poem becomes a form of redemption, a theme to which Becker often returns: redemption and solace for the Jew, the survivor, the lesbian, the outsider.

Becker's poetry travels toward a discovery of the self through an understanding of loss, living with it, and identifying what brings joy and peace. Her writing of displacement is also the urge to find a place, and the arms to hold one in that place.

Further Reading. *Selected Primary Sources:* Becker, Robin, *Backtalk* (Pittsburgh: University of Pittsburgh Press, 1982); ———, *Giacometti's Dog* (Pittsburgh: University of Pittsburgh Press, 1990); ———, *The Horse Fair* (Pittsburgh: University of Pittsburgh Press, 2000); ———, *Personal Effects* (Pittsburgh: University of Pittsburgh Press, 1977). *Selected Secondary Source:* Sewell, Marilyn, ed., *Claiming the Spirit Within* (Boston: Beacon Press, 1996).

Kate Gale

BEERS, HENRY AUGUSTIN (1847–1926)

Henry Augustin Beers was a poet and literary historian who focused on the style of the Romantic and pre-Romantic eras. Defining Romanticism as the reproduction in modern art or literature of the life and thought of the Middle Ages, he captured in his own writing the simple, sincere, natural forms of expression emblematic of this eighteenth-century era.

Beers was born on July 2, 1847, in Buffalo, New York. He attended Yale University, graduating with his bachelor's degree in 1869. That same year, he was initiated into the Order of Skull & Bones, a secret organization, founded at the university in 1832, for the elite children of the Anglo-American Wall Street banking establishment. Beers studied law in New York and, in 1870, was admitted to the New York state bar. However, he practiced law for only one year before returning to Yale as an English literature tutor from 1871 until 1874. He was named a professor of English at the university in 1875 and, following five months of study abroad, he attained full professorship in 1880. In his more than forty years of teaching at Yale, Beers wrote over twenty books, among them volumes of poetry including *Odds and Ends: Verses Humorous, Occasional, and Miscellaneous* (1878), *The Thankless Muse* (1885), and *Poems* (1921). In 1916 he was named professor emeritus at Yale. Beers died on September 7, 1926, in New Haven, Connecticut.

The bulk of Beers's writing centers on literature, including *A Century of American Literature* (1878), *An Outline Sketch of English Literature* (1886), *An Outline Sketch of American Literature* (1887), and *A History of English Romanticism in the Nineteenth Century* (1898). In addition to writing about and teaching the works of others, Beers was an accomplished poet in his own right. His verses resemble those written in the Romantic and pre-Romantic eras in that they express a deep appreciation of the beauties of nature with an emphasis on emotion and the senses.

This emotional sensation and predilection for the mysterious and otherworldly can clearly be seen in Beers's poem "Ecce in Deserto." Set in the shadowy woods, the verse follows the speaker on a trek to confirm knowledge about the divine wisdom and musical spirit that reside in nature. Amidst the roar of the pines on a windless day and the ghostly melodies that sweep the air, the listener and speaker pursue a mystical force that holds the forest's secret. Yet the presence is not to be overtaken and "to other woods the trail leads on, / to other worlds and new." The romance so prevalent in Beers's historical studies fully flowers in his "Biftek Aux Champignons," in which the speaker asks his beloved Mimi to recall a September outing in which they searched for mushrooms. Putting down his copy of Browning, the speaker looks on admiringly as his companion raises her skirt to search the pasture for the delectable morsels. Spontaneity and emotionality run high as the listener takes in the sights, sounds, and smells that envelop the couple on "that blue September day."

The preoccupation of the Romantics with the genius, the hero, the exceptional figure, and their interest in the artist as an individual, creative spirit is captured in Beers's ode "Posthumous." The verse relates a scene following the demise of a poet in which his survivors review his legacy and "his memory, whom we honored long." Recalling the vision that he imparted to them, the survivors realize that the writer's true legacy is not to be found among chairs, prints, tablecloths. He left no familial heirs to carry on his name. Instead, the poet's bequest, as the speaker comes to realize, is the artistry that he shared with his apprentices, one of whom may then "say: 'This phrase, dear friend, perhaps, is mine; / The breath that gave it life was thine.'"

Through his poetry, Beers conveys Romanticism's "spontaneous overflow of powerful feelings," as described in William Wordsworth's "Preface" to the second edition of Lyrical Ballads, the manifesto of the English Romantic movement in poetry. He exalts the roles of nature, love, and heroism, as revered in the days of medieval chivalry, and applies them in a late nineteenth-/early twentieth-century context. Thus, the emotional sensitivity and deeply felt personal responses to art and the natural world that marked the Romantic age transcend time and space to embrace an industrial period in which tenderness and compassion were threatening to become a thing of the past.

Further Reading. *Selected Primary Sources:* Beers, Henry Augustin, *A Century of American Literature* (New York: Holt, 1878); ———, *A History of English Romanticism in the Eighteenth Century* (New York: Holt, 1899); ———, *A History of English Romanticism in the Nineteenth Century* (New York: Holt, 1898); ———, *Odds and Ends: Verses Humorous, Occasional, and Miscellaneous* (Boston: Houghton, Osgood,

1878); ———, *An Outline Sketch of English Literature* (New York: Chautauqua, 1886); ———, *Poems* (New Haven, CT: Yale University Press, 1921); ———, *The Thankless Muse* (Boston: Houghton, Mifflin, 1878). **Selected Secondary Source:** Peacok, Scot, ed., *209 Contemporary Authors* (Detroit: Gale, 2003).

Roxanne Y. Schwab

BELKNAP, JEREMY (1744–1798)

Although mostly known for his prose work, the poetry of Jeremy Belknap, most notably his "Eclogue Occasioned by the Death of the Reverend Alexander Cumming A.M.," is worthy of study as the poem helps to solidify the genre of **pastoral elegy** in early America. Other Boston writers of the genre, such as **Joseph Green**, looked to Belknap for guidance in the form and even appropriated lines from Belknap, just as Belknap looked to **Joseph Seccombe**. Through this borrowing, we are afforded a glimpse into a network of early American poets. What we also find in Belknap's elegy is a blending of both the classical and Adamic mythoi. What we see is a writer deftly molding Christianity within a pagan form of art.

Jeremy Belknap—clergyman, historian, writer, patriot, poet, and teacher—was born June 4, 1744, and graduated from Harvard in 1762. After being ordained in 1767, he accepted a position at a New Hampshire congregation and was later appointed to the Federal Street Church in his hometown of Boston. Belknap is most widely known for his founding of the Massachusetts Historical Society and the publishing of his *History of New Hampshire*. He died in Boston on June 20, 1798. In recognition of his life and accomplishments, Belknap's name has been given to a county in New Hampshire.

While at Harvard, Belknap wrote in a journal, "Wherefore everyone who is in capacity to do good to others is bound both by the laws of God and nature to do it; and it behooves everyone to relieve those of his fellow creatures who stand in need of it" (Marcou, 13). As he believed in and was an ardent practitioner of this sentiment, it is of little wonder that he chose the genre of pastoral elegy in which to write his verse. In the pastoral elegy, it is the lament that "characterizes much of the form and content of the pastoral elegy," and "the author of pastoral elegies, then, is a physician helping to heal the grief of those suffering the loss of a loved one" (Shields, 131). It is Florio who deeply grieves for the passing of the minister in "An Eclogue Occasioned by the Death of the Reverend Alexander Cumming A.M." Florio is shocked that his friend Albinus finds the news of Cumming's death "amazing" and as something that thrills his "inmost soul." But it is not a mere loss that Albinus sees. Instead, the death of Cumming is the work of Divine Providence, and he recognizes that Cumming has gone to a better place. Why then, Albinus asks his

companion, should we mourn? And why should we wish Cumming back into "this gloomy Vale of Tears"? Through a biblical allusion to Job 1:21 ("The Lord gave and the Lord hath taken away") death is further established as a work of divine providence , which also melds Christianity into this classical form of poetry.

It is necessary here to diverge momentarily from the commentary to discuss the source for Belknap's poem. In "The Argument" section of the poem, which Belknap more than likely borrowed from Joseph Seccombe rather than Milton, who uses no "Argument" in his pastoral *Lycidas*, Belknap states that his "Eclogue" is formed "partly on the Plan of Virgil's Daphnis." Belknap does borrow the opening line of his poem from Milton's *Paradise Lost* ("Sweet is the Breath of Morn") and includes a reference to Alexander Pope's *Essay on Man, Epistle II*, so one may be apt to write off Belknap's "Eclogue" as nothing more than a slavish imitation of. It is important to remember, however, that it was fashionable during the time to quote texts readily available to the public. With the exception of the above-mentioned items, the "Eclogue" does just as Belknap suggests in that it owes a considerable debt to Virgil.

Belknap does make his own amendments to the pastoral elegiac form. Florio and Albinus, although they do spy "those flocks, that graze / On yonder Lawn," are not shepherds but men of learning. There is no formal invocation of the muse in Belknap's poem. Instead, it is a sign in nature, an oak tree shattered by lightning, that reminds Florio of his loss. One critic notes that Joseph Seccombe, in his pastoral elegy "On the Death of the Reverend Benjamin Colman, D.D. An Eclogue" (1747), also uses a natural disaster to institute remembrance of the dead.

The other notable amendment to the pastoral genre is Belknap's inclusion of a closing prayer, which echoes a hymn, in the closing line of the poem. Although he was a Harvard-educated minister, Belknap's use of the hymn warrants further discussion precisely because he was an ordained minister. The eighteenth century saw a major shift in the stylistics of hymn writing. As the Puritan influence began to wane, the hymn writer was no longer required to use literal translations of biblical psalms as subject matter. For example, the Englishman Isaac Watts, a noted nonconformist who opposed the literal translation of the psalms, published *Hymns and Spiritual Songs*, which appeared in America in 1739 and exhibited a new style of free paraphrase. As Belknap was intimately familiar with and had published a biography of Watts, and was the publisher of his own book of songs and hymns, there is little doubt that he knew of both the sacred past and the "nonconformist" variations taking place. As a result of Belknap's inclusion of a poetic form once reserved for summarizing biblical psalms into a classical form of poetry such as an eclogue, we see not only America's further departure from Puritan strictures, but also a clear blending of the classical and Adamic myths and a "christianization" of a classical form.

Along with the divergences from the conventions of pastoral elegy and the failure of Belknap to quote anything from the prime British model of pastoral elegy, Milton's *Lycidas*, one can see this New England writer attempting his own version of classical forms, with an interest in his contemporaries rather than in the poets of Great Britain.

Further Reading. *Selected Primary Sources:* Belknap, Jeremy, "An Eclogue Occasioned by the Death of the Reverend Alexander Cumming" (Boston: 1763); Marcou, Jane Belknap, *Life of Jeremy Belknap, D.D., the historian of New Hampshire. With selections from his correspondence and other writers. Collected and arranged by his granddaughter* (New York: Harper, 1847). ***Selected Secondary Sources:*** Kirsch, George B., "Jeremy Belknap: Man of Letters in the Young Republic" (*New England Quarterly* 54.1 [March 1985]: 179–196); Leary, Lewis, "Poetry as Payment: Jeremy Belknap" (*Early American Literature* 17.2 [Fall 1982]: 161–164); Shields, John C., *The American Aeneas: Classical Origins of the American Self* (Knoxville: University of Tennessee Press, 2001).

Raymond Yanek

BELL, MARVIN (1937–)

Since publishing his first volume of poetry in 1966, Marvin Bell has had a prolific career: sixteen books of poetry as well as *Old Snow Just Melting*, a 1986 volume of essays and interviews. Despite these publications, Bell remains surprisingly underread, especially since his poetry carries the common speech qualities of **William Carlos Williams** and is accessible in subject matter. His work bears the stamp of the generation following Williams, including **Robert Lowell**, **John Berryman**, and **Elizabeth Bishop**. Like the work of these poets, Bell's poetry elevates the deeply personal to the universal, inclusive of literary and political contexts. It fluctuates in form between syntactical experiment and the "plain speak" patterns of spontaneous utterance, evoking the defiant spirit of the **Beats** as well as the **experimental** qualities of poets like **John Ashbery**.

Bell was born in 1937 in New York City. His father was a Jewish immigrant from the Ukraine—an influence Bell readily acknowledges, and one that is most keenly felt in his poems exploring issues of Jewish-American identity. He grew up in Center Moriches, on the south shore of Long Island, and was an undergraduate at Alfred University in New York. At twenty-two, he moved to Chicago, where he received his MA from the University of Chicago. In 1965 Bell moved to Iowa City, Iowa, and joined the prestigious University of Iowa's Writer's Workshop, first taking his MFA in poetry and then join-

ing the faculty. Since 1985 Bell has divided his time between Iowa City and Port Townsend, Washington.

Bell published his first collection of poetry in 1966. His second collection, *A Probable Volume of Dreams* (1969), was given the Lamont Award from the Academy of American Poets, and his 1977 collection, *Stars which See, Stars which do not See*, was a finalist for the National Book Award. His other honors include fellowships from the Guggenheim and the National Endowment for the Arts, senior Fulbright appointments in Yugoslavia and Australia, and poetry prizes from the *American Poetry Review*, *Poetry*, and the *Virginia Quarterly Review*. In March 2000 Bell was named the first poet laureate of Iowa, and he is currently the Flannery O'Connor Professor of Letters at the University of Iowa. Among those in his impressive list of former students are **Rita Dove**, **James Tate**, **Joy Harjo**, and **Marilyn Chin**.

One way in which Bell engages the personal in his poetry is through his exploration of Jewish American identity. His engagement with this topic has been evident throughout his career, including his earliest works. For instance, his first collection of poetry, *Things We Dreamt We Died For* (1966), includes the poem "The Israeli Navy." In this poem Bell bridges the personal quest for identity with the political quest for nationhood. Recognizing that the Jewish navy, state, or self has been adrift since creation, the poem concludes, "For years, their boats were slow, / and all show" In a similar way, his 1969 poem "The Extermination of the Jews," from *A Probable Volume of Dreams*, conflates personal, familial survival with the universal survival of the Jews in the years immediately following the Holocaust: "We who have not forgotten, / our children shall outremember." Perhaps Bell's most poignant Holocaust poem, however, is "Getting Lost in Nazi Germany." Written in 1971, the poem asks, "Would you eat the fruit of the corpses?" and hauntingly answers, "You would." All of these poems prove timely to the challenges facing Jewish Americans in the decades following World War II.

As with Bell's work generally, these poems demonstrate his ability to capture the complexities of the human condition in a poetic language that, while conversational and accessible, is nonetheless multifaceted and nuanced. Bell is arguably at his best in poems like "Being in Love," from his 1974 collection, *Residue of Song*. Writing about the oft-repeated theme of unrequited love, he observes, "Being in love with you, who are not / in love with me, you understand my dilemma." Clearly reminiscent of **e.e. cummings** and Williams, the playful simplicity of these lines underscores Bell's talent for transforming the common and mundane into the unique and remarkable.

Although Bell's poems often embrace the quotidian—engaging conventional subjects such as love, family, and work—his poetic form is often decidedly unconventional.

As his first statement in "32 Statements about Writing Poetry" suggests, Bell firmly believes "every poet is an Experimentalist." And while the bulk of his poetry is marked by the experimental tendencies of **modernism** and **postmodernism**, nowhere is this penchant for experiment more evident than in his "Dead Man" poems—a form he is credited with inventing. According to Bell, the "Dead Man" poems derive from the Zen axiom, "Live as if you were already dead." Fluctuating between lines of prose and poetry, this form allowed Bell to escape the poetic limits of enjambed and end-stopped lines. He further claims that, "with one foot in life and the other in death," "Dead Man" poems "swe [ep] the horizon." They are, he says, his "way of studying the dark without turning on the light."

The first "Dead Man" poem appears in Bell's 1990 collection, *Iris of Creation*, and in 1994 he published an entire collection of "Dead Man" poems appropriately titled *The Book of the Dead Man*. In the preface to this collection, he reminds readers that "perfected fallibility" is the key to understanding these poems, and that through their form these poems transcend the binaries of positive and negative, right and wrong, poetry and prose, and life and death: The "Dead Man," writes Bell, "accepts all and everything." *The Book of the Dead Man, Volume II* appeared in 1997, and Bell's latest collection of poetry, *Rampant* (2004), again returns to this form. The final section of this collection, titled "Journal of the Posthumous Present," includes ten pieces that recall Bell's earlier "Dead Man" poems, and throughout the collection generally Bell continues to experiment with the poetic line. By expanding the line's length to such an extent that the boundary between prose and poetry begins to blur, he aligns himself with an American poetic tradition best exemplified by poems like **Walt Whitman**'s "Song of Myself," Williams's "Patterson," and **Allen Ginsberg**'s "Howl." An active poet for over forty years, with a long publishing career, Bell continues writing today.

Further Reading. *Selected Primary Sources:* Bell, Marvin, *The Book of the Dead Man* (Port Townsend, WA: Copper Canyon Press, 1994); ———, *New and Selected Poems* (New York: Atheneum, 1987); ———, *Old Snow Just Melting: Essays and Interviews* (Dearborn: University of Michigan Press, 1983); ———, *A Probable Volume of Dreams* (New York: Atheneum, 1969); ———, *Rampant* (Port Townsend, WA: Copper Canyon Press, 2004). ***Selected Secondary Sources:*** Bunge, Nancy, "Marvin Bell: 'The University Is Something Else You Do'" (*American Poetry Review* 11.2 [Spring 1982]: 8–13); Jackson, Richard, "Containing the Other: Marvin Bell's Recent Poetry" (*North American Review* 280.1 [Winter 1995]: 45–48).

Richard Hishmeh

BELL, ROBERT MOWRY (1860–19?)

Robert Mowry Bell's poetry mirrors that of the Romantics in that it seeks to portray the true, natural emotions of an ordinary individual with a meditative and feeling mind. His skilled physician's eye aids him in identifying and examining the universal questions for which most people continue to seek answers.

Robert Mowry Bell was born in 1860 in Chicago, Illinois. He graduated from the University of Minnesota and Harvard Medical School, in addition to undertaking several years of study in Europe. Bell practiced medicine in Minneapolis until 1893, when poor health necessitated his moving to a milder climate. He relocated to California, and eventually traveled to Germany to continue his studies, with an eye toward serving as an instructor.

Bell's verses, most of which were contributed to periodicals, are of an elevated order. His poem "The Tutelage" is a fresh vision of the shell theme of William Wordsworth and Walter Savage Landor. It is an optimistic summation of the questions involved. The poem opens with the uncertainty of the proposition of the ocean's sound being audible through a coiled shell. Some say that hope leads to this belief rather than the shell's capacity. The speaker contemplates the fact that the sea places this and many shells on land as a testament from nature, the message of which is "life ruled by love nor dies nor dissipates." "The Second Volume" takes up the theme of discovering a magical object, in this case "a little book, in choicest vellum bound" in the library of a tower. The text reveals a romance so powerful that it mesmerizes the speaker for several hours. Yet when the book ends, there is no additional volume to conclude the tale, despite the speaker's frantic search for one. After a troubled inventory of the soul, the speaker is certain that there must be more to look forward to. The concluding line, "Soul, soul, there is a sequel to thy tale!" is delivered with such heartfelt conviction that the listener cannot help but share the speaker's enthusiasm.

Comparable to the Romantic poems of Samuel Taylor Coleridge and William Wordsworth, Bell's verses convey delight in the powers of nature. They convince the listener to sympathize with the speaker because the words express the truth of nature. Using a physician's keen analysis, such as that displayed by **William Carlos Williams**, another physician poet, Bell communicates the passions of his subjects through detailed and sympathetic imagery.

Further Reading. *Selected Primary Source:* Bell, Robert Mowry, "A' Ordinary Man" (*Century* 56.6 [1898]: 1054). ***Selected Secondary Source:*** Stedman, Edmund Clarence, *An American Anthology, 1787–1900* (Grosse Point, MI: Scholarly Press, 1968).

Roxanne Y. Schwab

BENEDIKT, MICHAEL (1935–)

Best known for his collections of **prose poems** published in the 1970s, Michael Benedikt is a surrealist poet who explores the inexplicable absurdity of daily life. Although he has become somewhat less familiar to readers of contemporary poetry—most likely because he has not published a full-length collection since 1980—his was a considerable contribution to twentieth-century verse. In addition to his five collections of poetry, he is an anthologist and translator. One of the contemporary poets he most closely resembles is **James Tate**; like Tate, he fuses witty trivia with a nearly existential sense of purposelessness. His poems are energetic and humorous; he emphasizes the improbability of the physical world, how randomly the world functions and has evolved. Although he lacks the bittersweet melancholy of **John Ashbery**, he shows a similar sense of the ironic, the zany, and the unpredictable; he constantly melds the high and the low, participating fully in the creation of poetic antinomies. Also like Ashbery, his poems lack a reliable narrator, or sense of the poet's self as speaker. They are very far from autobiography. Like the prose poems of **Russell Edson**, Benedikt's work relies upon a sense of spontaneity as well as the creation of unlikely fictional landscapes to render truths about the precariousness of the human condition.

Born May 26, 1935, Benedikt grew up in New York. His father worked as an electronics engineer; his mother taught elementary school. He was educated at New York University and served in the army reserve while attending college. After receiving his BA in 1956, he went on active duty, eventually becoming a sergeant. Upon his discharge from the military, he attended graduate school, completing an MA in English and comparative literature at Columbia University in 1961. He wrote his master's thesis on **Wallace Stevens** and French surrealism. After completing his education, he worked for Horizon Press from 1959 to 1962; he then served as managing editor for the magazine *Locus Solus*. Benedikt also wrote for *Art News* and *Art International*, indicating his longstanding interest in visual art. In addition to his collections of verse, Benedikt has worked on many anthologies, co-editing *Modern French Theatre: The Avant-Garde, Dada, & Surrealism* (1964); *Post-War German Theatre* (1966); and *Modern Spanish Theatre* (1967). He single-handedly edited two major **anthologies** of twentieth-century poetry: *The Poetry of Surrealism* (1974) and *The Prose Poem: An International Anthology* (1976). Benedikt served as poetry editor for the *Paris Review* from 1975 to 1978. He has taught at Bennington College, Sarah Lawrence College, Hampshire College, Vassar College, and Boston University, where he held the Anne Sexton Chair in Poetry in 1975 and has been a visiting professor since 1977. He has received a Guggenheim, a grant from the National Endowment for the Arts, and a grant from the New York State Council on the Arts. He currently serves as contributing editor to the *American Poetry Review*.

Benedikt's first collection, *The Body*, emphasizes relationships between people and is more realistic than his later work. Less inclined to humor, the sensibility of the poems is subtle and seems almost neo-Romantic, and his language suggests a somewhat idyllic and idealistic perspective: "what you see is a permeated heaven / Of stars and lattices and everything flourishing." Still, however, the poems are suggestive of Benedikt's inheritance from French surrealism: "The wings of the nose," he writes, "I sense them fluttering / Making a passenger of the whole olfactory system." "The Wings of the Nose" is one of the better-known poems in the collection and it demonstrates the sense of distance between people, between the mind and body, and between the body and the landscape, that are the dominant themes of the collection. In the first poem, he writes, "Air, air, you are the distant-most thing I know."

Sky (1971) followed *The Body* and it is notable as a transitional moment in Benedikt's work. In the poems in *Sky*, it is possible to detect Benedikt's increasing movement toward surrealism, as well as a strong influence from the **New York School** poets, particularly **Frank O'Hara**. A poem titled "Coming and Going" is reminiscent of O'Hara's "Ave Maria": "Get the children of America out of Troy, New York!" The tone of the collection is more exhausted and resigned than that of his debut volume: "Nothing works," he writes. "The mind is manufacturing infinite and irrelevant amounts." This sense of resignation is key to Benedikt's eventual shift to total surrealism, as it represents the failure of realism to illuminate the problems and dilemmas of modern living as the poet experienced them.

Benedikt is best known for his two collections of prose poems, *Mole Notes* (1971) and *Night Cries* (1976). *Mole Notes* has been described by critic Louis Gallo as a book "which relate[s] the ruminations, experiences, feelings, or regrets of a fable-like persona and central consciousness called 'Mole'." "Mole" consciousness is at the heart of the book—in other words, the expression of the idea that there is no "real" world, there is only the world that is created within the mind. Critic Louis Gallo has further pointed out that Benedikt's principal method is to conflate the outer world with the inner by compounding metaphors. For example, from "Private Eye," the first poem in the book: "The private eye just accepted the challenging assignment!—that is, solving the mystery of why inner and outer are frequently unconnected." In *Night Cries*, the sense of futile despair evident in Benedikt's early work has been heightened; Louis Gallo refers to it as "ironic horror." The following example, "The Gift," amply illustrates this strain: "It's a specially designed pistol for committing suicide, with a muzzle at one end and on the other a bottle opener, in case you should decide to drink yourself to death."

Further Reading. *Selected Primary Sources:* Benedikt, Michael, *Benedikt: A Profile. With Critical Essays by Louis Gallo and Alan Ziegler, an interview by Naomi Shihab and a portfolio of 18 new poems and a preface by Michael Benedikt* (Tucson, AZ: Grilled Flowers Press, 1978); ———, *The Badminton at Great Barrington; or Gustave Mahler & the Chattanooga Choo-Choo* (Pittsburgh: University of Pittsburgh Press, 1980); ———, *The Body* (Middletown, CT: Wesleyan University Press, 1968); ———, *Mole Notes* (Middletown, CT: Wesleyan University Press, 1971); ———, *Night Cries* (Middletown, CT: Wesleyan University Press, 1976); ———, ed., *The Poetry of Surrealism* (Boston: Little, Brown, 1974); ———, *Sky* (Middletown, CT: Wesleyan University Press, 1970). *Selected Secondary Sources:* Gallo, Louis, "Contemporary Parables" (*Modern Poetry Studies* 7.3 [Winter 1976]: 249–251); Howard, Ben, "Comment" (*Poetry* 130.5 [August 1977]); Martz, Louis L., "Recent Poetry: Visions and Revisions" (*Yale Review* 60.3 [Spring 1971]: 415–416); McGann, Jerome, "The Virtues of Prose" (*Times Literary Supplement* [23 July 1976]: 911).

Amy Newlove Schroeder

BENÉT, STEPHEN VINCENT (1898–1943)

In the first line of "John Brown's Body," his **epic** poem on America's Civil War, Stephen Vincent Benét invokes the "strong and diverse heart" of the "American muse" to be his source, a muse that the rest of his invocation identifies as embodied in every bit of the American landscape and in every inhabitant, native or immigrant, of that landscape. He wrote five novels and scores of short stories, but Benét always saw himself as a poet. For the primary subject matter of that poetry and much of the prose, he chose American history: American legends and myths; American persons, both real and fictional; and American ideals and dreams.

Benét's American muse sang in folk songs, ballads, and spirituals as well as in the formal forms of poetry in English—dramatic dialogues like Robert Browning's, blank verse, heroic couplets, quatrains, fourteen-liners, and **free verse**. Probably the English writer whose work most influenced Benét's poetry was William Morris, whom Benet read extensively as a boy and young man. He copied Morris's technique of integrating ballads and songs into narrative verse; and, like Morris, he used octosyllabic couplets for narrative passages (Stroud, 24). He learned to write **Walt Whitman**'s free lines and **Vachel Lindsay**'s heavily rhythmic ones (Izzo, 4). The roots of Benét's poetry were imbedded in the nineteenth century. Perhaps because of that continuity, he was possibly the most widely read American

poet of his day. Politically, Benét was a liberal, a strong supporter of Franklin Roosevelt's New Deal policies. In literary forms and subject matter, he was far more conservative. Sometimes, however, as in *Burning City* and in his short tale "By the Waters of Babylon," his vision is an apocalyptic one of a civilization destroyed.

Benét was born into a military family on July 22, 1898, in Bethlehem, Pennsylvania, where his father was stationed at the time. He was the youngest child of Captain James Walker Benét and Frances Neill Benét. He grew up in a number of states—Pennsylvania, New York, Illinois, California, and Georgia. It seems likely that his movable home stimulated in him a national consciousness of his country rather than a narrower, regional one. Although both his father and his grandfather, for whom Stephen Vincent was named, were West Point graduates and career ordnance officers, the family was a literary one in their home. All three children—William Rose, Laura, and Stephen—became poets and writers.

In 1915, when he was only seventeen, Stephen sold his first poem to the *Nation*. He also published his first book of poems, *Five Men and Pompey*, and he entered Yale. Yale was significant to his continuing development as a poet. Its university press published Benét's second book of poems, *Young Adventure*, in 1918. He wrote for and chaired the *Yale Literary Magazine*. He also wrote for Yale's satirical *Record*. He was a member of the Elizabeth Club. The writers **Archibald MacLeish**, Thornton Wilder, and Phillip Barry were his close friends at Yale and then for life. So, too, was John C. Farrar, who later became Benét's editor and then his publisher. After graduating in 1919, Benét stayed on at Yale to study for a master's degree, which he received in June 1920. As his thesis, he presented a set of poems that were published later that year as *Heaven and Earth*. Yale also granted him a traveling fellowship for the next academic year. He went to Paris and there completed his first novel, *The Beginning of Wisdom*.

In Paris Benét also met Rosemary Carr, an American journalist writing for the *Chicago Tribune*. They were married in November 1921. The marriage was "the great love story behind the rest of his work and life" (Izzo, 4). Benét's second novel was published in 1922, and a third in 1923. Benét was writing prose to ensure an adequate income for his growing family. In 1926 he won a Guggenheim fellowship, the first awarded to a poet, for the purpose of researching and writing a long poem on the American Civil War (Monroe, 91). To make the money last for two years, the Benéts moved to Paris. "John Brown's Body" was published in 1928 and won the Pulitzer Prize for poetry in 1929. The epic was the Book of the Month Club's choice for August 1928; in the following two years its publisher, Doubleday, sold over 130,000 copies. Benét's second Pulitzer for poetry was a posthumous one for *Western Star*, the first book of a projected second epic about the relentless push of the frontier from the East to the West Coast. Unexpectedly, in 1943, Stephen Vincent Benét, only forty-four years old, died of a heart attack in his wife's arms.

Benét was an unusually prolific writer of both prose and poetry. He took up prose primarily to earn his living and had to teach himself to write prose. He wrote five novels; the first three, appearing in rapid succession—*The Beginning of Wisdom* (1920), *Young People's Pride* (1922), and *Jean Huguenot* (1923)—concerned problems of youth, romantic love, and ambition. Parry Stroud finds that the three are marked by structural disunity and by Benét's preference for romanticism over realism (97). The fourth novel, *Spanish Bayonet* (1926), is set in pre-Revolutionary Florida. The hero is a young New Yorker investigating the sinister colony of New Sparta near St. Augustine. Stroud finds it to be a "technically a competent novel," unified in structure and consistent in style but marred by "cookie-cutter characterizations" and the synthetic aura of "costume romance" (99–100). Benét published his last novel, *James Shore's Daughter*, in 1934. The primary scene is New York society in the early 1900s. Benét examines the plutocracy created by American wealth and power after the closing of the frontier.

Benét's short stories are at their best when he weaves American history and myths into his imaginative plots. Of these many tales, the finest is "The Devil and Daniel Webster." It is an American Faustian story in which a hard-pressed young New England farmer, Jabez Stone, contracts with an American Mephistopheles named Scratch to pay with his soul for ten years of prosperity. Daniel Webster saves the young man's soul by reminding a jury of twelve American ghosts, including Judge Hathorn and Benedict Arnold, that the they were once men who made morally condemnable mistakes but who also contributed to bringing something new into history—the concept and reality of the free individual (Lincoln Konkle, "American Reincarnations"; Izzo, 175). "The Devil and Daniel Webster" seems to be a parable about America itself. Benét later revised it into a one-act play, then into a libretto for an opera. In 1941, the tale became a highly successful film.

One last prose work, "By the Waters of Babylon," should be noted because some critics consider it to be a forerunner of science fiction stories and films of apocalypse (Toby Johnson, "Stephen Vincent Benét in the Twilight Zone"; Izzo, 213). The setting is sometime in the future following a holocaust, a great burning that has destroyed all the world's civilizations. The narrator goes on a long journey to the "Places of the Gods," which turn out to be the ruins of Washington, D.C., and New York City. He does not learn the why of the great burning, but he comes to realize that these were cities of men, not gods, and what men had destroyed, men could rebuild. Benet returns to the themes of apocalypse in four poems in *Burning City* (1936). In each poem New York is either destroyed or being destroyed. Morton Dauwen Zabel warns Benét against prophecy because "it is the surest way of deluding a valid ambition to poetry" (282).

Benét published his ballads and **lyrics** as single poems in magazines and in collections. One of his ballads, "American Names" (1922), is familiar to readers today. He wrote it in Paris when he was working on "John Brown's Body" and missing the American landscape. The speaker warns that if you bury his body in Sussex or bury his tongue Champmedy, "I shall not be there, I shall rise and pass. / Bury my heart at Wounded Knee" (*Selected Works*, I, 368). Wounded Knee is the site in South Dakota where, in 1890, the Seventh Cavalry massacred a gathering of the Lakota Sioux. It was the final clash between the U.S. Army and Native Americans. Benét knew this history when he wrote that final line and image. Dee Brown further enriched the image when, in 1970, he used the line as the title of his Indian history of the American West.

The "Ballad of William Sycamore" (1922) is, on the other hand, an idealized portrait of an American frontiersman from his birth in 1790 until his death in 1871 (a later edition changes his death date to 1880). Thus William Sycamore's life comes very close to spanning the whole push to settle the frontier from the original colonies to the West Coast. Sycamore's nemesis is not the Native Americans around him or in front of him, but rather the ever-encroaching towns at his back. Stroud praises the narrative ballad for its use of colloquial speech, its inclusion of folk lyrics, and its ability to capture the rhythms of country fiddle playing (28).

Both these ballads are intimately related to Benét's major work, "John Brown's Body." The push westward was part of the genesis of the Civil War, and the massacre at Wounded Knee had its inception in that war. Benét's epic of almost 15,000 lines begins, after its invocation, with John Brown's raid on Harper's Ferry and ends with President Abraham Lincoln's death and General Robert E. Lee's surrender at Appomattox. Only to a limited extent does Benét follow the epic structure of Homer and Virgil; he divides his poem into books, but only eight rather than twenty-four. Benét's characters include a significant range of historical persons—Lincoln, Jefferson Davis, Lee, Ulysses S. Grant, Stonewall Jackson, and John Brown—as well as a range of fictional characters, some representing the Northern side and some the Southern. Gary Grieve-Carlson notes that the epic has "genuine strengths," particularly in "its cataloguing of vivid emotional images" ("*John Brown's Body* and the Meaning of the Civil War"; Izzo, 130). These vivid images appropriate the senses, especially the visual and aural. Benét narrates his stories of the Civil War by revealing them to the reader in dramatic vignettes. The poem itself refers to its structure as a cyclorama, a pictorial representation on a circular wall with the viewer in the center (Stroud, 48). **Harriet Monroe** recognizes that Benét's poem is a "kind of cinema epic, brilliantly flashing an hundred different aspects of American character and history on the silver screen" (91). F.O. Matthiesson interprets Monroe's use of "cinema epic" as a negative, reductive appellation parallel to his own reductive description of the poem as "a novel in a variety of verse forms" (*Literary History of the United States*, 1350). Monroe also describes the poem as a "super-journalistic epic" (91). On the other hand, she finds much to praise, especially "the poet's whole-hearted abandonment to his 'American Muse'" (92–93).

It is this very abandonment that Morton Dauwen Zabel criticizes in his review of *Burning City*, a collection of poems published in 1936. Zabel argues that Benét's enthusiasm leads to a diminished focus on meaning in the word, the metaphor, and in the whole poem. He classifies Benét as a bard, a "romantic fabulist," spinning "legends out of any stuff . . . Biblical, historical or fantastic" (277). Benét is one of a long line of bards, extending through Vachel Lindsay back to **Henry Wadsworth Longfellow**. For Zabel, *Burning City* illustrates the difference between bard and poet. The bard has no need to refine his language to exact meanings and no interest in an economy of structure or in personal references. The bard indulges the reader by making the reading easy. Benét's poems in *Burning City* on the cruelties of the totalitarian regimes of Europe produce "passable verse journalism" but lack anything "memorable as poetic meaning."

Paul Engle, reviewing *Western Star*, Benét's final work, partially answers Zabel's criticism of Benét. He suggests that just as America is diverse in its geography and people, so, too, its art must be diverse, able to incorporate both **T.S. Eliot** and **Robert Frost**. Benét's early death was "a particular loss" because he added the historical narrative to American poetry's variety. Engle defends Benét's "deep regard for the U. S. A.," pointing out that Benét understood the "misery and corruption" of our history, but he believed this country to be "remarkable" in permitting human freedom and in translating the concept of freedom to individual rights and intellectual "exemption" (160). Engle, however, does echo one of Zabel's observations about Benét's lack of concern for exact meaning. Engle finds that Benét too often and too readily accepted the word or phrase, writing that came easily to hand. However, Engle also ends with praise, writing that *Western Star* "expands the types of our poetry" with its verse narratives about individuals searching "for a home and an emblem" (162).

Further Reading. *Selected Primary Source: Selected Works of Stephen Vincent Benét*, 2 vols. (no editor) (New York: Farrar & Rinehart, 1942). *Selected Secondary Sources:* Engle, Paul, "The American Search" (*Poetry*, LXIII [December 1943]: 159–162); Izzo, David Garrett, and Lincoln Konkle, *Stephen Vincent Benét: Essays on his Life and Work* (Jefferson, NC: McFarland, 2003); Monroe, Harriet, "A Cinema Epic" (*Poetry*, XXXIII [1928]: 91–96); Stroud, Parry, *Stephen Vincent Benét* (New York: Twayne, 1962); Zabel, Morton Dauwen, "The American Grain" (*Poetry*, XLVIII [August 1936]: 276–282).

Helen Deese

BENNETT-COVERLY, LOUISE (1919–)

Regarded by many as the first **Caribbean** woman "dub" poet, Jamaica's leading folklorist Louise Bennett-Coverly (affectionately called "Miss Lou") is known for her linguistic and political stance in operating exclusively within the Jamaican Creole idiom, forcing and forging its acceptance as a national language. On the one hand, her championing of the Jamaican dialect accounts for the scant recognition Bennett-Coverly received nationally and internationally in the early years of her career. On the other hand, it has earned her numerous awards, including the Jamaica Order of Merit, the Institute of Jamaica's Musgrave Silver and Gold Medals, and the Most Excellent Order of the British Empire, bestowed by Queen Elizabeth in 1960 for the poet's outstanding contribution to the arts and culture of Jamaica. Embedded in the oral tradition, much of Bennett-Coverly's work is social commentary and criticism on political, social, and economic issues affecting ordinary people. University of the West Indies' (Mona) chancellor Rex Nettleford underscores the uniqueness of Bennett-Coverly's work, noting that although this uniqueness presents problems of classification and description, the poet's most valuable asset is originality.

Born on September 7, 1919, in Kingston, Jamaica, Louise Bennett-Coverly adopted a stance of self-acceptance and national pride from her widowed mother, a dressmaker, and her grandmother. She revealed a knack for poetry and storytelling around age seven and wrote her first dialect poem at age fourteen. Married for almost fifty years to Eric Winston Coverly, a well-known theatre personality in Jamaica, Miss Lou was widowed in 2002. She has a son and several adopted children and resides in Toronto, Ontario.

Bennett-Coverly is best known for her book of poetry, *Jamaica Labrish* (1966). In 1979 she published another book of poetry, *Anancy and Miss Lou*, and in 1993 her first collection of monologues in prose, *Aunty Roachy Seh*. Among her numerous recordings are "Jamaica Singing Games" (1953), "Jamaica Folksongs" (1953), "Miss Lou's Views" (1967), "Listen to Miss Lou" (1968), "Carifesta

Ring Ding" (1976), "The Honorable Miss Lou" (1981), and "Miss Lou Live" (1983). Her composition "You're Going Home Now" won a nomination from the Academy of Canadian Cinema and Television for the best original song in a movie (*Milk and Honey*) in 1998.

Absorbed in grassroots tradition, Bennett-Coverly brings both sympathy and satire to the ordinary but complex lives of common people. Her advocacy of women's rights is apparent in her poem "Bans o' Ooman," in which once silenced women are given voice by the newly created Jamaica Federation of Women (*Jamaica Labrish*, 1966). Bennett-Coverly also celebrates black pride and the quest for racial equality, an emphasis dating particularly from the 1948 visit to Jamaica by Paul Robeson. Issues of nationality and nationhood are developed in poems such as "Dear Departed Federation," "Jamaica Elevate," and "Independance" (*Jamaica Labrish*). In the latter she writes that the desire for independence is intrinsic in human nature and that "she glad fe see dat Govament / Turn independant to" (*Jamaica Labrish*, 169). Jamaica's progress and independence are viewed in the final section of the book, "Jamaica—Now an' Then." While the "then" of the title reflects nationhood and identity, the "now" signals a new generation and a new movement: "migrancy." With the advent of emigration, a reverse colonization, so to speak, comes the invention of a new home space. Britain and America are seen both as the "new" promised land and as imperial powers (Britain as former and America as present) in the poems "Colonisation in Reverse," which refers to England, and "America." Most fittingly, this section of *Jamaica Labrish* ends with Bennett-Coverly's obsession: the politics of language. She questions the validation of one form of language, standard (British) English, over another, Jamaican English, arguing that both are derivatives of dialect. She addresses the speakers of standard English when she refers to this speech as "Dah language weh yuh proud o', weh yuh honour and respeck," noting that this language, too, "spring from dialect!" (*Jamaica Labrish*, 218).

This linguistic concern continues in Bennett-Coverly's collection of monologues in prose, *Aunty Roachy Seh* (1993), epitomized in the call-and-response format suggested by the title. Bennett-Coverly invokes the storytelling tradition at the beginning of each story with the phrase "listen, no!" The concerns of *Aunty Roachy Seh* include gender relations, female exploitation, equality, classism, and racism. The resilience and resistance of women are embodied in the eighteenth-century heroine and female leader of the maroons, Hero Nanny. Sharing a platform with Nanny, Bennett-Coverly reveals herself as a revolutionary also, having revolutionized the Jamaican language, lending credence and visibility to the vernacular.

Further Reading. *Selected Primary Sources:* Bennett-Coverly, Louise, *Anancy and Miss Lou* (Kingston, Jamaica: Sangster's Book Stores Ltd., 1979); ———, *Anancy Stories and Dialect Poems* (Kingston, Jamaica: Gleaner, 1944);———, *Aunty Roachy Seh*, ed. Mervyn Morris (Kingston, Jamaica: Sangster's Book Stores Ltd., 1993); ———, *Children's Jamaican Songs & Games* (sound recording) (New York: Folkways, 1957); ———, *Jamaican Dialect Verses by Louise Bennett* (Kingston, Jamaica: Gleaner, 1942); ———, *Jamaican Folk Songs and Stories* (sound recording) (Kingston, Jamaica: Sangster's Book Stores Ltd., 1966); ———, *Jamaica Labrish* (Kingston, Jamaica: Sangster's Books Stores Ltd., 1966); ———, *Jamaican Poems* (Kingston, Jamaica: Gleaner, 1943); ———, *Laugh with Miss Louise: Poems, Folksongs, Stories in Jamaican Language* (Kingston, Jamaica: Pioneer Press, 1960); ———, *Lawd the Riddim Sweet* (sound recording) (Kingston, Jamaica: Sangster's Book Stores Ltd., 1999); ———, *Miss Lou and Friends* (video recording) (Paris: UNESCO, 1990); ———, *Selected Poems* (Kingston, Jamaica: Sangster's Book Stores Ltd., 1982); ———, *Songs from Pantomime* (Kingston, Jamaica: Gleaner, 1949); ———, *Yes M'Dear* (video recording) (London, 1983). ***Selected Secondary Sources:*** Beckwith, Martha Warren, *Jamaica Proverbs* (New York: Negro Universities Press, 1970); Cooper, Carolyn, *Noises in the Blood: Orality, Gender, and the 'Vulgar' Body of Jamaican Popular Culture* (Durham, NC: Duke University Press, 1995); Dance, Daryl Cumber, ed., *Fifty Caribbean Writers* (New York: Greenwood Press, 1986); DeCaires Narain, Denise, *Contemporary Caribbean Women's Poetry: Making Style* (London: Routledge, 2002); Jekyll, Walter, ed., *Jamaica Song and Story: Annancy Stories, digging sings, ring tunes, and dancing tunes. With new Introductory Essays by Philip Sherlock, Louise Bennett and Rex Nettleford* (New York: Dover, 1966); Ramazani, Jahan, *The Hybrid Muse: Postcolonial Poetry in English* (Chicago: University of Chicago Press, 2001).

Simone A. James Alexander

BERG, STEPHEN (1934–)

Stephen Berg is a poet, translator, editor, and anthologist whose work helped establish the mainstream of American poetry in the early 1970s. Berg can be seen as a representative poet of his times: He first emerged as a practitioner of a post-confessional **free verse** mode influenced by **Theodore Roethke**, **Stanley Kunitz**, and **Robert Lowell**. His later poetry took greater formal risks and moved toward prose and longer forms without abandoning the autobiographical impulse that has guided much of his writing. As a translator of "versions" from numerous traditions, Berg has contributed to the internationalization of American poetry that began in the 1960s and has continued to the present. Finally, beginning with *Naked Poetry* (1969) and continuing through his editorship of the *American Poetry Review* (founded 1972), Berg's work as an editor has been perhaps more influential than his poetry, reconciling differences and creating reputations.

Stephen Berg was born in Philadelphia, Pennsylvania, and was educated at the University of Pennsylvania, Boston University, the University of Indiana School of Letters, and the State University of Iowa (BA, 1959). The bulk of his career has been spent in Philadelphia, where he has taught at Temple University, Princeton University, and Haverford College; since 1967 he has been professor of humanities at the University of the Arts in Philadelphia. Berg has received awards and fellowships from numerous institutions, including the Guggenheim and Rockefeller foundations and the National Endowment for the Arts.

Stephen Berg's early poetry arises within the autobiographical free verse tradition that began with **Walt Whitman** and continued through Robert Lowell and **James Wright**. Often focused on domestic subjects, including his wife and daughters and the death of his father, Berg's early work tends toward an elegiac seriousness. Sometimes the influences are obvious; "A Wife Talks to Herself," from *The Daughters* (1971), clearly derives from **William Carlos Williams**'s poem "The Widow's Lament in Springtime." But elsewhere the ancestry is less apparent, though in retrospect it is clear that Berg is assembling his own voice out of multiple influences. In American poetry, these influences include Williams, Lowell, the American surrealism of Wright and **Robert Bly**, the plainspoken negativity of **Alan Dugan**, and numerous poets who emerged in the 1960s.

Other influences included the stories of Anton Chekhov and the poetry of the Russian Anna Akhmatova. In *Grief* (1975), Berg fashioned several poems after Chekhov stories even as the primary theme of the book—mourning his father's death—remained autobiographical. The book as a whole is an autobiographical text of mourning, but it does not disavow its literariness. Indeed, "With Akhmatova at the Black Gates," a poem born out of both mourning and reading, identifies Berg's own grief with Akhmatova's personal and political isolation. In his next book, also titled *With Akhmatova at the Black Gates* (1981), Berg extends this technique through an entire sequence that transforms the poems and biography of Akhmatova into something neither translation nor entirely original. In these poems, the dialogue between the source text and the biography of the poet doing the translating blends into a single voice.

Although *With Akhmatova at the Black Gates* is not really a **translation**, even his more conventional translations are fairly free. Berg, who calls his translations "versions" (much as Robert Lowell called his "imitations"), frequently works from the literal translations of others to make a new poem. In *The Steel Cricket: Versions 1958–1997* (1997), Berg collects versions of poems and songs originally composed in Spanish, French, Italian, Hungarian, Japanese, and other languages (including Eskimo). In a preface and notes, he explicitly acknowledges the sources of these poems in translation and maintains a "commitment to free invention."

With *In It* (1986), Berg moves back into the postconfessional lyric, but with a looser, more prose-like line and with renewed confidence in his own voice. In these poems Berg's career as a teacher enters the poems explicitly as one in a number of autobiographical details: The speaker of "Sad Invective" speaks of "never being afraid of anyone—no academic deans, no Presidents great at fund-raising, no strict English Department Chairmen," and the title poem matter-of-factly mentions "teaching all day at the university." In earlier poems, Berg's affiliation as an academic had tended to be represented in terms of textuality itself, either in the intertextual dialogues of the Chekhov or the Akhmatova poems or in the instructions to the reader in "Page 256" (from *Grief*). Here, however, the poet is comfortable in his role as a teacher and represents it simply and directly as a job.

Berg's *New and Selected Poems* (1992) ends with "Homage to the Afterlife," a seventeen-page poem in which each long, Whitmanic line begins with the anti-Whitmanic "Without me"—as though the poet were testing the absence of self within American poetry's most self-directed tradition. (If, however, the "me" in the opening phrase of each line "Without me" is the afterlife, the poem is testing the possibilities of a world without illusions: "Without me, the world became what it was what it always is.") "Homage to the Afterlife" is not quite prose, but it approaches prose; Berg continues to explore the possibilities of prose, as well as the longer line, in his later books *Oblivion* (1995), *Shaving* (1998), *Porno Diva Numero Uno* (2000), and *X=* (2002) (a book which, like "Without Me," plays with oracular possibilities of anaphora in the tradition of Whitman and **Allen Ginsberg**).

Berg has also worked tirelessly as an anthologist and editor. *Naked Poetry: Recent American Poetry in Open Forms* (1969), co-edited with **Robert Mezey**, may be seen as an attempt to tame **open form** poetry (represented most famously by Donald Allen's 1960 anthology, *The New American Poetry*) by printing under one cover a variety of poets writing in free verse from **Robert Creeley** to **Sylvia Plath**. It excluded the most tendentious and theoretical advocates of open form (such as **Robert Duncan** and **Charles Olson**) in order to advocate a more relaxed notion of literary quality.

The unifying mission of *Naked Poetry* was in a sense extended in 1972 when Berg founded the *American Poetry Review*, which became one of the most important literary magazines of the late twentieth century. From its founding, *APR* was distinguished both by its format (large pages, author photos accompanying poems) and by its openness to a wide variety of forms and genres. In addition to original poetry by American authors, *APR* published interviews, reviews, essays, and translations. Although *APR* was sometimes accused of representing only a fairly narrow range of academically embedded, free-verse poets (and although it was generally hostile to explicit poetic movements such as **New Formalism** and **Language poetry**), in fact it has published both formal and experimental verse and can make a claim to being the representative magazine of the diversity of American poetry at the end of the twentieth century.

Further Reading. *Selected Primary Sources:* Berg, Stephen, *The Daughters* (Indianapolis: Bobbs-Merrill, 1971); ———, *Grief* (New York: Grossman, 1975); ———, *In It* (Urbana: Univerity of Illinois Press, 1986); ———, *New & Selected Poems* (Port Townsend, WA: Copper Canyon Press, 1992); ———, *Oblivion* (Urbana: University of Illinois Press, 1995); ———, *Shaving* (Marshfield, MA: Four Way Books, 1998); ———, *The Steel Cricket: Versions 1958–1997* (Port Townsend, WA: Copper Canyon Press, 1997); ———, *With Ahkmatova at the Black Gates* (Urbana: University of Illinois Press, 1981); ———, *X =* (Urbana: University of Illinois Press, 2002); Berg, Stephen, ed., with David Bonanno and Arthur Vogelsang, *The Body Electric: America's Best Poetry from the American Poetry Review* (New York: Norton, 2000); Berg, Stephen, ed., with Robert Mezey, *Naked Poetry: Recent American Poetry in Open Forms* (Indianapolis: Bobbs-Merrill, 1969). *Selected Secondary Sources:* Digges, Deborah, "Translation and the Egg" (*Field: Contemporary Poetry and Poetics* 39 [1988]: 27–31); Lieberman, Laurence, "The Passion of Mourning," in *Beyond the Muse of Memory: Essays on Contemporary American Poets* (Columbia: University of Missouri Press, 1995), 129–169.

David Kellogg

BERNARD, APRIL (1956–)

Author of a novel, a screenplay, and numerous literary and topical essays, April Bernard is best known for her three collections of poetry, which have been praised for addressing the aesthetic and moral turmoil of the age with startling urgency. Of her three books, the first, *Blackbird Bye Bye*, depicts that turmoil in the most extreme terms; the book received the 1988 Walt Whitman Award from the Academy of American Poets. Her second collection, *Psalms* (1993), depicts a similar world with broader vision and a more open heart. *Swan Electric* (2002) reflects knowingness, maturity, and self-acceptance.

April Bernard was born in Williamstown, Massachusetts, and raised in New England. She received a bachelor's degree from Harvard University and did graduate work at Yale University before leaving academe for New York City. After working for years in magazine publishing, Bernard began her full-time teaching career in the early 1990s. In 2003 she was awarded a Guggenheim grant in poetry. She currently teaches at Bennington College in Bennington, Vermont.

Predominantly urban, Bernard's poems are also set at the sea shore and in woodlands. Whatever their external settings, the poems focus on fragmented and uneasy inner landscapes. Opposing this focus, in her first two books, especially, is a struggle for wholeness and moral clarity that finds some degree of resolution in *Psalms* and to a greater degree in *Swan Electric*. Despite her occasionally ironic stance, Bernard does not set herself apart from the people and situations her poems explore; she locates herself among them, introducing a collective undertone.

Each of Bernard's collections evolves from the previous one thematically and stylistically, yet each is in some way distinct. In *Blackbird Bye Bye* a strong voice is already evident, as are Bernard's characteristic concerns. At the same time, the book bears hallmarks of a first collection, including a small group of poems that clearly allude to literary predecessors and a poem responding to a professor's comment about landscape poetry. *Blackbird Bye Bye* includes a wide variety of subject matter, from "Prayers and Sermons for the Stations of the Cross," which ends with the speaker's failure to "be persuaded," to "The Score," a shorter sequence about a robbery narrated with journalistic objectivity, to the title poem, which opens with the image of a drunken boy in a soldier's cape, explores personal memory and the contemporary zeitgeist, and ends with a plea that the "you" the poem addresses speak back about "these bad times."

The opacity reviewers have observed in Bernard's work is most evident in this collection. This feature does not represent absence of meaning; it reflects lack of contextual information, lack of syntactical connections, and the use of disparate metaphors for the same object or idea. Rather than fight toward understanding, the reader might prefer to follow the advice **Laura (Jackson) Riding** gave for reading her own poems; that is, do so repeatedly, allowing meaning to surface. This approach foregrounds the texture of Bernard's language and sensory details, rather than sacrificing them to the construal of sense.

The thematic transition from Bernard's first collection to her second, *Psalms*, is seamless. Whereas *Blackbird Bye Bye* ends with an allusion to "these bad times," *Psalms* opens with their depiction: a bleak winter cityscape peopled by one man with feet bound in rags. The speaker of "Psalm of the City-Dweller Gone Home" is moved to comment, "If I wandered with bloody feet on this bitter night and asked for God / I would be afraid to find him." All the poems in this collection, except those in "Part Five: Lamentations and Praises," include the word "psalms" in their titles, which, given the book's range of subjects, suggests both cultural and individual spiritual struggles. The poems move between the despair expressed in the first poem, the outright denial declared in "Psalm of a Dark Day," which opens with the statement that "There is no God," and the faith revealed in "Lamentations and Praises Two," which ends with the observation that "You [God] have become my favorite reader." With this sentence, an impediment has been overcome. That New York, the "most sagrada of cities," is the home of would-be murderers as well as those who pray that "the sweet taste" be taken from "the violent thought," home of a man who uses "rags to bind his feet" as well as a person who worries about the placement of a vase, suggests that faith, if achieved, requires acceptance of the world as it is.

Psalms shares several tonal elements with *Blackbird Bye Bye*, including irony, despair, and mixed diction. At the same time, the poems in *Psalms* are more coherent, and a notable feature in the collection is its imagery. "Part Five: Lamentations and Praises" is written in prose rather than verse lines. The numerous allusions to specific biblical psalms suggest the timelessness of the fight for belief. The songs themselves may be new, as the book's epigram "Sing unto the Lord a new song" suggests, but their inspiration is an ancient one.

Swan Electric, April Bernard's third collection of poems, is distinctive for the sense of perspective that informs its view of the past, and for the controlled intelligence that comments on the difficult present. The tone of *Swan Electric* is its unifying element and is a marked change from the urgency of the earlier collections. While it is apparent from the first poems of the book, the quality of calm directness is particularly noticeable in Part Two, the long sequence "Song of Yes and No," which comprises a poetic memoir of the New York City of the poet's young adulthood and, we surmise, her artistic youth and that of her friends. The largest difference between *Swan Electric* and Bernard's two earlier collections may be the somewhat sad wisdom that pervades this sequence; passion and innocence have given way. God is not mentioned; there is a sense that the poet has put aside questions of faith for the time being at least. The other sequence in the book, "Eidetica," recounts dreams or fantasies. They are narrated in the same straightforward way as are the incidents in "Song . . .," and they also reflect a degree of self-knowledge, and acceptance of self and others, that the earlier books do not, although the poems are by no means complacent.

The more even-toned quality of *Swan Electric* is also detectable in the book's technical elements. Part One comprises sonnets "disheveled" because they are not in iambic pentameter and do not follow the traditional rhyme pattern, yet sonnets because they are fourteen lines long and do follow the sonnet's rhetorical pattern, which Bernard describes as "This, and this, but this; and moreover" (quoted in Livingston). Internal and end rhymes are used throughout the book, making the texture of language congruent with meaning rather than oppositional. The poems in *Swan Electric* are not staid or unsurprising, however. Lines such as "fwup, fwup, fwup, shouts the copter / bulging blue head in the inky sky" and "I sit combing the spite from my hair" and "There's a sport: longing" reveal Bernard's provocative tone. *Swan Electric* does not alarm or lament so much as it confides. The difference between these is the journey Bernard's poetry traces.

Further Reading. *Selected Primary Sources:* Bernard, April, *Blackbird Bye Bye* (New York: Random House, 1989); ———, *Psalms* (New York: W.W. Norton, 1993); ———, *Swan Electric* (New York: W.W. Norton, 2002). ***Selected Secondary Sources:*** Doty, Mark, "Most Sagrada of Cities Sky-Lit" (*Parnassus: Poetry in Review* 19.2 [1994]); Livingston, Reb, "Interview: April Bernard by Reb Livingston" (*Post Road* 7 [2003]); Skloot, Floyd, "Bearing Sorrow" (*Southern Review* 39.1 [Winter 2003]); Vendler, Helen, "Four Prized Poets" (*New York Review of Books* 36.13 [17 August 1989]).

Bea Opengart

BERNSTEIN, CHARLES (1950–)

To date the beginning of a poet's authority one often looks to the poet's first book, which in Charles Bernstein's case is *Asylums*, published in 1975. Bernstein's effect on American poetry, however, really began in 1978, when with **Bruce Andrews** he started *L=A=N=G=U=A=G=E* magazine, which ran until 1981. Practically at the same time, then, Bernstein's presence was announced both as a poet and as someone orchestrating new means of community (re)formation. In the last quarter century, he has lived both roles simultaneously as a refutation of the idea that poets write in isolation. His poetry and his community work have walked in step with each other, neither one possible without the other. Alongside the publishing of well over twenty books of poetry, Bernstein started or helped to start two reading series (Ear Inn in New York, and Wednesdays @ 4 Plus in Buffalo), a website (Electronic Poetry Center), an e-mail discussion list (Poetics@), and an academic book series on Modern and Contemporary Poetics (with University of Alabama Press). His provocative essays have now been collected three times, in *Content's Dream* (1986), *A Poetics* (1992), and *My Way* (1999), and he has edited or co-edited numerous collections of essays, including *The Politics of Poetic Form: Poetry and Public Policy* (1990) and *Close Listening: Poetry and the Performed Word* (1998). Playing on **Robert Creeley**'s well-known expression of the relationship between form and content, one could say with Bernstein's career as an example that poets are never more than extensions of their community. With that in mind, one had better work to help create a vibrant community—which Bernstein has surely done.

Born in New York on April 4, 1950, Bernstein has held to the noisy city as his permanent place of residence except for a period from the late 1960s to the early 1970s. In those years Bernstein studied philosophy at Harvard University, where he wrote a thesis on **Gertrude Stein** and Ludwig Wittgenstein; afterward, with Susan Bee, whom he had met in high school, he moved to Vancouver, Canada, and then to Santa Barbara, California. With Bee, a painter and collage artist, he had a daughter in the late 1980s and a son in the early 1990s. Bernstein remained in New York even after starting a teaching career in 1990 at SUNY–Buffalo, where he was the director of the Poetics Program and David Gray Chair of Poetry and Letters until 2003, when he moved to the University of Pennsylvania. As Bernstein said at the celebration for **Robin Blaser**'s seventieth birthday in 1995, it was during his time in Vancouver in 1973 that writing poetry became a central part of his life. He took a course then on **Emily Dickinson** with Blaser, but it was Blaser's own poetry and involvement in the "New American Poetry" community that determined Bernstein's poetic sensibilities. His undergraduate thesis had started him thinking about experimental writing and language philosophy in the early twentieth century; Blaser and **Ron Silliman**, whom he visited while living in California, introduced him to the poets of the postwar period. Once back in New York, Bernstein immersed himself in the literary, visual and performance art, film, and music worlds there; and in the years before becoming an English professor, he supported himself by doing writing and editing work for commercial and non-commercial organizations, and with fellowships from the National Endowment for the Arts and the Guggenheim Foundation.

Readers can glean an understanding of a poet's work through knowing where and how that work has been published; throughout his career, Bernstein has worked with small magazines and **small press publishers** to make his poetry public. Before being collected for book publication, most of his poems appear first in print and online magazines that are edited by other poets. Such distributors, while they do have their own aesthetic and political agendas, are more agile and more open to new poetries than are commercial ones. In fact, small magazines and presses often come into existence solely to ensure that interesting work not go unpublished. So instead of poets writing to suit a publisher's established criteria for success, the opposite happens: Small venues build an identity out of the work they promote. In that way *L=A=N=G=U=A=G=E* magazine began. Bernstein has commented that in 1978 both he and Andrews were

insisting "on the value of nonexpository essays and also our rejection of received and beloved notions of voice, self, expression, sincerity, and representation" (*My Way*, 249). Such a comment does define their stance, but it has caused some misunderstanding. Rejected outright was the idea that poetry should have any "beloved notions"; yet voice, self, and so on can never be entirely snuffed out. Instead, all conventional notions must be continuously tested. The point of the magazine, Bernstein has said, "was not to define its own activity or to prescribe a singular form of poetry, but rather to insist on particular possibilities for poetry and poetics" (*My Way*, 249). So many poets became contributors to the magazine or were linked with its "poetics of possibility" that the magazine's name was quickly used as the label for a generation of writers who from that time on have been best known as "**Language**" poets. Bernstein arguably has been this group's foremost representative.

Following **Ezra Pound**, who said that poets give the best criticism of other poets' work, Bernstein has offered dozens of essays on twentieth-century poets, including **William Carlos Williams**, **Laura (Jackson) Riding**, **Jackson Mac Low**, and **Hannah Weiner**. His essays, like those of Pound and **Marianne Moore**, have saved scholarly prose from its own worst tendency to write only of a poet's accomplishments; Bernstein would rather point out for other writers what a poet has done that remains useful or interesting. Implied in his essays is a challenge to readers that they produce something in response, and that approach carries over into the classroom. From 1990 to 2003 at SUNY–Buffalo, Bernstein, along with **Susan Howe**, Robert Creeley, and Dennis Tedlock (and others, as faculty changed over the years), ran the Poetics Program, an informal program composed mostly of students in the English Department's master's and doctoral degree programs. Buffalo has an immense library collection of first editions and manuscripts covering the field of twentieth-century poetry; as well, the program's funding brings visiting writers each week to Buffalo, and students are able to organize reading series and start small presses. Although Buffalo has all of these poets on staff, it offers neither a BFA nor an MFA. Bernstein's courses, while they attract people interested in what is typically known as "creative writing," are not workshop courses; instead, he offers "Wreading" courses, which have extensive reading lists. Students in this context write essays and poems simultaneously, so that the creative and critical minds work in tandem. The result is the production of poet/scholars.

Two of Bernstein's major books were recently published by an elite academic press; with its ability to distribute books more widely than small presses are able to, his influence has expanded even further. *My Way: Speeches and Poems* (1999) and *With Strings: Poems* (2001) are companion books, not only because they are both collections of work from the mid 1980s to the late 1990s but because the contents of *My Way* deliberately cut across genres: His essays and poems are co-extensive of each other. "What is the difference," he asks in the preface to *My Way*, "between poetry and prose, verse and essays? Is it possible that a poem can extend the argument of an essay or that an essay can extend the prosody of a poem?" (xi). To the latter question, readers of Bernstein's work will answer "yes," especially those familiar with one of his most often cited pieces, "Artifice of Absorption," a lineated essay first published in 1987. In "Artifice" he has given the essay form the advantage of poetry's quickness and inclusiveness, its privilege to ask questions without always having to offer answers. He asserted in his 1990 preface to *The Politics of Poetic Form* that "poetry remains an unrivaled arena for social research into the (re)constitution of the public and the (re)construction of discourse" (viii). In other words, with poetry we can test the limits and uses of community and language. A *social* poetry addresses these and other questions: Who speaks and how? Who will read this poem and why?

"Artifice of Absorption" historicizes the first decade of **Language poetry**. Bernstein reviews the work of a number of his peers through an evaluation of the degree to which it resists "absorbing" the reader, singling out **Steve McCaffery**'s as perhaps the most anti-absorptive. These Language poets, Bernstein notes in this hybridization of a poem and an essay, have allowed us to question "what we are normally / asked to be absorbed into" (*A Poetics*, 54). Texts that absorb readers are "illusionistic," written so that readers will recognize what is in the poem as "real"; they will, in other words, feel that they are looking over the poet's shoulder. In the theater, a similar relationship occurs when the performers on stage act as if a fourth wall separates them from the audience. Thus, when poetry "breaks the fourth wall," readers will actively confront rather than passively overhear texts. Bernstein refers to the shift around 1795 toward a Romantic poetry that promoted the existence of "irreducible human values" and naturalized artifice to the extent that it became invisible to the common reader; such poetry has continued to be popular for many readers and academic critics. In contrast, Bernstein prefers a poetry that draws attention to its artifice. Both absorptive and anti-absorptive works require artifice, Bernstein argues in this poem-essay, "but the former may hide / this while the latter may flaunt / it" (*A Poetics*, 30). Theoretically, readers aware of the artifice of all poetry will regard any claims about "human values" with some skepticism. Poetry presents not "the truth" but theater.

As much as "Artifice of Absorption" calls attention to the problem of the reader's passive absorption into a text, this essay/poem concludes by arguing for an "intensified, technologized" absorption that would absorb the reader "into a more ideologized / or politicized space" (53). In fact, Bernstein claims that his poetry oscillates between "absorption & impermeability / [which] are the warp & woof of poetic composition" (86). Marjorie Perloff has referred to his technique of juxtaposing the two modes as an "art of adjacency." In his own description he refers to the medical term "dysraphism," which, he notes, "means congenital misseaming of embryonic parts" (*A Poetics*, 23). In a "dysraphic" poem, the reader has a heightened sense of poetic artifice: The parts stay parts, instead of blending into a harmonious whole. Faced with such a text, the reader feels outside, at a distance. As familiarity with this poetry grows, however, that distance diminishes. At one point Bernstein offers an illuminating analogy: His thoughts on absorption remind him of **Susan Howe**'s analysis of a "captivity narrative" as told by a seventeenth-century New England woman (25). A captive of Native Americans for three months, Mary Rowlandson experienced both a fear of becoming absorbed into an "other" culture *and* an attraction. This is the ambiguity Bernstein wants his readers to experience: English speakers may recognize the language in his poems as disturbingly different and resist plunging in; with time, though, they will notice themselves becoming "native" readers of the once-strange language. Then, and most important, when they "return" to "normal" English, they will be conscious of the artifice of "normal." No language practice should be taken for granted or assumed to be the only one.

Bernstein addressed this connection between poetry and fear in his 1990 poem "Autonomy Is Jeopardy," in his *Republics*, where he expressed his own fear at the "virtual (or ventriloquized) / anonymity" of poetry, in which there is no protection against "its pervasive / purposiveless." Bernstein's poetics of artifice aims to place both the writer and reader in that condition of anonymity. In his "Today's Not Opposite Day," in *With Strings*, a call-and-answer poem, the final stanza includes a nod both to his collection *My Way* and to Dickinson: "What will you say? / I'm just a nobody making my way." Dickinson's 1861 poem begins "I'm Nobody! Who are you? / Are you—Nobody—too?" (Franklin #260). Writer and reader thus make a pair of nobodies. In a sense, Rowlandson became a nobody during her captivity (or absorption), neither English nor Native American; and the poem, like the "Wilderness" in which she traveled, is a space that encourages a divestment of the interfering ego. A nobody: somebody with an open identity. In Bernstein's poem "The Lives of the Toll Takers," from his collection *Dark City*, the poet explains that the poems he writes are not about him "though they / *become me*"; and a few lines later he adds: "I'm a very becoming guy." The poet is like a spiritual medium, channeling what comes from "outside." The reader should follow suit, and realize that the "things I read are not about me though they *become me*."

Bernstein's major books of poetry include *Controlling Interests* (1980), *Islets/Irritations* (1983), *The Sophist* (1987), *Rough Trades* (1991), *Dark City* (1994), and *With Strings* (2001). *Republics of Reality: 1975–1995* (2000) usefully reprints Bernstein's early work, as well as some from the early 1990s. *Republics* begins with *Parsing*, the title a description of the poet's task: "this parsing of the world / to make worlds & worlds." In isolated passages the voice seems personal ("I'm not going to change my language") but it shifts between and sometimes within lines so much that the poet must be read as performing the "I" from a multitude of positions. There are sequences as well that play on the various uses of a word: "turning a bed down / or a deaf ear," for instance; and moments that reflect on decentered movement in language, as where Bernstein writes that what we have is a network "and that's all / a sequence of camping sights." In *Parsing*, then, one can see already the wide range of formal experimentation that characterizes all subsequent Bernstein books, a range that includes fractured and dysraphic poems, collage and quotation poems, "New Sentence" poems (in which a semantic gap exists between sentences), song-like poems, and typo poems. His immense capacity for comedic play, as in these lines from his collection *Controlling Interests*, for instance, "conveyor belts / incapacitated for several weeks with psychomimetic complaints," is even more obvious when he performs his poems for an audience. Opportunities to hear him read are not to be missed, for they make clear the profound energy inherent to language.

In Bernstein's dysraphic poems, the line break often signals a shift or the shift occurs within the line. In "Live Acts," from *Controlling Interests*, we find that our reading process as Bernstein traces it through several lines is "redaction," "promise," "conversion," "revulsion," and "encounter." Meaning is thus not held to an exclusive moment but is dispersed throughout the poem. Lines in "Pinot Blanco," from *With Strings*, have a "New Sentence" quality: "Slowly but surely I felt a rumor in my pain (succor in her refrain, a groomer in my brain). As for instance salt tastes salty, pepper hot, sugar sweet, apples tart."

The language in a Bernstein book often modulates between relatively impermeable passages and transparent or absorbable ones, as in these lines from "Emotions of Normal People," from *Dark City*: "Moreover, all systems components / Are easy to install & reconfigure." Composed entirely in the language of advertising, self-help books, thank-you letters and so on, "Emotions" exposes, when juxtaposed with his other poems, the artificial techniques at work even in our everyday language; the everyday has been made strange.

The **modernist** English poet Basil Bunting's comment that "we lose very little by not knowing what the words mean, so long as we can pronounce them" struck a chord with Bernstein (quoted in *A Poetics*, 58). Bunting was thinking of how, in his experience, people reading or listening to a foreign language can still enjoy or even understand some of it. Bernstein's poem "Egg Under My Feet," from *With Strings*, tests that possibility: "Fogem / frumptious besqualmitity / voraxious flumpf" (*With Strings*, 80). Ostensibly a mess of typos, these words can be pronounced. A reader could produce a homophonic translation (choosing English words that sound like those in the original) of this poem—as Bernstein sometimes does with poems in other languages.

Again, one finds abundance in a Bernstein book; adjacent to poems that seem far from a personal expression of the poet are ones that display an enacted self in social space, the self dramatized. Many aspects of the poet's identity—his social status as a New York intellectual, his position as a husband and father, his Jewish heritage, his gender—are parsed. An ironic voice in "The Influence of Kinship Patterns upon Perception of an Ambiguous Stimulus," from *Dark City*, observes that nobody wants to hear "about the pain we men feel / Having our prerogatives questioned." Another voice says that a "poem bleeds / Metaphorically, just like I do"; and a few pages later comes the question "What color blood came out?"

The effect that Charles Bernstein's books and teaching have had on writers, critics, and students constitutes only a part of what has made his presence in American poetry so substantial. There is his promotion of new media in the 1980s, when he argued that poets needed to look at how writing on a computer would extend what had already been made possible in the shift from the pen to the typewriter. Much of his work has been made freely available online. In addition, he has fostered exchanges between American poets and poets in other countries (Canada, especially, and countries in Central and South America and Europe). More recently he has written librettos for concert hall musicians; his interest in performance led to a role in a Hollywood film (*Finding Forrester* [2000]) and a series of radio and TV commercials (for Yellow Pages). In "Artifice of Absorption" Bernstein quotes Veronica Forrest-Thomson's idea that poets should write so that it becomes "impossible as well as wrong for critics to strand poems in the external world" (*A Poetics*, 10). Made of and in the world, Bernstein's poems have not been left stranded. His "Live Acts" poem, from *Controlling Interests*, ends by contending that these "projects"—poems or essays—contain "the person, binding up in an unlimited way what / otherwise goes unexpressed." In "an unlimited way," his way.

Further Reading. *Selected Primary Sources:* Bernstein, Charles, *Controlling Interests* (New York: Roof, 2004);

———, *Dark City* (Los Angeles: Sun & Moon, 1994); ———, *My Way: Speeches and Poems* (Chicago: University of Chicago Press, 1999); ———, *A Poetics* (Cambridge, MA: Harvard University Press, 1992); ———, ed., *The Politics of Poetic Form: Poetry and Public Policy* (New York: Roof, 1990); ———, *Republics of Reality: 1975–1995* (Los Angeles: Sun & Moon, 2000); ———, *With Strings: Poems* (Chicago: University of Chicago Press, 2001). ***Selected Secondary Sources:*** Beach, Christopher, "Reappropriation and Resistance: Charles Bernstein, Language Poetry, and Poetic Tradition," in *ABC of Influence: Ezra Pound and the Remaking of American Poetic Tradition* (Los Angeles: University of California Press, 1992, 237–251); Lazer, Hank, "Charles Bernstein's Dark City: Polis, Policy, and the Policing of Poetry" (*American Poetry Review* 24.5 [September 1995]: 35–44); Mark, Alison, "Poetic Relations and Related Poetics: Veronica Forrest-Thomson and Charles Bernstein," in *Assembling Alternatives: Reading Postmodern Poetries Transnationally*, ed. Romana Huk (Hanover, NH: Wesleyan University Press, 2003, 114–127); Reinfeld, Linda, "Bernstein's Pharmacy," in *Language Poetry: Writing as Rescue* (Baton Rouge: Louisiana State University Press, 1992, 50–85); Silliman, Ron, "Controlling Interests," in *The New Sentence* (New York: Roof, 1987, 171–184).

Logan Esdale

BERRIGAN, EDMUND JOSEPH MICHAEL "TED," JR. (1934–1983)

Ted Berrigan came to New York with the other members of the so-called Tulsa Group: **Joe Brainard**, Dick Gallup, and **Ron Padgett**. He occasionally referred to himself as the last **Beat poet** but is normally identified as one of the leaders of the second generation of the **New York School** poets, which also included **Anne Waldman** and Lewis Warsh. They were based in the Lower East Side of Manhattan and were one of the groups central to the founding of the Poetry Project at St. Mark's Church. Berrigan was first convinced of the possibility of being a writer through reading Thomas Wolfe, but it was **Jack Kerouac** and **Frank O'Hara** who were decisive stylistic influences. Berrigan's reputation as a voluble and influential poet was built through his numerous books and chapbooks of poetry, his collaborations with illustrators and poets, and his unflagging encouragement of poets in both informal and formal venues. Possessing a generous and offbeat sense of humour, Berrigan supported younger poets through letters, his journal "*C*," and his teaching of poetry writing courses at Northeastern Illinois, Naropa, the Stevens Institute, Iowa, Yale, Michigan, and Essex.

Edmund Joseph Michael Berrigan was born in Providence, Rhode Island, on November 15, 1934. He served with the U.S. Army in Korea from 1954 to 1957, before going to the University of Tulsa on the G.I. Bill, where he received a BA in 1959. He also earned an MA there in 1962 but returned the certificate along with a letter claiming that he was the master of no art. In order to establish himself as a writer, in 1960 Berrigan moved to New York City, where he co-founded and edited "*C*" magazine and "*C*" Press. Despite the wishes of her parents, he married Sandra Alper in 1962 after meeting her on a trip to Florida. Together they had two children, David and Kate. and she also collaborated with him in his writing, as well as publishing her own poems. From 1966 to 1967 Berrigan taught in the poetry workshop at the St. Mark's Poetry Project, New York, and in the course of the following decade at a number of other institutions across the United States and Great Britain. In 1971, after his first marriage had ended, Berrigan married **Alice Notley**, later an accomplished and well-respected poet, with whom he had two children, Anselm and Edmund. He died on July 4, 1983, of liver complications after years of health problems exacerbated by amphetamine use, long-standing but undiagnosed hepatitis, and the inability to afford medical care.

Berrigan's first success—and most famous book—was his 1964 publication, *The Sonnets*, for which he received the Poetry Foundation Award. It is a sequence of seventy-seven poems that deal with his daily life, his loves, and the sonnet form itself. Although the sonnets he uses are a far cry from Donne or Shakespeare, the sequence traces Berrigan's own poetic education, and, as a result, his treatment of the sonnet form is more sympathetic than might be expected from an experimental Beat poet. Berrigan showed that the sonnet is not necessarily about iambic pentameter, but rather is a form dependent upon certain intimate relationships of rhythm and understandings of the world. To effect these relationships he borrows liberally from the world and the poets around him. The sequence contains translated but unattributed verse from Rilke and Rimbaud, snatches of conversation from the world around him, and recycled lines of his from earlier in the series.

The sequence is a deliberate quilting of impressions, imitations, and pastiches of these seminal poets as he learns about them and is influenced by them. These influences include **John Ashbery**'s *Some Trees*, **Ezra Pound**'s *Cantos*, and some **T.S. Eliot**, but the tone, especially unlike the latter, is curious instead of weary, humorous instead of despairing, and continuously forward moving in search of new lessons and new experiences. Whereas Eliot and Pound looked to high culture for their starting point, Berrigan scavenged from everything: canonical poets, recent poets, his own sonnet sequence in the writing, his friends, his conversations, and letters. This has led to a criticism of his writing as mechanical or method driven, but this is only true inasmuch as it is a record of his developing method of learning about, and through, poetry.

Berrigan's technique, though tempered through his engagement with the sonnet form, often appears unorthodox or derivative and his subject matter mundane or self-indulgent. From at least *The Sonnets* onward, however, he is self-consciously concerned with poetic form and with his own ongoing performance as the writer. His lines are like the lines of a sketch, or artist's brushstrokes, which, like their equivalent in visual art movements, can be repeated or rearranged to achieve a desired effect. Indeed, as a critic for *Art News* over many years, Berrigan's knowledge of artistic theory and practice deeply informed his poetry. Although often identified as an Expressionist poet following William Saroyan in the American Expressionist tradition, perhaps the label Abstract Expressionist poet would fit him better, as he owes more to Willem de Kooning than even to Frank O'Hara, from whom he also borrowed subject matter and phraseology.

In addition to de Kooning, Berrigan was influenced by the playfulness and fractured texts of Marcel Duchamp and the arch iconoclasm of William Burroughs. He noted how Duchamp in art, **John Cage** in music, and Burroughs in prose identified traditional forms before thoroughly disrupting and expanding them. Berrigan, a great believer in the expansion of form, argued that it operated on far more subtle levels than critics and poets generally realized or acknowledged. Although he was also influenced by **Kenneth Koch** and **Paul Blackburn** in his own generation, his choice of artistic lineage and his own self as a subject dogged his reception throughout his career.

Bean Spasms (1967) is a good example of Berrigan's early collaborative work—there were not many rules, but he and Ron Padgett alternated lines, trying to guide the poems out, playing games, making meaning, learning words. With Joe Brainard's deliberately childlike drawings, it looks like a children's book, but it belies the appearance with its adult language and subject matter ("If I fall in love with my friend's wife, she's fucked"), its dedication ("to **Allen Ginsberg**") and its opening poem (a translation of a poem by the French proto-surrealist poet Guillaume Apollinaire). Again, as in *The Sonnets*, Berrigan returns to his own lines, cutting and re-pasting them until he achieves the desired effect for the particular part of the book. Although intensely thoughtful and densely filled with allusions, the book's humor and childlike delight in language (the "Sonnet for Andy Warhol" comprises thirteen lines of z's) as well as the conundrums and difficulties of the world gives it a lightness that speeds the reader through the events and thoughts of the book.

Also published in 1967—although written over a longer span of time—*Many Happy Returns* shows Berrigan playing with form throughout the early 1960s. The layout changes drastically between sections, showing

quite graphically Berrigan's movement between poems with compact lines and poems in open form. "Tambourine Life" is best known of the **open-form** poems, because **Paul Carroll** included it in his important anthology, *The Young American Poets* (1968). Seeming to imply that poets who choose other subjects are somehow disingenuous, Berrigan again places himself squarely as the subject of his poetry. In "Tambourine Life" he discusses his friends, his experiences, his reflections on politics and painting, and other overlapping snatches of his life. The seventy loosely connected sections that reflect seven years of work end with the surprisingly simple reflection: "Joy is what I like, / That, and love."

The early 1970s were a period of reflection for Berrigan but not of slowing down. His books and chapbooks of poetry were still published regularly, sometimes two or three a year. These years, however, saw a melancholic tinge to his poetry. Although he continued to use both traditional and open form for *In the Early Morning Rain* (1970) and *A Feeling for Leaving* (1975), these forms no longer are in sole service of discovery but also record a sense of loss. Loss pervades *In the Early Morning Rain*. Whether it is the comment "I thought a lot about dying" of "Anti-War Poem," the passing present implied by "it will never make us laugh here again" ("Ann Arbor Song"), the list of "people who died" in the poem of the same name, beloved heroes of "Telegram—to Jack Kerouac" ("Bye-bye Jack. / See you soon"), or just the loss of meaning in the word "hello," which originally meant "be whole," the world that he was beginning to find in *Bean Spasms* and *The Sonnets* was already fading before him.

A Feeling for Leaving was published, like *Bean Spasms*, in a reader-friendly, large-format book, but the poems no longer burst with the childlike exuberance of the earlier book. In "I used to be but now I am," the speaker laments the premature arrival of the future: "I used to be the future of America, / But now I am America." Berrigan treats the discovery of new places with wonder; he begins "Peking" by saying, "These are the very garments of the poor," but place has ceased to be simply a form of excitement as in *Bean Spasms*. Speed now implies transience, as is made explicit in the reference to how the fleeting "landscape [is] rushing away." His journey to England, he remarks in "Old-fashioned air" (a poem to Lee Crabtree), has only taken him "back where we started from." His words are playing ironically with being in England, where "English" poetry began, but also reflect a sense of regret that, as a result of his transatlantic relocation, he has not somehow moved on.

Although Berrigan continued to experiment with form through the 1970s, critical reception of his work was sparse. Nor did his **prose poetry** appeal to many beyond a small coterie of poets and friends. Berrigan (and Padgett) had been experimenting with prose poems as a fertile extension of open poetic form since at least 1964, and it was a form to which he frequently returned. Several prose poems appeared as part of *In the Early Morning Rain*, including "Autobiography in Five Parts," ostensibly and ironically made up of four separate prose sections. *Clear the Range*, a novel created by substituting words in a popular Western, was published as a complete book in 1977 after having appeared little by little in *Angel Hair* for some years.

Despite the relative neglect of his individual publications, there a was critical audience for his work as a whole. His friends, students, and the worldwide community of poets who had come to meet at St. Mark's and Berrigan's unfailingly welcoming apartment created the demand for the publication of a volume of new and selected poems, *So Going Around Cities*, in 1980. The title of the selection comes from a line from *Rivers and Mountains* by John Ashbery and had been the title of a small collection of his poems in 1969. With a typically restless comment in the author's note, Berrigan suggests that it might rather have been called "As Much as Was Possible of the Story So Far." As it transpired, this belated recognition of his work came only three years before his death. In the intervening time he still wrote but became increasingly sick even as he did so. The book succeeded in bringing Berrigan's work together into a comprehensible oeuvre for the first time, and the framework of the collection provided a formal context for the sonnets, comic poems like "Winter" ("The Moon is Yellow. / My Nose is Red"), and more extended forays such as "Memorial Day," his 1971 collaboration with Anne Waldman. In circumscribing the output and framing the formal and human, *So Going Around Cities* has provided the model for later, posthumous, understandings of his writing.

Berrigan's oeuvre has provoked as much criticism as praise. The deliberate and continuous intertwining of his daily life with his poetry seemed too superficial or tangential to a community interested in deep psychological, spiritual, or political interventions. At the same time, as his subject matter veers off into the occasionally irrelevant or tangential seeming, his formal experiments never quite combine into the organic unity for which he seems to hope. Even Berrigan's commitment to a life lived as a poet, and writing his life through poetry, did not endear him to critics. He displayed too much of the quotidian and a level of lewd buffoonery that, whether part of life or not, is not to the taste of many critics. For Berrigan anything that is part of life is part of poetry—a stance that appears even more heroic in light of the Reagan and post-Reagan years that immediately followed his death. The high esteem in which he was held by friends, readers, and students has meant that though death has stopped his prolific output, it has not stemmed his publication: Six books of his work, in collaboration with others, have been published since his death. A second volume of *Selected Poems* appeared in 1994, and a new *Collected Poems*, edited by his second wife and their sons, was published by the University of California Press in 2005.

Further Reading. *Selected Primary Sources:* Berrigan, Ted, *Clear the Range* (New York: Adventures in Poetry/Coach House South, 1977); ———, *Many Happy Returns to Dick Gallup* (New York: Angel Hair, 1967); ———, *So Going Around Cities: New & Selected Poems, 1958–1979* (Berkeley, CA: Blue Wind Press, 1980); ———, *The Sonnets* (New York: Lorenz and Ellen Gude, 1964); Berrigan, Ted, and Joel Lewis, *On the Level Everyday* (Jersey City, NJ: Talisman House, 1997); Berrigan, Ted, and Ron Padgett, *Bean Spasms* (New York: Kulchur Press, 1967); Ratcliffe, Stephen, and Leslie Scalapino, *Talking in Tranquility: Interviews with Ted Berrigan* (Bolinas, CA: O Books, 1991). ***Selected Secondary Sources:*** Berrigan, Ted, and Anne Waldman, *Nice to See You: Homage to Ted Berrigan* (Minneapolis, MN: Coffee House Press, 1991); Carruth, Hayden, "Making It New" (*Hudson Review* 21 [Summer 1968]: 399–412); Clark, Tom, *Late Returns: A Memoir of Ted Berrigan* (Bolina, CA.: Tomboctou Books, 1985); Foster, Edward, *Code of the West: A Memoir of Ted Berrigan* (Boulder, CO: Rodent Press, 1994); Hoover, Paul, "Fables of Representation: Poetry of the New York School" (*American Poetry Review* 31.4 [July/August 2002]: 20–30); Padgett, Ron, *Ted: A Personal Memoir of Ted Berrigan* (Great Barrington, MA: The Figures, 1993); Rifkin, Libbie, *Career Moves: Olson, Creeley, Zukofsky, Berrigan, and the American Avant-Garde.* (Madison: University of Wisconsin Press, 2000).

Dan Friedman

BERRY, WENDELL (1934–)

Wendell Berry is essentially a **lyric** poet and a traditionalist, showing little influence either from **modernism** or **postmodernism**. Berry's fundamental belief that poetry should be rooted in a particular place underpins his work. The prolific author of more than thirty books—novels as well as collections of essays and poems—Berry has worked as a farmer and writer for most of his life. His work reflects a deep love of land, strong agrarian sensibilities, and profoundly Christian (but never triumphalist) spirituality.

Wendell Berry was born in 1934, the first of John and Virginia Berry's four children. Both sides of his family have deep roots in Henry County, Kentucky, which may explain Berry's own fierce attachment to his native soil. Berry always wanted to farm like his father, a founder of the Burley Tobacco Growers Cooperative Association. In "Remembering my Father" (*Entries*, 1994) Berry writes that his father taught him "the difference / between good work and sham." Schooled at Millersburg Military Institute, he pursued a BA in English at the University of Kentucky at Lexington, where he studied with Thomas B. Stroup and Hollis B. Summers. There he coedited *Stylus*, the university's literary magazine. In 1957 he completed a master's degree in English, also at the University of Kentucky; later that year he married Tanya Amyx.

In 1958 Berry received a Wallace Stegner fellowship and studied creative writing at Stanford University, where he later taught. In 1960 he and Tanya returned to the Berry family farm. Awarded a Guggenheim fellowship, Berry took his family to Europe in 1961 through 1962. He also taught at New York University before moving back to Kentucky on July 4, 1965. For decades thereafter he taught at the University of Kentucky and at Centre College in Danville.

Berry has been a prolific writer by any standard, publishing novels and short story collections; volumes of essays, among them *The Long-Legged House* (1969) and *The Art of the Commonplace* (2002); and ten collections of poetry, along with numerous limited-edition volumes and chapbooks. *The Broken Ground* (1964), his first verse collection, consists of lyric poems colored by the regional earth in which they grew. His third collection, *Farming: A Hand Book* (1970), celebrates the pleasures of rural life. Here Berry introduced the Mad Farmer, a bizarre figure who dances in the streets, speaks surprising sense in "Prayers and Sayings of the Mad Farmer," and recurs in several later collections.

Berry's writing is characterized by a strong regional sensibility. His poems are often written in first person from the perspective of a Kentucky farmer-husband. Many poems quietly glorify the virtues of husbandry: both animal husbandry/land stewardship and the respect, caring, and connection implicit in marriage, which he regards as an essential aspect of human society.

His desire is to redeem the fallen world through honest work. Through work, his poems argue, we can repair and care for our hills and fields—and the source of life that works through us can repair and care for us. Christian theology permeates his poems, particularly the Sabbath poems written on his solitary Sunday morning walks. *Sabbaths* (1987) and *A Timbered Choir* (1998) collect these to strong effect. In his preface to *A Timbered Choir*, Berry observes that his Sabbath poems were "written in silence, in solitude, mainly out of doors" and exhorts his readers to read them "slowly, and with more patience than effort" (xvii).

In engaging with small details of the natural world, Berry finds and creates resonance. In "The Old Elm Tree by the River" (*The Country of Marriage*, 1971) Berry describes a regal old tree: "That is a life I know the country by. / Mine is a life I know the country by."

Most of Berry's poems are small, spare, and resonant, similar in tone to those of **Jane Kenyon**; in contrast, the Mad Farmer poems evoke **Walt Whitman**, with long,

rolling cadences like a preacher standing on a Kentucky mountaintop. In "Manifesto: The Mad Farmer Liberation Front," Berry urges his readers to do one thing daily "that won't compute. Love the Lord. / Love the world. Work for nothing." The poem closes with the exhortation "Practice resurrection." Berry means that in every possible way: the resurrection of crops in the field, the resurrection of the cared-for earth, and also the bodily resurrection his theology promises at the end of days.

"The themes of home, work, husbandry, rootedness, stewardship, responsibility, thrift, order, memory, atonement, and harmony resonate through his work," observes Andrew J. Angyal in his 1991 volume, *Wendell Berry* (ix). In an interview with Angyal, Berry argued that "[o]ur permanent condition is a condition of dependence on the land and on each other" (142). His poems prove, and praise, that interdependence.

Berry's nonfiction serves as an articulate defense of farming. For Berry, Angyal observes, farming and writing are both spiritual disciplines that can temper the human impulse toward carelessness. Many of his essays explore agrarianism, which in *The Art of the Commonplace* Berry calls "a way of thought based on land" (239). The agrarian mind thinks locally; is interested in particularities, not abstractions; and is ultimately a religious mind that "prefers the Creation itself to the powers and quantities to which it can be reduced" (240). Berry's concerns about the disappearance of farming and rural life are both economic and moral.

Berry's poetry arises out of the same agrarian passions as his nonfiction, though he naturally expresses them differently in verse than in prose. In "The Farmer" (*The Country of Marriage*) he refers to the earth as "the beloved body." In "Below" (*A Part*) he asserts, "What I stand for / is what I stand on."

His themes remain consistent in his most recent collection, *Entries* (1994), which is characterized by his trademark love of landscape and detail, his reverence for life's natural rhythms and for aging, and his quiet awe at the unfolding of marriage over time (as in "The Blue Robe," where he asserts, "We belong to one story / that the two, joining, made").

Howard Hinkel has observed that Berry follows in the steps of William Wordsworth, writing "in a prophetic role," and notes that Edward Abbey called Berry a "contemporary Isaiah" (49). Berry's poems exhibit careful pacing, genuine emotion, wry humor, and trenchant observations of his world, in service of the spirituality and stewardship he experiences as natural outgrowths of genuine grounding in the physical world, and in which he exhorts his readers to join him.

Further Reading. *Selected Primary Sources:* Berry, Wendell, *The Art of the Commonplace: Agrarian Essays* (New York: Counterpoint, 2002); ———, *The Broken Ground* (New

York: Harcourt Brace & World, 1964); ———, *The Country of Marriage* (New York: Harcourt Brace Jovanovich, 1973); ———, *Entries* (New York: Pantheon, 1994); ———, *Farming: A Hand Book* (New York: Harcourt Brace Jovanovich, 1970); ———, *The Long-Legged House* (New York: Harcourt Brace & World, 1969); ———, *A Part* (San Francisco: North Point Press, 1980); ———, *Sabbaths* (San Francisco: North Point Press, 1987); ———, *A Timbered Choir* (Washington, DC: Counterpoint, 1998). **Selected Secondary Sources:** Angyal, Andrew J., *Wendell Berry* (New York: Twayne, 1991); Hinkel, Howard, "Prophets of Nature: Wordsworth's Environmental Second Selves" (*Wordsworth Circle* 34 [Winter 2003]: 49); Merchant, Paul, ed., *Wendell Berry* (Lewiston, ID: Confluence Press, 1991).

Rachel Barenblat

BERRYMAN, JOHN (1914–1972)

John Berryman distinguished himself by writing some of the most inventive and original poetry in English during the second half of the twentieth century. His major work is *The Dream Songs,* published as one collection of 385 poems in 1969, but first appearing in two separate installments as *77 Dream Songs* (1964) and *His Toy, His Dream, His Rest* (1968). Prior to this **long poem,** Berryman published *Homage to Mistress Bradstreet* (1956), a highly stylized yet **modernist** work that anticipates the unusual syntax and language of *The Dream Songs,* as well as a major sonnet sequence originally titled *Sonnets to Chris,* written in 1947–1948 but not published until 1967 under the title *Berryman's Sonnets.* These are Berryman's major works, but he also published three other significant volumes of verse and a collection of critical essays, and left an unfinished novel at the time of his death. A collection of critical essays, *The Freedom of the Poet* (1976), and an unfinished novel, *Recovery* (1973), appeared posthumously. More recently, a scholarly edition of his *Collected Poems* (1989), including all of his major work in verse except for *The Dream Songs,* as well as *Berryman's Shakespeare* (1999), a volume of his critical work on Shakespeare, have been published. Berryman scholar and biographer John Haffenden, editor of *Berryman's Shakespeare,* also published a small collection of previously unpublished "Dream Songs" as *Henry's Fate & Other Poems* (1967–1972) in 1977.

Berryman was born John Allyn Smith, Jr., on October 25, 1914, in McAlester, Oklahoma, and was named for his father, a banker. His mother, Martha Shaver Little Smith, was a schoolteacher. Berryman was raised a Catholic, serving as an altar boy in his family's church. Catholicism plays a role in his mature poetry in several ways. In *The Dream Songs,* the concept of sin and guilt is a recurring theme, treated alternately with seriousness and whimsicality. Later in his career, in two shorter poetic

sequences, Berryman undertakes a serious exploration of the spiritual quest. These poems are "Eleven Addresses to the Lord" from *Love and Fame* (1970) and "Opus Dei" from *Delusions, Etc.* (1972).

Shortly before his eleventh birthday, Berryman and his younger brother were placed in a Catholic boarding school when his parents, lured by the Florida land boom, moved to Tampa along with his maternal grandmother, where they purchased and operated a restaurant. The boys were soon brought to Florida to join the family and placed in public schools. By 1926 the Florida market had bottomed out, and the family was forced to sell the restaurant and relocate to an apartment in Clearwater. Berryman's mother began an affair with the apartment building's owner, John Angus Berryman, twenty years her senior. Despondent over his financial situation and his wife's affair, the future poet's father died of an apparent suicide by gunshot (although there was some evidence of foul play) on June 26, 1926, just outside the apartment. Ten weeks later, Martha married John Angus Berryman in New York City and relocated the family to the borough of Queens, changing her son's name to John Allyn McAlpin Berryman. The name change did not become official until 1936. Ultimately, the themes of identity and the absent father would come to haunt much of Berryman's major poetic work. Berryman continued as a public school student in New York before being enrolled in South Kent School, a Connecticut preparatory school for boys. Although his years at the school were not happy ones, Berryman, always a good student, distinguished himself academically to the degree that he became the first student in the prep school's history to skip the sixth form in order to enter college. In 1932 Berryman returned to New York City to attend Columbia, where he worked with his most influential teacher, Mark Van Doren. He published his first poems in Columbia's student literary magazine, graduated in 1936, and became the first American to be awarded the prestigious Kellett fellowship to study at Cambridge University. Berryman went to Clare College, Cambridge, in 1936, studying there for two years, focusing primarily on Shakespearean studies, a lifelong passion. While in England, he managed to meet **W.H. Auden,** Dylan Thomas, and W.B. Yeats. Several poems in *Love and Fame* recount Berryman's experiences at Cambridge. Upon returning to the United States in 1938, he had some early poems published in the *Southern Review.* At that time, he began a long career as a teacher, work that would take him to several appointments, including Harvard, Princeton, the University of Iowa, and ultimately, the University of Minnesota, where he would teach for the last thirteen years of his life.

In 1940 **James Laughlin** published a handful of Berryman's poems in a New Directions volume, *Five American Poets,* a book that also included poems from **Randall**

Jarrell, who would become a close friend of Berryman. Two years later, Laughlin would publish a thin collection of Berryman's poems titled *Poems* (1942). In that same year Berryman married Eileen Mulligan, the first of his three wives. The couple separated in 1953 and divorced in 1956, and later Eileen, under the name Eileen B. Simpson, published a chatty memoir about their years together, *Poets in Their Youth* (1982). The memoir also describes Berryman's burgeoning friendship with **Robert Lowell**, the poet who would become a major rival and the most gifted of a talented circle of writer friends that included Jarrell and **Delmore Schwartz**. In 1947 Berryman began an extramarital affair, chronicling the relationship in a highly accomplished sonnet sequence, *Sonnets to Chris*, which was not published until 1967. The sonnets, numbering 117, most of them in the Petrarchan form, explore the relationship of eros to language. Individual lines point to Berryman's mature mastery of tense and unusual syntax that would distinguish *Homage to Mistress Bradstreet* and *The Dream Songs*: "You, Chris, *contrite* I never thought to see." The sonnets also employ, though to a lesser degree, some of the humor of *The Dream Songs*, as well as the major Berryman themes of desire, longing, loss, and the exploration of the inner psyche.

In the years since their publication as *Berryman's Sonnets* in 1967, the sonnets have received mixed reviews from Berryman scholars. While most commentators agree that the poems were his first successful attempt at using his life as art, the success of Berryman's engagement with the sonnet form and its long tradition has been debated. Some feel that the sonnets are so rhetorical as to be devoid of genuine passion, but in a 1983 article, David K. Weiser argues that the poems demonstrate both a mastery of Renaissance sonnet conventions and a discomfort with the traditional content of the form. Others have similarly noted how Berryman simultaneously embraces and plays with the parameters of traditional sonnet form, a tendency also apparent in *Homage to Mistress Bradstreet* and *The Dream Songs*.

In 1948 Berryman published his first major collection, *The Dispossessed*, containing fifty poems divided into five sections. The book was not widely or enthusiastically reviewed, but Randall Jarrell, in a detailed, albeit lukewarm, review in the *Nation* (Mariani, 210–211), noted the promise suggested by some of the stronger poems and predicted great work from Berryman once he learned to rein in his emotions. Among the significant poems in *The Dispossessed*, "The Ball Poem" introduces one of Berryman's central themes, the need to cope with loss. In his identification with a boy who has lost his ball, the poet suggests the more complex forms inhabiting the psyche of others that would be crucial to the success of both *Homage to Mistress Bradstreet* and *The Dream Songs*. A similar approach characterizes "The Nervous Songs," a

sequence of nine poems within *The Dispossessed*, often seen by scholars as an important precursor to *The Dream Songs*. Using the flexible form of three 6-line stanzas that he would perfect in *The Dream Songs*, "The Nervous Songs" are spoken by an array of characters enduring various situations of stress and longing. The poems experiment with a unique syntax designed to explore the speakers' thought processes. This preoccupation with psychological processes is reflected not only in Berryman's early poetry, but also in his *Stephen Crane* (1950), a psychoanalytic biography of the American writer.

Berryman actually wrote the opening stanzas of *Homage to Mistress Bradstreet* in 1948 but stalled on the poem for several years. He completed it in 1953, and it was published in *Partisan Review* that same year. Farrar, Straus and Giroux, the company that would publish all of Berryman's poetry volumes from this point on, published the poem as a book in 1956. *Homage to Mistress Bradstreet* remains one of the most unique poems in American literature, with Berryman perfecting the odd, convoluted syntax that would become his hallmark as a poet. The poem is essentially a dialogue with the spirit of America's first poet, **Anne Dudley Bradstreet**, including an attempted seduction of Anne by the poet-speaker, as well as a memorable section where Anne speaks during childbirth: "Drencht & powerful, I did it with my body!" The form of the poem is numbered sections, each an eight-line stanza, a form that Berryman said he adapted from Yeats, and one allowing flexibility, narrative movement, and lyric intensity. Nominated for the Pulitzer Prize, *Homage to Mistress Bradstreet* is a remarkable chronicle of a poet's search for inspiration, style, and voice as he engages and attempts to enter into the tradition of American verse. Edmund Wilson called it "the most distinguished long poem by an American since *The Waste Land*" (quoted in CLC 62 [1991]: 72).

The mid-1950s were a vital time for Berryman. Not only did *Homage to Mistress Bradstreet* appear and secure his reputation as a highly innovative and learned American poet, but he also met and fell in love with Ann Levine, who would become his second wife and mother of his son Paul, who was born in 1957. Having been in and out of psychoanalysis for nearly a decade, Berryman now undertook an analysis of some six hundred pages of journals he had been keeping of his dreams. He had thought of working the dream analyses into a publishable book, but instead their language began to make its way into a new sort of poem he had begun writing: poems of three 6-line stanzas, spoken by a persona in a jazzy, nervous, streetwise but intellectual idiom. These are the poems that would eventually appear as *77 Dream Songs* (1964) and *His Toy, His Dream, His Rest* (1968), brought together in one volume titled *The Dream Songs* in 1969. It took Berryman a few years to settle on the form of the poem and to decide that it would revolve around a central character who would speak and perform all of the poems.

In 1958 Berryman published a small chapbook, *His Thought Made Pockets & the Plane Buckt*, where he experimented with the nervous voice of *The Dream Songs*, but the book hardly drew notice. Nevertheless, convinced that this new type of poem represented his breakthrough, he continued to write exclusively in the new idiom and form, almost to the point of obsession. He continued to teach, travel, and share drafts of Dream Songs with friends and fellow poets, particularly Robert Lowell, who encouraged him to arrange some of the Songs for publication. By the spring of 1959, just over two years after their marriage, Berryman and Ann Levine divorced. In early 1961, while working at the University of Minnesota, where he had begun teaching in 1955, he met Kate Donahue, then twenty-two. They were married in September of that year and would remain married until Berryman's death eleven years later. Berryman had two daughters with Kate, Martha (born 1962) and Sarah Rebecca (born 1971).

By the early 1960s Berryman had written hundreds of Dream Songs and finally published *77 Dream Songs* in 1964. Anticipated by "The Nervous Songs" in *The Dispossessed* and by some of the dense language of *Homage to Mistress Bradstreet*, the Dream Songs explore the unconscious and give voice to the id and to oedipal tendencies, as well as to intense feelings of and response to loss, particularly the deaths of his father and of fellow writers. At the same time that they are frequently poignant and sad, the Songs employ humor to a degree almost unparalleled in American poetry. The poems are spoken by a character named Henry, described by Berryman in the foreword to *His Toy, His Dream, His Rest* as a white, middle-aged man who has suffered an "irreversible loss" and who speaks incessantly about himself in first, second, and third person. Henry has a friend who appears and plays the straight man in some of the poems, at times questioning Henry, at times cajoling, and at other times comforting him. The friend is never named but refers to Henry as "Mr. Bones," or humorous variations of that name. While *77 Dream Songs* puzzled most reviewers on its initial appearance, the power and originality of the new poems were recognized, particularly by the poet **Adrienne Rich**, whose review in the *Nation* commented on the "surrealistic quality" of the work and the importance of the character Henry as the collection's organizing figure. *77 Dream Songs* was awarded the Pulitzer Prize, and four years later *His Toy, His Dream, His Rest* won both the National Book Award and the Bollingen Prize for poetry.

The themes that run throughout *The Dream Songs* include love, death, fame, history, politics, and the self in relation to society. However, it is not so much theme as it is the voice and character of Henry and the unique style of the poems, driven by Henry's humor, depression, learnedness, and free-associative thinking that have compelled readers. Berryman himself compared the work to that of Walt Whitman in *Leaves of Grass*, in terms of placing an individual within his national culture and history, and recording their interaction. Moreover, taken as one long poem, the 385 Dream Songs extend the tradition of the long poem in American letters, combining the autobiographical impulse of **confessional poetry**—the movement Berryman is most often associated with—with an attempt to capture a tumultuous era of American social and political history.

In *Love & Fame* (1970), Berryman reflects on his past in a looser, more anecdotal style than ever before. While the volume does conclude impressively with "Eleven Addresses to the Lord," overall it lacks the dynamic voice, fresh humor, and structural unity of *The Dream Songs*. One aspect of *Love & Fame* that is carried over from *The Dream Songs*, however, is Berryman's ongoing conversation with the literary works that shaped his thinking and art.

By this time Berryman's alcoholism had taken an enormous toll on his health, both physical and mental. While he struggled valiantly to conquer his addiction during the final years of his life by joining Alcoholics Anonymous, an experience chronicled in the uncompleted novel *Recovery*, he ended his life early on January 7, 1972, by jumping from the Washington Avenue Bridge in Minneapolis onto the banks of the Mississippi River. Later that year, *Delusions, etc.* his final full volume of poems, appeared. The volume begins with "Opus Dei," the impressive nine-poem sequence of spiritual quest, but on the whole this collection, along with *Love & Fame*, suggests that Berryman's power as a poet had diminished significantly after *The Dream Songs*. He does return to the Dream Song form in two particularly haunting poems from *Delusions, etc.* "Henry by Night" and "Henry's Understanding" return to insomnia and the contemplation of suicide, revealing some of the poet's physical and mental anguish. While the scholarly edition of Berryman's *Collected Poems* did not elicit a rush of critical studies, important essays and book chapters on Berryman's work continue to appear, and his status as a major, original American poet seems secure.

Further Reading. *Selected Primary Sources:* Berryman, John, *Collected Poems 1937–1971*, ed. Charles Thornbury (New York: Farrar, 1989); ———, *The Dream Songs* (New York: Farrar, Straus and Giroux, 1969); ———, *The Freedom of the Poet* (New York: Farrar, 1976); ———, *Henry's Fate & Other Poems, 1967–1972* (New York: Farrar, 1977). ***Selected Secondary Sources:*** Blake, David

Haven, "Public Dreams: Berryman, Celebrity, and the Culture of Confession" (*American Literary History* 13.4 [Winter 2001]: 717–736); Kelly, Richard J., and Alan K. Lathrop, eds., *Recovering Berryman: Essays on a Poet* (Ann Arbor: University of Michigan Press, 1993); Smith, Ernest J., "John Berryman's 'Programmatic' for *The Dream Songs*, and an Instance of Revision" (*Journal of Modern Literature* 23.3/4 [Summer 2000]: 429–439); ———, "'Approaching Our Maturity': The Dialectic of Engagement and Withdrawal in the Political Poetry of Berryman and Lowell," in *Jarrell, Bishop, Lowell, and Co.: Middle Generation Poets in Context*, ed. Suzanne Ferguson (Knoxville: University of Tennessee Press, 2003, 287–302); Thomas, Harry, ed., *Berryman's Understanding: Reflections on the Poetry of John Berryman* (Boston: Northeastern Univerity Press, 1988); Travisano, Thomas, *Midcentury Quartet: Bishop, Lowell, Jarrell, Berryman, and the Making of a Postmodern Aesthetic* (Charlottesville: University of Virginia Press, 1999); Vendler, Helen, "John Berryman: Freudian Cartoons," in *The Given and the Made: Strategies of Poetic Redefinition* (Cambridge, MA: Harvard University Press, 1995, 31–57).

Ernest Smith

BERSSENBRUGGE, MEI-MEI (1947–)

An important innovative poet, Mei-mei Berssenbrugge's work does not easily fit into the standard maps of contemporary American poetry. She has clear alliances with **Language poetry**, yet her work holds a strong connection to lyric poetry and its attention to individual subjectivity. She maintains conversations with the New York visual and performance art scene, and has worked on several collaborations with Asian American arts groups such as the Morita Dance Company and Basement Workshop, yet her writing shows little overt connection to social or cultural questions. Hers is not an experimentalism of radical form, identity politics, or social critique but an experimentalism of embodied subjectivity and the phenomenology of affective and perceptual life. Challenging the narrative and lyric conventions that transform the experience of seeing into passive description, she argues that perception is always situated and embodied and that language is always constitutive of experience. As such, her work links in important ways both to the **phenomenology** of Merleau-Ponty and to recent work in **feminist** theory.

Mei-mei Berssenbrugge was born in 1947 in Beijing, China, to Chinese and Dutch American parents set adrift by Mao's revolution. Though she grew up in Massachusetts and changed her language to English at the age of nine months, her first memories, her first language, and her mother were Chinese. Berssenbrugge learned early the relativity of language, and her work has been strongly influenced by a Chinese sense of

"nature-plus-thinking." She also identifies strongly with her mother's and her grandmother's feminism, closely tied to the matriarchal part of Chinese culture. Having published more than a dozen books of poetry and collaborations, her work has received two NEA fellowships, two American Book Awards, and book awards from the Asian-American Writers Workshop and the Western States Art Foundation. She has been a contributing editor of *Conjunctions* magazine since 1978 and has taught at Brown University and the Institute of American Indian Arts. Once an associate of Georgia O'Keefe, she has lived in rural New Mexico for the past twenty-five years with artist Richard Tuttle and their daughter, and now also lives in New York.

A poet of careful observation, meticulous detail, and sensuous meditation on the immediacies of place, Berssenbrugge's poems are marked by a heightened impulse "to look again and then look" ("The Swan," *Empathy* [1989]). At the same time, her poems stage a rigorous questioning of the act of perception itself. Through a shifting examination of spaces occupied and empty, of sizes and scales, transparencies and frames, intervals and invisible entities, the poems in *Empathy* seek to create an experience of space rather than a representation of it— "a sense of spaciousness for things to take place" ("The Carmelites"). "The Margin" attends to "the pulls and weights of the body in motion," while "Fog" uses the experience of fog—as something you have to see in order to see through—to explore the blurred boundaries between subject and object, inside and outside, and one self and another.

Continuing her careful attention to the experience of perception, the title poem of *Sphericity* (1993) investigates how "the state of mind touches an object" and how images in the mind differ from perceptions in the world. In "Value" she attends to how language shapes our ways of seeing, observing that "the sentence is her concrete experience of time along a scapula or the sag of his belly beside her." Her poems are composed of long, expansive lines with no stanzas, often with each sentence seeming to stand by itself, creating a very spatial and tactile experience of the page. Unlike many **experimental poets** who emphasize the materiality of language over its transparency, the language of her poems ties us to the physical world in what Linda Voris calls "a densely layered referentiality" (69), but the physicality of language and of her books—often produced in collaboration with visual artists—is an important part of her poetics.

In her book poem *Endocrinology* (1997) Berssenbrugge situates her exploration of the bodily-ness of knowing and seeing in the interior landscape of the human body, exploring the complex relationship between the endocrinal system and our subjective experience of ourselves and others. The poem is saturated with explorations of different kinds of porous, interpenetrating relationships:

the flows of hormones and vascular circulation, the shared bodies of mother and child during pregnancy, the intimate bodies of two lovers, and the sensuous openness of the body to the physical world. The circulation through space peculiar to endocrinology re-imagines the minute ways in which the phenomenal world enters our language use, and how the materiality of experience diffuses into language. The physiological nature of these relationships challenges our deeply rooted habit of thinking about the subject in psychological terms—"Because she's in a body, it makes decisions."

Lurking within the images of *Endocrinology* is a concern that shared circulation communicates damage—a concern that Berssenbrugge explores in the title poem of her book *Four Year Old Girl* (1998). Beginning with the difference between genotype and phenotype, the poem explores the question of inheritance, both psychological and genetic, and the possibility of changing one's fate. Just as fate becomes at once an abstraction and a material, molecular reality, the poems of this book explore how "to formally express ethereal existence" in concretely material and experiential terms ("Daughter").

In her most recent work, *Nest* (2003), Berssenbrugge backed away from the beauty of *Four Year Old Girl*, opting instead for a self-consciously flat style that continues her exploration of the isolated sentence as a medium of attention. The nest acts as a central motif throughout the book, exploring architecture, metaphysics, and social relationships. Haunted by spaces, there is a sense of emptiness and dislocation that arises from the individual's search for a permanence in social relationships, as in "The Retired Architect" when she writes, "I tried to complete a life circumstance like a building I aspired to, loose in space on used land."

Further Reading. *Selected Primary Sources:* Berssenbrugge, Mei-mei, *Empathy* (Barrytown, NY: Station Hill Press, 1989); ———, *Endocrinology*, art by Kiki Smith (Berkeley, CA: Kelsey St. Press, 1997); ———, *Four Year Old Girl* (Berkeley, CA: Kelsey St. Press, 1998); ———, *The Heat Bird* (Providence, RI: Burning Deck, 1983); ———, *Nest* (Berkeley, CA: Kelsey St. Press, 2003); ———, *Sphericity*, drawings by Richard Tuttle (Berkeley, CA: Kelsey St. Press, 1993). *Selected Secondary Sources:* Altieri, Charles, "Intimacy and Experiment in Mei-mei Berssenbrugge's Empathy," in *We Who Love to Be Astonished: Experimental Women's Writing and Performance Poetics*, ed. Laura Hinton and Cynthia Hogue (Tuscaloosa: University of Alabama Press, 2002); Simpson, Megan, *Poetic Epistemologies* (Albany: State University of New York Press, 2000); Tabios, Eileen, *Black Lightning: Poetry-in-Progress* (New York: Asian American Writers Workshop, 1998); Voris, Linda, "A 'Sensitive Empiricism': Berssenbrugge's Phenomenological Investigations," in *American Women Poets in the 21st Century*, ed. Claudia

Rankine and Juliana Spahr (Middletown, CT: Wesleyan University Press, 2002).

Greg Kinzer

BIBLE AND AMERICAN POETRY

Occupying a central place in the American poetic tradition, the Bible reflects the complex trajectory of spiritual and **religious** perspectives that span the gamut from the Calvinistic poetry of the Colonial Puritans to the **postmodernist** dismissal of traditional doctrines and organized churches. As such, the Bible provides an index to American culture that no other text, sacred or secular, can rival. The extent of its presence and usage in American verse provides invaluable commentary about the cultural clime and religious persuasions of the times.

No American poets relied more heavily on the Bible as a core text than those of the Colonial Puritan epoch. Scriptural quotes, allusions, and references appear in virtually every substantive work. For the Puritans, both the Hebrew and Christian testaments, as translated in the Geneva Bible, provided typological evidence for the strict Protestant mores that grounded their daily lives. Accordingly, works such as **Anne Bradstreet**'s thirty-three–stanza *Contemplations* evidence the indispensable connection between the Bible and Puritan belief. Stanza 11, for example, reinforces Calvin's stance on humankind's absolute depravity since from "Eden fair" was "glorious Adam" driven:

To get his bread with pain and sweat of face.
A penalty imposed on his backsliding race.

Bradstreet's poetry keenly reflects her desire to maintain faith in times of acute sufferings, even after the catastrophic loss of her house to fire on July 10, 1666. While narrating the tragic details in "Verses upon the Burning of Our House," Bradstreet inserts scriptural allusions or references that remind her, and by extension her reader, that God's will, however inexplicable, must be accepted with faith, making the poem a didactic sermon on perseverance in the face of trials, as in these lines, which allude to the book of Job:

And when I could no longer look,
I blest His name that gave and took.

Bradstreet ends the work by reaffirming her conviction that heaven is her real home. The final couplet, though rarely recognized as an allusion to the Gospel, clearly echoes the Sermon on the Mount, where Christ advises that riches be stored not on earth, but rather in heaven (Matthew 6:19–21):

The world no longer let me love,
My hope and treasure lies above.

An equally vital example of biblical saturation is found in **Michael Wigglesworth**'s *The Day of Doom*, in which virtually all of the work's 224 eight-line stanzas incorporate an astonishingly wide range of scriptural passages. Stanza 180 offers multiple allusions that Wigglesworth uses to defend Calvin's doctrine of unconditional election:

Such you shall have; for I do save
none but Mine own elect.

Edward Taylor, meanwhile, follows Wigglesworth's strategy in supporting creeds with scriptural evidence. In his series of "Preparatory Meditations"—designed to function as a contemplative prelude for administering the Lord's Supper—sections generally begin with scriptural epigraphs, primarily from the Gospels, aimed at reinforcing the particular dogma that follows.

As the rigid Puritan communities began to wane with the influx of rationalism, with a few exceptions the Bible's role in American verse began to shift and decrease. Deism's lack of dogma and creeds appealed to a growing Colonial population that preferred the reason of the Enlightenment over New England's constrictive Calvinism, fueling a decline in scriptural references. Deists such as **Philip Freneau** and **Joel Barlow** searched for the divine in nature, not in the Bible, while focusing on themes that espoused the cause of liberty. **Phillis Wheatley**, the nation's first major black poet, was a curious exception to this trend. While she, too, made the revolution a theme, her verse remained scripturally centered, concentrating on the Christian ethics she acquired as a slave raised in a Puritan household. In "On Being Brought from Africa to America," Wheatley references the mark of Cain while lecturing white Christians on the status of her race within the doctrine of Unconditional Election:

Remember, *Christians, Negroes*, black as *Cain*,
May be refin'd, and join th' angelic train.

Nonetheless, Wheatley's generous use of scriptures remains atypical, and it would not be until the influence of British Romanticism that the Bible's role in American verse would rebound significantly. Traditional and accessible, **Henry Wadsworth Longfellow** used both biblical allusions and quotations in such well-anthologized works as "A Psalm of Life" and "A Jewish Cemetery at Newport." In "The Arsenal at Springfield," Longfellow rails against war by warning that Cain's curse awaits those who slaughter their brothers:

It's hand against a brother, on its forehead Would wear
forevermore the curse of Cain!

These awful sounds of war, in time he prays, will yield to "solemn, sweet vibrations" as we hear "once more the voice of Christ say, 'Peace!'"

John Greenleaf Whittier, while not overtly religious in either his life or verse, said of his youth, "the moral and spiritual beauty of the holy lives I read of in the Bible and other books also affected me with a sense of my falling short and longing for a better life." As such his frequent use of Biblical references lent support to his larger political ideal: the abolition of slavery through nonviolence. "Laus Deo" (Latin for "Praise be to God") was written specifically to mark passage of the Constitutional amendment ending slavery and includes allusions from Exodus, Job, Isaiah, and the Gospel of Luke. The concluding stanzas display the connection between divine intervention and the moral imperative, celebrating the broken chains of sin: "*It is done! . . . It shall belt with joy the earth!*" The final lines profess the sovereignty of God:

Tell the nations that He reigns,
Who alone is Lord and God!

Emily Dickinson's Bible may indeed be "an antique Volume—"; nonetheless, it served as an invaluable resource for her intense theological struggles—in particular, the way in which her verse was affected by the fracturing New England Protestantism of the later nineteenth century. While her claims and questions about the deity tended to be multifaceted, she often employed specific scriptural allusions to support her inquiries. In poem 1545, "The Bible is an antique Volume—," she succinctly lists and renames the text's major subjects from "Eden—the ancient Homestead—" to "Sin—a distinguished Precipice." She concludes by claiming that "*Boys that 'believe' are very lonesome—Other boys are 'lost'—*" but "*Had the Tale a warbling Teller—All the Boys would come—.*"

Meanwhile, in poem 1651, the Incarnation and the Christian rite of Holy Communion lead Dickinson to contemplate the relationship between Christian doctrine and the nature of language itself. Referencing the Gospel of John's "the Word was made flesh and dwelt among us," she asks if it is possible that "*such condescension be / Like this consent of Language.*"

Finally, Poem 59, a midrashic retelling of the story of Jacob and the Angel, seems especially revealing of the poet's own struggles with faith and the divine as she depicts Jacob's refusal to end the struggle: "*'Except thou bless me'—Stranger!*" As the morning light reaches "*'Peniel Hills beyond,'*" she concludes the brief narrative:

And the bewildered Gymnast
Found he had worsted God!

Dickinson's contests with God transcend the personal; indeed, they portray the intricacies and caveats of a religious dialectic that marks a fading tradition while anticipating the crisis of faith that will characterize the periods that follow.

Pressing questions about belief undermined the role of religion in the early twentieth century and deeply affected the emergence of **modernism**. Movements such as realism and naturalism not only fueled far-reaching anxiety about traditional institutions but served to further problematize a poetic movement that articulated widespread disillusionment or, in rare instances, battled against it. The Great War only exacerbated this growing distrust of staple institutions while the broken confidence in governments, churches, communities, family, and the autonomy of the self become thematic fodder for the period's strongest voices. Ironically, as the subjects of faith and religion remained central, the Bible's role once again shrank—as demonstrated by such major figures as **Edwin Arlington Robinson**, **Robert Frost**, **Ezra Pound**, **T.S. Eliot**, **Wallace Stevens**, and **Hart Crane**.

The **epic** impulse of the period helped produce such groundbreaking works as Pound's *The Cantos*, Eliot's *The Waste Land*, and Crane's *The Bridge*. While all are richly allusive, Eliot stood virtually alone in using the Bible as copiously and effectively as his nineteenth-century predecessors. In the "The Burial of the Dead" section of *The Waste Land*, references range from the Bible to Wagner's opera *Tristan und Isolde*. Eliot addresses the "Son of man," in a language of spiritual alienation and loss:

> You cannot say, or guess, for you know only
> A heap of broken images, where the sun beats.

Here "the dead tree gives no shelter . . . the dry stone no sound of water. Only / There is shadow under this red rock," and with "your shadow at evening rising to meet you; I will show you fear in a handful of dust."

Crane, meanwhile, preferred to employ biblical characters as metonyms on behalf of his thematic objectives or, more directly, his attempt to fulfill the Whitmanian vision that, through the Brooklyn Bridge, might "lend a myth of God." While examples from Crane's work are plentiful and varied, "Southern Cross," the first of "The Three Songs" from *The Bridge*, uses Eve, Mary Magdalene, and the Virgin Mary as central characters charged with symbolic fertility. His "nameless Woman of the South . . . lifts her girdles from here, one by one," as he asks if it is "Eve! Magdalene! / or Mary, you?"

Such examples, however, are rare, as the Bible's importance in American poetry continued to dwindle through the mid- to late twentieth century despite several culturally driven attempts at spiritual resurrection. The poetry of the **Harlem Renaissance**, although replete with Christian language and undertones, demonstrated this trend as the inspired works of **Countee Cullen**, **Langston Hughes**, and Gwendolyn Bennett connected the spiritual quest to ongoing battles for justice and equality, not necessarily a specific Christian agenda.

Robert Lowell, conversely, is another notable exception, as he made ample use of scriptures to complement his frequent use of mythological allusions. Ironically, Lowell's best examples, such as "Waking Early Sunday Morning," point to the Bible's fading role in both American culture and, by extension, its literature. Here the Bible is "chopped and crucified / in hymns we hear but do not read," as "they sing of peace and preach despair":

> yet they gave darkness some control,
> and left a loophole for the soul.

By the end of twentieth century, the religious and spiritual diversity of American culture had all but decentered the issues of faith and belief from their traditional Judeo-Christian roots. For the first time in the American poetic tradition, the Bible, once a primary resource, yielded to secular texts. With the exception of midrashic verses, scriptural references become relegated to the confessional and personal, as seen by **Anthony Hecht**'s poem about his first son, Adam, the child of a broken marriage. "Our Father in heaven" spoke to "his first, fabled child, / The father of us all," and here the speaker tells "the words over again / As innumerable men . . . have done" since antiquity.

And while spiritual, moral, and ethical inquiries rage on in the verse of the most celebrated modern voices— **Adrienne Rich**, **W.S. Merwin**, **John Ashbery**—the conversation has moved away from the scriptures. Perhaps no poem illustrates this phenomenon more strikingly than the ironic sonnet "Saint Judas" by **James Wright**, a Christian midrash that twists the story of the Bible's chief metonym for betrayal. "Banished from heaven," Wright's Judas "found this victim beaten, / Stripped, kneed, and left to cry," which compels him to drop his rope before, he says, "I remembered bread my flesh had eaten," concluding:

> The kiss that ate my flesh. Flayed without hope,
> I held the man for nothing in my arms.

Thus this sacred referential text, which possessed a central place in a cultural tradition for over two hundred years, has dimmed into virtual obscurity. The trend appears to be indicative of a postmodern culture that, with the exception of mainstream Judeo-Christian communities of worship, has divorced the spiritual enterprise from traditional sacred texts. So while the Bible's historical importance as an integral literary reservoir remains secure, American poetry, at least for the time being, has moved away from the scriptures as a primary canonical resource for its most pressing conversations.

Further Reading. *Selected Secondary Sources:* Bercovitch, Sacvan, ed., *Typology and Early American Literature* (Amherst: University of Massachusetts Press, 1972); Bloom, Harold, *The Bible, Bloom's Modern Critical Views* (New York: Chelsea House, 2003); Neusner, Jacob, *What is Midrash?* (Philadelphia: Fortress Press, 1987).

John P. Wargacki

BIDART, FRANK (1939–)

Through seven volumes to date, Frank Bidart has written an intensely original and widely acclaimed poetry that maps not only his own life but also the lives of other personae—selves and anti-selves who, consumed by their own fates, struggle to find clarity. He is a poet famous for opening up psychologies uncomfortable to witness, much less inhabit. He has, as he writes in "Curse," a poem about 9/11, *"the imagination to enter / the skin of another."* Bidart's poetry might be called **confessional** were it not that these poems go well beyond the psychological exhibitions that characterize the poetry we label as such; rather, as Helen Vendler has written, "Bidart is compelled—or condemned—to the relational as an instance of the metaphysical, and even of the theological" (*New Yorker* [10 June 1991]: 104).

The unusual content of Bidart's work is matched by an immediately recognizable style, virtually devoid of those elements traditional to poetry: figurative language, imagery, or formal devices of verse. Instead, Bidart creates a prosody of his own, particularly in his earlier books, deploying widely varied lines and spacing, typographic resources such as fonts (boldface, italics) and capitals, and mixtures of punctuation in an effort to "score" the poetry as one might a piece of music. Such a strategy has allowed him to represent his internal experience of a voice: "some way to get down the motions of the voice in my head" (*In the Western Night*, 224). Moreover, Bidart's diction, while conventional among educated English speakers, is unusual in poetry: It is sparse but contemplative, intellectual, and seldom imagistic. Finally, Bidart employs little or none of the irony identified with **postmodern** poetry, preferring instead to engage large ontological questions: the thwarted search for meaning, the relation between mind and body, the anxiety induced by the knowledge of death, and the ravages of guilt, loss, and love. Bidart's is a poetry of discourse rather than of a mimesis of the kind espoused by the two generations of poets who followed **William Carlos Williams**'s dictum of "No ideas but in things." Though in most regards unlike any other poet of his time, he is, like a few of his contemporaries—**Louise Glück**, **C.K. Williams**, **Jorie Graham**, and **Charles Wright**, among others—a poet of abstraction even more than of the physical world. The conditions of the world as

lived and sensed demand, for Bidart, the "necessary thought" that constitutes his poetry (*In the Western Night*, 232).

Frank Bidart was born in 1939 in Bakersfield, California, the son of a successful potato farmer who dreamed of being a cowboy, and a mother who, according to the poet, entertained dreams of being a Hollywood beauty. Both appear in Bidart's first book of poems, *Golden State.* Bidart grew up in Bakersfield and Bishop. He was educated at the University of California–Riverside, where he first became interested in writing, giving up his earlier ambition to be a film director; and at Harvard University, where he studied under **Robert Lowell**. The two poets eventually became close friends, Bidart offering the sounding board that the older poet needed at a pivotal point in his career, helping particularly to edit and shape Lowell's last four volumes of poetry. Upon Lowell's death in 1977, Bidart became the literary executor of Lowell's estate. He is also co-executor of the estate of **Elizabeth Bishop**, another close friend and mentor. Bidart is the editor, with David Gewanter, of Lowell's *Collected Poems* (2003). Since 1972, Bidart has taught literature and poetry writing at Wellesley College. His permanent home has continued to be Cambridge.

Frank Bidart's books include *Golden State* (1973), *The Book of the Body* (1977), *The Sacrifice* (1983), *In the Western Night: Collected Poems 1965–1990, Desire* (1997), *Music Like Dirt*, a chapbook (2002), and *Star Dust* (2005), which begins with the fourteen-poem sequence of *Music Like Dirt.* Bidart's books have been nominated for the Pulitzer Prize, the National Book Award, and the National Book Critics' Circle Award. Among his numerous awards are the Wallace Stevens Award from the Academy of American Poets, the Shelley Award from the Poetry Society of America, and the Theodore Roethke Memorial Poetry Prize, for *Desire.*

From the publication of his first book, it has been clear that Bidart's voice was to be like no other in contemporary poetry. While Robert Lowell's example was inevitable, particularly that poet's influential turn toward writing about his personal life from the late 1950s onward, Bidart's emphasis was not to be on the concretely remembered world Lowell set out in *Life Studies*, but on a world still unformulated, in order, as Bidart has said, "to express a drama of processes, my attempts to organize and order, and failures to organize and order" (*In the Western Night*, 237).

Three principal themes characterize Bidart's work from its beginnings to the present: the question of the body and "nature," the question of desire and fate, and, most recently, the question of making, whether of art or life.

The Body

Bidart's poetry acts out the drama of a doomed need for self-determination, a desire exacerbated to the point that the poems' speakers frequently express the longing to be free of the body, which is seen as a recalcitrant if not treasonous bulk, inhibiting self-realization. The burden of the body occupies speakers such as the anorexic Ellen West (in "Ellen West," *The Book of the Body*), the amputee of "The Arc" (*The Book of the Body*), the murderer and necrophiliac Herbert White ("Herbert White," *Golden State*), and the speaker of the poem "Luggage" (*Music Like Dirt*). One of the patients in the amputee's ward ("The Arc"), for example, says she wants to be free of any identity, yet the speaker remembers her as embodied: "even in my mind," he says, "she wears a body." In "Confessional" (*The Sacrifice*) the speaker repeats of his mother, "THERE WAS NO PLACE IN NATURE WE COULD MEET." And yet, "ALL WE HAD WAS NATURE."

"Ellen West," still Bidart's best-known poem, is also the most thorough treatment of the body as other. The title is a pseudonym for the anorexic whose treatment Ludwig Binswanger documented in *The Case of Ellen West* in 1944. Binswanger's notes form part of this highly dialogistic poem, as do nonhistorical sections such as Ellen's meditations on the opera diva Maria Callas, and the suicide letter that closes the poem. When, early in the poem, the narrator asks her doctors why she is a female, they tell her that it is a "given." Ellen, however, wants no givens; she wants her body to be "the image of her soul." Observing her aging mother, Ellen says, "I *loathed* Nature." Of Maria Callas's dramatic weight loss toward the end of her life, she says that Callas's spirit "loathed the unending struggle / to *embody* itself." While Ellen eventually concedes that one cannot know oneself without a body, her ultimate insistence is upon a self "anterior / to name; gender; action . . . MATTER ITSELF." Perhaps more clearly than any other poem in Bidart's oeuvre, "Ellen West" represents both the genre Bidart has created—a multiply narrated, past-tense recounting of desire and loss, shot through with extensive theoretical ruminations—and that genre's chief themes.

Desire

Although Bidart has written many short poems, he has specialized in long sequences, particularly dramatic monologues such as the one just discussed. The longest of these are three poems, each about thirty-five pages, which are better considered jointly than in their individual volumes: "The First Hour of the Night" (*In the Western Night*), "The Second Hour of the Night" (*Desire*), and "The Third Hour of the Night" (*Star Dust*). The titles of and concepts behind the poems derive from the Egyptian Book of the Night, which is divided into twelve sections by vertical lines of text called "gates," representing the twelve hours of night that the sun must pass through before rising. The three poems are part of a sustained effort to analyze Western conceptuality and one's life in

relation to it. In the course of these three poems, all of the themes under discussion come into play, but particularly the theme of being shaped and indeed fated by ineradicable desire.

"The First Hour of the Night" begins with a visit to the son of a deceased friend, in the course of which the son expresses remorse over his father's death. The speaker responds with his own story, concerning a miniature colt to which he was devoted as a child, but which he outgrew and which later died. Years afterward, the horse visits him in dreams, beseeching him to come back to it. Anguished at this memory, he nevertheless tells the son that the guilt they share is not their fault; rather, it is built into human relations.

Unconsoled by his own argument, the speaker retires for the night and is visited by a dream in which he finds himself inside Raphael's fresco *The School of Athens*, a reproduction of which hangs over his bed, placed there by his old friend. This twenty-two–page section of the poem surveys Plato, Aristotle, Heraclitus, Euclid, Descartes, and many other philosophers with the purpose of finding "*UNITY OF THOUGHT*." Instead, the philosophical views proliferate until the "ground DISAPPEARS" beneath the philosophers' feet, and the temple collapses. The speaker realizes that every society that has held an unshakable conviction has used its power and priesthood to launch wars and commit atrocities to validate it. Nothing that one might grasp out of history, the speaker finds, can "lodge safe /in *unhistorical* existence."

He wakes in despair, then sleeps again, this time dreaming that he is carrying on his back, and has carried all his life, the entrails of his childhood pony, a burden so customary he has hardly noticed it. Peering into a deep pit, he sees his pony at the bottom, looking up at him. He climbs down, lays the pony's entrails on the ground, and watches as the pony eats them. Then he mounts the pony and rides up out of the pit. At this point the speaker wakes and, though unable to relate his two dreams, experiences a feeling of "beneficence," which transforms what earlier had "overwhelmed / consciousness, lying SLEEPLESS between dream and dream." The poem concludes: "This is the end of the first hour of the night." (A parallel line, mutatis mutandis, will end the subsequent two poems of the series.)

"The First Hour of the Night" is an attempt to clear the ground for the exploration of transgressive desire, by means of the speaker's failure to locate a perspective within Western thought and, perhaps more important, by his successful exorcism of a disabling childhood guilt. The next two poems, written years apart, will more explicitly take up the issue of that transgressive desire.

"The Second Hour of the Night" again borrows from classical sources, this time retelling Ovid's story of the fatal desire of Myrrha for her father, the king Cinyras. Myrrha's own explanation for her desire—"I *fulfill* it, because I *contain* it— / it *prevails*, because it is *within me*"—suggests Heraclitus's idea that "character is fate," that man's daimon (ethos, moral climate, or "guardian angel") determines the course of his life. The consequences of Myrrha's sleeping with her father—veiled and brought as a gift by Hippolyta, a family servant—are the murder of Hippolyta, the suicide of Cinyras, and the exile of Myrrha, pregnant with his child, to a distant island. There she begs the gods to make her into something not human, neither alive nor dead, a request the gods grant by transforming her into a tree. Her blood and tears become the sap (myrrh, with its aphrodisiac and anodyne properties) that the tree exudes. From this tree, the child Adonis is born.

Myrrha's story concerns the sources, consequences, and inscrutability of desire. Like Ellen West or Herbert White, Myrrha is helpless in the grip of her longing, which is—in the same language the poet uses in "Ellen West"—a "given" of her existence. ("Every tragedy," Bidart remarked in another interview, "starts from an irremediable radical given" [Rathmann, 22].) Toward the end of the poem comes an apostrophe that seems to echo Eliot's "Phlebas the Phoenician" from *The Wasteland*, in which the speaker addresses the reader who can look into the mirror with gratitude at the lawfulness of his desire, advising him to anoint his body "*with myrrh / precious   bitter resin*" (spacing and italics in the original). The lines suggest both the comfort of norms and the necessity for the normal, if it would escape its own blindness, to absorb into itself the experience of the other.

"The Third Hour of the Night," originally published in *Poetry* magazine in 2004, appears in Bidart's *Star Dust*. The poem's chief sources are the autobiography of Benvenuto Cellini, a book on the principles of Cellini's sculpture, and an essay on Australian black magic. The idea of desire as an inhabiting demonic fate appears almost immediately, as the speaker refers to a "beast" within oneself that "can drink till it is / sick, but cannot drink till it is satisfied." This beast alone knows oneself, and it "does / not wish you well." For the sculptor Cellini, the beast within that is at odds with him—also seen as a God-granted "vision" guiding his work—is transgressive homoerotic desire, for which he is eventually imprisoned.

"The Third Hour of the Night," more than its two predecessors in the sequence, ties together the questions of transgressive desire and artistic creativity. Cellini, more than the narrators and subjects of the earlier long poems (Berlioz, Myrrha, the Greek philosophers) sees desire as inextricable from the drive to create, a drive frustrated at every stage by failure, as the human creator in time struggles to make something outside of time. In the end, the poem makes a case for art as the difference between life and death—whether in Cellini's bloody and thwarted career or—in the last section of the poem, where Bidart shifts to a very different source: the even bloodier black magic rite in which a woman is eviscerated, her uterus filled with mud, and made to live for two days, to prove the sorcerer's power to bury within a being "the hour it ceases." In both cases the emphasis is on the making: "After sex & metaphysics,— / . . . what? / What you have made." The final, italicized section, following the black magic narrative, returns us to the overriding need to make something out of the "corruptible" body, to create a new body of one's making.

Making

This concern for making pervades Bidart's poetry, often as a commentary on poetics in the root sense and as an exploration of the relation between body and art. Ellen West contemplates this relation when she says of Maria Callas's vulnerability "that to struggle with the *shreds* of a voice / must make her artistry subtler." Nijinsky says that his long training in classical ballet, which taught him to seek the illusion of effortlessness and poise, was of no avail in his life, which had none of these qualities. Cellini's meditations in "The Third Hour of the Night" echo Nijinsky's: Cellini studied to create in art an equilibrium of warring forces, forces that remained unresolved in his own life.

Music Like Dirt, which consists of fourteen poems, subsequently collected in *Star Dust*, on the theme of making, is the sequence that most explicitly addresses this issue, particularly in "Advice to the Players," which begins with the observation that humans need to recognize their need to make. In "Young Marx," similarly, Bidart notes that the problem of modern man is "*[t]hat where he makes what he makes he is / not: That when he makes, he is not.*" "Lament for the Makers" concerns Bidart's parents, whose grief was, he says, not to have made with clarity. The poem begins with sentences adapted from Marx, arguing that many creatures make "but only one must seek / within itself what to make." As the poet earlier wrote in "Homo Faber" (*Desire*), "Whatever lies still uncarried from the abyss within / me as I die dies with me."

"Insanity is the insistence on meaning," says the narrator of "The Arc." Bidart's speakers insist on finding meaning, and they fail. But to be engaged in that search—to be *making*— is the only thing that matters; the search is an expression not of the "Nature" that narrators such as Ellen West abhor, but of the "nature" of *homo faber*. The poems trace the arc of their search—posing and often exploding the questions raised, the perspectives offered. The nonmastery before the opacity of the world that is illuminated in these poems, coupled with the refusal to give up the search, is the madness that recommends and endears them to us. As Bidart writes in "The Confessional" (*The Sacrifice*), "*Man needs a metaphysics; / he cannot have one.*"

Further Reading. ***Selected Primary Sources:*** Bidart, Frank, *Desire* (New York: Farrar, Strauss and Giroux, 1997); ———, *In the Western Night: Collected Poems, 1965–1990* (New York: Farrar, Straus and Giroux, 1990); ———, *Music Like Dirt* (Louisville, KY: Sarabande, 2002); ———, ed., with David Gewanter, *Robert Lowell: Collected Poems* (New York: Farrar, Straus and Giroux, 2003); ———, *Star Dust* (New York: Farrar, Straus, and Giroux, 2005). ***Selected Secondary Sources:*** Gray, Jeffrey, "'Necessary Thought': Frank Bidart and the Postconfessional," *Contemporary Literature* 34.4 (1993), 714–739; Halliday, Mark, "An Interview," in *In the Western Night*, 223–241; Hammer, Langdon, "Frank Bidart and the Tone of Contemporary Poetry" (*Southwest Review* 87.1 [2002]: 75–91); Pinsky, Robert, *The Situation of Poetry: Contemporary Poetry and Its Traditions* (Princeton, NJ: Princeton University Press, 1876); Rathman, Andrew, and Danielle Allen, "An Interview with Frank Bidart" (*Chicago Review* 47.3 [2001]: 21–24); Sewell, Lisa, "Frank Bidart," in *American Writers: A Collection of Literary Biographies, Supplement XIV*, ed. Jay Parini (Farmington Hills, MI: Scribner's Reference/The Gale Group, 2004).

Jeffrey Gray

BIERCE, AMBROSE (1842–?)

Ambrose Bierce is better known as the author of the vitriolic definitions in *The Devil's Dictionary* and his melodramatic story "An Occurrence at Owl Creek Bridge" than as a poet, but all his life he admired poetry and wrote a considerable amount of it.

Ambrose Bierce was born on June 24, 1842, in Ohio. He worked as a printer's apprentice before enlisting in the Union Army, where he served as an officer during the Civil War. After the war, he turned his hand to journalism, serving as editor of the *San Francisco News-Letter* and *California Advertiser.* He became a respected critic and columnist, especially noted for his column "The Prattler."

Bierce was best known for his biting wit. His mastery of the epigrammatic flair that helped make *The Devil's Dictionary* something of a classic can be felt and heard in all of his poems, many of which are short, articulate, and sharpened by an astringent wit, as evidenced in his poem "Insectivora," where in response to a "chorus of admiring preachers" who praise the munificence of Providence, a gnat states, "His care . . . even the insects follows: / For us He has provided wrens and swallows."

The Gilded Age and its aftermath were a perfect milieu for a satirist possessed of a Swiftian *saeva indignatio*; and "Bitter Bierce," as he was known in his San Francisco days, was fascinated by the vulgarity, sentimentality, and silliness of the period. Indeed, he was so much a man of late-nineteenth-century America that one cannot conceive of his living in any other place and time. The jingoism of the day inspired his parody of

"My Country 'Tis of Thee," which many believe has a greater claim than "The Star Spangled Banner" to being America's true national anthem, thus inspiring the flat-footed pun in its title ("A Rational Anthem"): "My country 'tis of thee, / Sweet land of felony." Although the meanings of "A Rational Anthem" are accessible to any generation, its full satiric force would have been most appreciated in the days of Boss Tweed, Tammany Hall, and, indeed, some of Bierce's very own neighbors, the giddy land pirates of San Francisco, where this parody was first published.

Justice Oliver Wendell Holmes once pointed out that for all its faults, American-style democracy was simply the best government that had ever been devised—a judgment Bierce might well have shared, for his misanthropy was more cosmopolitan than patriotic. He was so steeped in pessimism regarding the essential cussedness and stupidity of the human species that he scorned all doctrinaire convictions, such as the idea that happiness can be attained simply by fussing with a political system or, even less probable, creating one out of the the adolescent idealism that is the source of such miasmas.

Other men were often the targets of Bierce's wrath, for he was gifted in acrimony, and lusted to lampoon the deserving. His capacity for outrage was impressive. The poem "Compliance," in honor of John D. Rockefeller and his son, typifies his approach. Here the poem's sardonic politicized social humor is underscored by the heavy-handed rhythm and end-rhymes: "Said Rockefller, junior, to his dad: / 'I never do a single thing that's bad.'" Some of Bierce's most memorable poems are supplements to the definitions in *The Devil's Dictionary*, as in the lines regarding the "megaceph," described as "[a] man who to all things under the sky / Assents by eternally voting, 'I.'"

Bierce thought of a true poet as "a king of men." Indeed, his idealization of the poetry was such that he was disgusted with the great majority of popular verse produced in late-nineteenth-century America. This is manifest in his definition of poetry as "A form of expression peculiar to the Land beyond the Magazines." Not all of Bierce's poetry is witty or didactic, however. When he was deeply touched, he could take on the mantle of piety and wear it as convincingly as most Victorian poets. In "The Death of Grant," the persona's opening apostrophe is deliberately ambiguous, inclusive of both God and the dead general, who is virtually apotheosized in what follows: "Father! Whose hard and cruel law / Is part of thy compassion's plan."

During his years as a Union officer in the Civil War, Bierce had witnessed such horrors that the scars on his mind never healed. But there was one thing Bierce devoutly believed in: the beauty and perfectibility of language. Precision of word usage was for him a moral obligation, and he was from the beginning intent upon his personal version of "purifying the language of the tribe"—his own language included. In 1913, Bierce went to Mexico and was never seen again. His exact date of death is unknown, although some believe he died in the battle of Ojinaga in 1914.

Further Reading. ***Selected Primary Sources:*** *The Collected Works of Ambrose Bierce*, 12 vols. (New York: Neale, 1909); Duncan, Russell, and David J. Klooster, eds., *Phantoms of a Blood-Stained Period: The Complete Civil War Writings of Ambrose Bierce* (Amherst: University of Massachusetts Press, 2002); Grenander, M.E, ed., *Poems of Ambrose Bierce* (Lincoln: University of Nebraska Press, 1995); Hopkins, Ernest Jerome, ed., *The Enlarged Devil's Dictionary* (New York: Doubleday, 1967). ***Selected Secondary Sources:*** Davidson, Cathy N., *Critical Essays on Ambrose Bierce* (Boston: Hall, 1982); Gale, Robert L., *An Ambrose Bierce Companion* (Westport, CT: Greenwood Press, 2001); McWilliams, Carey, *Ambrose Bierce: A Biography* (Hamden, CT: Archon, 1967).

Jack Matthews

BIERDS, LINDA (1945–)

A poet of exact and empathetic imagination, Linda Bierds uses images and figures from the past—Thomas Edison, Philip V of Spain, lacemakers, Gregor Mendel—to plumb instances of transformation and discovery. Her richly meditative poems seek answers to philosophical questions by investigating the particularities of a moment. Bierds does not embody the past she writes of but strives to examine it with precision, thereby revealing its significance. She says she is "not interested in the dramatic monologue . . . but in the soliloquy, the interior conversation" (*Bellingham Review*, 23). Bierds presents readers an opportunity to know a poet not through details of autobiography but through her steady, outward gaze. Publishing a book of poems about every three years since 1982, Bierds's clear, **lyric** voice and unique, historic perspective has earned her, among other honors, a 1998 MacArthur Foundation grant.

Born in Wilmington, Delaware, Bierds grew up in the Seattle area. She was the first of her family to finish high school and earned both her bachelor's and master's degrees at the University of Washington, where, after working as an editor for a credit union and an information specialist, she became a lecturer in 1989 and teaches creative writing to this day. Bierds has not published memoir, fiction, or essays; her sole focus has been on her work as a teacher of poetry and a maker of poems.

From her first full-length collection, *Flights of the Harvest-Mare* (1982), Bierds knew her subject: historic moments of transformation. Each book since has pushed forward the craft of individual poems and the possibilities of a collection. *The Stillness, the Dancing* (1988) is popu-lated with poems that center on ideas of exploration, and in *Heart and Perimeter* (1991) the poems are unified by the idea and imagery of bells. These early books cement Bierds's loyalty to the lyric narrative—a poem that tells a story in a manner that privileges sound and image.

The influence on Bierds of **Elizabeth Bishop** and **Norman Dubie** must be acknowledged as among the most important—Dubie for his historic detail, vivid voices, varied line lengths, strong enjambment, and dense syntax; Bishop for her exquisite precision, willingness to let detail convey story, and restraint. Another influential poet is **William Carlos Williams,** whose lines broken across the sense of a sentence shift a reader's focus from the narrative and favor instead a lyric sense of perception, something often seen in Bierds's work.

Bierds writes slowly and steadily, crafting one poem at a time, line by line. Not one to draft and redraft, she seldom revises and says that her poems grow organically, dictating their own conclusion as they are made. Images are her primary point of entry into a poem. When Bierds comes upon "orphaned images," she writes them in her notebook; then, from that mote and from associated details, sounds, and stories that she uncovers, a poem begins to form.

After her first three books, Bierds began to write collections in which the whole gives depth to the parts. The poems of *The Ghost Trio* (1994) center on the intertwined lives of Charles Darwin, Josiah Wedgewood, and several miners, exploring through them what earth can offer. *The Profile Makers* (1997) is even more tightly unified. Framed by Civil War photographer Matthew Brady's portraits, the poems examine both Brady's picture making and, more generally, the idea of an image—what it captures and what it leaves out, what power it holds. Such questioning leads Bierds to Muybridge, Silhouette, and Daguerre and invites the reader to consider the poet as image maker as well. When asked whether she worries that historic subjects make her poems inaccessible, Bierds says she strives to provide enough information to give readers access without footnotes or endnotes. Because her poems are so sensual and detailed, what emerges through her work is not the distance between readers and the subjects of her poems, but their shared perception and thus humanity. Bierds takes the question of what there is to both praise and critique in our history to even greater lengths in her next two books.

"Into what shape will our shapelessness flow?" is the question repeated in *The Seconds* (2001). Bierds looks for answers through music and through the various meanings of seconds: as time, dueling backups, and discarded remnants. As in her other books, Bierds's form is consistent: The poems are generally about fifty lines long; are shaped into irregular lines and stanzas; and use enjambment, alliteration, hyphenated phrasing, and anaphora to move down the page. Her stance is consistent as well. Bierds does not vary her diction or syntax to enter the various ages and geographies of her poems even when the characters speak, thus foregrounding the lyric narrator and unifying her various subjects through the questions asked of them.

In *First Hand* (2005), Bierds retains all her strengths and adds exciting new formal and conceptual elements to her poems. The collection focuses on Gregor Mendel and asks how faith and science resemble one another in their hope and disquietude. But Bierds does not stay in the past. She explicitly connects Mendel's work with modern genetics, particularly in a poem about Dolly, the first cloned sheep. She uses techniques not seen in her earlier work: persona poems; short, incantatory non-narrative lyrics; and a crown of sonnets broken into two voices—Mendel's and Bierds's—with the repeating lines moving from one speaker to the other, bridging time, gender, and technology, bridging indeed the gap between scientist and poet, something latent in Bierds's other work but never so directly and arrestingly expressed. Bierds has used an autobiographical voice before, particularly in poems from *The Ghost Trio*, but never in collusion with the history that inspires her. *First Hand* elevates the work of observation and connection making done by both scientists and artists through curiosity and spiritual wonder. Bierds's humanism, her generous attention to the world's stories, moves here into a larger realm and promises that her next book will amplify and make even more essential her intelligent, lyric voice.

Further Reading. *Selected Primary Sources:* Bierds, Linda, *First Hand* (New York: Putnam, 2005); ———, *Flights of the Harvest-Mare* (Boise: Ahsahta Press, 1985); ———, *The Ghost Trio* (New York: Henry Holt and Co., 1994); ———, *Heart and Perimeter* (New York: Henry Holt and Co., 1991); ———, *The Profile Makers* (New York: Henry Holt and Co., 1997); ———, *The Seconds* (New York: G.P. Putnam's Sons, 2001); ———, *The Stillness, The Dancing* (New York: Henry Holt and Co., 1988). ***Selected Secondary Sources:*** Baker, David, "Kinds of Knowing" (*Kenyon Review* 15.1 [1993]: 184–192); Marshall, John, "Unassuming Linda Bierds a 'Genius' in Our Midst" (*Seattle Post Intelligencer* 20 [April 2000]: E1); Marshall, Tod, "Linda Bierds," in *Range of the Possible: Conversations with Contemporary Poets* (Spokane: Eastern Washington University Press, 2002); Slease, Markus, and Jennifer Whetham, "The Grand Outline: An Interview with Linda Bierds" (*Bellingham Review* 25.2 [2002]: 19–24).

Elizabeth Bradfield

BIRNEY, EARLE (1904–1995)

Although Earle Birney did not become a serious and powerful poet until his mid-forties, he did, nonetheless, enjoy one of the most diverse and intriguing careers in **Canadian poetry**. From his first **Auden**-esque volumes of poetry in the years following World War II to his playful, **concrete poetry** of his later years, Birney's work runs the gamut of styles and approaches to verse. The breadth of stylistic strength that his work displays is always undercut by a serious sense of irony, something that he acquired as a Chaucerian scholar. Although the scholar in Birney may have helped him to acquire technical mastery of everything from Anglo-Saxon alliterative structures to a **Black Mountain**–inspired frankness in his **free verse**, his hallmark remains that of the creative, itinerant inquirer. The persona of his poetry is that of a traveler and lover whose sense of social justice is tempered by a profound and influential understanding of English language poetic approaches and structures.

Born in Calgary when that city was in its pre-provincial days as part of the Northwest Territories, Birney never lost his sense of delight in the rugged landscapes and verbal rhythms of his childhood. His mother, a stern Scot, taught him the poetry of Robert Burns early in his life, and his later delight in both alliteration and a sharp-edged music to language can be traced back to her influence, especially in such mock Anglo-Saxon alliterative poems as "Anglo-Saxon Street." When Birney was seven, his rural life was changed for that of the mountains when his family relocated to Banff. The mountain experiences of Banff, and its surrounding, fir-lined slopes, would recur many times in Birney's poetry, especially in touching comparisons between his second, much younger wife, Wailan Lo, and trees, and in his early narrative masterpiece "David."

"David," which garnered Birney the prestigious Governor General's Award for his first collection (also titled *David*, 1942), tells the story of two friends who share a mutual love of hiking, mountain climbing, and wilderness adventure. When the two young men are climbing one day, David slips from his hold and plunges to a plateau where he lies broken and near death. Realizing that he will never experience the same sort of freedom and breathless adventure that the life in the wild had given him, the crippled David requests that the narrator push him off the ledge in an act of mercy killing. After much suffering and deliberation, the narrator consents, thus freeing David's spirit from a broken body. Birney was accused, later in life, of having killed the actual David of the poem (a grave mistake on the part of one critic who confused fiction with reality in the reading of the poem). In a playful act of literary touché, the poet not only won a successful lawsuit against the critic but also produced the individual who was the model for David in a National Film Board documentary on the poet's life and work.

Birney's sense of the free spirit that expresses itself in both his poetic playfulness and his deep-seated love of nature was hard won from a rough period in his early life. Following his father's return from the Great War and the conclusion of his early education, Birney worked as a bank clerk, a farm laborer, a scaler (one who scrapes the coal build-up from the bunker of a steamer), and a seaman throughout the 1920s and the 1930s. His sense of Conradian adventure took him, via the seaman's life, to the Far East, India, and throughout the Pacific.

His formal education began in 1922, when he enrolled in chemistry at the University of British Columbia, then a fledgling series of huts and scattered buildings on a peninsula not far outside Vancouver. As Birney recounts in his all-too-brief memoir, *Spreading Time*, he switched to English at the beginning of his second year and met such early-twentieth-century Canadian poets as Bliss Carman at the university while serving as editor of the campus literary magazine, *The Ubyssey*. Following his undergraduate studies at the University of British Columbia, Birney received his master's in English from the University of Toronto, where he was a contemporary of such poets as A.J.M. Smith and Roy Daniels. He went from the University of Toronto to the University of California–Berkeley, but left Berkeley to take up a lectureship at the University of Utah. The transition from student to faculty member was not an easy one for Birney, and he recorded his experiences and the foibles of academic life in his second novel, *Down the Long Table* (1955), a book that also deals with Birney's adventures in Trotskyite ideology during the 1930s. However he was received at Utah, his wanderlust soon caught up with him.

During the 1930s, Birney spent significant time in Mexico and Norway with the exiled Russian political leader, Leon Trotsky, and with such soon-to-be luminaries from the world of art and literature as Malcolm Lowry (author of *Under the Volcano*) and the filmmaker Luis Bunuel. Bunuel and Birney co-authored a script for a film that was never made. Lowry and Birney formed a very strong friendship that spanned several decades, Lowry's bout with excessive drinking, and two continents. Birney eventually loaned Lowry his cottage on an inlet in British Columbia, and there the expatriate British novelist completed his masterpiece, *Under the Volcano*, while facing, each evening, the broken neon sign of a Shell refinery that flashed on and off, missing its letter "S."

By the 1930s, Birney had completed his doctorate on Chaucerian irony at the University of Toronto and settled into the life of a roving academic. Birney's years in Toronto during the late 1930s, which ended with the coming of World War II and his enlistment in the Canadian army, was a productive turning point in his life. During this time, his left-leaning politics led him into a circle of friends that included the noted Goethe translator Barker Fairley, who brought Birney aboard as poetry editor for his noted national magazine the *Canadian Forum*. It was also during this period that Birney formed a close friendship with the literary critic (and also *Canadian Forum* editor and writer) Northrop Frye. Frye's connections to Victoria College at the University of Toronto and close association with the then Canadian poet laureate, E.J. Pratt, led to Birney's involvement as poetry editor for the *Canadian Poetry Magazine*, which, at the time, was the leading voice for poetry in Canada. Birney's role as "the" major editorial force on the Canadian poetry scene ended with the coming of the war.

Northrop Frye recalled that a group of Canadian poets gathered one evening in Birney's Toronto apartment just before the poet's departure for duty overseas. The University of Toronto was on the verge of being shut down because of the war, and, as Frye noted, the casualty lists were pouring in following the debacle at Dunkirk. The gathering on that particular evening included Birney, Frye, Pratt, and the poet and framer of Canada's current constitution, F.R. Scott. Each of the poets read something from their works. E.J. Pratt unveiled his miniature **epic** poem "The Truant," a poem about a small man standing up to a great totalitarian "panjandrum." Birney read one of his most memorable poems, "Vancouver Lights," a prophetic poem that predicts the coming of the atomic bomb. "Vancouver Lights," as Birney noted, was based on an actual experience in the West Coast city at the beginning of the war when the poet climbed a mountain overlooking the metropolis just as the first blackout erased suburb after suburb of the city. The final, assertive line, "there was light," is both a chronicle of the darkness falling over civilization and a demand for humanity in the face of the rising tide of barbarism. Frye later recalled that "that evening was what got me through the war. I knew then and there that we would win the struggle."

In his war service, Birney was spared the vicious experience of actual combat, and he served his time as a senior officer overseeing personnel selection. His experiences as a personnel officer, encountering uneducated, simple young men who had no idea of what they had gotten themselves into with their armed services duty, led to Birney's penning his first novel, *Turvey* (1949). *Turvey* is a picaresque story of a bungling Canadian soldier who blunders from adventure to adventure. On returning to Canada, Birney found that his place at the University of Toronto was gone. He worked for a brief period as supervisor of the International Service of the Canadian Broadcasting Corporation (CBC) before accepting a professorship at the University of British Columbia. His return proved to be a fruitful experience for both Birney and the university. While he was teaching medieval literature, he founded Canada's first **creative writing program**, a department that remains a major Canadian venue for the study of the practice of literary arts.

For Birney, the 1940s was an important decade of literary development and production. Away from the pressures of literary management duties, he penned his first two books, *David* (1942) and *Now Is Time* (1945), both of which won the Governor General's Award for poetry. In these books, Birney displays a careful sense of prosodic craft, a craft that he later perceived as too caring and too stiff. Many of his successful early poems, such as the sonnet "Alaska Passage," were reinvented during the 1960s and 1970s as either concrete poems or **sound poems**. His poems from this period, although formal in their structure, possess an acerbic wit that often examines and questions the Canadian identity, or lack of it.

In "Canada: A Case History: 1945," he presents the nation as a disturbed child who has been driven to the point of madness by his bilingual and bicultural parents—the nation as product of a broken home. In "Can.Lit," Birney offers a stinging critique of Canadian literature in comparison with American literature. The lack of an apparent tradition (a theme echoed by Birney's contemporary Douglas Le Pan in "Country Without a Mythology") suggests that the national literature is suffering from an absence not only of tradition but of spirit. Canada, Birney points out, never had a **Walt Whitman** (although Whitman did spend almost a year living in London, Ontario, in the late 1880s) or an **Emily Dickinson** to define the poles of its poetic voice. He concludes with the observation that Canadian literature is haunted by its lack of ghosts, and the poem amounts to a plea for an articulate national spirit that could find expression in credible verse.

As a social commentator, Birney often looked at Canadian society with a candor or wry grimace. In "Anglo-Saxon Street," he depicts Toronto's Cabbagetown district, at the time the largest white slum in the world. The poem uses Birney's familiarity with Anglo-Saxon rhythms and language to paint the slum as something frightening and strange, and as a place that transcends itself through the power of the poet's descriptive language. The world of "Anglo-Saxon Street" is a world rife with the politics of rage and hatred, a divisive place as uncertain as the marshy worlds of *Beowulf* and as uncompromisingly cold and unwelcoming as the world found in such early English poems as "The Wanderer" or "The Seafarer."

As Birney's career progressed through the 1950s and the 1960s, his work acquired an international flavor. The old wanderlust of the 1930s was still very much in his blood and still very evident in his poetry as he explored Europe, and in particular the East. Poems such as "Bear on the Delhi Road" and "A Walk in Kyoto" are among Birney's finest in that they blend the aestheticism of the East with the rhythms, forms, and verse structures of Western poetry that are so ingrained in Birney's sense of expression. In "A Walk in Kyoto," Birney sees himself as a gullible Gulliver, staring wide-eyed at a world that seems to lie beyond the reach of pure logical explanation. The weary traveler's mind is literally ablaze with defined, pure images as he tires at the end of a day of exploration; yet within that same mind there is a profound sense of oneness, of integration, and of a transcendence of the physical realm where the action has taken place. The same sense of mystical "unreality" is at play in "A Bear on the Delhi Road," where, as a traveler in India, the poet attempts to reconcile the cruel treatment of the bear with the failed desire to see the bear dance and create a moment of human joy. For Birney, the experience of this paradox dissolves into a pathos that he expresses for all nature as it suffers the self-inflicted and humiliating fate of mankind.

The later poems of Earle Birney are marked by both a desire to transcend the strictures of the linear elements of the line and page, and to rise above the expectations of the art to explore a giddy second childhood of love and other possibilities. This late phase had a tremendous impact on such experimental poets as bill bissett and **bp Nichol**, who recognized a poetic leadership in Birney's abandonment of capital letters and playful fusion of language and image. In poems such as "Alphabirney," where the poet sketches his face using the letters of the alphabet, there is a tremendous sense of self-parody, as if somehow the process of deconstructing himself as both a poet and a poetic voice would undo time itself. This later period, in which he either rewrote or restructured many of his early poems, marked a phase in his opus of experimentation where sonnets became sound poems, where tightly wrought lyrics leapt into visual or concrete poems, and where his sense of second youth was expressed in his love for Wailan, a woman considerably his junior. In "Evergreen," he laments that his love is young but that he is old, and he feels the presence of mortality creeping up on him. As a love poet devoted to his muse, Wailan, Birney celebrated her beauty and her youthfulness in a poetry that is grand for its simplicity and imagistic clarity. In "She Is," for example, he declares that he is "at peace in her." In his final book, *Last Makings* (1991), written while the poet was in the hospital as the result of several severe heart attacks, Birney works toward a kind of simplicity that he appears to have sought throughout the long voyage of his life as he took in the world and tried to order and understand it through his verse.

Further Reading. *Selected Primary Source:* Birney, Earle, *Spreading Time: Remarks on Canadian Writers and Writing, 1904–1949* (Montreal: Vehicule Press, 1989). ***Selected Secondary Sources:*** Aichinger, Peter, *Earle Birney and His Works* (Toronto: ECW Press, 1984); Cameron, Elspeth, *Earle Birney: A Life* (Toronto: Viking Press, 1994).

Bruce Meyer

BISHOP, ELIZABETH (1911–1979)

A little more than a decade after Elizabeth Bishop died, an outpouring of literary criticism sealed her reputation as among two or three of the most significant poets to emerge in her generation. In 1995 Thomas Travisano called the immense attention the poet garnered "the Elizabeth Bishop phenomenon" (4). Despite her Pulitzer Prize in 1956, she was known only narrowly through a few poems, repeatedly anthologized. The darling of other poets, she was praised for her apparently seamless mastery of craft, yet for decades there was only one slim volume on the poet's work and life, written by Anne Stevenson. The relative paucity of scholarship emerged chiefly from the difficulty in fully understanding the subtly unsettling quality of Bishop's poems. She has been called a **modernist**, a formalist, a **postmodernist**, a **feminist**, and even a **confessional poet**, yet none of these categories are adequate to her achievement.

The modernist poet **Marianne Moore** (whom Bishop met in 1934), clearly shaped some of Bishop's most cherished aesthetic practices, namely, an arduous crafting of poetry (rather than calling upon inspiration) and a close scrutiny of the natural world. She inherited Moore's ability for hyper–close-up examination (in fact, Bishop was known for having better than 20/20 vision). Bishop's significance as a major poet in part revolves around her perspicacious vision; however, such vision is ultimately the means of creating resonant interior landscapes, as David Kalstone early on observed. In some sense, she embodies the ability to express "felt thought," what **T.S. Eliot** designated as the union of intellect and sensation in the Metaphysical poets, a union that had, for Eliot, become obsolete in modern poetics.

Bishop's literary output was generally slow and painstaking; one reason for this was her continual efforts at revision (she spent almost fifteen years working on "The Moose," one of the masterpieces in *Geography III* [1976]). Bishop's formalist sensibility, reflecting **W.H. Auden**'s influence, emerges in her impeccable metrical sense and deft handling of poetic forms, particularly the villanelle and sestina. Yet, in postmodern fashion, she also calls attention to her reinvention of these forms. In her hands, they become "home-made" (to use a touchstone word from "Crusoe in England" in *Geography III*). Rather than "stays against confusion," as **Robert Frost** would have it, or transcendent art objects, they become more permeable testimonies to the interaction of life and art. Moreover, one of Bishop's signature devices is the inclusion of her own self-revisions—changing her mind midstream, revealing the process of consciousness. Thus, in looking at one of her uncle's sketches in "Poem," she purposely discloses a lack of surety in distinguishing an object: "A specklike bird is flying to the left. / Or is it a flyspeck looking like a bird?" (*Geography III*). Such interruptive moments lend a highly personal and quietly self-conscious character to her inventively meditative poems.

While Bishop's poems have been frequently called impersonal and reticent, their skillful acuity of understatement, silence, and negation evoke or more intensely confront imperative emotional and philosophical crises or impasses. In fact, her poetry and autobiographical prose galvanized **Robert Lowell**'s breakthrough to a more open, fluid style in *Life Studies* (1956), a landmark in the confessional movement; he claimed that her writing helped him relinquish some of his armor. Nonetheless, Bishop shunned restrictive literary categories, and her stated dislike of confessionalism has obscured the autobiographic imperatives in her work. Bishop, however, increasingly integrated personal experience and memories into her poems, and more than any other poet of her generation (except perhaps **James Merrill**) reflected upon the making of lived experience into art as well as the reverse. In effect, she furthered what Auden had begun—infusing finely crafted poems with an acute awareness of personal struggles with love, sexuality, loss, and mortality. Her homey, deceptively transparent language often belies, but ultimately reveals, an obsession with larger questions of existence and epistemology.

The motifs of loss and displacement that permeate Bishop's writing emerge directly from her biography. She was born on February 8, 1911. Her father died of Bright's disease when Bishop was only eight months old. For the next five years, her depressed and grieving mother, Gertrude Bulmer, originally from Great Village, Nova Scotia, was in and out of sanitariums, moving Elizabeth between Great Village (where her maternal grandparents resided) and Worcester (where Bishop's wealthy paternal grandparents lived). In the autobiographical story "In the Village," written in 1952, Bishop memorialized her childhood rural life in Great Village, as well as the final catastrophe of the nervous collapse that in 1916 caused her mother to spend the rest of her life in the Nova Scotia Hospital in Dartmouth. The story opens with a scream that converts the landscape into an emblem of inconsolable loss, a scream that paradoxically awakens the child's poetic sensibility. After this breakdown, Bishop never again saw her mother, who died in May 1934, the same year Bishop graduated from Vassar College. (Her anxieties over this loss, the fear of mental illness, as well as guilt led to a lifelong problem with alcoholism.) For the most part, Bishop considered her maternal grandparents her family during her formative early years. When she was six years old, Bishop was uprooted from Nova Scotia when her paternal grandparents took her to live in Worcester. There she suffered intense homesickness as well as numerous physical ailments—asthma (which

Bishop struggled with all her life), bronchitis, and eczema. Her Aunt Maud (her mother's sister) offered a reprieve from Worcester, and her spirits and health apparently improved while she lived with Maud in Boston.

Bishop's childhood displacements reverberated in the poet's adult life. She traveled and inhabited diverse locations (among them New York, Paris, Spain, Mexico, Seattle, and Boston), never making any of them, except for Brazil in 1951, a permanent residence. When she set sail for South America, she had no idea that she would remain in Brazil for fourteen years. Detained in her travels because of an allergic reaction to a cashew fruit, she was nursed back to health by the Brazilain Lota de Macedo Soares (whom she had briefly met in New York). Her longest intimate relationship turned out to be with Lota. Just prior to her trip to South America, Bishop had been consultant in poetry at the Library of Congress (1949–1950). Her expatriation to Brazil in the 1950s can be seen as partly a result of the cultural climate of the Cold War and the extreme hostility to homosexuality in America. It is also no wonder that Bishop "hid" her lesbianism from the public.

Her "Brazil period," her most productive period of writing, was achieved while she had a measure of security in love that she had not before experienced. Being an expatriate also allowed her to draw upon her early experiences in Nova Scotia. In 1957 she translated the *Diary of Helena Morley*, an adolescent's account of growing up in a pre-industrial Brazilian town, a kind of mirror for her own developing personal narrative. In 1966, Bishop returned to the United States to teach in Seattle. The following year, the exhausted Lota (who had been in charge of planning a vast public park in Rio) committed suicide, contributing to Bishop's lengthy catalogue of losses. During the 1970s, until she died of a cerebral aneurysm on October 6, 1979, Bishop taught at Harvard University. Bishop published five collections of poetry, included in *The Complete Poems: 1927–1979*, which also contains *New Poems*, unpublished poetry, and translations from the French, Portuguese, and Spanish. Her published stories and essays are gathered in *The Collected Prose*. Along with *The Diary of Helena Morley*, she also authored the *Time/Life* edition on Brazil in 1961. Bishop's unpublished poems and drafts continue to appear posthumously. The prodigious *One Art: Selected Letters*, edited by Robert Giroux, was published in 1994.

Bishop's first publication in a book appeared in the anthology *Trial Balances* (1936), where Moore introduced her, praising the emerging poet for her debts to John Donne and Gerard Manley Hopkins as well as for her syntactic and verbal inventions. Featured in *Trial Balances*, "The Map" became the first poem in Bishop's debut book, *North & South*, awarded the Houghton Mifflin Poetry Prize in 1945 and published the following year. This volume, like subsequent publications, broadly

concerned itself with movement and travel, as the title suggests. She composed the poems over the course of a decade, during which time she traveled with Louise Crane to Paris in 1936 and then to Florida for fishing, where she discovered Key West. In 1937 she traveled back to France, where she was involved in a terrible car accident, memorialized obliquely in "Quai d'Orléans," a poem dedicated to her friend, Margaret Miller, who lost an arm. Bishop would try for years to write a poem from the point of view of the amputated arm, but finally this poem registered the agonized muteness in the face of severe trauma: "We stand as still as stones to watch / the leaves and ripples" (*North & South*). From 1938 to 1941 she lived in Key West; its dramatic thunderstorms form the backdrop for the unpublished love poem beginning "It is marvelous to wake up together" (written to Marjorie Carr Stevens).

These various landscapes—Paris, Florida, Key West— are the touchstones of *North & South*. The inability to find a home spurs the poet on in her sometimes "romantic" quests: "We'd rather have the iceberg than the ship, / although it meant the end of travel" ("The Imaginary Iceberg"). As a first book, it tries out and remakes previous poetic models, drawing upon poets as diverse as George Herbert (she claimed to carry his volume in her suitcase at all times), Auden, Moore, T.S. Eliot, and **Wallace Stevens**.

"The Map" (written New Year's Eve 1934) establishes mapping as emblematic of her poetic activity and inaugurates a series of poems that construct a variety of artist figures (*North & South*). All of these figurations valorize the indeterminate, the subjective and instable, as does "The Map." The first lines of the poem offer an interaction between perceiver and object that depends upon visual and verbal slippage, "shadows" that could be "shallows": "Land lies in water, it is shadowed green. / Shadows, or are they shallows, at its edges." The questions that follow begin with Bishop's preferred conjunction, "or," perpetuating alternatives: "Or does the land lean down to lift the sea from under, / drawing it unperturbed around itself?" "The Map" animates the apparently impersonal object with its "tugging" and lifting; likewise, the map enlivens the observer into a passionate engagement: "We can stroke those lovely bays." In the end, "The Map" provides only provisional substantiality, and Bishop introduces what will become one of her key vocal registers—the child voice asking the most obvious and difficult questions in *Geography III*. Here she asks with unassuming simplicity, "Are they assigned, or can the countries pick their colors?" The last two lines, epigrammatic and decisively destabilizing, expose how the map's artifice and flatness manifest the relativity of place and home (as *Questions of Travel* later interrogates): "Topography displays no favorites; North's as near as West. / More delicate than the historians' are the map-makers' colors." The mapmaker is Bishop as watercolorist, operating without the strict, rigid lines that must be drawn by the historian. Bishop wanted to be a painter almost more than a poet and painted numerous watercolors. Her visual style is not, however, naturalist; rather, as her work as a whole suggests, she is precise about imprecision, about the inability to pin an object down.

A significant influence upon Bishop is surrealism, particularly evident in the poems she wrote while in France, such as "Chemin de Fer," "Love Lies Sleeping," "Sleeping on the Ceiling,"and "Paris, 7 A.M.," where she makes "a trip to each clock in the apartment" and looks down into the courtyard: "It is like introspection / to stare inside, or retrospection" (*North & South*). "Cirque d'hiver" presents the poet identifying with the "melancholy soul" of a "little circus horse," a mechanical toy: "Facing each other . . . we stare and say, 'Well, we have come this far.'" Bishop never explains the "desperation," yet it circulates the poem.

Like her "Gentleman of Shalott," who finds "the uncertainty" an "exhilarating" state (*North & South*), Bishop exults in "the sense of constant re-adjustment" ("Gentleman of Shalott"). Her landscapes and personae frequently partake of extremes and altered states of consciousness, and like "The Map" highlight the blurred division between internal and external experience. Her fantastical, grimly giddy "Gentleman of Shalott" lives with a mirror down his middle ("he's in doubt / as to which side's in or out"), in perpetual crisis, never knowing if it will slip ("he's in a fix"). Similarly, another hybrid, surreal artist figure, "The Man-Moth," presents an urban poet, at home only in the underground subways: "Each night he must / be carried through artificial tunnels and dream recurrent dreams." This perverse creature, slightly inhuman, "always seats himself facing the wrong way." Many of Bishop's early poems fashion isolated male personae (partly as poetic mask) who bear resemblance to herself, such as the Man-Moth, who fears "a disease / he has inherited the susceptibility to." The poem points toward Bishop's credo of confessing by not confessing: The Man-Moth "palms" his "one tear, his only possession," and the poem warns, "and if you're not paying attention / he'll swallow it."

The poet, keen on the experience of perception itself, often stares (a word recurrent in *North & South*) at an image until it turns into temporary "vision," what she called in a letter to Stevenson, "glimpses of the always-more-successful surrealism of everyday life, unexpected moments of empathy (is it?), catch a peripheral vision of whatever it is one can never really see full-face but that seems enormously important" (quoted in *Elizabeth Bishop and Her Art*, 288). Bishop's "peripheral vision" remains tentative, limited, and often suddenly foreclosed. Her Man-Moth, for instance, "stares back, and

closes up the eye." Her early sestina "Miracle for Breakfast" (1936) provides lucid details to both conjure up and deflect the visionary (*North & South*). The quotidian "makings of a miracle"—"one lone cup of coffee" and "one rather hard crumb"—transmute into "galleries and marble chambers." A hyperbolic imbibing of "gallons of coffee" precedes deflation: "A window across the river caught the sun / as if the miracle were working, on the wrong balcony."

"The Fish" is often held up as exemplary of Bishop's talent for description, yet she provides an unreasonably protracted look at the caught fish: its "brown skin hung in strips"; it is "speckled with barnacles" and "infested / with tiny white sea-lice" (*North & South*). The speaker ultimately empathizes with the studied creature, even if it would "not return [her] stare." The fish becomes, nevertheless, a testament to survival—"a five-haired beard of wisdom / trailing from his aching jaw." Through her intricate scrutiny of the fish, the poet exposes the limitations of our ability "to see" or comprehend otherness. By the end, after she has "stared and stared," the "little rented boat" provides a visionary moment: The oil in the boat has spread into a rainbow, and everything "was rainbow, rainbow, rainbow! / And I let the fish go." Such an overflowing is earned by painstaking vision (as well as through the accident of light and bilge). This poem, with its aleatory style, differs from Moore's of the same title that restricts itself to syllabics, yet it shares the mode of ethical allegory with its predecessor: Observation with empathy leads to an anticipatory act of losing (letting the fish go), which becomes a "philosophy" of renunciation in the later "One Art" (*Geography III*).

Bishop's second volume, *A Cold Spring* (1955), was originally published with *North & South* in *Poems*. In *Cold Spring*, she continues to consider the way objects retain or reflect back our emotional states, but abandons the testing of poetic models and focuses upon intimate relationship. She subdues the Romantic undercurrent that would make her prefer the iceberg to the ship, or to risk sleeping "on the top of a mast / with his eyes fast closed" ("The Unbeliever," *North & South*). By closely recording the external world, she finds correlatives—fluid as they are—for internal conditions. In small print under the title, the words "[On my birthday]" give only the slightest indication that "The Bight" (one of the volume's key poems) has any personal resonance. Bishop assiduously keeps the first person out of this poem of uneven, asymmetrical lines, yet in avoiding pronouns altogether (except a single "one"), she need not pretend to false objectivity. Like many in this volume, the inlet immersed in water is paradoxically "absorbing, rather than being absorbed." In depicting a scene of excavation ("the little ocher dredge at work off the end of the dock"), she invokes Baudelaire's poem, "Correspondences," and its belief in language achieving a unity of the senses through synesthesia; but rather than imagined unities, her landscape is "littered with old correspondences." The "little white boats" that "lie on their sides" are "like torn-open, unanswered letters." Unlike Baudelaire, Bishop reveals no faith in the world as ultimately legible or transcendent; in fact, the scene is decidedly not sublime, with the work of dredging (a parallel for poetic thinking) implicitly linked to the pelicans with their "humorous elbowings" and the "frowsy sponge boats" that "keep coming in / with the obliging air of retrievers." The final image of the dredge—it "brings up a dripping jawful of marl"—points toward Bishop's obsessive orality (in the title as well) along with her un-Romantic rendering of the act of writing as "untidy activity," always dissonant, often unanswered, "awful but cheerful."

"The Bight" is itself a kind of letter in a volume that can be read as a series of correspondences with significant others, expressing a desire to connect. For instance, "Letter to N.Y." (for Louise Crane) explicitly demands continued intimate exchange: "In your next letter I wish you'd say / where you are going and what you are doing" (*Cold Spring*). And her "Invitation to Miss Marianne Moore" reiterates, "Please come flying." This kind of passionate invocation culminates in "The Shampoo," the last poem of *Cold Spring*. After a fairly elaborate conceit, describing her lover's hair as "spreading, gray, concentric shocks" that "have arranged / to meet the rings around the moon," she requests, "—Come, let me wash it in this big tin basin, / battered and shiny like the moon." "Insomnia," one of Bishop's most overt expression about her sexuality, imagines an inverted world, "where left is always right / where the shadows are really the body." This poem has the surreal atmosphere evoked in *North & South*, but it is now attached to a desiring body in an alternate universe "where we stay awake all night." The poems, then, in *Cold Spring*, are often intimate and domestic, even when tinged with anxiety or frustration.

The centerpiece in *Cold Spring* is "At the Fishhouses," which appears at first to be an intense and detailed description of the sea as it decorates and warps all that it comes into contact with: "All is silver: the heavy surface of the sea, swelling slowly as if considering spilling over, / is opaque." At the same time, the lobster pots, the rocks, the old buildings, and the wheelbarrows are all "of an apparent translucence." As the reader gradually descends into the poem, lulled and hypnotized, like the narrator, to the water's edge, "where they haul up the boats, up the long ramp / descending into the water," the poem turns into one of Bishop's most overtly philosophical, meditating as it does upon the "cold dark deep and absolutely clear." Fronting this "element bearable to no mortal," she entertains a "seal" who is "curious about [her]." Bishop interjects her wry humor, singing to the

seal a Baptist hymn, and claiming their kinship: "like me a believer in total immersion." The poem reaches a crescendo, where epistemology becomes deliquescence; the water, burning with coldness, "is like what we imagine knowledge to be: dark, salt, clear, moving, utterly free," and thus an unlimited and proximate entity. We are bound only to "the cold hard mouth" of temporality "since / our knowledge is historical, flowing and flown." She articulates a position akin to Heraclites, that of continual change, epitomizing her aesthetic distaste for the transcendent. In a similar gesture of making and withholding grand claims, the later "Santarém," with its "conflux of two rivers," seems to ask for "literary interpretations / such as: life/death, right/wrong, male/female," but "such notions would have resolved, dissolved, straight off / in that watery, dazzling dialectic" (*New Poems*).

Bishop avoids overweening "literary interpretation" in preference for the soluble and the vacillating. Thus she intentionally never resolves her central dialectic between home and travel. "The Prodigal" suggests that exile might be more thrilling than homecoming (*Cold Spring*). Bishop's third volume, *Questions of Travel* (1965), intently meditates upon this dichotomy. The volume was originally published with the story "In the Village," a bridge between a section called "Brazil" and another titled "Elsewhere," containing poems that deal with her New England past. The ending line of the first poem in *Questions*—"we are driving to the interior"—signals a shift toward more personal writing that will follow from her questions of travel, related to ethnocentrism and colonialism. Oddly, these questions emerge as she attempts to settle down and make a home in Brazil. Even so, she is aware that such stability can only be imagined, just as one's contact with another culture often involves projection. She states this conundrum most lucidly in the poem "Questions of Travel," where, after cataloguing the exoticism and difference of Brazil, she italicizes and quotes as an entry from a traveler's notebook: "*Is it lack of imagination that makes us come / to imagined places, not just stay at home?*" She answers her own questions paradoxically and with another question, "*No. Should we have stayed at home, / wherever that may be?*"

As an American in another culture, she appreciates her status as outsider and even criticizes the shallowness of herself as tourist. "Arrival at Santos" humorously reveals her own cultural insulation and naivety: She sees the country's flag, and recognizes that she "somehow never thought of there *being* a flag." Throughout this volume, she connects the dangers of imagined knowledge with the dangers of appropriation, of the "immodest demands for a different world, / and a better life, and complete comprehension" ("Arrival in Santos"). That her concerns are political in this volume emerges in

"Brazil, January 1, 1502," when she traces out the conquest as a parallel to the act of making nature into art: "Januaries, Nature greets our eyes / exactly as she must have greeted theirs." Naturalism inevitably fabricates; vision itself participates in colonial incursion. Finally, the moment of conquest becomes an act of rape where the soldiers "ripped away into the hanging fabric, / each out to catch an Indian for himself—." The women of this poem, however, evade capture: "Those maddening little women who kept calling" are "retreating, always retreating." Other poems in the "Brazil" section of *Questions of Travel* reveal Bishop's social concerns, most striking in "The Burglar of Babylon," a ballad that features the hunting down of a criminal, among the many "poor who come to Rio / And can't go home again." These kinds of concerns recur in "Pink Dog," begun in the 1960s and not finished until just before her death in 1979, with its hairless female dog, compared to other outcasts hidden from society, and who is encouraged by the speaker to dress up for Carnival: "Tonight you simply can't afford to be a- /n eyesore" (*New Poems*). The line is purposefully imperfect as Bishop slips into wry irony, informing us that beggars who are drowned, "go bobbing in the ebbing sewage, nights / out in the suburbs, where there are no lights."

In the "Elsewhere" section of *Questions of Travel*, Bishop's "Sestina," perhaps the greatest poem to use this particular form, relies upon ritual repetition, not only as an aesthetic device, but also as method of reliving and covering over painful experiences. The form, as with the later "One Art," is the theme—the poem's very gut or crux. Its six chosen words—the simple unassuming nouns (house, grandmother, child, stove, almanac, tears) magically revolve and incant. "Sestina" recreates a childlike perspective, animating homey objects (as in "The Map"): "The iron kettle sings on the stove"; the almanac is "clever," and even "the house / feels chilly." While the *specific* sorrow guiding the poem remains inexplicit, we can assume from the grandmother's sadness as well as her masking of it ("laughing and talking to hide her tears") that "Sestina" pivots on the poet's early events of loss, her mother's insanity ("the teakettle's small hard tears / dance like mad") and subsequent removal. The almanac commands, "*Time to plant tears.*" The sestina form becomes a formula for transmuting the self and its losses, creating a tentative shelter for revisited grief.

"Elsewhere" gives us other places besides the sites of Bishop's mourning (such as "First Death in Nova Scotia"), but her emerging *direct use* of autobiography informs even the most seemingly incongruous landscapes. Thus, "Filling Station" points toward the absent mother in the "oil-soaked, oil-permeated" station where the oil cans are arranged as a cry of help and a soothing iteration: "ESSO—SO—SO—SO." Or even "Visits to St. Elizabeth's," recording her visits of Pound in the "house of bedlam" with the template of "the house that Jack built," has her own name in it, perhaps touching upon her "hereditary susceptibility" ("The Man-Moth"). "Sandpiper" is a self-portrait in quatrains identifying the poet with the creature who "runs to the south, finical, awkward / in a state of controlled panic." The poem recreates both her aesthetic of indeterminacy ("The world is a mist. And then the world is / minute and vast and clear") and her almost painful propensity for particulate vision where there exists "no detail too small" so that the "obsessed" bird keeps "looking for something, something, something" amid the "millions of grains" of multicolor sands.

Bishop's last published book before she died, *Geography III* (1976), confirms her talent for revealing psychological intensity in muted yet piercing language. Here she underscores, in postmodern fashion, that to remember is always, in some sense, to create. In considering a "minor family relic," her uncle's humble "little painting" of a Nova Scotia landscape in "Poem," she discovers a legacy of shared experience "cramped" on a "Bristol board" so that "life and the memory of it so compressed / they've turned into each other." "Which is which?" she asks, reflecting her ongoing sense of permeable boundaries. As memory confirms loss throughout this volume, she constructs a poetics of the "homemade," the shaping of an adaptable imagination. The volume opens with fragments of lessons taken from an 1884 geography primer with such seemingly self-evident questions such as "What is the shape of the Earth?" They orient us (like "The Map") to the disorientation that ensues from trying to place the self within the unnavigable vastness of "blue black space" ("In the Waiting Room").

The first poem in the volume, "In the Waiting Room," recreates Bishop's "real" experience of accompanying her Aunt Florence to the dentist three days before her seventh birthday in 1918. This event turns out, retrospectively, to be an ontological crisis in the child's life—the moment she recognizes having a self ("you are an *I*, you are an *Elizabeth*"), as well as the relativity of that self ("Why should I be my aunt, / or me, or anyone?"). She also realizes (or the poem does) the illusory nature of time and space. It begins apparently on solid ground, as do so many of Bishop's poems, giving us clear, straightforward language: "I went with Aunt Consuelo / to keep her dentist's appointment." But quickly the poem begins to shift the boundaries of inside and outside, using prepositions to displace us. The child's aunt "was inside / what seemed like a long time," and it is one of the poem's key intentions to make vivid how we abide inside temporality, stranded in the "waiting room" of our mortality.

Consciousness of mortality necessarily comes through language. In fact, the child is proud that she can read the *National Geographic*—"(I could read)"— but her reading of the journal's photographs of "the inside of a volcano" that is "spilling over" and of African women with naked breasts (they "were horrifying") begins her sense of unmoored identity. Her aunt's scream of pain from the next room comes from "inside" and plunges her into vertigo: "I was my foolish aunt, / I—we—were falling, falling." The sudden sense of fusion with her "foolish, timid" aunt emerges as part of her recognition of her own femaleness and New England whiteness; at the same time, she is linked to the "the breasts" of the African women, who are only apparently "outside" her fragilely delimited terrain. Markers of "north" and "south" (as we learned from "The Map") are after all arbitrary impositions.

The self is not only a "homemade" one, but one dependent upon the relations of difference and sameness ("the family voice"); by marking the self in time through language—"I said to myself: three days / and you'll be seven years old," Elizabeth hopes to halt "the sensation of falling off / the round, turning world, / into cold blue-black space." The "cry of pain that could have / got loud and worse but hadn't" unfurls a legacy of loss (echoing her mother's scream of "In the Village") and knowledge of time that conjoins "us all together." The discovery of self converts to a discovery of female sexuality, a find that inextricably connects humans with one another.

This notion returns less as a crisis and more as an "indrawn affirmative" in "The Moose," which describes a long, hypnotic bus journey. The sudden appearance of the "homely" and "towering" animal in the New Brunswick woods draws the disparate passengers temporarily together and to question why we all feel "this sweet / sensation of joy?" "The Moose," one of Bishop's most evocative pieces, composed over a long stretch of time and knit together through dense aural repetitions, allows us to view the self as not limited to individual existence but as bound to a larger communal "dreamy divagation," an "old conversation," emerging from somewhere, / back in the bus."

If the "deaths, deaths, and sicknesses" resound in the stories reiterated in the back of the bus ("The Moose"), "Crusoe in England" rewrites Defoe's novel (which she found boring) into an **elegy** for lost connection. The shipwrecked self relies apparently only upon imagination. Forced into making his own "home-brew" and "home-made flute," her Crusoe cries out, "Home-made, home-made! But aren't we all?" However, what makes "Crusoe," in part, a major American poem is its orchestration of multiple strands: personal, political and literary. First of all, the island landscape reflects Bishop's travels (both literal and imagined) to many islands, including Aruba, the San Juan Islands, and, of course, England, as it also integrates the landscapes of Swift and Darwin; second, she rejects the mythic depiction of Crusoe as expert exile, finding in Defoe a prototypic colonialist text: "None of the books has ever got it right," the first stanza asserts; next, it explores Bishop's sense of an amnesiac relationship to a primarily masculine tradition ("The books / I'd read were full of blanks"); third, she explores the question of free will and self making: "Was there / a moment when I actually chose this?" Crusoe asks; and most important, framed as a retrospective memory told from the point of view of Crusoe back at "home" drinking his "real tea" in England, it functions as an elegy for the beloved (most likely for Lota).

Crusoe functions creatively while alone, although he suffers from guilt-ridden nightmares and indulges in self-pity: Sitting at the edge of one of the island's craters, he reassures himself, "'Pity should begin at home.' So the more / pity I felt, the more I felt at home." What finally makes the island "home," however, is the arrival of Friday, whose appearance in the poem cannot be overestimated. With Bishop's characteristic understatement, Crusoe marks Friday's appearance with telling restraint: "Friday was nice. / Friday was nice, and we were friends." Instead of the slave Defoe makes of him, Bishop makes him the desired other, and subversively refers to lesbian passion by Crusoe's exclamation "If only he had been a woman!" The first introductory dashes forewarn Friday's supreme importance: "— Pretty to watch; he had a pretty body," a line followed by an islanded one, poignant in its omission of feeling: "And then one day they came and took us off." The poem's last line makes it stunningly evident that Crusoe's time has been measured by grief, by the loss of Friday: "—And Friday, my dear Friday, died of measles / seventeen years ago come March."

In contrast to the somewhat meandering narrative of "Crusoe," "One Art," like the earlier "Sestina," uses the compact villanelle to inscribe the inextricable link between language and loss. The poem confesses its denial, as if commenting on poetic form itself as the supreme means of this denial, that the repeated "art of losing isn't hard to master." Art, as this elaborate formal structure insists, requires careful precision as well as the loss and return of its key words, here "master" and "disaster." Bishop instructs, "Lose something every day," and in the third stanza, "then practice losing farther, losing faster." The tercets build from the apparently small (a lost key, "the hour badly spent") to the big ("some realms I owned, two rivers, a continent"), and the items lost become increasingly personal: "I lost my mother's watch. And look! My last, or / next-to-last, of three loved house went." The reader is drawn into the very process of loss ("And look!"), heightened here with the "flowing, and flown" ("At the Fishhouses") character of the enjambed lines linked by "or."

We may believe the hard-boiled speaker's self-convincing refrain, until Bishop makes the denial of "disaster" transparent and finally impossible through subtle formal readjustments in the last stanza. As with the most significant moment in "Crusoe," she introduces the first line with a rupturing dash, "—Even losing you," a phrase followed by the parenthetical "(the joking voice, a gesture / I love)," reinforcing Bishop's "negative" poetics, understating the most important elements. We are no longer concerned with an object such as the timepiece standing in for the mother (like the "things" in "Crusoe" that have no real meaning apart from their emotional context). Furthermore, the stanza erodes the declaration of mastery with the addition of "not too": "the art of losing's not too hard to master / though it may look like (*Write* it!) like disaster." There is an intentional mistake in the doubling of "like" to convey a loss of control, while the fiercely whispered "(*Write* it!)" is another way of saying "don't lose it." But writing reveals a duplicity: Language may tentatively "hold" or remember, but for Bishop it inevitably foregrounds displacement and loss. Rhyming, dashing, parenthesizing, joking—all these are meant to contain, but even in emphatic practice are subordinated to Bishop's "art of losing." In other words, the mastery of disaster cannot be *the* function of art. Bishop lets slip the "next-to-last, of three loved houses," knowing homes to be only provisional.

Bishop's work has many postmodern elements, including her deft play with language ("I'd time enough to play with names," her Crusoe says) and her sense that names are arbitrary, flexible, without "essential" meanings. Thus, a single letter can convert one thing into another, so that her Crusoe interchangeably calls his volcano "*Mont D'Espoir* or *Mont Despair*." In matters of gender, a simple change in "headgear" can give aunts and uncles a "transvestite twist" ("Exchanging Hats," *New Poems*). Bishop's scrutiny of language *as language* runs throughout her work so that her "Over 2,000 Illustrations and a Complete Concordance," musings over the stories in a family Bible, notes the inability to gain a solacing, overseeing perspective beyond bare conjunctions: "Everything only connected by 'and' and 'and'" (*Cold Spring*). Art for Bishop is a matter of finding what will suffice: "the little that we get for free, / the little of our earthly trust" ("Poem," *Geography III*). Hers is not a monumental poetics, but this is precisely how Bishop achieves her greatness, like her moose, "towering" and even "otherworldly" in her unqualified brilliance.

Further Reading. *Selected Primary Sources:* Bishop, Elizabeth, *The Collected Prose* (New York: Farrar, Straus and Giroux, 1984); ———, *The Complete Poems 1927–1979* (New York: Farrar, Straus and Giroux, 1979; ———, *One Art: Letters, Selected and Edited*, ed. Robert Giroux (New York: Farrar, Straus, and Giroux, 1994). *Selected Secondary Sources:* Costello, Bonnie, *Questions of Mastery* (Cambridge, MA: Harvard University Press, 1991); Goldensohn, Lorrie, *Elizabeth Bishop: The Biography of a Poetry* (New York: Columbia University Press, 1991); Kalstone, David, *Five Temperaments* (New York: Oxford University Press, 1977); Lombardi, Marilyn May, ed., *Elizabeth Bishop: The Geography of Gender* (Charlottesville: University Park of Virginia, 1993); McCabe, Susan, *Elizabeth Bishop: Her Poetics of Loss* (University Park: Pennsylvania State University Press, 1994); Millier, Brett, *Elizabeth Bishop: Life and the Memory of It* (Berkeley: University of California Press, 1993); Schwartz, Lloyd, and Sybil P. Estess, eds., *Elizabeth Bishop and Her Art* (Ann Arbor: University of Michigan Press, 1983); Stevenson, Anne, *Elizabeth Bishop* (New York: Twayne, 1966); Travisano, Thomas, "Elizabeth Bishop Phenomenon" (*New Literary History* [July 1995]: 3–29); ———, *Elizabeth Bishop: Her Artistic Development* (Charlottesville: University of Virginia Press, 1988).

Susan McCabe

BISHOP, JOHN PEALE (1892–1944)

John Peale Bishop wrote criticism, fiction, and poetry that received considerable attention in the 1920s and 1930s. He is probably best remembered now as a peripheral figure in the group of lost generation writers. Close friends and admirers of his literary abilities included Ernest Hemingway, F. Scott Fitzgerald, **Archibald MacLeish**, and Edmund Wilson. Bishop served as the model for Tom D'Invilliers, the highbrow writer in Fitzgerald's *This Side of Paradise*. Indeed, critics and biographers most often cite him as an *inspirateur* rather than a formidable literary talent in his own right. Unlike his more famous associates, he was utterly nonpolitical in his writings and avoided taking a position on issues that, in 1930s America, were central for friends such as Jon Dos Passos. In many respects Bishop was a poet both inspired by and trapped in the past. Despite sporadic attempts to rehabilitate his reputation since his death, he remains largely a name associated with dubious adjectives in the vein of "second rank," "minor," or "neglected."

Bishop was born May 21, 1892, in Charles Town, West Virginia. He enjoyed an upper-middle-class youth and began writing poetry as a teenager. His first published poem appeared in *Harper's Weekly* in 1912. While attending Princeton he forged lifelong friendships with classmates F. Scott Fitzgerald and Edmund Wilson. Bishop's work appeared regularly in the *Nassau Literary Magazine*, and his first volume of poetry, *Green Fruit* (1917), was published prior to his graduation and subsequent acceptance of an Army commission. Bishop saw action in Wold War I, most notably in the battle of the Argonne. Following the war, he lived in New York and took an active role in the city's literary life. After serving for two years as contributing editor to *Vanity Fair*, he published a second book of verse, *The Undertaker's Garland* (1922), with co-author

Edmund Wilson. Bishop soon married Margaret Hutchins, and the couple spent most of the next ten years in France. During this period he published two books: a volume of short stories, *Many Thousands Gone* (1931), and a book of verse, *Now With His Love* (1933). By the mid-1930s the Bishop family had permanently returned to America, eventually erecting a grand estate on Cape Cod. Two works were published in 1935: a novel, *Act of Darkness*, and a book of poetry, *Minute Particulars*. The death of his close friend F. Scott Fitzgerald in 1940 prompted the **elegy** *The Hours* and other poems thought to be among his best. Bishop published his *Selected Poems* in 1941. The final years of his life were marked by poor health, and he died April 4, 1944, in a Massachusetts hospital.

Critics tend to agree that for the greater part of his career, Bishop wrote imitative verse. He would borrow the tone, idiom, or convention of various predecessors or contemporaries at the expense of developing a truly individual voice. Depending upon the critic, this mode of imitation is used to point up Bishop's poetic deficiencies or, alternatively, his ability to adopt a wide variety of forms and styles to good effect. His first book, *Green Fruit*, is a collection of rather unsuccessful emulations of Swinburne, Baudelaire, and Gautier. The next volume, *The Undertaker's Garland*, shows a more mature poet with an increasing sense of control. "The Death of a Dandy" is considered the strongest poem in the collection, and the reader can trace the influences of **T.S. Eliot** (especially "Gerontion" and *The Waste Land*) in many of Bishop's lines: "Behind the shrunken eyelids, what apparitions? / What pebbles rattle in a dry stream?" **Modernist** themes running throughout the poems in *The Undertaker's Garland* include the banality of middle-class life, man's struggle to deflect and transcend the ravages of time, and the notion that tradition and the best of high art can temporarily stay the progression of cultural decay.

Moving home after ten years of expatriation in France (a period in which he wrote little and published nothing), Bishop turned his poetic eye to America in the collection *Minute Particulars*. The poems are mainly concerned with shortcomings of American culture and the opposed value systems of myth (Christianity) and modern science. Many of the entries demonstrate Bishop's continued imitation of celebrated poets (most notably at this time W.B. Yeats and **Hart Crane**). However, he also begins to exercise an individual voice and talent in poems such as "Experience in the West." This four-part poem critiques the idea of Manifest Destiny and the whitewashed legend of an American frontier. Each of the sections explores the settling of the continent as a march of desecration and destruction. The pioneers are portrayed as infected with a lust for dominance: "A continent they had / To ravage, and raving romped from sea to sea." Bishop rejects the myth of

the American West that was being celebrated at the time by such diverse figures as **Carl Sandburg** and John Steinbeck.

Late in life Bishop wrote what are considered to be some of his strongest poems. Most of these deal with sensual love, heroic action, the failings of modern culture, and reflections upon his childhood. Among these works appears the elegy for F. Scott Fitzgerald, "The Hours," published in *Selected Poems*. Critic Robert L. White refers to this poem as one of the best produced in the twentieth century. In its form and truly moving pathos, it shows Bishop at the top of his game: "Dark, dark. The shore here has a habit of light. / O dark! I leave you to oblivious night!" Written a year after this poem, "A Subject of Sea Change" (published posthumously in *The Collected Poems* [1948]) is both a deeply personal and public work. Set against the backdrop of World War II, it laments the chaos of the modern moment while asserting that humankind can locate meaning in existence if people are willing to assume the burden of time. Bishop intimates that all individuals must come to terms with their own relationship to history: "Time is man's tragic responsibility / . . . / Both the prolific and destroying years." The past glories and tragedies of human civilization are key to developing a moral code: Each act must convey "[n]ot merely his own, but human, dignity." While history has not seen fit to accord John Peale Bishop the accolades enjoyed by several of his close friends, his strongest poems are worthy of praise and deserve a certain standing in literary history.

Further Reading. *Selected Primary Sources:* Bishop, John Peale, *The Collected Poems* (New York: Charles Scribner's Sons, 1948); ———, *Minute Particulars* (New York: Alcestis Press, 1935); ———, *Selected Poems* (New York: Charles Scribner's Sons, 1941); ———, Bishop, John Peale, and Edmund Wilson, *The Undertaker's Garland* (New York: Knopf, 1922). ***Selected Secondary Sources:*** Spindler, Elizabeth Carroll, *John Peale Bishop: A Biography* (Parsons, WV: McClain Printing Co., 1980); White, Robert L., *John Peale Bishop* (New York: Twayne, 1966).

Jason Spangler

BLACK ARTS MOVEMENT

While the Black Arts Movement (ca. 1965–1975) produced enduring work in all literary genres, the poetry of the movement may prove to be its finest legacy. Much of the poetry was inspired by the era's political climate, especially by the widespread support for black political and cultural nationalism among writers, visual artists, musicians, and the wider black public. Amid calls to articulate a new "black aesthetic," poets of the period benefited from the emergence of several major independent black presses and small-circulation periodicals that were distributed in major cities. Responding to the widening interest in African American writing, established national presses became more willing to publish and promote emerging poets. Major poets such as **Amiri Baraka**, **Nikki Giovanni**, **Michael S. Harper**, **June Jordan**, **Audre Lorde**, Haki Madhubuti, **Clarence Major**, **Sonia Sanchez**, **Lorenzo Thomas**, and Alice Walker reached a national audience during this era.

The period also helped re-energize the career of black poets who were well established before the start of the movement, particularly **Gwendolyn Brooks** and **Sterling Brown**. Many other poets made memorable contributions to the movement, among them **Jayne Cortez**, Mari Evans, Carolyn Rodgers, **Bob Kaufman**, Ted Joans, and **Etheridge Knight**. While some of their original work has fallen out of print, they remain familiar to scholars and readers with an interest in the period. Several **anthologies** and critical studies of **African American poetry** must be noted as landmark accomplishments of the period as well. Examples include *The New Black Poetry*, edited by Clarence Major (1969); *The Black Poets*, edited by **Dudley Randall** (1971); *Understanding the New Black Poetry*, edited by Stephen Henderson (1972); and *Drumvoices*, by Eugene Redmond (1976).

Black Nationalism: Influence on Black Arts Movement Poetry

The Black Arts Movement took shape in the wake of the Civil Rights Movement's successes and crises in the mid-1960s. Supporters of the Black Arts Movement argued that a program of civil rights not only failed to defeat white supremacy on the political front but also offered no viable model for black artistic production and aesthetic criticism. Independence movements on the African continent in the 1950s and early 1960s were an early influence on the movement, inspiring curiosity about African cultural forms and a desire for radical political change in the United States. The rise of black political nationalism domestically (embodied by the life and death of Malcolm X and the emergence of the Black Panthers) and the popularity of soul and **jazz** music also influenced the work of emerging poets. The movement took its name from the Black Arts Repertory Theater, founded by Amiri Baraka in 1965 to produce works that had a black revolutionary sensibility.

The movement, however, was controversial from its beginnings. Political tensions and generational differences are exemplified in two poems by Dudley Randall and Nikki Giovanni. Randall's "Ballad of Birmingham" offers a tribute to the four young girls murdered in the infamous 1963 bombing of the 16th Street Baptist Church. Giovanni's "The Funeral of Martin Luther King, Jr." is written in both tribute and anger shortly after the death of the famed civil rights leader. Randall, a towering figure and elder statesman of the Black Arts

Movement, uses his poem to dramatize the humanity of a grieving black mother through third-person description and carefully composed dialogue. In the closing lines, the mother of a bomb victim digs through the rubble of the church in a desperate search for a trace of her child: "O, here's the shoe my baby wore, / But, baby, where are you?" (quoted in Henderson, 234).

The Giovanni poem, however, foregrounds the speaker's anger using a plain style and indicts the white supremacist culture that has enabled and sanctioned the murder of Dr. King: "His tombstone said 'Free at last, free at last' / But death is a slave's freedom" (quoted in Randall, 144). Younger poets, including Giovanni herself in other poetic texts, are often harshly critical of the politics of assimilation advocated by earlier generations of black leaders. Poets Amiri Baraka, Haki Madhubuti, and Askia Touré repudiated their "slave names" to suggest their reclaiming of a black cultural and political heritage. Such actions linked their artistic work with nationwide efforts among activists to assert that "black is beautiful," and to raise awareness of black cultural history.

Some poets from the period, however, were skeptical of black political nationalism in its most visible forms and took their inspiration from other sources in black cultural life. Alice Walker, for instance, opposed revolutionary black nationalism, which she felt reinforced patriarchal thinking at the expense of black women. In *Revolutionary Petunias* (1973), Walker's poem "Nothing Is Right" declares that "it was our essence that / never worked" (36), repudiating nationalist claims that racial essentialism could lead to progressive change. Walker's epigrammatic approach and innovative uses of slant rhyme and other sound devices are distinctive in her work.

Another prominent poet from this period, Audre Lorde, also challenged nationalist orthodoxies on issues of gender, sexuality, and the nature of oppression. Her early work was published by Dudley Randall's Broadside Press, a groundbreaking publisher of the "new black poetry" during the era. Poems in *New York Head Shop and Museum* (1975) use imagery and a reflective speaker to describe the cultural geography of the New York City. Lorde's poetry calls for a radical critique of color and gender caste systems that exist in black communities. The opening lines of "Revolution Is One Form of Social Change" demonstrate Lorde's expansive view of who suffers due to racial oppression. She suggests that distinctions in complexion are unimportant "when the man is busy / making niggers" (38).

Other poets were influenced by stylistics of the **avant-garde**, using African American cultural memory as well as current controversies for subjects. "Dear John, Dear Coltrane" by Michael Harper suggests that both black angst and black achievement have deep roots in the cultural past (quoted in Henderson, 238). Bob Kaufman also wrote often and well about musical subjects, including the jazz artist Charlie Parker. Kaufman maintained a vow of silence during much of the period between the Kennedy assassination and the end of the Vietnam War, a powerful and distinctive act of protest in an era of fiery rhetoric. Clarence Major and **Ishmael Reed** also published poems that are distinctive in terms of craft, and made important contributions to the era's writing through their editing projects. Their work testifies to the diversity of style and subject that is sometimes overshadowed by the public prominence of the nationalist standpoint.

Manifestos and Major Statements

The Black Arts Movement produced audacious poetic statements by Amiri Baraka, Haki Madhubuti, and Sonia Sanchez, among others. Their work is fully engaged in the era's cultural politics, weighing in on the side of black nationalism. Amiri Baraka rose to prominence as a colleague of **Beat** writers and their avantgarde sensibility, but his manifesto, "Black Art" (1969), repudiates much of his artistic history before that time and remains the best-known poem of the period. "Black Art" stridently calls for a new aesthetic challenge to white supremacy with writing that was symbolically deadly: "We want 'poems that kill.' / Assassin poems" (quoted in Gates, 1883). The poem also calls for "words of the hip world life flesh & / coursing blood," a sentiment that seems consistent with the emphasis during the movement on musical styles identified with African Americans, and on the efforts of movement partisans to rescue art from the enshrinement and entombment they associated with classical art. The poem's ethnic slurs and scatological references have also been sources of continuing controversy.

In the title poem to her 1970 collection, "We a BadDDD People," Sonia Sanchez invokes one of the most common tropes of the period's verse—a poetic voice speaking for black masses. Her poem typifies the wider efforts of movement activists to appeal to mass audiences rather than literati. The mood of the poem implies action and engagement rather than the contemplation one might expect in literary poetry from earlier in the century. Innovative line structure, extensive use of black vernacular, and a rhetoric of collective consciousness in the poem are hallmarks of the movement's stylistics: "We gots some bad/N A T U R A L S" (52).

Haki Madhubuti's collection of poems, *Don't Cry, Scream* (1969), evokes independence of spirit and a strong interest in black cultural traditions. Like the collection by Sanchez, *Don't Cry, Scream* was published by Broadside Press, with an introduction by Gwendolyn Brooks, who observes that Madhubuti (then Don Lee) "has no patience with black writers who do not direct their blackness toward black audiences" (9). The title poem is dedicated to John Coltrane and uses onomatopoeia to mimic the sound of a saxophone; symbolically, black masses

move from the passive act of crying to the aggressive act of screaming in response to racism. In "a poem for negro intellectuals," the term "Negro" is repudiated in favor of "Black," and the speaker calls for a new birth among "a people deathliving /in /abstract realities" (41).

Legacies of Black Arts Movement Poetry

Contrary to its early dismissal by many critics, poetry of the Black Arts Movement remains compelling both for its stylistics and the variety of subjects it treats. The streetwise and performative character of the work formed a foundation for later artistic work in the styles of hip-hop and spoken word. A number of poets from the period have become household names, among them Amiri Baraka, Audre Lorde, Clarence Major, Sonia Sanchez, and Alice Walker. While the volume of published scholarship has probably not done justice to the quality of work from the period, some book-length critical studies are now available, such as *A Nation Within A Nation: Amiri Baraka and Black Power Politics* by Komozi Woodard (1999), and *Wrestling with the Muse: Dudley Randall and the Broadside Press* by Melba Joyce Boyd (2003). An impressive range of poetry from the Black Arts Movement remains to be read and discussed. This poetry has much to teach about trends in recent African American writing as well as strategies for change and contested issues in the volatile racial climate of the 1960s and 1970s.

Further Reading. ***Selected Primary Sources:*** Henderson, Stephen, *Understanding the New Black Poetry* (New York: William Morrow, 1973); Lorde, Audre, *New York Head Shop and Museum* (Detroit: Broadside, 1975); Madhubuti, Haki, *Don't Cry, Scream* (Detroit: Broadside, 1969); Randall, Dudley, *The Black Poets* (New York: Bantam Books, 1971); Sanchez, Sonia, *We a BadDDD People* (Detroit: Broadside, 1970); Walker, Alice, *Revolutionary Petunias* (San Diego: Harcourt, Brace, 1973). ***Selected Secondary Sources:*** Boyd, Melba Joyce, *Wrestling with the Muse: Dudley Randall and the Broadside Press* (New York: Columbia University Press, 2003); Gates, Henry Louis, *Norton Anthology of African American Literature* (New York: Norton, 1997); Major, Clarence, *The New Black Poetry* (New York: International Publishers, 1969); Neal, Larry, *Visions of a Liberated Future* (New York: Thunders Mouth Press, 1989); Redmond, Eugene, *Drumvoices: The Mission of Afro-American Poetry* (New York: Anchor, 1976); Reed, Ishmael, *Yardbird Reader* (Berkeley, CA: Yardbird Publishing, 1972); Woodard, Komozi, *A Nation Within A Nation: Amiri Baraka and Black Power Politics* (Durham: University of North Carolina Press, 1999).

David Jones

BLACK MOUNTAIN SCHOOL

The Black Mountain School is a term that refers to the work, predominantly poetry, of a group of writers associated in the 1950s with Black Mountain College, an experimental school in the mountains of North Carolina. For some critics, the term refers to the work of writers who taught or studied at the college; for others, it refers, more broadly, to writers published in the *Black Mountain Review* (1954–1957), a journal that appeared as just seven issues but survived beyond the college's demise and exerted considerable influence on the canon of post–World War II American poetry; most often, Black Mountain School refers to the ten poets published under this designation in Donald Allen's seminal **anthology**, *The New American Poetry: 1945–1960*, only six of whom had any connection to the college. The poetics of the Black Mountain School tends to be even less clearly delineated than its membership, often indicating little more than a general commitment to **open form** and a conscious awareness of the contingent or spontaneous nature of the act of composition. Nonetheless, for many readers and practitioners of **experimental poetry**, especially in the1960s and early 1970s, the poetry associated with Black Mountain provided one of the most compelling alternatives to the restrictive dogmas of the **New Critics** and to the reactionary cultural politics of **modernists** like **Ezra Pound** and **T.S. Eliot**.

By any accepted measure of institutional success, Black Mountain College itself was a dismal failure. The school was founded in 1933 by a group of iconoclastic professors who had left Rollins College in a dispute over academic freedom. Like their more famous successors on the Black Mountain faculty, the founders valued intellectual rigor over academic convention. They were particularly committed to eliminating distinctions between "curricular" and "extracurricular" and to establishing the arts at the center of the curriculum. Throughout its existence, Black Mountain College suffered from low enrollment, financial shortages, and physical decline. This institutional peril was especially acute in the early and mid-1950s—the years in which a Black Mountain School of poetry emerged—when there were fewer than two dozen students enrolled. But fortunately for American poetry, many of the leading figures of Black Mountain College were indifferent to, even defiant of, accepted measures of success. And for this brief time, artistic innovation—in music, painting, dance, crafts, and perhaps most of all poetry—flourished on the verge of institutional extinction. Just as the college expired in 1956, its writers began to be recognized as a rising avant-garde.

The writer most closely associated with the Black Mountain School of poetry, **Charles Olson**, arrived at Black Mountain College from the Yucatan in 1951 to become the school's rector—that is, its "senior administrator." In this role, he presided over both the school's demise—occasionally selling off property rather than compromising his educational vision—and the poetic

movement's initial recognition. A towering presence, literally and figuratively (by most scholarly estimates, he stood somewhere between 6'7" and 6'9"), Olson wrote the closest thing to a Black Mountain manifesto in his 1950 essay "Projective Verse," famously declaring his opposition to "that verse which print bred" and (often in capital letters) his conviction that "FORM IS NEVER MORE THAN AN EXTENSION OF CONTENT" and "ONE PERCEPTION MUST IMMEDIATELY AND DIRECTLY LEAD TO ANOTHER" (*Selected Writings,* 15–17). In other words, he called for a "kinetic" poetry that would be responsive to the intensity, immediacy, physicality, and unpredictability of human experience, as opposed to a "static" poetry subservient to proscribed forms or deduced from intellectual premises. For all his stylistic idiosyncrasies, Olson was able, in a handful of essays and letters, to articulate a set of directions that could lead American poetry past the nearly hegemonic influence of Eliot's high modernism.

Beyond that, Olson began to sketch an alternative to the philosophical tradition inherited from Europe which, in his view, devalued the "actual" world (a term by which he suggested both "real" and "active"), thus impeding personal action and social change. Often drawing from the philosophical writing of Alfred North Whitehead, especially *Science and the Modern World* and *Process and Reality*, Olson sought to circumvent the influence of the metaphysical tradition epitomized by Plato and Descartes. Many of the various writers influenced by "**projective verse**"—and by Olson's related proclamations in "Quantity in Verse, and Shakespeare's Late Plays," "Human Universe," "Proprioception," *The Mayan Letters*, and *The Special View of History*—described their poetry as "open," that is, revealing its subject matter or "material," and its unique form, in the act of composition.

The fullest realization of Olson's poetics—and the most common reference in most discussions of Black Mountain Poetry—is his **epic** *The Maximus Poems*, begun in 1950 and published in three book-length volumes between 1960 and 1975. Olson's persona of Maximus, based loosely on two second-century philosophers, Apollonius of Tyana and Maximus of Tyre, provides a figure of unconstrained humanity; at the same time, it provides Olson with a means of locating his poem in a particular place and historical context, his home town of Gloucester, Massachusetts. Yet, as several of Olson's critics have noted, Maximus often seems to be not so much a particular man as a figure for a way of living in the world, characterized by an openness to experience, a willingness to reconstruct the past, and a desire to create a radically different future. Olson constructed his epic as a series of letters to the citizens of Gloucester, and this rhetorical focus reflects the poem's primary concern: to discover the conditions of a vital "polis," a community in which citizens live according to their "attention and care" for the "common world." In this project, Olson was largely guided by his ambivalent view of his poem's two most important forerunners, Pound's *Cantos* and **William Carlos Williams**'s *Paterson*. These earlier modern epics provided him with methods of using historical references, or "time material," in order to replace the lyric poetry of the "individual as ego" with the epic poetry of a thriving polis.

The ideas and interests shared by the poets associated with the Black Mountain School are not often obvious in their poetry, even in the work of the school's two other highly recognized figures, **Robert Creeley** and **Robert Duncan**. Creeley and Duncan both taught briefly at Black Mountain College. Creeley also edited the *Black Mountain Review* (initially from Majorca, briefly from Black Mountain, and finally from San Francisco) and sustained a monumental correspondence with Olson (now published in nine volumes) in which the two poets worked out most of their formative ideas about poetry. Most important, in dialogue with Olson, Creeley developed a poetic alternative to the traditional English **lyric** by writing improvisational poems that, with their attention to immediate perceptions, counteract humanity's estrangement from the "common world"—the world of temporality, physical process, and the body. On a very superficial level, Creeley's short, narrow poems have sometimes been mistaken for more conventional lyrics; but when they are read with sufficient attention to their lines and sounds, these poems can be seen to continue Olson's rebellion against the lyric tradition's desire for transcendence. More than Olson, Creeley found exemplary models in William Carlos Williams's shorter poems of the 1950s; and even more than Williams, he used small lines and stanzas to produce halting, shifting, syncopated rhythms. Especially in his books from the 1960s and early 1970s—like *Words* (1967), *Pieces* (1969), and *Thirty Things* (1974)—Creeley also found significant influences in **jazz**, most of all Charlie Parker's bebop of the 1940s, and in painting, particularly Abstract Impressionism. There, he found an improvisational spontaneity that had been lacking in the American poetry of his time.

Duncan shared Olson's and Creeley's commitments to open form, to the poem as process, and—especially in his powerful earlier volumes, *The Opening of the Field* (1960) and *Roots and Branches* (1964)—to reclaiming for poetry the experience of the immediate physical world. More than any other poet associated with the Black Mountain School, however, he also became increasingly interested in a religious and poetic mysticism derived largely from Dante, Blake, and most of all **H.D.** (Hilda Doolittle). Following the demise of Black Mountain College just about a year after his arrival, Duncan began to explore an idiosyncratic neo-Platonism very different

from Olson's rejection of metaphysics. Some of his later books, beginning with *Bending the Bow* (1968) and *Dante* (1974), can be just as difficult as *The Maximus Poems*, with eccentric allusions and dramatic disjunctions, but they demonstrate a very different sensibility—more fluid, less aggressively masculine, and often softly musical. In some respects, though, Duncan maintained commitments to the common world: He was among the most outspoken American poets in his opposition to the Vietnam War and, with his generous eclecticism, he forged some of the most productive links between the Black Mountain School and other poetic movements of his time, including the **Beat** movement and the **New York School**.

Critics tend to view Black Mountain poetry as a predominantly, if not exclusively, male movement. In many accounts, the only woman mentioned is **Denise Levertov**. Levertov never even visited Black Mountain College, but she is often associated with the Black Mountain School, partly because her poetry was published, early on, by **Cid Corman** in his journal *Origin*—an important forum for Black Mountain writers, especially in its initial series in the 1950s—and by Creeley in the *Black Mountain Review*, and partly because of her friendship and poetic affinities with Creeley and Duncan. The most enduring of these affinities is the one least typical of the Black Mountain School—the mysticism Levertov shared with Duncan, though her poetry tends toward a more sacramental view of the physical world. More significantly, what gets lost in most accounts of the Black Mountain School is the poetry of **Hilda Morley**. Morley was married to one of the most influential members of the Black Mountain College faculty, the composer Stephan Wolpe. The couple lived at Black Mountain in the critical years for the emergence of a poetic movement, 1952 to 1956; for a time, when Olson took a leave of absence, Morley took his place as writing teacher. Though Morley wrote a number of striking poems at Black Mountain, she became much more productive after Wolpe's death in 1972; when she published her first major volume, *To Hold in My Hand* in 1983, some of the poems she included were nearly thirty years old. The main concern of her poems of this period is a constant re-interpretation of the figure of the artist: Her work includes poetic commentaries on Olson himself, in a beautiful yet critical **elegy**, and on other artists such as Verdi, Cézanne, Goethe, Tolstoy, and Matisse.

In various ways, the legacy of Black Mountain College has been maintained by several of its students who have had long and productive careers as poets, including **Joel Oppenheimer**, **John Wieners**, **Jonathan Williams**, and **Edward Dorn**. The poetry of this second generation follows even less of any "party line"—and for the most part shows few obvious similarities—but these poets do extend many of their teachers' more interesting experiments. For instance, Oppenheimer's poetry examines the relationship between personal and collective experience, sometimes in terms of Jungian psychology. Like Creeley, Wieners explores the poetic possibilities raised by abstract expressionism and jazz. Dorn's poetry includes a brilliant tribute to Olson, "From Gloucester Out," and the multi-voiced epic *Gunslinger*, which ranges in its references from Olson's favorite pre-Socratic philosophy to Mister Ed. In addition, these poets share their predecessors' firm commitment to creating forums for experimental poetry in a literary culture increasingly dominated by MFA programs and large-market publishers. Beginning at Black Mountain, Williams has worked tirelessly as a publisher and promoter of poetry influenced by the Black Mountain School and the Beat movement. In the 1960s, Oppenheimer was the first director of the St. Mark's Church Poetry Project in New York. Through the 1980s, Dorn edited the wildly satiric newspaper *Rolling Stock*.

In the past twenty-five years or so, the Black Mountain School has not had the influence on contemporary poetry that many critics expected when, for instance, Olson completed *The Maximus Poems* and Creeley published his *Collected Poems*, or when their correspondence began to appear, volume after volume. A number of solid, book-length studies, most of them focusing primarily on Olson, appeared between 1978 and 1981, but not much since then. Much remains to be studied, for example, about the productive relationships established at Black Mountain between the poets and the artists working in other media. Beginning in the mid-1940s, the experimental composer **John Cage**, the dancer Merce Cunningham, and the "comprehensive designer" Buckminster Fuller all taught at the college for considerable periods, on and off, and the visual artist Robert Rauschenberg was a student. In addition, a remarkable array of musicians and visual artists—including Walter Gropius, Robert Motherwell, Willem de Kooning, and Franz Kline—visited for the school's summer institute. Viewed in this larger context, the Black Mountain School provided American poetry's most interesting effort to bring the arts together in a community designed to encourage collaboration and experimentation.

Further Reading. *Selected Primary Sources:* Allen, Donald, ed., *The New American Poetry* (Berkeley: University of California Press, 1999); Creeley, Robert, ed., *Black Mountain Review* (New York: AMS Press, 1969); ———, *Collected Prose* (Normal, IL: Dalkey Archive, 2001); ———, *Selected Poems* (Berkeley: University of California Press, 1996); Dorn, Edward, *Gunslinger* (Durham, NC: Duke University Press, 1989); Duncan, Robert, *Selected Poems*, ed. Robert Bertholf (New York: New Directions, 1997); Morley, Hilda, *To Hold in My Hand: Selected Poems* (New York: Sheep Meadow, 1983); Olson, Charles, *The Maximus Poems*, ed. George Butterick (Berkeley: University of California Press, 1983); ———,

Selected Writings, ed. Robert Creeley (New York: New Directions, 1966). ***Selected Secondary Sources:*** Christensen, Paul, *Charles Olson: Call Him Ishmael* (Austin: University of Texas Press, 1979); Conniff, Brian, "Reconsidering Black Mountain: The Poetry of Hilda Morley" (*American Literature* 65.1 [March 1993]: 117–130); Duberman, Martin, *Black Mountain: An Exploration in Community* (Gloucester: Peter Smith, 1988); Harris, Mary Emma, *The Arts at Black Mountain College* (Cambridge: Massachusetts Institute of Technology Press, 1987); Paul, Sherman, *Olson's Push: Origin, Black Mountain, and Recent American Poetry* (Baton Rouge: Louisiana State University Press, 1978); von Hallberg, Robert, *Charles Olson: The Scholar's Art* (Cambridge, MA: Harvard University Press, 1978).

Brian Conniff

BLACKBURN, PAUL (1926–1971)

Paul Blackburn is best known for poems similar in style and structure to the **Black Mountain** poets, represented by **Robert Creeley, Charles Olson,** and **Denise Levertov**. Blackburn was extremely active in the Greenwich Village, New York, poetry scene in the 1960s, organizing and attending readings by nearly all the major figures of the era, including **Allen Ginsberg, Amiri Baraka, Frank O'Hara, Diane Di Prima,** and other members of the **Beat, New York School,** and Black Mountain poetry movements. His enthusiasm and organization of poetry readings are often recognized as influencing the creation of the Poetry Project at St. Marks Church on the Bowery in New York City.

Blackburn published thirteen books of poetry during his lifetime. His most famous poems are anthologized in Donald Allen's *The New American Poetry* (1960). Poems such as "The Continuity" and "The Assistance" emphasize spacing and enjambment while playing with the formal properties of the page. His poetic process is most commonly associated with Charles Olson's **projective verse** which argues for an emphasis on the author's breath as a unit of poetic meter. Using the page as if it were a "field," the projective poet places words, ideas, and narratives on the page as they occur spontaneously to him, capturing the accidental genius of the creative moment. Marked by placement of words and phrases outside traditional linear structures, margins, and justified spaces, projective verse works to pressure language so that the reader can reconstruct the emotional and technical moment of the poem's genesis.

Like those of his contemporary Frank O'Hara, Blackburn's poems are at times funny and at times incredibly poignant, pressuring the traditions of poetry by exploring unconventional subjects through unconventional narrative forms. His poems emphasize the pace and cadences of ordinary speech, working to place images and ideas in complex relationships to one another, gradually building to a well-constructed metaphoric moment, or image, that the poet **Ezra Pound** described as an "intellectual and emotional complex in an instant of time." He saw himself as composing his poetry from the found materials of his daily life, calling his creative process, like that of Frederico Garcia Lorca, *duende*, which according to Blackburn "is that faculty of making into which you subsume yourself, your nickel, your dime, your cruzeiro, your peso, your five-dollar gold piece, your talent, silver mark, or denier, a goddam ha'penny, if that's all you're carrying around in your pocket that day." Blackburn's poetry stands as a testament to one person's expression of his place in the world, warts and all, through the seemingly spontaneous record of that experience.

Blackburn's ties with Charles Olson, Robert Creeley and the *Black Mountain Review*, which he edited for a short time, led to a rather misguided association with the Black Mountain School of poetry. Blackburn never attended or taught at Black Mountain and has gradually carved out a place of his own as definitions of postwar American poetry become clearer. Blackburn championed all kinds of poetry, often acting as a conduit for younger poets and valuable ally to more established writers.

Born in St. Albans, Vermont, on November 24, 1926, Blackburn attended New York University and the University of Wisconsin, where he received his BA in 1950. While completing his undergraduate degree at the University of Wisconsin, Blackburn became interested in the troubadour style of **French lyric poetry** known as provençal. He would go on to spend a good deal of his life researching and translating provençal poetry. He won a Fulbright scholarship in 1954 to study in Paris after publishing a volume of translations entitled *Proensa*. Along with provençal poetry, Blackburn is known for his translations of the **epic** Spanish poem *El Cid* and of South American writers such as Lorca and Julio Cortazar.

Throughout his life Blackburn was a nomadic figure, living in Spain and Morocco, New York and Wisconsin. He held a variety of jobs: working for encyclopedias, poetry editor for the *Nation*, and teaching at the University of Toulouse, the University of Wisconsin, and the State University of New York in Cortland. Often criticized for being misogynist and overusing obscene language, Blackburn's poetry is largely ignored by the critical canon of postwar poetry in America, his significant contribution often reduced to the role of proxy agent for other, more recognizable contemporaries. He notes in his introduction to *The Cities* that "every man's stand be his own. [My poetry] is a construct, out of my own isolations, eyes, ears, nose, and breath, my recognition of those constructs not my own that I can live in" (11). In 1971 Paul Blackburn died of cancer in New York at the age of forty-four.

Further Reading. ***Primary Sources:*** Blackburn, Paul, *Against the Silences* (New York: Permanent Press, 1980); ———, *The Assassination of President McKinley* (Mt. Horeb, WI: Perishable Press, 1970); ———, *Brooklyn-Manhattan Transit: A Bouquet for Flatbush* (New York: Totem Press, 1960); ———, *By Ear* (New York: # Magazine, 1978); ———, *The Cities* (New York: Grove, 1967); ———, *The Collected Poems* (New York: Persea Books, 1985); ———, *The Dissolving Fabric* (Palma de Mallorca: Divers Press, 1955); ———, *Early Selected y Mas: Poems 1949–1966* (Los Angeles: Black Sparrow, 1975); ———, *Gin: Four Journal Pieces* (Mt. Horeb, WI: Perishable Press, 1970); ———, *Halfway Down the Coast* (Northampton, MA: Mulch Press, 1975); ———, *In—On—Or About the Premises* (New York: Grossman/Cape Goliard, 1968); ———, *The Journals*, ed. Robert Kelly (Los Angeles: Black Sparrow, 1975); ———, *The Journals: Blue Mounds Entries* (Mt. Horeb, WI: Perishable Press, 1971); ———, *Lorca/Blackburn: Poems of Federico García Lorca Chosen and Translated by Paul Blackburn* (San Francisco: Momo's Press, 1979); ———, *The Nets* (New York: Trobar, 1961); ———, *Poem of the Cid* (New York: American R.D.M., 1966; reissued by University of Oklahoma Press, 1998); ———, *Proensa* (Palma de Mallorca: Divers Press, 1953); ———, *The Reardon Poems* (Madison, WI: Perishable Press, 1967); ———, *The Selected Poems of Paul Blackburn* (New York: Persea Books, 1989); ———, *The Selection of Heaven* (Mt. Horeb, WI: Perishable Press, 1980); ———, *Sing-Song* (New York: Catapillar Press, 1966); ———, *16 Sloppy Haiku and a Lyric for Robert Reardon* (Cleveland: 400 Rabbit Press, 1966); ———, *Three Dreams and an Old Poem* (Buffalo, NY: University Press, 1970); ———, *Two New Poems* (Madison, WI: Perishable Press, 1969); Cortázar, Julio, *Cronopios and Famas*, trans. Paul Blackburn (New York: Pantheon, 1969); ———, trans., *End of the Game and Other Stories* (New York: Pantheon, 1967); ———, trans., Picasso, Pablo, *Hunk of Skin* (San Francisco: City Lights, 1968). ***Selected Secondary Sources:*** Dembo, L.S., "An Interview with Paul Blackburn" (*Contemporary Literature* 13 [Spring 1972]: 133–143); Fredman, Stephen, "Paul Blackburn the Translator" (*Chicago Review* 30 [Winter 1979]: 152–156); Rosenthal, M.L., *The New Poets* (New York: Oxford University Press, 1967); Sorrentino, Gilbert, "Singing, Virtuoso" (*Parnassus* 4 [Spring–Summer 1976]: 57–67); Woodward, Kathleen, *Paul Blackburn: A Checklist* (San Diego: Archive for New Poetry, 1980).

David N. Wright

BLACKMUR, R.P. (1904–1965)

Although known predominantly as a **New Critic**, R.P. Blackmur published three volumes of poetry in the late 1930s and 1940s. Of the three, the first, *From Jordan's Delight* (1937), is generally considered the most accomplished. For the most part, however, Blackmur's poetry can best be read as illustration of his critical principles.

R.P. Blackmur was born in 1904 to struggling middle-class parents who moved from Springfield, Massachusetts, to New York and back to Cambridge, Massachusetts. His education was unusual: Home-schooled for his first three years, he attended grammar school and high school in Cambridge until he was expelled at age fourteen. Afterward, he earned his living working in and managing bookstores while attending occasional courses in Harvard. In 1928 he became the editing manager for *Hound and Horn*, an influential little magazine. During his tenure, the magazine published poetry by **Ezra Pound** and **Wallace Stevens**, among others. In 1930, however, he lost the job. In the same year, Blackmur married Helen Dickson, a painter; they divorced in 1951. For the next ten years Blackmur worked as an independent scholar and poet while he and his wife struggled financially. Blackmur took a one-year position at Princeton University in 1940 and thereafter held various appointments and fellowships until 1948, when he became an associate professor. At Princeton, Blackmur directed the Christian Gauss Seminars in literary criticism. He is best remembered for his critical examinations of twentieth-century American poets, continental novelists, and Henry James.

Arguably some of Blackmur's better poetry was only put into verse by **John Berryman**, who quoted the following sentence in tribute: "The art of poetry is amply distinguished from the manufacture of verse by the animating presence in the poetry of a fresh idiom: language so twisted and posed in a form that it not only expresses the matter in hand but adds to the stock of available reality" (*Language*, 364). Even without Berryman's line breaks, one can see the inherent poetry in Blackmur's prose.

Much of Blackmur's own poetry reflects the principles that guide his criticism, and his best work carries with it the musicality of his prose. He felt that a poet should combine personal insight and cultural convention in such a way as to be anonymous and authoritative. Anonymity allows the poet and reader to communicate through the poem without inhibiting or obscuring it; authority allows the poet to present ideas through art without slavish devotion to, or unintelligible deviation from, contemporary poetics. In his criticism, Blackmur also emphasized the craft of poetry, searching for the techniques and devices best suited to clear communication of poetic themes through "a fresh idiom" of "language twisted and posed in a form." Blackmur's poetry likewise follows many traditional conventions and forms, notably rhyme, alliteration, and regular rhythms. Its linguistic play tends to show through inverted or unusual syntactical structures, archaic words, and neologisms. James Bloom has pointed out that the principle poetic influences on Blackmur were W.B. Yeats and **T.S. Eliot** (10).

Blackmur's first collection, *From Jordan's Delight*, shows the poet's interest in the sea as metaphor for death and desire, as well as his fascination with religious symbolism of evil and the complexities of human desire. The title poem presents eleven scenes of an island off the Atlantic coast, juxtaposing rustic images, reminiscent of **Robert Frost**'s, with allusions to Shakespeare's works. The island is "a place of exile," the site of shipwrecked ancestors, eccentric lobstermen, and "jilted" fishermen struggling with the twin dangers of desire and loss. "Sea Island Miscellany" continues Blackmur's study of isolation and exile. In one section, the poet sees the image of a mountain, "sun yellow and sea-green." He concludes, despite being told it is a mirage, "there I have been living ever since." "Of Lucifer" and "Judas Priest" examine the force and necessity of evil. The latter poem presents a Judas who, unlike Pilate, "had a wakened mind" during the crucifixion of Christ, knowing the suffering he would cause. Judas was, however, necessary for the process of human redemption, a "willed looker-on." Blackmur treats sexual desire in "Simulacrum Deae," in which a woman who "had been half handsome stranger, half / casual friend" becomes "newly flesh" through the poet's desire. "A Labyrinth of Being" treats human desire more globally, following a man from the tentative stages of youth through marriage, fatherhood, separation, and renewed, elderly love.

Blackmur's next two collections, *The Second World* (1942) and *The Good European* (1947), together are less weighty than his first. The most engaging poem of the middle volume is "Before Sentence Is Passed," which presents a trial of conscience, in which the defendant, guilty, addresses the judge and jury to explain the importance of having an uncomfortable engagement with morality. At the poem's center is the play on "conviction" as both guilt and belief. Thus, righteousness that is asserted is "avowed guilt," the prisoner's situation is the "guilty reward" of the jury's situation, and people search for the "hope of new guilt." Yet the speaker complains of an "erosion" of good and evil with "no tension to hold them together." The final collection offers Blackmur's response to World War II. "Three Poems from a Text: Isaiah LXI: 1–3" mourns the loss of a friend, "killed in Italy on a high road." This and other later poems are infused with Christian imagery and themes, evidenced not only by direct references to scripture but also by allusions to Gerard Manley Hopkins: The speaker has been "selfed [sic] just so before, and drained." The title poem, "The Good European: 1945" posits a kind of Christian renewal as a positive response to the pain of the previous years, but the imagery is vexed and uncertain, and the poem concludes, "God does not make, does keep, man's vow." By the mid-1950s, Blackmur had shifted his critical attention largely to prose, and he published few poems. Posthumously, his poetic work was collected in *Poems of R.P. Blackmur* (1977).

Further Reading. *Selected Primary Source:* Blackmur, R.P., *Poems of R.P. Blackmur,* ed. Dennis Donoghue (Princeton, NJ: Princeton University Press, 1977). *Selected Secondary Sources:* Blackmur, R.P., *Language as Gesture* (New York: Harcourt, Brace, 1952; reprint Westport, CT: Greenwood Press, 1977); Bloom, James D., *The Stock of Available Reality: R.P. Blackmur and John Berryman* (London: Associated University Presses, 1984); Fraser, Russell, *A Mingled Yarn: The Life of R.P. Blackmur* (New York: Harcourt Brace Jovanovich, 1981).

Benjamin Harder

BLASER, ROBIN (1925–)

As a core participant in the **San Fransisco Renaissance** and a deep-reaching theorist and practitioner of seriality, Robin Blaser has enriched both **Canadian** and American poetry and **poetics** since his debut as a poet in the late 1940s. In particular, Blaser, along with **Robert Duncan** and **Jack Spicer**, played a central role in the Berkeley-based San Fransisco Renaissance—a movement that made possible his and Spicer's articulation of seriality, an aesthetic as well as a politically, socially, and ethically informed mode of writing that has fundamentally influenced both American poets (**Robert Creeley, Charles Bernstein, Susan Howe, Charles Olson,** and **Louis Zukofsky**) and Canadian poets (**bp Nichol**, George Bowering, and Daphne Marlatt). However, despite having such a decisive impact, the more philosophically challenging aspects of Blaser's work in conjunction with a dual Canadian and American citizenship (making him indigenous to neither country) have resulted in a dearth of critical attention to his work.

Born in Denver, Colorado, Blaser was raised in numerous small towns throughout Idaho by his father and maternal grandmother, Sophia Nichols; in *Astonishments* (a series of autobiographical tapes from 1974), Blaser recalls his grandmother's attempts to keep "duty and love alive" in arid, working-class railroad towns. Funded by his grandmother, Blaser went on to attend Northwestern University and the College of Idaho before beginning a nine-year-long career at the University of California in 1944. It was here at Berkeley that Blaser, alongside Spicer and Duncan, took courses with medieval political philosopher Ernst Kantorowicz and participated in Duncan's "anti-university" social events, which attracted like-minded poets, artists, and students. As Robert Creeley puts it in the foreword to Blaser's *The Holy Forest,* Berkeley at this time was not only significant for the presence of this San Fransisco "school" of writers but it also represented a place "where learning for oneself and discovering the appropriate teacher . . . had still a singular value" (xii).

Blaser left Berkeley in 1955 to accept a position in Harvard's Widener Library—the point that he marks as the beginning of his unique poetic vision as reflected in such early books as *Earlier, 1956–1958: The Boston Poems.* As Blaser writes in "The Fire" (1967), "I have worked since 1955 to find a line which will hold what I see and hear, and which will tie a reader to the poems, not to me" (242). Subsequently, between his stay in Boston and his acceptance of a position at Simon Fraser University in 1966, Blaser published his first substantial works: *The Moth Poem* (1964) and *Les Chiméres: Translations for Fran Herndon* (1965). However, it was not until the publication of his major work, *Image-Nation* (1962–1993)—a work that has appeared alongside other individual poems in *Syntax* (1983) and *Pell Mell* (1988) and culminates in the appearance of *The Holy Forest* (1993)—followed by *The Truth Is Laughter* (1979–1988) and *Great Companions* (1971 and 1988), that Blaser established himself as one of the most crucial practitioners of philosophically informed seriality.

The openness and inherently processual nature of seriality has allowed Blaser to continually work out issues such as the relationship between the imaginary and the real, self and other, public and private, all the while incorporating conflicting points of view. Moreover, the nature of the serial form is also perfectly suited to Blaser's concern with relationality itself as well as the forgoing of authorial control. As he revealingly writes in "The Fire," "This is a narrative which refuses to adopt an imposed story line, and completes itself only in the sequence of poems, if, in fact, a reader insists upon a definition of completion which is separate from the activity of the poems themselves" (237). While *Image-Nation* is clearly the most challenging and deeply searching example of such work, it is worth noting that even *The Holy Forest* itself (in which the *Image-Nation* poems are collected along with the most important works in Blaser's oeuvre) reflects such indeterminacy, as the poems and books are inextricably bound together in a constantly shifting and recurring set of themes such as love, companionship, the everyday, the sacred, and "the fold." Gilles Deleuze is the most contemporary, and perhaps most appropriate philosopher that Blaser draws on in *The Fold: Leibniz and the Baroque.* Deleuze claims the fold is the ideal trope for a philosophy based on process, interrelationality, and flux.

Literally folded into *The Holy Forest,* the *Image-Nation* poems, then, take up Blaser's primary aesthetic and ethical preoccupations. Building on Leibniz's belief in a world knowable only from endless and diverging points of view, as well as drawing on thinkers such as Hannah Arendt, Alfred North Whitehead, Maurice Merleau-Ponty, and Michel Serres, these poems incorporate a multitude of images and voices to formulate a notion of image and nation. As the source of vision, images for Blaser are necessary to present public, private, political, social, and linguistic life and future action; as he writes in "Particles" (1969), "Greek and

Roman political experience argues that to act intelligently in the public realm requires a vision of things. The words themselves, vision and things, are telling. Vision, full of that sense of seeing and image, which [is] basic to knowing." (36). Moreover, without images, we are left homeless and living out inhuman lives—"as the image wears away / there is a wind in the heart" ("Image-Nation 5 (erasure)"); in connecting us to a sense of home, images are also bound to our sense of nationhood. It is important to note, however, that nation and home cannot be defined from a transcendent point of view, since a world built on flux and relationality is one in which difference (and so particularity) reigns and unity and logical consistency are unsustainable. As Blaser writes in "Image-Nation 15 (the lacquer house)," "the point is transformation of the theme— / enjoinment and departure—."

Further Reading. *Selected Primary Sources:* Blaser, Robin, *Astonishments* (audio recording) (Contemporary Literature Collection, W.A.C. Bennett Library, Simon Fraser University Library, 1974); ———, "The Fire," in *The Poetics of the New American Poetry*, ed. Donald Allen and Warren Tallman (New York: Grove Press, 1974, 235–246); ———, *The Holy Forest* (Toronto: Coach House Press, 1993); ———, *Les Chimères: Translations of Nerval for Fran Herndon* (San Fransisco: Open Space, 1965); ———, *The Moth Poem* (San Fransisco: White Rabbit Press, 1964); ———, *Syntax* (Vancouver: Talonbooks, 1983); ———, *Pell Mell* (Vancouver: Talonbooks, 1988). *Selected Secondary Sources:* Nichols, Miriam, *Even on Sunday: Essays, Readings, and Archival Materials on the Poetry and Poetics of Robin Blaser* (Orono, ME: National Poetry Foundation, 2002); Truitt, Samuel R., "An Interview with Robin Blaser" (*Talisman: A Journal of Contemporary Poetry and Poetics* 16 [1996]: 5–25); Watts, Charles, and Edward Byrne, eds., *Recovery of the Public World: Essays on Poetics in Honour of Robin Blaser* (Vancouver: Talonbooks, 1999).

Lori Emerson

BLEECKER, ANN ELIZA (1752–1783)

In some ways, Ann Eliza Bleecker typifies the most melancholy strands of sentimental poetry of a type lampooned in the nineteenth century, most famously by Mark Twain in the figure of *Huck Finn*'s Emmeline Grangerford. Bleecker's life and work, however, belie the parody, offering insight into the power of **sentimental** poetry at the end of the eighteenth century and displaying a breadth of theme and tone that has largely gone ignored by critics. In the span of a short life that included a great deal of drama, Bleecker managed to be fairly prolific, participating both in the **genteel** tradition of manuscript circulation (writing for friends and family) and in the emerging commercial print sphere, where her work appeared in New York City periodicals. Bleecker represents, then, both a neglected moment in poetic history and a transitional moment in the history of authorship.

Born into two prominent early New York families, the Van Wycks and the Schuylers, Ann Eliza Bleecker lived a quiet life as a young woman, pursuing her interest in literature as a hobby and marrying John Bleecker in 1769. With her husband, Bleecker settled in a small village near Albany called Tomhanick. During the Revolution, raids by the British and the Native Americans threatened the Bleeckers' home on a number of occasions. In 1777, while John Bleecker was away, the British troops under the command of General Burgoyne moved through the area, and Bleecker fled with her two daughters, Abella and Margaretta. Traveling on foot without supplies and with two children, Bleecker suffered intensely on this journey, an event that was to color the rest of her life, at least as her biography was later to be interpreted by her elder daughter. Her younger daughter, Abella, died during their flight. In 1781 John Bleecker was imprisoned by the British; he was eventually released. In the years following the Revolution, Bleecker continued to write, but according to her daughter (also her biographer), she destroyed much of her writing, sometimes almost as quickly as she wrote it. Bleecker suffered multiple health problems, including serious depression, for the rest of her short life, dying in 1783 at the age of thirty-one. Her novel, *The History of Maria Kittle* (1791), and her *Posthumous Works* (1793) were published by her daughter, **Margaretta Faugeres**.

Bleecker has often been invoked as an emblem of the melancholy turn of much sentimental poetry. That image certainly was courted by Margaretta Faugeres in her published biography of her mother. For that reason, Bleecker's poem "Written in the Retreat from Burgoyne" (1777) has been her most anthologized and commented-upon work. The poem, which depicts in heroic couplets Bleecker's flight from the British and the death of her younger daughter, is indeed an undiluted expression of grief. To a modern sensibility the rhyme and regular meter may seem inappropriate; nonetheless, read with an open mind, the poem comments on grief in ways that are meaningful. When the poet talks of her friends encouraging her to bear up stoically under her loss, speaking of "souls serene and Christian fortitude," she finds this attitude (actually more typical of religiously inflected elegies of the period than is Bleecker's inconsolable grief) heartless. She ends the poem with a stubborn refusal to be comforted: "Nor shall the mollifying hand of time, / Which wipes off common sorrows, cancel mine." Compared with the willing resignation of **Anne Bradstreet** or **Edward Taylor** in response to the death of children, Bleecker presents an intensity of emotion more typical of the British Romantic poets.

On the other hand, in spite of the image of Bleecker as constantly depressed, much of her poetry is more light-hearted, even humorous. Her poetic exchanges with a neighbor find Bleecker working in a mock heroic strain, mixing classical references with homely tales of local livestock and light-hearted references to her correspondent's love life. In those same poems, Bleecker offers commentary on the poetry of John Donne and its differences from neoclassical poetry, demonstrating her awareness of English poetic tradition. In a poem like "To Mr. Bleecker" (1793), Bleecker demonstrates both her awareness of poetic convention and her humor: The entire poem describes a fanciful attempt at invoking the muses, followed by invocations of other classical figures. In other poems, such as "Joseph" (1793), a retelling of the Old Testament story, Bleecker works in less personal and more serious modes. To survey the poems collected in Bleecker's *Posthumous Works* is to recognize a poet familiar with the conventions of neoclassical poetry, able to work within those conventions as well as playfully work at the boundaries of them, and writing on a broad spectrum about the human condition—far from the maudlin, tear-drenched sentimental stereotype often evoked by a knowledge of her struggles with depression.

Further Reading. *Selected Primary Sources:* Bleecker, Ann Eliza, *The Posthumous Works of Ann Eliza Bleecker . . . To Which is Added, a Collection of Essays, Prose and Poetical, by Margaretta V. Faugères* (New York, 1793); Harris, Sharon, ed., *American Women Writers to 1800* (New York: Oxford University Press, 1996; Lauter, Paul, ed., *Heath Anthology of American Literature*, 3rd ed., vol. 1 (Boston: Houghton Mifflin, 1998). ***Selected Secondary Sources:*** Ellison, Julie, "Race and Sensibility in the Early Republic: Ann Eliza Bleecker and Sarah Wentworth Morton" (*American Literature* 65 [1993]: 445–474); Giffen, Allison, "'Till Grief Melodious Grow': The Poems and Letters of Ann Eliza Bleecker" (*Early American Literature* 28 [1993]: 222–241).

Angela Vietto

BLOEDE, GERTRUDE (1845–1905)

A native speaker of German, Gertrude Bloede decided to become an English-writing poet at the age of sixteen. In 1865 she had her first poem published under the male pseudonym of Stuart Sterne (as were all subsequent publications), which was followed by some one hundred fifty short poems until her book *Angelo* (1878) established her as an American poet. *Angelo* was Bloede's first and most successful effort at a number of long, narrative poems written in blank verse. These **long poems** showed little structure, but Bloede was considered, above all, a dramatic talent. Despite her belief that no writer of florid prose ever became more than a minor poet, she published a novel and some short stories in her later years.

Bloede concealed herself from public attention, and little is known about her private life. Interest in her work, always limited, declined after her death.

Bloede was born in Dresden, Germany, in 1845. Her father, Gustav, had participated in the 1849 Saxon uproar, after which he was forced to emigrate with the family in 1850. After living briefly in Philadelphia and nearby places, they settled in Brooklyn in 1860, where Bloede spent most of her life. It was here, in the proximity of New York, that her mother, Marie Bloede, also a poet, made contact with **Bayard Taylor** and other writers of the Genteel Circle and encouraged the younger Bloede to write poetry. Gustav Bloede, having become an editor of the *New Yorker Demokrat*, urged his daughter to follow the Republican Party. At the same time, Gertrude fell under the influence of the speeches of Massachusetts senator Charles Sumner and began to advocate the principles of universal freedom and universal love, values that defined her work thereafter. However, being "too much a woman to labor even in a great cause without an individual representative of the same to love and admire" (*Journal* [1 January 1864]), Bloede fell in love with the senator, despite his remoteness.

After a major crisis in the 1870s caused by personal troubles as well as by her growing dissatisfaction with her poetry, Bloede turned back to her German literary origins, to Goethe in particular. She began to write less about her personal feelings and more about historical personalities. Having started her career as a contributor to the *Boston Commonwealth*, she returned to a Massachusetts newspaper in her later years as a writer, publishing poems and short stories in the *Springfield Republican*, and befriending Charles G. Whiting and Chester T. Stockwell, also on the staff of that newspaper. Considering the consequences of the Spanish-American War, she supported the campaign of William Jennings Bryan in 1900 and joined the Anti-Imperialistic League. Having suffered from rheumatism since her Philadelphia years, Bloede lived her last years in severe physical pain. She died in Baldwin, Long Island, in 1905.

When Bloede started writing professionally, she was influenced by the Irish American poet John A. Dorgan, to whom she dedicated a number of pieces in her first published volume, *Poems* (1874). However, most of the poems were inspired by love, especially "the love of a woman for a man, which is given with no reserve of pride, not to say of calculation or even of prudence," as a perceptive critic wrote without knowing who the poet was (*Galaxy* [May 1875]: 718).

Angelo, her next publication, did not reveal the poet's identity either, since its subject was Condivi's *Life of Michelangelo*, in which Michelangelo cannot conceal his passionate love for Vittoria Colonna. Vittoria, however, refuses to abandon the religion that has consoled her since the death of her beloved husband. After some inner struggle, Angelo devotes himself to an *imitatio Christi*, which finds its expression in one of his most famous statues.

The theme of human love elevated to the heights of religious experience would subsequently be treated in other historic scenarios by Bloede, such as Venice at the time of Giorgione in *Giorgio and Other Poems* (1881), or Florence at the time of Savonarola in *Piero da Castiglione* (1890). In the latter, Piero renounces his profound love for Maria, under the influence of the zealous Fra Giro-lamo, who claims all human love to be *amor dei*. Piero decides to become a priest, while Maria, still clinging to Piero, shows the attitude that the author saw as her own—and indeed her gender's—principal conflict: God himself, she believes, has decreed that she must follow Piero's voice until that time when her soul too "shall be / Among his own elect."

Bloede published another volume of poems, *Beyond the Shadow and Other Poems* (1888), anonymously. The book was posthumously dedicated to Sumner "through whom has come to me a deeper comprehension of life, death, and eternity" (n.p.). *Beyond the Shadow* takes the form of a dialogue and is reminiscent of Goethe's *Faust* in regard to both form and subject. Voices from above and below reveal the redemption of a man through a woman, who pardons all the deception and ill treatment she has endured from him. Bloede here establishes a scenario of the Unknown, which evokes the major conflict in the life of her father; having been a rigid materialist in Germany, later he joined the movement of American spiritualism.

On January 11, 1891, Bloede revealed a few details about herself and her work in an interview with the *Brooklyn Daily Eagle*. Everything written about the poet since that time is based on these revelations. The last poems for the Springfield paper took Bloede's love for Sumner as their subject. In *Berkshire* (1902) the poet wanders through the natural landscape, imagining a man by her side who never knew about her love other than as an indistinct metaphor in her early poems.

Further Reading. *Selected Primary Sources:* Bloede, Gertrude, *Journals*, 10 vols. (1857/1898) (in possession of Dieter Langee); ———, *Angelo: A Poem* (Boston: Houghton, Mifflin, 1878); ———, *Beyond the Shadow and Other Poems* (Boston: Houghton, Mifflin & Co., 1888); ———, *Giorgio and Other Poems* (Boston: Houghton, Mifflin, 1881); ———, *Piero da Castiglione* (Boston: Houghton, Mifflin, 1890); ———, *The Story of Two Lives* (New York: Cassell, 1891); Sterne, Stuart, *Poems* (New York: Patterson, 1874).

Dieter Lange

BLOOD, BENJAMIN (1832–1919)

If ever now made mention of, Benjamin Blood is referred to as the philosopher of nitrous oxide and mys-tical experience obtained under anesthesia. Although his poetry appeared occasionally from 1854 until his death, his preferred forms of writing were prose on aspects of speculative philosophy and letters, many to correspondents and admirers of more enduring fame, such as **Ralph Waldo Emerson**, William James (see Ralph Barton Perry, *The Thought and Character of William James* [Boston: Little, Brown, 1935], for their letters), and Alfred, Lord Tennyson. His letters to local newspapers ranged, in the words of H.M. Kellen in his introduction to *Pluriverse*, "from petty politics or the tricks of spiritual-ist mediums to principles of industry and finance and profundities of metaphysics" (xxi).

Benjamin Blood was born on November 21, 1832, in Amsterdam, New York, the only child of John Blood, a prosperous landowner. Writing of his youth, Blood said, "I . . . went a good deal my own way," blazoning an eclectic career, which ran from inventing a swathing reaper to gambling under the Tweed regime, and from boxing to farming, but he claimed he was "much idle," during which time he read widely and wrote (Perry, 228). "Of ubiquitous grasp, as he was to have ubiqui-tous interests," Blood wrote admiringly of Napoleon, ruefully implying that if he, Blood, could not make "the iron of nature redden under his Titan blows," he could follow his polymath idol in revealing the "inscriptions in the elements of things, recorded at the founding of the world" (*Napoleon I*, 5). Yet it was because of Blood's attachment to metaphysics and because of his considerable means that he never saw fit to leave his native upstate New York environs for any extended time. After a long life, long enough to earn him the nickname "the healthy mystic," Blood died on January 15, 1919.

His most recognizable prose works concern his four-teen-year experimentation with nitrous oxide, first related in a pamphlet, *The Anesthetic Revelation and the Gist of Phi-losophy*, which he self-published in 1874, and later in his posthumous book *Pluriverse: An Essay in the Philosophy of Pluralism*. He found that invariably when he was "coming to," he was afforded insight into the "genius of being" (*Pluriverse*, 204), an experience confirmed by William James, who named Blood as an essential spur to his own writing of *The Varieties of Religious Experience*. By the time of his death, Blood had completed a full articulation of his "pluralistic" philosophy, which cast him in an Emerson-ian and Hegelian light, for he spoke of the need for "tergi-versation *between* the static and dynamic viewpoints" (*Pluriverse*, 15–16), of the One and the Many, and of the operations of chance. Swedenborg and Kant were other major figures who ultimately echoed, for Blood, what Napoleon exclaimed at his abdication: "From the sublime to the ridiculous is but a step" (42).

Blood completed, some twelve years apart, two lengthy poems: *The Bride of the Iconoclast* and *The Colonnades*. *Bride of the Iconoclast* is a soul-quest told in Spenserian quatrains but maintaining parallels to Romantic poetry, such as the dream genesis and dreamlike language of Coleridge's "Kubla Khan" and the quest language of Tennyson's "Ulysses." The hero, Barron, seeks to bring his bride, Hermia, home. After an argument about love, the couple is soon cast into a "new world" to contend with it and with the pirates that seem the only other inhabitants; the romance is cut short by both of their deaths. Comfortable with other voices, such as those of the squabbling pirates and besotted lovers, Blood confirms his love of Shakespearean characters, noble and common. *The Colonnades* continues this mimicry through conversations with and imitations of Socrates, Aesop, Swedenborg, Byron, Burns, Pope, and others.

Interpreting *The Colonnades* in light of Blood's experimentation with nitrous oxide is a tempting proposition. The bulk of the poem is composed of dramatic dialogues engendered by the poet's dream of a descent into Hades, mirroring the ancient trope of *nekyia*; it is clear, however, that any visionary insight will be atypical, for Charon, the first being he encounters, is cast as counter to the "decrepit churl whom poets feign," instead having an eye "mellow as a lake at evening." In their ensuing conversation, the poet expresses his yearning for and, as we come to see, his need to *be* a "sunrise bard" whose "shout shall ask no hush of Academe / To gape its welcome." The poet also longs for origins, for those whose hands "curved the eyelids of the Sphinx" and who "dug the cellars of the pyramids." As such imagery suggests, and as three other poems collected posthumously in *Heirlooms*—"The Lion of the Nile," "In Egypt," and "Thyreus"—indicate, Blood was deeply interested in Egypt (though he had never been there), as part of a general flurry of interest in hieroglyphs and matters Egyptian in the first half of the nineteenth century (see John Irwin, *American Hieroglyphics: The Symbol of the Egyptian Hieroglyphics in the American Renaissance* [New Haven, CT: Yale University Press, 1980]). The breadth of Blood's learning is also evident in *The Colonnades'* extended exchange between, on the one side, Plato and Praxiteles, and on the other, an Egyptian youth, precocious and demanding. The poem, true to Blood's ever-expanding list of interests to be unified under his pluralistic philosophy, covers alchemy, aesthetics, and more.

Heirlooms, a collection of shorter lyrics Blood published in *Scribner's* and other New York newspapers, stands as a too-short testament to Blood's talent in the mode, especially as underlying Blood's poems is a confidence that each letter of the alphabet has "in some sense a suggestive character of its own," much as **Edgar Allan Poe** and Arthur Rimbaud believed (*Pluriverse*, 249). William James's high praise for "Lion of the Nile" concludes, "Who of us all handles his English vocabulary better than Mr. Blood?" (quoted in John Edmund Willoughby, Preface to *Heirlooms*, n.p.). Other poems work with the raw material of Shakespeare, as Tennyson does in "Mariana," redramatizing and somewhat understating; some of these poems seem precursors to the dark simplicities of **Robert Frost** and **Edwin Arlington Robinson**.

Blood's historical sense and anesthetic revelations never altered his Christian faith, which was earned, as it were, through the course of writing an early work on the nature of justice between God and man, a study that ultimately left him with the sense that the "hint of initiation—the hint that NOW YOU KNOW," was spoken by what was long known to him—he says without a trace of irony—as *"the voice of the blood"* (*Pluriverse*, 206).

Further Reading. ***Selected Primary Sources:*** Blood, Benjamin Paul, *The Anesthetic Revelation and the Gist of Philosophy* (Amsterdam, NY: Benjamin Paul Blood, 1874); ———, *The Bride of the Iconoclast; Suggestions toward the Mechanical Art of Verse* (Boston: James Munroe, 1854); ———, *The Colonnades* (Amsterdam, NY: Benjamin Paul Blood, 1868); ———, *Heirlooms: A Book of Poems* (Albany: F.S. Hills, 1924); ———, *Optimism: The Lesson of the Ages* (Boston: Bela Marsh, 1860); *Napoleon I: A Historical Lecture* (Amsterdam, NY: C.P. Winegar, 1868); ———, *Pluriverse: An Essay in the Philosophy of Pluralism* (Boston: Marshall Jones, 1920). **Selected Secondary Sources:** Nelson, Christopher A.P., "The Artificial Mystic State of Mind: WJ, Benjamin Paul Blood, and the Nitrous-Oxide Variety of Religious Experience" (*Streams of William James* 4.3 [2002]: 23–31); Tymoczko, Dmitri, "The Nitrous Oxide Philosopher" (*Atlantic Monthly* [May 1996]: 93–101); Wright, A.J., "Benjamin Paul Blood: Anesthesia's Philosopher and Mystic," in *The History of Anesthesia: Third International Symposium, Proceedings, Atlanta, Georgia, March 27–31, 1992* (Park Ridge, IL: Wood Library–Museum of Anesthesiology, 447–456).

Douglas Basford

BLUES

Blues song, born in the heart of African American culture, is one of the United States' most important contributions to the history of music. Blues songs are rooted in and inextricable from African music, spirituals, and work songs. The genre emerged in the early twentieth century and continues to thrive into the twenty-first century in traditional forms and in a range of other hybrids and manifestations. Many forms of jazz and rock and roll, for example, are based structurally and stylistically on the blues.

In addition to its wide diffusion and influence as music, the blues has played a central role in the landscape of twentieth-century **African American poetry** and of American poetry in general. It has also had a major impact on perspectives in literary criticism, particularly on African American literary theory. It has a central role in the course of twentieth-century African American poetry and also emerges in the work of white poets. In the 1920s poets began to incorporate into their work the lyrics, imagery, and archetypal protagonists of blues songs and to structure their poems based on the rhythms and rhymes and other musical elements of the blues.

A blues song typically includes one voice and one or more instruments, such as the guitar or piano. Characteristically, a song is a twelve- or eight-bar sequence comprising the progression of the one, four, and five chords. Each verse, typically, is three lines with four beats each: The first line is repeated in the second line, and the third line contains the same end word or rhyme. Although there are many variations on this structure, blues songs characteristically use "blue" or flatted notes of the third, fifth, and seventh tones of the major diatonic scale and include slides in pitch from note to note. Various blues styles developed in particular locations, such as the Mississippi Delta area and Chicago, St. Louis, New Orleans, and Memphis.

Traditionally, blues musicians, incorporating verbal and musical formulaic phrases, have had little use for musical scores. A song's wit, irony, and humor, and a performer's improvisational skills are valued by his or her audience. A song, from the first person point of view, typically, complains of a bad situation and may express sadness, anger, frustration, or restlessness. The person may be alienated, leaving a bad situation or a bad place, and heading for the next train.

Blues figures of speech and improvisational sequences are quintessential qualities in African American folk tradition. In addition, the raw blues lyrics and sexual double-entendres, the brilliant improvisational prowess of some singers and instrumentalists, and the nightclub setting for performance contribute to the image of the blues performer as someone alienated from mainstream white society and the American dream. Thus, the blues has captured the imagination of African American poets and has steered discussions on African American aesthetics, beginning with the New Negro Movement in the 1920s. For Houston A. Baker and Henry Louis Gates, two major contemporary scholars and literary theorists, blues expression epitomizes the vernacular tradition, which is at the core of their perceptions of African American literary theory, culture, and history. Blues songs have also been the source of imagery and stanzaic forms for white American poets in the tradition of **Walt Whitman**, who praised the music of the American people, and for poets, disaffected from mainstream American social or political values, who identify with the mythic image of the blues musician or song protagonist.

Blues elements are rendered into poetry in a variety of ways. A poem may imitate standard blues stanza forms, include the images and phrases of blues songs, or attempt to capture thematically an aspect of the spirit of the blues. Whereas many poems combine these elements, others represent highly individualized treatments of the blues. Finally, blues songs themselves are included in some poetry anthologies.

The blues idiom was of great interest to writers of the **Harlem Renaissance** or New Negro Movement (1919–1940), including **Langston Hughes** and **Sterling A. Brown**. In the 1920s African American arts began to flourish as artists pursued an aesthetic free from the limitations and demands of outside forces. Oral folk arts were adapted and incorporated into literary texts and thereby undercut the stereotyped figures and racist appropriation of these arts found in minstrel shows. Hughes was the first writer to merge the blues and poetry. He also wrote a number of blues songs, collaborated with various musicians, and read his poems to jazz/blues accompaniment. Several collaborations were recorded in the 1950s and 1960s, including the album *The Weary Blues and Other Poems*. In *Langston Hughes & the Blues*, Steven C. Tracy devotes a chapter to defining the blues and makes the point that the "term is complex because it refers to a number of entities—an emotion, a technique, a musical form, and a song lyric" (39). He discusses specific blues sources, compares particular poems to songs, and treats poems that are, by strict definition, associated with bebop and other jazz forms.

The musical pulse and the central metaphors of many of Hughes's poems are adaptations of blues and jazz figures, including the following: the lyrics of blues songs; the rhythmic phrasing of boogie-woogie music, a style related to blues though more upbeat with fast-moving bass clef octave chords played on the piano; the phrasing of bebop, a jazz style that emerged in the 1940s, which was freer in structure than the blues and played by a small ensemble employing numerous improvised passages; and the phrasing of free-form jazz, a genre characterized by extensive improvisation, melodic dissonance, and rhythmic discontinuity. Hughes borrowed from the blues in form, diction, and theme in his collections *The Weary Blues* (1926); *Fine Clothes to the Jew* (1927), and *Shakespeare in Harlem* (1942); from boogie and bebop in *Montage of a Dream Deferred* (1951); and from free-form jazz in *Ask Your Mama: Twelve Moods for Jazz* (1961).

Through his poetry and prose, Hughes helped construct a foundation for an African American aesthetic, partly based on an oral folk art, in a cultural environment that mocked it and favored artistic expression based on white American social values and traditional European definitions of art. Early in his career, Hughes wrote in the seminal essay "The Negro Artist and the

Racial Mountain" (1926) that when the black artist "chooses to touch on the relations between Negroes and whites in this country with their innumerable overtones and undertones surely, and especially for literature and drama, there is an inexhaustible supply of themes at hand." He continued that the artist can apply to these themes his "heritage of rhythm and warmth, and his incongruous humor that so often, as in the Blues, become ironic laughter mixed with tears" (57).

Also aligning style in music to a sociopolitical sphere, in *Collected Poems*, Hughes wrote the following about his extended poem *Montage of Dream Deferred* (1951): "In terms of current Afro-American popular music and the sources from which it progressed—jazz, ragtime, swing, blues, boogie-woogie, and be-bop—this poem on contemporary Harlem like be-bop is marked by conflicting changes, sudden nuances, sharp and impudent interjections, broken rhythms, and passages, sometimes in the manner of a jam session, sometimes the popular song, punctuated by the riffs, runs, breaks and distortions of the music of a community in transition."

The poems in this volume, and others throughout Hughes's career, brilliantly approximate musical gesture. Several poems are strongly interlinked and convey variations and improvisations on various themes. "Dream Boogie," "Boogie: 1 a.m.," "Lady's Boogie," "Deferred," "Nightmare Boogie," "Likewise," "Dream Boogie Variation," "Harlem," "Good Morning," and "Same in Blues" echo each either through the repetition and recapitulation of motifs in various combinations. The phrase "dream deferred" and "good morning daddy" appear in a variety of contexts that carry over from poem to poem so that the figures resonate incrementally. The "dream deferred" addresses racism in America and treats the image of self, the relationship between men and women, and the intense experiences of joy and sorrow. "Boogie: 1 a.m." defies paraphrasing. Through multiple musical references and its connections to other poems in the sequence, in eight short lines it portrays life in Harlem and elsewhere. It presents a profound sense of frustration and growing impatience, and it conveys an avenue of momentary escape: "Boogie: 1 a.m." refers to "The boogie-woogie rumble / Of a dream deferred" and continues with references to musical instruments. While imitating the boogie-woogie twelve-bar musical structure, Hughes also echoes the traditional blues song "Good Morning Blues." The blues singer's personal experience of various kinds of dissatisfaction, however, is transformed by Hughes into a potent summation of the social, psychological, and political ramifications of racism in America.

Sterling A. Brown, Hughes's contemporary, also addresses oppression through the blues trope. Poems in his collection *Southern Road* (1932) and elsewhere incorporate blues meter and rhyme and include names and phrases from blues and folk songs. Brown's country protagonists respond in a variety of ways to life in a separate and unequal America. "Odyssey of Big Boy" (1927) is one of his frequently discussed poems. Written from the first-person point of view in five-line stanzas rife with strong stresses, Brown presents a litany of jobs held by an African American laborer, including rice and tobacco field work and dock work. The balladeer, who has done them all, identifies with Casey Jones and John Henry, who were folk heroes and the subjects of many songs.

Other poems criticize oppression in American society and white stereotyping of African Americans. Five poems—"Slim Geer," "Slim Lands a Job?" "Slim in Atlanta," "Slim Hears 'The Call,'" and "Slim in Hell"—present Slim, a trickster who overcomes various obstacles and foes with his fast talking, fast thinking, and fast living, qualities depicted in blues songs. "Slim Geer" tells the tale of his tricking a white woman who thinks he is from Europe. By the time "the crackers" come after him, assuming he is black because he plays the blues so well, Slim is gone. "Slim Jim Lands a Job?" treats the impossible working conditions imposed by white employers on black workers. However, unlike the down-and-out blues song complaint, Slim prevails. "Slim in Atlanta" mocks the Jim Crow laws through a humorous, outrageous tale, and again Slim is victorious. In "Slim in Hell," through a tall tale of the protagonist's descent into hell where the devil turns into a sheriff, Brown identifies the segregated South with hell. In "Slim Hears 'The Call'" the poet mocks hypocrisy in the church, a theme dealt with in the blues song "Preachin Blues," sung by Son House and other blues musicians.

Brown's "Ma Rainey" (1930), about the great singer known as "the mother of the blues," is written in the diction of a blues song from the perspective of an admiring member of the audience. The poem reads like a folk ballad about Rainey and includes lyrics to her songs. The black community's pleasure in listening to brilliant blues performers is celebrated by the poet.

A number of Brown's poems mention blues in the title, such as "Kentucky Blues," "River Bank Blues," "New St. Louis Blues," "Tin Roof Blues," "Rent Day Blues," and "Long Track Blues." "Memphis Blues" (1931) merges elements of the blues, the folk ballad, spirituals, and the sermon. The poem ends with a powerful political statement suggesting that modern Memphis will come to destruction like the biblical city and that ultimately this makes no difference to African Americans.

"Tin Roof Blues" closely resembles a blues song with its three-line stanzas, the first two lines' end-word repetition, and the third line's end rhyme. It speaks about abandoning the city and returning to the country. "Long Track Blues," written from the first-person perspective, bears a striking resemblance to Robert Johnson's "Love in Vain," which was recorded in the mid-1930s. Both the song and the poem recount the speaker missing his woman, who has taken a train and left him. Johnson sings, "When the train, it left the station—with two lights left on behind. / Well, the blue light was my blues—and the red light was my mind" (*Robert Johnson*). Describing a similar situation, Brown writes, "Went down to the yards" and continues, "Red light in my block / Green light down the line." Brown's adaptation of the blues in his poetry was an important component in his commitment to African American folk traditions. In addition, he wrote influential cultural and literary histories and edited major anthologies of African American literature.

Melvin Tolson, a contemporary of Brown and Hughes, worked on a book-length poem, *Harlem Gallery* (1965), in the 1930s. The twenty-four–part poem, comprising sections titled by letters of the Greek alphabet, represents a brilliant fusion of New Negro Movement aesthetics and **modernism**. Its protagonist and main narrator is a Harlem Gallery curator, an art historian. Parts of the poem are in the voices of other characters, including "the poet laureate of Harlem," Hideho Heights. *Harlem Gallery* is packed with allusions to high culture and African American culture, and among various themes, it addresses definitions of African American art and concepts of the artist. Tolson devotes considerable space to the voice of Hideho Heights, who uses jazz lingo and celebrates the blues world and its legendary heroes. The poem's multiple voices and references recall Pound's technique, but with the wit, irony, and playfulness of the African American oral tradition.

Harlem Gallery was published in the mid-1960s in a period when new definitions of art were being pursued in the **Black Arts Movement** or New Black Aesthetic. **Amiri Baraka** (LeRoi Jones) poet, playwright, essayist, and revolutionary made important contributions to that movement, including founding the Black Arts Repertory Theater/School and co-editing *Black Fire: An Anthology* (1968). In his early influential essay "The Myth of 'Negro Literature'" (1962), Baraka argues that the sources of great African American literary expression are in the blues, among other African American musical forms, rather than in well-worn conventional English poems.

The Black Arts Movement advocated black art for an African American audience, pride in Africa, Black Power, and revolution in America. Although innovative jazz forms were of greater interest, references to the blues appear in poetry by **Nikki Giovanni**, **Sonia Sanchez**, **Ishmael Reed**, and other writers. **Gwendolyn Brooks**, who became interested in the movement, echoed the blues in her early poems from the 1940s.

A contemporary of Brooks, **Robert Hayden** also borrowed from the blues. "Shine Mister?" (1940) and "Bacchanale" (1940), employing stanza structure and language reflecting blues songs, treat the lives of hard-working laborers. "Homage to the Empress of the Blues" (1949), for Bessie Smith, uses unrhymed strophes to celebrate the singer and portrays some of the societal conditions of poverty and oppression that were experienced by many in her audience. Hayden alludes to the blues and jazz in a number of later poems that also confront these conditions.

Sherley Anne Williams, a novelist, playwright, poet, and critic, was influenced by both the New Negro Movement and the Black Arts Movement. Williams devotes a third of her book of poems *Some One Sweet Angel Chile* (1982) to Bessie Smith. The section titled "Regular Reefer" is made up of several voices, including Smith's, Ruby Walker's (a niece and close friend who performed with the singer), and the poet's. Early in the sequence Ma Rainey is evoked by Smith, thus presenting a theme of a maternal artistic legacy. The sequence treats such themes as Smith's passion for music, her experiences of love, and her tragic death, the result of Jim Crow laws when a Mississippi hospital refused to admit her for treatment. "Regular Reefer" is an important voice in the history of blues poetry because of its strong feminist and womanist perspective.

Williams addressed the subject of the blues in poetry in her essay "The Blues Roots of Contemporary Afro-American Poetry," which appeared in *Chants of Saints: A Gathering of Afro-American Literature, Art, and Scholarship*, the important collection edited by the critic Robert B. Stepto and the poet **Michael S. Harper**. Music in general but jazz in particular has had a major role in Harper's poetics and poetry. However, in his first collection, *Dear John, Dear Coltrane* (1970), and in subsequent books, his poems resonate with blues references. Harper edited *Sterling A. Brown's Collected Poems* in 1980, and in 1994 he edited an anthology of African American poetry since 1945.

In anthologies of recent African American poetry, the legacy of the blues continues with young poets' frequent references to musicians and their songs. The music and the culture of the blues have also had a significance presence in the poetry of white writers. For example, **Beat poetry** (by white and black writers) embraces the improvisation of the blues and jazz. In this poetry the term "blues" becomes a trope for a profound alienation from American society and the rejection of its values. **Jack Kerouac** authored books of extended poem/choruses—*Book of the Blues* and *Mexico City Blues*—and **Allen Ginsberg** wrote blues poems and blues songs. A short list of other poets who have borrowed from the blues in stanza form or in theme, or who celebrate blues music, includes **Robert Creeley**, **Jonathan Williams**, and **Muriel Rukeyser**. Finally, **Hayden Carruth**, who published a book of essays on blues and jazz, alludes to the blues in a number of his poems.

Further Reading. *Selected Primary Sources:* Brown, Sterling A., *The Collected Poems of Sterling A. Brown*, ed. Michael S. Harper (Evanston, IL: Northwestern University Press, 1980); Hughes, Langston, *The Collected Poems of Langston Hughes*, ed. Arnold Rampersad and David Roessel (New York: Knopf, 1994); ———, "The Negro Artist and the Racial Mountain," in *Within the Circle: An Anthology of African American Literary Criticism from the Harlem Renaissance to the Present*, ed. Angelyn Mitchell (Durham, NC: Duke University Press, 1994, 55–59); Tolson, Melvin, *Harlem Gallery and Other Poems by Melvin B. Tolson*, ed. Raymond Nelsen, intro. Rita Dove (Charlottesville: University of Virginia Press, 1999); Whitehall, Dave, and Scott Ainslie, eds., *Robert Johnson: At the Crossroads, the Authoritative Guitar Transcriptions* (Milwaukee: Hal Leonard, 1992); Williams, Sherley Anne, *Some One Sweet Angel Chile* (New York: Morrow, 1982). *Selected Secondary Sources:* Baker, Houston A., *Blues, Ideology, and Afro-American Literature: A Vernacular Theory* (Chicago: University of Chicago Press, 1984); Gates, Henry Louis, *The Signifying Monkey: A Theory of African American Literary Criticism* (New York: Oxford University Press, 1988); Harper, Michael S., and Robert B. Stepto, eds., *Chants of Saints: A Gathering of Afro-American Literature, Art, and Scholarship* (Urbana: University of Illinois Press, 1979); Tracy, Steven C., *Langston Hughes and the Blues* (Urbana: University of Illinois Press, 1988).

Kathy Rugoff

BLY, ROBERT (1926–)

Poet, translator, critic, journal editor, anthologist, public figure, and sometime cultural gadfly, Robert Bly has occupied a major position in the international literary scene for over half a century. He is frequently seen as the central figure in a new poetic movement of the 1960s and 1970s. Variously categorized as "**Deep Image**" poetry, the "new surrealism," or "subjectivist" poetry, it was sharply differentiated from the **modernist** poetry that preceded it and from the contemporaneous "**confessional**" **poetry**. Bly's accomplishments as an editor, critic, and translator are as noteworthy and influential as his achievements as a poet. As founder and editor of the Fifties Press, which later became the Sixties, Seventies, and Eighties Press, Bly greatly influenced the direction of contemporary American poetry. The main reason Bly founded the press was to introduce American audiences to the poetic imagination of certain European and South American writers. Scandinavian poets such as Tomas Tranströmer and Rolf Jacobsen, Spanish and South American poets such as Juan Ramón Jiménez, Pablo Neruda, and Cesar Vallejo, and the German poet Georg Trakl were translated into English by Bly and others, often for the first time, in the pages of Bly's journal and in books published by his press. Other poets translated by Bly over the course of his career include the ancient Indian poet Kabir, the Japanese poets Matsuo, Basho, and Issa Kabryashi, the French poet Francis Ponge, and the celebrated German poet Rainer Maria Rilke, among others. In addition to translations of foreign poets, Bly published American poets such as **Louis Simpson** and **James Wright**, whose work exemplified the concern with imagery that Bly endorsed and who received some of their earliest recognition in the pages of his journal. In his role as critic, especially as the irascible "Crunk," Bly wrote lengthy essays analyzing the achievements of Simpson, Wright, **Robert Creeley**, and **Denise Levertov**, among others, and attacked the work of modernists such as **Robert Penn Warren** as well as contemporaries such as **Robert Lowell** and, in an essay famous for its vituperation, **James Dickey**.

Robert Elwood Bly was born on December 23, 1926. Descending from a long line of farmers, he grew up on his parents' farm in Madison, Minnesota. During his early years, the love for the land so obvious in his poetry developed. After graduation from high school, Bly enlisted in the Navy. Stationed in Chicago, Bly made friends with literary enthusiasts, and his own passion for books was kindled. Discharged from the Navy in 1946, Bly enrolled at St. Olaf College in Northfield, Minnesota, but, in search of a more intense literary life, transferred to Harvard after only one year. Among his Harvard classmates were **Donald Hall**, **John Ashbery**, **Frank O'Hara**, and **Kenneth Koch**. Bly's poems, fiction, and book reviews were published in the *Harvard Advocate*, which Bly edited during his senior year. Shortly after graduating magna cum laude in 1950, Bly moved to New York City, where he lived for three years in virtual solitude, years that proved to be his true literary apprenticeship. Bly spent two years at the University of Iowa Writers' Workshop, where he earned an MA degree in creative writing in 1956, and two Fulbright years in his ancestral Norway, where he translated Norwegian literature into English. In 1958 Bly returned to the family farm in Madison with his first wife, Carol, whom he married in 1955, not to work the land but to become a poet. That year, Bly founded the Fifties Press with William Duffy, enhancing his reputation as poet, translator, editor, and critic. In 1966 Bly began his political activism, founding Poets Against the Vietnam War and organizing public poetry readings protesting America's involvement in Vietnam. During this period, Bly wrote the powerful *The Teeth Mother Naked at Last* and the political poems that appeared in *The Light Around the Body*. When he won the National Book Award for *Light* in 1968, he turned the award money over to the anti-war movement. Bly's anti-war fervor has not abated, and in 2004 he published *The Insanity of Empire: A Book of Poems Against the Iraq War*.

In 1979 Robert and Carol Bly were divorced, and the following year Bly married Ruth Ray, moving with Ruth's two boys and his own younger children to a farm near Moose Lake, Minnesota. In the early 1980s, Bly began conducting workshops and conferences for men, introducing material that eventually found its way into the unlikely international best seller *Iron John: A Book About Men* (1990). In 1989 Bly was the subject of a popular Bill Moyers PBS documentary, *A Gathering of Men*, which, along with *Iron John*, brought Bly and his men's work wide public visibility. Now in his seventies, Bly remains active and vigorous, continuing to produce new poetry, conduct men's conferences, and lead, with his wife, Ruth, and others, the Annual Conference on the Great Mother and New Father, which Bly began in the 1970s and which focuses on poetry and ritual. The importance of Bly's poetry has been confirmed by a series of awards and honors. In addition to the National Book Award for *The Light Around the Body*, Bly has been the recipient of Fulbright, Guggenheim, and Rockefeller fellowships, as well as a grant from the National Institute of Arts and Letters. In 1987 he was inducted into the American Academy of Arts and Letters.

Renouncing both the wasteland of modernism and the self-conscious reflexivity of **postmodernism**, Robert Bly's poetry reveals a certain moral intensity and attentiveness that subsequently releases a wide realm of generosity and expansion. Although Bly's 1980s poetry resumed a more overt interest in formal concerns, his earlier poetry should be seen as a marked departure from the aesthetic distance and objectivism undergirding modernist platforms. Nonetheless, while departing from earlier precedents and resisting certain rhetorics, even Bly's early poetry never lacked formal commitment. His sound systems, line velocities, and constructions of a lyric speaker—as formal innovations or departures—may be the most obvious elements that are critical to an informed reading. Since Bly regards rationality as only part of the total psyche, its privileged position in the **New Criticism**, as well as in Western consciousness at large, promotes to him a fragmentation based on the fraudulent assumption that objectivism is the only path to authenticity. His poetry, then, salient for its subjectivism, attempts to regain what he considers to be neglected features of life: emotion, intuition, and spirituality. Although Bly bypasses technical linguistic or postmodern theoretical vocabularies in his poetry and essays, his assertions and commitments reveal a continuum of complex interrelations, usually insistent upon constant internal and external passageways. While Bly's work is wide ranging, it springs from coherent motivations. Almost always the motive is recuperative, striving for union with that which has been neglected through lack of vision or bad intention. Each poem serves as a corrective, privileging some forgotten, imperialized, or brutalized person, sex, quality, natural or supernatural element, or historic or mythic event. Unifying and enlarging, each poem augments the next, where the focus shifts again.

Bly's poems must therefore be read as an ongoing journey addressing some previously unacknowledged aspect of existence, each piece in some ways adumbrating the next. The error most often committed when reading Bly is to mistake his stance in a given poem for a satisfied ontological conclusion. Bly's desire for unity, his holistic gesture, although singular in purpose, is vast in implication. Each individual collection is bonded to the next, but also contains departures and different endeavors; at times there may be seen a conscious weaning from previous positions. In this special sense, renunciation is as much a characteristic procedure as recuperation. To recognize that which is most significant in Bly, then, one must be aware of what underlies apparent self-contradiction. However, any attempt to confine Bly to single categories will fail because the "self" is in process, and the negotiation between a man of such keen worldly intellect and deep spiritual insight resists complacency and paradigmatic adherence. Bly is at once a Lutheran and a believer in pagan mythic figures and Jungian archetypal tendencies. He is simultaneously a vociferous reader of canonical literature and one who imbibes and deserts some of the formulaic modes of reception. Bly, the intellect, is searing, often vexing current assumptions from vastly different professional idioms—politics, biology, psychiatry, sociology. Bly, the intuitive, penetrates deeply beneath the cultural resonances, often with astounding associations and astonishing insight. One needs to pay attention to this interactive resonance to understand Bly's breadth and depth.

In *Silence in the Snowy Fields* (1962), Bly's first book, the poet associates light with what might be called "day consciousness," darkness with "night consciousness." Whereas the former is tied to traditionally Western modes of perception and suggests rationality, objectivism, and the world of distinctions that such perception insists upon, the latter is relatively Eastern in its perceptual mode, thereby suggesting intuition, subjectivity, and holism. Ultimately, this vision does not exchange night for day consciousness, but incorporates both into a single point of view. Divided into three sections, *Silence* records the poet's gradual attainment of what might be called an incorporative consciousness. An initial intuition of heightened night consciousness announces itself in section one; the weight of day reasserts itself before becoming transformed and expanded into a dark psychic milieu near the end of section two; finally, in section three, the poet's serenity results from his arrival at a different plateau of consciousness. The world of *Silence in the Snowy Fields*, then, consists both of the particular and the natural, the universal and the arcane. Bly saturates the land with darkness, an atmosphere both of night and vision, and portrays a speaker in natural harmony with his landscape and in spiritual communion with this nightscape. The physical setting becomes a different milieu, which is born of the interaction between the speaker and his world, this interaction investing both speaker and world with new powers. The speaker illuminated in darkness sees harmony, spirituality, and serenity in the universe.

"Three Kinds of Pleasure," the first poem in the volume, describes a midwestern landscape, but the three-part poem progresses from a relatively casual description of the public physical landscape to a more intense portrayal of private subjective vision. This private landscape becomes saturated with a quality unaccountable in the public one. The landscape of the final lines includes images somehow invested both with horizontal and vertical dimensions, black and white, spiritual and physical. Such inclusion comes not by objectively noticing dark things, as in the first stanza, but by vision through darkness. Such vision incorporates the seer and his milieu, thus overcoming the dualistic, objective, rational Western landscape. The intuition increasingly permeating this poem, then, goes hand in hand with the darkness increasingly permeating the landscape of the poem, the poet, and the reader.

The dark qualities of permeation and transformation that begin this book also conclude the collection. Bly provides both dark and light imagery in the final poem, "Snowfall in the Afternoon." Oncoming snow, which seems to be a white blanket, accompanies the oncoming evening. At the conclusion of the poem, surface imagery ("on deck") becomes symbolic of superficiality in its limitation to physicality. The speaker brings whiteness down and inward, and then sees through this dark ambience. Such inward vision transforms the natural setting into a spiritual landscape. With a more comprehensive vision, the speaker brings the natural scene to such life that, finally, anyone who by this time cannot see inward is proclaimed to be "blind." Indeed, the speaker has guided his readers far enough to persuade them that "A darkness was always there, which we never noticed." Such transformative darkness, he says, has always existed for those who are prepared to take notice. By the end of the poem, the singular "I" joins a visionary "we" that also weds the material world to spiritual cosmic motion. The storm sets the barn in motion "like a hulk blown toward us in a storm at sea." Water imagery suggests a fluidity that has greater strength than the more rigid physical forms. The storm gathers energy, as does the vision, until at last this force is released and opened up for the proclamation concluding the volume: "All the sailors on deck have been blind for many years." To the speaker, it appears that a man "on deck," on the surface of sensory and physical land, is blinded to truth. This truth does not abide in the storm; the storm, rather, is a symbolic preparation required for initiating the speaker (and the reader). Attending to and enduring the storm prepares him for the arrival, at darkness, of illumination.

He calmly asserts the superficiality of life "on deck," transforming that landscape into one that is part of the many dimensioned universe.

The rigor required for new life might perhaps best be seen in the metamorphic volume *The Light Around the Body* (1967), in which Bly reveals, often through a collage technique, a horrific society captured by externalism. A sense of exhaustion fills the volume, especially in its anti–Vietnam War poems. Disenchanted with a perverse and aggressive society, Bly ridicules President Kennedy in "Listening to President Kennedy Lie About the Cuban Invasion," a poem in which Bly senses "a bitter fatigue adult and sad." The energy in the cities is largely physical, not spiritual—"Here is a boiling that only exhaustion subdues"—and weary and unclean: "A bitter moiling of muddy waters." Here, the poetry censures male domination developed for imperial strength. When in "The Current Administration" Bly concludes, "Steps coming! The Father will soon return!" he has found an effective shorthand for the loss of those interior qualities cherished and portrayed in *Silence in the Snowy Fields*. The land of *The Light Around the Body* is populated by external humankind, where "children end, in the river of price fixing, / Or in the snowy field of the insane asylum" ("Sleet Storm on the Merritt Parkway").

Bly anguishes frankly in "Hatred of Men with Black Hair," since "underneath all the cement of the Pentagon! There is a drop of Indian blood preserved in snow!" A penchant for cruelty was evident in the founding of America, when victory meant death for the Native American. Bly believes that this bloodshed persists in the psyche and must be confronted. Instead, "the trail now lost," Americans pursue war and victory through power, at the expense of interior life. Filled with weltschmerz, the speaker in "The Fire of Despair Has Been Our Savior" concludes, "Not finding the road, we are slowly pulled down." Though seemingly disconsolate, Bly restores balance by plumbing depths resistant to defeat. An incandescent glow lights the end of the volume, when in "Looking into a Face" the speaker undergoes a spiritual metamorphosis and "rises to a body! Not yet born, / Existing like a light around the body! Through which the body moves like a sliding moon." Moonlight powers and waters reappear, along with hermits and women, an imagery auguring a more harmonious atmosphere. Near the conclusion, the speaker in "Moving Inward at Last" finds that "mountains alter and become the sea." With a resurgence of interior perceptual strength, he perceives a landscape symbolically oceanic, liquid, feminine, without boundaries, loaded with hidden elements for new life.

Growth continues in *This Body Is Made of Camphor and Gopherwood* (1977), in which Bly turns to the prose poem, adopting a Sufi form, he says, because of the intimacy and directness that it affords. According to

Bly, the prose poem appears when poetry has become too abstract. Bly's prose poems attempt to remedy abstraction by attending to singular manifestations within a larger unit. The form's capacity for absorbing detail and resisting categorical thought accommodates Bly's stance as a subjectivist who wishes to grasp the universal by perceiving the particular. The volume's strength comes partially from renunciation, a refusal to rely upon inherited structures. Opening *This Body Is Made of Camphor and Gopherwood*, "Walking Swiftly" portrays pilgrimage to new places. Reiterating the journey motif from *Silence* as well as the imagery of waking and sleeping, consciousness and unconsciousness, the poem declares artistic action to be both interior and exterior. The body's camphor and gopherwood are the house and energy of the poem. The body, filled with heat, centripetally pulls inward as it "knots into will," then centrifugally pours outward "into generosity." This reflection of the oyster that closes and opens all questions becomes more apparent when Bly resolves all in the human body's capacity for "mad love that lasts forever." Since the body has potential for gathering and releasing great energy, its greatest success may be in crossing boundaries. Bly goes beyond corporeal limitation with the centripetal and centrifugal energies of the human body, and resolves even their implicit dualism with "mad love."

In *The Man in the Black Coat Turns* (1981), Bly pauses on the road to look back and, typically, to collect that which may have been thus far too carelessly attended. Many of the poems derive from autobiographical occasions; grounded in the particulars of his experience, they are not limited to his inner life. In "Written at Mule Hollow, Utah," for example, Bly focuses on his own public persona. The existential irony regarding his relationship to language seems to pierce Bly centrally: He is a man of words who values silence, a poet of solitude whose living depends in part on public talk. "After three days of talk," the poems begins, "I long for silence." Bly here confronts the word as armor, concealment, part of the duplicitous face we prepare to meet the faces that we meet. But if the stony, prolix, public male of "Mule Hollow" is one of language's heirs, Bly the poet—aesthetic heir to Pablo Neruda, from whom he inherits the boundariless water element—is quite another. In poems such as "Words Rising," the liquid word cherished by the inward man, the maker of words, sluices through time and space, myth and history, not masking but interweaving. Such an unbounded, interactive element, a liquid plain, can be found in the elegiac "Mourning Pablo Neruda." The speaker in this poem undergoes an important change: Here he appears sympathetic to those who are undeveloped, finding reasons for inadequacies and gratitude for his path. Nonjudgmental, this voice seems more humble than Bly's familiar bardic manner. Char-

acteristic of his poems of the 1980s, Bly focuses less on the ego's attempt to empty itself of intentionality and more on the tug and haul of human relationships.

In particular, Bly portrays with great empathy the grief of men, tracing the history of men in one man, depicting a collective consciousness that, while it engenders potential, also delimits, as seen in "The Prodigal Son," who bears traces of "father beyond father beyond father." Whereas grief in the earlier poems had been generalized, archetypal rather than personal, the autobiographical overtones of poems such as "My Father's Wedding" or "In Rainy September" hint at localized suffering. The poems in this volume speak of shame and anger, of dishonor and loneliness, of prodigal sons and disaffected fathers. Such subjects, Bly seems to have concluded, require new forms that increase rather than relax tensions. This conclusion in turn led to Bly's experiments with sound and line in his poems of the 1980s. Bly's interest in form (an interest which he disavowed earlier in his career) and his shifting interest to the male at this point in his career should seem neither surprising nor contradictory. Bly's feminism had always involved the incorporation of the elemental female into his own psychic economy. For Bly, however, individuation never implies the simple exchange of elemental characteristics. Quick to dismiss dichotomous thinking, even (especially?) his own, as lacking the complexity of a more comprehensive understanding, always seeking completion, ever continuing to address neglected features in culture and the psyche, Bly turned naturally toward the forgotten male in his work of the 1980s.

Bly's next book, *Loving a Woman in Two Worlds* (1985), may be seen as a companion text to *Black Coat* for several reasons. Many of the poems in this volume are of the same length and continue the narrative quality of *Black Coat*. But whereas *Black Coat* primarily concerns men, here the focus is on a particular woman as Bly continues his poetic and spiritual odyssey by moving, in the 1980s books, to an emphasis on community, family, and sexual love. In *Black Coat*, Bly supplements the female consciousness developed in solitude with what he calls father consciousness, which he associates with the Jungian shadow. Only after working through "male grief," Bly believes, can a man love a woman in the manner celebrated in *Loving a Woman*. In this book, the archetypal feminine of the earlier poems is supplemented with an actual woman and, in such poems as "In the Time of Peony Blossoming" and "The Whole Moisty Night," with sexual love. One of the volume's signal poems, "Out of the Rolling Ocean, the Crowd . . . ," whose title is appropriated from Whitman, traces a transformation from the physical to the perceptual to the noumenal, and successfully blends emotional, physical, and intuitive responses, powers associated with both the archetypal male and female, in a celebration of a universe that is fully participatory.

Throughout the 1990s and the early years of the new century, Bly has continued to write and grow. In 1992 *What Have I Ever Lost by Dying?* brought together in a single collection all his prose poems that had not appeared in *This Body. Morning Poems* (1997), with an apparent move away from the rhetorics of the West, augments the quietness of some earlier volumes with a clearer sense of humanity and a spiritual beyond. Here are poems of wisdom, expansive with humility, gratefulness, and generosity. *Meditations on the Insatiable Soul* (1994) include poems primarily concerned with the relationship between Bly and his father's aging and death (and, surely, cast more broadly, both the archetypal and contemporary sociological mark of the father upon the son). Especially notable in this volume in the long poem, "Anger Against Children," and a visionary sequence of "Not Caring" poems. *Eating the Honey of Words* (1999), Bly's second volume of collected poems—his first, *Selected Poems*, appeared in 1986—contains two hundred poems, including over two dozen not previously published in any of Bly's volumes, that reveal a fairly comprehensive overview of Bly's continuing and shifting investments. The familiar titles, however, should not be the stopping place, since many of the previously published poems have been revised considerably. Although his surreal imagery, political outrage, and deep spirituality are clearly recognizable, this book further demonstrates the career of a poet unwilling to stagnate, even resisting the closure of previously published poems. Here, at times, Bly introduces himself more than he did in his *Silence in the Snowy Fields*, explains more lucidly some of the surreal juxtapositions of *Light Around the Body*, and at times seems to engage the reader through the use of more current content as well as being tactically more dialogical. Note, for example, how "Galloping Horses" shifts from its earlier version in *This Body Is Made of Camphor and Gopherwood*:

The horses gallop east, over the steppes, each with its rider, hard. (1977)
Let's imagine that the soul is made up of twenty horses and their riders. (1999)

While the first version carries starker juxtapositions, the second seems more inviting and appropriate to a moment when it may seem necessary to more explicitly state that the subject is spiritual discourse. Here, involvement is signaled with these cues about the domain being spiritual, as well as with a sense of mutuality more clearly felt because of the opening invitational gesture.

For *The Night Abraham Called to the Stars* (2001), Bly earned the Maurice English Poetry Award for a distinguished book of poems published in the preceding calendar year by a poet over fifty. Whereas Bly's generosity has been established, the sense of gratitude—a related sentiment—emerges increasingly as a dominant impulse. In *The Night Abraham Called to the Stars*, Bly continues to show his investment in the poetic forms of other cultures. Here, Bly uses his versions of the Islamic ghazal form—primarily represented by versions of Rumi and Hafez. Bly has stated that he loves the independence of the separate stanzas, a motif that correlates nicely with his own leaping imagery. The sense of boundlessness, however, that one derives from such juxtaposition is contained within a broader spiritual ground. This seems an apt form for someone whose signature mode displaces the binary between spiritual and material values. In the eponymous poem "The Night Abraham Called to the Stars," for example:

the ordinary realm expands into the extraordinary; the clarity of that which is materially close is apparently the precedent for the vision that goes beyond that which is sensory, the continuum made possible by efforts of care and attentiveness. Here is the same poet who could say in his second book that he has wandered in a face for hours ("Looking into a Face," *Light*), and the quiet regard that penetrates the psyche as a mode enables a different kind of vision.

Further Reading. *Selected Primary Sources:* Bly, Robert, *Eating the Honey of Words: New and Selected Poems* (New York: Harper, 1999); ———, *The Insanity of Empire: A Book of Poems Against the Iraq War* (St. Paul, MN: Ally, 2004); ———, *Iron John: A Book About Men* (Reading, MA: Addison-Wesley, 1990); ———, *Selected Poems* (New York: Harper, 1986); ———, *What Have I Ever Lost by Dying? Collected Prose Poems* (New York: Harper, 1992). *Selected Secondary Sources:* Davis, William Virgil, *Critical Essays on Robert Bly* (New York: G.K. Hall, 1992); ———, ed., *Understanding Robert Bly* (Columbia: University of South Carolina Press, 1988); Harris, Victoria Frenkel, *The Incorporative Consciousness of Robert Bly* (Carbondale: Southern Illinois University Press, 1992); Jones, Richard, and Kate Daniels, eds., *Of Solitude and Silence: Writings on Robert Bly* (Boston: Beacon, 1981); Nelson, Howard, *Robert Bly: An Introduction to the Poetry* (New York: Columbia University Press, 1984); Peseroff, Joyce, ed., *Robert Bly: When Sleepers Awake* (Ann Arbor: University of Michigan Press, 1984); Sugg, Richard P., *Robert Bly* (Boston: G.K. Hall, 1986).

Victoria Frenkel Harris

BODMAN, MANOAH (1765–1850)

Best known for the eight-part poem *Oration on Death* (1817), Manoah Bodman occupies a unique if somewhat obscure place in American poetry. *Oration*, which contains both prose and poetry, represents Bodman's original perceptions about the afterlife. As with many American poets of his era, Bodman's obvious influence by earlier English neoclassicism—in this case, the hymns of Isaac Watts, whose metrical alteration between three and two beats was taken up by Bodman—has deceived critics into underestimating the differences in philosophy and attitude among the poets concerned. Bodman's hallucinations and night visions inhabit a psychological continuum somewhere between **Edgar Allan Poe** on the one hand and **Jones Very** on the other. Although Bodman writes in conventional meter, the views in his poetry are far from orthodox.

Manoah Bodman was born January 28, 1765, in Sunderland, Massachusetts. The name "Manoah" comes from Samson's father in the biblical book of Judges; it is also prominent, under slightly different spelling, in Milton's *Samson Agonistes*. Bodman was also known by the name of a more familiar biblical character, Noah; this was probably a contraction of his real first name. Bodman grew up during the tumultuous years leading up to the American Revolution and the war itself, but western Massachusetts was seldom directly affected by the fighting. At the age of fourteen, the Bodmans moved to Williamsburg, in what are now called the Hidden Hills of western Massachusetts. Two of Bodman's uncles accumulated considerable power in the town, and Bodman thus had the prestige of being the town eccentric without much of a concomitant stigma. An eccentric he certainly was: Exhibiting a socially acceptable zeal following "the Second great Awakening" of Calvinist revival in the late 1770s and early 1780s, after his younger brother's death in 1784 Bodman began to experience disturbing hallucinations. This vascillation between the sanctioned and the unheard-of in Congregationalist doctrine and preferred conduct persisted throughout Bodman's life. Long thought unmarriageable, at the age of thirty-three Bodman married Theodosia Green. She died in 1799 after only a year of marriage. Though Bodman's depression was made even more acute by this tragedy, all of his published work was issued after that date, including his major poem, *Oration on Death*, and three pamphlets, *Oration on Birth of Our Savior* (1826), *Washington's Birthday, an Oration* (1814)—interesting as an excursus on national themes during the great New England discontent with the War of 1812—and *Oration Delivered at Williamsburg*, July 4, 1803. Bodman practiced law briefly, but Satanic apparitions that both disturbed his soul and moved him to write continued to preoccupy him.

In *Oration On Death*, while using metaphors of light and of participation similar to Platonic mystical poetics, Bodman is quite anti-Platonic in insisting on resurrected bodies and heavenly material in general, retaining a difference in heaven not just assimilated to a monadic spirit. With a kind of mystical Aristotelianism inflected by the American **sublime**, Bodman makes the major argument of "Oration of Death" that, just as God, in the biblical creation account, created many different creatures with different functions, he will retain this created difference in the afterlife. Surely, argues Bodman, spirits cannot be denied the blessings of variety that God gives to lower creatures. There will be no "dull conformity" in heaven. Heaven will not be a soporific utopia where nothing ever happens. Spirits will "different see" and this difference will be a blessing. Bodman's spirituality does not need standardization as a kind of insurance. It is so confident, so fervid, so unable to be dissuaded from the intensity of its visions that it can accommodate plurality. This confidence, in some ways foreshadowing **Emerson** (particularly in Bodman's sense both of his own greatness and his own smallness), partakes generally of Romanticism's celebration of idiosyncrasies, and it is utterly different from a death-obsessed English contemporary of Bodman, Thomas Lovell Beddoes. Bodman was terrified by death but not haunted by it. He was obsessed with it, but he did not make a fetish out of death.

Bodman had to balance his perceived eccentricities with the normative expectations of a small New England town, which he never left. This entailed not only a vigilance with respect to possible unorthodoxy—Bodman, for instance, asserted that his visions had *not* been supernatural, that he had *not* been specially visited by God or by angels, but by natural, if spiritual, visionary inducements—but also assurances about the public utility of what could be seen as morbid fantasies best kept private. This self-censorship inhibited the surface of Bodman's work, but released its depths.

An Oration On Death was Bodman's last major work, though he lived thirty-three more years, as far as the midpoint of the nineteenth century. He spoke of, though apparently never attempted, a work that would prove the divinity of Jesus on the basis of the Old Testament alone, exemplifying an obsession with the Hebrew scriptures characteristic of American Protestantism in general but reaching an apogee in such American literary works as **John Pierpont**'s "Airs of Palestine" and the prophetic visions of the founder of Mormonism, Joseph Smith.

There are many other nineteenth-century poets equally obscure and almost as talented, but Bodman was fortunate to have a latter-day champion in the contemporary poet Lewis Putnam Turco, who has written about Bodman and edited a selection of his poems. With a good sense of Bodman's place in both the spiritual and formal traditions of American poetry, Turco has brought Bodman back into the literary conversation.

Further Reading. *Selected Secondary Sources:* Foster, Edward Halsey, "Manoah Bodman," in *Companion to*

Encyclopedia of American Poetry: The Nineteenth Century, ed. Eric Haralson (Chicago: Fitzroy Dearborn, 1998); Turco, Lewis, *The Life and Poetry of Manoah Bodman* (Washington, DC: University Press of America, 1999); ———, *Visions and Revisions of American Poetry* (Fayetteville: University of Arkansas Press, 1986).

Nicholas Birns

BOGAN, LOUISE (1897–1970)

Louise Bogan's poetry is distinguished by its strict and formal elegance and its singular adherence to the English lyric tradition during a period of avant-garde experimentation and that tradition's degeneration. Bogan exacted the same austerity from her poetic oeuvre as from her individual lyrics, including only 105 poems in her final book of collected poetry, *The Blue Estuaries, Poems 1923–1968*. As the poetry reviewer for the *New Yorker* for thirty-eight years, Bogan is as well known for her criticism as for her slim and perfected poetic oeuvre. Although she always championed the historical and contemporary development of female poets, Bogan questioned the idea of women's poetry as a separate cultural field of study with its own canon and standards of evaluation. Her reputation is secured by the poets she influenced, including **Theodore Roethke**, **May Sarton**, **William Meredith**, and **Sylvia Plath**. She benefited from close and enduring friendships with Rolfe Humphries, Edmund Wilson, John Hall Wheelock, and William Maxwell. As a poetry critic, she was in many ways responsible for the shaping of twentieth-century public taste in poetry. Her technical virtuosity and formal complexity won her deserved respect as a poet, yet also consigned her reputation to that of inheritor rather than innovator, although she was consistently both, as the poems demonstrate throughout her career.

Louise Bogan was born in Livermore Falls, Maine, on August 11, 1897 into an Irish Catholic family, descendants of a Portland sea captain, as she liked to make known. The daughter of a New England mill-town foreman, Bogan was raised in a lower-middle-class household where she learned firsthand the prejudices and exclusions of class. The habits of privacy upon which Bogan later insisted were formed early on through her experience of the insidious gossip common to small town life. Her parents' marriage was an unhappy one, characterized by frequent relocation, constant quarrels, and her mother's intermittent affairs and absences from the home. The violence and betrayals of Bogan's early childhood became the core of experience to which she would return repeatedly in her work. One of the central figures of this experience is her mother, a proud and, in Bogan's words, arrogant woman whom Bogan both resisted and emulated.

After her family's move to Boston in 1909, Bogan was educated at the Girls' Latin School, where she received excellent training in English composition, Latin, Greek and French. In 1915 she attended Boston University for one year before marrying a soldier, Curt Alexander, whom she followed, four months pregnant, to the Panama Canal Zone the next year. Bogan returned to Boston after the birth of her only child, Mathilde (Maidie) Alexander, and separated from her husband in 1919. Her second and final marriage in 1925 to the poet Raymond Holden lasted through Bogan's two emotional breakdowns and hospitalizations in the 1930s until their divorce in 1937, after which Bogan never remarried. She made her home in New York City where she spent the majority of her adult life, with brief interludes in New England, and began her career as a poet with the publication of five poems in *Poetry* magazine in 1921. Bogan published six books of poetry: *Body of This Death* (1923), *Dark Summer* (1929), *The Sleeping Fury* (1937), *Poems and New Poems* (1941), *Collected Poems 1923–1953* (1954), and *The Blue Estuaries: Poems 1923–1968* (1968). From 1931 to 1969 she wrote poetry reviews for the *New Yorker*, publishing two books of selected reviews and one book of criticism, *Achievement in American Poetry, 1900–1950* (1951). The recipient of numerous prizes including two Guggenheim Fellowships, the Bollingen Prize, and awards from the Academy of American Poets and the National Endowment for the Arts, Bogan also served as a fellow in American letters at the Library of Congress in 1944 and as the Chair of Poetry at the library from 1945 to 1946. After 1950 Bogan began to spend time lecturing at universities as a visiting professor and translating German and French literature. During her lifetime she published translations of works by Johann Wolfgang von Goethe, Ernst Jünger, and Jules Renard, and produced with William Jay Smith an anthology of children's poetry, *The Golden Journey: Poems for Young People* (1965). She died in 1970 in her apartment in Washington Heights, a year after her retirement from the *New Yorker*.

Influenced by the French symbolists, in particular Stéphane Mallarmé and Paul Valéry, as well as the English metaphysical poets (to whom she is often compared), Bogan was a fierce adherent to traditional lyric form and to the symbol in her writing. She considered form not a remnant of convention against which to rebel or a restriction of freedom, but rather as the basis for experimentation, the principle of rhythm being common to not only artistic creations but also the physiological functions of our bodies. Lyric intensity must be derived from real emotion, Bogan believed, but needed prosody to discipline experience into art. She had no tolerance for what she saw as the surrealists' primitive use of dream images; though the "translucent depths beneath fear," the subconscious, played a large part in her poetry, her poems appear as if carved into crystalline forms, striking a contrast between irrational and ambiguous symbols and strictly rational forms. She described the sustained treatment of symbols from the subconscious in poetry as a journey not to be undertaken lightly, a developmental and artistic journey that resulted in profound changes in comprehension of one's psyche and evolution in one's art.

In Bogan's early poetry the solitary self, be it man or woman, is always engaged in a struggle, yet the voice of the poems comes from a place beyond struggle, a separate peace found in distance from the object of emotional crisis. "Come let us counsel some cold stranger / How we sought safety, but loved danger," sings the speaker of the poem "Last Hill in a Vista" from Bogan's first book of poetry, *Body of This Death*, published in 1923. Solace comes from separation, turning away from passion to learning how "trees make a long shadow / And a light sound." At times, the consolations seem as fleeting as the pleasures of the rhymes that produce them. Danger is often viewed as the excesses of emotion, and safety a narrow selvage from emotion into rhetorical structures like irony or satire. The natural world is the setting of retreat from the fleeting impermanence and pain of human relations, but in the end it too serves as the ultimate reminder of transience. The title, *Body of This Death*, refers to St. Paul's Epistle to the Romans, in which "the body of this death" stands for the weight of sin, the struggle between the mind and the flesh. In the poem "The Alchemist," the quest for a "passion wholly of the mind" is denied through an alchemical process of "utter fire." In a brilliant choice of adjective, Bogan conveys the disappointment of the quest with the resultant "unmysterious flesh," found to be "still / Passionate beyond the will." Some feminist critics point to the male protagonist of the book's opening poem, "A Tale," as indicative of Bogan's reluctance to champion the female voice, to feature a woman as initiator of a quest. Yet Bogan is nothing if not playful with gender distinctions in the book, freely using a male voice in the poems "The Frightened Man" and "Juan's Song" to satirize love from a male point of view. She proves herself early on as an accomplished writer of satiric verse, at times bitter, as in "My Voice Not Being Proud," and at times witty, as in "Chanson Un Peu Naïve."

The single symbols in the poems of *Body of This Death*, such as the concluding images of willow leaves in "Betrothal" and shadows of trees in "Knowledge," or the initiatory crows in "The Crows" and the last hills in "Last Hill in a Vista" are developed into entire conceits in Bogan's second book, *Dark Summer* (1929). Landscape is no longer merely a setting in which one finds certain objective correlatives; instead the landscape is entirely suffused with emotion. As surely as the landscapes are unique to the emotion expressed in each poem, so are the varied cadences. "The Drum" is composed of five quatrains of insistent iambic dimeter, whereas the lilting meter of "Come, Break with Time" is an exhortation that shifts into a dialogue both on the thematic level (between two speakers) and the prosodic level (between dactyls and anapests). Bogan broadens her formal repertoire in *Dark Summer* and experiments with a more developed dialogue poem between two voices in "Summer Wish." In the poem "Didactic Piece" she tries her hand at longer lines and greater stanza forms, free of the local setting and hard condensation of some of her shorter lyrics, thereby allowing herself the range necessary for greater abstraction, the lists of like objects, expostulations, and parallel syntax.

In 1930 Bogan received *Poetry* magazine's John Reed Memorial Prize, and she wrote to the editor of *Poetry*, **Harriet Monroe**, that the prize touched her deeply and provided her with a renewed belief in her work. Attuned throughout her life to the aspirations, infighting, and rumors generated by any specialized or delimited society, Bogan had feared integration into the literary scene and had privately renounced poetry after several brief and vicious encounters. Though the prize caused Bogan to take heart once again in her artistic capabilities, she turned to writing mostly short stories during the next several years, in addition to poetry. The majority of Bogan's short stories appeared in the *New Yorker* during the years from 1931 to 1935. The stories are psychological studies in human behavior, intention, and emotion, using an event or incident, in place of the symbols in her poetry, to reveal aspects of the human psyche. Ultimately Bogan believed the story form to be deficient in the exactitude and formal precision that only poetry could produce. In a letter to Ruth Benedict in 1925, she protested that "prose is so terribly unsatisfactory. Everything in it could be said in any number of ways. While a poem is itself, inevitably, unerringly" (*What the Woman Lived*). Her short story writing was short-lived. Bogan's lasting prose contributions were not her stories, but her reviews. **W.H. Auden** called Bogan the best poetry critic in America. Her training in criticism began under Edmund Wilson's instruction. In addition to reviews of individual American and British poets and their volumes of poetry, she wrote about the condition of American verse at mid-century, about experimentalism in poetry, about folk art, French and German literature, and women. Her essay "The Pleasures of Formal Poetry" was a timely defense of form defined as rhyme and rhythmic principle. In the essay she traces poetry's aural roots in speech and song, and warns against poetry becoming "encased—one might almost say embalmed—in print" (*A Poet's Alphabet*). She bemoans the loss of emotion and the **sublime** in poetry, topics that terrify young poets, she finds, because of the impossibility of approach without the controlling reins of form.

Bogan's third book, *The Sleeping Fury*, was published in 1937, eight years after *Dark Summer*. In the interim,

Bogan had suffered from emotional illness for which she was hospitalized in 1931; had spent a summer in Europe on a Guggenheim fellowship (1933), which failed to produce any poems; had separated from her second husband, Raymond Holden; and was again hospitalized for depression in 1934. By 1935 she was emerging from this dark period, and her poems shift in kind toward greater philosophic distance. In a letter to her friend, the critic Morton D. Zabel, Bogan described the final arrangement of her book, *The Sleeping Fury*, in characteristically self-deprecating and witty terms, as a four-part movement from "Bogan in cothurnus" to "Bogan in flat heels." The first section of the book contains poems composed from 1930 to 1933. These are poems written from Bogan's experiences of despair and neurosis and her struggle with alcoholism during this period. The poem "Hypocrite Swift" was a poem of recovery, begun as an exercise and ending as a technically accomplished variation of the Sapphic stanza that explores through the character of Swift the dangers of the renunciation and denial of love, whose resulting sterility can only be overcome by wit in words, by choosing to "live by stealth." The title poem of the volume, "The Sleeping Fury," recalls Bogan's earlier poem "Medusa," where the image of an avenging mythological female figure is also central. In the poem "Medusa," the speaker is a victim turned into "a shadow / Under the great balanced day" The "dead scene" is yet visible, but incapable of interrogation or resolution. In "The Sleeping Fury" Bogan projects herself into the scene again, no longer as a victim, but as a witness: "You are here now, / . . . Alone and asleep, and I at last look long upon you." The poem ends on a note of calm that becomes the tenor for the remainder of the volume. Tones of sensuality and mysticism also enter into the later poems. The last poem of the book, "Song for a Lyre," is perhaps Bogan's singular apostrophe to love that is devoid of resistance, of the notes of disappointment and cynicism toward love that her earlier poems obsessively sounded. Though set in autumn, the poem invokes love as a constant without seasons: "O love, though once I lay / Far from its sound, to weep, . . . Night to your voice belongs."

The Sleeping Fury was Bogan's last book of new poetry. She continued to write poetry in the last three decades of her life, but only a fraction of the output of her earlier years. Her first collected volume, *Poems and New Poems*, published in 1941, contains sixteen new poems (two of which were translations), including some of her most important works, such as "Animal, Vegetable and Mineral," "The Dream," "Come, Sleep . . ." and "The Daemon." Auden wrote to Bogan that though he abhorred making comparisons between living poets, he found the new poems of her collection to be the finest English lyrics of their kind presently being written. **Stanley Kunitz**, in reviewing *Poems and New Poems*, pronounced

that at last Bogan's imaginative world, "the sunk land of dust and flame" to which she had only eluded previously in fragmentary glimpses, was laid bare in all of its beauty and terror. Kunitz considered "The Dream" one of Bogan's best poems, equal in intensity of image to "Medusa" and "The Sleeping Fury."

Bogan's last two volumes, *Collected Poems 1923–1953* and *The Blue Estuaries: Poems 1923–1968*, contain only three and ten new poems, respectively. Among the best of her work here is the lyrical series "After the Persian I–V" and the poems "Song for the Last Act" and "Night." They seem more poems of old age than of the middle age Bogan was at the time of their composition. They are poems of peace achieved after long battle, poems which contain images of translucency, fluidity, and release. Bogan wrote once that she imagined her reader of the "After the Persian" series carrying the poems through a desert. The speaker of "After the Persian V," cries out at the end: "There was so much to love, I could not love it all;/ I could not love it enough." These are uncommon lines for a Bogan poem and all the more insistent for it.

Bogan was never a political poet. She had great distaste for the posturing of the 1930s and the allegiances and betrayals devised in the name of politics. For some critics, Bogan's reticence, both personal and poetic, is seen as self-marginalization, and her thematic and formal discipline is regarded as repression. Furthermore, her adherence to modern prosody has earned her the epithets of both victim and perpetrator of the patriarchal tradition. The fate of Bogan's reputation rests not in the classroom and scholarly monographs, but in poetic circles of readers and writers, in their continued esteem for the quality of her work, and their ability to appreciate the pleasures of formal excellence and emotional depth.

Further Reading. ***Selected Primary Sources:*** Bogan, Louise, *The Blue Estuaries, Poems 1923–1968* (New York: Noonday Press, 1995); ———, *A Poet's Alphabet: Reflections on the Literary Art and Vocation*, ed. Robert Phelps and Ruth Limmer (New York: McGraw-Hill, 1970); ———, *What the Woman Lived: Selected Letters of Louise Bogan 1920–1970*, ed. Ruth Limmer (New York: Harcourt Brace Jovanovich, 1973). ***Selected Secondary Sources:*** Bowles, Gloria, *Louise Bogan's Aesthetic of Limitation* (Bloomington: Indiana University Press, 1987); Frank, Elizabeth, *Louise Bogan: A Portrait* (New York: Alfred A. Knopf, 1985); Ridgeway, Jaqueline, *Louise Bogan* (Boston: Twayne, 1984); Upton, Lee, *Obsession and Release: Rereading the Poetry of Louise Bogan* (Lewisburg, PA: Bucknell University Press, 1996).

Susan Barba

BÖK, CHRISTIAN (1966–)

Christian Bök has emerged as one of Canada's most important experimental poets in recent years. His published books so far include *Crystallography* and *Eunoia*, the latter earning him the Griffin Prize for Poetic Excellence in 2002. Bök is also renowned for his virtuoso performances of **sound poetry** (particularly Kurt Schwitters's *Ursonate*) and his conceptual art, which includes a series of poems constructed of twenty-seven Rubik's cubes and a book made entirely out of Legos. Bök insists that poetry must create "unholy hybrids," synthetic and contradictory "jerry rigging contraption[s] that fuse old parts with new ideas." His poetic practice is indebted to a complex nexus of avant-garde literary strategies, including the mannerist techniques of the Oulipo, the pataphysical theories of Alfred Jarry, and the non-referential writings of the **Language poets**. His work signals a rejection of post-confessional lyricism and the hegemony of **free verse** in favor of an emphasis on process and formal constraint. In this regard, his work is best understood within the context of such contemporaries as **Kenneth Goldsmith** and Darren Wershler-Henry, poets who challenge the boundaries of literary form and who reflexively interrogate the process of poetic composition.

Christian Bök was born on August 10, 1966, in Etobicoke, Ontario, Canada. He grew up in a working-class family: His mother, Sandra Evoy, was a bookkeeper at a car dealership and his father, George Book, made his living as a plumber. The poet began to write seriously during his undergraduate career at Carleton University in Ottawa, but it was not until he encountered **Steve McCaffery**'s *The Black Debt* that he abandoned early attempts at conventional lyric poetry for the radically experimental verse of his soon-to-be mentor. Bök returned to Toronto in the early 1990s to take a Ph.D. at York University, where McCaffery and other influential **Canadian poets** like **Christopher Dewdney** lived and taught. He was also fortunate enough at this time to establish a mutually supportive friendship with another aspiring poet, Darren Wershler-Henry, who Bök affectionately referred to as "the more user-friendly version" of himself. Both writers, along with Kenneth Goldsmith and Brian Kim Stefans, belong to an international collective of experimental poets known as the "Ubu Group"; originally a reference to Alfred Jarry's play (*Ubu Roi*), the name derives from Goldsmith's website, www.ubu.com, where much of their work is collected. Since the publication of *Eunoia*, Bök has received unprecedented acclaim, but his work has also generated controversy among members of the mainstream literary community because of his anti-Romantic view of poetry.

Bök's inaugural book of poems, *Crystallography*, investigates the normally antagonistic relationship between the discourses of poetry and science. *Crystallography*, according to Bök, is a "pataphysical encyclopedia that misreads the language of poetics through the conceits of geology." If a crystal is a mineral "jigsaw puzzle" that

"assembles itself out of its own constituent / disarray," then a "word is a bit of crystal in formation." The text as a whole is better understood as a constellation of intersecting elements (rather than as a poetic sequence), charting and transposing literary coordinates onto scientific ones. The poems in this collection possess a remarkable verbal economy and formal unity, announcing its goal to achieve "an aesthetic of structural perfection" that mirrors the intricate patterns found in the crystalline structures of the natural world. Bök responds to a long tradition of nature poetry, but the comfortable boundaries between nature and culture are breached. Indeed, those without "mineralogical experience" might easily mistake the symmetry of a crystal as the "artificial product of a precision technology." In many ways, the variety of formal experiments found in *Crystallography* prepared the author for his next book, a more sustained and concentrated use of formal constraint.

Eunoia's immediate critical acclaim quickly made it the best-selling book of experimental poetry in Canadian history. Its title, *Eunoia*, is the shortest word in the English language that contains all five vowels; it literally means "beautiful thinking." Indebted to the procedural methods of the French Oulipo group (Ouvroir de Littérature Potentielle), *Eunoia* is a univocal lipogram, which means that the text omits all but one vowel in each of the book's five chapters. Here are two examples from Chapter A and I respectively: "Awkward grammar appalls a craftsman" and "Writing is inhibiting. Sighing, I sit, scribbling in ink this pidgin script." Bök explained in an interview with *Brick Magazine* (Spring 2002) that he proceeded by reading through the dictionary five times to extract all the univocal words; he then arranged the words according to parts of speech, and then into topical categories, in order to determine "what stories the vowels could tell." He soon learned, however, that he was able to employ a series of subsidiary rules. Each chapter is divided into paragraphs that use the same number of lines, all chapters must self-reflexively allude to the "act of writing," describe a "culinary banquet," a "prurient debauch," a "pastoral tableau," and a "nautical voyage." Furthermore, the text must exhaust the English lexicon, using at least 98 percent of all available words. The result is an intensely euphonic poem that exploits internal rhyme and syntactical parallelism wherever possible. Consider an example: "I print lists, filing things (kin with kin, ilk with ilk) inscribing this distinct sign. . . . I find it whilst skindiving in Fiji. I find it whilst picnicking in Linz." Not only does this passage conform to its initial univocal constraint, it also observes precise syntactical symmetry. Notice that each of the two sentences in the latter part of the passage have the same relationship between predicate and object, both have seven words, and both have an equal number of letters in each of the verbs and nouns. The text makes a "Sisyphean spectacle" of its own poetic process, yet it is important to understand that the formal constraint for Bök is no mere act of verbal athleticism. Rather, the constraint demonstrates that despite the most extreme and hostile restrictions placed upon language, it is nonetheless resilient and flexible enough to produce a comprehensible—even sublime—narrative.

In addition to his two published books, sound poetry performances, and conceptual artworks, Bök has created two artificial languages for science fiction television shows: Gene Roddenberry's *Earth: Final Conflict* and Peter Benchley's *Amazon*. This is perhaps more relevant to his multivalent poetic practice than it would first seem, demonstrating the poet's obsessive attention to the structures of language. At present Bök is working on a long sound poem titled *The Cyborg Opera.*

Further Reading. ***Selected Primary Sources:*** Bök, Christian, *Crystallography* (Toronto: Coach House, 1994); ———, "Bibliomechanics," in *Poetry Plastique* (New York: Marianne Boesky, 2001); ———, *Eunoia* (Toronto: Coach House, 2001). ***Selected Secondary Sources:*** Perloff, Marjorie, "The Oulipo Factor: The Procedural Poetics of Christian Bök and Caroline Bergvall" (*Jacket* 23 [August 2003], http://www.jacketmagazine.com/23/perlof-oulip.html); Jaeger, Peter, "Of Crystallography" (*Open Letter* 10.1 [Winter 1998]: 77–79).

Stephen Voyce

BOKER, GEORGE HENRY (1823–1890)

During the period that would come to be known as the American Renaissance, George Henry Boker was one of the least "American" of American poets. Eschewing the literary nationalistic rhetoric of his period, Boker's poetry and plays evince a recurrent interest in, and fascination with, early modern European literary traditions. Best known as the playwright of *Francesca da Rimini* (1853), Boker was perpetually frustrated in his attempts to secure fame as a poet; in the words of his poem "The Lesson of Life," Boker too often felt the "nipping blast / Of cold neglect." Devoted to established poetic forms and conventions, Boker's verse addressed the always-complex relationships between the physical and the metaphysical, the part and the whole, the individual and the collective. Boker's most significant contribution to American poetry came posthumously with the 1929 publication of *Sonnets: A Sequence of Profane Love.* This collection, which includes 313 of the nearly 400 sonnets Boker wrote during his lifetime, offers a sustained and occasionally startling meditation on the interpenetrations of physical and spiritual love.

George Henry Boker was born October 6, 1823, to a wealthy banking family in Philadelphia, Pennsylvania.

Boker graduated from Princeton in 1842, where he trained as a lawyer. In 1844 Boker married Julia Riggs, with whom he had one child, George, who lived to adulthood. In addition to his work as poet and playwright, Boker served as Minister to Turkey (1871–1875) and Envoy Extraordinary and Minister Plenipotentiary to Russia (1875–1878). Boker returned to Philadelphia in 1879, where he lived until his death in 1890.

Much of Boker's early verse appeared in periodicals such as *Grahams's, Lippincott's,* and *Sartain's,* and was first collected in 1848's *The Lesson of Life and Other Poems.* This otherwise unremarkable volume betrayed Boker's Anglophilia and suffered from trite diction and forced rhymes. That said, the volume's lengthy title poem does demonstrate a strong command of blank verse, and its five sonnets show an early mastery of the Italian form. *The Podesta's Daughter and Other Poems* followed in 1852 to little fanfare. In an attempt to enliven his fledgling career as a poet, the thirty-three-year-old Boker published his collected words, *Poems and Plays,* in 1856. This diverse collection included his most popular plays (e.g., *Anne Boleyn* [1849], *Francesca da Rimini*) alongside his lesser-known poems. Following the tepid critical response to *Plays and Poems,* Boker took a respite from writing.

However, the American Civil War inspired Boker and gave rise to some of his best and most popular verse. Between 1861 and 1865, he worked ceaselessly for the Union cause, helping to form the Union League of Philadelphia, campaigning for President Lincoln's reelection, and publishing a series of timely poems and satires. During the war years, Boker read widely and wrote quickly, often rushing his poems to print in newspapers and broadsides, thus exploiting a vibrant Union print culture. The best known of these poems were the satires "Tardy George" (1862) and "The Queen Must Dance" (1862), which—despite Boker's chummy relationship with the Lincoln administration—parodied General George McClellan and First Lady Mary Todd Lincoln, respectively. Several of Boker's occasional poems appeared in 1864's *Poems of the War,* a volume that included ballads (e.g., "The Black Regiment"), songs (e.g., "Hooker's Across"), a handful of sonnets, one superb elegy ("Dirge of a Soldier"), and two odes. Of these, "Ode to America" is among his most celebrated of poems, having been described as one of the best rhapsodic poems in American literature. The ode programmatically lays out Boker's Civil War–era poetic project: "No more of girls and wine, / No more of pastoral joys . . . My country, let me turn to thee." Yet, even as he wrote occasional verse about a specifically American conflict, these sentimental and jingoistic poems continued to look to, and gesture toward, European literary traditions. Nonetheless, Boker's poems received the praise of many eminent Northerners—among these

Oliver Wendell Holmes—and sold better than any other volume of Boker's verse. (Indeed, *Poems of the War* outsold both **Herman Melville**'s *Battle-Pieces, and Aspects of the War* [1866] and **Walt Whitman**'s *Drum-Taps* [1865].) Enjoyingwide public acceptance of his poetry for the first time, Boker emerged alongside Holmes, **James Russell Lowell**, and **John Greenleaf Whittier** as one of the Civil War's most widely read poets.

Such wartime poetic popularity was, however, short-lived. Boker's uneven and uninspired collection *Königsmark; the Legend of the Hounds; and Other Poems* was published in 1869. Essentially a hodgepodge of errant verse, the collection's most noteworthy poem is "Ad Criticum," in which Boker defends his Anglophilic interests and spells out his resistance to American literary nationalism. Bitterly disappointed by muted critical and popular response to his poetry, he would publish only one other collection of verse during his lifetime: *The Book of the Dead* (1882), a collection of caustic poems about the legal battles that attended his father's 1858 death.

Were it not for biographer Sculley Bradley, George Henry Boker's career as a poet would have remained an obscure one. In the process of researching his biography of Boker, Bradley discovered a manuscript collection of 313 sonnets, which the biographer subsequently published as *Sonnets: A Sequence of Profane Love*. Written between 1858 and 1887 and circulated in a limited way to his mistress and a coterie of intimate friends, all but two of the sonnets were unpublished. Throughout, Boker's sonnets insist on the indissoluble and interdependent relationship between the spiritual and the physical. As one sonnet opines, "The fervid kiss, the interlocked caress— / Is heavenly pure to love's most dainty sense" ("CCLXIII"). Vaguely reminiscent of John Donne's holy sonnets, these frank and sensual poems are suffused with an awareness of the metaphysical implications of human companionship and contact. Likewise, the sonnets' emphasis on corporeality and fluidity—"the firery current in my veins / With longings wild, mixed thrills of joys and pains" ("LXXII")—would be familiar to any reader of Boker's contemporary Walt Whitman. Although not a particularly innovative sonneteer—he made fairly traditional use of the Italian sonnet form—Boker can be praised for his ability to achieve climax at the end of the octave. Finally, though, *Sonnets* proves uneven as a sequence, the broad scope of experience it records is extraordinary. As Bradley's important scholarship suggests, *Sonnets: A Sequence of Profane Love* is the only known American sonnet sequence of the nineteenth century. Marking perhaps the first attempt to translate the Elizabethan sonnet sequence tradition to an American idiom, *Sonnets* anticipates later "sequences" by **John Berryman**, Mark Jarman, **Edna St. Vincent Millay**, **Elinor Wylie**, and others. Thus, with the assistance of a posthumous publication, George Henry Boker emerged as one of the most prolific and important of early American sonneteers, and he gained in death the literary fame he so earnestly desired in life.

Further Reading.   ***Selected Primary Sources:*** Boker, George Henry, *The Book of the Dead* (Philadelphia: J.B. Lippincott, 1882); ———, *Königsmark; the Legend of the Hounds; and Other Poems* (Philadelphia: J.B. Lippincott, 1869); ———, *The Lesson of Life and Other Poems* (Philadelphia, G.S. Appleton, 1848); ———, *Plays and Poems* (Boston: Ticknor and Fields, 1856); ———, *Poems of the War* (Boston: Ticknor and Fields, 1864); ———, *Sonnets; a Sequence on Profane Love*, Sculley Bradley, ed. (Philadelphia: University of Pennsylvania Press, 1929). ***Selected Secondary Sources:*** Bradley, Sculley, *George Henry Boker, Poet and Patriot* (Philadelphia: University of Pennsylvania Press, 1927); Evans, Oliver H., *George Henry Boker* (Boston: Twayne, 1984).

Coleman Hutchison

BOLAND, EAVAN (1944–)

Widely considered the leading Irish female poet, Eavan Boland's stature was enhanced with the publication of her memoir, *Object Lessons: The Life of the Woman and the Poet in Our Time* (1995). Boland has argued that the still dominant Irish nationalist historical narrative has largely ignored the personal lives of women, children, and even men by privileging the story of an emergent nation above all else. Her most recent work that rejects the mimicry inherent in a largely invented nationalism succeeds her earlier poetry that explored the tangled relations among women's personal lives and Irish history.

Boland was born the daughter of the Irish diplomat F.H. Boland on September 24, 1944, in Dublin. She was educated in London and New York and later did university work at Trinity College, Dublin. Married to the novelist Kevin Casey, she has two daughters and continues to split time between the Dublin suburb of Dundrum and Stanford, California, where she is a professor of creative writing. Her suburban, liminal locale has enabled her to escape the fierce allegiance to Dublin held by earlier Irish writers such as Sean O'Casey and to avoid the sometimes idealized portrayals of the rural landscape by other Irish authors such as Yeats.

After Boland moved to London from Dublin at the age of five, she was isolated and adrift in a foreign land. Throughout her poetry, she registers her ambiguity as latter day Anglo-Irish, born and brought up in England, America, and Ireland. Boland's poems register her geographic and national ambiguity through the use of rhetorical questions—a construction often employed by William Butler Yeats. Boland has identified strongly with Yeats's cultural hybridity and even cowrote a critical study of Yeats with Micheal Mac Liammoir in 1971.

Boland's poetry, almost exclusively written in free verse, often focuses upon concrete objects that lead to more expansive musings. A signature Boland poetic device is her habit of inserting herself as first person into poems that began in third person in an effort to more closely identify with her subject, as she does in poems such as "Lava Cameo," from her 1995 volume, *In a Time of Violence.* This poem focuses her reflections on history through the filter of distance. "Lava Cameo" typifies Boland's poetry: It represents both her search for her feminine, Irish past and her attempts to insert herself into that past poetically.

After moving to New York City at the age of eleven, Boland met the Irish writer Padraic Colum and felt more connected to the poetry and culture of Ireland. The final phase of her exile came with her return to Ireland at fourteen. Although she was a native, her moves to London and New York had conspired to erase her sense of place and of the past. Unable to remember her childhood in Ireland, Boland began to imagine events from her past there and embellish family stories about relatives such as her grandmother, who she recalls in "Lava Cameo." Hers was a particularly vexed form of exile, further complicated by a move to Dundrum, a Dublin suburb, after she married.

Her first volume of poetry, *New Territory* (1967), contains mostly poems written in college dealing with Irish history and myth. Boland's "Yeats in Time of Civil War" came out in this volume and clearly plays on Yeats's title for his poetic sequence "Meditations in Time of Civil War." Whereas she had earlier imagined an Irish childhood for herself as an Irish exile, now her imagination was fired by that of the elder Yeats.

Boland's second volume, *The War Horse* (1975), includes her first political work (the title poem) and other poems on Irish history and life in suburbia. Written in the early 1970s, during a time of widespread violence in Northern Ireland, the volume's title poem simultaneously registers current atrocities and references past ones through its disturbing images called up by a wandering horse "stumbl[ing] on like a rumour of war." Increasingly, Boland has come to explore her own place as a suburban Irish woman, and that of women generally, and has infused these explorations into political poetry. Her realization upon writing "The War Horse," then, is a crucial act of recovering herself and women from the position of objects and transforming them into subjects, or independent beings. This discovery and subsequent call to action form the thesis of *Object Lessons.*

In her angry third volume, *In Her Own Image* (1980), and in her more reserved, domestic volume, *Night Feed* (1982), Boland explores the varying ways in which women experience their bodies, examining anorexia, breast cancer and mastectomies, and motherhood. *The Journey and Other Poems* appeared in 1986 and was the Poetry Book Society Choice in 1987. *Outside History* (1990) focuses upon a variety of women, none more representative of her ongoing concerns with the intersection of women and nationhood than "The Achill Woman," the first poem in the sequence "Outside History." The poem features a woman living on Achill Island, off the western coast of Ireland, bringing water to Boland in the cottage where she is vacationing. She is of a piece with the natural world and her rural reticence contrasts markedly with the talkative, urban Boland. At the time, the meeting makes little impression on Boland and she returns inside and reads the book of English Court poets she brought with her. The old woman's eventual function as muse arises from her literal, though inherited, association with defeated, pre-independence Ireland. This woman might seem to be exactly the kind of feminine symbol for Ireland that Boland felt male Irish poets had objectified, but, somehow, she is sufficiently her own woman to be the subject of Boland's poem. Her private encounter with the Achill woman gave her a sense of the horrible suffering of women, and of Ireland, in a way that most public poetry written by masculine Irish poets had not.

In a Time of Violence (1994) features a series of poems on the intersection of objects with history. For example, "The Dolls Museum in Dublin" is Boland's rewriting of Yeats's "Easter, 1916." She replaces the elder poet's extended, finally elegiac, descriptions of the Irish rebels with the mute dolls' witnessing of the moment immediately before the Easter Rising in Dublin. Their status as inanimate objects renders them as mute as the Irish women who had promenaded with British soldiers; their past, Boland suggests, has been superseded by Irish nationalist history. "The Dolls Museum in Dublin" represents the utter reality of the past. In the space of each glass case, the dolls resist history—nationalist, revisionist, and otherwise. They exist to display a record of silences in Ireland's history, specifically here in history written about the Easter rebellion. The full story, Boland suggests, is much more than that enacted by sixteen men and various hangers-on; women and children had hopes and dreams too at that time, about the nation, about their future mates, about their playthings. Only when the past reanimates history can reality be truly depicted. Thus, for Boland, one part of the "postcolonial" legacy in Ireland is the vast elision of the personal lives of women, children, even men, by a narrative that privileges the story of an emergent nation above all else.

The Lost Land (1998) emerged from Borland's ongoing vexed relationship with Ireland and England. This volume is characteristically hybrid, divided into two parts, "Colony" and "The Lost Land." A number of poems in "Colony" feature images of personal and political wounds, whereas several poems of "The Lost Land" conflate Boland's lament for Ireland's Gaelic past with her mourning for her daughters who had recently left home. In the opening poem to the volume, "My Country in Darkness," Boland laments the dead bardic order after the Flight of the Wild Geese in the late 1690s.

A number of successive poems in the first half of this volume feature images of wounds, personal and political. For example, in the sixth poem in this section, "The Scar," Boland writes of the worn profile of "Anna Liffey . . . on the old Carlisle bridge." We learn in stanza two that Boland's own head was scarred at the age of five. After she muses upon the Liffey and its history of "the long ships, the muskets and the burning domes" on misty autumn days, she asks, "If colony is a wound what will heal it? / After such injuries what difference do we feel?" Although there is no answer, the concluding lines of the poem suggest the hint of one: "I turn to you as if there were— / one flawed head towards another." This private exchange represents another example of Boland's attempt to recuperate the past, not history per se. Somehow, her own scar enables her to identify with both the previous scarring caused by Ireland's invasions and with its scarred and objectified female representation in the profile of Anna Liffey. In this poem and a later one from this section, "A Habitable Grief," a new "language" is both a site of injury and of resilience, out of which can come a national identity. Both the immigrant woman and Boland learned a new dialect of Irish-English out of the collision between Irish-influenced English and English spoken in England, the first of which they were able to speak successfully and which has flourished in Ireland and its literature.

As the volume shifts from poems of "Colony" in the first section to poems of "The Lost Land" in the second one, Boland's lament for Ireland's Gaelic past, for an Ireland relatively unsullied by British influence, is conflated with, then replaced by her lament for her daughters, who have left her house. Nowhere is this shift more evident than in the title poem of this section, "The Lost Land," in which she recalls her two daughters and her attempt to make her suburban location truly her own. The poem ends with a remarkable series of italicized disyllabic words, underscoring the ache of national and personal dispossession: "Ireland. Absence. Daughter."

By the end of the volume, Boland is alone with only her work to sustain her. It concludes with a poem entitled simply "Whose?" in which the patriot from an earlier poem in this section, "Heroic," appears and whispers, "Beautiful land," to Boland. She has, however, recognized his nationalistic contribution—representative of history—and turned away, looking inward to her individual story, more important than any historical narrative. Boland paints a picture of herself as a solitary writer in the frozen suburbs of Dublin where "Shadows

iced up. Nothing moved. / Except my hand across the page. And these words."

An Origin Like Water: Collected Poems 1967–1987 appeared in America in 1996. Boland's most recent volume is *Against Love Poetry*, published in 2001 in America. She is past member of the International Writing Program at the University of Iowa and was the Hurst Professor at Washington University and Regent's Lecturer at the University of California at Santa Barbara. She currently is the Bella Mabury and Eloise Mabury Knapp Professor in Humanities and the Melvin and Bill Lane Professor in English at Stanford University.

Further Reading. *Selected Primary Sources:* Boland, Eavan, *Collected Poems* (Manchester: Carcanet, 1995); ———, *The Lost Land* (Manchester: Carcanet, 1998; New York: W.W. Norton, 1999); ———, *New Collected Poems* (Manchester: Carcanet, 2005); ———, *Outside History: Selected Poems 1980–1990* (New York: W.W. Norton, 1990); ———, *An Origin Like Water: Collected Poems 1967–1987* (New York: W.W. Norton, 1996); ———, *Prose: Object Lessons: The Life of the Woman and the Poet in Our Time* (New York: W.W. Norton, 1995). *Selected Secondary Sources:* Allen-Randolph, Jody, "A Backward Look: An Interview with Eavan Boland" (*Colby Quarterly* 35.4 [December 1999]: 292–304); Auge, Andrew J., "Fracture and Wound: Eavan Boland's Poetry of Nationality" (*New Hibernia Review/ Iris Éireannach Nua: A Quarterly Record of Irish Studies* 8.2 [Summer 2004]: 121–141); Maguire, Sarah, "Dilemmas and Developments: Eavan Boland Re-Examined" (*Feminist Review* 62 [Summer 1999]: 58–66).

Richard Rankin Russell

BONTEMPS, ARNA (1902–1973)

Better known as a writer of fiction for children and adults, as well as for his careful African American historiography, Arna Bontemps received his first literary prizes for poetry during the **Harlem Renaissance**. His lifelong friendship with **Langston Hughes** and their collaboration on plays, translations, children's books, and especially poetry anthologies make him an important figure in the development of **African American poetry**.

Born October 13, 1902, in Alexandria, Louisiana (the site is now a museum), Bontemps moved with his family to Los Angeles three years later. His early years were marked by the strong influence of the Seventh Day Adventist Church. Obtaining his BA in 1923 from Pacific Union at Angwin, he moved to Harlem in 1924 to begin his teaching career in the church's Harlem Academy. His first published poem appeared in *Crisis* in 1924, and he regularly published in *Crisis* and *Opportunity* in the 1920s. He married Alberta Johnson in 1926, and Langston Hughes portrayed his early family years in *The Big Sea*. Bontemps published his first novel, *God Sends Sunday*, in 1931.

The Depression sent him looking for sustenance elsewhere, and he taught at Oakwood Junior College in Huntsville, Alabama, before finding himself unemployed (but still writing) in his parents' home in Los Angeles. Hired to work on the Illinois Writer's Project, Bontemps moved to the South Side of Chicago, living at East 50th Place. In 1936 he collaborated with Langston Hughes on a play performed by the Gilpin players: *When Jack Hollers*. In February of the same year, Bontemps, Hughes, and Richard Wright were all keynote speakers at the first National Negro Congress. Recipient of two Rosenwald fellowships (1938 and 1942), he completed an MA in library science at the University of Chicago. In 1943 he received an appointment to the Fisk University Library. When the George Gershwin Memorial Collection of Music and Musical Literature opened at Fisk, in April 1947, Hughes, Carl Van Vechten, and Charles S. Johnson were there. Bontemps served as a judge for Whitney Foundation fellowships, and Hughes wrote in a letter to Van Vechten that he was "always on the lookout for new young writers for them to consider" (June 28, 1957). Upon retirement from Fisk in 1965, Bontemps taught at the University of Illinois, and then curated the James Weldon Johnson Collection at Yale from 1969 to 1971. He accepted a writer-in-residence position at Fisk and returned to Nashville, where he died on June 4, 1973.

Some of Bontemps's poems were anthologized (in *American Negro Poetry*, for example), but Ronald Primeau rightly suggests that his poetry has been unjustly overlooked (248). One small volume gathers together twenty-three poems: *Personals* (1963, 1973). Its introduction conveys the atmosphere of the Harlem Renaissance days, when the "New Negro" was thought to embody the saving graces of primitivism by white patrons. "The Return," a poem of six stanzas, has a natural music and begins with a "you and I" listening to rain, the birds, "and summer trembling on a withered vine." The following stanzas offer a primitivist decor with the vines and the drums of the jungle, but the poem ends uneasily in a loss of words: "A question shapes your lips, your eyes glisten / retaining tears, but there are no more words." Nostalgia for Africa is a central motif, even though the healing pool does no healing in "Nocturne at Bethesda" (1926), where the narrator says, "I shall be dying for a jungle fruit." The appealing lyricism of "Prodigal," "Idolatry," and "Lancelot" and their similarities in form (quatrains with regular rhymes) suggest they can be read together. "God Give to Men" is altogether different in tone. It is an angry supplication, asking for what each race already possesses: Those with blue eyes should have swivel chairs in tall buildings, ships at sea, and "on land, soldiers / and policemen." In these poems, Christianity is attuned to the African American experience. In "Golgotha Is a Mountain", the mountains of the world pass in review, and the ending suggests an identification with Christ in the narrator's suggestion of his own tomb that will be like a mountain: "I think it will be Golgotha." Bontemps could also be interacting here with Hughes's 1926 essay, "The Negro Artist and the Racial Mountain," also suggesting the price the African American artist pays for a poetic affirmation of identity.

Bontemps was a *passeur*, a bringer of the poetry to the people. Critical essays such as "Negro Poets, Then and Now" (1950), which suggests his admiration of Langston Hughes's use of popular music, "Famous WPA Authors" (1950), or *The Harlem Renaissance Remembered* (1972), which contains his "The Awakening: A Memoir," allow readers to get a sense of the African American poetic landscape during the Harlem Renaissance of the 1920s and the Chicago Renaissance of the 1930s and 1940s. *The Book of Negro Folklore*, a joint project with Hughes that was published in the 1950s, contains a discussion of Harlem jive and bop. The introductory essays to anthologies he edited are equally insightful. In one case Bontemps notes the role of the musical influence on African American poetry, yet insists "Phillis Wheatley wrote with some success before it existed" (*American Negro Poetry* xx).

The historical preservation efforts of Bontemps may have inspired some of Langston Hughes's historical poems, and they continue to provide poets with raw material. With Jack Conroy, founder of *The Anvil*, the proletarian magazine that published Hughes, Wright, and **William Carlos Williams** during the 1940s, Bontemps composed *Anyplace But Here* (originally *They Seek a City* [1945, 1966, and 1996 reprint]) which contains, among other treasures, an account of the 1943 Detroit riot (300–302) and a chapter called "Du Sable: Man of the Midlands" (12–20). He also edited the autobiography of W.C. Handy (1944). His 1968 introduction to the 1936 novel *Black Thunder* about an 1800 slave revolt in Virginia reveals his passion for history: "I began to read extensively about slave insurrections and to see in them a possible metaphor of turbulence to come" (viii). In order to recreate the scene, Bontemps's creative expression turned to prose. He explains, "Discovering in the Fisk Library a larger collection of slave narratives than I knew existed, I began to read almost frantically" (xii). Historical research resulted in *100 Years of Negro Freedom* (1961) and *Great Slave Narratives* (1969, edited by Bontemps), as well as various accounts for children, including *The Story of the Negro* (1953), in which he quotes William Wordsworth's sonnet on Toussaint L'Ouverture (76–77).

Further Reading. ***Selected Primary Sources:*** Bontemps, Arna, ed., *American Negro Poetry* (New York: Hill & Wang,

1963, rev. ed. 1974); ———, *Black Thunder* (1936; reprint Boston: Beacon Press, 1968); ———, "Dirge" (*Crisis* 32 [May 1926]: 25); ———, "Famous WPA Authors" (*Negro Digest* 8.8 [June 1950]: 43–47); ———, ed., *Golden Slippers: An Anthology of Negro Poetry for Young Readers* (New York: Harper, 1941); ———, ed., *Great Slave Narratives* (Boston: Beacon Press, 1969); ———, ed., *The Harlem Renaissance Remembered* (New York: Dodd Mead, 1972); ———, ed., *Hold Fast to Dreams: Poems Old and New* (Chicago: Follett, 1969); ———, "Holiday" (*Crisis* 32 [July 1926]: 121); ———, "Hope" (*Crisis* 28 [August 1924]: 176); ———, "Negro Poets, Then and Now" (*Phylon* 11.4 [1950]: 355–60); Bontemps, Arna, and Langston Hughes, eds., *The Poetry of the Negro, 1746–1949* (Garden City, NY: Doubleday, 1949, rev. enl. *The Poetry of the Negro, 1746–1970*, Doubleday, 1970); Nichols, Charles H., ed., *Arna Bontemps–Langston Hughes Letters, 1925–1967* (New York: Paragon House, 1990). **Selected Secondary Sources:** Brown, Sterling, *Negro Poetry and Drama* (New York: Atheneum, 1969); Primeau, Ronald, "Frank Horne and the Second Echelon Poets of the Harlem Renaissance," in *The Harlem Renaissance 1920–1940*, ed. Cary D. Wintz (New York: Garland, 1996, 371–391); Reagan, Daniel, "Achieving Perspective: Arna Bontemps and the Shaping Force of Harlem Culture" (*Essays in Arts and Sciences* 25 [October 1996]: 69–78).

Jennifer Kilgore

BOOTH, PHILIP (1925–)

As Philip Booth put it in a 1989 interview, he wishes to transmit through his poetry the "restorative powers" of nature as a means of "mak[ing] the world more habitable" (Barghash, 37). Using natural landscapes metaphorically to work through the self's struggle to find its place in the world, Booth draws heavily on the national legacy of **Robert Frost** and **Henry David Thoreau**. He has been called a neo- or post-Transcendentalist, signaling the ways in which he takes the transcendental tradition in new formal and thematic directions by keeping his poetry relevant to the contemporary moment in which he is writing.

Phillip Booth was born in Hanover, New Hampshire, in 1925. His father, a professor of English at Dartmouth College, taught him from an early age to respect the written word. In his mother's family home in Castine, Maine, Booth spent the summers of his childhood immersing himself in the talk of the wharfs and exploring the coastline by sailboat. Booth served in the Air Force from 1944 until the end of World War II. After his return, he married Margaret Tillman in 1946. He then devoted himself to his education, receiving his AB from Dartmouth in 1948, where Robert Frost was one of his teachers. He went on to study under Mark Van Doren at Columbia University, and he was awarded an MA in 1949. Booth began writing poetry seriously in 1950,

after a short stint as a teacher at Bowdoin College in Brunswick, Maine. He disliked his institutional talk as a teacher and wanted to discover a language of his own making. Over the next four years, he worked on the poems that would fill his first book. By 1954 he had settled himself for the next seven years in Lincoln, Massachusetts, with his wife and three daughters, teaching English at Wellesley College. Booth quickly received critical recognition for his poetry, winning the *Poetry* magazine Bess Hokin Prize in 1955 for his poem "Letter from a Distant Land." For his poetry collection of the same name, he was awarded the Lamont Poetry Selection in 1956. In 1961 he began his professorship at Syracuse University, and remained both professor and poet-in-residence there until his retirement in 1986. Booth has published eleven books of poetry and continues to receive many honors, notably two Guggenheim fellowships, nominations for both the National Book Award in Poetry and the Pulitzer Prize, and most recently, the Poet's Prize from the Academy of American Poets (2001). Booth found his way back to his family house in Castine, where he continues to write poetry.

The Maine coastline haunts both the form and the content of Booth's poetry. Keeping with the transcendental tradition, the coast is both a physical and metaphysical location. But Booth adds a modern formalist twist as he uses the shoreline to unify his form and content through the tidal rhythms of his poetic line. Furthermore, Booth takes the coast in a particularly postmodern sense as a generative in-between space, a borderland between man and nature, experience and innocence, self and other. In his first poetry collection, *Letter from a Distant Land* (1956), there are already signs of the transcendental importance he attaches to the sea as he encourages his daughter in "First Lesson" to trust in the tidewaters of the ocean: "lie back, and the sea will hold you." His poem "Letter from a Distant Land" is a blank-verse epistle addressing Thoreau. Here, he discusses his placement on the metaphoric shoreline halfway between a military airfield and Walden Pond, between a fallen state borne by the technological potential for war, and the Edenic power he reaches for in the wilderness. In his second collection, *The Islanders* (1961), Booth begins to develop the sparse, taut style, with very short lines and few/no stanza breaks, that would become a trademark of his work. Calling himself in 1976 "Puritan to the bone," Booth attempts to trim away any unnecessary signs of linguistic indulgence. "The Tower," the longest poem in the collection, narrates a town's symbolic fall from innocence. The form of a poem straddles the border between linguistic restraint and indulgence: On the one hand, the succinctness of his lines signal a Puritan attempt to avoid falling into babble, yet on the other hand, the lines stack long and narrow, forming a Tower of Babel across several pages.

The titles of his next two collections indicate his continued concern with in-between spaces: *Weathers and Edges* (1966) and *Margins* (1970). Exemplary here is a poem published in both volumes, "The Man on the Wharf." In this poem, after losing his wife, a man teeters on the edge between land and sea, life and death, as the ocean calls to him: "The sea is all he can ask." In the 1970s, with *Available Light* (1976) and *Before Sleep* (1980), Booth begins to experiment with the disposition of line fragments, letting words and phrases slip down the space of the page, in a manner reminiscent of **William Carlos Williams**. Thematically, the temporal margin between life and death becomes increasingly insistent. "The House in the Trees" describes the artistic legacy that might survive beyond the poet. But the poem ends with the dark inevitability, "before it [the house] could ever be done / he would have, finally, to leave it." His collections *Selves* (1990) and *Pairs* (1994) continue his theme of margins by exploring the ways in which two separate entities—selves, animals, people—interconnect with each other; even a self can be divided: "he's stayed outside half / his life already." *Lifelines* (1999), his last major collection of poetry, brings together selected poems from throughout his life and adds some new ones. His recent work attempts to deal with new technologies, like cyberspace, and the apocalyptic threat of the new millennium. He still tries to reconcile the human and natural worlds, though the human world often wins out. In 2001 he reprinted a poem, "Crossing," from his first collection in the form of an illustrated children's book; and so his writing returns full circle, bridging the margin between past and present, beginning and end.

Further Reading.   *Selected Primary Sources:* Booth, Philip, *Before Sleep* (New York: Viking, 1980); ———, *The Islanders* (New York: Viking, 1961); ———, *Letter from a Distant Land* (New York: Viking, 1957); ———, *Lifelines: Selected Poems, 1950–1999* (New York: Viking, 1999); ———————, *Margins: A Sequence of New and Selected Poems* (New York: Viking, 1970). **Selected Secondary Sources:** Barghash, Rachel, "Philip Booth: An Interview" (*American Poetry Review* 18.3 [1989]: 37–39); Rotella, Guy, *Three Contemporary Poets of New England: William Meredith, Philip Booth, and Peter Davison* (Boston: Twayne, 1983).

Michael LeBlanc

BOUCHER, JONATHAN (1738–1804)

Recognized primarily as the best-known Loyalist of the American Revolution, Jonathan Boucher was an articulate political analyst, historian, preacher of Tory doctrines, teacher, philologist, and lexicographer of the British and American dialects. "Absence, a Pastoral: drawn from the life, manners, customs and phraseology of planters (or, to speak more pastorally, of the rural swains) inhabiting the Banks of the Potomac, in Maryland" (ca. 1775) is generally agreed to be Boucher's major contribution to poetry, although some of his poems had occasionally appeared in the *Maryland Gazette*. His reputation as a literary scholar, however, rests mainly on *A View of the Causes and Consequences of the American Revolution* (1797), a collection of sermons published after his return to England.

Boucher was born March 12, 1738, to a poor family in the village of Blencogo in Cumberland County in England. Despite his family's difficult financial situation, Boucher was a hard-working child who taught himself to read and write at a very early age. His extensive reading secured him a temporary teaching position at the age of sixteen and in two years he became usher at Saint Bees School, whose headmaster, the Reverend John James, would become his lifetime mentor and patron. His career as an Anglican clergyman and preacher was launched by James, who recommended the young man as a tutor to a planter's family in Virginia, and at the age of twenty-one, Boucher left his hometown for America. It was at the time of his residence in America and during a short trip to England in 1762 that he was ordained by the Bishop of London.

While still in America and before he became vigorously involved in the political controversies of his time, Boucher turned to literature and theater and gained fame for himself as a lover of art. His occasional poems, which appeared in the *Maryland Gazette*, and his passion for recording the peculiarities of the American dialect eventually brought him to the attention of those in literary circles. During this time, Boucher was taking careful notes of the Chesapeake dialect; this material was used and put together later on, in his years of exile in England, as a supplement to Dr. Johnson's *Dictionary*. Boucher's best-known work in verse, "Absence, a pastoral," hardly recognized as a poem, is based upon Virgil's *Eclogues*. The intention behind writing the poem as expressed by the poet himself was to incorporate in it as many words as possible that were peculiar to those parts of America he was familiar with. The poem is generally believed to be void of any literary value, but in terms of its contribution to the fields of lexicography and philology, it is one of the major works of its type and has been valuable in helping scholars identify colonial American speech patterns. The poem, written before 1775, includes explanatory notes appended to it by Boucher in 1800. The following are some representative words Boucher describes in footnotes to the poem: "*Pacosen*: an Indian term for a swamp, or marsh," "*Fall, mall* and *tote*: i.e., *fall*, or cut down, a tree; split, or rive it, by means of *mallets* and wedges, into rails, clapboards, staves, shingles, firewood, or any other purpose for which it may be fit and wanted, and then *tote*, or carry it to some pile or heap, from whence it may be carted away," "*Cushie*: a kind of pancake, made of Indian meal," and "*Egg-nogg*: a heavy and unwholesome, but not unpalatable strong drink, made of rum beaten up with the yolks of raw *eggs*."

By 1770, almost twenty years after his migration to America, Boucher had become a rising yet controversial figure in politics and a respected minister whose contentious sermons eventually led to his exile; he had to leave America for England finally in 1775. It was after his return that his literary career flourished. He contributed several essays to William Hutchinson's *History of the County of Cumberland* (1794); wrote his autobiographical work, *Reminiscences of an American Loyalist 1738–1789* (not published in full until 1925); and composed *A View of the Causes and Consequences of the American Revolution* (1797).

Boucher's literary fame rests upon *A View of the Causes and Consequences of the American Revolution* (1797). It is significant to note that, between 1763 and 1775, at the time of his residence in America as a preacher, Boucher had declared some of his radical views in relation to the divine right of kings. He had also expressed his unwavering faith in constitutions and legal processes, and his views on the absurdity of democracy. *A View of the Causes and Consequences of the American Revolution* (1797), consisting of thirteen chapters, is based on these sermons but rewritten in a less belligerent tone. Boucher is believed to have significantly moderated his political and social views after he left America. The book has a ninety-page preface and is dedicated to George Washington. The preface is thought to be the most significant part of the book; surprisingly, it deals less with the causes of the American Revolution than with those of its French counterpart. Boucher showed particular interest in the works of the French, especially Montaigne and Voltaire. In addition, he is known to have read the sermons of Massillon in French.

Poetry, according to Boucher, was not recognized as a major literary genre in America, and in a letter published in the *Maryland Historical Magazine* he indicates that people in his part of the country treated poetry as merely "exotic." During the time of his residence in the country, Boucher found Americans to be innovators in all areas, including language, and he fully expected them to develop an independent language bearing no similarity to English—an expectation that has come true, although not necessarily to the extent that he anticipated.

Further Reading. *Selected Primary Sources:* Boucher, Jonathan, *Reminiscences of an American Loyalist, 1738–1789* (New York: Houghton Mifflin, 1925); ———, *A Supplement to Dr. Johnson's Dictionary of the English Language*, Part 1 (London: Longman, Hurst, Rees & Orme, 1807); ———, *A View of the Causes and Consequences of the American Revolution* (London: G.G. & J. Robinson, 1797). ***Selected Secondary Sources:*** Bailyn, Bernard, *The Ideological Origins of the American Revolution* (Cambridge, MA: Harvard University Press, 1967); Gummere, Richard M., *The American Mind and the Classical Tradition* (Cambridge, MA: Harvard University Press, 1963); Zimmer, Anne Y., *Jonathan Boucher: Loyalist in Exile* (Detroit: Wayne State University, 1978).

Manijeh Mannani

BOYLE, KAY (1902–1992)

Poet, short story writer, novelist, journalist, teacher, and, perhaps most prominently, political activist, Kay Boyle was one of the earliest experimental writers and prominent poets of the **expatriates** during the 1920s and 1930s. A contemporary of **William Carlos Williams**, **Gertrude Stein**, James Joyce, **Archibald MacLeish**, **Djuna Barnes**, Ernest Hemingway, and Robert McAlmon, Kay Boyle was recognized by **Ezra Pound** as one of the more important writers of the female expatriates, and considered by many to be one of the most political of the avant-garde **modernist** movement. Boyle's memoir, *Being Geniuses Together 1920–1930*, co-authored with McAlmon, is an account of their lives in Paris as writers and expatriates.

Boyle was born in St. Paul, Minnesota, but spent her childhood years in Philadelphia, Washington, D.C., Cincinnati, and Atlantic City, in addition to traveling extensively with her family. Before moving to France in 1922 with her first husband, Richard Brault, she worked for the experimental literary magazine *Broom*. When her marriage ended, Boyle became involved with Ernest Walsh with whom she spent a year in Grasse, France, prior to his death and her return to Paris. In Paris Boyle became a part of the social and artistic world of the expatriates, and her work began to appear in literary magazines, one of which, *transition*, also published the "Revolution of the Word," a twelve-point manifesto that expressed the artistic strategies adopted by the signers for freeing literary works from conventionality and reader expectation, of which Boyle was a signer (Spanier). Both before and after her marriage to Laurence Vail in 1931, she published fiction and poetry, publishing novels of social and political protest, such as *Death of a Man* in 1932, a novel remonstrating against Nazism. She married Baron Joseph von Franckenstein in 1943 and returned to the United States. Boyle had six children from her various liaisons. She worked as a writer, teacher, and lecturer, having taught at San Francisco State College as a member of the faculty from 1963 to 1979, Northwestern State University in Spokane (1981), and Bowling Green State University (1986); she was a fellow at Wesleyan University (1963), as well as Radcliffe Institute for Independent Study in 1965.

Although she published fourteen novels and ten short story collections, Boyle always thought of herself as a poet first, and indeed her first creative publication was a poem. Boyle told a reporter that William Carlos Williams always referred to her as a poet and claimed it was a mistake that she had ever written prose (McCarthy). Boyle's **lyric poetry** reflected her activism as much as her novels had criticized the war and politics. In her poems, she continued to fight anti-Semitism, defend women and minorities, and support unpopular causes such as the peace movement, civil rights, and equality for gays and lesbians. Boyle's publishing career began with a letter to the editor, published in Harriet Monroe's *Poetry: A Magazine of Verse* in 1921, in which she "[decried] the gap in innovation between the music and the poetry of the day" (Spanier 9). This outrage at the establishment of her day continued throughout her life, beginning with the publication of the "Monody to the Sound of Zithers" in *Poetry* (1922) and "Morning" (1923) in the literary magazine *Broom*. During her Paris years, Boyle was published in *This Quarter*, edited by Ernest Walsh, and *transition*, edited by Eugene Jolas. Boyle's *Collected Poems* was published in 1962 and dedicated to William Carlos Williams. Her final book of poetry, not generally considered to be her best, but considered by many to be her most passionate work, *Testament for My Students and Other Poems* was published in 1970.

Further Reading. ***Selected Primary Sources:*** Boyle, Kay, *American Citizen: Naturalized in Leadville, Colorado* (New York: Simon & Schuster, 1944); ———, *Collected Poems of Kay Boyle* (Port Townsend, WA: Copper Canyon Press, 1995); ———, *A Glad Day* (New York: New Directions, 1938); ———, *The Lost Dogs of Phnom Pehn* (Berkeley: Two Windows, 1968); ———, *A Poem for February First 1975* (Waltham, MA: Quercus Press, 1975); ———, *A Statement* (New York: Modern Editions Press, 1932); ———, *Testament for My Students and Other Poems* (New York: Doubleday, 1970); Boyle, Kay, and Robert McAlmon, *Being Geniuses Together 1920–1930* (New York: Doubleday, 1968). ***Selected Secondary Sources:*** Madden, Charles F. ed., *Talks with Authors* (Carbondale: Southern Illinois University Press, 1968); McCarthy, Joanne, *Dictionary of Literary Biography, Volume 48: American Poets, 1880–1945*, ser. 2, ed. Peter Quartermain (Detroit: Gale Group, 1986, 45–51); Spanier, Sandra, *Kay Boyle Artist and Activist* (Carbondale: Southern Illinois University Press, 1986).

Pat Tyrer

BRACKENRIDGE, HUGH HENRY (1748–1816)

Best known for the picaresque novel *Modern Chivalry*, Brackenridge was also a poet, magazine and newspaper editor and publisher, legislator, and jurist. Though never an accomplished poet, Brackenridge published poems and essays on various topics in newspapers such as the *Pittsburgh Gazette* and the *Tree of Liberty* (Pittsburgh), and collected his newspaper writing in *Gazette Publications*. Brackenridge also wrote on legal topics, the most substantial of which was the 1814 *Law Miscellanies*, a consideration of differences between English and American law.

Born in the Scottish village of Kintyre, Hugh Henry Brackenridge's family emigrated to the United States when he was five years old. He settled with his family in York County, Pennsylvania. Brackenridge was admitted to the College of New Jersey (now Princeton) in 1768 at age twenty. In 1769 he and his friends (**Philip Freneau**, James Madison, and John Bradford, Jr.) organized the Whig Literary Society, a rival of the Cliosophic, or Tory, Society. After graduation, Brackenridge became master of Somerset Academy in Somerset County, Maryland. He received his master's degree from Princeton in 1774. In 1776 Brackenridge left Somerset Academy to serve as an (unordained) chaplain in Washington's army. Feeling he had a calling for the literary life, Brackenridge moved to Philadelphia in 1778, there establishing the short-lived *United States Magazine*, a journal of politics and literature. In 1780 he was admitted to the Philadelphia bar, and the following year settled in the frontier village of Pittsburgh.

In Pittsburgh, Brackenridge carried on a successful law practice, established the *Pittsburgh Gazette*, and in 1786 was elected to the state assembly, where he served one term. During the late 1780s and 1790s Brackenridge began *Modern Chivalry*, the first two volumes of which were printed in Philadelphia in 1792, the third in 1793. Brackenridge played a central role in the Whiskey Rebellion of 1794, the result of armed resistance to federal taxes on whiskey. He managed to anger both the rebels (by urging moderation) and the federal troops (by his perceived defense of the rebels). The accusations of treason levied against Brackenridge found their way in fictional form into the fourth volume of *Modern Chivalry*, published in 1797.

In a final return to politics, Brackenridge became the western Pennsylvania leader of Jefferson's Republican Party, and in December 1799 he was appointed an associate justice of the state supreme court, a position he held until his death in 1816. Two years after his appointment to the bench, Brackenridge moved from Pittsburgh to Carlisle, Pennsylvania. There he composed a new volume of *Modern Chivalry*, published in 1805, and continued his involvement in contentious state party politics. From 1805 to the end of his life, Brackenridge focused his energies primarily on various legal issues, including a study of Pennsylvania law that he called a "Pennsylvania Blackstone," published in 1813.

Brackenridge dabbled in a variety of genres and forms, never settling into a single one during his prolific career. His literary career began at Princeton, in his collaboration with Philip Freneau on two pieces. The first was *Father Bombo's Pilgrimage to Mecca in Arabia*, a prose fiction satire (perhaps the first work of prose fiction written in America) that provides comic glimpses into eighteenth-century American life. In 1771 he and Freneau again collaborated, this time on a patriotic poem, "The Rising Glory of America." Brackenridge read the poem aloud at the September 1771 Princeton commencement exercises. It was issued in 1772, the first published work of both authors. Brackenridge later wrote a second poem on similar themes, "A Poem on Divine Revelation" (1774) also delivered at Princeton commencement exercises. During the Revolutionary War, Brackenridge composed two heroic dramas for his students at Somerset Academy. The first, in 1775, was titled *The Battle of Bunkers-Hill*. The second, *The Death of General Montgomery*, was written in 1777.

Brackenridge's literary reputation rests primarily on *Modern Chivalry*; the first volume was published in 1792 and the first collected edition, in four volumes, was published in 1815. The collected edition was republished in Philadelphia in 1846, with illustrations by Darley. *Modern Chivalry* follows the exploits of Captain Farrago, Brackenridge's spokesman, and his servant, Teague O'Reagan, an Irish "bog-trotter." The novel is a political and social satire, generally good-natured, often reflecting Brackenridge's disillusioning involvement with Pennsylvania politics. *Modern Chivalry* is concerned about the excesses of democracy—or, what might be more charitably called the deviation from what Brackenridge considered rational democracy. *Modern Chivalry* sheds light on the trials and tribulations of democracy in the early republic—tensions and strains that have persisted through the twenty-first century.

In addition to *Modern Chivalry* and his early poetry, Brackenridge published essays, poetry, and longer prose works throughout his life. In 1795 Brackenridge published a defense of his own role in the Whiskey Rebellion, the rather hastily composed *Incidents of the Insurrection in the Western Parts of Pennsylvania, in the Year of 1794* (1795). Brackenridge died in 1816.

Further Reading. ***Selected Primary Sources:*** Brackenridge, Hugh Henry, *Modern Chivalry: Containing the Adventures of Captain John Farrago and Teague O'Regan, his Servant* (originally published as 4 vols., 1792–1797; rev. ed. 1805; final ed. 1815) (New Haven, CT: College & University Press, 1965); ———, *A Poem on Divine Revelation; being an exercise delivered At the Public Commencement at Nassau-Hall, September 28. 1774. By the same Person, who on a similar occasion. Sept. 25. 1771. delivered a small Poem on the rising Glory of America* (Philadelphia: printed by R. Aitken, 1774); Brackenridge, Hugh Henry, and Philip Freneau, *A Poem, on the Rising Glory of America; being an exercise Delivered at the Public Commencement at Nassau-Hall, September 25, 1771*

(Philadelphia: printed by Joseph Crukshank [etc.], 1772); Marder, Daniel, ed., *A Hugh Henry Brackenridge Reader, 1770–1815* (Pittsburgh: University of Pittsburgh Press, 1970). ***Selected Secondary Sources:*** Heartman, Charles F., *Bibliography of the Writings of Hugh Henry Brackenridge* (New York: The Compiler, 1917; reprint New York: Burt Franklin, 1968); Marder, Daniel, *Hugh Henry Brackenridge* (New York: Twayne, 1967); Newlin, Claude Milton, *The Life and Writings of Hugh Henry Brackenridge* (Princeton, NJ: Princeton University Press, 1932).

Ann M. Brunjes

BRADFORD, WILLIAM (1590–1657)

William Bradford was a historian and the founder of Plymouth, Massachusetts. Although not a practicing poet per se, in the latter years of his life Bradford produced a small body of poems to articulate his concerns about religion and New England. These verses typify the general range and aesthetic properties associated—except for the major poets—with New England Puritanism; they are generally marked by rhythmic balance, attentiveness to diction, impersonal sobriety and piety, a plain-spoken prophetic strain, and a biblically and classically informed background. Because of his small output of verse, and because only one short poem was published in the seventeenth century, his poetic influence may be considered negligible.

Born in Austerfield, Yorkshire, to a yeoman farmer, Bradford was orphaned by age five. He experienced an extended illness at about age twelve; he used his convalescence for extensive reading, especially in the Geneva Bible. At about this time, he began attending sermons by nonconformist minister Richard Clyfton in nearby Babworth. By 1606 he had formally joined the Separatist congregation at Scrooby led by William Brewster and John Robinson, a commitment he honored for the remainder of his life. Bradford left for Holland with the congregation in 1608, settling first in Amsterdam, then in Leyden. Bradford was part of the splinter group that departed in 1620 to establish Plymouth in New England. Bradford was elected governor on the death of John Carver during the catastrophic first winter; he frequently served in that capacity until his death, which made him instrumental in colony affairs. Additionally, with Edward Winslow he co-authored *Mourt's Relation* (1621), an early account of Plymouth. He is best remembered for his classic prose history *Of Plymouth Plantation* (composed 1630–1650; first publication, 1856), a manuscript he worked on from 1630 to about 1650. After abandoning work on the history, Bradford turned to composing prose dialogues of ecclesiastical polemic (two of three of which survive) and to topical didactic verse. At the time of his death from natural causes at age sixty-seven, Bradford was the wealthiest individual in Plymouth Colony.

Seven posthumously published poems have been attributed to Bradford. The earliest is a twenty-four–line elegy in common measure on the death of the Reverend John Robinson, the church's beloved minister who died in 1625 before he could make passage to Plymouth; the poem first appeared anonymously in the Plymouth church records, begun in 1680. The remaining poems are believed to have been composed in the early-to-mid-1650s, after Bradford had discontinued work first on his history and then on the dialogues. With the exception of part of "Some Observations," they survive only in an unreliable, incomplete copy made by then fifteen-year-old John Willett (son of one of the executor's of Bradford's will) shortly after Bradford's death. In octosyllabic couplets, "On the Various Heresies" catalogs erroneous sects (such as Antinomians, Familists, Ranters, et al.) and concludes with a call for unity to combat the heretics. Bradford's alarmist position is consistent with that of English heresiographers of the 1640s (especially Ephraim Pagitt), but it is difficult to assess how much of Bradford's account stems from personal exposure to the sectarians denounced. Certainly, Bradford does not offer a New England context for these errors.

Next is a group of three brief verse jeremiads, or prophetic laments, given as "words" addressed respectively to New Plymouth, Boston, and New England. These poems notably take up in miniature certain themes and imagery developed in book II of *Of Plymouth Plantation*, but Bradford also contextualizes his criticism in terms of seventeenth-century European religious wars as witnessed from a distance. These allusions, drawn from pamphlets and other sources, indicate that the Plymouth Separatists were neither uninformed nor uninvolved. The "words" to New England and Boston are especially significant for Bradford's endorsement of colonies he could have taken as threatening to Plymouth's existence.

The most ambitious of Bradford's poems, "Some Observations" (1654), is the final poem in the Willett manuscript; most of it survives also in Bradford's own handwriting. At 431 lines, it most closely approximates *Of Plymouth Plantation* in narrative sweep and polemical thrust, albeit with significant omissions and gaps; additionally, it is the only Bradford poem written in decasyllabic couplets. The poem opens by targeting Native Americans as lawless, godless, tyrannical, "brutish and savage." Next, the poem takes on the tone of a promotional tract as Bradford catalogues the material produce of New England; for example: "Onions, melons, cucumbers, radishes, / Skirrets, beets, coleworts, and fair cabbages." The poem then recounts the material prosperity of the 1630s resulting from the Great Migration, as well as the subsequent depression. Far above this, though, Bradford nostalgically celebrates the spiritual benefits of "Well ordered churches" and "a learn'd ministry" as well as a "prudent magistracy" that defended the civil and ecclesiastical order. Yet, despite signs that some New Englanders maintain these values, he prophetically bemoans "some great change at hand, / That, ere long, will fall upon this poor land," due to the decay of virtue and "true godliness" so present among the founders. He adopts here much of the nostalgic, apologetic, defensive, and prophetically critical tone that pervades portions of *Of Plymouth Plantation*, attributing corruption and declension to human vanity, material prosperity, and especially to the "mixed multitude" that followed the New England saints into the wilderness. At the end, Bradford reserves special wrath for the "most desp'rate mischief" of trading guns with the natives, a charge he had also brought against Thomas Morton. Bradford finally calls on God to "take pity on thy people poor; / Let them repent, amend, and sin no more."

In addition to the Willett copy, "Epitaphium Meum" also appeared in Nathaniel Morton's *New England's Memorial* (1669). Most likely composed in the closing days of his life, it is the most personal of the poems. Bradford describes himself as a "pilgrim" and a "man of sorrows" who has witnessed the full panoply of human experience with "[c]onsolations" and consequent pious wisdom to share with his children.

Further Reading.   ***Selected Primary Sources:*** Bradford, William, *The Collected Verse*, ed. Michael G. Runyan (St. Paul, MN: John Colet, 1974); ———, *Of Plymouth Plantation, 1620–1647*, ed. Samuel Eliot Morison (New York: Knopf, 1952). ***Selected Secondary Sources:*** Jantz, Harold S., *The First Century of New England Verse* (*Proceedings of the American Antiquarian Society* 53 [October 1943]: 219–508; reprint New York: Russell & Russell, 1962); Smith, Bradford, *Bradford of Plymouth* (Philadelphia: J.B. Lippincott, 1951); Westbrook, Perry D, *William Bradford* (Boston: Twayne, 1978).

Michael G. Ditmore

BRADLEY, MARY EMILY NEELEY (1835–1898)

Mary E. Bradley's poetry, while no longer frequently in publication, was popular enough in its time to be printed in various journals, including *Harper's Weekly* and *Appleton's Journal*. Her poems often evoke Christian themes of life and death mixed with romantic images of nature. From the late 1850s to the 1890s, Bradley wrote poems as well as short stories and books for children, often with religious morals. A product of antebellum America and industrialization, Bradley's poetry, although written in the latter half of the nineteenth century, has a transcendental, romantic quality interwoven with **sentimental** images of nature and life.

Mary Emily Neeley was born in Easton, Maryland, in 1835, and later married George T. Bradley. The couple resided in New York City and other places in the eastern part of the United States during Bradley's lifetime. She cultivated a friendship with renowned editor and writer Richard Henry Stoddard, who encouraged her to write poetry. As a result, Bradley published short stories for children, particularly girls, and poems about children and nature. Although she published many poems separately in journals, she only published one book of her poetry: *Hidden Sweetness* (1886), which was reviewed very favorably by *Harper's Weekly*. Dorothy Hilroyd's illustrations of flowers and birds complemented Bradley's poetry in the book.

Some of Bradley's earlier works include *Bread upon the Waters* (1856); *Douglass Farm* (1857); *Arthur, and other stories in prose and rhyme* (1860); and *The Infant Catechism* (1862). *Douglass Farm* renders what farm life was like for children growing up in Virginia. In *Arthur, and other stories*, Bradley writes many moral-based stories and poems that instruct children to obey their parents and be good Christians. According to the inscription in *The Infant Catechism* (1862), Bradley had four children of her own: Cornele, Tom, Bobbie, and Leonard. She wrote numerous poems as well as over twenty short stories and novels for children.

Bradley's poetry often intertwines images of nature, death, family, and Christianity. Although not printed in *Hidden Sweetness*, one of her most published poems, "A Chrysalis," exemplifies Bradley's main themes and style. The poem reveals the tale of a "little Mädchen" (German for little girl). The little Mädchen finds a chrysalis, or butterfly's cocoon, and her mother, the poem's speaker, says that she has discovered a "baby butterfly." The little girl excitedly asks if she will see the butterfly hatch from its shell; the poem ends on a somber note, however, as the speaker reveals that before the butterfly can take its first flight, her daughter has died. The mother mourns the loss of her daughter, but she compares her to the chrysalis and reasons at the end of the poem: "And Death that robbed me of delight / Was but the radiant creature's flight!" In several poems, such as "The First Snow-Drop" and "Heartsease," Bradley's verse tells the story of a sweet child who dies too young. In "A Chrysalis," she reconciles this tragedy with the consolation that the child is now redeemed by an everlasting life in heaven. This therapeutic characteristic is often evident in her poetry. Furthermore, it may be that this theme had some autobiographical elements to it: Bradley inscribed in *The Holy Days of the Church* (1861) the words "In Memory of a Lamb of the Flock who died 1/15/1860," which suggests that one of her own children died at an early age.

Many of Bradley's works reveal her passion for nature and flowers. The changing seasons and blossoms appeal to her senses, as evident in "My Grape-vine" in *Hidden Sweetness*. Bradley intriguingly relies on the Victorian language of flowers when penning her poems about certain blooms. For instance, at the beginning of "Mignonnette," the symbol of the flower is presented, noting the *Language of Flowers* definition: "Your qualities surpass your charms." In the poem the speaker chooses the mignonette over the rose, pansy, lily, and many more exotic flowers. For the speaker, the mignonette symbolizes the "innocence" and "modest graces" of a "little maid" that was close to her heart. At the closing of the poem the speaker notes, "Therein, while suns shall rise and set / To bloom unchanged, my mignonette!" This ending suggests that like the previous poems mentioned, the speaker believes that the little girl lives eternally, but not on earth.

Bradley's strong Christian faith is apparent, both in her work and in her affiliations with certain publishers. Many of her poems and prose were first published by Christian publishers such as the General Protestant Episcopal Sunday School Church Book Society. Often these books of verse and prose were intended to teach children about Christianity and its traditions. For instance, *The Holy Days of the Church* (1861) guided young children through the Christian calendar year with explanations of each religious celebration and excerpts on Christian saints. Throughout her works for these Christian publications, Bradley interweaved prose and poetry, engaging children in remembering biblical promises and advice through her clever rhymes.

Although her church publications make up a large portion of her writing, Bradley's mainstream poetry and prose should not be overlooked by readers of nineteenth-century literature. Indeed, her early poetry as well as her collection of poems, *Hidden Sweetness*, provides valuable insight into the nineteenth-century woman's life and concerns. She died in Washington, D.C., in 1898.

Further Reading. ***Selected Primary Sources:*** Bradley, Mary E.N., *Bread upon the Waters* (New York: Gen. Prot. Episcopal Sunday School Union, 1856); ———, "A Chrysalis," "In Death," "Beyond Recall," "A Spray of Honeysuckle," in *An American Anthology: 1787–1900*, ed. E.C. Stedman (Boston: Houghton Mifflin, 1900); ———, *Douglass Farm* (New York: D. Appleton, 1857); ———, "The First Snow-Drop," in *Arthur, and other stories in prose and rhyme* (New York: Gen. Prot. Episcopal Sunday School Union and Society, 1860); ———, "Heartsease," "Mignonnette," "In the Night," in *The Female Poets of America*, ed. R.W. Griswold (Philadelphia: Carey & Hart, 1848); ———, *Hidden Sweetness* (Boston: Roberts Brothers, 1886); ———, *The Holy Days of the Church* (New York: Gen. Prot. Episcopal Sunday School Union, 1861); ———, *The Infant Catechism, or Questions and Answers in Rhyme for the Little Children of the Church* (New York: Gen. Prot. Episcopal Sunday School Union, 1862).

Allison Kellar

BRADSTREET, ANNE DUDLEY (1612–1672)

Anne Bradstreet, by most historical and critical accounts, retains her status as the first significant English poet published in the New World, the first woman poet in the "American" tradition, and, along with **Edward Taylor** and possibly **Michael Wigglesworth**, one of the only seventeenth-century New England poets to have maintained a popular and critical reputation into the twenty-first century. Bradstreet's extraordinary book *The Tenth Muse, Lately Sprung Up in America* (1650), published without her knowledge by her brother-in-law during a trip to London, marks the beginning of a poetic tradition that combines the Puritan quest for spiritual transcendence with the unique experiences and features of the New England landscape, the concrete details of everyday life, and Bradstreet's own experience as a woman, wife, and mother. Hers is a distinctive lyric poetry that is considered by many to be the foundation of a unique American aesthetic—one that would not be fully realized until at least the mid-nineteenth century. Bradstreet's influence extends from her younger contemporary, Taylor (whose copy of *The Tenth Muse* was the only volume of poetry in his collection), to **John Berryman**, whose *Homage to Mistress Bradstreet* (1953) enshrines her as both a spiritual and literary mentor, and **Adrienne Rich**, who looks to Bradstreet as an important forebear to her own modern **feminist poetics**. Although Bradstreet's reputation as a poet and her place in the critical canon have undergone numerous reevaluations and interpretations over the centuries, it is unlikely that she'll ever again be displaced or forgotten as an important early voice of the New World.

Anne Dudley Bradstreet was born in 1612 to Thomas Dudley and Dorothy Yorke Dudley, in Northhamptonshire, England. Her father was steward to the Earl of Lincolnshire, on whose estate Anne was raised from the age of seven until the family made its way to America in 1630. Her father's circumstances and appreciation for education, as well as his access to the earl's extensive library, allowed Anne and her siblings a solid early education in languages, literature, and music, as well as in the Puritan religious traditions that the Dudley's embraced. This education, although not unusual for young women of her situation during and immediately after the reign of Elizabeth I, would stand in stark contrast to that of subsequent generations in the New World. Some of her early literary influences may have included the works of Spenser, Shakespeare, George Herbert, John Donne, and Sir Philip Sidney, to whom she later dedicated an elegy. No doubt she also absorbed those important religious texts and theological writings that were central to the Puritan tradition, including the **Bible**, and later, the ***Bay Psalm Book***, from which she would draw much of her poetic inspiration.

When she was sixteen, Anne survived a severe case of smallpox, and shortly afterwards, married her father's young assistant, Simon Bradstreet. Their marriage would eventually produce eight children, all of them born in the New World. In 1630 she, her husband, and her parents sailed to America aboard the *Arbella* with John Winthrop's Massachusetts Bay Colony. Bradstreet writes movingly in an epistle, "To My Dear Children," of her ambivalence about the journey and her first impressions of "a new world and new manners, at which my heart rose" (all quotations from the Hensley edition of *Works*, 241). However, she also indicates her willingness to submit to the will of God and to her place in the community. The family settled first in Newtown (Cambridge), then moved to Ipswich, and later Andover, where Anne would spend the rest of her life. Her father was selected as the second governor of Massachusetts, a position that her husband would also hold, seven years after her death. Bradstreet was well aware of the privilege and responsibility that her relationship to these men brought, and it was no doubt an important factor both in her ability to pursue poetry as a vocation and in her reluctance to fully embrace it as an identity. As a daughter, wife, and mother of prominent status, Bradstreet adopted without complaint the public and private duties that went along with these roles in Puritan society. Indeed, she often found great strength and comfort in them, even when they inhibited her ability to write or reflect. It is likely that she never entertained the notion of a "conflict" between these various roles, seeing them, as most Puritans did, as the worldly extensions of a larger spiritual mission: the nurturing and cultivation of Christian souls, including her own and that of her children. This is not to say that Bradstreet didn't struggle with her faith—her letter to her children, as well as her poetry, reveals an intelligent, educated, and thoughtful woman who has, at least, entertained the notion that other faiths (particularly Catholicism) may not be devoid of truth.

It is also clear from her poetry, her careful revisions, and her preservation of her writing, that despite its secondary status in her daily life, Bradstreet took great pride in her work, going so far as to refer to it (humorously, but at least half-seriously) as one of her "offspring." Self-conscious though she was, and probably a bit annoyed by her brother-in-law's well-meaning but unauthorized publication of her work, Bradstreet nonetheless seems to have drawn encouragement from the public approval that the poems received. In "The Author to Her Book," Bradstreet captures both the chagrin that she feels at having sent this child "out of door" without proper attire, and the grudging affection and humble hopes that she maintains for it. In fact, some critics suggest that the success of *The Tenth Muse* may have opened a tenuous creative door for Bradstreet, which allowed for the writing of her later, more personal, concrete, and uniquely "American" poems that have since sealed her critical reputation. She continued to write and revise her work until the last years of her life, allowing for the posthumous publication of a second edition, *Several Poems*, in 1678. A number of unpublished manuscripts, including the letter to her children mentioned above, and several occasional poems, have been added to her *Works* in later editions.

Bradstreet's early poems, many of them presented to her father as a gift, reflect those Puritan values and interests that were central to her community—the virtues of piety, patience, duty, obedience, and self-examination, and the need for didacticism and practical learning in literary works. One long series of poems, which take up the bulk of *The Tenth Muse*, includes such titles as "The Four Elements," "The Four Ages of Man," "The Four Seasons," and the unfinished "Four Monarchies." These quaternions (poems made up of four books each) are modeled on popular scholarly or poetic works of the time, notably Joshua Sylvester's translation of Guillaume Du Bartas's *His Divine Weekes and Works* (1605), Sir Walter Raleigh's "History of the World" (1614), and even her father's own lost work, "On the Four Parts of the World" (date unknown), and were meant to serve as poetic catalogues of learning and wisdom drawn from centuries of European scholarship, often fitted into the paradigms of the Christian creation story. Some see these poems as indications of a desire to hold on to an Old World identity and historical ties, especially to England, that helped to counter the sense of separation and loneliness evoked by New World frontier life. Recent criticism, though, suggests that Bradstreet may have also utilized these historical and scientific narratives to challenge many of the Puritan assumptions about women's roles and capacities as rational or moral beings, political leaders, and artists (Harvey, 2000). For example, by including accounts of various historical queens, including Cleopatra and Elizabeth I, Bradstreet seems to set them on par (at least) with their male counterparts, and to suggest that their accomplishments might be due not merely to exceptional natures or divine blessing, but to the cultural attitudes of their time. In her prologue to these poems, Bradstreet notes that the Greeks not only recognized the creative capacity of women, but in fact, identified the Muses themselves as female. Though she deferentially laughs off the judgment of the Greeks, and concedes that "Men can do best, and women know it well"(16), it is difficult to read this line as anything but irony or disingenuousness—she knows, of course, that her point has already been made! In another poem dedicated to Elizabeth, "In Honor of the High and Mighty Princess Queen Elizabeth of Happy Memory," Bradstreet makes her critique of "masculinist" history even more clear: "Nay masculines, you have thus taxed us long, / But she, though dead, will vindicate our wrong" (198).

These implicit tensions between religious or cultural values and the experienced truth of a woman's life have become one of the more interesting avenues of critical thinking on Bradstreet's work in recent years. In particular, those later poems that deal more concretely with the everyday realities of her life—marriage, motherhood, illness and family hardships, the loss of loved ones, and so forth—offer fertile ground for re-thinking the relationship between communal values and individual experience in Puritan New England. In an unpublished poem "Upon the Burning of Our House" (1666) Bradstreet recounts the loss of her home, and, metaphorically, of all the worldly memories associated with it. The loss is severe and painful, leading the speaker to return again and again to the ruins, in an almost Freudian act of melancholia—though she also chides herself for her lack of gratitude to God and appreciation for his divine purposes. Fully half the poem is a catalogue of losses, and yet the conclusion looks ahead to eternity, where all these transient attachments will be compensated—curiously, by "house on high erect" (292). That her material losses are so concretely returned to her suggests some lingering attachment, at least to the forms of earthly life—a poignant, understandably human need, but one that may work subtly against the utter submission and acceptance that her faith demands.

It would be a mistake, though, to suggest that Bradstreet rejects Puritan values or aspirations on the whole. Indeed, most of her poems maintain a commitment to the Christian narratives of repentance, conversion, spiritual transcendence, and rejection of worldly materialism. In the earlier poems, these commitments often take the form of a dialogue or argument between competing perspectives or entities, as in "The Flesh and The Spirit" or "The Vanity of All Worldly Things," in which worldly concerns are presented as pale and transient in comparison to the eternal rewards of heaven. Many of her eulogies also seem to re-enact a process of Christian mourning—sorrow, reflection, justification, and acceptance—albeit in a more intensely personal and emotional language. And some of Bradstreet's later poems, like "By Night When Others Soundly Slept" or "In My Solitary Hours," make the argument in nearly erotic terms, suggesting that the relationship between speaker and Christ rivals and surpasses even the passion of her marriage (particularly when her husband is away—an almost scandalous portrayal!). In one of her last poems, "As Weary Pilgrim" (1669), Bradstreet envisions salvation or transcendence as an ultimate escape from earthly suffering and loss: "Oh, how I long to be at rest/ And soar on high among the blest" (294).

In these poems the promise of her religious faith more often than not overcomes the inevitable doubts and uncertainties that experience brings. Many critics note that it is precisely through the self-conscious narration of suffering and doubt, followed by acceptance and then joy, that Puritan writers express their faith most deeply.

Questioning, in this context, is not a sin or an aberration, but religious duty, insofar as it is a part of the process of conversion and salvation.

But if the story of suffering, questioning, and ultimate grace is, in itself, not original or startling in Bradstreet, her specific modes of expressing it may be. Unlike most male writers, including the poets, of her time, who tend to linger in the abstract, the universal, and the grandiose, Bradstreet's later verse makes use of the intimate details, concrete realities, and the humble everyday struggles that were particular to seventeenth-century women's lives. She offers eulogies to lost friends and family members, prayers for deliverance from illness, protection from the elements and the dangers of travel, and reflections on the anxiety of childbirth and motherhood—all subjects that might have seemed hardly "poetic" to the great male authors that she so admired. Poems of the body, such as "Upon a Fit of Sickness" or " Upon Some Distemper of the Body," are among the earliest American writing to wrestle with issues of the flesh in a language drawn not merely from philosophical or theological discourse, but from first-hand experience of the fevers, agues, and injuries that frontier life entailed. It was a harsh reality with which many later generations of American pioneers (and poets) might readily identify.

Similarly, Bradstreet's depth of emotion and the passion of her relationships—not often publicly expressed by Puritan women—become clear in both the eulogies and in poems such as "Before the Birth of One of Her Children," in which she reflects not only on the constant presence of death, particularly in and around the time of childbirth, but also on her anxiety about the fate of her children should her husband be left alone, or worse, remarry, leaving them at the mercy of a harsh "step-dame" (224). This poem, and a number of others that address concerns for her children and grandchildren, is notable for its placement of the mother-child relationship at the center of communal and personal life, and its emphasis on parental affection as a necessary and irreplaceable element of child-rearing (Watts, 1977). The poem is also a somewhat morbid, but sincere, love letter to her husband, for whom she feels an abiding attachment, even jealousy, as she prepares for the possibility of her own death. Bradstreet's love for and subtle teasing of her husband takes on even more passionate, even erotic, tones in poems such as "To My Dear and Loving Husband" and in a series of verse letters penned during his frequent journeys away from home. In these poems she challenges other women to "Compare with me . . . if you can" (225); she scolds him for his absences, imagines herself a widow, pleads for his return, and laments the "strange effect" that causes her to grow weary and weak in his absence (226). Her sometimes melodramatic longing and erotic playfulness often echo the qualities of her earlier Elizabethan influences—Shakespeare, Donne,

or Marvell—more so than her Puritan "fathers." That a Puritan woman might express such a complex range of emotion—fear, desire, jealousy, loneliness, anger, and ironic humor—in poetry and in print still surprises many modern readers more familiar with the stately eloquence of a John Winthrop or the dire fervor of a **Cotton Mather**.

Some have even seen Bradstreet's emotionalism as an early precursor to the nineteenth-century Romantic revival of emotion and **sentimentality** in American writing, though by that time, Bradstreet herself was shrouded in the obscurity of a critical disregard for Puritan writing in general, and early women's writing in particular (Dolle, 1990). Still, it isn't the only element in Bradstreet that seems to foreshadow later developments in American literature. One of her most highly regarded long poems, "Contemplations," has been frequently examined for its reflections on the American landscape and its similarities to pre-Romantic nature poetry. In it, Bradstreet's speaker wanders through an autumnal New England landscape, reflecting on the sensual beauty of the scene, its relationship to spiritual or heavenly objects, and its capacity to inspire thought and praise: "My humble eyes to lofty skies I reared, / To sing some song, my mazed Muse thought meet" (206).

The poem even expresses some qualified sympathy with pre-Christian forms of nature worship: "No wonder some made thee deity; / Had I not better known, alas, the same had I" (205). Ultimately, though, the speaker does "know better," and finds in nature an affirmation of her faith in a divine creator, a spiritual "current," and the transience of even the most enchanting natural beauty. Identifying herself with the fabled Philomel (nightingale), but inverting its traditional association with loss and mourning, the speaker turns away from her earthly vision and hearkens to the call for spiritual transcendence—"I judged my hearing better than my sight, / And wished me wings with her a while to take my flight" (212).

The poem has been read as everything from an offshoot of the English "emblematic" tradition (the transformation of personal experience into timeless natural symbols drawn from the literary tradition), to a treatise on natural theology (deductions of God from nature), to a proto-Transcendentalist meditation, all of which can be seen as elements of a larger American **sublime**—an aesthetic based on the immense awe, terror, sensual power, and spiritual efficacy of our encounter with Nature—elaborated almost two centuries later by such figures as **Ralph Waldo Emerson**, **John Greenleaf Whittier**, **Edgar Allan Poe**, and **Emily Dickinson** (Dolle, 1990).

These last two comparisons—to Poe and Dickinson—suggest one final element of identification between Bradstreet and the nineteenth century (or beyond): her self-reflexive position as a writer, particularly as a woman writer. Though most lyric poetry in the English tradition speaks from the position of a subjective "I," it is often an assumed conceit that reveals little about the author, her life, her creative process, or her attitude toward her own work and its place in the larger context of historical experience. But as a Puritan author, steeped in the Augustinian traditions of self-examination and confession, and as a woman sharply aware of the freedoms and limitations of her time, it is not entirely surprising to see a different dynamic at work in Bradstreet's poetry. It is not only her willingness to incorporate direct autobiographical material but her sometimes self-conscious, observing, and critiquing presence in the poems, and the awareness of her position as an object of scrutiny for others, that makes these poems unusual. In her poem "Prologue," she self-mockingly refers to her "foolish, broken, blemish'd Muse," by way of asserting that very Muse as worthy to endure the inevitable scrutiny and judgment that she faces as a female poet. In "The Author to Her Book," she directly ties the process of poetic production to the various other kinds of "production" required of her—motherhood, nourishment, clothing and educating the young, and so forth. And in "Contemplations," she humbly mourns her "imbecility" as an artist, but notably, only in comparison to the profound creative capacities of God and Nature, not to other poets! It is Bradstreet's conscious, purposeful assertion of her need for and right to self-expression, and the careful craftsmanship that allows her to make this assertion within the framework of a sometimes stifling cultural context, that has caught the attention of modern feminist critics and others interested in the historical interactions between art and identity. The impact of such re-reading on poets like Adrienne Rich has already been noted, though one could easily extend the scope of analysis to include many of the poets of the **confessional** school, the **Beat poets, gay and lesbian** writers, and the various minority authors who have followed Bradstreet in closely examining their tenuous place as "American" poets within their own writing.

Further Reading.   ***Selected Primary Sources:*** Bradstreet, Anne, *Several Poems . . . by a gentlewoman in New England* (Boston: John Foster, 1678); ———, *The Tenth Muse, Lately Sprung Up in America* (London: Stephen Bowtell, 1650); ———, *The Works of Anne Bradstreet*, ed. Jeanine Hensley (Cambridge, MA: Belknap Press/Harvard University Press, 1967). ***Selected Secondary Sources:*** Dolle, Raymond, *Anne Bradstreet, A Reference Guide* (Boston: G.K. Hall, 1990); Harvey, Tamara, "'Now Sisters . . . Impart Your Usefulnesse, And Force': Anne Bradstreet's Feminist Functionalism in *The Tenth Muse* (1650)" (*Early American Literature* 35.1 [2000]: 5–28); Martin, Wendy, *An American Triptych: Anne Bradstreet,*

Emily Dickinson, and Adrienne Rich (Chapel Hill: University of North Carolina Press, 1984); Stanford, Ann, *Anne Bradstreet: The Worldly Puritan* (New York: Burt Franklin, 1975); Walker, Cheryl, *The Nightingale's Burden: Women Poets and American Culture before 1900* (Bloomington: Indiana University Press, 1982); Watts, Emily Stipes, *The Poetry of American Women from 1632 to 1945* (Austin and London: University of Texas Press, 1977).

John Edward Martin

BRAINARD, JOE (1942–1994)

The poet Joe Brainard was primarily a visual artist who painted and drew, made collages and assemblages, collaborated on comic books, did cover art and design for hundreds of books, and created posters, theatrical sets, and costumes. His output, enormous and fueled by amphetamines and an unapologetic addition to cigarettes, was so varied that critics have difficulty identifying a Brainard style. He can be considered a pop-artist for his use of commercial logos and consumer goods. He created small and huge assemblages using materials such as religious statuettes, lace, beads, artificial flowers, price tags, feathers, bottle caps, sequins, plastic dolls, and cigarette butts. Like Roy Lichtenstein, he appropriated cartoon characters to star in his paintings. He particularly liked Ernie Bushmiller's round-faced little girl, Nancy, painting her into campy situations—imagining her as a proud boy exposing under a flipped-up dress a little cartoon penis, or as an ashtray with a gigantic cigarette stubbed out in her mouth. Brainard wanted most to master painting, but thought in the end that he hadn't, though his "overall" paintings of flowers startle and delight and his still lifes of scallions, blueberries, cherries, and flowers in vases are carefully observed, light-hearted, and colorful. He painted many portraits of Whippoorwill, a dog belonging to his long-time friend, sometime lover, and collaborator, **Kenward Elmslie**. These paintings, which contrast intensely white fur with usually green backgrounds of grass or fabric, depict, skillfully and attentively, the many moods and poses of the beautifully streamlined dog, with its black, watchful eyes. Brainard's friend, the poet and art critic **John Ashbery** thought the most radical aspect of Brainard's work was that one could return to it "again and again finding something that is new, bathing in its curative newness" (Lewallen, 2).

Brainard befriended poets like breathing, beginning with **Ron Padgett**, with whom he shared a Tulsa, Oklahoma, boyhood and his first enchanted introduction to New York City. He became the artist of choice for poem-painting collaboration, comic book collaborations, drawings or paintings for book covers, and what Bill Berkson calls that "beautiful luxury item, a book of illustrated verse." Elmslie's books *The Champ* (1968) and

Sung Sex (1989) reach more eloquently to their readers because his wild poetic hijinks are set beside Brainard's elegant, cleanly executed, black and white line paintings. Ashbery's poems on the right-hand pages of *Vermont Notebook* (1975) enhance and balance Joe Brainard's illustrations of roads, rain, windows, leaves, a burning cigarette, a dandelion shedding seeds, newspapers, cups of coffee, a toilet, a shirt, bacon and eggs on a plate, a photo of a poodle, a beach, flies, a naked young man. Brainard worked also with Padgett, Ashbery, Berkson, Tom Clark, **Anne Waldman**, **Ted Berrigan**, **Robert Creeley**, **Jonathan Williams**, LeRoi Jones (**Amiri Baraka**), **Frank O'Hara**, **Kenneth Koch**, Edwin Denby, Lewis Walsh, and Tony Towle. Tom Clark wrote of his stint of collaboration, "Briefly drifting into Joe's quiet, charmed, living-and-working orbit was the most graceful thing I've ever been given to do. It was sheer luck" (http://jacketmagazine.com/16/br-clar.html).

Brainard seemingly loved language as much as he loved paint, poetry as much as images. He wandered the landscapes of the sister arts, and found their common ground. Fluent in both dialects, he translated each for the other, setting up possibilities all around of intermedial dialogue. He wrote poetry, and can take credit for having invented a twentieth-century poetic form, a casual prose-poem, in which every line begins with the phrase "I remember," followed by a short memory recalled from Brainard's past—sometimes from childhood or adolescence, sometimes from yesterday or this morning, sometimes narrative, sometimes lyrical, often trivial, lackadaisical, funny, moving, strange, always direct, somehow both sophisticated and naive. This proved an open-ended form for its creator, resulting in what Jim Cory has dubbed "the longest catalog poem in the language": the initial *I Remember* (1970) was followed by *I Remember More* (1972), *I Remember Christmas* (1973), and *More I Remember More* (1973), all gathered into one volume in 2001. Brainard accumulates the smallest of events, sensations, and half-thoughts typically considered beneath notice, not material worthy of poetry. He *will* bring back into his reader's memory an astonishing assemblage of things forgotten, the substrata of the past, the precious presentness and nonsense of lost daily life. "I remember," he writes, "Halloween and the annual problem of whether to wear a mask or to see. (Glasses.)" "I remember trying to put on a not quite dry bathing suit. (Ugh.)" "I remember day dreams of committing suicide and of the letter I would leave behind." "I remember when green black-boards were new." "I remember a *very* deluxe Crayola set that had gold and silver and copper." Hundreds of these accumulate into autobiography, and into American cultural history.

Brainard's poetry appeals with a curious, persistent modesty. It doesn't rise to big emotions, like rage or love or despair, but simmers along on anxiety, embarrassment, mild amusement or surprise, late-afternoon revelations, and diffident concessions to the clichés by which we live. It seems odd to aspire to a poetics of self-deprecation, but lines like "others have already written what I would like to write," and "the 'so what' in me wins again" give this impression, as does the title of his collection, *Nothing to Write Home About* (1981). There are poems that chart exactly how low low-key can get: The poem titled "Poem" reads in its entirety: "Sometimes / everything / seems / so / oh, I don't know." One can't help but admire the confessional effrontery of such ennui and such linguistic disinclination, topped off with the blasé flourish of such an honorific title. There is surely a direct line from **William Carlos Williams**'s domestic post-it note "This Is Just to Say," through Frank O'Hara's "I do this, I do that" poems, to these laconic, gently celebratory, deadpan observations of a poet-painter's ways and days. The poem as dilatory diary-entry is a Brainard staple: "After an unsuccessful night, going around to queer bars, I come home and say to myself, 'Art.'" And "The only thing that is wrong with people is that they don't smoke enough. I smoke four packs a day and am proud of it. Why not?"

Often his poems are irreverent, loving tributes to other artists. A poem called "Andy Do It" repeats fifteen times "I like Andy Warhol" only to conclude "And that is why I like Andy Warhol." This kind of Steinian repetition and tautology reads as very close to the comic spirit of Warhol's art, an ekphrasis that, in stating "Andy Warhol paints Andy Warhols. And I like that" performs in poetry an act of unpretentious critical appreciation. Brainard also wrote "Ten Imaginary Still Lifes" that might have been painted, but exist only in words, dependent on the reader's inner visual resources. This feels like Brainard's famous generosity, his wish not to limit or intrude. Perhaps, he seems to imply, we might take more pleasure in imagining "something copper. (A tea pot with missing lid.) And dried cornflowers in an earthenware pot" than we would in seeing it fully realized on canvas and framed, a "Brainard" rather than an image partly our own, conjured up from our own stock of ordinary, beautiful mental objects. He can do the same with word portraits. Here is James Schuyler: "surprise—yellow socks. The body sits in a chair, a king on a throne, feet glued to the floor," and here, Frank O'Hara, particularly his walk: "Light and sassy. With a slight bounce and a slight twist. . . . Confident. 'I don't care.' and . . . 'I know you are looking.'"

Brainard stopped producing art and poetry around 1989, and he died in 1994 of complications from AIDS. His legacy to American poetry will no doubt be his unswerving candor, his refusal to use language in acts of aggrandizement, and his working assumption that the visual and the verbal arts are intimate and natural companions. The catalogue of the Berkeley Art

Museum's retrospective of his work, published in 2001, with a lively green, yellow, and white still life of flowers on the cover, samples generously from his career in art and in poetry, and includes important essays by John Ashbery, Constance M. Lewallen, and Carter Ratcliff.

Further Reading. *Selected Primary Sources:* Brainard, Joe, *I Remember* (New York: Granary Books, 2001); ———, *Joe Brainard: A Retrospective* (New York: Granary Books, 2001); ———, *Nothing to Write Home About* (Los Angeles: Little Caesar Press, 1981); ———, *Selected Writings* (New York: Kulchur, 1971); ———, *Ten Imaginary Still Lifes* (New York: Boke Press, 1997). *Selected Secondary Sources:* Berkson, Bill, "Working with Joe" (Joe Brainard feature) (*Jacket* 16 [March 2002], http://jacketmagazine.com/16/br-berk.html); Clark, Tom, "My Joe Brainards" (Joe Brainard feature) (*Jacket* 16 [March 2002], http://jacketmagazine.com/16/br-clar.html); Lewallen, Constance M., ed., *Joe Brainard: A Retrospective* (New York: Granary Books, 2001).

Sara Lundquist

BRAITHWAITE, WILLIAM STANLEY (1878–1962)

An **African American poet** who believed in "art for art's sake," William Stanley Braithwaite lived by the philosophy that social and racial issues should not be a concern in poetics. In his preface to *The Book of American Negro Poetry*, another African American poet, **James Weldon Johnson**, said of Braithwaite, "He has written no poetry motivated or colored by race . . . . race has not impinged upon him as it has upon other Negro poets. In fact, his work is so detached from race that for many years he had been a figure in the American literary world before it was known generally that he is a man of color" (99). A man ahead of his time, he wanted to go beyond race to a universal artistic appreciation of poetry. Toward this end, not only was he a poet, he was an anthologist, editor, critic, publisher, and mentor. Even though he was very influential and prolific during the first half of the twentieth century, Braithwaite has been virtually ignored by the poetic field at large. Furthermore, African American literary scholars tend to dismiss him because of his controversial viewpoints. In actuality, Braithwaite helped many now famous poets such as **Langston Hughes** and **Carl Sandburg** get recognition. Probably no one helped further poetry as an art form during the first half of the twentieth century more than Braithwaite.

Braithwaite was born on December 6, 1878, in Boston to Emma De Wolfe, whose family were former slaves, and William Smith Braithwaite, a West Indian of mixed ancestry from a prominent and prosperous family. As a result, Braithwaite lived in genteel wealth and was homeschooled. At the age of eight his father died, leav-

ing the family destitute, and his mother had to start working. Braithwaite had to leave school at twelve to support his family. From that moment on, he worked very hard to educate himself. His education got plenty of assistance when he became an apprenticed typesetter. This position led to his lifelong love and appreciation of literature, especially poetry. The British poetry of William Wordsworth, John Keats, and Robert Burns particularly inspired him to start writing his own poems. He also borrowed books from the Boston Public Library to further his education.

However, his literary career did not start until after he married Emma Kelly in June 1903. Ultimately, they had seven children together. His first poetry volume, *Lyrics of Life and Love*, which intentionally echoed **Paul Lawrence Dunbar**'s previous volume title *Lyrics of Love and Laughter* (1903), appeared in 1904. He also submitted poetry to various publications and wrote articles for *Colored American Magazine*. In 1906 his second volume, *The House of Falling Leaves*, was published. That same year he was elected to the Boston Authors' Club. Despite the publication of these two volumes, most of Braithwaite's poetry and other pieces appeared in various publications and have yet to be collected in one volume.

Besides being a poet, Braithwaite was one of the first successful African American poetry critics, as shown in his column in *Boston Transcript* starting in 1905. Despite his aesthetic and mainstream inclinations, Braithwaite fully supported African American poets through critical reviews and by publishing their poems in his anthologies. He may not have agreed with some of their methods, such as the use of dialect, and he may not have approved of racial or social subjects, but he still admired their work. Braithwaite of course was fully aware of the racism that shaped his time period, but he decided to fight racism by stressing that African Americans could become mainstream poets. In his criticisms, he gained a reputation for being evenhanded and impartially focused on examining and cultivating the careers of new poets. At different times in his life, Braithwaite started a journal and his own publishing company. Although both ventures failed, his contributions through his yearly *Anthology of Magazine Verse* were very successful. He helped such African American poets as **Georgia Douglas Johnson**, James Weldon Johnson, and **Countee Cullen** and others such as **Edgar Lee Masters**, **Robert Frost**, **Wallace Stevens**, and **Vachel Lindsay** get published.

In 1935 Braithwaite moved to Atlanta to become a professor of creative literature at Atlanta University and taught there for ten years. During this time, he served on the editing board of *Phylon*, an African American literary journal of major import. His *Selected Poems* were published in 1948, and his biography on the Brontës titled

The Bewitched Parsonage: The Story of the Brontës appeared in 1950. After retiring, he moved to Harlem and died on June 8, 1962. In 1972 *The William Stanley Braithwaite Reader* was published.

As a poet, Braithwaite's stylistic technique was precise and exact; his work was not known for its emotional impact. Although he experimented with sonnets, the lengths of his poems tended to be short, and his favorite topics seemed to be mysticism, whimsy, and dreams. In his poem "Rhapsody" Braithwaite focuses upon the connection of art with nature and expresses his gratitude for "the gift of song." In other words, he thanks God, nature, and/or the universe for his ability to write poetry, even when time's change and things do not turn out for the best. He loves life regardless of what happens. The rest of the poem concentrates on Braithwaite's gratitude for his imagination, which not only helps him survive the agony and ecstasy of life but helps him write as well. Another poem, "Sic Vita," which means "yes, life" in Latin, continues in the same vein. Braithwaite's overwhelming exuberance and admiration for nature is his way of demonstrating his love for life. This poem exhibits both Braithwaite's positive outlook and the inspiration for his poetic artistry.

Although he was a prolific poet and his poems appeared in countless journals and anthologies, Braithwaite is known more for his attempts at legitimizing mainstream American poetry. Even though opinions about him and his viewpoints are mixed, no one can deny his numerous contributions to making poetry a unifying force accessible to all, regardless of racial, artistic, or social differences. His work may have become partially obscured over time, but his impact upon modern poetry as a result of helping up-and-coming poets get published can not be minimized.

Further Reading. *Selected Primary Source:* Johnson, James Weldon, ed., *The Book of American Negro Poetry* (San Diego: Harvest, 1969). *Selected Secondary Sources:* Gross, Dalton, and Maryjean Gross, "Braithwaite, William Stanley Beaumont" in *American National Biography*, vol. 3, ed. John A. Garraty and Mark C. Carnes (New York: Oxford University Press, 1999). Schulze, Robin G., "Braithwaite, William Stanley," in *The Oxford Companion to African American Literature*, ed. William L. Andrews, Frances Smith Foster, and Trudier Harris (New York: Oxford University Press, 1997). Williams, Kenny J., "William Stanley Braithwaite," in *Dictionary of Literary Biography*, vol. 50, ed. Trudier Harris and Thadious M. Davis (Detroit: Bruccoli Clark, 1986).

Devona Mallory

BRATHWAITE, EDWARD KAMAU (1930–)

Edward Kamau Brathwaite—poet, historian, and cultural critic—is perhaps the Caribbean's most innovative Anglophone poet. Ranging from his early trilogy *The Arrivants* (1973) to *Magical Realism* volumes 1 and 2 (2002), Brathwaite's work explores the Caribbean's encounters with slavery, colonization, and what Timothy Reiss calls "desperate post-colonial catastrophe" (xlv). While always conscious of the region's public and private chaos, Brathwaite creates landscapes of the imagination where self, community, and nation come into being. In the past, literary critics have often placed Brathwaite in opposition to St. Lucian poet and Nobel laureate **Derek Walcott**, presenting Brathwaite as essentially Afrocentric in sensibilities and Walcott as the Caribbean's most prominent English poet. Such a distinction, however, underestimates both poets' awareness of their dual heritage.

Born in Bridgetown, Barbados, in 1930, Kamau Brathwaite graduated from Harrison College in 1950, then left for Cambridge University, where he studied history. Between 1955 and 1962 he taught in Ghana. These early years of Ghana's independence, under the leadership of Kwame Nkrumah, moved Brathwaite, who had grown up in a colonial society, to acknowledge and explore his African ancestry. In Ghana, Brathwaite's intuitive connections between ancestral and New World experiences became realities. This reaching out for cultural connections was also fermenting in the Caribbean, and Brathwaite's yearnings for African groundings were inspired by George Lamming's *In the Castle of My Skin* (1953). Brathwaite also spent several years in Jamaica. In 1980 he was named Professor of History at the University of the West Indies. Since 1991 Kamau Brathwaite has been Professor of Comparative and Caribbean Literature at New York University. In 1994 he was awarded the Neustadt International Prize for Literature.

In *Pathfinder: Black Awakening in the Arrivants of Edward Kamau Brathwaite*, Gordon Rohlehr, commenting on *The Arrivants* (1973), describes its intricacy and range and recognizes its rootedness in the Caribbean vernacular. This trilogy chronicles the Africans' violent uprooting from their origins and sources, their traumatic Middle Passage journey, and their tortured steps on the plantations of the New World where, in "O Dreams O Destinations," "trapped in flesh, / [they] litter the landscape with their broken homes" (61). In Brathwaite's second trilogy, *Mother Poem* (1977), *Sun Poem* (1982), and *X/Self* (1987), he re-imagines a Caribbean space grounded in a collective memory of Africa. Although this space remains one of dispossession and dread, in "Xango" Brathwaite's poetic landscape has a vitality and an acceptance of living moments that suggest change and regeneration are possible: "He will shatter outwards to your light and calm and history / your thunder has come home."

The Zea Mexican Diary (1993), *Barabajan Poems* (1994), and *DreamStories* (1994) see the development of a new stage in Brathwaite's poetry. In his early works, he experimented with what he terms his "video-style." In these works, he has honed this style into what has become the unique inscription of his art. "Video-style" is his use of various computer fonts and sizes of type that move far beyond conventional representations of words on a page. He describes it, on the back cover of *Dream-Stories*, as "trying to create word sculpture on the page, word sculpture in the ear." As a result, the poetic text becomes theater. Words gain other lives and appear and disappear on the white space of the page. *The Zea Mexican Diary* (1993) recounts Brathwaite's encounter with personal grief and terror. For the first time, the poet permits entrance into the painfully traumatic world of his interior consciousness as he tries to come to terms with the imminent death of his wife: "why—I know I will not only lose my life my love my love—my very very very friend—and there are o too few of these" (*Barabajan Poems*, 78). Loss and the scarcity of human companionship are mirrored in the diminution of the text. Brathwaite equates the loss of his wife to the loss of his creative inspiration and descends to the very pit of despair.

Barabajan Poems, on the other hand, records the poet's ascent to a place where he recognizes the power of self and the sanctity of the poetic task. The text is a meditation on the development of an artistic self, and the creative/destructive forces community brings to bear upon the artistic sensibility. Brathwaite, in examining early influences on his work, permits entry into the sacred places where his words come into being. It is a gathering together of moments in time and the creation of an imaginative space that permits the poet to explore his experiences, reorder them, and impose upon them his vision of the world. As he states in "Vèvè": "the Word becomes again a god and walks among us" (*Barabajan Poems*, 259). Brathwaite refashions identity and creates Caribbean icons, thus giving birth to a text essential to the development of Caribbean aesthetics.

Barabajan Poems is an intricate multilayered composition of personal, communal, and national experiences. Here, seamlessly intertwined, is the poet's autobiographical journey into voice and related references and quotations from works by other Caribbean writers. The notes and appendices to the text come into their own as a theoretical exploration of autobiographical form and the Barbadian vernacular. An additional subtext is a list the poet compiles of "Bajan Poets" from 1661 to 1987. Although each element of this text has its own internal rhythmic pattern and a sometimes random arrangement and interplay, the work is an organic whole. The text mirrors the Caribbean-centered philosophy Brathwaite has developed as a way of discussing Caribbean reality. His theory of "tidalectics," which he describes as "dialectics with [his] difference," is such an example. He suggests that dialectics, with its structured reasoning and identifiable lines of argument, if applied to Caribbean philosophy would, by the narrowly defined space it identifies, moves discussion away from a Caribbean worldview. On the other hand, tidalectics, by mirroring the fluctuation of tides, captures the circular nature of the Caribbean's history and culture. Brathwaite creates a mythology that explains the sounds and movements of the Caribbean: "the pebbles of the pan, the plangent syllables of blue, the on-rolling syncopation, the rhythmic tidalectics" (*Barabajan Poems*, 118). He preserves and celebrates the language of the Caribbean and makes it both visual and aural.

Whereas the landscape of *Barabajan Poems* is ultimately one of possibility in that it chronicles the steps of the poet's coming into being, *DreamStories* plunges relentlessly into landscapes of dread. It is a journey into the Caribbean's heart of darkness where Brathwaite explores the psyche of oppressor and oppressed. At the center of this prose poem, Brathwaite meditates on the question: How is a new world to be created out of ruins and fragments? In this collection the shifting and illusory landscapes and dream visions testify to a state of impermanence. The slave plantations of the past surface as the factories and cane fields of the present; the character of evil appears fixed and eternal. Brathwaite takes public sins seriously; he believes that the politician's mission is to create a world where people can be virtuous. The poet's relentless excavations of the grotesqueries of the past are uneasy reminders of the repetitions of the horrors of history. In "4th Traveller," he probes the deeply complex psychic responses to the region's violent origins: "the canefield of womb or escape must have been a great gushing tumour." Brathwaite also focuses on the "tumour[s]" that devour personal relationships. For him, the turbulence governing personal relationships is the private reenactment of public violence, and it is nowhere more clearly seen than in "Grease," where relationships have no possibility for survival in the grim "ungovernmental yard." Symbolically, the body of the female protagonist is the battleground upon which the history of the Caribbean is enacted. She is married to a plumber. Ironically, she attempts, in an extramarital relationship with a locksmith, to find release from the prison house of her marriage. In Brathwaite's imaginary landscapes, the desecration of the female body is analogous to the physical and cultural exploitation of the Caribbean historically. It is also analogous to the contemporary plunder of the Caribbean by local governments and their global allies.

Unlike *DreamStories*, where Kamau Brathwaite confronts dread in its various manifestations, *Magical Realism* volumes 1 and 2 move far beyond Brathwaite's video-style as manifested, for example, in *DreamStories, Barabajan Poems*, or *Conversations with Nathaniel Mackey* (1999). *Magical Realism* is an important work in Brathwaite's oeuvre. Here video-style foregrounds the word and transforms it into sign and symbol; it is tangible and sacred. In addition to creating various sizes of type and symbols, maps and graphics are given primacy on the page; in addition, the poet's own chartings and intricate designs strive to make tangible the manifestations of the abstract world of his poetic consciousness. In the two volumes of *Magical Realism*, Brathwaite explodes conventions of prose, poetry, and critical exegesis. Such a gathering together of genres, where words work in ways ranging from the habitual to the magical, results in a text that requires of the reader a peculiar engagement of the visceral and the commonplace. Words are characters in the theater of the poet's text and they bring forth worlds of dread and wonder. Words serve also to bring to public hearing the frenzied cries of the anguished and the dispossessed. Some pages of the text are devoted to a single symbol. On other pages text appears enclosed in diagrams of varying shapes. The text may be composed of words reproduced by using fonts of various sizes, a series of symbols, or even figures in miniature. The compression or expansion of signs and symbols and their irruption upon the stage of the text challenge the reader to confront the world Brathwaite constructs in the text, and, through the kaleidoscopic landscapes of his imagination, enter into his poetic consciousness.

The focus of the text is an identification of the elements of magical realism in the literature of the Caribbean. Brathwaite in *Magical Realism* 1 describes the work as "a black caribbean blues perspective on post-cosmological disruption & redemption in the new millennium" (*MR*, 1:11). This work locates the concept of magical realism beyond Latin America and the Caribbean. *Magical Realism* is a complex interconnected text, a web of interlocking poetic, narrative, and visual strands. Grounded in the text is a talk on magical realism given to Brathwaite's class on magical realism at New York University by Chilean artist, poet, and filmmaker Cecilia Vicuña. To Vicuña, magical realism is rooted in the collision between the Europeans and the inhabitants of the New World that resulted in human devastation as well as marvelous creations. Brathwaite's text appears at a particularly apocalyptic moment in human history; therefore, it is not surprising that dread and awe lie at the heart of his treatise. Returning in time to the very beginnings of the world, its cosmography and cosmology, the poet locates the central tropes of his poetic world, missile and capsule. For example, a sketch of the Eiffel Tower occupies one page of the text, and on the facing page a poem diagrams the tower's outline (*MR*, 1:173).

While maps and diagrams illustrate the result of the encounter between missilic European cultures and capsulic African cultures, Brathwaite locates a space that moves beyond visual and diagrammatic representations. In this space he enlarges words into symbols that surge

and shrink on the page. These techniques are clearly illustrated, for example, in the section of the text where he retells the story of three gunmen who break into his house in Kingston, Jamaica, and by chance fail to murder him: "for this is the alive— / the spirit of the room— / my **nam**—" (*MR*, 2:416–417). As the poet concentrates on the interior terror, words enlarge and expand; they appear in bold outline, a testimony to the dread of the moment. The word "nam," which Brathwaite defines as man's fundamental essence, is reduced in size and fixed on the territory of the page, symbolizing a mysterious force, a brooding consciousness painfully waiting to be liberated from the territory of dread. Brathwaite's poems radiate a powerful intensity and, as in "Cosmos," cry out for a return to wisdom: "**corruption failure & xtinguishment / will be the opposite of who I am**" (*MR*, 1:229). Building imaginative art out of contrary elements, Brathwaite weaves together abstract theories: for example, Einstein's theory of relativity and his studies of the space-time continuum, together with what he terms "the death of God" and the deterioration of the sacred in society. To the poet, this deterioration leads to the further development of missilic secular cultures. He suggests that magical realism is the Caribbean's literary response to a reclamation of the cultural and the spiritual inspired by the region's gods and sacred places.

Magical Realism 1 and 2 are key texts in the development of Caribbean poetics. Brathwaite merges past and present, and ancient myths and modern truths, and he penetrates time, history, and mythology in his yearning for a new world. His imagination is consumed by his desire to inspirit the Caribbean space with markers of the region. To this end, he distinguishes between the terms Sisyphus and Dorado; Dorado is the mythic Eldorado. In his words, "Sisyphus . . . is that mainly or characteristic anglophone(?) Caribbean xpression that sees the task of liberation . . . as a surely pessimistic toil." Eldorado "remains close to the hope? the dream of a ?NewWorld" (*MR*, 1:81). Brathwaite's imaginary landscapes offer no stark division between the two. His poetic consciousness ranges from an acknowledgment of the centrality of certain cultural symbols—for example, the Asian pagoda, the African circles, and the Western missile—to a presentation of what he terms "the Classic(al) Missilic Ladder of Reason Faith and Progress" (*MR*, 1:182). He identifies each rung from Aristotle's *Organon* through Edward Long's *History of Jamaica* to Karl Marx's *Das Kapital*. The poet transforms this ladder into a symbol of the universal human experience. At the foot of the ladder he buries the traumatic experience of slavery, the dread of the Middle Passage, and the experiences of personal and collective colonial trauma.

In *Magical Realism* 1 and 2 Brathwaite gathers together the worlds of wonder and dread. The text is a testament to the concept of magical realism that he locates at the center of the apocalyptic meeting between Europe and the New World. The text is also unique in that Brathwaite engages the critical theories of magical realism as well as the works that epitomize them. He links forms of art ancient and modern, and weaves them through place and time. The *Odyssey* and the *Aeneid* join *Gilgamesh*, *Beowulf*, and *Roland*, *The Arabian Nights*, moralities, miracles, mysteries, Miss Queenie, *The Pilgrim's Progress*, Ti-Jean, and *Mission Impossible*. In this partial listing, there is a coming together of disparate entities. The reader, at one with the poet's prophetic vision, is challenged to negotiate past and future. Brathwaite's visionary world is comparable to the visionary world of the Guyanese novelist Wilson Harris. Like Harris, Brathwaite journeys into the world of the imaginary in an attempt to transform the world and bring a new one into being. Both writers create constantly shifting landscapes of consciousness where space and time are transformed by the magical power of the word.

Magical Realism 1 and 2, like his other works, confirm Kamau Brathwaite as a poet of experimentation and innovation. More than any other poet from the Caribbean, he explores and explodes language and form, creating new genres in which to rewrite the region's turbulent past and envision its future possibilities.

Further Reading. *Selected Primary Sources:* Brathwaite, Kamau, *The Arrivants: A New World Trilogy* (Oxford: Oxford University Press, 1973); ———, *Barabajan Poems* (New York & Kingston, Jamaica: Savacou North, 1994); ———, *Magical Realism*, vols. 1 and 2 (New York & Kingston, Jamaica: Savacou North, 2002). ***Selected Secondary Sources:*** Bobb, June D., *Beating a Restless Drum: The Poetics of Kamau Brathwaite and Derek Walcott* (Trenton, NJ: Africa World Press, 1998); Reiss, Timothy J., ed., *For the Geography of a Soul: Emerging Perspectives on Kamau Brathwaite* (Trenton, NJ: Africa World Press, 2001).

June D. Bobb

BRAUTIGAN, RICHARD (1935–1984)

Richard Brautigan wrote poetry for seven years to prepare to write novels. By 1960 he had published four books of verse and established himself as a minor figure in the **San Francisco Renaissance**. That year he also began work on his first novel, employing the spare style, offset by wildly imaginative figurative language, that he had honed as a poet. Upon publication seven years later, this novel, *Trout Fishing in America* (1967), became a literary emblem of the flourishing counterculture movement. Brautigan gained an international audience and returned to writing poetry—this time for its own sake. He would publish six more books of poems, but his readership would decline with the waning of the counterculture movement.

Brautigan was born in Tacoma, Washington, in 1935, shortly after his parents had separated. Accounts from family members indicate that his childhood was marked by loneliness, neglect, and poverty. He began writing as a teenager and was determined to become successful. Poverty added urgency to this goal, as he felt writing was his only skill. After graduating from high school in Eugene, Oregon, in 1953, he began publishing his poems in national magazines. In 1958 he settled in San Francisco at the height of the Beat movement and befriended many of the **Beat poets** including **Lawrence Ferlinghetti**, **Michael McClure**, and **Philip Whalen**. His poetry began appearing in major Beat publications such as the *Evergreen Review* and *City Lights Journal*. His first published novel, *A Confederate General from Big Sur* (1964), sold poorly, but *Trout Fishing in America* quickly sold two million copies. Brautigan's reclusive lifestyle and aversion to the drug culture made him an unlikely hippie icon, but the candor, idealism, and whimsical nature of his work appealed widely to that generation. The author nurtured this association by the free distribution of *Please Plant This Book* (1968), eight poems printed on seed packets suggesting the reader prolong the life of the poem by transplanting it into the earth. But his popularity dropped dramatically in the mid-1970s, by which time he became relegated to cult status. Brautigan did not adjust well to this decline, and his later years were characterized by alienation and alcoholism. In the summer of 1982, he secluded himself in his Bolinas, California, ranch house to write his final novel, published posthumously as *An Unfortunate Woman* (2000). His body was discovered on October 25, 1984, several weeks after he had died of a self-inflicted gunshot wound.

Brautigan's verse is pervaded by a preoccupation with time. Generally, if he is not lamenting the erosive effects of time, he is celebrating and attempting to preserve ordinary moments before they are lost to oblivion. Whether his poems are despairing or ecstatic, their effect tends to rely on irony and innovation. His first book, a broadside titled *The Return of the Rivers* (1957), introduces this concern with time. The poem alludes to Ecclesiastes, acknowledging the perpetual ebb and flow of the earth's waters but noting the presence of spring, which does not, for the moment, "dream of death." Brautigan's early poems often feature surreal anachronisms. In "To England" from *Lay the Marble Tea* (1959), the poet imagines mailing a letter back to a time when John Donne's "grave hasn't been dug yet." He imagines Donne greeting the postman, who approaches with a glass cane. The new poems in Brautigan's first major collection, *The Pill Versus the Springhill Mine Disaster* (1968), which includes nearly all the poems of his earlier books, resemble the concise, conversational poetry of **William Carlos Williams** ("Widow's Lament") and recall the word play of **e.e.**

cummings ("The Shenevertakesherwatchoff Poem"). In the title poem, one of many that allude to a historic tragedy as an analogue for personal loss, "all the people lost" due to a girlfriend's use of birth control are compared to the victims of a mining catastrophe. Brautigan's poems frequently use dates to harness more firmly an ephemeral moment. In "Alas Measured Perfectly," a snapshot of two seemingly happy women, taken on August 25, 1888, becomes a metaphor for the poem itself, which has captured what is "all gone." His next collection, *Rommel Drives on Deep into Egypt* (1970), includes a few poems with only titles, the blank page suggesting something forgotten. "1891–1944," for example, refers to the lifespan of General Rommel, who, as Brautigan notes in the book's title poem, has "joined the quicksand legions / of history." In "The Memoirs of Jesse James," the poet compares his school teachers to the legendary outlaw "for all the time they stole" from him. Often the composition of a poem is itself the subject, as in "April 7, 1969," where Brautigan wishes to commemorate how bad he feels with "any poem, this/ poem."

The title poem of his next collection, *Loading Mercury with a Pitchfork* (1976), conveys the poet's frustration in trying to capture the essence of experience. But in "Seconds" he notes that with "such a short amount of time to live and think" he has spent the proper number of seconds observing a butterfly: "twenty." In the introduction to his final collection, *June 30th, June 30th* (1978), Brautigan credits the Japanese haiku poets for teaching him to concentrate "emotion, detail, and image" to create "a form of dew-like steel." He also acknowledges the frequent criticism that his work is uneven, stating "the quality of life is uneven." In this book, which chronicles a stay in Japan, Brautigan emphasizes that his art not only preserves poetic moments but also validates his existence. In "Tokyo / June 11, 1976" he remarks that his passport and his poetry "are the same thing." Brautigan's final poem, "The Past Cannot Be Returned" lacks the optimism of "The Return of the Rivers." The "umbilical cord" broken, he notes, life cannot "flow through it again."

The 1990s saw nine of Brautigan's books, including *The Pill*, reissued in America and many more throughout Europe. The discovery of his earliest poems, published in *The Edna Webster Collection* (1999), shows that Brautigan's experimental style and his concern with the transience of experience colored his work from the start.

Further Reading. *Selected Primary Sources:* Brautigan, Richard, *The Edna Webster Collection of Undiscovered Writings* (New York: Houghton Mifflin, 1999); ———, *June 30th, June 30th* (New York: Dell, 1978); ———, *Loading Mercury with a Pitchfork* (New York: Simon & Schuster, 1976); ———, *The Pill Versus the Springhill Mine Disaster* (San Francisco: Four Seasons Foundation, 1968); ———, *Rommel Drives on Deep into Egypt* (New York:

Dell, 1970). *Selected Secondary Sources:* Abbot, Keith, *Downstream from Trout Fishing in America: A Memoir of Richard Brautigan* (Santa Barbara: Capra Press, 1989); Foster, Edward Halsey, *Richard Brautigan* (Boston: Twayne, 1983); Malley, Terrence, *Richard Brautigan* (New York: Warner, 1972).

John Cusatis

BRITISH POETRY

In the famous and deliberately provocative preface to the first edition of *Leaves of Grass* (1855), **Walt Whitman** declares his nationalist agenda: "The Americans of all nations . . . have probably the fullest poetical nature. The United States themselves are essentially the greatest poem." Whitman's declaration of America's poetical supremacy was met with derisive sneers by most of his English reviewers. "But what claim has this Walt Whitman to be considered a poet at all?" asks one critic, before going on to describe him as a "Caliban throwing down his logs" and his poetry as merely the monstrous offspring of English poetical supremacy (Anonymous review of *Leaves of Grass, The Critic* 1 April 1856, n.p.) Although what is ostensibly at stake here is a definition of poetry and the poetic, the panache and obstinacy of the rhetoric on both sides makes apparent the degree to which a consideration of transatlantic poetic relations can, in fact, be seen as a measure of Britain's and America's ideological entanglements. From this encounter it is clear that the poetic relationship between Britain and America is profoundly engaged with—indeed helps to encode—debates about the formation of national and cultural identity. The rhetorical framing of these debates and this relationship, moreover, indicates two things. First, it shows the susceptibility to change of the terms (the poetic, the national) in which such debates are grounded. Second, it reveals the underlying tension from which such debates might be seen to arise: the partial (in both senses) understanding of each side of this relationship by the other.

The ways in which British and American poetries have related to and influenced one another, then, have important repercussions for thinking about wider transatlantic relations. Rather than simply valorizing the sorts of narrowly prescriptive—and pretty much fixed—ideas of nationhood that have dominated readings of Whitman and of Anglo-American literary relations, it might be argued that it is precisely when this wider debate is carried out in terms of "poetical natures" that it reflects more accurately (or at least sets up more accurate terms for an investigation of) the difficult and contested dynamics of transatlantic exchange. The idea of the poetic, in other words, is a useful ideological index of the mutual fascination and mutual antagonism of Anglo-America's "special relationship."

The history of the relationship between British and American poetries is, therefore, a history of continually changing structures of cultural power. It plays out a series of "double-edged discourses" that are, as Paul Giles has argued, "liable to destabilize traditional hierarchies and power relations, thereby illuminating the epistemological boundaries of both national cultures" (*Virtual Americas*, 5). In broad terms, a history of Anglo-American poetic relations (from the colonial period up to the twenty-first century) witnesses a marked, though gradual, power shift in the double-edged discourse of poetic influence. Initially American poetry was under the powerful sway of English poetic influence. But, since the early years of the twentieth century, English poetry's power of influence over American has steadily declined. Despite this broad pattern of declining English influence and increasing American, there remains a sense of cagey unease about the mutual influence and relationship between the two poetic traditions. Effectively the relationship between both poetic traditions has always been one of destabilization, in which each tradition feels itself ill-defined by—because it is always, to some extent, in comparison to—the other. In this context, then, the linking of nationhood with an idea of the greatest poem introduces into the Anglo-American compact precisely that "element of strangeness" that constitutes, according to Giles, transatlantic cultural relations. This means that although at times one tradition may make a claim to various forms of cultural or ideological superiority over the other, and at other times it may seem to ignore them, both are continually engaged in a cultural dynamic that inescapably defines their (national) poetics. Throughout the history of Anglo-American poetic relationships, this sort of negotiation has more frequently—certainly more visibly—taken place at the margins of each poetic culture, at their respective epistemological boundaries. Indeed, it has been the avant-gardes in both traditions that have embraced, challenged, and made specific use of each other in ways that have, ultimately, come to re-invigorate the whole tradition. In contrast, the poetic mainstreams in America and Britain, then, confirm their mutual importance and influence largely by ignoring (or dismissing as irrelevant and strange) one another.

In terms of nationality, of course, England and the American colonies were one and the same until 1776. Despite this, some of the earliest poetry written in the American colonies is especially marked by its sense of difference from English verse. It is already produced within a poetics of American nationalism, one that quite explicitly hypostatizes its own elements of strangeness. Indeed, the key terms in the efforts of early American poetry to define its own grounds are its relationship to, and influence by, English poetry. Such terms come to be carried over, via the developing idea of an American poem, into cultural (and ultimately political) debates between the Old and New worlds. The first phase of influence between English and American poetry can therefore be seen to run throughout the colonial period. If the poetry of this phase is characterised by a sort of religious utopianism and Puritan zeal on both sides of the Atlantic, it is in America that such strands begin to become markers of cultural difference, of burgeoning republicanism and democratic hope.

The first poet who can probably be considered "American" in any meaningful sense is the Puritan **Anne Bradstreet**. Her poetic career exemplifies, in many interesting ways, the struggle of America to define itself as a culture separate from (but in relation to) England. The publication of her first book of poems in 1650 demonstrates this. Because of copyright laws and literary markets at the time, the best place for an aspiring author to publish was London (or, possibly, Edinburgh). Bradstreet's poems were, apparently without her knowledge or initial consent, first published in London at the insistence of her brother-in-law, John Woolbridge. As if to emphasize the specialness of her work, by marking it as exotically different, the volume was titled *The Tenth Muse Lately Sprung Up in America*. From the start, then, Bradstreet's poems were marketed on their qualities of "strangeness": not only were they by a woman, but by an American woman. Many poems in this volume are conventional exercises that seek to expand, without radically changing, the bounds of poetic decorum. The poem "In Honour of Queen Elizabeth," written in heroic couplets, depicts Elizabeth as a "Phoenix queen" modeled on classical examples and who expanded the bounds of English Empire into the "terra incognita" discovered by Drake. Though entirely conventional, this image has a peculiar and distinctive resonance in a poem written in New England. Such qualities in Bradstreet's work signal the beginnings of an American poetic sensibility. These are heard most often in her later less epic, more personal lyrics. A set of figures that appears often in Bradstreet's lyric poems is that of issues of family, the domestic, and motherhood. Although these denote her status as woman-poet, they also come to signify her other difference from English poetic influences, her Americanness. "The Author to Her Book" written to preface the second (1666) edition of *The Tenth Muse*, is a conventional poetic disclaimer at the start of a work (like Milton at the start of *Lycidas*). However, by describing her poems here as "ill-form'd offspring" she sets in motion a way of thinking about American poetry as though it were the hideous progeny of the mother poetry of England. Much subsequent evaluation of the relationship between English and American poetry has—as we have already seen in the case of Whitman—either explicitly or implicitly drawn on this image as its model of influence.

In other ways, too, the poetry of Puritan New England draws on, and then away from, the influence of English poetry. **Edward Taylor**'s devotional lyrics develop a homespun, plain-speaking idiom that has often been used since to distinguish between American and English poetries. As Donald Davie has demonstrated, Taylor's plainness of diction is deeply influenced by Isaac Watts and English hymnody. However, it is in the particular social circumstances from which Taylor's poems arise that his Americanness can be felt. George Herbert and John Donne also provide models of poetic devotion for Taylor, if only through Taylor's writing against them. The intricacy of their poetic wit stems from precisely the sort of hierarchical power relations (of the Anglican Church) that is inimical to the Congregationalist tenor of Taylor's New England experience. Plainnesss of diction and clarity of idiom thus become markers of a distinctively American poetics not simply to distinguish it from English poetics but because of the different social and religious circumstances from which it arises. This can be seen particularly powerfully in the ***Bay Psalm Book*** (1640). Written specifically for the religious devotions of the people of the Massachusetts Bay colony, its aim was to translate the Psalms into the everyday "plain" idiom of the colonists. The *Bay Psalm Book* embodies, therefore, the poetics of difference and influence of America's nascent sense of national identity.

As American poetry moved into the eighteenth century the need to define itself against the influence of English poetry became ever more pressing. Marius Bewley has argued that the largest problem facing the American writer is "the nature of his separateness from, and the nature of his connection with . . . English culture." And by the early 1700s, following the restoration of the monarchy and changing trading patterns across the Atlantic, this problem became especially pressing for American writers. In terms of poetic influence, though, the dominant voice on both sides of the Atlantic in this period was that of John Milton. Milton's epic, *Paradise Lost* (1667), had special resonance in the colonies. It provided America with a poetic model of the perfect Christian republic by authorizing a sense of the heroic ethics of American nationalism. In many ways, then, Milton's powerful influence over American poetry at this time was due to his perceived separateness from English culture that resulted from his own position of Calvinist dissent. Following Milton's example (though not necessarily his politics) various American poets attempted to write an American **epic**: **Joel Barlow**'s *Vision of Columbus* (1787) and **Philip Freneau** and **Hugh Henry Brackenridge**'s "On the Rising Glory of America" (1771) are perhaps the best-known examples. The emancipatory utopianism of Milton's epic poetics also had a decisive influence on the work of black poets and former slaves **Phillis Wheatley** and **Jupiter Hammon**, though Hammon's "An Evening Thought: Salvation by Christ, with Penetential Cries" (1760) is indebted to English ballad tradition, too.

Neoclassical English poets such as Dryden, Pope, and Swift were also dominant influences on American poets at this time. American poets were aware that they were writing for English as well as American audiences, and they found that the forms of satire and the satirical impulse of such English models suited their sense of cultural doubleness. So, if Milton provided American poetry with one style for its own sense of political and cultural dissent, the mock-epic style of English satirists provided America with a different style, and tone, for its poetics of dissent. Written in 1708, **Ebenezer Cooke**'s *The Sot-Weed Factor* satirizes English stereotypes of America, and especially of its merchant classes. Cook's poem is a particularly vibrant example of American poetry's ability to capitalize resourcefully on an English poetic model. Based on the form of Samuel Butler's biting satire of Puritans, *Hudibras* (1653–1680), it turns the tables on the transatlantic relationship. By taking on the voice of a member of the English elite—the sot-weed factor, or tobacco merchant—it deftly satirizes his snobbish attitude toward Americans, whom he sees as morally destitute and culturally backward. American readers would easily have recognized the merchant's ignorance of America and its culture, and delighted in his inaccurate assumptions about America. Another famous example of American poetry's adoption for its own purposes of the mock-epic form is Barlow's *The Hasty Pudding* (1796), which celebrates a native American dish, cornmeal mush, in the high style of heroic epic. Such mock epics derive their cultural power as expressions of American concerns precisely because they challenge and disturb the dominant paradigm of power (English verse) that they adopt as their influence. To a degree, then, this indicates the highly self-conscious nature of America's sense of its relation to English poetics. This means that because American poetry, right from its earliest moments, has always consciously seen itself in a productive dialogue with English poetry, it has always had a particularly acute sense of its poetics as a political tool, the means of declaring cultural independence.

The dominant poetic models and influences over the course of the eighteenth century—epic and satire—are, of course, public modes. In some regards this might sit uneasily with the mode of lyrical introspection and self-analysis that has now come to be seen as the "typical" mode of American poetics. However, the lyric mode in America (as with Bradstreet and Taylor) has always arisen from political and cultural circumstances, from the contested ground between personal and public expression. This sense of lyric contestation is another marker of how American poetry has introduced an element of strangeness into its relationship with English poetics. One way of thinking about this conscious making strange of sources, for political purposes and in terms of America's lyric energies, is the use of songs and ballads in the Revolutionary period. As rallying cries to both patriot and loyalist causes such songs share a common assumption about what constitutes a specifically "American" poetics. Whether pro- or anti-English, such lyrics all assume that America is different from England, and thus they are based on a poetics of exchange in which traditional English folk songs are adapted to current American circumstances. This is remarkably similar to the underlying assumption of the *Bay Psalm Book*: In effect, the political pressures of America's difference from England call for a different set of words, though the forms may remain remarkably similar. The particular political bite of "Yankee Doodle," to pick the most famous example of this tendency, lies in a strategy of defamiliarization whereby new words, signaling new contexts and assumptions, are sung to the tune of a traditional folk song. Indeed, up to the early years of the American nation, American poetics might well be summed up as the singing of new words to old tunes, for a distinct set of political purposes. Because this strategy very deliberately seeks to destabilize existing power structures, it is a useful model of the relationship between English and American poetics, demonstrating as it does how American poetics is more than a simple parody of English poetics. This sense of an interweaving system of mutual relationship and influence has profoundly colored ways of thinking about discourses of American democracy over the years, and on both sides of the Atlantic. By the turn of the nineteenth century, however, there was a strongly felt need in American poetry for not just the words, but the old tunes themselves to be changed.

The nineteenth century, then, posed a new set of challenges for poetic relations across the Atlantic. Although America was now a new nation testing the terms of its independence from England, its poetry in the early years of the century still remained dependent upon, and felt itself to be subservient to, English poetry. What the age demanded was a radical breaking of the old models of poetic influence. Writing in the wake of the wars of 1812 and 1815, Edward Tyrell Channing described America's need for a "a literature of [its] own" in terms of the overbearing influence of English literature. "Our literary delinquency," he notes, is the result of "our dependence upon English literature" ("Reflections on the Literary Delinquency of America," *North American Review*, 1815). It would seem that Channing's fears about the straitjacket of English literary influence was remarkably prescient. Interestingly, in terms of Anglo-American poetic relations, those American poets who rose to popular prominence at the time, such as **William Cullen Bryant**, **Henry Wadsworth Longfellow**, **John Greenleaf Whittier**, and even **Lydia Sigourney**, were decisively influenced by English poetry. This gives some

indication of the dominance not only of the British literary marketplace and publishing houses at the time but also of English critical attitudes. Simply put, those poets who best fit English models were hailed as embodying the real spirit of American poetry.

In the first half of the century, for example, Bryant was felt to be America's brightest poetic hope because his "beautiful and affecting simplicity" came closest to poets in the English **pastoral**-landscape tradition such as Cowper, Gray, and Southey. Bryant's most celebrated poem, "Thanatopsis," is heavily influenced by English Romantic poetry, particularly the Wordsworth of the *Lyrical Ballads* (1798). The American details of this poem—"lose thyself in the continuous woods / Where rolls the Oregon"—seem merely incidental to Bryant's exercise in poetic imitation of English masters. Whittier and Sigourney drew on slightly different traditions. As with his major influence, Robert Burns, Whittier's verses arose from an experience of childhood poverty and poor education. Ironically, the sensationalism with which he expressed his anti-slavery views derived from the English sentimental tradition. Sigourney, too, was praised for her similarity to the women poets who influenced her—Felicia Hemans, Charlotte Smith, Mary Robinson, Anna Letitia Barbauld—but (because she was a woman) was felt not to quite match up to the "manly" strengths of the male Romantics. The most interesting of these American poets in terms of his sense of poetic influence and its importance to issues of poetic nationality is Longfellow. His most famous work, *The Song of Hiawatha* (1855), is an exercise in making strange his sources in order to make them fit peculiarly American circumstances. Longfellow adopts the verse form of the Finnish epic poem *The Kalevala* for *Hiawatha*, an epic based on Native American stories. Tellingly, Longfellow's English poetic antecedents are less apparent than is the case for most of his contemporaries. By the second half of the century, Longfellow was widely held to be—on both side of the Atlantic—America's best, and most representative, poet. America's poetic tradition was starting to break free of English influence.

It was only in the second half of the century that Whitman and **Emily Dickinson**—who now epitomize and define a radically different American poetics (one of new words set to new tunes)—began their poetic careers. Despite their prominence now in any history of American poetry they were, for the most part, not considered part of the mainstream during their lives. The turnaround in the posthumous poetic fortunes of Whitman and Dickinson can be attributed to changing attitudes about the relationship between English and American poetry, and about what actually might constitute a "truly" American poetry. In retrospect, Whitman and Dickinson seem absolutely central to the idea of an American poetics because of their characteristically

"American" voices (and this despite Dickinson's debt to the Brontës, Elizabeth Barrett Browning, and Christina Rossetti). Although their different poetic voices kept them at the epistemological margins of American poetry during the nineteenth century, it is precisely this sense of the different voice of American poetry that continues to dominate a consideration of the relation and influence between American and British poetry in the twentieth century and beyond.

By and large, since the early twentieth century the poetic mainstream in Britain and America has dismissed the other as irrelevant to its poetic and cultural concerns. It is at the poetic margins that the most lively and productive transatlantic poetic exchanges have taken place. In a historical turnaround that matches America's political rise to global preeminence in the century, it has mostly (though not exclusively) been American poetry that has influenced and re-invigorated English. Just how complicated these mutual relations and influences have been is intimated at the start of the century by the careers of **modernist** poets such as **Ezra Pound, T.S. Eliot**, and **H.D.** All three were American born, and their poetry has had a huge impact in both America and Britain, so quite properly they should be seen as important American poets. However, their major works were all written outside America. Perhaps it is precisely because this underscores the problems and ambiguities of thinking about a national poetry that subsequent modern poetry in both America and Britain has tended to ignore the transatlantic dynamic in its definition of its own poetry. In America, for example, the homespun modernity of poets such as **William Carlos Williams, Wallace Stevens, Hart Crane**, and **Carl Sandburg** avoids English influences in order to develop its own, specifically American poetics. And a similar pattern of avoidance can be seen in British poetry for most of the century. Modern English poets such as **W.H. Auden**, Stephen Spender, Louis MacNeice, and the Movement poets (dominated by Philip Larkin) seem especially English in their cultural sensibilities and their concern to avoid "contamination" by American poetic ideas. Indeed, British commentators scornfully derided Auden's settling in New York in 1939. Only Auden and Dylan Thomas can seriously be thought of as mainstream British poets who had any a real influence on American poets in the twentieth century—Auden on the crisp ironies of **James Merrill** and the early work of **John Ashbery**, and Thomas on the **Beats** (and, of course, **Bob Dylan**).

It is, however, the experimental poetries of Britain and America that have most consciously and deliberately embraced their mutual relationship to, and influence upon, each other. The Beats, and especially **Allen Ginsberg**, had a radically galvanizing effect on the British avant-garde in the early 1960s at a time when British poetry was dominated by the modes of introspective gloom practiced by Movement poets. The Mersey Beats—Liverpool poets Brian Patten, Roger McGough, and Adrian Henri—popularized poetry and brought about a thriving performance poetry scene in Britain. A telling moment in the history of Anglo-American poetic relations was the reading, organized by Michael Horowitz at the Albert Hall in 1965, in which British and American poets, Ginsberg included, appeared together. For many British poets this opened up their poetry to the energetic possibilities they could see in the work of their American counterparts. Important voices in British experimental poetry, including Roy Fisher, Lee Harwood, Edwin Morgan, Tom Raworth, and Gael Turnbull, to name a few, saw poetic possibilities emerging from their interrelation with American experimental poetry at the time. All of these poets have acknowledged their debt to Don Allen's groundbreaking anthology *The New American Poetry* (1960). Another vital figure in British experimental poetry since the late 1960s has been J.H. Prynne. His complex and difficult, but necessary, poetry is deeply influenced by American modernist poetics and, especially, **Charles Olson** and the **Black Mountain School**. Via Prynne a new generation of British experimental poets have been made to account for the place of American poetics within their own practices. The **New York School** poets, **Language poets**, and other groupings of American **postmodernists** have all had a profound influence on those contemporary British poets for whom the idea of a fixed and traditional sense of British poetry is shorthand for poetic and cultural complacency. Throughout its history, the negotiation of complex and difficult relationships and influences within Anglo-American poetry and poetics has helped, therefore, to provide a rich point of energetic and self-questioning renewal for poetic practice in both Britain and America. It has also helped shape those double-edged discourses that make up transatlantic cultural relations.

Further Reading. Bradbury, Malcolm, *The Expatriate Tradition in American Literature* (Durham, UK: British Association for American Studies, 1982); Clark, Steve, and Mark Ford, eds., *Something We Have That They Don't: British and American Poetic Relations Since 1925* (Iowa City: University of Iowa Press, 2004); Giles, Paul, *Transatlantic Insurrections: British Culture and the Formation of American Literature, 1730–1860* (Philadelphia: University of Pennsylvania Press, 2001); ———, *Virtual Americas: Transnational Fictions and the Transatlantic Imaginary* (Durham, NC: Duke University Press, 2002); Lease, Benjamin, *Anglo-American Encounters: England and the Rise of American Literature* (Cambridge: Cambridge University Press, 1981); Mengham, Rod, and John Kinsella, eds., *Vanishing Points: New Modernist Poems*

(Cambridge: Salt, 2005); Tuma, Keith, *Fishing by Obstinate Isles: Modern and Postmodern British Poetry and American Readers* (Evanston, IL: Northwestern University Press, 1998).

Nick Selby

BROCK-BROIDO, LUCIE (1956–)

Lucie Brock-Broido is a poet of daring appropriation, channeling what seems, at times, an anachronistic voice through an array of personae, both personal and historical. She has an archaeologist's fascination with relic, as well as with how the arcane and archaic pertain to contemporary American culture and idiom. Brock-Broido is most directly a descendent, in ideology if not in mannerism, of **Wallace Stevens**, **John Berryman**, and **Emily Dickinson**, as well as of Thomas James, a lesser-known American poet, whose work she champions. She is also a decorated teacher of poets, formerly at Harvard and, since 1992, as director of the poetry concentration in Columbia University's graduate writing program.

Born in 1956, Brock-Broido grew up in Pittsburgh, leaving to attend the Johns Hopkins University. As an undergraduate there, she largely wrote fiction, studying with John Barth and Edmund White, but she entered the university's graduate writing seminars as a poet. There she studied with **Richard Howard**, who would become, along with the critic Helen Vendler, perhaps the most important supporter of her work. In 1979 Brock-Broido enrolled in Columbia University's MFA program, studying with **Stanley Kunitz** and **Charles Simic**. After graduating in 1982, she began publishing her poems in a number of prominent journals and, in quick succession, won fellowships from the Fine Arts Work Center in Provincetown and the National Endowment for the Arts, as well as a Hoyns fellowship at the University of Virginia. In 1983 she moved to Cambridge, Massachusetts, where she taught at various colleges. With the publication of her first book, *A Hunger* (1988), she became Briggs-Copeland Lecturer in Poetry at Harvard, a position she held from 1987 to 1992. At Harvard she developed an important relationship with colleague **Seamus Heaney**, from whom Brock-Broido's poetry would inherit a sensibility for the physical landscape.

From the start *A Hunger* displays several trademark characteristics of Brock-Broido's writing. Its syntax and lexicon are, intermittently, colloquial and baroque: Its opening poem, "Domestic Mysticism," begins, "In thrice 10,000 seasons, I will come back to this world / In a white cotton dress." Brock-Broido's speakers are disenfranchised yet ecstatic, often longing for some aspect of the past and future, while uneasy with their present. Much of this is accomplished with changing idiom; "Domestic Mysticism," for example, ends using the current vernacular: "I've got this mystic streak in me." It is her capacity to intermingle the archaic and the colloquial in language that infuses her poems with such unrest. Both the opening poem and the collection as a whole convey the poet's interest—spiritually, creatively, and idiomatically—in reincarnation. *A Hunger* is peppered with personae poems, its assumed identities diverse and unlikely as Oyewolffe Momar Puim ("Birdie Africa"), a fourteen-year-old survivor of the MOVE cult, whose building was firebombed by the Philadelphia police; Edward VI ("Edward VI on the Seventh Day"), who became king of England at the age of nine in 1553 (and died six years later); and June Gibbons ("Elective Mutes"), one of two institutionalized twin sisters who, as children, stopped speaking to anyone but each other, and ultimately plotted one another's murders. However, no matter whom her medium, the voice that pervades *A Hunger* is distinctively, idiosyncratically Brock-Broido's own, her attraction to her speakers borne more out of what seems a sense of kindred spirit than an impulse to reproduce their distinctive parlances. In "Jessica, from the well," for instance, a poem in the voice of a girl who, at eighteen months, spent several days trapped at the bottom of a Texas well shaft, the speaker describes "[t]he noise of my own form against the loosening / walls as I am born into the dark / rococo teratogenic rooms of the underground." The poems in *A Hunger* were occasionally dismissed by some as ornamental and out of step with a contemporary American readership, but they are in fact highly preoccupied with the contemporary American experience, particularly that of the restless Midwest of the poet's childhood, as in poems like "Ohio & Beyond" ("Towns pass you by like pretty girls / you wish you left behind") and "A Little Piece of Everlasting Life." In "Autobiography" the speaker refers to "the autoerotic sounds of my American voice," perhaps as clear a declaration of self-description as there is of *A Hunger*'s aesthetic: It is a book which over and over reveals Brock-Broido as a poet enthralled by the timelessness of language and how it can render a moment in time both foreign and intimate.

It was nearly a decade before the publication of Brock-Broido's second book, *The Master Letters* (1997). In it, the psychic synthesis of poet and personae becomes even more pronounced, the landscape, both physical and verbal, even more exotic. Inspired by three letters written by Emily Dickinson to a nameless master, the poems, many in the form of epistles, are addressed to their own mysterious mentor: "To a Strange Fashion of Forsaking" begins "*Master*— / I hardly know to address you; you are—a man?" Indeed, the collection overflows with cryptic allusion, as its omnipresent, singular speaker, an irrepressible acolyte, seeks clarity from among her own erudite, at times gaudy, psyche. The mysteriousness of this project— the compulsive (occasionally multilingual) interrogation of an unidentifiable muse-mentor—results in a collection that, though poignant, is more arcane than *A Hunger*. Still, although some reviews dismissed the book as esotericism, on the whole *The Master Letters* was deemed a metaphysical triumph.

With her third book, *Trouble in Mind* (2004), written after a three-year hiatus, Brock-Broido produced her most accessible and powerful collection to date. While retaining the extravagance and strangeness that won her first books critical acclaim, it subtly incorporates a greater aspect of the personal, compelled by the deaths of the author's mother and her dear friend, the writer Lucy Grealy, to whom the book is dedicated. The poems are pithier; even the endnotes to the poems, so elaborate in the first two volumes, are fewer and more solemn. The collection emphasizes neither personae nor master, declaring in "Dire Wolf," "To you, / I am not speaking anymore," before asking, rhetorically, "Whom/ Shall I address?" Like her muse, Wallace Stevens (whose notebook of potential poem titles inspire a number of the poems in *Trouble in Mind*), Brock-Broido seems to be curbing (to great effect) some of her instinct for adornment as she moves into mid-career.

Further Reading. ***Selected Primary Sources:*** Brock-Broido, Lucie, *A Hunger* (New York: Alfred A. Knopf, 1988); ———, *The Master Letters* (New York: Alfred A. Knopf, 1997); ———, *Trouble in Mind* (New York: Alfred A. Knopf, 2004).

Gabriel Fried

BRODSKY, JOSEPH (1940–1996)

Properly characterized as a Russian American poet, Joseph Brodsky led a life nearly evenly divided between the two countries. His expulsion from the former Soviet Union occurred in 1972, when Brodsky was thirty-two years old. Thereafter he resided in the United States, becoming an American citizen in 1977. Having taught himself English while in his teens, he began after his exile to produce poems in both Russian and English, and criticism and essays in English. In 1987 he was awarded the Nobel Prize in Literature. He served as Poet Laureate of the United States in 1991–1992, where his chief aim was the furtherance of the American Poetry and Literacy Project he founded with Andrew Carroll. This project, which continues, was meant to make a reality of Brodsky's belief that poetry should be ubiquitous—available in gas stations, supermarket checkout lines, hospitals, and hotel rooms. Brodsky formally introduced this idea in his acceptance speech to the Library of Congress, titled, "An Immodest Proposal." Thousands of volumes of poetry have been distributed as a result.

Joseph Brodsky was born May 24, 1940, in the city of Leningrad. He was largely self-taught as a scholar and a poet. He left school after completing the eighth grade, took a wide assortment of jobs, and began to read widely and write verse. He soon gained recognition, coming to the attention of his contemporaries and such major figures as Anna Akhmatova. His work also came to the attention of the authorities. After various questionings, detentions, and arrests, in 1963 Brodsky was sentenced on the charge of social parasitism to five years hard labor in the Archangelsk province of Siberia. Through the intervention of literary figures in the Soviet Union and abroad, Brodsky's sentence was commuted after eighteen months. He was later to look back on his time of exile as a time of happiness that united him with the farm people of his country and showed him another, more private way to live. On June 4, 1972, Joseph Brodsky was permanently exiled from the Soviet Union. **W.H. Auden** helped to arrange Brodsky's immigration to the United States and his first teaching position at the University of Michigan. Brodsky quickly established himself as a force in American literary circles, forming close friendships with such major figures as **Seamus Heaney**, **Robert Lowell**, **Mark Strand**, and **Derek Walcott**. He achieved renown as a teacher at several major institutions, spending the last fifteen years of his life as a professor at Mount Holyoke College. Brodsky's students were devoted to him, in spite of the requirement to memorize hundreds of lines of poetry that kept all but the most stalwart away. His courses consisted of the poet talking about poetry and the poets read in such a way that it was all brought to the level of the familiar. His students felt the poetry was something palpable, real, and alive, and the people who wrote it, many of whom Brodsky knew, were equally so. Brodsky continued to teach, lecture, and read until the very end of his life. He was, in fact, due back at Mount Holyoke the day after his death to start the spring semester. Brodsky died of a heart attack at his home in Brooklyn on January 28, 1996.

In the essay "A Poet and Prose," Brodsky wrote that poetry was language in its "highest form of existence." Few who read his trial transcripts could forget that when he faced down the judge who asked him what he believed made him a poet, he told him he believed it must come from God. For Brodsky, poetry was a form of religion, and he practiced it with an absolute devotion akin to faith. It was such single-mindedness that caused many to believe that he was not so much a poet as the very embodiment of the poet.

In traditional forms with a novel and inventive use of rhyme, Brodsky explored motifs of love, loss, and the plight of the individual. The first of Brodsky's works to be published in America was *Selected Poems* (1973); this volume, translated by George Kline, includes a foreword by W.H. Auden. Auden wrote that Brodsky is a "traditionalist in the sense that he is interested in what most lyric poets in all ages have been interested in, that is, in personal encounters with nature, human artifacts, persons loved or revered, and in reflections upon the human condition, death, and the meaning of existence." *Selected Poems* includes Brodsky's "Elegy for John Donne"(1963); several poems addressed to M.B., including his "New Stanzas to Augusta" (1964); and a number of the poems composed while he served his sentence of hard labor. The volume concludes with "Odysseus to Telemachus," the poem Brodsky wrote as a goodbye to his four-year-old son, Andre, after he learned of his impending exile from Russia.

Although the bulk of his work has not yet been translated from the Russian, Brodsky produced a number of volumes in English or in translation, many done by himself or under his supervision. *Collected Poems in English* (2000) contains *A Part of Speech* (1977), *To Urania* (1984), *So Forth* (1996), and previously uncollected poems. *A Part of Speech* is in two parts, "A Song to No Music" and "A Part of Speech." The first section comprises poems written while still in Russia; the second half begins the poems of exile. It includes one of his earliest poems written in English, "Elegy: for Robert Lowell."

To Urania includes "The Fifth Anniversary," written to commemorate five years of exile. Brodsky usually composed poems to mark important dates such as his exile, his birthday, and the Christmas and New Year holidays. The final two lines of "The Fifth Anniversary" reveal Brodsky's continued preoccupation with space, which often extends to the question of where his body will eventually lie: "I don't know anymore what earth will nurse my carcass / Scratch on, my pen: let's mark the white the way it marks us." "Afterward" revisits his relationship with M.B., the mother of his son Andre. As in many poems addressed to or about her, the holy family is invoked: the mother and child, and Joseph, the father, who lies somewhat outside the mystery shared by mother and child. The poet says that he no longer remembers the events that passed between them, just providing a catalog of where they might have taken place. What seems most important is found in one phrase where the poets says, "I am speaking to you," something he was to continue to do for most of his life, even though they were not to meet again. "May 24, 1980," one of Brodsky's most widely quoted poems, was written to mark his fortieth birthday. He presents the reader with an overview of his forty years in only twenty lines. Filled with what most of us would deem tragedy, he attempts to shrug it all off as something that simply happened. To summon the image of his three open-heart surgeries, Brodsky writes only that he has "thrice let knives rake my nitty-gritty." He concludes that for all of it, until the end of his life, there will be no complaints heard from him, "only gratitude." "Gorbunov and Gorchakov" is printed in *To Urania* in its entirety. This verse drama in fourteen cantos depicts a conversation between two inmates in a mental hospital. Brodsky con-

ceived it when he himself was institutionalized by the Soviet authorities.

So Forth was completed by the author but not published until after his death. In it, Brodsky seems preoccupied with his mortality and keenly aware of his impending demise. The title refers not only to one of the common phrases employed by Brodsky when conversing in English but also to the movement forward to the death he was sure was soon to come. Many of the poems seem to project that death, using figures like centaurs or the mythical Daedalus to stand in for the poet. Brodsky also attempts, it seems, to bring to a close his involvement with M.B., whom he addresses again in "Brise Marine." Again he seems to protest too much, writing, "your body, your warble, your middle name, / now stir practically nothing." The choice of characteristics he includes, in their specificity, suggests otherwise. But among the concern with endings there is a nearly equal portion of hope in the form of celebration of new love and new life in poems such as "Song," "New Life," "Nativity," "Lullaby," "Love Song," "Song of Welcome," and "To My Daughter." The list above is heavy with songs, and the rest of the volume makes this more explicit, for there are also poems such as "Anthem," "Reveille," "Blues," and the final poem, "Taps," his own goodbye song, which was also chosen to be the back cover of the *Collected Poems in English*. He writes there that he knows he will soon "dwindle into a tiny star."

Nativity Poems (2001) collects those poems that Brodsky wrote yearly at the Christmas and New Year season; they form an extended meditation on the Christian mythos and the sense of hope that these beliefs might represent to the individual, with their emphasis on forgiveness, birth, beginnings, and the love of the father, in this case another Joseph. Although it might strike some as strange that Brodsky, a Jew, would produce what is essentially a Christmas book, Brodsky was enamored with the beauty of the story of the Nativity and the family unit of mother, father, and child.

Brodsky's essays have been deservedly cited for praise. Collected in two volumes, *Less Than One* (1986) and *On Grief and Reason* (1996), these serve as an introduction to the poet, his poetics, and his wide and various influences. *Less Than One* was given the National Book Critics Circle Award. In this collection of essays, Brodsky largely looks back to Russia, focusing on his parents, his native city, and his literary predecessors. In the essay "To Please a Shadow," he recounts buying his first English language typewriter in 1977, in order to compose a poem to W.H. Auden in his native language, thereby, perhaps moving closer to him, though Auden was four years dead.

On Grief and Reason includes essays on **Robert Frost** and Thomas Hardy that provide examples of what

Brodsky's classroom was like; it also includes his Nobel acceptance speech and lecture, "Uncommon Visage." The book takes its title from the essay on Frost, where Brodsky does a line-by-line reading of "Come In" and "Home Burial." In addition to these works, also available in English are Brodsky's verse play, *Marbles* (1986); a book-length essay on Venice, *Watermark* (1992); and a children's book, *Discovery* (1999). In 1996 Farrar, Straus and Giroux released *Homage to Robert Frost*, a volume containing essays on Frost by Brodsky, Seamus Heaney, and Derek Walcott.

No discussion of Joseph Brodsky would be complete without mention of him as a reader, or singer, of poems. He believed that poetry was still a melic art, that poems were to be sung. Anyone in attendance at one of his readings would immediately recognize that the atmosphere differed from that of a typical poetry reading, resembling nothing so much as a religious service, with poems taking the place of prayers. Fortunately there are recordings and videos that capture this experience for posterity.

Since Brodsky's death in 1996 there has been no dimming of his reputation. Worldwide there have been memorial services; the list of those who have elegized Brodsky is long and the names on it are esteemed. The Joseph Brodsky Memorial Fellowship provides fellowships for Russians to study in Italy, a country he loved and thought essential to the development of the intellect and aesthetic sensibility. There has been talk of releasing a volume of his sketches. Eventually, more of his Russian poems will be translated, and America will know more of this poet.

Further Reading. *Selected Primary Sources:* Brodsky, Joseph, *Collected Poems in English*, ed. Ann Kjellberg (New York: Farrar, Straus and Giroux, 2000); ———, *Discovery* (New York: Farrar, Straus and Giroux, 1999); ———, *Less Than One: Selected Essays* (New York: Farrar, Straus, and Giroux, 1986); ———, *Marbles* (New York: Noonday, 1989); ———, *Nativity Poems* (New York: Farrar, Straus and Giroux, 2001); *On Grief and Reason: Essays* (New York: Farrar, Straus, and Giroux, 1995); ———, *A Part of Speech* (New York: Farrar, Straus and Giroux, 1980); ———, *Selected Poems* (New York: Harper & Row, 1973); ———, *So Forth* (New York: Farrar, Straus and Giroux, 1996); ———, *To Urania* (New York: Farrar, Straus and Giroux, 1988); ———, *Watermark* (New York: Farrar, Straus and Giroux, 1992); Brodsky, Joseph, Seamus Heaney, and Derek Walcott, *Homage to Robert Frost* (New York: Farrar, Straus and Giroux, 1996). ***Selected Secondary Sources:*** Bethea, David, *Joseph Brodsky and the Creation of Exile* (Princeton, NJ: Princeton University Press, 1994); Loseff, Lev, and Valentina Polukhina, *Brodsky's Poetics and Aesthetics* (New York: St. Martin's Press, 1990); MacFadyen, David, *Joseph Brodsky and the Soviet Muse* (Montreal: McGill-Queen's University Press, 2000); Polukhina, Valentina, *Joseph Brodsky: A Poet for Our Time* (New York: Cambridge University Press, 1989).

Anna Priddy

BROMIGE, DAVID (1933–)

As a poet, David Bromige has a genius for variety. He has published thirty books, each one so different from the others as to seem to be the work of a different author. Bromige is often associated with the **Language poets**, but this connection is based mainly on his close friendships with some of those poets. It is difficult to fit Bromige into a slot. He departs from Language poetry in the thematic unity of many of his poems, in the uses to which he puts found materials, in the romantic aspect of his lyricism, and in the sheer variety of his approaches to the poem.

Bromige was born in London, England in 1933. At an early age, he showed signs of being tubercular and was sent to an isolation hospital, but after four months his condition improved and he was discharged. "However," he writes in an unpublished memoir, "I would not speak to my parents, or my sister, for weeks." That hospital was the first of several crucial interludes that molded his adult life. The second of these interludes came during the London blitz. A stick of bombs falling in their customary sequence appeared likely to destroy the Bromiges' house, with them inside: "I swore on my soul that, if we were spared, I would be someone else." The next interlude involves his schooling and work experience. When the war ended, Bromige won a scholarship to Haberdashers' Aske's Hamstead and a chance to study at a socially superior school. After completing his school certificate, Bromige accepted an offer to be a dairyman on a farm in southern Sweden. Each of these interludes changed him. The first made him suspicious of his family; the bombing made him vow to be someone else; work and study gave him the worldly experience to be a poet.

He met other poets at the University of British Columbia—George Bowering, Frank Davey, David Dawson, Jamie Reid—and they encouraged him to write and publish his work. At the 1963 Vancouver Poetry Festival, Bromige met **Robert Creeley**, **Charles Olson**, **Denise Levertov**, **Allen Ginsberg**, and **Robert Duncan**. The festival made Bromige rethink his poetic philosophy: "I had to think of a new way to write; I had to think until I came out the other side of thinking."

The result of this endeavor was the publication of many poems. **Robert Hass**, the chairman of the Western States Book Award Committee, wrote glowingly of his work and chose his 1988 book, *Desire: Selected Poems, 1963–1987* to win the first prize for poetry. He has twice been honored by the Poet's Foundation, once with a $3,000 prize and again with a $10,000 prize. And he has twice been honored by the National Endowment for the

Arts. He won the college prize for the first poem he ever published. "This not only won me $50, which was about $300 at today's rates," he writes, "but it secured me the editorship of the campus literary journal."

Three years later, Bromige won a Woodrow Wilson scholarship. The rules stated that he had to do his graduate work at a different university. He chose Berkeley after graduating from the University of British Columbia. It was 1962. "I do remember *some* of the 60's," he says. For instance, after reading from his first book, *The Gathering*, at the Berkeley Poetry Conference in l965, he remembers that Robert Duncan told him, "Don't stop at the end of each line like Creeley. It's bad enough that he does it. Find your own way to read. Read freely."

In 1968 his third book, *The Ends of the Earth*, was published by Black Sparrow Press. It was the beginning of a twenty-three–year partnership that produced eleven of his books. The poems in this book have a ghostly tone, as though Cocteau were doing a very detailed description of Bromige's life. The change, apparent in his fifth book, *Threads*, is startling. It reads as though the ghostly presences from *The Ends of the Earth* had fleshed out and learned to speak a language from the various lives whose talk fills the book.

Then came seven books in two years. This is Bromige at an early peak. *Ten Years in the Making* begins it. This book consists of some of his early poems, going back to 1960, work engagingly open to the average reader. Then came selections from *The Gathering*, followed by poems from *Threads*. Next was *Birds of the West*, from Victor Coleman of Coachhouse Press in Toronto. This book consists of three sections: a journal of gardening and visitors; a section of more finished poems, filled with a landscape of Western Sonoma County; and a single **long poem** written in sparse triplets to reflect a white-tail kite's hovering flight.

Soon afterward *Tight Corners and What's Around Them* was issued by Black Sparrow. Bromige has stated that it was the most interesting to him of this clutch of books: "I was using a fairly familiar sort of sentence, in prose, with a last line that either boosted sales or fell flat as a flapjack. I didn't care. Banal or brilliant, it made no difference in the world I was living in. Besides, sometimes the banal turned brilliant as I listened."

He also did three pint-sized books about this time for the Sparrow series. As he explains, "I like twelve-page books. Most books should be about that size." In 1974 he also published a book of "occasional" poems, *Spells and Blessings.*

Bromige continued to publish prodigiously in magazines, and in 1980 published a book called *My Poetry.* "Ron Silliman said to me it was perfect, so I found some faults with it, but not many. I thought it was good enough to be my last book, but then Lynn Hejinian asked me to write a Tuumba book for her series. I

thought I had a good idea, but someplace I lost it. I was far fonder of a trio of tales I wrote about Hung Chow, who was somewhat older than I, in exile in London and teaching a class in Buddhism. I meant to write more of those," he said, "and just this summer of '04, I did."

The 1980s started with a Pushcart Prize for *My Poetry* and ended with the Western States Poetry Award for his selected poems, *Desire*. In between, Bromige devoted himself to his wife and young daughter while carrying a full-time professor's responsibilities in the English Department at Sonoma State University (SSU). He coordinated poetry conferences at SSU, published a collaboration with Opal Nations, wrote an analysis of Allen Fisher's four-day residency at Langton Street in San Francisco, and was himself the subject of an issue of Tom Beckett's *The Difficulties*. In 1990 John Martin, who had moved Black Sparrow Press to Santa Rosa, published *Men, Women & Vehicles*, a book of selected prose.

Bromige retired early from SSU, in 1993, and he continued to publish and give readings. *Tiny Courts in a World Without Scales* is a book of fifty short poems, showing Bromige at his droll and sarcastic best. He had fun with *They Ate*, a cut-up from a turn-of-the-century detective novel, before producing *A Cast of Tens*. The poems in *Cast* are made up of ten-line stanzas, but in each poem the lines are distributed variously. *The Harbormaster of Hong Kong* came next, with many kinds of writing in it, including a perfect sonnet. Bromige's final book from the 1990s was *Vulnerable Bundles*, which appeared in a limited edition of thirty.

Bromige returned to teaching part-time at the University of San Francisco, and he also began writing what would later be *As in T as in Tether*, which was awarded Best Book of the Year (2003) recognition from Small Press Traffic. He published *Indictable Suborners* and *Behave or Be Bounced* in 2003. Finally, Bromige has been collaborating with poet and dPress editor Richard Denner on *100 Cantos*. Even at this stage of his career, he continues to experiment with poetic forms in new and interesting ways.

Further Reading. *Selected Primary Sources:* Bromige, David, *As in T as in Tether* (Tucson, AZ: Chax Press, 2002). ———, *Desire: Selected Poems 1963–1981* (Santa Rosa, CA: Black Sparrow Press, 1988); ———, *The Harbormaster of Hong Kong* (Los Angeles: Sun & Moon Press, 1995); ———, *My Poetry* (Berkeley, CA: The Figures, 1980); ———, *Selected Prose* (Santa Rosa: Black Sparrow Press, 1991); ———, *Threads* (Los Angeles: Black Sparrow Press, 1978); ———, *Tight Corners and What's Around Them* (Los Angeles: Black Sparrow Press, 1974).

Richard Denner

BRONK, WILLIAM (1918–1999)

In its profound skepticism, embodied in acutely refined statements, William Bronk's poetry holds a unique place in the history of American letters. His poetry is philosophical on its face, and by turns it can be angry or tender as it plumbs the depths of the problem of how human beings can come to know their world, and whether or not they can ever rest contented with what it is that they come to believe they know. Bronk takes up the problem of language, and alternately the problem of the mind, and he can twist one around the other to remarkable effect. Overall, his view of the human condition is extraordinarily austere, and his writing style, concise and elegant, is equally and appropriately austere. Bronk's language is subtle, balanced in tone and diction, and, in embodying his poetic vistas, is extraordinarily distilled. In addition, Bronk is always explicit visually and resonant musically. It is both difficult and easy to contextualize him. He writes in keeping with a New England poetic tradition: He evokes natural landscapes and the seasons—winter most of all—as he delves into the nature of reality or truth. These themes were explored in the nineteenth century by **Henry David Thoreau** (an especially strong influence on Bronk), **Ralph Waldo Emerson**, and **Emily Dickinson**, and the focus was firmly established early in the twentieth century by the New England poets **Robert Frost** and **Wallace Stevens**, and later by—along with Bronk—**Robert Creeley** and **George Oppen** (who was not a New Englander although he spent many years in New York). Bronk can also be thought of as related to the **Black Mountain School** of poets (including Creeley and **Charles Olson**); he started publishing in the pages of two magazines associated with this group, *Origin* (edited by **Cid Corman**, who published Bronk's first collection, *Light and Dark*, in 1956) and *The Black Mountain Review* (edited by Creeley). In terms of writing style, Bronk can also be usefully compared with the **Objectivist poets**; Oppen was prominent for Bronk among them, had a productive relationship with him, and was instrumental in the publication of a second collection, *The World, the Worldless* (1964).

Bronk was born February 17, 1918, in Fort Edward, near Hudson Falls, New York, where he lived his entire life except during his student years at Dartmouth College and Harvard University, a period of military service during World War II, and a brief turn as an instructor at Union College. Even after he gained a wide readership, Bronk kept himself out of the spotlight and concentrated on his immediate surroundings. Nevertheless, Bronk won the American Book Award in 1982 and the Lannan Prize for his life's work in 1992. While at Dartmouth, he met Robert Frost, and his fellow student and friend was Samuel French Morse, who became a well-known authority on Wallace Stevens. Stevens was an influence Bronk eventually felt he could ill afford (indeed, many critics have likened the two). In middle age, Bronk divested himself of all of the Stevens books he owned to avoid rereading them and to develop his own distinct point of view and style, although, stylistically, Bronk and Stevens are very different, the latter flamboyant, the former ascetic. Perhaps Bronk's way of living is best typified by his poem "The Abnegation" (1971), in which he proclaims his unwillingness to compromise not only his poetic vocation but his entire existence. He writes, "I will not / be less than I am to be more human." He believes that what he knows of the world is, at best, only a semblance of the truth; reality exists and he is able to intuit its existence, but it is finally beyond his grasp. Language can only offer a shadow of the real, but it is what he has to work with.

At the heart of Bronk's work lies paradox. His elegant poetic statements—never a word more than is necessary to create a poetry of statement—purport to describe the facts of life; and yet Bronk constantly writes about the elusiveness of any fact. In "The Rain of Small Occurrences" (1955) he notes, "The world is not quite formless; we lean down / and feel the massive earth beneath our feet." The earth is tangible. Even so, the closest to factuality Bronk can come is the poem itself, ultimately a poem that, in its sureness, in its reliability of diction, meter, and outlook, insists on a reality that finally will lie beyond his comprehension. Faced with such a daunting epistemological dilemma, Bronk is forced to live fiercely in the present, as the poem "On the Failure of Meaning in the Absence of Objective Analogs" (1971) suggests: "There is only this whatever this may mean / and this is what there is and nothing will be."

Some things are knowable in limited ways—desire especially. To be sure, desire is, as Norman Finkelstein has commented, the "single great constant" in Bronk's work. So what is it that Bronk desires? Impossibly, he desires "the world." But knowing the world, all in all, is beyond his capacity. In any case, knowledge is only a logical realization. Of course, the human condition is not predicated on reason alone. "Despite the self-limiting fact that consciousness is aware of its inability to experience this totality, it continually struggles for the achievement of its goal. Cut off from any ground of belief, secure only in its desire, consciousness therefore creates a world, which despite its insufficiency in metaphysical terms nevertheless allows for the rendering of form—the poem" (Finkelstein 481).

In "The Inference" (1972) Bronk allows that there are "reassurances" in life; these are "the far trips / the mind can make." Our peregrinations occur within this world of desire, a world tantalizingly unknowable. All the same, there may be "a world we know from inference. / It isn't here and yet we go to it." Imbued by desire, then, human existence is never absolutely grounded in certainty and therefore is without a real identity, as Bronk explains in the preface to his book of collected essays, *Vectors and Smoothable Curves* (1983). Who and what, and where, are we? We attempt to find ourselves as a way of knowing who we are; the problem here is that no matter how "direct and immediate our awareness may be it is also devoid of external reference and its strength and centrality is uncertain." We are like vectors, merely "proposals of location and force whose only referential field is internal—not ultimately oriented. We can be grateful for their stabilities even aware as we are of an arbitrariness with them." To live with these propositions means we must recognize the tenuousness of life. In other words, "Reality is brought to mind by the inadequacy of any statement of it, the tension of that inadequacy, the direction and force of the statement" (n.p.).

Some things are provisionally knowable. Bronk's poem "Some Musicians Play Chamber Music for Us" (1955), in a phrase reminiscent of Stevens, claims that "all we will know are fragments of a world," even through the arts. In "The Mind's Landscape on an Early Winter Day" (1955), a poem whose evocation of winter rivals winter poems by Frost, Bronk writes, with an unparalleled bleakness that in turn evokes a delicate beauty, of what he calls the "winter mind, the ne'er do well," his alter ego, a "poor blind" that "is always lost and gropes its way . . . even when the senses seize the world." The best comforts against the sense of being lost are the stories we live and the metaphors that we are. Hence, Bronk's poem "The Wanted Exactitude" (1991) ends in a single-line stanza: "let our metaphor be accurate." Metaphor is as close to reality as he can come. In "The Mind's Limitations Are Its Freedom" (1972) Bronk asks, "What else but the mind / senses the final uselessness of the mind?" The irony in this statement is not, of course, lost on Bronk, and so it might be a surprise to realize that his contemplation of the human mind is joyful even though "the mind of man" is "frail, deep / in disorder" and "always pushed by the falsenesses / of unreality." It is this unreality that is predicated by desire, and so Bronk has no choice but to embrace that desire. "I want to be that Tantalus," Bronk proclaims in "The Abnegation," "unfed forever." He asks that he be spared all compassion and that his reader notice how humankind "takes handouts, makeshifts, sops for creature comfort." These he refuses.

Even physical love is undermined by this restlessness. In "Wants and Questions" (1985), Bronk accuses his lover, naked beside him in bed, of taunting him simply by "[wearing] those skins and bones." Who is this person, and who is he? As Paul Auster has commented, "Bronk's poetry stands as an eloquent and often beautiful attack on all our assumptions, a provocation, a monument to the questioning mind" (30). Ultimately, Bronk's greatest struggle may be with the fact of death, which defines his life, although he will forgo the opportunity to acknowledge death's sway. Indeed, in his towering poem, "The Smile on the Face of a Kouros" (1969), he purposely undermines death in a rhetorical strategy that rivals, in its stature, John Donne's sonnet "Death Be Not Proud." Bronk considers the statue of a young athlete. Looking at it, he observes that "The boy was dead, and the stone smiles in his death / lightening the lips with the pleasure of something achieved"; what has been achieved is the coming "to death / as an end"—but more than this, coming with "the full / weight of his strength and virtue, the prize with which / his empty hands are full." This poem presents "the interrelationships among beauty, death and form," Burt Kimmelman has commented, in order make a "major aesthetic and philosophical statement" (90). Form is underwritten by death. Death gives shape to art and life both. In what amounts to a statement of his own poetics, which might describe his austere poetry, Bronk concludes his poem by stating that he refuses to offer up to death any creation—since he refuses to acknowledge death's power—except that the essentially paradoxical nature of his life is evidence of his very existence. At the conclusion of this poem, its persona's apostrophe sums up the uncompromising repudiation that becomes the most authentic way to live: "I tell you death, expect no smile of pride / from me. I bring you nothing in my empty hands."

Life, as demarcated by death, is overwhelming, and the trick is to avoid ineffability. Here, indeed, Bronk succeeds. And he can marvel at life's conditions, even reveling in them at times. In "The Various Sizes of the World" (1964) we find Bronk looking through a telescope at the night sky. The mind is marvelous in that it can seemingly travel the great distances to the stars, thanks to science and technology—the telescope, the mathematician's slide rule, and so on. The "sensitive plate / of a telescope has fixed a light so far / we never knew." Even a galaxy's huge breadth is made relative. Still, Bronk is driven to ask, "What address ever really finds / us in the endless depths the world acquires?" All measurements are ultimately futile, all attempts at positioning. "No," he must end up saying, "here's an incongruous world, too large, too far."

Even so, Bronk realizes himself as a human being through his recognition of his limits. Given the provisional nature of all perception and knowledge, the lack of fixity in the physical world, and so on, Bronk constructs a vision in which centrality is key. In "Of the All with Which We Coexist" (1969) he relies on a single image, that of the eye, which is meant to signify perception. He can see as far as the eye can see, yet he knows "the sky goes farther," and instruments such as a telescope confirm this understanding—however, as in "The Various Sizes of the World," instruments are also of limited use. Finally Bronk must turn back upon himself, since no journey outward will tell him anything sure about the world; there is nothing that cannot be qualified. His self-locus becomes what is most significant for him, what he can best rely upon. "If I am not central to the world, then it fails / to make any difference whatever I feel," he insists. He realizes that he is "the instrument of the world's passion." He finally instructs his reader: "Feel." To be a sentient being is to live at the center of things.

Bronk's is a poetry of rigorous statement and yet it is musical, refined, and deeply ruminative, as it advances the most troubling human inquiries that by definition cannot be answered. The questions, then, become supremely important. Bronk, over the course of a long life, wrote poetry that was consistent in style and discourse. It is almost as if he were a cipher, writing down what some divine force had dictated, so of a piece, and simultaneously disturbing and beautiful, is virtually all of his work.

Further Reading. ***Selected Primary Sources:*** Bronk, William, *Life Supports: New and Collected Poems* (Jersey City, NJ: Talisman House, 1997); ———, *Selected Poems*, ed. Henry Weinfield (New York: New Directions, 1995); ———, *Vectors and Smoothable Curves: Collected Essays* (Jersey City, NJ: Talisman House, 1997). ***Selected Secondary Sources:*** Auster, Paul, "The Poetry of William Bronk" (*Saturday Review* [8 July 1978]: 30–31); Clippinger, David, ed., *The Body of This Life: Essays on William Bronk* (Jersey City, NJ: Talisman House, 2001); Ernest, John, "William Bronk," in *Dictionary of Literary Biography*, vol. 165, ser. 4, ed. Joseph Conte (London/ Detroit: Bruccoli Clark Layman/Gale Research, 1996), 69–80; Finkelstein, Norman, "William Bronk: The World as Desire" (*Contemporary Literature* 23.4 [1982]: 480–492); Kimmelman, Burt, *The "Winter Mind": William Bronk and American Letters* (Madison, NJ: Fairleigh Dickinson University Press/ London: Associated University Presses, 1998).

Burt Kimmelman

BROOKS, CHARLES TIMOTHY (1813–1883)

Charles Timothy Brooks occupied a place among the New England intellectual elite, and like a number of his peers and friends from his Harvard days—including, J. Lathrop Motley, **Oliver Wendell Holmes**, and **Theodore Parker**—he was a man of letters. Brooks was known in his own day primarily for his religious writing, sermons (he wrote at least 1,350 in his lifetime), pamphlets, essays, and of course for his poetry, but he is primarily remembered today as a translator of German poetry and drama.

Born in Salem, Massachusetts, on June 14, 1813, Charles Timothy Brooks joined a long line of respected Puritans. In 1832, at the age of only eighteen, already showing an interest in religion, partly as a result of his earlier exposure to **Ralph Waldo Emerson**'s sermons, Brooks graduated from Harvard, where he had distinguished himself as leader of the *Hasty Pudding Club* and

as class poet. Also, to his good fortune, during his time at Harvard, Brooks had the opportunity to study under Carl Follen, a highly respected German scholar of his time. Directly following his graduation, Brooks chose to pursue a Unitarian education at Harvard Divinity School, from which, to no one's surprise, he graduated three years later with honors.

Soon after his graduation from divinity school, Brooks began to travel—as a sort of pastor at large—but his wandering was short-lived. In 1837 he received the call to become the pastor for a newly formed church in Newport, Rhode Island. He was officially ordained a short time later by **William Ellery Channing** (Channing also presided at Brooks's wedding). Brooks would remain Newport's pastor for thirty-seven years. Later that same year, Brooks married Harriet Lyman Hazard, and together they had four children, two girls and two boys. However, little is known of his life with Harriet and their children.

In 1859 Brooks published *The Simplicity of Christ's Teaching*, a collection of his sermons explicating his thoughts and beliefs concerning the new admixture of religion, culture, and science that was Transcendentalism. The early to mid-nineteenth century also found the intellectual elite of New England enjoining a sensibility that celebrated the German culture.

Brooks took from Harvard confidence in his gifts as well as his studied expertise in the art of **translation**. Over the course of Brooks's post–divinity school life, he translated Schillers's *William Tell* and the first English translation of Goethe's *Faust* to be published in America, works by Richter, and numerous pieces by minor German writers—in order to introduce more of the German culture, the German sensibility, to the American reading public (von Klenze, 4, 5).

Brooks was unhealthy as a child and also as an adult. When he was seriously ill, he often traveled, yet he seldom used his time away for rest; rather, he would often preach at other Unitarian churches. At the age of twenty-nine and again nine years later, while suffering from a particularly serious bout of respiratory problems, Brooks appears to have nursed his way back to health by delivering sermons to the Unitarian Society, a small group of Unitarians outside Mobile, Alabama. Brooks would leave his duties in Newport three more times before his death. The first, to India in 1853, was due to illness; then in 1865–1866 he left on a long-awaited tour of Europe. The last time was when he retired in 1871 (Brooks was so beloved by his parishioners that it was not until 1873 that his resignation was accepted by his congregation).

When Brooks sailed for India on the first of his trips away from Newport, he was so ill he thought that only a long sea voyage might affect a cure. He was at sea for ten months, but it was another year before he could return to his duties as pastor. In 1854, still in India,

Brooks finally regained his health, and he also managed to publish a few articles in *Harper's Monthly*. During his excursions across the Atlantic, both to India and Europe, Brooks was able to establish friendships with many of the great minds of his day, among them William H. Channing, Elizabeth Gaskill, and Thomas Carlyle, for whom Brooks had great respect.

By far, the majority of Brooks's poetry was published in periodicals. His choice of rhyme and meter schemes was seldom seen as an artistic stretch. His two most remembered poems, "Our Island Home" and "Lines: Composed at the Temples of Maralipoor," stand as examples (Hollander, 626–628); both use repetitive *ABABCDCD*. . . rhyme schemes, eight-beat end-stopped lines, and four-line stanzas. "Aquidneck" (1848), on the other hand, written to be read at the one hundredth anniversary of the Redwood Library in Newport, poses as a short **epic** poem, but uses only a few of the more obvious epic conventions: rhymed couplets and iambic pentameter. The poems in *Songs of Field and Flood*, his first full-length book of poetry, also rely on the simple meters of his time. All but three of the thirteen poems are rhymed couplets: two follow the traditional *ABAB* rhyme scheme, while the other is a translation of a sailor's song, a limerick of sorts, rhymed *AABBB*.

Although Brooks's poetry could be rightly accused of propagating the mundane and received little critical approval in its day, his work was known and consumed by the populace at large. What popularity he did enjoy was based on his being a recorder of the times; he wrote accessible poetry about the shifting times of the Restoration, the loosening of the Puritanical religious chains, our relationship to nature and each other, and politics and patriotism, both shaken to their roots by the Civil War. Brooks ends *Songs of Field and Flood*, with "Toll! Toll! Toll!" a poem at once recalling the majesty of George Washington and linking Washington's noble image to the tolling of a church bell. His verse encourages the reader to remember Washington, "the noble soul," who via the monument at Mt. Vernon, "speaks peace for ever more."

After his official retirement from the pulpit, and almost blind, Brooks settled into his last years as a writer. During that time he published numerous new translations, including "The World Priest" (1873) and "Of the Wisdom of the Brahmin" (1882). In these translations, as in all his other works, Brooks was communicating his Transcendentalist/Unitarian ideals. Brooks died one June morning in 1883. Although his death was quiet and peaceful, it did not go unnoticed; he was mourned both by his neighbors and past parishioners, and by his friends and colleagues across the world.

Further Reading. *Selected Primary Sources:* Brooks, Charles Timothy, *Aqidneck; A Poem Pronounced on the Hundredth Anniversary of the Incorporation of the Redwood Library Company, Newport, R. I. August XXIV, MDCCCXLVII. With Other Commemorative Pieces* (Providence, RI: Charles Burnett, Jr., 1848); ———, *Songs of Field and Flood: A Volume of Poems* (Newport, RI: John Wilson and Son, 1853); Hollander, John, ed, *American Poetry: The Nineteenth Century*, vol. 1 (New York: Library Classics of the United States, 1993); Wendte, Charles W., *Poems, Original and Translated* (Boston: Roberts Brothers, 1885). ***Selected Secondary Sources:*** Cooke, George Willis, *Unitarianism in America: A History of Its Origin and Development* (Boston: Scholarly Press–American Unitarian Association, 1902); Eliot, Samuel A., ed, *Heralds of a Liberal Faith: The Preachers*, vol. 3 (Boston: American Unitarian Association, 1910); Klenze, Camillo von, *Charles Timothy Brooks: Translator from the German and the Genteel Tradition* (Boston: D.C. Heath–MLA, 1937).

Thomas L. Herakovich

BROOKS, GWENDOLYN (1917–2000)

The literary life of poet Gwendolyn Brooks spans seven decades and several literary and political movements. In her more than thirty books, the impact of racial discrimination and poverty upon everyday urban black people remains her most prominent theme. Gwendolyn Elizabeth Brooks was the first African American writer to win the Pulitzer Prize, and is best known for her mastery of language and **poetic forms**, her contributions to the **Black Arts Movement**, and her commitment to mentoring young poets.

Brooks was born on June 7, 1917, in Topeka, Kansas, although she lived most of her life in Chicago, and much of her work chronicles life in the black neighborhoods of the city's South Side. Brooks took an early interest in reading and writing, and her first poem, "Eventide," was published in *American Childhood Magazine* in 1930, when she was sixteen years old. Upon graduating from high school, Brooks had a portfolio of over seventy-five published poems. Her first collection, *A Street in Bronzeville*, appeared to critical acclaim in 1945. Her second collection, *Annie Allen* (1949), was honored with the Pulitzer Prize, and Brooks was named Poet Laureate of Illinois in 1968, a post she held until her death. Brooks served as Consultant in Poetry to the Library of Congress from 1985 to 1986 and received countless honorary degrees and awards over the course of her career, including fellowships from the Guggenheim Foundation and the Academy of American Poets; the Frost Medal; a National Endowment for the Arts Lifetime Achievement Award; the Shelley Memorial Award; and the National Book Foundation Award for Distinguished Contribution to American Letters. Brooks was also named Jefferson Lecturer by the National Endowment for the Humanities, the highest award given by the U.S. government for achievement in the humanities.

Brooks's work can be divided into three distinct yet interconnected phases. Her early poetry, with its emphasis upon language and form, is characterized as an expression of the American **modernism** of the **Harlem Renaissance**. After attending the Second Black Writers Conference at Fisk University in 1967, Brooks became deeply involved in the Black Arts Movement, changing her publisher from the mainstream Harper & Row to Broadside Press, the Chicago-based publishing house run by Black Arts poet **Dudley Randall**. At this point, Brooks's poetry and activism were related to the black cultural nationalism associated with the Black Arts and Black Power movements of the 1960s. In the later stages of her career, although retaining her commitment to writing poetry "by Blacks, for Blacks, about Blacks," Brooks was most actively a poetic mentor. In this capacity she worked toward an aesthetic associated with the idea of poetry as a popular mode of expression available to all members of society, not simply to intellectuals and academics.

The major works associated with Brooks's early publishing career include *A Street in Bronzeville*, a chronicle of black life in Chicago's South Side, specifically in a neighborhood known as "Bronzeville" in reference to the racial identity of the majority of its inhabitants. This collection of poems presents portraits of ordinary people making their way through the complex realities of black, urban life, struggling to overcome poverty and racism as they raise families, run businesses, attend church, and keep house. Marked by the technical mastery of form for which Brooks received acclaim, the poems make use of alliteration ("The Sundays of Satin Legs Smith"), rhyme, and poetic forms including the sonnet, the ballad, and even the **epic**. Portraits of people located in a specific time and place (the urban poor in the post–World War II era), the poems employ the black vernacular, situating Brooks in the tradition of Harlem Renaissance poets **Langston Hughes** and **James Weldon Johnson**. In the early poem "When Mrs. Martin's Booker T.," for instance, Brooks presents vernacular speech as a direct quote from Mrs. Martin about her disappointment in her son. She declares that she doesn't want to know if "he's dyin'" or if "he's dead." She wants to know only one thing: "'But tell me if'n he take that gal / And get her decent wed.'" Here the vernacular situates the poem as a narrative piece squarely located in the time and the place of the black urban "folk." In contrast, Brooks also experimented at this early stage of her career with antiquated language, diction, and form, acknowledging in this arena the influence of **Emily Dickinson**.

The comparison with Dickinson is also relevant to the subject of gender in Brooks's work, as many of her poems examine the complexities of gender relations within the larger frame of race and class divisions in the twentieth-century United States. Both *Annie Allen* (1949) and *Maude Martha* (1953) offer sustained explorations of the psyches of black women struggling against racial standards of beauty and the difficulty of sustaining a marriage in the face of poverty, racism, and the poor treatment of black servicemen during and after World War II. The long **narrative poem** "The Anniad" has been categorized by critics as a "mock epic." That is, focused upon characters and forces that participate in shaping a society, allusive and elevated in its language, "The Anniad" is shorter than a traditional epic and its tone is satirical. Indeed, its "heroine," Annie, has been cited by critics as an example of Brooks's concern with the "unheroic"; that is, with characters whom critic Claudia Tate asserts "exemplify the unjustly defeated in whose fall others can locate and avoid qualities that are likely to bring similar defeat on them" (xxiv). Annie struggles to come to consciousness as a black woman faced with white standards of beauty and other oppressive forces that seek to define her. Similarly, the "dearest wish" of the title character of Brooks's only novel, *Maud Martha* (1953)—a girl who is "the color of cocoa straight"—is "to be cherished." The novel chronicles the pragmatics of that wish as it unfolds in the life of a black woman who marries a grocery clerk and lives her life in a tenement with a "whole lot of grayness." This life contrasts sharply with her dreams of "what she felt life ought to be. Jeweled. Polished. Smiling. Poised." In these works, Brooks dramatizes **W.E.B. DuBois**'s notion of "double consciousness" (the psychic struggle of experiencing a specifically African American consciousness at odds with the majority U.S. culture in which it is situated). She also explores how this racial double consciousness is complicated by gender roles in the black community.

In these early works, including *The Bean Eaters* (1960), Brooks demonstrates the mastery of poetic form and technique required to achieve critical success in the dominant culture. *The Bean Eaters* contains the often anthologized "We Real Cool," perhaps the best known of Brooks's poems. This tightly crafted eight-line poem is written in the voices of young black men poignantly articulating the danger and violence characterizing black street life. Importantly, these early poems reveal the seeds of protest that dominate Brooks's literary output in the 1960s and 1970s. For instance, "Negro Hero: to Suggest Dorie Miller" critiques the treatment of black servicemen who fought in World War II and suffered segregation and violence at home. The "Ballad of Pearl May Lee" explores the subject of lynching from the perspective of a white woman who makes a false rape claim against a black man, and "kitchenette building" responds to Langston Hughes's poem "A Dream Deferred," with a portrait of tenement life unable to accommodate the "giddy sound" of a word like "dream." However, her

1968 collection, *In the Mecca*, based upon her experiences working in a Chicago tenement of the same name, is widely considered to be the text that marks her transition from a focus upon form to a deeper interest in content. Moving away from the constraints of the sonnet and ballad forms, and loosening her strict rhythm and rhyme schemes, Brooks employs **free verse** in this collection that pays tribute to black activists and nationalists such as Medgar Evers, Malcolm X, and the Blackstone Rangers. Brooks's own comment upon her aesthetic and political shift is that "the forties and fifties were years of high poet-incense; the language-flowers were thickly sweet. Those flowers whined and begged white folks to pick them, to find them lovable. Then—the sixties: Independent fire!" (*Artful Dodge*).

The Black Arts Movement, anticipated by Malcolm X in his call for a Black Arts Center in Harlem before his death, was actualized by poets and writers such as **Amiri Baraka** (then called LeRoi Jones), Ron Karenga, Eldridge Cleaver, and Larry Neal. Dudley Randall was a major Black Arts presence in Chicago, and Brooks switched to his Broadside Press with the publication of *Riot* (1969) as an expression of her solidarity with Black Arts and Black Power. Later, Brooks eschewed the 1980s nomenclature "African American" as watered down, championing the power and beauty of "blacks" and "blackness" through the rest of her career and titling a collection of her works released in 1987 *Blacks*. But while the Black Arts Movement in its close alliance with Black Power groups such as the Black Panthers sometimes advocated violence in its manifestoes (LeRoi Jones's "Black Art" called for "poems that kill," or, as Larry Neal asserts, for "poems [as] physical entities: fists, daggers, airplane poems, and poems that shoot guns"), Brooks's poems call for protest without violence, intoning instead an empowered celebration of black life. The preacher of *In the Mecca*'s "Sermon on the Warpland" proclaims that one should "Build with lithe love": "With love like morningrise. / With love like black, our black—." This is not to obscure the important fact that Brooks wrote extensively about violence perpetrated against black people around the globe and that she called for radical change; however, she describes violence—both the violence of white brutality and the violence of black protest—without necessarily *calling* for it as a response to oppression.

In the 1970s and 1980s, Brooks expanded her focus on African American life to develop a highly diasporic African consciousness. A great many of her later works are dedicated to African heroes such as Steven Biko or the children of Soweto who fought and died in a South African township for the right to learn in their own languages, or to ordinary Africans in poems such as "A Welcome Song for Laini Nzinga" or "The Near-Johannesburg Boy." Brooks employs the spelling "Afrika" in her later work to denote an authentic or essential African consciousness and heritage. However, as the subtitle of her poem "To the Diaspora: you did not know you were Afrika" (1981) indicates, Brooks locates that *essence* of Afrika *within* diasporic black people, revising the pervasive idea that American and European black people needed to journey "home" to Africa to find that consciousness.

As Brooks's connection with black people grew internationally, so did her poetic activism. Having had her own important experience with mentoring through poetry workshops held on Chicago's South Side when she was a teenager, Brooks believed deeply in the role of the mentor and in the capacity of poetry to help young people to secure successful, powerful futures. In a 1979 interview, Brooks identifies her "three stages of creativity," starting with the "express myself" phase and then the "integration" stage. As for the third stage, Brooks articulates that "I'm trying very seriously now to create for myself, develop for myself a kind of poem that will be immediately accessible and interesting, immediately interesting, to all manner of blacks, not just college students though they're included too. That kind of poem will feature song, will be *songlike*" (*Artful Dodge*). The emphasis upon song—manifested early through Brooks's skill with rhythm and rhyme—becomes part of her diasporic consciousness, a celebration of African and African American oral cultures and traditions, as well as a way to make poetry available to all readers, rather than to a select few.

Several of Brooks's later collections reflect her interest in mentoring young people, including *Young Poet's Primer* (1981), *Very Young Poets* (1983), and *Children Coming Home* (1988). Much of Brooks's work late in her life had to do with increasing the visibility of poetry and encouraging young poets. Most famously, Brooks mentored Black Arts poet Don L. Lee, but she also encouraged generations of young writers when in 1969 she founded the Young Poet Laureate Awards, an annual event honoring twenty young poets in Illinois. That same year, Brooks succeeded **Carl Sandburg** as Poet Laureate of Illinois, holding that title until her death. Critics such as Kalamu ya Salaam credit her with inspiring the newest African American poets, a claim most significantly substantiated in the historic conference "Furious Flower: A Revolution in African American Poetry" at James Madison University in 1994. This conference, preserved as a four-tape video anthology released by conference director Joanne Gabbin, was titled after a line in Brooks's "Second Sermon on the Warpland": "The time cracks / Into furious flower."

Gabbin reads "furious flower" as a metaphor for poetry itself, and the conference celebrated this "furious flower" by gathering three generations of **African American poets**—including a group of new or "third-stream" black poets performing in the genres of spoken word, hip-hop, and **jazz** poetry—to read, perform, and talk about poetry. The conference, inspired by and dedicated to Brooks, has been critically praised as the most important gathering of third-stream black poets, and its spirit—the spirit of poet, activist, and mentor Gwendolyn Brooks—continues for young poets and students at the Furious Flower Poetry Center, established in 1999 at James Madison University.

Further Reading. *Selected Primary Sources:* Brooks, Gwendolyn, *Blacks* (Chicago: Third World Press, 1991); ———, *Maud Martha* (Chicago: Third World Press, 1993); ———, *Report from Part One: An Autobiography* (Chicago: Broadside Press, 1972); ———, *Selected Poems* (New York: Perennial, 1999); ———, *To Disembark* (Chicago: Third World Press, 1981); Cape, Scott, *Artful Dodge: Interview with Gwendolyn Brooks* (1979, http://www.wooster.edu/artfuldodge/interviews/brooks.htm). *Selected Secondary Sources:* Kent, George E., *A Life of Gwendolyn Brooks* (Lexington: University Press of Kentucky, 1990); Mootry, Maria K., and Gary Smith, eds., *A Life Distilled: Gwendolyn Brooks, Her Poetry and Fiction* (Urbana: University of Illinois Press, 1987); Tate, Claudia, ed., *Black Women Writers at Work* (New York: Continuum, 1983); Wright, Stephen Caldwell, *On Gwendolyn Brooks: Reliant Contemplation* (Ann Arbor: University of Michigan Press, 1996).

Elizabeth Goldberg

BROOKS, MARIA GOWEN (1795–1845)

Maria Gowen Brooks, also known as Maria del Occidente, was a native New England poet who lived in virtual self-exile in Cuba for much of her literary career. She is most noted for the highly autobiographical and exotic nature of her work. Unlike many of her nineteenth-century American contemporaries, her work did not center on domestic New England life—a way of life she despised for its patriarchal bounds—but on life classically imaginative and otherworldly. Although not well received publicly, especially in the United States, due partly to her perceived British Romantic styling in a time when America was very much claiming its own literary identity, Brooks's work, especially her epic *Zophiel, or, The Bride of Seven* (1833), garnered attention from the best known among literary circles in the United States, England, and Cuba. Her personal relationships included such notables of the time as Washington Irving, Robert Southey, and Rufus Griswold. Southey praised Brooks in the *London Quarterly Review* as "the most impassioned and imaginative of all poetesses," and Charles Lamb, upon reading *Zophiel,* exclaimed, "Southey says it is by some Yankee woman: as if there had ever been a woman capable of any thing so great!"

Born Abigail Gowen into a wealthy Medford, Massachusetts, family, Brooks, well connected to privilege, was heavily influenced by her father's literary connections to Harvard. Highly intellectual, the young Brooks studied the literatures of several languages and, although she is often narrowly defined as a Romantic, a mighty classical influence permeates her work. Brook's charmed life changed drastically when her father, William Gowen, died when she was only fourteen or fifteen; she was taken under guardianship by John Brooks, a fifty-year-old, wealthy Boston merchant and family friend who paid for her schooling and then proposed marriage. By all accounts, she was miserably married to Brooks for thirteen years until he died in 1823 after suffering financial setbacks. It is this unhappy period in her life, however, that seemed to most shape her writing and fuel the persona of a tormented inner spirit so evident in her work. After her husband's death and an unsuccessful relationship with a Canadian officer that led her to attempt suicide twice, Brooks moved her family, consisting of her two sons, Edgar and Horace, and two stepsons, to her maternal uncle's coffee plantation in Matanzas, Cuba. She inherited the property when her uncle, William Cutter, died. Known for always wearing white and placing a passion flower in her hair, Brooks lived the rest of her life in Cuba, once again wealthy and privileged—and seemingly ambivalent in regard to politics. Her ambivalence toward the slave labor on her plantation is particularly noted. However, in her psychological novel *Idomen: or The Vale of Yuri* (1843) Brooks is anything but ambivalent as she speaks directly and unsympathetically in regard to Cuba's dependence on African slave labor, noting that "the sable laborers" were much better suited for the heavy toil of plantation work than "the gentle and highly civilized Peruvian."

In 1820, while still married to John Brooks, Brooks anonymously published her first collection of poems, *Judith, Esther, and Other Poems,* in Boston. In the preface to *Zophiel,* first published in Boston by Richardson and Lord in 1825 under the name Mrs. Brooks, she noted, "my lyre has been a solace when everything else has failed." She eventually traveled to Europe with her brother in 1830, where she met Southey, who named her Maria del Occidente and was responsible for getting the revised *Zophiel, or, The Bride of Seven* published in London in 1833. Brooks's final work, *Idomen: or The Vale of Yumuri,* was first published serially in the *Boston Saturday Evening Gazette* in 1838, but no commercial publisher would print the thinly veiled autobiographical novel that related Brooks's troubled domestic life and two suicide attempts as well as her detached perspective on slavery as a necessary fate. Brooks issued a private edition of the novel in New York in 1843. At the age of fifty, Brooks died in Matanzas, Cuba, on November 11, 1845, after contracting a tropical fever.

Zophiel, or, The Bride of Seven, based loosely on the story of Sara in the Book of Tobit in the Apocrypha, relates in six cantos the story of the fallen angel Zophiel and Egla, the bride of seven. A deep sense of sorrow wallowing in the sweet aroma of tropical life permeates this story of Zophiel's possessive pursuit of the fair and virginal Egla, who at age twenty is pressured by her parents to marry and carry forth the race. The classic virtue of *pietas* is evident throughout the work, and as Egla, against her will, honors her parents' wish for her to marry in accordance with Hebrew law, every suitor falls under the spell of Zophiel, who is intent on having Egla as his own bride. The elegance of Brooks's poetry as well as the explanation for her attachment to the passion flower is illustrated as Zophiel gently addresses Egla, "Here's for thy hair a garland: every flower/That spreads its blossoms, watered by the tear/Of the sad slave in Babylonian bower,/Might see its frail bright hues perpetuate here." Paula Bernat Bennett notes, "As a tale of death and erotic obsession, Zophiel is without parallel among the works of nineteenth century American women poets" (24).

The true depth of Brooks's work, especially *Zophiel,* has yet to be recognized. Zophiel uniquely balances the mythological virtues of classicism with the spiritual aesthetics of Romanticism. Her work is rich with her deep admiration for Cuba's picturesque, as well as a desire to bask in all its natural splendor and to shelter her female spirit from an unjust earthly life. Beneath the finely measured and musically fluid verse is a nineteenth-century portrait of a life of contrasts between women and men, Cubans and Americans, Africans and Anglos, rich and poor—a wealth of social commentary virtually unexplored.

Further Reading. *Selected Primary Sources:* Brooks, Maria Gowen, *Judith, Esther, and Other Poems* (Boston: Cummings and Holland, 1820); ———, *Idomen: or The Vale of Yumuri* (New York: S. Colman, 1843); ———, *Zophiel, or, The Bride of Seven* (London: Hillard, Gray, 1833). ***Selected Secondary Sources:*** Bennett, Paula Bernat, ed., *Nineteenth-Century American Women Poets: An Anthology* (Oxford: Blackwell, 1998); Gruesz, Kirsten Silva, *Ambassadors of Culture: The Transamerican Origins of Latino Writing* (Princeton, NJ: Princeton University Press, 2002); Walker, Cheryl, ed., *American Women Poets of the Nineteenth Century: An Anthology* (New Brunswick, NJ: Rutgers University Press, 1992).

Deborah Adams Renville

BROSSARD, NICOLE (1943–)

A prolific and **experimental** writer whose work encompasses (and often crosses) the genres of poetry, fiction, and theory, Nicole Brossard has influenced several specific writing communities: French-Canadian, **postmodern, feminist,** and lesbian. Her often-cited call for an "écriture au féminin" (writing to/of the feminine) has been heard across linguistic and national boundaries, leading to increased interest in her work in the United States and Europe. Brossard is positioned as both mother and inheritor of a tradition of women writing about women's lived experience and in the process trying to refashion language to remove patriarchal biases or "fictions" about women, as well as trying to find an honest, non-phallocentric way to use words to invoke an erotic, woman-centered consciousness. Thus, her work links her with such earlier writers as Colette, Djuana Barnes, and **Gertrude Stein**; near-contemporaries like **Adrienne Rich** and **Audre Lorde** in the United States; and **Canadian** writers including Daphne Marlatt, Betsy Warland, Louky Bersanik, and Erin Mouré. Although some have called her poetry "formalist," it is not, at least not in the usual sense of the term (as referring to the use of established forms). Rather, she experiments with form, playing with genre conventions, **prose poems**, poetic prose, typographical devices, white space, puns, fragmentation, and ellipsis to create a form elastic and sensitive enough to accommodate her thoughts and emotions. The success of her efforts has been acknowledged by two Canadian Governor-General's Awards for poetry, the Grand Prix de la Poésie de la Fondation des Forges, and other awards.

Brossard was born November 27, 1943, in Montréal, part of a well-known family that included a Supreme Court judge. During her lifetime, Quebec was transformed from a highly Catholic, xenophobic society ruled by the repressive premier Maurice Duplessis to a liberal and hedonistic culture that has nurtured French language and literature despite the English media onslaught. In 1965 Brossard published her first poetry collection (*Aube à la Saison* or *Dawning Season*) and co-founded the influential journal *La Barre du Jour.* A year later, she married and also published a second book of poems. After graduating from university, she taught high school for two years, and then published her first fiction. By 1974 she had fallen in love with a woman, given birth to a daughter, and transformed herself into a radical feminist and lesbian. Much of the rest of her writing reflects her struggle to find forms in poetry and fiction that give a voice and vocabulary to other women who made similar choices. The collection *Mecanique jongleuse,* translated by Larry Shouldice as *Daydream Mechanics,* won her a Governor-General's Award for poetry. In 1980 she co-directed a documentary film, *Some American Feminists.* She began her "lesbian trilogy" with *These Our Mothers or The Exploding Chapter* (*L'Amèr*) (1977) and continued with *Lovhers* (*Amantes*) (1980) and *Surfaces of Sense* (*Le Sens Apparent*) (1980). Her collected poems were published in *Double Impression: Poemes et Textes 1967–1984.* She collaborated with Daphne Marlatt on *Character/Jeu de lettres*, which appeared in 1986. Now the author of more than two dozen books of fiction, poetry, and theory, she has been a visiting writer and lecturer at universities and colleges in Canada and the United States, and continues to write (in French, although occasionally venturing into English).

In *These Our Mothers*, Brossard declares, "To write *I am a woman* is full of consequences." In her poetry, these consequences include an exploration of the eroticism she senses in everyday women's lives, as well as in the acts of writing and speaking. In the poem "Knowledge" (*Installations*, 70) she writes, "my darling, I'm writing so you'll show me / your sex in a fine mood." It also requires a refashioning of language; in French, every noun is either masculine or feminine. Brossard has "feminized" the noun "*l'amant*" (lover) by adding a terminal "e"; this shift is represented by her translators as "lovhers." She counters poetic and narrative linearity ("the world files off / before her in a completely straight line according to the law of patriarchal heritage" (*Lovhers*, 87) with radical disjunctions, so that a poetic sequence may contain sensations, philosophical statements, allusions, and puns. In *Lovhers*, she proposes the symbol of the spiral and the sensation of vertigo as part of an alternative poetics of explosion and excess. The divisions between poetry, fiction, and prose are of little interest to her, and many of her books contain either poetic outbursts arising from paragraphs of prose, or prose-poem–like blocks, either maintaining a fiction or building a poetic series. She is also, by writing of and in the body, confronting a history of violence the world has imposed on women: "THE (male) politics of the gaze of sexual bliss is also the silence of bodies elongated by hunger, fire, dogs, and the bite of densities of torture" (99). One of her characteristic poetic devices (which seldom translates effectively into English) is a shift between words occasioned by similarity of sound, much like "excess/access" or "sight/site" in English. Consider the lines from her chapbook *Sous la langue/Under the Tongue*, where "*langue*" means both "language" and the physical tongue: "Fricatelle ruiselle essentielle aime-t-elle le long de son corps la morsure." The association between the initial words in this phrase is the third-person feminine pronoun "*elle*." Translator Suzanne Lotbiniere-Harwood renders these lines as "Does she frictional she fluvial she essential does she all along her body love the bite." Not accidentally, this page resolves with another list: "dans la flambée des chairs pendant que les secondes s'écoulent cyprine, lutines, marines" (translated as "in the blaze of flesh to flesh as seconds flow by silken salty cyprin"— the last word referring to female sexual secretions.

Another interesting aspect of Brossard's technique is her acknowledgment of artificiality and the constraints of the printed page, shown in her use of nonverbal devices such as extended long dashes, spaces, even empty boxes on the page, and written gestures to the reader-as-reader (for example, "turn the page"). Reinforced by such experimental techniques, Brossard's writing, straddling many communities and affiliations, rewards readers with a rich, challenging, and distinctive feminist poetics.

Further Reading. ***Selected Primary Sources:*** Brossard, Nicole, *Amantes* (Montreal: Editions Quinze, 1980), translated by Barbara Godard as *Lovhers* (Montreal: Guernica, 1986); ———, *Double Impression* (Montréal: Hexagone, 1984); ———, *Installations, avec et sans pronoms* (Montreal: Éditions Ecrits des Forges, 1984), translated by Robert Majzels and Erin Mouré as *Installations with and without Pronouns* (Winnipeg: The Muses' Company, 2000); ———, *Museé de l'os and de l'eau* (Montreal: Éditions du Noroit and Cadex Éditions, 1999), translated by Robert Majzels and Erin Mouré as *Museum of Bone and Water* (Toronto: Anansi, 2003). ***Selected Secondary Sources:*** Godard, Barbara, "Producing Visibility for Lesbians: Nicole Brossard's Quantum Poetics" (*ESC* 21.2 [June 1995]: 125–137); Lévesque, Claude, "Le Proche et le lointain" in *Garder vive l'émotion* (Montreal: VLB éditeur, 1994, 130–137); Lundgren, Jodi, and Kelly-Anne Maddox, eds., "Revisiting Nicole Brossard: Québécois Feminist Subjectivity in the 21st Century" (*How2* 2.3 [Spring 2005], http://www.departments.bucknell.edu/stadler_center/how2/current/index.shtm).

John Oughton

BROUMAS, OLGA (1949–)

Though she has received little critical attention since the acclaim surrounding her first book published in the United States, Olga Broumas has served as a pioneer among **feminist** lesbian poets for nearly thirty years. Repeatedly reinventing what it means to write from one's body, she fills her poetry with an erotic sisterhood that celebrates both women and sexuality, mingling the sacred and the sensual in her verse. Although occasionally accused of esotericism in her writing, Broumas's experiments with language and music have helped to shape a generation of poets concerned with the erotic.

Born in 1949 in Hermoupolis, Greece, Broumas immigrated to the United States in 1967, a year after publishing her first collection of poetry in Greece. Broumas studied architecture at the University of Pennsylvania, where she received her BA, and she went on to attend the University of Oregon, from which she received an MFA in creative writing. Broumas remained at the University of Oregon to teach English and women's studies, and during this time she composed her first book in English, which won the Yale Younger Poets Award in 1977. Since then, in addition to writing, she has taught at a number of universities, including the University of Idaho, Goddard College, Boston University, and Brandeis University, where she is currently Fanny Hurst Poet-in-Residence and Director of Creative Writing. Broumas was also a founding member of FREEHAND, a community of women writers and photographers that has since disbanded, and for over twenty years she has been a licensed bodywork therapist practicing in Cape Cod, Massachusetts. In addition to her own poetry, Broumas has written in collaboration with other authors and has translated numerous works by Greek Nobel Laureate Odysseas Elytis.

Beginning with O (1977), the collection for which Broumas is best known, is primarily made up of revisions of Greek myths and fairy tales that celebrate lesbian love and sensuality in fluid lines that often reference imagery of the sea. In the first section, "Twelve Aspects of God," Broumas includes a cycle of **ekphrastic** poems based on the oil paintings in Sandra McKee's *Ma Mata Cycle,* which portrays contemporary women as mythic Greek figures. Perhaps the most notable poem in this section is "Artemis," from which the collection's title comes; in this poem, Broumas declares herself committed to "a politics / of transliteration" in which women must "find words / or burn." "The Knife & the Bread," the collection's middle section, deals both with marital and martial relations, combining the personal and the political in poems commemorating both the breakup of her marriage and the women of Cyprus who were violated during the invasion by the Turks in 1974. The third section of the collection, "Innocence," like **Anne Sexton**'s *Transformations,* plays off of traditional fairy tales and recasts them in a new light. Broumas's version of "Cinderella," for instance, shows the title character forsaking the new privileges she acquires in her life with the prince in order to rejoin her sister.

In *Soie Sauvage* (1979), Broumas's second full-length work in English, Broumas continues to attempt the nullification of the distinction between body and soul, as in the long poem "Namaste," in which she declares that her work is "to force the holy back / into the flesh." In these poems, her tone is often subdued and introspective, as the poet works her way through the self-imposed solitude she began after the publication of her previous book. Focusing on the Oregon landscape and on a landscape of the self, the poems in *Soie Sauvage* include prayers and Zen-like meditations frequently free of punctuation. In these poems, dedicated to **Gary Snyder**, among others, Broumas attempts, more quietly than in her previous collection, "To love / the body to love its work."

Pastoral Jazz (1983) is perhaps the most abstract of Broumas's work and relies less on narrative than on a seemingly spontaneous composition to guide the poems. The influence of **jazz** on her work is certainly evident in this collection, as she riffs and improvises complex rhythms throughout the book. In these poems, Broumas, a self-taught musician, draws on both the visual and the musical to create poems in which lines play off one another but never quite form a singular, coherent meaning. In these "lush jazz massages, piercings made / each moment by the riddling light," Broumas taps into the emotion of her earlier collections but disperses it here into a performance of sound that dwells in the moment: "It's like with making love / It does no good to *remember.*"

Returning to the more direct voice of *Beginning with O, Perpetua* (1989) moves from haunting lyrics through sexual narratives to poems that make use of **John Cage**'s musical silences. Whereas the first section of the collection works in an **elegiac** and memorial mode, often meditating on the death of Broumas's father, in the second section, Broumas's trademark eroticism is evident in narratives that are sometimes teasingly ironic, as in the poem "Attitude," which opens, "I let them whip and fuck me," and ends, "We went to the movies on other nights." The third section, "Lumens," with its extremely short lyric poems, links the work of *Pastoral Jazz* to the collaborative work Broumas would soon undertake.

Sappho's Gymnasium (1994), co-authored with classical scholar T. Begley, Broumas's partner, is composed of numerous brief, untitled poems, each occupying its own page, as though the poems collected were the remaining fragments of Sappho's own work. The primary portion of the book, "Prayerfields," contains fifty pages of short lyrics that display an undercurrent of violence, incest, and imprisonment, but are always layered with a sense of healing and wholeness oriented around the body of the beloved. Although the poems in "Prayerfields" delve into the traumatic, they are often worshipful in tone and underscore how the "work of grace makes us visible," even after the most soul-shattering events. In these poems, helplessness and agency are so thoroughly intertwined that the subject of the poem is not simply a source for pity or outrage but for a polyphonic chorus in which anger, witness, and celebration can all speak with one voice.

Rave: Poems 1975–1999 (1999), winner of a Lambda Literary Award for Lesbian Poetry, offers a retrospective of Broumas's work, including selections from the previously mentioned collections as well as other, lesser-known pieces. Among these are, most notably, *Black Holes, Black Stockings* (1985), a collaboration with Jane Miller, and *Caritas* (1976), a self-published chapbook that speaks in a Whitmanian voice and demonstrates the attention to landscape and the body that would become such an imperative part of her later work.

Further Reading. *Selected Primary Sources:* Broumas, Olga, *Beginning with O* (New Haven, CT: Yale University Press, 1977); ———, *Caritas* (Eugene, OR: Jackrabbit Press, 1976); ———, *Pastoral Jazz* (Port Townsend, WA:

Copper Canyon Press, 1983);———, *Perpetua* (Port Townsend, WA: Copper Canyon Press, 1989); ———, *Rave: Poems 1975–1999* (Port Townsend, WA: Copper Canyon Press, 1999); ———, *Soie Sauvage* (Port Townsend, WA: Copper Canyon Press, 1979); Broumas, Olga, and Jane Miller, *Black Holes, Black Stockings* (Middletown, CT: Wesleyan University Press, 1985); Broumas, Olga, and T. Begley, *Sappho's Gymnasium* (Port Townsend, WA: Copper Canyon Press, 1994). ***Selected Secondary Sources:*** Hammond, Karla, "An Interview with Olga Broumas" (*Northwest Review* 18.3 [1980]: 33–44); Horton, Diane, "'Scarlet Liturgies': The Poetry of Olga Broumas" (*North Dakota Quarterly* 55.4 [Fall 1987]: 322–347); Ingram, Claudia, "Sappho's Legacy: The Collaborative Testimony of Olga Broumas and T Begley" (*Tulsa Studies in Women's Literature* 19.1 [Spring 2000]: 105–120).

Jennifer Perrine

BROWN, STERLING A. (1901–1989)

Widely hailed as the dean of African American letters, Sterling Allen Brown, poet, scholar, cultural critic, ethnographer, teacher, and raconteur, devoted his career to the accurate representation of African American life and culture. Culling from overlapping yet distinct literary and cultural heritages, reshaping Western prosody, black vernacular, and folk idioms, Brown helped to create a completely new artistic and poetic vocabulary. Through his exploration of the expressive possibilities of African American folk culture and its myriad responses to American modernity, he, in effect, recreated the conception and representation of African Americans and blackness for a modern age. Thus Brown wrote in response to racist caricature and stereotypes. From advertising to cartoons, to film and "serious" literary art, American culture traded on stereotypes such as the mammy, the sambo, the pickaninny, and the coon, often delivered through minstrel dialect and the plantation tradition. In response, Brown's poetry proves that not only is black vernacular and folk idiom capable of expressing the full complexity of black lives, they serve as profound responses to the conundrum of being black in modern America. As heirs to citizenship and the very sign of American democratic failure, African Americans, for Brown, existed in the liminal space between the ideal of democratic equality and the reality of racial oppression. In response, African American folk culture fully captures the paradox of black life in modern America, and thus Brown's poetry, based on folk idiom and form, reflects the inherent modernity of African American folk culture. Brown's larger vision for his poetry and prose finds its greatest resonance in the context of the New Negro movement, and its literary wing, the **Harlem Renaissance**.

Born May 1, 1901, to a prominent middle-class black family in Washington, D.C., Brown was heir to the struggles of his parents and their generation as they strived for equality. His father, Sterling Nelson Brown, was born a slave yet worked his way through Fisk University, then Oberlin Seminary College, and became a professor of religion at Howard University and the pastor of Lincoln Temple Congregational Church. Brown's mother, Adelaide Allen, graduated from Fisk as well, and championed the arts and education as a means of racial advancement. Together the Browns created a household dedicated to racial uplift. Indeed, their social circles included Frederick Douglass, Alexander Crummell, John M. Langston, and Kelly Miller; they were all children of Reconstruction and took full advantage of the educational opportunities newly accorded blacks. They also championed the goal of political equality. They witnessed the subsequent dismantling of Reconstruction and the country's reneging on the guarantees of the Thirteenth, Fourteenth, and Fifteenth amendments. In response, this generation bequeathed to their children the ongoing struggle for full citizenship.

This struggle largely shaped New Negro ideology, and Brown's career in particular. Brown's generation, born toward the turn of the twentieth century, inherited the promise of Reconstruction legislation *and* the brutal exclusion from political participation. They also witnessed a dramatic transformation in African American life, as blacks migrated from the country to cities (in both the North and South) and became wage earners. Such dramatic changes necessarily altered African American culture, giving life to modern **blues** and gospel, for example. In response to both political and cultural changes, New Negroes created and sustained organizations such as Marcus Garvey's Universal Negro Improvement Association (UNIA), the NAACP, and the Urban League.

In short, New Negroes struggled to make real the constitutional guarantees of Reconstruction. In terms of literary, graphic, and performing arts, the Harlem Renaissance contributed to the larger project of democratic access through a comprehensive attention to black representation. In every arena artists attempted to reclaim black representation and imbue it with depth, complexity, and humanity. Literature in particular took on a central role as *Opportunity* (the literary magazine of the Urban League) and *Crisis* (the official magazine of the NAACP) aggressively promoted young writers and their literature as a means of combating racism.

Furthermore, a group of younger Harlem Renaissance writers that included Brown—in particular, **Langston Hughes**, Zora Neale Hurston, and **Jean Toomer**—looked to African American folk culture and the black vernacular as a basis for their art, indeed as reference for a more insightful portrayal of modern black life. And although Brown disagreed to a degree with Hughes's and Hurston's approaches—Hughes's portraits lacked emotional depth and range, whereas Hurston's portrayals ignored stoicism and bitterness—Brown was fully invested in the radical position that black vernacular and folk idiom should stand at the center of New Negro artistic expression.

For Brown's part, he held that immersion into folk culture was a prerequisite for its representation. Thus, after completing his MA at Harvard University, Brown embarked upon an odyssey across the rural South. From 1923 to 1929 he taught at various black colleges and universities: Virginia Seminary and College, Lincoln University in Missouri, and Fisk University. With these schools as his base, Brown ventured into the countryside in order to learn first-hand the patterns of speech, the variety of folk forms, and the general ethos of African American folk culture. He encountered Slim Greer, Calvin "Big Boy" Davis, and Mrs. Bibby, among others, all of whom would become central figures in his folk myth cosmology. He frequented churches, bars, juke joints, and parties, interacted with the rural folk, and thus forged a deeper understanding of defining forms such as the blues, spirituals, work song ballads, hollers, tale tales, and signifying.

Brown began publishing his poetry in prominent New Negro magazines and anthologies: *Opportunity*, *Crisis*, **James Weldon Johnson**'s *Book of American Negro Poetry* (1922 and 1931), **Countee Cullen**'s *Caroling Dusk* (1927), and V.F. Calverton's *Anthology of Negro American Literature* (1927). His first collection, *Southern Road* (1932), soon followed; and although *The Last Ride of Wild Bill and Eleven Narrative Poems* would not appear until 1975, and *No Hiding Place* would be published in *The Collected Poems of Sterling A. Brown* (1980), the bulk of this poetry was written between 1928 and 1940. *Southern Road* chronicles the multiplicity of voices, forms, and mythic figures that populated the black Southern landscape of the 1920s and 1930s; the collection registers the Afro-modern milieu largely in folk form as the mythic road lends both access and metaphor to the scene. Riffing on the spiritual that proclaims there will be no hiding place on the Day of Judgment, *No Hiding Place* depicts the ubiquitous and murderous nature of white supremacy and racism. Where in *Southern Road* the irrepressible black voice takes center stage, in *No Hiding Place* the daunting realities of Southern peonage threaten to subsume the heretofore hopeful voices. Finally, *The Last Ride of Wild Bill and Eleven Narrative Poems* presents heroism, in the black masculinist tradition, as a rejoinder to racial oppression. Here Brown presents ballads celebrating black men in the life-and-death struggle for dignity and personhood in the racist South. Across all of his poetry Brown reinvents dialect accurately to represent black vernacular. Where James Weldon Johnson had proclaimed that due to **minstrelsy** black dialect could render only humor and pathos, Brown proved that the vernacular could convey the fullest range of human emotions and psychological states.

Furthermore, folk forms themselves—particularly the blues, spirituals, work songs, and ballads—proved to be rich poetic forms *and* media through which the folk expressed their modernist sensibilities. So, too, mythic figures, such as John Henry or Stagolee, immortalized through folk forms, also reflect the inherent modernity of folk culture, and thus shape Brown's seminal poems. Put more succinctly, Brown's poetry portrays modern folk life by stressing, among others, three overarching qualities: subjectivity, historicity, and the perpetual paradox of being black in modern America. First, Brown's poetry underscores folk culture's display of black subjectivity; not simply that blacks possess rich and complex interior lives, but that black subjectivity continues to assess and inform its surroundings. Second, over and against stereotypes asserting stasis or a-historicity, blacks are historical beings, necessarily changing over time, and thus they are perpetually in the process of becoming. And finally blues, work songs, spirituals, and so forth directly address the conundrum at the heart of modern black life. They are both the sign and the address of the chronic indeterminacy that results from white supremacist brutality and systemic disfranchisement, indeed from life in the liminal space on the fringes of citizenship.

For example, three of Brown's most successful poems, "Odyssey of Big Boy," "Southern Road," and "Ma Rainey," aptly illustrate his larger Afro-modernist aesthetic. "Odyssey of Big Boy" is a blues ballad that emphasizes the future rather than the past. The speaker, Calvin "Big Boy" Davis, emerges in the perpetual process of performance and vocalization in the pursuit of transcendent meaning. As he sings his personal chronicle of work and love, he compares his life to folk cultural gods such as John Henry and Stagolee, and asks that his deeds be sufficient for equal immortal status. Where this vocal odyssey toward myth and immortality relies on interpretation of his deeds, it also depends upon the form of the vocalization itself: here the folk ballad of John Henry. Davis reconstructs himself poetically in the form of John Henry and so presents himself both as subject and object, the voice of creation and its referent. Indeed in terms of stanza form—number of lines, rhythm, rhyme scheme, and repetition—Davis replicates the folk ballad form that Brown would later anthologize in *Negro Caravan* (1941).

Playing on the dramatic tension between past and future, the poem dramatizes the perpetual black subjective moment. Through performance, Davis reshapes his folk heritage and thus himself in order to envision an expansive, indeed transcendent, future. Furthermore, Davis, as both musician and poet, emerges as metaphor for the artist and his or her ability to recreate experience to envision possibilities beyond immediate oppressive circumstances. Thus Davis, improvisationalist, lyricist, and blues hero, signals the modernity of folk culture. His ability to synthesize idioms, voices, traditions, and forms in order to create meaning in a context that deems black life essentially meaningless establishes the vocabulary, process, and artistic vision for *Southern Road*, if not the entire Brown corpus.

The title poem itself, "Southern Road," further illustrates this use of idiom and voicing as a means of portraying black modernity. The poem takes the folk form of the work song, whose steady rhythm and sharp punctuation helped to coordinate group manual labor. The folk form usually comprises loosely connected verses, related through depictions of hard, tedious work. As such, they usually do not convey linear progression. Here Brown appropriates both the form and the ethos of the work song, but reworks the idiom to convey narrative content: the life and tragic events of the speaker. As he chronicles the loss of his family and his own incarceration, the "hunh" at the end of the first and third lines of each stanza punctuates his physical exertion and the tragedy of his circumstances. Ironically the poem never mentions a road, and indeed suggests eternal stasis rather than travel; nevertheless the poem incorporates the major theme for the collection. As the Southern road serves as access and witness to the Southern black milieu, "Southern Road" depicts a tragically common sight in the Deep South of the 1920s and 1930s: black men working on a chain gang. Yet where context suggests chronic stasis, both idiom and voice invoke the possibility of resistance. Just as Big Boy Davis reassembles the shards of a potentially meaningless life, the speaker of "Southern Road" uses the work song to reshape the chaotic, the brutal and the absurd into an art form over which he exercises control, of which he is indeed the creator. The speaker confronts and reviews the potentially crushing circumstances of his life, and through art makes them livable. Here "Southern Road" presents the contextualized black subject, both victim and agent, incarcerated and (rhetorically) free, again in the perpetual process of reshaping his life, of responding to the relentless pressures of black modernity.

Ultimately "Ma Rainey" makes explicit the blues ritual shaping much of Brown's poetry. Marking a performance by the "Empress of the Blues," the poem narrates the gathering and the reaction to her singing. As high priestess of the blues ritual, she embodies both the pain and transformative possibilities of the form. Thus she sings "'bout de hard luck / Roun' our do'": the vicissitudes of modern black life, here made concrete in the 1927 Mississippi flood. Performing her famous "Backwater Blues," she laments the death, destruction, and ultimate existential crisis the flood occasions. On a "high ol' lonesome hill" she can see the desolation the flood has wrought, desolation similar in force and capriciousness

to Southern white supremacy. Yet as the people gather to hear her tale of woe, she "jes' gits hold of us dataway." The ritual process through which she leads them does not result in despair, but rejuvenation and transcendence. As Ralph Ellison puts it, the blues here serves as a means of reducing chaos to order, while art becomes a way of reaping lyricism from the chronic pain and potential despair of black life in the South. In a similar sense, "Strong Men," "Sister Lou," "Virginia Portrait," the Slim Greer series, "The Ballad of Joe Meek," and many more poems portray personae in the process of culling from their folk traditions in order to make sense of the absurdity of modern black life. Brown's poetry ultimately discovered agency and vitality in black vernacular and folk culture, and thus created a new artistic vision that anticipated Ellison and the black writers of the 1950s, as well as the cultural nationalism of the **Black Arts Movement**.

Further Reading. *Selected Primary Sources:* Brown, Sterling A., *The Collected Poems of Sterling A. Brown*, ed. Michael S. Harper (Chicago: TriQuarterly, 1980); ———, *A Son's Return: Selected Essays of Sterling A. Brown*, ed. Mark A. Sanders (Boston: Northeastern University Press, 1996). ***Selected Secondary Sources:*** Benston, Kimberly W., "Sterling Brown's After-Song: 'When de Saints Go Ma'ching Home' and the Performance of Afro-American Voice" (*Callaloo* 5.14–15 [February–May 1982]: 33–42); Gabbin, Joanne V., *Sterling A. Brown: Building the Black Aesthetic Tradition* (Westport, CT: Greenwood, 1985); Henderson, Stephen, "The Heavy Blues of Sterling Brown: A Study of Craft and Tradition" (*Black American Literature Forum* 14 [Spring 1980]: 32–44); Kutzinski, Vera M., "The Distant Closeness of Dancing Doubles: Sterling Brown and William Carlos Williams" (*Black American Literature Forum* 22 [Spring 1982]: 19–25); Lewis, David Levering, *When Harlem Was in Vogue* (New York: Oxford University Press, 1981); Sanders, Mark A., *Afro-Modernist Aesthetics and the Poetry of Sterling A. Brown* (Athens: University of Georgia Press, 1999).

Mark A. Sanders

BRUCHAC, JOSEPH (1942–)

Joseph Bruchac is a prolific American Indian (Abenaki) poet and writer. His career began in the early 1970s, and he has published in a wide variety of genres, including poetry, fiction, and nonfiction. He has also edited numerous collections of poetry and fiction, many featuring other American Indian poets and writers whose careers he has been instrumental in promoting. His most important anthologies have been *Songs from This Earth on Turtle's Back: Contemporary American Indian Poetry* (1983), *Returning the Gift: Poetry and Prose from the First North American Native Writers' Festival* (1994), and *Smoke Rising: The Native North American Literary Compan-*

ion (1995). In his own poetry, Bruchac focuses on a number of important American Indian themes, including issues surrounding identity and culture, the role of the past in contemporary lives, and creating and sustaining a significant connection to the natural world within an American Indian cultural and spiritual framework.

Bruchac was born October 16, 1942, in Greenfield Center, New York, a small town in the foothills of the Adirondack Mountains. His father was Slovakian and his mother was of English and Abenaki descent. He was raised by his maternal grandparents, Marion Bowman and Jesse Bowman, from whom he traces his American Indian heritage. He earned a BA degree from Cornell University, an MA degree in literature and creative writing from Syracuse University, and a Ph.D. degree in comparative literature from the Union Institute of Ohio. He has worked as an educator, including eight years directing a college program for Skidmore College inside a maximum security prison, an environment that served as a setting for many of his early poems.

In the early 1970s Bruchac, along with his wife, Carol, founded the Greenfield Review Literary Center and the Greenfield Review Press, a **small press** that has been instrumental in introducing new voices not only in the field of **Native American poetry**, but also **Asian American poetry**, **African American poetry**, and a wide range of material from a variety of people and groups often alienated from more mainstream presses. Among other notable successes, Greenfield Review Press published **Leslie Marmon Silko**'s first collection of poetry, *Laguna Woman*, as well as several important anthologies, including *Breaking Silence: An Anthology of Contemporary Asian American Poets*.

Bruchac himself has appeared in some five hundred publications and anthologies, from *American Poetry Review* to *Smithsonian Magazine* to *National Geographic*. He has authored seventy books for adults and children, including fiction, poetry, picture books, young adult fiction, and nonfiction for both children and adults. Much of his work has centered around Abenaki culture and traditions, including collections of Abenaki tales and stories taken from Abenaki history. But his themes are often wider, encompassing American Indian subjects as far-ranging as an account of the Lakota warrior Crazy Horse titled *Crazy Horse's Vision*, to collections of Iroquois stories such as *New Voices from the Longhouse*, to an anthology of Alaskan native writers titled *Raven Tells Stories*. As well as being a writer, Bruchac is an accomplished storyteller and singer. He, along with his sister Margaret and his two adult sons, James and Jesse, performs traditional and contemporary Abenaki music as the singing group Dawnland Singers.

Bruchac's poetry career began in 1971 with the publication of *Indian Mountain and Other Poems*. Many other volumes followed during the 1970s and early 1980s, including *The Buffalo in the Syracuse Zoo and Other Poems* (1972), *Flow* (1975), *The Road to Black Mountain* (1977), *Entering Onondaga* (1978), *There Are No Trees Inside the Prison* (1980), *Remembering the Dawn* (1983), *Walking with My Sons and Other Poems* (1986), and *Near the Mountains: New and Selected Poems* (1987). Most of his early poetry centers on the American Indian experience, and much of it is autobiographical. But the poems are also concerned with the loss of nature and the difficulty of maintaining ties to the land in the face of social conflict and change.

His three latest works, *No Borders* (1999), *Above the Line* (2003), and *Ndakinna (Our Land)* (2003) represent a poet who has matured in his craft and taken his place as a strong voice in the field of Native American poetry. *No Borders* is a collection of narrative poems that chronicle American Indian experience from a wide range of perspectives, from "Snowshoeing across Lake Champlain" to "Desert Tortoise in the Rain" to "Geese Flying over a Prison Sweat Lodge." Bruchac's lyric narratives depict a land where political boundaries have little meaning and where the only thing that truly matters is the "consciousness of life in motion[,] spirit in place."

In *Above the Line*, Bruchac continues with strong images from the natural world, and his poetry is often still specifically autobiographical, as in the title poem of the collection, in which he recalls a trip he took as a child to the segregated South with his great-grandparents. But the poems in this collection also attempt a number of interesting **postmodern** juxtapositions of traditional Indian culture and contemporary society. His humorous poem "Coyote's Car Wash," in which Coyote transforms himself into a 1978 Ford Mustang, and his meta-poetic "New Hope for Dead Indians" explore the possibilities of existing in both worlds simultaneously, as a traditional Indian and a full participant in postmodern America.

Ndakinna (Our Land) begins with a rather long section that amounts to an extended prayer to the natural world. Each poem in the section is connected to specific sites on traditional Abenaki land or to the specific creatures or plants found there. In the second section, titled "Traveling Stories," Bruchac demonstrates how to maintain these spiritual connections to the land and nature as you move out into the world, encountering new and different landscapes. In short, the collection functions as a primer for maintaining an Indian sensibility grounded in nature even as you live and function in the larger society.

Further Reading. ***Selected Primary Sources:*** Bruchac, Joseph, *Above the Line* (Albuquerque, NM: West End Press, 2003); ———, *Flow* (Austin, TX: Cold Mountain Press, 1975); ———, *Ndakinna (Our Land)* (Albuquerque, NM: West End Press, 2003); ———, *No Borders* (Duluth, MN: Holy Cow! Press, 1999); ———,

Walking with My Sons and Other Poems (Buffalo, NY: White Pine Press, 1987). **Selected Secondary Sources:** Alderdice, Kit, "Joseph Bruchac: Sharing a Native-American Heritage" (*Publisher's Weekly* 243.8 [February 19, 1996]); Bodin, Madeline, "Keeping Tradition Alive" (*Publisher's Weekly* 239.54 [December 14, 1992]); Craig, Patricia, "Sage Spirit: Abenaki Storyteller Joseph Bruchac Tells Tales" (*Library of Congress Information Bulletin* 53.22 [November 28, 1994]); Di Spoldo, Nick, "Writers in Prison" (*America* 148.1–3 [January 22, 1983]).

Edward Huffstetler

BRYANT, WILLIAM CULLEN (1794–1878)

William Cullen Bryant was one of the first and most distinguished American Romantic poets. Sometimes called the "American Wordsworth," he transcends this derivative label in his best work, which mixes eighteenth-century Calvinism with early nineteenth-century Romanticism and literary nationalism. He achieved success as a poet while he was in his twenties, and most of his best work was written before 1840. Although his early poems were fresh and original, his restrained public persona and his conventional later work cemented his reputation as a staid "fireside" or "schoolroom" poet. His poems had begun to fall from critical favor by the time of his death in 1878, and by the end of the twentieth century, most critics pronounced him "minor" when they took note of him at all. However, as one of the first American poets equally admired on both sides of the Atlantic, Bryant is an important figure. His elegant, accessible poems reflect the flowering of a self-consciously American branch of Romanticism—a Romanticism rooted in the forests, waterfalls, and prairies of the New World.

Bryant was born November 3, 1794, in Cummington, Massachusetts, a small town centered—like so many New England towns—around its Congregational church. He was descended from John and Priscilla Alden, and his father, Peter Bryant, was a cash-poor but distinguished physician and legislator. Bryant was a precocious versifier, self-publishing two satirical pamphlets of poetry while still in his teens, and composing the bulk of his most famous poem, "Thanatopsis," when he was just seventeen. His first national recognition as a poet came in 1817 when **Richard Henry Dana** published an early version of "Thanatopsis" in the *North American Review*. His first full-length collection, *Poems*, appeared in 1821. It was well received, establishing his reputation as a rising American poet. An expanded 1832 edition of *Poems*, edited by Washington Irving, was widely praised in Britain and further bolstered his American reputation. His subsequent poetry books included *The Fountain and Other Poems* (1842), *The White-Footed Deer and Other Poems* (1844), and translations of the *Iliad* (1871) and the *Odyssey* (1872), as well as numerous editions of *Poems*. *Poetical*

Works of William Cullen Bryant, edited and compiled by the author in 1876, has become the standard compact edition.

In 1821 Bryant married Frances Fairchild; they eventually had one daughter, Fanny. After an abortive career in law ended in 1825, he turned to journalism, becoming editor-in-chief and part owner of the New York *Evening Post* in 1827. He held this editorial position for over fifty years, weighing in as a progressive (though never a radical) on the issues of the day. Bryant supported the nationalist revolts in Greece and Italy abroad, and at home he promoted prison reform, the Free-Soil movement, and ultimately, the Republican Party. In 1860 he introduced and moderated Abraham Lincoln's famous anti-slavery speech at Cooper Union. He continued to produce poetry into the 1870s, but his output was modest, hampered by his heavy civic and professional commitments. He died in 1878 shortly after delivering a public address in Central Park—a park that he had helped to establish.

Bryant's poems can be approached from many angles: They register a transition from Calvinism to religious liberalism (while stopping short of Transcendentalism); they echo the literary nationalism of Bryant's New York contemporaries, Washington Irving and James Fenimore Cooper; they celebrate nature, complementing the expansive vistas of the Hudson River School of painters; and they are often explicitly didactic, reflecting Bryant's philosophy (shared by most of his admirers) that poems should improve and elevate readers. His output, while not voluminous, was broad; he wrote occasional poems and introspective sonnets, Gothic ballads and political verses, fairy-tale poems and hymns. He was also a significant translator of European poetry, particularly from the Spanish. Today, his most widely anthologized poems tend to be "nature" poems, broadly conceived; these include "Thanatopsis," "The Prairies," "To Cole, the Painter, Departing for Europe," "To the Fringed Gentian," and "To a Waterfowl."

"Thanatopsis," Bryant's first major poem, is also one of his most striking pieces. It anticipates his mature style, and yet it is startling and strange in a way that the later, more conventional, Bryant could never match. "Thanatopsis" is written in a plain style, reminiscent of a Puritan sermon. He derives his blank verse form most immediately from Cowper's "The Task," another famous meditation on death. And yet Bryant's take on this theme is distinctive, despite its roots in the English "graveyard school." The poem begins benignly enough: "To him who in the love of Nature hold / Communion with her visible forms, she speaks / A various language." Quickly, however, it devolves into an almost visceral depiction of a Calvinist's "darker musings" on death, which is seen as "stern agony, and shroud, and pall, / And breathless darkness, and the narrow house." The obsession with physical burial, and the narrow space of the coffin, is countered, however, by a sudden turn—not toward God, but toward Nature. The old Puritan terrors—death, perdition, isolation—are counteracted by a more reassuring image of death as a series of reunions, with the earth, with the "wise, the good" patriarchs of the past, and with the beauty of nature. Bryant's vision of death dispenses with the Judgment Day; instead, when we die, we regain our innocence, joining "the tribes" that slumber in "the earth's bosom." And yet, like **Emily Dickinson**, a slightly later apostate from the same Calvinist faith, Bryant refuses—at least in this poem—to imagine paradise as the solution to the problem of death. Instead, the all-consuming earth is offered as an Edenic alternative to Heaven, a place of beauty that serves to decorate "the great tomb of man." The idea of the earth itself as a vast cemetery—a leveling funeral urn, containing all of mankind in the end—is Romantic and democratic: All will join the "innumerable caravan," regardless of their status in life. Death descends on all, unbidden and unearned, rendering questions of judgment, predestination, and providence moot. Calvinism is mutating into liberal Unitarianism—and indeed, when Bryant joined a church in adulthood, it was a Unitarian church. Yet, although the poem's outlook is liberal, its diction retains a post-Puritan starkness that distinguishes it from Bryant's later, more flowery, verses. Critical debates have attempted to fix Bryant's theological position in "Thanatopsis"; some have called it Deist, some Pantheist, and some Wordsworthian. The poem evades easy pigeonholing, blending an eighteenth-century naturalist's attention to physical decay with a nineteenth-century Romantic's faith in the regenerative power of nature. Surely, however, the poem is notable for its refusal to consider the afterlife as supernatural; it insists, rather, on the sacred properties of the natural world.

The last nine lines of "Thanatopsis" were added early in 1821, after the poem's first appearance in the *North American Review* but before its publication in Bryant's first book. These lines are controversial because they appear to compromise the starkly funereal effect of the poem, advising the reader to "approach thy grave, / Like one who wraps the drapery of his couch / About him, and lies down to pleasant dreams." This ending domesticates nature's "rock-ribbed" embrace, equating death to a cozy nap on the sofa. However, it does fit with the poem's Romanticism, in the sense that the "moral" it offers is affective: It tells people how to feel, not how to act. This is consistent with Bryant's theory of Romantic "suggestiveness," which stipulates that readers should be swayed by a poem's emotional force, rather than by its ideas.

Such attention to emotion allies Bryant with **Lydia Sigourney**, whose "A Versification of a remark by Pliny" appeared in the same issue of the *North American Review* (September 1817) as "Thanatopsis." Sigourney, even more than Bryant, took the problem of death—and its partial, though not sufficient, consolations—as her central concern. Although her work was long derided as **sentimental** (while Bryant's was venerated), both poets are responding to the collapse of Calvinist certainties and revising the Puritans' terrifying vision of death into a more palatable and marketable nineteenth-century form. And yet death continues to be terrifying—in "Thanatopsis," if not in Bryant's later, more fully romantic poems—because it is not explicable. The poem speaks in the voice of Nature, advising its readers to accept death, but it offers no reason for this apart from death's inevitability: *memento mori*, the poem seems to remind its readers, eschewing the progressive optimism that made many of Bryant's later poems easy—perhaps too easy—for nineteenth-century readers to swallow.

After the publication of "Thanatopsis," Bryant moved to New York City and took up his public career as an editor. There, he was associated with the Knickerbocker school, and many of his poems from the 1820s and 1830s are steeped in a self-conscious literary nationalism that he shared with Cooper and Irving. His other major blank verse poem, "The Prairies," was written in 1832 after he visited his brother, John Howard, in Illinois, and it reflects his interest in fashioning a distinctly American literature. "The Prairies" begins:

These are the gardens of the Desert, these
The unshorn fields, boundless and beautiful,
For which the speech of England has no name—

Bryant's assertion that British English "has no name" for the American sublime landscape places his vision firmly in the New World even as he draws on the British tradition of topographical poetry. At the same time, the "gardens of the Desert" evoke the biblical realm of the Fertile Crescent, or even the Garden of Eden. Bryant thus posits himself as an American Adam, able to "take in," and to name, the "eternal vastness" of the prairies.

Just as the opening lines use an old image to describe a new world, so too does the rest of the poem balance an awareness of historical and natural cycles with a sense of immediate wonder. As he rides his horse across the "verdant waste," he recalls how the mound-building civilizations were supplanted by "roaming hunter tribes," noting that now these tribes have in turn departed to seek "a wilder hunting-ground." Bryant's narrative pictures the hunter tribes massacring the mound builders, but makes the "red man's" ultimate departure from the prairies both voluntary and natural. "The Prairies" implicitly supports Andrew Jackson's Indian Removal policies, which were based on the assumptions of manifest destiny. In place of the Indian, Bryant imagines future generations of white settlers; in the hums of bees and insects, he hears "the sweet and solemn hymn / Of Sabbath worshippers." All of these people, however—mound builders, hunter tribes, and white settlers alike—are embedded in the landscape, a landscape that registers the eternal power of nature. As in "Thanatopsis," nature in the "The Prairies" is a source of endless renewal, and humans return to that source when they die.

Nature in "Thanatopsis" is mostly abstract (generic woods, unspecified flowers) but in "The Prairies" it is minutely described. As Michael P. Branch points out, Bryant had a scientific bent, and he was a pioneering figure in the field of environmental journalism. "The Prairies" teems with bison, prairie-wolf dens, dam-building beavers, vultures, and hawks. At the end of the poem, when Bryant's visions of cyclical civilizations recede, he writes, "All at once, / A fresher wind sweeps by, and breaks my dream, / And I am in the wilderness alone." By this moment in the poem, "the wilderness" has been established as a valuable or even sacred place in its own right; it is not just a source of raw materials for pioneers. Bryant's romantic valuation of wildness works against his manifest destiny ideologies, and it is not surprising that naturalists from **Henry David Thoreau** to John Burroughs admired Bryant's work.

The expansive vistas in "The Prairies" also echo the paintings of the Hudson River School. Asher B. Durand's 1848 painting *Kindred Spirits* portrays Bryant and the painter Thomas Cole on Table Rock in the Catskills, surrounded by lush trees, crags, and waterfalls. In his sonnet "To Cole, the Painter, Departing for Europe" (1830), the poet both praises the painter's "glorious canvas" and succinctly advances his own theory of American exceptionalism. Bryant advises Cole to keep a "living image" of America in his heart. The difference between Europe and America, he suggests, is that Europe is picturesque and civilized—"everywhere, the trace of men"—whereas America is an "earlier, wilder" place. Here Bryant, like a true Romantic, locates the sublime wilderness in the landscape but also in the consciousness; Cole can remain true to his nationalist vision through introspection and memory.

Bryant's panoramic visions in poems such as "Thanatopsis," "The Prairies," and "To Cole" are complemented by more microscopic observations in his brief lyrics. In "To the Fringed Gentian" (1829) the poet apostrophizes the last flower of the season, the gentian, that comes "when woods are bare and birds have flown" and is so blue it is "as if that sky let fall / A flower from its cerulean wall." From the image of the flower's blue eye, the poet draws a moral; he ends the poem wishing that, as he approaches death, he will feel hope blossom within him and "look to heaven" like the gentian. The poem is perfectly balanced; its images (sky, flower) reinforce each other, and its prosody advances an idea of perfect order in which all parts of creation echo one

another. The moral is not a didactic blunder but rather an artful reflection of Bryant's philosophy of poetry; as he put it in his "Lectures on Poetry":

> Among the most remarkable of the influences of poetry is the exhibition of those analogies and correspondences which it beholds between the things of the moral and of the natural world. I refer to its adorning and illustrating each by the other—infusing a moral sentiment into natural objects, and bringing images of visible majesty and beauty to heighten the effect of moral sentiment. (McDowell, 198)

Here again, remnants of his Calvinist heritage put pressure on Bryant's Romanticism, so that his admiration of the natural world is tempered by a belief in orderly purposes and correspondences, as well as by a determination to make poetry morally uplifting.

Bryant's distinctive blend of passion and order reaches its apotheosis in "To a Waterfowl," a poem that Matthew Arnold once called the best short poem in English. The poem addresses a bird that is flying into the sunset, asking, "Whither . . . dost thou pursue / Thy solitary way?" The bird's "visible majesty and beauty" is both precise and panoramic as Bryant offers the reader a sublime landscape, but trains his eye on one moving object within that landscape. In this poem, it quickly becomes evident how the natural world corresponds to what Bryant would call the "moral" world, the world of the interior self. As Albert McLean has argued, the image of the bird corresponds to the observer's soul: Both fly into darkness, both are pursued by death, and yet both are guided by a "Power / Whose care" guides them along "that pathless coast / The desert and illimitable air." Is the power a Christian God, or some less personal force? The poem is ambivalent on this point—just as many early-to-mid-nineteenth–century American readers were unsure about the nature of God.

Like "To the Fringed Gentian," Bryant's apostrophe "To a Waterfowl" ends by explicitly stating its moral: The power that guides the flight of the bird will will also "[i]n the long way I must tread alone / . . . lead my steps aright." This typically didactic ending marks Bryant's distance from many of his British contemporaries; a poet such as Keats also maps correspondences between himself and a bird in "Ode to a Nightingale," but he does not end with such an explicit moral. Bryant's moralism is part of what makes him a distinctly American poet; he absorbed transatlantic Romantic influences while retaining a faint strain of Calvinist didacticism.

Bryant's reputation continues to evolve. "To a Waterfowl" was memorized and recited by generations of schoolchildren up until at least the 1950s, so in some sense he remained a popular success. At the same time, proponents of the modernist aesthetic, such as **Harriet Monroe**,

Buckley, Christopher (1948–)   215

tended to dismiss Bryant as they valorized the more innovative work of **Walt Whitman** and Emily Dickinson. However, Whitman himself understood Bryant to be an innovative and important poet. In *Specimen Days*, he praises Bryant for writing "the first interior verse":

—[T]throbs of a mighty world—bard of the river and wood, even conveying a taste of the open air, with scents as from hay-fields, grapes, birch borders—always lurking fond of threnodies—beginning and ending his long career with chants of death, with here and there through all, poems or passages of poems, touching the highest universal truths, enthusiasms, duties—morals as grim and eternal, if not as stormy and fateful, as anything in Aeschylus. (267)

Bryant's strength, as Whitman suggests, lies in the way he mixes enthusiasms and duties. In his best work, opposing forces—wilderness and civilization, passion and order—fuse to produce romantic poems that still convey "a taste of the open air."

Further Reading. *Selected Primary Sources:* Bryant, William Cullen, *Poetical Works of William Cullen Bryant* (New York: D. Appleton & Co., 1876); Bryant, William Cullen II, and Thomas Voss, eds., *Letters of William Cullen Bryant* (New York: Fordham University Press, 1975); McDowell, Tremaine, ed., *William Cullen Bryant: Representative Selections* (New York: American Book Company, 1935). *Selected Secondary Sources:* Brown, Charles H., *William Cullen Bryant* (New York: Scribner's, 1971); Krapf, Norbert, *Under Open Sky: Poets on William Cullen Bryant* (New York: Fordham University Press, 1986); McLean, Albert F., *William Cullen Bryant* (New York: Twayne, 1964); Morris, Timothy, "Bryant and the American Poetic Tradition" (*American Transcendental Quarterly* 8.1 [March 1994]: 53–71); Ostrowski, Carl, "'I Stand Upon Their Ashes in Thy Beam': The Indian and Bryant's Literary Removals" (*American Transcendental Quarterly* 9.4 [December 1995]: 499–513); Whitman, Walt, "My Tribute to Four Poets," in *Specimen Days, Prose Works*, vol. 1 (New York: New York University Press, 1963).

Angela Sorby

BUCKLEY, CHRISTOPHER (1948–)

Christopher Buckley grew up near Santa Barbara, California, in a lush and vibrant landscape he credits with forming an aesthetic focused on place and on those ephemeral moments when the natural world invites the individual to explore the metaphysical. His interest in the connection between nature and the desires that drive the human heart has produced a poetry that asks the reader to see small matters of daily life as potentially sacred. The poems carry the burden of this inquiry gracefully; Buckley's sense of humor and his keen memory of growing up

in the 1950s and 1960s provide a setting and tone that is lively and engaging. Buckley has been a prolific writer and an energetic force for creating and showcasing California poetry. He has actively aligned himself with the Fresno poets, notably **Philip Levine** and **Larry Levis**, producing both critical work and anthologies on California poets, and, even more locally, Fresno poets.

Except for what he deems an exile to the east early in his teaching career, Buckley has lived his whole life in California, mainly Southern California. He was born on January 14, 1948, and grew up in Montecito, just outside Santa Barbara, when it was an affordable place for a working-class family. His father was a radio disc jockey and his mother was a secretary. In *The Geography of Home* (1999), an anthology he also edited, Buckley describes his childhood as largely carefree: "It's hard to imagine a better childhood environment. . . . We were happy, healthy, and free as light." His elementary, high school, and undergraduate college years were spent in Catholic institutions, but surfing and beach life seem to have made at least as serious an impression. In an interview in *Poetry Santa Cruz* he tells of opening *Surf Guide* to find a photo of a perfectly formed wave with a stanza from Swinburne's "The Garden of Proserpine" superimposed on it. After college Buckley went first to San Diego State University, where he studied with Glover Davis, and then to University of California at Irvine, where he earned an MFA. After teaching for a few years in Kentucky and Pennsylvania, he returned to Southern California. He now teaches in the University of California–Riverside, **Creative Writing Program**. Buckley lives with wife, the artist Nadya Brown, in Lompoc, California.

Buckley has published thirteen volumes of poetry and numerous chapbooks. The poems are permeated by landscape—usually Southern California but occasionally a European venue. The ocean, the blossoming trees, the ever-changing cloudscape are both background and character in his poems, at times even serving as a sort of spiritual guide. In his third book, *Other Lives* (1985), the poem "Blossom" opens with the line "Today, Sunday I am all right." The speaker's sanguinity seems directly due to the landscape's example: "the lime trees seem less worried / with winter, its basket of less and less." The poet figures that since the "sand-colored birds / are ramshackle at the feather" his tattered sleeves don't matter much, and the poem ends with the philosophical point of view that underwrites many of Buckley's poems: Things are better than they may at first seem "Because riches fall / even to the least of us."

But this almost idealistic position is occasionally undercut by life's disappointments, and in his tenth book, *Fall from Grace* (1998), Buckley finds himself writing not only about life's riches but also the frustrations and limitations of a teaching poet's career. "20 Years of Grant Applications and State College Jobs" is a poem that pokes fun at aspiring to prizes and lasting fame while arguing for loving the quiet good life of friends, a life by the sea, "Zinfandel and a bowl of Spanish olives" and "a Pavarotti aria holding off death, / drifting out the kitchen window onto the ambered light." In this work Buckley seems to call out his vocation as a poet—"my notes scrawled in the margins where I've tried to locate / the trace elements of God"—but still seems to envy the immediacy of youth, which is joyful even "in uncertainty, not enough gas in the tank to get out of town." The reader feels some of the discipline that the poet must bring to bear to maintain his sense of values. This theme occurs regularly in Buckley's work, as if he must go to nature again and again to remember the grace of daily living.

In praising Buckley's work **Gerald Stern** has said, "Buckley's subject is radiance. So he hates fascism and believes we are more than dust" (back cover, *Fall from Grace* and *Sky*). His poems of praise, filled as they are with lush description and frank admiration for the physical landscape he loves, have an interest in the **sublime** and a sense that the appreciation of what is beautiful in the outer world can shape the inner landscape of the attentive. Buckley seems to feel this influence is productive of good even, and perhaps especially, when absorbed unconsciously as children. Although his Catholic school education surfaces in many Buckley poems, the power of that experience is portrayed as easily undercut by nature's glory. In "The Lost Catechism of the Clouds," from *Blue Autumn* (1990), Buckley recounts a class visit from a priest who quizzed students on the holy order of the words. Buckley claims that even after naming *The Five Near Occasions of Sin* "we so loved ourselves" that a natural windy updraft made the students head to the beach "and there in our indolence refute grammar/and the formulas for grace until dusk."

Buckley's prolific writing career continues, as does his work as a critic. His poems are published widely (*New Yorker, American Poetry Review, Nation*) and have garnered prizes and praise. It is telling that he titled one volume of reviews *Appreciations: Selected Reviews, Views & Interviews*. In his poems and his criticism Buckley demonstrates the impulse and talent to appreciate what is present and gorgeous in life, which his poems claim is fleeting and not to be missed.

Further Reading. *Selected Primary Sources:* Buckley, Christopher, *Camino Cielo* (Alexandria ,VA: Orchises Press, 1997); ———, *Dark Matter* (Providence, RI: Copper Beech Press of Brown University, 1993); ———, *Fall from Grace* (Kansas City: BkMk Press, 1998); ———, *A Short History of Light* (Davis, CA: Painted Hills Press, 1994); ———, *Sky* (Riverdale-on-Hudson, NY: Sheep Meadow Press, 2004); ———, *Star Apocrypha* (Evanston, IL, TriQuarterly Books, Northwestern University Press, 2001). ***Selected Secondary***

Sources: Long, Alexander, "A Review of Christopher Buckley's *Fall From Grace*" (*Montserrat Review* [2004], http://www. themontserratreview.com); Paul, Maggie, "A Higher Lyric Pitch—An Interview with Christopher Buckley" (*Poetry Santa Cruz* [2004], http://www.baymoon.com/~poetrysantacruz/interviews/buckley.html).

Deborah Bogen

BUKOWSKI, CHARLES (1920–1994)

During the 1960s, Charles Bukowski methodically rose to literary prominence. He published beautifully designed books like *It Catches My Heart in Its Hands* (1963) and *At Terror Street and Agony Way* (1968). However, his initial wide popularity came from short stories and first-person narratives he wrote and published in radical tabloids like *Open City* in Los Angeles and *NOLA Express*. Bukowski's readership embraced his anarchistic, independent, cynical, and brutally frank philosophy. He wrote contrary to polite ideals and his work fell outside the limits of all academic poetry. Shunning literary movements, he published his sarcastic, anti-authoritarian poems in underground literary publications such as the *Wormwood Review* and mimeo magazines such as *Ole*. The raw vigor of his unique, impudent, and independent point of view and his eccentric lifestyle won him a wide and loyal readership. His influence was immense, and between the late 1970s and the early 1990s nearly all outlaw and **small press** poetry was derivative of his work. A counter-culture literary hero, he remains one of America's mostly widely read yet rarely praised poets.

The son of an American soldier and German mother, Henry Charles Bukowski, Jr., was born August 16, 1920, in Andernach, Germany, and brought to Los Angeles in 1922. As a young man he worked an endless series of menial jobs and lived on skid row. In 1955, after prolonged alcohol abuse, he was hospitalized with a severe bleeding ulcer. Shortly after this near-death experience, he began to write and publish poetry prolifically and to work for the U.S. Postal Service. He published his first book, *Flower Fist and Bestial Wail*, in 1960. In 1965 he met John Martin, whose Black Sparrow Press became Bukowski's primary publisher. At age fifty, Bukowski took Martin's offer of a small stipend, quit his job, and began to write full time. The last decades of his life were marked by relative emotional peace. His screenplay *Barfly* (1987) was made into a major motion picture. He married Linda Lee Beighle, drove expensive cars, and owned a home in San Pedro, California. He published large collections of poetry, including *You Get So Alone at Times That It Just Makes Sense* (1986) and *Septuagenarian Stew* (1990), and novels such as *Hollywood* (1989) and *Pulp* (1994). After publishing more than sixty books in a dozen languages, he died of leukemia in 1994. The majority of his books remain in print. A decade after his death, new volumes of unpublished poems and letters continue to appear.

There is no hallmark poem or single book that best exemplifies Bukowski's poetic achievements. His work evolved over his fifty-year career. His early poetry is intensely pondering, introspective, and influenced by poet **Robinson Jeffers**. In his poem "The Tragedy of the Leaves" (1962), he writes about waking up to find "my woman was gone/ and the empty bottles like bled corpses/ surrounded me." The poem concludes with the dark and somber thought that age crushes youthful idealism and love and leaves the individual in an unsalvageable state of emotional pain.

The second phase of Bukowski's poetry began in the mid-1960s. He admired and perfected spontaneity, and his poetry illustrates unrestrained Dionysian passion and melodramatic sensation. His collections *The Days Run Away Like Wild Horses over the Hills* (1969) and *Love Is a Dog from Hell* (1977) feature poems that appear to be mere gesture compositions, but are highly honed and perfected poetry. Semi-autobiographical, Bukowski's poetry is a measured form of spoken language, rich in cadence, with uneven lines and odd line and stanza breaks. It illuminates the poetry in the mundane (shaving, for instance) and makes vapid the sacred (such as meeting famous authors). Stripped of most metaphor, the rhythmic language delivers poetry rife with humor, irony, and sarcasm. Bukowski equated his talent with the artistic courage he acquired living in a feral state. Being unrestrained allowed him to express, satisfy, and satiate his desires without restraint. Therefore, Bukowski's poetry celebrates volatility and animalistic acts such as defecation and copulation, the desire for intoxication and, for Bukowski, the need to create.

In the 1980s he entered his final phase. The poems became reflections on daily events and memories that he enhanced with biting commentary. Confronting death and the rejuvenation he experienced in writing are themes explored in *The Last Night of the Earth Poems* (1992). In his poem "Only One Cervantes" (1992) Bukowski notes, "writing has been my fountain / of youth." Death, which appears as a cigar-smoking specter or as a woman, is stalled by the creative act. Writing furiously in his waning years, he amassed thousands of poems now collected into volumes like *Sifting Through the Madness for the Word, the Line, the Way* (2003). The book concludes with the poem "Like a Dolphin," in which he writes of his "lost childhood," which "leaps like a dolphin / in the frozen sea."

Bukowski also wrote prose. *Notes of a Dirty Old Man* (1969) was an early substantial collection of short stories, and *Post Office* (1971) was his first novel. Stylistically, his poetry and prose were influenced by Ernest Hemingway's clear, quick, and unadorned language. It was also in his narrative poetry and prose that Bukowski manifested his greatest literary achievement in the form of his alter ego, his persona Henry Chinaski, a hard-living, cantankerous, self-obsessed character drawn from the works of Ferdinand Celine, Fyodor Dostoyevsky, and John Fante. Bukowski admired exaggerated, eccentric personalities and fashioned his own persona to follow suit. Chinaski is a menacing and sensitive figure and a wise fool. He was an embellished version of Charles Bukowski. Chinaski's outrageous adventures through the nether regions and lowest rungs of American society were, in the end, imaginary adventures. Bukowski's narrative poetry and prose were not so much depictions of reality as they were the autobiography of his imagination.

Further Reading. ***Selected Primary Sources:*** Bukowski, Charles, *At Terror Street and Agony Way* (Santa Rosa, CA: Black Sparrow Press, 1968); ———, *The Days Run Away Like Wild Horses over the Hills* (Santa Rosa, CA: Black Sparrow Press, 1969); ———, *Flower Fist and Bestial Wail* (Eureka, CA: Hearse Press, 1960); ———, *Hollywood* (Santa Rosa, CA: Black Sparrow Press, 1989); ———, *It Catches My Heart in Its Hands* (New Orleans: LouJon Press, 1963); ———, *The Last Night of the Earth Poems* (Santa Rosa, CA: Black Sparrow Press, 1992); ———, *Love Is a Dog from Hell* (Santa Rosa, CA: Black Sparrow Press, 1977); ———, *The Movie: "Barfly"* (Santa Rosa, CA: Black Sparrow Press, 1987); ———, *Notes of a Dirty Old Man* (North Hollywood: Essex House, 1969; reissue San Francisco: City Lights Books, 1973); ———, *Open All Night: New Poems* (Santa Rosa, CA: Black Sparrow Press, 2000); ———, *Post Office* (Santa Rosa, CA: Black Sparrow Press, 1971); ———, *Pulp* (Santa Rosa, CA: Black Sparrow Press, 1994); ———, *Run with the Hunted: A Charles Bukowski Reader*, ed. John Martin (New York: HarperCollins, 1993); ———, *Septuagenarian Stew* (Santa Rosa, CA: Black Sparrow Press, 1990); ———, *Sifting Through the Madness for the Word, the Line, the Way*, ed. John Martin (New York: HarperCollins, 2003); ———, *War All the Time* (Santa Rosa, CA: Black Sparrow Press, 1984); ———, *You Get So Alone at Times That It Just Makes Sense* (Santa Rosa, CA: Black Sparrow Press, 1986). ***Secondary Sources:*** Brewer, Gay, *Charles Bukowski* (New York: Twayne, 1997); Cherkovski, Neeli, *Hank: The Life of Charles Bukowski* (New York: Random House, 1991); Harrison, Russell, *Against the American Dream* (Santa Rosa, CA: Black Sparrow Press, 1994).

Michael Basinski

BURKARD, MICHAEL (1947–)

Michael Burkard has published nine full-length collections of poetry as well as several chapbooks. His considerable poetic output (which first gained significant attention with the publication of *Fictions from the Self* in 1988) has a high degree of consistency. Some elements of his work bear a kinship to **confessional poetry** and other aspects resemble the poets of the **Deep Image** school. Yet Burkard's writing does not fall comfortably within either of these categories. His poetic influences include the abstract, painterly writings of **Wallace Stevens** and **John Ashbery**, while his deployment of the poetic line and his frequently anxious persona owe a dept to the writing of **Robert Creeley**. Burkard writes in a highly varied **free-verse** style, with approaches to the line ranging from short-lined poems to longer, looser lines to **prose poetry**; his poems are examples of **open form**. Like several of his contemporaries (including **Jean Valentine** and Jane Miller), Burkard explores some of the linguistic possibilities offered by avant-garde poetry without abandoning his lyric themes. His detractors (such as **Fred Chappell**) find his poetry vague and unfocused, but his advocates discover a rigorous interrogation of the imagination in the poems' self-reflective abstractions and intensely psychological landscapes.

Burkard was born in Rome, New York, in 1947 and educated at Hobart College (BA, 1968) and the University of Iowa (MFA., 1973). He has taught at a number of colleges and universities, including Sarah Lawrence College, the University of Iowa, the University of Louisville, and Syracuse University, and he has long been affiliated with the Fine Arts Work Center in Provincetown, Massachusetts. He has also worked in the mental health field; from 1969 to 1971 he was a psychiatric aide, and in the 1990s he worked as an alcoholism counselor for children.

From the beginning, Burkard's poetry has been characterized by a simultaneous interest in abstraction and psychological dynamics, tendencies that struggle for priority in the work. For example, by beginning with the words "I remember shame," the poem "Shame" in *Ruby for Grief* (1981) seems to evoke a confessional stance. Yet the word "shame" becomes abstracted from personal history by being repeated (along with "ashamed") seventeen times in a short lyric; eventually, shame and the speaker of the poem become inextricably entangled and even identified. In these poems, a single word is used in a painterly, gestural way that evades concrete reference, and indeed some poems in *Ruby for Grief* (such as "Klee") explicitly reference painters in ways that recall the abstract expressionist traditions of the **New York School**. In "Envy," this use of gesture and abstraction controls a short narrative in which the speaker witnesses a conversation between two people he cannot hear while a third throws stones at a car driving away. The speaker can say nothing about the content of the conversation or about what motivates the stone-thrower, but he is not interested in such things in any event. What interests him is the scene as an abstract map of a set of relationships and a test of the poet's imagination: The conversation between the couple "burns out," Burkard writes, "because I say it does."

Burkard's abstract yet subjective landscapes become fully realized in *Fictions from the Self* (1988) and *My Secret Boat* (1990), a pair of books that develop similar themes

and even exchange lines: "a lamp explodes / in my grandmother's grave" reads a line in "The Blue Paradise" (from *My Secret Boat*), making a verse paragraph out of a line in "North and South" (from *Fictions*). The structures of both *Fictions* and *My Secret Boat* suggest the presence of a narrative dimension to the work. *Fictions*, a relatively long collection of poems, divides its three sections by date of composition; the subtitle of *My Secret Boat* is *A Notebook of Prose and Poems*, implying a sequential order as well. The poems in these books frequently seem like rapid-fire associations, exemplifications of the principles of speed articulated in **Charles Olson**'s open-form manifesto "Projective Verse." Through both books, a set of elemental images cycles, including self, amnesia, father, sister, hatchets, wells, lamps, boats, and rent. In one sense, these images illustrate the themes of the poems, but in another sense the term "theme" is inadequate to describe the kinds of compulsive repetition in which these poems engage. Indeed, repetition itself —in the Freudian sense of compulsively repeated and inadequately understood behavior —is perhaps the principle theme, along with family, memory, and money. The title of *Fictions from the Self* suggests not confessional reconciliation but defensive projections; the knowledge that they *are* fictions gives these defenses their characteristically open-ended, self-undermining quality. The last two lines of "Strangely Insane" (from *Fictions*) illustrate this stance well: "I could not each much as a child. / Go away, go away, go away." In a similar fashion, Burkard writes "I securely fasten my cap / to the door of my nervousness" in "The Blossoms" (from *Fictions*), as though this secure fastening is a form of security countering the nervousness itself.

Burkard's recent poetry, although not confessional, seems more at ease with autobiographical detail. In particular, the image of the poet as recovering alcoholic unifies the poems of *Entire Dilemma* (1998) and *Pennsylvania Collection Agency* (2001). The poem "Your Sister Life," from *Entire Dilemma*, imagines the lure of drinking as the Siren of an alternate life, a life abandoned in favor of a continually reaffirmed "She's there. / You don't have to let her in." Many poems in *Entire Dilemma* attempt to represent the cost of alcoholism: "Before the Dark" assesses a relationship with Fred that was lost in part to alcohol. But here as well, the characteristic dreamlike abstraction of the poem retrieves it from melancholy regret: Fred, the poem concludes, "is one / of many names." Just so, the book concludes with "But Beautiful," a poem where many names are retrieved and affirmed as beautiful "one by one, / and one for all."

Unsleeping (2002) contains a wide range of poems illustrating all of Burkard's tendencies, including some (such as "Hat Angel") showing him at his most humanistic and tender, others (such as "Talking") displaying a diaristic quality reminiscent of *My Secret Boat*, and some (such as the sequence "Notes about My Face") exemplifying Burkard at his most open-ended and fragmentary.

Further Reading. *Selected Primary Sources:* Burkard, Michael, *Entire Dilemma* (Louisville: Sarabande Books, 1998); *Fictions from the Self* (New York: Norton, 1988); ———, *My Secret Boat* (New York: Norton, 1990); ———, *Pennsylvania Collection Agency* (Kalamazoo, MI: New Issues Poetry Press, 2001); ———, *Ruby for Grief* (Pittsburgh: University of Pittsburgh Press, 1981); *Unsleeping* (Louisville: Sarabande Books, 2001). ***Selected Secondary Sources:*** Chappell, Fred, "Fictions from the Self" (*Georgia Review* 43.2 [1989]: 386–388); Gallagher, Tess, "Inside the Kaleidoscope: The Poetry of Michael Burkard" (*American Poetry Review* 11.3 [1982]: 34–41); Gervasio, Michael, "My Secret Boat: The Poetry of 'Before'" (*Denver Quarterly* 28.3 [1994]: 76–79).

David Kellogg

BYER, KATHRYN STRIPLING (1944–)

Although she grew up in the southwest Georgia flatlands, Kathryn Stripling Byer is best known as a poet of the Appalachian Mountains. Her first book, *The Girl in the Midst of the Harvest* (1986), probes and celebrates her south Georgia background. However, within that book several poems already point to the Appalachian world that dominates her next two collections, *Wildwood Flower* (1992) and *Black Shawl* (1998). In them, Byer tunes in the bygone voices, silenced by geographical obscurity and economic hardship, of women from the mountains of western North Carolina. "How to get through—," Byer writes in her essay "Time Lines," "isn't that the most urgent question one can ask?" Her best work to date has developed from the imaginative encounter with these historically "silent" women. Although a departure from her Appalachia, her most recent book, *Catching Light* (2002), keeps its focus on culturally undervalued women, examining from a contemporary woman's perspective the challenges of aging while also questioning "how to get through." In all of her books, Byer expands the boundaries of American poetry by exploring regions and populations often overlooked in the canon.

Byer was born in Camilla, Georgia, in 1944; after her early years in Camilla, she attended Wesleyan College in Macon, Georgia, then earned an MFA. from the University of North Carolina–Greensboro. There she studied, most notably, with poets **Allen Tate** and **Fred Chappell**. She chose to remain in the North Carolina mountains, settling in the small town of Cullowhee in 1968. She and her husband, Jim, have one daughter, Corinna. Byer served as poet-in-residence at Western Carolina University from 1988 until 1998. In 2005 the governor of North Carolina named her the state's poet laureate.

In *The Girl in the Midst of the Harvest*, the speaker tests her identity as daughter and granddaughter, wife and mother, Southerner and poet. The opening poem, "Wide Open, These Gates," is an acknowledgment of her past, as well as an acerbic assessment of how others might judge it: "I've come a long way / from what's been described as a mean and starved / corner of backwoods America." Rather than have it described for her, she will articulate her life: "The gnats sing, and I'm going / to sing. One of these days I'll be gone." These final lines of the poem startle with their matter-of-fact existentialism. The speaker accepts the responsibility to make meaning for herself, accepts human contingency, and vows "to sing." The philosophical poise of this speaker (and others) is one of the revelations of Byer's work. One critic refers to the "kitchen existentialism" of a poem from this collection (Richman, 40), but it is, in fact, a stance that defines all of her books, countering stereotypes of "backwoods America." One need not be an urban intellectual to evaluate life profoundly, the poems suggest. They are not grim, however, and some are celebratory, but her speakers ultimately reject what they see as illusory consolation. Near the end of this first book, Byer places "Prayer." She inventories the heaven her grandmother would want, and it is the essence of the life she lived, not an alien paradise. The grandmother wakes up on Saturday morning, the consummate Byer heroine, "wide-awake among what she has lost."

The choice to be "wide-awake" shapes *Wildwood Flower* and *Black Shawl*. In the former, themes from her first book gain more focus through the life of a single character, Alma. Byer initiates the existential theme in the first poem, "Wildwood Flower," and then develops it with variations throughout the collection. The poem opens with a woman strenuously at work ("I hoe thawed ground / with a vengeance"), and so the book begins with urgent necessity, an awareness of contingency. Later in the poem the speaker tells how once she climbed to the top of a ridge to look beyond her life of hard work. What she saw, however, did not comfort her: "Beyond me the mountains continued / like God. Is there no place to hide / from His silence?" She quickly shifts from uncomfortable abstraction and asserts, "A woman must work / else she thinks too much." Near the end of the poem, Byer emphasizes "nothing," a key word in her existential Appalachia: "I hoe / this earth until I think of nothing." The stanza breaks before the line continues, "but the beans I will string, / the sweet corn I will grind into meal." This shifting between faith in the creative force of work and the fear of thought's abnegation is one of the collection's main rhythms.

By the end of the book, however, Alma looks more steadily at "nothing," discarding conventional religious consolation in particular. In "Easter," she observes that "the preacher *shouts* death has no victory" (my emphasis).

She also is forced to see past the myth of romantic love. Her husband leaves on a trip early in the collection and never returns. Invoking an image that becomes the central symbol in Byer's next book, Alma recalls in "Trillium" his courtship voice: "I should have covered my head with my shawl / and kept silent!" The poem "Black Shawl" appears near the end of *Wildwood Flower*, and a section of it serves as an epigraph for Byer's third book, *Black Shawl*. The clothing comes to Alma from her grandmother and conveys a tradition of women knitting protection for themselves and teaching those who come after how to do the same. In this third book, Byer's form of **feminism**, tempered by an existential outlook, is fully represented by this symbolic shawl.

Black Shawl is not inflected by one woman's voice but rather weaves in the voices of a community of women. One of the most important is Delphia. Her name conjures allusions to the Delphic oracle, but she makes no claims to have answers for what she calls "the big questions." Therefore, it is she to whom the poet looks for an existential role model. In "Delphia," the older woman's oracular identity emerges in her discussion of quilt making, the art of piecing together remnants, which Byer often uses as a symbol of "how to get through," how to make meaning from one's experience. "Don't ask me the big questions / none but a fool tries to answer / straight," Delphia chides as she quilts. "All I can tell you of why / you were born is to take your own time / once the needle's been threaded." It is through "her window" in "The Morning of the First Day" that the speaker first consciously recognizes "the world outside / me. What has always / refused to hold still." And it is Delphia who wraps the symbolic shawl around the young girl in a ritualistic gesture that confirms her initiation into the awareness of contingency. "The Morning of the First Day" is not the day of physical birth, but of birth into awareness. A visible sign of mourning, the shawl also gives comfort and protection. Seeing life clearly is a kind of comfort and a kind of protection, the poem implies, even though it requires acknowledgment of life's tragic dimension. Delphia is one of several female characters Byer summons as a model of how women empower each other in one place and time.

Her most recent collection, *Catching Light*, enters the world of contemporary women's concerns, especially that of aging, perhaps in response to criticism that her work had lodged itself too firmly in the past (Makuck 174). Whatever the motivation, in a poem like "Vanity" Byer connects the musing of a contemporary woman with that of the mythical Eve, asserting a continuum from past to present. The woman in the poem "tends the image / she sees in her glass." It is an image that she alone must come to terms with, and as the word "tends" suggests, care for. In the final lines, she is thus associated with Eve "who dared eat / from her own hand / the fruit of self-knowledge." The sort of daring scrutiny that this poem

honors is the guiding principle of the collection and connects it powerfully with Byer's other books in which women struggle to stay "wide-awake" in the midst of loss.

Further Reading. ***Selected Primary Sources:*** Byer, Kathryn Stripling, *Black Shawl* (Baton Rouge: Louisiana State University Press, 1998); ———, *Catching Light* (Baton Rouge: Louisiana State University Press, 2002); ———, *The Girl in the Midst of the Harvest* (Lubbock: Texas Tech Press, 1986); ———, "Time Lines" (*Carolina Quarterly* 51.2 [1999]: 68–76); ———, *Wildwood Flower* (Baton Rouge: Louisiana State University Press, 1992). ***Selected Secondary Sources:*** Howard, Julie Kate, "'Having Become Their Own Voices': The Third Stream in Kathryn Stripling Byer's *Black Shawl*" (*Asheville Poetry Review* 6.1 [1999]: 37–44); Makuck, Peter, "Threads of a Dark Design" (*North Carolina Literary Review* 8 [1999]: 173–177); Richman, Ann, "'Singing Our Hearts Away': The Poetry of Kathryn Stripling Byer," in *Her Words: Diverse Voices in Contemporary Appalachian Women's Poetry*, ed. Felicia Mitchell (Knoxville: University of Tennessee Press, 2002).

James M. Smith, Jr.

BYLES, MATHER (1706/7–1788)

Seldom discussed and usually criticized negatively, Mather Byles is a poet whose significance in helping to establish American literary independence is probably underestimated. Although this Congregationalist clergyman is considered by many modern readers to be little better than a derivative imitator of his British contemporary Alexander Pope, readers in Byles's own time revered him as one of the best poets in the American colonies, and he therefore warrants at least some attention. Byles not only actively sought and garnered fame as a poet but he also helped to establish, edited, and contributed regularly to America's first newspaper devoted strictly to literature, the *New England Weekly Journal*. It was in this periodical that Byles published one of the first pieces of American literary criticism, "Bombastic and Grubstreet Style: A Satire"(1727), an essay in which he aimed to help "form and embellish the [writing] style of our ingenious Countrymen." Byles's stated purpose may seem banal upon first glance; however, given the fact that the Puritan "plain style" had been the predominant mode in which all writing, not simply poetry, had been composed, it becomes apparent that Mather Byles hoped to usher in a new, more aesthetically oriented era in American belletristic writing, a mode which was to be judged by good taste. Incorporating both British and Classical influences in his effort to create a distinctive style of his own, Byles produced a body of work that is as experimental as it is eclectic.

Born March 15, 1707, in Boston, Byles was reared by his mother, Elizabeth Mather, and his uncle, the famed preacher and poet **Cotton Mather**. After attending the

North Latin School, where the youngster was steeped in classical literature, Byles went on to attend Harvard University, receiving his AB in 1725 and his AM in 1728. Although there was never any doubt that Byles's vocation would be the ministry, his pursuits in the literary arena must have been sparked at an early age. Byles had access to, and would later inherit, his uncle's library of over two thousand volumes, and he attended Harvard University shortly after it had completed its shift to a more literary curriculum. It was in these college years that Byles would compose the bulk of his poetic works, publish essays in the *New England Courant*, and write the first literary criticism dissertation on record in America. During a three-year gap between his graduation and his acceptance of the pulpit at the Hollis Street Church, Byles published numerous essays and poems in his *New England Weekly Journal*. Not until 1744, however, did his two collections of poetry, *Poems on Several Occasions* and *A Collection of Poems by Several Hands*, get published. More than thirty years later, after the lines had been drawn between Loyalists and Revolutionaries, Byles was dismissed from his pulpit, put on public trial, and sentenced to banishment for his Tory sympathies. The sentence, however, was lessened to house arrest, which was then lifted entirely two years later. What Byles seems to be most remembered for, besides his poetry, are his wit and his love of practical jokes and puns. Charles Eaton, Byles's sole biographer, includes an entire chapter devoted exclusively to the minister's brand of humor. For example, upon being asked by a friend in terrible pain where he might get a tooth "drawn," Byles instructed the man to find his way to the Beacon Hill home of John Singleton Copely, not a dentist but an artist. Eaton also includes the story of Byles's chance meeting with a fellow minister in the street on a day of fasting. Both were on horseback, and when Byles saw his friend in the distance, he began riding as fast as his horse would go. When his friend asked why he was in such a hurry, Byles quickly replied that it was a "fast day."

Although Byles believed that, politically, America was better off as a part of the British Empire, a close reading of two of his more famous poems, "Written in Milton's *Paradise Lost*"(1727) and "To an ingenious Young Gentleman, on his dedicating a Poem to the Author"(1726), reveals his conviction that, artistically, America needed to cultivate a voice of its own. Ironically, these two works, both of which seem manifest paeans to British poets (John Milton and Alexander Pope, respectively) are the ones most often cited in the criticism that Mather Byles did little more than poorly mimic those famous poets from the other side of the Atlantic.

"Written in Milton's *Paradise Lost*" is 184 lines of blank verse on the subject of John Milton's 1667 epic. A cursory reading may reveal that this poem is basically a summary of various episodes from *Paradise Lost*. He describes first the terrifying vision of hell, Satan, and death; goes on to relate the battle in heaven, the heroic exploits of Michael and Christ; and then swiftly changes gears in order to detail the sights and smells of the Edenic landscape and the virginal beauty of Eve. In the last stanza, Byles instructs his muse to shake off the "imaginary Trances . . . vain Illusions" of attempting Milton's praise, admitting that his own verse pales in comparison to that of his subject. Interestingly, there appear two earlier occasions in which the poet seems to concede defeat. After relating Satan's fall through chaos into the pits of hell, the poet claims that he cannot maintain such heights, and that only Raphael or Milton could possibly do justice to the story of Satan's defeat and fall. Once again, immediately following his description of Eve, the poet asks his "fair Mother" to forgive him his "Redundance of Expression." Given Byles's apparent reticence regarding his poetic abilities, one could make the argument that the poet probably would have been better off had he never attempted to retell Milton's work. However, Byles has no intention of merely sketching his predecessor's masterpiece, and his three stops reveal not a poet who feels as though he is not up to the task so much as one who is keenly aware of the dangers of overt imitation and repetition.

Indeed, this poet's purpose is rather an original one, for he seeks not to retell the story of *Paradise Lost* or merely to try his hand at blank verse, but to relate the feelings of aesthetic rapture into which Milton's work casts him. What Byles illustrates is the "joyful dread, the terrible Delight" (the feeling of the sublime) ensnaring him as he reads of the angelic host defeating the rebel angels, or how he is "charm'd and ravish'd by Milton's rendering of Eden. That Byles speaks in terms of aesthetics rather than in terms of religious rapture has a larger significance, insofar as the nature of his own reading is patently different from the common one in Britain at the time. (Thanks in large part to Joseph Addison's *Spectator* essays, *Paradise Lost* became, for some time, devotional Sunday reading material.)

That the poet emphasizes John Milton's method over his religious theme does not indicate that Byles in any way avoided themes of piety or reverence and awe before God, subjects that permeate his *Poems on Several Occasions*. In much the same way that Byles praises Milton for his rendering of Christian content and imagery, he lauds the anonymous writer of the poem "Eternity" in "To an ingenious young gentleman, on his dedicating a Poem to the Author." In brief, Byles's poem can be broken down into three parts. First, Byles praises the young poet's person as well as his abilities in the art of numbers; second he describes in great detail the conflicting emotions—envy and pride—that arise as a result of being touted as the young man's poetic mentor; third, he concedes that praise is due not to him, but to Alexander Pope, the true instructor and beacon of light, whose radiance Byles merely reflects; and finally Byles urges this young poet to continue writing, instructing his protégé to continue directing his poetic efforts toward the spiritual.

"To an ingenious young gentleman," however, is much more than the sum of its parts, as a closer reading reveals further evidence of and desire for American literary independence. What must be understood in order fully to comprehend the significance of this work is that the author of "Eternity," the ingenious young gentleman, is none other than Mather Byles himself. Byles literally sings his own praises as a poet who "fly[s] aloft, unfettered, unconfined." Returning briefly to "Written in Milton's *Paradise Lost*," the primary method through which Byles praises his predecessor is by concession that his own rendering of the master's art falls short. Byles praises his own work in much the same way by stopping short his homage to "Eternity" (1726) (the ingenious gentleman's alleged masterpiece and object of Byles's praise) lamenting that "The Beauties which I strive to praise I wrong." Considering that one of the principal traits of a culturally independent nation is self-reference, this work must certainly qualify as an early expression of autonomy, even if the work being referenced is the poet's own.

Still, Byles exhausts forty-four lines in supplicatory praise of Alexander Pope, the "wondrous Bard," for whom "evr'y Clime project[s] a laurel Grove." But to admire and learn from a great poet, even though he or she might be a British one, must not be condemned as seeming derivation. Indeed, two additional observations temper Byles's statement that "Pope's are the Rules which you, my Friend, receive." The first observation requires one merely to read the two lines immediately following the stanza dedicated to Pope. In them Byles commands, "Go on, sweet Poet, charm our list'ning Ears / Infuse new Joy, and scatter all our cares." Even if Byles as mentor may instruct the next generation of writers to attend to the virtues of prior works, he does anything but advocate simple poetic parrotry. Second, Byles's own stated method of inspiration and composition reflects his desire for originality. Pride for being lauded by the young poet and envy for having been outdone clash, and cause Byles's "catching passions to strike a sudden flame." Comparing his method of writing to a sudden and unstoppable torrential downpour, a "vent" for his consuming passions, he clearly forges new ground. Byles, sometime before 1726, composed verse that is "the spontaneous overflow of powerful feelings" long before William Wordsworth would define it as such in the preface to the second edition of *Lyrical Ballads*, a document largely held as the primary work marking the paradigm shift from neoclassicism to Romanticism.

The two works discussed above, then, reveal an author whose method of composition and overall significance to American literary history may be generally misunderstood. Byles certainly admired the works of his British predecessors and contemporaries; he did not, however, simply copy their styles and subject matter. Rather, Mather Byles used his sources generatively in what seems to be an effort to contribute to as well as to foster a nascent independent American poetry.

Further Reading. *Selected Primary Sources:* Byles, Mather, "Bombastic and Grubstreet Style: A Satire" (*New England Weekly Journal* 5 [24 April 1727]); ———, *Poems on Several Occasions* (New York: Columbia University Press, 1940); ———, *Works: Compiled with an Introduction by Benjamin Franklin V.* (Delmar, FL: Scholars' Facsimiles and Reprints, 1978). *Selected Secondary Sources:* Eaton, Arthur Wentworth Hamilton, *The Famous Mather Byles: The Noted Tory Preacher, Poet and Wit 1707–1788* (Freeport, NY: Books for Libraries Press, 1971); Kyper, Peter Thomas, "The Significance of Mather Byles in the Literary Tradition of America: A Study of his Poems on Several Occasions and his Literary Criticism" (Ph.D. diss., Auburn University, 1974); Shields, John C., *The American Aeneas: Classical Origins of the American Self* (Knoxville: University of Tennessee Press, 2001).

Patrick Moseley

BYNNER, WITTER (1881–1968)

A poet, scholar, and translator, Witter Bynner's reputation was nonetheless made as a hoaxer. Apart from his role in the infamous "Spectra Hoax," he is now remembered most prominently as a translator of Chinese poetry, particularly the work of Lao Tzu, and as the founder of one of the preeminent foundations supporting contemporary American poetry.

Bynner was born August 10, 1881, in Brooklyn, New York, and educated at Harvard, where he was appointed to the staff of the Harvard *Advocate* by **Wallace Stevens**. This was the first of many associations with the major literary figures of his time, from Henry James to O. Henry, and including **Edna St. Vincent Millay**, to whom he once proposed marriage. Millay accepted, but later both thought better of it and the engagement was canceled. Upon his graduation from Harvard in 1902, he joined the staff of *McClure's* magazine, where he gave A.E. Housman his first American publication. After a four-year stint at *McClure's*, he left the working world to write full-time, though in 1910 as a consultant to the publishing house of Small, Maynard, and Co. he arranged for the publication of **Ezra Pound**'s first collection.

In 1916 he made his first trip to Asia, which was to have a lasting impact on his aesthetic. In 1922 he moved to Santa Fe, New Mexico, where in 1923 he played host to D.H. and Freida Lawrence on their first trip to New Mexico. He remained in Santa Fe for the rest of his life, along with his longtime companion, Robert Hunt. He devoted himself to his writing, the development of a literary circle, and the rights of minorities and women. He died in 1968 after a series of debilitating illnesses. A bequest in his will established the foundation that bears his name, which supports poets, translators, and poetry programs.

Bynner was a prolific poet, whose work underwent a series of transformations throughout a long and productive life. His early poetry was powerfully influenced by his Harvard experience. His first collection, published in 1907, was *An Ode to Harvard and Other Poems*, later reprinted in 1925 as *Young Harvard*. Yet its literary influences are elsewhere: In its evocation of youth and place, the early work has been compared to Housman, and in its democratic openness, to Whitman.

Although Bynner was instrumental in getting Pound his first publication, the **Imagists** and followers of similar movements—**Vorticism**, Futurism—grew irksome to Bynner. He and his friend Arthur Davison Ficke decided to parody them. They created a literary hoax—a movement called Spectrism, made up out of whole cloth. The Spectrist manifesto concocted by Bynner and Ficke made reference to breaking the image into fragments similar to the effect of a prism on the colors of the spectrum, and to the development of "spectres"—images that existed in shadowy relationship to real objects. In short, the manifesto was a justification for writing poetry that cohered virtually not at all. Bynner chose the pseudonym Emanuel Morgen, and Ficke was Anne Knish. Their book, *Spectra*, was published in 1916.

The hoax both made and undid Bynner's reputation. The Spectrists gained a notoriety of their own, and when the hoax was finally revealed, some critics who had been fooled declared that they liked Emanuel Morgen's work better than Bynner's. Perhaps more interesting, Bynner had created in Morgen a doppelganger of his poetic self who never entirely disappeared. His next book under his own name, *The Beloved Stranger* (1919), which represents some of his best work, has a looseness and allusiveness that owes much to the Asian poetry he had begun studying, but also to the spectral allusions of Emanuel Morgen. However, the modernists whom Bynner had lampooned rapidly became the central force in American poetry, and Bynner came to be considered a fringe figure. Nevertheless, he continued to write and produced a varied and always interesting body of work. *Pins for Wings* (1921) and *Guest Book* (1935) contain portraits, sometimes devastating, of his friends and contemporaries.

In 1929 Bynner published two books. *The Jade Mountain* is his free translation of Chinese poetry from the T'ang dynasty, and marks, in an important sense, his break with Emanuel Morgen. The *Spectra* hoax had given Bynner the freedom to explore the quirks of his imagination; the T'ang poetry brought him back to the unembellished simplicity of the lyric. In *Indian Earth*, often considered his best book, he used the techniques of Chinese poetry to describe the Native American cultures of Mexico and New Mexico. *The Way of Life According to Laotzu*, Bynner's translation of the *Tao Te Ching*, appeared in 1944. It became his most commercially successful book, and it is the only one still in print. His last poems, collected in *New Poems 1960*, were written in longhand when he was virtually blind. They are spare of words, and all were written in one draft. They show a mind and a poetic sensibility that had not yet finished engaging the world.

Futher Reading. *Selected Primary Sources:* Bynner, Witter, *The Beloved Stranger* (New York: Alfred A. Knopf, 1919); ———, *Indian Earth* (New York: Alfred A. Knopf, 1930); ———, *The Way of Life According to Laotzu* (New York: Perigee Books, 1995); Morgan, Emanuel (pseud. for Witter Bynner), and Anne Knish (pseud. for Arthur Davison Ficke), *Spectra* (New York: Mitchell Kennerley, 1916). *Selected Secondary Sources:* Smith, William Jay, *The Spectra Hoax* (Middletown, CT: Wesleyan University Press, 1961); Kraft, James, *Who Is Witter Bynner? A Biography* (Albuquerque: University of New Mexico Press, 1995).

Tad Richards

BYRD, WILLIAM, II (1674–1744)

William Byrd II is known primarily for his prose works about the colonial frontier. As a man who spent roughly half his life in London and half at his Westover plantation in Virginia, Byrd introduced urbanity and belles lettres to the tidewater colonies. At the time of his death, Byrd possessed one of the largest libraries in the North American colonies. Admittedly, Byrd's contribution to poetry is not at all significant. He published merely a few short, uninteresting poems praising ladies at the English spa Tunbridge in an annual miscellany dedicated to that subject in 1719, and he wrote a song for Colly Cibber's play *The Careless Husband* in 1704, all of which are collected by Maude Woodfin in *Another Secret Diary* (1941). As a gentleman, Byrd would not have been concerned with publishing, but rather with participating in an elite culture, and most of his known works are manuscripts written for the amusement and edification of friends. Although he wrote his panegyric and satiric poems while in London, not in America, the elements of such literary exercises are clearly present in his unique prose works about Virginia.

Born in Virginia in 1674, Byrd was the son of William Byrd I, one of the leading members of Virginia's House of Burgesses. When he was seven years old, his father sent him to England to get a good education. Eventually, in 1692, he began studying law at Middle Temple. There he met such literary figures as William Congreve and such champions of new scientific thought as Robert Boyle. He became a member of the Royal Society and eventually contributed to its proceedings an article about an African slave with white splotches on his skin.

In 1696 he came back to Virginia, but then returned to London after only one year to represent Virginia's interests to the Crown and the Board of Trade. While in London, Byrd pursued a position as secretary of Virginia as well as an English heiress, Lady Elizabeth Cromwell. He failed at both pursuits. This pattern of ambition and failure would plague Byrd for much of his life. His self-portrait written at this time, "Inamorato L'Oiseaux," is a candid examination of his strengths and weaknesses, whereas his song for *The Careless Husband* is a shallow attack on beautiful women who reject their suitors.

In 1704 his father died, and Byrd returned to Virginia to assume responsibility of the plantation and the political position of auditor and receiver general. In Virginia, he married Lucy Parke and raised two daughters. Conflict between himself and the governor, as well as personal debts, prompted Byrd to return to London in 1715 to resolve his difficulties. After his wife died in 1716, Byrd spent the next ten years primarily in London, pursuing heiresses and political appointments. It was at this time that he wrote the poems about fashionable ladies at the Tunbridge spa. Finally, in 1724, still in debt, he married Maria Taylor, and returned to Virginia. Soon after, he was asked to join the expedition for which he is most famous—the surveying of the dividing line between Virginia and North Carolina. From his journal of the expedition, he wrote two narratives. His satirical *Secret History of the Line* employs the genre of character sketch that he had practiced while in England to reveal the political squabbles between the different surveyors. His larger *History of the Dividing Line betwixt Virginia and North Carolina* synthesizes such character sketches with natural history to paint a broader, depersonalized portrait of Virginian and Carolinian character. His prose works were never published, but circulated among his friends both in Virginia and England. For the remainder of his life, Byrd developed his plantations and participated in Virginia politics.

Byrd's poetry and prose use rhetorical flourishes, especially antithesis, to draw satiric or panegyric portraits of his acquaintances. In several letters to "Minonet" he wrote that satire is easier than panegyric, because human nature easily reveals another's faults in contrast to any ideal. To bestow beauty, the painter of such portraits needs a beautiful mind himself, so that praising another is a social performance that reflects back upon the painter. Perhaps not surprisingly, then, in his Tunbridge spa poems, he devotes most of his lines to the impossibility of capturing the lady's true beauty. For example, in his poem "On the Lady Charlotte Scott" he admits that "Nature frowns to see me dare aspire, And poorly spoil what she has left entire." At other times, however, he is more specific, such as when he praises Lady Percival for her good sense and encourages her to participate in conversation. In these poems as in all his writing, Byrd is performing the role of an English gentleman, a role he tried hard to cultivate throughout his life. For many modern readers, Byrd seems to be a male chauvinist, and critics have either excused Byrd as a product of his times or criticized Byrd as an exemplar of eighteenth-century patriarchy. To do so, however, in some ways misses Byrd's fondness for paradox and for writing as a reflective process. For example, his satire on women "The Female Creed," which lampoons women for their superstition and inconstancy, is also a critique of men, for the ultimate stupidity of women that concludes the "creed" is that they trust men and mistakenly believe men to be consistent. Although in many of his letters and prose works Byrd repeatedly fantasizes about himself as literally "one of the [biblical] patriarchs," he also sometimes undercuts this fantasy with self-mockery. The question before contemporary readers is whether Byrd's self-mockery subverts the logic of patriarchy or merely reinscribes patriarchy through a gentlemanly performance of praise and satire.

Further Reading. *Selected Primary Sources:* Woodfin, Maude H., ed., *Another Secret Diary of William Byrd of Westover, 1739–1741, with Letters and Literary Exercises, 1696–1726* (Richmond, VA: Dietz Press, 1941); Wright, Louis B., *The Prose Works of William Byrd of Westover* (Cambridge, MA: Harvard University Press, 1966). ***Selected Secondary Sources:*** Berland, Kevin, Jan Kirsten Gilliam, and Kenneth Lockridge, eds., *The Commonplace Book of William Byrd II of Westover* (Chapel Hill: University of North Carolina Press, 2001); Marambaud, Pierre, *William Byrd of Westover, 1674–1744* (Charlottesville: University Press of Virginia, 1971).

Steven Thomas

C

CAGE, JOHN (1912–1992)

Probably the most influential composer in the history of American music, John Cage worked in graphics, theater, dance, and other art forms as well. Much of his poetry appears in five collections of his writings: *Silence* (1961), *A Year from Monday* (1967), *M: Writings '67–'72* (1973), *Empty Words: Writings '73–'78* (1979), and *X: Writings '79–'82* (1983). Two lengthy, late works were published separately: *Anarchy* (1988) and *I–VI* (1990). Many of his poems remain uncollected, scattered in record brochures, **small press** editions, and little magazines of his time.

Born in Los Angeles, Cage in his twenties studied composition with Henry Cowell and Arnold Schoenberg. In 1942 he and his wife, Xenia, settled in New York City. When they separated three years later, Cage became the lifelong professional and personal partner of the choreographer Merce Cunningham. Ever experimenting—and ever controversial—he composed hundreds of works for every imaginable instrument (including cactus plants), and performed and taught worldwide, from Tokyo to Caracas to Darmstadt. He died in New York on August 12, 1992, after suffering a stroke in the spacious loft he and Cunningham shared for forty years.

In devising his poems Cage often applied to language the techniques of his musical compositions. His "45' for a Speaker" (1954) uses the same rhythmic structure as his slightly earlier "34' 46.776 for Two Pianists," the structural units in both works being assigned the same time length in performance. In writing the dance chants for his effective "Series re Morris Graves" (1973), he arranged syllables from *The Gospel of Sri Ramakrishna* according to metrical patterns in his *Quartet for Percussion* (1935). In his self-reflexive "Lecture on Nothing" (1959) and similar works, he took over from his music what he called micromacrocosmic structure, with each unit of the poem (or composition) having the same number of measures that the entire poem has of units.

All of Cage's poems echo varieties of twentieth-century experimental writing—*poésie concrète* (**concrete poetry**), **Objectivism**, *hörspiel*, **Language poetry**—but also distinctively depart from them. Only a (needed) book-length study could make clear the evolution of his poetics. The poem's statement usually interested him less than its structure. As he put it, "What I am calling poetry is often called / content." He, on the other hand, referred to it as "form." That is, Cage often turned the Romantic doctrine of organic form inside out: Instead of form arising from content, content arises from form. Most of his poems are not so much written as invented, the outcome of ingeniously intricate methods of treating language. As he restated the matter, "we're / no longer making objects / but processes."

One of Cage's favorite types of process poem was the mesostic, a sort of pattern poetry he began writing around

1968. Mesostics resemble acrostics, except that the vertically spelled words appear in capital letters not at the beginning of the line but, as the term suggests, in the middle. Cage often wrote simple mesostics for friends, using for the spine JASPER JOHNS, say, or AARON COPLAND. A few are affecting, such as his mesostic **elegy** on the composer Ben Webster (1979), recalling their continued closeness despite their musical disagreements. Some are amusing, such as "Sports" (1989), twenty-one mesostics on fishing, the roller coaster, flirting, and other diversions, each spelling ERIK SATIE down the spine. A few he set to music, in effect turning them into songs, such as "Mirakus²" (in French), instructing the vocalist, "The lines of the music should be sung as lines of poetry."

Ever re-inventing himself and his work, Cage increasingly complicated his mesostics. He made some of them syntactical, others not, and distinguished among what he termed 25 percent, 50 percent, and 100 percent mesostics. He gave up the brief haiku-like form based on a proper name and began writing mesostics structured around vertically spelled sentences or lengthy statements. The first may have been "James Joyce, Marcel Duchamp, Erik Satie: An Alphabet" (1982), a mesostic playlet in which, among other delightful imaginings, the ghost of Satie argues with the ghost of Houdini. He created a variant, too, called the "Autoku" (presumably "automatic haiku"). Here the entire source text forms the spine, which also supplies the wing words, making for fugue-like repetition: "All that gets said in the lines is the same thing over and over again," he explained; "the poem . . . consumes itself" (MUSICAGE, 66).

Cage also began turning other writers' books into mesostic essay poems and lecture poems. Usually he did so with the help of computer programs made especially for him. Should he want to, he said, "I could every day, every hour or every minute make a new poem on the same subject . . . as though poetry was put on the stove and was cooking" (Kostelantetz, 160)

In his poems, as in most of his music after 1950, Cage used what he called "chance operations." To determine pitch, duration, and other sound events he sometimes consulted the random imperfections in a sheet of paper, or more often tossed coins according to the elaborate coin oracle method described in *I Ching*, the ancient Chinese Book of Changes; he eventually used made-to-order *I Ching*–based computer programs, particularly MESOLIST and IC. Much influenced by Zen ideas of egolessness, he regarded such devices as means of freeing himself from subjectivity and habitual ways of thinking. He applied chance operations similarly in his process poems to determine what material to draw from a source text for subject matter; whether to select words, phrases, sentences, or all three; how many sections, lines, and characters per line to create; and the tempo, volume, and other aspects of reading the poem aloud.

Cage viewed chance operations as the means to a further end as well. He assayed in his music to let sounds "be themselves" rather than serve the purposes of harmony, counterpoint, or melody. Similarly, he wished to let words and phrases "be themselves," freed from grammar, syntax, and signification. "I hope to let words exist," he told an interviewer, "as I have tried to let sounds exist" (*For the Birds*, 151). By following *I Ching* methods, he said, he could create "a language that can be / enjoyed without being understood"—an expressive medium between poetry and music (*M*, 215).

This intermedium can be clearly seen and heard in "Mureau" (1970) and the closely related **"Empty Words"** (1974–1975). For the content of "Mureau" Cage used the entries about music, sounds, and silence in the journals of **Henry David Thoreau**. Subjecting them to chance operations produced a mix of separate or run-together syllables, words, and phrases, an asyntactical process prose poem. He shredded Thoreau's language still more finely in the four-part "Empty Words," setting the *I Ching*–generated verbal fragments on the page in differing typefaces and sizes, with zigzagging marginations and drawings by Thoreau. The language becomes increasingly less referential, ending as what Cage called "language saying nothing at all" (*Empty Words*, 51). Thoreau's text is gradually pulverized into clusters of letters ("r e et ii om l h artess oung s rktttth") and blank spaces representing silences—a metamorphosis, as Cage put it, "from language to music" (*Empty Words*, 76, 65).

Except for the experimental typography, much of "Mureau" and "Empty Words" looks and sounds like *Finnegans Wake*. In fact, Cage's year-long labor on "Empty Words" led him to seriously investigate *Wake*, which became his favorite literary work. He made five "writings-through'" of the book (ca. 1978–c. 1982), turning its "verbivocovisual" words and phrases into repeated mesostics spelling JAMES JOYCE. His final writing-through, entitled *Muoyce* (music + Joyce), almost completely transforms language into sound ("m ranns r y have dP midst uration oye"). It also splashes Joyce's commas, exclamation points, periods, and other punctuation around the page—seemingly at random but actually in *I Ching*–dictated patterns. Cage contrived similar writings-through for **Ezra Pound**'s *Cantos* (1981) and **Allen Ginsberg**'s *Howl* (1986), and planned one for the King James Bible, using an electronic concordance.

Cage came to view such disjunctive process works as having a valuable social dimension. Approving his friend Norman O. Brown's remark that syntax is the arrangement of the army, he lent himself to what he called "the *demilitarization* of language: a serious musical concern" (*Empty Words*, 184. By changing language he might help to change hierarchical ways of thinking. Something of the course of his political and social ideas can be traced in his *Diary: How to Improve the World (You Will Only Make Matters Worse)*.

Cage began *Diary* in 1965 to celebrate the technological utopianism of another friend, Buckminster Fuller. Planning to produce ten installments, he completed eight by 1982, plus a lengthy micromacrocosmic interlude that uses as mesostic spines the Latin names of mushroom species. (Cage was a passionate mycologist.) Chance operations prescribed for him how many diary entries to write each day, how many words per entry, and which of twelve different typefaces to use in printing it. For later sections of *Diary* he greatly expanded the range of typography, using a Letraset kit to fashion full-page *poésie concrète–*looking mesostic ideograms. "[W]e / give each letter undivided attention," he explained, "setting it in unique face and size; / *to read* becomes the verb *to sing.*"

This shape-shifting polyvocal visual prose poem is at the same time a genuine diary. The mosaic of remarks takes in his day-to-day thinking about music and the other arts; personal anecdotes (losing his billfold, driving a Jaguar); and observations on Watergate, solar energy, communist China, and other public affairs that reflect his deepening interest in Fulleresque "world improvement."

Social philosophy dominates several of Cage's late works, such as *Anarchy* (1988). Here he reworked thirty quotations bearing on the idea that government is not merely unnecessary, but harmful and immoral. MESOLIST and IC transformed the quotes into eighty printed pages of mesostics, the first spine being PETER KROPOTKIN. Cage's "Overpopulation and Art" (1991)—mesostics on deschooling society and abolishing nation-states—was reprinted in Germany in connection with a "squat," the takeover by demonstrators of an empty house.

The most ambitious process work of Cage's last years is *I-VI*, shorthand for a mostly asyntactical 420-page epical lecture poem whose full title is *Method Structure Intention Discipline Notation Indeterminacy Interpenetration Imitation Devotion Circumstances Variable Structure Nonunderstanding Contingency Inconsistency Performance* (1990). Cage regarded the fifteen categories as aspects of his artistic development, some of them treated earlier in *Composition in Retrospect* (1981, 1988). The headings serve as spines for a *Cantos*-like collage of mesostic narrative and rumination—"as though I am in a forest," he said, "hunting for ideas" (*I-VI*, 2).

Cage hunted even more hermetically than usual. Chance operations determined that seven mesostics on the same heading would appear—six making sense, the seventh not—and decided which pages of which books of Ludwig Wittgenstein would be quoted, and which dates of which newspapers. Considering *I-VI* "a kind of poetry"—specifically in "the way of the breathing and . . . changing or not changing of sounds"—Cage also conceived a notation for directing the pronunciation of the lectures when read aloud (*I-VI*, 403–4).

Cage himself often gave public readings of his process poems. They were not always well received. At a notorious performance of *Empty Words* in Milan in 1977, his mostly young audience responded with a ceaseless, jeering concatenation of rhythmic handclapping, firing of cap pistols, and cries of "Go Home!" During his delivery at Harvard of the first part of *I-VI*, more than a third of the audience reportedly walked out.

Yet Cage's writings as well as his music have generated lasting interest and admiration internationally. The poet **Clark Coolidge** remembered the publication of *Silence* as "a tremendous turn-on. . . . *Everyone* was influenced by Cage. Everyone read *Silence*" (Doherty, 5). Artists in various media—Frank Gehry, Ellsworth Kelly, Merce Cunningham—have acknowledged being inspired by Cage's aesthetic. So have such poets as **John Ashbery**, **Ted Berrigan**, and the experimentalist **Jackson Mac Low**; members of **Fluxus** and of the Brazilian Noigandres group; and New York's Lower East Side poets of the 1950s and 1960s. Poems of homage to Cage have been written by, among others, Octavio Paz.

Commercial recordings and videos exist of Cage reading/singing some of his longer process poems, including an eight-CD performance of *Diary*. Cage being Cage, he "musicated" the printed version, translating its typographical changes into changes of volume and stereophonic position of the voice, passing on to the sound engineer nearly 2,000 instructions. Hearing this or Cage's other varicolored readings of his poems affords a sense of the latent musicality and verbal beauty of their chance-determined language.

Further Reading. *Selected Primary Sources:* Cage, John, *Empty Words: Writings '73–'78* (Middletown, CT: Wesleyan University Press, 1979); *For the Birds: John Cage in Conversation with Daniel Charles* (Boston: Marion Boyers, 1981); ———, *I-VI* (Cambridge, MA: Harvard University Press, 1990); ———, *M: Writings '67–'72* (Middletown, CT: Wesleyan University Press, 1973); ———, MUSICAGE. Ed. Joan Retallack (Middletown: Wesleyan UP, 1996); ———, *Silence* (Middletown, CT: Wesleyan University Press, 1961). ***Selected Secondary Sources:*** Bernstein, David W., and Christopher Hatch, eds., *Writings Through John Cage's Music, Poetry, + Art* (Chicago: University of Chicago Press, 2001); Doherty, Tyler, "A Conversation with Clark Coolidge" (*Jacket* 22 [May 2003]); http://jacketmagazine.com/22/doher-cooli.html; Gena, Peter, and Jonathan Brent, eds., *A John Cage Reader* (New York: C.F. Peters, 1982); "John Cage" (*Revue d'Esthétique* 13–15 [1987–1988]]); Kostelanetz, Richard, ed., *Writings about John Cage* (Ann Arbor: University of Michigan Press, 1993); Nicholls, David, ed., *The Cambridge Companion to John Cage* (Cambridge, UK: Cambridge University Press, 2002); Perloff, Marjorie, and Charles Junkerman, eds., *John Cage: Composed in America* (Chicago: University of Chicago Press, 1994).

Kenneth Silverman

CAMPO, RAFAEL (1964–)

Rafael Campo positions his work at the nexus of two equally ancient human practices: poetry and healing. He has published four volumes of poetry, including the Lambda Award–winning *What the Body Told* and two volumes of prose. He also received the National Hispanic Academy of the Arts and Sciences Annual Achievement Award and was a PEN Center West Literary Award finalist. Indeed, when one considers Campo's work, one immediately thinks of American poet/physician **William Carlos Williams** and the poet/healer **Walt Whitman**. Campo's work explores the complicated intersections between nation, culture, race, sexuality, and gender. He tests the limits of language as a tool of healing and healing as a foundation of poetry.

Rafael Campo was born in Dover, New Jersey, in 1964 to parents who migrated there as Cuban exiles. Campo left New Jersey for the Ivy League (first Amherst, and then Harvard Medical School) and chose a dual vocation of medical doctor and poet. Thus, almost as if by design and not just by some strange coincidence, Campo intersects the company of two other New Jersey poets: William Carlos Williams, the doctor-poet, and Allen Ginsberg, the activist-poet. Campo continues to channel these two voices in his poems and in his work as a physician. In the medical field, Campo continues to work to bring humane practices back into an institutional machinery that he believes treats patients increasingly as obstacles to profit rather than as human beings in need. At Harvard Medical School (where he has taught) he worked to promote a shift in the bio-cultural model that medical schools use to train their students. Currently, he is a doctor at Beth Israel Deaconess Medical Center in Boston, where he treats mainly gay/bisexual/lesbian/transgendered persons, Latinos, and persons with HIV/AIDS. In his poems, Campo challenges readers to experience the intimacy, sensuality, empathy, and frankly sexual nature of ourselves in sickness and in health. As to the question of how Campo manages to connect these seemingly disparate worlds, he sees them as inextricably connected under the banner of *healing*, to the extent that he often uses one name for both his vocations: "healer."

Despite his admiration for Williams, Campo does not work within the grain of Williams's **modernism**. Instead, he has remained one of the most accomplished technicians of traditional poetic forms, especially with his masterful use of the sonnet, while invigorating these forms with new content. This is not to suggest that Campo's work merely champions a **New Formalism**. Rather, Campo treads the line between traditional forms and their inevitable breaking points. His work compresses the powerful ecstasies of bodily and spiritual revolt until they cause the forms he uses to nearly (and sometimes fully) crumble. Witness, for instance, the singsong, ballad-like end rhymes of "The Abdominal Exam" (*Diva*). In this poem, the lines "Before the glimmer of his sunken eyes / What question could I answer with my lies?" give way to a break in the rhyme when the doctor/speaker finds the "lump." Immediately, the end rhyme changes as the speaker's hand goes "limp." In this moment, life and death are linked by the speaker's inability to make "limp" rhyme with "lump," and thus the poem refuses to resolve the fact of this "lump" through purely formal means; language must attend to the realities of the world and the hard facts of illness. Yet the poem must still find a way to "heal" even if it cannot remake the world in its own image of ideal harmony and ideal rhyming.

When working in less formally rigid modes, Campo's language remains true to its subjects by allowing the form to reveal the tensions and complexities of a situation without merely imposing form onto those situations. Take for instance "Route 17," where the speaker's deep homosexual longing for an older man he works with at a diner reveals itself at the same moment a car wreck occurs on the highway outside the diner (*What the Body Told*, 4). Here the juxtaposition of these events moves the poem toward revelation: The older man, Al, contracts HIV and AIDS and dies from a similar contingent collision of two bodies in space. These incidents do not rhyme in the sense of end rhymes, but the poem's form opens up to allow the contents to, in a sense, "rhyme" themselves in a powerful poetic argument. The argument is formal enough in itself: Campo's poem knows that bodies and psyches, our bodies and psyches, are led inexorably along paths of pleasure and pain.

Campo's poems focus not only on the ecstasies of the other but also on the ecstasies of the self. The self that is revealed through Campo's lyric is, like the formal structures he employs, varied and complex. The egos that emerge are by turns frightened and frightening, vulnerable and powerful, passive and aggressive. In some of the finest of Campo's poems, the speaker reveals his or her desire beyond the ego's knowledge of itself. "Revulsion" serves as a particularly striking example of how the desire that moves through the speaker's language exceeds the knowledge of the speaker. In "Revulsion" the narrator tells the story of a man in drag who "fooled" an ostensibly straight man into loving her, and the man ended up beating her to death. As the poem progresses, the speaker's confusion about how to describe the gender of the love object (the "MALE PROSTITUTE / FOUND DEAD") is mirrored in the confused desire that the speaker projects. It is palpably clear at the end of the poem that the speaker is unaware of his own desire toward the love object even as the inklings of elegy undercut the speaker's sexism and homophobia. Thus, the speaker is rendered aggressive *and* vulnerable—aggressive to the point of violence, but vulnerable in that this violence also does him violence.

When Campo waxes more autobiographical, the ego that emerges is a complex interplay of racial, cultural, national, and gender identities. Moreover, Campo's work that directly addresses sexual identities has produced some of the finest gay love poems in contemporary literature. One such poem is "Before Safe Sex," where poetry, medicine, AIDS, and homosexual love intersect in a complex web of emotion and sensation (*What the Body Told*).

Often, Campo's poems, autobiographical and otherwise, follow a constellated logic wherein the speaker will believe that "writing poetry is just as queer [as drag]" and "illness is a form of drag: / [t]he body dresses in the gossamer / [o]f death" and that "[e]ach has everything to do with dreams" (*What the Body Told*). Consequently, the poems always seek to narrate the power of these complexities *as complexities*, whether addressing the political injustices and powerful emotions that surround HIV/AIDS and other illness, the complexities of multicultural identity, or the ultimately fluid character of actual gender and sexual identities as opposed to cut-and-dried cultural norms. Campo's language maintains a fidelity to boundless compassion and thus powerfully renders desires, bodies, and psyches in their most exuberant, tender, and ragged moments.

Further Reading. *Selected Primary Sources:* Campo, Rafael, *The Desire to Heal: A Doctor's Education in Empathy, Identity, and Poetry* (New York: Norton, 1997); ———, *Diva* (Durham, NC: Duke University Press, 1999); ———, *The Healing Art: A Doctor's Black Bag of Poetry* (New York: Norton, 2003); ———, *Landscape with Human Figure* (Durham, NC: Duke University Press, 2002); ——— *The Other Man Was Me: A Voyage to the New World* (Houston: Arte Publico Press, 1993); ———, *What the Body Told* (Durham, NC: Duke University Press, 1996). ***Selected Secondary Sources:*** Lima, Lázaro, "Haunting the Corpus Delicti: Rafael Campo's *What the Body Told* and Wallace Steven's *(Modernist) Body*" (*Wallace Stevens Journal* 25.2 [Fall 2001]: 220–232); Rendell, Joanne, "A Very Troublesome Doctor: Biomedical Binaries, Worldmaking, and the Poetry of Rafael Campo" (*GLQ: A Journal of Lesbian and Gay Studies* 9.1–2 [2003]: 205–231).

Mikel Parent

CANADIAN POETRY

George Bowering's 1974 poetry chapbook *At War with the U.S.*, written in a prosody he developed in part from his readings of U.S. **Black Mountain** and **Beat** generation poets, and displaying on its cover a Greg Curnoe drawing of a Canadian fighter jet shooting down a U.S. P-51 Mustang, embodies some of the ambiguities one finds in the relationship between Canadian and U.S. poetries, as well as between Canadian and U.S. cultures. Always latent in Canadian culture are the facts that Canada's roots began in dissent from the United States, and

that Canada has been repeatedly reaffirmed by U.S. citizens themselves as the alternative North American nation, especially during such times as the First and Second World Wars (when they went north early in those wars to enlist in the Canadian armed forces), during the McCarthy period, during the Vietnam War, and during the current "war on terrorism." Canada's first wave of English-speaking immigrants were United Empire Loyalist refugees from the American Revolutionary War. Canada's formation as a nation in 1867 was in part a response to the large U.S. armies created by the Civil War. Just as Canadian governments have been restricted by this complex cultural history in the extent to which they have been able to affiliate themselves with U.S. policies, Canadian poets have necessarily been both unconsciously and consciously selective in their associations with U.S. poetries and **poetics**. In general, Canadian poets have avoided association with hegemonic U.S. poetries or poetries that have celebrated the U.S. nation. Canadian poets, such as Daryl Hine, David Wevill and **David Bromige**, who have expatriated themselves and their writing to the United States, have often been effectively erased from the Canadian literary institution. Most Canadian links to U.S. poetries have been to ones that have themselves dissented from the economic, political, and nation-state ideologies that have been dominant in that country. Thus Canadian poets have linked themselves overtly to **Emerson**, but not to **Holmes** and rarely to **Whitman**, whose celebration of U.S. Manifest Destiny has been particularly noted and whose expansive prosody appears to have often been read in Canada as enacting U.S. expansionism. They have linked themselves to **Pound**, **Williams**, and **Hughes**, but not often to **Frost** or **Ransom**; to **Olson**, **Ginsberg**, **Bukowski**, **Levertov**, **Plath**, and **Rich**, but not to **Lowell**, **Wilbur**, **Snodgrass**, or **Kennedy**; to the **language poets** but rarely to the **New Formalists**.

Throughout the nineteenth and early twentieth centuries, Anglophone-Canadian poets' closest relationships were with British poetry, and Francophone-Canadian poets with **French poetry**. Much as one frequent theme of the Anglophone poetry was the establishment of an even more prosperous and just version of Britain on Canadian soil, its formal aims were to write at least as well as British poets while naturalizing the latter's diction to the Canadian context. Both these elements are evident in Oliver Goldsmith, Junior's *The Rising Village* (1825)—written in emulation of his great uncle's *The Deserted Village*—as well as in Thomas Cary's *Abram's Plains* (1789), Standish O'Grady's *The Emigrant* (1841), and Charles Sangster's *The St. Lawrence and the Saguenay* (1856), in which the poetic models range from Burns to the landscape poems of Wordsworth. It is also present in Isabella Valancy Crawford's **long poem** "Malcolm's Katie" (1884), in which the prosody and narrative structure seem derived from Tennyson but in which the personifications of Amerindian mythology suggest considerable awareness of **Longfellow**.

The first significant contact between Canadian and U.S. poetry came with the Confederation poets of 1880–1920 (Charles G.D. Roberts, Archibald Lampman, Bliss Carman, and Duncan Campbell Scott)—a group so named because they were all born in the decade preceding the 1867 confederation of Britain's Canadian colonies. Generally regarded as late-Romantic poets who created the most discursively Canadian poetry written to that time, they chose poetic models that were largely British, and that ranged from the Romantics to the pre-Raphaelites. Roberts and Carman, however, were cousins and both related to Emerson through his grandfather, Daniel Bliss, after whom Carman was named. Their familiarity with Emerson's work, and through him with that of **Channing** and **Thoreau**, brought Emerson's ideas into circulation in the Canadian intellectual community of the 1880s and 1890s. The most strongly influenced by Emersonian Transcendentalism was Lampman, especially in some of his best-known poems, such as "Heat," "The Clearer Self," and "Among the Timothy." On April 22, 1893, Lampman wrote in the now famous "At the Mermaid Inn" literary column of the Toronto newspaper *The Globe* that more Canadians ought to read Emerson's poems because within them "is the freedom, the vitality, the fertility, the inexhaustible permutation, the godlike optimism of nature herself."

From the earliest times, book publication in England had been the preference of Anglophone-Canadian poets, both for copyright reasons and because of the widely held belief—one that persisted until the 1960s—that only recognition abroad could certify a Canadian poet's achievement. Roberts and Carman were the first Canadian poets to publish most of their books initially with U.S. publishers; Scott and Lampman published major collections in Boston. Their publishing choices reflected an ongoing shift in the Canadian book market toward a North American orientation. The lack of international copyright agreements throughout most of the nineteenth century tended to push most Anglophone-Canadian writers toward either Britain or the United States. Only first publication in one of these markets could give their work copyright protection within that market; first publication in Canada left their work open to piracy in both markets. Canada's 1887 accession to the Berne Copyright Convention (which the United States did not sign until 1989) gave Canadian authors reciprocal copyright protection in most European and British Empire countries; however, protection ·in the United States was not achieved until the two countries signed a bilateral agreement in 1924.

Carman lived in New England most of his life, writing with New York poet Richard Hovey the enormously popular *Songs of Vagabondia*, published in Boston, which went through numerous editions between 1894 and 1935. Like most of Carman's work, *Vagabondia* favored the faux medievalism of the British fin de siècle ballad stanza, but in the popular theme of its title offered a genteel version of Whitman's open road (an influence also evident in his controversial and subsequently uncollected "Marjory Darrow," published in New York in the *Independent*, September 1, 1892). Roberts, who lived in New York from 1897 to 1907, and Carman both had close friendships with Hovey, and may have shared his interest in French and Belgian *symbolisme* (see Bentley 1999). In 1927 Carman edited the *Oxford Book of American Verse*, producing a collection that essentially reified the nineteenth-century canon of **Longfellow**, **Bryant**, **Holmes**, and **Whittier**, while slightly elevating **Whitman** and **Dickinson** and largely ignoring the emerging **modernist** poetries of **Eliot**, Pound, **Stevens**, **Moore**, **Williams**, **Crane**, and **cummings**.

Modernism in Anglophone Canadian poetry, which emerged relatively late—notably in the mid-1920s poetry of A.J.M. Smith and F.R. Scott, and with a left-of-center politics that continued through the 1930s—brought Canadian poets only moderately more into contact with their U.S. colleagues. The roots of modernism for Smith and Scott were European and pan-national. As Brian Trehearne has demonstrated in his *Aestheticism and the Canadian Modernists*, Canadian modernism drew on late nineteenth-century aestheticism, the Decadents, 1920s dandyism, as well as the poetries of Rimbaud, Baudelaire, Laforgue, Verlaine, Eliot, Hulme, and Pound. The American poets the Canadians of the 1920s knew best were those who had gone to Europe—Eliot, Pound, and **Stein**—although they were also peripherally aware of poets such as Moore and Williams because they read much of the new poetry in U.S. journals such as the *Dial* and *Poetry* (Chicago). Smith wrote an MA thesis on Yeats and the Symbolist poets at Montreal's McGill University (1926), and a doctoral thesis on John Donne at Edinburgh (Ph.D. 1931) under H.J.C. Grierson, editor of the highly influential 1912 edition on Donne. He had most likely been attracted to Donne by his readings of Eliot in 1924–1926. Unable to find a permanent teaching position on his return to Canada, he took up a position at Michigan State University in East Lansing, which he held until retirement. Although he became both a naturalized American and for three decades the major historical editor of Canadian poetry (largely through his 1943 University of Chicago Press anthology *The Book of Canadian Poetry*), and became in the early 1960s poet-in-residence at Michigan State, his formal links to U.S. poetry were relatively slight. These included his co-editing with M.L. Rosenthal the college anthology *Exploring Poetry* (1955, 2nd ed. 1973). The U.S. influences on his complex and witty poems seem to have been mostly through the poems of Eliot's Prufrock and Sweeney periods. In his extensive critical essays on Canadian poetry, however, his clear preference for a "pure" poetry suggests influence as well by the poets of the **New Criticism**.

This Canadian modernist perception of U.S. poetry as a relatively small part of international poetry continued throughout the 1920s and 1930s. In his essays Smith frequently offers cosmopolitan lists of poets—"Eliot, Pound, the later Yeats, and **Auden**, . . . Baudelaire, Rimbaud, and Rainer Maria Rilke" (*Towards*, 185). The two leading Canadian leftist poets of the 1930s, the Stalinist Dorothy Livesay and the Trotskyist **Earle Birney**, tended to be more concerned with ideology than poetics; Birney once remarked that his reading of U.S. literature was mainly the fiction of Steinbeck, Farrell, and Dos Passos, and that his reading of contemporary poetry was mostly confined to Auden, Spender, and Day Lewis: "I did not read an equivalent amount of Americans at that time and this was bad for me in developing contemporaneity, because Auden, Spender, and Lewis were not really contemporary in the way that Pound was or many people" (quoted in Davey 1971, 19). Livesay has written that she learned her early **Imagist** style in the late 1920s from the work of Pound, **H.D.**, Aldington, and **Amy Lowell** that appeared in *Poetry* (Chicago) (90); discovered Auden, Spender, and Day Lewis in a Greenwich Village bookstore in 1935; and wrote her major Marxist poem of that decade, "Day and Night," later that year in Newark under the influence of black spirituals and Cole Porter's "Night and Day" (131).

This Canadian perception of U.S. poetry began to change rather quickly in the 1940s. The first development was the deployment by Montreal-based poet and editor John Sutherland of U.S. poetry against British poetry in an argument that the modernist poetry of A.J.M. Smith's generation had been colonial because of its British influences. In an attack on Smith's 1943 anthology, *The Book of Canadian Verse*, he declared that Canada was a North American nation, and that to date "Canadian poetry struggles to follow the American example even while its dominant bias remains British." Calling Smith's term "cosmopolitan" a code word for "colonial," he forecast that

the American example will become more and more attractive to Canadian writers; that we are approaching a period when we will have "schools" and "movements" whose origin will be American. And perhaps it is safe to say that such a period is the inevitable halfway house from which Canadian poetry will pass towards an identity of its own. (18)

It is now apparent that Sutherland's criticisms of Smith were more tactically than intellectually founded—that they were part of a growing turf war in Canadian poetry both between generations and among younger writers. In particular, Sutherland wished to advance the work of three young leftist poets, Irving Layton, Raymond Souster, and Louis Dudek, whose poems he had been featuring in his little magazine *First Statement*, and who had not been included in Smith's anthology. However, Sutherland's general perception that the influence of British poetry in Canada was waning, and that of American poetry growing, was prescient. Birney's biographer, Elspeth Cameron, in describing the cultural landscape that faced him shortly after his return from World War II service in Holland, writes, "It was clear by the 1950s that American poets had superseded their British counterparts. John Crowe Ransom, William Carlos Williams, Wallace Stevens, e.e. cummings: these were the names to know" (415).

The first fruitful direct relationship between Canadian and U.S. poetry began in 1949, when Louis Dudek, who had now temporarily left Montreal to complete a doctorate at Columbia, wrote to Ezra Pound at St. Elizabeths. Although Dudek visited Pound only once, his letter began a long correspondence (published by Dudek in 1974 as *D/k: Some Letters of Ezra Pound*) and spurred Dudek to write over the next two decades several important long poems, one of which (*Europe*, 1954) A.J.M. Smith dismissed as mere "Pound cake" (Dudek 1991, 17). Dudek's interest in Pound and in Pound's ideas about U.S. commercialism led him not only to defend Pound in two radio presentations broadcast nationally by the Canadian Broadcasting Corporation (1955 and 1956) but also to found the little magazines *CIV/n* (titled after a Pound quotation) and *Delta*, and found or co-found three **small presses**, the enormously influential Contact Press, and the smaller Delta Canada and DC Books—each inspired by the Poundian idea that in an age of such commercial corruption writers needed to control the means of literary production and dissemination. Dudek's relationship with Pound led him into contacts with Williams, **Paul Blackburn**, **Harold Norse**, and **Charles Olson**, and to bring copies of **Cid Corman**'s magazine *Origin* to the attention of poets in Montreal and Toronto (Davey 1980, 10). Dudek's eventual Toronto partner in Contact Press, Raymond Souster, was so influenced by Dudek's gift to him in 1951 of *The Collected Later Poems of William Carlos Williams* that in 1966 he wrote that because of that gift his "world of poetry [had] assumed its present shape" (quoted in Davey 1980, 11).

Souster, who had founded and edited two limited-circulation magazines (*Direction*, 1943–1946, and *Enterprise*, 1948), founded a similar magazine, *Contact*, in late 1951 and, supplied with U.S. names and addresses by Dudek, was soon publishing work by **Judson Crews**, Blackburn, and Corman, and being introduced by Corman to French, German, Italian, and other U.S. poets. In the following three years *Contact* would publish work by Gottfried Benn, Blackburn, **William Bronk**, Jean Cocteau, **Robert Creeley**, René de Obaldia, **Larry Eigner**, **Theodore Enslin**, Vincent Ferrini, Denise Levertov, Hugh MacDiarmid, Samuel French Morse, Charles Olson, **Kenneth Patchen**, Octavio Paz, Jacques Prévert, George Seferis, Chad Walsh, and Williams. Souster and Corman would begin a long and still unpublished correspondence (including 109 letters from Souster to Corman).

Also conducting a correspondence with Creeley, who was then in Mallorca, Souster sent Creeley copies of two recent Irving Layton books; he was so engaged by them that he wrote to Layton at once, in February 1953, to invite him to submit a manuscript to his Divers Press. The book that resulted from Creeley's editing and subtle counseling of Layton, *In the Midst of My Fever*, received in Canada the most favorable reviews that Layton had yet received. Ekbert Faas and Sabrina Reed, who edited the 1953–1978 correspondence of Layton and Creeley, note that this, "the first of Layton's collections of verse not financed by the poet himself" (xiii), was the one that for Northrop Frye "settled 'the question of whether Mr. Layton is a real poet or not'" (iv). The collection led to Layton's publication in Corman's *Origin* and to three further collections of his poems being published by **Jonathan Williams**'s Jargon Press—the last of which, *Red Carpet for the Sun*, was co-published by Canada's largest commercial press, McClelland & Stewart, and won for Layton the prestigious Canadian Governor-General's Award for Poetry. He was also invited by Olson and Creeley in 1957 to teach at Black Mountain College, an invitation he had to decline, because his late 1930s leftist writings had caused him to be barred from entry by the U.S. Immigration Service. *Red Carpet for the Sun* was Layton's last U.S. book publication. Over the next twenty years he would publish a poetry collection almost every other year with McClelland & Stewart and be one of Canada's most popular poets. Creeley's recognition of him had been important, but Layton perceived Canada to be the base from which he would now try to build an international reputation.

Dudek, Souster, and Layton co-founded Contact Press in 1952, naming it, like Souster's recently founded magazine *Contact*, after Williams's and Robert McAlmon's 1920s magazine, *Contact*. Over its sixteen years Contact Press published mostly poetry written in the colloquial language and speech measures pioneered by Williams and argued for as potentially "Canadian" by John Sutherland, and—in Dudek's view—opposed the archetypal post-Eliot poetry being written in the 1950s by Canadian poets influenced by Northrop Frye. Founded on U.S. modernist models, Contact became the most important Canadian poetry publisher of its period, but

distributed its limited-edition books almost exclusively within Canada. Souster, however, continued to think internationally, and in the 1950s founded in Toronto the Contact reading series, bringing U.S. poets such as Corman and Olson to their first Canadian audiences.

Layton's focusing of his publications on a Canadian audience after his Jargon Press successes signaled a significant shift that distinguished Canadian poetry of the 1960s and 1970s from that which preceded it. While most earlier Anglophone poets had hoped for publication and critical recognition in Britain or the United States, and Francophone-Canadian poets had hoped (with much more success) for publication and recognition in France, most of the poets who began writing after Layton perceived international reputations to be produced more by imperial politics than aesthetics, and preferred recognition within Canada. While Earle Birney had lamented that his visits to New York made him realize that he was "an average 2nd-rate poet" (quoted in Cameron, 503) and had been demoralized by having book manuscripts rejected by Wesleyan University Press (Cameron, 425) and by **Lawrence Ferlinghetti**'s City Lights (Cameron, 425), most of the 1960s and 1970s generation saw U.S. publication as irrelevant and published there only if invited. Many of the poets published by Contact Press—Eli Mandel, D.G. Jones, **Al Purdy**, Milton Acorn, John Newlove, and Gwendolyn MacEwen—became major figures in Canadian poetry while being virtually unknown in the United States.

The next significant interaction between Canadian and U.S. poetries again involved the poets of the Black Mountain group. Following a reading by **Robert Duncan** in Vancouver, British Columbia, in the spring of 1961, young poets there paid his travel expenses to return and deliver a week of lectures on modernist poetry; they founded the monthly poetry newsletter *Tish* almost immediately after. In the decades that followed, several of the *Tish* editors—George Bowering, Frank Davey, Daphne Marlatt, **Fred Wah**—have become nationally important writers. Other consequences of Duncan's visit include the hiring of Robert Creeley to teach poetry and creative writing at Vancouver's University of British Columbia for 1962–1963; a three-week summer poetry seminar in 1963 at which Olson, Duncan, Creeley, Ginsberg, and Denise Levertov conducted workshops and gave numerous public readings and lectures, and in which U.S. poets **Philip Whalen**, Carol Bergé, **Michael Palmer**, and **Clark Coolidge**, as well as Canadians Bowering, Marlatt, Wah, Bromige, and Lionel Kearns also participated (Cameron, 440–441; Bergé, 1); **Jackson Mac Low**'s visit and performance of fall 1963; and **Jack Spicer**'s "Vancouver lectures" of 1965.

Bowering's winning of the Governor-General's Award for Poetry in 1970 sparked a very public anti-American backlash in which these American visits to Vancouver were characterized as "invasions" and Bowering as a writer who was propagating an "American brand of liberal anarchist individualism" (Mathews 1978, 306). The backlash, which was covered by the Canadian national media, was led both by Irving Layton, who helped raise money to have a substitute "People's Prize" awarded to an arguably more "Canadian" poet, and by critic Robin Mathews, whose long series of attacks on the *Tish* writers culminated in his book *Treason of the Intellectuals* (1995). Interestingly, although the *Tish* poets' interest in the work of these U.S. writers (much like Dudek's interest in Pound and Souster's in Williams) was largely founded on their critiques of U.S. nationalism and their dissenting positions vis-à-vis established U.S. poetries, Mathews's persistent arguments have created the impression in Canada that the Black Mountain poets have been the hegemonous U.S. poets of the last half-century, and have made them until recently the only U.S. poets widely known in Canada. Noteworthy also is how "U.S. poetry" has been for Canadian poets since Sutherland's time as much a term through which to gain political leverage as it has been the name of a body of texts to be read.

Emerging in Toronto within five years of *Tish* was another internationally conceived Canadian poetry movement—one focused on visual poetry, linguistics, and sound poetry, and on re-exploring the potential of the poetics of the **Dadaists** and of Gertrude Stein. Of the young writers of this movement—David Aylward, **bp Nichol**, **Steve McCaffery**, Paul Dutton, and Hart Broudy—only Nichol and McCaffery went on to have substantial careers. Nichol published prolifically in the late 1960s and 1970s small presses of Canada, the UK, and the United States, establishing links with the Noigandres **concrete poets** of Brazil, with Bob Cobbing and Ian Hamilton Finlay in the UK, and d.a. levy, **Dick Higgins**, Emmett Williams, Ron Caplan, Clark Coolidge, and Karl Young in the United States. As contributing editors of the Canadian poetics and theory journal *Open Letter*, itself a successor to *Tish*, Nichol and McCaffery also established close links to **Charles Bernstein**, **Bruce Andrews**, and **Ron Silliman** of the U.S. Language poets, in 1973 publishing some of that group's early manifestos as "The Politics of the Referent" section of that journal, and in 1982 arranging the publication of the first widely circulated and professionally printed issue of the U.S. group's own journal, *L=A=N=G=U=A=G=E*, as a special issue of the better-funded *Open Letter*. Following early collaborations with Nichol, McCaffery produced a large body of "non-referential" poetry throughout the 1970s and 1980s and wrote two books of poetic theory, both published in the United States by presses friendly to Language poetics. These books discuss the poetics of a number of U.S.

poets, most frequently Olson, Mac Low, **John Cage**, and Ron Silliman. Although McCaffery's work is relatively unknown in Canada, despite most of his poetry collections having been published there, it has become one of the touchstones of Marjorie Perloff's recent books on U.S. avant-garde poetics.

Extremely important as well to Canadian poetry's relationship to U.S. poetry in the 1970s and 1980s was McCaffery's main Canadian publisher, Toronto's Coach House Press, edited for most of its early years by Victor Coleman, who had close ties to New York poetry and whose own poetry was indebted to that of **Frank O'Hara**, **John Ashbery**, and Jack Spicer. During Coleman's editorship the press published books by **Ron Padgett**, Allen Ginsberg, and Robert Creeley; the latter two manuscripts were essentially gifts from the poets in support of the press. It also published a pirated edition of Spicer's *After Lorca*. Spicer's importance in Canada rested on his three high-profile "Vancouver lectures" of 1965 and on the later presence in Vancouver of San Francisco poets **Robin Blaser** (Spicer's literary executor) and Stan Persky, who emigrated to Canada shortly after and became major contributors to the poetry and general culture of Vancouver— Blaser as a teacher and Persky as a Marxian cultural critic and founder of the New Star publishing house. Among the Canadian poets influenced by them, the most nationally important have been Erin Mouré and cultural critic Brian Fawcett.

Other connections between Canadian and U.S. poetry in this period were less significant in that they tended to confirm rather than alter or enlarge the writers' poetics and had little impact on other writing. Al Purdy, celebrated by some Canadian nationalist critics as the major Canadian poet of the 1970s, had a close relationship with Charles Bukowski, the U.S. poet he perceived as most similar to himself; they published in 1983 *The Bukowski-Purdy Letters: A Decade of Dialogue 1964–1974*. Daryl Hine, believing his own traditional poetic to be unfashionable in Canada, moved to the United States in 1967, and was editor of *Poetry* (Chicago) from 1968–1978. Interacting with the work of the gay formalists **Richard Howard** and **James Merrill**, he became one of the leaders in the emergence and recognition in the United States of homosexual poetry, but remains very little read in Canada.

French-language poetry in Canada showed little if any awareness of American poetry until the 1960s "Quiet Revolution" period in Quebec of rapid secularization of what had been a culture largely dominated by the Roman Catholic Church. But while Québécois novelists such as Victor-Lévy Beaulieu (*Jack Kerouac: essai-poulet*, 1972; *Monsieur Melville*, 1978) and Jacques Poulin (*Jimmy*, 1969; *Volkswagen Blues*, 1984) became intrigued by U.S. culture, there has been no equivalent interest among the poets. In 2005 one could still read thousands of pages of interviews with Canadian Francophone poets and essays on their works without encountering a single reference to U.S. poetry. The major exception is poet, editor, publisher and politician Gérald Godin, who in the 1960s became fascinated with Pound, reading him, however, not in the context of U.S. poetry but as the successor to Apollinaire and contemporary of Blaise Cendrars. He admired Pound for his "mixing of the humdrum with the sacred, the 'joual' of American soldiers with the culture of China or Venice," he has said. "I placed myself, 'poetry-wise,' . . . under his revolutionary umbrella" (quoted in Gervais, 75). It was mostly Pound's *Cantos* that Godin drew from, publishing *Poèmes et Cantos* in 1962 and *Les Cantouques* in 1967. The Beat poets—celebrated in Poulin's *Volkswagen Blues*—seem to have had some indirect presence in Quebec in the foregrounded orality of the mid-1960s sociopolitical poems of Michèle Lalonde. The Beats also influenced the planned hallucinogenic poetry performances of Claude Péloquin, who visited Ginsberg at Big Sur during the late 1960s.

With literary theorists and philosophers largely replacing poets in the last decades of the twentieth century as sources of poetic theory, recent links between Canadian and U.S. poetry have often been mediated through shared influence by theorists. The writing of Canadian **feminist poets** such as **Nicole Brossard** and France Théoret in Quebec and Erin Mouré and Daphne Marlatt in Anglophone Canada have reflected an influence by French feminist theorists Hélène Cixous, Luce Irigaray, Julia Kristeva, and Monique Wittig that is also evident in the work of some U.S. feminist poets. Similarly, racial minority poetry flourished in Canada in the 1980s and 1990s without much awareness of U.S. racial minority poetries but with considerable awareness of theorists such as Gayatri Spivak, Trinh Minh-ha, bell hooks, Henry Louis Gates, and Rey Chow. To some extent these mediations, and the Canadian poets' apparent lack of interest in the content of U.S. poetries culturally parallel to their own, reflect the very different situations and histories of Canadian writers and Canadian minorities from those of their American counterparts—for instance, that most African Canadians are of Caribbean or United Empire Loyalist origin, and that manyAnglophone-Canadian poets can read and speak French. One of the leading contemporary African Canadian poets, George Elliott Clarke, has argued, after giving up a position at Duke University to return to Canada, that "African America is its own pseudo-nation, and . . . like the American mainstream, solely self-absorbed. To be 'Black' and Canadian in that setting was to suffer the erasure of *Canadian* as a legitimate expression of black identity" (5). Although there have been some high-profile links between Canadian and U.S. poets such as between **Margaret Atwood** and **Carolyn Forché**, more meaningful ones have been evident in the frequent

citation by recent Canadian women poets of the work of **Audre Lorde**, **Adrienne Rich**, Gloria Anzaldùa, **Lyn Hejinian**, and Kathy Acker. There has been an especially close relationship in recent years between Rich and the Trinidad-born Canadian poet Dionne Brand. They have toured together to give readings, and in 1996 Brand, who is also a filmmaker, made the widely circulated film *Listening for Something: Adrienne Rich and Dionne Brand in Conversation*.

For the past decade the closest continuing relationship between the two poetries has been between the poets of the Canadian Kootenay School of Writers (also known as KSW) and the Language poets. The KSW writers emerged in British Columbia in the 1980s as descendants of the *Tish* group, strongly inflected—as was the language group—by poststructuralist language theory. First known through the writing of Jeff Derksen, Lisa Robertson, Catriona Strang, Deanna Ferguson, and Dorothy Trujillo Lusk, KSW now loosely includes a number of poststructuralism-influenced writers from across the country, among them **Christian Bök**, Peter Jaeger, Nicole Markotic, Louis Cabri, and Darren Wershler-Henry as well as the expatriate Canadians Dan Farrell and Kevin Davies. Their work is published in magazines and on websites associated with the two groups in both countries. The U.S. poets who are most closely linked to KSW and whose work has appeared in KSW-related publications in Canada and been available on its website include Bruce Andrews, Charles Bernstein, **Michael Davidson**, Barbara Einzig, **Carla Harryman**, Lyn Hejinian, **Susan Howe**, Michael Palmer, **Bob Perelman**, Ron Silliman, and **Barrett Watten**. Like the Black Mountain poets, these have become in Canada the most widely known U.S. poets of their generation.

For the KSW writers, however, it should be noted that their U.S. connections are a part of a thematic and strategic engagement with globalization related to their activities in Europe, an engagement not necessarily shared by their often more nationally oriented U.S. counterparts. Different perspectives on the national and the global are also evident in the case of **Anne Carson**, a Canadian who for most of her short career has resided in Canada but published almost exclusively in the U.S., and who has frequently been anthologized as an American poet, but whose direct aesthetic connections are with neither recent Canadian nor American poetry but with classical literature and European high modernism.

Further Reading. Bentley, D.M.R., *The Confederation Group of Canadian Poets, 1880–1897* (Toronto: University of Toronto Press, 2004); ———, "'The Thing Is Found to Be Symbolic': Symbolist Elements in the Early Short Stories of Gilbert Parker, Charles G.D. Roberts, and Duncan Campbell Scott," in *Dominant Impressions: Essays on the Canadian Short Story*, ed. Gerald Lynch and Angela

Robbeson (Ottawa: University of Ottawa Press, 1999, 27–51); Bergé, Carol, *The Vancouver Report* (New York: Fuck You Press, 1964); Bowering, George, *At War with the U.S.* (Vancouver: Talonbooks, 1974); Butling, Pauline, and Susan Rudy, *Writing in Our Time: Canada's Radical Poetries in English (1957–2003)* (Waterloo, ON: Wilfrid Laurier University Press, 2005); Cameron, Elspeth, *Earle Birney: A Life* (Toronto: Viking, 1994); Clarke, George Elliott, *Odysseys Home: Mapping African-Canadian Literature* (Toronto: University of Toronto Press, 2002); Davey, Frank, *Earle Birney* (Toronto: Copp Clark, 1971); ———, *Louis Dudek and Raymond Souster* (Vancouver: Douglas & McIntyre, 1980); Dudek, Louis, *D/k: Some Letters of Ezra Pound* (Montreal: DC Books, 1974); ———, *Europe*, rev. ed. (Erin, ON: Porcupine's Quill, 1991); Gervais, André, "Gérald Godin's *Cantouques*" (*Ellipse* 45 [1991]: 73–83); Golding, Alan, *From Outlaw to Classic: Canons in American Poetry* (Madison: University of Wisconsin Press, 1995); Layton, Irving, and Robert Creeley, *The Complete Correspondence, 1953–1978*, ed. Ekbert Faas and Sabrina Reed (Montreal: McGill-Queen's University Press, 1990); Livesay, Dorothy, *Journey with My Selves: A Memoir 1909–1963* (Vancouver: Douglas & McIntyre, 1991); Mathews, Robin, *Canadian Literature: Surrender or Revolution*, ed. Gail Dexter (Toronto: Steel Rail Educational Publishers, 1978); ———, *Treason of the Intellectuals: English Canada in the Post-Modern Period* (Prescott, ON: Voyageur, 1995); ———, "The Wacousta Factor," in *Figures in a Ground: Canadian Essays on Modern Literature Collected in Honor of Sheila Watson*, ed. Diane Bessai and David Jackel (Saskatoon, SK: Western Producer Prairie Books, 1978, 295–316); Perloff, Marjorie, *Poetry on & off the Page* (Evanston, IL: Northwestern University Press, 1998); ———, *Radical Artifice: Writing Poetry in the Age of Media* (Chicago: University of Chicago Press, 1991); ———, *21st-Century Modernism: The "New" Poetics* (Oxford: Blackwell, 2002); Smith, A.J.M., ed., *The Book of Canadian Poetry* (Chicago: University of Chicago Press, 1943); ———, *Towards a View of Canadian Letters: Selected Critical Essays 1928–1971* (Vancouver: University of British Columbia Press, 1973); Spicer, Jack, *The House That Jack Built: The Collected Lectures of Jack Spicer*, ed. Peter Gizzi (Hanover, NH: University Press of New England, 1998); Sutherland, John, "Introduction" in *Other Canadians: An Anthology of the New Poetry in Canada 1940–46* (Montreal: First Statement Press, 1947); Treharne, Brian, *Aestheticism and the Canadian Modernists: Aspects of a Poetic Influence* (Montreal: McGill-Queen's University Press, 1989).

Frank Davey

CANON FORMATION

One of the most contentiously debated terms in recent critical discourse, "the canon" in its literary sense represents the set of written works considered to be worth reading and interpreting. Alternatively, given that the original Greek word *kanon* meant "measuring rod," a canon also implies the rules or standards by which individual works are judged worthy of inclusion (or exclusion). Both definitions automatically imply that there are multiple canons: General worthiness as well as specific standards of worth are by nature inconstant. Indeed, although there do seem to be a significant number of canonical authors (Homer, Virgil, Dante, Shakespeare, etc.) whose works have remained continually relevant or important, there has been wide historical variation on which particular texts (and corresponding standards of judgment) are considered canonical. Dating from John Guillory's coinage in a 1983 article in *Critical Inquiry*, and elaborated in his influential 1993 book *Cultural Capital*, the process of how works and authors are canonized is now called *canon formation*. The dynamics of canon formation may be the most consequential issue in contemporary literary studies: All canons imply some kind of value, and in the **postmodern** era "value" has become a notoriously slippery and ill-defined category (Smith).

Although Guillory situates the prime force of canon formation in "the school," this institutional locus is one of at least four to be posited in the long conceptual history of "the canon" and its formation. The canon formation of poetry in the United States has embodied all four versions of the concept, which date from the classical era. None of the four conceptual phases has been definitively superseded; rather than forming an evolutionary sequence, all four of these diverse conceptions of what a canon is, and consequently how it is formed, are very much still with us:

1. *Canon as numbered list, formed arbitrarily.* The first canons were scriptural ones, the sacred works that were listed as acceptable; those outside this sacred circle are non-canonical or "apocryphal." In English, the earliest uses of "canonicity" and related word forms stem from Reformation debates over what texts and doctrines should be included in the biblical canon. The numbering of these sacred texts also assumed symbolic significance, as in the Hebrew Pentateuch (the "five scrolls"). The Septuagint, the canonical Greek translation of the Hebrew Bible, is said to have gotten its name when seventy translators independently arrived at identical wordings. In the classical era, there were numbered lists of canonical secular authors, such as "The Ten Attic Orators" and "The Nine Lyric Poets" (who was included in these lists could fluctuate). The scholars associated with the library of Alexandria, where Homer's poetry was critically edited for the first time, also assembled *pinakes* or "indices" of so-called included works. Quintilian's list of critically acceptable authors and works in *Institutio Oratoria* (first century A.D.) is organized by genre (from

most to least prestigious). In the Middle Ages, the lists were called *auctores* and included Christian and pagan authors appropriate for teaching.

In all of these cases, canon formation is arbitrary and thus variable, but the resulting canons assume a sacred or pseudo-sacred status nonetheless, since they purport to derive "from above." At the Council of Trent (1646), for instance, the Catholic Church listed a canon of the Bible that included books apocryphal for Protestants—and condemned anyone who thought differently (or who relied on any text other than the Latin Vulgate translation). The power of not only listing but *numbering* to supply a sense of authoritativeness cannot be overstated, especially when lines, chapters, and verses are numbered, implying that such texts deserve detailed commentary. Today, numbered canons are still very much with us: Syllabi for literature courses still constitute them, not to mention the plethora of collections or rankings by number, such as the Modern Library's marketing tool "The 100 Best Novels in English of the Twentieth Century" and William Harmon's *The Top 500 Poems* (1992). In American literature the numbered canon is already represented by eighteenth-century literary schoolbooks, which were essentially catalogues of satisfactory authors with short extracts.

2. *Canon as a masterpiece or a body of masterworks, formed by an authoritative voice.* The earliest use of "canon" in an artistic sense dates from the classical Greek sculptor Polyclitus (fifth century B.C.), who used the term to refer to both one of his statues and an accompanying manual, together intended to embody the perfection of statuary form. The statue was quickly imitated (and parodied) because it was recognized by other sculptors as authoritative. To this day, the concept of the canon as a set of masterworks inheres whenever an author's name is used metonymically to mean "the works of." Likewise in this canon, the *major* author is preferred to the *minor*, with major status implying longer and more impressive creations, ones that thus deserve further study and "authoritative" critical editions. The contemporary theory of poetic influence of Harold Bloom has enshrined an oedipal version of the masterwork as an attack on the fatherly predecessor ("strong poetry"). Bloom's *The Western Canon: The Books and School of the Ages* (1994) is thus short on "strong poets" from the early Middle Ages, when authorship was attributed to God ahead of human writers. Bloom's mostly modern canon of the masterwork reflects how since the eighteenth century "the author" has been resuscitated as a fully legitimate legal and artistic category.

Early attempts at canonizing American poetry naturally focused on major American-born voices as points of origin, such as **Philip Freneau** and **William Cullen Bryant**; the belated discovery of the poetry of **Edward Taylor** was welcomed since now America had an even

earlier (albeit British-born) "major voice." In the eighteenth century American poets like Bryant, **Ralph Waldo Emerson**, and **John Greenleaf Whittier** lent their authorial reputations to popular anthologies of American poetry. In the twentieth century, **New Criticism**, though associated with the "fallacies" of biography and intention (*see* **Intentional Fallacy**), did significant work toward canonizing the Metaphysical poets and certain modernists such as **T.S. Eliot** (much of whose criticism was likewise devoted to "individual talents"). More recently, the popular anthologies of Norton and other publishers have canonized the major author as a figure around which literature courses can be built. While many contemporary critics have rightly objected to the over-representation of "dead white males" among the canonized, those seeking to "open" the canon have often operated by locating suitable major voices within underrepresented traditions, such as African American and women's writing. Another modern advance in this kind of canon formation is the recognition of living (and younger rather than older) authors as also authoritative. It is also possible to recover once-slighted voices, as in the cases of **Walt Whitman** and **Emily Dickinson**, whose reputations have soared to the point that they are frequently the only American poets included in contemporary anthologies of world literature.

3. *Canon as classic, formed by "the test of time."* When the Romans inherited the Greek classics, they also came into the Greek idea that civilization was something that defined itself against a primitive and barbaric past. But rather than turning to contemporaries or early Latin exemplars, Virgil structured his poetic career after a "golden" Greek literary history, specifically the Greek poets Theocritus, Hesiod, and Homer, moving backward in time and higher in ambition through this sequence. The "classic" implies something "traditional" in the root sense of being worth passing down to future generations. This canon concept is thus most transparent whenever "the ancient" is preferred to "the modern," or vice versa; "the classic," whether new or old, is above all a civilizing agent. Since Virgil is perhaps the greatest embodiment of a "universal" classic, he plays a central role in statements by Charles Augustin Sainte-Beuve and T.S. Eliot on "What Is a Classic?" (1850, 1944). In Eliot's "The Tradition and the Individual Talent" (1919—itself a "classic"), the "tradition" was the historical series of great works and authors whom the modern "individual talent" must learn from in order to become "impersonal," the truest mark of the classic for Eliot and a strong contrast to the concept of canon as masterpiece. In the canonizing of American poetry, the concept of the classic has been difficult without reference to European models, and thus even **modernists** like Eliot and **Ezra Pound** allude frequently to earlier world literatures. While it is not precluded by the con-

cept of the classic, innovation is understood in this canon as adding something (usually small) to a long and well-understood tradition. As American literature has aged, however, it has become easier to locate a body of American literary classics. Nevertheless, an abiding legacy of "the classic" is the still-prominent place of British and world literatures in America's English curricula.

4. *Canon as institution, formed by ideology.* Just as the classic and the masterpiece are parallel concepts, the institutional canon recalls the sacred list. The first academic institution that controlled a canon of poetry was the library at Alexandria, but today the influence of the academy in poetic canon formation is unprecedented, since many important poets themselves hold visiting or permanent positions in prominent universities. Although poets have often benefited from various forms of patronage in the past, the current situation is ironic, since many living poets built their initial reputations as part of the (or an) avant-garde that opposed earlier institutionalized poetic canons. But such is the process of "ideology," to disarm the avant-garde and draw it unconsciously and inevitably into the "mainstream." Alternatively, through tenuring and other protections, the institution may empower and disseminate significant anti-institutional viewpoints, since any art produced under a dominant ideology can just as well subvert as perpetuate that ideology. Insofar as this means that important innovations eventually can be accepted, the institution can also be compared to the community (Beach), the social web in which all artistic production and reception must necessarily take place, including extra-institutional communities such as little magazines (Golding). In view of the extreme durability of the academy and the club in American history, it may be that both the institution and the community are poetry's best hopes, since a much smaller percentage of today's general population read poetry than in the past.

Given its insidious and unconscious nature, however, ideology should not be underestimated, especially since its canons are so easily masked. The influential canons of certain critics, for instance, hide significant institutional bias under appeals to the power of individual poetic genius. Likewise, many readers only experience poetry in one of the ubiquitous college literary anthologies, where the institutional formation of this canon (through committees of academic editors) is obscured by direct appeals to the concepts of the classic or the masterpiece. Timothy Morris has found that, contrary to respecting poets as irreducibly unique artists, successive waves in modern American literary studies have remade even major poets to fit the reigning critical mold.

In a sense, all four canon concepts discussed here are institutional in nature and must be respected for their power to persist, to metamorphose, and to intersect at many different points.

Further Reading. ***Selected Primary Source:*** Eliot, T.S., "Tradition and the Individual Talent" and "What Is a Classic?" ed. Frank Kermode, *Selected Prose of T. S. Eliot* (New York: Harcourt, 1975). ***Selected Secondary Sources:*** Beach, Christopher, *Poetic Culture: Contemporary American Poetry between Community and Institution* (Evanston, IL: Northwestern University Press, 1999); Golding, Alan, *From Outlaw to Classic: Canons in American Poetry* (Madison: University of Wisconsin Press, 1995); Guillory, John, *Cultural Capital: The Problem of Literary Canon Formation* (Chicago: University of Chicago Press, 1993); Morris, Timothy, *Becoming Canonical in American Poetry* (Urbana: University of Illinois Press, 1995); Smith, Barbara Herrnstein, *Contingencies of Value: Alternative Perspectives for Critical Theory* (Cambridge, MA: Harvard University Press, 1988).

Christopher M. Kuipers

CARIBBEAN POETRY

Poetry from the Caribbean includes the French-, Spanish-, and English-speaking West Indies. Collecting all these linguistic parts together for one study is problematic, as the region has historically been broken up along language/colonial lines that posit Cuba, Puerto Rico, and the Dominican Republic as Latin America, Guadeloupe and Martinique as part of France, and Haiti as its own "troublesome" space, while the Anglophone countries and territories have traditionally been studied in isolation.

One issue is certain, though, and that is that Caribbean poetry, be it in French, Spanish, English, Pampiamento—which is not covered here due to space—or Creole, has developed from Romanticism in the nineteenth century through Aimé Cesaire's surrealism to **negritude**'s **modernism**, to **postmodernism** and on to transnational diasporic identities and issues. While a history of colonization and slavery has brought the region together, it has also sought to separate it, particularly on the basis of language and politics. Haiti became the model for all black countries to follow as the first Black Republic, but it soon also became the model not to follow, with all its socially conscious, left-leaning poets in the early days.

If Caribbean poetry has any commonalities, they lie in its beginnings. Small groups of **expatriate** writers produced works that looked at the islands and territories as exotic, often inferior colonial outposts. This group was later followed by Creole writers, usually white colonials born in the New World of European or mixed parentage and often educated in Europe, in the various colonial centers—Paris, London, Madrid—before returning to the region of their infancy as cosmopolitan adults. The poetry produced by them was often very European in approach, material, and form, only diverging in its subject matter, the West Indies. Some poets are even more difficult to define, like **James Grainger**, whose poem *The Sugar-Cane*, is a celebration of the cane in Latin, but must be considered in any study of the development of Caribbean poetry.

If another trait can be traced over the region, it is the existence of an oral tradition that has developed mostly within the African Caribbean descendants of former slaves, as a precursor to a literary or scribal tradition. Many of these works include slave songs, hymns, rhymes, and tales that either would have been written down later in order to retain them as part of the scribal culture, or lost over time.

Two of the major developments in Caribbean poetry occurred almost simultaneously in the 1930s–1940s with the emergence in Haiti of what is called *indigenisme* or the nativist movement, with poets and writers like Jaques Roumain and Jaques Stephen Alexis. The next great movement in the region, which actually began in Paris, is negritude, with writers and poets like Aimé Césaire, who led the way in the French Caribbean with his poem *Un retour au pays natal.* A great deal of the early Caribbean verse has a common theme, the celebration of the land and of the native peasantry, along with a cry to put an end to the exploitation of that peasantry through unfair laws and practices.

There has always been a resistance to popular expression in the region, be it by the colonial authorities pre-independence or local governments post-independence. This resistance was met head-on by poets and performers like Louise Bennett in Jamaica, who spoke out against the denigration of the local in favor of the foreign/colonial.

A tremendous body of literature, literary movements, and trends produced in exile later returned to the Caribbean as if they had begun there, such as negritude. Works by Jean Rhys, produced mostly in Paris, and by John Agard and Wilson Harris, mostly produced in Britain, raise arguments as to whether their authors can be called Caribbean writers. Those like St. John Perse have to be Caribbean writers, on the other hand, as their work deals with the region.

Certainly, a discussion of Caribbean or Jamaican poetry cannot be complete without talking about Marcus Garvey, who influenced people like **Claude McKay** and later on, Oxford Rhodes Scholar Mervyn Morris. But there are names like Walter Rodney, who is famous not only for his poetry but also for his political activism and untimely death. Other prominent names in Jamaican letters are Tom Redcam, Jamaica's first poet laureate; Edward Baugh; and **Lorna Goodison**. There are also those famous for their oral poetry, better called dub poets, like Michael Smith. Again, one visible link is the development of social and literary movements like Garveyism, which spread from New York, through the region, and throughout the United States, and had a profound impact on poets and writers like McKay, who is best known for being a part of the **Harlem Renaissance**. Obviously, then, such trends do not respect national or geographic boundaries. One theme in Caribbean poetry for many decades was that race went hand in hand with nationalism. Guyana and its poets like Martin Carter are just as important to the changing face of Caribbean poetry and politics as are those from Barbados like **Edward Kamau Brathwaite**.

The Hispanic Caribbean has been just as active with its poetry movements and poets as the other islands and territories. In Puerto Rico each decade has a group or movement, such as *el grupo de los sesenta* (the group of the sixties) or *el grupo de los cuarenta* (the group of the forties). However, one of the more important literary movements in the Hispanic Caribbean is *negrismo*, the literary expression of cultural nationalism. The celebration of blackness or the heightened awareness of the African element in Caribbean culture came out of the 1920s, which gave rise to *negrismo* and the body of poetry produced with this philosophy in mind. Of course, social events have a great deal to do with literary movements, and the 1898 Spanish-American War marked the rupture between the old colonial self and the new vision of self in the Spanish-speaking Caribbean. The literature that followed this event also marked a new awareness of the threat of American imperialism that would simply replace Spanish imperialism.

The Second World War and its aftermath influenced literary production through an anti-rationalist ethos that developed in its wake. One aspect born of this ethos is the celebration of the senses and a focus on primitive aspects of culture (primitivism), which in turn produced negrophilism. While European movements produced images of the Black Caribbean, local cultural development began to articulate an African Caribbean ethos that was less representative and more honest about its cultural self. One aspect of this was *negrista* poetry. Similar trends were afoot in Haiti with a European-educated mulatto middle class who, for the most part, still did not see themselves as black.

While the *negrista* movement may have been an improvement on negrophilism, it did not break sufficiently with the cultural stereotyping of the latter and may have even further imbricated some of the undesirable literary stereotypes of the Negro while simultaneously establishing new ones. Unfortunately, then, *negrista* poetry often hinted at discriminatory aspects of the writers toward the Negro. This exoticizing of the Negro produced two enduring images: the image of the black man as intellectually inferior, primitive, and simply instinctual; and the sexualized black woman, or *la mulata sabrosa* (the hot, sexy, mulatta). Sadly, these images managed to survive the eventual decline of *negrismo* in the 1930s. Among some of the leading figures in the early years of *negrismo* are names like Julia De

Burgos, Luis Pales Matos, Ramón Guirao, José Tallet, Emilio Ballagas, and Manuel del Cabral. There were also New Yorrican writers and poets creating in New York.

Indeed, these images began to change in the Spanish-speaking Caribbean in general, and in Cuba in particular. Cuba's ideological change is mostly a result of the 1959 revolution's socialist philosophy. Such is particularly the case for the alterations in the literary images of Caribbean/Cuban women. The shift in discourse to a more positive one for Caribbean women is evident in the work of most Cuban writers of the early post-revolutionary period, both pro- and anti-Castro. While the revolution has taken great strides to break down the racist divide that existed in pre-revolutionary Cuba, racism is still present in the mythical raceless/classless state.

Inherent in most Caribbean cultural movements of the early period is the focus on cultural mixing or miscegenation and the assimilation of the European model. Also implicit in literary and cultural trends was a developing sense of nationalism, which often overwhelmed almost all other concerns. Poetry is most certainly bound up in this cultural development of a sense of nation or national identity as an answer to European imperialism and cultural colonization. In the Spanish-speaking Caribbean this would have been evident with the *mulatez* that underscores *negrismo*. This *mulatez* is, however, deconstructed in the French Caribbean negritude movement, with its exalting of blackness and the African heritage of the Caribbean. Thus, negritude represents a rupture with old, colonial ways and their replacement with a new way of articulating the African self.

The Hispanic Caribbean's *negrista* writers' ideology of African European or cultural hybridity does not go far enough in valorizing the African ethos or reality of Caribbean culture. It is significant that negritude as proposed by Césaire departs from this model and establishes a cultural paradigm that will later develop into poet and cultural theorist Édouard Glissant's coining of *Antillanité* and *Créolité*. With the work of the Martinican, *Antillanité* develops out of the space that negritude makes with its break from European models, but *Antillanité* fills in the gaps negritude creates with its essentialized blackness, as the former includes all aspects of Antillean identity and culture. Following in Glissant's footsteps is the *Creolité* group of Jean Bernabé, Raphaël Confiant, and Patrick Chamoiseau. While declaring that there is still no Creole literature, however, these men argue for a re-essentializing of Creole literature into indigenous Caribbean writing that is written in Creole, the language of Guadeloupe, Martinique, Haiti, and, to a lesser degree, some of the Anglophone islands. This despite the fact that French remains the official language of the first three countries and English the official language of the others.

A real concern for Caribbean literature/culture/poetry, though, has been the presence of women as poets and active participants in discourse and literary formation, or the lack thereof, particularly in the early period. For the most part, Caribbean poetry had been a male-dominated field at least until after World War II. If women's active participation was rare, then the public's recognition of them was more limited. Even in the 1980s, critical works that detailed men's achievement in poetry paid scarce attention to women's roles. This has changed, however, and women's involvement in, creation of, and recognition of poetry has been reflected in the publication of poetry collections, anthologies like *Her True, True Name*, and critical studies that focus solely on women or divide their attention between women and men. Of course, this trend has varied from country to country. A collective like Jamaica's Sitren, with Honor Ford Smith, breaks new ground with oral testimonies of life in *machista* Jamaica and **performance poetry** highlighting women's—particularly black women's—suffering. Such female expression follows in the spirit of earlier women poets.

The 1930s saw an assertion of female voices from Puerto Rico and Jamaica with Carmen Colón Pellot and Una Marson, respectively, who in their work about being black women dealt with myths of beauty and problems of racial and gender alienation. Cólon Pellot does this in *Amber mulatto* (1938) and Marson in "Kinky Hair Blues" (1937). Although color has always been a problem in Caribbean poetry, as seen above, the ways that it is articulated are changing. The discourse of the absent black identity can be seen throughout the region and particularly in Puerto Rico, where the phrase (¿y tu abuela, adonde está?) implies that the grandmother is the hidden link to Africa.

While pride in blackness is a trope in Afro-Cuban and Afro-Puerto Rican poets from the 1930s and on, black pride becomes one of the recurring themes in spoken poetry of the Anglophone Caribbean, in this case Jamaica, with Bob Marley's poetic lyrics for his oral discourse on emancipation of the black man from slavery in Babylon. Marley, with others like Jimmy Cliff, pushed the oral tradition into a new forum with the reggae protest music of the 1960s and 1970s. Some may not consider this poetry, but the lyrics to many reggae standards are poetry put to music, or what would become known as dub poetry in another incarnation, with artists like Mutabaruka, Peter Tosh, and Michael Smith.

While the oral tradition spans decades, it also crosses genres with post-independence arguments about what is acceptable English and what is not, and the cry for pride in what is Jamaican. **Louise Bennett** can be seen as embodying a celebration of this oral culture with her use of dialect, or what would become known as *nation language*, a phrase coined by Edward Kamau Brathwaite.

The performance poetry that comes out of this custom or culture is a quintessentially Jamaican expression, with performers like Michael Smith in "Me Cyan Believe It" and Jean Binta Breeze in "Dubbed Out." There is ongoing controversy in the English-speaking West Indies as to what language, including English, is to be spoken and written and what is not. Bennett and Brathwaite use nation language to deconstruct the narrow view of language's acceptability, arguing for national pride in what the folk speak. **Derek Walcott**, on the other hand, fits mostly into the group employing standard English in their work, while he West Indianizes European canonical classics like *The Odyssey* into *Omeros*. Jamaica's Carolyn Cooper is well known for her promotion of nation language. Cooper works in the oral/scribal tradition in order to undermine the high/low cultural divide and debunk any myths of inferiority still calcified in society.

A similar trend of oral expression and scribal tradition blending to form oral performance poetry is seen in Trinidad with the popularizing of English in Calypso. Artists like the Mighty Sparrow, the Mighty Chalkdust, and Lord Kitchener are representative of this art form, co-opting popular parlance, and often satirizing current events that have an impact on Trinidad society. Sparrow's famous and timeless songs "The Yankees Back" and "Jean and Dina" are examples of this satirizing of the American presence in Trinidad and the local society's response to it. Arguably, these are all examples of the Caribbean taking European poetic forms—willed to them by colonial forefathers—and converting them into vehicles that express their reality on their own terms.

If the 1804 success of the Haitian revolution was one moment that inspired poetic production and affected the face of Caribbean poetry, the Cuban revolution was another such moment. It also meant that there would be yet another split in Cuba's poetic production between the literature produced within the confines of the Castro revolution and that produced in exile, often in the United States, particularly in cities like Miami and New York, where large pockets of exiles settled, and produced new centers.

Poets who remained in Cuba and became important voices within the revolution are those like Nicolás Guillén and Nancy Morejón. In order to understand Guillén culturally, however, one must read Fernando Ortiz's extremely poetic *Contropunteo cubano del tabaco y azúcar*. Guillén became famous for his celebration of Cuba's ethnically mixed population in his poetry; this broke from a history of downplaying Cuba's blackness and celebrating its European blood. Of course, his poetry also questioned the right of the whites to dominate the country. **José Martí** is another influential poet, creating a vision of an America united under its *mestisage*. Martí's success also signaled a split, though, as anti-Fidelistas came to see him as inseparable from the socialist revolution and thereby unacceptable.

Poets in the Dominican Republic have also been a major force in the Spanish-speaking Caribbean's literary landscape. Writers like Pedro Muir and Tomás Hernández Franco illustrate the extremity of the racial situation in that country and the construction of color as a nationalist discourse under the Trujillo government that has still not been addressed. If blackness was seen and represented as ugly and exotic in Cuba, Puerto Rico, and Jamaica, it became depraved and "Haitian" in the Dominican Republic.

A more recent migration of voices has occurred in Caribbean poetry, one that is slightly different from the one that occurred between the Anglophone Caribbean and Great Britain when writers like Harris, Naipaul, and Selvon studied in England on scholarships in the 1950s. This second wave of migration has been focused more in North America and Canada and has produced a large number of women poets like Dione Brand and **Lorna Goodison**, among others. Britain, however, still produces a large number of Caribbean voices, Grace Nichols, Fred D'Aguiar, David Dabydeen, and Amryl Johnson among them. Meanwhile, Olive Senior and Lorna Goodison are among those who travel between the two spaces, the metropolis and the Caribbean. And there are those like Cyril Dabydeen who have become poets laureate in their adopted lands.

Caribbean poetry has seen another, more recent invigoration in Miami. The Caribbean Writers Summer Institute at the University of Miami from the early 1990s to 1996 promoted many young voices, such as Edwidge Danticat, although not as a poet. Others produced at the institute are Marzo Silén (Puerto Rico); Myriam Chancy (Haiti, Canada, United States), who, although better known for her critical work and novels, also writes poetry; L. Manoo Rhaming (Trinidad, Bahamas); Marion Bethel (Bahamas); and Nicolette Bethel (Bahamas). These are only a few of the names that the institute has brought together, generating more recognition for Caribbean poetry.

The incredibly rich fabric of Caribbean poetic expression has become transcultural in the twenty-first century. With new and booming diasporic communities in metropolitan centers like London, Paris, New York, Amsterdam, Miami, and Toronto, the oral/scribal, dialect/formal, Spanish/English collisions or elisions of New Yorrican poets or Cuban American poets are now commonplace. When Gustavo Pérez Firmat offers of Miami, "English is broken here . . ." we get the hint of a past of rigid conformation to European norms being deconstructed and a new literary landscape being created by Caribbean poets from Fred D'Aguiar to Pedro Pietri. The form has become as diverse as the expression, from the lyrics of Gloria Estefan's *Mi Tierra* to the stanzas of Rosario Ferré's *Language Duel Poems / Duelo del Lenguaje poemas*. Caribbean poetry is transnational and transcultural.

Carleton, Will(iam McKendree) (1845–1912)   241

It embodies what Glissant would call *Antillanité* as poets and performers no longer feel the need for language exclusivity or the "localness/locatedness" that the *Creolité* group holds as two of the most important tenets for defining Antillean literature/poetry.

Further Reading. Burnett, Paula, *The Penguin Book of Caribbean Verse in English* (London: Penguin, 1986); Chamberlain, J. Edward, *Come Back to Me My Language: Poetry and the West Indies* (1993; reprint Kingston: Ian Randle, 2000); Cooper, Carolyn, *Noises in the Blood: Orality, Gender and the 'Vulgar' Body of Jamaican Popular Culture* (London: Macmillan Caribbean, 1993); Williams, Claudette M., *Charcoal and Cinnamon: The Politics of Color in Spanish Caribbean Literature* (Gainesville: University Press of Florida, 2000).

Ian A. Bethell Bennett

CARLETON, WILL(IAM MCKENDREE) (1845–1912)

Will Carleton was a popular poet whose best-known narrative poems, in *Farm Ballads* (1873), *Farm Legends* (1875), and *Farm Festivals* (1881), focus on rural and farm life, especially the difficulties of rural poverty. Carleton recited his poems primarily to rural audiences, who lauded his works because they bolstered their prejudices against the lure of urban lifestyles and celebrated rural life. However, he is also considered a social activist because of his focus on the plight of the victims of poverty and social neglect.

Carleton was born and raised on a farm near Hudson, Michigan. He graduated from Hillsdale College in 1869 and made his living first as a journalist and later as a newspaper writer, lecturer, and reciter of his poetry, gaining fame from the popularity of performances akin to those of his contemporary, **James Whitcomb Riley**. In 1882 he married Adora Goodell and moved to Brooklyn, where he wrote *City Ballads* (1885), *City Festivals* (1892), and *City Legends* (1889). These poems present the difficulties of urban life, especially for rural people moving to the city. In 1894 he founded *Every Where* magazine, which continued until shortly before his death on December 18, 1912.

Nostalgic, sentimental, didactic, moral, and relational are all apt descriptors of Carleton's poems that celebrate rural life, especially the lives of farmers. Carleton tended to create stories that his rural audience would recognize, whether it was the crazy neighbor who escapes the poorhouse ("Rob, the Pauper"), the birth of a child to a crowded household ("The Christmas Baby"), or three young men competing for the affection of one girl ("The Three Lovers"). Carleton was famed for his poetic recitations and wrote poems with a humorous twist, whether it was a misunderstood joke ("Gone with a Handsomer Man"), a child running away with the circus but returning in the end ("Paul's Run off with the Show"), or a young man about to be executed who is saved when his purported victim gallops up at the hanging ("Death-Doomed"). To appreciate Carleton one must recognize the ways he used **sentimentalism** to evoke social change, as well as his work as a social activist for the poor and for women.

Carleton's most popular poems stand as political statements about how women should be treated. "Over the Hill to the Poor-House" and its sequel "Over the Hill from the Poor-House," are both in *Farm Ballads* (1873), and they tell the story of a "smart an' chipper" seventy-year-old woman trying to survive after her husband's death. Tension with her town-raised daughter-in-law forces her to move. For diverse reasons, she is then shuttled from one child's home to another until the last one sends her to the poorhouse. The poem concludes with the grandmotherly narrator piously praying that none should suffer as she has. Carleton rescues her from these dire straits in "Over the Hill From the Poor-House." Its narrator is the "black sheep" son who has served jail time and gone west. When he hears that his mother is in the poorhouse, he heads back east, buys her old house, fixes it up, and moves in with her. It concludes with an exhortation to do Christian good, like this prodigal son.

"Betsy and I Are Out" is the first poem in *Farm Ballads* and it opens with the surprising proclamation from the narrator that his marriage has ended: "Draw up the papers, lawyer, and make 'em good an stout; / For things at home are crossways, and Betsy and I are out." The narrator catalogues the build-up of marital tensions leading to the divorce and instructs the lawyer to divide their property equitably. The poem concludes with the speaker noting that he wants to be buried next to Betsy, where he hopes that in death they will find agreement. "How Betsy and I Made Up" relates that while driving home from the lawyers, the narrator concludes that he is to blame for many of their marital problems. After reading the divorce agreement, Betsy claims that he has given her too much and kisses him, "the first time in over twenty years!" The narrator responds by burning the agreement, and the pair talk all night. Thereafter, their relationship is stronger because they are more willing to give and less willing to fight.

Carleton's third book, *Farm Legends* (1875), uses popular stories that have become local legends, but no one can validate their veracity. "The School-master's Guests" is an excellent example. It is the story of a school board's surprise visit to a school because of rumors that students add "g's" to their "doin's", spell "musick" without a "k," drop the "u" out of "labour," and conjugate the verb "love" for grammar lessons. The visit is cut short when the stovepipe, which has been loosened by a student, falls down and spreads soot everywhere. In *Farm Festivals* (1881) Carleton experiments by using a diversity of first-person narrators in a single poem. To accomplish this, he sets his poem in public places where several people would naturally speak, including a pioneer meeting, a country store, a town meeting, and a school concert. This device allows Carleton to tell a story from multiple perspectives that modify one another and create a more complex understanding. Although he clearly labels shifts between speakers, the style does not change significantly, meaning that the performer of the work would have been the major creator of the persona, not the poet. This is a device that he uses in many of his later works.

Because he intended his poems to be performed for a popular audience, his narrative ballads are written with a heavily accented, rhymed style that precludes any possibility of their being remembered for their aesthetic qualities; rather, Carleton's works are those of an activist, one determined to alter contemporary attitudes toward the poor, the rural, and women.

Further Reading. *Selected Primary Sources:* Carleton, Will, *City Ballads* (New York: Harper and Brothers, 1886); ———, *City Festivals* (New York: Harper and Brothers 1892); ———, *City Legends* (New York: Harper and Brothers, 1889); ———, *Farm Ballads* (1873); ———, *Farm Legends* (1875); ———, *Farm Festivals* (1881); ———, *Poems* (1871). ***Selected Secondary Sources:*** Corning, Amos Elwood, *Will Carleton: A Biographical Study* (New York: Lanmere Pub. Co., 1917); Fallon, Jerome A., *The Will Carleton Poorhouse: A Memorial to a Man, a Dwelling, and a Poem* (Hillsdale, MI: Millsdale County Historical Society, 1989); "Will Carleton, Michigan's Poet" (*Michigan Historical Collections* 39 [1915]: 30–42).

Doug Werden

CARROLL, JIM (1950–)

By the 1978 publication of *The Basketball Diaries,* Jim Carroll had already established himself as a major figure in the New York poetry scene of the late 1960s and early 1970s. *The Basketball Diaries,* written from the diaries he kept when he was thirteen, tells the story of his becoming a highly touted basketball prospect in New York City and his subsequent addiction to drugs. By the time he was a teenager, Carroll had already marched alongside **Allen Ginsberg** in protest of the Vietnam War, kept company with **New York School** poets **Frank O'Hara** and **Ted Berrigan**, and become a member of Andy Warhol's Factory scene. At twenty-two years old, Carroll became the youngest poet in history to be nominated for the Pulitzer Prize. Such a prodigious beginning caused **Jack Kerouac** to say in an oft-quoted phrase, "At 13 years of age, Jim Carroll writes better prose than 89 percent of the novelists working today." Since the 1970s, Carroll has been a well-respected poet, writer, musician, actor, and spoken-word performer.

Carroll was born in New York City in 1950, the child of a working-class family. He was raised on the Lower East Side of Manhattan, but his basketball and academic talents landed him a scholarship to elite Trinity High School in uptown Manhattan, where he graduated in 1968. After reading Kerouac's *On the Road* (1957), Carroll began keeping a journal and writing poetry. At school, he also began experimenting with drugs. Carroll proceeded to live the life of a junky, becoming a thief and a hustler, and at age sixteen he spent three months in Riker's Adolescent Detention Center on a drug charge. For the next ten years Carroll struggled with heroin addiction, which, according to him, often sparked his creativity and fueled his poetry writing. Indeed, drugs and the New York urban culture were to become major thematic preoccupations of his poetry.

At age fifteen Carroll became involved in the St. Mark's-in-the-Bowery Poetry Project, where he attended workshops and met such notable New York poets as O'Hara, Berrigan, and **Anne Waldman**. Between the ages of sixteen and twenty he published two small books of poetry: *Organic Trains* (1967) and *Four Ups and One Down* (1970). His poetry and fiction also began appearing in such major publications as *Poetry* and the *Paris Review*, and he won the Random House Young Writer's Award for an excerpt in the *Paris Review* of what would later become *The Basketball Diaries*. But *Living at the Movies* (1973) was his breakthrough book, solidifying his reputation as a child prodigy; he was nominated for the Pulitzer Prize in poetry later that year. In this volume, his verse is pervaded by images of urban spaces, drugs, sexuality, and spiritual redemption. Perhaps the favorite subject of his work is New York City, "the greatest hero a writer needs," according to his diary of the time. Carroll's love for the city speaks through such poems as "Fragment: Little N.Y. Ode," "Leaving N.Y.C.," "Love Poem," "Birthday Poem," and "Highway Report." These poems usually describe New York as a space of unlimited possibilities, often reveling in the city's urban decay and nightlife. For instance, in "Fragment: Little N.Y. Ode" he speaks gleefully of sleeping on tar roofs and "screaming [his] songs," proclaiming once and for all that "this city is on my side."

Carroll's early poems are often loosely autobiographical, describing his life in New York, his friends and acquaintances, and, most frequently, his addiction to drugs. Documenting the underbelly of New York urban drug culture, some of his poems describe drug use with a tone of unapologetic experimentation (e.g., "Tonight we play with needles" from "In the Valley") whereas other poems describe drug use with a sense of remorse and stark desolation. "Withdrawal Letter," for example, employs a tone of emptiness and obsession, possibly alluding to a drug addict's withdrawal symptoms: "I think / all day about the likeness of heroin." These early poems also demonstrate the strong sense of poetic zeitgeist in Carroll's work, evoking the New York City poetry scene that was such a field of creative energy. His poem "New York 1970" is a meditation upon the deaths of O'Hara, Kerouac, and **Charles Olson**, which, as he says, may be seen as signaling the "death of poetry" itself. Carroll intertwines the deaths of these three poets with the death of the 1960s counter-culture, evoking a tone of spiritual and poetic stasis that marks the onset of the 1970s: "All my footprints of the 60's across N.Y.C.'s sidewalks / gone, so important now I realize."

Carroll's poems, with their strange and elusive metaphors, resemble the poetry of the surrealists, especially Arthur Rimbaud, and also recall the **postmodern** word play of New York School poets **John Ashbery** and O'Hara. While there has been little scholarly attention paid to Carroll, he has always remained an extremely popular poet. His appeal reached new audiences in the late 1970s, when he became interested in **performance poetry** and rock 'n' roll music. His vision of blurring the distinction between rock lyricist and poet became a reality when the Jim Carroll Band released its first album, *Catholic Boy* (1980). His popularity reached new heights in the 1990s with a film version of *The Basketball Diaries*, which made his book a *New York Times* best seller.

The 1980s and 1990s saw Carroll increasingly experimenting with both his poetry and other media. In 1986 he published *The Book of Nods*, in which he veered away from the surrealistic lyrics of his earlier work and started to experiment with a new form he called "Nods." These "nods" (street lingo for a heroin trip) were **prose poems** that combined fiction, autobiography, and poetry. In 1992 he released a spoken-word album, *Praying Mantis*. Spoken-word poetry, part of the emergent culture of **slam poetry**, attempts to blur the distinction between poetry as an elite cultural form and as a popular form. He was at the forefront of this new movement in poetry and was one of the first to perform spoken-word poetry on popular cable television stations MTV and VH-1. These performances, along with the enduring popularity of both the film and book versions of *The Basketball Diaries*, have introduced a new generation to his work. In 1993 Penguin Books collected the major works spanning his entire career and published *Fear of Dreaming: The Selected Poems of Jim Carroll*.

Further Reading. *Selected Primary Sources:* Carroll, Jim, *The Basketball Diaries* (New York: Penguin, 1978); ———, *The Book of Nods* (New York: Penguin, 1986); ———, *Fear of Dreaming: The Selected Poems of Jim Carroll* (New York: Penguin, 1993); ———, *Living at the Movies* (New York: Grossman, 1973). ***Selected Secondary Sources:*** Kuennen, Cassie Carter, "Jim Carroll: An Annotated Selective, Primary and Secondary Bibliography, 1967–1988" (*Bulletin of Bibliography* [June 1990]: 81–112); Malanga,

Gerald, "Review of *Living at the Movies*" (*Poetry* [December 1974]: 164); Milward, John, "Catholic Boy" (*Penthouse* [March 1981]: 141+); *The Jim Carroll Website* (http://www.catholicboy.com).

Jeremy Kaye

CARROLL, PAUL (1927–1996)

Paul Carroll, the trailblazing editor of *Big Table*, is best known for his affiliation with the **Beats**, whose verse he published liberally though not exclusively in this short-lived, influential periodical. As the perspicacious editor, too, of *The Young American Poets* (1968), a prophetic anthology of avant-garde writers under thirty-five, and the author of *The Poem in Its Skin* (1968), astute opinionated essays on ten poets, Carroll was pigeonholed as a rebellious, unconventional writer himself. Many of his poems of the 1950s and early 1960s, though, were carefully crafted and certainly did not fit the Beat label. While he denied being a Beat, his best-known poem, the five-feet foldout oral "Ode to Severn Darden," was. The versatility of Carroll's verse—or perhaps, the fact of his never finding his specific voice—led to his having to peddle his first manuscript, *Odes* (1969), for ten years before, despairing, he published it himself.

Paul Carroll was born in 1927 in Chicago to an Irish-Catholic magnate and his much younger wife. His father died when he was in high school, and he came to loathe his mother obsessively and incestuously, as is apparent from the piercingly cruel poem "Mother." The ghosts of his youth, however, were not laid to rest by such autobiographical poems, or by years of Freudian psychoanalysis, but were to haunt him all through his life, leading to self-destructive behavior. Having attended Catholic schools, he enlisted in the Navy during World War II but was not sent overseas. He received his MA in English from the University of Chicago, then taught at Notre Dame for a few years before returning to his alma mater for his Ph.D., which he did not finish. Besides teaching at Loyola University, Carroll became poetry editor, under Irving Rosenthal, of the University of Chicago's *Chicago Review*, publishing work by **Allen Ginsberg**, **Jack Kerouac**, and William S. Burroughs. Attacked for obscene content, the Winter 1959 issue was suppressed, and Rosenthal and Carroll published its contents in their quickly founded periodical *Big Table*. When Rosenthal left, Carroll went on to edit four more issues. After its demise, he worked for the magazine *WFMT Perspective*, then for Mortimer Adler's Institute for Philosophical Research. He founded Big Table Publishing Company in 1965 and published **Bill Knott**'s and **Andrei Codrescu**'s first books. The previous year he had married, and his son Luke, the central subject of the intimate, illustrated *Luke Poems* (1971), was born in 1970. By that time, Carroll was affiliated with the University of Illinois in his home city, where he founded the Program for Writers. His behavior and drinking worsened, and he was hospitalized and divorced. With his second wife, whom he married in 1977, he later left the city so pervasively present in his poetry, spending his last years in North Carolina.

Carroll's poetry is a fiercely honest attempt to describe his wounded psyche as precisely as possible. All through his career, certain images recur: masks, ghosts and shadows, clouds and angels, trees and parks, fellow poets and visual artists. In addition, Carroll often used odd juxtapositions and surreal images—shaped by the Catholic Church—to create an extravagant Dali-like dreamworld, simultaneously celebrating the conscious and the subconscious, the ordinary and the preternatural. Nevertheless, apart from a permanent predilection for alliteration and repetition, it is hard to categorize Paul Carroll's poetry, as he changed his style drastically every few years. The *Odes*, consisting of poems written over seventeen years and divided into five periods in reverse chronological order, demonstrate these changes. Part V consists of learned, controlled, and depersonalized poems, with saints and martyrs (Benedict Labre, Ignatius) as main characters, and with many classical references (for instance, "Tertullian Addresses the Men of Carthage"). In Part IV we still find references to historical figures, but painters (Klee, Duchamp) rather than saints have become Carroll's muses and voice his feelings. Most poems rhyme and revel in assonance and alliteration, as in "Winter," where a crow "crisscrosses across / this ice-cold sky." "Dinner Party," linking sex and death in shockingly unpredictable ways, looks ahead to the openly autobiographical and Freudian middle part of the book, written after Carroll had begun analysis. In "Father," a harsh tribute, he gets "sick" of the ghost of the man who called "Mayor Kelly crooked to his face," and "July 15," one of his birthday poems, starts "By now you know most of the complicated habits / heart contrives to commit its suicides."

These poems do not anticipate the sudden stylistic breakthrough, fueled by Carroll's editing of the Beats, in the exhilarating, sensory, oral pop poem "Ode to Severn Darden" in Part II. This reinvention of the ode, a Whitmanesque, campy commemoration of Carroll's main subject, contemporary America, fused in its long, limber lines popcorn and politics, angels and art. It ignited similarly nonselective associations of Carroll's subconscious, but he soon exhausted this particular style. Odes nevertheless remained his trademark; the collage "Ode to the Angels" in Part I, lauding his poet-heroes **James Dickey**, **John Logan**, **James Wright**, and Pablo Neruda, emphasizes that "each poem wears its own skin."

The odes in *The Luke Poems* range from the **minimalist** "Luke / sucks" (the complete "Ode of the Jealous Father") to the all-inclusive "Ode to the African Poets I–XX," the different subsections of which take up one-third of the book. Its first, page-long part is in the style of his surreal poems; section II is the one-liner "And the witches?," III is an empty page, and IV and XIV are virtually identical. These experiments, meant to shock the reader into feeling, pall; Carroll moves the reader most when he is stirred himself, as in "XVII: Ode of Gratitude to the Art Institute of Chicago" or in his references to Luke. The dedicatory poem "To My Son" makes poetry primary: "This book is your father's face. / Touch it."

The eleven new poems in *New and Selected Poems* (1978) and later, uncollected ones are equally varied and range from one-liners to the five-part "Ode to Darwin aboard the HMS Beagle," which welds lyrics and prose, showing that "Eden must be near"; in fact, it is "under that fat toadstool near your boot." In one of his last, better (because directly autobiographical) poems, "Body you've turned into my enemy," published in *Chicago Review* in 1998, he touchingly chides his body for having a urinary tract infection, and then celebrates it by observing that without his body he would never be able to see things like "that delicious / rump of the ASU co-ed biking." Paul Carroll died of bladder cancer in 1996.

Further Reading. *Selected Primary Sources:* Carroll, Paul, *The Luke Poems* (Chicago: Big Table, 1971); ———, *New and Selected Poems* (Chicago: Yellow Press, 1978); ———, *Odes* (Chicago: Big Table, 1969). *Selected Secondary Sources:* Hoover, Paul, "The Poet in His Skin: Remembering Paul Carroll" (*Chicago Review* 44.1 [Winter 1998]: 5–12); Poulin, A., Jr., "Carroll's Triple Skins: Three Decades of American Poetry" (*Shenandoah* 21 [Summer 1970]: 94–99); Schultz, John, "Or What Worse Evil Come" (*Ohio Review* 59 [1999]: 164–184).

Marian Janssen

CARRUTH, HAYDEN (1921–)

A New Englander immersed in the works of **Robert Frost**, **T.S. Eliot**, **Ezra Pound**, and **Wallace Stevens**, Hayden Carruth is likely to be remembered for his ability to echo those poets' voices without producing poetry that is derivative of these masters. For example, while Carruth celebrates the grandeur of the rural world in which he has spent much of his working life, he nonetheless rejects what he considers **Henry David Thoreau**'s "solipsistic view of nature" and calls for a more engaged and pragmatic view of the natural world. His **jazz** and **blues** poetry, and his volume *The Bloomingdale Papers* (1975), written about his time in a mental hospital, enrich readers' experience of music and their understanding of mental illness. Carruth has placed his imprint on contemporary poetry through his work as editor of *Poetry*, poetry editor for *Harper's*, and advisory editor for the *Hudson Review*, as well as through his work with the students of the Graduate Creative Writing Program at

Syracuse University. Carruth's anthology, *The Voice That Is Great Within Us* (1970), is one of the best-selling anthologies of twentieth-century American poetry. Pulitzer Prize–winning poet **Yusef Komunyakaa** reports that he carried a copy of this anthology with him during his tour of duty in Vietnam.

Hayden Carruth was born in Waterbury, Connecticut, and studied at the universities of North Carolina and Chicago. He was stationed in Italy during World War II, where he worked in the public relations office. Boring though the work was for Carruth, who had trained as a code breaker, it provided him with a typewriter on which he could work his earliest experiments as a poet. Back in the United States, Carruth married, fathered his first child, divorced, and underwent psychiatric treatment for depression. He later moved to Vermont and, for many years, scratched out a difficult living doing hack work and ghost writing while trying to pursue his own work as a poet. Carruth's struggles as a poet working outside the academic world, with its possibilities of grants, sabbaticals, and relatively comfortable workloads, have been addressed in a number of his poems and essays. When acclaim came to Carruth late in his life, it was not without costs. Overcommitted to a rigorous schedule of readings, Carruth found himself drinking too much and on the verge of another breakdown. He returned to his home, canceled his remaining engagements, and determined to live a more hermetic life, as he had done throughout the 1960s, 1970s, and much of the 1980s.

Although Carruth produced creditable poetry as early as 1959, some critics maintain that he found his voice with *Brothers, I Have Loved You All* (1978), which incorporates New England's physical and psychological landscapes into a distinctive voice. Individuals may be humbled, or even defeated, by circumstance and an unyielding environment, but in the poems of *Brothers, I Have Loved You All*, they refuse to give up. "Late Sonnet" from *Brothers* serves as an explanation of Carruth's aesthetic ideals at that time. In "Late Sonnet" Carruth's narrator concludes with the rueful acknowledgment that he has been an enthusiastic but inattentive listener to the music of Sidney Bechet, whose work asserts that "tone, phrasing, and free play" are more important than the originality for which the poet has strived. The poem in which this revelation is presented is itself a model of "tone, phrasing, and free play"; indeed, the constraints of the sonnet form weigh so lightly upon the poem that one might not notice that it *is* a sonnet without the help of its title.

Another distinctive volume, *Asphalt Georgics* (1985), highlights Carruth's ability to take enjambment to extremes, and to achieve rhymes through hyphenation. The hyphenation, however, is not capricious; indeed, Carruth's intimate knowledge of words, their construc-

tion, and their derivation make the poems taut and precise, despite the apparent idiosyncrasies of line length and enjambment. *Asphalt Georgics* is an example of poetry written by a craftsman who knows the tools of his craft well enough to subvert those tools, creating something unexpected and startling, but not superficial, modish, or simply shocking. "Tone, phrasing, and free play" take their place as primary considerations in the poems, although originality is certainly a characteristic of the volume as a whole.

Scrambled Eggs and Whiskey: Poems 1991–1995 (1996) ranges over such matters as aging, depression, love, poverty, the loss of a child, death camps, and the act of writing. "Saturday at the Border" appears at first to be a self-conscious meditation on the possible absurdity of writing one's first villanelle at the age of seventy-one, but it is also a commentary on the borders between youth and age, rich and poor, Mexico and the United States, inspiration and God's absence. The poem's narrator sees the wealthy bankers of Arizona spinning self-protective ideologies that cause violence and warfare throughout the world, and he suggests that the ascendancy of such ideologies represents the death knell of the world, even as time and infirmity ring the poet's own death knell. "Saturday at the Border" is politically engaged yet also witty and aware of the formal requirements of the villanelle.

Among other acknowledgments of his contributions to American poetry, Carruth won the National Book Critics' Circle Award for *Collected Shorter Poems, 1946–1991*, and the 1996 National Book Award for Poetry for *Scrambled Eggs and Whiskey* (1996).

Further Reading. *Selected Primary Sources:* Carruth, Hayden, *Asphalt Georgics* (New York: W.W. Norton, 1985); ———, *The Bloomingdale Papers* (Athens: University of Georgia Press, 1975);———, *Brothers, I Have Loved You All* (Riverdale, NY: Sheep Meadow Press, 1978); ———, *Reluctantly: Autobiographical Essays* (Port Townsend, WA: Copper Canyon Press, 1998); ———, *Scrambled Eggs and Whiskey: Poems 1991–1995* (Port Townsend, WA: Copper Canyon Press, 1996); ———, *The Voice That Is Great Within Us* (New York: Basic Books, 1970).

Angela M. Salas

CARSON, ANNE (1950–)

Anne Carson was a late arrival to contemporary American poetry, publishing her first two books of verse in her mid-forties, but her influence has been immediate and widespread. Her ambitious and original work is widely seen as having introduced a new classical dimension to North American poetry. Moreover, her writing challenges conventional distinctions not only between verse and prose but also among genres (poem, novel, and essay), as well as between original text, **translation**, and commentary. Her work combines a heady engagement with a variety of acknowledged sources (including **Sylvia Plath**, Emily Brontë, John Keats, Renaissance and modern painting, and a wide range of classical authors) with a bracing candor and fierce eroticism.

Anne Carson was born June 21, 1950, in Toronto, Ontario, Canada, and was educated at the University of Toronto, where she earned her Ph.D. in 1980. She taught classics for a number of years at McGill University and has also taught at Emory University, Princeton University, the University of California–Berkeley, and the University of Michigan. She has received numerous prizes for her writing, including a Guggenheim fellowship, a Lannan Literary Award for poetry, and the T.S. Eliot Prize for Poetry; in 2000 she was named a fellow of the John D. and Catherine T. MacArthur Foundation.

Carson's book of criticism *Economy of the Unlost* (1999) begins "There is too much self in my writing." This statement might seem startling coming from a writer whose work is characterized by its extraordinary erudition and whose books include minimal explicit biographical information (some dust jacket biographical statements consisted solely of the statement "Anne Carson lives in Canada"). But in fact from her first books Carson's poetry has included equal doses of classical allusion and autobiographical **confession**. The classical ironies of her highly allusive work are warmed, but not overwhelmed, by the occasional burst of confessional honesty; and the autobiographical forthrightness of some of her poetry is cooled, but not undermined, by the critical restraint of her analytical, quick-moving lines. Certain facts of biography (her father's mental deterioration, her mother's death, her own marriage and divorce) keep coming back until the reader is able to piece together the outlines of a life. Yet even such an outline is uncertain, given the obvious literariness of her enterprise: Moments of seeming candor are frequently transmuted, and autobiography itself may burst into an apparently fictional or critical context. This balance among competing forces applies to the forms of her writing as well: Each of Carson's books is marked by a different mixture of genres, combining prose, verse, original, translation, lyric, fiction, and confession. It is the contrapuntal effect created by the juxtaposition of these forms, rather than Carson's success at any particular form, that characterizes her contribution to contemporary North American poetry.

Carson's first two major books including original verse, *Glass, Irony and God* (1995) and *Plainwater: Essays and Poetry* (1995), were published nearly simultaneously. These books contained organizational strategies that would come to be seen as characteristic of Carson's approach. For example, rather than collect a number of short lyrics in the dominant manner of a contemporary poetry collection, the poems in these books were organized into longer sections or sequences. *Glass, Irony and God* is divided into five verse sequences followed by a

critical essay entitled "The Gender of Sound." The book opens with "The Glass Essay," a thirty-eight–page narrative poem recounting the end of a love affair while examining the possible sources of Emily Brontë's creative work in Brontë's own biography. The theme of this poem—the continuation of life after the end of love—occupies several of Carson's longer works. Moreover, Carson's speculations about the relationship between the biography of Emily Brontë and Brontë's creative work suggest a fictional dimension even to the acknowledged sources in Carson's biography: One section quotes a poem of Brontë's that refers to an "iron man" and follows the quotation with "Who is the iron man? / My mother's voice cuts across me." By bringing in the poet's mother, her nagging companion in the years following her divorce, Carson suggests that all representation, even if the iron man is entirely fictional, is determined by our experiences of others. Carson's identification with other writers who are subject to biographical speculation, such as **Emily Dickinson** and Sappho, is shaped in part by the fragmentary character of our knowledge and the teasing inconclusiveness of any evidence.

Other poems in this collection show Carson channeling radically different influences and stretching her capacities for telling a story in verse. Both "The Truth About God" and "Book of Isaiah" include God as a character and show influences from Blake to Ted Hughes; "The Truth About God" in particular seems influenced by Hughes's dark poetic sequence *Crow*. "The Fall of Rome: A Traveller's Guide" tells the story of a visit to a friend in Rome in seventy short sections. "TV Men," a sequence Carson revised and expanded in *Men in the Off Hours* (2000), tries to imagine the relationship between historical and literary figures and the medium of television. Some of these poems (such as "TV Men: Hector") represent the character of their title as though broadcast on a television show. In other poems, the relationship between television and poetic representation is more complex; "TV Men: Artaud" uses jump cuts and the interjection of private points of view to examine the public representation of madness itself. "TV Men: Sokrates," on the other hand, scrambles the zones of public and private by conducting a sort of TV-mediated visit with the supremely rational philosopher at the moment of his death.

Plainwater is even more ambitious and wide-ranging.. Dominated by writing in prose, *Plainwater* nonetheless expands the possibilities for American poetry. It begins with "Mimnermos: The Brainsex Paintings," a set of translations from an ancient Greek poet, translations so free they include references to Chicago and Berlin. Some of the translated fragments emphasize the syntactical ambiguity of the original, while others, such as fragment 22, "Half Moon," sound like a Greek version of

Ezra Pound's Chinese poems: "Half moon through the pines at dawn / sharp as a girl's ripcage." While both Pound's *Cathay* and his "Homage to Sextus Propertius" are ancestors of this sort of creative translation, there is nothing in Pound to prepare one for the essay and interviews with Mimnermos that accompany it. For an analogous project, one would have to look to **Armand Schwerner**'s *The Tablets* and the notes of Schwerner's fictive "scholar-translator."

Of the other parts of *Plainwater*, two are in verse and two in prose. The first verse section, "Canicula Di Anna," a multipart narrative poem set in Italy, has some things in common with "The Fall of Rome." The other section in verse, "The Life of Towns," is a sequence of poems each on a different town (such as "Holderlin Town" or "Town of My Farewell to You"). Superficially, they are characterized by an idiosyncratic punctuation in which each line ends with a period although the syntax of the sentence frequently insists on enjambment. Like miniature versions of Italo Calvino's "Invisible Cities," the towns suggest a landscape of longing and regret that harks back to the broken relationship of "The Glass Essay." Of the prose sections, "Short Talks" has an effect similar to "The Life of Towns": It consists of short titled paragraphs on different subjects, including writers (Dickinson, **Stein**, Plath), art, and philosophy. Each paragraph stands alone, but together the paragraphs combine to create a character portrait of the speaker and her desires that has little to do with the ostensible subjects of the paragraphs: "I am writing this to be as wrong as possible to you. Replace the door when you leave, it says. Now you tell me how wrong that is, how long it glows. Tell me" (*Plainwater*, 45)

The final section of *Plainwater*, a series of essays, **prose poems**, or **lyric** essays titled "The Anthropology of Water," occupies over half of the book. The main figures in this project are men: Carson's father, losing his mind to Alzheimer's disease; a significant lover; and Carson's brother, who disappeared as a young man. The title is suggestive of the complexities of a poet analyzing her own kinship structures; as she puts it in the introduction to a section called "Just for the Thrill," "I don't like romance and have no talent for lyrical outpourings—yet I found myself during the days of my love affair filling many notebooks with data. There was something I had to explain to myself" (*Plainwater*, 190). That she can refer to her own reactions to her lover as "data" suggests something of the attitude of these poems: self-critical, restless, inquiring, sharp-eyed. Yet the emotional investment (the "water" of her anthropological gaze) is no less personal for being subjected to analysis.

With *Autobiography of Red* (1998), which she called "a novel in verse," Carson reached her widest audience. The seeds for this project were clearly laid by the Mimnermos project in *Plainwater*, and the same elements are all here: freely translated fragments of an ancient Greek poet (Stesichoros), critical essays questioning the meaning and significance of those works, a faux interview with the poet himself. The title work, however, is an innovation entirely. Stesichoros's character, a winged monster named Geryon who is slain by the hero Herakles, is reimagined as a boy born into a modern human (and abusive) family who grows up to become a philosophy student and photographer (closely paralleling Carson's dual identity as academic and artist). Carson's verse novel has elements of magical realism (a man with wings is also the central character of Salman Rushdie's *The Satanic Verses*) but might best be classified as a homoerotic neoclassical bildungsroman. Rather than the hero who kills Geryon directly, as in the myth, Herakles here is Geryon's handsome and fickle lover who damages the fragile Geryon by coldly leaving him. Years later, Geryon encounters Herakles again in Argentina. Though Herakles by this time has a new lover, he and Geryon briefly resume their complex, fated relationship in a pilgrimage to a Peruvian volcano until Geryon transcends his loss in a moment of artistic (and literal) flight. In the final section, Geryon, Herakles, and Herakles's lover Ancash stare at a bakery oven resembling the mouth of a volcano: "We are amazing beings, / Geryon is thinking. We are neighbors of fire." The narrative is complex, and leaves many things unsaid. Some of Carson's long-standing themes (life after the end of love, classical myths reimagined, relationships between travel, pilgrimage, and loneliness) are here combined and reformulated in a book-length **narrative poem**. This is also the poem in which Carson's interest in volcanoes, which goes back to "The Glass Essay," is given the most sustained attention.

Men in the Off Hours (2000) may be Carson's most conventional book. Though it continues her practice of mixing genres, it is not broken up into discrete sections. It might be described as a lyrical diary of engagement with sources: Many of the short poems clearly emerge from the practice of reading. Some lyrics, though scattered throughout the book, can be collected to function as short sequences: There are, for example, several poems labeled "drafts" and seven "Epitaphs." Other sequences are contiguous: In addition to the reprise of "TV Men" from *Glass, Irony and God*, there is a sequence based on the paintings of Edward Hopper and a set of riffs on the Latin poet Catullus. Catullus, of course, has been the subject of poetic experiment before, most notoriously in **Louis Zukofsky**'s homophonic translations. Whereas Zukofsky paid overwhelming attention to sound, Carson improvises on a word or idea from the original. For example, her take on Catullus's poem 97 ("*Non Quicquam Referre Putavi*") consists almost entirely of an alphabetical list of synonyms for the word "anus."

With its domination by the short lyric and its recycling of previously published material, *Men in the Off Hours* gives the impression of an interregnum between more ambitious projects. And indeed, in *The Beauty of the Husband* (2001), Carson returns to the book of poetry as a single sustained work. Though subtitled "a fictional essay in 29 tangos," *The Beauty of the Husband* is a remarkably forthright narrative poem about the beginning, end, and aftermath of a marriage, a sort of **postmodern** version of George Meredith's *Modern Love*. The husband's fickleness and infidelity, a theme since "The Glass Essay," is brought into direct contact with his magnetism, which Carson imagines as she diagnoses her own hopeless attraction to him. Carson uses various techniques "to save these marks from themselves," or to keep the book from collapsing into self-pity: long, analytical, and sometimes funny section titles; cryptic epigraphs from the writings of John Keats; referring to herself at times as "the wife." In one section, the narrator notes that poets "prefer to conceal the truth beneath strata of irony / because this is the look of the truth: layered and elusive." This comment is made with respect to the question of whether the husband was a poet (the answer is "Yes and no"), but it could be made with regard to Carson herself. And in this formulation, the truth is both "beneath" the "strata of irony" and in the "layered and elusive" nature of the whole product.

In 2002 Carson published *If Not, Winter: Fragments of Sappho*, a new translation of the complete poetry of the ancient Greek poet Sappho. In many ways this marks the return of Carson to her classical roots as in her 1986 *Eros the Bittersweet*, a study of human desire through an examination of archaic Greek poets that began with a discussion of Sappho who, as Carson writes, "first called eros 'bittersweet'" (3). Readers of "The Brainsex Paintings" and *Autobiography of Red* were perhaps startled to find a fairly straightforward translation, with original text on facing pages and relatively no-nonsense explanatory notes. Unlike some other recent translations, Carson does not attempt to capture the prosody of the original (now called Sapphic meter), but she does pay homage to the fragmentary nature of the text by deploying a square bracket in what her introduction calls "an aesthetic gesture toward the papyrological event."

Further Reading. *Selected Primary Sources:* Carson, Anne, *Autobiography of Red: A Novel in Verse* (New York: Knopf, 1998); ———, *The Beauty of the Husband* (New York: Knopf, 2001); ———, *Decreation: Opera, Essays, Poetry* (New York: Knopf, 2005); ———, *Economy of the Unlost* (Princeton, NJ: Princeton University Press, 1999); ———, *Eros the Bittersweet: An Essay* (Princeton, NJ: Princeton University Press, 1986); ———, *Glass, Irony, and God* (New York: New Directions, 1995); ———, trans., *If Not, Winter: Fragments of Sappho* (New York:

Knopf, 2002); ———, *Men in the Off Hours* (New York: Knopf, 2000); ———, *Plainwater: Essays and Poetry* (New York: Knopf, 1995). *Selected Secondary Sources:* Hamilton, Jeff, "This Cold Hectic Dawn and I" (*Denver Quarterly* 32.1–2 [1997]: 105–124); Phillips, Adam, "Fickle Contracts: The Poetry of Anne Carson" (*Raritan: A Quarterly Review* 16.2 [1996]: 112–119); Rae, Ian, "'Dazzling Hybrids': The Poetry of Anne Carson" (*Canadian Literature* 166 [2000]: 17–41); Scroggins, Mark, "Truth, Beauty, and the Remote Control" (*Parnassus: Poetry in Review* 26.2 [2002]: 127–145); Stanton, Robert, "'I Am Writing This to Be as Wrong as Possible to You': Anne Carson's Errancy" (*Canadian Literature* 176 [2003]: 28–43); Tschofen, Monique, "'First I Must Tell About Seeing': (De)Monstrations of Visuality and the Dynamics of Metaphor in Anne Carson's *Autobiography of Red*" (*Canadian Literature* 180 [2004]: 31–50).

David Kellogg

CARVER, RAYMOND (1938–1988)

Primarily associated with the short story, Raymond Carver also wrote a fine and extensive body of poetry. Markedly autobiographical, Carver's poems drew from real-life concerns and from situations that pressed upon him, poems that offered a "rough, but true map of [his] past." His poetic terrain is thus often marked by privation, a frequent and intense focus on the negative stuff of his life. It also, however, renders an exploration of resilience and gratitude, a sense of regret about his past but also a sense of astonishment at having survived it and, in the process, having found a greater level of respect and responsibility for himself and for others. His poetry titles include *Near Klamath* (1968), *Winter Insomnia* (1970), *At Night the Salmon Move* (1976), the Levinson Prize–awarded *Where Water Comes Together with Other Water* (1985), and *Ultramarine* (1986). Published posthumously, *A New Path to the Waterfall* (1989) and *All of Us: The Collected Poems* (1996) perform and make available the coda to his poetic oeuvre.

Carver was born in Clatskanie, Oregon, on May 25, 1938, the son of a sawmill worker and a waitress and clerk. His formative years were spent primarily in Yakima, Washington, where the family's life was blighted by financial uncertainty. Married at age eighteen and the father of two children by the time he was twenty, Carver helped support his own young family with a number of low-paying manual jobs. After earning his AB degree from Humboldt State College and taking a brief period of study at the Iowa Writers' Workshop in the early to mid-1960s, Carver was employed as a hospital custodian. The ensuing years proved increasingly difficult. The Carvers filed for bankruptcy in 1967 and again in 1974. Shortly thereafter Carver found work as a textbook editor. It was around this time that his prolonged and well-documented battle with alcohol began.

A series of creative writing teaching jobs in the early to mid-1970s gave way to his growing alcoholism. After nearly a two-year period of unemployment and a number of hospitalizations, he stopped drinking on June 2, 1977. Living apart from his wife by this time (they would divorce in 1982), Carver spent the last ten years of his life with the poet and writer **Tess Gallagher**. During this time his literary reputation steadily increased, and he worked at a number of high-profile teaching jobs. In addition to several other honors, notably a Pulitzer Prize nomination for his story collection *Cathedral* (1983), he was the first recipient (along with Cynthia Ozick) of the prestigious Mildred and Harold Strauss Living Award (1983). He married Gallagher a matter of weeks before his death from lung cancer on August 2, 1988.

Carver's appreciation of a recognizable narrative in poetry, or "story poems," can be seen in his work from the earliest to the last. His poetry derives much of its effectiveness from having an evident story line, a clear forward motion that is combined with plain and often colloquial language to create accessible and even courageous work, the persona matter-of-fact. In the process he invoked a powerful and often disquieting poetry: a poetry of hard-lived domesticity that, for example, renders issues of marital tension, the demands of parenthood, matters of adultery, bankruptcy, and the diminishing and damaging effects of alcohol on the individual and those closest to him. In an essay titled "My Father's Life" (1984), Carver made plain the circumstances of his early environment, the ways in which, for example, he felt a sense of shame at the family's living conditions and, later, his acute sadness at the way his father, owing in part to the effects of alcoholism, fell victim to a physical and psychological breakdown (the results of which for the father were a period of electroshock treatments and, thereafter, six years of unemployment). Toward the end of the essay, in a poem called "Photograph of My Father in His Twenty-second Year" (1968), Carver offered a poignant if tentative consideration of his father's misgivings and, moreover, their respective struggles with alcohol.

Carver continued throughout to explore and articulate what he believed to be the oppressive and often malevolent contours of his life, to reiterate his own and the world's negative capacity, asking, "[W]hat am I to make of this?" In addition to the seemingly ordinary events used to anchor many of the poems, there is a dark and unsettling atmosphere at their parameters, a tacit yet palpable degree of apprehension. His poetry contains, for example, often startling meditations on death and the many dangers, mysteries, and inspiring abilities of the natural world. There are numerous instances when he relates his pleasure at fishing or hunting, or merely spending time in the outdoors. Yet he also portrays what he sees as nature's inexplicable forces, its ability to instill fear and confusion in the individual. Most often, the poems set in the natural world are in keeping with the overall mood of his poetic output, whereby moments of transitory contentment or happiness are balanced against more enduring, adverse demands. There is also, however, in this as with the rest of his poetry, a sharp awareness of and a compassion for the situations affecting people's lives, and moreover, their ability and determination to prevail.

In one of his later and finest poems, "This Morning" (1986), the speaker illustrates his clear appreciation of the outdoors as he goes for a walk—"All lovely"—yet finds his pleasure weighed against hurtful recollection: "The stuff I live with everyday." Even so, the poem ends on a relatively affirmative and resolute note, as the speaker describes the way birds emerged "from the gnarled trees. And flew / in the direction I needed to be going."

This note of relative affirmation becomes more apparent in the collections Carver published after he stopped drinking and settled into his relationship with Gallagher. The title poem of *Where Water Comes Together with Other Water*, for example, represents a far greater optimism than in years past, with the speaker declaring his love of rivers and "everything that increases me." The final poem in the collection, "For Tess," affirms Carver's love and gratitude for Gallagher's companionship: "I'm grateful to you, you see. I wanted to tell you." "The Gift," a poem dedicated to Gallagher in the subsequent collection *Ultramarine*, finds the speaker/Carver relating, "It's the tenderness I care about."

It would be wrong, however, to say that the general tenor of Carver's poetry diverges greatly from his middle to late work. What it does, rather, is maintain the directness and general quality of the previous years, and in the case of his final collection, *A New Path to the Waterfall*, render explicitly his relationship with his past, present, and imminent death. Assembled during his illness and composed of new and revised poems, in addition to lineated passages from writings that touched him during his last months, the book represents the culmination of an often difficult life afforded substantial poetic expression and, in the end, dignity: "To call myself beloved, to feel myself / beloved on the earth" ("Late Fragment," 1989).

Further Reading. *Selected Primary Sources:* Carver, Raymond, *All of Us: The Collected Poems* (New York: Vintage, 2000; London: Harvill Press, 1996); ———, *At Night the Salmon Move* (Santa Barbara, CA: Capra, 1976); ———, *Call if You Need Me: The Uncollected Fiction and Prose*, ed. William L. Stull (London: Harvill Press, 2000); ———, *Fire: Essays, Poems, Stories* (New York: Vintage, 1989); ———, *Near Klamath* (Sacramento, CA: English Club of Sacramento State College, 1968); ———, *A New Path to the Waterfall*

(New York: Atlantic Monthly, 1989); ———, *Ultramarine* (New York: Random House, 1986); ———, *Where Water Comes Together with Other Water* (New York: Random House, 1985); ———, *Winter Insomnia* (Santa Cruz, CA: Kayak, 1970). **Selected Secondary Sources:** Bethea, Arthur F., *Technique and Sensibility in the Fiction and Poetry of Raymond Carver* (New York: Routledge, 2001); Brown, Arthur A., "Raymond Carver and Postmodern Humanism" (*Critique* 31 [Winter 1990]: 125–136); Saltzman, Arthur M., *Understanding Raymond Carver* (Columbia: University of South Carolina Press, 1988).

Wayne Thomas

CARY, ALICE (1820–1871)

Alice Cary was a prolific writer who, during her lifetime, was one of the nation's most popular poets. Her oeuvre defies simple categorization. She wrote ballads, **lyrics**, hymns, and **narrative poetry** that express a range of irony, humor, consolation, and didacticism. As a professional writer, she was skilled in the language and cadence of **sentimental** verse that was often associated with, but not limited to, female poets of the period. Her poems express sympathy with the lives of common people, and she is often compared to **John Greenleaf Whittier**. Cary's poetry is best understood as bridging the traditions of nineteenth-century American Romantics and realists. While she employs the diction and tropes of Romantic writing, many of her poems are more realistic in their psychological portrayal of character and theme.

Cary was born on a farm outside of Cincinnati, Ohio, on the Western frontier. Her childhood was marked by the deaths of two sisters and her mother. Although she had little formal education, she showed an early interest in literature and a determination to become a writer. She published her first poem, "The Child of Sorrow," at the age of eighteen in a Universalist newspaper and continued publishing in regional and national papers, often with little or no payment. In 1849 Rufus Griswold included poetry by her and her younger sister, **Phoebe Cary**, in *Female Poets of America*. In a review of the book, **Edgar Allan Poe** made Alice famous by praising her "Pictures of Memory" as the "noblest poem in the collection." In 1850 the sisters published *Poems of Alice and Phoebe Cary* and traveled east, where they met Whittier, who memorialized Alice in his poem "The Singer." Later that year, Alice moved to New York City to fulfill her ambition to support herself as a writer, and she was later joined there by Phoebe. The two sisters earned enough money to buy their own house, where they lived together the rest of their lives. They became known for their popular Sunday afternoon salons, and Alice was the first president of Sorosis, a professional women's club. She also maintained a demanding daily writing schedule, and her many publications included a weekly poem in the *New York Ledger* for nearly a decade. During her lifetime, she published four volumes of poetry, three novels, three collections of short fiction, and two children's books. While modern critical scholarship focuses mainly on Cary's short stories, during her lifetime she was primarily known for her poetry.

Much of Cary's poetry emphasizes the importance of individuals, especially as they cope with loss. Structurally, many of her poems contain a narrative shift or an unexpected turn at the end, a factor that may have contributed to her popularity with a mass audience. Cary's sense of conclusion differentiates much of her work from the effusive, romantic lyrics of the period and also reflects her work as a writer of short stories. Even the sentimental "Pictures of Memory," praised by Poe, exhibits Cary's talent for narrative surprise. At first, the speaker extols the "violets golden" and "milk-white lilies" of the "dim old forest" that is her favorite "picture" in her memory. She explains, however, that she loves the forest memory not for these beautiful images, but because her little brother, whose "feet on the hills grew weary," died there in a "bed of the yellow leaves" that she had arranged. In the darkly comic "Maid and Man," two lovers enjoy an evening river sail. Inspired by the sight of a "modest, slim-necked flower / Nodding and nodding up to the sun," the pair collaborate on a song anthropomorphizing the flower as a young girl, singing "Be warned, my beauty—'t is not the fashion / Of the king to wed with the waiting-maid . . . The dew is a-tremble to kiss your eyes— / And there is but danger in the skies!" The real danger, however, is that the pair are so absorbed in their song that they do not realize they are about to go over a waterfall. The poem's speaker calls the lovers' song a "ditty," showing her disdain for their conventional warning to the single girl / flower and their "doleful pity." The flower is "safe on the shore" as the pair is lost over the fall, ironically singing, "There is danger! danger! frail one list!" Many of her poems offer variations on the popular theme of a woman waiting to be reunited with loved ones. In "The Seal Fisher's Wife," as in much of her poetry, Cary uses repetition to create melody, each stanza ending with a slight variation on the line "She cards the wool for her gown." The repetition of the line, unlike the poem's title, highlights the domestic work of the woman. The husband's boat is crushed in the icy sea, and in the morning she, too, is found "stiff and cold" in death, as her baby is "smiling up so sweet" in its cradle, kept alive and warm "[f]rom the carded wool of her gown." In "Watching," the speaker tries to cheer the weeping Elella, a young woman who is waiting for her husband to return. The speaker promises to share a "legend wild," raising expectations for an imbedded narrative that never develops as the poem turns again with the sounds of a dog baying and the wind "so like a foot-step near."

While readers may have expected the poem to end with news of the husband's death, the last line announces his return, thus doubly countering conventions by refusing to supply the happy reunion. In "The Bridal Veil," Cary writes one of her strongest critiques of marriage. Instead of a narrator telling a story, a young woman speaks directly to her new husband, telling him "you think you have won me" and challenging him to lift her white veil to truly "look on me." Rather than call attention to her beauty or purity, the bride states that she is "matter to vex you, and matter to grieve you, / Here's doubt to distrust you, and faith to believe you." Even though the veil has "flattened down" her "wings," she warns him, "I can slip like a shadow, a dream, from your hands." In the final rhymed couplet, she asserts that the veil can be a "cover for peace that is dead, or a token / Of bliss that can never be written or spoken." In the end, the veil becomes a shroudlike symbol of her loss of self as she is fated to be silenced by a deathlike peace or a wordless happiness, which seems especially ironic considering the speaker's powerful voice in the poem.

Further Reading. *Selected Primary Sources:* Cary, Alice, *Ballads, Lyrics, and Hymns* (New York: Hurd and Houghton, 1866); ———, *Lyra and Other Poems* (New York: Redfield, 1852); ———, *Poems* (Boston: Ticknor and Fields, 1855); ———, *Poems of Alice and Phoebe Cary* (New York: Redfield, 1850). *Selected Secondary Sources:* Fetterley, Judith, "Introduction," in *Clovernook and Other Stories* (New Brunswick, NH: Rutgers, 1987); Venable, Emerson, ed., *Poets of Ohio* (Cincinnati: Robert Clarke, 1909); Walker, Cheryl, ed., *American Women Poets of the Nineteenth Century* (New Brunswick, NH: Rutgers, 1992).

Denise Kohn

CARY, PHOEBE (1824–1871)

Phoebe Cary, a well-known poet during her lifetime, published ballads, hymns, lyrics, and parodies in the popular periodical press. As a professional writer, she wrote many poems that reflect the sentimental tastes of middle-class nineteenth-century readers. In her parodies and dialogues Cary shows a bold sense of humor and comedic wit, demonstrating her range of talent and the broader spectrum of popular poetry written by women during the period.

Cary was born on the then-Western frontier on a farm near Cincinnati, Ohio. She was the younger sister of the poet **Alice Cary**. Even though they had little formal education and grew up in a home with few books, Phoebe, like Alice, showed an early talent for writing poetry. In 1849, when Phoebe was twenty-five, her poetry was published in *Female Poets of America*, and afterward Horace Greeley visited the sisters in Ohio. Greeley remained a lifelong friend, and in 1868 he wrote an essay about them for his book *Eminent Women*

of the Age. In 1850 the sisters published *Poems of Alice and Phoebe Cary*, and the following year Phoebe joined her sister in New York City to earn her living as a writer. The two lived together the rest of their lives in the home they bought with their earnings, and for fifteen years they hosted a popular literary salon on Sunday afternoons. Both sisters were Universalists who supported abolition and woman's rights, and Phoebe worked briefly on the *Revolution*, the suffrage newspaper edited by Susan B. Anthony and Elizabeth Cady Stanton. Phoebe, who enjoyed taking time off from writing, was not nearly as prolific as Alice, and her poetry was collected in two volumes during her lifetime. Grief-stricken at the death of Alice in 1871, Phoebe died of hepatitis five months later.

In her dialogues and parodies, Cary uses humor to critique gender inequities. "Was He Henpecked?" is wry commentary on the ideology of separate spheres and male fears that voting would give women too much power. At the poem's beginning, the female speaker Mrs. Dorkling tells her husband that she is tired of the "chanticleer / Who crows o'er us so loudly" and suggests that women should be able to vote. Her husband replies with horror, stating "I like you in your proper sphere: / The circle of a hen's nest." Although the farmer insists suffrage is wrong because women must be protected from public politics, by the end of the poem he has expressed his true fear that voting will give his wife the power to "fly so high" and "roost above me!" In the dialogue "Dorothy's Dower," Cary looks at the problems married women faced in controlling their own finances. As newlyweds, the husband encourages his wife to do what she pleases with her money, even "spend it on sugar-candy," assuring her that the more money she asks for and spends, "[t]he better you will please me!" Later, though, he complains about her spending and needs to borrow money from her. After they have children, and expenses have increased, he accuses her of mismanaging money and tells her he would not have spent it on "sugar-candy" like a woman, to which she retorts, "I think the most of it / Went for cigars and brandy!" More conventional poems such as "The Rose" and "The Hunter and the Doe" show women as trusting figures who are hurt by the men they love. In other poems, however, women are safe from pain because they view their romantic love as idealistic, not realistic. In "Disenchanted," the female speaker remains happy despite her disillusionment with her lover because the "dear romance and the poesy / Were mine, and I have them still." In "Do You Blame Her," a young woman explains that she rejected her suitor because she realizes that her "fancy" gives her lover a "thousand graces," and that "I only like him when he is by, / 'T is when he is gone I love him." In her poetic parodies, Cary cheerfully satirizes some of the most famous poets of her time. **Edgar**

Allan Poe's sentimentally morbid "Annabel Lee" becomes the story of the prosaic "Samuel Brown." In "The City Life," a speaker speculates what will happen when his beloved moves to the city, a parody of **William Cullen Bryant**'s "The Future Life," a meditation about the loss of the beloved to heaven. Cary's success in poetic genres as disparate as hymns and parodies is important because it offers readers a more complicated view of popular nineteenth-century poetry and aesthetics.

Further Reading. *Selected Primary Sources:* Cary, Phoebe, *Poems and Parodies* (Boston: Ticknor and Fields, 1854); ———, *Poems of Alice and Phoebe Cary* (New York: Redfield, 1850); ———, *Poems of Faith, Hope, and Love* (New York: Hurd and Houghton, 1867). *Selected Secondary Sources:* Ames, Mary Clemmer, ed., *A Memorial of Alice and Phoebe Cary, with Some of Their Later Poems* (New York: Hurd and Houghton, 1875); Bennett, Paula Bernat, *Nineteenth-Century American Women Poets* (London: Blackwell, 1998); Walker, Cheryl, ed., *American Women Poets of the Nineteenth Century* (New Brunswick, NH: Rutgers, 1992).

Denise Kohn

CASSITY, TURNER (1929–)

Turner Cassity's work is known among poets for its campy erudition, uncompromising metrical mastery, and biting wit. Cassity came of age during **free verse**'s mid-century shift to the **confessional** but chose to cast a jaundiced eye on human foibles and to render them in formal verse. The combination of his strict adherence to metrical poetry, refusal to wallow in the lyric "I," sardonic view of human nature, and prolific publishing record makes Cassity an important American poet of the twentieth century. Critics less taken with his work have seen it as, by turns, arch, obscure, overly clever, and emotionally distant.

Allen Turner Cassity was born January 12, 1929, to Allen Davenport and Dorothy Turner Cassity in Jackson, Mississippi. His father, who died when Turner was four, came from a line of Southern timber farmers and gun manufacturers; his mother was a violinist for silent film theaters. As a child, he lived in the lumber town of Forest, where the main attractions for boys were gravel pits and chinaberry fights; later, he and his mother moved to a Jackson boarding house, where the young poet began his observations of humans behaving badly. His mother held Cassity's inheritance while schooling him in money management; when he turned sixteen, she gave him full control of his own money, which to this day he prides himself on having managed well.

Cassity's young adulthood was fairly conventional for a white Southern male. He drilled in ROTC and sold newspaper subscriptions door to door. Soon after graduation from a class notable for the number of murderers it produced, Cassity entered Millsaps College, where his work began to draw recognition. His poetry took first place two years running at the Southern Literary Festival, and he was cited for an informal essay, "The Beautiful Lady of Guadalupe Hidalgo." Of his graduation from Millsaps, Cassity writes, "I graduated on a Monday; on a Tuesday I bought a brand new convertible, and on Sunday I left for California. The most intelligent week, by a comfortable margin, I ever spent" ("A Little of Myself," 24–25).

As the Korean War heated up, Cassity immersed himself in Stanford's rigorous writing workshop led by **Yvor Winters** (and nicknamed the "frigidarium" for its icy criticism). When he was drafted the following year, he joined the Navy and was sent to Puerto Rico. There he served in two unusual capacities: as rifleman in a funerary firing squad for Puerto Ricans killed in action in Korea, and as a teacher of English as a Second Language. Cassity describes the M*A*S*H-style ESL pedagogy as "appropriate for the edification of Mynah birds," made even more hopeless by the "bewildering range of accents" among the teachers and by the fact that the trainees had lost their teeth from eating sugar cane all their lives ("A Little of Myself," 32).

Beneath the surface of such unblinking narratives as "Mainstreaming" (*Between the Chains*), a poem about an ill-fated attempt to place mentally retarded men in the U.S. Army, and "Clay Bertrand Is Alive and in Camelot," told in the persona of Clay Shaw, a gay New Orleans businessman caught up in the Kennedy assassination, lies a deep understanding of human foibles that could only come from close observation and empathy. Cassity peers at our darker natures through a lens ground by history, polished by meter, and tinted by Calvinism. His is a poetry of experience, not innocence: He has seen it all before, and, furthermore, points us to his myriad sources, should we care to look them up.

Some reviewers are put off by the demands of Cassity's historical and literary references, but Cassity observes the external world, not merely the psyche of the poet. Racial segregation, whether in Mississippi or in Johannesburg; silent film starpower or the oblique film noir milieu of pre-Stonewall gay life; the wonders of architecture and science fiction; daily life on and off the military base; humanists and demagogues—these are some of the subjects of his verse narratives.

Cassity's exacting metrical practice is integral to his poetics. Generally, he works within the confines of the short lyric, with heroic couplets being his favored scheme. However, in July 1970 he shocked many when his 1,200-line blank verse cycle of twelve poems, *The Airship Boys in Africa*, filled an entire issue of *Poetry*. Practically an ars poetica, "The Metrist at the Opera" (*No Second Eden*) compares the off-tuning of first and second violins, a ballerina's angled limbs, theatrical makeup, and perspective in visual art with the subtle substitutions and reversals that give the lie to meter as mere tick-tock: "A metronome confirms clockmaker's art, not this." The fourth-foot reversal from iamb to a trochee in that line suggests that indeed Cassity's meter is not mere clock-making.

The precision of Cassity's lines sometimes cuts into the syntax, even to the point of obscuring the sense. Richard Johnson, while admiring Cassity's linecraft, notes that at times "the economy goes past a point of diminishing returns, into crypticism" (197). John Ash finds that Cassity's form can become "rigid and monotonous," forcing him into "ugly linguistic contortions," yet grants that he is never guilty of the "maudlin and seemingly interminable free verse effusions" that fill contemporary American poetry magazines (19).

Yvor Winters thought that poetry should pass moral judgment on the poet's understood experience, without falling into effusiveness. Cassity has followed Winters, but on his own terms. What he best understands is irony and hypocrisy, colonial style—perhaps not surprising in a Southern poet. Cassity has a particular penchant for setting his poems in the "developing world." Whether writing of apartheid South Africa, U.S.-occupied Puerto Rico, or the World Trade Center attacks, Cassity reveals colonialism's moral bankruptcy. His most recent poem in this vein, "WTC," indicts American hubris and doublespeak, comparing the Twin Towers to Babel: "Our tongues so long confused / Must fail and be recused" (*No Second Eden*).

Cuddly and effusive Cassity is not. His is a poetry that almost without exception turns its back on the confessional "I." Timothy Steele sees this tendency against self-revelation as limiting—not, Steele insists, because the reader longs for scandal but "because I sense that the connection between the private man and the public colonial—between the needs of the individual and the demands his profession places on him—is an issue central to Cassity's concerns" (211). In *The Defense of the Sugar Islands*, however, Cassity's poems turn autobiographical, drawing on his Army service in Puerto Rico. Dana Gioia lauded the book as a breakthrough, because "for once the poems have as much emotional as intellectual force to them," crediting this to the persona's similarity to "the poet himself, rather than some figure from colonial history" (497). The final poem of Cassity's most recent book, *No Second Eden*, is—of all things—a free-verse love poem in the first person, "Laying It on the Line." In it, the "heart of stone" addresses a love for whom, "just once, I broke my meter." He proves he can be flexible, and admits to his emotional devastation, until the last iambic pentameter line: "But as you see, the beat keeps coming back."

Where other poets of his generation have foundered in angst or outrage, Cassity has reveled in exacting judgment: on himself, on history's footnotes, and on humanity's failings.

Further Reading. *Selected Primary Sources:* Cassity, Turner, *Between the Chains* (Chicago: Phoenix, 1991); ———, *The Defense of the Sugar Islands: A Recruiting Poster* (Los Angeles: Symposium, 1979); ———, *The Destructive Element: New and Selected Poems* (Athens: Ohio University Press, 1988); ———, *Hurricane Lamp* (Chicago: Phoenix, 1986); ———, "A Little of Myself" (Ts. 1988. Turner Cassity papers, MSS 642, Papers 1948–1991, Emory University Special Collections); ———, *No Second Eden* (Athens, OH: Swallow, 2002); ———, *Steeplejacks in Babel* (New York: David R. Godine, 1973); *Watchboy, What of the Night?* (Middletown, CT: Wesleyan University Press, 1966). *Selected Secondary Sources:* Ash, John, "A Brash Yankee and a Southern Dandy" (*New York Times Book Review* 20 [April 1986]: 19); Barth, R.L., *A Bibliography of the Published Works of Turner Cassity, 1952–1987* (Florence, KY: R.L. Barth, 1988); Davie, Donald, "On Turner Cassity" (*Chicago Review* 34:1 [Summer 1983]: 22–29); Gioia, Dana, "Poetry and the Fine Presses" (*Hudson Review* 35:3 [Autumn 1982]: 483–498); Johnson, Richard, "Actions Outdone" (*Parnassus* 3.1 [Fall/Winter 1974]: 192–203); Steele, Timothy, "Curving to Foreign Harbors: Turner Cassity's 'Defense of the Sugar Islands'" (*Southern Review* 17.1 [Winter 1981]: 205–213).

Robin Kemp

CASTILLO, ANA (1953–)

One of the foremost voices in Chicano writing today, Ana Castillo has written five novels, one critical theory text, one children's book, and six collections of poetry. While Castillo is probably best known for her novels, such as *So Far from God* (1993) and *The Mixquiahuala Letters* (1986), poetry has played an important role in her life and her work. In her introduction to *My Father Was a Toltec* (1995), Castillo discusses her first experience with poetry at the age of nine when her paternal grandmother died. "Instead of giving a boy a bloody nose or climbing on the monkey bars," recalls Castillo, "I wrote . . . short, roughly whittled saetas of sorrow" (xv). Today, Castillo's poetry still reflects her intensely personal experiences while exploring the lives of twentieth-century women of color.

Born and raised in a working-class Chicago neighborhood, Castillo credits her paternal grandmother and extended family for much of her formative influence, because her parents, Raymond and Raquel Castillo, often worked long hours at factory jobs to provide for the family. In 1975 Castillo earned her BA in art from Northeastern Illinois University, and in 1979 she received her MA in Latin American and Caribbean Studies from the University of Chicago. During her college years, Castillo became politically active in the struggles of Chicanos for social justice, and in the early 1970s she joined the Association of Latino Brotherhood of Artists. Certain that art was a way by which to challenge oppression and form coalition, Castillo self-published two chapbooks of poetry: *Otro Canto* (1977) and *The Invitation* (1979). Castillo also holds a Ph.D. in American Studies from the University of Bremen in Germany.

Written in both English and Spanish, Castillo's poetry often focuses on the central theme of Xicanisma, a term Castillo coined in *Massacre of the Dreamers* (1994). Xicanisma, as defined by Castillo, is an "ever present consciousness" Chicana women possess that helps them to challenge racial, sexual, and economic subjugation (226). "In My Country," from *My Father Was a Toltec*, is an excellent example of this consciousness as the poem addresses all the oppressions that never occur in Castillo's imagined country: "Men do not play at leaders," work is plentiful and pays well, violence is nonexistent, the air is clean, and women do not feel the need to "go artificially blonde" and are "not made ashamed / for being." As the poem progresses, Castillo turns her focus from her country to the world itself, remarking that, in her world, Africa is left alone and Arab women do not have to cover their faces, for "no one is prey." By using the present tense rather than the conditional, Castillo's poem imagines her country and her world into existence, demonstrating how Xicanisma can be used to challenge such oppressions.

Other poems portray the multiple hardships daily endured by Chicanos. "1975," from *Otro Canto*, for example, discusses the hours spent "talking proletariat talks" about "unpaid bills," "bigoted unions," "no-turkey Thanksgivings," "deportation," and "plants closing down," and warns that one day Chicanos will be "tired / of talking." Likewise, "Saturdays," from *My Father Was a Toltec*, describes a working mother who spends "from 5 to 5" on Saturdays washing and ironing—only to find her husband in "a tailor-made silk suit / bought on her credit" off to meet another woman. "Recipes for a Welfare Mother," from Castillo's most recent collection of poems, *I Ask the Impossible* (2001), further illustrates these daily sociopolitical hardships. Castillo describes the monotony of nutritionally poor meals based on lard, sugar, flour and "government cheese product"; the diseases these foods cause; and the limited options for women on welfare: One can "dissipate slowly" or wait for one's heart to explode "like an illegal firecracker"; one can stay at home or find minimum-wage work, but, regardless, "your diet will stay the same. / Your life will be the same." Above all, Castillo's poems place the reader directly into the lived experiences of those struggling in American society.

Castillo's poetry also explores female sexuality, contesting the persistent binary that women are either virginal and pure, or sexual creatures intended solely for men's pleasure. Indeed, her collection *The Invitation* focuses almost exclusively on works that celebrate women's sexuality and equate poetry with lovemaking to create "a Masterpiece" of "two bodies blending / into a poem / that never ends." Other poems, such as "Women of Marrakech" from *My Father Was a Toltec*, illustrate the conflicts women have in a society that punishes them for being "sex personified," leaving them with "no inheritance, no home, nothing." Like her earlier collections, Castillo's *I Ask the Impossible* explores female desire in poems like "Seduced by Nastassia Kinski," where Castillo writes about her obsession with the actress, or "When Women Part," which tells of the politics of an ending love affair between two women. Whether celebrating women's sexual experiences or contesting the limits placed on such experiences by society, Castillo's poetry challenges fixed definitions of female sexuality.

In 2000 Castillo's poetry was acknowledged in a reception to celebrate her inclusion in the Sears Tower mural honoring local writers. She currently divides her time between teaching at Chicago's DePaul University, writing, and serving as a guest editor for *3rd Woman*, a literary magazine she co-founded with Norma Alarcon.

Further Reading. *Selected Primary Sources:* Castillo, Ana, *I Ask the Impossible* (New York: Anchor Books, 2001); ———, *Massacre of the Dreamers: Essays on Xicanisma* (Albuquerque: University of New Mexico Press, 1994); ———, *My Father Was a Toltec and Selected Poems 1973–1988* (New York: Norton, 1995); ———, *Otro Canto* (Chicago: Alternativa Publications, 1977). ***Selected Secondary Sources:*** Agosin, Marjorie, and Cola Franzen, eds., *The Renewal of the Vision: Voices of Latin American Women Poets, 1940–1980* (Peterborough, ON: Spectacular Diseases, 1987); Alarcon, Norma, ed., *Chicana Critcal Issues* (Berkeley, CA: Third Woman Press, 1993); Spurgeon, Sara, *Ana Castillo* (Boise, ID: Boise State University Press, 2004).

Kristin Brunnemer

CATHER, WILLA (1873–1947)

Although Willa Cather is best known as a novelist, her first book was a collection of poetry, *April Twilights* (1903). This text was later republished as *April Twilights and Other Poems* (1923), with thirteen original poems omitted in favor of twelve more recent ones, along with textual revisions to some of the 1903 verses. A final poem, "Poor Marty," originally published in 1931, was included in all subsequent reissues of the collection (1933, 1938, and 1951). In addition to providing groundwork for her more famous fiction, Cather's poetry was popular among contemporary readers and favorably remarked upon by critics. Indeed, prior to 1912 she was best known as a poet (Slote, xliii). Perhaps most significantly, Cather continued to publish poetry throughout her career and took steps to ensure that her poetry would stay in print.

Willa Cather lived near Winchester, Virginia, until she was eight, when her family moved to Red Cloud, Nebraska. Her first poems were published in the University of Nebraska–Lincoln's student literary publication, the *Hesperian*. Between 1896 and 1912, Cather lived in Pittsburgh and then New York, working as a teacher, a journalist, and an editor while composing poetry and short stories that she published in magazines like *Scribner's* and *McClure's* and later releasing *April Twilights* (1903) and a collection of stories, *The Troll Garden* (1905). From 1912 to the end of her life, Cather wrote full-time, publishing eleven novels and two more collections of short stories.

The poems of *April Twilights* (1903) are **lyrics** written in closed form and utilizing traditional rhyme schemes. Their topics are abstract, romantic, and classical, including death, loss, and unrequited love. Few contemporary reviewers found the volume particularly groundbreaking, though most were taken by at least one poem, most often "Grandmother, Think Not I Forget" or "Prairie Dawn." Poems like "The Mills of Montmartre," "Paris," and "Asphodel" (an English sonnet) clearly sprang from Cather's recent trip to Europe and are generally considered derivative (O'Brien, 256–257); by contrast, "The Swedish Mother" draws on Cather's early memories of Virginia, while "Prairie Dawn" and "White Birch" have a western setting, though they do not yet reflect Cather's recognition of the value of her own prairie roots (Woodress, 169).

Cather claimed to have regretted publishing *April Twilights* and in 1908 tried to buy up and destroy all remaining copies. However, she chose to republish a number of these poems in *April Twilights and Other Poems* (1923). This volume is divided into two parts, original 1903 verses and those published afterward; here Cather replaced some of the more imitative 1903 poems with ones that seem to come more directly from her own prairie heritage, such as "Macon Prairie," "Prairie Spring," and "Going Home" (O'Brien, 261). She also removed the dedicatory poem and its accompanying dedication to her brothers, and replaced it with the dedication "To my Father for a Valentine."

Although in 1925 Cather spoke disparagingly of herself as a poet (Woodress, 164) and many modern critics dismiss her poetry as a detour in an otherwise stellar literary career, it is important to note that poetry was not purely a phase or apprenticeship for Cather. When compiling the Houghton Mifflin collected "Autograph Edition" of her work, Cather coupled the 1933 version of *April Twilights* with her first novel, *Alexander's Bridge*, as the third volume of the series; however, she chose to leave out her first volume of fiction. This suggests that Cather considered her early poetry significant enough to include, and made the conscious decision to anthologize it as part of her collected works.

Cather's poetic bent links her with other novelists who also produced poetry, including Thomas Hardy and William Faulkner (both of whom she read and both of whom were familiar with her work). Cather wrote her early stories and poetry simultaneously, and her poems contain sparks of what would be more fully fleshed out in prose (Slote, xliii). At the same time, poetry permeates her fiction, as in the case of *O Pioneers!* (1913), whose title comes from a **Walt Whitman** poem and whose epigraph is her own "Prairie Spring." Her prose has also been praised for its poetic qualities. While most people remember Cather the novelist, George Seibel, a lifelong friend and early champion, chose to eulogize Cather the poet. On July 5, 1903, Cather inscribed a copy of her poems "To Mr. George Seibel, the first and kindest critic of these verses"; approximately forty-five years later, Seibel entitled his eulogy "April Midnights." Although not necessarily her greatest work, Cather's poems are a memorable and important part of her corpus and still considered worthy of study both for what they teach us about Cather's fiction and for their own sake.

Further Reading. ***Selected Primary Sources:*** Cather, Willa, *April Twilights (1903)*, ed. Bernice Slote (Lincoln: University of Nebraska Press, 1968); ———, *April Twilights and Other Poems* (New York: Knopf, 1951). ***Selected Secondary Sources:*** O'Brien, Sharon, *Willa Cather: The Emerging Voice* (New York: Oxford University Press, 1987); Slote, Bernice, "Willa Cather and Her First Book" (Introduction), in *April Twilights (1903)*, by Willa Cather, ed. Bernice Slote (Lincoln: University of Nebraska Press, 1990, ix–xlv); Woodress, James, *Willa Cather: A Literary Life* (Lincoln: University of Nebraska Press, 1987).

Jessica G. Rabin

CAWEIN, MADISON JULIUS (1865–1914)

Prolific and well regarded, Madison Julius Cawein produced a body of work that brought into American letters, as much as **Thoreau**'s, the mysteries of the American landscape. Cawein drew most of his inspiration from his home state of Kentucky, commonly filling his poems with references to local flora with startling effect. As **William Dean Howells** noted, in his preface to Cawein's *Poems*, "He has the gift, in a measure, that I do not think surpassed in any poet, of touching some commonest thing in nature, and making it live, from the manifold associations in which we have our being, and glow thereafter with an indistinguishable beauty" (*North American Review* [1908], 2). Such capacity caused Cawein to be dubbed the "Keats of Kentucky."

Cawein was born in Louisville, Kentucky, to parents of German descent. His father, William, earned a living as an herbalist. His mother, Christina, considered herself something of a medium. After graduating from high school in 1886, he spent the next six years working in the nearby Newmarket Poolroom. At twenty-two he published his first collection of poems, *Blooms of the Berry*, which was positively reviewed by Howells. Cawein's next collection, *The Triumph of Music* was also dedicated to Howells. In 1903 Cawein married Gertrude Foster McKelvey, and soon after had a son, Preston.

As prolific as he was, publishing thirty-six collections of verse in his lifetime, Cawein made his living not through writing but rather by speculating in real estate and the burgeoning financial markets at the turn of the century. Much of what he earned was lost, however, in the San Francisco earthquake of 1906. Beyond Howells, his literary friendships included the poets **Edward Arlington Robinson** and **James Whitcomb Riley**. He died in 1914 when, after suffering a stroke, he fell and struck his head.

Without making too much of his upbringing, Cawein had in his parents a perfect marriage of the natural and supernatural worlds, an interplay one sees throughout his poetry. In Cawein's work one is likely to discover "the Earth's wild fairy-dance" ("The Unimaginative") or "Demon-World" ("Caverns") as frequently as red haws or rose hips. And not unlike the spiritualists of his day, Cawein locates in nature the seat of revealed knowledge.

The poet **Edwin Markham** noted in an introduction to a posthumous collection that had Cawein included more of the human in his work, he might have been regarded among the most gifted lyricists of his age. Howells countered that the interior or "human" experience is not absent from Cawein's poems but rather finds a voice in nature. In "Under Arcterus" the natural world acts as frame, an occasion for the revealed as a mimetic trope.

Spanning the nineteenth and twentieth centuries, Cawein's work is similar to that of one of his contemporaries, W.B. Yeats. Just as Yeats used Celtic mythology as a touchstone throughout his poetry, Cawein turned to the Arthurian legend, which was enjoying a revival in the period, in part due to the popularity of Sir Walter Scott's work. Several poems, including "The Dream of Sir Galahad" and "The Daughter of Merlin," take Arthurian figures for their subject. In these works the speaker moves beyond the immediate world into that of legend and myth. The daughter of Merlin provides, at the peak of a mountain, a portal beyond which those following her can hear "White music of silence and snow." Similarly, in "To One Reading the Morte D'Arthur," the narrator compares himself to the young female reader named in the opening lines, described as a "daughter of our southern sun," and wishes, with a hint of regret, that the "Romance—which on thee lays/The spell of bygone ages" was also able to hold him.

Wistfulness and nostalgia find fertile ground in the flora and mythology featured throughout Cawein's work. His is "The world of Yesterday/A faery world of memory," a place in which "the child I used to be/ Still wanders with his dreams" ("A Path in the Woods").

Further Reading. ***Selected Primary Sources:*** Cawein, Madison Julius, *Kentucky Poems* (London: G. Richards, 1902); ———, *Myth and Romance* (New York: G.P. Putnam's Sons, 1899); ———, *Poems of Nature and Love* (New York: G.P. Putnam's Sons, 1893); ———, *Triumph of Music* (Louisville, KY: J.P. Morton, 1888); ———, *Weeds by the Wall* (Louisville, KY: J.P. Morton, 1901). ***Selected Secondary Sources:*** Baskerville, William Malone, *Southern Writers* (New York: Gordian Press, 1970); Howells, William Dean, "Introduction" (North *American Review* [1908]); Rittenhouse, Jessie Belle, *The Younger American Poets* (Freeport, NY: Books for Libraries Press, 1968); Rothert, Otto Arthur, *The Story of a Poet* (Freeport, NY: Books for Libraries Press, 1971).

Anthony Lacavaro

CERAVOLO, JOSEPH (1934–1988)

Joseph Ceravolo remains one of the more enigmatic figures in what is now called the second generation **New York School** of poets. He wrote poems in a wide range of forms and on diverse themes, but he is best known for his mid- to late 1960s **lyric poetry**, much of which is collected in a posthumous collection, *The Green Lake Is Awake* (1994). His writing shows the influence of his workshop teachers, **Kenneth Koch** and **Frank O'Hara**, although his writing ultimately differs from theirs in its metaphorical intensity and in its lack of irony.

Ceravolo was born in Astoria, Queens, the son of a tailor and a seamstress. He would go on to graduate from City College and later take poetry classes at the New School. He served briefly in the Army in the late 1950s and traveled to Mexico, where he wrote some of the poems that would later be collected in *Transmigration Solo* (1979). By profession an engineer, he lived until his death with his family in Bloomfield, New Jersey. Although he was prolific in his poetic output throughout his life, he had less contact with the New York poetry scene after the 1960s.

Ceravolo's first book *Fits of Dawn* (1965), published by **Ted Berrigan** as a mimeograph, shows the influence of **John Ashbery**, Kenneth Koch, and Frank O'Hara, but it also departs from their models in its stylistic ambitiousness. *Fits of Dawn* is arguably one of the most challenging and experimental works produced in New York during the mid-1960s. In its use of neologisms, nonsequiturs, and fractured syntax, *Fits of Dawn* was every bit as unorthodox as Ashbery's *Tennis Court Oath* or O'Hara's "Second Avenue."

Like many of the second-generation New York School poets with whom he associated—such as Berrigan, **Ron Padgett**, **David Shapiro**, **Anne Waldman**, and **Ber-**

nadette Mayer—Ceravolo was strongly influenced by **Beat poetry** and by **William Carlos Williams**, as well as by O'Hara, Ashbery, and Koch. Unlike many of his peers, Ceravolo wasn't much of a bohemian. At a fairly young age he settled outside of Manhattan with his family. His poems often take family life, beaches, and parks for their settings. His poems are deeply experiential even if they reveal little biographical detail. *Fits of Dawn* was followed by a chapbook in 1967, *Wildflowers Out of Gas*, published by Tibor de Nagy. In 1968 Ceravolo's *Spring in this World of Poor Mutts* won the first ever Frank O'Hara Award, earning him publication from Columbia University Press. It is for these poems that Ceravolo is best known; they are dense, highly metaphorical, and verbally dextrous.

After *Spring in this World of Poor Mutts*, Ceravolo would not publish another book for over ten years. His last two books, *INRI* (1979) and *Millennium Dust* (1982), are particularly difficult to categorize. The increasing religiosity of these two books seems to have distanced him from his peers and from the New York scene in general, and he read and published infrequently during this period.

If Ceravolo seldom interacted with the poetry scene at large in the 1970s and 1980s, he nonetheless continued to be prolific in his poetic output until his death from pancreatic cancer in 1988. Though his work is well edited and selected in *The Green Lake Is Awake*, much of Ceravolo's poetry is no longer in print. More important, there is a substantial amount of his writing that has never been published. The mini-**epic** poem *Hellgate* (a recording of which was played at the memorial reading for him at the Poetry Project, and the title of which refers to the Hellgate Bridge in Astoria, where Ceravolo was raised) remains in manuscript, as do the poems that he was working on in the 1980s which he placed under the title *Mad Angels*. Ceravolo left little, if anything, in the way of criticism and there are few records (other than oral anecdotal ones) of his larger views on poetry and **poetics**. This may make him something of a poet's poet since his reputation depends entirely on his poems and not necessarily on his personality or on his role within a poetic movement. Unlike many of his peers, Ceravolo was not particularly interested in self-promotion or in publishing his fellow poets. Instead, throughout his lifetime he modestly and imaginatively pursued what his wife, Rosemary, called "his primary love," poetry.

Further Reading. ***Selected Primary Sources:*** Ceravolo, Joseph, *Fits of Dawn* (New York: "C" Press, 1965); ———, *The Green Lake Is Awake* (Minneapolis: Coffee House, 1994). ———, *Millennium Dust* (New York: Kulchur Foundation, 1982); ———, *Spring in This World of Poor Mutts* (New York: Columbia University Press, 1968); ———, *Transmigration Solo* (West Branch, IA: Toothpaste Press, 1979). ***Selected Secondary Sources:*** North, Charles, "Wild Provoke of the

Endurance Sky," in *No Other Way: Selected Prose* (Brooklyn, NY: Hanging Loose Press, 1998, 25–29); "Spring in This World of Mad Angels: The Poetry of Joseph Ceravolo," forthcoming in *Don't Ever Get Famous: New York Writing Beyond the New York School*, ed. Daniel Kane (Madison: University of Wisconsin Press, 2004).

Paul Stephens

CERVANTES, LORNA DEE (1954–)

Lorna Dee Cervantes is a poet whose ancestors originate from both sides of the U.S.-Mexico border and whose writing reflects her Amerindian roots, her vision of the world, and her political affiliations. The most anthologized Chicana poet to date, she has published three volumes of poetry: *Emplumada* (1981), *From the Cables of Genocide: Poems on Love and Hunger* (1991), and *Drive: The First Quartet* (2005). As the founding editor of Mango Publications, Cervantes first published several Chicana/o literary luminaries, including **Gary Soto**, Sandra Cisneros, and **Jimmy Santiago Baca**.

Lorna Dee Cervantes was born in San Jose, California, and later moved to the Mission District of San Francisco. Her poems often look back on both of these cities as important early life environments. Currently, she lives and teaches in Colorado. Cervantes began writing as a child, continued throughout her youth, and ultimately achieved national recognition with the publication of *Emplumada*. The word "emplumada"—deriving from the plumed serpent of pre-Columbian history—suggests the autobiography of the poet, in that much of what she conveys in her poetry relates to the history of the dispossession of California Indians and the legacy of colonization that impinges upon the destinies of Mexican and American Indian people in the United States. Her poetry strikes a strong political chord. While several of the poems of *Emplumada* are explicitly political and even acrimonious, Cervantes's work overall promotes the interrelationship of people and the environment. In this poetic world, however, U.S. institutions of dominance are seen as sources of oppression, impoverishment, and racism.

The poems of *Emplumada* often juxtapose a matriarchal figure against structures such as freeways and bridges. Within the urban and coastal settings of *Emplumada* the poet seeks a personal, spiritual, and social harbor in which her abilities can mature. For Cervantes, the exploitation of Mexican and Indian women is both personally embodied and socially conditioned. Overall, the poems address the violence and oppression of the barrio; yet the barrio is part of a native homeland, a place frequented by foes as well as mentors and peers, and a place containing hidden messages. For example, in *Emplumada* birds are spiritual beings conveying mystical knowledge to the poet, whose role is to decipher this knowledge for the purposes of self-preservation and poetic composition. Poetry, identity, and survival are interconnected, providing consistency and meaning.

The most famous poems of *Emplumada*—"For the Young White Man Who Asked How I, an Intelligent, Well-Read Person Could Believe in the War Between Races," "Beneath the Shadow of the Freeway," and "Uncle's First Rabbit"—are more narrative than most of Cervantes's poems, each retelling events from a life determined by the anti-Indian history of California. For the young Mexican American speaker of these poems, sexual violence and cultural genocide threaten survival in unpredictable ways. Poetry is one way to escape danger and proclaim a hard-won survival.

In *From the Cables of Genocide: Poems on Love and Hunger*, personal experience again evokes an oppressive history, particularly in longer poems such as "Drawings: For John Who Said to Write about True Love" and "Pleiades from the Cables of Genocide" These **epic**-like sequences take up issues such as divorce, Native American genocide, matrilineal sacred knowledge, and contemporary politics. The poems in this volume represent one of the major achievements of Cervantes's career to date—the amalgamation of personal and global topics, sensual and historical focuses, and physical and cosmic orientations.

References to the body in Cervantes's texts are often graphic, but they serve to amplify the importance of more global or historical issues. In "Santa Cruz," for example, Cervantes compares diminished love with species endangerment by alternating images of animals with those of female physiology. She associates the mouth ("the spit on my lip") with the lips of the vulva "pushing / fins and flash." In "Raisins," she compares raisins and nipples. Ultimately, the body, through its privileged access to experience and its motility, responsiveness, and impressionability, speaks the greater truth.

Such poems emphasize the connection between love and hunger, and reveal a physically based core of language, communication, and knowledge. For example, at the end of a long marriage the speaker announces that a final meal is over, saying that "both lips bit and shriveled," a phrase suggesting the breaking of a physical bond, the plosive "p" and "b" emphasizing the rupture. The poem is both a disquieting inquiry on the subject of divorce and the invocation of a mind-body unity.

In Cervantes's poetry, erotic and physiological frames of reference serve as portals through which to perceive the natural environment, the social world, and Native American cosmology. Poetry is a sacred act and often connotes blood sacrifice, as in "The Captive's Verses," a poem that interweaves divorce and Native American land dispossession; poetry and the land meld with the poet's own body. Cervantes writes that, with a nation "ruined," she is left with her "wash of it . . . wringing in the mud." The poem establishes a connection between the personal and the cultural aspects of the poet's life. Images of the natural world, particularly those of endangered animals and geographical features (such as fissures, rivers, and caves), the seasons, and astronomy supply the poems with much of their meaning and lyricism. Though Native Americans have been dispossessed of their former lands, nature—fauna, flora, and the earth itself—still provides the poet with a source of meaning and identity. In Cervantes's poetry, nature is not a passive template but rather a semiotic source that she, as bard, is called upon to decipher and disseminate.

Further Reading. **_Selected Primary Sources:_** Cervantes, Lorna Dee, *Drive: The First Quartet* (San Antonio, TX: Wings Press, 2005); ———, *Emplumada* (Pittsburgh: University of Pittsburgh Press, 1981); ———, *From the Cables of Genocide: Poems of Love and Hunger* (Los Angeles: Arte Publico Press, 1991). **_Selected Secondary Sources:_** González, Ray, "I Trust Only What I Have Built with My Own Hands: An Interview with Lorna Dee Cervantes" (*Bloomsbury Review* 17.5 [September–October 1997]: 3, 8); Monda, Bernadette, "Interview with Lorna Dee Cervantes" (*Third Woman (II)* 2.1 [1984]: 103–107); Savin, Ada, "Bilingualism and Dialogism: Another Reading of Lorna Dee Cervantes's Poetry," in *An Other Tongue: Nation and Ethnicity in the Linguistic Borderlands*, ed. Alfred Arteaga (Durham, NC: Duke University Press, 1994); Seator, Lynette, "Emplumada: Chicana Rites of Passage" (*MELUS: The Journal of the Society for the Study of the Multi-Ethnic Literature of the United States* 11.2 [Summer 1984]: 23–38); Wallace, Patricia, "Divided Loyalties: Literal and Literary in the Poetry of Lorna Dee Cervantes, Cathy Song and Rita Dove" (*MELUS: The Journal of the Society for the Study of the Multi-Ethnic Literature of the United States* 18.3 [Fall 1993]: 3–19).

Edith M. Vasquez

CHA, THERESA HAK KYUNG (1951–1982)

Theresa Hak Kyung Cha is best known for her poetry in *Dictée* (1982), but because her works span literature, photography, film, and the performance arts, they defy easy categorization. Cha's exploration of Korean women's experiences of racial marginalization, fragmented identity, and colonial domination help explain Korean and Korean American women's identities. *Dictée* is both autobiographical and biographical, committed to recovering Korean women's fragmented experience. Cha recognizes the limitations inherent in trying to rescue an identity that has been subjected to dictatorial patriarchy, Japanese colonialism, Catholic dogma, and racism. Cha's work also emphasizes the physicality and violence of language as a colonial apparatus. Trinh T. Minh-ha's discussion of *Dictée* in her groundbreaking book *Woman, Native, Other* (1989) marked the beginning of a broader critical reassessment of Cha's life and work.

Theresa Hak Kyung Cha was born in Pusan, Korea, where the war forced her seven family members to move repeatedly, settling in Seoul and then Hawai'i in 1962 and California in 1964. At the Convent of the Sacred Heart Catholic School Cha studied classics and excelled, attending first the University of San Francisco and then the University of California–Berkeley, where she received BA degrees in Comparative Literature and Art and then the MA and MFA, studying with sculptor and conceptual artist Jim Melchert. After a stay in Paris to study film in 1976, Cha returned to San Francisco to rejoin the community of Bay Area artists and filmmakers. She continued experimenting with representations of memory, history, immigrant experience, and displacement—themes that permeate *Dictée*. Cha moved to New York in 1980 and edited *Apparatus/Cinematographic Apparatus* (1980). In 1981 she taught at Elizabeth Seaton College and later traveled to Korea to begin the film project *White Dust from Mongolia*. In New York in 1982, on the heels of both her marriage and *Dictée*'s publication, Cha was murdered by a stranger.

Cha appropriates Western classical themes to tell alternative stories or histories. For example, she begins *Dictée* by quoting the Greek lyric poet Sappho as a representative of women's poetic voice in a cultural space where the thoughts, ambitions, desires and longings of women were rarely celebrated, explored, or voiced. Sappho's words "May I write words more naked than flesh, / stronger than bone, more resilient than / sinew, stronger than nerve" are appropriate because Sappho's work remains only in fragments, and it is fragmentary identity and words that are central to Cha's concerns.

Dictée is built around nine sections loosely associated with the nine Muses, but Cha replaces Euterpe, Muse of **lyric poetry**, with the fictional Elitere. Within the nine sections there is a diverse range of approaches used to represent the pressures that have transformed Korean and Korean American women's identities and to reconstruct their various histories, including Cha's own. The main "poetic" sections occur under the muse headings of Calliope (**epic** poetry), Erato (love poetry), Elitere (Cha's muse of lyric poetry), and Polymnia (sacred poetry). Each muse frames a reworking of a poetic genre. For example, the masculine epic of nation building and cultural identity found in Homer and Virgil reemerges as the tale of Cha's mother, an exiled teacher struggling to preserve her culture and identity while in Japanese-dominated Manchuria. Love poetry explores women silenced and circumscribed by patriarchy.

Dictée uses Korean (Hangul), Greek, Chinese, French, and English languages; dictation and **translation** exercises; a revision of the Demeter and Persephone myth as the story of a Korean woman exile; photographs of inscriptions in various languages (such as the etched *Hangul* script of Korean conscript workers shipped to Japanese coal mines); film stills; Catholic religious writings; portraits; and political documents. The translation, pronunciation, and recitation exercises illustrate how colonial and patriarchal power are imposed through the colonial languages, the devaluation of the pidgin speech of the native or immigrant, recitations of scripture, catechisms, and obligatory Catholic confessions. Cha demonstrates their ability to enforce the rules of culture, create truth, establish authenticity, and dictate both identity and positions of superiority and inferiority. Her confessing speaker admits her inferior position in the process of trading her deficient identity for a promise of being made whole: "I am making up the sins. For the guarantee of ab- / solution," but the catechist may translate or recite to the point of rebellion: "*God made me. To conspire in God's own Tongue.*"

The multiplicity of voices, experiences, acceptances, rebellions and confessions in *Dictée* and the uncertain speakers of the likely biographical and autobiographical lines demonstrate the difficulty of telling Korean and Korean American women's stories, recovering a usable history, and pulling together a coherent identity from the many fragments. Cha's enduring distinction may be her pioneering attempt to meet the challenge of fragmented identity directly and to voice the complexity of Korean and **Asian-American** women's experiences.

Further Reading. *Selected Primary Sources:* Cha, Theresa Hak Kyung, *Dictée* (New York: Tanam Press, 1982; Berkeley: University of California Press, 2001). ***Selected Secondary Sources:*** Cheng, Anne Anlin, "Memory and Anti-Documentary Desire in Theresa Hak Kyung Cha's *Dictée*" (*MELUS* 23.4 [Winter, 1998]: 119–133); Kang, Hyun Yi, Norma Alarcon, and Elaine H. Kim, eds., *Writing Self, Writing Nation: A Collection of Essays on* Dictée *by Theresa Hak Kyung Cha* (Berkeley: Third Woman Press, 1994); Minh-ha, Trinh T., *Woman, Native, Other: Writing Postcoloniality and Feminism* (Bloomington: Indiana University Press, 1989).

Eric Ashley Hairston

CHANDLER, ELIZABETH MARGARET (1807–1834)

Elizabeth Margaret Chandler was an abolitionist and is often credited with being the first American woman writer to focus her energies on anti-slavery essays and poetry. Her poems appeared in print almost a decade before **John Greenleaf Whittier**'s anti-slavery poetry. Chandler's writings were published in Benjamin Lundy's *The Genius of Universal Emancipation*, **William Lloyd Garrison**'s *The Liberator*, and various literary journals. She was a member of the Female Anti-Slavery Society of Philadelphia and the Ladies' Free Produce Society of Philadelphia. Within two years of moving to the Territory of Michigan, she formed the Logan Female

Antislavery Society in 1832. Chandler's writings influenced later female abolitionists and writers.

Elizabeth Margaret Chandler was born in Centre, Delaware, to Quaker parents Margaret Evans and Thomas Chandler. Chandler's mother, Margaret Evens, died two days after giving birth to Elizabeth. After Margaret's death, Thomas Chandler moved his family to Philadelphia and placed his daughter under the care of his deceased wife's mother, Elizabeth Evans. Three aunts, particularly Ruth Evans, were also instrumental in Chandler's upbringing. Chandler attended schools that were established and run by the Society of Friends. She excelled in her studies, particularly in the literary arts. Upon finishing school at the age of twelve or thirteen, Chandler continued her own course of reading and writing. Friends often solicited articles from her, which she began publishing when only sixteen. Her early pieces were published anonymously, as was the custom for women during this period.

Chandler's poem "The Slave Ship" (ca. 1825), for which she won an editor's award, was initially published in the *Casket*. It was later reprinted in Benjamin Lundy's the *Genius of Universal Emancipation*. Chandler claimed in a letter to a friend that "The Slave Ship" was the first piece she ever wrote on the topic of slavery. Upon learning, through a mutual acquaintance, that Chandler was the author of the poem, Lundy requested that she contribute more writings to his paper, which she did. Lundy soon asked Chandler to take over the editorship of the "Ladies' Repository" section of the *Genius of Universal Emancipation*.

Chandler's anti-slavery poetry is often representative of nineteenth-century **sentimental** poetry. Standard themes include the nobility of the slave, the suffering of the slave parent, the innocence of children, and inhumanity of slavery. Her poems are often melodramatic and heavy on moral instruction. However, some poems are also highly sensual and graphically charged with images of blood and gore. Chandler's poems that are more graphic center on themes such as the vengeful slave, the hypocrisy of American "freedom," and the sisterhood of white women with their slave counterparts.

In "The Confessions of the Year" (ca. 1825–1834), the narrator describes the torment of a slave who is mocked by the "eagle wing of Freedom" waving over his head as he toils in the fields. The slave compares the wealth and happiness of his master's home with his own lot. The desire for liberty burns within the slave until "the demon spark, in his bosom nursed, / Blazed up beyond control." The slave then revolts and kills the master's wife and infant. Those who have nightmares of the "vengeful slave" may take temporary comfort in knowing that "the slave was crush'd" and his fetters made more secure than before; however, the narrator asks whether those who keep the slave down know the greater the oppression, the "fiercer his rising hour." Slave owners can subdue the slave with force and "drench the earth with his blood," but they should realize that the "best and purest of their own" will also be destroyed." The only "hope for tranquil hearts," the narrator concludes, is for the slave masters to "let the oppress'd go free."

In both her essays and poetry, Chandler argued for white women to see black female slaves as their sisters. Because women were perceived as the primary purveyors of moral education at the time, Chandler hoped their influence would contribute to the end of slavery. In "The Kneeling Slave" (ca. 1825–1834), the narrator lists the luxuries that white ladies enjoy: loving parents, friends, and days spent frolicking among the flowers. The female slave experiences nothing of the kind and is at the mercy of her master's will. "She is thy sister, woman!" the narrator pleads and asks, "shall her cry, / Uncared for, and unheeded, pass thee by?" If the reader does not feel moved to help this woman, the narrator asks accusingly, is it because "thy heart grown selfish in its bliss, / That thou shouldst view unmoved a fate like this?"

In addition to the private, cultural influence that women wielded, Chandler argued that women could also have a direct economic impact on slavery. Chandler was a member of the Ladies' Free Produce Society of Philadelphia, and her essays and poems, such as "Slave Produce" (ca. 1825–1834), urged women to purchase goods that were produced outside the slave system. The hope was that a greater demand for non-slave products, such as wool instead of cotton, would contribute to the economic decline of slavery.

Chandler died in 1834 from either cholera or ague. Had she lived into maturity, there is little doubt she would have continued to play a major role in the abolitionist movement. Abolitionists used Chandler's poems as hymns in religious and social gatherings, and women wrote testimonials about the impact her writings had on their lives. More recently, historian Jean Fagan Yellin has noted that Chandler's work directly affected later generations of female abolitionists such as **Angelina Ward Grimke**.

Further Reading. ***Selected Primary Sources:*** Chandler, Elizabeth Margaret, *Essays, Philanthropic and Moral: Principally Relating to the Abolition of Slavery in America* (Philadelphia: Howell, 1836); ———, *Poetical Works of Elizabeth Margaret Chandler with a Memoir of Her Life and Character by Benjamin Lundy* (Philadelphia: Howell, 1836). ***Selected Secondary Sources:*** Mason, Marcia J. Heringa, ed., *Remember the Distance That Divides Us: The Family Letters of Philadelphia Quaker and Abolitionist and Michigan Pioneer Elizabeth Margaret Chandler, 1830–1842* (East Lansing: Michigan State University Press, 2004); Yellin, Jean Fagan, and John C. Van Horne, eds., *The Abolitionist Sisterhood: Women's Political Culture in Antebellum America* (Ithaca, NY: Cornell University Press, 1994).

Christina Wolak

CHANDRA, G.S. SHARAT (1935–2000)

Gubbi Shankara Chetty Sharat Chandra arrived in the United States from India in the late 1960s and drew on his memories and experiences of his native country, as well as on the more surrealistic elements of his life in America, to explore the world of the bicultural Indian **expatriate**. One of the first Indian poets to teach creative writing in American universities, Chandra refused the role of "ambassador of good will" for India, but instead frequently attacked the sexism and hypocrisy of his home country in his poetry while also poking fun at American bigotry and ignorance. Adopting the "open and easy style" of American poets such as **Robert Frost** and **William Carlos Williams**, Sharat Chandra mined the terrain of cultural bifurcation and the loss of communal ritual and custom.

Born May 3, 1935, into a prosperous family established in rural Nanjagud in Karnataka, India, G.S. Sharat Chandra was raised with literature. The family library consisted of selections from an English subscription service called the "Right Book Club," and he was raised on the classics of British literature such as Shakespeare, the Brontës, and George Bernard Shaw. He found an early inspirational figure in 1913 Nobel Laureate for Literature Rabindranath Tagore (1861–1941). Inspired by the success of his countryman and attracted to the poet's "versatility and mysticism," Sharat Chandra explored Tagore's Romantic sources in Shelley and Wordsworth, but for Chandra, writing in "their diction and language felt alien."

After he graduated with degrees in English and law from the University of Mysore, Chandra entered the civil service as a probation officer and as a private labor secretary for coffee and tea plantations. While working in the Indian countryside, Chandra took to reading **Ezra Pound** and Robert Frost. Chandra continued to find himself drawn to American poets such as **Hart Crane**, **Wallace Stevens**, and **William** Carlos Williams. Uninterested in a law career, Chandra left India to pursue a master's degree in English at the State University of New York, Oswego. However, he later earned a master's degree in law, specializing in comparative labor law, from Osgoode Hall Law School in Canada, and after obtaining the LLM. in 1966, he taught under a Law Society teaching fellowship. He came to the United States when he was twenty-seven after being accepted into the International Writing Program at the University of Iowa as its first Indian poet. Shortly after, Chandra transferred to the University of Iowa's Writer's Workshop, receiving his MFA in 1968.

Chandra credits the Writer's Workshop experience for the change in the direction of his work. Here he "shook off the lush romantic influence of Tagore" and became more influenced by "Latin American surrealists" as well as by the "open and colloquial idiom" of his favorite American poets (Vasudeva, 12). Also spurred on by the Vietnam War protests and the belief that "poetry plays a pivotal role . . . in bringing about sociopolitical changes," (Vasudeva, 12) Chandra's early work, by his own account, "was mostly about the proletarian hell in India and the Third World, from the point of view of an insider" (Vasudeva, 15). After publishing in magazines and chapbooks abroad, his first major collection, *Heirloom* (1982), featured poems that not only ponder personal dislocation, such as "In the Third Country," but also poems such as "Bangla (water-pipe) Desh," which reveals the plight of "Bengalis unnecessarily gifted away in the name of democracy" while lashing out at the gamesmanship of international diplomacy and its failure to relieve human suffering.

In 1983 Chandra settled in Missouri after joining the English Department of the University of Missouri–Kansas City as a professor of creative writing. From his vantage point in suburban middle America, Chandra treated his adopted environs as "a surreal country where I wander aimlessly and invisibly." His next book, *Family of Mirrors* (1993), reflects his poignant and ironic trials while negotiating difference as well as the cultural crossings between his Indian childhood and his life in America. The collection considers what reviewer Fred Marchant called the "double consciousness of holding on and letting go" of culture, custom, language, as well as of youth and fantasy, earning Sharat Chandra a nomination for the Pulitzer Prize for poetry.

The next shift in Sharat Chandra's poetry came from reading **Objectivist poets** such as **Robert Creeley**, **Charles Olson** and **Paul Blackburn**, from whom he drew ideas about how to "render Indian themes in a post-modern technique and voice." These are evident in his last book of poetry, *Immigrants of Loss* (1993–1994), which won both the Commonwealth Poetry Prize and the T.S. Eliot Poetry Prize. The manuscript moves through three sections documenting Sharat Chandra's journey of "looking for aimless / beginnings between streets." A 1989 Fulbright Award to Bangladesh helped facilitate the writing of the Bangladesh sequence, which provides a center for a collection of poems that finds a home in loss and "ordinary goodbyes."

Sharat Chandra published poetry steadily from the late 1960s and became a widely anthologized poet. With his last book, *Sari of the Gods* (1998), he switched to prose writing. His short story collection attracted favorable reviews in publications such as the *New York Times Book Review*. Two years later Chandra suffered a sudden brain hemorrhage after returning to Missouri from his second Fulbright award–related trip to the Indian subcontinent.

Further Reading. *Selected Primary Sources:* Chandra, G.S. Sharat, *Family of Mirrors* (Kansas City, MO: BKMK Press, 1993); ———, *Heirloom* (Oxford: Oxford

University Press, 1982); ———, *Immigrants of Loss* (Frome, UK: Hippopotamus Press, 1993–1994); ———, *Sari of the Gods* (Minneapolis, MN: Coffee House Press, 1998). **Selected Secondary Sources:** Das Kamar, Bijay, "Indian English Poetry by an Expatriate Indian: A Note on G.S. Sharat Chandra's *Heirloom*" (*Literary Half-Yearly* [January 1991]: 34–42); Marchant, Fred, "*Family of Mirrors*" (*Weber Studies* 11.2 [Spring/Summer 1994]); Miller, Philip, "*Immigrants of Loss*: The Pleasures of Mixed Prosodies" (*Literary Review* [Winter 1997]: 336–338); Vasudeva, Mary, "Swallowing for Twenty Years / the American Mind and Body": An Interview with G.S. Sharat Chandra (*Journal of Commonwealth and Postcolonial Studies* [Fall 1997]: 9–17).

Melissa Gabot Fabros

CHANNING, WILLIAM ELLERY (1780–1842)

William Ellery Channing, uncle of the poet **Ellery Channing**, led the liberal charge against New England's Puritan churches and became the intellectual and spiritual leader of the American Unitarian Church. Rejecting Calvinist doctrine on human depravity, Channing emphasized the innate divinity of the soul and found a sympathetic ear among young intellectuals like **Ralph Waldo Emerson**, who lionized him as "the star of the American church." While he never officially signed on to the movement, Channing remains a seminal figure in the emergence of American Transcendentalism, having been the first to articulate ideas that would later be adopted by **Emerson**, **Theodore Parker**, **Henry David Thoreau**, and **Margaret Fuller**. Channing's primary contribution to American poetry is in the influence his ideas have had on other writers. Both a friend and admirer of Samuel Taylor Coleridge, Channing called for "a poetry which pierces beneath the exterior of life to the depths of the soul, and which lays open its mysterious working, borrowing from the whole outward creation fresh images and correspondence, with which to illuminate the secrets of the world within us." In his "Remarks on American Literature" (1830) he argued against the ongoing English influence on American writers.

Channing was born in Newport, Rhode Island, in 1780, the second in a family of nine children. Channing's youth was marked by his parents' stern sense of duty and the conservative theology of New England Puritanism. After receiving his degree from Harvard in 1798, Channing served as a tutor in Virginia. In 1803, after a brief return to Harvard to study theology, Channing became pastor of Federal Street Church, Boston, where he would hold a post until his death in 1842. Though wary of sectarianism, Channing organized the conference of liberal Congregational ministers, which in 1825 became the American Unitarian Association.

By 1838 Transcendentalism had moved from an incipient idea into a full-blown movement. The publication of Channing's lecture *Self-Culture* had an immediate effect, and a number of its ideas were adopted by Emerson in his essay *Self-Reliance* (1841), and found their way into his poetry as well. As Channing's last major work, it outlines the process of spiritual growth and the responsibility of the individual to this process.

Channing shared many things with the Transcendentalists, including an intractable confidence in the capacity of the human soul and the conviction that materialism posed a major threat to individuals and democracy. But while sympathetic to many of the "new views," he never allowed himself to be called a Transcendentalist and expressed on numerous occasions misgivings about the mystical and pantheistic tendencies of Transcendentalism, the vagaries of Emerson's philosophy, and the extremism of **Amos Bronson Alcott** and Theodore Parker.

Likewise, the Transcendentalists had their own reservations. For Channing, reason represented the rational, studied process of differentiation and selection that enabled man to "look beyond the letter to the spirit." For the more politically minded Transcendentalists like Orestes Brownson, Channing's attention to the individual came at the cost of society, for while "self-culture is a good thing, it cannot abolish inequality, nor restore men to their rights." While the Transcendentalists were always quick to acknowledge Channing's importance, reservations about his continued influence led Emerson to comment in his journal in 1837, "Now we become so conscious of his [Channing's] limits and of the difficulty attending any effort to show him our point of view that we doubt if it will be worth while. Best amputate."

Nevertheless, Channing remains a seminal figure not only in the history of American Transcendentalism but also in the history of American letters. He was a prominent figure among the Boston intellectual elite, and many of his writings were translated into French and German during his lifetime. As a testament to his influence, collections of his works in six-volumes went through twenty-two editions by 1872, while his memoirs, published by his nephew William Henry Channing, reached ten editions by 1874.

Further Reading. *Selected Primary Sources:* *The Life of William Ellery Channing, D.D.* (Boston: American Unitarian Association, 1880); *The Works of William Ellery Channing, D.D.* (Boston: American Unitarian Association, 1891). ***Selected Secondary Sources:*** Brown, Arthur W., *Always Young for Liberty: A Biography of William Ellery Channing* (Syracuse, NY: Syracuse University Press, 1956); Mendelsohn, Jack, *Channing: The Reluctant Radical* (Boston: Little, Brown, 1971); Patterson, Robert L., *The Philosophy of William Ellery Channing* (New York: Bookman Associates, 1952).

Michael James Mahin

CHANNING, (WILLIAM) ELLERY (1817–1901)

Ellery Channing, nephew of the influential Unitarian minister **William Ellery Channing** (1817–1901), was born into New England royalty and, like his uncle, named for his great-grandfather, Rhode Island's signer of the Declaration of Independence. Though a minor poet, Channing remains an important figure within Transcendentalism as a confidante and close companion of such luminaries as **Nathaniel Hawthorne**, **Ralph Waldo Emerson**, **Henry David Thoreau**, **Amos Bronson Alcott**, and **Margaret Fuller**.

Born in Boston, Massachusetts, in 1817 to Walter Channing, professor of obstetrics at Harvard, and Barbara Perkins Channing, daughter of a wealthy mercantile family, Channing's youth was marked by his mother's death when he was five, and an intellectual exuberance and emotional moodiness that would characterize him throughout his adult life. In 1834 Channing entered Harvard but after only a few months returned home and sank into habitual idleness. During this period, which lasted almost five years, Channing made his first attempts at poetry, publishing a series of erratic poems under the pseudonym Hal Menge. After a failed attempt at homesteading in Illinois, Channing moved to Cincinnati in 1840 and that same year published his first poem in the *Dial*, a new journal edited by Emerson and Fuller. Over the next four years Channing became the journal's most frequent contributor, prompting Emerson to comment, "I have seen no verses published in America that have such inward music."

Channing's association with the literati of New England continued to grow and was secured when he met and quickly married Ellen Fuller, Margaret Fuller's sister, in 1841. Though Margaret had reservations about the engagement, she would later find in Channing a dear friend, insightfully describing him as "a great Genius with a little wretched boy trotting beside him."

This contrast between greatness and immaturity is a key characteristic not only of Channing's life but also his poetry. While Emerson found Channing's work "authentically inspired," a trait desperately lacking in American poetry, he also found his poems impatient and undisciplined. In a letter to Margaret Fuller, Emerson writes of Channing, "A true poet that child is, and nothing proves it more than his worst verses" and later to another friend, "He [Channing] has great self-possession. . . . If only he could master his negligent and impatient way of writing—this impatience of finishing, his sweet wise vein of thought and music would have no rival."

Public reception of his poetry was likewise conflicted. When Channing's first volume of poetry was published in 1843 under the title *Poems*, **Edgar Allan Poe** berated it, asserting that the book was full of mistakes "of which the most important is that of their having been printed at all," while Emerson and Thoreau, with whom he had become fast companions, recommended it to their friends.

The intuition of divinity that drove Transcendentalism to its highest metaphysical peaks was but a vague notion for Channing. Neither God nor the Transcendentalist "Oversoul" and the mystical presence of divinity ever provoked Channing's imagination, and unlike his closest friends Fuller, Emerson, and Thoreau, he believed that nature rarely points to more than itself.

Apart from the occasional examination of divinity in nature, which in his *Dial*-published poem "October" is reduced to a vague "Power," Channing preferred communion with nature, a sentiment he records in his poem "The Earth Spirit," when he writes, "I fall upon the grass like love's first kiss." As Robert Hudspeth writes, "Too interested in the immediate effect nature had on the emotions to probe metaphysics, [Channing's] curiosity stopped with phenomena; the human, not the divine, reality challenged him to write."

In his later writing, nature becomes the symbol of emotional security and stability, which, since the death of his mother and after the death of his wife, were absent from Channing's life. In his **narrative poem** *The Wanderer* (1871) autobiographical elements are thinly veiled as Channing records man's love of nature and the greater forces working against fulfillment of that **pastoral** ideal. "I hurry forward where the leafless trees / Are wrapped in silence" records a bleak winter moment in which the author nevertheless finds peace, exclaiming a few lines later, "how calm!" But the ideal crumbles under the intrusion of the "noisy train" and its "volleyed thunder on the iron rail." According to Hudspeth, *The Wanderer* realizes the values inherent in the American pastoral and stands as a climax to Channing's career. Paired with his biography of Thoreau, the two works represent a statement of his hopes and ideals about how full life could really be.

For both Emerson and Thoreau, Channing's gift was not in his poetic sense but as a friend and companion, leading Emerson to write, "I have found a true delight in his talk, and have been very sensible that there was no literature in these days up to the mark of his criticism. . . . His writing is unworthy [of] him." Thoreau characterized Channing's writing as "sublimo-slipshod" but thought so highly of his presence that he immortalized him as the "winter visitor" in *Walden*, who made "the house ring with boisterous mirth."

Of the nine books of poetry and prose that Channing published, none perhaps were as important to him as his biography of Thoreau. *Thoreau: The Poet-Naturalist* (1873) was published to mixed reviews but nevertheless stood for Channing not only as a way to honor his dear friend but also as "a note and advertisement that such a man lived—that he did brave work, which must yet be given to the world."

In 1853, unable to bear their increasing poverty and Channing's constant moodiness, his wife left, taking their four children. After two years she returned and a year later in 1856 gave birth to their fifth child. Shortly thereafter she died of consumption at the age of thirty-five. An initially caring and generous husband, by the time of his own death Channing hardly knew his own children. Having survived the deaths of all his friends and most of his contemporaries, Channing died in the home of his friend and publisher, F.B. Sandborn, where he had been living for ten years. After a sparsely attended funeral in late December 1901, Channing was buried next to Emerson and Thoreau in Sleepy Hollow Cemetery, in Concord, Massachusetts.

Further Reading. ***Selected Primary Sources:*** Channing, William Ellery, *The Collected Poems of William Ellery Channing the Younger* (Gainesville, FL: Scholars' Facsimiles, 1967); ———, *Poems of Sixty-Five Years* (Philadelphia and Concord: James Bentley, 1902); ———, *Thoreau: The Poet-Naturalist* (Boston: Goodspeed, 1902). ***Selected Secondary Sources:*** Hudspeth, Robert N., *Ellery Channing* (New York: Twayne, 1973); McGill, Frederick T., Jr., *Channing of Concord: A Life of William Ellery Channing II* (New Brunswick, NH: Rutgers University Press, 1967).

Michael James Mahin

CHAPPELL, FRED (1936–)

Raised in southern Appalachia, Fred Chappell draws extensively on its culture in his fiction and poetry, balancing this material with the wide-ranging interests of a scholar of literature. This combination of influences marks his poetry from the start, but it culminates most ambitiously and successfully in his book-length poem *Midquest* (1981), his single most significant contribution to American poetry. In contrast to that work's epic reach, he later published a book of epigrams. In fact, Chappell has explored a remarkable range of poetic forms during his career (many within *Midquest*); it is this virtuosity especially that distinguishes him from many contemporary poets, who rarely, if ever, venture beyond established **free verse** modes. A writer of dizzying comic talents, he deepens his humor with a serious register, shaping the complex voice of a moralist. Erudite without pretension, his literary criticism often champions Southern writers, including those from Appalachia. He deflects the charge of regionalism, maintaining that good poetry reveals the universal in the local.

Before he published a book of poems, Chappell wrote three novels, foreshadowing the role of narrative in much of his poetry. These early novels, however, were experimental, highly compressed, symbolic narratives. Chappell later criticized their obscurity. No less ambitious, his subsequent fiction is less cryptic in its material and manner and more committed to character and plot.

Even so, his realistic short stories and novels appear alongside various types of fantasy. In his fiction and poetry, he rarely settles into a single mode for long.

Born in Canton, a small papermill town in the North Carolina mountains, Chappell grew up working on his grandparents' farm, but by adolescence he had decided to be a writer. In 1959 he married Susan Nicholls, who appears often as muse in his poetry. They have one son, Heath. Chappell earned his BA in English from Duke University in 1961, and his MA in 1964. That year, he accepted a teaching position in the English Department at the University of North Carolina in Greensboro, assuming a major role in the MFA Writing Program after the death of **Randall Jarrell**, its most eminent teacher at the time. Chappell taught at Greensboro for forty years, retiring in 2004. From 1997 until 2002, he served as Poet Laureate of North Carolina.

Sharply critical of his early novels, Chappell expresses discontent, too, with his first collection of poetry, *The World Between the Eyes* (1971), faulting its lack of overall structure. Especially strong, however, are its long **narrative poems**, which develop the child's perspective of self within family, community, and the natural world: "The Father," "The Mother," "The World Between the Eyes," "February," "Sunday," and "The Farm"—these point to the triumphs of *Midquest*, poems centered on character, place, story. Opening his first book, "February" is an unflinching look at the communal work of hog slaughtering. It announces the poet's intention to assess hard realities, even when treating them with humor; like the child in the poem, who is "elated-drunk / with the horror." The mixed attitudes emphasize the complexity of material that Chappell never allows to devolve into mere regionalism.

A novel in 1973 followed this first collection of poems, but then Chappell launched a project that evolved into *Midquest*. *River* appeared first (1975), followed by *Bloodfire* (1978), *Wind Mountain* (1979), and *Earthsleep* (1980). The four books, representing the four elements, comprise one poem in the single volume *Midquest* (1981). In 1985 he shared the Bollingen Prize with **John Ashbery**, an ironic pairing. In his short preface to *Midquest*, Chappell declares his poem "to some degree a reactionary work" (x), one that does not automatically embrace "contemporary idiom" and "post-**Symbolist** advances in sensibility" (xi), although he can excel in both categories. Rather, in *Midquest* he seeks to recover qualities mainly lost to the contemporary poetry of his time: "detachment, social scope, humor, portrayal of character and background, discursiveness, wide range of subject matter" (x). Set against the example of Ashbery, Chappell resists **postmodern** dithering over what language signifies.

Like Dante, Chappell's speaker wakes up in the middle of his life and assesses his place in the cosmos. He covers the same day in each of the four books, his thirty-fifth birthday contemplated each time by way of a different element. This alignment with the ancient notion of the four elements puts the speaker's quest into the larger context of the search for meaning throughout human history. Readers will note many influences, some acknowledged by Chappell in his preface: "Chaucer, Dryden, Browning, Horace, John Gay, Byron, Hebbel" and fiction writers "Chekhov and Mann as always, but also **Sarah Orne Jewett** and Mary Wilkins Freeman" (x–xi).

The poem has the high seriousness of Dante but also the rollicking look at human nature found in Chaucer. Technically, it spans the range of poetic inventiveness. But the stakes are high; the poem is not merely gaming with language. The speaker, sometimes referred to as "Ole Fred" or "Uncle Body," a sort of everyman, quakes at mortality and looks for consolation. He turns, however, not only to literary and philosophical sources for direction but also to the folk tale and family narrative of Appalachian culture. "My Grandmother Washes Her Feet" carries the same authority as "In Parte Ove Non E Che Luca," an imitation of a canto by Dante.

Although subsequent collections do not have the scope of *Midquest*, they confirm Chappell's deft handling of verse forms, his double allegiance to the worlds of academic learning and folk culture, and his experimental tendency. A mix of genres (including allegory, fairy tale, Gothic tale, and science fiction fantasy), *Castle Tzingal* (1984) develops mainly through dramatic monologues from its various characters. Often as daunting as his early fiction in its symbolic method, the poem's essential story examines moral corruption and redemption. As the title *Source* (1985) connotes, the quest for meaning drives his next book, less sanguine than *Midquest*. Dark fantasy elements disturb, as do folk tale material with overtones of the Brothers Grimm. Three prayers appear in the opening section and a prayer concludes the volume, but in between, bitter meditations plumb the depths of human nature and destiny. *First and Last Words* (1989) provides some antidote to the anguish of *Source*. Most of its poems function as prologues or epilogues to major works of literature, art, music, philosophy, religion, and science. The learned persona of Fred Chappell evaluates and honors the power of human imagination to transform and elevate life, but he keeps the project on home ground as in the narrative poem, "An Old Mountain Woman Reading the Book of Job." With *C* in 1993, Chappell celebrated the compression of urbane epigrams (one hundred of them), counterweight to the Appalachian storytelling energy of his other books. Mastering such divergent methods, he exemplifies an active and flexible poetic intelligence.

Spring Garden: New and Selected Poems appeared in 1995, but Chappell has published two collections since that retrospective volume. He acknowledges *Family Gathering* (2000) as a sort of vacation into lighter material, but his portraits of a fictional "family" delight with their pithy analysis of human character. Far from lightweight, *Backsass* (2004) exploits contemporary idiom and idiocy in a fractious voice that finds its most sustained expression in two long epistles of rhyming couplets, imitations of the Roman poet Juvenal. These classically derived dissections of contemporary mores situate the entire book within the larger context of the rise and fall of civilizations. This most recent collection also reminds one of Chappell's citizenship in two worlds: the learned realm suggested here by ancient Roman satire, as well as the folk culture implied by "backsass," satire's Appalachian analogue.

Further Reading. *Selected Primary Sources:* Chappell, Fred, *Backsass* (Baton Rouge: Louisiana State University Press, 2004); ———, *Bloodfire* (Baton Rouge: Louisiana State University Press, 1978); ———, *C* (Baton Rouge: Louisiana State University Press, 1993); ———, *Castle Tzingal* (Baton Rouge: Louisiana State University Press, 1984); ———, *Earthsleep* (Baton Rouge: Louisiana State University Press, 1980); ———, *Family Gathering* (Baton Rouge: Louisiana State University Press, 2000); ———, *First and Last Words* (Baton Rouge: Louisiana State University Press, 1989); ———, *Midquest* (Baton Rouge: Louisiana State University Press, 1981); ———, *River* (Baton Rouge: Louisiana State University Press, 1975); ———, *Source* (Baton Rouge: Louisiana State University Press, 1985); ———, *Spring Garden: New and Selected Poems* (Baton Rouge: Louisiana State University Press, 1995); ———, *Wind Mountain* (Baton Rouge: Louisiana State University Press, 1979); ———, *The World Between the Eyes* (Baton Rouge: Louisiana State University Press, 1971). *Selected Secondary Sources:* Bizzaro, Patrick, ed., *Dream Garden: The Poetic Vision of Fred Chappell* (Baton Rouge: Louisiana State University Press, 1997); Lang, John. *Understanding Fred Chappell* (Columbia: University of South Carolina Press, 2000).

James M. Smith, Jr.

CHICANO POETRY

A discussion of Chicano poetry entails a discussion of Mexican American poetry, for Chicano poetry is but a "blip" in the literary history of Mexican Americans, whose literary production as Mexican Americans began in 1848, following the Treaty of Guadalupe Hidalgo, signed on February 2, 1848, which ended the U.S. war against Mexico (1846–1848). Mexicans who came with the dismembered territory brought with them a literary tradition that, from their Spanish forebears, stretched back to the beginnings of Spanish literature and had its roots in the Greco-Roman world. From their indigenous forebears, the literary tradition of Mexican Americans stretched back to the Mayan books of Chilam Balam (the book of the Jaguar Priest), long before the arrival of the Spaniards and the beginning of Aztec hegemony in the thirteenth century A.D. (Ortego, 1971a). Like the British roots in the new American soil, the Hispanic literary roots have yielded a vigorous and dynamic body of literature, which historically has been studied as part of a foreign enterprise rather than as part and parcel of an American heritage. Mexican American literature, its roots and traditions, constitute the forgotten pages of American literature.

As part of that tradition, Chicano poetry began in tandem with the Chicano movement, an ontological revolution that began circa 1960 and blossomed between 1966 and 1975, the years of the Chicano Renaissance (Ortego, 1971b), the period of its greatest efflorescence, much like the flowering of black poetry during the **Harlem Renaissance**. This is not to say that Chicano poetry defoliated in 1975. Far from it. This was just the period of greatest growth. As a consequence of this boom in the genre, the poetry of Chicanos continues the metaphoric characterization of this group as a diasporic people searching for their identity in the land of their forebears that treats them as strangers (Salazar, 1969).

The period of the Chicano movement was essentially one during which Mexican Americans, having grown weary of "searching for America," cast aside the expectations that the United States would "do right" by them. Instead, they proclaimed themselves agents of their own change. Chicano literature was percolating in the cauldron of Chicano nationalism and hammering out its agenda to identify the enemy, promote the revolution, and praise the people. That in its incunabula many of the early works of Chicano literature were inspired by ideology did not lessen the expectations among many Chicanos that the responsibilities of Chicano writers were ultimately to fashion a literature so essentially Chicano that it stood on its own merits apart from other literatures. As this literature emerged from the cauldron of Chicano nationalism, some Chicanos saw its role as reflecting Chicano life and values and drawing from a distinctively Chicano imagination. Like the disciples of Senchan Torpeist, the Irish poet of myth, who were sent out to recover the whole of the Tain—the great Irish saga—which none of them could remember entirely, Chicano writers were the disciples through whom the lost literary inheritance of the people would be recovered (Ortego, 2001). They would be the stewards of a Chicano message that had to be written down, explained, and defended as one would defend a beloved daughter.

The terms "Mexican American" and "Chicano/a" are interchangeable, but only to a point. Mexican Americans are the Mexicans who became Americans by fiat per the terms of the Treaty of Guadalupe Hidalgo that annexed more than half of Mexico's territory as a spoil of the U.S. war against Mexico. "Chicanos" was a pejorative term for "low-life" Mexicans. Just as many African Americans embraced the term "black" as a self-identifier, so too Mexican Americans embraced the term "Chicano." Originally, the term was meant to promote the concept of *Chicanismo* (brotherhood) among Mexican Americans. However, with the growth of the Chicano movement, the term became more ideologically laden. Thus, a Chicano/a is likely to be a Mexican American, but a Mexican American is not necessarily a Chicano/a.

Chicano poetry draws its images and metaphors from the social conditions of Chicano existence, which are viewed by Chicano poets as simply extensions of ancient settings and origins (Ortego, 1979). But the metaphor of Chicano existence is woven linguistically into the fabric of the political context in which the Chicano poet finds himself or herself. That is, in order to assert his or her ethnic identity in a context that seeks to eradicate that identity, the Chicano poet must marshal for Chicanos the splendor of their antiquity and show how that antiquity bears directly on the Chicano present. In "Aztec Angel," for example, **Luis Omar Salinas** welds the present to the past. He is "an Aztec angel," he tells us, criminal of a scholarly society doing favors for whimsical magicians where he pawns his heart for truth and finds his way through obscure streets of soft-spoken hara-kiris. "I am an Aztec angel / offspring / of a woman / who was beautiful." There is a defiant emphasis on the words.

Chicano poetry portends a shift from mainstream American poetry to a distinctively new **poetics** that embraces politics and sociology as well as new linguistic parameters, as evident in Alurista's (Alberto Urista's) "Mis ojos hinchados," one of the earliest productions of Chicano binary poetry, a mixture of Spanish and English sententially alternated, as linguistics describe the phenomenon: "Mis ojos hinchados / flooded with lagrimas / de bronce / melting on the cheek bones / of my concern." The binary line strengthens the binary metaphor, fusing English and Spanish in a logically concatenated or syntactically appropriate "string" to produce the intrasentential image. Spoken, this code switching is often referred to pejoratively as "Spanglish." But this binary phenomenon reflects the linguistic reality of Chicanos. Chicano writers, and Chicano poets in particular, have used code switching extensively in their works, demonstrating their identity as Chicanos and throwing down a gauntlet challenging the mainstream literary establishment.

This was the genesis of Chicano literature, its writers thumbing their noses at the mainstream literary venues that excluded them. In 1967 a cohort of Chicanos at Berkeley led by Octavio Romano organized *Quinto Sol* Publications to publish *El Grito: Journal of Mexican American Thought*, the first effort to create independent Chicano venues for Chicano writers. In that first volume of *El Grito* the editorial was actually a manifesto challenging the rejection of Mexican American writers by Anglo-American mainstream presses and their stereotyped works on Mexican Americans. In fact, "[o]nly Mexican Americans themselves can accomplish the collapse of" those pernicious rhetorical structures (Romano, i). The result was a rash of Chicano publications serving as countertexts to the mainstream texts that denigrated Chicanos through the misuse of social data, stereotype, and racial clichés. *El Grito* became the frontline publication of the Chicano Renaissance, "a forum for Mexican American self definition" (ibid.). By 1975 the *Premio Quinto Sol* for literature, awarded by the publisher of *El Grito*, became the most coveted prize in Chicano letters. A flood of ephemeral Chicano publications (mostly garage presses) emerged to give voice to Chicano letters, especially Chicano poetry.

In Chicano poetry, the epic poem "I Am Joaquin" by Rodolfo "Corky" Gonzalez, first published in 1967, became the hallmark of the genre. Joaquin became the Chicano everyman caught in the existential dilemma of identity: Is he Spanish? Indian? He realizes he is both. Despite the odds, as the embodiment of *la raza* (the people), he cries out at the end of the poem that he "shall endure" as the offspring of both Spaniard and Indian. For too long, society had foisted a choice on him, either/or, most often falling on the side of the Spanish, despite how John Steinbeck saw them—the color of a brown, well-polished meerschaum pipe (Ortego, 1973a). Then, as if to dispel any ambiguity about his survival, he says, "I will endure," changing the "possible" to an "imperative." It was in this declaration that Chicano poets found succor.

No poet of the early wave of Chicano poets is more reminiscent of **Walt Whitman** than Ricardo Sanchez (*Canto y grito my liberación*, 1971), to whom has been applied the sobriquet "poet laureate of Aztlan"—the mythical homeland of the Aztecs, said to be somewhere in what is now the Hispanic Southwest of the United States. In asserting their territorial priority in the construct of what is now the United States, Chicanos sought to "recover" their historical past by embracing the metaphor of Aztlan as a land of their own, a kind of Chicano Camelot, and by creating a history to believe in. These were not fabrications out of thin air. They were ideological constructs in the Chicano armory of survival. A literature draws from the history and myths of its people's past, and Chicanos turned to their Indian past for their most meaningful symbols and metaphors. More important, perhaps, the Chicano movement provided Chicano writers with the impetus to declare for themselves who they were and to challenge the mainstream's contention of who Chicanos were.

In this regard, one of the most remarkable poems of the Chicano movement and of the twentieth century, Abelardo Delgado's poem "Stupid America," best represents the angst of Chicano existence at the threshold of Chicano liberation in the 1960s (Ortego, 2004). In the fashion of Robert Browning, the persona of the poem speaks to Anglo-Americans. Like Emile Zola, Delgado berates them for their myopia toward Chicanos, for their failure to recognize the inherent artistry of a Chicanito standing with "a big knife / in his steady hand" instead of a paintbrush because "Stupid America" won't let him be who he can be, seeing him only as a threatening alien ragamuffin who has crossed its borders without benefit of documents. "Fear of the other," as Anna Quindlen aptly puts it, "is an enduring human handicap" (74). Or as Jose Limón informs us, "one of the mechanisms through which colonizers achieve a racial-cultural domination of colonized populations" is stereotype, "a process that parallels and reinforces the political and economic forms of domination" (259).

Unlike the work of Ricardo Sanchez, the avenging angel of Chicano poetry, in Abelardo Delgado's poetry there is a cosmic simplicity and, at times, an ineffable sadness about the plight of Chicanos facing an array of formidable forces opposing their upward mobility. Sanchez and Delgado were pivotal poets who vented the anger of the Chicano community in a range of protest poetry that Francisco Lomelí calls "instigative poetry with strong political overtones" (289). Two other Chicano poets of the time have also left their imprint on the genre: Jose Montoya (*El Sol y los de Abajo*, 1972) and Tino Villanueva (*Hay Otra Voz Poems*, 1972).

Like Sanchez and Delgado, Montoya produced poetry reflective principally of the Chicano experience. Villanueva, on the other hand, began his poetic efforts in the vein of what is commonly called "Movement poetry" (Ortego, 1973) but has since transcended that moment—not as an apostate but experientially. He writes now from an international Chicano vista, principally in Spanish, and in 1994 he received an American Book Award for his book of poems in English *Scene from the Movie Giant*.

Mexican American women have generated a profusion of Chicana poetry since the 1960s, inter alia Angela de Hoyos (*Arise Chicano and Other Poems*, 1975), Bernice Zamora (*Restless Serpents*, 1976), Ana Castillo (*Otro Canto*, 1977), Olivia Castellano (*Blue Mandolin, Yellow Field*, 1980), Cheri Moraga (*Living in the War Years*, 1983), Teresa Paloma Acosta (*Passing Time*, 1984), Naomi Quiñones (*Sueños de Colibri*, 1985). There are hundreds of Chicano and Chicana poets working in the genre today, which is surprising considering the current paucity of American poets and the general decline of poetry as a public medium of literary expression.

Currently, the most prominent Chicano/a poets are **Gary Soto** (*Elements of San Joaquin,* 1977), who works successfully "within the boundaries of Anglo-American literary conventions" and who has been compared to **T.S. Eliot; Alberto Rios** (*Whispering to Fool the Wind,* 1982), one of the "most technically sophisticated and complex" of the Chicano poets; Raul Salinas (*East of the Freeway,* 1995); Rosemary Catacalos (*As Long as it Takes,* 1984); Carmen Tafolla (*Curandera,* 1983), whose poetry is "rooted in a collective identity"; and **Pat Mora** (*Borders,* 1986). Perhaps because Chicana poets were overlooked and excluded early on from Chicano poetry, they have furiously eclipsed their male counterparts in the production of Chicano/a poetry. That production is a testament to their ardor and motivation and may be a cultural vestige from the years of the Conquest generation (1848–1912), when poetry was the paramount medium of cultural production for Mexican Americans.

Today Chicano poetry is grounded in language and culture and may or may not be anchored to ideology. Before 1960 most Mexican American poetry reflected the **pastoral** form and nostalgic function of mainstream Mexican poetry or mainstream American poetry, however much the latter rejected Mexican American literary production (Ortego, 1972). Since World War II Mexican American poetry has been transformed into Chicano poetry, full of the *sturm und drang* of the Chicano movement, repudiating American and Western aesthetics and touting the uniquely "binary line" in which both English and Spanish are mixed in syntactical structures.

Today more mainstream outlets are publishing the work of Chicano poets, but only those who satisfy the requirements of mainstream standards. This suggests that Chicano/a poets are part of a mold that produces only politically correct cookie-cutter poetry. This is far wide of the mark, for Chicano poets are not a homogeneous or monolithic group. They are poets who happen to be Chicano/a and who may or may not be poetic anarchists. That is, as with poets everywhere, one cannot put them all into one box. Like all literatures, Chicano literature is evolving day by day into what it will become. What that is, *quien sabe?*

Further Reading. Limón, Jose, "Stereotyping and Chicano Resistance" (*Aztlan: Journal of Chicano Studies* 4.2 [1974]); Lomelí, Francisco, "An Overview of Chicano Letters: From Origins to Resurgence," in *Chicano Studies: Survey and Analysis* (Dubuque, IA: Kendall/Hunt, 1997); Ortego y Gasca, Felipe de (Philip D. Ortego), *Backgrounds of Mexican American Literature* (Ph.D. diss., University of New Mexico, 1971a); ———, "Chicano Poetry: Roots and Writers" (*Southwestern American Literature* [Spring 1972] [presented at the first symposium of Chicano Literature and Critical Theory, Pan American University, Edinburg, Texas, November 1971]); ———, "The Chicano Renaissance" (*Journal of Social Casework* [May 1971b]); ———, "Fables of Identity: Stereotype and Caricature of Chicanos in Steinbeck's *Tortilla Flat*" (*Journal of Ethnic Studies* 1 [1973]); ———, "A Fire in the Heart: Abelardo Delgado–The People's Poet" *El Paso Times Online* [August 1, 2004]; ———, "Introduction to Chicano Poetry" in *Modern Chicano Writers: Twentieth Century Views* (New York: Prentice-Hall, 1979); ———, "The Labyrinth and the Minotaur: Chicano Literature and Critical Theory" (*Aztlan: Journal of Chicano Studies* [Spring 2001]); ———, ed., *We Are Chicanos: Anthology of Mexican American Literature* (New York: Washington Square Press, 1973); Quindlen, Anna, "Separate, Not Equal at All" (*Newsweek* [May 2, 2005]); Romano, Octavio V., ed., *El Grito: A Journal of Mexican American Thought* (1.1 [Spring 1968]); Salazar, Rubén, *Strangers in Their Own Land* (U.S. Commission on Civil Rights Clearing House Publication No. 19, May 1970).

Felipe de Ortego y Gasca

CHILD, LYDIA MARIA (1802–1880)

During the nineteenth century, American periodicals increased in number. Poetry and prose, fiction and nonfiction were popular, and Lydia Maria Child wrote extensively in all genres. Her numerous publications include the novel *Hobomok, A Tale of Early Times* (1824); the advice book *The Frugal Housewife* (1829); and the abolitionist work *An Appeal in Favor of That Class of Americans Called Africans* (1833). She also published children's literature, including *The Juvenile Miscellany* (1826–1834) and *Flowers for Children* (1844–46), each containing some of her poetry. Her poems also appeared in *The Coronal* (1832), *Letters from New York* (1843, 1845), and *Autumnal Leaves* (1857). Child's literary career spanned approximately fifty-five years, a period of turmoil in U.S. history and one that also encompassed some of the most significant intellectual and social movements of the period. The Romantic movement dominated poetry of the first two-thirds of the century, and much of Child's poetry shows its effects. Emanuel Swedenborg's ideas were also prevalent among many nineteenth-century American women poets, and Child adapted many of his concepts.

Lydia Maria Francis Child was born February 11, 1802, in Medford, Massachusetts. She had very little formal education, but after her mother's death and her move to Norridgewock, Maine Territory, she attended summer classes offered by students at Bowdoin College. Under the guidance of her brother, Convers Francis, a Unitarian minister, she also studied literature. Her sojourn in Norridgewock exposed her to the Native Americans' plight as well as the injustices of slavery, causes that she espoused throughout her life. She also taught school in Maine and in 1825 opened a girls' school in Massachusetts; concurrently, she published two novels, *Hobomok* and *The Rebels.* In 1826 she began *The Juvenile Miscellany*, a bimonthly magazine for children. It folded in 1834, when her anti-slavery stance cost her many subscribers. In 1828 she had married David Lee Child, lawyer, journalist, and impractical idealist. Ultimately, Child's writing supported them. She published extensively in periodicals, as well as publishing domestic advice books and anthologies of her prose and verse.

Child's marriage was not a success. David Child was imprisoned for libel of a state senator; his law practice disintegrated; and the *Massachusetts Weekly Journal* (variant titles), which he edited, failed. The Childs supported **William Lloyd Garrison** and the abolitionist movement, especially during the 1830s and 1840s. Child wrote anti-slavery tracts, pamphlets, and books. Simultaneously, David Child pursued poorly conceived ventures and even borrowed money from Child's father to buy a farm and grow sugar beets. Nothing succeeded. Finally, Child and her husband separated when, in 1841, she accepted the editorship of the *National Anti-Slavery Standard* in New York City, which she edited until 1843. She remained there and published *Letters from New York*, but in 1849 the couple reconciled and soon moved to her father's home in Wayland, Massachusetts. They lived a frugal, retired life, although Child continued to write and once again took up the abolitionist cause. David Child died in 1874, but Lydia lived there until her death, on October 20, 1880.

Although Child's poetry is less familiar than her prose, "A New-England Boy's Song About Thanksgiving Day," in *Flowers for Children II*, stands out with its familiar lines "Over the river and through the wood, / To grandfather's house we go." Each volume of *Flowers for Children* targets a particular age group. Volume 2, for children eight or nine years old, contains poems such as "The Spring Birds" and "Father Is Coming." Volume 3, for children eleven or twelve years old, introduces more complex topics, as in "The Hen and Her Ducks," in which a hen tries to rear a chick like a duckling. Most of Child's poetry is unsubstantial but charming. For example, in the Wordsworthian "To the Fringed Gentian," Child uses natural imagery to teach that "Thus buds of virtue often bloom / The fairest, mid the deepest gloom. / ... / To ripen in affliction's gleam." It appeared under varying titles in *The Juvenile Miscellany* (1828), the *Massachusetts Weekly Journal* (1828), and, finally, *The Coronal.*

Not all of Child's poetry was for children. "Lines, To Those Men and Women, Who Were Avowed Abolitionists in 1831, '32, '33, '34, and '35" lauds the abolitionists (*The Liberty Bell* for 1839). "Lines, Suggested by a Lock of Hair from Our Departed Friend, Catherine Sargent" eulogizes her fellow abolitionist (*The Liberty Bell* for 1856). Moreover, *Autumnal Leaves* contains six of her poems interspersed between the prose. The last piece, "The Kansas Emigrants," her powerful argument against

slavery in Kansas, is followed by the poem "I Want to Go Home." The narrator, musing on a child's premature death, laments, "Father! I'm *tired.* I want to go *home.*" Several poems are also included in the two series of *Letters from New York*, including one welcoming the return of Ole Bul, a violinist with whom Child became infatuated (*Second Series*). As a whole, Child's poetry employs conventional, sometimes simple rhythms and rhymes, frequently uses couplets, and just as frequently uses a four-line rhyming stanza (*abab, cd cd, . . .*). She avoids dense and complex diction and figures of speech in favor of a straightforward presentation of ideas. Her poetry demands little of its reader, but frequently leaves a charming impression.

Child wrote in many genres, but she was always guided by a democratic impulse advocating equality for all human beings. She marketed her works with a keen understanding of her audience and was one of the most prolific and renowned nineteenth-century American women writers. Although her poetry is little remembered, its charm and simplicity appealed to young and old, and the didactic poems for youth cloak their moral lessons within natural images and simple narrative. The sum total of her work renders her well deserving of William Lloyd Garrison's commendation naming her "the first woman in the republic."

Further Reading.   *Selected Primary Sources:* Child, Lydia Maria, *Autumnal Leaves: Tales and Sketches in Prose and Rhyme* (New York: C.S. Francis, 1857); ———, *The Coronal: A Collection of Miscellaneous Pieces, Written at Various Times* (Boston: Carter and Hendee, 1832); ———, *Flowers for Children, I, II, III* (New York: Charles S. Francis, 1844, 1844, 1847); ———, *The Juvenile Miscellany* (Boston: John Putnam, 1826–1834); ———, *Letters From New York, First Series* (New York: Charles S. Francis, 1843); ———, *Letters From New York, Second Series* (New York: Charles S. Francis, 1845). ***Selected Secondary Sources:*** Karcher, Carolyn L., *The First Woman in the Republic: A Cultural Biography of Lydia Maria Child* (Durham: Duke University Press, 1994); Osborne, William S., *Lydia Maria Child* (Boston: Twayne, 1980); Yellin, Jean-Fagan, *Women and Sisters: The Anti-Slavery Feminists in American Culture* (New Haven, CT: Yale University Press, 1989).

Mary Rose Kasraie

CHILDREN'S POETRY

English-language children's poetry in the United States has a rich history. It begins with the largely religious and didactic poetry of the European settlers of the seventeenth and eighteenth centuries, continues on to the rhymed narrative and light verse of the nineteenth century, and extends to more stylistically varied contemporary verse. Contemporary poetry, composed predominantly of secular work, is sometimes socially conscious, sometimes bawdy and nonsensical, sometimes didactic, and sometimes designed simply to delight and entertain.

The poetry read by eighteenth-century American children was diverse and included imported English poetry, such as Isaac Watts's *Divine Songs, Attempted in Easy Language for the Use of Children* (1715). Furthermore, children chanted and recited less religious (and often subversive) street cries and nursery rhymes. These they learned from parents, inexpensive chapbooks, and the oral folk traditions of their peers. However, the best-known and (though still indebted to English influence) most obviously American children's text is probably *The New England Primer*. First printed in Boston by Protestant dissenter Benjamin Harris in the 1690s, *The Primer* is a miscellany of poetry and poetical writings supporting New England Puritan values.

The most famous of *The Primer*'s contents is undoubtedly its rhymed alphabet, containing the oft-cited couplet "In *Adam's* Fall / We Sinned all." *The Primer* also includes lists like "The Dutiful Child's Promises," which strike contemporary ears as poetry, as do the various prayers and catechisms that appear throughout its many editions. The oldest surviving copy of *The Primer* is dated at 1727, although advertisements suggest it may have been in publication as early as the late 1680s. For over one hundred years *The Primer* was the dominant tool for teaching Anglo-American children to read, and, outside of English translations of the Christian Bible, it functioned as the American child's primary introduction to poetry. Millions of copies of *The Primer* were printed in its day, each printer revising its contents somewhat. Nevertheless, early editions are now scarce, probably due to its poor production quality and the rough handling of its child readers.

The American Revolution ushered in increasingly secular primers, such as Noah Webster's *A Grammatical Institute of the English Language* (1783) and, even later, *The Illuminated American Primer* (1844), which couches its still Protestant alphabet in overtly nationalistic images, including the rhyme "U is for Union,—this the good will approve: / V is for Virtue,—which I hope you will love." Within the shape of the letter U stands both a virtuous George Washington and a fluttering flag.

A boom in the publication of periodicals for children marked the nineteenth century; *The Youth's Companion* (1827) and *St. Nicholas* (1873) were among the most popular. Found in such magazines are a flood of domestically produced poems and rhymes, often composed by women. Predominant children's poets of this period include **Clement Clarke Moore**, to whom authorship of "A Visit from St. Nicholas" is commonly ascribed, although this belief has recently been cast into doubt by Don Foster, who suggests that poet Henry Livingston, Jr., is more likely the author. Another well-known children's poet, Eliza Lee Follen, collected *Little Songs, for Little Boys and Girls* (1833), a book that includes the popular "Three Little Kittens" (who "lost their mittens"), often erroneously attributed to her. **Sarah Josepha Hale** penned the celebrated (and often parodied) "Mary's Lamb," found in her *Poems for Our Children Designed for Families, Sabbath Schools and Infant Schools* (1830). Hale is also well known for editing the periodical *Juvenile Miscellany*, in which Mary and her famous lamb first appeared.

The line between poetry for adults and poetry for children blurred in nineteenth-century America, a state of affairs that would recur in the 1950s and 1960s, when poets like **Randall Jarrell** and **Theodore Roethke**, heavily influenced by nursery rhymes and fairy tales, composed works that resist easy classification. Well-known nineteenth-century poets like **William Cullen Bryant**, **Oliver Wendell Holmes**, **Henry Wadsworth Longfellow**, **James Russell Lowell**, **John Greenleaf Whittier**, and even **Edgar Allan Poe** produced adult poetry that was nonetheless deemed appropriate for children. Longfellow's "The Children's Hour" and Poe's "The Bells," for instance, are commonly appropriated by children and those who collect verse for them. The work of these nineteenth-century luminaries appeared regularly in periodicals produced for children.

Late-nineteenth-century children's poets in America favored nonsense, had a predilection for natural settings and animal characters, and aimed for a lightness of tone that would remain the norm until the mid-twentieth century. **Eugene Field** and Laura E. Richards wrote some of the period's most striking poems. Richards, who received the Pulitzer Prize for *Julia Ward Howe, 1819–1910* (1915), is best remembered for her last collection of verse, *Tirra Lirra: New Rhymes and Old* (1932), an overview of her career. Other poets of this period include Mary E. Wilkins Freeman, **Edith M. Thomas**, and Katherine Pyle.

Most poets writing verse for children during the first half of the twentieth century shared the aesthetic sensibilities of those in the previous century; **Sara Teasdale**, Elizabeth Madox Roberts, Elizabeth Coatsworth, and David McCord were among the most famous of those century-bridging poets. However, the experimental spirit of **modernism** did influence children's poetry to some degree. **Carl Sandburg**, famous for his rambling, rambunctious lines and marvelous *Rootabaga Stories* (1920), brought populist politics and a Whitmanesque poetic to children's poetry in 1930 with *Early Moon*, a lively collection set apart by Sandburg's frank "Short Talk on Poetry" that opens the volume. Composed in unrhymed **free verse** that embraces political subjects unflinchingly, the poems in *Early Moon* are quite different from most of the verse written for children at the time. "Street Window" is a characteristic piece, beginning "The pawn-shop man knows hunger."

Langston Hughes published *The Dream Keeper* in 1932. Like Sandburg, Hughes questions common assumptions regarding what is appropriate for children. *The Dream Keeper* includes ambiguous poems about death, old age, poverty, love, and, as the title suggests, dreams. Less formally experimental is **Countee Cullen**, who, like Hughes, is associated with the **Harlem Renaissance**. Though not written for children, Cullen's melancholy "Incident" is commonly anthologized for them. However, Cullen also wrote poetry especially for children. His *The Lost Zoo* (1940), which is more conventional children's fare, features nonsensical, rhymed verses involving fantastic, pre-diluvian animals.

Like Hughes, modernist **Gertrude Stein** questions mainstream conceptions of children's poetry. Her *The World Is Round* (1939) is a wildly experimental and underappreciated children's book. Although it can be read as an extended prose poem, *The World Is Round* also features more conventional, lined poetry, most famously the lines "I am Rose my eyes are blue / I am Rose and who are you." Stein also wrote a poetic alphabet book for children, *To Do: A Book of Alphabets and Birthdays*, which remained unpublished until 1959. Like much of Stein's work, *To Do* crackles with an energized mix of lined and **prose poetry**: "And that is the end of the sad story of N which is not as sad as the story of M which is much sadder and badder, of course it is." Stein wrote *The World Is Round* at the suggestion of Margaret Wise Brown, known for her publication work for the Bank Street School of Education. Although widely acknowledged as a capable picture book author, Brown is less commonly acknowledged as the fine poet she is. Counting among her influences Stein and Virginia Woolf (1882–1941), Brown crafts delicate, musical verse that suggests her experimental roots and is extraordinarily popular with children, as these lines from *Goodnight Moon* (1947) demonstrate: "And a comb and a brush and a bowl full of mush / And a quiet old lady whispering hush."

Another modernist, **Thomas Stearns Eliot**—nicknamed Old Possum by **Ezra Pound**—also tried his hand at children's poetry, composing *Old Possum's Book of Practical Cats* in 1939. Less formally experimental than Stein's work, Eliot's text features irrepressible characters like Macavity, a criminal cat who is "called the hidden paw / For he's the master criminal who can defy the law." Poet and artist Edward Gorey, who masterfully illustrated a regularly republished 1982 edition, played a role in invigorating *Old Possum*'s reputation, as did Andrew Lloyd Webber's immensely popular adaptation, *Cats*, playing from 1981 to 2002 in London and from 1982 to 2000 in New York. Perhaps no single book of children's poetry has proved as profitable or influential.

The publication of *The Cat in the Hat* (1957) by Dr. Seuss (**Theodor Seuss Geisel**), and *The Reason for the Pelican* (1959) by **John Ciardi** heralds an important change in both the market for and perspective on children's poetry in the United States. These poets, along with poet and illustrator Maurice Sendak, added a little vinegar to the oversweet verse common in the 1940s and 1950s. They reminded readers that children are sometimes naughty, even vicious people who delight in bad behavior and humorous verse devoid of moral or lesson, thereby paving the way for later poets like Jack Prelutsky and Shel Silverstein. Ciardi's wit and verbal skill often took aim at his child readers, mocking them playfully in poems like "Sleepless Beauty," concerning "a girl who never went to bed," ending "Some people might tell you, 'Well, now, serves her right!' / But what *I* feel most is: she just wasn't bright." Never cruel, Ciardi delights his readers by treating them as equals, by mocking and teasing as if he were one of the gang, evoking the tropes and commonplaces of childhood playground rhymes. Many of his books are illustrated by Gorey, his former student.

The late 1950s and early 1960s saw many adult poets begin to write for children: **Gwendolyn Brooks**, **Sylvia Plath**, William Jay Smith **May Swenson**, **Richard Wilbur**, and the aforementioned Ciardi, Jarrell, and Roethke. That these respected poets found the composition of poetry for children an aesthetically rewarding and professionally acceptable enterprise suggests that children's poetry was beginning to be taken seriously as literature. Doubtless the end of World War II had a great deal to do with this invigorated interest in childhood. As incomes grew, middle-class Americans began spending more on household goods and the children inhabiting those households. This period ushered in the youth market and the very notion of a youth culture.

Robert Frost got his start in children's poetry; before the publication of his first book, three of his early poems were published by *The Youth's Companion*: "Ghost House" (1906), "October" (1912), and "Reluctance" (1912). However, it was not until 1959 that Frost published *You Come Too: Favorite Poems for Young People*, his first and only book especially for children. After the publication of this book, Frost quickly became what might be called the United States' official school poet. His poems are regularly collected in children's poetry anthologies and commented upon in education textbooks. "Stopping by Woods on a Snowy Evening" remains one of the most commonly taught poems in U.S. schools. The edition illustrated by Susan Jeffers is a perennial winter favorite. Many of the adult poets who began writing for children during the late 1950s and early 1960s are closely associated with Frost. **X.J. Kennedy**, for instance, became a strong advocate for and writer of children's poetry, commenting on the subject in essays and editing with his wife, Dorothy Kennedy, *Knock at a Star* (1982 and 1999) and *Talking*

Like the Rain (1992), two successful anthologies of children's poetry. **Donald Hall**, one of the editors of the poetically conservative *New Poets of England and America* (1957)—for which Frost wrote an introduction—also edited the impressive *Oxford Book of Children's Poetry in America* (1985). He later refashioned this scholarly edition into a collection marked for young children, calling it *The Oxford Illustrated Book of American Children's Poems* (1999).

The more formally experimental poets of the 1960s also grew interested in writing for children and teaching them to write. **New York School** poets **Kenneth Koch** and **Ron Padgett**, for example, were active in the Teachers and Writers Collaborative, a landmark poets-in-the-schools program. Koch, Padgett's teacher at Columbia, wrote a pair of seminal works about teaching children poetry: *Wishes, Lies, and Dreams* (1970) and its companion anthology of poetry by children, *Rose, Where Did You Get That Red?* (1973). Over the next several decades, these books would spark much debate on how poetry should be taught to children, Koch's position that children are "natural poets" tackled most strenuously by Myra Cohn Livingston. However, Koch did not limit himself to teaching, for in 1985 he and Kate Farrell would edit *Talking to the Sun: An Illustrated Anthology of Poems for Young People.*

The late 1960s and early 1970s in the United States saw an unprecedented interest in poetic experimentation. This openness to new forms set the stage for the acceptance of **visual poetry**, a kind of verse in which the boundary between word and image is blurred or erased. Although visual poetry, or, as poet/critic Dick Higgins calls it, *pattern poetry*, has a long and complex history, America's interest in it was announced through the publication of two landmark anthologies for adults, Emmett Williams's *An Anthology of Concrete Poetry* (1967) and Mary Ellen Solt's *Concrete Poetry: A World View* (1968). Shortly thereafter, Robert Froman composed and published some of the first visual poetry for children in America, collected in his *Street Poems* (1971) and *Seeing Things: A Book of Poems* (1974).

A large number of visual poems for children were written in the 1970s, with even relatively conservative poets like Livingston trying their hand at visual work. Livingston's *O Sliver of Liver* (1979) contains several such pieces, "Winter Tree" and "Piano Lesson (Carissa)" among them. Furthermore, her "4-Way Stop," anthologized by the Kennedys in *Knock at a Star*, uses found and visual elements to interesting effect. Echoing the opinion of many critics, Livingston later decried such experimentation, championing the more formally conservative work of McCord, who, incidentally, also experimented with typography and visual elements in his poetry, particularly in "The Grasshopper" in *Far and Few* (1952) and "Summer Shower" in *For Me to Say* (1970).

Visual poetry for children is still being published today. Examples are found in J. Patrick Lewis's *Doodle Dandies: Poems That Take Shape* (1998), Sharon Creech's *Love That Dog* (2001), and Joan Bransfield Graham's *Splish Splash* (2001). However, more common are books in which the poems are highlighted by exceptional graphic design. For instance, the poems in Robin Hirsch's *FEG: ~~Stupid~~ Ridiculous Poems for Intelligent Children* (2002) may verge on visual poetry, but in fact they are simply accentuated by illustrator Ha's computer-generated art and layout. Maira Kalman's picture book *Max Makes a Million* (1990), about a dog poet who yearns for Paris, is another compelling example of the productive interface between graphic design and poetic text. Similarly, in *Poems for Children Nowhere Near Old Enough to Vote* (1999) Istvan Banyai's compelling visual designs radically refigure nineteen of Sandburg's previously unpublished children's poems.

Arnold Adoff also experiments with the elements of his children's poetry, creating work that is both visually and aurally arresting. As the late 1960s and early 1970s were marked by an interest in identity politics as well as formal experimentation, Adoff often combined radical politics with experimental form. His *Black Is Brown Is Tan* (1973), for instance, is the first picture book to feature an interracial couple. Adoff's *Slow Dance Heart Break Blues* (2003) extends his earlier visual experiments, typographic puns and other visual cues creating rich layers of meaning. A capable poet and outspoken advocate for poetry and childhood, Adoff is best known for his anthologies; *I Am the Darker Brother* (1968), a collection of poems written by African American poets, is perhaps his most famous.

Like Adoff, **Naomi Shihab Nye** is a poet and anthologist with her feet in two worlds, writing poetry for children and adults; her *19 Varieties of Gazelle: Poems of the Middle East* (2002) was a National Book Award finalist. Preoccupied with cultural difference and ethnic identity, Nye endorses the need for cross-cultural and intergenerational empathy. *Sitti's Secrets* (1994), a picture book illustrated by Nancy Carpenter, involves an American girl and her Palestinian grandmother. Separated by distance, by "many miles / of land and water . . . / . . . fish and cities / and buses and fields," they are nonetheless bound together by culture and family. Adoff's and Nye's insistence on social relevancy in children's poetry is by no means rare in contemporary children's poetry, though their high aesthetic standards are. The children's poetry of **June Jordan** and **Nikki Giovanni** also engages the political in complex and poetically rich ways. For instance, the speaker of Jordan's *Who Look at Me* (1969), originally titled "Portrait of the Poet as a Little Black Girl," returns the gaze of the adult—perhaps white—viewer; the poem ends with a direct challenge: "WHO LOOK AT ME?"

Many U.S. children first experience poetry through anthologies, most of which are, like Adoff's *I Am the Darker Brother*, thematic. Some of the best-known themed anthologies are Harold Bloom and Donald Hall's *The Wind and the Rain* (1961); Myra Cohn Livingston's *Why Am I Grown So Cold? Poems of the Unknowable* (1982); Lee Bennett Hopkins's *My America: A Poetry Atlas of the United States* (2000); and Paul B. Janeczko's anthology of visual poetry for children, *A Poke in the I* (2001). Other anthologies are more general, like Louis Untermeyer's *The Golden Treasury of Poetry* (1959). Stephen Dunning, Edward Lueders, and Hugh Smith's *Reflections on a Gift of Watermelon Pickle . . . and other Modern Verse* (1966), an attempt to acquaint young readers with modern poetry, contains a good deal of poetry not originally intended for children, a common characteristic of children's poetry anthologies. Other important U.S. anthologies include Prelutsky's *The Random House Book of Poetry for Children* (1983), perhaps the best selling of all U.S. poetry anthologies, and Elizabeth Hauge Sword and Victoria McCarthy's *A Child's Anthology of Poetry* (1995), its contents recommended by a thirteen-member advisory board comprising such well-known poets as **Louise Glück**, **Jorie Graham**, **Edward Hirsch**, and **Thylias Moss**. Liz Rosenberg, author of the young adult poetry collection *Heart & Soul* (1996) and a dedicated champion of poetry for adolescents, is also a well-respected editor and anthologist, responsible for such anthologies as *Light-Gathering Poems* (2000*)*, *Earth-Shattering Poems* (1998), *The Invisible Ladder: An Anthology of Contemporary American Poems for Young Readers* (1996), and others.

From the late 1970s to the turn of the century, the U.S. children's poetry scene has been dominated by the nonsense work of Prelutsky and Silverstein. These poets, borrowing from the gross-out traditions of playground rhyme, have developed irreverence to a fine art, although they sugar their irreverence with just enough didacticism to appeal to the adults who, more often than not, do the book buying. Nevertheless, Silverstein, who first made his name drawing cartoons for *Playboy*, is often challenged for developing inappropriate themes in his work, despite such sentimental verses as "Hug o' War," in which the narrator prefers hugs to tugs, because in a hug of war "everyone kisses, / and everyone grins, / and everyone cuddles, / and everyone wins." No other U.S. poet has so effectively balanced the coarse and the sweet.

Another trend in contemporary children's poetry is the novel in verse. With the rise of literacy programs and the desire to help so-called reluctant readers, the turn of the century has seen a proliferation of these largely free verse novels. Karen Hesse's *Out of the Dust* (1997) and *Witness* (2001) are the most successful, artistically and poetically. Other novels in verse include Creech's *Love That Dog*, **Ron Koertge**'s *Shakespeare Bats Clean-up* (2003), Maria Testa's *Becoming Joe Dimaggio*

(2002), and Jacqueline Woodson's *Locomotion* (2003). Perhaps better characterized as a biography in verse, **Marilyn Nelson**'s award-winning *Carver: A Life in Poems* (2001) stands out as one of the finest collections of its kind, setting a new standard for well-crafted narrative poetry.

However, the more things change, the more they stay the same: Stephen Michell's *The Wishing Bone and Other Poems* (2003), winner of the 2003 Lee Bennett Hopkins Award for U.S. children's poetry, is a collection of evocative and technically accomplished rhymes rooted in the nonsense of Laura E. Richards and Eugene Field. Doubtless the twenty-first century will see children's poetry continue to reinvent itself.

Further Reading. Hall, Donald, ed., *The Oxford Book of Children's Poetry in America* (New York: Oxford University Press, 1985); Styles, Morag, *From the Garden to the Street: An Introduction to 300 Years of Poetry for Children* (London: Cassell, 1998).

Joseph T. Thomas, Jr.

CHIN, MARILYN (1955–)

Marilyn Chin's poetry unravels the complexities of the immigrant experience through the convergence of Chinese cultural history, Chinese American familial/generational relationships, and contemporary urban landscapes, thus marking this poet as a powerful voice in American poetics and a significant presence in **Asian-American poetry**.

Born Mei Ling in 1955, Chin came to the United States from Hong Kong soon after her birth. Raised by her mother and grandmother, she grew up in Portland, Oregon, and in 1977 she graduated from the University of Massachusetts at Amherst; sheearned an MFA from the University of Iowa in 1981.

Besides editing an anthology of Asian-American writing, *Dissident Song: A Contemporary Asian American Anthology* (1991), Chin has published three volumes of poetry: *Dwarf Bamboo* (1987), *The Phoenix Gone, The Terrace Empty* (1994), and *Rhapsody in Plain Yellow* (2002). She has received two National Endowment for the Arts writing fellowships (1984–85); a MacDowell Colony fellowship (1987); a Yaddow fellowship (1990–94); a Josephine Miles Award, PEN (1994, 1995); and the Pushcart Prize (1994, 1995, 1997).

Chin's poetry solidifies her position as a poet who often renders the personal political. The theme of the immigrant's assimilation into white America recurs in her work. However, Chin also writes of loss and exile, cultural history and family relationships, sadness and sacrifice, as well as gender, and through her foregrounding of the complexity of assimilation, Chin refuses to render a one-dimensional depiction of this process, representing instead the fear, hatred, and "wonderful magic of it" (Moyers, 1996. Her poem "How I Got That Name: an essay on assimilation" (*The Phoenix Gone, The Terrace Empty*) reveals the violence that the process enacts on identity (a new name generated from her father's obsession with the blonde Marilyn Monroe, a gin and Nembutal– "swollen" white woman). This poem also illustrates Chin's concern with issues regarding gender: The father emerges as "a tomcat," "gambler," and "thug"; the mother unable to pronounce the "r" in her daughter's name inhabits the kitchen surrounded by children. In addition, "How I Got That Name" challenges white America's assumptions regarding Asians and Asian-Americans as it warns that "the 'Model Minority' is a tease" (17). Chin laments the loss of historical and cultural certainty (a generation of sons and daughters viewed as ugly by the ancestor the Great Patriarch Chin) and, finally, she celebrates the singularity of Marilyn Mei Ling Chin, marking herself an "am" rather than a "becoming," and "solid as wood," enthralled by what assimilation has given to her as well taken from her.

In *The Phoenix Gone*, as in her other poetry, Chin sounds a voice angry and compassionate, harsh and tender, declarative and questioning as she moves between ancient and contemporary Chinese history in poems such as "The Barbarians Are Coming," and "Barbarian Suite," or elegizes her friend in "Elegy for Chloe Nguyen." This voice continues as she pays homage to Diana Toy, a Chinese immigrant who dies in a mental hospital, in the ten poems that comprise the middle section of the book, or writes hauntingly of love in poems such as "Where Is the Moralizer, Your Mother?" "Urban Love Poem," and "And All I Have Is Tu Fu." The final section of *The Phoenix Gone*, "Beijing Spring," written in tribute to the Chinese Democratic Movement, resonates with a poignancy generated from startling instances of violence intertwined with memories and longings. "Floral Apron" tells of a woman wearing a floral apron preparing squid, who in the preparation teaches the young watchers about "the Asian plight," imparting what the speaker calls a "primal lesson" about courage, patience, and restraint. In "Tienanmen, the Aftermath," Chin has the speaker in bed when she learns of the carnage, the "blood and guts all over the road" (88). Seemingly unaffected, the speaker drifts off to sleep only to dream of and merge with a young girl crying. The poem concludes with a plea to "leave the innocent ones alone" (88). "Beijing Spring" speaks of yearnings and "what ifs": what if I could change the seasons, what if I could restore China's splendor, what if I could change the destiny of my mother and father? The poem ends at Tiananmen Square with the speaker wanting to restore life to a dead lover by breathing breath into his mouth, merging the personal and the political in this longing for restored life, rebirth, and new beginnings.

Rhapsody in Plain Yellow, Chin's most recent volume, is strikingly **postmodern** in the poet's experimentation with form and language and in its fusion of ancient Chinese history, contemporary American concerns, high and popular cultures, and East and West. The poems in *Rhapsody* explore the nature of loss in poems eulogizing the loss of Chin's mother and grandmother, "Hospital Interlude" and "Hospital in Oregon" among others. With the skill of a bricoleur, Chin borrows from grand narratives to create new stories, mocking, adapting, and rewriting traditional forms. The poems whisper with allusions to Chinese folk songs, ancient Chinese poetry and myth, Maoist dance drama, Confucianism, the poetry of **Emily Dickinson** and **William Carlos Williams**. In fact, the volume opens with an epigraph from Williams's "Love Song," with the yellow stain of love upon the world. "Hospital Interlude" points to the "eternal stain"of death found in an empty "unmade bed," and "Hospital in Oregon" echoes Dickinson's "I heard a fly buzz" as a deerfly enters the room of the dying grandmother, lands on the woman's ear, and "Together, they listen to the ancient valley" (41). This volume resonates with poetic traditions, East and West, as it reconfigures those traditions.

Rhapsody in Plain Yellow not only continues the thematic concerns of Chin's previous volumes of poetry but it also extends her experimentation with language and form. In all her work, Chin insists on pushing the limits of poetic expression by offering "hybrid forms" such as a mixture of epigrams and haiku, and she offers an eclectic mix of form and style while sounding a voice tinged with irony, wit, brashness, accusation, grief, compassion, and love.

Further Reading. *Selected Primary Sources:* Chin, Marilyn, *Dwarf Bamboo* (Greenfield, NY: Greenfield Review Press, 1987); ——, *The Phoenix Gone, the Terrace Empty* (Minneapolis, MN: Milkweed Editions, 1994); ——, *Rhapsody in Plain Yellow* (New York: Norton, 2003). ***Selected Secondary Sources:*** Gery, John, "'Mocking My Own Happiness: Authenticity, Heritage, and Self-Erasure in the Poetry of Marilyn Chin" (*Literature Interpretation Theory* 12.1 [2001]: 25–45); Moyers, Bill, *The Language of Life: A Festival of Poets* (New York: Doubleday, 1995, 67–80); Slowik, Mary, "Beyond Lot's Wife: The Immigration Poems of Marilyn Chin, Garret Hong, Li-Young Lee, and David Mura" (*MELUS* 25.3–4 [2000]: 221–242).

Catherine Cucinella

CHINESE POETRY

In 1970 a park ranger stumbled upon hundreds of Chinese poems carved into the crumbling walls of the long-abandoned **Angel Island** detention center in San Francisco Bay. Angel Island served as a holding facility for most hopeful Chinese immigrants, who were deported or confined for weeks, months, or in some cases, years on end after the passage of the Chinese Exclusion Act in 1882. The poems were composed in colloquial Cantonese, mostly by young Chinese men, and expressed dismay, depression, and often anger over their unlawful confinement. The poems draw upon many elements found in classical Chinese poetic forms, which enabled them to bring their political statements into pointed, often unsettling verse. While considered the earliest body of Chinese poetry composed in America, the Angel Island poems would not be the last body of American poetry to be influenced by classical Chinese poetic forms. At the same time these young Chinese immigrants were carving their poetry into the wooden walls of their holding cells, a young **Ezra Pound** was carving a new form of English verse from the literal Chinese translations and notes of the late **Ernest Fenollosa**. These translations and the **poetics** derived from them initiated a revolution in American poetry that would radically alter its course for the next century. While scholarship exploring this cross-cultural legacy usually centers on the controversial attempts of Fenollosa and Pound to incorporate Chinese poetic elements into American poetry, many American poets have followed in their footsteps, continually carving new poetic forms into the American **canon**. In 1913 Pound received the manuscripts of the late Fenollosa from his widow, **Mary McNeil Fenollosa**. Since the young Ezra Pound was already interested in the importance of the *image*, and the juxtapositional nature of Japanese haiku poetry (*see* **Japanese Poetry**), it is easy to see why Pound would have read Fenollosa's essay "The Chinese Written Character as a Medium for Poetry" as confirmation and further elaboration of a new method for English poetry based on juxtaposed images. Pound would later call this unique combinatory poetics his *ideogrammic method* because Fenollosa showed how both Chinese characters and poetry (which rarely uses linking verbs or particles) rely on juxtaposition as the principal compositional method.

Throughout much of Ernest Fenollosa's writings, one encounters his belief that Chinese ideograms visually reveal the ancient combinations of "things" and "images" that come to make up Chinese "words." While English words can also be broken down into their etymological units, the alphabetic nature of the language does not visually reveal a word's composite parts. Fenollosa erroneously believed that Chinese characters "wore their etymology on their faces" and, therefore, always visually suggested all the ancient metaphors that make up any given character. To find the irony in this assertion, however, one need not go farther than the word "irony" itself. Like irony, most Chinese characters are composed of phonetic elements that suggest meanings

wholly unrelated to the word at hand. Following Fenollosa's assertion, irony would have to be understood as a derivation of the word "iron." Nevertheless, the example of a language and poetic tradition that created meaning through an explicit combinatory or juxtapositional means provided Fenollosa, and later Pound, with a powerful new set of poetic and aesthetic values. In his essay "A Poet's Work," the poet Sam Hamill joins a large chorus of American poets and critics who argue that Ezra Pound's collection of Chinese translations *Cathay* (1915) "is the single most influential volume of poetry in [the twentieth] century"(76). In this volume we see for the first time the beginning of an ideogrammic method in practice. In his translation of Li Bai's poem "Taking Leave of a Friend," Pound begins to create juxtaposed structures by setting images upon one another with little grammatical mediation: "Blue mountains to the north of the walls/White river winding about them." However, Pound did not limit his ideogrammic method to his translations alone but also deployed it within his magnum opus, the *Cantos*. For example, in "Canto LXXIV" the poetic images come from the central character for learning and practicing (made up of feather-wings and white). Not only did Pound create juxtaposed structures within the *Cantos* but he went so far as to include untranslated Chinese characters in the text as well, conveying his belief that characters can be experienced as "ideogrammic vortexes" regardless of one's ability to understand written Chinese.

For later poets working out of what Laszlo K. Gefin calls the *ideogrammic stream*, the ideogrammic method represents far more than a poetic form like a sonnet or a haiku. Instead, this method represents a far-reaching concept of artful representation linked to other global movements from cubism to collage artists like Max Ernst and Kurt Schwitters, where image and meaning find forms outside normative conventions and syntaxes. Pound's cross-cultural assault on Victorian verse forms, therefore, have continually offered American poets a tradition through which even the basic conventions of English grammar can be effectively contested.

Yet Ezra Pound was not the only poet associated with the **Imagists** to publish translations of East Asian verse. **Amy Lowell** and later **William Carlos Williams** began translating and incorporating Chinese poetic elements into their own work. Like Pound, Amy Lowell never laid foot in Asia, yet the translation of Chinese poetry and use of East Asian themes and landscapes were central to her poetry. While East Asian themes appear in almost all of her published works, her later work begins to show a greater interest in the Far East, typified by her book of verse *Pictures of a Floating World* (1919). Her later collaboration with the amateur sinologist /translator Florence Ayscough on *Fir-Flower Tablets* (1921) went even further than Fenollosa's and Pound's valuation of the visual etymology of the characters, to create a method of translation that focused more than most on minute details of the originals. For example, the line 光细弦岂上, translated in an unadorned way by **Kenneth Rexroth** as "The Bright, thin, new moon appears" (Fung, 390) becomes, for Lowell, "Its light delicate, crescent of the First Quarter is about to rise" (Fung, 390). What most translators would translate as a "mirror" Lowell and Ayschough translate as a "water-chestnut mirror" (Lowell, 15) or a "gilded magpie mirror" (Lowell, 14) to bring out the particular visual elements within the poem's characters. The publication of *Fir-Flower Tablets* solidified Lowell's prominence as a populist of Asian verse and Orientalist aesthetics. Even though neither Lowell nor Pound read Chinese and both were poorly received by the sinological community, their translations helped usher in and popularize the century's interest in poetic translations, Asian verse, and Orientalist aesthetics.

Like **Marianne Moore**, **H.D.** (Hilda Doolittle), and Ezra Pound, William Carlos Williams showed an early interest in Chinese art and wrote positive reviews of Pound's *Cathay* in 1915. Williams's own work repeatedly alludes to the face of "Yang Guifei," the courtesan-beauty of Bai Juyi's 806 A.D. **long poem** *Changhenge*, which he had read through the translations of Herbert A. Giles published in 1901. While Williams's translations are not marked by the same emphasis on the visual etymological richness of Lowell's and Pound's own attempts, his earlier poetry works squarely within the idiogrammic stream. One can see Williams's use of bare, juxtaposed images in his canonical "Red Wheelbarrow" or in poems like "Nantucket": "Flowers through the window lavender and yellow/changed by white curtains smell of cleanliness."

Yet poets associated with Imagism were not the only Americans to find inspiration from their contact with Chinese poetry; several prominent figures associated with the **Beats** were heavily influenced by Eastern cultural, literary, and spiritual models as well. Of these poets, Kenneth Rexroth and **Gary Snyder**'s roles as translators and poets merit more attention.

Kenneth Rexroth's translations resisted Pound's looming influences by adopting a more relaxed, colloquial tone: "Every day on the way home from My office, I pawn another of my Spring Clothes" (*One Hundred Poems from the Chinese*, 14). The substitution of "office" for the more common "court" situated in the everyday syntax "on my way home from . . ." and the decidedly colloquial word "pawn" reveal Rexroth's idiosyncratic style. Yet one can still see that Rexroth's translations draw upon the **minimalist**, clear, and concrete qualities that not only characterize Pound's Asian translations but had by mid-century become quintessentially **modernist**: "The bright, thin, new moon appears" (*One Hundred*

Poems, 19). Ever since the publication of *One Hundred Poems from the Japanese*, his translations have been widely read, enjoyed, and criticized. Over his long career Rexroth translated several volumes of poetry from Japanese and Chinese (with a particular concentration on the Tang poet Du Fu). Yet, as with both Pound and Lowell, Rexroth's apprenticeship to **translation** influenced his own works as well. In a series literally titled, "Imitations of the Chinese," Rexroth writes his own "Chinese" poetry in English, as in his poem "Erinnerung": "The wind in the ancient ginkgo tree/Sounds like the rustle of brocaded silk."

While Pound found himself an apprentice to the Chinese poet Li Bai, and Rexroth found Du Fu, Gary Snyder found his model in Han Shan. Snyder took a great interest in formal cross-cultural experimentation while studying classical Chinese under Professor Chen Shih-hsiang at the University of California–Berkeley. Here Snyder began his translations of the eccentric Tang Chinese "mountain poet" Han Shan (Snyder), which reflect his sensitivity to the natural landscape of Han Shan's poetry: "What's beyond the yard?/White clouds clinging to vague mountains."

Snyder's own work often bears the imprint of Chinese's monosyllabic, visually rich style discovered through his early translation work: The title of one well-known work, *Earth House Hold*, for instance, consists of a series of uninflected monosyllabic nouns and verbs. This terse Imagistic verse can be found throughout Snyder's work. In a poem with a title longer than the poem itself, "24: JV:400075,3:30 PM, n. of Coaldale, Nevada, A Glimpse Through a Break in the Storm of the Summit of the White Mountains," we again see the imprint of classical Chinese prosody:

sky   cloud   gate   milk   snow
wind-   void-   word.

Unlike the Imagists before them, both Rexroth and Snyder brought out the celebration of wilderness found in classical Chinese verse by emphasizing (although some would say overemphasizing) the Taoist or Buddhist reverence for landscapes, which did not fear the wild or seek to domesticate it.

Translations of Chinese poetry continue to be published within both academic and nonacademic circles, and the ideogrammic method still holds a place of importance in contemporary American poetry and poetics. Today poets like **Arthur Sze** both translate Chinese poetry and integrate Chinese poetic themes and forms into their work. In Sze's collection *The Redshifting Web*, one finds selections from his earlier works *The Willow Wind* (1972) and *Two Ravens* (1976) that work squarely out of the "ideogrammic stream." Nevertheless, Sze's references to the great Chinese poets Wang Wei and Li Po reveal his own study of the

Chinese classics, which continue to reshape his English in ways not simply inherited from the Chinese influences on earlier generations. Sze's later work *Archipelago (1995)* reveals a rethinking more radical than Imagist juxtapositions, yet also more **lyrical** than most **Objectivist** parataxis and collage. Sze's style reflects a greater affiliation with the twentieth-century Chinese poets Wen I-To and Yen Chen, whom Sze has translated, or Gu Cheng and Bei Dao of the *Menglong* ("Misty") school. Sze, like so many American poets, was enriched by the Imagist revolution as well as the catalytic otherness that helped it blossom. Other poets, such as **Charles Wright**, explicitly note their doubled inheritance from both Pound's influence and their reading of Chinese poetry in their dependence on the resonant image and a reconfiguration of the poetic line. The ongoing translation of both classical Chinese poetry as well as contemporary poetry ensures the ongoing influence of Chinese poetry.

Further Reading. Hamill, Sam, "Sustenance: A Life in Translation," in *The Poem Behind the Poem: Translating Asian Poetry*, ed. Frank Stewart (Port Townsend, WA: Copper Canyon Press, 2004); Lowell, Amy, *Fir-Flower Tablets* (Boston: Houghton, 1921); Pound, Ezra, *Cathay* (London: Chaswick Press, 1915); ——— *The Cantos, Revised, Collected* (London: Faber and Faber, 1975); Rexroth, Kenneth, *One Hundred Poems From the Chinese* (New York: New Directions, 1971); ———, *The Complete Poems of Kenneth Rexroth*, ed. Sam Hamill and Bradford Morrow (Port Townsend, WA: Copper Canyon Press, 2003); Snyder, Gary, *The Gary Snyder Reader* (Washington DC: Counterpoint Press, 1999); Williams, William Carlos, *The Collected Earlier Poems* (New York: New Directions, 1951).

Jonathan Stalling

CHRYSTOS (1946–)

Chrystos is a Menominee poet whose commitment to both Native American and queer identities has produced a distinctive and compelling body of poetry. Her political poetry, evinced most famously in *Not Vanishing* (1988), is restless, cantankerous, and characterized by unexpected twists of humor. Her erotic poetry, particularly in the 1993 *In Her I Am*, reaches for a celebration of lesbian sexuality that is devotional in both its attention to the physical details of lesbian sex and its **Imagistic** associations. The coexistence of these two incarnations—the political and the erotic—links Chrystos to a larger project shared by many women poets of color—namely, as both **Audre Lorde** and Gloria Anzaldua have expressed it, the need to resist silence politically and to make use of the erotic politically.

Chrystos was born on November 7, 1946, in San Francisco, to a Menominee father and a Lithuanian/French mother. She has dedicated her life as a poet and activist to Native American, queer, and feminist causes. Though she says feminism has been "gutted by academia," she still considers herself a liberationist, particularly regarding sexuality. She has most often been anthologized as a queer Native American poet.

Locating her work within various traditions is an ongoing project of the poet herself. Her first collection of poetry, *Not Vanishing*, contains **prose poems** and **free verse** poems that express rage against the colonization and degradation of Native American people. Chrystos's facility for detail, in poems such as "I Was Over on the Rez," evokes for readers the claustrophobia, ugliness, aimlessness, and boredom that characterize reservation life. It is part of the "not vanishing" of the spirit, however, that the poems refuse to disintegrate into despair: Rage is used for insight, and insight is used for the development of a story line, and the story ends in a sort of bitter but compassionate and sensual humor. The speaker wanders on a hot Saturday, finding no place to go to walk her dogs in peace: All the best beachfront is taken by rich people, the bars are full of bloody fights, the rocks on the beach are littered with broken glass, and the local boaters hurl sexual insults at her. She intervenes when a blank-faced blonde boy harasses an intoxicated old man, but ends up angry at the victim because "he is old and I need to respect him." The anguish and rage of the experience keep twisting in on themselves, until she wishes she could get her own dog to bite her, "Just enough to place the pain." However, just as the poem seems about to end on this hopeless note, the speaker's lover comes up behind her, reads what she is writing, and bites the speaker herself: "& and we laugh with a / tinny taste of tears under our tongues."

In an interview in the feminist magazine *Off Our Backs*, Chrystos comments on the cantankerous quality of her writing as part of her commitment to

> talking about genocide and that's a nasty subject. . . . I don't write pleasant, what I call tom-tom poetry, which is a really derogatory thing, I shouldn't say that. But [it is the kind of poetry] you can read and enjoy all the little Indian feathers and bells and not ever feel responsible to find out what Indian country is really like. (7)

Yet what the Indian country is "really like" is precisely what is at stake for Chrystos as a Native American and queer artist, because though she wants to avoid reifying stereotypes of Native Americans, she does not relinquish the power that Native cultures draw from nature, from humor, from eroticism, and even from the madnesses that result from poverty and marginalization. Though she says her experiences in mental institutions have made her art "more bloody," she is less afraid of drawing upon the visionary aspects of art, calling her poems "lunatic celebrations of nature, just way, way out there, being the tree and things like that, and that kind of stuff is considered crazy" (7).

Where such a sensibility "fits in" and where it does not is a constant exploration for Chrystos. She is a lesbian poet who embraces sexual aggression and submission, the sublimation of emotional pain into seemingly dangerous scenarios acted out with lovers, and other practices that would make celebrants of "vanilla sex" squeamish. In an extended analysis of Chrystos's poem "I Like a Woman Who Packs" from *In Her I Am*, Deborah Miranda charts out the humor and celebratory sexuality of a speaker who describes her lover as a woman who uses a dildo and a leather strap around her wrist to satisfy her. The play of whispers and anticipation in the poem's sexual encounter climax in the speaker's experience of being penetrated by a dildo and "ridden" in a way that seems to echo male-to-female domination, but that is an act so focused on and controlled by female sexual desire and pleasure that the patriarchal associations of a penis-shaped sex toy are erased. According to Miranda, "the work of the erotic in this poem is not to punish but to ignore patriarchal presence by allowing the erotic to acknowledge itself. By doing this, the lover makes herself visible and patriarchal culture suddenly invisible" (143).

How a sex toy shaped like a penis can be used by two women to make patriarchy disappear and a specifically female sexuality more visible is one of those twists and turns Chrystos excels at in *In Her I Am*. It is also a creative/erotic/feminist exploration that has led to controversy and perhaps kept her audience, as she acknowledges in *Off Our Backs*, mostly Native American and queer. This is not, after all, "bells and feathers" Native American poetry, but a bracing, intellectually playful **poetics** that is as open to the places its erotic explorations can take its artist as the speakers in the poems are to the places sexual pleasure can take them.

The "use of the erotic" as a creative energy for cultural and spiritual survival, as Audre Lorde termed it, has appealed to many feminists as an idea, but its actual practices are not necessarily shared by the white feminist world. It is that world that Chrystos addresses in "White Girl Don't," from *Not Vanishing*, excoriating the "social/political tourism" of white women poets who speak of atrocities committed outside the United States while ignoring the atrocities committed by white people upon indigenous people in the United States. In "I Am Not Your Princess," she calls to account those white feminists who want to use her as a stereotypical fountain of Native American spiritual knowledge while trying to commodify her culture at the same time. She demands, in a series of funny and scathing callings to account, that they actually see *her*: "See my confusionlonelinessfearworrying about all our / struggles to keep what little is left for us."

That social, sexual, and political world of white feminists, while itself fuzzy and indistinct, is inescapable for Chrystos and must be dealt with. In "Water," from *Not Vanishing*, the speaker distrusts this world of vaporous women who "fought in words / concepts about all you couldn't see or grasp or cook with," but finds she must keep returning to this world because of the difficulties in the other worlds: homophobia in Native America, sexual and emotional cruelty among other lesbians of color. Yet among white "flowers," the Native American lesbian can only be exoticized in a way that leads to a terrible loneliness, further alienation, and disgust. The highly professionalized, privileged, and purblind world of mainstream feminists Chrystos implies, is not a world that can hold her intellectual attention or politically sustain her.

Because Chrystos does not let anyone off easily, politically, intellectually, sexually, or socially, her work can be as scathing and challenging as it is gorgeous, erotic, and funny. She refuses to celebrate bourgeois feminism as the center of the universe, and instead continues her commitments to the survival and well-being of native and queer people. Perhaps because of this, it can be difficult to locate her works outside the worlds of Native and queer anthologies. This absence represents a failure on the part of feminists of all colors and all sexualities. We have much to learn, for example, from the generosity shown in the closing poem of *Not Vanishing*, "Ceremony for Completing a Poetry Reading," in which part of the vision of "not vanishing," so to speak, consists in giving away: "I give you the seeds of a new way."

Further Reading. *Selected Primary Sources:* Chrystos, *Dream On* (Vancouver, BC: Press Gang Publishers, 1991); ———, *Fire Power* (Vancouver: Press Gang Publishers, 1995); ———, *Fugitive Colors* (Cleveland, OH: Cleveland State University Press, 1995); ———, *In Her I Am* (Vancouver, BC: Press Gang Publishers, 1993); ———, *Not Vanishing* (Vancouver, BC: Press Gang Publishers, 1988). ***Selected Secondary Sources:*** Bealy, Joanne, "An Interview with Chrystos" (*Off Our Backs* 33 [September–October 2003]: 7–11); Gould, Janice, "American Indian Women's Poetry: Strategies of Rage and Hope" (*Signs* 20.4 [Summer 1995]: 797–817); Miranda, Deborah A. "Dildos, Hummingbirds, and Driving Her Crazy: Search for American Indian Women's Love Poetry and Erotics" (*Frontiers* 23.2 [2003]: 135–148); theGULLY.com, "Chrystos on Queer America" (www.thegully.com/essays/gaymundo /020313_chrystso_native_gay_html); Zeleke, E. Centime, "Speaking About Language" (*Canadian Women's Studies* 16.2 [Spring 1996]: 33–35).

Evelyn Navarre

CHURCH, BENJAMIN (1734–1778)

Cursory examinations of Benjamin Church's poetry could relegate him to the status of another eighteenth-century imitator of the English Augustan poets. When studied more carefully, however, Church's work reveals an original and important American voice in poetry. Although Church does pay homage in some works to the Augustan poets, he Americanizes his poetry by using the American landscape and by writing about issues of concern to his contemporaries, factors that situate him as a poet of **literary independence**.

Church, born in 1734, believed himself a "Son of Honour" and "candidate for Fame." After graduating from Harvard in 1754, he studied medicine and earned a position at the first Army Hospital at Cambridge. During this time, Church continued the writing he had begun as a student. He published his most famous poetic work "The Choice" in 1757, and contributed to *Piatas et Gratulatio Collegii Cantabrigiensis* (1763), a collection of poems penned by Harvard alumni and undergrads mourning the death of King George II and praising his successor, George III. Church later became the chief satirist and propagandist for the Whig party and also gave *An Oration . . . to Commemorate the Bloody Tragedy of the Fifth of March, 1773*, in remembrance of the Boston Massacre. His quest for honor, however, ultimately ended in infamy. Church was accused of various acts of treason during the Revolution, and was court-martialed in 1775. He was allowed to leave Massachusetts in 1778, but the ship on which he was traveling, either to London or the West Indies, was lost at sea.

While "The Choice: A Poem after the Manner of Mr. Pomfret" owes its title and certain thematic elements to the British poet John Pomfret, Church diverges greatly from Pomfret's text, borrowing instead from other American writers of the time, most notably **Richard Lewis** and **William Livingston**, who were also writing in the **pastoral** genre.

Church's "Choice" is decidedly pastoral. The speaker hopes that if "human will might govern future Fate" he will soon find himself "Remote from Grandeur" and will "all the Glitter of a Court despise." The speaker, in search of "rural pleasures," will situate himself, as would Pomfret, in the traditional sequestered seat of pastoral poetry, yet near a town. His home, again as with Pomfret, will be frugal and, of necessity, devoid of the glamour he earlier decries. But Church does not begin his retreat to the country until line 153, whereas Pomfret's move to the country occurs five lines into the text. Church must first wait until the sun melts New England's "hoar winter with her rage."

It has been argued that Richard Lewis, in his "Journey from Patapsco" (1732), Americanizes the pastoral genre by blending the mythical, pastoral landscape with the American landscape. Church does the same. He includes "lofty Cherry Trees" in his pastoral orchard as does Lewis. Where Pomfret includes only lime and sycamore trees, Church finds himself "doubly blessed"

for he is "on native verdure laid, / whose field supports him and whose arbours shade."

In a nod to Livingston, the future governor of New Jersey, who also wrote a version of Pomfret's poem, titled "Philosophic Solitude" (1747), Church describes his cherry grove as a "blooming canopy of Love!" Pomfret mentions love only when describing what "amorous" Ovid knew and balks at bringing a wife into his pastoral landscape. Both Church and Livingston, however, do bring in mates. Indeed, Church compares his gardens to Eden and his mate to Eve, blending the Christian myth of Adam with classical forms.

Church breaks from both Pomfret and Livingston in regard to his general theme. The choice in Pomfret and Livingston is between rule by a monarchy and rule by representation, with Pomfret and Livingston taking opposing views. Church instead chronicles what an American man, in a society with more leisure time, could and should become. Enjoy leisure, he writes, but through the reading list he recommends, he implies that leisure should still serve a specific end, for "An active State," Church writes, "is Virtue's proper Sphere." Jeffery Walker's opinion is that these lines are a gentle throwback to seventeenth-century thoughts of industriousness. One also sees a suggestion that the colonies should avoid falling into the idleness of the European aristocracy, which leads to the loss of virtue.

Church in his untitled elegy for George II adopts the style of Virgil's fifth *Eclogue*. The poem begins by alluding to the classical pastoral convention in which Pollio (a name borrowed from the Roman orator, author, and poet) retreats to the "thick-embowering shades" of the country that, as a vague invocation to the muse, "shed poetic ease." Church then memorializes George by listing his accomplishments, focusing particularly on what George has done for the colonies. It was George, Church writes, who kept the Native American at bay. In further accord with the genre, Church suggests that Nature is given new life as he points toward George's successor and namesake, who has had the righteous George II to guide him. In this poem, Church again blends the Christian with the classical by referring to both the Christian "Heav'n" and the "Christian Mind."

Along with giving a distinctly American touch to a classical form, Church introduced contending Adamic and classical mythoi; in his later poems the Adamic conquers. Church distanced himself from the classics not because he favored the Adamic or New World emphasis, but because, given his desire for fame, Church could reach a wider audience by using the Adamic mythos.

Further Reading. *Selected Primary Source:* Walker, Jeffery Brian, *The Devil Undone: The Life of Benjamin Church (1734–1778) to Which Is Added, An Edition of His Complete Poetry* (Ann Arbor, MI: University Microfilms International, 1977).

Selected Secondary Sources: Bowden, Edwin, "Benjamin Church's Choice and American Colonial Poetry" (*New England Quarterly* 32 [1959]: 174–184); Shields, John C., *The American Aeneas: Classical Origins of the American Self* (Knoxville: University of Tennessee Press).

Raymond Yanek

CIARDI, JOHN (ANTHONY) (1916–1986)

Poet, critic, and anthologist John Ciardi is best remembered as a children's poet and the translator of Dante's *Divine Comedy*—his verse rendering of *The Inferno* (1954) remaining one of the most poetically energetic and accessible in English. Ciardi strove to write verse concerned with the lives of everyday people, verse that is neither condescending nor willfully obscure, combining wit, formal virtuosity, and humanistic pathos.

Born June 24, 1916, in Boston, Massachusetts, to immigrants Antonio and Concetta Ciardi, he spent his early years in a working-class neighborhood steeped in Old World Italian mores and custom. His father died just sixteen days after Ciardi's third birthday, leaving his mother to raise him with the financial help of his three older sisters. Excelling as a student, Ciardi was promoted early from the fourth to the sixth grade, gratifying his mother—who spoke little English—and setting a precedent for future intellectual accomplishments. Although his childhood was largely happy, it was rife with economic hardship and sibling rivalry, two facts perhaps at the root of the dark humor in his poetry.

As an adolescent, Ciardi was a physical laborer, digging ditches to save money for college. After a brief stint at Bates College, Ciardi transferred to Tufts, where he met his mentor, poet John Holmes, who inspired Ciardi to become a poet. Upon graduation, Ciardi applied for University of Michigan's $1,200 Hopwood Award. Under the tutelage of Professor Roy W. Cowden, Ciardi won the Hopwood, and strengthened his resolve to make poetry his vocation. While at Michigan, Ciardi honed his poetic craft, and in 1940 Henry Holt accepted his Hopwood manuscript, *Homeward to America*, for publication.

Ciardi served in the U.S. Army Air Forces from 1942 to 1945, seeing combat as a B-29 gunner during the Japanese air offensive. Returning stateside, Ciardi experienced further professional gains and publications. His Italian heritage served him well in his translation of Dante's *Divine Comedy*, which deftly captures both the beauty and the coarseness that marks Dante's work. Ciardi's translation of the final lines of Canto XXI looks forward to his children's poetry, particularly in his willingness to engage low comedy: "[The demons] stuck their pointed tongues out as a sign / to their Captain that they wished permission to pass, / and he had made a trumpet of his ass." The wordplay in the final couplet— the verb "pass" suggesting both "to go by" and "to pass gas"—is not in the original Italian, and thus is typical of Ciardi's desire both to translate faithfully and to craft interesting English poetry.

Ciardi married Judith Hostetter in 1946, and together they raised three children, Myra Judith, John Lyle Pritchett, and Benn Anthony. When first his nephews and then his own children began reading, Ciardi started writing children's verse. Between 1959 and 1966, Ciardi published nine books for children, among them the classic *Reason for the Pelican* (1959), a collection of nonsense acclaimed for its wit and originality; *The Man Who Sang the Sillies* (1961), winner of the Boys' Clubs of America Junior Book Award; and *You Know Who* (1964). His daughter Myra's difficulty learning to read inspired him to write *I Met a Man* (1961), an easy reader based on a first-grade reading vocabulary, an enterprise doubtlessly helped along by the success of Dr. Seuss's newly launched Beginner Books series.

Ciardi's fame and income were supplemented by his association with the prestigious Bread Loaf writer's conference and his regular and provocative column for the *Saturday Review*. His popularity on the lecture circuit led him to become the host of CBS's *Accent*, a weekly television program. An uncommonly famous public intellectual, he was unafraid of boasting, a tendency that perhaps estranged him from younger poets who were largely unaware of his working-class roots.

Ciardi's children's verse has been criticized for inappropriate obscurity and a morbid sense of humor. In this respect, Ciardi anticipated—and perhaps paved the way for—American children's poet Shel Silverstein, who, like Ciardi, did not balk at featuring violence and ill-mannered children in his poems. Books like *The Monster Den* (1963) caricature the genteel diction common in mid-century American children's poetry. Often featuring macabre humor, poems such as "Sit Up When You Sit Down," from Ciardi's *You Know Who* (1964), do not shrink from inflicting harm on their youthful subjects. Here the narrator threatens to beat a naughty child with "a stick" but discovers that all he has to do is show the child the stick, after which the child just *knows* "how to sit up when he sits down. / And now he's the very best boy in town." "About the Teeth of Sharks," collected in *You Read to Me, I'll Read to You* (1962), concerns a narrator whose curiosity leads the "you" of the poem to be decapitated by a shark: "Still closer—here, I'll hold your hat: / Has it a third row [of teeth] behind that? / Now look in and . . . Look out! Oh my, / I'll never know now! Well, goodbye." Recalling the puns and jokes of A.A. Milne and Lewis Carroll, these poems illustrate the language play common in Ciardi's children's verse (*looking out* and *looking in, sitting up* and *sitting down*) even as they highlight Ciardi's willingness to use the caricatured violence of playground poetry in the service of good-natured teasing.

Ciardi's surreal violence also imbues his adult work. "A Dream," from *39 Poems* (1959), one of his best-known books for adults, begins with the speaker having his arm bitten off by the tiger he is dancing with, then hearing a dance instructor say to his class, "'Note and avoid this dancer's waste of motion—more violence than observance,'" adding, as the suffering speaker dies, "'Dancing, my dears, is a selection of measures.'" Like **Theodore Roethke** (for whom he wrote an **elegy**), Ciardi was intrigued by the rhythms and nonsense of playground chant, adapting these tendencies in his children's and adult poetry. Though written for adults, "A Ballad of Teleologies" suggests these roots "Says Father Marx, who gave the Law, / 'I must confess, I'm left in awe: / it comes to more than I foresaw.'" Yet Ciardi's emotional range is wide, as poems like "At My Father's Grave," "Inscriptions for a Soldier's Marker," and "Massive Retaliation" demonstrate.

Having authored more than twenty collections of poetry for adults, twelve for children, and the popular textbook *How Does a Poem Mean?* (1959), Ciardi was a stalwart public intellectual and artist, remaining in the public eye through poetry readings, lectures, and appearances on television. Ciardi died of a heart attack in 1986. He will be remembered as a poet who strove to make poetry accessible to all, adults and children alike.

Further Reading. *Selected Primary Sources:* Ciardi, John, "About Being Born, and Surviving It," in *Contemporary Authors Autobiography Series* (Detroit: Gale Research Co., 1984); ———, *Ciardi Himself: Fifteen Essays in the Reading, Writing, and Teaching of Poetry* (Fayetteville: University of Arkansas Press, 1989); ———, *How Does a Poem Mean?* (Boston: Houghton Mifflin, 1959); ———, *The Inferno* (New Brunswick, NJ: Rutgers University Press, 1954); ———, *39 Poems* (New Brunswick: Rutgers University Press, 1959); ———, *You Read to Me, I'll Read to You* (New York: Harper & Row, 1962). *Selected Secondary Sources:* Cifelli, Edward M., *John Ciardi: A Biography* (Fayetteville: University of Arkansas Press, 1997); Krickel, Edward Francis, *John Ciardi* (Boston: Twayne, 1980); White, William, *John Ciardi: A Bibliography* (Detroit: Wayne State University Press, 1959).

Joseph T. Thomas, Jr.

CLAMPITT, AMY (1920–1994)

Written between 1960 and 1994, Amy Clampitt's poetry inhabits a tradition that extends beyond the confines of American poetry, engaging historical trauma of various times and places. Two ideas are crucial to her **poetics**: that the American landscape offers an unparalleled sense of hope, and that the traumatic history of the twentieth century negates that hope.

Given Clampitt's apparently idyllic youth, such historical realities as genocide and exile may seem unlikely inspi-

rations for her poetry. Clampitt spent her childhood in New Providence, Iowa, which she describes in "My Cousin Muriel" (1990) as "a farmhouse childhood, kerosene-lit, / tatting-and-mahogany genteel." Clampitt graduated from Grinnell College in Iowa in 1941, later moving to New York City, where she studied briefly at Columbia University and the New School for Social Research. Her most significant jobs included secretary and writer for Oxford University Press from 1943 to 1951 and reference librarian for the Audubon Society from 1952 to 1959. During this time, Clampitt pursued fiction writing; it was not until the 1960s that she turned from writing novels to writing poetry. In 1978 **Howard Moss**, poetry editor of the *New Yorker*, published her first poem, "The Sun Underfoot Among the Sundews." Clampitt has won such prestigious awards as a Guggenheim fellowship (1982), an Academy of American Poets fellowship (1984), and a MacArthur Foundation fellowship (1992). In 1994 she died of ovarian cancer.

Clampitt discovered material for poetry in both the American and the British literary traditions. In "A Hermit Thrush" (*Archaic Figure*, 1987), she resurrects the central symbol of **Walt Whitman**'s 1868 **elegy** to Abraham Lincoln, "When Lilacs Last in the Dooryard Bloom'd." In "The Burning Child" (1983), she emphasizes the significance of "lost particulars," drawing on philosophical concerns of **Wallace Stevens** and **Ezra Pound** but reaching back also to William Blake, who refers to "minute particulars" in his *Jerusalem: The Emanation of the Giant Albion* (1804). Clampitt's investment in the potential of Romantic poetry to inspire twentieth-century verse is nowhere more clear than in her treatment of John Keats. Her 1985 volume, *What the Light Was Like*, contains a section entitled "Voyages: An Homage to John Keats," in the last poem of which Clampitt writes, "the voyage, every voyage at the end is cruel," a line that unifies the idea of the psychic voyage with the voyage across a landscape. In some ways, the American landscape is what Clampitt writes best. Equally committed to the East Coast, the Midwest, and California, Clampitt revives the sense of Manifest Destiny and the hope that U.S. immigrants felt during their first decades in the New World.

For all these glimpses of hope, however, Clampitt's oeuvre possesses a haunting dimension. Clampitt has been characterized by Jahan Ramazani as a modern elegist—a poet who seeks not to console in her poetry but rather to "reopen the wounds of loss" through a melancholic approach to memory and literary forms (Ramazani, ix–xii, 322–333). Her first volume, *The Kingfisher* (1983), famously contains elegies both to her mother, "A Procession at Candlemas," and to her father, "Beethoven, Opus 111." Both poems, as Ramazani argues, do not offer celebrations of the deceased, but rather convey regret over certain failures. For example, in "A Procession," Clampitt calls memory "that exquisite blunderer," and in "Beethoven, Opus 111," she compares her father's dying to Beethoven's masterpieces, unheard even by himself.

Clampitt's "The Burning Child" is the last poem in that volume—a volume divided into six sections respectively entitled, "Fire and Water," "Airborne, Earthbound," "Heartland," "Triptych," "Watersheds," and "Hydrocarbon." As the last poem in the last section on water and carbon, combustion and burning, "The Burning Child" depicts the most extreme consequence of combining the inflammatory resources of the earth: genocide. In a direct reference to Sigmund Freud's dream of the burning child, Clampitt writes of "the whimper / of the burning child, the trapped / reprieve of nightmare," suggesting the specific human failure to awaken to the screams of children burning at Auschwitz. Thus, "The Burning Child" emphasizes the potential for poetry to bear witness to history, and reveals how dreams can, paradoxically, both *demand an awakening* and *neglect to awaken* the public to that history. For Clampitt, if the reality of the burning child is not awakened in history, it is destined to be repeated in dreams. As in many of her poems, Clampitt demonstrates her commitment to engaging traumatic history—a history buried within the landscape of hope in the American terrain.Early reviewers of Clampitt's poetry dismissed it for its difficult syntax and ideas, and its elaborate and archaic vocabulary. Mary Karr, for example, suggested that Clampitt's "purple vocabulary sounds . . . like a parody of the Victorian silk that Pound sought to unravel. [One passage] . . . could be Swinburne on acid or Tennyson gone mad with his thesaurus" (quoted in Spiegelman, 172). Moreover, as "A Burning Child" may suggest, for readers who look to poetry for consolation, Clampitt's offers little. In the title poem of *The Kingfisher*, Clampitt describes memory as "no porthole vista / but down on down, the uninhabitable sorrow." Similarly, the speaker in "A Hermit Thrush" suggests that "no point is fixed . . . there's no foothold."

In Clampitt's final collection, *A Silence Opens* (1994), it becomes clear just how focused on inhumanity in history her poetry has been all along. In the poem "Sed de Correr" ("Thirst to Run"), inspired by César Vallejo, the Peruvian poet who died in Paris in 1938, Clampitt identifies "the breaking / wave of displacement" that is at the heart of that thirst.

Further Reading. *Selected Primary Sources:* Clampitt, Amy, *The Collected Poems of Amy Clampitt* (New York: Alfred A. Knopf, 1997); ———, *A Homage to John Keats* (Louisville: Sarabande Press, 1984); ———, *Predecessors, Et Cetera: Essays* (Ann Arbor: University of Michigan Press, 1991). ***Selected Secondary Sources:*** Benfey, Christopher, "'Nowhere Wholly at Home'" (*New York Times Book Review* [9 November]: 1028); Goodridge, Celeste, "Reimaging 'Empire's Westward Course': Amy Clampitt's *A Silence Opens*," in *Women Poets of the Americas: Toward a Pan-American Gathering*, ed. Jacqueline Vaught Brogan and Cordelia Chávez Candelaria (Notre Dame, IN: University of Notre Dame Press, 1999, 159–175); Huesgen, Jan, and Robert W. Lewis, "An Interview with Amy Clampitt" (*North Dakota Quarterly* 58.1 [1990]: 119–128); Ramazani, Jahan, *Poetry of Mourning: The Modern Elegy from Hardy to Heaney* (Chicago: University of Chicago Press, 1994); Spiegleman, Willard, "What to Make of an Augmented Thing" (*Kenyon Review* [Winter 1999]: 172–181); Weisman, Karen A., "Starving Before the Actual: Amy Clampitt's *Voyages: A Homage to John Keats*" (*Criticism—A Quarterly for Literature & the Arts* 36.1 [1994]: 119–137).

Aimee L. Pozorski

CLEGHORN, SARAH NORCLIFFE (1876–1959)

Sarah Norcliffe Cleghorn began her poetic career by writing about the people and landscape of her Vermont home. After a turn to social causes in her twenties, she devoted her poems—and her life—to political activism. In 1913 Cleghorn became a Christian Socialist, and her sharply crafted writing expresses her passionate support for prison reform and equal rights for women and African Americans, as well as her critique of vivisection and child labor. Her poems appeared in popular magazines such as *Harper's* and the *Atlantic Monthly*, often provoking controversy. In addition to the poetry collection *Portraits and Protests* (1917), Cleghorn published *Poems of Peace and Freedom* (1945), several prose works, a play, and an autobiography. Despite a substantial readership during her life and a considerable impact, particularly in the fields of anti-war poetry and religious poetry, Cleghorn's work remains largely unknown to contemporary readers.

After her mother's abrupt death from pneumonia, the nine-year-old Cleghorn and her six-year-old brother Carl left their father in Minneapolis, Minnesota, to live with their Episcopalian aunts in the primarily Congregationalist town of Manchester, Vermont. Cleghorn's upbringing in Vermont and her religious faith provided the foundation for her poetry, which began with what Cleghorn called her "sunbonnet" poems— these consisted mainly of character sketches and illustrations of country life. Cleghorn would later abandon these more "traditional" subjects for her self-described "burning" poems, which expressed a more pointed political stance while maintaining the technical skill and sensitive attention to detail that Cleghorn had developed in her earlier poetry. In addition to establishing religion as an important aspect of Cleghorn's life, her two socially conscious aunts introduced her to political action (her Aunt Jessie was a leader in Manchester's animal rights effort). The combination of Cleghorn's growing awareness of radical politics and the development of her own spiritual beliefs was crucial to her eventual identification as a pacifist and a leftist Christian. Reacting to claims in the late nineteenth century that Christianity was aligned not with workers but with capitalist institutions, the Christian Socialist movement positioned itself at the intersection of society and economy. During her life Cleghorn taught at experimental schools in Vermont and wrote for the leftist Christian journal the *World Tomorrow*. A significant figure in Cleghorn's life and development as a writer was her friend Dorothy Canfield Fisher, whom Cleghorn met while studying at Radcliffe in 1895. Fisher and Cleghorn collaborated on the prose work *Fellow Captains* (1916), and later on a collection of short stories, *Nothing Ever Happens and How It Does* (1940). In 1934 Cleghorn wrote a play that she based on Fisher's book for children, *Understood Betsy* (1916). Among other works, Cleghorn published two novels, *The Turnpike Lady* (1907) and *The Spinster* (1916), and an autobiography, *Threescore* (1936). In the 1920s and 1930s, she produced a number of ballads for her students. These ballads focused on historical figures such as Harriet Tubman and Eugene Debs.

Cleghorn is perhaps best known for her striking four-line poem protesting child labor, "The Golf Links Lie So Near the Mill," which appears in *Portraits and Protests*:

The golf links lie so near the mill
That almost every day
The laboring children can look out
And see the men at play.

Several of her other political poems demonstrate Cleghorn's use of incisive wit and social critique. In the same year she wrote the "Golf Links" poem (1914), Cleghorn wrote "Comrade Jesus," which was first accepted by Max Eastman for publication in the *Masses*. The poem was later included in the *Portraits and Protests* collection and in *May Days: An Anthology of Verses from Masses-Liberator* (1925), edited by **Genevieve Taggard**. In "Comrade Jesus" Cleghorn depicts a Saint Matthew "who had been / At mass-meetings in Palestine" and a dues-paying, union card–carrying Jesus who sees his enemies' "childishness quite plain / between the lightnings of his pain."

Cleghorn's poem "The Poltroon," printed in the *New York Tribune* in the second year of World War I, was similarly inflammatory, in that it portrayed Jesus as a pacifist. The poem describes a man who did not volunteer but spoke of "a most unpatriotic peace"—a "milksop" who "never had the manhood to hit back." Cleghorn does not name her character until the poem's final piercing sentence: "His name was Jesus." This merging of religious and political beliefs in poetry was groundbreaking at a time when religion, politics, and poetics were a particularly explosive combination. Speaking of

Cleghorn's poetry in its historical context, Cary Nelson notes in *Repression and Recovery* that "the idealization of the poetic, in effect, gave special moral authority—and consequent outrage—to poems that linked politics and religion" (295).

Further Reading. ***Selected Primary Sources:*** Cleghorn, Sarah N., *Portraits and Protests* (New York: Henry Holt and Co., 1917); ———, *Threescore* (New York: Smith and Haas, 1936). ***Selected Secondary Sources:*** Nelson, Cary, *Repression and Recovery: Modern American Poetry and the Politics of Cultural Memory 1910–1945* (Madison: University of Wisconsin Press, 1989); Schroeter, Joan G., "Sarah Cleghorn and the Religious Left" (*Colby Quarterly* 31.3 [September 1995]: 214–227).

Becky Peterson

CLIFTON, LUCILLE (1936–)

Though she emerged as a poet during the heyday of the **Black Arts Movement** (BAM) and was influenced to a degree by its aesthetics, Lucille Clifton's poetry is not defined by that association. Clifton has written about race and gender in American society using a **minimalist** style that belies the complexity of her critiques. Without its being identified with any specific school of poetics or engendering a recognized group of disciples, her work has quietly garnered her some of American poetry's most prestigious awards and honors. Clifton uses her platform—as the author of twelve books of poetry, a widely sought-after reader, and, since 1999, a Chancellor of the Academy of American Poets, among other distinctions—to, in her words, "comfort the afflicted and afflict the comfortable." Recording the inspiring moments and disturbing truths of everyday life, in language that is at once imagistic and mythical, she both soothes and troubles a diverse readership.

Lucille Clifton (née Thelma Lucille Sayles) was born in Depew, New York, and lived there and in Buffalo until she was sixteen, when she matriculated at Howard University on an academic scholarship. Her parents were daily readers of the newspaper and instilled in Clifton a great appreciation for books, despite the fact that her father, Samuel L. Sayles, who was employed as a steelworker, and her mother, Thelma Moore Sayles, who worked as a launderer and a homemaker, had had very little schooling. Clifton spent two years as a drama major at Howard, where she met several people who were or would become significant literary figures, including **Sterling Brown**, LeRoi Jones (later **Amiri Baraka**), Chloe Wofford (later Toni Morrison), A.B. Spellman, and, briefly, James Baldwin, as well as her future husband, Fred Clifton, an educator and philosopher. She continued her studies at Fredonia State Teachers College, after which she married, moved with her husband to Baltimore, and began raising her six children.

Clifton often speaks about the difficulties she faced trying to write poetry while caring for her family, especially when her children, all very close in age, were young. The hectic pace of her days meant that she often had to memorize the lines she thought of until she could snatch a moment to write them down; in this way, she honed her craft. Her poems caught the attention of **Robert Hayden**, who entered them on her behalf in the 1969 YW-YMHA Poetry Center Discovery Award contest, which she won. With the award came the publication of her first book of poems, *Good Times* (1969), which commenced a prolific and illustrious career as both a poet and a writer of children's books. In addition to her poetry collections, Clifton has published a family memoir, *Generations* (1976), which was edited by Morrison, and more than twenty books for children, to date. Her honors and awards include two fellowships from the National Endowment for the Arts (1970 and 1973); designation as the Poet Laureate of Maryland (1979 to 1985); three Pulitzer Prize nominations, for *Two-Headed Woman* (1980), *Next* (1987), and *Good Woman: Poems and a Memoir 1969–1980* (1987), the last of which was a finalist; a Lila Wallace/*Reader's Digest* Award (1999); a nomination for the National Book Award in Poetry for *The Terrible Stories* (1995) and the Award itself for *Blessing the Boats: New and Selected Poems, 1988–2000* (2000); and an Emmy for her contributions to the television production of *Free to Be You and Me*. Clifton has taught at Coppin State College, Columbia University School of the Arts, George Washington University, University of California at Santa Cruz, Duke University, and St. Mary's College of Maryland, where she has been Distinguished Professor of Humanities since 1991.

The power of Clifton's poetry arises, in part, from her ability to transform personal experiences and preoccupations into poems that ring true not only for similarly situated people but also for those with other standpoints. Her identity as an African American woman born and raised in a working-class family is not incidental to her poems, yet she emphasizes that her work is about "human" experiences to which readers should be able to relate, regardless of their race, class, or gender. The wide-ranging appeal of her characteristically short poems may also be attributed to her deliberate effort to write in an accessible style—using unadorned diction and uncapitalized words—without compromising the complexity of the ideas. By combining the vernacular's most provocative ambiguities with resonant popular references, Clifton creates poems that reward not only the first reading but additional readings as well.

Several themes run through Clifton's work: family, the body (especially black and/or female bodies), racism and the legacies of slavery, sexism, spirituality and religion, and loss. Most of these themes make their appearance in her first book, *Good Times*. The title poem redefines the term "good times" by undoing the middle-class association of poverty with misery. Clifton depicts a working-class family in that joyous, if temporary, moment when there is enough money to cover the necessities of food and shelter, with a little left over for celebration. The extended family—including "grampaw" and "uncle brud"—have come together for food and drink "and dancing in the kitchen." Declaring that "these is good times," Clifton strikes a similar note to that found in **Nikki Giovanni**'s well-known poem, "Nikki-Rosa," which explicitly states what Clifton's poem deftly implies: that the wealth possessed by working-class African American families must be measured in terms of love and community, rather than dollars and goods. *Good Times* contains a number of poems, such as "in the inner city" and "miss rosie," that describe her family and community in terms revealing the beauty, dignity, and strength often invisible to white Americans. Although racial themes predominate in this book, Clifton's interest in creating empowering depictions of black women's bodies is established in "if i stand in my window," which envisions her naked body as able to send "the man" into a worshipful frenzy, "crying / praying in tongues."

The poems in *Good Times* and Clifton's second book, *Good News About the Earth* (1972), are those in which Clifton most directly embraces BAM aesthetics, which called for poets to write unapologetically about black experience from a perspective grounded in the black community's values. Her second collection includes a section entitled "heroes," in which the poems honor such well-known figures as Malcolm X, Angela Davis, and Little Richard, alongside Clifton's personal heroes, such as her father and husband. With this juxtaposition Clifton humanizes the cultural icons and teaches her readers that the most ordinary people have extraordinary potential. Clifton also writes a number of poems that condemn the behavior of whites and encourage African Americans to celebrate their blackness. But although she writes an "apology (to the panthers)" for "her whiteful ways," as she describes her behavior during the era preceding the revolution in black consciousness, she also defends the pre-BAM generations, in the poem "listen children," by instructing the younger ones to "all ways" remember that "we have never hated black," that "all ways / we loved us."

Within this same period, Clifton began writing the poems about women's experiences that have played an increasingly larger role in her oeuvre over time. *Good News* contains an oft-anthologized piece, "the lost baby poem," which lays bare the hard decision faced by a mother who simply cannot afford to bring another child into the world. The poem remains ambivalent about how to think of this "lost baby," the first-person speaker's addressee. Nonetheless, the mother of this "almost body" clearly feels a responsibility, if not to its life, to its memory, which she honors by vowing never to be "less than a mountain / for your definite brothers and sisters." Her punishment for breaking this vow, she says, should include being ostracized by "black men," which suggests that her duties as a mother are owed to the men of her race as much as to the children. Another such poem, "mary," appears in a section of poems that recast biblical figures from Adam and Eve to Lazarus as black. In this poem, Mary speaks of the experience of conceiving Jesus, and in so doing she eroticizes God's entrance into her body. The poem's ten short lines showcase Clifton's metaphorical economy; the final couplet—"between my legs / i see a tree"—suggests not only sexual penetration, but also the cross on which her child will be crucified. The reimagining of biblical stories is a motif in Clifton's work. Akasha (Gloria) Hull's observation that Clifton "(1) Africanizes, (2) feminizes, (3) sexualizes, and (4) mysticizes" the Bible in her poems highlights the convergence of her interests in race, gender, and spirituality in this context (273).

Mysticism appears in Clifton's work not only in relation to biblical matters but also in a broader realm of spirituality that is connected to the recurrence of loss in her life. Her mother's early death is particularly significant for Clifton. In a number of poems, beginning with the collection *Two-Headed Woman*, Clifton comes to terms with her mother's short life, in order to record the ancestral voices, including her mother's, that she begins to hear after Thelma Sayles's death. For example, in a section of the book called "the light that came to Lucille Clifton," the poet writes about feeling "the fingers of madness" upon her as she comes to realize that the voices she hears, which call themselves "the Light," are speaking from and of "a world" beyond this one. Clifton relates her awareness of this spiritual world to the biological marker of otherness that she shares with her mother and one of her daughters: all three were born with six digits on each hand. When initially questioning her sanity, she tells her mother that they ought to have known "a twelve-fingered flower / might break." Ultimately, however, she compares herself to Joan of Arc, another hearer of voices, and, like Joan, will not be talked out of believing what her own senses tell her. "They are there," she asserts finally, and speaking "the truth." In these poems, she pushes her characteristic combination of vernacular diction and extraordinary imagery to new levels, bridging the differences with biblical phrasings and echoes as well as stunning uses of synesthesia.

Although these autobiographical poems trace a thin line between speaker and poet, Clifton frequently writes in a dramatically different mode, using personae. As in the poem "mary," discussed previously, Clifton takes the voice of familiar figures and gives them words that unfold the flat characters into three-dimensional beings.

From biblical figures, such as Lucifer and Lazarus, to mythological ones, like Leda, to popular ones, such as the fictional Auntie Em and the real Lorena Bobbit, these speakers enable Clifton to remind us that the story depends upon who is telling it and where the teller chooses to end. We hear from a miraculously resurrected Lazarus who wants nothing more than to return to death, where he experienced "the only truth i know." And from Auntie Em, we learn that Dorothy, whose ruby slippers brought her back to Kansas, is still "clicking her heels." Such poems challenge us to look into and beyond the happy endings we construct, drawing their authority from Clifton's own recurring experiences of facing pain and fear.

Besides the devastating losses of loved ones, Clifton has confronted perhaps her greatest trials in the series of life-threatening illnesses she has sustained. Poems that begin to appear in the relatively recent collection *The Terrible Stories* concern her three bouts with cancer, as well as her kidney failure and transplant, and testify to her body's (and spirit's) powers of rejuvenation. Pieces such as "dialysis," "cancer," and "lumpectomy eve" have attracted the attention of not only poetry lovers but also medical professionals interested in connections between poetry and healing. Images in these poems range from almost matter-of-fact depictions of the daily horrors of sickness ("blood fountains from the blind man's / arm and decorates the tile today") to the charged language of rage ("i am alive and furious. / Blessed be even this?"). Her work on her illnesses is of a piece with her work on the subject of the black female body more generally. In "donor," she makes an explicit connection between the unhealthy body and the reproductive body—to set up not an analogy, but a continuum. A daughter she tried to abort has become the person who will donate a kidney to Clifton. The poem responds to the possibility that Clifton's "body / might reject" the vital organ. Clifton recasts the failed abortion as a sign of how this potential rejection will also end with the daughter's body "buckled in," regardless of any protest Clifton's body might make, "fastened to life like the frown / on an angel's brow." Clifton subtly declines to make the poem a condemnation of her younger self's decision, emphasizing instead the powerful will to live that ties mother and daughter together.

Thus, an appreciation for the miraculous nature of the body links the poems about illness to the widely read and reproduced poems (such as "poem in praise of menstruation" and "poem to my uterus") celebrating women's sexuality, including reproduction, which made *Quilting* (1991) such a well-loved book among feminist readers. In "to my last period," Clifton takes the female function that patriarchal custom often constructs as unclean and offensive and personifies it—"well, girl, goodbye"—referring to "her" lovingly as the "hussy" in the "red dress" who, after she is gone, is remembered for being "beautiful." Indeed, Clifton's willingness to address cultural taboos, such as menstruation, is a defining characteristic of her work. Another such taboo is incest, although Clifton is far from celebratory in her treatment of this topic. Some of her earliest work on incest, in the "shapeshifter poems," couches it in mythological terms, describing the way the full moon "follows some men into themselves" and gives them such "strange hands" that "their daughters / do not know them." Later poems on this theme take a more clearly autobiographical approach; "moonchild," for example, gains its power from Clifton's juxtaposition of the "giggling" rituals of girlhood with improperly acquired sexual knowledge.

Despite the fact that African American women writers have frequently kept silent on the subject of sexuality, to shield themselves from racist stereotypes of black women as promiscuous or sexually aggressive, Clifton has written famously about her own desire and sexual potency. One of her trademark poems is "homage to my hips," in which she rejoices that her "big hips" have the power "to put a spell on a man and / spin him like a top!" By emphasizing that they are "free hips" that "have never been enslaved," she again calls attention to the intersection of race and gender in her understanding of her sexuality.

Although in recent years she has been identified more with her poems about women's issues than with those about race, Clifton resists the drawing of such false oppositions. She has remained consistently interested in exploring the legacies of slavery and the operation of racism. Notable in this regard is the poem "slaveships," which echoes Hayden's "Middle Passage" in highlighting the ironies in the names of these vessels. She writes of people "loaded like spoons / into the belly of Jesus" or "chained to the heart of the Angel." Similarly, she exposes the double vision that comes with African American double consciousness in an untitled poem from her latest collection, *Mercy* (2004). The poem responds to the implied accusation that she never writes about nature by spinning out a pretty line about the "knotted branches" of the trees, only to interrupt it with the reminder that "an other poem"—presumably about lynching—lies underneath the nature poem.

Mercy also weaves the other thematic threads that have occupied Clifton throughout her career. The series of poems written in the wake of the September 11 attacks marks her concern with contemporary world events, even as another series devoted to the voices that spoke to her in the 1970s shows her continued engagement with a timeless, spiritual other-world. The recent publication of the first book of literary scholarship devoted to Clifton's poetry suggests that the academy may finally be catching up with her popular audience in appreciating the cultural range, linguistic nuance, and spiritual generosity of her ongoing body of work.

Further Reading. ***Selected Primary Sources:*** Clifton, Lucille, *Blessing the Boats: New and Selected Poems 1988–2000* (Rochester, NY: BOA Editions, 2000); ———, *The Book of Light* (Port Townsend, WA: Copper Canyon Press, 1993); ———, *Good Woman: Poems and a Memoir 1969–1980* (Brockport, NY: BOA Editions, 1987); ———, *Mercy* (Rochester, NY: BOA Editions, 2004); ———, *The Terrible Stories* (Brockport, NY: BOA Editions, 1996). ***Selected Secondary Sources:*** Holladay, Hilary, *Wild Blessings: The Poetry of Lucille Clifton* (Baton Rouge: Louisiana State University Press, 2004); Hull, Akasha (Gloria), "In Her Own Images: Lucille Clifton and the Bible," in *Dwelling in Possibility: Women Poets and Critics on Poetry*, ed. Yopie Prins and Maeera Shreiber (Ithaca, NY: Cornell University Press, 1997, 273–295); Mance, Ajuan Maria, "Re-locating the Black Female Subject: The Landscape of the Body in the Poems of Lucille Clifton," in *Recovering the Black Female Body: Self-representations by African American Women*, ed. Michael Bennett and Vanessa Dickerson (New Brunswick, NJ: Rutgers University Press, 2001, 123–140); Ostriker, Alicia, "Kin and Kin: The Poetry of Lucille Clifton" (*American Poetry Review* 22.6 [November–December 1993]: 41–48); Rushing, Andrea Benton, "Lucille Clifton: A Changing Voice for Changing Times," in *Coming to Light: American Women Poets in the Twentieth Century*, ed. Diane Wood Middlebrook and Marilyn Yalom (Ann Arbor: University of Michigan Press, 1985, 214–222).

Evie Shockley

CLOSURE

Poets have been less drawn to techniques of closure than fiction writers because poetry has less of an investment in narrative. Conventionally, texts that foreground narrative have a beginning, middle, and end, a tri-stage structure that corresponds to the human life: childhood, adulthood, and death. One would think that the normal avoidance of death would produce a desire for texts that also resist closure; in fact, however, readers have long preferred closed texts, ones in which the end signals that the chaotic events of the beginning and middle have been resolved, if not happily then in a way that can be accepted as plausible or just. People do not love things that end; instead, desiring control of their own fate, they are comforted by examples of power. At the turn of the nineteenth century, William Wordsworth formalized and popularized the tendency of that period toward a poetry that presented a "recollection" of a past experience. Knowing the end of a narrative thus allowed for control of the end. **Edgar Allan Poe**, in "Philosophy of Composition" (1846), affirmed Wordsworth's idea when he recommended that writing begin only after the ending has been decided; in other words, write as if you were remembering something that has happened.

Often poems do tell stories, but by the twentieth century many American poets had replaced the idea of "poetry as recollection" with that of "poetry as composition," an approach that made poetry more structurally and thematically open. The change occurred when poets rejected narrative structures as well as traditional poetic forms and devices: sonnets or balanced antithesis, for instance. A traditional form was tied up with a conventional content; therefore, to say something different the poet needed to construct a new form. Poets began espousing an **open form** poetics. The two great American poets of the later nineteenth century, **Walt Whitman** and **Emily Dickinson**, although they sometimes tell stories and adhere to some aspects of conventional poetry, were defiant: Whitman kept expanding his *Leaves of Grass* (1855), and Dickinson refused to publish, a decision that allowed her to revise her poems without ever settling on one definitive version. The open, or "democratic," form (as Whitman called it) of their poetry and their statements (in essays and letters) about a poetry that embodied present circumstances, including the act of composition itself, were foundational for the **modernist** poets of the early twentieth century. In general, modern (since 1800) poems have tended toward open form, while the degree of closure in the content varies widely.

Closure appears most clearly in "genre fiction" (detective or romance novels, for instance). The teleology inherent to detective fiction (which Poe helped to define) demands that the narrative end with the revelation of the murderer. Closure in poetry, however, happens in degrees and never entirely. Even tightly defined forms like the sonnet or the elegy have a content that often plays up ambiguity or irony, so that as a whole the poem may be open. Moreover, "closure" and "stability" are to be distinguished. A poem can be full of unresolved antitheses ("Love is painful *and* pleasurable") or test the limits of intelligibility and still put forward a stable meaning. One method of achieving this is to end the poem with a statement that the reader will accept as a self-evident truth. In *Poetic Closure* (1968)—still the only book-length study of the subject—Barbara Smith notes that "the conditions which contribute to the sense of truth are also those which create closure" (154). The best example of a closed poem remains John Keats's "Ode on a Grecian Urn" (1819): In the last two lines of a poem consisting of five tightly wrought ten-line stanzas, the immortal urn tells each succeeding generation that "Beauty is truth, truth beauty," and the poet adds "—that is all / Ye know on earth, and all ye need to know." Truth can be messy, but if stated succinctly and authoritatively at the end, as in this Keats poem, the reader should feel a sense of closure.

In the twentieth century **Gertrude Stein**'s work stands as perhaps the most insistent case for "poetry as composition," not "recollection." Her poetry starts with a phrase and then responds to what its terms propose. The laws of genre are irrelevant because the poet owns no stock in what has been done in the past; all that matters begins now on the page; the poem defines itself only in the process of being written. Stein did not see beginnings or ends, only middles: poems open *in medias res* and stay there, instead of returning to the beginning and winding things up at the end, as John Milton's *Paradise Lost* (1667) had done. In her *The Geographical History of America* (1936) Stein states that "any one writing knows that there is no finishing finishing in writing" (480). A poem thus remains unfinished even after a poet has stopped adding to a poem; one poem starts up where another had left off. Balachandra Rajan, in *The Form of the Unfinished* (1985), distinguishes between a "fragment" and something "unfinished." Many Romantic poets were fond of publishing their work as fragments, and labeled them as such; modernist poets, in contrast, published unfinished work. To say "fragment" connotes that the poem was once part of something whole, or aspired to be whole, whereas an unfinished poem defers wholeness. Stein and writers sympathetic to her made poetry a perpetually unfinished project, with new poetry (and new truths) being needed as time goes on.

A poem composed "in the now" does not aim to present the truth about something because arriving at the truth usually depends on time having passed and on reflecting on the difference between then and now. Twentieth-century poets more typically present their "observations" on what they are seeing, feeling, or reading, and they pass on to readers their vivid experiences with language as a highly charged and surprising medium. In a highly literate society nothing is, paradoxically, more taken for granted than language, and poets attempt to dispel that complacency. **Charles Olson**'s "Projective Verse" (1950) was a call to poets to build on the work of **Ezra Pound** and **William Carlos Williams**, work that got "rid of the lyrical interference of the individual as ego" (247). Poetry for them still held a special position in the world, but poets were to be regarded as craftspeople who refused to be complacent when they handled language. Olson's essay defines his principle of "composition by field": According to Olson, the poem must be an open and self-aware thing of energy that knows its direction only after it is under way. **Susan Howe**, by the 1970s, was seeing the page as a field of energy, with each word an object at play in relation to the other words. Other poets, to reduce "lyrical interference" and go beyond the habits of the self, were using aleatory procedures or particular constraints: For instance, **Christian Bök**'s *Eunoia* (2001) includes poems in which every word contains the vowel "e" and only that vowel (conversely, for similar reasons, the French writer Georges Perec wrote his 1969 novel *La Disparation* without once using the vowel "e").

Concurrent with Olson's call, ideas about "serial poetry" were emerging. **Jack Spicer**, in a 1958 letter to

Robin Blaser, asserted that the point was "not to search for the perfect poem, but to let your way of writing of the moment go along its own paths, explore and retreat but never to be fully realized (confined) within the boundaries of one poem." A "poem is never by itself alone," he concludes (54–55). Spicer learned this from **Robert Duncan**, who taught that poets should write books, not individual poems; in these books were "serial poems." More recently, in "The Rejection of Closure" (1983), **Lyn Hejinian** has observed that poems open themselves by involving the reader in the production of meaning; in contrast, a closed poem claims to be sufficient on its own, asking only that the reader give witness. Parataxis, disjunction, and "the swerve" (nonlinearity) are techniques that open the poem. Hejinian notes that the modernist poets let the content determine the form; doing so allowed the broken or incipient materials of the poem to overwhelm any tendency in the form toward closure. Finally, according to Hejinian, poems end without reaching closure because of the impossibility of matching word and world, the word and the thing it represents; what poems reach for in their words will always be ungraspable. And when writing *is* thinking (or listening), and no end to thinking exists, closure will again be deferred.

Proposals in the last century and a half about democratic, unfinished, **projective**, aleatory, and serial poetry were all made by writers considering the politics of poetic form: Poems were not to be (closed) commodities but spaces open to all manner of language practices, not just "the poetic," and to people historically excluded from elite literary culture. An "open form" **poetics** became the popular choice in the last part of the twentieth century, though one must note the artificiality of the binary "open/closed" and maintain a healthy skepticism regarding those who claim that an "open" poem by definition beats a "closed" one. At the same time, critics of open form must keep in mind that an open form poetics does not advocate formlessness; instead, each poem demands its own form, one that suits the occasion of the writing and the content being expressed.

Further Reading. *Selected Primary Sources:* Hejinian, Lyn, "The Rejection of Closure," in *The Language of Inquiry* (Los Angeles: University of California Press, 2000, 40–58); Olson, Charles, "Projective Verse," in *Collected Prose*, ed. Donald Allen and Benjamin Friedlander (Los Angeles: University of California Press, 1997, 239–249); Smith, Barbara H., *Poetic Closure: A Study of How Poems End* (Chicago: University of Chicago Press, 1968); Vincent, John, *Queer Lyrics: Difficulty and Closure in American Poetry* (New York: Palgrave Macmillan, 2002). ***Selected Secondary Sources:*** Rajan, Balachandra, *The Form of the Unfinished: English Poetics from Spenser to Pound* (Princeton, NJ: Princeton

University Press, 1985); Spicer, Jack, "Letters to Robin Blaser: 1955–1958" (*Line* 9 [Spring 1987]: 26–55); Stein, Gertrude, *The Geographical History of America or The Relation of Human Nature to the Human Mind*, in *Gertrude Stein: Writings 1932–1946*, ed. Catharine R. Stimpson and Harriet Chessman (New York: Library of America, 1998, 365–488).

Logan Esdale

CODRESCU, ANDREI (1946–)

Andrei Codrescu is a Romanian-born poet, essayist, radio commentator, literary magazine editor, and documentary filmmaker. Despite the relatively wide audience for his frequent commentaries for National Public Radio, he remains a dissenter and an outsider. He employs various styles and voices in his poetry, which is often labeled surrealist. His poems frequently display his discomfort both with the communist society of want from which he emigrated and the capitalist society of excess in which he settled. Particularly in his early poems, he adopts a variety of poetic personae ranging from Julio Hernandez, an imprisoned Puerto Rican, to Alice Henderson-Codrescu (which is also the name of the poet's wife), who becomes Codrescu's feminine alter ego. The poems "written" by these personae were initially assembled in *License to Carry a Gun* (1970) and *The History of the Growth of Heaven* (1971). In addition to writing, Codrescu began and continues to edit the underground literary magazine *Exquisite Corpse*. Founded in 1983 as a traditional paper magazine and now an online journal, *Exquisite Corpse* publishes a variety of often **avant-garde**, surrealist, and **Dadaist** essays and poems.

Andrei Codrescu was born Andrei Perlmutter in Sibiu, Romania, on December 20, 1946, the child of two Jewish photographers who divorced before Codrescu was born. He immigrated to the United States in 1966 and within four years had written his first volume of poetry in English. After living and writing first in New York and then California, where he taught poetry at Folsom Prison, Codrescu, his wife Alice Henderson, and their two young sons settled for several years in Baltimore. There, Codrescu obtained his first college teaching appointment, at Johns Hopkins University; began writing essays for National Public Radio; and founded his literary magazine *Exquisite Corpse*. In 1984 Codrescu began teaching at Louisiana State University in Baton Rouge. He now maintains residences in both Baton Rouge and New Orleans. He has won several awards and grants, including National Endowment for the Arts fellowships for poetry, editing, and radio.

Andrei Codrescu asserts that for about four years before his immigration from Romania to the United States, he wrote in Romanian, and after learning just a few words of English (or "American," as he styles it), he had begun to string those words together into poems.

These first English poems, published as *License to Carry a Gun* (1970), include the eponymous poem, supposedly written by an incarcerated Puerto Rican named Julio Hernandez. He writes that because of his criminal record, "they will forever refuse you the license to carry a gun," so he must envision a weapon of his own: "but when the lights go out in these cells, / they are my loaded darkness." The darkened lights in his prison cell thus become a metaphor for the potential power of the gun he cannot have. The personae he adopts in these early poems allow Codrescu to explore the lives of various inhabitants of his new country—people of assorted genders, ethnicities, and occupations.

In the mid-1970s, Codrescu began experimenting with **prose poems**. Many of these poems feature a narrator who seems either delusional or extraordinarily gifted, experiencing brilliant visions. In "Evening Particulier" (1974), the narrator acknowledges that he will never be like asparagus, a piano, or an onion, and perceives the imagination that allows him to wonder about what it would be like to be an inanimate object as both a blessing and a curse: "Imagination is my grace and I am tired of her constant / presence!" Other poems find Codrescu disturbed by the body rather than the mind. In "Body Blues," the poet curses the demands of his body for food, sex, exercise, and entertainment: "body, what do you want now?" Food, especially the anxiety of excess produced by the bewildering array of products available in America, emerges repeatedly as a theme and an image in Codrescu's poems of this era. In "Jingling the Cookery," Codrescu declares, "More food! The food of anxiety! The vivacious / spiralling appetite of progressing paranoia!" whereas "In the Supermarket," a surrealist prose-poem, asserts the loneliness of solitude among plenty, "I was left to do my shopping alone and a great sadness tore at my innards."

Codrescu's poems of the 1980s feature increasingly bizarre imagery, while desire and eroticism, always prominent themes, develop still greater importance. "The Operations of Desire" lists several events, headline-style, including "The Lamp Post Child Whore" and "The Manhole Steam Dancing Nude Nun," then reports that it is to these things "I owe my present ability / to eroticize the world." Rather than abilities, Codrescu celebrates inabilities in "Horse Power," where he observes that despite living in a materialistic, destructive society, he is a holdout of anti-consumerism; addressing himself, he notes: "You don't know how to shop / You don't know how to drive"; nevertheless, a sense of superiority is not possible, as he discovers that "Everyone I know does harm" to the environment, "screwing the earth & its fauna."

Codrescu's most recent poems, collected in *Belligerence* (1991) and *it was today* (2003), are varied in theme and structure. Many of the poems in *Belligerence* feature dreamlike, disconnected, yet often political images. In the **long poem** "Mnemogasoline," for instance, a man has sex with a prostitute and falls asleep; when he awakens, he finds himself in the midst of a protest against Apartheid. Food imagery recurs here, too: The sleeping bodies of the protesters look like "tempura dishes in the windows of Chez Japan." *it was today* consists of three parts; the first includes lighter poems, the last contains poems that comment on contemporary social and political issues, including "9/11," which begins "9/11, I can barely remember you, they've buried you in so much hype!" The second part of this volume, however, is a long poem, "Lu Li & Weng Li." Ostensibly poems written by thirteenth-century Chinese lovers, the preface to the poems observes both that "Lu Li was a courtesan at the imperial court, Weng Li was a warrior" and, later, that Lu Li and Weng Li are poetic creations of Andrei Codrescu. This adoption of literary personae echoes the early part of Codrescu's career, in which much of his poetry was either spoken through an alternative persona or written as collaborations with other writers.

As a poet, Andrei Codrescu has brought an Eastern European worldview and a humorous and surrealist experimentalism to American letters. As an editor of *Exquisite Corpse*, he has provided a venue for many artists who might otherwise have remained unread, and as a National Public Radio commentator, he has brought his wry observations of American life and popular culture to the general public.

Further Reading. *Selected Primary Sources:* Codrescu, Andrei, *Alien Candor: Selected Poems 1970–1995* (Santa Rosa, CA: Black Sparrow Press, 1996); ———, *Belligerence* (Minneapolis, MN: Coffee House Press, 1991); ———, *it was today* (Minneapolis, MN: Coffee House Press, 2003); ———, *License to Carry a Gun* (Chicago: Big Table, 1970); ———, *Selected Poems 1970–1980* (New York: Sun, 1983). ***Selected Secondary Sources:*** Lehnert, Tim, "Codrescu versus America: A Postmodern Poet Turned Loose" (*Xavier Review* 20.2 [Summer 2000]: 31–42); Marin, Noemi, "The Rhetoric of Andrei Codrescu: A Reading in Exilic Fragmentation," in *Realism of Exile: Nomadism, Diasporas, and Eastern European Voices*, ed. Domnica Radulescu (Lanham, MD: Lexington, 2002, 87–106); Orlich, Ileana Alexandra, "Song of My Emerging Self: The Poetry of Andrei Codrescu" (*Melus* 18:3 [Fall 1993]: 33–40).

J. Robin Coffelt

COFER, JUDITH ORTIZ (1952–)

Judith Ortiz Cofer is a poet of feeling and of personal relationships. Like the Romantics, she values heartfelt intuition, although unlike the Romantics she celebrates the sustaining connections between individuals. Coming from a Spanish-speaking southern island to live first in the North of the United States and then in the South, she writes with a surprising clarity of perspective in which honesty of expression combines with lucid insight. Cofer's characteristic insight is the force that carries her poems, which tend to engage issues of human kinship, both with reference to family and to the common bonds of all humans. Her technique is unpretentious, and most of her poems consist of sequences of cadenced sentences in which the aesthetic impact results from powerful figurative language.

Born in Hormigueros, Puerto Rico, in 1952, Judith Ortiz moved to the United States with her parents, living in New Jersey before relocating to Augusta, Georgia, in 1967. She married John Cofer in 1971 and received a BA in English from Augusta College in 1974. She then attended Florida Atlantic University, receiving an MA in English in 1977. Her interest in poetry led to the publication of a sequence of chapbooks in the early 1980s, followed by some collections of poems. Since 1990, she has published much more prose than poetry, and her prose works include some notable novels, short stories, and essays. Since 1999 she has been Franklin Professor of English and Creative Writing at the University of Georgia. For her poetry, she was awarded a National Endowment for the Arts fellowship in 1989, and her prose has received extensive acclaim. She continues to lecture widely.

A representative Cofer poem is "Quinceañera" from her 1987 book *Terms of Survival*. (The Spanish word *quinceañera* refers to the celebration of a girl's maturing to womanhood at age fifteen.) The speaker is a fifteen-year-old girl who has just crossed the threshold from childhood to womanhood. Her mother has just pulled her hair back painfully. She muses over her mixed emotions, puzzles over her physical sensations, and finally compares herself to the crucified Christ, concluding "I am wound like the guts of a clock, / Waiting for each hour to release me."

This final simile connects the earlier theme of winding—the mother's affectionate but vigorous twisting of the girl's braids—with the alarming suspense of waiting for her moment of release. The phrase "like the guts of a clock" echoes the sound of winding an old-fashioned clock, and though the poem is sympathetic it is also humorous. One has both the amusing image of a girl being given her last rites of childhood (wound like an alarm clock by her mother's twisting hands) and the sense of intense internal pressure and an impending countdown to an unknown release. This combination of sympathy and wit occurs often in Cofer's poems.

In two other poems from *Terms of Survival*, the wit is grim. In "Esperanza" and "Socorro," Cofer reflects upon women who bear these names, which translate respectively as "Hope" and "Help." Esperanza, whose mother died in childbirth, is hated by her father as a result, and the irony of her name is emphasized by her own hope-lessness. The futility of her efforts to clear away the past is clear in the final image, in which she holds a broom in her hands but "[i]n my heart— / ashes, ashes." Like Esperanza, Socorro suffers from a loss, that of her one child, and though she is mocked by children because of her name, she survives by raising chrysanthemums to sell. Rejected by those around her, Socorro is comforted by the presence of death, portrayed as a "gentleman" who helps her cross the street every morning and waits for her patiently, "in her corner / smelling her flowers." These poems of incongruity and loss allow an implicit reversal of the irony of the women's names in that neither Esperanza with her broom or Socorro with her gentleman friend is hopeless or helpless.

"Night Driving," from *Peregrina* (1986), is a solitary meditation on personal relations and an assessment of the relation of courage to love when courage is in short supply. Yet even here the intellectual predicament is formulated playfully as a game, and the uncertain night journey reaches its moment of nearest certainty as the narrator contemplates a hypothetical threat to her child and says "with almost no hesitation / I extend my body like a bridge." The lonely solitude provokes a sense of the power of fear, as the word "almost" is an honest concession to the abiding parental nightmare of threats to offspring. As the "other voices" fade at the close of the poem, the reader is left uncertain as to what comfort the narrator has ended her game with. The impression that remains is that of the directness with which the prospect of fear is confronted. The passing mile markers bring to mind murdered nuns in violent places, but the response, instead of a domestic complacency, is the internal question of the extent to which fear can be faced. The implied devotion of the dead nuns provokes an analysis of devotion itself, and the wry result seems to be a fatigued concession that perfect devotion is no easy matter.

Further Reading. *Selected Primary Sources:* Cofer, Judith Ortiz, *Among the Ancestors* (Louisville, KY: News Press, 1981); ———, *The Latin Deli* (Athens: University of Georgia Press, 1993); ———, *The Year of Our Revolution: New and Selected Stories and Poems* (Houston: Arte Público Press, 1998); ———, *Latin Women Pray* (Florida Arts Gazette Press, 1980); ———, *The Native Dancer* (Pteranodon Press, 1981); ———, *Peregrina* (Golden, CO: Riverstone Press, 1986); ———, *Reaching for the Mainland* (Tempe, AZ: Bilingual Review Press, 1987); ———, *Terms of Survival* (Houston: Arte Público Press, 1987). ***Selected Secondary Sources:*** Davidson, Phebe, "Judith Ortiz Cofer: Drawn to the Outsider," in *Conversations with the World: American Women Poets and Their Work* (Pasadena, CA: Trilogy Books, 1998); Gordon, Stephanie, "An Interview with Judith Cofer" (*AWP Chronicle* 30.2 [1997]); Rangil, Viviana, "Pro-Claiming a Space: The Poetry of

Sandra Cisneros and Judith Ortiz Cofer" (*MultiCultural Review* 9.3 [2000]).

Robert W. Haynes

COLE, HENRI (1956–)

Henri Cole has a complex position in American poetry. His poems consistently resist being pinned to national markers. "Nationality," Cole himself has said, "has no supreme claim on me" ("What's American"). As a **lyric poet**, he is a singer who recreates universal emotions in a specific context, eschewing more common American and modern identifications, including regionalism and, later, social and cultural emphases. With a lyric eye on the shape of feeling, primary emotion, and meticulous craft, Cole's poems look to self-breeding states of transition between nature and art, human beings and other animals, the single human being with itself. In those acts of travel, Cole's poems find ancestry in the piercing panoramas of **W.H. Auden** and Philip Larkin, satirists either looming or squatting over potential luminous states. But Cole's dogged acts of looking, instances of what he has called "aparthood," ("How I Grew") lead the poems more often to release, which if modulated, nonetheless remains surprisingly literal, and American. In lyric fashion, Cole's eye lingers on a feeling of wonder: It can "find" and found "the world luminous and waiting." Although the findings of that world have roots in European Romanticism and the visuals of international **Modernism**, the speech acts of declaration in forging that world, of making it so, turn the poetic wheel toward an American idiom of autobiography and self-consciousness: the world found may be luminous, but the acts of both finding and founding it—stringent and spare—remain inseparable from exile—watching, waiting, and desire.

Cole's poems have their ancestry in the English language. His modern eye convenes with the sly voyeurism of **Walt Whitman**, the panning of **Hart Crane**, the montage of **William Carlos Williams**, the satiric portraiture of **Robert Lowell**, and the fierce modesty of **Elizabeth Bishop**. Sliding back and forth—between the mundane and monumental, or the "I" as "I" and the "I" as "you"—Cole's lyricism follows these American eyes, which both frame human displacement and, then, assess the miraculous rebound. Thus, Cole's poems are modern and self-conscious and unsettling, but not essentially ironic; his voice is American, solitary, and domestic, but interconnected with other nations, including the nations of animals or other silent souls.

Born in Fukuoka, Japan, in 1956, and raised in a lower-middle-class family, Cole grew up in Virginia. In his house, English, French, and Armenian were spoken, but Cole spoke English primarily. By his own account, tone at this early stage of separation was important, a "signal to meaning." (For several years, he lived in a tree house in the woods apart from his house ["How I Grew"].) He began writing poems during his junior year at William and Mary and graduated in 1978. In his poems, discipline, violence, and love, informed by Roman Catholicism, the military, and homosexuality, can shape language of the castaway or wanderer: first, separation or dislocation, and then again "beyond all this" a web of social relations containing and releasing "me." After he received his MA from the University of Wisconsin–Milwaukee in 1980, he was granted his MFA from Columbia University in 1982. Cole has held teaching positions and residencies at institutions including Columbia University, Reed College, Yale University, the University of Maryland, Brandeis University, and Smith College. He was named a Briggs-Copeland lecturer at Harvard University from 1993 to 1999. Among numerous fellowships and prizes, he has received the Amy Lowell Poetry Travelling Scholarship in 1989 and the Rome Prize in Literature from the American Academy of Arts and Letters in 1995. Nominated for a Pulitzer Prize in 2004, he has been praised by critic Harold Bloom as "a master poet, with few peers" (*Middle Earth*).

From 1982 to 1988, Cole was executive director of the Academy of American Poets. Rich with what he names the "Apollonian in body and Dionysian in spirit" ("An Interview by Christopher Hennessy," 43), his first collection, *The Marble Queen* (1986), is marked by the technical astonishment found in poets such as **James Merrill** and Hart Crane. It is especially concentrated in the eye, a blaze of stanzaic repertoire, technicolor camera action, and dramatic mask. What would become a characteristic movement of the eye appears in concentration here; initial displacement—and, then, "unexpected" release—careens self-consciously across species ("Of Island Animals," "The Octopus Orchid," or even "The Limo-Angel"), sexualities ("Father's Jewelry Box), and eras of the sun and sonless ("Desert Days on the Reservoir"). This form of self-recognition is opened out in Cole's second book, *The Zoo Wheel of Knowledge* (1989), which pushes lyric representation to social conditions, importantly AIDS, in which listening (to others, nature, oneself) is added to conditions of seeing and being, in a developing nerve of self-recognition. The book begins with the characteristic "dilated / pupil"; it ends in another dislocation and relocation, of man with beasts, "who see those that flee / from them" and, somehow accustomed, "listen tirelessly."

His third book, *The Look of Things*, came out in 1995. In it the dislocated, solitary, but periscopic eye is reunited with the biblical, particularly the parable, and with narrative time. A litany of interruptions on the landscape by the Angel of History (death and, worse, suffering) appear, as the very same infection that binds, and releases, human imagination. Together these three books establish Cole's lyric correlatives, his vision of the relative kinships among a "zoo wheel" of people, animals, the land, and the self. "Seeing and being," in his own words, conspire in his poems toward social solitariness and ascension, like a spire, organized along a characteristic spine of the conjunction "as": "I watch the roses trellised against the porch . . . as the sun drops free of her captive" in *The Marble Queen*, or from *The Look of Things*, "On the windowsill, / red tulips / stopped their grieving . . . as something stirred / beneath the sheet." That wisp of a connection "as," gentle but probing, in these first three books especially, bolts together ornament and brevity, cause and effect, the atemporal and the domestic, producing a vast and mysterious sum of interrelations.

In Cole's fourth book, *The Visible Man* (1998), and fifth book, *Middle Earth* (2003), that sum is broken into its two parts: the eye as artifice, and the eye as organic. The trope of seeing and being persists in *The Visible Man*, peaking in the Apollonian and classical element. Roman Italy, Roman Catholicism, the god of art and religion who loves and hates the visible man, and his human, gay, animal mouth—all mark the mix of eternity with the human body, the "bath where faith, hope, & charity / toss against spent semen, saliva, & tears." An epigraph from Plato in Section II locates the human gaze at the center of the examined transition between visibility and invisibility: "And, if the soul is about to know itself, it must gaze into the soul." But a Dionysian note roars back in Cole's fifth volume, *Middle Earth*, which he worked on while a Berlin Prize Fellow in 2000, during which time he was the Fannie Hurst Poet-in-Residence. Litanies that appear in *The Visible Man*, characteristic of Western cataloguing and biblical parataxis, in *Middle Earth* spread out into Eastern meditative repetition, silences, and landscape painting. Here, the "I" is nothing but—and is exactly—the small figure noted in the forms of nature. Whether in the poem "Kayaks" or "Necessary and Impossible," the non-egocentric and yet inevitable emergence of "I" from its surroundings, whether of memory or nature, comes from a newfound emotional and rhetorical transparency, and occasional humor. This new realism is familiar, however, finding edges, boundaries, and middles to harbor, if not risings, then the very blur of connection, "licking my paws, licking my throat," satiation. Even the last line, drawn from the West, East, and in-between, fills in the sense of things, the "odors of the soft black earth." Released in 2003, *Middle Earth* received the prestigious Kingsley Tufts Poetry Award in 2004.

Across Cole's poems, the lyric self-examination of "trying and trying to be lifted" holds. There are moments: rising of friendship from the ashes ("Supper with Roy" in *The Look of Things*), of man from the sea, of comfort from the earth. And there are descendings,

along with attempted reclamation, on the occasion of self-pity or doubt. Cole's scope is more wide with wonder and the silence of this travel than **Wallace Stevens**'s or **John Ashbery**'s **modernist** American eye. It is also more solemnly humble and human. Still, though human and graphic in guilt, sex, and social critique, Cole's poems resist easy categorization in tempting current political and literary scenes, American or international. Though topical, they are not essentially topical. Like lyric poets **William Logan**, an American, or Adam Zagajewski from Poland, or Thomas Kinsella of Ireland, Cole locates specific contexts of landscape, gender, war, sexuality, religion in larger vision—the art of change, combined with surprising human moments of monument. Cole incorporates even the act of writing into the plane of kinship. "This evening, as I write, through my desk window, across the park, I see one man embrace another on a rooftop terrace," he comments simply. "What I witness unexpectedly is the invisible, the true, which is what poems are, what mine strive to be" ("First Loves").

Further Reading. ***Selected Primary Sources:*** Cole, Henri, "First Loves" (American Poetry Society of America, www.poetrysociety.org/journal/articles/firstloves.html #Henri); ———, "How I Grew" (*Borzoi Reader Online*, www.randomhouse.com/knopf/authors/cole/poetson poetry.html); ———, *The Look of Things* (New York: Alfred A. Knopf, 1995); ———, *The Marble Queen* (New York: Atheneum, 1986); ———, *Middle Earth* (New York: Farrar, Straus and Giroux, 2003); ———, *The Visible Man* (New York: Alfred A. Knopf, 1998); ———, *The Zoo Wheel of Knowledge* (New York: Alfred A. Knopf, 1989). ***Selected Secondary Sources:*** Hennessy, Christopher, "An Interview by Christopher Hennessy" (*APR* 33.3 [May/June 2004]: 43–46); Vendler, Helen, "A Dissonant Triad" (*Parnassus* 16.2 [1991]: 391–404); "What's American about American Poetry?" (*American Poetry Society of America* [1999], http://www.poetrysociety.org/cole.html).

Page Richards

COLEMAN, WANDA (1946–)

Perhaps one of the most prolific writers of her age, Wanda Coleman is a novelist, essayist, scriptwriter, editor, journalist, short-story writer, and poet. A fellowship recipient from the Guggenheim Foundation and the National Endowment for the Arts, Coleman was awarded the 1999 Lenore Marshall Poetry Prize for *Bathwater Wine* (1998) and was a finalist for the 2001 National Book Award in Poetry for *Mercurochrome* (2001). Although Coleman's work is highly acclaimed, she has not received much scholarly attention beyond interviews and short reviews of her work. Coleman, nevertheless, remains an active figure in her hometown of Los Angeles, where she has hosted a local radio program on poetry, and her work is often anthologized in collections of **feminist**, **African American**, and **postmodern** poems.

The daughter of a seamstress and an advertiser, Coleman was born in Watts, a district of Los Angeles, California, on November 13, 1946. After attending two years of college, Coleman joined Studio Watts, a program that brought together musicians, actors, writers and visual artists from the local area. The Studio Watts manifesto, to create cultural, social, and economic change through artists and their artistry, has had an enduring effect on Coleman's work, which often focuses on the conditions experienced by black women at the intersections of race, gender, class, and history. In an article titled "On the Poetics of Wanda Coleman," for the summer 1990 edition of *Catalyst Magazine*, Coleman once wrote of herself, "I am a minority within a minority within a minority—racially, sexually, regionally" (37).

This spirit of the marginalization and determined survival of African Americans, particularly African American women, dominates the whole of Coleman's poetry. Coleman's *Mad Dog Black Lady* (1979) addresses these issues most directly in the poem "Women of My Color," where Coleman writes about the "particular light" in which men see her. Here, she considers the various roles black women are asked to play: to be sisters, saints, mothers and whores for black men while concurrently being regarded as "exotic" and as "enemies" by white men. Likewise, in "No Woman's Land" from the same collection, Coleman intertwines various U.S. political institutions with the politics of sexism, condemning how both "napalm my dreams of black womanhood," producing "détente for them, defeat for me." By juxtaposing the personal and the political throughout her poetry, Coleman demonstrates her interest in lived condition of African American women.

Although Coleman's poetry often focuses on the contemporary, her work equally evokes a sense of how history affects the present. In "Emmett Till," from *African Sleeping Sickness* (1990), Coleman laments the fourteen-year-old's murder in 1955 for his "smooth long all-american hallelujah whistle" at a white woman. Beginning with the biblical River Jordan, Coleman interupts her retelling of Till's brutal slaying with an alphabetical list of U.S. rivers that are now "blood river born" with his body. In so doing, Coleman shows that the "hate-inspired poverty" of Jim Crow resides throughout these American rivers, and hence the entire United States, not only the South. In "Ethiopian in the Fuel Supplies" from *Hand Dance* (1993), Coleman, borrowing the phrase from one of W.C. Fields's racial slurs, addresses the historical role of skin color in the black community. Discussing complexion with her son, who is called a "zebra" in school for mixed heritage, Coleman reviews the color lines in African American history, from "yellow," to "ogalala Sioux." Playing with the old adage of

"sticks and stones," Coleman writes, "if yah stick me hard baby / i'll gush blood blue," thereby demonstrating the power of words to be like swords. The poem, which opens with a playground challenge to her son to prove he is "human," ends with Coleman comforting her son with the equation that "hue" plus "man" does indeed mean "human."

Language play is another facet that exemplifies Coleman's work. Often compared with **Amiri Baraka** and **Charles Bukowski**, the latter of whom she claims to be an early influence on her work, Coleman is known for her rhythmic use of language and intertexuality. Like the equation and repetition in "Ethiopian in the Fuel Supplies," Coleman's "Essay on Language" from *Heavy Daughter Blues* (1987) offers equations such as ""black skin + new money = counterfeit" and "colorlessness + glibness = success." Coleman also plays with childhood word games, beginning the nursery rhyme "who stole the cookie from the cookie jar," intermixed with "the middle passage." The product is a postmodern poetry that concurrently discusses the issues of identity, history, cultural memory and popular culture.

The title poem of Coleman's *African Sleeping Sickness* (1990) further demonstrates Coleman's ability to interweave these topics. In the poem, Coleman's "petite white man" doctor diagnoses the African American condition as "four centuries of sleep." Intermixing medical terms and historical conditions, such as "the encephalopathy of slavery," Coleman makes dreamlike references to childhood memories: her father singing "My Blue Heaven," "kryptonite," and "the six o'clock news." Coleman also references **Langston Hughes**'s "The Negro Sings of Rivers," as she repeatedly writes, "sing me rivers" and "sing to me of rivers." Likewise, many of her recent poems also reflect this use of intertextuality. "Thirteen Ways of Looking at a Bluesbird," from *Bathwater Wine* (1998), for example, models itself in verse and form upon **Wallace Stevens**'s "Thirteen Ways of Looking at a Blackbird."

Much of Coleman's poetry also derives from her experiences in Los Angeles. Her collection *Imagoes* (1993) most particularly centers on images of Los Angeles with works such as "Flight of the California Condor," a poem dedicated to Los Angeles that compares life for the African American in Watts to the endangered bird. Coleman's later poems from *Mercurochrome* (2001) also explore regions of the city, such as Hollywood, El Camino Real, and Union Station.

In "Word Game," from *Mad Dog Black Lady* (1979), Coleman begins the poem with the line "once upon a time, I a poet, transformed myself into a poem." As so much of Coleman's identity and experiences make their way into her poetry, one can easily concur with Coleman that her life is indeed poetry transformed. Today, Coleman continues to write and perform her poetry, and she recently released her latest collection of poems *Ostinato Vamps* (2003) to solid reviews.

Further Reading. Selected Primary Sources: Wanda Coleman, *African Sleeping Sickness: Stories and Poems* (Santa Rosa, CA: Black Sparrow Press, 1990); ———, *Bathwater Wine* (Santa Rosa, CA: Black Sparrow Press, 1998); ———, *Hand Dance* (Santa Rosa, CA: Black Sparrow Press, 1993); ———, *Heavy Daughter Blues* (Santa Rosa, CA: Black Sparrow Press, 1986); ———, *Imagoes* (Santa Barbara, CA: Black Sparrow Press, 1983); ———, *Mad Dog Black Lady* (Santa Barbara, CA: Black Sparrow Press, 1979); ———, *Mercurochrome* (Santa Rosa, CA: Black Sparrow Press, 2001). **Selected Secondary Sources:** Brown, Priscilla Ann, "What Saves Us (An Interview with Wanda Coleman)" (*Callaloo* 26.3 [Summer 2003]: 635–662); Magistrale, Tony, and Patricia Ferreira, "Sweet Mama Wanda Tells Fortunes: An Interview with Wanda Coleman" (*Black American Literature Forum* 24.3 [Fall 1990]: 491–508).

Kristin Brunnemer

COLLIER, MICHAEL (1953–)

Michael Collier has had an important place in American poetry since the early 1990s, based on the four collections of poems he has published, as well as his work as a prominent teacher, editor, and director of literary institutions. Since his debut with *The Clasp and Other Poems* in 1986, Collier has been committed to the art of the actual. His is an aesthetic that seeks transcendence not through linguistic experimentation or surreal imagination, but through controlled, meticulously crafted language and keen attention to the physical world. His enduring concern with the subject of memory and his quiet, precise style mark Collier as an heir to the literary mentors with whom he is often associated, **William Meredith** and William Maxwell. Although his books have established him as an important voice in his generation, Collier has also had an active role in shaping the direction of twenty-first–century American poetry, as the editor of an influential poetry series at Houghton Mifflin, and as the sixth director of the Bread Loaf Writers' Conference.

Collier was born in Phoenix, Arizona, in 1953, and raised in a suburban West that is chronicled in many of his poems. After graduating from the Jesuit Brophy College Preparatory School in Phoenix, Collier came east to Connecticut College, where he studied under the poets William Meredith and **Robert Hayden**. Meredith also introduced Collier to William Maxwell, the fiction writer and famous editor at the *New Yorker*. These older writers became mentors and friends to Collier, and their emphasis on clarity and precision is apparent in his poems. He is among a generation of poets trained in the Iowa-style creative writing programs that flourished in the 1970s, and after finishing his undergraduate degree, Collier enrolled at the University of Arizona, receiving his MFA in 1979. At Arizona, and later at the Fine Arts Work Center in Provincetown, Collier formed bonds with many young writers who would go on to distinguished careers, including **Alberto Rios**, David Wojahn, William Olsen, Tom Sleigh, **Michael Burkhard**, **Lorna Dee Cervantes**, and John Skoyles.

By the mid-1980s Collier was teaching in the University of Maryland's MFA program and had made his mark with the publication of *The Clasp and Other Poems* (1986). His second book, *The Folded Heart* (1989), received the Alice Fay di Castagnola Award of the Poetry Society of America, and by the time his third collection, *The Neighbor* (1995), was published Collier was an established voice in American poetry, and an increasingly prominent editor and director of literary programs. He was chosen by Wesleyan University Press to edit *The Wesleyan Tradition: Four Decades of American Poetry* in 1993, and then in 1994 he was named as the sixth director of the Bread Loaf Writers' Conference, which has been the preeminent summer writing symposium in the country since its founding in 1926. The conference, whose list of former faculty is a veritable who's who of American literature, has thrived under Collier, who broadened its horizons by welcoming writers from a wide range of aesthetic camps, from previously underrepresented minority groups, and from countries around the world. Collier has received fellowships from the Thomas J. Watson Foundation, the National Endowment for the Arts, and the Guggenheim Foundation, and served as Poet Laureate of the State of Maryland from 2001 to 2004. His fourth collection, *The Ledge* (2000), was a finalist for the National Book Critics Circle Award and the *Los Angeles Times* Book Prize.

In an age often characterized by experimental poetry and postmodern irony, Collier's poems are remarkable for their quiet authority. The aesthetic that governs his work, even as Collier has broadened his thematic and formal range over the years, is one of careful attention, as the poet draws connections between vividly rendered narratives and the hard truths that lie beneath the surface of human lives. In one of his best early poems, "V-8" (*The Folded Heart*), Collier writes of a huge motor that hung for decades "tarp-covered and lashed with rope" in a neighbor's backyard. When the neighbor confronts the fact that he will never rebuild the engine and finally sells it to a younger man, Collier transforms the object into an emblem, freighted with all the complex emotions that are the real subject of the poem. As the man hoists the V-8 into a truck, his mixture of bitterness and love is not named so much as embodied, as Collier describes the motor "settled in the bed, tilted on its side, / leaking a puddle of oil, dark and latent."

Such combinations of empathy and hard realism recur in many of the poems, which can be at once tender and brutal. When the poet remembers a childhood friend crying himself to sleep in the poem "Bread Route" (*The Neighbor*), he depicts love not as an abstraction but an experience, inseparable from the flawed world of things in which it occurs. For the boy crying on his first night away from home, Collier writes, "love is dark, a parent arriving in the night or leaving / each morning: a father's boot, a van door sliding shut."

At his best, Collier writes on this border between the personal and the universal, the particular and the mythic, and although he looks upon the brutality of the world unflinchingly, he also documents the dignity of those moments when we strive to overcome it. In a recent poem, "Brave Sparrow" (*The Ledge*), he revitalizes the conventional subject of the bird at the poet's window, depicting a sparrow in a hostile garden of hawks and robins "patrolling the yard like thugs." Collier gives voice to his sympathy and hope for the sparrow, even as he reminds himself that its situation is hopeless. To the cornered, starving thing, he can offer only an impossible prayer: "Stay where you are you lit fuse, / you dull spark of saltpeter and sulfur." Here, as in so many of his lyrical narratives, the poet finds an emblem for the ineffable in the world of "things as they are." It is a form of attention Collier learned well as a student of Meredith and Maxwell, a way of seeing the doomed sparrow as both a metaphor for our plight and, at the same time, as the actual, beautiful thing that it is.

Further Reading. ***Selected Primary Sources:*** Collier, Michael, *The Clasp and Other Poems* (Middletown, CT: Wesleyan University Press, 1986); ———, ed. and tr., *Euripides' Medea* (Oxford: Oxford University Press, 2005); ———, *The Folded Heart* (Middletown, CT: Wesleyan University Press, 1989); ———, *The Ledge* (New York: Houghton Mifflin, 2000); ———, *The Neighbor* (Chicago: University of Chicago Press, 1995); ———, ed., *The New American Poets: A Bread Loaf Anthology* (Lebanon, NH: University Press of New England, 2000); ———, ed., *The Wesleyan Tradition: Four Decades of American Poetry* (Middletown, CT: Wesleyan University Press, 1993); Collier, Michael, Charles Baxter, and Edward Hirsch, eds., *A William Maxwell Portrait* (New York: W. W. Norton, 2004); Collier, Michael, and Stanley Plumly, eds., *The New Bread Loaf Anthology of Contemporary American Poetry* (Lebanon, NH: University Press of New England, 1999). ***Selected Secondary Sources:*** Baker, David, "The Ledge (Book Review)" (*Kenyon Review* 24:2 [Spring 2002]: 150–165); Bang, Mary Jo, "The Neighbor" (*Boston Review* [February 1996]); Biespiel, David, "Free Verse Styles" (*Sewanee Review* 111.3 [2003]: 470–479); Collins, Floyd, "Poetry and the Primacy of the Imagination" (*Gettysburg Review* [Autumn 2003]: 471–484); Guereschi, Edward, "Bridesmaids and Veterans" (*American Book Review* 12.5 [November 1990]); Hatch, James, "Transformations" (*American Book Review* 22.3 [March 2001]); Redmond,

John, "Stirring Your Tea . . ." (*London Review of Books* [6 July 1995]: 18–19).

Patrick Phillips

COLLINS, BILLY (1941–)

Billy Collins writes poetry that he identifies as "hospitable" to the reader. Like many contemporary poets, Collins insists that poetry be a "thing" of the people, and he works to make poetry public property through his transparent, accessible style and his commonplace subjects. As U.S. Poet Laureate (2002–2004), Collins worked to increase interest in the field through his Poetry 180 project, which offered a poem a day to schools throughout the United States. The "guidelines" for this project suggest a broad range of readers, including teachers, students, administrators, and staff, and discourage discussion of the poetry unless students initiate it. Collins stresses the importance of hearing poetry free from academic requirements.

Traditionally, and perhaps paradoxically, commercial and popular success often taints a literary reputation. Collins, however, proves the rare exception, as his significance to American poetics rests squarely on his popularity as a literary voice, a voice that speaks clearly and often humorously. He writes smart, engaging, comic, and complex poems that appeal to both the first-time, occasional reader and the experienced reader of poetry.

Collins, born in New York City, now lives with his wife, Diane, an architect, in Westchester County, New York. A Distinguished Professor of English at Lehman College, City University of New York, Collins is also a writer-in-residence at Sarah Lawrence College, New York. He attended Holy Cross College in Massachusetts and earned a Ph.D. from the University of California–Riverside.

Collins has published seven books of poetry: *Nine Horses: Poems* (2002); *Sailing Alone Around the Room: New and Selected Poems* (2001); *Picnic, Lightning* (1997); *The Art of Drowning* (1995), a finalist for the Lenore Marshall Poetry Prize; *Questions about Angels: Poems* (1991), selected by Edward Hirsh for the National Poetry Series; *The Apple That Astonished Paris: Poems* (1988); *Pokerface* (1977); and in 1997, *The Best Cigarette*, a CD on which Collins reads thirty-three of his poems. In addition, his poetry regularly appears in textbooks, anthologies such as the Pushcart Prize anthology and *The Best American Poetry*, and periodicals such as *Poetry*, *American Poetry Review*, *American Scholar*, *Harper's*, *Paris Review*, and the *New Yorker*.

The New York Foundation for the Arts, the National Endowment for the Arts, and the Guggenheim Foundation have all awarded fellowships to Billy Collins, and he has won the Oscar Blumenthal Prize, the Hokin Prize, the Frederick Bock Prize, and Levinson Prize (all awarded by *Poetry* magazine). Collins has also served as a "Literary Lion" for the New York Public Library.

In interviews, Collins explains his views regarding the readers of his poems. He imagines the reader as someone in the room with him, someone intimately engaged in the writing of the poem. This awareness of the reader makes Collins's poetry accessible (an adjective found in most all the reviews of Collins's work), not surprisingly, they also often address and instruct the reader. For example, in "Introduction to Poetry" from *The Apple That Astonished Paris*, the poet bids the reader to look at, listen to, and probe the poem while "water-ski[ing] / across the surface of a poem." Collins closes "Introduction" by regretfully acknowledging that readers insist on tying up, torturing, and beating the poem in order to have it confess its meaning. In "Workshop," from *The Art of Drowning*, the speaker, a participant in a poetry writing workshop, comments on a poem, providing the perspective of both poet and reader. Here Collins satirizes unnecessary ambiguity and obscure meaning as he advocates a clear poetics that moves the reader through a poem. This insistence on clarity emerges also in "Night Letter to the Reader," the opening poem in *Nine Horses*, as the poet tells the reader what he *wishes* to tell him or her, twice using "tell" and three times directly addressing the reader as "you." Midway through the poem, the poet muses on the importance of the poetic renderings, likening them to "flecks of ash, tiny chips of ice."

Collins's poetry almost always conveys a sense of movement as it contemplates the daily and the ordinary. Poem after poem delineates a journey of thought and imagination. In fact, when asked about his poems, Collins likens poetry and poetry writing to travel. His poems provide mini-journeys into musings about death and aging, writing and reading, words and meaning, love and desire, comfort and contentment. Generally, his poems begin in small places or with ordinary objects, and through carefully chosen details, Collins renders the ordinary extraordinary. For example, in "Osso Buco" (*The Art of Drowning*), the speaker muses on the bone on the plate, the risotto, the soft meat and marrow that make up the meal. From the comfort and confines of the kitchen, the poem moves to a contemplation of contentment ending at the center of the "earth itself." "The Death of Hats" (*Picnic, Lightning*) memorializes the poet's father as it is he who wears a hat of sky, clouds, and wind. In this poem the simple everyday object "hat" becomes a metaphor for a lifetime journey.

The metaphors of life as a journey through time and time as motion stand as dominant themes in *Nine Horses*, in poems such as "Velocity," "Albany," "Rooms," and "The Parade." This volume brings together many of Collins's poetic preoccupations: the writing and reading of poetry ("Night Letter to the Reader," "Royal Aristocrat," "The Return of the Key," Writing in the Afterlife," and "Poetry"); the importance of observation and the moment ("Today," "Roadside Flowers," "Albany," and "Ignorance"); musings on aging, absence, and death ("Obituaries," "Birthday," and "The Listener"). In *Nine Horses*, as he does throughout his entire oeuvre, Collins sounds a particularly American voice, using the commonplaces of our lives to invite us into a poetry that offers possibilities for the imagination.

Further Reading. ***Selected Primary Sources:*** Collins, Billy, *The Apple that Astonished Paris* (Fayetteville: University of Arkansas Press, 1988); ———, *The Art of Drowning* (Pittsburgh: University of Pittsburgh Press, 1995); ———, *The Best Cigarette* [audio CD] (Cielo Publishing, 1997); ———, *Nine Horses: Poems* (New York: Random House, 2002); ———, *Picnic, Lightning* (Pittsburgh: University of Pittsburgh Press, 1997); ———, *Pokerface* (Philadelphia: Kenmore Press, 1977); ———, *Questions about Angels: Poems* (Pittsburgh: University of Pittsburgh Press, 1991); ———, *Sailing Around the Room: New and Selected Poems* (New York: Random House, 2001). ***Selected Secondary Sources:*** Lund, Elizabeth, "Poet Laureate Promotes 'Events for the Ear'" (*Christian Science Monitor* [25 April, 2002]: Features, 15); Merrin, Jeredith, "Art over Easy" (*Southern Review* 38.1 [2002]: 202–214); Reeve, F.D. "Inadequate Memory and the Adequate Imagination" (*American Review of Poetry* 32.3 [2003]: 11–13).

Catherine Cucinella

COLMAN, BENJAMIN (1673–1747)

Benjamin Colman was an American Colonial minister, essayist, and poet. More widely published in prose than poetry, Colman's poetical accomplishments are primarily **elegies** and expressions in verse of his religious vision. He was well known as an elegant, poetical prose stylist as well as a competent poet in the popular eighteenth-century heroic style.

Benjamin Colman was born on October 19, 1673, in Boston, Massachusetts, the son of William and Elizabeth Colman. His education began at an early age and continued through two degrees at Harvard College, in 1692 and 1695. Shortly after the completion of his MA, Colman embarked on a voyage to England to seek opportunities to practice his vocation. During the trip, French pirates waylaid the ship and imprisoned its crew and passengers for several months, but Colman did eventually reach England and preach at Ipswich, Cambridge, and Bath. In 1699, Colman, having been ordained in England, returned to Boston to preside over the Brattle Street Church, established as an alternative to the Second Church. The remainder of his career and life was occupied by the practical and literary duties inherent in his position as church leader and important figure in the religious and intellectual life of Boston. He attained a degree of international fame, was awarded an honorary Doctor of Divinity from the University of Glasgow in

1731 and was associated with the leading American religious thinkers of his time. He married three times, surviving his first two wives and all three of his children. Colman died on August 28, 1747, writing and publishing essays and sermons until the year before his death.

Colman was known to be a reader and admirer of Alexander Pope's works, and his poetry shows a stylistic influence, though Pope tended to write satire and Colman's poetry is far more devotional. Colman's allusions were biblical rather than classical, and his verse less intended to instigate or protest political action, in keeping with his general conservative tendency as regarded church doctrine. His greatest innovations in both prose and poetry were in linguistic style. Colman embraced relatively plain language and eschewed obscure metaphors. He did include in his works some of the conventions of the heroic style, such as the invocation of the Muse, and he did maintain some expression in language that was consistent with poets such as Pope and themes such as those of John Milton, whom he also admired. On the whole, however, he achieved considerable clarity in his verse, rendering it remarkably readable today.

Colman's elegies couched the tribute to the deceased in terms of the religious ideals of his faith. In "Another to Urania" (1700), a poem about a mother who loses a child, Colman compares the mother's prayers to him as a minister to those of the Shunamite woman's to the prophet Elisha in 2 Kings 4; his closing message to the mother is to seek to accept the will of God as the Shunamite woman did, as that faith was her son's salvation. In "A Poem on Elijah's Translation, Occasion'd by the Death of the Reverend and Learned Mr. Samuel Willard" (1707), Colman refers to the history of the prophet Elijah, Elisha's father, whose ascent to Heaven in 2 Kings 2 was preceded by Elisha's request to receive from his father a double share of his spirit. Colman implies again that he places himself in the poem, this time in the Elisha role, to Willard's Elijah, as the next generation of holy man in need of strength.

In the twentieth century, a small amount of scholarly work has been done on Colman's life and writings, but there is no current published biography, and the scholarly essays tend to be historical or comparative rather than critical, focusing on the sermons rather than the poetry. It has been nearly two decades since any critical work has appeared at all, including listed dissertations. But the sheer volume of publications in Colman's own time suggests the magnitude of his influence in pre-Enlightenment Boston, and his linguistic gifts render both his prose and verse accessible to contemporary historical and literary scholars.

Further Reading. *Selected Primary Sources:* Benjamin Colman's papers are available for microfilm viewing at the Massachusetts Historical Society in Boston, MA: "Another to Urania" (Boston, 1749); "A Humble Discourse on the Incomprehensibleness of God" (Boston, 1714); "A Poem on Elijah's Translation, Occasion'd by the Death of the Reverend and Learned Mr. Samuel Willard" (Boston, 1707). *Selected Secondary Sources:* Adams, Howard C., "Benjamin Colman: A Critical Biography" (Ph.D. diss., Penn. State University, 1976); Toulouse, Teresa, "'Syllabical Idolatry': Benjamin Colman and the Rhetoric of Balance" (*Early American Literature* 18.3 [Winter 1983–1984]: 257–274); Turrell, Ebenezer, *The Life and Character of the Reverend Benjamin Colman, D. D.* (Boston, 1749; reprint Delmar, NY: Scholars' Facsimiles and Reprints, 1972).

Nicole Roussos

COMMONPLACE BOOK

A commonplace book is a notebook in which the keeper enters textual memorabilia, usually by hand. The items recorded in the books are called "commonplaces"; commonplaces include maxims, excerpts from literature or philosophy, bits of scientific data, excerpts from friends' letters or other writing, and records of oral conversation. In addition to the record of quotations, the commonplace book often includes commentary by its keeper. The act of recording commonplaces in a book is called "commonplacing." Commonplace books served many functions: they were scrapbooks, containers for memories; they were pedagogical tools in early modern schools; they were sites of self-improvement.

The commonplace book was used in colonial and revolutionary American schools for young gentlemen to accomplish pedagogical goals. For example, students were encouraged by their instructors to condense and transcribe their lessons into commonplace books to develop memory. Students studied and transcribed classical rhetorical styles in order to develop skills in argument and to have a collection of rhetorical topics for future use. Thomas Jefferson began his literary commonplace book at the beginning of his formal education. However, rather than ceasing to record commonplaces at the end of his schooling, Jefferson continued to make entries through his late twenties.

The commonplace book of **William Byrd II** reveals that he too continued to use his commonplace book as a site of education throughout his life. According to his diaries, Byrd recorded in his commonplace book regularly, as part of his daily routine. Much of what he recorded derived from his private readings at the time. He also recorded ideas for self-improvement and scientific observations. Significantly, the book functioned as a site of reflection, "an instrument of confession and self-realization."

Sur Plusiers Beaux Sujects, the commonplace book of **Wallace Stevens**, provides a more contemporary example of the keeping and using of a commonplace book. In his book, Stevens collected both thoughts from his own imagination and ideas he encountered in his life and readings. The significance of the book to his work as a writer is obvious: Of the 104 entries in the book, 22 he either quoted directly or paraphrased in his poetry. Additionally, he repeats in his formal writing themes developed in other entries.

The commonplace books that survive today are useful artifacts for contemporary readers for many reasons. A commonplace book provides insights into the private life of its keeper, similar to those provided by a diary. In studying the life of Thomas Jefferson, a public figure who guarded his privacy, his literary commonplace book is vital for learning about his inner life and thoughts. Perhaps most significant, the surviving commonplace books that were kept by women provide a record of colonial and revolutionary women's lives and writings that would never have come to light otherwise. For example, the commonplace book of **Elizabeth Graeme Fergusson** contains the only extant copies of much of the poetry written by her niece, **Anna Young Smith**. Had Fergusson not transcribed Smith's poetry into her commonplace book, only Smith's few published poems would have survived today. The commonplace book of **Milcah Martha Moore** also preserves much writing by American women of the revolutionary period.

Further Reading. *Selected Primary Sources:* Byrd, William, II, *The Commonplace Book of William Byrd II of Westover*, ed. Kevin Berland et al. (Chapel Hill: University of North Carolina Press, 2001); Jefferson, Thomas, *Jefferson's Literary Commonplace Book*, ed. Douglas L. Wilson (Princeton NJ: Princeton University Press, 1989); Moore, Milcah Martha, *Milcah Martha Moore's Book: A Commonplace Book from Revolutionary America*, ed. Catherine La Courreye Blecki and Karin A. Wulf (University Park: Pennsylvania State University Press, 1997); Stevens, Wallace, *Sur Plusiers Beaux Sujects: Wallace Stevens' Commonplace Book*, ed. Milton J. Bates (Stanford, CA: Stanford University Press, 1989). *Selected Secondary Source:* Stabile, Susan M., *Memory's Daughters: The Material Culture of Remembrance in Eighteenth-Century America* (Ithaca, NY: Cornell University Press, 2004).

Katie Rose Guest

CONCRETE POETRY

The birth of the concrete poetry movement gave a new impetus to **visual poetry**. Dating from 1955, the name was adopted by the Swiss poet Eugen Gomringer and Decio Pignatari, a Brazilian instructor of industrial design and communication theory, who agreed to join forces. Like Gomringer, Pignatari and his colleagues Augusto and Haroldo de Campos were heavily influenced by Stéphane Mallarmé. In addition, the Brazilians greatly admired **Ezra Pound**, with whom they corre-

sponded. Significantly, they called themselves the Noigandres group, after a passage in Pound's *Canto 20* in which the Old Provençal scholar Emil Levy despairs of ever deciphering this enigmatic word. Although the Brazilians have tended to be more concerned with sociopolitical problems, concrete poets on both sides of the Atlantic contend that their poetry has a practical value. Gomringer suggested installing signs in airports and other public places, for instance, that would be universally intelligible. The Brazilians also insist concrete poetry can provide useful, linguistic solutions to various problems.

If linguistics stops at the sentence, as Roland Barthes once remarked, concrete poetry stops at the word. Like the sentence in linguistics, the word is the largest unit within the scope of concrete poetry's field of inquiry. It is conceived not only as a fundamental building block but also as an independent entity. The traditional sentence, in concrete poetry, is reduced to a few basic words (even at times to one word) that tantalize the reader with their brevity. Because they must bear the whole weight of the composition, these words tend to denote objects and/or operations. Like the futurists before them, who also abolished traditional syntax, the concrete poets show a predilection for verbs and nouns. Whereas traditional poetry operates on the conceptual level, concrete poetry is based on perception. In contrast to traditional poetry, which occupies a virtual dimension, concrete poetry possesses an undeniable presence. It differs from conventional verse in its ability to translate abstract ideas into visual images. In addition to condensation, concrete poetry is distinguished by spatialization. Having abolished conventional grammar, the poem employs a spatial syntax. Words are liberated from the tyranny of the sentence on both the syntagmatic and the paradigmatic axes. They are free to combine with each other visually as well as verbally, vertically as well as horizontally.

Visual syntax presents the reader with multiple choices at every turn. One can proceed from left to right, from top to bottom, or diagonally in any direction. Because words are free to establish multiple relations, concrete poetry is by definition indeterminate. This does not mean it is unstructured but rather that the concept of structure has been redefined. From a circumscribed entity focused inward upon itself, the poem has been transformed into a work that opens outward to embrace multiple possibilities. What the concrete poem communicates above all, Pignatari and his colleagues declare, is its structure, which is projected onto the visual plane for everyone to see. Unlike conventional works, which attempt to obscure their underlying mechanisms, concrete poetry has nothing to hide. Each poem is conceived as an autonomous object, as the sum of its various signifiers. Seen in this light, concrete poetry is all surface.

Concrete poetry has proved to be phenomenally popular in America. Emmett Williams, Mary Ellen Solt, **Dick Higgins**, **Aram Saroyan**, and the Canadian **bp Nichol** were among numerous poets who initially experimented with this genre. Two anthologies were influential and helped to publicize the international movement: Williams's *An Anthology of Concrete Poetry* (1967) and Solt's *Concrete Poetry: A World View* (1970). Among the many heirs of the first generation of concrete poets, **Johanna Drucker** and the Canadian poet **Steve McCaffery** have been especially active. The widespread availability of computer and xerographic technology is transforming the genre in several radically different ways. Liberated from previous constraints, concrete poets possess an unprecedented freedom in selecting their materials and in devising ways to combine them. At present, half a dozen websites exist in North America devoted to concrete poetry and related subjects. Current experiments are so varied and so abundant as to virtually defy description. Some poets are attracted to hypertext technology, for example, wheras others prefer to construct kinetic poems. An exhibition of Eduardo Kac's works in 1998 featured a hologram, two videos, a set of Iris inkjet prints, and a computer terminal where visitors could operate six programs.

Further Reading. Bohn, Willard, *Modern Visual Poetry* (Newark:University of Delaware Press, 2001); Jackson, K. David, Eric Vos, and Johanna Drucker, eds., *Experimental—Visual—Concrete: Avant-Garde Poetry Since the 1960s* (Amsterdam and Atlanta: Rodopi, 1996); Solt, Mary Ellen, ed., *Concrete Poetry: A World View* (Bloomington: Indiana University Press, 1970); Williams, Emmett, ed., *An Anthology of Concrete Poetry* (New York: Something Else, 1967).

Willard Bohn

CONFESSIONAL POETRY

The term "confessional poetry" was coined by the critic M. L. Rosenthal in his review of **Robert Lowell**'s 1959 volume *Life Studies* for the *Nation* magazine in the September 10, 1959, issue. Although the term was generally associated with the poet's exploration of deep personal and family issues, and was sometimes regarded as equivalent to writing therapy, the poets associated with the movement nonetheless demonstrated a keen concern with social issues of the day such as the Cold War, the nuclear threat, and cultural diseases such as racism and sexism. Although the movement has often been denigrated by critics for the tendency of some of the more gifted poets to employ both subject matter and style for effect, nearly a half-century after the movement's peak, it seems safe to say that confessional poetry redirected American poetry's impulse toward autobiographical writing understood in its broadest possible terms, opening new areas of subject and voice for poetic expression.

In addition to Robert Lowell, the poets most often associated with the movement are **John Berryman**, **Sylvia Plath**, **Anne Sexton**, and **W.D. Snodgrass**. Other poets closely associated with the middle generation such as **Elizabeth Bishop**, **Randall Jarrell**, and **Theodore Roethke**, although close friends with members of the movement, are generally not classified as confessionals, although their poetry shares aspects of the autobiographical impulse. Although none of the "confessional" poets ever embraced Rosenthal's term (Lowell disliked it, Rosenthal himself later worried about its misuse, and John Berryman once answered an interview question by saying that he responded to the term "with rage and contempt"), the term stuck, and critics have continued to use it to describe one of the most vital and dynamic movements in twentieth century American poetry.

One aspect of the movement that has yet to be fully explored is the connection between confessional poetry and the **Beat** movement. Lowell said it was when he became aware, while on a West Coast reading tour, of the breakthrough of **Allen Ginsberg**'s "Howl," that he began to feel the ponderousness of his own well-received earlier work, from *Lord Weary's Castle* (1946) onward. So, according to Lowell, he began to relax the **New Critical** tension that had been a hallmark of his initial volumes. As Christopher Beach notes, "The mode of confessionalism—whether one approved of the term or not—served as a model for poets who chose to reject modernist difficulty and New Critical complexity in favor of a more relaxed or personal voice" (155). Other poets schooled in the New Critical aesthetic followed suit, with John Berryman moving from a highly dense and allusive verse to his jazzy, polyvocal idiom of *77 Dream Songs* (1964), and younger poets such as Sylvia Plath moving from regular stanzas and long lines into the volatile, more irregular personal lyrics of *Ariel* (1965).

Alongside Lowell's *Life Studies*, scholars point to a lesser-known volume, W.D. Snodgrass's *Heart's Needle* (1959), as an early work in the movement. Snodgrass had studied with Lowell and then Berryman at the University of Iowa Writers' Workshop in the mid-1950s, and *Heart's Needle* chronicles the birth of the poet's daughter, his subsequent divorce and remarriage, in frank, direct, emotional terms, exposing his fears and vulnerabilities to the reader. Lowell's *Life Studies*, published in the same year, is arguably, along with Ginsberg's *Howl and Other Poems* (1956), the most influential volume of poetry of the period. Organized into four sections, the book begins with several poems concerning cultural upheaval on a global scale, dealing with large subjects such as history, religion, and war, but with a focus on individuals as representative of societal anxiety, as in the poem "A Mad Negro Soldier Confined at Munich." A crucial component of the book is its second part, a personal memoir titled "91 Revere Street," where Lowell details the conflicts between his parents and his childhood response to those tensions. Alternately humorous, poignant, and lacerating, Lowell began the prose work as an autobiography, but decided to turn to poetry as his vehicle for exploring family and other aspects of his personal history. The prose memoir sets the stage for the fourth and final section of the volume, the sequence of poems titled "Life Studies." Preceding them are four brief poems dealing with modern writers with whom Lowell identifies, artists who struggled to gain recognition in an indifferent or even hostile world. Then comes the sequence of autobiographical poems, including many of Lowell's greatest achievements in verse, such as "My Last Afternoon with Uncle Devereux Winslow," where he explores his youthful initiation into the stark reality of human mortality, and "Memories of West Street and Lepke," with the poet recalling his days spend in jail as a conscientious objector. The volume concludes with what is probably Lowell's most anthologized poem, "Skunk Hour," with its famous line "My mind's not right." Writing about the poem, Lowell's friend and rival John Berryman described it as a poem detailing a psychological breakdown, and Lowell later admitted that Berryman was correct in his reading. Concluding his review of *Life Studies*, Rosenthal places the volume in a thematic line running through twentieth-century verse: "To build a great poem out of the predicament and horror of the lost Self has been the recurrent effort of the most ambitious poetry of the last century" (113). In his subsequent volumes, Lowell would continue to explore the personal, but would increasingly link the personal to public life, in landmark volumes such as *For the Union Dead* (1964) and *History* (1973).

Like Lowell, his friend John Berryman was erudite and schooled in the rich tradition of English poetry. His early work was largely unrecognized, but he broke through into his own unique voice and style with the poem *Homage to Mistress Bradstreet* (1953), an interior monologue in the voice of early American poet Anne Bradstreet. Shortly after publishing this poem, Berryman began to experiment with shorter lyrics in six-line stanzas where he used a consistent persona, a character named Henry, who speaks incessantly about himself in terms of loss, yearning, and boredom in a convoluted syntax, alternating between humor and sadness. Berryman did not publish these poems until 1964, when he brought out *77 Dream Songs*, and then in 1968, when he published *His Toy, His Dream, His Rest*. A year later he brought the two collections together as *The Dream Songs* (1969), totaling 385 poems. Despite the poet's insistence to the contrary, Berryman's Dream Songs are clearly autobiographical, chronicling

Berryman's obsession with his father's suicide, the death of fellow poets, lust and alcoholism, marriage and parenthood. Combining slang, Shakespearean rhetoric and syntax, attempts at minstrel dialect, and even baby talk, Berryman created a unique idiom and voice, spoken through the compelling persona of Henry, at various points called Huffy Henry, Henry Hankovich, and Henry House. Lowell was a great admirer of Berryman's breakthrough, and it was at his urging that Berryman finally gathered a sequence of the Songs for the initial volume in 1964, which brought Berryman the Pulitzer Prize. The 1968 volume would achieve the rare distinction of earning both the National Book Award and Bollingen Prize. In a poem elegizing Berryman, who died a suicide in 1972, Lowell wrote of how the two poets shared a similar educational background and interests, but singled out Berryman's humor as the feature that distinguished his poetry. Indeed, none of the other confessional poets ever come close to Berryman's irreverence, all the more striking in a long sequence of poems whose major theme is loss.

Sylvia Plath, born in 1932, was of a younger generation than Lowell and Berryman, but both she and Anne Sexton studied briefly with Lowell at Boston University in the 1950s. Although her career was quite brief, cut short by her suicide in February 1963, it is possible to discuss her work in terms of the early as opposed to the late stage, because there is a striking difference between her pre-1960 poems and the poetry she wrote in the year preceding her death, most of it included in *Ariel*, for which she is best known. Plath's work written during the 1950s, some of which appeared in *The Colossus* (England 1960; U.S. 1961), was dense, highly allusive, indebted to mythology, Shakespeare, and the iambic pentameter tradition. Yet within this early work, a reader detects her alienation following her father's death when she was eight years old, her struggles with a controlling mother, a passionate literary ambition, cultural constraints on a young woman growing up in 1950s America, and other autobiographical elements. But by the early 1960s, in the wake of her difficult marriage and subsequent estrangement from the British poet Ted Hughes, and the two children she was left to care for, her poetry takes on a more urgent, and at times angry, tone. Yet even in poems where she treats her own suffering, such as the well-known "Daddy" and "Lady Lazarus," she remains in careful control, using personae to speak the highly dramatic, charged poems. Unlike Berryman's jazzy, often careening persona of Henry, Plath's women speakers stage a taut, high-toned struggle against patriarchal oppression. Her intensely charged language, held in such tight rein, is unmistakably her own, a voice that has not been duplicated in American poetry.

Plath's friend Anne Sexton wrote poetry that is often more relaxed and almost always more explicit than that of Plath. Sexton began writing poetry as therapy, and in her first book, *To Bedlam and Part Way Back* (1960), she wrote directly about her "madness" and suicide attempts, her mother's terminal illness, her estrangement from her daughter, and ongoing conversations with her therapist. At the same time, she probed with a feminist's keen eye the culturally inscribed roles available to women, and the power of resistance, in poems such as "Her Kind." She would go on to treat heretofore taboo subjects such as abortion and masturbation. In addition to her subject matter, Sexton, like Berryman later in the decade, brought the art of the poetry reading into the forefront of the confessional movement. Her readings were performative events, playing to packed houses, and Sexton played up the dramatic aspects of both her own magnetic personality and the explicit subject matter of her poetry. A writer who reworked several fairy tales into verse, she consistently cast poetry as an enchanted realm, or as she put it in one poem's title, "The Black Art," where she wrote "A woman who writes feels too much."

The work of other poets often associated with the confessionals is also autobiographical, but not as explicit in personal detail as that of Berryman, Lowell, Plath, Sexton, and Snodgrass. The poems of Randall Jarrell, a close friend of both Lowell and Berryman, have only recently begun to be reassessed and brought out from under the shadow of his influential criticism. A college classmate of Lowell's, Jarrell was, like Lowell and Berryman, educated by the poet-critics who codified New Criticism. In his second and third volumes, *Little Friend, Little Friend* (1945) and *Losses* (1948), he wrote poignant elegies concerning his experience in World War II, and like most of the confessionals, he struggled with depression; like Berryman's, Jarrell's primary motif was loss, his primary mode the elegiac. In addition, by writing so poignantly about childhood, he opened up a perspective fully explored by other confessional poets. In his later volumes such as *The Woman at the Washington Zoo* (1960) and *The Lost World* (1965), he continued to explore personal loss and longing in autobiographical verse, at times writing in the persona of a woman.

Theodore Roethke was another influential figure for many of the confessionals, particularly Plath. Roethke projected into his poems extreme psychological states, whether of ecstasy or of despair. Elegized by Berryman in one of his Dream Songs as "the garden master," his poetry of the 1940s and 1950s also explored the realm of childhood, and looked to the natural world as both a source of primitive instincts as well as possible transcendence.

In her essay "What Was Confessional Poetry?" the critic Diane Wood Middlebrook points to the resistance by this group of poets not just to the Eliotic dictate of impersonality, but also to the cultural pressure to conform. This is another way in which the confessionals,

sometimes criticized for solipsism, engaged the sociopolitical climate of their day. In addition, nearly all of these poets underwent psychotherapy, so the exploration of self in relation to family became a natural tendency in their thinking, or, as Middlebrook writes, "Confessional poems sought to expose the poverty of the ideology of the family that dominated postwar culture and to draw poetic truth from the actual pain given and taken in the context of family life, especially as experienced by children" (648). Succeeding generations of poets extended this theme, including poets such as **Louise Glück**, **Sharon Olds**, **C.K. Williams**, and countless others. Poignant and unabashed in their treatment of the personal, the confessional poets implicitly insist on the value and responsibility of poetry's engagement with the cultural pressures of the day. Their work demonstrates how the personal voice need not be sacrificed in order to write a poetry of social engagement.

Further Reading. Axelrod, Stephen Gould, *Sylvia Plath: The Wound and the Cure of Words* (Baltimore: Johns Hopkins University Press, 1990); ———, ed., *The Critical Response to Robert Lowell* (Westport CT: Greenwood Press, 1999); Beach, Christopher, *The Cambridge Introduction to Twentieth-Century American Poetry* (Cambridge: Cambridge University Press, 2003); Ferguson, Suzanne, ed., *Jarrell, Bishop, Lowell, and Co.: Middle Generation Poets in Context* (Knoxville: University of Tennessee Press, 2003); Middlebrook, Diane Wood, "What Was Confessional Poetry?" in *The Columbia History of American Poetry*, ed. Jay Parini and Brett C. Millier (New York: Columbia University Press, 1993); Travisano, Thomas, *Midcentury Quartet: Bishop, Lowell, Jarrell, Berryman, and the Making of a Postmodern Aesthetic* (Charlottesville: University Press of Virginia, 1999).

Ernest Smith

COOKE, EBENEZER (CA. 1667–CA. 1732)

Ebenezer Cooke wrote one of the most interesting and important satires in American writing before 1820. First published in London in 1708, Cooke's *The Sot-weed Factor* took aim at colonists and their English detractors alike and, in the process of skewering both, provided readers with a new way of imagining being English in America. The poem gained new life in the nineteenth and twentieth centuries when historians, literary critics, and novelists saw in this satire the foundation for a distinctly Southern brand of humor and worldview.

We know few details regarding Cooke's life. Like many colonial poets, he was born, around 1667, in England. Records suggest that he first came to the New World sometime around 1694. His movements between Maryland and London are difficult to track for the next twenty-five years or so, but it is likely that he went back and forth across the Atlantic before settling in Maryland sometime in the 1710s until his death sometime after 1732. During his time in Maryland, he seems to have worked various jobs at various times. Records suggest that he was a land agent, a deputy of Henry Lowe II, a receiver-general of the province, and an attorney. Between 1722 and 1732, his name appears only on his poems. No other public records have been found bearing his name during this period. His last poem in 1732 marks Cooke's final appearance on the public stage, and scholars consider it likely that he died soon after its publication.

The Sot-weed Factor is Cooke's first known published writing. The poem combines satiric conventions well known to eighteenth-century English readers. First, the narrator, the eponymous sot-weed factor, or tobacco merchant, appears to be straight out of the classical models of satire eighteenth-century English writers used as a structural blueprint. He casts himself as a Juvenalian narrator who decries vice and error, which are no less heinous for being ridiculous. Stylistically, the narrator uses what had become known as Hudibrastic doggerel, named after the seventeenth-century satire by Samuel Butler. Further, the colonist-as-savage was already a common satiric figure by the time *The Sot-weed Factor* appeared in the early eighteenth century. The poem follows the merchant on his trip through the rough and tumble world of colonial Maryland, a world where the colonists have adapted so well to the local environment that, to the narrator at least, they seem more like Indians than English. The judges in this world are illiterate, the colonists seem to drink more often than work, and their food is uneatable by those with refined tastes. Indeed, whereas the colonists are mocked for being not English enough, the narrator is lampooned for being too English in that he demonstrates a palate so delicate that a drink of local water renders him immobile for six months. In the end, the poem imagines English identity in terms of exchange and transformation rather than an unchallengeable purity of bloodlines.

After *The Sot-weed Factor*, Cooke's work was published only in the colonies. He published several occasional poems in Maryland in the 1720s and another long poem in 1730, *Sot-weed Redivivus*. *Redivivus* is a 540-line poem divided into three cantos, all in the Hudibrastic style. Where the humor of Cooke's earlier poem *The Sot-weed Factor* grows directly out of the often ridiculous twists and turns of its admittedly simple but nonetheless crucial plot, *Sot-weed Redivivus* could be said to forgo such seemingly obligatory narrative devices as plot entirely. Indeed, much of the poem consists of a conversation between the narrator, who has a rather different personality than he has in the earlier *The Sot-weed Factor*, and one of his hosts from the earlier poem with whom he has met up again. Although the poem's explicit subject relates to contemporaneous debates over tobacco and

monetary policy in Maryland, the poem uses those debates to re-imagine English identity through images of American trading goods. In Cooke's writing, images of exportable products and paper money are used to challenge conventional notions of identity.

In 1731 the local printer William Parks brought out a collection of Cooke's poems, *The Maryland Muse*. This collection included what was labeled a "third edition" of *The Sot-weed Factor*, substantially unchanged from the 1708 version except for its concluding lines, which seem to soften the satire on the colonists. Whether a "second edition" of the poem ever appeared in London or in Maryland remains doubtful, but the subject has been of interest to scholars of the period since at least the middle of the nineteenth century. In addition to the revised *Sot-weed*, Cooke's collection included another satire, "The History of Colonial Nathaniel Bacon's Rebellion." This poem of approximately 1,300 lines mocks the leader of the late-seventeenth-century rebellion.

Further Reading. ***Selected Primary Sources:*** Cooke, Ebenezer, *The Maryland Muse* (Annapolis, 1731); ———, *Mors Omnibus Communis. An ELOGY on the Death of Thomas Bordley, Esq.* (Annapolis, 1726 or 1727); ———, *The Sot-weed Factor* (London, 1708); ———, *Sot-weed Redivivus* (Annapolis, 1730). ***Selected Secondary Sources:*** Egan, Jim, "The English Common Body as Commodity in Ebenezer Cooke's *The Sot-weed Factor*" (*Criticism* 41 [1999]: 385–400); Lemay, J.A. Leo, *Men of Letters in Colonial Maryland* (Knoxville: University of Tennessee Press, 1972); Wroth, Lawrence C., "The Maryland Muse by Ebenezer Cooke" (*American Antiquarian Society Proceedings* 44 [1934]: 267–335).

James Egan

COOKE, ROSE TERRY (1827–1892)

Rose Terry Cooke's poetry both does and does not fit the pattern of the women poets who dominated the literary scene in the mid- to late nineteenth century. Like the poetry of **Sarah Morgan Piatt**, another complicated case, it ponders the waste of women's lives and at times uses irony to offset the darker emotions of pain and disillusionment that women poets of the period often expressed. However, again like Piatt, Cooke violated the decorum of the Nightingale tradition by writing poems of such power and subtlety that they confused contemporary critics and had to wait until the late twentieth century for readers more attuned to their peculiar demands.

Rose Terry was born on a farm near Hartford, Connecticut. Her father was a landscape gardener like **Lydia Sigourney**'s, but Rose had a distinguished pedigree. Her grandparents on both sides were prominent people involved in federal, state, and local government, banking, insurance, and the shipbuilding industry. When she was six, her parents moved into the Terry mansion in Hartford, and throughout her life she retained fond memories of this brief period of comparative ease when she and her family were able to live a life of middle-class comfort.

Intellectually she blossomed in an environment that seemed to favor women's education. Required to memorize a page of the dictionary each day, Cooke accumulated a large vocabulary, which she later felt helped her to become a poet. She also attended the Hartford Female Seminary and graduated at sixteen with one of the best secondary educations then available to young women. After graduation she joined the Congregational Church, went to work as a teacher and then a governess, lived with a married sister, and later came home to take care of her parents in their final years.

However, like her mother, Rose Terry harbored strong feelings that were not entirely consistent with the Victorian model of women as pious, pure, domestic, and submissive. Of Anne Terry, Rose would later write: "My mother was nursed by a gypsy, and in her were the oddest streaks. Severer in her Puritanism than ever I was, there was a favorable wildness about her" (Walker 1992, 144). The same could no doubt have been said about her daughter.

Against the wishes of her family, Rose married Rollin Cooke, a widower with two daughters, when she was forty-three and he a mere thirty. Accounts vary concerning the happiness of this union but, however well-matched this couple might have been, it is clear that her husband and father-in-law squandered the small inheritance that had allowed Rose time to devote to perfecting her writing. Like her father, Rollin Cooke went from job to job, and the last years of her life seem plagued by perennial moves and desperate attempts to use her pen to support the family. Due to the continual need to earn money, Rose Terry Cooke wrote feverishly for children's magazines and parochial journals as well as the more mainstream publications she preferred: *Harper's*, *Putnam's*, and the *Atlantic Monthly*. In her article on **Harriet Prescott Spofford** for a book called *Our Famous Women* (1886), edited by Elizabeth Stuart Phelps, she complained, "Women who are driven by the necessities of their lives to write, as others are to sew, to teach, or to nurse, do not cease their labors till the pen drops from their weary hand, and the exhausted brain refuses to feed the laboring fingers. 'Work! Work! Work!' is not only the 'Song of the Shirt,' but the song of the Woman, and under that stringent cry we reel off pages of fiction, overridden by the dreamy facts of need, like the spider, spinning out not only our dwellings, but our grave-clothes from our own breasts" (538). Rose Terry Cooke died six years later at the age of fifty-five.

Until quite recently, Cooke was remembered, if she was remembered at all, for her realist short stories, praised by Van Wyck Brooks in the 1940s, Jay Martin in the 1960s, and Elizabeth Ammons (among others) in the 1980s. Her poetry was not as well received, one critic after another bemoaning it as sentimental, conventional, and undistinguished. Recently, however, readers have found Cooke's work worth another look as feminist literary criticism has helped to provide new contexts and perspectives from which to survey nineteenth-century women poets.

Cooke published two books of poetry during her lifetime: *Poems* (1860) and a revised and expanded edition of *Poems* (1888). She was held in high esteem by her contemporaries, including **Thomas Wentworth Higginson** (**Emily Dickinson**'s mentor), **John Greenleaf Whittier**, **Sarah Orne Jewett**, and Harriet Prescott Spofford, though Spofford, like **James Russell Lowell**, never quite understood what Cooke was doing in her poetry and admitted to a preference for her prose. The poems for which Cooke was best known in her lifetime were "The Trailing Arbutus" and "The Two Villages"—both Victorian set-pieces that do seem conventional and sentimental by today's standards.

"The Trailing Arbutus" describes this forest flower as fair and lonely: "Veiled from Nature's heart, / With such unconscious grace as makes the dream of Art!" The poem suggests an association between the pursuit of art and the passionless, regressive desire so often associated with women at the time. It was first published in 1851 in the *New York Tribune*. Similarly conventional is "The Two Villages," which sets side-by-side one town under the hill, where people go about performing their daily tasks with little sense of the preciousness of their lives, and a second "village" on the hilltop, where

All the villagers lie asleep;
Never a grain to sow or reap;
Never in dreams to moan or sigh;
Silent and idle and low they lie.

One thinks of Oliver Goldsmith's eighteenth-century classic "The Deserted Village."

However, there are other poems in this collection that show a far different poet at work. Cooke's "Semele," for example, is closer to Emily Dickinson's "Wild Nights" than anything else. In it the young female speaker openly expresses her desire for erotic consummation, enjoining the "Exulting, rapturous flame" whose name she "dare not breathe" to "come, in all matchless light." It is worth remembering that in the Greek myth, Semele (who has been badly advised by a disguised Hera) asks Zeus to appear to her in all of his radiant divinity; when he does so, she is consumed by the fire of his lightning. Cooke's Semele chooses the fiery consummation, however, rather than finding herself its victim.

Like Emily Dickinson, Rose Terry Cooke toys with violent imagery in several of her most powerful poems. "Basile Renaud" uses the ballad form to tell a gruesome story in which three sisters collaborate to murder a man who betrayed one of them in order to pursue her sibling. "Fantasia," which Spofford picked out as among Cooke's best, luxuriates in the sensuality of violence, imagining a spirit who torments mariners at sea, and "After the Camanches" recommends scalping Native Americans who have stolen a white woman on the verge of marriage: "The bridemen danced to bullets, / The wild dogs ate the feast." Cooke's so-called frontier ballads drew commendation from James Russell Lowell, who said they possessed the "true game flavor" of the West.

One poem, however, has haunted generations of readers, from R.H. Stoddard, who updated Rufus Griswold's nineteenth-century anthology of women poets in 1873, to John Hollander and the editors of *The New Anthology of American Poetry* (Rutgers University Press, 2003) in our own time. "Blue-beard's Closet" has a tormenting dactylic meter that seems halfway between **Edgar Allan Poe**'s poem "The Haunted Palace" and the hoofbeat rhythm of "After the Camanches." The woman addressed in the poem is advised to "Cover the portal, / That eyes may not see," and to "Get thee to market, / to wedding and prayer." With such advice, "Blue-beard's Closet" positions itself among a number of male texts—*Hamlet*, Robert Browning's "My Last Duchess," Poe's "The Fall of the House of Usher," and fairy tales by the Brothers Grimm. But its subject seems to be violence against women and its implied audience is female. Cooke ends the poem on a despairing note, suggesting that no matter where the woman wanders, her misery and constraint are certain: "Flying or staying / The chamber is there!"

The anti-moralism of this side of Cooke's work seems to derive from two sources: her willingness to expose an anarchic quality in female sensuality (in addition to "Semele" see "In the Hammock") and her vengeful fantasies stimulated by anger at patriarchal oppression. This Rose Terry Cooke possesses the wild subversiveness that David S. Reynolds (in *Beneath the American Renaissance*) located in other nineteenth-century writers such as **Herman Melville**.

However, the more conventional Rose Terry Cooke did not consider herself a feminist and blamed women as often as men for the troubles between the sexes. It is hard to reconcile the Gothic feminist with the conservative Puritan who was outspoken in opposing divorce. Given the lack of material about her life, we cannot recreate her psyche. But it is instructive to place her work next to that of Emily Dickinson, who also vacillated between the bloody-minded persona of "My life had stood a loaded gun" and that more filial figure whose life was governed by duties and obligations. Rose Terry Cooke was not a **modernist** before her time like Emily Dickinson. But in her wildness as well as her manipulation of Victorian conventions, she remains an interesting example of nineteenth-century contradictions.

Further Reading. *Selected Primary Sources:* Cooke, Rose Terry, *Poems* (Boston: Ticknor and Fields, 1861); ———, *Poems* (New York: Gottsberger, 1988). *Selected Secondary Sources:* Downey, Jean, *A Biographical and Critical Study of Rose Terry Cooke* (Ph.D. diss., University of Ottawa, 1956); Kilcup, Karen L., "Rose Terry Cooke," in *Encyclopedia of American Poetry: The Nineteenth Century*, ed. Eric L. Haralson (Chicago: Fitzroy Dearborn, 1998, 97–100); Walker, Cheryl, "Rose Terry Cooke" (*Legacy: A Journal of American Women Writers*, 9.2 [Fall 1992]: 143–150); ———, "The Whip Signature: Violence, Feminism, and Women Poets," in *Women's Poetry, Late Romantic to Late Victorian*, ed. Isobel Armstrong and Virginia Blain (New York: St. Martin's Press, 1999, 33–49).

Cheryl Walker

COOLBRITH, INA (1841–1928)

Renowned in the late nineteenth century as a Western woman writer with considerable talent, Ina Coolbrith led an adventurous life, beginning with her frontier travels as a child from Illinois to St. Louis and then, via the Overland Trail, to California. She was born Josephine Smith, the niece of Joseph Smith, founder of the Mormon Church. She grew up in Los Angeles when it was still a town of Mexican pueblos and, as one of the few eligible white women in a mostly Latino town, she attracted the attention of Robert Carsley, a local businessman. After a brief and abusive marriage, she was divorced from Carsley and relocated to San Francisco, where she attempted to forget her past, adopting her mother's maiden name of Coolbrith.

There she began to publish her poetry in local journals and gained a reputation, eventually drawing the attention of **John Greenleaf Whittier**, **Edmund Clarence Stedman**, and even George Meredith, who called her "a genius" particularly sensitive to nature's moods. "In touch with every human emotion," Meredith wrote, "she has suffered; an echo of sadness rings in her work" (Rhodehamel and Wood, 308). Though she never remarried, her life was not devoid of incident. The many trials she faced reinforced both her sense of her own talents and her melancholy belief that it was her fate to miss out on life's keenest joys.

As a member of the local intelligentsia of Oakland and San Francisco, she held a weekly salon that attracted such figures as Mark Twain, Bret Harte, Joaquin Miller, Jack London, and John Muir. Among her female friends, she could count writers and artists such as **Helen Hunt Jackson**, Isadora Duncan, **Mary**

Austin, and Gertrude Atherton. At one time she was considered the foremost female literary figure in the San Francisco area, part of the so-called Golden Gate Trinity with Bret Harte and Charles Warren Stoddard.

Nevertheless, she was also hemmed in by the limitations of her sex. She had to work long hours six days a week as a librarian in order to support herself and several children (a castoff mixed-race child of Joaquin Miller, a niece, and a nephew) all of whom she raised by herself. Though she was an early feminist and campaigned for women librarians, she eventually saw herself replaced not only by a man but specifically by the nephew for whom she had made many sacrifices. In 1906 the San Francisco earthquake and the subsequent fire destroyed her home, many books and manuscripts, and she was forced to accept the charity of friends. Even the honor of being named California's first poet laureate was not sufficient to offset the disappointments of a lifetime. She saw her work as limited, explaining that "in a life of unremitting labor, 'time and opportunity' [for serious literary endeavors] have been denied" (Rhodehamel and Wood, 314).

Ina Coolbrith is generally remembered for her poems about the West, especially "The Mariposa Lily"; her melancholy lyrics of disappointment such as "Withheld" and "When the Grass Shall Cover Me"; and her spirited poems of historical commentary. "The Captive of the White City" is especially worth rereading today. This poem addresses the Native American who was exhibited, along with his cabin, at the Columbian Exposition of 1892. He was reputed to be Custer's killer though no one actually knows who was responsible for Custer's death at the Battle of Little Bighorn. Coolbrith's poem expresses sympathy for both sides: "Alas, for the death-heaped plain! / Alas, for slayer and slain!" However, she extends her sympathy especially toward the Native American: "From the wrongs of the White Man's rule / Blood only may wash the trace. . . . Alas for your blood-stained hands / O Rain-in-the-Face!" (*Songs from the Golden Gate*). This poem probably shows the influence of her friend Helen Hunt Jackson, whose concern for Native American wrongs was the driving force of her later life.

Coolbrith's earlier books, *A Perfect Day, and Other Poems* (1881) and *The Singer by the Sea* (1894), were more concerned with her emotions and place her firmly in the Nightingale tradition that flourished in the mid-nineteenth century, a group of poets influenced by the English poet Felicia Hemans, whose poetry often focuses on limits and longings. *Songs from the Golden Gate* (1896), which contains "The Captive of the White City" as well as reprintings of her earlier work, shows a greater interest in current events. A final volume, called *Wings of Sunset*, was published posthumously in 1929 by Houghton Mifflin and contains a memoir by Charles Philips.

Wings of Sunset also includes the poem she wrote to her adopted city, "San Francisco," written after the earthquake when Coolbrith felt the need, as many did in New York after September 11, 2001, to express her love for her ruined urban environment. She looks forward to its rebuilding—"Thy wraith of pearl, wall, minaret, and spire, / Framed in the mists"—calling it, in a rhythmic incantation, "Lost City of my love and my desire."

Another late poem in that final volume is "Concha," a 900-line **narrative poem** about the daughter of an American father and a Spanish mother. Concha is presented as a mixed-race child who questions the legitimacy of white hegemony. She is also bitter about being prevented from getting an education. But Concha has many moods—she is passionate, demure, modest, and outspoken by turns, as Coolbrith herself was. One can see many possible influences at work here: Bret Harte's "Heathen Chinee" which she helped to edit, Helen Hunt Jackson's *Ramona*, and possibly **Rose Terry Cooke**'s "In the Hammock," which also features a transgressive Latina. Coolbrith began the poem in 1920 when she was almost eighty, but its ideas show the influence of modern feminism, possibly the result of her friendship with Isadora Duncan and other New Women.

Coolbrith is an interesting historical figure, but, taken as a whole, her work is minor. She was not as outspoken or subtle as **Sarah Piatt**, not as chillingly powerful as Rose Terry Cooke, not as lyrically adept as **Louise Imogen Guiney** or Helen Hunt Jackson, and her work seems pale beside that of **Emily Dickinson**. Nevertheless, as a Western woman poet of the late nineteenth and early twentieth centuries, she deserves a place in literary histories.

Further Reading. ***Selected Primary Sources:*** Coolbrith, Ina, *Songs from the Golden Gate* (Boston: Houghton Mifflin, 1895); ———, *Wings of Sunset* (Boston: Houghton Mifflin, 1929). ***Selected Secondary Sources:*** Laurence, Frances, *Maverick Women: 19th Century Women Who Kicked Over the Traces* (Carpinteria, CA: Manifest, 1998); Rhodehamel, Josephine DeWitt, and Raymund Wood, *Ina Coolbrith: Librarian and Laureate of California* (Provo, UT: Brigham Young University Press, 1973); Walker, Cheryl, "Ina Coolbrith and the Nightingale Tradition" (*Legacy: A Journal of Nineteenth-Century American Women Writers* 6.1 [Spring 1989]: 27–33).

Cheryl Walker

COOLIDGE, CLARK (1939–)

Clark Coolidge's writing was informed early on by his reading of **Jack Kerouac**'s novel *On the Road*. In addition to Kerouac, he has claimed **modernists** such as Samuel Beckett, **Gertrude Stein**, and **Louis Zukofsky** as influences. His early work drew from and was associated with the poetry of the **New York School**. This work was also an important influence on some of the poets later associated with **Language poetry**. **Barrett Watten** published several of Coolidge's early books. In addition, his work has been discussed and anthologized by poets such as **Charles Bernstein** and **Michael Palmer**. Although Coolidge's poetry cannot fully be described in terms of a particular poetic movement, his work has continued to take innovative approaches to poetic language, making him an important figure for subsequent generations of experimental poets. A great deal of his work draws on his background as a **jazz** drummer. An interest in improvisation and in the sound structures of language is consistent throughout his poetry.

Coolidge was born in Providence, Rhode Island, on February 26, 1939. From 1956 to 1958 he attended Brown University, where he studied geology. In 1958 Coolidge relocated to New York City. He moved between New York, Providence, and finally San Francisco over the course of the next decade. During this time, he met **Ted Berrigan**, edited the magazine *Joglars* with Palmer, continued to perform as a drummer, and produced a weekly poetry program for KPFA radio in Berkeley. In 1970 Coolidge moved to Hancock, Massachusetts, where he remained until moving to Petaluma, California, in 1997. He gave up performing as a musician for most of this period and began a prolific period as a poet that continues to the present. Over the years, he has collaborated with numerous poets, including Larry Fagin, **Michael Gizzi**, **Bernadette Mayer**, **Keith Waldrop**, and **John Yau**. His collaborations with the artist Philip Guston were published in the book *Baffling Means: Writings/Drawings* (1991).

Coolidge's earliest work is collected in *Space*, his first and only book published by a major publisher. *Space* was part of a series by Harper & Row that broadly identified Coolidge and a number of other poets as second-generation New York School poets. Like older poets such as Berrigan and **John Ashbery**, Coolidge sought a break with the confessional and personal modes of mainstream American poetry. Coolidge wrote the poems with the aid of a dictionary in an attempt to avoid the conventions of poetic language and syntax. The poems in *Space* consist largely of words that may initially seem unrelated. The words are brought together on the page, but they are not organized into sentences. The words, which in these circumstances become composite materials, cannot retain or import their existing meanings. The poem's elements, brought together spatially, must be read in terms of their particular relation with and resistance to one another. Coolidge is also interested in the meaning that occurs at the level of sound. This is not to say, however, that his poetry rejects meaning. The words, associated by their proximity rather than by the logic of statement, establish new meanings.

Coolidge's early work had an important influence on the Language poets. His books of the 1970s, several published by Watten through This Press, reflect his affiliation with some of these poets. Coolidge's work of this period continues to deal with language as it does in *Space*. Works such as *The Maintains* (1974) use a reductive syntax, which allows Coolidge to use words in unfamiliar ways. The poems rarely produce conventional sentences, but develop their own criteria for reading by directing one's attention to the groups of words that make up each line. Coolidge's method in these works is to encounter words as new, as if they were abstract forms such as one finds in the art of Guston or Willem de Kooning, rather than referential language.

The book-length poem *Polaroid* (1975) foregrounds and builds from pronouns, demonstratives, and prepositions, often leaving out the subjects or antecedents that one might expect to find. Lines in *Polaroid* such as "when thus of so what then," revise the terms by which these words ordinarily make meaning. In his essay "Total Syntax: The Work in the World," Watten suggests that this aspect of Coolidge's early work performs an inquiry about language rather than describing an external world. "The meditation on semantics," Watten writes, "is enacted in the way the words are placed on the page" (93).

The word that Coolidge used to describe his early work is "arrangement." As he explained in a talk at the Naropa Institute in 1977, the poem can be understood as a spatial arrangement like that of a geologic formation or like that of notes in a musical sequence. Coolidge suggests that a poem changes depending on its "arrangement," rather than being thematically or formally restricted. Although Coolidge does not proceed anywhere in his work to make the political claims that the Language poets ultimately do, he anticipates the concern that those poets have with work that insists upon its own materiality rather than presuming an external world about which the work simply reports.

Beginning with the prose poems in *Own Face* (1978), Coolidge's work makes a significant shift to a more autobiographical or lyrical mode. Rather than the clusters of words that comprise the earlier work, Coolidge begins to write poems that are more sentence based. These poems often contain a speaking subjectivity, or what some have called a lyric "I." This speaker is present in much of the collection *Solution Passages: Poems 1978–1981* (1986). Despite this shift, Coolidge remains interested in a certain amount of invention in his language. His sentences, although they are often syntactically correct, continue to question semantic meaning rather than provide a clear narrative about the "I" writing the poem. Our tendency to seek semantic meaning at the expense of language's other registers of meaning is still challenged, as in the poem "Noon Point," in which Coolidge writes "I think I wrote a poem today but I don't know well."

Within the sentence, Coolidge continues to use words in terms of their relation rather than their reference. *The Crystal Text* (1986), published the same year as *Solution Passage*, takes as its subject a piece of quartz on Coolidge's desk. The poem's many disparate sections result from the single constraint that the poet write about the crystal. Like Stein, Coolidge remains interested in the change that undergirds the act of writing. Although the writing remains engaged with one thing, the words continue to have different meanings each time they are used. *The Crystal Text* insists that it is not strictly a report about its subject but a record of what results from the concentration and engagement that governs the writing of the poem.

Even in Coolidge's more autobiographical writing, he remains concerned with formal experimentation. In the long poem *At Egypt* (1988), which draws on Coolidge's trip up the Nile River, and the collection *Odes of Roba* (1991), written during a residency in Rome, Coolidge allows experience to influence his writing. Neither book, however, offers a narrative. The relationship of the language to Coolidge himself, or to particular events, is indeterminate. In addition, these books emphasize the effects of foreign languages on the writing. Coolidge does not translate the languages spoken around him, but allows them to inform his writing by being attentive to their sound. The experience in each case allows for linguistic play rather than autobiography. As is common throughout Coolidge's work, the experience is not allowed to obscure the work that results. The influence that Rome and Egypt exert on the writing cannot be separated from the writing itself.

For Coolidge poetry remains most concerned with the act of its own writing. Consequently, his interest in Kerouac, particularly Kerouac's improvisational prose, has informed his poetry throughout his career. Coolidge's writings on Kerouac are collected in *Now It's Jazz: Writings on Kerouac and the Sounds* (1999). He points out that Kerouac was interested not only in writing about jazz improvisation, but in finding a form analogous to improvisation in writing. Kerouac is often most successful as an improviser, Coolidge suggests, not when he is writing about jazz, but when he becomes involved with and attentive to the act of writing. Coolidge writes in *Now It's Jazz*, "[i]t is as if hidden somewhere in his books there is a writing that hasn't been written yet and will never be finished" (18). Coolidge suggests that Kerouac's writing must not be read only in terms of its narratives. Improvisation in Kerouac is not simply about music. Kerouac attempts instead to find a way of writing that, like jazz improvisation, is appropriate to its medium.

This sense of improvisation has continued to play a role in Coolidge's poetry. His poems often have a partic-

ular subject or derive from a set of sources. At the same time, they insist that their relationship to an event or source is incidental. *On the Nameways, Volume 1* (2000) and *Volume 2* (2001) are drawn from a large series of poems that Coolidge wrote while watching movies on satellite television. The poems combine the titles, names, and dialogue from these movies, with the language Coolidge produces spontaneously while watching television. As in *At Egypt*, *The Crystal Text*, and *Odes of Roba*, the work is not determined by any particular constraint other than the condition for writing. The poems themselves are written spontaneously, but the names and titles that enter them are put to new uses, their meanings not limited to their previous contexts.

In this sense, Coolidge remains interested in the composition by arrangement that characterizes the early work. His approach to writing as an empirical process produces increasingly sophisticated poetry. Although the words in the early work are treated as physical forms, Coolidge's more recent work focuses on their arrangement as sound. Improvisation remains an important concern, not only as it relates to sound but also to the invention that Coolidge wants consistently in his poetry.

Further Reading. *Selected Primary Sources:* Coolidge, Clark, "Arrangement," in *Talking Poetics at Naropa Institute*, ed. Anne Waldman and Marilyn Webb (Boulder, CO: Shambhala, 1978, 143–169); ———, *At Egypt* (Great Barrington, MA: The Figures, 1988); ———, *The Crystal Text* (Great Barrington, MA: The Figures, 1986); ———, *The Maintains* (San Francisco: This Press, 1974); ———, *Now It's Jazz: Writings on Kerouac and the Sounds* (Albuquerque, NM: Living Batch Press, 1999); ———, *Odes of Roba* (Great Barrington, MA: The Figures, 1991); ———, *On the Nameways, Volume 1* (Great Barrington, MA: The Figures, 2000); ———, *On the Nameways, Volume 2* (Great Barrington, MA: The Figures, 2001); ———, *Own Face* (Lenox, MA: Angel Hair Books, 1978); ———, *Polaroid* (New York: Adventures in Poetry, 1975); ———, *Solution Passage: Poems 1978–1981* (Los Angeles: Sun and Moon Press, 1986); ———, *Space* (New York: Harper & Row, 1970); Coolidge, Clark, and Guston Philip, *Baffling Means: Writings/Drawings* (Stockbridge, MA: O-Blek Editions, 1991). ***Selected Secondary Sources:*** Bernstein, Charles, "Maintaining Space: Clark Coolidge's Early Work," in *Content's Dream: Essays 1975–1984* (Los Angeles: Sun and Moon Press, 1986, 259–265); Lewis, Joel "'Jazz Is the Endless Conversation': Some Notes on Clark Coolidge's Prosodics" (*Talisman* 3 [Fall 1989]: 55–59); Orange, Tom, "Arrangement and Density: A Context for Early Clark Coolidge" (*Jacket* 13 [April 2001]); Watten, Barrett, "Total Syntax: The Work in the World," in *Total Syntax* (Carbondale: Southern Illinois University Press, 1985); Ziarek, Krzysztof, "Word for Sign: Poetic Language in Coolidge's *The Crystal Text*" (*Sagetrieb* 10.1–2 [Spring–Fall 1991]: 145–166).

Patrick Farrell

COOPER, JANE (MARVEL) (1924–)

"What I need is a new medium," Jane Cooper writes in her poem "Olympic Rain Forest," first published in *The Flashboat: Poems Collected and Reclaimed* (2000), "one that will register / . . . / how slowly a few hours passed"; and since the late 1940s Cooper has attempted to create that "new medium" in poems that meditate on the function of time in the work of twentieth-century women writers and artists. In her foreword to *The Flashboat*, Cooper suggests that the way her poems' "self-definitions have been subject to some redefinition . . . is part of a lifelong effort to be more honest, to understand a fluid nature in the grip of a difficult century. And perhaps after all the pattern is not so unusual for a woman artist of my generation." Like her friend and contemporary **Adrienne Rich**, Cooper is dedicated to a **feminist poetics** in which her own changing "self-definitions" are an integral part of her poems' fabric. Cooper's work runs the gamut of formal possibilities available to twentieth-century American poets: Her first book, *The Weather of Six Mornings* (1969) is composed almost entirely of strictly rhymed and metered lyrics and sequences, although in the late 1960s she began writing in looser, more open-ended forms, and her most recent full-length collection, *Green Notebook, Winter Road* (1994), contains traditional lyrics, long-lined **free-verse** poems, a **blues** poem, **prose poems**, and longer biographical poems.

Jane Cooper was born in Atlantic City, New Jersey, the daughter of John Cobb and Martha (Marvel) Cooper, and spent her early years in Jacksonville, Florida. When she was nine her family moved to Princeton, New Jersey. Cooper's father became a specialist in aviation and space law, while her uncle, Merian C. Cooper, made pioneering documentary films in the 1920s, worked for a time as John Ford's Hollywood partner, and conceived, produced, and co-directed the original *King Kong*. (Cooper writes about this aspect of her background in the poem "Seventeen Questions About King Kong" from *Green Notebook, Winter Road*). In her most recent work, Cooper has written extensively about her family and childhood in order, as she suggests in a 1995 interview published in the *Iowa Review*, "to extend the individual consciousness through history and mythology" (92). In her prose poem "The Past," from *Green Notebook, Winter Road*, for instance, Cooper muses, "It seemed, when I was a child, as if you could just reach back and rummage in the 19th century. . . . How have we come so far? How did we live through (in the persons, for me, of my father, of my uncle) radio, aviation, film, the conquest through exploration of Equatorial Africa, Persia, and Siam?" whereas in "Hotel de

Dream," she wonders "how to relish yet redress" her "sensuous, precious, upper-class, / unjust white child's past."

Cooper attended Vassar College and the University of Wisconsin, graduating from the latter with a BA in 1946; she studied at Oxford University in 1947 and saw first-hand the devastation of postwar Europe. In 1950 she began teaching creative writing at Sarah Lawrence College, on whose faculty she would remain until retiring in 1987 as Poet-in-Residence Emerita, having mentored several generations of young poets and having helped to develop Sarah Lawrence's well-regarded creative writing program. Cooper spent the 1953–1954 academic year earning a BA in English at the University of Iowa, where she participated in poetry workshops taught by **Robert Lowell** and **John Berryman**; her classmates included poet and painter Shirley Eliason Haupt, on whose paintings Cooper would meditate in numerous later poems, **W.D. Snodgrass**, **Donald Justice**, and **Philip Levine**. At Sarah Lawrence Cooper's colleagues and close friends included **Grace Paley**, **Jean Valentine**, and **Muriel Rukeyser**. The extent of Cooper's quiet but persistent influence on postwar American poetry may be recognized only when her papers—drafts of poems, an extensive correspondence, journals, and teaching notes—which are housed at the New York Public Library's Berg Collection of English and American Literature, are fully explored by researchers. Cooper, who lived most of her adult life in New York City, now lives in Newton, Pennsylvania.

The Weather of Six Mornings, which received the Lamont Award of the Academy of American Poets, contains poems written between 1954 and 1967, many of them about her mother, who appears in one poem as "[m]y young mother, her face narrow / and dark with unresolved wishes" in the "middleaged" speaker's dream, "calling me from sleep after decades." Cooper had been writing seriously well before the mid-1950s. *Maps & Windows* (1974) contains both poems written between 1968 and 1973 and "Mercator's World," a selection of poems written between 1947 and 1951 with an accompanying essay, "Nothing Has Been Used in the Manufacture of this Poetry That Could Have Been Used in the Manufacture of Bread," which meditates on why Cooper "gave up poetry" at twenty-six and suppressed her early work. Citing one early poem she asks, "I can't help speculating on what it might have meant to other women had it come out when it was composed." *Scaffolding: New and Selected Poems* (1984), similarly presents a number of "reclaimed" poems that she had written and discarded, some of which—"Blind Girl," for instance—rank among her best work. *The Flashboat* furthers this process of reclamation by including still more unpublished work. Although these "reclaimed" poems are worthy on their own terms, they also illuminate Cooper's previously published work in unexpected and exciting ways (compare "Holding Out" with "95°," for instance).

"Threads: Rosa Luxemburg from Prison," which was first published as a chapbook in 1978 and later included in *Scaffolding,* is the first of Cooper's long biographical poems collaged together from primary sources, in this case Luxemburg's *Prison Letters to Sophie Liebknecht.* After "Threads" Cooper spent ten years researching and writing the four-part "Vocation: A Life," later published in *Green Notebook, Winter Road,* a poem about **Willa Cather** that incorporates quotations from writing by and about Cather in which, Cooper suggests in the *Iowa Review* interview, she attempted to "explore how a woman artist feels about her art at different ages—in youth, childhood, middle age, and old age" (100). "Vocation: A Life" stands as the capstone to Cooper's lifelong attempt to "create a new medium" in poetry that can confront the role of time in women artists' lives: "When we try to sum up a life, events cease to matter," she writes. "What we came away with was never written down." Both "The Winter Road," a shorter sequence about Georgia O'Keefe, and "Vocation: A Life" allowed Cooper, as she suggests in the same interview, "to meditate on some of the themes that most concern me: the survival of the earth, the importance of relationship, the nature of solitude, whether enforced or self-imposed, what it means to grow older, what it means to be a woman who breaks the mold" (102).

Throughout her long career Cooper has received many honors and awards, including a Guggenheim fellowship in poetry, an Ingram Merrill Foundation grant, and the Maurice English Poetry Award. With the publication of *Green Notebook, Winter Road* and the *The Flashboat,* Cooper's importance to American poetry has become increasingly apparent. In 1995 she received the Walt Whitman Citation of Merit as New York State Poet, a post she held for two years. Cooper's poetry has created the testing ground for its own integrity, which makes her ongoing reclamation of previously unpublished poems all the more illuminating. Characteristically self-effacing, Cooper's poems are no less masterful for their quietude, their calmly forceful insistence on the interrelation of aesthetics and ethics, and their commitment to apprehending what *Scaffolding*'s "Conversation by the Body's Light" calls "[t]he still-not-believed in / Heartbeat of the glacier."

Further Reading. *Selected Primary Sources:* Cooper, Jane, "Acceptance Speech for Walt Whitman Citation of Merit as New York State Poet, December 19, 1995," http://www.albany.edu/writers-inst/cooperja.html; ———, *The Flashboat: Poems Collected and Reclaimed* (New York: W.W. Norton, 2000); ———, Foreword to Muriel Rukeyser, *The Life of Poetry* (1949; reprint Williamsburg, MA: Paris Press,

1996). ***Selected Secondary Sources:*** Gudas, Eric, "An Interview with Jane Cooper" (*Iowa Review* 25.1 [Winter 1995]: 90–110); Hadas, Rachel, "'An Ecstasy of Space'" (*Parnassus: Poetry in Review* 15.1 [1989]: 217–239); Silman, Roberta, "'A Radiance of Attention'" (*Virginia Quarterly Review* 7.4 [Autumn 2001]: 745–749).

Eric Gudas

CORMAN, CID (1924–2004)

Cid Corman began writing poetry in the 1940s. His poetry is characterized by its economy, its Japanese influence, and its Buddhist stress on the importance of the present moment. His contribution to American poetry extends beyond his own writing to include his translations, his editing, his small press publishing, and his ability to bring other poets together. Living much of his life in Japan and publishing much of his work in little magazines and chapbooks may have limited the number of American readers familiar with his work; however, Corman had a tremendous impact on the work of other poets, and remains an important figure in American arts and letters.

Born in Boston, Massachusetts, on June 29, 1924, to Abraham and Celia Kravitz Corman, Sidney Corman was the second of four children. He attended Boston Latin School and then earned a BA from Tufts University in 1945. He studied literature in a graduate program at the University of Michigan but left just before earning his MA. He then studied briefly at the University of North Carolina–Chapel Hill. Corman published his first poem in 1941, and wrote consistently from that time on. He also worked energetically to circulate the poetry of other writers. In 1949 he began a poetry radio program in Boston that was on the air for three years, and in 1951 he began editing the first series of *Origin,* a literary journal of poetry and essays. In 1954–1955 he received a Fulbright fellowship to study at the Sorbonne, and afterward he continued to travel abroad. He had already visited Mallorca in the early 1950s, and in 1956 he accepted a position as an English teacher for a British school in Bari, Italy. He left, however, after one term for another position in Naples. Corman traveled to many parts of Italy including Florence, and his experiences led to the poems that comprised *Sun Rock Man* (1962). After accepting another teaching position, this time in Kyoto, Corman left for Japan, stopping at many places along the way, including Egypt, India, Vietnam, and China. Once settled, Corman focused on writing and publishing including producing the second series of *Origin.* In 1960, he returned to the United States for a two-year visit, starting in San Francisco where he spent time with Beat Poets and members of the San Francisco Renaissance including **Jack Kerouac**, Lew Welch, and **Phillip Whalen**. He continued on to Boston to visit family and friends including **Louis Zukofsky** and an aging **William**

Carlos Williams before returning to Japan, where he married Shizumi Konishi. Corman and his wife relocated to Boston from 1970 to 1982. During this time he was finally able to meet Lorine Niedecker, with whom he had a longstanding correspondence and for whom he later became literary executor. He also published more of his work including books of poetry such as *Once and For All*, translations of other texts such as Matsuo Basho's *Back Roads to Far Towns*, and collections of critical prose such as *At Their Word*. The Cormans then returned to Japan to live permanently in Kyoto, with occasional visits to the United States for poetry readings and conferences. Corman continued working with *Origin* and writing on a daily basis, developing the compressed lines, attention to syllabics, and the keen perceptions that formed the basis for his poetics. Short collections of his work as well as longer books appeared consistently from small presses, including his own, and from larger publishers, including New Directions. In 2003 he was preparing a sixth *Origin* series to be published online; however, on December 31, Corman suffered a heart attack and went into the hospital. After kidney failure and pneumonia, he was finally able to have surgery to install a pacemaker in January 2004, but he never recovered his strength and was in a semi-comatose state. He passed away March 12, 2004.

Much of Corman's effort went into promoting the work of other poets, especially through his radio program, his journal, and his small press. Corman began the program *This Is Poetry*, in 1949 on the Boston station WMEX. For fifteen minutes each week, he read poems by other writers, and many programs focused on writers visiting or living in the region such as John Ciardi, John Crowe Ransom, and Theodore Roethke. He started *Origin* in 1951. The first series contained twenty issues, and it continued, although not annually, through the sixth series Corman was preparing at the time of his death. The final issue focuses on Bob Arnold as the featured poet, and plans were under way to include Charlie Mehrhoff as the featured poet of the second issue. Corman used *Origin* to publish his own poetry and essays as well as the work of many important poets over the years, including William Bronk, Robert Creeley, Larry Eigner, Denise Levertov, and Charles Olson. Origin Press accomplished a similar goal. Many of Corman's own books appeared under its imprint, as did work by other poets including Louis Zukofsky's *A 1-12* and the first edition of Gary Snyder's *Riprap*.

In addition to circulating poetry through his efforts as a radio host, editor, and publisher, Corman also brought the work of many poets to a wider readership through his translations and his transvisions. He rendered works from German, French, Chinese, and Japanese into English. At times he worked with co-translators, such as his collaboration with Susumu Kamaike on Shimpei Kusano's *Selected Frogs*. The majority of his translations were of Japanese poems, including tanka from the ancient *Manyoshu* anthology, haibun by Basho, and haiku by Basho, Issa, and other haiku masters. Some of these translations appeared in their own collections; others were published within books of Corman's original poetry. Corman also employed a creative process of translating that he described as "transvising," examples of which are his versions of Lao Tzu's verses in *How Now*. The word "transvising" was his attempt to develop new terminology that would reflect his belief that to change one word of a poem was to create a new poem.

In developing his own poetics, Corman explored and mastered many traditional forms only to move away from them in his own poetry. His graduate work contributed to his knowledge of literary history; he read widely, and he was always in contact with other poets. However, his primary means of honing his craft came from continuous writing. Books such as *Sun Rock Man* demonstrate his ability to use a range of formal approaches to create a unified collection. Corman used varied line lengths and stanzaic structures, including quatrains and poems without stanzas, to convey his emotional response to his time in Italy. He states at the beginning of the collection, "What I saw, what I learned, what I felt, my relations to others there and that of earth and air, fire and water, to them and to myself, should be implicit, if not explicit, in the poems that follow." The poems range from descriptions of landscape and architecture to considerations of children and workmen to a remembrance of a girl saying goodnight to him on his first night in town. Most of the poems in *Sun Rock Man* were not pared down to the extent of his later work; however, many of them reflected his growing preference for a certain style of poem: long, slender verses composed of short and often enjambed lines broken into three-line stanzas.

Many other Corman poems resemble Japanese haiku and senryu. For instance, "It was all / rain until / the sky came," a three-line poem in *Nothing Doing*, conveys the brief line length and natural imagery of haiku. The shift in the middle line builds a sense of surprise into the conclusion much as the pivot line in a haiku allows for a moment of awareness by shifting the poem away from the reader's expectations. Other poems, including "Life is re- / membering / and don't you / forget it," reflect the humor of Corman's work, a humor at times structured around the foibles of human nature. The similarities between Corman's poetry and Japanese poetic forms are not surprising given his many years of residence in Japan, his translations of Japanese poetry, and his own original haiku. In fact, Corman's relocation to Japan profoundly influenced his style of writing beyond the formal characteristics of his poems. The Buddhist belief in the interconnectedness of all things and the importance of the present moment informed the central tenet of Corman's poetics: livingdying.

Corman coined "livingdying" as a way to express his belief that each moment of living is simultaneously connected to a moment of dying, that the present moment immediately expires and merges into the next new moment. He wrote of livingdying in his correspondence and spoke of it in his interviews, and he published a book of poems under this title, as well. Numerous collections of Corman's work attempt to present new ways of communicating this belief. As he states in an untitled poem in *Nothing Doing*, "It all comes / back to this. / In fact—it / never left," and again in *Just For Now*, "Even this/passes and/becomes this." For Corman, a poem conveys the experience of the present moment. It foregrounds the fact that the experience of the poem itself is, at that moment, everything. Many of his poems convey this point through their content. The speaker directly addresses the reader or another person and makes a short, philosophic claim about the brevity of life, the reality of death, or the no-nonsense basics of human experience. The didacticism of these poems, however, is tempered by humor, such as "Remembering how / much I've forgotten reminds / me of this moment." Corman's puns and wordplay combine with his economical lines, allusions, and use of white space to create short poems that present dense poetic moments. The poems formally model the message they attempt to convey.

Corman claimed that he wrote poetry every day since 1941, and although not all of his verse appeared in print, his poetry circulated in literary journals such as *Poetry*, in broadsides such as *Nothing More* (1999), in chapbooks such as *Together* (1991), and in larger books such as *And the Word* (1987). His published books and chapbooks are estimated to number in the hundreds, many from established publishers and many others from small presses around the world. Even Corman's correspondence contained poetry written in the letters and on the envelopes. Because so many of his books were produced in limited editions, most of his work is out of print and in private collections, although new chapbooks continue to be published. At present there is no selected or collected edition of his work.

Further Reading. ***Selected Primary Sources:*** Corman, Cid, *And the Word* (Minneapolis, MN: Coffee House Press, 1987); ———, *How Now* (Boulder, CO: Cityful Press, 1995); ———, *Livingdying* (New York: New Directions, 1970); ———, *Nothing Doing* (New York: New Directions, 1999); ———, *Sun Rock Man* (New York: New Directions, 1970). ***Selected Secondary Source:*** Taggart, John, *A Bibliography of Works by Cid Corman* (New Rochelle, NY: Elizabeth Press, 1975).

Ce Rosenow

CORN, ALFRED (1943–)

Alfred Corn's work has attracted the attention of critics and writers with widely differing aesthetic sensibilities and temperaments. His first book, tellingly titled *All Roads at Once*, drew the attention of and glowing reviews from **John Ashbery**, Harold Bloom, **James Merrill**, and **Richard Howard**, among others. His mastery of meter and **pastoral** tone has been pleasing to the ears of advocates of traditional verse, at the same time that he has been read as **postmodern** because of his sense of *jouissance* and his widely cast points of reference.

Alfred Dewitt Corn III was born on August 14, 1943, in Bainbridge, Georgia, to Grace Lahey Corn and Alfred Dewitt Corn, his namesake. After a childhood spent almost entirely in Valdosta, Corn went on to complete degrees in French at Emory University (BA 1965) and Columbia (MA 1970). Corn's marriage to Ann Rosalind Jones in 1967 lasted less than four years; he gradually came to understand and write about his homosexuality, particularly after meeting his long-time partner, poet **J.D. McClatchy**, in 1975. Their relationship rested in part on a mutual commitment to taste, cosmopolitanism, and aesthetic sensibility. Corn has received fellowships from the Guggenheim Foundation, the National Endowment for the Arts, and the Academy and Institute of Arts and Letters, and prizes from the Academy of American Poets and *Poetry Magazine*.

Corn's editorship of *Incarnation: Contemporary Writers on the New Testament* (1990) raised, as he acknowledges in the introduction, somewhat surprised if not hostile responses from acquaintances; it was precisely in order to argue against the conflation of fundamentalism and spirituality that led Corn to bring together such renowned literary figures as **Anthony Hecht**, **Amy Clampitt**, **John Updike**, Annie Dillard, Reynolds Price, and **Jonathan Galassi** to discuss the relevance of the sacred texts to contemporary creative practice. His own essay, reminiscing on his childhood in relation to the Second Letter of Paul to the Corinthians, moves beyond the defensive posture caused by widespread distrust of Christian influence by pointing to "just how syncretistic and evolutionary Christianity is, the product of ages of religious practice in many different circumstances" (133). Ultimately, though, he seems more interested in the problem of "trying to establish personal legitimacy," which he says necessarily involves a listener's "will to contradiction" (138). If St. Paul knew his impending visit to Corinth meant that he would need to speak in "more than *propria persona*," then a poet, upon entering the public arena, must be prepared to do the same (146).

Corn has also written two books of prose, the first a collection of essays, *The Metamorphosis of Metaphor* (1987), which contains ruminations primarily on the poetry of **Wallace Stevens**, **John Ashbery**, **Robert Pinsky**, **Robert Lowell**, **Elizabeth Bishop**, Hart Crane, C.P.

Cavafy (whose work is dear to both him and McClatchy), Eugenio Montale, **John Hollander**, **Charles Tomlinson**, and L.E. Sissman, among others. His second book, a manual of prosody, *The Poem's Heartbeat* (1997), makes a startling claim for scansion that accounts for subtlety of stress: Instead of assigning stressed and unstressed syllables, he suggests numbering each syllable in order of relative stress.

Corn's early work in *All Roads at Once* (1976), *A Call in the Midst of the Crowd* (1978), and *The Various Light* (1980) established him as a poet of talent and vision. One of his central influences is **Hart Crane**. There are also hints of **W.H. Auden** at his most serious in "Promised Land Valley, June '73" and liberal borrowings from the Orientalist tendencies of **Marianne Moore** in "Chinese Porcelains at the Metropolitain" (with the familiar concatenated list of hyphenated terms—"Glazes: *claire-de-lune, mirror-black, tea-dust,* / . . . *Fish-roe crackle,* and *blue-and-white*"— in looser nonce stanzas than Moore wrote). Critics like **Dana Gioia** took to *The Various Light* for its greater "concentration" that didn't lose the informality of Corn's speaking voice (624). This can be seen in Corn's condensations and distillations—for example, in "Prime Minister in Retirement," where "Past, present, they boil down to much the same." Similarly, the clipped sestina "Audience" (with five-line stanzas and a two-line envoy, indicating a playfulness with form he appears to derive from Auden) admits that art presents "A program that's too rich, maybe, / For every day."

Notes from a Child of Paradise (1984) is Corn's most transparently autobiographical book. Tracing the course of Corn's marriage to Ann Jones, and modeled after Dante's *Divine Comedy*, the tripartite book wrestles mightily but humorously with what Harold Bloom calls "belatedness": "Great Freud! Since you teach men self-disabuse: / Who makes us house our loves in Grecian urns?" The pitch-perfect verse letter to Ann, in which he says of her and her new partner, "You and Peter sound chryselephantine—Good" is ultimately a poet's self-inoculation against future criticism. In language evoking Wordsworth, Byron, Baudelaire, and **John Berryman**, the poem traces Ann and the poet's journey through the vagaries of 1960s daily life, the pop culture, the anti-war movement, and events such as "the First Central Park Be-In," all set against the backdrop of earlier history: Lewis and Clark provide a counter-narrative to the aimless "spindrift comedy" (an echo of Crane).

Corn's middle body of work to this point, composed of four books—*The West Door* (1988), *Autobiographies* (1992), *Present* (1997), and Corn's selected poems *Stake* (1999)— shows a surer handling of pathos and wit, from the rueful line "The unused ticket spins to the ground" ("The Jaunt") to the pop-cultural excess of "a just-kids lifestyle / Whose central shrine is the shopping mall—K-Mart, hail to thee!" ("Contemporary Culture and the Letter 'K'").

"An Xmas Murder" and "1992" continue Corn's established presence as a major poet of the medium-length poem.

Corn's *Contradictions* (2002) confirms his Whitmanian calling to "contain multitudes" without chagrin. Corn's contribution to AIDS/HIV literature in "To a Lover Who Is HIV-Positive" has the appeal of work by **Mark Doty** and others, but a poem adjacent to it in the collection, in which John Coltrane "knocks one same note eight times / to say, 'This is over, over, over,'" better represents his management of pent-up tension.

Further Reading. *Selected Primary Sources:* Corn, Alfred, *All Roads at Once* (New York: Viking, 1976); ———, *Autobiographies: Poems* (New York: Viking, 1992); ———, *A Call in the Midst of the Crowd* (New York: Viking, 1978); ———, *Contradictions* (Port Townsend, WA: Copper Canyon Press, 2002); ———, *Incarnation: Contemporary Writers on the New Testament* (New York: Viking/Penguin, 1990); ———, *The Metamorphosis of Metaphor: Essays in Poetry and Fiction* (New York: Viking/Elizabeth Stifton, 1987); ———, *Notes from a Child of Paradise* (New York: Viking, 1984); ———, *The Pith Helmet: Aphorisms* (Omaha, NE: Cummington Press, 1992); ———, *The Poet's Heartbeat: A Manual of Prosody* (Brownsville, OR: Story Line Press, 1997); ———, *Present* (Washington, DC: Counterpoint, 1997); ———, *Stake: Poems, 1972–1992* (Washington, DC: Counterpoint, 1999); ———, *The Various Light* (New York: Viking, 1980); ———, *The West Door* (New York: Viking, 1988); Proust, Marcel, *L'Indifférent*, trans. Alfred Corn (New York: Sea Cliff, 1992). *Selected Secondary Sources:* Henry, Brian, "On Alfred Corn" (*Iowa Review* 28 [1998]: 183–188); Aboritz, Richard, "The Traveler: On the Poetry of Alfred Corn" (*Kenyon Review* 15.4 [1994]: 204–216); Gioia, Dana, "The Various Light" (*Hudson Review* 33.4 [Winter 1980–1981]: 624–626).

Douglas Basford

CORRIDOS

In the American Southwest, traditional Spanish ballads, dating back to the first European settlers in the region in 1598, shed considerable light on the popular mind of the Mexican and Mexican American people. Morality and ethics, human triumphs and defeats, and political, social, and religious views are all revealed in folksongs. Folklorists such as Aurelio M. Espinosa, Arthur L. Campa, Jovita González, J. Frank Dobie, and Charles F. Lummis collected *romances, décimas, corridos, coplas,* and *canciones* at the turn of the twentieth century in efforts to preserve this poetic expression within a rapidly changing North American way of life. Of all these genres, it is the *corrido* that has received the most attention from scholars in recent years. Vicente Mendoza and Merle Simmons suggest that a direct line of descent from the Spanish *romance* is responsible for the evolution of the *corrido,* whereas Américo Paredes argued that the tradition of the *corrido* began approximately in the middle of the nineteenth century along the Lower Rio Grande region.

Paredes's theory is the most persuasive when one considers a "tradition" of *corridor* within a given area and time frame as opposed to a random collection of *corridos* throughout Mexico and Latin America. Along the Lower Rio Grande region, as Paredes shows in *"With His Pistol in His Hand": A Border Ballad and Its Hero* (1958), these early ballads describe the cultural conflict between the westward expansionist aims of Anglos and Mexican residents that sparked the Texas Revolution (1835–1836) and later the U.S.–Mexican War (1846–1848). Paredes believed that, at the time, U.S./Mexican Border balladry was working its way "toward a single type: toward a single form, the *corrido*; toward one theme, border conflict; toward one concept of the hero, the man fighting for his right with his pistol in his hand" (149). Gregorio Cortez Lira, on whom the famous ballad "El Corrido de Gregorio Cortez" is based, was a ranch hand in Gonzalez, Texas, who, falsely accused of stealing a horse, killed a sheriff in a gun battle in 1901. The ballad tells the story of his flight, pursuit, and imprisonment. It continues to be sung along the Mexican border. (The story was made into a Hollywood film starring Edward James Olmos in 1988.) Like most *corridos*—and indeed like most traditional British ballads—this one consists of four-line octosyllablic stanzas, or quatrains, and a rhyme scheme of *abcb*:

En el condado del Carmen
Tal desgracia sucedió,
murió el Sheriffe Mayor
no saben quién lo mató.
[In the County of Carmen
Such a sad event,
The head Sherriff died
And nobody knows who killed him.]

The folksong, through its refining process, manages to relate a long story rapidly and swiftly. The formal opening of the *corrido* presents the scene and tone of the narrative and sets up the interrogation. It begins in medias res (in the middle of the story) to capture the listener's attention. The performer's role in the narration is that of a spectator, too, who calls for the attention of his audience. He is an anonymous actor, and his creative act involves the re-creation of an event. At the time of the song, heightened with the accompaniment of music, the imperfect tense is used to create a fluid present in which singer, audience, and event are all present at once.

If the independent quatrains of the *corrido* serve as imaginary, moving pictures (accompanied by music) for an oral community, the written stanzas serve as narrative "sketches" for readers of literature. Analogous to the *corrido,* the "sketches" suggest a shifting of scenes, point of view, and time frame within the narration to offer multiple views of a particular event. The scenes swing back and forth, and the point of view moves from protagonist, to adversaries, to common people. The time frame can either be early, late, or in the middle of the story. The dialogue and drama within these compact scenes, moreover, allow the story to move swiftly and easily. Since the border *corrido* is a composition in most cases (excluding broadside publications) of and for the folk, it possesses a local interest rather than a nationalistic agenda. The language is hybrid, and familiar places are observed within the narrative to reflect community interests. These local interests generally make use of universal themes, such as honor, respect, infidelity, and betrayal.

Yet, aside from the content, language, and form of this folk poetry, it is not complete if the performance element is not included in the analysis. Américo Paredes examined this aspect, too, in one of his early essays entitled "Some Aspects of Folk Poetry" (1964, 1993), in which he linked poetic form with performance. He studied folk poetry on its own terms to demonstrate its value and uniqueness in spite of its simplicity in comparison to "sophisticated" literature. For the Mexico-Tejano performer, written poetry was more complex and multifaceted because it had removed itself farther and farther from the spoken word. A tendency of sophisticated literature, therefore, was toward individual modes of expression that attempted to be striking and original. Thus the interaction between the poet and public that characterizes folk poetry was no longer necessary. The process now involved the "act of private communication between poet and reader" (127).

Folk poetry, on the other hand, made use of a highly conventional language and a simple, balanced, binary structure. It had to retain a sense of immediacy for one reason: it was performed. For Paredes, this factor was essential to folk poetry because the performer made all the difference with regard to his material:

[T]he performer . . . is an actor, a personality. In the comic song he may play the clown. In the folksong of high seriousness he will be serious; he will take a detached attitude toward himself as performer. But he is far from detached in respect to his subject. On the contrary, it is a supreme involvement that gives him the intense style that is often called impersonality. (126)

Like the writer of sophisticated literature, the folk poet was an artist, and Paredes underscored the importance of the performer and the context of performance to highlight some of the conditions necessary to understand folk poetry. At family gatherings or in intimate settings, folksongs were given temporary life through performances, and it was the performer's interpretation of this material that gave it a power and passion often lost in written poetry. In the end, in "Some Aspects of Folk Poetry," Paredes wanted to do away with preconceived notions of value that separated sophisticated literature from folk poetry.

Although the *corridor* is still popular today in Mexico and the United States, times have changed, and the topic of border or revolutionary heroes is no longer a central issue within this ballad type. Drug trafficking, specifically cocaine and marijuana, has created a subgenre within the *corrido* legacy known as *narco-corridos*. These songs pay homage to Mexican drug lords, such as *El Guero* Palma, Rafael Caro Quintero, and Ernesto Fonseca, who in recent years have gained social and cultural legitimacy within specific sectors of the Mexican and Mexican American population. This is not to suggest that Mexican society in general condones drug smuggling and its ring leaders, but that the use and trafficking of narcotics is a fact of life and that there will be those—in keeping with this ballad tradition—who will find drama in the characters involved and will wish to sing about them.

Further Reading. *Selected Primary Sources:* Herrera-Sobek, María, "The Theme of Smuggling in the Mexican *Corrido*" (*Revista Chicano Riquena* 7.4 [1979]: 49–61); McDowell, John Holmes, "The *Corrido* of Greater Mexico as Discourse, Music, and Event," in *"And Other Neighborly Names": Social Process and Cultural Image in Texas Folklore*, ed. Roger D. Abrahams and Richard Bauman (Austin: University of Texas Press, 1981, 44–75); Paredes, Américo, *"With His Pistol in His Hand": A Border Ballad and Its Hero* (Austin: University of Texas Press, 1958); Ramírez-Pimienta, Juan Carlos, *"Del corrido de narcotráfico al narcocorrido: Orígenes y desarrollo del canto a los traficantes"* (*Studies in Latin American Popular Culture* 23 [2004]: 21–41). ***Selected Secondary Sources:*** Campa, Arthur L., *Spanish Folk-Poetry in New Mexico* (Albuquerque, NM, 1946); Herrera-Sobek, María, *Northward Bound: The Mexican Immigrant Experience in Ballad and Song* (Bloomington: Indiana Unversity Press, 1993); Paredes, Américo, *A Texas-Mexican Cancionero: Folksongs of the Lower Border* (Austin: University of Texas Press, 1976).

José R. López Morín

CORSO, GREGORY (1937–2002)

Gregory Corso brings to American poetry a unique blend of surreal imagery and comic timing blended into an idiom that combines both hipster and archaic language. Made famous through his association with the Beat Generation, particularly his friendships with **Jack Kerouac** and **Allen Ginsberg**, Corso wrote poetry that resembles that of no other American poet.

His association with the Beats fueled both his inspiration and his wider public acceptance. This was especially the case between 1958 and 1963. In those years, Corso became a media icon for Beat poetry, making regular appearances in daily papers in New York, Chicago, and San Francisco, and regularly appearing in such national magazines as *Time*, *Newsweek*, and *Life*. Part of what led to Corso's celebrity in these years was his ability to capture in poetry the tensions and problems associated with a number of established American institutions. Corso became, for his time, the poetic voice of dissident youth, notable particularly for such poems as "Bomb," "Power," "Police," "Army," "Hair," and "Marriage." In these and other poems Corso, in both comic and deadly serious terms, investigates the possibility of redemption and grace in a modern world of institutionalized repression.

Gregory Corso was born on March 26, 1930, in a small flat on top of a funeral home on the corner of Bleecker and MacDougal in Greenwich Village, New York City. His mother, Michelina Colonni Corso, was sixteen, and his father, Fortunato Samuel, was seventeen. Shortly after the birth, his parents separated; his mother returned to Italy, and his father gave the baby up to foster care. In 1940, when his father remarried, the ten-year-old returned home. When the United States entered World War II, Corso's father was drafted into the Navy. Unhappy with his stepmother, Corso ran away and began a life on the street. He was soon arrested. Eventually, he would serve time in a New York City prison. In jail, he was beaten and abused by the older prisoners. At one point, he was sent to the Children's Observation Ward of Bellevue Hospital. There, he ended up in the ward for the seriously demented for three months. Ultimately, he was confined to prison in upstate New York and would not be released until he was nineteen.

Once out of prison, Corso went back to New York, where he fell into the bohemian world of coffeehouses, bars, and literary bookstores that defined Greenwich Village in the early 1950s. There, he met the poet Allen Ginsberg. At the time, Ginsberg was already the center of a vibrant if still unknown group of young writers, which included Jack Kerouac and William S. Burroughs. This group welcomed Corso, but it was a short-lived adventure. By 1952, Corso, like Ginsberg, Burroughs, and Kerouac, had left the city. Corso spent time as a reporter in Los Angeles; he then joined the Merchant Marine and traveled to South America and Africa.

Eventually, he found his way, through his Beat friends, to Cambridge, Massachusetts. There, he became part of a poetry scene associated with Harvard University and centered around **Frank O'Hara**. Corso published his first book during this period, including lyrics of his childhood experiences, prison years, and experiences with his Beat friends. This book, *The Vestal Lady of Brattle* (1976), refers to Brattle Street, one of the main roads in Cambridge. The book was not a commercial venture, however; Richard Burkenfeld privately printed it in an edition of three hundred copies, financed by selling subscriptions to Corso's friends, roughly fifty students from Harvard and Radcliffe who, according to biographer Barry Miles, "clubbed together to raise the money." Corso, however, mailed review copies to established poets and to the literary media of the era and won a surprisingly receptive audience. Not only did *Poetry* magazine review his collection but so, too, did **Randall Jarrell**, then the Consultant in Poetry to the Library of Congress (a position now called Poet Laureate) and a noted poet and critic of the day. Jarrell was so impressed he invited Corso to Washington, D.C., for a visit.

After this debut, more travel followed, taking Corso to San Francisco, Mexico City, and finally Europe. In 1957, he again settled down with his Beat friends, this time in Paris in a hotel at 9 Rue Git-le-Coeur, that he named the Beat Hotel. There, he lived in a small triangular attic room, sporting a cape and occasionally carrying a cane. These Beat Hotel years were by far his most productive. During this period (1958–1964) he published the poems and books by which he is known today. The first book to come from the Paris years was *Gasoline* (1958). Published by **Lawrence Ferlinghetti**'s City Lights press, with an introduction by Ginsberg declaring the book to be "a box of crazy toys," it also had, on the back cover, a blurb from the newly famous Jack Kerouac whose novel *On the Road* (1957) had just been published to wide acclaim. For its epigraph, Corso chose a sentence from one of his own essays, "How Poetry Comes to Me": "It comes, I tell you, immense with gasolined rags and bits of wire and old bent nails, a dark arriviste, from a dark river within." Altogether, in thirty-two poems Corso moved his readers from darkness to light, from cruelty to pleasure, from hell to heaven as he transformed his experiences in New York, Mexico, Rotterdam, and Paris into a surreal poetry of shocking images and bizarre diction.

Following that book, Corso then wrote his two most famous poems, "Bomb" and "Marriage." "Marriage," in fact, remains his most anthologized poem. Corso also briefly returned to the United States in 1959, where he became the image and icon of the Beat Generation, a youth movement the media had suddenly discovered. Whenever the media did a story on this youth movement, they reprinted Corso's poetry and often included his picture. In one such example, *Newsweek* quoted Corso as saying: "Everything but the BG [Beat Generation] stands amid the ordeals of life. The BG is the happy birthday of death." Under their photo of Corso was the caption "Gloomy Corso: Birthday of Death" (*Newsweek* [29 June 1959]: 83).

Not surprisingly, his next book, which was published soon after he returned to Europe, was called *The Happy Anniversary of Death* (1960). The title refers to the fact that the book was finished on the anniversary of the dropping of the atomic bombs on Japan. It also contained the famous poem "Bomb." That poem was printed as a centerfold with typography that took the shape of a mushroom cloud. This and the book's other poems emphasize Corso's unique blend of mockery and gravitas. As the critic Michael Skau says, Corso is "disrespectful while still serious because he refuses to encounter death with solemnity. Virtually without exception, his tone is mocking and derisive" (79). Other notable long poems from this volume also question political, social, and cultural phenomena with both satire and solemnity. For critics, the most notable are "Army," "Police," "Hair," "Clown," and most famously "Marriage."

Corso's facility with long **free-verse** poems often using surreal imagery continued in his next poetry collection, *Long Live Man* (1962). After publishing that collection, Corso returned to the United States, where in 1963 he married Sally November, a schoolteacher. Following his marriage, he took a number of odd jobs, including working in his father-in-law's flower shop. Then, on the strength of his poetic reputation, Corso was hired by the State University of New York's Buffalo campus to teach in the English department. This position soon ended, however, when he refused to sign a loyalty oath required of all faculty in this Cold War era. Fired for this refusal, Corso went back to Europe and began what one biographer, Bruce Cook, calls "his longest ramble . . . favoring the eastern Mediterranean, the Aegean islands, and Greece." Also in these years, his first child was born. Meanwhile, his marriage to Sally November ended in divorce. In 1968 he married Belle Carpenter, with whom he had two children.

Almost ten years would elapse before his next collection of poetry. The new collection, *Elegiac Feelings American* (1970), continues his turn to the long poem, and although maintaining his characteristic style it also broke new ground. For all the biographical turmoil of the eight years of poetic silence, critics note that this 1970 collection was the most innovative of the poet's books. Divided into three sections, the first contains five poems, including **elegies** to Jack Kerouac (who died in 1969), Native American civilization, and John F. Kennedy. There follows a second experimental section that explores Egyptian mythology. Rather than appear in typeface, this section of the book reproduces Corso's handwriting through more than thirty-one pages and includes revisions, drawings, notes, graphs, and other working papers abundantly illustrated with hieroglyphics, drawings, and a wide array of symbols. The book's third section contains twenty-nine poems ranging from impressionist plain-spoken anecdotes familiar from his Beat years to his typical blend of surreal imagery and arch wit.

An even longer silence of eleven years followed this book, resulting in *Herald of the Autochthonic Spirit* (1981). This slim book of fifty poems in fifty-seven pages marked a retreat from the experimental, surreal, and beat idiom that had marked each of his previous books. Critics noted that these poems were far more "confessional" and openly autobiographical. As the literary critic Gregory Stephenson says, "Many of the poems in this collection have a spare, pared-down feel to them in comparison to the more expansive and extravagant poems of the preceding volumes. The poems here are . . . less exuberant and more subdued, more austere" (76). In terms of their theme, he notes that the poems are "retrospective, introspective and prophetic" (69).

Corso's final collection appeared eight years later: *Mindfield: New and Selected Poems* (1989). This collection contained selections from each of his previous collections and included a substantial number of unpublished poems, many from the late 1980s. Critics agree that the most important of those newer poems was a long extended meditation, "Field Report." They note that the poem reads as a poetic last will and testament, and serves as his ars poetica. Ultimately, then, these selected poems would serve as Corso's poetic legacy, ensuring that his vision and style would continue even after his death. The book's foreword by Allen Ginsberg summarized his friend as follows: "Gregory Corso's an aphoristic poet, and poet of ideas," adding "As poetic craftsman, Corso is impeccable. His revision process, which he calls 'tailoring,' generally elision and condensation, yields gist-phrasing, extraordinary mind-jump humor." This essay was then followed by "Introductory Notes" by William S. Burroughs, who singles out "Gregory's voice. . . . It will be heard so long as there is anyone there to listen."

On January 17, 2001, in Robbinsdale, Minnesota, attended by his daughter Sheri Langerman, a nurse, Gregory Corso died of prostate cancer. He was seventy. The *New York Times* obituary recalled how "Mr. Corso would delight his fans and inflame his critics by muttering into a microphone disconnected thoughts like 'fried shoes,' 'all life is a Rotary Club' and 'I write for the eye of God.'"

Further Reading. *Selected Primary Sources:* Corso, Gregory, *The American Express* (Paris: Olympia Press, 1961); ———, *Elegaic Feelings American* (New York: New Directions, 1970); ———, *Gasoline* (San Francisco: City Lights, 1958); ———, *Gasoline and the Vestal Lady on Brattle* (San Francisco: City Lights, 1976); ———, *The Happy Birthday of Death* (New York: New Directions,

1960); ———, *Herald of the Autochthonic Spirit* (New York: New Directions, 1982); ———, *Long Live Man* (New York: New Directions, 1962); ———, *Mindfield: New and Selected Poems* (New York: Thunder's Mouth Press, 1989); ———, *Selected Poems* (London: Eyre Press, 1962); ———, *The Vestal Lady on Brattle* (Cambridge, MA: Richard Bruckenfield, 1955); Corso, Gregory, Sinclair Beiles, William S. Burroughs, and Brion Gysin, *Minutes to Go* (Paris: Two Cities Press, 1960; reprint San Francisco: Beach Press, 1968). ***Selected Secondary Sources:*** Cambell, James, *This Is the Beat Generation* (Berkeley: University of California Press, 2001); Cook, Bruce, "An Urchin Shelley," in *The Beat Generation* (New York: Scribner's, 1971, 133–149); Foster, Edward Halsey, *The Beats* (Columbia: University of South Carolina Press, 1992, 128–149); Hartman, Geoffrey, "No Marvelous Boys" (review of *Long Live Man*) (*Kenyon Review* 25.2. [Spring 1963]: 374–375); Honan, William, "Gregory Corso: A Candid Voiced Beat Poet Dies at 70" (*New York Times* [19 January 2001]); Miles, Barry, *The Beat Hotel* (New York: Grove, 2001); *Newsweek* (29 June 1959: 83); Skau, Michael, *A Clown in a Grave: Complexities and Tensions in the Works of Gregory Corso* (Carbondale: Southern Illinois University Press, 1999); Stephenson, Gregory, *Exiled Angel: A Study of the Work of Gregory Corso* (London: Hearing Eye Press, 1989).

Jonathan N. Barron

CORTEZ, JAYNE (1936–)

Jayne Cortez is a poet best identified by her rhythmic, blues-inflected poetry and her inspired performances. She is a crucial link for contemporary poetry to the worlds of jazz and blues music. She is especially important for keeping the tradition of the Delta blues storyteller accessible to a poetic audience that may be unfamiliar with the poetry of blues music. To date, she has released numerous recordings and books of poetry, many of which have been published by Bola Press, a **small press** she founded in the early 1970s.

Jayne Cortez was born in May 10, 1936, in Fort Huachuca, Arizona, and spent her formative years in California. In 1979–1980 and again in 1986 she was the recipient of a National Endowment for the Arts for creative writing. Her book *Mouth on Paper* won the 1980 American Book Award. She has also received the 2001 Langston Hughes Medal from the City College in New York and the International African Festival Award.

She has lectured at universities and been the invited performer at international conferences and festivals. She has crafted poems on such topics as the Vietnam War, African American pride, the New York City police, environmental pollution, and nuclear proliferation, the latter of which can be found in "Endangered Species List Blues." Her poetry is about empowerment and pride, as exemplified in "Find Your Own Voice" published in her book *Somewhere in Advance of Nowhere*: "Find your own voice & use it / use your own voice & find it." Her poems on visiting Africa express awe at the continent's natural beauty, balanced with her unique ability to capture social and political ineptitude. Her poetry repeatedly seeks subjects that expose the negative impact of oppression, bigotry, and injustice. She has crafted a body of liberal poetry that is unashamed and surrealistic.

Although a native of the West Coast, Cortez is closely identified with the urban pulse of New York City. A resident of New York for nearly forty years, she is recognized for her poem "I Am New York City," an anthem for capturing the spirit of the city, likening it to a woman's fertile and resilient body. She writes of her "docks red with grenadine / and jelly madness in a flow of tokay." In "Bricks" also, she addresses the city, "your face of plaster / your scaffolds of greetings."

It is in Cortez's live performances that the artistry of her layered poems comes alive. Cortez relishes the role of poet as "band leader" as she fronts her band, the Firespitters. It is impossible to extricate the influence of the **jazz** and **blues** cadence from her **performance poetry**. She follows in the tradition of Koko Taylor, Big Mama Thornton, and Etta James. In *Taking the Blues Back Home*, one might mistake the recording for a blues song, rather than a poet's performance. The repetition of select lines changes the written poem's meaning with slight variations of intonation. Cortez delivers the lines in a rhythmic voice that penetrates through the music. She says that she is "taking the blues back home before Robert Johnson comes from the graveyard to say the blues has been crapped on. . . . I am taking the blues back to the bush." Her urban and political poetry hovers over the juke-joint sounds of saxophone, guitar, and harmonica.

Both *Jazz Fan Looks Back* and *Mouth on Paper* exemplify Cortez's weaving of blues and jazz influences, the love of New York City, the African American pride movement, the feminist movement, and her social consciousness. In "For the Poets—Christopher Okigbo & Henry Dumas" she interjects monosyllabic sounds at the end of each line to augment the existing rhythm: "I need cockroaches ah / congo square ah / a can of skokian ah / from flaming mouth of a howling wolf ah." Her incorporation of such vocal elements, associated more with music than with written poetry, suggests her strengths in both genres, her roots in the performative dimension of language, and her drive to reveal the relations between these worlds.

Further Reading. *Selected Primary Sources:* Cortez, Jayne, *Celebrations and Solitudes* (recording) (New York: Strata East Records, 1975); ———, *Coagulations* (New York: Thunder Mouth's Press, 1984); ———, *Festivals and Funerals* (New York: Bola Press, 1971); ———, *Firespitter* (New York: Bola Press, 1982); ———, *Jazz Fan Looks Back* (New York: Bola Press, 2002); ———, *Mouth on Paper* (New York: Bola Press, 1977); *Pisstained Stairs and the Monkey Man's Wares* (New York: Phrase Text, 1969); ———, *Scarifications* (New York: Bola Press, 1973); ———, *There It Is* (recording) (New York: Bola Press, 1982); ———, *Unsubmissive Blues* (recording) (New York: Bola Press, 1980); Cortez, Jayne, and the Firespitters, *Taking the Blues Back Home* (New York: Harmolodic/Verve, 1996). ***Selected Secondary Sources:*** Feinstein, Sascha, "Returning to Go Someplace Else: An Interview with Jayne Cortez" (*Brilliant Corners* 3.1 [1998]: 53–71); Melhem, D.H., "A Melus Profile and Interview, Jayne Cortez" (*Melus* 21.2 [1996]: 71–79).

Diane Marie Ward

COTTON, JOHN (1584–1652)

John Cotton was the "teaching" minister in the Boston church from 1633 until his death in 1652, and a leading exponent of the New England Way of non-separating congregationalism; as such, he was extraordinarily influential as well as a prolific author of prose defenses. As regards his poetry, although his output was small and occasional, Cotton's primary contribution consists of his involvement in the **Bay Psalm Book** (*The Whole Booke of Psalmes*, 1640), both in translating biblical psalms for congregational singing but especially in the preface of that book, and in *Singing of Psalmes a Gospel-Ordinance* (1647), wherein he outlines what can be construed as the earliest poetic criticism in the British American colonies. Additionally, he was the subject of a memorable funeral **elegy** by John Fiske.

Born in Derby, Derbyshire, England, Cotton received his BA from Cambridge in 1602 and MA from Emmanuel College in 1606; he stayed at Emmanuel until 1612, in a variety of positions. Under the influence of William Perkins and especially Richard Sibbes, he converted in 1609 to Puritan theology and, later, to plain-style preaching, to the consternation of his audience (in turn, this led to the conversion of John Preston). In 1612 he was appointed vicar of St. Botolph's Church, Boston, Lincolnshire, where he served until shortly before his emigration in 1633. Cotton skillfully managed to hold to nonconformist practices and his pulpit until 1632 when, to avoid a summons to appear before the High Commission and Archbishop Laud, Cotton went underground. In September 1633 he arrived, along with Thomas Hooker and Samuel Stone, in Boston and shortly after was invited to become teacher for the church there. Cotton maintained this position despite suspicion and embarrassment to his reputation—in England and New England—caused by the Antinomian controversy, which rocked the Boston church in 1637 and centered around a parishioner named Anne Hutchinson. Cotton's career as an author commenced in the 1640s in several sermon collections and treatises defending the New

England Way of congregationalism and theology (of which Cotton was a chief architect); additionally, he sparred in print with Roger Williams through several volumes on the nature of religious toleration and liberty of conscience. He also drew up Massachusett Bay's first attempt at an abstract of civil law, which, though rejected, influenced the formative laws of New Haven and Southampton, Long Island. He died of natural causes in 1652.

Cotton's poetic output is limited to five known short poems and an early fragment, composed over four decades and scattered in five books by different authors; clearly, neither production, publication, nor circulation much mattered to Cotton. The poems hew closely to Puritan aesthetics in terms of plainness, ardent piety, brevity, didacticism, and providential consolation. The earliest of the group is a fragment on moral versus ceremonial Puritans; it is thought to have been composed around 1611, before Cotton's own conversion. Another poem reflects his thoughts "upon his removal" from England in 1633, which he interpreted as a personal purgation and purification by God as well as a lesson to the people of Boston about their pride. Next is an elegant elegy on Thomas Hooker, followed by three stanzas inscribed in an almanac on the deaths of two of his children in winter 1649. In 1651 there appeared a eulogy for Hartford minister Samuel Stone, filled with wordplay and biblical reference, for example, "Like *Samuel's Stone*, erst *Eben-Ezer* hight." Finally, "A Thankful Acknowledgment of God's Providence" was probably composed in the year of Cotton's death and is the most successful of the group. In Davidic tones, the stanzas are a thanksgiving for the various blessings of his life, concluding that "[t]his is the Heavn' on Earth, if any be: / For this, and all my soul doth worship Thee."

Given that the average seventeenth-century New Englander's contact with formal poetry most commonly came in the form of weekly congregational psalm singing, Cotton's contributions to the *Bay Psalm Book* are noteworthy. It is likely that Cotton helped organize the group of translators that produced the book (and probably produced some of the translation himself); he has also been credited (by Zoltan Haraszti) with penning the preface that described and justified the nature and procedure of the book. In doing so, Cotton briefly touches on aspects of translation, hermeneutics, and inspiration within the boundaries of Puritan orthodoxy. Having concluded, first, that Bible psalms (and not humanly invented hymns) alone are acceptable for corporate worship, Cotton next considers the problem of adapting Hebrew verse to an English worship setting. Having concluded that translation is a necessity, Cotton argues that the verses may be rendered "that soe wee may sing the Lords songs, as in our english tongue soe in such verses as are familiar to an english eare are commonly

metricall." Cotton further explains that "the true and proper sence of Davids words" were not violated in this adaptation. Somewhat famously, Cotton also apologizes for any possible consequent crudeness: "If therefore the verses are not always so smooth and elegant as some may desire or expect; let them consider that Gods Altar needs not our pollishings"; the translators "attended Conscience rather than Elegance, fidelity rather than poetry" in the effort.

Despite the fact that the *Bay Psalm Book* became the standard church songbook in New England Congregational churches until well into the eighteenth century, it was not without its contemporary detractors, as evidenced by Cotton's *Singing of Psalmes a Gospel-Ordinance* (1647), a further and more elaborate defense addressed to an unnamed objector. In justifying the use of English meter, he notes that "the Lord alloweth us to sing them in any such grave, and solemne, and plaine Tunes, as doe fitly suite the gravitie of the matter, the solemnitie of Gods worship, and the capacitie of a plaine People."

Further Reading. ***Selected Primary Sources:*** Cotton, John, and Thomas Shepard, *Singing of Psalmes a Gospel-Ordinance* (1647); Meserole, Harrison T., ed., *American Poetry of the Seventeenth Century* (University Park: Pennsylvania State University Press, 1985). ***Selected Secondary Sources:*** Craig, Raymond A., "Polishing God's Altar: Puritan Poetics in John Cotton's *Singing of Psalms*" (*Studies in Puritan American Spirituality* 5 [1995]: 1–33); Emerson, Everett, *John Cotton* (rev. ed. Boston: Twayne, 1990); Haraszti, Zoltan, *The Enigma of the Bay Psalm Book* (Chicago: University of Chicago Press, 1956); Ziff, Larzer, *The Career of John Cotton: Puritanism and the American Experience* (Princeton, NJ: Princeton University Press, 1962).

Michael G. Ditmore

COULETTE, HENRI (1927–1988)

Henri Coulette has the odd distinction of enjoying a cult, or underground, reputation as an exemplar of what is often considered the most conservative mainstream of American poetry—the form-conscious, ironic, academic poets of the 1950s, strongly influenced by the **New Critics**. Coulette's career foundered after the bizarre and accidental destruction of nearly every copy of his second book, but because of support from important admirers, and the resurgence of formalism in the 1980s and 1990s, he has come to be regarded as a poet's poet.

Coulette was born November 17, 1927, in Los Angeles, California, where he would die sixty-one years later on March 26, 1988, of apparent heart failure. After graduating from Los Angeles State College (later California State University at Los Angeles) in 1952, he enrolled in the University of Iowa Writers' Workshop, where he became a member of **John Berryman**'s class, which also included **Philip Levine**, **Donald Justice**, and **W.D.**

Snodgrass. He was included in the seminal *New Poets of England and America* anthologies (1957 and 1962), edited by **Donald Hall**, Robert Pack, and **Louis Simpson**, the second of which included sections from the sequence that became the title poem of his first book, *The War of the Secret Agents and Other Poems* (1966), winner of the Lamont Poetry Award from the Academy of American Poets. Coulette's second book, *The Family Goldschmitt* (1971), received almost no distribution, and he did not publish another. In the introduction to a posthumous collection, *The Collected Poems* (1990), editors Donald Justice and **Robert Mezey** explain that virtually the entire first printing was accidentally destroyed in the publisher's warehouse, and the book was never reprinted.

Although his background included a Hollywood stint in the publicity department of RKO Studios (where he is said to have saved the publicity stills for *Citizen Kane* from the fate that befell his own book), most of Coulette's working life was spent in academia. He taught for many years at California State University–Los Angeles, where he was teaching at the time of his death.

Coulette may have worked within the careful, formalist tradition which the **Beats** and their followers were to associate with poetic and aesthetic timidity, but he could not be said to have trusted the world of academia—or any other world, for that matter. In "The Academic Poet," he offers a savage, mocking self-portrait of the professor/poet hemmed in by the humdrum, the hopeless, and the painfully (but distantly) significant. In "The War of the Secret Agents," his best-known work, he adapts a true spy story of World War II into a meditation on identity and betrayal, in which love, friendship, loyalty, patriotism, and literary reputation (**T.S. Eliot** makes an appearance in the poem, as the editor of the nonfiction spy book) are all traduced, but the betrayals of love and friendship are the most painful to the survivors who try to understand what happened to them.

Coulette once said he wanted to make a world "as real and vital as television . . . except in good language," but reality is flickering and elusive in his poems, like the laughter of the dead in the laugh track of a thirty-year-old TV show ("Situation Comedy"). The characters in "The War of the Secret Agents" are drawn from a book none of its readers will have read; their referents are real, but unreachable. *The Family Goldschmitt* derives from a name forced on Coulette by an obstinate landlady—a fictional family that doesn't exist in reality and doesn't exactly exist in the poems either. "French Leave" finds the poet taking "long walks, imagining / Himself imaginary," and finally coming home to a waiting shadow in a black chair. Che Guevara ("Che") disappears into a universe in which the earth is only a blue star; a couple of poems later ("The Land of the Blue") the Nixon family are exposed under blue light.

After *The Family Goldschmitt*, Coulette wrote next to nothing for about seven years, then, in the last decade of his life, became prolific again. In the poems that Justice and Mezey collected as *And Come to Closure*, Coulette engages literary ambition ("bereft of title page,/vanity without signature or spine— / is that so bad?"). Though only in his fifties, he surveys the territory of death, particularly in the near-perfect "Petition," an **elegy** for his cat, with a concreteness he did not often find in life. He quotes a favorite fellow Californian, mystery novelist Ross McDonald, in "Confiteor," with the image of life as a blue hammer, the pulse at the wrist.

Zbigniew Herbert saw Coulette as a major poet, not only for his technical control but more importantly for his instinct for "thematic material of central importance to the modern world." Even more impressive, perhaps, is his gift for suggesting a larger context, rather than insisting on it. This last virtue may have contributed to the shrinking of his reputation, as American poetry entered an era in which the grand gesture gained the upper hand, and subtlety came to be seen as a dead end.

But Coulette's work was always incisive, insightful and accessible. His formalism was never showy or forced. When he worked in rhyme and meter, he gave the impression that they were his native tongue. He explored themes of identity, loss, and erotic longing, which frequently seemed to be different aspects of the same whole: double lives, betrayals, resignation, people goaded onward by need more than hope.

No one would choose to have the pulped remains of an important book as his escutcheon. Yet it seems hauntingly appropriate for Coulette, a poet of messages not received, of secret agents and secret agendas, whose words spoke under the radar screen of their time, but clearly and with emotional precision.

Further Reading. *Selected Primary Sources:* Coulette, Henri, *The Collected Poems*, ed. Donald Justice and Robert Mezey (Fayetteville: University of Arkansas Press, 1990); ———, *The Family Goldschmitt* (New York: Charles Scribner's Sons, 1971); ———, *The War of the Secret Agents* (New York: Charles Scribner's Sons, 1966). ***Selected Secondary Source:*** Santos, Terry, "Remembering Henri Coulette" (*Kenyon Review* 14.1 [1992]: 137).

Tad Richards

COWDERY, MAE VIRGINIA (1909–1953)

Although lesser known than other poets of the **Harlem Renaissance**, Mae Virginia Cowdery was one of only a handful of black women writers of the period to publish a full volume of poetry. Cowdery's poems address natural images and the complexities of love, but what makes her work stand out is her treatment of the erotic. Sometimes in **free verse**, sometimes in rhyme, Cowdery uses coded language to broach themes of lesbian desire, butch-femme gender roles, and the power struggles of all sexual relationships. In "Longings," for example, Cowdery approaches both the issue of blackness and that of lesbian sexuality obliquely and through metaphor. Her narrator is dark-skinned and achieves a metaphorical orgasm with a lover of lighter hue, as she speaks of her "brown body" plunging into a "golden pool."

Mae Virginia Cowdery was an only child, born into the middle class in Philadelphia in 1909. Her father was a postal worker and clerk, her mother a social worker and the director of the Bureau for Colored Children. Cowdery received her secondary education at the Philadelphia High School for Girls, a school that catered to scholastically gifted students. During Cowdery's senior year, three of her poems were accepted for publication in the 1927 spring issue of *Black Opals*, a Philadelphia-based monthly publication that attempted to rival **W.E.B. DuBois**'s *Crisis*. According to Vincent Jubilee, "the black intellectual and creative community [of Philadelphia] offered hopeful ground for nurturing the seeds of the Renaissance spirit that drifted down from the exuberant Harlem of the mid-20s" (3). *Black Opals* never achieved the critical success of *Crisis*, yet it did serve to connect Philadelphia's poets and writers, like Mae Cowdery and fellow gay writer Alain Locke, to Harlem's black literati. From Cowdery's publication in *Black Opals* came recognition as well as the Krigwa Poem Prize for "Longing," which brought a purse of $150 and publication in *Crisis* in 1927. Beyond her sporadic trail of publications, little is known about Cowdery. She was befriended by **Langston Hughes** and Alain Locke, and encouraged by them to submit her poetry to other black magazines. Between 1927 and 1930, Cowdery's verse appeared in *Crisis*, *Opportunity*, *Unity*, and *Carolina* magazines, as well as in anthologies such as Braitewaite's *Anthology of Magazine Verse: 1928*, Charles S. Johnson's *Ebony and Topaz*, and *The Negro Genius* by Benjamin Brawley. Cowdery also published one fictional piece, "Lai-Li," which was published in *Black Opals* in the spring of 1928. Between 1931 and 1935, there is no record that Cowdery published anything, but in 1936 she published *We Lift Our Voices and Other Poems*, a fifty-five–page volume, and her only published book.

Cowdery's poem "Dusk," first published in Charles Johnson's *Ebony and Topaz* in 1927 and later collected in her own volume, echoes a theme we find in the poetry of many black women writers of the time: that one's true self can be embraced only in the shadows. But Cowdery's cloaked, ambiguous images of female sensuality and sexuality, in poems such as "Longings" and "Dusk," gave way to more explicit treatments in later work. "Insatiate," Cowdery's most unapologetic and brazenly sexual poem—which went unpublished until her collection in 1936—brings human desire out of

darkness and obscurity. Although some of the images are stock—with lips as "rubies red" and eyes as "sapphires blue"—the laughter at the foibles of desire is explicit: "They would not be enough, / To fill the coffers of my need."

William Stanley Braithwaite writes, in the introduction to *We Lift Our Voices*,

> Miss Cowdery made her bow as a very youthful, and fugitive, poet during that Period . . . the Negro literary Renaissance. . . . I call her a fugitive poet, for she was one of a dozen young colored men and women, and much the youngest too, for she was still when the Renaissance flowered, in high school. (1–2)

Braitewaite's term "fugitive poet" does not refer to the famed fugitive poets of Vanderbilt but rather describes Cowdery's position as a marginalized writer: Even though she was published in well-respected African American magazines like *Crisis* and *Opportunity*, as well as in the white-run *Carolina Magazine*, she remained unacknowledged by most of her literary contemporaries. Mae V. Cowdery took her own life at age forty-three, and much of her work still remains in critical obscurity. Through her oblique and unusual metaphors and, for the time, disruptive choice of poetic personae, Cowdery allows the reader to hear the voice of the early twentieth-century African American lesbian.

Further Reading. ***Selected Primary Source:*** Cowdery, Mae V., *We Lift Our Voices and Other Poems* (Philadelphia: Alpress, 1936). ***Selected Secondary Sources:*** Honey, Maureen, ed., *Shadowed Dreams: Women's Poetry of the Harlem Renaissance* (New Brunswick, NJ: Rutgers University Press, 1989); Jubilee, Vincent, *Philadelphia Afro-American Literary Circle and the Harlem Renaissance* (Ann Arbor, MI: Dissertation Abstracts International, 1980); Patton, Venetria K., and Maureen Honey, *Double-Take: A Revisionist Harlem Renaissance Anthology* (New Brunswick, NJ: Rutgers University Press, 2001); Roses, Lorraine E., and Ruth E. Randolph, eds., *Harlem's Glory: Black Women Writing 1900–1950* (Cambridge, MA: Harvard University Press, 1996).

Lorna Wheeler

CRADOCK, THOMAS (1718–1770)

Thomas Cradock composed Christian devotional poetry, satirical poems imitating classical models, and a neoclassic verse drama on the death of Socrates, while serving as an Anglican clergyman in colonial Maryland. Although only some of his works survive, mostly in manuscript and often with only tentative attribution, Cradock published some devotional poetry in the *American Magazine* and two versions of psalm translations in book form, one in London (1754) and another in Annapolis, Maryland (1756), which became the second-most-common Maryland imprint in the colony's libraries. Cradock is the best known of a social and literary group called the Baltimore Bards, satirized by Alexander Hamilton in his chronicle of the Tuesday Club, a rival group meeting in Annapolis, which Cradock occasionally attended. Cradock's work typifies the belletristic writing of the leading figures in the active intellectual life of the colonial tobacco-producing settlements along the Chesapeake Bay. His published sermons, delivered to his own congregation and to other congregations of Anglicans, Lutherans, and Moravians throughout Maryland and Pennsylvania, show his involvement in the social issues of the day. For example, his sermon in Philadelphia attacked Benjamin Franklin's proposals to secularize education. In addition, his sermon at the opening of the Maryland General Assembly session in October 1753 records his long-standing but unsuccessful advocacy, in direct opposition to the Bishop of London and the Maryland proprietary governor, for a colonial bishopric to increase the quality of the colonial clergy and to improve the spiritual care of members of the Anglican church, Maryland's established church since 1702.

Thomas Cradock was born in Trentham, Staffordshire, England, to a family claiming descent from Welsh princes. His ancestors included prosperous merchants, the first governor of the Massachusetts Bay Company, and an archbishop of Dublin. After completing his early education, Cradock matriculated at Magdalen Hall, Oxford, in 1737 but did not take his degree, returning home instead for ordination and serving briefly as a schoolmaster before emigrating to Maryland in 1744. Various financial and romantic reasons have been proposed for his emigration, but his well-documented attentiveness to the spiritual nurture of his parishioners suggests colonial evangelism as a primary motivation. Upon arrival, he served as chaplain to the Maryland officials negotiating with the Iroquois Confederacy, an experience that would sour his view of the colonial treatment of Native Americans. He then became the first rector of the new St. Thomas' Church, also known as the Garrison Church, established to serve settlers in the forests west of Baltimore. During his twenty-five-year pastorate, Cradock established prayer societies similar to groups being formed by his Methodist and evangelical contemporaries in England. His ministry cut across social ranks, another departure from contemporaneous Anglican practice. In 1764, Cradock married Catherine Risteau, daughter of a prominent landholder connected to Lord Baltimore. They raised four children and established an estate that remained in the family for two centuries.

The devotional poems attributed to Cradock include, in addition to the psalm translations, elegies, hymns, and conduct poems in imitation of Horace. Two poems, "To Thyrsis" and "A Fragment," closely imitate Horace's Second Epode, a favorite in eighteenth-century America, by defining the happy or blessed man by means of a classical priamel, or negative catalog, which lists the material circumstances unnecessary to a life of virtue. "To Thyrsis" describes life as a "thorny Wilderness" and advises specific actions appropriate to a life of piety and charity. "A Fragment" more closely follows the Horatian model but similarly counsels contentment with modest means and virtuous social relations.

Cradock's satires, entitled "Maryland Eclogues in Imitation of Virgil's" follow the English Augustan Age practice of using the structure of ancient Roman authors to present contemporary settings and issues. Although Virgil had examined the impact of the Roman civil wars on social structures and rural land ownership, his critiques emphasized the cognitive and emotional dissonance experienced by his poems' characters due to this social upheaval. As in the traditional pastoral mode, Virgil's external landscapes often symbolize the characters' internal responses to displacement, drawing contrasts between desire or expectation and lived experience. However, Cradock, like his English contemporaries, uses the Virgilian structure to draw contrasts between the behavior of individuals and societal expectations of individuals in those roles, locating the dissonance in the observer.

The "Maryland Eclogues" satirize the behavior of colonial Marylanders focusing on two senses of the word pastoral: rural and ecclesiastical. The nine poems contrast the immorality of some Maryland colonists with the innocence that pastoral myth projects into the rural colonial landscape and contrast the irreligious lifestyle of some Maryland clergy with the moral rectitude expected of the pastoral vocation. The first poem imitates the dialogue structure of Virgil's first eclogue, renaming the two speakers "Crape," probably a reference to clerical vestments made of expensive fabric, and "Split-text," likely a reference to an improper limiting of the clerical role to preaching without further spiritual involvement with the congregation. Crape has been removed from his post for immoral living, "Guzzling" and "Folly," whereas Split-Text has retained his position due to social connections among the colonial aristocracy. Their conversation, like that of Virgil's speakers, presents the irony that the rural beauties and abundance can be enjoyed only by those who please the urban powers that be. Cradock's subsequent eclogues similarly attack colonial social practice, including miscegenation by slaveholders and perfidious treatment of Native Americans by colonial governments. Cradock's fourth eclogue makes reference to Annapolis schoolmaster and poet **Richard Lewis** as a teacher of unorthodox British deistic ideas. The eighth eclogue satirizes the thrifty behavior of a Scottish immigrant physician, perhaps

Alexander Hamilton, who jilts a faithful lover to marry a wealthy heiress. Each eclogue contributes details to our understanding of colonial Marylanders' social structures and daily lives.

The Death of Socrates is the title given by David Curtis Skaggs to a five-act, blank verse tragedy surviving only in a partial manuscript in handwriting like Cradock's. The play is the first known serious drama written in Maryland and the only known attempt at long poetic drama in America prior to 1765. Although it strictly follows the conventions of eighteenth-century verse drama, it introduces effective innovations, such as placing Plato at the execution and attributing important speeches to female characters. The play presents Socrates as a model of intellectual honesty and moral virtue and as a pre-Christian prophet of the soul's immortality, linking it to Cradock's other poetic writings.

Further Reading. ***Selected Primary Sources:*** Cradock's papers are held primarily at the Maryland Historical Society in Baltimore and at Saint Thomas's Parish in Owings Mills, Maryland. Cradock, Thomas, *The Poetic Works of Thomas Cradock, 1718–1770* (Newark: University of Delaware Press, 1983). ***Selected Secondary Sources:*** Davis, Richard Beale, *Intellectual Life in the Colonial South, 1585–1763* (Knoxville: University of Tennessee Press, 1978); Lemay, J. A. Leo, *Men of Letters in Colonial Maryland* (Knoxville: University of Tennessee Press, 1972); Skaggs, David Curtis, "Part I: Thomas Cradock and the Golden Age of Chesapeake Culture," in *The Poetic Works of Thomas Cradock, 1718–1770* (Newark: University of Delaware Press, 1983).

Nanette C. Tamer

CRANCH, CHRISTOPHER PEARSE (1813–1892)

Christopher Pearse Cranch ranged widely through the western world of the nineteenth century. At various points in his life he lived in Virginia, Kentucky, Ohio, Missouri, New York, Massachusetts, France, and Italy. He could include in his list of friends **Ralph Waldo Emerson**, **Theodore Parker**, John Sullivan Dwight, **James Russell Lowell**, James Freeman Clarke, Frederic Henry Hedge, **Margaret Fuller**, Robert and Elizabeth Barrett Browning, and William James. Cranch was at various times a poet, preacher, painter, an expatriate, amateur musician, a writer and illustrator of children's books, journal editor, and member of the Transcendental Club. Today he is best remembered as a Transcendentalist poet placed solidly in the company of Emerson, Fuller, **Henry David Thoreau**, and **Jones Very**.

Cranch was born on March 8, 1813, in Alexandria, Virginia, where his father, William Cranch, a conservative Unitarian and Federalist from New England, served

as a judge appointed to the District Court by President John Adams. Young Pearse Cranch first attended Columbian College (now Georgetown University) and then, after a move to Cambridge, Massachusetts, graduated from Harvard Divinity School. Some years later, as an itinerant Unitarian minister, Cranch found himself filling James Freeman Clarke's pulpit in Louisville, Kentucky, and assuming for a time in the late 1830s Clarke's editorship of *The Western Messenger*, a Transcendentalist-Unitarian literary monthly. Cranch began during this time to contribute his first poetic efforts to this periodical, and when he returned to New England in 1839, he continued to publish poems, most notably in the Transcendentalist journal the *Dial*. From this beginning, while living at various times in the United States and Europe, Cranch would go on to publish, among other works, three major volumes of poetry: *Poems* (1844); *The Bird and the Bell, with Other Poems* (1875); and *Ariel and Caliban with Other Poems* (1887). In 1971, almost eighty years after the poet's death on January 20, 1892, *Collected Poems of Christopher Pearse Cranch* appeared.

Both thought and theme in much of Cranch's early poetry derived from Emerson, to whom *Poems* (1844) was dedicated. "Enosis" is generally cited as typical of early Transcendentalist poetry and of this period in Cranch's development as a poet. The transcendent notion of unity or of combination into one, enosis, drives the poem thematically. At the outset, the poem claims intuition as the way of knowing spiritual truths: "THOUGHT is deeper than all speech, / Feeling deeper than all thought."

Moreover, the separation of humanity into individuals is only apparent: "We are columns left alone, / Of a temple once complete." Through transcendence—both rising above separateness and returning to a spiritual time before separation occurred—humans can become whole again. Here the architectural metaphor changes to one of raindrops pooling together. This unification—this "flowing into one"—is the realization of Emerson's concept of the Over-Soul portrayed in *Nature*, "The Divinity School Address," and other essays, works with which Cranch was familiar.

Of the thirty-one years that separate *Poems* from 1875's *The Bird and the Bell*, Cranch and his family spent thirteen living an expatriate life in Italy and France—one stay of three years, one of ten. During this same thirty-one–year period, Cranch experienced the birth of his two sons, George and Quincy; the death of George, the eldest, of a fever; and the horrors of the American Civil War. He also developed friendships with the Brownings and Lowell. Although the poems written during this long period of living tend to be somewhat inconsistent, collected together in *The Bird and the Bell*, many reveal Cranch's growth as a poet. They are more creative and concrete and less bound to the abstractions of Transcendentalism. Broader experience brings the poems' ideas and ideologies to life through more insightful use of language, image, narrative and character.

In 1887 Cranch published *Ariel and Caliban, with Other Poems*, his final volume of poetry. This collection represents what the poet believed to be his best work in both execution and maturity. In the title poem, a closet drama, Cranch imagines the lives of Shakespeare's creations after Prospero has left the island. Ariel and Caliban—at first antagonists, as of old—develop a relationship that seems to cause each to become more human. Cautious friendship soon transforms into brotherly love, and in the end, they too sail away from the magical island, their destination a new land that, as Ariel describes having seen it from afar, appears to be much like the United States.

This final volume also represents the culmination of Cranch's work in the sonnet, a form he made substantial use of in both earlier collections as well. Fifty-seven sonnets appear in *Ariel and Caliban*. Several form cycles—ten sonnets "To E.P.C." (his brother Edward), seven for "The Seven Wonders of the World," eight for "Life and Death." Others stand alone. Cranch most often used the Italian sonnet as his basic form, consistently adhering to its octave structure of rhyming lines—*abbaabba*. Variations usually occurred in the sestet, which he often kept close to the Italian form but sometimes substituted with variations of the final quatrain and couplet of the Spenserian sonnet.

Cranch seems to sum up his own career in *Ariel and Caliban*'s "Ars Longa, Vita Brevis." This first-person poem concerns itself with the process and value of his art and his lifelong interest in transcendent nature. Along his "lonely road," he and his "few companions" are "on one high purpose bent": "To live for Nature, finding truth / In beauty, and the shrines of art." Despite these lofty aims, however, Cranch correctly assesses his minor position in the history of American poetry. As he continues to write worthwhile verse, he is overtaken on "the mountain road" by a "younger throng with voices loud" and ultimately finds himself still moving forward but "lost amid the crowd."

Further Reading. *Selected Primary Sources:* Cranch, Christopher Pearse, *Ariel and Caliban, with Other Poems* (Boston: Houghton, 1887); ———, *The Bird and the Bell, with Other Poems* (Boston: Osgood, 1875); ———, *Collected Poems of Christopher Pearse Cranch*, ed. Joseph M. DeFalco (Gainsville, FL: Scholars' Facsimiles & Reprints, 1971); ———, *Poems* (Philadelphia: Carey & Hart, 1844); ———, *Satan: A Libretto* (Boston: Roberts, 1874). ***Selected Secondary Sources:*** Armitage, Shelly, "Christopher Pearse Cranch: The Wit as Poet" (*American Transcendental Quarterly* 1.1 [March 1987]: 33–47); Levenson, J. C., "Christopher Pearse Cranch: The Case History of a Minor Artist in America" (*American Literature* 21.4

[January 1950]: 415–426); Lind, Sidney E., "Christopher Pearse Cranch's 'Gnosis': An Error in Title" (*Modern Language Notes* 62.7 [November 1947]: 486–488).

Michael Cody

CRANE, HAROLD HART (1899–1931)

One of the central American poets of the first half of the twentieth century, Hart Crane became almost as famous for his personal excess and intensity, reminiscent of some of the French **Symbolists**, as for his brilliant contribution to poetry. Crane's poetry, particularly his famous epic poem "The Bridge," is characterized by a unique admixture of Romantic intensity and ambition with modernist complexity and allusiveness. Nonetheless, Crane's legacy remains problematic while his place among his **modernist** contemporaries, as well as within the American **canon** at large, continues to spur critical debate.

This stems in part from the brevity of Crane's life. Despite a large and complex body of verse, the poet's suicide at the age of thirty-one left twentieth-century critics to speculate as to whether his potential was ever fully realized. The completion of his most ambitious endeavor, *The Bridge* (1930), only served to fuel the argument due to its mixed and, at times, disparaging reviews. Nevertheless, *The Bridge* persists as a vibrant and relevant work in the United States, Europe, and around the world.

Deeply marked by both British and American Romanticism and French Symbolism, Crane's poetry reveals dense and often obscure meters and highly stylized metaphors. Allusive and lyrical, his poems of all subjects and lengths (as well as the multiple drafts that precede them) reflect the work of an obsessive craftsman who states in a letter to **Harriet Monroe** that poetry is primarily a "predetermined and objectified" undertaking. Among Crane's many influences, the strongest is **Walt Whitman**. The persistent optimism of Whitman drives the spirit of *The Bridge*—the **epic** poem that was Crane's contribution, in 1930, to the innovative epic impulse of the 1920s, and which stands as perhaps the era's most ambitious attempt to versify the American experience since *Leaves of Grass*.

Born in Garretsville, Ohio, on July 21, 1899, Crane initially appeared an unlikely contender to ascend the ranks of his modernist contemporaries. The only child of Grace Hart and Clarence Arthur Crane (a prolific businessman and inventor of Lifesavers candy), Crane had a somewhat privileged upbringing that digressed into a familial horror show. By the time he was nine, his family had moved to Cleveland and, shortly after, Harold was sent to live with his maternal grandmother in an attempt to spare him from what he described as the "bloody battleground" of his childhood. Nonetheless, Grace and Clarence contended for their son's allegiance following their stormy divorce in 1916, leaving Harold's loyalties irreparably divided.

Through his teens, Crane's defenses and diversions against this domestic turbulence foreshadowed his adult life. He escaped into alcohol abuse, sexual escapades, and twice attempted to take his own life. Ironically, it is this same tortured existence that also served to ground and nurture his poetic gift—a talent that became for him at once a craft, distraction, and means of sheer survival. Hence the great dialectic of Crane's poetry is cast: a battle between the dark verses that both chronicle and assuage his emotional wreckage set against his grand artistic and spiritual vision. What prompts his pen is not so much reclamation, but rather affirmation, both for himself and the nation. He envisions the dawn of an epiphanic age of Whitmanian proportions, an age of spiritual awakening in America, built not upon obsolete Judeo-Christian mythologies, but upon his own brand of neo-Transcendentalism. Furthermore, Crane declares that he will play a major part in bringing forth this transcendental epiphany. Toward this end, his project is epic; his medium, poetry—specifically his theory of the "Logic of Metaphor." In the short essay that outlines his poetics, "General Aims and Theories," Crane writes:

> I am concerned with the future of America, but not because I think that America has any so-called par value as a state or as a group of people. . . . It is only because I feel persuaded that here are destined to be discovered certain as yet undefined spiritual quantities, perhaps a new hierarchy of faith not to be developed so completely elsewhere. And in this process I like to feel myself as a potential factor; certainly I must speak in its terms and what discoveries I may make are situated in its experience. (219)

Throughout his tempestuous adolescence, it did not appear likely that Crane would become a "potential factor" in much of anything. After dropping out of high school, he would substitute vigilant and diversified reading for a formal education. Although this helped prepare him as a young poet, it could not insulate him from his home life. In order to distance himself completely from Garretsville, seventeen-year-old Harold moved to New York City four days after Christmas in 1916, immersing himself thoroughly in Manhattan's stimulating atmosphere. He had already published two poems, leaving aside all of his undergraduate verse from Cleveland. Making New York City the locus of his new life, Crane's migration effectively distanced him from his painful home life, though he did not confess to his parents that becoming a poet was the true purpose behind his exodus.

Manhattan not only situated Crane in the epicenter of America's literary life, it would, just as important, link him to the sea—a central trope for his own verse and a major tether to Whitman. Crane honed his skills, hoping to emerge as a formidable verse-maker. And though he would never be wholly free from his divided family, he would at least be free from the corrosive effects of its battleground. His allegiance was at last nominally decided after Grace Hart chastised her son for his omission of "Hart" when publishing "Annunciations" and "Fear" (inspired partly by **T.S. Eliot**'s "Prufrock") the following April in the *Pagan*. A despondent Grace inquired in writing whether he was ignoring the Hart side of his family completely. He responded by signing his very next poem "Harold H. Crane," and from then on "Hart Crane." As Crane biographer **Paul Mariani** observed, "His father was not impressed" (35).

Despite a series of immediate successes, Crane's dismal financial situation chased him back to Cleveland in 1918, forcing him to exchange his days of studying and writing for a series of dead-end office jobs that supplied little more than a steady income. By 1919, the desperate poet resigned to put aside his pen temporarily and begrudgingly agreed to work as a clerk in one of his father's Akron stores. The next inevitable melee, however, would separate him and his father irrevocably and Crane returned to New York.

His return was made possible when editor, author, and literary critic Gorham Munson and his wife, Lisa, provided him with lodging. Still, he remained unable to support himself—let alone his indulgences—by the pen alone. And it was not until he secured a job with a local advertising company that the hospitable Munsons were at last relieved of their erratic though creative house guest. Crane required visual inspiration to begin work on his epic and found it by renting the Roebling Room in April of 1924, where the view from his window looked out upon the "harp and altar" of his poetic quest: the Brooklyn Bridge. "Just imagine looking out your window on the East River with nothing intervening between your view of the statue of Liberty, way down the harbor, and the marvelous beauty of the Brooklyn Bridge close above you on your right," he wrote to Grace. The majestic scene later inspired the opening lines of "Poem: To Brooklyn Bridge": "How many dawns, chill from his rippling rest / The seagull's wings shall dip and pivot him."

Satisfactorily situated but hardly well off, Crane tried to convince New York banker Otto Kahn to sponsor his literary enterprises. Kahn agreed, helping Crane in 1926 to at last publish the first of his two volumes of poetry, *White Buildings*, a collection that met initially with enthusiastic reviews, especially from Crane's circle of mentor supporters. "I withdraw all minor objections I have ever made to your work," **Yvor Winters** wrote to Crane. "I have never read anything greater and have read very little as great." Other reviews were far less generous, most notably Kay Boyle's scathing attack in *transition*. The poet reacted furiously to Boyle's review while Winters defended him in a sharp letter to the magazine. Such difficulties with reviewers, even among editors who encouraged his work, would become a pattern with Crane. Anxious for the money, he permitted **Marianne Moore** to change the title of "The Wine Menagerie" while reworking parts of it for publication in the *Dial*. Moore found the poem impenetrable otherwise, but Crane literally wept over her alterations.

That Crane strove for aesthetic complexity is clear enough. His **poetics** reflect a mixture of stylized neoclassical structures together and a high Romantic impulse. Like Keats, he strives to produce the well-wrought urn of a poem via his own verbal "scaffolding." His self-proclaimed "Logic of Metaphor" accounts for an "organic principle . . . which antedates our so-called pure logic, and which is the genetic basis of all speech, hence consciousness and thought-extension" ("General Aims," 221). Such "logic" then transcribes a matrix for building not one bridge, but many—bridges between America's past and present, between the human and divine, indeed a bridge that might facilitate his personal transport to salvation from ruin and despair. In spite of these worthy objectives, often realized with astonishing effect, his dense metaphoric compressions and richly allusive lyrics tended to leave even some of his most ardent readers dazed and confused.

Despite its weaknesses, *White Buildings* displays a number of Crane's finest poems, showcasing the young poet's thematic and imagistic networking that foreshadowed a formidable career. Driven by personal passion, the collection's verses often depict a soul in the forlorn anguish of unrequited desire in the Romantic terms that Crane borrowed from his major precursors after Whitman: Herman Melville, **Emily Dickinson**, and, of course, Shelley. "At Melville's Tomb," for instance, situates the titanic Melvillean and Whitmanian poles of the American Renaissance: "Monody shall not wake the mariner. / This fabulous shadow only the sea keeps. As with the connection between American history and the sea in the "Ave Maria" section of *The Bridge*, where Crane recounts Columbus's historic journey back to Spain, he attempts here to isolate America's literary identity through the same fertile image. The mighty sea inspires, seduces, sustains, and, finally, takes all "beneath the wave" never to return as "only the sea keeps."

The trope persists in the equally powerful and poignant "Voyages," whose second part remains the strongest of the sequence. Replete with sequences of birth, death, rebirth, desire, and unrequited love, the sea both unifies and perpetuates each succeeding cycle. "Voyages II" includes a litany of Crane's finest instances of phrase-making: "This great wink of eternity," "Adagios of

Islands," "Vortex of our grave," and "The seal's wide spindrift gaze toward paradise." Nevertheless, as a series, "Voyages" displays an anti-synergistic quality as particular moments often exhibit a brilliance that outshines the sum of the six parts (a characteristic criticism of *The Bridge*).

Yet, all told, this miniature epic journey of love, desire, death, and, ultimately, rebirth, remains a potent erotic confession as well as a shrewd witness to the poet's own "imaged Word" as a creative force—a power that returns with an "unbetrayable reply." In the end, however, this intense sensual pleasure, the very zenith of erotic ecstasy, has purchased only uncertainty. The poet reborn in the flames of such passion does not realize the promise of the "improved infancy" from "Passages" but is left to wallow in its intense negation, "Waiting, afire, what name unspoken, I cannot claim:" Indeed, this poet knows all too well that "The bottom of the sea is cruel."

Defining the place of *The Bridge* in the American canon is no less difficult than calculating the epic project's obsessive role in its author's brief life. That the work consumed its creator seems clear enough, as Crane toiled to fulfill his own prophecy concerning the new epiphanic age of American modernity and, perhaps more important, his own spiritual reclamation. In its entirety, *The Bridge* is at once, as Crane notes in "General Aims and Theories," the "new *word*, never before spoken" (221) as well as the poet's most generous contribution toward helping to bring about that "new hierarchy of faith"—those "spiritual qualities" that he forecast would only be found in America (218). Long after Crane's suicide, his former lover, Emil Opffer, noted that Crane sometimes remarked, "The whole world is a bridge." The metaphor seems to speak to Crane's aesthetics as well as to his personal existence.

To secure additional funding from Kahn, Crane mapped out the project's "general method of construction," teasing his patron with trailer-like pieces of finished sections, and describing others not yet written. Even for the poet, this proved to be a maddening exercise. Although his holistic vision propelled him throughout the seven-year odyssey of orchestrating the project's eight sections, the journey, not surprisingly, was fraught with constant revision and delay. In a letter to Kahn, Crane described the venture as nothing short of "handling the Myth of America," and achieving that lofty objective would remain his constant goal and burden.

Though its climactic section, "Atlantis," was actually written first, the poem begins with the overture-like "Proem: To Brooklyn Bridge," an eleven-quatrain invocation that not only posits the Bridge as the poet's subject and muse but also serves to deify the structure as a sacred link between the human and divine. As the concluding lines plead, "Unto us lowliest sometime sweep, descend / And of the curveship lend a myth to God."

The first section that follows the "Proem," "Ave Maria," reaches back through time and space, recalling Columbus's first voyage back to Spain while braving a tempest to return with the "incognizable Word / Of Eden" found across the sea, our passage to the Chan." This moment, poeticized by Crane to mark the birth of the American continent, segues to the longest and most complex section, "Powhatan's Daughter." Composed of five interrelated parts, "Powhatan's Daughter" transports the poet from his Greenwich Village loft ("Harbor Dawn") on a journey westward, before venturing south to where "The Mississippi drinks the farthest dale." Meanwhile, the poet establishes Powhatan's daughter, Pocahontas, as a key unifying icon. She is the sexually charged "well-featured but wanton yong girle," the "Princess whose brown lap was virgin May," while her dusky red skin symbolizes for Crane the fertile American soil. In this paradigm, brutal confrontations between the natives and western cultures culminate in a dance: "Now is the strong prayer folded in thine arms, /The serpent with the eagle in the boughs."

"Cutty Sark" and "Cape Hatteras," the third and fourth sections, respectively, serve to close one half of *The Bridge* and begin the second. Having journeyed westward, the poet begins another metaphorical voyage, another sea quest, depicted this time through the drunken sailor narrating through "Cutty Sark." While "walking home across the Bridge," an array of nineteenth-century clipper ships appears from the East River to the poet/narrator, reinforcing the epic's nautical theme. As the longest single poem of *The Bridge*, "Cape Hatteras" begins with an epigraph from Whitman: "The seas all crossed, / weathered the capes, the voyage done." Establishing Whitman as the dominant figure of the section, the quote also recalls the sea voyages that began with Columbus and concluded with "Cutty Sark." The "dorsal change" between the sections is marked dramatically by the shift from the land and sea to the air, from the horizontal mode of travel and a linear view of history, to the vertical "Ascensions" that unlock the corporal self, as well as the heavens, to the unbound soaring spirit. Although Crane employs such conceptual tropes to illustrate this transformation, vibrant images appear throughout the section on the history of flight, crystallizing in one of the poet's most dramatic invocations of the entire work: *Panis Angelicus*—the Medieval Catholic hymn through which the aircraft, Whitman's voice, and the Whitmanian vision of America all converge: "Afoot again, and onward without halt, — / Not soon, nor suddenly,—no, never to let go." The section concludes as Crane links hands with his precursor, Whitman. Crane's journey home continues with Whitman's vision of communion solidly established, recognized, and reinforced, as Crane endeavors to become the "divine literatus" Whitman defined and prophesized in *Democratic Vistas*:

View'd today, from a point of view sufficiently overarching, the problem of humanity all over the civilized world is social and religious, and is to be finally met and treated by literature. The priest departs, the divine literatus comes. Never was anything more wanted than, today, and here in the States, the poet of the modern is wanted, or the great literatus of the modern. (457–458)

"Three Songs" subsequently posits discrete odes to Eve, Mary Magdelene, and "blue-eyed" Mary, while preparing the reader for the descending sections of "Quaker Hill" and especially "The Tunnel," where the visage of **Edgar Allan Poe** appears to haunt the rider/narrator's journey beneath the East River. Once there, a hellish scene unfolds, in which the "phonographs of hades in the brain" unleash the despair that threatens any promise of ascension: "Are tunnels that re-wind themselves, and love / A burnt match skating in a urinal." From this literal and thematic nadir, the epic climaxes explosively in "Atlantis." Returning to the foot of the bridge, the subject-object of the project has been transformed into an epicenter of spiritual unity. Crane's Brooklyn Bridge fully transcends its concrete and metal to become "steeled Cognizance," an "intrinsic Myth, Forever Deity's glittering Pledge." "Thy pardon for this history," ever present, and "beyond time." "Unspeakable Thou Bridge to Thee, O Love. / Thy pardon for this history, whitest Flower." Calling his bridge the "Answerer of all—Anemone," the stanza concludes: "(O Thou whose radiance doth inherit me) / Atlantis, —hold thy floating singer late!" The poet asks ultimately if this "One Song, one Bridge of Fire!" is truly Cathay. Have we at last closed the circle of the globe, the circle of the sea, the circle of time and returned to that vision of paradise—not in our mythologies—but in this all-encompassing future, where we find "the serpent and eagle in the leaves"? The bridge, in something of a reply, "whispers antiphonal in azure swing." With this imperfect grammar, in which the nouns and verbs seem interchangeable, we are left to wonder if the journey is finally completed, the mission accomplished, the Epiphany proclaimed. Has Cathay, four hundred years later, at last been reached? Despite its deliberate vagueness, the phrase may be for Crane a personal utterance of completion. It may be the final "incognizable Word" of his lengthy quest through time and space, a whisper of deeply subjective hope rather than purely an empirical forecast.

That this epiphanic moment arrived neither for Crane nor America should not detract from the literary and national achievement that is *The Bridge*. In terms of the poet's uniquely American experience, the epic in its entirety becomes the "*new* word, never before spoken and impossible to actually enunciate," the new word that embodies the qualities of the American consciousness. Yet this new epic-logos was achieved at a very high price, for no project both occupied and consumed Crane so thoroughly as *The Bridge*. If Harold Bloom is accurate in describing Crane as "a prophet of American Orphism, of the Emersonian and Whitmanian Native Strain in our national literature" then this epic becomes a bold and costly effort to resurrect that spiritual awakening in those terms.

In order to create this transcendental quality, Crane developed a sophisticated relationship between the creative word of the poet and the redemptive "Word" of God throughout. Incarnation, therefore, becomes a prominent subtext in which the bridge itself is transformed into a type of portal between the human and divine. It is not, of course, the literal fact of the Brooklyn Bridge that empowers this transformation, but Crane's "Logic of Metaphor" that sustains the rhetorical progression for the edifice from structure to symbol to viable presence.

As Lee Edelman states in his introduction to *Transmemberment of Song*, "Thus for Crane, in the beginning was neither word nor world, but the rhetorical logic of association that would call forth and shape them both" (14). As such there are really two types of "words" at work in *The Bridge*. The first is the object of his pilgrimage, the poet's own realization of the "word made flesh," a tangible, physical presence that makes the bridge simultaneously the means and the end, the signifier and the signified. The second word is the poem itself, the portal of language through which the first visionary word might be made known.

Throughout *The Bridge* and the poetry surrounding it, Crane strove to reconcile the influence of two American giants, one his precursor, the other his contemporary. The struggle with Walt Whitman is not against his poetics, as much as it manifests itself in the desire to rekindle and extend his idol's ambitious themes. On the other hand, allusions from *The Waste Land, The Love Song of J. Alfred Prufrock*, among other lyrics by T.S. Eliot, punctuate Crane regularly. Here, however, he wrestles against Eliot's dark version of modernity. Indeed, if Crane begins his epic by distinguishing his more "positive" tones from "Eliotic despair," he concludes it in the midst of a feverish battle to rescue himself from a *Waste Land*–like existence that appears to be subsuming his own. In the end, ironically, it is only the poem, and not the poet, that is saved.

In a letter to Gorham Munson dated January 10, 1923, Crane betrays great respect for Eliot's genius while departing from his themes:

There is no one writing in English who can command so much respect, to my mind, as Eliot. However, I take Eliot as a point of departure toward an almost complete reverse of direction. His pessimism is amply justified, in his own case. But I would apply as much of his erudition and technique as I can absorb and assemble toward a more positive, or (if [I] must put it so in a sceptical age) ecstatic goal. . . . I feel that Eliot ignores certain spiritual events and possibilities as real and powerful now as, say, in the time of Blake. Certainly the man has dug the ground and buried hope as deep and direfully as it can ever be done. (114–115)

In Eliot, the dark angst of the modern world possesses the power to overwhelm sensibility, drown consciousness, while reducing language to a state of incoherent utterances. And although Crane's own dark digressions are essential to the nature of his quest, his lowest moments parallel Gethsemane, the cross, the descent—scenes that may ultimately serve as preludes for a personal, though secularized, resurrection.

Despite the ebullient climax of "Atlantis," Crane's private disintegration reaches new depths. Even his energized island verse, replete with the liberating freedom associated with the tropical culture, can neither save the poet from his demons nor cast them from his memory. In "O Carib Isle!" while standing before a graveyard of coral, the poet calls into question the creative enterprise itself, wondering if, like the hurricanes that menace the region, nature obliterates even our most sublime attempts to order her. "You have given me the shell, Satan, —carbonic amulet / Sere of the sun exploded in the sea. Ironically appropriate perhaps, one of Crane's last poems, "The Broken Tower," depicts his unsuccessful attempt at a heterosexual union with Peggy Baird Cowley. Written in Mexico in 1932 and couched in contending religious and sexual imagery, the poet uses the stark oppositions and erotic tensions ("My word I poured") to unite his poiesis and his passion: "Whose thigh embronzes earth, strike crystal Word / In wounds pledged once to hope, —cleft to despair?"

Juxtaposed against the rhetorical question that climaxes *The Bridge*, this "Matrix of the heart" ends not with uncertain hope but uncertain achievement, as the poet here seems to acknowledge his own waning prowess. Crane marks the poem complete on Good Friday, March 25, with no Resurrection in sight at the end of the journey. The dark and conflicted tenor recalls Crane's powerful affinity to Emily Dickinson, who follows only Whitman in influencing him. Acknowledging the genius of Dickinson, his "sweet, dead Silencer," he says that the harvest she "descried" and understood "[n]eeds more than wit to gather, love to bind. / Some reconcilement of remotest mind." For Crane, however, such reconciliation would not come.

Crane's legacy as one of the most innovative and romantically visionary American poets of the twentieth century endures in the minds of influential critics.

Bloom places him among Whitman, Dickinson, and **Wallace Stevens** as one of the four pillars of the American tradition, claiming that Crane was "perhaps more gifted than any of them." Mariani, meanwhile, contends

> However we sum up the age, however we read Whitman and Stevens, Pound and Eliot, however we read Frost, or Moore, Plath or Bishop, Berryman or Lowell, Hughes or Wilbur, Merrill or Ashbery, Levine or Justice, or so many other extraordinary voices, Crane seems destined to have a central place in any serious assessment of the age. (14)

On April 27, 1932, a drunken Crane leapt from the stern of the *Orizaba*, ten miles east of the Florida coast. Whether or not he had deliberately tried to commit suicide remains uncertain, but what seems clear is that this act was not so much a moment of lapsed judgment as much as it was the final act of a spirit that had long been in serious decline. In the end, his completion of *The Bridge* seemed a great relief to Crane instead of the glorious expression of the American vision that he had longed to see fulfilled. In the end, his epic neither redeems the American nation nor re-creates the "spiritual qualities" he so ardently believed in. Nevertheless, the poem remains a testament to the imaginative inner journey that may still lead to a type of redemption, perhaps even atonement, even if it could not rescue Crane from his own tortured existence. The strength of *The Bridge* both complements and affirms the astonishing body of work he yielded in so short a time, identifying Crane with a supremely rich moment in the American poetic tradition.

Further Reading. *Selected Primary Sources:* Crane, Hart, *The Complete Poems and Selected Letters and Prose*, ed. Brom Weber (New York: Anchor Press, 1966); ———, *The Complete Poems of Hart Crane*, ed. Marc Simon (New York: Liveright, 2001); ———, *The Letters of Hart Crane and His Family*, ed. Thomas S. Lewis (New York: Columbia University Press, 1974); ———, *O My Land, My Friends: The Selected Letters of Hart Crane* (New York: Avalon, 1997); ———, *White Buildings* (New York: Liveright, 2001). ***Selected Secondary Sources:*** Bloom, Harold, *Hart Crane* (New York: Chelsea House, 1986); Brunner, Edward, *Splendid Failure: Hart Crane and the Making of* The Bridge (Chicago: University of Illinois Press, 1985); Butterfield, R.W., *The Broken Arc: A Study of Hart Crane* (Edinburgh: Oliver & Boyd, 1969); Edelman, Lee, *Transmemberment of Song: Hart Crane's Anatomies of Rhetoric and Desire* (Stanford, CA: Stanford University Press, 1987); Giles, Paul, *Hart Crane: The Contexts of* The Bridge (Cambridge: Cambridge University Press, 1986); Irwin, John T., "Hart Crane's 'Logic of Metaphor,'" in *Critical Essays on Hart Crane*, ed. David R. Clark (Boston: G.K. Hall, 1982); Mariani, Paul, *The Broken Tower: The Life of Hart Crane* (New York: W.W. Norton, 1999); Nilsen, Helge Normann, *Hart Crane's Divided Vision: An Analysis of* The Bridge (Oslo: Haugesund Bok & Offset A/S, 1980); Paul, Sherman, *Hart's Bridge* (Chicago: University of Illinois Press, 1972); Tate, Allen, "Hart Crane," in *The Merrill Studies in* The Bridge, ed. David R. Clark (Columbus, OH: Charles E. Merrill, 1970); Winters, Yvor, "The Progress of Hart Crane," in *Critical Essays on Hart Crane*, ed. David R. Clark (Boston: G.K. Hall, 1982); Yingling, Thomas E., *Hart Crane and the Homosexual Text: New Thresholds, New Anatomies* (Chicago: University of Chicago Press, 1990).

John P. Wargacki

CRANE, STEPHEN (1871–1900)

Although he achieved widespread fame for *The Red Badge of Courage* (1895) and is still known primarily for this novel of the Civil War, Stephen Crane highly valued his poems, or as he called them, his "lines." In a 1987 letter to John Northern Hilliard, Crane insisted that he liked his poetry better than the *Red Badge* and that it contained his philosophical ideas, rather than relating a "mere episode," as he claimed his fiction had done. During his lifetime Crane published 105 poems in two volumes: *The Black Riders and Other Lines* (1895) and *War Is Kind* (1899). His poems were often panned or parodied by reviewers, who found his break with tradition laughable. A notable exception is Elbert Hubbard, who in a March 1896 *Lotus* review of *Black Riders* praised Crane as a genius. Although Crane's poems have been republished in several editions, with another thirty-one added posthumously, they have been the primary subject of only one book of criticism and a few journal articles. Some critics, however, argue that the poems are undervalued and are important experimental forerunners of the later **modernist** movement.

Born on November 1, 1871, in Newark, New Jersey, Stephen Crane was the fourteenth and last child of the Reverend Jonathan Townley Crane and Mary Helen Peck Crane, the daughter of a prominent Methodist minister. Following in the family tradition of his father, author of religious tracts; his mother, a correspondent for Methodist newspapers; his sister Agnes, a short story writer; and his brother Townley, a newspaper reporter, Crane showed an interest in writing at an early age. He wrote in a wide variety of forms, including novels, short stories, newspaper reports, and poetry. As the youngest child in a large family, he was likely coddled and spoiled, but he was forced into early independence by the deaths of those closest to him. Only eight when his father died, the boy had a great deal of freedom as his mother busied herself with church and temperance work and his beloved sister Agnes tried to forge a career as a teacher. Four years later Agnes died, and when Crane was twenty, his mother died.

Stephen Crane attended Pennington Seminary, a Methodist boarding school, from 1885 to 1887 and then enrolled in Claverack College and Hudson River Institute, a coeducational military school. In the fall of 1890, he entered Lafayette College as a mining engineering student, but after one semester he transferred to Syracuse University. There he began his novel *Maggie: A Girl of the Streets* (1896) and soon became more interested in exploring the slums of lower Manhattan and writing about what he saw there than in going to class. In 1894 Crane showed **Hamlin Garland** some of his "lines," which Garland found to be highly original. The meeting proved to be advantageous because it led to Crane's friendship with **William Dean Howells**, who attempted to interest *Harper's Magazine* in the poems. Although that venture was unsuccessful, Howells remained an important literary friend and contact; Copeland and Day later agreed to publish the first volume of Crane's poetry.

The philosophy of life that Stephen Crane insisted his poems reveal has its basis in his early religious training and his freedom to experience the seamier side of society. Perhaps because of the gap he discerned between the doctrines of the church and the realities of poverty and licentiousness, Crane in his poetry often presents two sides or two ways of looking at one situation. As a journalist and writer, he spent his adult life exploring different facets of contemporary issues. With approval from Police Commissioner Theodore Roosevelt, he investigated social conditions in the Tenderloin district of New York City, but he lost favor when he criticized police and defended in court a prostitute, Dora Clark, who had brought charges of false arrest. He toured the Western United States to see how that section of the country differed from the East. In an effort to view war in Cuba, he booked passage from Jacksonville, Florida, on the filibustering steamer *Commodore*, whose sinking inspired his masterpiece short story, "The Open Boat" (1897). He later reported on wars in Greece and Cuba to see if his Civil War novel had presented combat experience realistically. During the last few years of his short life, he settled in England, where he was able to view America itself from a different perspective. There he was befriended by such prominent writers as Joseph Conrad, Henry James, Harold Frederic, and Ford Madox Ford, who accepted his openly living with Cora Taylor as husband and wife, even though she was not divorced from her current husband. Before his death from tuberculosis at the age of twenty-eight, Crane the reporter investigated various points of views, and Crane the poet strove to articulate that variety.

Stephen Crane's first book of poetry, *The Black Riders and Other Lines*, demonstrates his insistence on multiple points of view and his rebellion against custom. In this book, the first indication of his break with traditional poetry, and with traditional ways of seeing, is the poetic

form itself. The poems, or lines, have no titles, are identified only by roman numerals, and are written mostly in free verse—innovations that some critics have connected to the influence of **Emily Dickinson** and others to that of **Walt Whitman.** Crane's poems deal with subjects ranging from the ambiguity of perception, to the difficulty of poetic representation, to morality and religion, to war and love.

The ambiguity of perception is the subject of many poems in *Black Riders*, where Crane presents truth as being ephemeral, with different characters perceiving different truths. In "'Truth,' said a traveler," one traveler sees truth as "a mighty fortress, a rock," whereas the other sees it as a "shadow, a phantom" whose presence can never be fully verified. The narrator sides with the second traveler, who cannot equate truth with anything as reliable as a fortress or firm as a rock. Even a change in location influences truth or reality. In "A man saw a ball of gold in the sky," the man views a sphere in the sky as being made of gold when it is at a distance and seems unattainable. After a long, strenuous climb, he discovers the ball is made of clay. Paradoxically, once on the ground again, he sees the ball as made of gold. The poem suggests that truth is not absolute but is a function of perspective. Truth, or reality, in Crane's poetry is fluid, dependent on the observer, the observer's world view, the location, or the situation.

When a poetic character operates within a system of didactic judgment, his perception is restricted. A man in "Think as I think" issues this command and then adds, "Or you are abominably wicked; / You are a toad." At this point the narrator ponders the implications of the command and tells the man he will, then, "be a toad." The man, unwilling to acknowledge other truths, considers the divergent thinker evil.

Other narrators in *Black Riders*, instead of condemning sinners, seem to identify with them. The title poem introduces the first of these reprobates with a noisy flourish: "Thus the rush of sin." The poem connects the black riders to the reality of imperfection and suggests the apocalypse, as the horsemen arrive from the sea with much clanging and clashing and shouting. The noise and the energy of this poem invite the reader to share in this experience. The poem "I stood upon a high place" further explores the universality of sin as it presents many devils carousing below the highly positioned narrator. Looking up at the narrator, one of the demons greets him as an equal, calling him "Comrade! Brother!" In another poem populated by blades of grass, God asks one blade what good it has performed during its lifetime. When the blade answers that he can think of nothing, God replies, "Oh, best little blade of grass!" The blade's recognition of its own imperfection marks a step toward goodness.

Some poems in *Black Riders* deal with such modernist concerns as the difficulty of poetic representation. The poem "Three little birds in a row" depicts three birds noticing a man passing by. They say about him, "He thinks he can sing." Then they laugh at such a spectacle, as the narrator turns the tables by proclaiming the birds to be "curious." This word choice suggests that the narrator is as skeptical of the birds' opinion as the birds are skeptical of the man's singing ability. In "Yes, I have a thousand tongues," the narrator avers that he has 1000 tongues, but that 999 of them "lie." Still he strives "to use the one" remaining, which he says "will make no melody at my will, / But is dead in my mouth." Another poem, "In the desert," depicts both the pain and the pleasure of writing poetry. The bestial creature in the desert is eating his own heart, much as the poet metaphorically consumes his heart in his poetry. When the narrator asks if the heart is good, the creature answers:

> I like it
> Because it is bitter
> And because it is my heart.

In this figurative agony of poetic representation, Crane anticipates the later modernist exploration of the process of writing itself.

In another move toward modernist concerns, Crane articulates his deliberate break with prevailing philosophy and literature in "Tradition, thou art for suckling children." The narrator realizes how difficult that break is by concluding with the admission that "alas, we all are babes." Crane's rupture with tradition included a rejection of the rigid church as he had known it and the idea of God as an actor in human affairs. Crane presents instead a god who sits back and watches the world he has fashioned so carefully sail rudderless along its way. Worshipers in some of the poems imbue the gods with negative characteristics. In "A man went before a strange god," the man goes to the "god of many men," who is "sadly wise," full of rage, and punitive. Then the man goes to another god, the "god of his inner thoughts," who is kind and compassionate. Although some critics accused Crane of being atheistic, the poems in this volume affirm the existence of a deity but condemn those hypocritical in their worship and judgmental of their fellow humans.

John Blair points out that Crane assumes the posture of a bohemian in *Black Riders* and that he seems to revel in creating as much "anarchy" as possible. Published only a few years later, Crane's other volume of poetry, *War Is Kind*, includes poems that indicate a wider perspective, perhaps due to his broader experience and travel. Still rejecting tradition, these poems present a more complicated, thoughtful assault on the issues of worship, war, and social institutions and practices. As Blair observes, the Crane of the later poems is more mature, more an observer than a poseur.

The poems in *War Is Kind* tend to be longer and more imagistic, and the narrators in even the short, simple works seem to be more thematically aware of the complications of life near the end of the nineteenth century and to anticipate the fractured existence of the twentieth. In the poem beginning "When the prophet, a complacent fat man," the seer has lost the polarized vision of *The Black Riders*. Instead of finding the "good white lands" and the "bad black lands," he discovers that "the scene is grey." This short poem avoids limiting perception to two opposing sides and intimates that every issue is complex.

These poems still refuse popular methods for defining God. In one poem the narrator asks, "You define me God with these trinkets?" In another he disparages the listener's definition of God by telling him, "this is a printed list, / A burning candle and an ass." Crane as poet does not reject God but rejects humanity's definition or restriction of God. Ambiguous in its reference, the term "ass" forcefully concludes this three-line poem. The word could refer to God, or to the animal depicted as bearing Mary and her child, but likely it refers to the listener who attempts to limit the concept of God with the trappings of traditional worship.

Other poems in *War Is Kind* directly attack social problems such as war, yellow journalism, and the accumulation of wealth during the period of the Gilded Age. In the title poem, first published in *Bookman* in 1896, Crane uses irony to undercut the glory of war. The narrator addresses a maiden, a child, and a mother with the refrain of "Do not weep. / War is kind." These obviously ironic lines of comfort to the three who have lost loved ones in battle contrast with longer passages depicting the thrill of war. In "A newspaper is a collection of half-injustices," Crane decries the sensationalism of the press, a poignant critique given his own reporting for such publications. A poem beginning "The impact of a dollar upon the heart" juxtaposes images of "pimping merchants" and "baubles" with that of a "cryptic slave," who makes such riches possible.

Concluding this volume is the "Intrigue" suite of ten poems, which deal with the difficulty of romantic love. These poems all address a lover, probably Crane's common-law wife, Cora. According to Fredson Bowers, the first five poems in this suite were written before Crane left Cora in England and went to Cuba in 1898 (212–214). The narrator in these poems, a lovesick young man, revels in the torture of his love and jealousy. Although he expresses doubt in his lover, knowledge of her other affairs, and concern for his own peace, he is obviously infatuated with this object of his adoration.

In the sixth poem, the first written or revised in Havana, the tone darkens dramatically. The narrator remembers when he had thought himself to be a "grand knight," who had swaggered and called his beloved "Sweetheart." The poem then ends abruptly with an image of despair:

And we preserved an admirable mimicry
Without heeding the drip of the blood
From my heart.

The image of the dripping blood implies more than the disillusionment of a romantic lover. Instead, it suggests the very real problems that Crane faced in his relationship with Cora. His continuous money worries and the need to keep Cora in style in an English household including servants and a constant stream of visitors had exacted a heavy toll on Crane's freedom and his creative activity.

This disillusionment appears even stronger in a disturbing poem written probably in 1898 and unpublished in Crane's lifetime. Beginning with the line "A naked woman and a dead dwarf," the poem tells of a dead dwarf whose last sight is of a naked woman, referred to as "the eternal clown." The "poor dwarf" dies amid "bells and wine" while he endures the sight of the clown/woman, the embodiment of subterfuge. The dwarf had imagined himself in an exalted position with "foolish kings," but this final joke on the dwarf belies his previous visions of grandeur and power and renders him helpless as he dies with "a desperate comic palaver." The clown/naked woman remains "eternal," enduring before and after the dwarf's existence and waiting to exhibit herself for the next victim.

The poet may have equated himself with the dwarf, as Stephen Crane left Cuba on December 28, 1898, and sailed from New York to England on New Year's Eve. Cora's desperate pleas for his return and his highly developed sense of responsibility forced him to turn out as much hack work as possible. During 1899 his debts mounted as his health worsened, with a tubercular hemorrhage following an extravagant Christmas party at Brede Place, the manor house Cora had leased during his absence. The beginning of the twentieth century found the young writer extremely ill. Perhaps, like the dwarf, he could only observe the comedy of his life and feel the treachery of a relationship that had drained his finances and his creativity. He continued to write, but his body and his spirit were fractured by the pressures on his physical and psychic energy and the tuberculosis that killed him on June 5, 1900.

To the emerging modernist movement in poetry, Stephen Crane contributed his insistence on multiple points of view, his rebellion against traditional mores and cultural absolutism, his techniques of juxtaposition, his deceptively simple form, and his attention to the act of writing itself. Still largely neglected even by Crane scholars, a handful of his poems are often anthologized, but his poetic innovations are generally ignored.

Further Reading. *Selected Primary Sources:* Crane, Stephen, *The Complete Poems of Stephen Crane*, ed. Joseph Katz (Ithaca, NY: Cornell University Press, 1972); ———, *The Works of Stephen Crane, Poems and Literary Remains*, Vol. 10, ed. Fredson Bowers (Charlottesville: University of Virginia Press, 1975). ***Selected Secondary Sources:*** Blair, John, "The Posture of a Bohemian in the Poetry of Stephen Crane" (*American Literature* 61.2 [May 1989]: 215–229); Colvert, James, "Introduction," in *The Works of Stephen Crane, Poems and Literary Remains*, Vol. 10, ed. Fredson Bowers (Charlottesville: University of Virginia Press, 1975); Gandal, Keith, "A Spiritual Autopsy of Stephen Crane" (*Nineteenth-Century Literature* 51 [March 1997]: 500—530); Hoffman, Daniel, "Many Red Devils upon the Page: The Poetry of Stephen Crane" (*Sewanee Review* 102 [Fall 1994]: 588–603); ———, *The Poetry of Stephen Crane* (New York: Columbia University Press, 1957).

Joyce C. Smith

CRAPSEY, ADELAIDE (1878–1914)

Adelaide Crapsey, a little-known **modernist** master, was a close and perceptive observer of nature, adept at relating exterior scenes to interior realities. Although she sometimes wrote of joy and exultation, she always sensed the presence of death in herself and her world. This haunting awareness led her to focus on the experiences of illness, depression, loss, and pain. She also wrote female-centered poems suggesting the independence of women's spirit and the gratifications of affectional bonds among women. Crapsey knew the tremendous power of the unsaid. She had an uncanny ability to make her silences as eloquent as her words. Despite or because of the omnipresence of death in her work, she constructed imaginative spaces that served as a source of pleasure, health, insight, and freedom—of compensation and redemption.

Inspired by **Japanese** tanka and haiku and Native American "charms," Crapsey invented an entirely new verse form called the cinquain, arguably the first wholly original poetic form to emerge from the United States. The cinquain is a five-line poem in which the number of stresses in each line are, respectively, one, two, three, four, and one. Crapsey's cinquains and other short poems suggest a huge interior life registered in small textual shards. These poems—both beautiful and unsettling— mirror her brief, painful, yet triumphant life. They invite us to read the resonances, to share an intimacy, and to recognize a psychic landscape at once strange and familiar. Crapsey's poems, written in illness and social isolation between 1910 and 1914, complemented the more celebrated **Imagist** poems being composed at about the same time by **H.D.**, **Ezra Pound**, and **Amy Lowell**. Like the other poets, none of whom she knew personally, Crapsey wrote poems notable for their verbal economy, formal innovation, vivid imagery, and aura of modernity. These poems are as astonishing today as the day they were written.

Crapsey's life was filled with private accomplishment. She was born in Brooklyn and raised in Rochester, New York, one of nine children in a free-thinking Episcopal clergyman's family. Dr. Crapsey, influenced by John Henry Newman, Charles Darwin, and Karl Marx, believed that caring for the underprivileged mattered more than the doctrine of the Virgin Birth. As a result of such unorthodoxies, he was deposed from his rectorship in 1906. Adelaide, a brilliant student, attended Vassar College and did further study at the School of Archaeology in Rome. She started a career teaching English, first in private academies and then at Smith College. All the while she worked on the poetry for which she is now known and on a scholarly treatise concerning meter. She was particularly interested in the formal aspect of poems. One of her students later commented, "She never let poetry be only feeling. It had form; it had technique. . . . A rondel had meaning because of its very form, a ballad became alive like a person—it had its own body."

For most of her adult life Crapsey suffered from poor health. After teaching at Smith during weekdays, she would spend weekends lying in bed, exhausted from the physical strain. Doctors could not diagnose her condition. Some claimed that her infirmity resulted from too much indoor study and advised brisk walks in the country. Finally, while visiting a friend in the Berkshire Mountains in 1913, she collapsed. After extensive tests, two lung specialists diagnosed her condition as advanced tuberculosis. She spent the last year of her life wasting away and suffering great physical pain before she died at the age of thirty-six.

Although Crapsey had previously been unsuccessful in publishing her work, she did place one poem, "The Witch," in *Century Magazine* shortly before her death in 1914. She had thus lived long enough to see her first poem accepted, though she was dead by the time it appeared. With the help of two friends, Jean Webster and Esther Lowenthal, Crapsey prepared a manuscript of poems for publication. Titled simply *Verse*, it was published by a family friend in 1915, a year after her death, and then it was republished by Alfred Knopf in 1922. Her scholarly work, *A Study in English Metrics*, was also published by Knopf, in 1918. Although Crapsey has not yet achieved the posthumous fame of **Emily Dickinson**, her name and work have been known to subsequent generations.

In addition to its stress pattern of 1-2-3-4-1, the cinquain form often possesses a regular syllabic count of 2-4-6-8-2. This form may imply a pattern of incremental growth and sudden contraction that parallels Crapsey's own brief life. "November Night," for example, exemplifies the genre's normal pattern of stresses and syllables:

> Listen.
> With faint dry sound,
> Like steps of passing ghosts,
> The leaves, frost-crisp'd, break from the trees
> And fall.

"November Night" also possesses the plangent imagery that is the form's hallmark. The sight and sound of dried autumn leaves detaching and falling suggest an emotional complex of loss, grief, regret, resignation, and awe. The poem invites us to "listen" rather than to watch, and to listen to the virtually imperceptible sound of leaves breaking from their branch. It asks us to stretch our awareness to its limits and beyond. Line four intimates the sought-after sonic event in its rapid succession of *t*, *p*, *b*, and *k* sounds. The poem's precise auditory and visual imagery is complemented by one telling simile: The sound is as faint and apparitional—and frightening—as the "steps of passing ghosts." Such poems are at once a source of aesthetic pleasure and an immersion into the subjective world of perception, emotion, and spirit. Crapsey believed that the great dramas of life resided not in outward events but in the resonances between outward and inward.

Many of Crapsey's poems, though ostensibly about the natural scene, evoke the fragility and power of the female body. Consider, for example, "Niagara: Seen on a night in November":

> How frail
> Above the bulk
> Of crashing water hangs,
> Autumnal, evanescent, wan,
> The moon.

In this nature poem, the initial adjective, "frail," has to wait the full length of the poem to discover its missing noun, "the moon." By exclaiming "How frail," "Niagara" begins by suggesting the vulnerability of an object ultimately revealed as a heavenly body traditionally freighted with feminine associations. The modifier "frail" itself suggests illness and weakness—features that popular discourse commonly applied to women. The poem's second and third lines change the subject abruptly, however, pushing the silent feminine figure out of the way to evoke the assertive sound and movement of the masculine falls. Initially, the forceful waters seem to have overpowered the sickly moon as she barely "hangs" on in space. In the fourth line, the poem returns to the still unnamed moon, though continuing to describe it as pallid and peripheral. But the moon recovers her centrality in the poem's dazzling final syllable, triumphantly zooming into focus, dominating the poem after three verses of deferral. At the very end of the poem, the falls fall away, and there is only one figure that matters, the previously sidelined but always implicit "moon." Despite the poem's title, this poem is not about Niagara Falls at all—that bulky, "crashing" bore. This poem is a meditation on the *moon*, a celebration of its hidden power. And through the image of the moon, the poem meditates and celebrates the female body, including perhaps the poet's own body, shining through illness.

Crapsey at times focused even more directly on the female body and female affectional ties. In her personal life, her closest emotional bonds were with women. Her sister Emily was an object of deep affection as well as a competitor for their mother's approval. Emily's stereotypical femininity and domesticity contrasted sharply with Adelaide's more adventurous spirit. At Vassar, Crapsey roomed with Jean Webster, who became her lifelong friend. Later, Webster used Crapsey as the model for the rebellious yet innocent protagonist of her first novel, *Daddy Long Legs*. Webster sat by Crapsey's bedside when she was dying, as did Esther Lowenthal, Crapsey's housemate and colleague at Smith, who later described their relationship as "brief but intense." Both friends had read Crapsey's poems in draft, and both helped arrange their posthumous publication.

In a poem Crapsey wrote while vacationing with Webster on the last day of well-being before her health permanently collapsed, she played with concepts of the female body and desire. "Laurel in the Berkshires" celebrates the pleasing sensations of a warm New England summer's day. The speaker envisions herself as two mythic figures: first Aphrodite arising from the sea-foam and then a mermaid lounging on the rocks. She projects a female self of agency, activity, and health. Her physical prowess is matched by her imaginative ability to dream herself into a mythic form. The daring spondee of the ending line—"Gold flood"—indicates Crapsey's creative self-confidence. In conjunction with the poem's innovative cinquain form, it also suggests her rebellion against gender and sexual norms, since formal disruption may signal a willingness to break with social conventions as well. "Laurel in the Berkshires" resists patriarchal notions of women by inscribing a powerful and independent female figure, happy without a male complement. Indeed, the phrase "dream me mermaid" in the fourth line may mean not only that she wishes to dream *herself* a mermaid but also that she aims to dream a mermaid as her companion—another female figure with whom to bond and identify.

Crapsey wrote poems in which every word counts. Beneath a surface of reserve, they evoke the tragedy and evanescence of life, as well as the shimmering beauty of the fragile world around us, the necessary quest for pleasure, and the joy of words and creativity. No poet has ever done more with less.

Further Reading. ***Selected Primary Source:*** Crapsey, Adelaide, *Complete Poems and Collected Letters*, ed. Susan Sutton Smith (Albany: State University of New York Press, 1977). ***Selected Secondary Sources:*** Alkalay-Gut, Karen, *Alone in the Dawn: The Life of Adelaide Crapsey* (Athens: University of Georgia Press, 1988); *Amaze: The Cinquain Journal*, www.amaze-cinquain.com; Axelrod, Steven Gould, Camille Roman, and Thomas Travisano, "Adelaide Crapsey," in *The New Anthology of American Poetry, Volume 2: Modernisms 1900–1950* (New Brunswick, NJ: Rutgers University Press, 2005, 129–137); Smith, Susan Sutton, "Introduction," in *Complete Poems and Collected Letters* by Adelaide Crapsey, ed. Susan Sutton Smith (Albany: State University of New York Press, 1977, 1–58).

Rise B. Axelrod
Steven Gould Axelrod

CRASE, DOUGLAS (1944–)

Douglas Crase's sole collection of poems to date, *The Revisionist* (1981), has established him as one of the major poets of his generation. A book of sweeping ambition and vast rewards, *The Revisionist* takes as its theme nothing less than the history and future of America—a mighty topic that Crase brings down to earth in the local, lovingly described landscapes and dense internal arguments of the poems themselves.

Crase was born in 1944 in Battle Creek, Michigan, and grew up on a nearby farm. After graduating with a BA from Princeton, he enrolled in law school at the University of Michigan but dropped out in order to write campaign speeches for the state's Democratic candidate for governor. He moved to Rochester and for three years worked as a speech-writer for Eastman Kodak. He then relocated to New York City, where he wrote poems and supported himself as a freelance writer. His collection of poems, *The Revisionist*, was published by Little, Brown in 1981 to rave reviews: The critic David Kalstone remarked that it appeared "with that sense of completion of utterance and identity that must have come with the first books of **Wallace Stevens** and **Elizabeth Bishop**," **James Merrill** called Crase "a marvelous new poet," and **John Hollander** hailed *The Revisionist* as "the most powerful first book I have seen in a long time." It was nominated for both the American Book Award and the National Book Critics Circle Award. Crase has since published two more books: *AMERIFIL.TXT* (1996), a **commonplace** book of quotations from favorite American authors; and *Both* (2004), a study of the lifelong friendship between the English botanists

Rubert Barneby and Dwight Ripley. Crase has also written the introduction to an edition of **Emerson**'s essays and has published poems and essays—on such writers as **John Ashbery**, **Lorine Niedecker**, and James Schuyler—in numerous journals. He has received a Guggenheim fellowship, a MacArthur fellowship, a Whiting Writer's Award, and the Witter Bynner Prize from the American Academy and Institute of Arts and Letters. He currently lives in New York City and Honesdale, Pennsylvania.

The Revisionist is from start to finish a deeply American book, as can be seen not only from the poems' titles—"Six Places in New York State," "The One Who Crossed the Hudson," "Chelsea Square," "When Spring Comes First to West 21st Street"—but also from the parade of influences on display: **Walt Whitman** and **Hart Crane**, with their visionary expansiveness; Wallace Stevens, with his cerebral jauntiness; and, as Crase has himself attested, John Ashbery, from whose tonal variety—his ability to sound playful one minute and prophetic the next—Crase has clearly learned much.

But what separates Crase from other Ashbery-influenced poets, not to mention Ashbery himself, is the exhilarating (though hard-won) optimism that leaps from every page of *The Revisionist*. Crase certainly expresses continual dismay over what America has become: a place whose "energies of terrible belief" mean that "temperance, drunkenness hold camp meetings / Close at hand" ("The Lake Effect"); a site of deadening commercialism where "the once individual rooms / Close rank in a take-it-or-leave-it portfolio" ("The Elegy for New York"); a sadly paradoxical "lovely country where the streets are emptier / For being so well lit" ("Abraham Lincoln in Cleveland"). But he also constantly reminds us of the saving "revisionism" of which the country and its inhabitants are capable. In the title poem, claiming that "My ambition wraps tighter and tighter / Around your name," Crase expresses a desire to form "a sediment of history rearranged" and to "tap / The native energies you've never seen." And in poem after poem he puts this desire to work: A river inspires us "with prospects of an extended world / And not its narrow origins" ("The Day Line"). Another poem urges us to remember "The invisible volume of richness within our grasp" that "Is unfathomable unless we retrieve it / In peculiar experience" ("Summer"). Crase rejects crippling nostalgia in favor of a confrontation with "the toughest past whose moments unfasten / In confusion with the active land" ("In Memory of My Country"); and he insists on the perpetual need to try new things, since "the 'as ifness' of the world is real, / Productive, wherever it comes from can't be ignored" ("Gunpowder Morning in a Gray Room"). He reminds us to be open to the unexpected moments when "the ordinary, / Though not what you were looking for . . . turns / Like the leaves into discovery before your eyes"

("In the Fall When It's Time to Leave"). And he praises the comforts and pleasures of surprise, the moments when "The cows / Are freshening off schedule again. There is nothing to fear" ("There Is No Real Place in the World"). Revision and reinvention, whether at a national or personal level, haunt Crase's collection like promises of grace, making it vital and inspiring reading.

With a few exceptions, the form of Crase's poems is the same: sprawling Whitmanesque lines and single long stanzas. In *Ecstatic Occasions, Expedient Forms* (1996), he has described this style as "the 'civil meter' of American English . . . the meter we hear in the propositions offered by businessmen, politicians, engineers, and all our other real or alleged professionals." It may also, of course, reflect Crase's own background as a speech-writer; in any case, he frankly weighs its strengths and weaknesses when he remarks, "If you write in this civil meter, it's true you have to give up the Newtonian certainties of the iamb. But you gain a stronger metaphor for conviction by deploying the recognizable, if variable patterns of the language of American power." This uniform style can yield rich and unexpected results, as in the poem "Experience and What to Make of It," which is structured as the outline of a scientific experiment: The "*Statement of the Problem*" is that "experience has been bewildered by the landmarks of / Spent meanings"; the "*Results*" are that significance seems "to have attached itself with pathogenic consequences / By the time of second experience," and so on. But alongside this deliberate journalistic blandness, there emerges a conclusion that belies the gloom from which it comes: Although "all experience is equally meaningless," we are left with a bold injunction to "go on with the harvest expecting intermittent relief / From infection and nothing more. *Tables of evidence.*"

On the sometimes rough waters of Crase's poetry—he is clearly following not just Ashbery's example, but also **T.S. Eliot**'s insistence (in "The Metaphysical Poets") that modern poetry be difficult—powerful descriptions float like gratifying buoys: Crase describes a "legato lake" ("Pultneyville"); compares himself to "a vengeful Johnny Appleseed" ("The Revisionist"); conjures a house where "constitutions vibrate in the blockfront drawers" ("America Began in Houses"); recalls a date "Like a Roman arch when stone and keystone met / To frame this vista I can't throw off" ("Creation Du Monde"); or simply delights in a litany of American place names: "*Maumee, Menominee, Michilimackinac*" ("The Continent as the Letter M").

Until Crase graces the world with a second collection, readers can find new poems in journals such as *LIT* and the *Paris Review* as well as in easily accessible anthologies like *The Best of the Best American Poetry* (1998) and *The KGB Bar Book of Poems* (2000). In one recent poem, "True Solar Holiday," Crase declares to an unnamed speaker, with characteristically refreshing optimism, that "Out of the whim of data . . . I've determined the trend I call 'you' and know you are real."

Further Reading. *Selected Primary Sources:* Crase, Douglas, *AMERIFIL.TXT: A Commonplace Book* (Ann Arbor: University of Michigan Press, 1996); ———, *Both: A Portrait in Two Parts* (New York: Pantheon, 2004); ———, Essay on John Ashbery, in *Beyond Amazement: Essays on John Ashbery*, ed. David Lehman (Ithaca, NY: Cornell University Press, 1980); ———, "Introduction," in Ralph Waldo Emerson, *Essays: First and Second Series* (New York: Vintage/Library of America, 1990); ———, *The Revisionist* (Boston: Little, Brown, 1981). ***Selected Secondary Sources:*** Michael Schiavo, "Douglas Crase's *The Revisionist* and *AMERIFIL.TXT*" (*Tin House* 17 [Fall 2003]); Vernon Shetley, Review of *The Revisionist* (*New York Review of Books* [29 April 1982]).

Rachel Wetzsteon

CREATIVE WRITING PROGRAMS

Creative writing programs are academic courses of study designed by colleges and universities to support the artistic development of poets, fiction writers, playwrights, screenwriters, and nonfiction writers. Creative writing, in its origins as an academic discipline, was the sibling of composition and rhetoric. In the 1880s, Harvard University began to offer classes in advanced composition; these classes contained elements of a pedagogy that, a century later, would become common in creative writing programs. Harvard's early classes in composition were partly a reaction against philology, a kind of scholarly research, as most English departments had codified it, that analyzed works of literature as sets of linguistic and historical artifacts. Whereas literary scholars aspired to bring scientific rigor to their study of the classics and the evolution of the English language from its Northumbrian, Mercian, West Saxon, Latin, Greek, German, and French roots, the teachers of writing hoped to shepherd their students to effective practical writing and to an appreciation of artistic accomplishments. Whereas scholars of philology emphasized historical research and linguistic and theoretical analysis, the writing teachers emphasized a more pragmatic use of English—frequent practice in the craft of writing—as well as the aesthetics of literary form and content. In addition to exercises in rhetoric, the writing teachers assigned their students exercises in writing stories, verse, and descriptive or impressionistic prose. Barrett Wendell, Le Baron Briggs, and Charles Townsend Copeland were among the early pioneers of this new, anti-philological mode of literary instruction, in which literature was studied from the writer's point of view, rather than from the linguist's or the literary historian's. Le Baron Briggs taught a class on the history and principles of versification in 1889. As the

students of Wendell, Briggs, and Copeland graduated and became teachers themselves, creative writing classes began to appear at a few other institutions, including public and private schools for grades 6–12. The University of Iowa, another pioneering institution in developing creative writing as a discipline, offered a class in verse-making in 1897.

These innovative classes at Harvard and Iowa were duplicated at other universities, but generally academe was reluctant to approve classes that allowed the study of literature to be an artistic practice. In 1940, the poet and critic **Allen Tate** complained, "We study literature today as if nobody ever again intended to write any more of it. The official academic point of view is that all the literature has been written, and is now a branch of history" (Myers, 127). Partly to reconcile critical and artistic views of literature and partly to apply literature to practical uses as well as to historical study, Norman Foerster established the first graduate program in creative writing at the University of Iowa in 1931. The program awarded MA degrees and Ph.D. degrees to its graduates; it accepted "a piece of imaginative writing" for the thesis. Foerster, however, did not intend for the program to be a vocational program for the training of professional writers. He intended for the program to stage a revolutionary synthesis of humanistic endeavors previously in conflict: criticism and historical analysis versus creativity and artistic innovation. The program was dedicated to improving the nation's general culture through the enlightenment of graduates and academic professionals. Nonetheless, Iowa's program soon began to emphasize artistic training; in 1939, it offered the Master of Fine Arts (MFA) degree, which had been previously established as the appropriate terminal degree for dancers, painters, and actors. The poet Paul Engle became director of the program in 1942; under his direction, the Iowa Writers' Workshop concentrated on providing artistic mentors, a literary education, financial aid, and apprenticeships for young writers.

The writing workshop is typically a seminar of approximately a dozen students who critique one another's work under the guidance of a writer-professor. The workshop became the core of creative writing curriculum; it was complemented with courses in the study of literature, especially seminars, often taught by writers, in which literature was studied from a writer's point of view, examining artistic choices in craft and form. In justifying this kind of academic study, Paul Engle wrote,

> After all, has the painter not always gone to an art school, or at least to an established master, for instruction? And the composer, the sculptor, the architect? Then why not the writer? . . . Right criticism can speed up the maturing of a poet by years. More than that, tough and detailed criticism of a young writer

can help him become his own shrewd critic so that, when he publishes, the critics will not have to be tough on him. (Wilbers, 84)

After the end of World War II, other graduate creative writing programs were established: at Johns Hopkins in 1946, at Stanford in 1947, at the University of Denver and Cornell in 1948.

The Iowa Writers' Workshop became famous enough to warrant an article in *Time* magazine in 1957. **Robert Bly**, **Marvin Bell**, **Henri Coulette**, **Jane Cooper**, **Donald Justice**, **Peter Everwine**, **W.D. Snodgrass**, **Philip Levine**, and **Charles Wright** were among the many poets to study at Iowa during the workshop's early days. As Iowa's graduates garnered national esteem as authors, academe became more accommodating to graduate writing programs, and they began to flourish in the 1960s. In 1967, a former teacher of the Iowa Writers' Workshop, R.V. Cassill, established a professional association, which became the Association of Writers and Writing Programs (AWP). AWP was formed to provide publishing opportunities for young writers, to share information and ideas among peers, and to support the MFA degree as the appropriate terminal degree for writers who teach. Fifteen writers representing thirteen institutions comprised the nascent organization in 1967. By 2004, 380 colleges and universities, 60 writers' conferences, and 24,000 individuals had joined AWP, including more than 300 graduate programs in the United States, Canada, and the United Kingdom. Undergraduate classes and minor or major courses of study in creative writing are now available in most of North America's 2,700 two-year and four-year colleges.

As the programs proliferated, they became an economic and cultural force that has shaped the literary audiences and professions of authors in North America. Writing programs provided thousands of professions, especially for poets, where none existed before. The programs made poetry readings and the lecture circuit a regular part of a poet's livelihood. By the 1980s and 1990s, the majority of the Pulitzer Prize–winning poets had made their livelihoods as teachers of creative writing and literature. Creative writing programs have influenced the way hundreds of thousands of college graduates study fiction, poetry, and nonfiction. These programs provide, each decade, apprenticeships for 20,000 to 30,000 young writers. The programs have created literary communities in many regions throughout North America whereas, before 1940, most literary activity was concentrated in only a few major cities. The programs and their many graduates, as part of the improved access to higher education at public universities, have helped to democratize literature, so that all races and classes and women as well as men are better represented in literature's subject matter, instruction,

and authorship. The majority of poets published in *The Best American Poetry* and most anthologies of contemporary poetry have academic affiliations.

As the influence of creative writing programs upon the careers of poets became stronger, criticism of creative writing programs became ubiquitous in literary reviews, essays, little magazines, and books. In their magazine *The Reaper* (1981–1989), Mark Jarman and Robert McDowell rebelled against what they believed to be the programs' indoctrination poets who wrote in the same style of **Imagistic**, lyrical **free verse**, a limited and monotonous style, they argued, that had neglected the powers of formal and narrative verse. In "Poetry and Ambition" (1983), **Donald Hall** called the workshop "the institutionalized café," a trivial simulacrum for the centers of intellectual life that flourish in European cities and New York; Hall indicted writing programs as franchises that mass-produced "McPoems," a poetry of modest ambitions and mediocre results. In "The Catastrophe of Creative Writing" (1986) Greg Kuzma portrayed creative writing as a crisis of careerism that has misplaced its artistic values. In "Theory and/in the Creative Writing Classroom" (1987), Marjorie Perloff suggested that writing programs served as purveyors of the naive, oppressive, retro-garde thinking of the **New Critics**; this failure of writing programs, according to Perloff, was largely due to the indifference or hostility with which most writer-teachers regarded literary theory. In "A Failing Grade for the Present Tense" (1987), William Gass accused the programs of being harbors for intellectual laziness, narcissism, and facile mimicry. Joseph Epstein amplified many of the above criticisms in "Who Killed Poetry?" (1988); Epstein argued that growing careerism and academic specialization was duplicating lackluster and obscure poetry along with disingenuous book reviewing and meek criticism, all of which had estranged the reading public. In *Creative Writing in America* (1989), a collection of essays, many writers proposed alternatives to the workshop, which they found sadly lacking in pedagogical effectiveness. **Dana Gioia** revisited Joseph Epstein's line of inquiry in "Can Poetry Matter?" (1992). Gioia argued that academe had incarcerated poetry in a subculture, removing it from the public's interest. In what is so far the most comprehensive history of writing programs, *The Elephants Teach* (1995), D.G. Myers argued that the programs had betrayed Foerster's revolutionary intention to unite criticism and creativity to establish a more coherent and fruitful humanism. And because every avant-garde needs an establishment against which it can rebel, creative writing programs soon became typecast as the mainstream or establishment against which many poets and critics did battle, especially practitioners of the **postmodernist** school of **Language poetry**. Christopher Beach in *Poetic Culture: Contemporary American Poetry Between Community* *and Institution* (1999) amalgamated many long-standing criticisms against the alleged academic mainstream of poetry while he championed the work of Language poets.

The numerous critiques of writing programs are intertwined with enduring debates about poetry's role—central or inconsequential—in North America's culture. Controversies over writing programs have also thrown into high relief a few mutually irreconcilable poetics. Some poetics advocate that the finest poems must dramatize political awareness; other poetics advocate that the finest poems must embody pleasure, beauty, and the past spirits of poetry—an aesthetic experience that is only debased by politics. The theory-infused criticism of **Charles Bernstein** and Marjorie Perloff, on the one hand, and the retrospectively appreciative criticism of **J.D. McClatchy** and **Tom Disch**, on the other, are representatives of these two opposing camps, both of which, nonetheless, blame creative writing programs for thwarting the appreciation and success of their agendas.

Some of the anxieties about writing programs and poetry's health were also inseparable from the democratization of poetry and all the arts, as multiculturalism, or identity politics emerged in contemporary letters. Because North America's vast system of public education made itself accessible to students of all races, cultures, and economic classes, creative writing programs, as part of public education, accelerated poetry's democratization and diversity. As the works and careers of poets such as **Philip Levine**, **Rita Dove**, **Carolyn Kizer**, **Annie Finch**, **Yusef Komunyakaa**, and many others made clear, the study of literature had become more accommodating to the experiences of women, the blue-collar working class, and minorities. Writing programs were among the cultural forces enabling a new literary pluralism to supplant the supposed universalism of the Western **canon** of literature. Some writers believe that this diversity has enlarged literature's aesthetic and moral possibilities whereas others have argued that it has debased poetry and lowered artistic and educational standards with political bromides. Like the dominance of three major TV networks that reigned in the 1950s but soon faced a hundred successful competitors, the dominance of only a few literary gatekeepers and a single literary canon has become overwhelmed by many venues and values of literature competing in a democratic culture. As these political and cultural changes become more widely understood, detractors and apologists of writing programs have fashioned more nuanced and complex arguments about what poetry and literary education should be in the twenty-first century; but writers and critics continue to examine the role of creative writing as an academic discipline, now that it has become a major economic and cultural force in North American literature.

Further Reading. Association of Writers and Writing Programs, *The AWP Official Guide to Writing Programs* (Paradise, CA: AWP and Dustbooks, 2004); Beach, Christopher, *Poetic Culture: Contemporary American Poetry Between Community and Institution* (Evanston, IL: Northwestern University Press, 1999); Epstein, Joseph, "Who Killed Poetry?" (*Commentary* 86 [August 1988]: 13–20); Gioia, Dana, *Can Poetry Matter? Essays on Poetry and American Culture* (St. Paul, MN: Graywolf Press, 1992); Hall, Donald, *Poetry and Ambition: Essays 1982–1988* (Ann Arbor: University of Michigan Press, 1988); Moxley, Joseph M., ed., *Creative Writing in America* (Urbana, IL: National Council of Teachers of English, 1989); Myers, David Gershom, *The Elephants Teach: Creative Writing Since 1880* (Englewood Cliffs, NJ: Prentice-Hall, 1996); Stegner, Wallace, *On the Teaching of Creative Writing* (Hanover, NH: University Press of New England, 1988); Wilbers, Stephen, *The Iowa Writers' Workshop* (Iowa City: University of Iowa Press, 1980).

D.W. Fenza

CREELEY, ROBERT (1926–2005)

Robert Creeley's terse, highly enjambed, and rhythmically intricate lines recording the ordeals of human relationships and the tenuousness of self-knowledge began to etch themselves into the bedrock of contemporary American poetry in the mid-1950s. The poet's New England roots—a childhood spent in Massachusetts with strong family connections through his mother to Maine—helped to situate him early in the lyrical tradition of **Emily Dickinson** and **Edwin Arlington Robinson**, as well as to bind him to **Charles Olson**, his nearly constant interlocutor throughout the 1950s and 1960s. The **modernist** experimentation of **Ezra Pound**, **Hart Crane**, and **William Carlos Williams** proved decisive in shaping the poet's address to form (which he famously defined in a letter to Olson as "never more than an extension of content"). In Williams's late work especially, Creeley was able to find validation for the poetics of intimate scale and interpersonal subject matter toward which he was by temperament drawn. As he writes in his *Autobiography*, "All that would matter to me, finally, as a writer, is that the scale and the place of our common living be recognized, that the mundane in that simple emphasis be acknowledged" (55). Coming to prominence in 1960 with the publication of **Donald Allen**'s *New American Poetry* anthology, in which fourteen of his poems were featured, Creeley's reputation was consolidated in 1962, when Scribner's published *For Love: Poems 1950–1960*. Although it is to this volume that many anthologists still turn when representing Creeley's contribution to American poetry, his prolific output—amounting to more than sixty volumes of poetry—and his emphatically restless life, which has included many travels (France, Majorca, Guatemala, Australia, Finland), scarcely stops with that first major volume nor with the initial set of categorizing identifications—such as the **Black Mountain School**, the **San Francisco Renaissance**, and **Beat poetry**—that steered his early reception. Indeed, for many poets it was with the sequence of books immediately following *For Love*—namely, *Words* (1967), *Pieces* (1969), and *A Day Book* (1972)—that Creeley earned his status as one of the most consequential figures of his generation. Known primarily for his poetry, Creeley's accomplishment as an editor—most notably of the pathbreaking *Black Mountain Review* (1954–1957)—is also formidable, and his work in prose (he abjured the label "fiction") has influenced several generations of prose poets and experimental writers, including the language-centered writers of the 1970s and 1980s. His critical essays, resolutely nonacademic in tone, helped to advance the reputations not only of immediate peers like Olson and **Edward Dorn** but also of neglected elders such as **Louis Zukofsky**. Collaboration with artists in many mediums has been a constant throughout his long career. By working with musicians (most notably the jazz saxophonist Steve Lacy), sculptors (Marisol), and others visual artists (his second wife Bobbie Louise Hawkins, Francesco Clemente, Robert Indiana, Jim Dine, Elsa Dorfman, and others), Creeley has pushed the linguistic medium of poetry into revelatory contact with the nonlinguistic arts and their audiences.

Robert White Creeley was born in Arlington, Massachusetts, on May 21, 1926, to Genevieve Jules Creeley and Oscar Slate Creeley. His father was a well-established physician twice previously married, and his mother a nurse who was thirty-nine at the time of her son's birth. His older sister, Helen, had been born four years earlier. A freak accident befell Creeley at the age of two, when a lump of coal dislodged from a passing truck struck the passenger window of the family car and sent shattered glass into his face, badly lacerating his left eye. Creeley soon received another blow: his father's death from pneumonia in 1928. Not long after, his mother determined that the injured eye was too great a risk as a source of infection and had it surgically removed—without forewarning—on what had seemed to the boy an ordinary trip to the hospital where his mother worked. Creeley's boyhood was spent on a farm in West Acton, Massachusetts, in the primary company—especially after his maternal grandfather's death—of women: his mother, his maternal grandmother, his Aunt Bernice, and his sister. This fact of his upbringing later seemed a source of persistent questions as to "what constitutes manhood," as he would put it in his 1990 *Autobiography*. Creeley began attending the Holderness School in Plymouth, New Hampshire, in 1940 and entered Harvard University in 1943. His studies were interrupted by a stint in the American Field Service in 1944–1945, during which time he served as an ambulance driver in India and Burma. Though he returned to Harvard in 1945 and was active in the literary community there, Creeley withdrew one semester prior to his anticipated graduation date in 1947 and moved first to Cape Cod and then to New Hampshire with his first wife Ann MacKinnon.

After a failed attempt at subsistence farming outside Littleton, New Hampshire, the Creeleys and their two small children moved to Aix-en-Provence in France, hoping to live on the modest income Ann received from a trust fund. A year later the family moved again, this time to the island of Majorca off the coast of Spain, where Robert and Ann founded the Divers Press and brought out handsome small editions of work by **Paul Blackburn**, **Robert Duncan**, Charles Olson, and others, including Creeley's own *The Kind of Act Of* (1952) and *The Gold Diggers* (1954), a collection of stories. In March of 1954, Creeley left his rapidly deteriorating relationship to take up a teaching position at Black Mountain College in Asheville, North Carolina, at the invitation of Olson, who had in 1951 become the third—and, as it would happen, the final—rector of the experimental college founded in the midst of the Great Depression by John Rice and for a long time defined by the presence of the Bauhaus émigrés Josef and Anni Albers. His time in Asheville was in many ways bleak. As Martin Duberman remarks, "What Creeley found at Black Mountain was a group of 'highly volatile and articulate people in a rather extraordinary circumstance of isolation,' people who matched and echoed his own personal extremity. He found a community at a peak of intensity—and on the verge of disintegration" (*Black Mountain: An Exploration in Community*, 419). By the time that disintegration came about—Olson shut the college down in 1957—Creeley had already departed, first back to Majorca for a futile attempt at reconciliation with Ann, then to San Francisco, where he intersected with the active San Francisco Renaissance and Beat scenes, whose poets he would anthologize in the seventh and final issue of *Black Mountain Review* (1957), which featured work by **Jack Kerouac**, **Allen Ginsberg**, **Michael McClure**, **Gary Snyder**, **Philip Whalen**, **Edward Dorn**, and others. When he moved to New Mexico in 1956 and met and married Bobbie Louise Hoeck (later known as Bobbie Louise Hawkins), with whom we would remain until 1976, Creeley had in many ways completed the first phase of his life. He had, at thirty years of age, met many of the writers whose "company" (this term out of Hart Crane—"the visionary company of love"—has occupied a key place in Creeley's lexicon throughout his life) he would most rely on and in later years most remember. His first poems and stories had been written and had earned him the recognition of writers he respected. His editorship of *Black Mountain Review* demonstrated the breadth of his commitments and interests, provided a vital counter-argument to the then-ascendant academicism best typi-fied by **New Criticism**, and helped to bring definition to an emergent field of poetry that Donald Allen's *New American Poetry* would organize for much broader con-sumption just a few years later.

The poems preceding *For Love* (1962), later gathered for publication under the title *The Charm* (1967), mark Creeley's apprenticeship to his various masters (Ezra Pound, D.H. Lawrence, Hart Crane, William Carlos Williams), his interest in reinterpreting traditional lyric modes (the alba, the lay, the canzone, etc.), and the first articulation of many of his abiding themes and tones. In "Stomping with Catullus," Creeley translates the Latin poet's forthright erotic utterances into contemporary **jazz** vernacular ("My old lady is a goof at heart" or "that's the gig / make it, don't just flip your wig"), sound-ing a tone that he would use well into the 1960s, most famously in the cryptic hep-talk of "A Wicker Basket" (1956–1958). In "The Sentence," also from *The Charm*, the linguistic fact of syntax is made a metaphor for erotic union ("There is that in love / which, by the syntax of, / men find women and join / their bodies to their minds") before shading, in a second and concluding quatrain, into the juridical meaning of the title, with its implica-tion that such union can become punitive if extended beyond its originating moment ("it must / be one's own sentence"). The handling of enjambment and internal rhyme in this eight-line poem is typical of Creeley's practice throughout his career, and the linguistic theme looks forward to his protostructuralist insights in impor-tant later poems like "The Language" and "The Pattern" (both from the 1967 volume *Words*). A third poem from *The Charm*, "The Method of Actuality," sounds another abiding theme of Creeley's—his ambivalent identifica-tions with, and strivings for differentiation from, the mother who bore and raised him, and by extension, women in general: "I see myself in long & uncombed hair / bedridden, sullen, and face to face, a face of hair. My mother's son." Here the threat of reincorporation into the mother is figured visually. The speaker sees himself in the abject maternal body—indeed sees him-self *as* that body—and the mirroring deeply unsettles him, just as, in the much later volume *Mirrors* (1983), the echo of his mother's voice will haunt him in a poem like "Mother's Voice."

The first of the three sections in Creeley's 160-page first collection *For Love* (1962) consists of poems dated between 1950 and 1955, and there are many continuities between it and the work in *The Charm*. Best known of the thirty-eight poems in the opening section are "The Immoral Proposition," "I Know a Man," "The Warn-ing," and "The Whip." The first of these poems begins with the assertion that "If you never do anything for anyone else / you are spared the tragedy of human rela-tion- / ships" and concludes with the axiom "The unsure

/ egoist is not / good for himself." The "unsure egoist" is a recurrent figure in Creeley's corpus, a crystallization of the ways in which self-absorption and uncertainty snare the mind into a solipsistic circuit that cannot admit the facts of otherness and intersubjectivity. It is easy to see the speaker of "I Know a Man" as just such an "unsure egoist"—with his incessant chatter ("because I am / always talking"), his apparently obtuse inattention to names ("John, I / sd, which was not his / name"), his bleak assessment of the situation ("the darkness sur- / rounds us"), and his oddly American decision to solve an existential crisis through the purchase of an automo-bile ("shall we & / why not, buy a goddamn big car")—and as the poem's fourth and final three-lined stanza concludes on a warning to "for / christ's sake, look / out where yr going," the reader is hardly consoled to find such a figure at the wheel. This sense of desperate, potentially self-destructive careening is as vivid an ele-ment of this poem as the idiosyncratic contractions ("sd" for "said," "yr" for "you're") and surprising line breaks are, and it is easy to understand why the poem might have captured the imagination of readers also attuned to Jack Kerouac's contemporaneous *On the Road*.

Both "The Warning" and "The Whip" address the ambiguities of heterosexual love in a foreboding tone of impending violence. The former is a first-person apos-trophe in two quick, impeccably balanced quatrains: It opens with the title words of the collection as a whole ("For love") followed immediately by a dash and then a threat: "I would / split open your head and put / a can-dle in / behind the eyes." This brutal image lingers across the stanza break and into the second stanza, which attempts—not entirely convincingly—to convert the misogynistic threat into an example of how love must constantly seek renewal in "quick surprise." In "The Whip," the first-person speaker spends "a night turning in bed," pulled by desire for his lover next to him ("a flat / sleeping thing") and also for another woman, whom he had addressed himself to "in / a fit she / returned." The poem is a marvel of compression and overdetermination, and as the five sentences of which it consists snake across nine distiches in highly coiled tension, the image of the "whip" comes to describe not just the conjugal hand unconsciously laid on the speaker's back by his sleeping wife—which stings like the whip of monogamy itself—but also the poem's own snapping movement.

The second section of *For Love* consists of forty-seven poems dated between 1956 and 1958, after the dissolu-tion of Creeley's first marriage and the end of his brief tenure at Black Mountain College. In this grouping are "A Wicker Basket" and "The Ballad of the Despairing Husband," both of which employ end rhyme and ballad meter to comical effect, as well as more serious poems such as "Heroes," "The Door" (dedicated to Robert

Duncan), and "The Hill." If in *The Charm* Creeley's speaker uses a poem's title to announce that he is "held by the fear of death," in "Heroes" a demystifying reading of Virgil's *Aeneid*—one attentive to the "humanness" to be discovered even within the heroic scale—yields the insight that "death also / can still propose the old labors." This recognition of death as a generative force in the fashioning of human projects ("the old labors") resonates not only with the existentialism in vogue in the 1950s but also with Whitman's hard-won embrace of mortality in "Out of the Cradle Endlessly Rocking."

Twenty-one quatrains long, "The Door" is the most sustained of the poems in *For Love*, and it is a curious blend of familiar tropes—the supplication to a "Lady," the tormented relationship of the speaker to his own consciousness—and surprising, quasi-mystical passages ("Mighty magic is a mother") more typically associated with the poem's dedicatee, Berkeley Renaissance and Black Mountain poet Robert Duncan, than with Creeley's more secular-minded poetic. In lines like "My knees were iron, I rusted in worship, of You," the poem would seem to be struggling with the **lyric** inheritance, from the troubadours through the Elizabethans to present, that poses the masculine speaker at the service of his unattainable feminine ideal, even as the speaker himself struggles to understand his place within an "absurd" and "vicious" psychic economy he longs to leave behind. The poem swerves from hopefulness to despair and back again, but it comes to no resolution beyond that of the penultimate quatrain, "I will go to the garden. / I will be a romantic. I will sell / myself in hell, / in heaven also I will be." When all is said and done, the rustling vision of "the Lady's skirt," beheld in the final quatrain, still exerts its transcendent, but (or because) intangible power over the speaker.

Similar themes animate the sixteen stanzas of "For Love," the title poem of the collection and the final poem both of the third section (fifty poems dated 1959–1960) and the book as a whole. But whereas the mythic resolution sought in "The Door" fails to materialize, the acute tensions and painful ambivalences accumulated over the course of "For Love" are ultimately able to be absorbed—in a strained but consoling fashion—in the last two lines: "Into the company of love / it all returns." The heroism, including the heroic suffering, of courtly love here yields to a more commonplace, but also more humanly scaled, love, and though the poet continues to "stumble" toward it in the mode of an unsure egoist—wracked by guilt, endlessly digressive, tediously self-regarding, and strangely incapable of simple solicitude—it is possible to imagine that in the person of the addressee, Creeley's second wife Bobbie (note the mirroring of names), the poet has actually found an answering term.

Of the many fears articulated in "For Love," the most anxious-making of all is the fear of displacement that the poet confesses to when he claims, "Nothing says anything / but that which it wishes / would come true, fears / what else might happen in / some other place, some / other time not this one." The displacements here enumerated are many: the human subject is displaced into reification ("nothing" speaks in its place) and, in a nod to Freudian theory, unconscious wishes are seen as systematically warping all discourse to their own ends. Most important, the embodied particularity of the masculine speaker is usurped by an intangible "voice" from elsewhere, whereas the woman's place is doubly removed from self-presence: "an echo of that only in yours." Tracing the logic of such displacements comes to occupy Creeley increasingly in the books after *For Love*, and two poems from *Words* (1967), "The Language" and "The Pattern," demonstrate his scrupulous approach to the phenomenon with special clarity.

"The Language" opens with a strange imperative: "Locate *I* / *love you* some- / where in / teeth and / eyes." The italicized phrase is a commonplace of incredible import that the poem treats as a fixed syntagm, a fixture of the linguistic system that can only with difficulty actually be attached to the physical presence of another ("teeth and eyes"). At the hinge point of the poem—in the fourth of eight tristichs—the preponderance of language over the speaking subject is registered in the sentence "Words / say everything." Little is left for the amorous subject to say: The language has gotten there before him, and love itself seems but a side-effect of a self-enclosed discursive system.

In the opening lines of "The Pattern"—"As soon as / I speak, I / speaks"—the addition of a single morpheme ("s") effects a change on the first-person subject that might be likened to the change Arthur Rimbaud worked in his famous phrase from the "Seer Letter": "Je est un autre" ("I is an other"). The poet implies that as soon as a speaker accedes to the first-person pronoun "I," it is that linguistic shifter, rather than the concrete individual making use of it, that takes control of the utterance. In other words, language speaks us, rather than our speaking language. And all that language can tell us about is itself, as in the tautological formula "Let / x equal x, x / also / equals x."

It is possible to view Creeley's work in *Words, Pieces* (1969), and the "In London" section of *A Day Book* (1972) as describing an arc of sorts, as an increasingly intense focus on the linguistic substratum of poetry works to pulverize the units of the poem into smaller and smaller fragments linked now into disjunctive series. This manner of describing Creeley's development helps connect his work of the late 1960s and early 1970s to the radical linguistic experiments of the second generation **New York School** and to the nascent tendency called language-centered writing (later, **Language poetry**), key figures of which—such as **Robert Grenier** and **Clark Coolidge**—studied Creeley's work closely. It also helps link him to the structuralist and poststructuralist trends in the humanities more generally, with their emphasis on the constitutive role played by language in human experience. But Creeley's own interest in Ludwig Wittgenstein and other philosophers of language notwithstanding, it is probably most accurate to say that his immanent investigation into the materials of his medium—words, syntax, rhythm—led him to insights concordant with, without being dependent upon, such external discourses.

After the first major phase extending from *For Love* to *A Day Book*, the middle phase of Creeley's career extends from 1972 forward to the publication of his *Collected Poems: 1945–1975* by the University of California in 1982 and includes his first fifteen years or so (of more than thirty in all) on the faculty of the University of Buffalo, where he taught from 1966 to 2002. This middle phase witnessed Creeley's divorce from Bobbie Louise (1976), the travels to New Zealand and other places documented in *Hello* (1976), and the poet's third and longest-lasting marriage, to Penelope Highton. The poetry of this phase is less well attended to, perhaps because the formal and thematic concerns remain relatively constant, and perhaps also because Creeley's address to the political upheavals of the day remained relatively oblique.

Unlike Duncan, **Levertov**, and Olson, let alone the **Black Arts Movement** activist LeRoi Jones/**Amiri Baraka**, Creeley declined to incorporate political position taking into his **poetics**, which is what makes a poem like "Ever Since Hitler," from the "Helsinki Window" section of his 1990 volume *Windows*, something of an exception in his oeuvre. This taut, syntactically intricate, fifteen-line poem simultaneously names a historical epoch ("ever since Hitler") and questions that act of naming ("or well before that"). What the poem attempts to confront is "the fact of human appetite" as manifested in politically organized murder, torture, even cannibalism ("or ate / the same bodies they / themselves had"). And it traces the spectacular acts of political violence perpetrated by the fascists—including the death camps—to a horrific "concentration" in which we continue to be implicated: "we ourselves / had plunged into density / of selves." The extinguishing of simple human singularity is recorded in the closing lines: "no possible way / out of it smile or cried / or tore at it and died / apparently dead at last / just no other way out." The inevitable but no less painfully wrenching existential displacements chronicled in so many other Creeley poems here are situated within a historical and political horizon that—unlike the facts of death and physical suffering—could be altered by human agency.

Like William Carlos Williams before him, Creeley has in the latter decades of his life provided readers with a candid and subtle phenomenology of aging. The poem "Age" from *Windows* describes the feeling of a narrowing trap in which one has gotten stuck and in which "any movement /forward simply / wedges one more." The humiliations visited upon the body not merely by its own failing processes, but also by a callous medical establishment, are frequent themes, as is the persistent worry carried over from earlier works that all that will be left to the poet is empty and inauthentic speech. In "Mother's Voice," from the 1988 volume *Mirrors*, the trope of the supplanting voice—already encountered in "For Love" and other poems—reappears in a new context as the poet hears his mother Genevieve's voice underneath (and undermining) his own and experiences his needs and desires being canceled by a phrase etched into his mind by her repetitions of it: "I won't / want any more of that" she repeats. Such memories, echoes, and anecdotes concerning departed friends and fellow poets, often rendered in quatrains that recall even while subtly defying conventional metrical patterns, are typical of Creeley's work in the 1990s and early 2000s.

In the twenty-seven poems collected in 1998 under the title *Life & Death* (the ampersand is to be taken emphatically), Creeley continues to take the measure of a life full of passion and contradiction, intelligence and suffering, as it passes into and again inevitably out of "the company of love." His methods remain more or less unchanged: the elemental cadences give the impression of immutability; the lexicon is restricted, resonant, precise; and the ethical stakes are sharply, but never rigidly, discerned. His occupations have likewise remained insistent: what is out there, what is other, what the mind will allow, what love has and has not provided for. The only other postwar writer to bring such pitiless and ceaseless self-monitoring to so humane, and often darkly humorous, a resolution in irreducible poetic rhythms is Samuel Beckett.

In *Life & Death*, the long sequences "Histoire de Florida" (twenty-one sections, thirteen pages) and "The Dogs of Auckland" (eight section built of expansive distiches covering eight pages) are the obvious masterworks: located, luminous, devastating. But the shorter sequences and single lyrics—their singularity always immanently mediated by thematic seriality, by their revisiting of a "commonplace" of the life's work—are exceptional as well. "Echo," "The Mirror," "Goodbye," "Help," "Edges," and "Mitch" all transcend the deprecating rubric "Old Poems, Etc.," and the poems in the latter third of the book, originating in collaboration with the painter Francesco Clemente, move with determined grace through the Dantean constraint of end-rhymed tercets in "Inside My Head," weave alternating melodic lines in "There," and balance memories of boyhood libidinousness and already-looming death in sharply pivoted nine-line stanzas in the title sequence "Life & Death."

Still, the works of longer duration do permit a different rhythm of elaboration and reversal to occur, as can be seen in the crucial seventh section of "The Dogs of Auckland."

Returning to a site vaguely remembered because poorly understood in the first place, Creeley sketches in distended couplets a series of anecdotes, memories, and present-tense observations in the first half-dozen sections of the poem. The seventh section opens with an inversion, redistributing the attributes normally assigned to objective spatial reality and subjective experience: "Empty, vacant. Not the outside but in." From there the nine couplets proceed with near-brutal clarity through a series of assumption shattering reversals.

Throughout this volume the severest self-assessments—confessions of envy, of cowardice, of arrogance, of reticence—carry a searing intensity that memory, family, domesticity, sexuality are enlisted to soothe. These figures of reconciliation involve their own contradictions, however. In the beautiful closing lines of "Goodbye," Creeley writes with great longing for "home." But "home" can never be a utopic condition of reconciled forces, as some brisk quatrains from earlier in the book show, when he accuses himself of leaving out of his writing what was most important, even while he thought he *was* writing it: "You've left it out / Your love / your life / your home / your wife / . . . No one is one . . . / No world's that small." Poetry, darkly envisioned here as a space of structural exclusions and killing unity, is itself, of course, not that small, not that unitary. If the canine gaze offers a "simple valediction" in "The Dogs of Auckland," a complex but no less authentic valediction emerges in the memory-assembled chorus of Zukofsky (whose "love lights light in like eyes" is the poetic formula for reconciliation within difference), Wallace Stevens, William Wordsworth, T.S. Eliot, Goethe, Dante, and others, whose lines permeate, punctuate, and conspire with Creeley's own.

In 1999, the same year he was elected a Chancellor of the Academy of American Poets, Creeley was awarded the prestigious Bollingen Prize by the Yale University Library, first awarded to Ezra Pound in 1949. In 2001 he was awarded the Lannan Lifetime Achievement Award. He has also received the Frost Medal, the Shelley Memorial Award, a National Endowment for the Arts grant, a Rockefeller Foundation grant, and fellowships from the Guggenheim Foundation. He served as New York State Poet from 1989 to 1991 and as Samuel P. Capen Professor of Poetry and Humanities at the State University of New York–Buffalo from 1989 until 2003, when he accepted a distinguished professorship at Brown University.

Further Reading. *Selected Primary Sources:* Creeley, Robert, *The Collected Essays* (Berkeley: University of California Press, 1989); *The Collected Poems* (Berkeley: University of California Press, 1982); ———, *The Collected Prose* (Berkeley: University of California Press, 1987); ———, *Just in Time: Poems 1984–1994* (New York: New Directions, 2001); ———, *Life & Death* (New York:

New Directions, 1998); ———, *So There: Poems 1976–1983* (New York: New Directions, 1998); *Tales Out of School: Selected Interviews* (Ann Arbor: University of Michigan Press, 1993). ***Selected Secondary Sources:*** Altieri, Charles, "Robert Creeley's Poetics of Conjecture," in *Self and Sensibility in Contemporary American Poetry* (Cambridge: Cambridge University Press, 1984, 101–131); Fredman, Stephen, "A Life Tracking Itself: Robert Creeley's *Presences: A Text for Marisol*," in *Poet's Prose: The Crisis in American Verse* (Cambridge: Cambridge University Press, 1990, 57–100); Terrell, Carroll F., ed., *Robert Creeley: The Poet's Workshop* (Orono, ME: National Poetry Foundation, 1984); Wilson, John, ed., *Robert Creeley's Life & Work: A Sense of Increment* (Ann Arbor: University of Michigan Press, 1987).

Steve Evans

CREWS, JUDSON (1917–)

A prolific and idiosyncratic poet, printer, editor, and publisher, Judson Crews was an important part of the avant-garde **literary magazine** network for almost three decades. Author of more than two dozen books and chapbooks, Crews employs a fluent, unadorned vernacular, producing short **lyric poems** focused on philosophical meditation, protest of war and brutality, close observation of the natural world, and celebration of erotic attraction. Crews developed his aesthetic in the late 1930s, when a friend advised him, "You all want to watch that your poetry isn't poetry for poetry's sake." In this view, art strives to record truth and becomes "beautiful" by "taking part in the movement to make life less sordid for the whole world" (*ST*, 16).

Judson Campbell Crews, son of Noah George Crews and Tommie Farmer Crews, was born June 30, 1917, in Waco, Texas. Though dyslexic, he was educated at local schools and graduated with a bachelor's degree in sociology from Baylor University in 1941. He served in the U.S. Army as a medic from 1942 to 1944 and then returned to Baylor, where he earned an MA with honors. He moved to Taos, New Mexico, in 1946 and married Mildred Tolbert, a writer and artist, in 1947. They were, she said, part of a group of "culturally deprived, artistically inclined misfits, tempered by the Depression and World War II" (29).

Although Crews and Scott Greer had been involved in literary activities in Texas, moving to Taos placed Crews squarely in an avant-garde literary setting that he both enjoyed and energized. Crews was among the liveliest editors on the national literary magazine scene of the 1950s and early 1960s. He edited a series of daringly iconoclastic journals including the *Flying Fish, Motive, Suck-Egg Mule*, the *Deer and the Dachshund, Poetry Taos*, and the *Naked Ear*. His little magazines published young writers such as Norman Macleod, **Robert Duncan**, and

Alan Swallow. His press also produced books by Michael Fraenkel, and, as owner of the Motive Book Shop in Taos, Crews actively engaged in protest against the banning of literary works by D.H. Lawrence, Henry Miller, and others. Crews admitted that he reveled in "accumulating a patina of ill-repute."

Crews's iconoclasm was evident early in his career. *The Southern Temper*, a prose work published in 1946, registered his dismay at class exploitation and the segregated racial status quo in Texas. Written in alternating casual and prophetic tones, this small jeremiad offers vignettes of a cross-section of citizens and recounts their grim anecdotes. "I picture fragments of the South," writes Crews, "neither for beauty, nor yet for horror; that at last, at last, the people might know. Can knowledge of this forever, forever go unheeded?" (12). Crews not only published many chapbooks and collections of his own poems and contributed to numerous literary magazines, but he also wrote prolifically under a series of pseudonyms. In fact, he created biographical details to fill out these noms de plume. The husband and wife poets Trumbull Drachler and Cerise Farallon (the pseudonym of Mrs. Lena Johnston Drachler) are two such inventions; and editors have suspected the same regarding the **African American poet** Mason Jordan, supposedly a close friend of Crews. As Crews has written, these little magazines of the 1950s "never published more than a few hundred copies—yet half of these arrived on the doorsteps of significant people" (14).

The books and literary journals that Crews printed were often illustrated with what he called "found art"—old photographs, pressed tree leaves, or pictures torn out of magazines—so that each copy was somewhat different from the others. **Robert Creeley** saw this as an attempt—like Crews's "twists of language"—to "shock the mind awake" (198).

Many of Crews's taut lyrics deal with what he calls "nagging love," while others offer explicit celebrations of erotic encounters that also seem to reinforce the idea of female inscrutability. Woman appears as temptress, talking tough, dressed in "Dancing shoes, her heels beating hell up from the floor." In "The Rape," included in his collection *Inwade to Briney Garth* (1960), Crews assess the damage sustained from a violent sexual assault—but the toll calculated is the aggressor's, not the victim's. "Homage to Melpomene" (1960) and other, more conventional love poems announce Crews's disruptive intentions by naming body parts that usually appeared in print during that era only in medical textbooks.

Crews's poems have an ideogrammatic impact and are difficult to paraphrase. In his poem "Of the Self Exceeded" (1960), Crews writes, "The bird is perfection of air, of air / but the mind is lost short of meaning." These lines and others in the poem suggest both a fine lyrical touch and a distrust of rationalization, a theme often addressed in his work. "What Babylon Was Built About" (1954) begins as Crews contemplates his own typewriter and printing presses and then the whole prospect of a poetic vocation. "My mind," he writes, "is not a mechanical mind / my precision is only the heart's precision." Suggesting a crucial opposition of social control and personal possibility, the poem ends with a striking image of an overdetermined society collapsing under its own weight, a society in which "no dream can flower in their frozen field." "Aftermath of War" (1960) also cautions against hubris. Humans are not the center of the universe but are caught in a "maelstrom of reality": "The rubble is alive with dung and with sparrows / there god is resting and he is among his own." This insistence on challenging society's unexamined beliefs and this reminding us of self-aggrandizing dangers characterizes all of Crews's best work.

Further Reading. *Selected Primary Sources:* Crews, Judson, *The Clock of Moss*, ed. Carol Bergé (Boise, ID: Ashata Press, 1983); ———, Judson Crews Papers, Harry Ransom Humanities Research Center, University of Texas, Austin; *Nolo Contendere*, ed. Joanie Whitebird (Houston: Wings Press, 1978); ———, "Shoe String Publisher" (*Southwestern American Literature* 11 [Fall 1985]: 5–15). ***Selected Secondary Sources:*** Anderson, Wendell B., *The Heart's Precision: Jordan Crews and His Poetry*, ed. Jefferson R. Selth (Carson, CA: Dumont Press, 1994); Creeley, Robert, "Ways of Looking" (*Poetry: A Magazine of Verse* 98 [June 1961]: 192–198).

Lorenzo Thomas

CRUZ, VICTOR HERNÁNDEZ (1949–)

Victor Hernández Cruz started writing poetry as a teenager. By 1975, he had published four books of poetry and garnered recognition as a key figure of the Nuyorican poets. A year later, Cruz published his verse, *Tropicalization* (1976), which uses bilingual diction and explores Puerto Rican and American cultures. This text helped propel Cruz as a prominent literary figure of cultural exploration. Cruz's poems have been translated into more than five languages and have been included in more than fifteen anthologies. He is also a recipient of the National Endowment for the Arts fellowship, Latin American Guggenheim fellowship, and New York Poetry Foundation award. His multicultural and multilingual audience has continued to grow with his five subsequent books of poetry.

Victor Hernández Cruz was born on February 6, 1949, in Aguas Buenas, Puerto Rico. Due to harsh financial circumstances, his family moved to Spanish Harlem in New York City in 1955. Around the age of fourteen, Cruz started to write poetry. He finished his first compilation of poems, *Papo Got His Gun! and Other Poems* (1966), at seventeen. A year later, the New York magazine *Evergreen Review* published some poems from the compilation. With his literary career developing, Cruz quit high school and co-created the East Harlem Gut Theater, a group of Puerto Rican actors, musicians, and writers. He also became an editor for *Umbra* magazine in 1967. Cruz's poems began to appear frequently in several other literary journals, such as *Confrontations* (1971), *Yardbird Reader* (1972), and *Mundus Atrium* (1973). The anthologies *The Puerto Rican Poets* (1972) and *You Better Believe It* (1973) also showcased his poems. During this period of the 1970s, Cruz became a member of the Nuyorican poets and met fellow poets **Miguel Algarín** and Pedro Pietri. This group featured second-generation Puerto Rican writers who primarily spoke English and lived in New York. Cruz blended English and Spanish diction in *By Lingual Wholes* (1982) and *Red Beans* (1991). He later explored the theme of displacement in *Panoramas* (1997), a collection of poems, essays, and stories. Cruz's popularity soared in 2001, due to the critical acclaim received by *Maraca: New and Selected Poems, 1965–2000* (2001). After teaching at the University of California–Berkeley, the University of California–San Diego, San Francisco State College, and the University of Michigan, Cruz continues to lecture at several academic institutions throughout the United States. He divides his time between Puerto Rico, New York, and Morocco.

Cruz's poems often depict life in Spanish Harlem and make use of both the English and Spanish languages. They are often narrative and are usually infused with rhythm and repetition. His first book, *Papo Got His Gun! and Other Poems*, presents the reality of death in a dangerous environment. In "Louis Is Dead," Cruz grieves over the death of a young friend; in "A Letter to Jose," Jose "has been killed" by city life. The poems in Cruz's first major collection, *Snaps* (1969), continue this examination of death and the power of poetry. "The Eye Uptown & Downtown" captures the brutal violence in major cities and in "IS A DEAD MAN" death is the failure to accomplish the American dream; however, the dream is unattainable because America is a "dead world." Cruz presents poetry as a form of social change, as in "today is a day of great joy." In this poem, poetry has the power to "knock down walls" and cause reform.

Cruz's second book of verse, *Mainland* (1973), moves away from life in the city and follows the narrator across the United States. He describes his observations of urban development in "The Ways of San Francisco," the congestion of traffic in "Chicago/3 Hours," and the fast pace of gambling in "Las Vegas." He eventually returns to Puerto Rico in "Aguadilla," to recall a house in the northwest town in which "the stove was burning / And the soft yellow smell of banana" lingers.

Cruz's next collection, *Tropicalization* (1976), returns to his depiction of urban life but with a touch of humor. In "Side 6" Cruz describes the harsh cold weather of New York. The frigid temperature keeps "Doctor Willie" from picking up a dollar bill on the ground. In "Side 3" the frigid weather has a "heavy overcoat" and wants "a cigarette" to keep warm. Similarly, in "Three Songs from the 50s" Cruz recalls living inside the tenements during winter and suffering because of the lack of heating. To get warm, he daydreams of his uncle who lives in Puerto Rico.

Cruz's next collection, *By Lingual Wholes*, turns more explicitly to political questions. "*Merengue* in History" describes the colonization of Puerto Rico, "Bacalao and Society" examines the colonialism of the Portuguese, and "Borinkins in Hawaii" explores the situation of Puerto Rican migrant workers in Hawaii. Here too he mixes English and Spanish as in "Ver-sion / cion."

In *Red Beans* Cruz changes themes again to examine **poetics** and poetic figures. In particular, he looks at **William Carlos Williams**'s influence on his poetry in "An Essay on William Carlos Williams." In *Panoramas* also, Cruz writes of William Carlos Williams in "Water from the Fountain of Youth," treasuring Williams's book in his pocket and recognizing his cultural link to Williams, whose mother was Puerto Rican.

Cruz has published two major collections of poetry selected from earlier books, *Rhythm, Content and Flavor: New and Selected Poems* (1988) and *Maraca: New and Selected Poems, 1965–2000*. These works highlight Cruz's bilingualism, his effort to depict city life in concrete detail, his political consciousness, and his use of rhythm and repetition.

Further Reading. ***Selected Primary Sources:*** Cruz, Victor Hernández, *By Lingual Wholes* (San Francisco: Momo's Press, 1982); ———, *Mainland* (New York: Random House, 1973); ———, *Maraca: New and Selected Poems, 1965–2000* (Minneapolis, MN: Coffee House Press, 2001); ———, *Panoramas* (Minneapolis, MN: Coffee House Press, 1997); *Papo Got His Gun! and Other Poems* (New York: Calle Once Publications, 1966); ———, *Red Beans: Poems* (Minneapolis, MN: Coffee House Press, 1991); ———, *Rhythm, Content and Flavor: New and Selected Poems* (Houston: Arte Público Press, 1988); ———, *Snaps* (New York: Random House, 1969); ———, *Tropicalization* (New York: Reed, Cannon and Johnson, 1976). ***Selected Secondary Sources:*** Dick, Bruce Allen, *A Poet's Truth: Conversations with Latino/Latina Poets* (Tucson: University of Arizona Press, 2003); Turner, Faythe E., ed, *Puerto Rican Writers at Home in the U.S.A.: An Anthology* (Seattle: Open Hand Publishing, 1991).

Dorsía Smith Silva

CULLEN, COUNTEE (1903–1946)

In 1925, his *annus mirabilis*, Countee Cullen was one of the nation's most popular poets, second only to **Edna St. Vincent Millay**. Though this fame engulfed him upon the appearance of his first book, Cullen was prolific during the early years of his career in the 1920s, and his work remains central to understanding the artistic upsurge known as the **Harlem Renaissance** or "New Negro" movement. Insisting on his connection to the centuries-long heritage of English-language poetry, Cullen called himself "conservative," prizing skilled performance—highly polished artifice and artistry—above technical experiment or ethnic authenticity. His best poems, notable for precise diction, wit, and fluent rhythmic effect, remain in anthologies and many textbooks studied at every grade level.

Though he enjoyed celebrity for at least a decade of his life, not much is known about his earliest years. Born May 30, 1903, Countee Porter (if that was his original surname) was raised for a time by his grandmother Elizabeth Porter and then adopted, perhaps in 1914, by Rev. Dr. Frederick Asbury Cullen and Carolyn Belle Mitchell Cullen. Rev. Cullen was a prominent civic leader, pastor of Salem Methodist Episcopal Church, the second largest African American congregation in New York City. Mrs. Cullen was active in efforts to "uplift" the poor through culture and education.

Cullen began writing and publishing poetry in national journals while attending DeWitt Clinton High School and New York University. In 1925 he won the Witter Bynner Poetry Prize, *Poetry Magazine*'s John Reed Memorial Prize, and awards in contests sponsored by *Opportunity*, *Crisis*, and *Palms*. Elected to Phi Beta Kappa, he earned his bachelor's degree in the spring and published *Color*, his first book-length collection of poems, in the fall of that year. He earned a master's degree at Harvard University in 1926. Other books rapidly appeared, including *Copper Sun* (1927), *The Ballad of the Brown Girl: An Old Ballad Retold* (1927), *The Black Christ and Other Poems* (1929), and *The Medea and Some Poems* (1935).

The high rate of productivity begun in 1925 continued as Cullen wrote a monthly column for *Opportunity Magazine* and edited an anthology titled *Caroling Dusk: An Anthology of Verse by Negro Poets* (1928). A brilliant elocutionist, he was in demand for poetry readings and lecture tours.

In 1928, with full celebrity press coverage and gossip, in the company of 1,500 invited guests, Cullen married **W.E.B. DuBois**'s daughter Yolande. The extravagant "wedding of the century" was soon followed by equally spectacular gossip about their divorce. Cullen remarried, more happily, in 1940. He and his second wife, Ida Mae Roberson Cullen, were together until his death.

A Guggenheim Foundation fellowship in 1928 allowed Cullen to spend two years in Paris writing and studying at the Sorbonne. While there he became associated with **expatriate** African American artists such as sculptor Augusta Savage and painter Palmer Hayden. For the next decade he spent summers in Paris and traveling in France.

Enthusiastic critical response for *Color* and the appearance of his **long poem** "Heritage" in Alain Locke's anthology *The New Negro* (1925) made Cullen a major figure of the dynamic literary movement known as the Harlem Renaissance. Shaped by Locke, **James Weldon Johnson**, Charles S. Johnson, and W.E.B. DuBois among others, the movement was an energetic attempt to ameliorate race relations in the United States by gaining greater public respect for African Americans by promoting their accomplishments in education and the arts. Though to a large public he might have been representative of a movement, Cullen's work is that of a complex individual who resists categorization. Cullen hoped to be judged for his own work simply as a poet, not as a member of a particular ethnic group. This desire, however, did not mean that he turned his back on writing poems of protest on behalf of black Americans. Similarly, though he was a minister's son, Cullen maintained a problematic relationship with religion.

Cullen mastered traditional English-language stanza forms such as ballads, sonnets, and rime royal, looking to the Romantic poets as models. His ambition was that his poems would join the **canon** of those he admired. Regardless of the subject matter addressed or the emotion explored, Cullen was interested in the musicality of language that poetry makes possible. In "The Black Christ" (1929) Cullen expressed his faith in the power of art, which is the "one spark of spirit God head gave / To all alike." Art, for Cullen, is the identifying marker of the human soul, its power such that despots should stand in fear of it: "Tell them each law and rule they make, / Mankind shall disregard and break / (If this must be) for beauty's sake."

Race and religion are major themes in Cullen's work. He vigorously protested **segregation** and the inferior caste status imposed on black people in the United States by law and social custom. The poem "Incident" (1925) documents the virulence of racial prejudice; an often-quoted sonnet ironically praises God as "good, well-meaning, kind" but then declares, "Yet do I marvel at this curious thing: / To make a poet black, and bid him sing!" The purpose of many of Cullen's poems is pointing out contradictions exemplified by a supposedly democratic society that unfairly limits the ability of its people to exercise their talents. He also explores this theme from a psychological or introspective perspective of individual frustration resulting from social restrictions determined entirely along the "color line" established by racial prejudice.

The magnificent poem "Heritage" (1925) seems at first to address racial heritage and the legacy of slavery. Speaking as "One three centuries removed / From the scenes his fathers loved," Cullen plangently asks, "What is Africa to me?" Seeking his answer leads to a consideration of cultural atavism and a reinvestigation of the idea that slavery served as a means of introducing Christianity to

African pagans. Cullen feels compelled to question divine purpose in allowing such suffering. Gerald Early has noted that Cullen's major poems "could only have been produced by a Christian consciousness." "Heritage" presents these weighty ideas in a tightly rhymed and metered poem reminiscent of Poe's "The Raven."

Although "Heritage" is a lyric that explores individual subjectivity by delineating an interior state of mind, it is not merely a psychological portrait of repression. Some critics have noted how Cullen's depiction of the nobility and natural beauty of ancient Africans resonates with the ideas popularized by contemporaries such as the leaders of Marcus Garvey's Universal Negro Improvement Association (UNIA). Modern African Americans, conversely, as represented by the poem's persona, their options circumscribed by racism, are shown to be tormented by a religion that seems to offer psychological constraint instead of spiritual deliverance.

Cullen's long poem "The Black Christ" (1929), again combining the issues of race and religion, elicited controversy from several quarters by treating a Southern lynching as equivalent to the crucifixion of Christ and incorporating cyclical motifs from pagan myth. The poem aspires to and achieves a Miltonic eloquence in the poet's attempt to understand the hatreds and violence of American life. Composed primarily of rhymed tetrameter couplets, this work revisits the religious doubt that characterized "Heritage."

In fact, an ambivalent response to Christian faith is evident everywhere in Cullen's poetry. The early "Black Magdalens" (1925) is a fluent expression of compassion for women working as prostitutes, and the biblical allusion to the woman taken in adultery (John 8: 1–11) serves, as might be expected, to suggest that some of the cruelties of antiquity are still present in our society. In this poem, however, Cullen charges that the blame might not be placed solely on the self-righteous mob. The poet being merely a witness, such women in the modern age have lost their defender. Cullen's brutally ironic description of Christ's resurrection as somehow a turning away from human suffering is a shockingly powerful element of a poem in brisk quatrains that might otherwise be seen as merely a technical tour de force of consonance and careful rhyme. Here, as in earlier poems, the deeper implication is that unbelief is not a viable alternative; and, in "The Black Christ," Cullen has to admit that wretchedness is the condition of those who do not believe "in something more than pain or grief."

Even if Cullen's work is not perceived as direct political protest—as the writing of contemporaries such as **Claude McKay** and **Langston Hughes** undoubtedly is—poems such as "Heritage," "Yet Do I Marvel," "Pagan Prayer," and "Simon the Cyrenian Speaks" present dramatic situations and compelling metaphors that register the deep resentment felt by black Americans regarding the social mistreatment they were forced to endure.

Indeed, Cullen's poems often seem to portray African Americans, denied privilege in every social sphere, as victims of an unfair racial system so powerful and pervasive that, as in the allegory of "The Ballad of the Brown Girl" (1927), its effects persist even beyond the grave. This poem also includes other recurring Cullen themes. As in "The Black Christ" and many of Cullen's love poems, the idealized female figure is a type of the Greek Medusa or *la belle dame sans merci*, a figure of death in life. This theme, a convention in medieval and Romantic European literature, can be found throughout Cullen's work. "Counter Mood" (1929), despite awkwardly complex diction, engages another of Cullen's favorite conventional topics, forcefully questioning the assumptions of poetry and philosophy. "I who am mortal say I shall not die," writes the poet while admitting that he has no supporting evidence and knows not "whence this arrogant assurance springs."

Although Cullen was especially sensitive to the power of words to do harm, as one sees in "Incident" (1925), where a child's racial slur proves unforgettable, and "The Black Christ," where harsh words "feast upon the mind," he also fully understood the power of words to create hopeful scenarios and promote improved social relations—the very purpose, according to Alain Locke and W.E.B. DuBois, of the New Negro Renaissance that Cullen's poetry helped to create. In the final analysis, Cullen, like **Edgar Allan Poe**, appreciated poetry as the language most suitable for expressing human suffering. In "Colored Blues Singer" (1927) the voice of the nightclub entertainer may recall "the mellow-bosomed maids / Of Africa," but it also evokes the opera diva who "breaks her heart / On symbols Verdi wrote." Both singers are performers, representing sorrow in a theatrical manner. What is most important is Cullen's equation of the artistry of the African American musician and the classically trained opera star. Implicit here is the idea that those who can express themselves with equal eloquence cannot be judged culturally inferior. Indeed, many felt that Cullen's own successful career as poet underscored the point.

Cullen published a novel, *One Way to Heaven* (1931), and settled into a job teaching French, English, and creative writing in New York City junior high schools. He translated the Greek tragedy *Medea*, which was published as a book in 1935. Avant-garde composer Virgil Thomson later set some of the poems from that work to music. Cullen also published two books for children, *The Lost Zoo* (1940) and *My Lives and How I Lost Them* (1942), "co-authored" by the poet and his pet Christopher Cat.

From his earliest days, Cullen had been interested in writing for the stage but did not achieve much success in that field during his lifetime. Controversy again engulfed Cullen in 1945 regarding *St. Louis Woman*, a collaboration with poet and novelist **Arna Bontemps** (1902–1973). Based on Bontemps's novel *God Sends Sunday* (1931), the project (written as the libretto for a musical score by Johnny Mercer and Harold Arlen) was attacked almost as soon as it was announced by critics who felt it misrepresented black working-class characters and employed degrading images reminiscent of the minstrel stage. When the show reached Broadway for a short run in 1946, after Cullen's death, *St. Louis Woman*'s most notable impact was that it included Arlen's song "Come Rain or Come Shine" and served as a vehicle for singer Pearl Bailey's theatrical stage debut. *St. Louis Woman* was revived in 1998 and later adapted as *St. Louis Woman: A Blues Ballet* by Michael Smuin for the Dance Theatre of Harlem at the 2003 Lincoln Center Festival.

In the last days of World War II, Cullen also worked collaboratively with poet and Howard University drama professor Owen Dodson on a commission from choreographer Mura Den. "The Third Fourth of July," published in August 1946, is experimental in staging and structure. The play depicts two mirror-image families—one black, one white—who have sons in the army overseas. A fateful telegram reporting the death of a soldier in action is delivered to the wrong family, allowing them to truly understand the vulnerability and humanity of the other. The play pointedly contrasts patriotic self-sacrifice and segregation but ends on a hopeful note. It was Cullen's last literary project.

The poet died of uremia on January 9, 1946. *On These I Stand*, Cullen's own selection from his published poetry, appeared in 1947. His fame has continued as new readers confront his rich, complex, and technically gifted poetry. Countee Cullen, commited to ideals of beauty in art and standing apart from now more popular Harlem Renaissance poets such as Langston Hughes, spoke eloquently to his own era, his personal dilemmas, and the struggle faced by his people.

Further Reading. *Selected Primary Source:* Cullen, Countee, *My Soul's High Song: The Collected Writings of Countee Cullen, Voice of the Harlem Renaissance*, ed. Gerald Early (New York: Anchor Books, 1991). ***Selected Secondary Sources:*** Ferguson, Blanche E., *Countee Cullen and the Negro Renaissance* (New York: Dodd, Mead, 1966); Perry, Margaret, *A Bio-Bibliography of Countee P. Cullen, 1903–1946* (Westport, CT: Greenwood Press, 1971); Shucard, Alan R. *Countee Cullen* (Boston: Twayne, 1984).

Lorenzo Thomas

CUMMINGS, E.E. (1894–1962)

As a poet, Cummings belongs to the generation that came to the foreground between the two world wars, a generation that includes **Wallace Stevens** and **William Carlos Williams**; that follows **Ezra Pound**, **Robert Frost**, **Carl Sandburg**, **Vachel Lindsay**, **Amy Lowell**, and **T.S. Eliot**; and that precedes **W.H. Auden**, **Robert Lowell**, **Randall Jarrel**, **Sylvia Plath**, and **Anne Sexton**. In other words, Cummings was a key figure in the emergence and hegemony of literary **modernism**, but he was a rebel against that movement as well. His place in literary history is thus complex: On the one hand, he is a modernist in his artistic experimentalism, his rejection of middle-class values, and his corresponding elitism; on the other, he is a Romantic anti-modernist in his rejection of intellectualism and his emphasis on feeling, love, spring, children, and the individual. Cummings has been accused by modernist critics of **sentimentality** and by anti-modernist critics of unintelligibility. It may be best to view him on his own terms in order to understand his significance. Such an approach is appropriate for one who saw himself as a maverick.

Edward Estlin Cummings was born in Cambridge, Massachusetts, on October 14, 1894, to Rebecca Haswell Cummings and Edward Cummings. A sister, Elizabeth, was born in 1901. His mother was a warm and loving presence who encouraged Estlin's drawings and writings from an early age; his imposing father was a Harvard sociology professor who later became a Unitarian minister. The family acquired a summer place in the country near Silver Lake, New Hampshire, where Cummings was able to develop a feeling for rural as well as urban life and landscape. He attended private and public grammar schools in Cambridge and was able to draw upon the family's large collection of books at home. He entered the Cambridge Latin School in 1907, the college preparatory side of Cambridge High, where he studied Latin, French, and Greek, as well as English, algebra, and geometry. He entered Harvard College in 1911, where he studied Greek and English literature, taking the BA in 1915 and the MA in 1916. He also studied Dante, whose *Divine Comedy* gave him the scheme for organizing his journal *EIMI*.

It was at Harvard that Cummings began to turn away from the genteel Victorianism of his background and education and toward the rebelliousness, both in art and life, that was emerging in America in the early decades of the twentieth century. He began publishing his poems in the college **literary magazines**, and he formed friendships with other bright young men of the time, such as John Dos Passos, S. Foster Damon, Scofield Thayer, and J. Sibley Watson. He became fascinated by popular arts such as vaudeville and the circus, and particularly with performers—clowns, acrobats, and chorus girls. As he learned about revolutions in art and literature, he was searching for his own poetic style and voice, experimenting with the spacing of a poem on the page; with typography; with departures from standard diction, grammar, and syntax; and with unconventional subjects and attitudes. At the same time, he did not abandon tradition: He made use of rhyme, meter, stanza, and traditional diction and themes when it suited him.

After taking his master's degree at Harvard in 1916, Cummings moved to New York City in hopes of developing his dual career as writer and artist, but World War I brought a temporary halt to his development, and he volunteered, as did many young men at that time, for service abroad with the Norton-Harjes Ambulance Corps in April 1917. During the shipboard Atlantic crossing, he met William Slater Brown, with whom he became lifelong friends and with whom, in France that June, he was assigned to duty at the Noyon sector on the Western Front. Because Brown's letters home expressing criticism of the French war effort were intercepted by the French Army censors, both men were arrested in the fall and sent to a detention camp at La Ferté Macé in the northwestern part of France, 125 miles from Paris. There they spent three miserable months, from September to December, under extremely difficult conditions.

Much the worse for wear, Cummings returned to New York in January 1918 but was then drafted into the American Army and sent to a training camp at Fort Devens, 40 miles northwest of Boston, until the Armistice of November 1918, whereupon he once again returned to New York to resume his writing and painting. He began work on *The Enormous Room*, an account of his experiences in France the previous year, and he met and fell in love with Elaine Orr Thayer, the wife of his well-to-do friend, Scofield Thayer. They had an affair in the open-marriage spirit of the 1920s, and their daughter Nancy was born in 1919. *The Enormous Room* was published in 1922, and Cummings's first book of poems, *Tulips and Chimneys*, appeared in 1923 in a rather truncated version of the original manuscript. Elaine divorced Thayer, and she and Cummings were married in March of 1924, but the relationship did not survive; they were divorced in December of that year. Cummings was devastated and suffered suicidal despair for a time.

He was nevertheless able to continue his career, winning the *Dial* Award in 1925 and publishing *is 5*, his first book of poems since *Tulips and Chimneys*, in 1926. Another doomed marriage—this time to Anne Barton—followed in 1927, ending in divorce in 1934. Meanwhile he had met Marion Morehouse, a fashion model, actress, and photographer, in 1932, and they formed a relationship that lasted for the rest of his life, she serving as his caretaker and archivist.

HIM, a play about the tensions within an artist between marriage and work, was published in 1927 and produced by the Provincetown Playhouse in Greenwich Village in 1928, and *No Title*, "a book without a title," containing surrealistic narratives, was published in 1930. The year 1931 was a busy one, including Cummings's trip to Stalinist Russia; the publication of *CIOPW* (a

book of artworks in charcoal, ink, oil, pencil, and watercolor); and his third book of poems, titled *ViVa*. The year 1933 saw the publication of *EIMI* (Greek for "I am"), the journal of his trip to the Soviet Union, and the receipt of a Guggenheim fellowship.

Given the publication of more than half a dozen creatively exciting and significant works and the receipt of numerous prestigious awards, Cummings's career would seem to have been in full flight as he approached the age of forty; nevertheless, his next book of poems was rejected by fourteen publishers. He consequently arranged, with the financial assistance of his ever-generous mother, to have it published by the Golden Eagle Press, a private operation headed by his friend Max Jacob, and he entitled it, significantly enough, *No Thanks*, listing the fourteen publishers in the shape of a funeral urn after the title page. Because the time was the middle of the Great Depression, because the book contained much experimental work, and because Cummings's politics ran counter to the leftism of artists and intellectuals of that era, the book was a risky venture for any commercial publisher.

Far from being discouraged, Cummings continued to write and publish, bringing out seven titles in the fifteen years between 1935 and 1950: *TOM* (1935), *Collected Poems* (1938), *50 Poems* (1940), *Anthropos* (1944), *1 X 1* [One Times One] (1944), *Santa Claus* (1946), and *Xaipe* (1950). Fittingly enough, he also won the Harriet Monroe *Poetry Magazine* prize, an Academy of American Poets fellowship in 1950, and a second Guggenheim in 1951. From this point on, Cummings's career flourished. He held the Charles Eliot Norton Lectureship at Harvard for 1952–1953, publishing the lectures subsequently as *i: SIX NONLECTURES*. He became the Boston Arts Festival Poet and won a Bollingen Award in 1958; that year saw also the publication of *95 Poems* and Firmage's collection of Cummings's prose pieces in *A Miscellany* (1958; rev. ed. 1965), and he received a Ford Foundation grant in 1959.

Cummings died unexpectedly from a stroke a few years later, in 1962, at the age of sixty-eight. *Adventures in Value*, a collection of photographs by Marion Morehouse with captions and commentary by Cummings, was published in 1962. *73 Poems* was published posthumously in 1963, and *Fairy Tales* (illustrations by John Eaton) came out in 1965. Although a preliminary *Complete Poems 1923–1962* was published by Harcourt in 1972, the definitive *Complete Poems 1904–1962*, edited by George Firmage, was published by Liveright in 1991.

Cummings's first appearance in book form was in 1917 with the publication of *Eight Harvard Poets*, a collection compiled by Stewart Mitchell, a classmate of Cummings, which was subsidized by the contributors and published by the Little Bookshop Around the Corner on East 29th Street in Manhattan. The other poets were S. Foster Damon, John Dos Passos, Robert Hillyer, Dudley

Poore, Cuthbert Wright, and William Morris. The collection included eight poems by Cummings, but it was not until six years later, in 1923, that he was able to see his first book of poems in print: *Tulips and Chimneys*, published by Thomas Seltzer. Unfortunately, as George Firmage informs us, this volume had a tangled publication history, for Seltzer reduced the size of the original manuscript to a little less than half, and the omitted poems were subsequently published by Cummings in *&*[AND] (1925), *XLI Poems* (1925), and *is 5* (1926). "However, the publication, in 1937, of the Archetype edition . . . restored the original manuscript number and arrangement of the poems" (*Bibliography*, 6ff.). *Complete Poems 1904–1962* (Liveright, 1991), the edition used here, represents the original edition. It has restored the original ampersand to *Tulips & Chimneys* (1922), which is followed by what was left of *&* [AND] (1925), amounting to forty-one out of the original eighty-six poems.

From the perspective of eighty or ninety years, the most memorable poems from these first five years (1917–1922) are "in Just- / spring" (27), "O sweet spontaneous / earth" (58), "Buffalo Bill's / defunct," (90), "the Cambridge ladies who live in furnished souls" (115), "let's live suddenly without thinking" (159), "Paris; this April sunset completely utters" (183), "Spring is like a perhaps hand" (197), and "i like my body when it is with your / body" (218). These early poems reveal the emergence of Cummings's characteristic themes and styles, among them the use of typography and spacing on the page; the tendency toward unusual diction; the recurrent focus on the natural seasons, cityscapes, and landscapes; the poems of praise and satire; the emphasis on sexual love; the admiration of human skill; and the sympathy for children and their experience.

One senses in *is 5* (1926) a growing and deepening grasp of these themes and techniques, but the volume begins with an unusual group of five sonnets entitled "Five Americans," each devoted to a different denizen of a brothel—Liz, Mame, Gert, Marj, and Fran. The sonnets present, individually and collectively, an unpleasant picture, and it is difficult to see what Cummings intended other than a desire to make art out of ugliness in the manner of some of the paintings of Henri de Toulouse-Lautrec. The young poet had an interest in exploring urban lowlife, perhaps in reaction to the high-minded upbringing of his youth. So we have "workingman with hand so hairy-sturdy," "now dis 'daughter' uv eve(who ain't precisely slim)sim," "she being Brand- / new," "on the Madam's best april the," "poets yeggs and thirsties," and so on. The language leaves the impression of the son of a Unitarian minister exploring the demimondes of New York, Boston (and "sinful Somerville"), and Paris, simultaneously fascinated and repelled by what he finds.

This volume has other moods and topics, however. Most significantly, it begins to develop that strain of satire that emerged with "the Cambridge ladies" of the first volume. "POEM, OR BEAUTY HURTS MR.VINAL" (228–229), the only mature poem with an actual title, is a deservedly well-known parody of commercial advertising that piles cliché upon cliché. And, as if to balance out the unsavory portrayal of sex in "Five Americans," there are poems from the other side, most notably "since feeling is first" (291) and "if i have made,my lady,intricate" (307). The former is an authentic innovation both in style and substance. In just sixteen **free-verse** lines, apportioned into five "stanzas," and based on a subtle yet consistent polarity between the language of "feeling" ("kiss," "fool," "spring," "flower," etc.) and that of reason ("syntax," "wisdom," "brain," etc.), the speaker invites his lady to laugh and accept his embrace, "leaning back in my arms / for life's not a paragraph / And death i think is no parenthesis" (291). The "romantic" message—*Vivamus, mea Lesbia, atque amemus*—is embodied in the "classical" framework of the consistently controlled structure of the poem. It is this tension that characterizes Cummings's "modernity," a tension that evolves further as he matures and develops a philosophical debate between a transcendental vision and the strictures of ordinary human existence, involving also the tension between the individual and society.

The poems of the 1930s, including *W(ViVa)* (1931), *No Thanks* (1935), and *New Poems* (from *Collected Poems*, 1938), clearly reflect the poet's response to the doldrums of the times. *Entre les deux guerres*, the postwar time of the Great Depression, is reflected in such poems as "i sing of Olaf glad and big" (340), "sonnet entitled how to run the world" (390), "IN) / all those who got / athlete's mouth jumping / on&off bandwagons / (MEMORIAM" (404), "when muckers pimps and tratesmen / delivered are of vicians" (405), "kumrads die because they're told)" (413), "this little bride & groom are" (470), and "my specialty is living said" (473).

As usual, however, there are the more personal, counterbalancing moods, in poems such as "if there are any heavens my mother will(all by herself)have / one" (353), and the perennially exquisite love poem "somewhere i have never travelled, gladly beyond / any experience, your eyes have their silence," which concludes, startlingly, "nobody, not even the rain, has such small hands" (367).

When modernist critics complain of Cummings's alleged sentimentality, they often fail to note the profound discipline upon which his art is based, for not only did he labor assiduously on draft after draft of each poem, he also experimented tirelessly with texture and structure, with diction, syntax, imagery, typography, spacing, and punctuation, searching endlessly for the right effect—contrary to the throwaway appearance of some of his poems on the page. The casual effect was the result of intense labor.

The charge of sentimentality is also based on Cummings's ostensible lack of self-doubt, on his complicity with the very aspects of modern life he pretends to deplore, and on his exaggeration of the struggle of "you-and-i" against "mostpeople." Although there is some truth to this critique, it is not entirely justified, for Cummings demonstrates self-doubt often enough in the poems. A late example would be the lines "a total stranger one black day / knocked living the hell out of me— // who found forgiveness hard because / my(as it happened)self he was" (*Complete Poems*, 730; from *95 Poems* [1958]). An early example is the play *HIM* (1927), which reveals an entire run of self-doubt on the part of the protagonist, a would-be playwright, who feels he is a failure—not only as an artist but also as a man. Significantly, the play ends with the birth of the child that he and his wife, Me, have been expecting, and with his ensuing "cry of terror" (144). (One recalls that a daughter, Nancy, was born to Cummings and Elaine near the end of 1919.) Nor do we find in this play that the poet justifies his failure by portraying the wife unsympathetically—quite the reverse.

Cummings published two more books of poetry in the 1940s—*50 Poems* (1940) and *1 X 1* (1944)—containing such favorites as "anyone lived in a pretty how town" (515), "my father moved through dooms of love" (520–521), "ygUDuh" (547), "plato told" (553), and "what if a much of a which of a wind" (560). These books represent a maturing of both vision and art, which combined to produce poems of greater structural regularity yet without any loss of verbal and imagistic inventiveness. One sign of this unique blend is found in the last-mentioned poem, whose theme is the survival of man through the most unimaginable disasters: "—when skies are hanged and oceans drowned, / the single secret will still be man . . . /all nothing's only our hugest home; / the most who die, the more we live" (560). We are reminded of the perennial theme in Cummings: the way down is the way up, a theme also used, as we shall see, in the design of *EIMI*, a journal of the poet's trip to the Soviet Union during the Stalinist period.

Xaipe (1950) and *95 Poems* (1958) bring us into the next decade, with Cummings's by now characteristic praise of love, nature and natural process, nonconforming people, and his displeasure with "manunkind"'s unnatural ways and inability to achieve integration. Cummings writes of the three sisters Soul, Heart, and Mind: "three wealthy sisters swore they'd never part: / Soul was(i understand) / seduced by Life; whose brother married Heart, / now Mrs Death. Poor Mind" (621). In this somewhat didactic scenario, Soul is taken over by Life, while Heart marries Death, leaving Mind isolated among abstractions. Cummings has come far from "let's live suddenly without thinking" (159), a line from *Tulips & Chimneys*, about twenty-five years earlier.

Another significant development is the overflowing sense of spiritual joy found in nature, as in "i thank You God for most this amazing / day" (663), "when faces called flowers float out of the ground" (665), "now all the fingers of this tree(darling)have / hands" (667), and "luminous tendril of celestial wish" (669). This last example begins a description of the new moon, which concludes "teach . . . me the keen / illimitable secret of begin." These 1950s books also demonstrate Cummings's ever-evolving treatment of love, as, for example, in "the great advantage of being alive" (664), a poem in which there is an equally ever-evolving variation on the refrain "that love are in we,that love are in we": "(for love are in we am in i are in you)," "for love are in we are in love are in we," and "For love are in you am in i are in we." Although typical of the kind of play for which Cummings is well known, these lines constitute an extraordinary rhythmic and verbal device for the thought and experience of unity created by the love between two people.

95 Poems (1958) begins with the oft-cited "leaf falls" poem (673), arranged slenderly down the page as if it were itself a leaf falling; it is a poem that, like Guillaume Apollinaire's *calligrammes*, demonstrates the way in which a poem can pictographically or typographically enact the very thing it is saying. *95 Poems* also contains the charming "maggie and milly and molly and may" (682), in which Cummings's theme of self-knowledge emerges as "whatever we lose(like a you or a me) / it's always ourselves we find in the sea." Cummings's developing mastery of irony, paradox, and ambiguity, qualities much valued by the **New Critics**, some of whom nevertheless disparaged Cummings as sentimental, is further seen in "in time of daffodils(who know)" (688), which concludes "and in a mystery to be/ (when time from time shall set us free)/ forgetting me, remember me." The concluding poem, "being to timelessness as it's to time, / love did no more begin than love will end," goes on to assert that love is "the hope which has no opposite in fear," and concludes "—do lovers love?why then to heaven with hell / Whatever sages say and fools, all's well" (768).

Published just after his death, Cummings's last book of poems was *73 Poems* (1963), following the title format established in *50 Poems* (1940) and *95 Poems* (1958). Typography, the city, seasons, love, and transcendence continue to occupy the poet, and his vision continues to deepen. Number 30 begins "one winter afternoon// (at the magical hour / when is becomes if) / a bespangled clown" gives him a flower; it concludes "—i thank heaven somebody's crazy // enough to give me a daisy" (802). The poem is an example of Cummings's vision in that the dying of the day is redeemed by the clown's "crazy" gesture, an unexpected act of generosity by means of the otherwise commonplace flower. Number

61 depicts a snowflake falling upon a gravestone, with Cummings's spacing of words, syllables, and letters revealing the connections between "one" and "gravestone" as well as the visual resemblance between the falling snowflake and the print falling down the page in a pattern of "lines" and spaces (833).

There follows a five-stanza meditation of six trimeter lines each, rhyming ababcc, which begins "now does our world descend / the path to nothingness," and pursues that despairing theme until it reaches the nadir "where everything's nothing," and concludes with an upward turn in the final line, "—arise, my soul; and sing" (834). The book—and, it suggests, the poet's career—concludes with Number 73: "all worlds have halfsight, seeing either with" life's eye or death's. "Only whose vision can create the whole / . . . he's free into the beauty of the truth" (845).

Cummings's five major prose works are *The Enormous Room* (1922), *HIM* (1927), *EIMI* (1933), *Santa Claus* (1946), and *i: SIX NONLECTURES* (1953). *The Enormous Room* and *EIMI* are both accounts based on personal experiences of the poet, experiences that were difficult and painful. As Cummings himself noted, his stay in the USSR was an experience of a more enormous room. And yet, separated as these two books are by more than a decade, they are also greatly different—in substance, style, and feeling. *HIM* and *Santa Claus* are both dramatic works, but they too are quite different from each other, *HIM* being presented in prose as a literal experience, however intermixed with fantasy, whereas *Santa Claus* is written in blank verse as a morality play.

i: SIX NONLECTURES consists of lectures written for delivery to an audience in Harvard's Sanders Theatre in Memorial Hall, and represents the poet's attempt to "avoid lecturing" while at the same time living up to the honor bestowed upon him by the Charles Eliot Norton Professorship. His solution, of course, was to talk about his life and works, thus continuing on a more literal level the autobiographical ventures in *HIM*, *The Enormous Room*, and *EIMI*. (*Santa Claus*, in dealing with a father's loss of his daughter, has an autobiographical basis as well.) Thus, it is possible to say that Cummings's art was in large part a series of attempts to understand and come to terms with the key dilemma of his life: on the one hand, his conflicted relationship with his parents and hence his compensatory image of himself as free and open, unconstrained by the usual responsibilities and tasks of "mostpeople"; and on the other, his very private, dependent, and self-protective nature. Cummings himself later came to understand and articulate this latter nature, in his private notebooks as well as in certain of the published writings.

This conflict in Cummings, although not always entirely beneficial to him, fortunately bears fruit in works such as *The Enormous Room* and *HIM*, his chief masterpieces of the 1920s. In the first, in a prose style that alternates between formal narration and impressionistic stream of consciousness, he portrays his incarceration as something almost willed, as if, along with Slater Brown, he were embarked upon a jolly adventure. He had been sick of dealing with the chief of his ambulance unit anyway. And he manages to keep up his spirits and treat the experience as a lark until almost the end, when Brown is released before he is. At this point he declines physically and emotionally, but he too is released not long after.

The experience is structured and deepened by the parallels Cummings builds into it to Bunyan's *Pilgrim's Progress*. Thus the director of the facility is "Apollyon," some of the inmates are "Delectable Mountains," and the entire experience is presented as a "Pilgrimage," concluding with an almost visionary experience of sailing into New York Harbor: "The tall, impossibly tall, incomparably tall, city shouldering upward into hard sunlight." Cummings's body and spirit have been sorely tried, and he emerges a wiser and more complete man than when he originally volunteered at the age of twenty-three for ambulance duty at the front.

HIM, coming five years later, continues the evolution of the man and artist. Here too we find a startling mixture of styles—the real and the surreal—and an alternation of literal scenes between Him, the would-be playwright, and Me, his discontented wife, with phantasmagorical interludes representing the play Him is trying to write, and depicting in symbolic terms what is going on in the literal action. The literal action is based on two interrelated problems: the conflict between Him and his wife over his apparent neglect of their relationship because of his obsession with this art, and the corresponding difficulty he is experiencing in trying to write this play. A boxes-within-boxes structure, no doubt influenced by the experimental theatre movements of the 1920s both in the United States and abroad but nevertheless sui generis: Cummings is writing a play (1927) about a man trying to write a play while at the same time trying to deal with his relationship with his wife three years after Cummings himself lost Elaine and Nancy (1924). Indeed, the concluding apotheosis of the play reveals the figure of Me holding in her "*arms a newborn babe at whom [she] looks fondly,*" whereupon "HIM *utters a cry of terror*" (144). It is hard not to believe that this terror was not also Cummings's own during his actual experience of unexpected fatherhood. But at the same time we must appreciate that Cummings as *author* of the play is becoming more able to deal with this major tragedy of his early manhood by the very act of organizing it in artistic form—a form that shows Him coming face to face with his own limitations. And the actual concluding scene shows the difficulty Him is having in believing that this room and the couple in it are real, as if Cummings were telling himself, "you *better* believe!"

The curious thing is that he married Anne Barton around the same time the play was published, and indeed the title page carries these lines attributed to her: "looking forward into the past or looking / backward into the future I / walk on the highest / hills and / I laugh / about / it / all / the way." They were separated, however, in 1932, and divorced in 1934. It was in 1932 that Cummings met Marion Morehouse, showgirl and fashion model, a dozen years his junior, with whom he remained for the rest of his life. It is probable that it was her caretaking presence that enabled him to give precedence to the soft mother-identified side of his nature as a relief from and a compensation for the sufferings his masculine side had been enduring in prison, in his previous two marriages, and his only partially-successful attempts to earn a living while devoting himself to his arts.

His trip to the Soviet Union in 1931, however, represents a watershed: On the one hand, it continues the original outgoing impulse that impelled Cummings to come to grips with the world, but on the other, it brings up the countervailing impulse to distrust and retreat from the world. For what he saw there seemed to be a mechanized state where people were turned into robots. The journey on which *EIMI* is based begins on May 10 and ends on June 14, thus totaling thirty-six days, a little more than five weeks, and its telling is based on Dante's *The Divine Comedy,* just as *The Enormous Room* is based on *Pilgrim's Progress.*

The book can be divided into three parts: Moscow (twenty-two days), Odessa (eight days), and Istanbul (six days). In Moscow he visits a prison, the Bolshoi and Moscow Art Theatres, Lenin's Tomb (which represents the Dantesque pit of Hell), the movies, and a circus. In Odessa he visits the Potemkin Stairs and the bathing beaches, and in Istanbul he does some sightseeing before embarking for home. What impressed him more than anything else in the Soviet Union, however, was the dreary sameness in the look of the people, the lack of femininity in the women, the absence of joy.

This experience reinforced and confirmed for him his philosophy and vision of life, as he wrote in his introduction to the 1934 Modern Library edition of *The Enormous Room*: "Russia, I felt, was more deadly than war; when nationalists hate, they hate by merely killing and maiming human beings; when internationalists hate, they hate by categorying and pigeonholing human beings." And he adds: "Eimi is the individual again; a more complex individual, a more enormous room" (viii).

Just more than a dozen years later, in 1946, *Santa Claus* appeared, a very complexly organized plot in blank verse in which the two main characters, Santa Claus and Death, meet, interact, and exchange masks and costumes several times. According to Kennedy's useful analysis, the play falls into two parts, "the first of which uses the Faust story of a good person tempted by evil in order to gain additional powers. The second part tells the story of the Lost Loved Ones Reunited" (*E.E. Cummings revisited*, 120). Thus in the first part the good person is Santa Claus, who has lost his wife and child (echoes of Cummings's own loss of Elaine and Nancy), and the evil one is of course Death; whereas in the second part Santa Claus, unmasked as a young man, is reunited with the Woman, who refuses Death's embrace, and the Child.

There is, finally, *i: SIX NONLECTURES* (1953), so-called because Cummings didn't want to be seen as a teacher, someone who knows, but rather as an "authentic ignoramus" who seeks to learn. The solution was in the first three lectures to explain how he came to be a writer and painter, and in the last three to speak through his writings of what he came to learn. In the first nonlecture he talks of his parents, and he has only good to report, for he sees himself as having grown past his too-close attachment to his mother and too-troubled relationship with his father. In the second he speaks of his childhood as having been happy, and in the third deals with what he saw as the crucial turning point of his life, involving his youthful experiences of Harvard, Cambridge, Somerville, Boston (where he developed a taste for burlesque shows), New York, and Paris. The fourth nonlecture begins his treatment of the final three, which deal with his writings as embodiments of the transcendental values learned in the first three. Thus the fourth presents his "purely personal values," the fifth shows how they are embodied in *Him*, and the sixth discusses contemporary politics in terms of these values. At the end of this series he provides a concluding answer to the opening question of "who,as a writer,am I?": "I am someone who proudly and humbly affirms that love is the mystery-of-mysteries, and that nothing measurable matters 'a very good God damn': that 'an artist, a man, a failure' is . . . a naturally and miraculously whole human being—a feelingly illimitable individual; whose only happiness is to transcend himself, whose every agony is to grow" (110–111).

Cummings has left a permanent legacy—for readers as well as for poets. For poets he has exemplified the possibilities of typography and the look of the poem upon the page, of the open yet disciplined expression of feeling, of the interplay of structure and anti-structure, of the varieties of linguistic device, of the flexibility of levels of diction and of experiments in syntax, and of freedom in the choice of subject matter. For readers, in addition to the pleasure of experiencing these turns and twists of art, Cummings offers a voice telling us, often in dazzling ways, that we can do no better than to listen to and becoming better acquainted with our selves.

Further Reading. *Selected Primary Sources:* Cummings, E. E., *Adventures in Value: Fifty Photographs by Marion Morehouse, Text by E. E. Cummings* (New York: Harcourt, Brace & World, 1962); ———, *AnOther E.E. Cummings*, ed. Richard Kostelanetz (New York: Liveright, 1998); ———, *Anthropos: The Future of Art* (Mt. Vernon, NY: Golden Eagle Press, 1944); ———, *CIOPW* (New York: Covici-Friede, 1931); ———, *Complete Poems 1904–1962*, ed. George J. Firmage (New York: Liveright, 1991); ———, *EIMI* (New York: Covici-Friede, 1933; New York: Grove Press, 1958); ———, *The Enormous Room*, ed. George C. Firmage (New York: Liveright, 1978); ———, *Fairy Tales* (New York: Harcourt Brace Jovanovich, 1965); ———, *HIM* (New York: Liveright, 1927); ———, *i: SIX NONLECTURES* (Cambridge, MA: Harvard University Press, 1953); ———, *A Miscellany*, ed. George C. Firmage (New York: Argophile Press, 1958; rev. ed. New York: October House, 1965); ———, *[No Title]* (New York: Covici-Friede, 1930); ———, *Santa Claus: A Morality* (New York: Henry Holt, 1946); ———, *Selected Letters of E. E. Cummings*, ed. F. W. Dupee and George Stade (New York: Harcourt, Brace & World, 1969); ———, *TOM* (New York: Arrow Editions, 1935). *Selected Secondary Sources: I. Bibliographical and Scholarly Aids:* Firmage, George C., *E.E. Cummings: A Bibliography* (Middletown, CT: Wesleyan University Press, 1960); McBride, Katherine W., *A Concordance to the Complete Poems of E.E. Cummings* (Ithaca, NY: Cornell University Press, 1989). *II. Biographical and Critical:* Cohen, Milton, *POETandPainter: The Aesthetics of E.E. Cummings' Early Work* (Detroit: Wayne State University Press, 1987); Friedman, Norman, *E.E. Cummings: The Art of His Poetry* (Baltimore: Johns Hopkins Press, 1960); ———, *E.E. Cummings: The Growth of a Writer* (Carbondale: Southern Illinois University Press, 1964); ———, ed., *E.E. Cummings: A Collection of Critical Essays* (Englewood Cliffs, NJ: Prentice-Hall, 1972); Heusser, Martin, *I Am My Writing: The Poetry of E.E. Cummings* (Tübingen: Stauffenburg-Verlag, 1997); Kennedy, Richard S., *Dreams in the Mirror: A Biography of E.E. Cummings* (New York: Liveright, 1980); Kidder, Rushworth M., *E.E. Cummings: An Introduction to the Poetry* (New York: Columbia University Press, 1979).

Norman Friedman

CUNNINGHAM, J.V. (1911–1985)

Perhaps the most striking apprentice-master relationship in twentieth-century American poetry was that of J.V. Cunningham to **Yvor Winters**. Winters, a critic who was ultimately more acclaimed for the vividness of his passion than the strength of his aesthetic, inspired more poets than he influenced. Cunningham became the most important poet to actually absorb the Winters aesthetic and base his poetic style on it. And because Cunningham, unlike Winters, devoted the bulk of his professional life to poetry rather than theory or criticism (though he wrote some distinguished essays and books on both), he can reasonably be said to be, even more than his mentor, the foremost poet of this school.

Cunningham was born on August 23, 1911, in Cumberland, Maryland, but his family moved to Billings, Montana, when he was three. He spent most of his childhood in Montana, and always considered it his home state. His father, James Joseph Cunningham, was a steam-shovel operator working in railroad construction; he died in an accident while Cunningham was still in high school.

The young Cunningham had shown great promise as a scholar, and his mother, Anna Finan Cunningham, moved the family to Denver, where the schools were better. He studied the classics at Regis High School, a Jesuit institution, and finished the Latin and Greek program by the time he was fifteen. During this same period, he first made the acquaintance, by correspondence, of Winters, then a graduate student at Stanford. They were brought together by a mutual friend who was interested in contemporary poetry, and nurtured the same interest in the youthful scholar.

But Cunningham's education was cut short. First his father died, and he postponed college to get a job as a messenger boy at the Denver Stock Exchange. Then he lost that job after the stock market crash of 1929. He became a hobo, traveling the West and Southwest working odd jobs—including the occasional writing job for a local newspaper. He had never completely given up on the idea of writing, or of scholarship, and finally, while down and out in Arizona in the winter of 1931, he wrote Winters asking for help. Winters responded with the offer of living quarters in a shed on his property, and Cunningham moved to Palo Alto, California, and enrolled at Stanford.

Like **Donald Justice**, another poet deeply influenced by the eccentric poet/critic, Cunningham never actually studied with Winters. But he did finish his education at Stanford over the next fifteen years, receiving an BA degree in classics in 1934 and a doctorate in English in 1945.

He remained in academia, teaching at the University of Chicago, the University of Hawaii, Harvard University, the University of Virginia, and Washington University. In 1953 he joined the faculty of Brandeis University, where he remained until his retirement in 1980. He was twice a Guggenheim fellow, in 1959–1960 and 1966–1967, and a fellow of the Academy of American Poets in 1976. He won grants from the National Institute of Arts and Letters in 1965, and the National Endowment for the Arts in 1966. He was married three times, to poet Barbara Gibbs in 1937 (divorced 1943), Dolora Gallagher in 1945 (divorced 1949), and Jessie Campbell in 1950. He died in 1985.

He published several books in his lifetime, among them *The Helmsman* (1942), *The Judge Is Fury* (1947),

Doctor Drink (1950), *Trivial, Vulgar, and Exalted: Epigrams* (1957), *The Exclusions of a Rhyme* (1960), *To What Strangers, What Welcome* (1964), and *Some Salt: Poems and Epigrams* (1967). But for all that, his total output was relatively slight, totaling less than two hundred poems, most of them short (some only two lines). Cunningham became known as a master of the epigram, probably *the* master in twentieth-century America, where few poets have taken the form seriously. **Mark Strand, e.e. cummings**, and **Richard Wilbur** have written epigrams, but for the most part, the epigram has been the province of light versifiers like **Dorothy Parker** and **Ogden Nash**. Interestingly, the line of demarcation between the literary and the light is so stringent in American poetry that Cunningham's work does not appear alongside these figures in anthologies of light verse, though his work is as witty and accessible as theirs, as in the poem about the reader who "Dislikes my book, calls it to my discredit / A book you can't put down before you've read it."

Winters's influence on Cunningham included formal rigor, anti-modernism, and a sense of poetry as an important part of a culture's moral dialogue, although Cunningham's moral lessons were frequently touched with more ribaldry than Winters's ("Lip was a man who used his head . . . With either sex at either end" [noting that he goes to bed with his friend and the friend's wife]). But other influences were important, too. His early Latin and Greek studies drew him to the classical Roman epigrammists, especially Martial (whom he translated). He drew a passion for argument and precise moral distinctions from his Jesuit training and his own Roman Catholic upbringing (although he was to lose his faith, which he lamented in his poetry).

Cunningham was to frustrate some admirers for the tenacity with which he stuck to his aesthetic code. He was criticized for emotional detachment; as **Louis Simpson** said of him, "You cannot show the triumph of discipline over disorder unless you also show the disorder." Critic J. Bottum praised his epigrams for achieving "everything the epigram can do," but pointed out that there is more to poetry than what the epigram can do, and suggested that Cunningham, with his gifts, could have done much more. Even Winters demurred from Cunningham's assertion that sensory images have no place in poetry.

In 1997 an important re-release of Cunningham's work, edited and with an introduction by poet **Timothy Steele**, revived his reputation and stirred new interest in his work.

Further Reading. ***Selected Primary Sources:*** Cunningham, J.V., *The Collected Poems and Epigrams of J.V. Cunningham* (Denver: Swallow Press, 1971); ———, *The Exclusions of a Rhyme* (Denver: Swallow Press, 1957); ———, *The Helmsman* (San Francisco: Colt Press, 1942); ———, *The Judge Is Fury* (New York: Swallow Press and William Morrow, 1947); ———, *The Poems of J.V. Cunningham*, ed. Timothy Steele (Athens, OH: Swallow Press and Ohio University Press, 1997); ———, *To What Strangers, What Welcome* (Denver: Swallow Press, 1957); ———, *Trivial, Vulgar, & Exalted: Epigrams, 4 Poems* (San Francisco: Poems in Folio, 1957). ***Selected Secondary Sources:*** Bottum, J., "America's Best Forgotten Poet" (*Weekly Standard* [16 February 1998]: 31); Rathman, Andrew, Review of *The Poems of J. V. Cunningham* (*Chicago Review* 43.3 [1997]: 107–109; Winters, Yvor, *The Poetry of J.V. Cunningham* (Denver: Swallow Press, 1961).

Tad Richards